NUKUORO LEXICON

PALI Language Texts: Polynesia
(Pacific and Asian Linguistics Institute)

NUKUORO LEXICON

Vern Carroll
and
Topias Soulik

The University Press of Hawaii
Honolulu

The publication of this book is subsidized by the government of the Trust Territory of the Pacific Islands.

Library of Congress Catalog Card Number 73-78975
ISBN 0-8248-0250-0
Manufactured in the United States of America

DEDICATION

De hagalava o de beebaa nei go de hagaodi o de hegau amaau ne daamada laa i taamada o taadeu nnoho hagabuni i honga Nukuoro.

E ssoa dangada ne malangilangi ga dugu mai olaadeu masava ga hai hegau hagammahi ama de hagadaubale mahamaha i de hai o de beeba nei. Gidaadeu alodahi ne hai gi adaadeu me ne mau. Gai tee maua i de hai gi llava me alodahi. Gimaau e dangidangi adu ai i me haisala ama me tee hagapuni ange.

Gai gidaadeu e hagalodolodo age bolo e tilo de aamuli i odaadeu dua ga loage ga hagapuni ange ama de hai gi kii ange i de mahamaha taadeu beebaa. Gai de masava nei gai gimaau e llodo bolo taadeu beëbaa nei gi hanu ono haigamaiana mai gi gidaadeu hugado. Iai laa muna o taadeu henua odaadeu e vvasu ai laa ama de aloha ai. Adaadeu e dee llodo laa bolo gi ngalo i odaadeu daha i dahi laangi.

Gimmau e dangidangi adu gi goodou gi aude haihaia i de mmule o de lava o taadeu beebaa.

CONTENTS

PREFACE

This Lexicon is designed for use by the Nukuoro people in establishing a lexicographic tradition, and in helping school children standardize their spelling of Nukuoro and learn to express themselves better in English. It is also for the use of scholars interested in the relationships among Polynesian languages. With these uses in mind we have included a Root List in which all the forms derived from a root are listed together (forms whose roots are unknown are listed at the end of that section). We have omitted foreign loan words, names of recently introduced plants, recently coined phrases, names for persons and places, and Nukuoro words known only to a single informant. We have not attempted an English-Nukuoro dictionary: the English-Nukuoro section of this work is merely a reverse listing of the English keywords which occur in the glosses provided for Nukuoro entries. The emphasis has been on listing as many traditional Nukuoro forms as possible, and not on providing extensive gloss information. In fact, gloss information has been omitted altogether for many derived forms (as explained in Appendix 1).

The introductory material has been limited to that which is essential to interpretation of the Lexicon entries. Reference material that expands the published literature on Nukuoro grammar (Carroll 1965) has been included in the appendices.

ACKNOWLEDGMENTS

Many people have helped us compile this Lexicon, yet it has many limitations of which we are painfully aware. We regard this as a preliminary effort, to be continued by Nukuoro students of their own language.

Nearly every person on the atoll contributed materially to this project. In addition to those who helped with early efforts to compile word lists, or with later efforts to verify words of which we were uncertain, many adults and school children helped collect specimens of flora and fauna that were sent to taxonomists for identification. Although there is insufficient space to record the names of all these generous people, we must mention the following persons who were especially helpful: Adisa, Adonisi, Aginesi, Aidele, Alege, Anton, Augusi, Bamala, Bodegi, Dala, Debalalo, Debola, Edelina, Ele, Eliodi, Gininga, Hagadau, Hellena, Hosea, Ioela, Iosua, Ivede, Madili, Maea, Nett, Otto, Salina, Sisugo, Sosese, Sulae, Uisili.

Topias Soulik began the compilation of this Lexicon, on a volunteer basis, during 1963 - 1966 while I was engaged in anthropological research on Nukuoro Atoll. We worked together during 1967 - 1969 at the Pacific and Asian Linguistics Institute, University of Hawaii, where he held the position of research associate. The final editing and writing of the introductory material and appendices were done by me during the summers of 1971 and 1972 at the Department of Linguistics, University of Hawaii, under the sponsorship of the Pacific and Asian Linguistics Institute.

Systems design and programing assistance were most ably provided by Robert Hsu and Ann Peters of the Pacific and Asian Linguistics Institute. The clerical labor of this project, during 1967 - 1969, fell on the able shoulders of Elaine Sommer; Jean Miyano and Gary L. Smith (through the courtesy of Freda R. Hellinger) provided additional, much needed, help in the summer of 1971. In the summer of 1972 I was fortunate to have the help of Ann Ikuta, Sharon Watanabe, Karen Young, and Cynthia Dalrymple.

Many taxonomists were generous with their time in identifying specimens. Nukuoro birds were identified from specimens by Robert W. McFarlane of the Department of Zoology, University of Florida. Nukuoro plant specimens were identified by F. Raymond Fosberg of the Smithsonian Institution. Shell specimens were identified by Alison Kay, Department of General Science, University of Hawaii. Fishes were identified, to the extent possible from color slides, by Gareth J. Nelson, Robert S. Jones, and William Van Heukelam — all of the Department of Zoology, University of Hawaii. Identification of miscellaneous marine invertebrates was provided (from color slides) by Lucius G. Eldredge of the Department of Zoology, University of Guam. Insects were identified from specimens by Setsuko Nakata of the Bernice P. Bishop Museum, Honolulu, and by her collaborators: W. A. Steffan (mosquitos), H. Sima (flies), and J. W. Beardsley (scale insects).

My work on this Lexicon in 1963 - 1966 was done during the tenure of a predoctoral fellowship from the U.S. Public Health Service (National Institutes of Mental Health). In the summer of 1967 further assistance was provided by the Graduate School Research Fund of the University of Washington. The major portion of the project was completed in 1967 - 1969 with the assistance of a research grant (GS - 1831) from the National Science Foundation, during the tenure of a postdoctoral fellowship from the American Council of Learned Societies and a visiting appointment at the Pacific and Asian Linguistics Institute (PALI) of the University of Hawaii. I am grateful to the director of PALI at that time, Howard McKaughan, for his extraordinary efforts on my behalf. During the summer of 1971, my work was supported by the Department of Education, Trust Territory of the Pacific Islands.

My colleagues at PALI and in the Department of Linguistics at the University of Hawaii have invariably provided an invigorating and cheerful environment in which to work. The PALI office, under the able direction of Joanne Nakagawa, was unfailingly helpful.

Publication of this work was made possible by the Department of Education, Trust Territory of the Pacific Islands; and by the Pacific and Asian Linguistics Institute, through the good offices of its current director, Donald Topping, without whose help and encouragement this work might never have appeared.

Editorial suggestions of great value were provided by Byron W. Bender, Raymonde Carroll, George W. Grace, Michael D. Lieber, and Donald M. Topping.

VERN CARROLL

Pacific and Asian Linguistics Institute
University of Hawaii
August 1972

ORTHOGRAPHY

The Nukuoro alphabet uses the following letters (the form in parentheses is the orthographical representation of doubling):

Consonants	labial	dental	velar
stops	*b (p)*	*d (t)*	*g (k)*
fricatives	*v (vv)*	*s (ss)*	*h (hh)*
nasals	*m (mm)*	*n (nn)*	*ng (nng)*
flap		*l (ll)*	

Vowels	front	central	back
high	*i (ii)*		*u (uu)*
mid	*e (ee)*		*o (oo)*
low		*a (aa)*	

English alphabetical order is followed in this Lexicon, *except* as follows: p follows b; t follows d; k follows g; ng follows nu; nng follows nnu (see chart above).*

Although this orthography does not fully conform to any of the orthographical traditions that have been imposed upon Polynesian speech communities, it is used here for the following reasons: It was devised on Nukuoro Atoll more than half a century ago, and all the Nukuoro people are familiar with it; it is also acceptable to local

*The order in which the Nukuoro alphabet is usually recited is as follows: a, e, i, o, u, m, n, k, b, p, t, g, v, s, l, d, ng, h. Consonants are recited by adding / i /, except to g, which takes / e / .

educational and administrative authorities. Further, this orthography faithfully represents the sounds of Nukuoro (i.e., it is fully phonemic).

HOW TO INTERPRET ENTRIES

EXAMPLE 1: ENGLISH-NUKUORO

SAMPLE ENTRIES	EXPLANATIONS
breechclout Breechclout: *huna; malo huna; malo sabo** [1]	[1] Archaic words are marked with asterisks.
Bruguiera [2] Plant sp.: oriental mangrove *(Bruguiera gymnorhiza* (L.) Lam.)[3]: *donga.*	[2] Plant and animal genera (but not species) names are invariably listed. [3] Binomials are listed only for plant and animal species which have been identified by taxonomists.
butterfly Butterfly: *bebe*$_2$[4] **butterfly fish** Fish sp.: butterfly fish[5]: *dihidihi.*	[4] Numerical subscripts distinguish homonyms. [5] English species names not accompanied by binomial identification indicate that positive identification was possible only to a generic or higher degree, owing to the lack of a suitable specimen.

SAMPLE ENTRIES	EXPLANATIONS
buttocks Buttocks: *dae*$_3$[6] Having flat buttocks, ugly (because not plump): *biihingi*.	[6]Note that not all meanings of each Nukuoro word are given in the English-Nukuoro section. *Dae*$_3$, for example, also means 'guts, intestines'. The additional meanings of a word, also information on word class and derivation are found in the Nukuoro-English section.

EXAMPLE 2: NUKUORO-ENGLISH

SAMPLE ENTRIES	EXPLANATIONS
a-$_3$[1]. PLURAL PREFIX. [2] *mf*.	[1] Numerical subscripts distinguish homonyms. (The hyphen indicates that this is a prefix.)
	[2] Grammatical designations and grammatical information appear in small capitals.
aapulu. (E--[3] ABULU) Sink all at once.[4] *a*[5].	[3] Derivation information (between parentheses): this consists of a "derivative-type code" and the root (see page 487, under which related forms may be found in the Root List.
aapuluanga. (E-1 ABULU) *n*.[6]	[4] Gloss.
	[5] "Word-class code" (see page xxiii).
	[6] There is no gloss for this word because normal derivatives are not glossed (see Appendix 1).
aada.[7] Easily startled, skittish, wild (of animals). *a*.	[7] Bases (always single words, by definition) have no derivation information if the base form is identical to the form of the root. For related forms consult the Root List under the form of the base.

Sample Entries	Explanations
aadea moana[8] Unobstructed.	[8] Idioms (always two or more words, by definition) have no derivation information. For related forms consult the Root List under the root form of each constituent word.
aduhale. (ADU_4[9], HALE) Village, compound (aggregation of houses); go from house to house. *a.*	[9]Compound words list their constituent roots and no derivative-type code.
amuamu (R-- AMU) —;[10] small and useless particles, leftovers. *v.*	[10]A dash in the gloss section indicates that this form has the meanings of a normal derivative (see note 6 above) in addition to those listed. (See also note 5 in example 3 below).
ana_2 [var. of *kana*].[11] *mt.*	[11] Comment by the compilers is enclosed in brackets. The listing of variants is arbitrary in that either one could be listed as a variant of the other.

EXAMPLE 3: ROOT LIST

SAMPLE ENTRIES		EXPLANATIONS
ADU $_4$ [1]		[1] Roots which are spelled the same but have different patterns of affixation are numbered apart.
B [2]	**adu** $_4$. *n*[3]. Conglomerate, islet.	[2] Derivative-type code.
XCO	**adudau.** *n.* Sand spit.	[3] Word-class code.
. . . .		
ADU $_{4a}$ [4]		[4] Compounds which have many derivatives are given a letter subscript for convenience in organizing the associated entries. The choice of root under which such forms are listed is arbitrary.
B	**adugau.** *v.* Arrangement of things into a straight row.	
B 1	**adugauanga.** *n.* — [5]	[5] Normal derivatives are not glossed (see Appendix 1).
B 2	**adugaua.** *v.* —.	
B 2	**adugaulia.** *v.* —.	
BE	**hagaadugau.** *v.* Arrange things in a row or line.	
BE 1	**hagaadugauanga.** *n.* —.	
BE 2	**hagaadugaua.** *v.* —.	
BE 2	**hagaadugaulia.** *v.* —.	
ID	**adugau daane.** Part of the plug of the pandanus.	

HOW TO INTERPRET CODES

A. TYPES OF CODES.In addition to the abbreviations used in the English gloss section (see List of Abbreviations below), there are two sorts of codes used in this work: word-class codes, and derivative-type codes.

Word-class codes classify single words (but not compounds or idioms) according to their Nukuoro grammatical category. A list of these is presented below. (See Appendix 4 for word-class definitions.)

Derivative-type codes classify words and phrases according to their relationship to a base form (the form in a series of related forms which is closest in form to the root). Derivative-type codes are written in three columns:the symbol in the first column indicates the type of stem; the symbol in the second column indicates the prefix, and the symbol in the third column indicates the type of suffix. A summary list is presented below. (Further information on the meaning of these distinctions is contained in Appendix 1.)

B. SUMMARY OF DERIVATIVE-TYPE CODES

Col. 1: Stem types

- B Base form
- C Variant of a base form
- E Emphatic form
- P Plural concord form
- R Reduplicated form
- S Second reduplicated form
- T Partially reduplicated form
- X Compound word

(If col. 1 is blank refer to the section on Additional forms below.)

Subtypes XCO compound word
XE XCO + the prefix *haga-* (see below under Prefixes)
XFL name of an animal or plant species
XG name of an item of native manufacture

U Unclassified

Col. 2: Prefixes

C *ma-* RESULTATIVE PREFIX
D *he-* RECIPROCAL PREFIX
E *haga-* CAUSATIVE PREFIX
F *haga-+ma-* (E+C, above)
G *haga-+he-* (E+D, above)
(A blank in this column means that the stem is uninflected.)

Col. 3: Suffixes

1 *-nga* NOMINAL SUFFIX
2 *-a* PERFECTIVE SUFFIX
3 *-a+nga*
(A blank in this column means that the stem is uninflected.)

Additional forms

ID An idiom
CF Compare the above with the following form, which may be related to this root.

C. WORD-CLASS CODES

A Adjective
AN Numeral
B Base surrogate
D Dependent word
I Interjection
M . . . Minor Morpheme
MA Article
MC Numeral Classifier
MF Prefix
MI Introductory Word
MP Preposition
MR Relational Particle
MT Tense-aspect Marker
MV Adverb
MZ Suffix
N Noun

NA Adjectival Noun
NL Location Word
NN Name of a Person
NP Place Name
NT Time Noun
P... Pronoun
- PI Independent Pronoun
- PP... Possessive Pronoun
- PD... Dependent Pronoun
- PT... Distributive Pronoun

U Unclassified
V Verb

LIST OF ABBREVIATIONS

The following abbreviations are used in the English gloss sections. Abbreviations for word-class codes and derivative-type codes are listed on pages xxii-xxiv.

[adj.]	adjective, as in English grammar
[dp]	a Nukuoro dependent form that always precedes a base
[ds]	a Nukuoro dependent form that always follows a base
Eng.	English
esp.	especially, . . .
ex.	except, . . .
[excl.]	exclusive (of the person spoken to) — a grammatical and semantic category which applies to Nukuoro first-person pronouns.
[incl.]	inclusive (of the person spoken to) — a grammatical and semantic category which applies to Nukuoro first-person pronouns.
incl.	including . . .
indep.	independent form
intrans.	intransitive
lit.	literally, . . .
opp.	the opposite of
[pl.]	plural (in number)
prob.	probably, . . .
[sing.]	singular (in number)
sp.	species (singular)
spp.	species (plural)
[trans.]	transitive (of verbs)

var.	variant of
[1]	pertaining to a single object
[2]	pertaining to just two objects
[3]	pertaining to three or more objects

Note also: an asterisk following a Nukuoro word indicates that the word is archaic.

NUKUORO-ENGLISH

a_1.
RELATIONAL PARTICLE 2. *mr.*

a_2.
PERSONAL ARTICLE. *ma.*

a-$_3$. (B-- A_3)
PLURAL PREFIX. *mf.*

aa_1.
The sound of hesitation noise. *i.*

aa-$_2$. (B-- AA_2)
FUTURE TIME PREFIX. *mf.*

aabi.
Room (of a house). *n.*

aabida.
Make a coil of dried pandanus leaves. *v.*

aabidanga. (B-1 AABIDA)
n.

aabo. (P-- ABO)
a.

aabonga. (B-1 ABO)
n.

aabongi. (P-- ABONGI)
a.

aabulu. (P-- ABULU)
a.

aabuluanga. (P-1 ABULU)
n.

aapulu. (E-- ABULU)
Sink all at once. *a.*

aapuluanga. (E-1 ABULU)
n.

aada.
Easily startled, skittish, wild (of animals). *a.*

aadea.
Clear (easily seen), unobscured. *v.*

aadea moana.
Unobstructed.

aadiidii. (B-- DII_a)
Dry (something) by artificial heat. *v.*

aadiidiia. (B-2 DII_a)
v.

aadiidiinga. (B-1 DII_a)
n.

aagai. (B-- GAI_{2a})
Continually wanting to eat. *a.*

aagainga. (B-1 GAI_{2a})
n.

aago. (P-- AGO_1)
v.

aagoa. (P-2 AGO_1)
v.

aagona. (P-2 AGO_1)
v.

aagonga. (P-1 AGO_1)
n.

aagonga i lalo*.
Social class of those who know the black arts.

aagonga i lunga*.
Social class of chiefs and priests.

aagunga. (B-1 AGU)
n.

aahe. (P-- AHE)
v.

aahee. (B-- HEE_{2a})
When? (indefinite future). *b.*

aahee ai.
Then which?

aahee ange.
What else?

aahee donu.
Exactly which?

aahee huu.
Then which?

aahee laa.
Which were those?

aahee loo.
When? (distant future).

aahee maa.
About when? (future); about how much?

aahee naa.
Then what? (distant future).

aahee nei.
Then what? (immediate future).

aahenga. (P-1 AHE)
n.

aahu.
The intense pain resulting from having one's skin punctured by a poisonous fish. *a.*

aahulu.
To leave food cooking overnight. *v.*

aahunga. (B-1 AAHU)
n.

aala. (P-- ALA_2)
a.

aalali.
Coral sp.: a type of coral which grows on the lagoon bottom. *v.*

aalanga. (B-- $LANGA_a$)
Member (of the body, a house, etc.). *n.*

aalinga.
Moving around just under the water. *a.*

aalingaanga. (B-1 AALINGA)
n.

aalo. (E-- ALO_1)
Come by paddling. *v.*

aaloa. (B-2 ALO_1)
v.

aalo dahi.
Do at one time.

aaloha. (P-- ALOHA)
a.

aalohi. (P-- ALO_{3a})
The portion of the atoll lagoon just lagoonward of the fringing reef. *n.*

aalohi modu.
Lagoonward of the islets of the atoll.

aalo lo te moana.
A disturbance (local) of air.

aalonga. (B-1 ALO_1)
n.

aalu. (E-- ALU)
Intercept; send for. *v.*

aalua. (E-2 ALU)
v.

aalukaba. (P-- ALU_a)
v.

aalunga. (E-1 ALU)
n.

aamanu. (B-- $MANU_a$)
Coral (growing live on the reef); coral head. *v.*

aamia.
Sufficient for the purpose or need. *v.*

aamua. (B-- MUA_a)
High-ranking. *a.*

aamua ange.
Higher.

aamuli. (B-- $MULI_{1a}$)
Descendants (in all inferior generations). *n.*

aamunga. (B-1 AMU)
n.

aanu. (P-- ANU)
v.

aanumanga. (P-1 ANU)
n.

aanunga. (B-1 ANU)
n.

aanga. (P-- $ANGA_1$)
a.

aangahia. (P-2 $ANGA_1$)
v.

aasanga. (B-- $SANGA_a$)
A watercourse between islets on the atoll. *v.*

aasasi.
Flee (of a small school of fish). *a.*

aasasinga. (B-1 AASASI)
n.

aasii.
Drum (native). *n.*

aasolo. (B-- SOLO)
Mollusk sp.: clam sp. (a type of *baasua*). *n.*

aasunga. (B-1 ASU)
n.

aau.
Remove. *v.*

aaua. (B-2 AAU)
v.

aauaau. (R-- AAU)
v.

aauaaua. (R-2 AAU)
v.

aauaaunga. (R-1 AAU)
n.

aau ai naa.
More so.

aaunga. (B-1 AAU)
—; the incompletely burned earth oven fuel remaining when the oven is uncovered. *n.*

aausa.
Wake (of a ship). *v.*

aausa ina.
A sea condition resembling that resulting from a ship leaving a wake.

aausanga. (B-1 AAUSA)
Way of leaving a wake. *n.*

abaaba. (B-- BAA_{4a})
Door; cover (something, e.g., to protect it from the elements). *v.*

abaabai.
Carry a canoe in shallow water; carry half lifting. *v.*

abaabaia. (B-2 ABAABAI)
v.

abaabainga. (B-1 ABAABAI)
n.

abadai.
European [adj.]. *na.*

abasasa.
European. *na.*

abasasa huu.
European in manner or appearance.

abe. (B-- BE_a)
"Or, to cite just one more example...". *mi.*

abi. (B-- ABI_2)
Fish sp.: tang. *n.*

abiabi. (R-- ABI_1)
Pull up slowly or gently with one's fingers. *v.*

abiabia. (R-2 ABI_1)
v.

abiabinga. (R-1 ABI_1)
n.

abitala.
Eave (of a house). *n.*

abo.
Capable; correct (suitable), true; feel comfortable. *a.*

aboabo. (R-- ABO)
Become accustomed to. *a.*

aboabongi. (R-- ABONGI)
Easily capsizable. *a.*

abo ange.
Good at.

abo donu.
Good (not evil or false); real, true; well (not sick); considerate, kind, generous.

abo manu.
To correct someone without justification.

abongi.
Capsize. *a.*

abongi baasi.
Capsize sideways.

aboo. (B-- BOO_{2a})
Tonight. *b.*

aboo nei.
Tonight (future).

abo sala.
Mean (by nature), unkind.

abuabulu. (R-- ABULU)
Easily sinkable. *a.*

abulu.
Sink (until submerged). *a.*

abuluanga. (B-1 ABULU)
n.

ada_1.
Picture, image, reflection, shadow. *n.*

ada_2.
CONJECTURAL PREFIX. *mf.*

ada_3.
Each person's several. *pta.*

adaada. (R-- ADA_1)
Dawn (first light). *a.*

adaada age.
The first light of the moon.

adaadamai. (R-- ADA_{1a})
Recall slightly. *a.*

adaadamaia. (R-2 ADA_{1a})
v.

adaadamainga. (R-1 ADA_{1a})
n.

adaadeu.
Our [incl. 3] several. *ppa.*

adaau.
Our [incl. 2] several. *ppa.*

adamai. (ADA_{1a}, MAI_1)
Recollect or recall past events or persons, etc. *v.*

adamaia. (B-2 ADA_{1a})
v.

adamai gauligi.
Remember childhood experiences.

adamainga. (B-1 ADA_{1a})
n.

ade.
Liver. *n.*

adi.
Relate news or gossip. *v.*

adia. (B-2 ADI)
v.

adiadi. (R-- ADI)
Relate repeatedly. *v.*

adiadia. (R-2 ADI)
v.

adiadinga. (R-1 ADI)
n.

adidi.
Plant sp. (not native — drifts ashore — used for making perfume). *n.*

adigai.
Luckily did not —, fortunately it did not —; if more; almost. *mi.*

adigai huu.
Were it not for; fortunately, luckily —.

adilo. (B-- $DILO_{2a}$)
The core of a body boil; the beginning of a fire. *n.*

adi longo.
To tattle.

adinga. (B-1 ADI)
n.

adi saele.
Disseminate information.

adu_1.
Toward hearer. *mv.*

adu_2.
Fish sp.: skipjack tuna. *n.*

adu_3.
Fish club (priest). *n.*

adu_4.
Conglomerate, islet. *n.*

adu ange laa.
The one following the one in question.

adu-balebale-i-dai.
Fish sp.

adu-balebale-i-dua.
Fish sp.: bonito.

adudai. (ADU_4, DAI_1)
"Islands to the west of Nukuoro" (the Mortlocks?). *n.*

adudau. (ADU_4, DAU_3)
Sand spit. *n.*

adugau. (ADU_{4a}, GAU_1)
Arrangement of things into a straight row. *v.*

adugaua. (B-2 ADU_{4a})
v.

adugauanga. (B-1 ADU_{4a})
n.

adugau daane.
Part of the plug of the pandanus.

adugaulia. (B-2 ADU_{4a})
v.

aduhale. (ADU_4, HALE)
Village, compound (aggregation of houses); go from house to house. *a.*

aduhenua. (ADU_4, HENUA)
Group of islands or atolls; archipelago. *n.*

aduisiisi. (?)
One's first spouse. *n.*

adu laa.
After tomorrow, the one after the next one.

adumodu. (ADU_4, MODU)
Group of islets; atoll (collection of islets). *n.*

adumua.
Pregnant and almost ready to deliver; first among a group of pregnant women to deliver. *v.*

atangada. (B-- $DANGADA_a$)
Generation, age set. *n.*

ataula. (B-- $DAULA_a$)
Anchor rope. *n.*

aga.
Root (of a tree or plant). *n.*

agaaga. (R-- AGA)
Having lots of roots. *n.*

agai. (B-- GAI_{3a})
And then, finally... *mi.*

agau.
Reef (the portion which is sometimes under water). *n.*

age.
Up. *mv.*

ageageli. (R-- AGELI)
v.

ageagelia. (R-2 AGELI)
v.

ageagelinga. (R-1 AGELI)
n.

ageli.
Pick head lice. *v.*

agelia. (B-2 AGELI)
v.

agelinga. (B-1 AGELI)
n.

agiagi. (R-- AGI)
Bird sp.: fairy tern (*Gygis alba*). *n.*

agiagilau. (R-- AGILAU)
v.

agiagilaua. (R-2 AGILAU)
v.

agiagilaunga. (R-1 AGILAU)
n.

agilau.
Pugnacious. *v.*

agilaua. (B-2 AGILAU)
v.

agilau gee.
Extremely pugnacious.

agilaunga. (B-1 AGILAU)
n.

agina.
To it, for it. *mv.*

ago. (B-- AGO_1)
Learn, teach. *v.*

agoa. (B-2 AGO_1)
v.

$agoago_1$. (R-- AGO_1)
Learning, teaching. *v.*

$agoago_2$. (R-- AGO_2)
Taro fibers. *v.*

agoagoa. (R-2 AGO_1)
v.

agoagona. (R-2 AGO_1)
v.

agoagonga. (R-1 AGO_1)
n.

ago i tua.
Learn by heart.

ago i me.
Copy, imitate.

agona. (B-2 AGO_1)
v.

agonga. (B-1 AGO_1)
n.

agu_1.
Say or tell (esp. in confidence). *v.*

agu_2.
My several. *ppa.*

agua. (B-2 AGU)
v.

agu age.
Say out loud.

aguagu. (R-- AGU)
v.

aguagua. (R-2 AGU)
v.

aguagule. (R-- AGULE)
v.

aguagulea. (R-2 AGULE)
v.

aguagulenga. (R-1 AGULE)
n.

aguagulia. (R-2 AGU)
v.

aguagunga. (R-1 AGU)
n.

agu bau.
Methinks.

agu iho.
Say to oneself.

agule.
Pick head lice. *v.*

agulea. (B-2 AGULE)
v.

agulenga. (B-1 AGULE)
n.

agulia. (B-2 AGU)
v.

agu made.
Perhaps, maybe;.

aha. (B-- AHA_1)
What? *v.*

aha ai.
What for?

aha-bagua.
Driftwood sp. (resembles *bagua*).

aha-dea.
Driftwood sp. (white in the center).

aha goi.
What next?

aha goi delaa.
What was I going to say?

aha laa.
I wonder why?

aha naa.
Let's (later).

aha nei.
Let's (now).

ahangi.
Lagoon. *n.*

ahe.
Return, go back. *v.*

ahe age.
Start again, reoccur.

aheahe. (R-- AHE)
Keep returning. *v.*

aheahelia. (R-2 AHE)
v.

aheahenga. (R-1 AHE)
n.

ahee. (HEE_{2b}, A_3)
Which? *b.*

ahee oo dagodo?.
How are you?

ahe iho.
Diminish (in intensity).

ahe ina.
Wind around completely once.

ahelia. (B-2 AHE)
v.

ahenga. (B-1 AHE)
n.

ahi. (B-- AHI_1)
Fire. *n.*

ahiahi. (B-- AHI_{1a})
Late afternoon and early evening. *a.*

ahiahi danuaa.
Good afternoon! Good evening!

ahi dangada.
A (mat) wrapping for dead persons who are disposed of in the sea [a precontact custom].

ahi tugi.
Ignite a fire by making sparks with a stone.

ahi malo.
A mat wrapping for clothes.

ahinga.
Armpit. *n.*

aho.
Fishing line of the sort used for *adu fishing*. *n.*

ahu.
Islet. *n.*

ahulu.
Fish sp.: goat fish (= *madulilau sisisi*). *n.*

ai.
PREDICATE COMPLEMENT. *mv.*

aigimea. (?)
Plant sp.: wedelia creeper (*Wedelia biflora* (L.) DC.). *n.*

ailaa.
Today (sometime). *b.*

ala_1.
A section of a mat. *v.*

ala_2.
Be awake, be open; bloom (of flowers). *a.*

ala_3.
The name of a name-group. *n.*

alaa. (LAA_{1a}, A_3)
Those over there. *b.*

alaa ai.
Those only.

alaa ai huu.
Those there only then.

alaa ai laa.
Those there then were.

alaa ai loo.
Those there then are.

alaa ange.
And those there.

alaa ange huu.
That there [pl.] much more only.

alaa ange maalie.
Those there are exactly right.

alaa ange naa.
About that [pl.] (over there) much more.

alaa dagodo.
Those there are the circumstances...

alaadeu.
Their [3] several. *ppa.*

alaa donu.
Those there only.

alaa huu.
Those (there) only are the ones.

$alaala_1$. (B-- ALAALA)
Fish sp.: jack (2 sorts) (= small *tulua*). *n.*

$alaala_2$. (R-- ALA_2)
Sleep fitfully. *a.*

alaa laa.
Those (there) which were there.

alaala dangada.
False labor pains (of a pregnant woman).

alaaladi. (R-- $LADI_a$)
v.

alaaladia. (R-2 $LADI_a$)
v.

alaaladinga. (R-1 $LADI_a$)
n.

alaa loo.
Those (there) were the ones.

alaa maa.
Those there were about (approximately).

alaa muhuu.
How about those there?

alaa muna.
Word [= *dalaa muna*].

alaa naa.
Those only?

alaa naa loo.
Those there seem to be.

alaa nei.
Those now.

alaange. (B-- ALA_{2a})
Allowed to, permissible. *a.*

alaa sili.
Those there were enough.

alaau.
Their [2] several. *ppa.*

aladi. (B-- $LADI_a$)
Initiate, begin. *v.*

aladia. (B-2 $LADI_a$)
v.

aladinga. (B-1 $LADI_a$)
n.

aladoidoi.
Iron (a piece of). *n.*

ala galigi.
A method of mat making.

alahage. (B-- ALA_{2b})
Wake up (from sleep). *a.*

alahenua. (B-- $HENUA_a$)
Plot of (bush) land, acreage. *n.*

Alamooi. (B-- ALAMOOI)
June. *n.*

alasala. (ALA_2, $SALA_2$)
Vicious. *a.*

alava.
Fish sp.: shark sp.? *n.*

alelo.
Tongue. *n.*

alelo-hatuli.
Mollusk sp.: pearly nautilus shell.

aliali. (R-- ALI)
The barely formed gelatinous layer inside the immature coconut. *v.*

alialinga. (R-1 ALI)
n.

aligi.
Priest (of a cult). *a.*

alili.
Mollusk sp.: *Turbo argyrostoma*. *n.*

alo-. (B-- ALO_2)
Coloring of coconut meat. *d.*

aloalo$_1$. (R-- ALO_1)
To paddle (a canoe). *v.*

aloalo$_2$. (R-- ALO_2)
Becoming colored (of coconut meat only). *d.*

aloalo$_3$. (R-- ALO_3)
Chest, front (opposite of back — e.g.,lagoon shore as opposed to seaward reef shore). *n.*

aloaloa. (R-2 ALO_1)
v.

aloalo gaadinga.
The part of a coconut's meat next to the sap.

aloalo me.
The current nearest to the (seaward) outer reef of the atoll.

aloalo-mea. (ALO_2, MEA)
Becoming red (of fully mature coconut meat). *a.*

aloalonga. (R-1 ALO_1)
n.

aloalo-uli. (ALO_2, ULI_1)
Becoming dark (of fully mature coconut meat). *a.*

alobagi. (XCO ALO_3)
A lagoonward sand spit next to a channel between islets on the atoll. *v.*

alodahi.
All. *n.*

alodahi hugadoo.
Everything, everybody; each and every.

aloha.
Compassion, affection. *a.*

aloha ai.
Feel sorry for or sympathetic toward.

aloha gelo.
Profound affection.

alohaha. (XCO ALO_3)
Throat (of fish only). *n.*

aloha iho.
Self-love.

aloha ina.
Helpful toward.

alohanga. (B-1 ALO_1)
A streak of smooth water in the sea. *n.*

alohi. (B-- ALO_{3a})
Anything forming a semi-circle. *n.*

alohi lima.
Palm (of the hand).

alohi vae.
Sole (of the foot).

alo-malie. (ALO_2, MALIE)
Coconut meat (fully mature) of good quality for eating. *a.*

alomasige.
Hasten to go or come. *a.*

alomasigeanga. (B-1 ALOMASIGE)
n.

alo-mea. (ALO_2, MEA)
Reddish color (of fully mature coconut meat). *a.*

aloo anahee.
For how long has this been going on?

alo-uli. (ALO_2, ULI_1)
Dark color (of fully mature coconut meat). *a.*

alu$_a$. (CF $GABA_3$)
v.

aluala. (R-- ALU)
— (ex. 'intercept' meanings). *v.*

alualua. (R-2 ALU)
v.

alualukaba. (R-- ALU_a)
v.

alualumanga. (R-1 ALU)
n.

alualumia. (R-2 ALU)
Send away [no meaning 'intercept' as *alualua*]. *v.*

alualunga. (R-1 ALU)
n.

alukaba. (B-- ALU$_a$)
Leave quickly (usually under duress). *v.*

alukabaanga. (B-1 ALU$_a$)
n.

alumanga. (B-1 ALU)
n.

alumia. (B-2 ALU)
v.

ama$_1$. (B-- AMA)
Outrigger float. *n.*

ama$_2$. (B-- MA$_{1a}$)
And, among other things,... *mi.*

amaadeu.
Our [excl. 3] several. *ppa.*

amaau.
Our [excl. 2] several. *ppa.*

amo.
Lift up. *v.*

amoa. (B-2 AMO)
v.

amoaa. (B-2 AMO)
v.

amoaanga. (B-3 AMO)
n.

amoamo. (R-- AMO)
Keep lifting one thing after another. *v.*

amoamoa. (R-2 AMO)
v.

amoamoaa. (R-2 AMO)
v.

amoamoaanga. (R-3 AMO)
n.

amoamoanga. (R-1 AMO)
n.

amoamoea. (R-2 AMO)
v.

amoamoeanga. (R-3 AMO)
n.

amoamonga. (R-1 AMO)
n.

amoanga. (B-1 AMO)
n.

amoea. (B-2 AMO)
v.

amoeanga. (B-3 AMO)
n.

amonga. (B-1 AMO)
n.

amu.
Twirl fibers (with *ina*); fibers for the manufacture of rope or cloth, etc. *v.*

amuamu. (R-- AMU)
—; small and useless particles, leftovers. *v.*

amuamuia. (R-2 AMU)
v.

amuamu iho.
Drizzle.

amuamulia. (R-2 AMU)
v.

amuamunga. (R-1 AMU)
n.

amuia. (B-2 AMU)
v.

amulia. (B-2 AMU)
v.

amu ligi.
Fine threads or hairs or fibers (in feather or leaf, etc.); fine-feathered.

ana-$_1$. (B-- ANA$_1$)
PAST TIME PREFIX. *mf.*

ana$_2$.
[Var. of *kana*]. *mt.*

ana$_3$.
His several, her several, its several. *ppa.*

anaa. (NAA$_{1a}$, A$_3$)
Those (away from the speaker). *b.*

anaa ai.
These (there) only.

anaa ai huu.
Those only then.

anaa ai laa.
Those then were those.

anaa ai loo.
Those then are.

anaa ange.
And these (there).

anaa ange huu.
That [pl.] much more only.

anaa ange maalie.
Those are exactly right.

anaa ange naa.
About that [pl.] (here) much more.

anaa dagodo.
Those are the circumstances...

anaa donu.
Those only.

anaahi. (AHI_{1b}, ANA_1)
Yesterday. *b.*

anaa huu.
Those only are the ones.

anaa laa.
These (there) which were there.

anaa loo.
These (there) were the ones.

anaa maa.
Those were about (approximately).

anaa muhuu.
How about those?

anaa naa.
These (there) only?

anaa naa loo.
Those seem to be.

anaa nei.
Those now.

anaange laa hanu.
A little while ago.

anaa sili.
Those were enough.

anaboo. (B-- BOO_{2b})
Last night. *b.*

anaboo taiao.
Early this morning.

anaboo nei.
Tonight (past).

anataiao. (ANA_1, DAIAO)
This morning.

anahee. (HEE_{2c}, ANA_1)
When? (past time). *b.*

anailaa (nei).
Today (in the past).

anailaa laa.
It was today that.

aneane. (R-- ANE)
To desire physically a member of the opposite sex. *n.*

aneanea. (R-2 ANE)
v.

aneanenga. (R-1 ANE)
n.

anei. (NEI_a, A_3)
These. *b.*

anei ai.
These (here) only.

anei ai huu.
These only then.

anei ai laa.
These then were those.

anei ai loo.
These then are.

anei ange.
And these (here).

anei ange huu.
This [pl.] much more only.

anei ange maalie.
These are exactly right.

anei ange naa.
About this [pl.] much more.

anei dagodo.
These are the circumstances...

anei donu.
Only these are the ones.

anei huu.
These (here) only are the ones.

anei laa.
These (here) which were there.

anei loo.
These (here) are the ones.

anei maa.
These were about (approximately).

anei muhuu.
How about these?

anei naa.
These (here) only?

anei naa loo.
These seem to be.

anei nei.
These now.

anei sili.
These were enough.

anengenenge.
Mollusk sp.: *Conus chaldaeus.*

anu.
To dance. *v.*

anu age.
To dance below people.

anuanu. (R-- ANU)
v.

anuanumanga. (R-1 ANU)
n.

anuanumia. (R-2 ANU)
v.

anuanumia age.
Visibly bobbing up and down in the sea.

anuanunga. (R-1 ANU)
n.

anumanga. (B-1 ANU)
—; dancing party. *n.*

anumia. (B-2 ANU)
Bobbing in the water. *v.*

anga$_1$.
Pay attention to (notice), be aware of. *a.*

anga$_2$.
The span of the outstretched thumb and little finger; a measurement of one span. *v.*

anga$_3$ --. (B-- ANGA$_3$)
Prototype, model (something from which a copy can be made). *d.*

angaa. (B-2 ANGA$_2$)
v.

angaanga$_1$. (R-- ANGA$_1$)
Aware, alert. *a.*

angaanga$_2$. (R-- ANGA$_2$)
Measure by spans (*anga*). *a.*

angaanga$_3$. (R-- ANGA$_3$)
Body. *n.*

angaanga dabuvae.
Toenail.

angaangahia. (R-2 ANGA$_1$)
v.

angaanga madannia.
Fingernail.

anga-baabaa.
Mollusk sp.: spider conch.

anga-dogi.
Mollusk sp.: *Cerithiidae.*

anga dua.
An adze blade which is set at a right angle to its handle.

anga gee.
Turn one's attention away from.

anga gi lodo.
An adze blade which is set at less than a right angle to its handle.

angahia. (B-2 ANGA$_1$)
v.

anga iho.
Self-awareness.

anga-mea.
Fish sp. (= large *dada*).

ange.
Away from both the speaker and hearer; more, farther; again. *mv.*

angeange. (R-- ANGE)
Again. *mv.*

angeange laa.
The one following the one in question.

ange gi.
According to —.

ange laa.
The next but one.

angi.
Blow gently (of wind); a disturbance (of the water). *v.*

angia. (B-2 ANGI)
Blow away, cause to move (in the water). *v.*

angiangi. (R-- ANGI)
Blow with increasing force (wind); blow continuously (wind); fan. *v.*

angiangia. (R-2 ANGI)
v.

angiangina. (R-2 ANGI)
v.

angianginga. (R-1 ANGI)
n.

angina. (B-2 ANGI)
v.

anginga. (B-1 ANGI)
n.

ango*.
The carapace of the hawksbill turtle; pearl. *n.*

ao$_1$.
Daylight. *v.*

ao$_2$.
Sufficient. *a.*

aoa$_1$.
Plant sp.: tree sp.: banyan tree (*Ficus prolixa* Forst.). *n.*

aoa$_2$.
Misshapen fruit. *v.*

aoa$_3$. (B-2 AO$_1$)
To inadvertently remain up until daybreak. *v.*

ao age.
Daybreak (become daylight).

aoa-laosedi.
Gorgonian (Coelenterate), false black coral.

aoao$_1$. (R-- AO$_1$)
Becoming daylight. *v.*

aoao$_2$. (R-- AO$_2$)
Continuously sufficient. *a.*

aoaoa. (R-2 AO$_1$)
Habitually remain up until daybreak. *v.*

aoaonga. (R-1 AO$_1$)
Way of staying up until daybreak. *n.*

ao de me.
Daytime.

ao ina.
Inadvertently remain up until daybreak (=*aoa*).

aonga. (B-1 AO$_1$)
Sort or degree of daybreak. *n.*

aoo.
A kind of sound, indicating surprise. *i.*

aso. (B-- ASO$_1$)
Fish sp.: white-tip shark. *n.*

asu.
Scoop up (liquids only), spoon. *v.*

asua. (B-2 ASU)
v.

asuasu. (R-- ASU)
v.

asuasua. (R-2 ASU)
v.

asuasulia. (R-2 ASU)
v.

asuasunga. (R-1 ASU)
n.

asulia. (B-2 ASU)
v.

au$_1$.
(The generic term for the major types of) currents in the open sea. *v.*

au$_2$.
I. *pi.*

au$_3$.
Your several. *ppa.*

aude.
NEGATIVE PRESCRIPTIVE ASPECT MARKER *mt.*

audee. (C-- AUDE)
[Var. of *aude*]. *mt.*

aude haia.
No kidding?

aude vaavaa.
Don't talk about this to anyone!

au dili dai.
An ocean current flowing away from land.

au dili uda.
An ocean current flowing toward land.

au doga.
A confluence of ocean currents, or a circular current in which drifting objects remain stationary.

au taadaaia.
Don't rush! Take it easy!

au e dee gai naa loo.
I'll bet you can't!

au e hai bolo.
"I thought that —".

au ga humai nei.
"I'm going on my way now...".

au ga sano*.
I give up!

augau.
Pus. *v.*

augaua. (B-2 AUGAU)
Infected. *v.*

augaunga. (B-1 AUGAU)
The appearance of an infected area. *n.*

au hagi.
An ocean current which turns away from the reef.

au hebaledage.
A confluence of ocean currents (on the surface only).

au madua.
A type of ocean current far from land in which drifting objects collect.

ava$_1$.
Passage, channel. *v.*

ava$_2$.
Relief, be relieved. *a.*

ava$_3$.
Fish sp. (= large *tonu*, also = large *hagaodalolo*). *n.*

avaava. (R-- AVA$_1$)
Full of holes. *v.*

avaavaanga. (R-1 AVA$_1$)
n.

baa$_1$.
Touch (two or more things), be in contact, make contact with uniformly. *a.*

baa$_2$. (B-- BAA$_3$)
Mollusk sp.: pearl oyster. *n.*

baa age.
Shallow (e.g., waters).

baa ange.
Close to, near to.

baabaa$_1$. (R-- BAA$_1$)
Continuously touch or slap lightly, pat. *a.*

baabaa$_2$. (R-- BAA$_4$)
Flat, board. *a.*

baabaa ama.
To steer a canoe to its outrigger side (opp. of *baabaa gadea*).

baabaa gadea.
To steer a canoe to the side away from its outrigger (opp. of *baabaa ama*).

baabaa luu lima.
Clap hands.

baabaanga. (R-1 BAA$_4$)
n.

baabaasi. (R-- BAASI)
A fishing method (angling with the side of a flying fish as bait). *v.*

baabaasianga. (R-1 BAASI)
n.

baabanga. (B-1 BAA$_4$)
—; an impression left by a hard object pressing on a soft one. *n.*

baabaoa. (R-- BAOA)
Wash up on shore continually; ghost (children's language). *v.*

baabaoanga. (R-1 BAOA)
n.

baabunga. (B-1 BABU)
n.

baabuu.
Lie down [baby talk]. *a.*

baabuunga. (B-1 BAABUU)
n.

baa donu.
Skillful at fighting (opp. of *baa sala*).

baadunga. (B-1 BADU)
—; punishment. *n.*

baatai. (P-- BADAI)
a.

baataianga. (P-1 BADAI)
n.

baa galele.
Fishing lure of pearl shell, used in *galele* fishing.

baagava. (XCO BAA$_5$)
Violent in word or action. *n.*

baageaa.
Weak (of a person). *a.*

baageaa ange.
Attracted to.

baageaa iho.
Weakening (becoming weaker).

baageaanga. (B-1 BAAGEAA)
n.

baagia. (B-2 BAA_5)
Move sideways while moving forward (as a canoe slipping in the water); slap. *v.*

baagia age.
To be carried to the shore (of a canoe) by a current or the wind.

baakuu. (P-- BAGUU)
a.

baakuunga. (P-1 BAGUU)
n.

baa hagasalau.
Make contact with while not aligned.

baa huu i --.
Just like.

baa i de madangi.
Be hit (usually forcefully) by wind.

baa iho.
Low (in altitude).

baa lahalaha.
Broad-chested.

$baalanga_1$. (B-1 BALA)
n.

$baalanga_2$. (B-- BAALANGA)
Metal (any kind) [from Trade Malay?]. *n.*

baalanga dua hale.
Metal roofing.

baalanga tea.
Stainless steel.

baalanga tugi.
Nail (of metal).

baalanga mmea.
Copper or brass or other reddish metal.

baalanga sauaa.
Magnet.

baalanga uli.
Cast iron.

baalasa.
Ballast for an outrigger [from Eng. 'ballast'?]. *v.*

baalasaanga. (B-1 BAALASA)
n.

baalasi.
Press down or against; sit on (as chicken hatching eggs). *v.*

baalasi ange.
Compete hard against (as in team sports).

baalasi de ada.
To take a picture.

baalasi mai (adu).
Shine a flashlight toward me (you).

baalasinga. (B-1 BAALASI)
n.

baalasi ngago.
Incubation of eggs (by a hen).

baalasi saele.
Shine a flashlight indiscriminately on people.

baalau.
Sticky, greasy. *a.*

baalaunga. (B-1 BAALAU)
n.

baalea. (B-2 $BALE_2$)
v.

$baalenga_1$. (B-1 $BALE_1$)
n.

$baalenga_2$. (B-1 $BALE_2$)
n.

baalunga. (B-1 $BALU_1$)
n.

baanab.
Stone (from Banaba [Ocean Is.]) used for trolling lure. *n.*

baani.
Lie down. *a.*

baaninga. (B-1 BAANI)
n.

baanginga. (B-1 $BANGI_1$)
n.

baangoa. (P-- BANGOA)
a.

baangoaanga. (P-1 BANGOA)
n.

baa sala.
Be clumsy (in physical contest).

baasanga. (B-1 $BASA_1$)
Manner of speaking, idiolect, dialect. *n.*

baasanga tugi ange muna.
Talk back.

baa sege.
Carom off.

baasi.
Side, half. *nl.*

baasi e haa o de langi.
The four quadrants of the sky.

baasi gi taiao.
Forenoon (from dawn to noon).

baasi lua.
Having two useful sides.

baasi madau.
Right side, right-handed.

baasi masui.
Left side, left-handed.

baa ssalu.
Carom off violently.

baasua.
Mollusk sp.: *Tridacna maxima.* *n.*

baaua.
Fish sp.: rabbitfish. *n.*

$baba_1$. (B-- BAA_4)
Level (not bumpy); (any sort of) flat base (esp. the board on which mats are plaited), the consolidated reef under water or sand; the back of a human; the shell of a turtle, crab, etc.; to be ready. *a.*

$baba_2$. (B-- BAA_4)
Fish sp.: squirrelfish. *n.*

babaa. (T-- BAA_2)
A cracking sound, the sound of continuous explosions. *a.*

baba age.
Be decided about.

baba ange.
Ready for.

baba donu.
Properly settled.

babaiangi.
A type of cloud formation (dark but not threatening rain). *v.*

babaiangi ina.
Cloudy, with clouds of the *babaiangi* type.

baba iho.
Recently settled.

babalia. (B-2 BAA_4)
a.

baba odi.
To have been settled for some time.

babu.
The noise of one hard object struck against another (as the snapping of fingers). *a.*

babu-daaea.
Fish sp.: snapper (= small *daea*).

babu-honga-agau.
Fish sp.: wrasse (2 sorts: 1 white, 1 red).

babulia. (B-2 BABU)
v.

bapaba. (R-- BAA_4)
Flutter against (as a hooked fish). *a.*

bapabaanga. (R-1 BAA_4)
n.

bapabu. (R-- BABU)
The staccato sound of one hard object being struck against another. *a.*

bapabuanga. (R-1 BABU)
n.

badabaatai. (U-- BADAI)
[Pl. form of *badabadai*]. *a.*

badabaataianga. (U-- BADAI)
[The nominal form of *badabaatai*]. *n.*

badabadai. (R-- BADAI)
Having a tendency to meddle in others' affairs. *a.*

badabadaianga. (R-1 BADAI)
n.

badai.
Meddle in others' affairs. *a.*

badaianga. (B-1 BADAI)
n.

badai gee.
Extremely meddlesome.

badii.
Fish sp.: scad? *n.*

badioda.
The residue remaining after coconut oil has been heated; the residue remaining after arrowroot starch-making. *v.*

badiodaanga. (B-1 BADIODA)
n.

badodi. (B-- $DODI_a$)
To jerk to a stop (as at the end of a tether); stumble, trip (fall). *v.*

badodia. (B-2 $DODI_a$)
v.

badodi gee.
To jerk violently.

badodinga. (B-1 $DODI_a$)
n.

badotodi. (R-- $DODI_a$)
Move jerkily. *v.*

badotodianga. (R-1 $DODI_a$)
n.

badu.
Hit or tap with the hand or foot; kick. *v.*

badua. (B-2 BADU)
v.

badubadu. (R-- BADU)
v.

badubadunga. (R-1 BADU)
n.

badulia. (B-2 BADU)
v.

bae.
An arrangement of rocks to make a retaining wall or pier, etc.; push aside (in all directions). *v.*

baea. (B-2 BAE)
v.

baeao.
Husk of the mature coconut. *n.*

baebae. (R-- BAE)
—; a row of stones. *v.*

baebaea. (R-2 BAE)
v.

baebaenga. (R-1 BAE)
n.

baelia. (B-2 BAE)
v.

bae mamu.
Fish weir.

baenga. (B-1 BAE)
n.

bagekege.
Move jerkily (as when stumbling). *v.*

bagekegeanga. (B-1 BAGEKEGE)
n.

bagekegelia. (B-2 BAGEKEGE)
v.

bagi.
Gun or any weapon of similar nature. *n.*

bagia. (B-2 BAGI)
Be hit (by wind, bullet, spear, etc.). *v.*

bagiaanga. (B-3 BAGI)
n.

bagibagi. (R-- BAGI)
[Occurs only in phrases]. *n.*

bagibagia. (R-2 BAGI)
v.

bagibagiaanga. (R-1 BAGI)
n.

bagibagi de me.
All of a sudden (violent actions).

bagi mada lagolago.
Machine gun.

bagobago. (R-- BAGO)
a.

bagu.
Scab, crust. *n.*

bagua.
Plant sp.: tree sp.: pandan tree (*Pandanus dubius* Spreng.). *n.*

baguu.
Fall over (as a felled tree); tip over; lean (in one direction). *a.*

baguu de laa.
Past noon.

baguunga. (B-1 BAGUU)
n.

bakau.
Shoulder (the whole joint), wing. *n.*

bakau dahi de manu.
Not to go fishing when other groups are going.

bakau doo.
A dislocation of the shoulder joint.

bahhaa.
To make a sound, like that of a turtle gasping for breath; the sound of air exhaled suddenly. *a.*

bahhaanga. (B-1 BAHHAA)
n.

baieu.
Mollusk sp.: clam sp. *n.*

bala.
Soft, mushy, offering no resistance. *a.*

balaagula. (P-- BALAGULA)
a.

balaagulaanga. (P-1 BALAGULA)
n.

balaavini. (P-- BALAVINI)
a.

balabala. (R-- BALA)
Very soft or weak (of things only). *a.*

balabalagula. (R-- BALAGULA)
Habitually clumsy. *a.*

balabalagulaanga.
(R-1 BALAGULA) *n.*

balabalasi. (R-- BAALASI)
v.

balabalasia. (R-2 BAALASI)
v.

balabalasinga. (R-1 BAALASI)
n.

balabalavini. (R-- BALAVINI)
Clumsy by nature; awkward by nature. *a.*

balapigi. (BALA, $BIGI_1$)
Drenched. *v.*

balagelage.
Crippled and unable to walk. *a.*

balagelageanga.
(B-1 BALAGELAGE) *n.*

balagelage gee.
Severely crippled.

balagia.
Fish sp.

balagia-a-de-gaga.
Fish sp.: parrot fish.

balaginagina. (B-- $BALA_a$)
Be squashed. *a.*

balagula.
Clumsy. *a.*

balagulaanga. (B-1 BALAGULA)
n.

bala i de --.
Covered with — (of skin only).

balala.
The sound of sucking liquid; the sound of coitus. *v.*

balalaanga. (B-1 BALALA)
n.

bala langi.
Rain.

balangi.
Fish sp.: tang. *n.*

balasia. (B-2 BAALASI)
—; be crushed. *v.*

balaulau.
Ugly-looking, messy, sloppy. *a.*

balaulaunga. (B-1 BALAULAU)
n.

balavini.
Clumsy, awkward (e.g., in carriage). *a.*

$bale_1$.
Help, assist, aid (with effort or advice, etc.). *v.*

$bale_2$.
Steer (e.g., a canoe). *v.*

balea. (B-2 $BALE_1$)
v.

baleao.
Fish sp.: milkfish. *n.*

$balebale_1$. (R-- $BALE_1$)
v.

$balebale_2$. (R-- $BALE_2$)
v.

$balebalea_1$. (R-2 $BALE_1$)
v.

$balebalea_2$. (R-2 $BALE_2$)
v.

$balebalenga_1$. (R-1 $BALE_1$)
n.

balebalenga$_2$. (R-1 BALE$_2$)
n.

baledilo.
The stage of plant growth at which immature leaves appear. *v.*

bale-masevaseva.
[Var. of *bani-magevageva*].

bali.
Immature coconut palm leaves. *n.*

balia.
Master navigator (having also the ability to forecast the weather). *a.*

baliaanga. (B-1 BALIA)
n.

balu$_1$.
To bring one's hands and arms (or wings) down or back once (as in waving, swimming, or the flapping of a bird's wings). *v.*

balu$_2$.
Fish sp. *n.*

balua. (B-2 BALU$_1$)
v.

balubalu. (R-- BALU$_1$)
v.

balubalunga. (R-1 BALU$_1$)
n.

balu-daaea.
Fish sp.

balu gauanga.
Trembling of legs.

balu-malau.
Fish sp.

balu moso.
Constant movement of the hands and feet, as when struggling (resembling the movements of a young starling).

baluu.
Coconut crab. *n.*

balu-udu.
Fish sp.: snapper.

bane.
The flat top of the shark's snout. *n.*

bani. (CF BAANI)

banibani. (R-- BANI)
Sea cucumber (many spp.). *n.*

bani-gegeva.
[Var. of *bani-magevageva*].

bani-magevageva.
Fish sp. (rare).

banuunu.
A type of basket. *n.*

bangabanga$_1$. (R-- BANGA$_1$)
Skinny, shrunken. *a.*

bangabanga$_2$. (R-- BANGA$_2$)
Fish sp. *n.*

bangabanga mai.
Become skinny, become shrunken.

bangadala. (CF BANGA$_2$)
Fish sp.: sea bass. *n.*

banganga.
Fish sp.: wrasse. *n.*

bangi$_1$.
Pinch (with the fingers). *v.*

bangi$_2$.
A type of prepared food (made from dried breadfruit). *n.*

bangia. (B-2 BANGI$_1$)
v.

bangibangi. (R-- BANGI$_1$)
v.

bangibangia. (R-2 BANGI$_1$)
v.

bangibanginga. (R-1 BANGI$_1$)
n.

bangi dua beau.
A certain way of pinching with the fingers.

bangi mada aasanga.
A certain way of pinching with the fingers.

bangoa.
Slow down, be exhausted (physically), feel unenergetic. *a.*

bangoaanga. (B-1 BANGOA)
n.

bangobangoa. (R-- BANGOA)
—; unenergetic. *a.*

bangobangoaanga. (R-1 BANGOA)
n.

bangongo.
Fish sp.: rabbitfish. *n.*

bangulu.
A part of the traditional loom. *n.*

bao.
Room, compartment. *n.*

baoa.
Wash up on shore. *v.*

baoa age.
Wash up on shore and beach thereon.

baoanga. (B-1 BAOA)
n.

basa₁.
Speak, talk, say. *v.*

basa₂ --. (B-- BASA₂)
Very many —. *d.*

basaa. (B-2 BASA₁)
Be talked into. *v.*

basa ange.
Answer, reply.

basabasa. (R-- BASA₁)
—; saying. *v.*

basabasaanga. (R-1 BASA₁)
n.

basabasalia₁. (R-2 BASA₁)
Be talked about frequently. *v.*

basabasalia₂. (R-- BASALIA)
v.

basabasalaanga. (R-1 BASALIA)
n.

basa baubau.
Speak badly of someone.

basa pada.
Speak harshly.

basa dau donu.
Speak moderately.

basa degidegi.
Speak disconnectedly with rage.

basa dua nnui.
Speak undiplomatically.

basa too gee.
Speak ungrammatically.

basa gauligi.
To imitate a child's manner of talking; baby talk.

basa gee.
Speak (or express oneself) strangely.

basa gelo.
Speak sagely.

basa gi lunga.
Speak loudly.

basa hagaeaea.
Stutter.

basa hagamalaia.
To curse (someone).

basa hagamao lalo.
Speak humbly.

basa hagamao lunga.
Speak arrogantly.

basa hagasengasenga.
Speak in riddles or aphoristically or in parables.

basa hagassee.
Speak so as to change the impression one's previous words have made.

basalia₁. (B-2 BASA₁)
Be talked about (one person or thing only). *v.*

basalia₂. (BASALIA, SALI)
Seep (of water). *v.*

basaliaanga. (B-1 BASALIA)
n.

basa lilo.
Speak indirectly (so that the meaning is vague).

basa maalie.
Speak moderately.

basa madua.
Speak as an elder (treating the hearer as a child).

basa senga.
Speak senselessly.

basa soe.
Say what is on one's mind; speak directly (so that one's meaning is clear).

bau. (B-- BAU₁)
To be worth it. *a.*

baua. (B-2 BAU₁)
Figure out, determine. *v.*

bauanga. (B-1 BAU₁)
Worth, value. *n.*

bau ange.
Capable of, be the equal of.

baubau₁. (R-- BAU₁)
Be capable at. *a.*

baubau₂. (R-- BAU₂)
Bad. *a.*

bau iho.
Capable only of looking after oneself (not others).

baulia. (B-2 BAU₁)
Figure out, determine. *v.*

baunga. (B-1 BAU₁)
Worth, value. *n.*

be.
Or, either. *mi.*

be...be.
Either...or.

beabeau. (R-- BEAU)
Choppy seas. *v.*

beabeaua. (R-2 BEAU)
v.

beabeaunga. (R-1 BEAU)
n.

beaha. (AHA₁, BE)
To be in a serious condition, critically ill or injured. *a.*

be aha naa huu.
Whatever; if ever.

beau.
A wave, the surf. *v.*

bebe₁.
Nervous, anxious (for reasons not connected with other people). *v.*

bebe₂.
Butterfly. *n.*

bebea. (B-2 BEBE₁)
Be very nervous, be very anxious. *v.*

bebeanga. (B-1 BEBE₁)
n.

bebe de lodo.
Anxiety state (psychological condition).

bebee. (T-- BEE)
Be flatulent. *a.*

bebeeanga. (T-1 BEE)
n.

bebela.
Prowler. *n.*

bebelia. (B-2 BEBE₁)
Be very nervous, be very anxious. *v.*

bedage.
Shallow (bowl, basket, etc.). *v.*

bedageanga. (B-1 BEDAGE)
n.

bedage ina.
Shallow on the inside.

bedi.
Fat (of, e.g., a person); plump (tending toward fat). *a.*

bedianga. (B-1 BEDI)
n.

bedibedi. (R-- BEDI)
Getting fat. *a.*

bedibedianga. (R-1 BEDI)
n.

bee.
Flatus, the sound of flatulence. *n.*

bega.
A sound indicating surprise. *i.*

be goai (naa huu).
Whoever.

behee.
Like what?

be hia.
How many (according to someone)?

bei.
Be like, be the same as. *a.*

beibei. (R-- BEI)
More-or-less alike. *a.*

bei tagodo.
For instance, for example; just like —.

bela.
Plot of taro bog, boggy soil. *n.*

belabela. (R-- BELA)
Dirty (like *bela*). *v.*

belabelaanga. (R-1 BELA)
n.

belu.
Lizard sp. *n.*

belubelu. (R-- BELU)
Fish sp.: scad? *n.*

be ne.
If there might be —.

benu.
A pandanus plug after it has been chewed; seed of the pandanus. *n.*

bese.
One of the harmony parts in old chants. *n.*

bibi. (B-- BIBI$_1$)
Mollusk sp.: *Cyclotinella remies*, also *Tellinidae* spp. *n.*

bibi-gabugabu-tai.
Mollusk sp.: a bivalve.

bibi-maadau.
Mollusk sp.: *Arcophagia scobinata.*

bido.
End (extremity); bit (of something); to complete an act later [p]. *nl.*

bidoa. (B-2 BIDO)
Lift or hold one end of something. *v.*

bido abongi.
Capsize eventually.

bidobido. (R-- BIDO)
Useless pieces. *d.*

bido dagi.
Follow in order to spy on.

bido gamu.
Uselessly short.

bie.
Plant sp.: Polynesian arrowroot (*Tacca leontopetaloides* (L.) O.K.). *n.*

bige.
A strip of land extending into the sea or a swamp. *n.*

bigi$_1$.
Be caught between two or more other things. *a.*

bigi$_2$.
Close to (in meaning); about to (in time). *a.*

bigi ange.
Just about like —.

bigibigi$_1$. (R-- BIGI$_1$)
—; gum (to chew), sap (of trees). *v.*

bigibigi$_2$. (R-- BIGI$_2$)
More-or-less close to. *a.*

bigibigia. (R-2 BIGI$_1$)
Covered with something sticky. *v.*

bigibiginga. (R-1 BIGI$_1$)
n.

bigi lima.
Hold hands.

biginga. (B-1 BIGI$_1$)
n.

bigo.
Bent; bedridden with illness. *a.*

bigobigo. (R-- BIGO)
Bent up (having several bends). *a.*

bigobigonga. (R-1 BIGO)
n.

biho.
Head; body of a trolling lure. *n.*

biho ngaalulu.
Headache.

biho o de agoago.
Topic of a sermon.

bii.
Semen, ejaculate. *a.*

biia. (B-2 BII)
Get wet. *v.*

biianga. (B-1 BII)
n.

biibii. (R-- BII)
Ejaculate repeatedly. *a.*

biibiianga. (R-1 BII)
n.

biigia. (E-2 BIGI$_1$)
Be stuck to completely. *v.*

biiginga. (E-1 BIGI$_1$)
n.

biigonga. (B-1 BIGO)
A curve, way of being bent. *n.*

biihingi.
Having flat buttocks, ugly (because not plump). *v.*

biininga. (B-1 BINI)
n.

bii o madahasi.
A certain kind of phosphorescence in seawater at night.

bili. (B-- BILI$_1$)
Be caught or hung up on something so as unable to fall (as a felled tree). *a.*

bilibili. (R-- BILI$_1$)
Having a tendency to be *bili.* *v.*

bilibili-hadu. (BILI$_1$, HADU$_2$)
Fish sp. (*Trachinotus bailloni*). *n.*

bili i de lodo.
Unforgotten.

bili makaga.
Love.

binaaina.
Cowardly (owing to weak-mindedness); afraid to assert oneself; not live up to one's obligations. *a.*

binabinaaina. (R-- BINAAINA)
a.

bini.
Braid (rope or hair, etc.), wrap with rope. *v.*

binia. (B-2 BINI)
v.

binibini. (R-- BINI)
v.

binibinia. (R-2 BINI)
v.

binibininga. (R-1 BINI)
n.

bini dali gadaha.
A method of braiding *dali* into string to make a bird snare; six-ply braiding (of rope).

bini daubemala.
A method of making flower headdresses.

bini gaahanga.
Three-ply braiding (of rope).

binga.
Be named, be called; regarded as. *a.*

bingabinga. (R-- BINGA)
The repeated use of a term or name in conversation. *a.*

bingibingi. (R-- BINGI)
Plant sp.: tree sp.: Hernandia tree (*Hernandia sonora* L.). *n.*

boa.
Record catch (of fish) by an individual during his lifetime on any one fishing expedition. *n.*

boaa.
Be caught in a storm. *v.*

boaa ina.
Be caught in strong wind or heavy rain.

boaa ina mai.
Prevented from coming by being caught in a storm.

boaanga$_1$. (B-1 BOO$_1$)
A period (of time) during which many people require massage (for fractures). *n.*

boaanga$_2$. (B-1 BOAA)
n.

bobo.
Rotten. *a.*

boboanga. (B-1 BOBO)
n.

bopobo. (R-- BOBO)
Deteriorated. *a.*

bopoboanga. (R-1 BOBO)
n.

boda.
Straggly (hair or feathers). *v.*

bodaanga. (B-1 BODA)
n.

bodobodo. (R-- BODO)
Short [sing.]. *a.*

bodobodoanga. (R-1 BODO)
n.

bodu. (B-- BODU$_1$)
Spouse. *n.*

bodubodu. (R-- BODU$_2$)
Particles of rotting wood or thatch, etc. *v.*

boduboduanga. (R-1 BODU$_2$)
n.

bodubodu-o-uda.
Insect sp.

bogi.
To plant taro slips. *v.*

bogia. (B-2 BOGI)
v.

bogibogi. (R-- BOGI)
v.

bogibogia. (R-2 BOGI)
v.

bogiboginga. (R-1 BOGI)
n.

bogo. (B-- BOGO$_1$)
Take something, steal something. *v.*

bogoa. (B-2 BOGO$_1$)
v.

bogoanga. (B-1 BOGO$_1$)
n.

bogobogo$_1$. (R-- BOGO$_1$)
v.

bogobogo$_2$. (R-- BOGO$_2$)
Pushed out of shape (as a tin can), rumpled, crumpled. *v.*

bogobogoa. (R-2 BOGO$_1$)
v.

bogobogoanga$_1$. (R-1 BOGO$_1$)
n.

bogobogoanga$_2$. (R-1 BOGO$_2$)
n.

bogobogolia. (R-2 BOGO$_1$)
v.

bogolia. (B-2 BOGO$_1$)
v.

boi.
Abnormal [sing.]. *a.*

boi a eidu.
Temporarily abnormal.

boialiali. (ALI, BOO$_2$)
The light just before daybreak. *n.*

boibala. (BALA, BOI, BOO$_{1a}$, I)
Watery (of prepared food). *a.*

boiboi. (R-- BOI)
Repeatedly displaying signs of abnormality; dizzy. *a.*

boiboinga. (R-1 BOI)
n.

boi dugidugi.
Idiot.

boi gadagada.
Laugh all the time at nothing.

boi malangilangi.
Laugh abnormally.

boinga. (B-1 BOI)
n.

bole.
Bawl out, be angry; be mad (as indicated by one's movements). *a.*

bolebole. (R-- BOLE)
Trembling [sing.]; shaking [sing.]; inclined to bawl out. *a.*

bolebolenga. (R-1 BOLE)
n.

bole gi de gai.
Eat ravenously.

bolengia. (B-2 BOLE)
Do something without reflection. *v.*

boli.
Take special care of. *v.*

bolia. (B-2 BOLI)
v.

boliboli. (R-- BOLI)
v.

bolibolinga. (R-1 BOLI)
n.

bolili*. (XCO LILI$_{1a}$)
A type of prepared food [small taro, prepared for the cult priests]. *n.*

bolo$_1$.
According to —. *mi.*

bolo$_2$.
Make a will (for oneself or others). *v.*

boloa. (B-2 BOLO$_2$)
v.

bolo ange.
Bequeath.

bolobolo$_1$. (B-- BOLOBOLO)
A type of basket. *n.*

bolobolo$_2$. (R-- BOLO$_2$)
v.

boloboloa. (R-2 BOLO$_2$)
v.

bolobolo a Sogo.
A type of basket.

bolobolonga. (R-1 BOLO$_2$)
n.

bolo iho.
To make oneself the beneficiary of a will which one has made for another.

bona.
A knot tied at the end of a rope or a string to prevent its unravelling. *n.*

bonaa ua.
The sheath of the turtle's neck.

bonabona. (R-- BONA)
Fear (as perceived somatically); having many *bona*. *a.*

bonabona age.
Become fearful.

bonabona age lodo.
Feel fearful.

bonabonaanga. (R-1 BONA)
n.

bono.
To close (something); to mend (clothes); to cover something (e.g., a pot); to block (the way). *d.*

bono aasanga.
A method of fishing (by blocking the channel at high tide).

bonobono. (R-- BONO)
v.

bonobonodia. (R-2 BONO)
v.

bonobononga. (R-1 BONO)
n.

bonodia. (B-2 BONO)
v.

bonga.
Bent, curved, defective (of fruit). *a.*

bongaa --. (B-- $BONGA_a$)
That which is hollow. *d.*

bongaa hala.
Any long and hollow object (e.g., a pipe or a hose).

bongaa manu.
Large, exposed roots (e.g., of the breadfruit tree).

bongaa usu.
Nostril.

bongabonga. (R-- BONGA)
Bent up. *a.*

boo_1.
Grab (with one's hand); hold (in one's hand); capture. *d.*

boo_2.
Night; birthday. *a.*

boo_3.
A type of sound, indicating surprise. *a.*

boo adu laa.
Day after tomorrow at night.

boo aleduu.
Tomorrow night.

$booanga_1$. (B-1 BOO_1)
n.

$booanga_2$. (B-1 BOO_3)
n.

boobodo. (T-- BODO)
Occurring at short intervals. *a.*

boobodoanga. (T-1 BODO)
n.

$booboo_1$. (R-- BOO_1)
a.

$booboo_2$. (R-- BOO_{1a})
A type of prepared food (made from taro or breadfruit). *n.*

boobooanga. (R-1 BOO_1)
n.

booboogia. (R-2 BOO_1)
v.

booboo me.
Massage (as a medical treatment).

boobosu. (T-- BOSU)
[Pl. of *bosu*]. *a.*

boobua.
Insect sp.; dragonfly. *n.*

boo dabeo.
A night which is rainy and stormy.

boo danuaa.
Good night! Good evening!

boo dolu de gulu.
The third day after breadfruit has been picked (after which it is not good to eat).

boo taiao.
Early morning.

boo ga dae laa.
My goodness!

boogia. (B-2 BOO_1)
v.

boogia mai.
Be caught doing something wrong.

boo gi dai.
The period when the quarter moon appears in the west just after sunset.

boo gi de gai.
Continually wanting to eat.

boo gi dua.
The period when the quarter moon appears in the east just before sunrise.

boo gi me.
Acquisitive (and acting on acquisitive impulses).

booginga. (B-1 BOGI)
n.

boo hagadanu małama.
The nights on which the quarter moon is obscured by rain.

boo hagalele mouli.
A night on which the making of noise is permitted (i.e., on certain holidays).

booi. (B-- BOO_{1a})
A type of prepared food (made from mashed taro and coconut juice). *n.*

booiaa (!). (B-- BOI_a)
Do something shameful (for shame!). *a.*

boo iho.
The following night.

boo i lalo o tangada.
The last days of a person's life.

boolaa. (XCO BOO_3)
A type of sound, indicating surprise. *a.*

boolaa ange.
Say *boolaa* to.

boolenga. (B-1 BOLE)
n.

boolinga. (B-1 BOLI)
n.

boolleiee. (XCO BOO_3)
A type of sound, made to frighten someone. *a.*

boolonga. (B-1 $BOLO_2$)
Testament. *n.*

boo mai ange laa.
The second night following.

boo manu.
To weed (a garden).

boonei.
Fish sp.? : damselfish? *n.*

boononga. (B-1 BONO)
n.

boongia. (B-2 BOO_2)
Be caught by darkness unexpectedly. *v.*

boo seniseni.
A type of children's game (played in the water, like tag).

bosu.
Be satiated with food [sing.]. *a.*

bosuanga. (B-1 BOSU)
n.

bou.
Mast (of a canoe). *n.*

bouli.
Darkness (of or pertaining to). *a.*

boulianga. (B-1 BOULI)
n.

bouli gee.
An alternative mode of existence (such as the world of ghosts).

bua.
Plant sp.: tree sp. (*Guettarda speciosa* L.). *n.*

buaalali.
Flood tide. *v.*

buaalalianga. (B-1 BUAALALI)
n.

buada.
Sling. *v.*

buadaanga. (B-1 BUADA)
n.

buadalia. (B-2 BUADA)
Cast with a sling. *v.*

bualeu. (BUA_a, LEU)
Ovaries and fallopian tubes. *n.*

bua moe.
Immature girl.

bubu.
Move about. *a.*

bubuanga. (B-1 BUBU)
n.

bubu donu.
Move skillfully.

bubu sala.
Move unskillfully.

bupubu. (R-- BUBU)
Make a lot of noise (not vocal). *a.*

bupubuanga. (R-1 BUBU)
n.

budu.
The appearance of many fish (or birds, or animals which are good to eat) after a death. *n.*

budubudu. (R-- BUDU)
Crowded together. *a.*

budubudunga. (R-1 BUDU)
n.

buga.
Plant sp.: tree sp. (*Pisonia grandis* R.B.). *n.*

bugaliaa.
Plant sp.: tree sp.: Indian mulberry tree (*Morinda citrifolia* L.).

buge.
A bump on a tree trunk. *n.*

bugolo.
Coral sp.: faviid coral. *n.*

bugu.
Mons veneris. *n.*

bugubugu. (R-- BUGU)
Swollen [sing.]. *a.*

bugubugunga. (R-1 BUGU)
The slope of a swelling or protuberance. *n.*

buibui. (R-- BUI)
Keep in (e.g., pigs); keep out (e.g., wind); soak (in water). *v.*

buibuia. (R-2 BUI)
v.

buibuinga. (R-1 BUI)
n.

bula.
A flash (e.g., of light); a quick glance; to light (a torch). *a.*

bulaanga. (B-1 BULA)
n.

bulabula. (R-- BULA)
Testicles; look here and there; to have a lot of spots; twinkling (of many stars or phosphorescent insects, etc.). *a.*

bulabulaanga. (R-1 BULA)
n.

bulada.
Banana tree fibers (for making cloth). *n.*

bula de ganomada.
Get mad.

bulaga*.
Plant sp.: swamp taro (*Cyrtosperma chamissonis*). *n.*

bulaga-a-leo. (CF BULAGA)
Fish sp.: tang. *n.*

bule.
Vertebra; mollusk sp.: cowry shell (many spp.). *n.*

bule dango.
Button.

buli.
Grab up. *v.*

buliaamou.
Long for, homesick. *a.*

buliaamounga. (B-1 BULIAAMOU)
n.

bulibuli. (R-- BULI)
Grab up one thing after another. *v.*

bulibulia. (R-2 BULI)
v.

bulibuliaamou. (R-- BULIAAMOU)
Prone to long for. *a.*

bulibuliaamounga.
(B-1 BULIAAMOU) *n.*

bulibulinga. (R-1 BULI)
n.

bulobulou. (R-- BUULOU)
To net flying fish. *v.*

bulobuloua. (R-2 BUULOU)
v.

bulobulounga. (R-1 BUULOU)
n.

bulu.
The short fibers of the mature coconut husk. *n.*

bulubulu. (R-- BULU)
Useless (things or matters). *d.*

bulubulu dangada.
Unimportant person.

bulubuludi. (R-- BUULUDI)
Keep hugging. *v.*

bulubuludia. (R-2 BUULUDI)
v.

bulubuludinga. (R-1 BUULUDI)
n.

bulubulu hegau.
Unimportant work.

bulubulu maanadu.
Incomplete idea.

bulubulu malo.
Rag.

buludia. (B-2 BUULUDI)
v.

bulu giidagi.
A type of caulking compound, made from *bulu* and sap.

bunaa.
The trail left behind a canoe paddle in the water (or a similar disturbance of the water). *n.*

bunaa hoe.
An eddy left by a paddle stroke.

bunana.
Conjunctivitis. *a.*

bunehulu.
Slow in running or walking. *a.*

bunehuluanga. (B-1 BUNEHULU)
n.

bunei.
Fish sp.: batfish? *n.*

buni.
Closed up, be together (in a group, or of two individuals). *a.*

buni ange.
Agree with; join, close up (something,e.g., a hole); close up to.

buni ange gi de gelegele.
To have been dead for a long time.

buni ange lodo.
Paralyzed by fear; acute anxiety attack.

bunibuni. (R-- BUNI)
Be more-or-less together. *a.*

buni de ua.
To be very thirsty.

buni lunga ma lalo.
A pitch black night.

bunua.
A young bird (of any sp. suitable for being raised as a pet). *n.*

bungaadogi. (P-- BUNGADOGI)
a.

bungaadogianga.
(P-1 BUNGADOGI) *n.*

bungaaleu. (P-- BUNGALEU)
a.

bungaaleunga. (P-1 BUNGALEU)
n.

bungabungadogi.
(R-- BUNGADOGI) *a.*

bungabungadogianga.
(R-1 BUNGADOGI) *n.*

bungadogi.
Unskillful (at difficult activities). *a.*

bungadogianga. (B-1 BUNGADOGI)
n.

bungaleu.
Unskillful (at difficult activities). *a.*

bungaleunga. (B-1 BUNGALEU)
n.

bungubungu. (R-- BUNGU)
Plump [sing.]. *a.*

bungubunguanga. (R-1 BUNGU)
n.

busi.
Blow (with the mouth). *v.*

busia. (B-2 BUSI)
v.

busibusi. (R-- BUSI)
v.

busibusia. (R-2 BUSI)
v.

busibusinga. (R-1 BUSI)
n.

buu$_1$.
Bladder, balloon, ball; the head of the octopus; a net on a long handle; a conch shell trumpet; or any other round, hollow, inflatable object. *n.*

buu$_2$. (B-- BUU$_4$)
Come out from (like smoke or pus); be forced out of. *a.*

buu$_3$.
Be greasy. *a.*

buuanga$_1$. (B-1 BUU$_3$)
n.

buuanga$_2$. (B-1 BUU$_4$)
n.

buubudu. (T-- BUDU)
Crowded together closely. *a.*

buubudunga. (T-1 BUDU)
n.

buubuu$_1$. (R-- BUU$_2$)
Divination. *v.*

buubuu$_2$. (R-- BUU$_3$)
a.

buubuu$_3$. (R-- BUU$_4$)
a.

buubuua. (R-2 BUU$_2$)
To divine (for omens). *v.*

buubuu a lada.
A type of puzzle.

buubuuanga. (R-1 BUU$_2$)
n.

buubuulia. (R-2 BUU$_2$)
To divine (for omens). *v.*

buubuunga. (R-1 BUU$_2$)
n.

buubuusagi. (R-- BUUSAGI)
v.

buubuusaginga. (R-1 BUUSAGI)
n.

buu de mama.
Air filled with *mama.*

buudunga. (B-1 BUDU)
Pile of, group of. *n.*

buu tangada.
An omen of death (when a certain kind or size of fish is caught).

buugani.
Be (in fact) slow-moving (while attempting to hurry). *a.*

buuganianga. (B-1 BUUGANI)
n.

buuganga*.
A trip for a festive or recreational purpose. *n.*

buu goede.
Worthless or useless ['like an octopus without a head'].

buugunga. (B-1 BUGU)
Conformation of a *bugu.* *n.*

buu-kangi-de-muli.
Mollusk sp.: *Cymatiidae* spp., also *Bursa bubo.*

buu hale moni.
Mollusk sp.

buuia. (B-2 BUU$_4$)
Be struck with something shot out from something else. *v.*

buu-ili.
Fish sp.

buulei.
Ring (for a finger). *a.*

buulia. (B-2 BULI)
v.

buulinga. (B-1 BULI)
n.

buulou.
Cover up (by wrapping up with one layer); to catch by scooping up (e.g., with a net or basket). *v.*

buuloua. (B-2 BUULOU)
v.

buulounga. (B-1 BUULOU)
n.

buuludi.
Hug. *v.*

buuludinga. (B-1 BUULUDI)
n.

buuninga. (B-1 BUNI)
n.

buusagi.
An eddy caused by a current. *v.*

buusaginga. (B-1 BUUSAGI)
n.

buusagisagi. (S-- BUUSAGI)
To be laden with scent (of air). *a.*

buusinga. (B-1 BUSI)
n.

buu unga.
An empty seashell; one of (a pair of) diving goggles.

buu useahi.
Blurred.

paa$_1$. (P-- BAA$_1$)
a.

paa$_2$. (P-- BAA$_2$)
Explode, burst. *a.*

paa age.
Explode from below.

paa de hatuli.
Rolling of thunder.

paa de hoa.
Happy (lit., 'to slap one's sides').

paa de mahedua.
Sneeze loudly.

paa i daalinga.
Move in closely (of birds) to *daalinga.*

paa i tua tinae.
Have an empty stomach.

paa iho.
Explode from above.

paalanga. (P-1 BALA)
n.

paa ono pagola.
Punished for his bad deeds.

paa ono maahana.
Receive one's punishment, suffer.

paba. (P-- BAA$_4$)
a.

pada.
Be coarse in texture, grain, weave, etc. *a.*

padaanga. (B-1 PADA)
n.

pagi. (E-- BAGI)
[Occurs only in phrases]. *d.*

pago. (E-- BAGO)
The sound of any sudden violent contact; the sound of an explosion. *a.*

pagola. (E-- BAGOLA)
Bad luck; punishment. *n.*

pagolia. (E-2 BAGO)
v.

pai.
A type of cloud formation like *babaiangi.* *v.*

pala. (P-- BALA)
a.

pala boo maasina.
The time of the month when rain is most likely to occur (1st quarter).

pala de langi.
It's raining!

pala ivi.
Work beyond one's endurance.

pale. (P-- BALE$_2$)
v.

pale age (iho).
Steer toward (away from) land.

palo. (E-- BALO)
A watery area extending into a land area (e.g., a bay). *n.*

panava.
Scrotum (one side only). *n.*

panga. (P-- BANGA$_1$)
[Pl. form of *bangabanga*]. *a.*

pasa. (P-- BASA$_1$)
v.

pasalia. (P-2 BASA$_1$)
Be talked about (many persons or things). *v.*

pau. (P-- BAU$_1$)
a.

pedi. (P-- BEDI)
a.

pedianga. (P-1 BEDI)
n.

pee. (E-- BEE)
Pass wind (flatus). *a.*

peeanga. (E-1 BEE)
n.

pena. (E-- BENA)
Take precautions. *v.*

penaanga. (E-1 BENA)
n.

pigi. (E-- BIGI$_1$)
Be stuck. *a.*

pigo. (P-- BIGO)
a.

pii. (E-- BII)
Splashed, sprinkled. *a.*

piianga. (E-1 BII)
n.

piigonga. (P-1 BIGO)
n.

pili$_1$. (P-- BILI$_1$)
a.

pili$_2$. (E-- BILI$_2$)
Be bored. *a.*

pilo. (E-- BILO)
Stink. *a.*

pilo bopobo.
Musty smell.

pobo. (P-- BOBO)
a.

poboanga. (P-1 BOBO)
n.

poda. (P-- BODA)
v.

podo. (P-- BODO)
a.

podoanga. (P-1 BODO)
n.

pogo. (E-- BOGO$_2$)
Crumpled up. *v.*

pogoanga. (E-1 BOGO$_2$)
n.

poi. (P-- BOI)
a.

poinga. (P-1 BOI)
n.

pole. (P-- BOLE)
—; shaking [pl.]; trembling [pl.]. *a.*

pono. (E-- BONO)
—; a cover (which closes) ; to block (the way) [as a single act]. *v.*

pono age de manava.
Be unable to breathe.

Pono-haanau. (BONO, HAANAU)
The name of a spirit. *nn.*

pono iho.
Put a cover on.

ponga. (P-- BONGA)
a.

poo. (E-- BOO$_1$)
Grab or catch in a single act. *a.*

pooanga. (E-1 BOO$_1$)
n.

poo ange.
Touch (someone or something with the hand).

poolenga. (P-1 BOLE)
n.

poo mai.
A unit of measurement (from the end of the extended thumb to the other side of the clenched fist).

pugu. (P-- BUGU)
Swollen [pl.]. *a.*

pula. (E-- BULA)
Open one's eyes widely; to light up suddenly; insect sp.: a phosphorescent insect. *a.*

pulaanga. (E-1 BULA)
n.

pula-laalaa. (?)
Fish sp.: shark sp.? *n.*

pula luu mada.
Excited with joy.

puli. (E-- BULI)
Grab up all at once. *v.*

pulu.
To be dry and smooth; satiated; be able to withstand. *v.*

puluanga. (B-1 PULU)
n.

puni. (P-- BUNI)
Closed up [pl.], be together (three or more things). *a.*

pungu. (P-- BUNGU)
Plump [pl.]. *a.*

punguanga. (P-1 BUNGU)
n.

puu. (P-- BUU$_4$)
a.

puugunga. (P-1 BUGU)
The slopes of swellings or protuberances. *n.*

daa (dau).
Chanting (of old chants).

daa$_1$.
To make a sharp turn [sing.]; a back-handed slap or jerking of

anything which moves (e.g., a hand, foot, tail, tongue, etc.); to tattoo; hit, strike, beat; to kill; to wash clothes; scoop up (liquids or solids); to bail (a canoe). *v.*

daa. (B-- DAA$_3$)
A bunch. *n.*

daa$_3$. (B-- DAA$_4$)
Fish sp.: squirrelfish. *n.*

daa age.
Go toward land (from the lagoon).

daabasi.
Angling for tuna. *v.*

daabasinga. (B-1 DAABASI)
n.

daabeduge.
Work seriously. *v.*

daabeduge adu ange.
Take a lot of.

daabedugeanga.
(B-1 DAABEDUGE) *n.*

daabeduge mai.
Bring a lot of.

daabeduge saele.
To bat around.

daabui. (B-- BUI$_a$)
Enclose. *v.*

daabuia. (B-2 BUI$_a$)
v.

daabuinga. (B-1 BUI$_a$)
n.

daadaa$_1$. (R-- DAA$_1$)
v.

daadaa$_2$. (R-- DAA$_2$)
Sweat [noun], perspiration. *n.*

daadaa$_3$. (B-- DAADAA)
Sibling (mostly children's talk). *n.*

daadaabasi. (R-- DAABASI)
v.

daadaabasinga. (R-1 DAABASI)
n.

daadaabeduge. (R-- DAABEDUGE)
v.

daadaabedugeanga.
(R-1 DAABEDUGE) *n.*

daadaaia. (R-2 DAA$_1$)
—; rush (usually preceded by *dee*). *v.*

daadaaia ange.
Be in a hurry to.

daadaaligi. (R-- DAA$_{1a}$)
v.

daadaaligidanga. (R-1 DAA$_{1a}$)
The way of being moved about in the air. *n.*

daadaaligidia. (R-2 DAA$_{1a}$)
v.

daadaalo. (R-- DAALO)
v.

daadaaloa. (R-2 DAALO)
v.

daadaalonga. (R-1 DAALO)
n.

daadaanga. (R-1 DAA$_1$)
—; appearance of (i.e., 'way in which made'). *n.*

daadaanga sala.
Ugly-looking.

daadaangia. (R-2 DADA$_1$)
Pull continuously. *v.*

daadaavalo. (R-- VALO$_1$)
a.

daadaavaloanga. (R-1 VALO$_1$)
n.

daadanga. (B-1 DADA$_1$)
n.

daadaohi. (R-- DAOHI)
v.

daadaohia. (R-2 DAOHI)
v.

daadaohinga. (R-1 DAOHI)
n.

daa de --.
Let's —.

daa de +NUMBER.
It is — o'clock.

daa de alelo.
Cluck one's tongue.

daa de baalanga.
Ring the bell.

daa de gaehala.
To swing a jump rope made of *gaehala*.

daa de hagallogo.
Perform certain old religious ceremonies or chants.

daa de hia?.
What time is it?

daa de masavaa.
Time's up! It is time for...

daa donu taahili.
Sing on-key.

daa taahili.
Sing a melody.

daatugu.
To curse (someone). *v.*

daatuguanga. (B-1 DAATUGU)
n.

daatugulia. (B-2 DAATUGU)
v.

daaea.
Fish sp.: snapper (= large *babudaea*). *n.*

daa gaiaa.
To murder someone so that others don't see.

daagami*.
Bodyguard, soldier. *n.*

daaganga$_1$. (B-1 DAGA$_1$)
Way of travelling. *n.*

daaganga$_2$. (B-1 DAGA$_2$)
n.

daaganga$_3$. (B-- DAAGANGA)
Kind (of), sort (of), variety (of). *n.*

daa gee taahili.
Sing off-key.

Daagelo. (B-- DAAGELO)
February. *n.*

daagina. (E-2 DAGI$_1$)
Towing; dragging. *v.*

daagunga. (B-1 DAGU$_1$)
n.

daakai. (P-- DAGA$_{1C}$)
a.

daakainga. (P-1 DAGA$_{1C}$)
n.

daakodo. (P-- DAGODO)
Be in place [pl.]; lie down [pl.]. *a.*

daakodoanga. (P-1 DAGODO)
n.

daakodolia. (P-2 DAGODO)
Be slept upon for a long time [pl.], be in place for a long time [pl.]. *v.*

daahaa.
A drinking coconut; to have drinking coconuts (of a tree); the stage of development of the coconut between *dahaa mada balabala* and *dahaa mada makaga*. *a.*

daahaa mada balabala.
The stage of development of the coconut between *mugamuga* and *daahaa*.

daahaa mada giigii.
The stage of development of the coconut between *daahaa mada makaga* and *modomodo*.

daahaa mada makaga.
The stage of development of the coconut between *daahaa* and *daahaa mada giigii*.

daa hatau.
Beat unmercifully.

daa hagabodobodo.
Make a quick trip.

daa hagapodo.
[Pl. of *daa haga bodobodo*].

daa hagalele.
Unscheduled, unplanned.

daa hagasaalei.
Make a striped design in tatooing.

daahanga.
Fool (someone), deceive. *v.*

daahanga ange.
Give pleasure to someone by giving him something.

daahangadia. (B-2 DAAHANGA)
v.

daahangalia. (B-2 DAAHANGA)
v.

daahea. (P-- DAHEA)
a.

daaheaanga. (P-1 DAHEA)
n.

daa hhali.
An adze stroke, used to chip out the interior of a bowl, canoe, etc.

daahia. (E-2 $DAHI_2$)
Clean off. *v.*

daahido. (P-- DAHIDO)
n.

daahili.
Song; sing. *v.*

daahili daumaha.
A church song.

daahili dau soa.
A love song.

daahili hagadaahao.
A song which is for amusement only (one which is not 'serious', i.e., not religious).

daahili lo te gohu.
A popular (secular) song.

daahinga. (B-1 $DAHI_2$)
Way of brushing off or sweeping. *n.*

daahuli. (P-- $HULI_a$)
a.

daahulianga. (P-1 $HULI_a$)
n.

daahulinga. (P-1 $HULI_a$)
n.

daahunga. (B-1 DAHU)
n.

daaia. (B-2 DAA_1)
Wash clothes completely; scoop up completely. *v.*

daa iho.
Go toward the lagoon (from land).

$daalaa_1$. (B-2 $DALA_1$)
v.

$daalaa_2$. (B-2 $DALA_3$)
v.

$daalanga_1$. (B-1 $DALA_1$)
n.

$daalanga_2$. (B-1 $DALA_2$)
n.

$daalanga_3$. (B-1 $DALA_3$)
Way of telling; legend, story. *n.*

$daalea_1$. (B-2 DALE)
v.

$daalea_2$. (P-- DALEA)
Tired [pl.]. *a.*

daaleaanga. (P-1 DALEA)
n.

daalenga. (B-1 DALE)
n.

daalia. (B-2 $DALI_1$)
v.

daaligi. (B-- DAA_{1a})
Do something seriously; be moved about; a jerky movement, caused by the wind (e.g., the flapping of a sail); work seriously. *v.*

daaligidanga. (B-1 DAA_{1a})
The slope of a canoe's keel. *n.*

daaligidia. (B-2 DAA_{1a})
To have been moved about by the wind. *v.*

$daalinga_1$. (B-1 $DALI_1$)
n.

$daalinga_2$. (B-- DAALINGA)
An area near the flowering part of the coconut tree (where birds perch). *n.*

daalo.
Stab, skewer. *v.*

daaloa. (B-2 DAALO)
To have been stabbed (esp. accidentally by *hanga*). *v.*

daalonga. (B-1 DAALO)
—; a wound (on the body, from a spear, etc.). *n.*

daamada.
Start; the beginning (of an event). *v.*

daamada age.
Start again.

daamadaa-sele.
Insect sp.: water bug.

daaminga. (B-1 DAMI)
n.

daa mouli.
Take life away from.

daane.
Man, male; thing [in some contexts only]. *n.*

daane abo donu.
Gentleman, person who is good.

daane dagidahi.
A person having unique skills or traits of personality.

daane dau.
A person of importance (specially accomplished).

daane dee lahilahia.
A very special one (rarely seen).

daane e manege.
A person who is capable at almost anything.

daane gasia.
A person who is useful to others.

daane hai moni.
Sailor, seaman.

daane hebagi.
Soldier.

daane honu.
A person of many accomplishments.

daane i lalo.
A person who fails at everything he tries.

daane mada daua.
Bravest in war.

daane mada duulanga.
A person able to do things others cannot.

daane masana.
Good one.

daane sauaa.
A person of extraordinary ability; shark (euphemism).

daane ssili dala.
Special one, important one.

daanunga. (B-1 DANU)
—; grave (for burial). *n.*

daanga. (B-1 DAA_1)
n.

daangage. (P-- $DANGA_a$)
v.

daangageanga. (P-1 $DANGA_a$)
n.

daangenge.
Meaty (not having much fat). *v.*

daangia. (B-2 $DADA_1$)
v.

daanginga. (B-1 DANGI)
n.

daasele. (B-- $SELE_{1a}$)
To swing a rope (in a jump rope game) so as to cause the jumper to trip. *v.*

daaselea. (B-2 $SELE_{1a}$)
v.

daaseleanga. (B-1 $SELE_{1a}$)
n.

daasissisi. (DAA_1, $SISI_1$)
Striped (with stripes). *v.*

daa sseu.
A way of forming the body of a canoe.

daasugi. (DAA_1, $SUGI_2$)
Struggle to get free; jerking of the tail. *v.*

daava.
Brackish (water); taste strange (of liquid). *v.*

daavaanga. (B-1 DAAVA)
n.

daavalo. (B-- $VALO_1$)
Make a great deal of noise (vocal). *a.*

daavaloanga. (B-1 $VALO_1$)
n.

daba.
A flash of light, a blink of an eye. *a.*

dabaanga. (B-1 DABA)
n.

dababa.
Fish sp.: shark sp. *n.*

dababa-gabugabu-tai.
Fish sp.: lizard fish?

$dabadaba_1$. (R-- DABA)
Twinkling, flashing, winking. *v.*

$dabadaba_2$. (R-- DABA)
Slipper lobster. *n.*

dabadabaanga. (R-1 DABA)
n.

dabadaballahi. (R-- $LAHI_a$)
More-or-less thin. *a.*

daba de ganomada.
Instantaneous, in the blinking of an eye.

dabaduu.
Fish sp.: (a small *suulee* or a var. of *suulee*).

dabagau.
A type of floor mat. *n.*

daballahi. (B-- LAHI$_a$)
Thin (of long flat object) [sing.]. *a.*

dabanimeeli.
Payment for medical treatment. *a.*

dabeo.
Unclean, unkempt. *v.*

dabeoanga. (B-1 DABEO)
n.

dabu. (B-- DABU$_1$)
Forbidden, awesome. *a.*

dabuanga. (B-1 DABU$_1$)
n.

dabudabui. (R-- DABUI)
v.

dabudabuia. (R-2 DABUI)
v.

dabudabuinga. (R-1 DABUI)
n.

dabu de --?.
Why not —?

dabui.
To splash water on something with the hand. *v.*

dabuia. (B-2 DABUI)
To *dabui* at one time. *v.*

dabuinga. (B-1 DABUI)
n.

dabula.
Lizard sp. *n.*

dabuna.
Part of the female genitalia. *n.*

dabuvae. (DABU$_2$, VAE$_2$)
Toe, footprint. *n.*

dabuvae madua.
Big toe.

dabuvae sisi.
Little toe.

dada$_1$.
Pull. *v.*

dada$_2$.
Fish sp. (= large *datada*, also = small *angamea*). *n.*

dada$_3$.
Each person's one. *pta.*

dada alohagi.
Trolling.

dada de ava.
A strong current in the channel.

dada de uila.
An electrical storm.

dada gaehala.
Picking even small breadfruit (to avoid having to change one's position, which would be necessary in order to pick breadfruit of the proper size).

dada mamu.
An impatient fisherman.

dada manu.
To snare birds (with a loop on the end of a pole).

dada me.
To obtain taro (by pulling up the tubers).

dada moni.
To beach a canoe without using runners [considered bad practice].

dadangi. (T-- DANGI)
Make noise repeatedly. *a.*

dadango. (T-- DANGO$_1$)
Repeatedly fall upon. *v.*

dadangolia. (T-2 DANGO$_1$)
v.

dada saele.
Always being borrowed.

dada saiolo.
To hoist a sail.

dada soosoa.
To put *soosoa* on the canoe.

dadau. (T-- DAU$_3$)
Hit repeatedly (on one occasion). *a.*

dadaunga. (T-1 DAU$_3$)
n.

datada₁. (R-- DADA₁)
To jerk repeatedly; an intermittent sharp pain. *v.*

datada₂. (R-- DADA₂)
Fish sp.: snapper (= small *dada*). *n.*

datadaanga. (R-1 DADA₁)
n.

datada de galomada.
Twitching of an eye.

datane-uli.
Fish sp.

datanu. (T-- DANU)
Fish sp. (a sort which burrows in the sand). *n.*

dae₁.
Hand net. *n.*

dae₂.
Arrive at. *a.*

dae₃.
Guts, intestines; buttocks. *n.*

daea. (B-2 DAE₂)
To have arrived at. *a.*

dae banibani.
The white excretion of the *banibani.*

daedae₁. (R-- DAE₁)
To catch continuously with a hand net. *v.*

daedae₂. (R-- DAE₂)
To reach many places. *a.*

daedaea₁. (R-2 DAE₁)
v.

daedaea₂. (R-2 DAE₂)
Have reached many places. *a.*

daedaenga₁. (R-1 DAE₁)
n.

daedaenga₂. (R-1 DAE₂)
n.

dae de lodo.
Be satisfied completely.

dae de ua.
Have a good time.

daegalala. (XCO DAE₃)
Internal organ of fish (long and dark) — *n.*

dae gi oona.
Be tops.

daelodo.
Number, figure; the outrigger boom between the *giado madua* and the *giado manu.* *n.*

daelodo dau.
A large enough number to "count".

daelodo dee odi ange.
Odd number.

daelodo gi lunga.
A large number of.

daelodo odi ange.
Even number.

dae maduu.
A method of pulling flying fish into the canoe with a hand net.

daemaha.
Heavy, oppressive, hard to take. *a.*

daemahaanga. (B-1 DAEMAHA)
Heaviness, sadness, unhappiness. *n.*

daemahadia. (B-2 DAEMAHA)
Heavy, oppressive, hard to take. *v.*

daemahalia. (B-2 DAEMAHA)
Heavy, oppressive, hard to take. *v.*

daenga. (B-1 DAE₂)
n.

daga₁.
Go from one place to another in a group. *v.*

daga₂.
Loosely clinging to a surface (outer or inner); coconut meat which has formed in the nut with no sap. *v.*

dagaa. (B-- DAGA₁b)
A leader (for a fishline, made of *olonga*). *v.*

dagaa de maadau.
To tie a leader to a fish hook.

dagaanga. (B-1 DAGA₁b)
Way of tying the leader to a fish hook. *n.*

dagabe.
Fish sp.: snapper. *n.*

dagabuli. (DAGA₁a, BULI)
Gather together in a group. *v.*

dagabulianga. (B-1 DAGA₁a)
n.

dagadaga$_1$. (R-- DAGA$_1$)
v.

dagadaga$_2$. (R-- DAGA$_2$)
v.

dagadagaanga$_1$. (R-1 DAGA$_1$)
n.

dagadagaanga$_2$. (R-1 DAGA$_2$)
n.

dagadagabuli. (R-- DAGA$_{1a}$)
v.

dagadagabulianga. (R-1 DAGA$_{1a}$)
n.

dagadagahi. (R-- DAGA$_{1e}$)
v.

dagadagahia. (R-2 DAGA$_{1e}$)
v.

dagadagahinga. (R-1 DAGA$_{1e}$)
n.

dagadagai. (R-- DAGA$_{1c}$)
Tending to *dagai*. *a.*

dagadagainga. (R-1 DAGA$_{1c}$)
n.

dagadagalia$_1$. (R-2 DAGA$_1$)
Heavily travelled. *v.*

dagadagalia$_2$. (R-2 DAGA$_2$)
v.

dagadagasala. (R-- DAGA$_{1d}$)
Be always blamed for. *v.*

dagadagasalaanga. (R-1 DAGA$_{1d}$)
n.

dagahi. (B-- DAGA$_{1e}$)
Step on, kick with one's heel. *v.*

dagahia. (B-2 DAGA$_{1e}$)
v.

dagahia de agau.
Reef which has been trampled previously by lobster hunters (and therefore is poor for lobstering).

dagahi ange gi de --.
Serve as a side dish for.

dagahinga. (B-1 DAGA$_{1e}$)
n.

daga holiage.
Surrounding area; to cut or make a ring around.

dagai. (B-- DAGA$_{1c}$)
Move jerkily, flail (one's legs), flounder about. *a.*

dagainga. (B-1 DAGA$_{1c}$)
n.

dagalia$_1$. (B-2 DAGA$_1$)
Trampled down (from people walking on); thoroughfare. *v.*

dagalia$_2$. (B-2 DAGA$_2$)
v.

dagaligiligi. (DAGA$_2$, LIGI)
Broken into small pieces. *a.*

dagalonga*. (B-1 DAGA$_1$)
Path, route. *n.*

dagamanga*. (B-1 DAGA$_1$)
Path, route. *n.*

dagasala. (B-- DAGA$_{1d}$)
Blame (for something); guilt; fault, crime. *n.*

dagasalaanga. (B-1 DAGA$_{1d}$)
n.

dagasisi. (DAGA$_2$, SISI$_1$)
Scoop out by inserting a knife between the meat and the shell (e.g., in cutting copra). *v.*

daga ula.
Go lobster catching.

dagelo. (B-- GELO$_a$)
Bottom, foundation. *n.*

dagi$_1$.
Lead, show the way, leader (of a group); extend to. *v.*

dagi$_1$. +NUMBER. (B-- DAGA$_2$)
— each. *mc.*

dagia. (B-2 DAGI$_1$)
v.

dagi ala.
Go around aimlessly.

dagidagi. (R-- DAGI$_1$)
—; carry in one's hands. *v.*

dagidagina. (R-2 DAGI$_1$)
v.

dagidaginga. (R-1 DAGI$_1$)
n.

dagidogoisi. (DAGI$_2$, DOGO$_{2a}$)
Very few for each one. *a.*

dagitilo. ($DAGI_1$, $DILO_1$)
Watchful, be on the lookout, keep an eye on. *v.*

dagi gee.
Lead away from.

dagihia. ($DAGI_2$, HIA)
How many for each?

dagilagolago. ($DAGI_2$, $LAGO_1$)
Many for each. *a.*

dagilanea. ($DAGI_2$, LANEA)
Each having a lot. *a.*

dagimomo. ($DAGI_2$, MOMO)
Few for each one. *a.*

dagina. (B-2 $DAGI_1$)
v.

daginga. (B-1 $DAGI_1$)
n.

dagisoa. ($DAGI_2$, SOA)
Many (people) at each (time or place, etc.). *a.*

dago.
Ritual activities, religious activities. *n.*

dagodagonga. (R-1 DAGO)
n.

dagodo.
Situation, circumstance; lie down [sing.]; be in place [sing.]. *a.*

dagodo adu.
Appear there (from here).

dagodoanga. (B-1 DAGODO)
—; expose oneself to the sun. *n.*

dagodo be --.
It seems that...

dagodo daudahi.
Having the same characteristics, be alike.

dagodo gee (ma).
Another thing altogether; different (from); recuperating (after an illness).

dagodo hai sala.
Fornication.

dagodo lalo.
Seriously ill and not improving.

dagodolia. (B-2 DAGODO)
Be slept upon for a long time [sing.]; be in place for a long time [sing.]. *v.*

dagodo mahamaha.
Nice, pleasing.

dagodo mai.
Appear from yonder.

dagoobala.
Fall on something and smash it. *v.*

dagoobalaanga.
(B-1 DAGOOBALA) *n.*

dagosala. (DAGO, $SALA_2$)
Death, die (of a person). *v.*

$dagu_1$.
Speak, pronounce, utter (words). *v.*

$dagu_2$.
My one. *ppa.*

$dagua_1$. (B-2 $DAGU_1$)
v.

$dagua_2$. (B-- DAGUA)
Fish sp.: yellow fin tuna (3 sorts?). *n.*

dagua-bodo.
Fish sp.: tuna sp.

dagua de --.
Not only the —, but think also of the — !

dagu age.
Say out loud.

dagua-loa.
Fish sp.: tuna sp.

dagu bau.
Methinks.

dagudagu. (R-- $DAGU_1$)
—; give commands. *v.*

dagudagua. (R-2 $DAGU_1$)
v.

dagudagulia. (R-2 $DAGU_1$)
v.

dagudaguna. (R-2 $DAGU_1$)
v.

dagudagunga. (R-1 $DAGU_1$)
n.

dagugu.
Fish sp.: (The native term is applied to many spp.): damselfish, snapper. *n.*

dagu hahine.
My "daughter" or "mother" (not one's natural mother).

dagu hai bolo.
"One would have thought that —".

dagulia. (B-2 DAGU$_1$)
v.

dagu made.
Perhaps, maybe.

daguna. (B-2 DAGU$_1$)
v.

daguu.
Axe. *n.*

daguu kalo.
A thin straight-bladed (easily sharpened) axe blade.

daha.
Outside, away, around. *nl.*

dahadaha. (R-- DAHA)
An embankment around a taro plot. *v.*

daha de hia maa.
About what time is it?

dahea.
Drift [sing.]. *a.*

dahea age.
Drift toward place where speaker is.

dahea gee.
Drift away.

dahea gi lalo.
Sink (completely).

dahea iho.
Drift toward the place where the speaker is not.

dahedahea. (R-- DAHEA)
Drift aimlessly. *a.*

dahedaheaanga. (R-1 DAHEA)
n.

dahi$_1$.
One, a. *an.*

dahi$_2$.
A stroking motion with something in the hand; shave, sweep, brush off (once). *v.*

dahi$_3$. (C-- DAI$_2$)
[Var. of *dai*$_1$ — only recently used]. *mt.*

dahia. (B-2 DAHI$_2$)
Shave [trans.]. *v.*

dahidahi. (R-- DAHI$_2$)
v.

dahidahia. (R-2 DAHI$_2$)
v.

dahidahinga. (R-1 DAHI$_2$)
n.

dahi de gumigumi.
Shave one's beard.

dahido.
Stem, base, foot (e.g., of a hill), stump. *nl.*

dahido lima.
Upper arm.

dahido mada.
Inner corner of the eye.

dahidonga. (CF DAHIDO)
Grandfather. *n.*

dahido vae.
The back of the thigh.

dahi tali.
Depend on (e.g., to come), rely on.

dahi i daho dangada.
Very popular.

dahi ma dahi.
Each individual.

dahi-malali.
The first number of a counting game played to determine who is "it".

dahinga. (B-1 DAHI$_2$)
Way of shaving. *n.*

daho.
Side of (part away from), with. *nl.*

dahola.
A method of fishing (night fishing on the reef with torches). *v.*

daholaa.
Whale. *n.*

Daholaa$_a$. (B-- DAHOLAA$_a$)
December. *n.*

daholaanga. (B-1 DAHOLA)
n.

dahu.
Start a fire (or an engine); build a fire. *v.*

dahua. (B-2 DAHU)
v.

dahudahu. (R-- DAHU)
v.

dahudahua. (R-2 DAHU)
v.

dahudahulia. (R-2 DAHU)
v.

dahudahunga. (R-1 DAHU)
n.

dahuli. (B-- $HULI_a$)
Turn back; change one's mind. *a.*

dahulia. (B-2 DAHU)
v.

dahulianga. (B-1 $HULI_a$)
n.

dahuli de lodo.
Change of heart, change one's mind, repent.

dahuli de madangi.
A change of wind direction.

dahuli de vae.
Dislocated ankle.

dahulihuli. (R-- $HULI_a$)
Keep shifting direction. *a.*

dahulihulianga. (R-1 $HULI_a$)
n.

dahulihuli donu.
Be careful! [said to someone going fishing].

dahulihulinga. (R-1 $HULI_a$)
n.

dahulinga. (B-1 $HULI_a$)
Custom, habit. *n.*

dahuli saboneálo.
The odor of overripe breadfruit.

dahuuhuu.
The topmost part of the house. *n.*

dai (tigi) lago --.
Becoming more — (but not quite).

dai_1.
Lagoon, sea, salt. *nl.*

dai_2.
Almost, nearly. *mt.*

daia. (B-2 DAA_1)
To *daa* completely (excepting meanings 'make a sharp turn', 'wash clothes', 'scoop up', 'bail'). *v.*

daia e de hegau.
Overworked.

daia e tuaadai.
Seasick.

daia e tulidaa.
Urgency in micturation.

daia e sseni.
Very sleepy.

daiao.
Morning, tomorrow. *n.*

daiao age.
The following morning.

dai beau.
Rough seas at a certain time.

dai bigi.
Almost (finished or done, etc.); just about.

dai deai.
Hardly any.

dai deeai.
Almost none.

dai deeai donu.
Almost none at all.

daihadu. (B-- $HADU_{2a}$)
Hardwood in the tree trunk. *v.*

dai hieunu.
Thirsty.

dai hiigai.
Hungry.

daina.
Brother, sister, sibling, cousin. *n.*

daina daane.
Brother, male cousin.

daina hahine.
Sister, female cousin.

Dai-nei. (DAI_1, NEI)
"Islands to the west" (the Mortlocks?). *np.*

dai sagana iho goe.
Watch out!

dai seni.
Sleepy.

$dala_1$.
Unfasten, undo, untie. *v.*

dala$_2$.
Tame [sing.]; not be timid or uneasy in another's presence [sing.]. *a.*

dala$_3$.
Tell, say to, relate. *v.*

dala$_4$.
Appendage, fin, spine (extending from a fish, etc.). *n.*

dala$_5$.
Bird sp.: tern? (a vagrant sp., rarely seen). *n.*

dala$_6$.
Plant sp.: shrub sp. (*Ximenia americana* L.). *n.*

dalaa. (B-- DALA$_{4a}$)
(Small) piece of, part of. *n.*

dalaa mada.
[= *dalaa umada*].

dalaa manu.
Piece of broken glass.

dalaa muna.
Word, phrase.

dalaa ubu.
Charcoal from the coconut shell.

dalaa umada.
Prow spray of a ship.

dalabaimanugadele. (B-- ?)
Sharp (as a knife). *a.*

daladala$_1$. (R-- DALA$_1$)
v.

daladala$_2$. (R-- DALA$_2$)
a.

daladala$_3$. (R-- DALA$_3$)
Say again and again. *v.*

daladala$_4$. (R-- DALA$_{4b}$)
Rough in texture (as perceived over time); fish sp.: squirrelfish. *a.*

daladalaa$_1$. (R-2 DALA$_1$)
v.

daladalaa$_2$. (R-2 DALA$_3$)
v.

dala-dalaa-moa.
Plant sp.: *Lycopodium phlegmaria* L.

daladalaanga$_1$. (R-1 DALA$_1$)
n.

daladalaanga$_2$. (R-1 DALA$_2$)
n.

daladalaanga$_3$. (R-1 DALA$_3$)
n.

daladalaehala. (R-- DALAEHALA)
v.

daladalaehalaanga.
(R-1 DALAEHALA) *n.*

dalaehala.
Pricked. *v.*

dalaehalaanga. (B-1 DALAEHALA)
n.

dala-galoi.
Fish sp.: puffer.

dala gaogao.
The part of the human body between the hip and the ribs.

dala-hagalulu-madangi.
Bird sp.: tern? (a vagrant sp., rarely seen).

dalahalu.
Plant sp.: tree sp. (*Allophylus timorensis* (DC.) Bl.). *n.*

dala hhua.
Eruptions on the skin (e.g., hives, insect bites, etc.).

dala-loa.
Fish sp.: squirrelfish.

dala malo.
Change clothes.

dala mmea.
Redness or inflammation of the skin (e.g., a welt).

dala-moana.
Bird sp.: tern? (a vagrant sp., rarely seen).

dalanga a kai.
A story which is not true.

dalangasau.
Be quick-witted in an emergency. *v.*

dalangasauanga.
(B-1 DALANGASAU) *n.*

dale.
Touch (two or more things being in contact); strike (a match). *v.*

dalea.
Tired [sing.]. *a.*

daleaanga. (B-1 DALEA)
n.

daleba. (B-- $LEBA_a$)
Flap briskly in the wind. *v.*

dalebaanga. (B-1 $LEBA_a$)
n.

dalebaleba. (R-- $LEBA_a$)
v.

dalebalebaanga. (R-1 $LEBA_a$)
n.

dalebu.
Turbulent (air or seas). *v.*

dalebua. (B-2 DALEBU)
n.

dalebuanga. (B-1 DALEBU)
n.

dalebulebu. (R-- DALEBU)
v.

dalebulebua. (R-2 DALEBU)
v.

dalebulebuanga. (R-1 DALEBU)
n.

dalepagi. (BAGI, DALE)
Fight hand-to-hand. *a.*

dale pilo.
A game (like tag), to leave something unfinished after having tried only slightly.

daledale. (R-- DALE)
Repeatedly touch lightly. *v.*

daledalenga. (R-1 DALE)
n.

dale gaiaa.
Provoke a fight by banging against someone (as children do); hit and run.

$dali_1$.
Wait for, along with. *v.*

$dali_2$.
Fibers of the coconut leaf rachi. *n.*

dalia.
Plant sp. *n.*

dalia-dodo.
Mollusk sp.: *Chlamys schmeltzi.*

dalia-mea.
Mollusk sp.: *Mitra mitra.*

dalidali. (R-- $DALI_1$)
v.

dalidalia. (R-2 $DALI_1$)
v.

dalidalinga. (R-1 $DALI_1$)
n.

dali hagavagavaga.
[= *hagavagavaga*].

dalimasanga. ($DALI_2$, SANGA)
Way of tying (rope, etc.). *v.*

$dalinga_1$.
Ear. *n.*

$dalinga_2$.
Fish sp.: mullet. *n.*

dalinga bobo.
Having a runny ear (with pus).

dalo. (B-- $DALO_2$)
Plant sp.: taro (*Colocasia esculenta*), also the corm of this plant. *n.*

dalodalo. (R-- $DALO_1$)
Pray. *v.*

dalodaloa. (R-2 $DALO_1$)
Pray for. *v.*

dalodaloanga. (R-1 $DALO_1$)
n.

dalodalo keli.
Pray earnestly.

dalodalo i de lodo.
Pray silently.

dalodalosia. (R-2 $DALO_1$)
Pray for. *v.*

dalogo.
A type of prepared food (prepared from grated coconut, coconut apple, and coconut juice). *n.*

dama.
Child. *n.*

damaa. (B-- $DAMA_a$)
DIMINUATIVE PREFIX; slowly, gently, skillfully, etc. *d.*

damaa dae.
Skillful at catching flying fish.

dama-a-de-galabe.
Fish sp.: goby?, sleeper?

damaa dogi.
Skillful in the use of an adze.

dama adu hale.
A child who wanders around to the homes of others.

damaa tili.
Sharpshooter.

damaa hine.
Girl, young woman, daughter.

damaa hungi.
Skillful at *hungi.*

damaa-manu.
Bird sp.: sharp-tailed sandpiper (*Erolia acuminata*).

damaa me.
Small [sing.]; little; tiny.

damaa velo.
Good at spearing fish.

dama pala.
A foetus which has been aborted, ugly [said jokingly].

damadaa. (B-2 DAAMADA)
To have started it; to have begun it. *v.*

dama daane.
Boy, young man.

dama dagidahi.
The only child of a couple.

damadanga. (B-1 DAAMADA)
—; origin, source. *n.*

dama daohi.
An adopted child.

dama de bialodo.
Deformed foetus [lit., 'looking like an animal'].

dama de gaehala.
A rain cloud (dropping its rain) seen in the distance.

dama doe.
The fourth child born to a couple.

dama donu.
A natural child.

dama doo.
A foetus which has been aborted.

dama gaiaa.
To hang around someone's house in the expectation of being served food [considered bad manners].

dama hodooligi.
Children of the chief [and of the chief's relatives?].

dama iai.
A person who has done something praiseworthy.

dama lalo.
A person who has visited other far-away lands.

dama legalega*.
Baby, infant.

dama madua.
Eldest child.

dama moemoe sala.
A foetus out of the proper position (in the womb) for delivery.

dama muli bee.
The twelfth child born to a couple.

damana.
Father, uncle, senior male relative, male elder, person in a fatherly relationship. *n.*

dama naale.
A talkative, deceitful person.

damana mai i daha.
Stepfather.

dama ssala.
An adopted child.

dama ssege.
A foetus which has been aborted.

dama ulungi.
A man good at catching tuna with a fishing pole.

dami.
Close one's jaws; closing of the two halves of a clam shell. *v.*

damia. (B-2 DAMI)
v.

damidami. (R-- DAMI)
v.

damidamia. (R-2 DAMI)
v.

damidaminga. (R-1 DAMI)
n.

dana.
His one, her one, its one. *ppa.*

dane. (B-- DANE$_1$)
A fungus infection of the skin (consisting of superficial white spots). *v.*

danea. (B-2 DANE$_1$)
To have *dane.* *v.*

daneaanga. (B-3 DANE$_1$)
n.

danedane. (R-- DANE$_1$)
An extensive infection of *dane.* *v.*

danedanea. (R-2 DANE$_1$)
Be covered with *dane.* *v.*

danedaneaanga. (R-3 DANE$_1$)
n.

danngaho.
Stomach. *n.*

danu.
Buried [sing.]; sunken from view [sing.]. *v.*

danuaa.
Good ! Hello! Good-bye! *a.*

danuaa age.
Improved, better.

danuaa ai loo.
Well, OK! (this time, but next time watch it!).

danuaa ange.
Good for, better than.

danuaa huu.
It's still OK! No wonder!

danuaa loo.
OK! (good).

danuaa mai i hee.
Good according to whom?

danuaa sili.
Good enough!

danu bela.
Spade in organic matter (to enrich taro plantings).

danudanu. (R-- DANU)
To bury a great many, to keep going down (so that it becomes hidden from view). *v.*

danudanumanga. (R-1 DANU)
n.

danudanumia. (R-2 DANU)
v.

danu de bela.
Spade up taro plots, adding mulch.

danu de laa.
The setting of the sun.

danu de maasina.
The setting of the moon.

danumanga. (B-1 DANU)
n.

danumia. (B-2 DANU)
v.

dangada.
Person, human being, relative [when preceded by a possessive pronoun]. *n.*

dangada abadai.
European persons (including Americans).

dangada abasasa.
European persons (including Americans).

dangada agoago.
Teacher, preacher.

dangada baoa.
Dead person buried at sea who washes back up on shore.

dangada dau duadae.
A sucker (a person who is easily fooled).

dangada de henua.
Natives of Nukuoro.

dangada duaagau.
An avid fisherman.

dangada gaiaa.
Thief.

dangada gai dangada.
Cannibal.

dangada gohu.
Ignorant person.

dangada haangoda.
Fisherman.

dangada hagao me.
Storekeeper.

dangada haigamaiana.
Worthwhile person.

dangada henua gee.
Foreigners, strangers.

dangada lo te gohu.
Unenlightened person.

dangada madua.
Old person, adult.

dangada mai i daha.
Relatives by marriage or adoption, etc.

dangadanga. (R-- DANGA)
Loose (not tight) [sing.]; sieve [which is shaken to make *bie*]. *a.*

dangadangalebu. (R-- $DANGA_b$)
Becoming rougher (of seas). *v.*

dangadangalebua. (R-2 $DANGA_b$)
v.

dangadangalebunga. (R-1 $DANGA_b$)
n.

dangada ngauda.
A person who rarely goes fishing, landlubber.

dangada ssigo.
Clever person.

dangada ulu.
Companions or friends who share the same interests, and who get along well.

dangada vai gelegele.
A person of filthy appearance or habits.

dangage. (B-- $DANGA_a$)
Raise one's head up or back. *v.*

dangage age.
Raise up one's head from a lowered position.

dangageanga. (B-1 $DANGA_a$)
n.

dangage dua.
Bend one's head backwards.

dangalebu. (B-- $DANGA_b$)
Rough or choppy sea condition. *v.*

dangalebua. (B-2 $DANGA_b$)
v.

dangalebu de me.
Bad weather.

dangalebu de moana.
Rough or choppy seas.

dangalebunga. (B-1 $DANGA_b$)
n.

dangaligi. (B-- $DANGA_c$)
A type of basket. *n.*

$dangaloa_1$.
Plant sp.: silver bush (*Sophora tormentosa* L.).

$dangaloa_2$.
Earthworm.

$dangaloa_3$. (B-- $DANGA_d$)
Shooting star. *n.*

dangau-paava.
Fish sp.: snapper.

dangau-daa-sissisi.
Fish sp.: snapper.

dangau-dongi.
Fish sp.: snapper.

dangau-laha.
Fish sp.: snapper.

dangau-ngudu-aahua.
[Var. of *dangau dongi*].

dangau-sissisi.
[Var. of *dangaudaasisisi*].

dange.
Mollusk sp.: giant clam (*Tridacna squammosa*). *n.*

dangi.
Cry. *a.*

dangi a beini*.
To have smelled ripe pandanus.

dangi buada.
The noise made by a fast-moving projectile.

dangidangi. (R-- DANGI)
Cry a lot; beg, apologize; a type of aboriginal chant. *a.*

dangidangi ange.
Ask permission of, apologize to.

dangidangi keli.
Beg, apologize, or ask permission in an insistent manner; pray fervently; beseech.

dangidanginga. (R-1 DANGI)
n.

dangi daudau.
Cry uncontrollably (for a long time).

dangi de musu.
Hear whispering (of others).

dangi talinga.
Tinnitus, a ringing sound in the ear [an omen].

dangi hagaeaea.
Wail (when crying).

dangi hagahadihadi.
Wail loudly (when crying).

dangi hhadu$_1$.
Cry for effect.

dangii.
Fish sp. (= small *valu*). *n.*

dangi iho.
Cry to oneself.

dangi see.
Cry aloud for a long time, wail.

dango$_1$.
Grab (in order to restrain, e.g., a person), fall upon. *v.*

dango$_2$.
Cat's-eye (of a shell); operculum of a gastropod. *n.*

dangoa. (B-2 DANGO$_1$)
Grabbed, fallen upon. *v.*

dangoanga. (B-1 DANGO$_1$)
n.

dangodango. (R-- DANGO$_1$)
Repeatedly grab. *v.*

dangodangoa. (R-2 DANGO$_1$)
v.

dangodangoanga. (R-1 DANGO$_1$)
n.

dangodangolia. (R-2 DANGO$_1$)
v.

dango de langi.
Downpour (of rain).

dangolia. (B-2 DANGO$_1$)
Grabbed, fallen upon. *v.*

dao$_1$.
Bake. *v.*

dao$_2$.
A spear, branch of (part of). *n.*

dao$_3$.
A method of calculating the relative maturity of coconuts by comparing the size of the upper (immature) ones on the tree with the lower (mature) ones; the second of a pair (e.g., *dao dogai*). *n.*

daoa. (B-2 DAO$_1$)
v.

dao badu.
Ridge pole (upper).

dao bagu.
Dry out (fish or food to preserve it).

dao beau.
The wave following the highest one.

dao bou.
Ridge pole support (end).

dao dahuuhuu.
Ridge pole (lower).

daodao$_1$. (R-- DAO$_1$)
v.

daodao$_2$. (R-- DAO$_2$)
Fish sp.: wahoo. *n.*

daodaoa. (R-2 DAO$_1$)
v.

daodaolia. (R-2 DAO$_1$)
v.

daodaonga. (R-1 DAO$_1$)
n.

dao de laangi.
Celebrate.

dao tili.
A spear or harpoon to which a line is attached.

daogave. (XCO DAO$_3$)
A type of coconut tree [bears seasonally]. *n.*

daogili.
[Var. of *daogoli*].

daogoli.
Plant sp.: swamp taro (*Cyrtosperma chamissonis*), also the corm of this plant.

daogubu. (DAO$_3$, GUBU)
Waist, circumference. *n.*

dao hadu.
Cover up (by putting on layer after layer); give too much (e.g., work) to.

dao hagaahulu.
To leave an earth oven covered, even after the food is cooked.

dao hagamaadau.
A spear with a barb.

dao haiava.
Path (a minor, not major, thoroughfare).

daohi.
Hold, restrain, keep (from). *v.*

daohia. (B-2 DAOHI)
v.

daohi age.
Donate, contribute.

daohi ange dahi hai.
Argue against.

daohi taelodi.
Keep a record of.

daohi i tua.
Learn by heart.

daohinga. (B-1 DAOHI)
n.

dao huge.
To open an earth oven as soon as the food is cooked.

daolia. (B-2 DAO_1)
v.

dao malui.
A spear with a hinged barb.

dao me hholu.
Arrow (for a bow).

daonga. (B-1 DAO_1)
—; feast. *n.*

dao o de nui.
(Topmost) roof support poles, wall plates (from the size of which one can estimate the maturity of those below).

dao o gasoni.
A type of a cloud formation [indicates that a storm is imminent].

dao ssanga.
Roof support (top) poles, wall plates.

dau (umu). (B-- DAU_6)
A cover for an earth oven. *n.*

dau_1.
Count, read; be included; of importance. *v.*

dau_2.
To fasten (a rope, etc.) between two points; hung up, suspended from. *v.*

dau_3.
Be hit; to beach (a canoe), arrive at. *a.*

dau_4.
Occurring in great numbers. *d.*

dau_5.
Chant (ancient). *n.*

dau_6.
Your [1] one. *ppa.*

$daua_1$. (B-2 DAU_1)
— ['count' and 'read' meanings only]; productive, yield a great amount of. *v.*

$daua_2$. (B-2 DAU_2)
v.

$daua_3$. (B-2 DAU_3)
War, battle. *v.*

dauaa.
Wrinkled. *v.*

dauaabulu. (ABULU, DAU_7)
Nearly sunk. *v.*

dauaadea. (AADEA, DAU_7)
Clear (with nothing in the way); unobstructed; cleared (of obstructions). *v.*

dauaahe. (AHE, DAU_2)
Gather or pleat in material; feathers of a rooster standing out on its neck (when angry); festooned with (e.g., flags). *a.*

dauaalo. (ALO_1, DAU_1)
Steady paddling. *v.*

dauaalu. (ALU, DAU_4)
Always borrowing or begging. *v.*

$dauaanga_1$. (B-3 DAU_1)
n.

$dauaanga_2$. (B-1 DAUAA)
n.

dau age.
To beach (a canoe) on land; reach land.

dau age de inai.
Be in the lee of the atoll while fishing (i.e., in a place protected from the wind).

dauagi. (B-- DAU_{2a})
Dry in the sun. *v.*

dauagia. (B-2 DAU_{2a})
v.

dauagina. (B-2 DAU_{2a})
v.

dauaginga. (B-1 DAU_{2a})
n.

dau ama.
The mast stay tied to the outrigger boom.

dau ange.
Depend upon (e.g., for sustenance).

dau balabala.
Slack (of rope).

daubasa. ($BASA_2$, DAU_4)
A great many. *na.*

daubeemala. (?)
A method of braiding flower headdresses or necklaces made from *manu-mala.* *v.*

daubodobodo. (BODO, DAU_1)
Short (in duration). *a.*

dau bodobodo.
To tie at the end of a short tether.

dau bodu.
Married man or woman.

daubulebule. (B-- $BULE_a$)
Spotted (covered with spots). *a.*

daubulebuleanga. (B-1 $BULE_a$)
n.

daudahi. ($DAHI_1$, DAU_1)
Only, alone (just one). *a.*

daudai. (DAI_1, DAU_7)
Skillful fisherman. *a.*

daudali. (XCO $DALI_{1a}$)
Follow (someone). *a.*

daudali i lodo.
Follow another's will.

daudau₁. (R-- DAU_1)
—; well-known, famous. *v.*

daudau₂. (R-- DAU_2)
v.

daudau₃. (R-- DAU_3)
—; wrestle. *a.*

daudaua₁. (R-2 DAU_1)
v.

daudaua₂. (R-2 DAU_2)
v.

daudauagi. (R-- DAU_{2a})
v.

daudauagia. (R-2 DAU_{2a})
v.

daudauagina. (R-2 DAU_{2a})
v.

daudauaginga. (R-1 DAU_{2a})
n.

daudaulia₁. (R-2 DAU_1)
v.

daudaulia₂. (R-2 DAU_2)
v.

daudaunga₁. (R-1 DAU_1)
n.

daudaunga₂. (R-1 DAU_2)
n.

daudaunga₃. (R-1 DAU_3)
n.

dau de madangi.
Be hit by (usually a strong) wind.

dau dinae.
A period during which many women are pregnant at the same time.

daudonu. (DAU_1, $DONU_1$)
If, in the case that; gentle, mild-mannered, soft-spoken. *a.*

daudu.
Fish sp.: spiny puffer. *n.*

dau duadae.
Be a sucker, be fooled easily.

dau gadea.
Boom lanyard (of a canoe).

dau gai.
The season in which seasonally available food is abundant.

dau gulu.
Breadfruit season.

dau haanau.
A period during which many children are born.

dau hala.
The season during which pandanus fruit of the same type matures.

dau honu.
The season during which tides are highest.

dau hoohanga.
The season during which birds lay eggs.

dauhuli (ange). ($HULI_b$, DAU_3)
Always criticizing (someone) to (his) face. *n.*

dau i tua.
Memorize.

daula.
Rope (heavy); anchored (of ship). *v.*

dau laagii.
To put on an ornament for a special purpose.

daula baalanga.
Cable, wire (heavy).

daula de boo.
A rope carried in the canoe (esp. at night) for anchoring or tying canoes together in case of strong wind.

daula de gona.
A cord between the naval and the genitals [according to Nukuoro anatomical lore].

daula duu nui.
A rope used to lower a bunch of coconuts to the ground.

daula gage.
A rope used to assist the climber of a breadfruit tree.

daula hagalevaleva.
A swing (made of rope).

daula luu hadu.
Testicle cords.

daula mada lau nui.
A rope for tying palm fronds together to make a *belubelu* seine.

daulanga. (B-1 DAULA)
Port (for ships); harbor (place where boats anchor). *n.*

dau langi.
Rainy season.

dau lango.
The season during which flies are most numerous [coincides with the breadfruit season].

dau laohie.
Dry season.

daula sele nui.
A rope used to pull a coconut tree in the desired direction when felling it.

dauleelage. (?)
Fish sp.: blenny. *n.*

daulia$_1$. (B-2 DAU$_1$)
—; popular. *v.*

daulia$_2$. (B-2 DAU$_2$)
v.

daulooloa. (XCO DAU$_1$)
Long time. *a.*

dau looloa.
To tie at the end of a long tether.

dau maagau.
A period during which many people die.

daumada. (DAU$_1$, MADA$_3$)
Stare at, observe closely. *v.*

dau magi.
Epidemic.

dau makaga.
Tightly stretched (not slack).

daumaha. (DAU$_{1C}$, MAHA)
Church (services); religious observance; religion. *v.*

daumaha daahili.
Song service (in church).

daumaha daamada.
The morning prayer service (before the major church service).

daumaha dalodalo.
Prayer service (church).

daumaha de manu.
Christmas Eve fete in the church at which "Santa Claus" appears.

daumaha haangoda.
Prayer service held while visiting others' houses [in the hope of getting converts].

daumaha hagadaahao.
Social activities which are held in the church under church auspices.

daumaha hagatoo donu.
Church service of dedication (in which the members renew their vows).

daumaha hagalava.
Evensong (last service of the day).

daumaha hagasaele.
A meeting of church members for business.

daumaha hagaulu.
The church service at which new members are accepted.

daumaha laanui.
The main Sunday religious observance in the church.

dau malino.
An area of the sea which is dead calm.

dau mamu.
The season in which fish are abundant.

dau manu.
Flock of birds (feeding on a school of fish).

dau masa.
The season during which tides are lowest.

dau me.
The sheath of the flower of the coconut tree.

daunadi.
Would it be better if (implying disagreement)?... *u.*

dau namu.
Mosquito net.

daunga$_1$. (B-1 DAU$_1$)
n.

daunga$_2$. (B-1 DAU$_2$)
n.

daunga$_3$. (B-1 DAU$_3$)
n.

dau ngaadahi$_1$.
Equally apportioned.

dau ngaadahi$_2$.
Equally stretched (of two or more ropes).

daungaangalu. (DAU$_3$, NGALU, DAU$_7$)
High-water mark. *n.*

dauoni.
Fish sp. *n.*

dauoni-baabaa.
Fish sp. (a rare school fish which looks like *saniba*).

dau soa.
Boyfriend, girlfriend; couple (not married); going steady (of an unmarried couple).

dauulu. (B-- ULU$_{2a}$)
Verdant (indicating growing well). *v.*

dauulunga. (B-1 ULU$_{2a}$)
n.

davage.
Bird sp.: white-tailed tropic bird (*Phaethon lepturus*). *n.*

davaia*.
The largest sort of tuna. *n.*

de.
The one. *ma.*

dea.
d.

deaamonga. (XCO AAMONGA)
[Var. of *seaamonga*]. *n.*

deadea. (R-- DEA)
Becoming lighter in color. *a.*

deadeaanga. (R-1 DEA)
n.

de aha.
Which is it?

deai.
None, no —, nothing. *a.*

deai ange.
No more, no other.

deai ange loo soo savaa.
Now I've got you!

deai ange soo laangi.
I'll get you!

deai donu.
None at all.

deai donu angaanga.
Nothing at all.

deai loo me.
I doubt it!

deai ma gi dahi.
None at all as you should very well know! [prob. = *deai maua gi dahi*].

deai me ao ai.
Useless.

deai me hagalongolongo.
Do unhesitatingly.

deainga. (B-1 DEAI)
Nothingness. *n.*

de baasi gee.
The opposing side.

debedebe. (R-- DEBE)
The folds of skin around the waist. *v.*

debedebenga. (R-1 DEBE)
n.

dee.
NEGATIVE ASPECT MARKER. *mt.*

dee abo.
Uncomfortable (esp. socially).

dee adagaigaina.
A great many; serious.

dee adahaia.
Very; very bad.

dee ahe mai.
Incurably ill.

deeai. (E-- DEAI$_a$)
[An emphatic form of *deai*]. *a.*

deeai donu.
Positively no!

dee anga.
Forgetful, absent-minded.

dee baa tae.
Stay for only a very short time.

dee beaha.
All right! It's nothing!

dee daea donu.
Unexpectedly.

dee dagua --.
It goes without saying that — is better!

dee dau ia.
It's OK!

dee dolia.
Impossible to find the equal of (*dehors concours*).

dee tala mai!.
Don't tell me!

dee gagu.
Uncouth.

dee galemu.
Never mind!, Don't bother!

dee galo.
Perhaps.

dee gamalie.
Do very attentively.

dee gide.
Blind.

deeginga$_1$. (B-1 DEGI$_1$)
n.

deeginga$_2$. (B-1 DEGI$_3$)
n.

dee kai laa dangada.
So, it's not so after all (just as we believed at first)! No wonder!

dee kasi.
Perhaps.

dee kona.
Easily.

dee haaoa i de gai.
Gluttonous.

dee hagabaulia.
Underestimate, misjudge.

dee hai gee.
Be tied (e.g., in a footrace).

dee haihai donu.
That's for sure!

dee hanga.
Don't move away from the reef! [an instruction heard when fishing for flying fish].

deehehee.
To make a certain pattern of sounds to call attention to oneself. *v.*

deeheheeanga. (B-1 DEEHEHEE)
n.

dee heloongoi.
Misunderstand one another; mismated (not matched properly); not fit; not able to get along with.

dee hemuu.
Not on speaking terms.

dee hilihili.
Indifferent.

de eidu pale.
Fortunately, luckily.

dee lago --.
Not quite —.

dee lago dae.
Not really good or sufficient, etc.

dee lahilahia.
Big (and therefore good), strong, tremendous.

deelenga. (B-1 DEḶE)
n.

dee madaladala de langi.
Raining without let-up.

dee maeva.
Not present, absent.

dee mahana tae.
Stay for only a short time.

dee manava age.
Do earnestly.

dee masae de leo.
Lose one's voice (from straining one's vocal cords).

dee modu.
Continually.

dee ni dago.
Never mind!

deengaa.
Let's — right away! *d.*

deengaa gamalie.
Let's do it attentively!

dee ngado mai.
Forever, eternally.

dee sao age.
Always fail or be defeated.

dee savaa (naa) de --.
Soon —.

dee savala.
Uninterested in; not enjoy.

dee vaagidee.
Ugly, awful; extremely disappointing.

dee vaaseegina.
Hardly able to wait for.

dee vasu.
Fearless (socially); inconsiderate.

de gai i mua.
Favorite food.

deganoe.
A part of the female genitalia. *n.*

de gau duuli sou.
Gilbertese people.

dege.
Corner. *nl.*

degedege. (R-- DEGE)
To wiggle the hips repeatedly. *v.*

degi$_1$.
To jerk; get something quickly. *v.*

degi$_2$. (B-- DEGI$_3$)
Kind, generous, forgiving. *a.*

degia. (B-2 DEGI$_1$)
v.

degi ange.
Forgive (someone), pardon (someone).

degidegi$_1$. (R-- DEGI$_1$)
To jerk repeatedly; bawl out (speak harshly to). *v.*

degidegi$_2$. (R-- DEGI$_2$)
Ticklish. *a.*

degidegi$_3$. (R-- DEGI$_3$)
Having a kind or generous nature. *a.*

degidegia. (R-2 DEGI$_1$)
v.

degidegingaa$_1$. (R-1 DEGI$_1$)
n.

degidegingaa$_2$. (R-1 DEGI$_2$)
n.

de heduu o taiao.
Morning star.

dehee. (B-- HEE$_{2d}$)
Which? *b.*

de hia.
Which number?

de-hine-aligi$_1$.
Insect sp.: cockroach sp. (black — foul smelling). *n.*

De-hine-aligi$_2$. (ALIGI, HINE)
The chief female spirit on Nukuoro (in legendary times). *nn.*

de hine dabeo.
A menstruating woman.

de hine hagahaanau.
Midwife.

de hua nei.
This size.

dehui. (B-- HUI$_2$)
Tens of coconuts [cf. *ngahui*]. *n.*

de huu de henua.
The layer of consolidated sand (without coral rubble) next to the reef base under the island.

de ia.
The, thing, it.

delaa. (B-- LAA$_{1d}$)
That one (over there). *b.*

delaa ai.
Therefore (with respect to that there).

delaa ai huu.
That was it (as before)!

delaa ai laa.
That there was it!

delaa ai loo.
That was it at last!

delaa ange.
That there is another one!

delaa ange maalie.
That there is exactly right!

delaa ange naa.
About that [sing.] (over there), much more.

delaadeu.
Their [3] one. *pp.*

delaa donu.
That there is it for sure!

delaa tagodo.
That there is the situation...

delaa tee madea.
Hard to tell apart from; resemble closely.

delaa huu.
That was it just as before.

delaa laa (?).
That there was it (was that it?).

delaa loo.
That was it.

delaa maa.
That there was about (approximately).

delaa muhuu.
How about that one there?

delaa naa (?).
That there will be it (will that be it?).

delaa naa loo.
That there could be it.

delaa nei (?).
That there is it (is that there it?).

delaa sili.
That there is enough.

delaau.
Their [2] one. *pp.*

dele.
Move from one place to another; to sail (a canoe); be transmitted; slip out of one's hands (e.g., a line on which a big fish has been caught). *v.*

delea. (B-2 DELE)
v.

dele de ada.
Dawn (first light).

dele de boialiali.
Daybreak.

dele de gada.
Smile.

deledele. (R-- DELE)
—; move swiftly. *v.*

deledele kau.
Walk proudly [culturally disapproved], strut.

deledele hainga a me.
Rush because of an emergency.

deledelenga. (R-1 DELE)
n.

deledele saele.
Walk around aimlessly; be spread all over (of news).

dele de longo.
Spread news or rumors.

dele de maahaa.
Daybreak.

dele de mahaa.
Starting to crack.

delengia. (B-2 DELE)
v.

deleulu. (DELE, ULU_1)
Good at catching tuna. *v.*

demaadeu.
Our [excl. 3] one. *pp.*

demaau.
Our [excl. 2] one. *pp.*

denaa. (B-- NAA_{1b})
This one (near you); that one (near you); That's right! *b.*

denaa ai.
Therefore (with respect to this, there near you, or concerning, you).

denaa ai huu.
That is it then!

denaa ai laa.
That was it!

denaa ai loo.
That is it (which has been decided upon).

denaa ange.
This there is another one!

denaa ange maalie.
That is exactly right!

denaa ange naa.
About that [sing.] (here), much more.

denaa donu.
That is it for sure!

denaa tagodo.
That is the situation...

denaa huu.
That is it still.

denaa laa (?).
That is it there (is that it there?).

denaa loo.
That was the one.

denaa maa.
That is about (approximately).

denaa muhuu.
How about that one?

denaa naa (?).
That will be it. (Will that be it?).

denaa naa loo.
That seems to be it; that could be it.

denaa sili.
That is enough!

denei. (B-- NEI$_b$)
This one. *b.*

denei ai.
Therefore (with respect to this here).

dnei ai huu.
This is it still.

denei ai laa.
This is that then.

denei ai loo.
This then is —.

denei ange.
This is another one!

denei ange maalie.
This is exactly right!

denei ange naa.
About this [sing.], much more...

denei au.
It is I!

denei donu.
This is it for sure!

denei tagodo.
This is the situation...

denei huu.
This is it still.

denei laa (?).
This is that (is this that?).

denei loo.
This is it at last.

denei maa.
This is about (approximately).

denei muhuu.
How about this one?

denei naa (?).
This will be it. (Will this be it?).

denei naa loo.
This seems to be.

denei nei (?).
This is it! (Is this it?).

denei sili.
This is enough!

denga$_1$.
The (several); each of —. *ma.*

denga$_2$.
A hump on a tree trunk (where a branch failed to flower). *n.*

dengaa. (B-- DENGA$_{1a}$)
The (several) I have in mind; each of — I have in mind. *ma.*

dengadenga. (R-- DENGA$_2$)
Having many *denga.* *v.*

denga hhuge --.
Upward current.

de ulu hagabolebole.
Topmost part of any standing object.

devedeve. (R-- DEVE)
Standing out all over (of feathers, etc.). *a.*

devedevenga. (R-1 DEVE)
n.

diadia. (R-- DIA)
To make a cover for something (e.g., a coconut shell) by plaiting or lashing around it. *v.*

diadiaanga. (R-1 DIA)
n.

diadialia. (R-2 DIA)
v.

diba$_1$.
Not level, tipped to one side. *a.*

diba$_2$.
Portion, share (of something); part (of something); fraction (in arithmetic). *n.*

dibaa dodo.
A clot of blood.

Diba-dahi. (XCO DAHI$_1$)
The name of a person in a traditional story. *nn.*

dibadiba. (R-- DIBA$_1$)
Unsteady (as a ship on the sea). *a.*

dibadibaanga. (R-1 DIBA$_1$)
n.

dibadibalia. (R-2 DIBA$_1$)
v.

Diba-dolu. (XCO DOLU)
The name of a person in a traditional story. *nn.*

Diba-haa. (XCO HAA$_3$)
The name of a person in a traditional story. *nn.*

Diba-hidu. (XCO HIDU)
The name of a person in a traditional story. *nn.*

diba iho.
To tip down; go away from the atoll.

dibalia. (B-2 DIBA$_1$)
v.

Diba-lima. (XCO LIMA$_a$)
The name of a person in a traditional story. *nn.*

Diba-lua. (XCO LUA)
The name of a person in a traditional story. *nn.*

Diba-madaangahulu. (XCO HULU$_3$)
The name of a person in a traditional story. *nn.*

Diba-ono. (XCO ONO$_1$)
The name of a person in a traditional story. *nn.*

Diba-siva. (XCO SIVA)
The name of a person in a traditional story. *nn.*

Diba-valu. (XCO VALU$_2$)
The name of a person in a traditional story. *nn.*

dibidibi. (R-- DIBI)
A square ball (for tossing about) plaited of pandanus leaves. *n.*

dibo.
Infant. *n.*

dibononi. (DIBO, NONI)
The youngest child of a couple. *n.*

didi. (B-- DIDI$_1$)
Grass skirt (of hibiscus fiber or palm leaf); to wear a grass skirt. *a.*

didianga. (B-1 DIDI$_1$)
The manner of wearing one's *didi*. *n.*

ditidi. (R-- DIDI$_2$)
To skim across the surface of land or water. *a.*

ditidianga. (R-1 DIDI$_2$)
n.

dige.
Roll over or about, turn (as of a wheel), spin, revolve, rotate. *a.*

dige de belubelu.
A circuit made by a school of *belubelu*.

digedige. (R-- DIGE)
a.

digedigelia. (R-2 DIGE)
v.

digedigenga. (R-1 DIGE)
n.

digelia. (B-2 DIGE)
v.

diha.
Move something by using a lever (esp. a pole) on a fulcrum; contradict. *v.*

dihaanga. (B-1 DIHA)
n.

dihadiha. (R-- DIHA)
v.

dihadihaanga. (R-1 DIHA)
n.

dihidihi. (R-- DIHI)
Fish sp.: butterfly fish (The native term is applied to many spp.). *n.*

dii.
Shine (sun). *v.*

diianga. (B-1 DII)
n.

dii ange.
A method of fishing in which the lure at the end of the pole is jerked to attract fish.

diibanga. (B-1 $DIBA_1$)
n.

diibanga goo dii.
A game played by children (to determine who is "it").

diibanga o de henua.
The categories of ancient custom.

diibuli.
A doll representing a spirit (from the story of *duudebaabaa*). *n.*

diidegaehala*. (CF DII)
The sixth child of a couple. *n.*

dii de laa.
The shining of the sun.

$diidii_1$. (R-- DII)
v.

$diidii_2$. (B-- DIIDII)
Penis; urinate. *a.*

diidiianga. (R-1 DII)
n.

diidii ange.
Urinate against.

diidiinei. (R-- DIINEI)
v.

diidiineia. (R-2 DIINEI)
v.

diidiineinga. (R-1 DIINEI)
n.

diidiinga. (B-1 DIIDII)
Manner of urinating. *n.*

diidiingia. (R-2 DII)
Be frequently exposed to the sun's rays. *v.*

diigenga. (B-1 DIGE)
n.

diihagaai*. (CF DII)
The eighth child of a couple. *n.*

diilaulauhai*. (CF DII)
The seventh child of a couple. *n.*

diilevalevanoa*. (CF DII)
The fifth child of a couple. *n.*

diilinga. (B-1 DILI)
n.

diilonga. (B-1 $DILO_1$)
n.

diiloo. (E-- $DILO_1$)
Look after; look at attentively. *v.*

diimadamadanoa*. (CF DII)
The ninth child of a couple. *n.*

diimolalaaidu*. (CF DII)
The tenth child of a couple. *n.*

diinei.
To extinguish (e.g., a fire, or the life of a plant, or the heat of the sun — as by clouds); to smooth rough edges. *v.*

diineia. (B-2 DIINEI)
v.

diinei de lodo.
Become calmer (after being angry).

diinei de madangi.
A decrease of wind velocity.

diinei de manu.
To kill off plants.

diinei mai.
Make smaller; decrease.

diinei mai dege.
To round off a sharp edge.

diineinga. (B-1 DIINEI)
n.

diinonga. (B-1 $DINO_1$)
A spirit which is worshipped; bad character (of a person). *a.*

diinonga eidu.
An idol representing a spirit.

diinonga-o-salo.
Fish sp.

diingia. (B-2 DII)
To be exposed to the sun's rays. *v.*

dili.
Shoot at; shine (e.g., a flashlight) on; let go, throw away, lose something; disregard; steady beating (as of a heart); a steady stroke (as of an adze). *v.*

dilia. (B-2 DILI)
v.

dili aalanga.
Exhausted (physically or mentally).

dilia ange.
Give fish to.

dili bala.
Collapse (of persons).

dili dagidahi.
Happening continually but one at a time.

dili dagidahi age.
Release one at a time or intermittently or sporadically.

dili dai.
Any current flowing away from the atoll.

dili dangada.
To fail to discharge one's obligations to help (esp. one's kin).

dili de lima.
To swing one's arms (when walking).

dilidili. (R-- DILI)
v.

dilidilia. (R-2 DILI)
v.

dilidili-dogi.
Bird sp.: Polynesian tattler? (*Heteroscelus brevipes*).

dilidilinga. (R-1 DILI)
n.

dili ebuebu.
Exhalation of air under water (forming bubbles).

dili gaiaa.
Sneak a look.

dilimangali. (DILI, MANGALI)
To catch flying fish [from the Ponapean *indilmenger*?]. *v.*

dili uda.
An ocean current which comes towards the shore (and carries in driftwood, etc.).

dilo$_1$.
Look at (inspect). *v.*

dilo$_2$.
The immature leaf of any plant, except of the coconut; a coconut leaflet midrib after scraping, soaking and drying. *n.*

dilodilo. (R-- DILO$_1$)
v.

dilodilonga. (R-1 DILO$_1$)
The manner in which one looks at one's reflection or appearance. *n.*

dilo gaiaa.
Sneak a look.

dilongaagau. (DILO$_1$, GAU$_{1d}$)
Voyeurism. *v.*

dinae.
Belly; the edible white part of clam meat. *n.*

dinae o de laa.
Ballooning of a sail.

dinae o ssaiolo.
[= *dinae o de laa*].

dinana.
Mother, aunt; senior female relative, person in a mothering, or motherly, relationship. *n.*

dinana donu.
Natural mother.

dinana mai i daha.
Stepmother.

dinihu.
Industrious, hardworking. *v.*

dino$_1$.
A share of, allotment, portion. *a.*

dino$_2$ + NUMBER (B-- DINO$_2$)
NUMERAL CLASSIFIER (BY TENS) FOR PERSONS. *mc.*

dinoanga hulu*.
A council (of ten) formerly having broad legislative and judicial powers on the atoll.

dino boo.
Nights (2) when the full moon appears just after sunset.

dingale.
Secretion of the genitalia (male or female); the milky sap on some pandanus plugs. *n.*

doa.
Giant. *n.*

doa agalala.
Very big giant.

doadoa.
The sound made to attract chickens. *v.*

doadoaanga. (B-1 DOADOA)
n.

dodi.
Have a limp (physical condition). *a.*

dodinga. (B-1 DODI)
n.

dodo$_1$. (B-- DODO)
Blood. *v.*

dodo$_2$.
Each person's one. *pto.*

dodo ina.
Bloody [of garments, etc.].

dotodi. (R-- DODI)
Limping (as an action). *a.*

dotodinga. (R-1 DODI)
n.

dotodo. (R-- DODO)
Bloody (of a person). *v.*

dotodoanga. (R-1 DODO)
n.

dotodolia. (R-2 DODO)
v.

dotonogaa. (?)
Fish sp.: goby. *n.*

doe.
Left over, remain. *a.*

doea. (B-2 DOE)
a.

doedoe. (R-- DOE)
Still remaining, still left over. *a.*

doedoea. (R-2 DOE)
a.

doedoenga. (R-1 DOE)
n.

doenga. (B-1 DOE)
n.

doga$_1$.
Land on (as a bird lands on the branch of a tree). *a.*

doga$_2$*.
A (live) coral formation. *n.*

dogaa.
Bashful, ashamed, shy, embarrassed. *a.*

dogaa ange.
Feel shy in the presence of.

dogaanga$_1$. (B-1 DOGA$_1$)
n.

dogaanga$_2$. (B-1 DOGAA)
n.

doga de manu.
Nesting of *gadada*, or *gaalau*, or *gailulu*.

dogadoga. (R-- DOGA$_1$)
a.

dogadogaa. (R-- DOGAA)
Having a tendency to be *dogaa*. *a.*

dogadogaanga$_1$. (R-1 DOGA$_1$)
n.

dogadogaanga$_2$. (R-1 DOGAA)
n.

dogadogalia. (R-2 DOGA$_1$)
v.

dogai.
Transverse tie beam [rests on *ssanga*]. *n.*

dogalia. (B-2 DOGA$_1$)
v.

dogi.
Adze; a tapping movement. *n.*

dogia. (B-2 DOGI)
Be wet from the rain. *v.*

dogiaanga. (B-3 DOGI)
n.

dogi daadaa.
A type of adze (with a small blade, for light chipping).

dogi hakolona.
A type of adze (with a curved blade of *Terebra* shell).

dogi hoda.
A type of adze (heavy — for hollowing out logs, etc.).

dogi hulihuli.
[= *sauligi*].

dogo$_1$.
To punt (propel a canoe by poling); punt pole. *v.*

dogo$_2$ + NUMBER. (B-- DOGO$_2$)
NUMERAL CLASSIFIER FOR PERSONS (by ones). *mc.*

dogoa. (B-2 DOGO$_1$)
v.

dogodoganga*. (R-1 $DOGO_1$)
Plant sp. [archaic name of *manugilimaau*]. *n.*

dogodogo. (R-- $DOGO_1$)
v.

dogodogoa. (R-2 $DOGO_1$)
v.

dogodogoisi. (R-- $DOGO_{2a}$)
Becoming fewer and fewer. *a.*

dogodogolia. (R-2 $DOGO_1$)
v.

dogodogona. (R-2 $DOGO_1$)
v.

dogodogonga. (R-1 $DOGO_1$)
n.

dogoduli. ($DOGO_1$, $DULI_2$)
Crouch on all fours. *a.*

dogo duu.
To punt while standing up on the stern gunwales of a canoe.

dogo huadia.
A way of punting a canoe.

dogoisi. (B-- $DOGO_{2a}$)
Few. *a.*

dogoisi loo huu.
Very few.

dogoisi mai.
Decreasing (in number).

dogolia. (B-2 $DOGO_1$)
v.

dogona. (B-2 $DOGO_1$)
v.

dogonogo.
Tip of the spine (caudal vertebrae). *n.*

dogu.
My one. *ppo.*

doha.
To spread out (something). *v.*

dohaa. (B-2 DOHA)
v.

dohaanga. (B-1 DOHA)
n.

dohadoha. (R-- DOHA)
v.

dohadohaa. (R-2 DOHA)
v.

dohadohaanga. (R-1 DOHA)
n.

dohadohalia. (R-2 DOHA)
v.

dohalia. (B-2 DOHA)
v.

dohe.
Mollusk sp: a bivalve sp. *n.*

dohi.
d.

dohi dilo.
To strip *dilo* (to make plaited hats, etc.).

dohidohi. (R-- DOHI)
—; divide up. *v.*

dohidohia. (R-2 DOHI)
v.

dohidohinga. (R-1 DOHI)
n.

dohi lau.
To strip pandanus leaves (to make mats, etc.).

dohu.
Sufficient, enough; able to cover a given area. *a.*

dohu ange.
Sufficient for.

dohu de angaanga.
Covered (all over the body) with —.

dohu de gili.
Covered all over (skin) with.

dohudohu. (R-- DOHU)
a.

dohudohunga. (R-1 DOHU)
n.

dohulia. (B-2 DOHU)
v.

dohu lodo.
Full to capacity.

doi.
Stain (permanent); any of a number of hardwood saps [found in driftwood] from which perfume is made. *v.*

doi-avaava.
The sap of a hardwood sp. which drifts ashore (used for making perfume).

doidoi. (R-- DOI)
v.

doidoinga. (R-1 DOI)
n.

doi-giva.
The sap of a hardwood sp. which drifts ashore [used for making perfume].

doi-lesi.
The sap of a hardwood sp. which drifts ashore [used for making perfume].

doinga. (B-1 DOI)
n.

dola.
Erection (of penis). *a.*

dolaanga. (B-1 DOLA)
n.

doladola. (R-- DOLA)
v.

doladolaanga. (R-1 DOLA)
n.

doli.
To obtain as many as one can; to defeat all comers. *v.*

dolia. (B-2 DOLI)
v.

doli age.
Obtain the smallest first.

doli de henua.
To defeat all comers.

dolidoli. (R-- DOLI)
v.

dolidolia. (R-2 DOLI)
v.

dolidolinga. (R-1 DOLI)
n.

doli iho.
To obtain the biggest first.

dolinga. (B-1 DOLI)
n.

dolo$_1$. (B-- DOLO)
Creep (a very slow movement over the ground). *a.*

dolo$_2$. (B-- DOLO)
Plant sp.: sugarcane [several varieties]. *n.*

dolo$_3$. (B-- DOLO$_a$)
The name of a name-group. *n.*

doloa.
The name of a name-group. *n.*

dolo bala.
To climb a coconut tree without using a rope (on one's hands or feet) for assistance.

dolodolo. (R-- DOLO)
—; logs on the sides of the house floor (to retain gravel); the bulge on the side of a knife blade. *a.*

dolodolohi. (R-- DOOLOHI)
v.

dolodolohia. (R-2 DOOLOHI)
v.

dolodolohinga. (R-1 DOOLOHI)
n.

dolodolo manu ligi.
The physical sensation (like bugs crawling on one) after one's leg, etc., has been asleep.

dolodolona. (R-2 DOLO)
Often flooded. *v.*

dolodolonga. (R-1 DOLO)
n.

dolodolo o de ava.
[= *luu dolodolo*].

dolohia. (B-2 DOOLOHI)
v.

doloinui. (DOLO, NUI$_1$)
A hard lump inside a female's stomach [tumor?]; a coconut of the youngest stage of development. *a.*

dolo-mea.
Spiny starfish.

dolona. (B-2 DOLO)
Flooded, washed out. *v.*

dolonoa. (XCO)
[Var. of *olonoa* (sea cucumber)]. *n.*

dolu.
Three. *an.*

dolu-inoha.
The third number of a counting game played to determine who is "it".

dona.
Wart, mole (raised). *v.*

donadona. (R-- DONA)
Covered with *dona*. *v.*

dono.
His one, her one, its one. *ppo.*

donu$_1$.
Real, really. *mv.*

donu$_2$. (B-- DONU$_{1a}$)
Understand; truth, right, correct. *a.*

donu$_3$. (B-- DONU$_2$)
Fish sp.: sea bass (= small *ava*). *n.*

donu ange.
Understand (someone or something).

donudonu. (R-- DONU$_{1a}$)
Understand somewhat. *a.*

donudonuanga. (R-1 DONU$_{1a}$)
n.

donu gee.
Misunderstand.

donu huu.
Only, just (no more than).

donu iho.
Realize, understand.

donu sala.
Misunderstand.

donga.
Plant sp.: oriental mangrove (*Bruguiera gymnorhiza* (L.) Lam.). *n.*

dongi.
A spot (e.g., on the skin); point at; peck at; a method of fishing for flying fish in which torches are extinguished on alternate legs of the canoe track. *v.*

dongia. (B-2 DONGI)
v.

dongi ange.
Appoint.

dongi de gelegele.
To peck at the sand (as do some kinds of fish when they are searching for food).

dongi de lae.
A spot on the forehead [worn in ancient religious ceremonies].

dongidongi. (R-- DONGI)
Spotted (covered with spots); to keep pointing at or peeking at. *v.*

dongidongia. (R-2 DONGI)
v.

dongidonginga. (R-1 DONGI)
n.

doo$_1$.
Get down, get off; take up a string figure (from another's hands); fall; plant (something); drop down. *v.*

doo$_2$.
An evil scheme. *n.*

doo$_3$.
Your [1] one. *ppo.*

dooa. (B-2 DOO$_1$)
Planted. *v.*

doo ade.
[A joking expression: lit., 'your liver'!].

doo ai me.
[= *doo me ai*].

dooanga. (B-1 DOO$_1$)
—; row of plants. *n.*

doopeva*.
Trick, prank. *v.*

doo dai.
Appearing from lagoonward; to come from lagoonward; wind direction from the west.

doo de --.
Transfer of a string figure from hand to hand.

doo de gai me.
Miss a meal or meals (leading to nausea when eating is resumed).

doo de gauanga.
Dislocated thigh bone.

doo de gulabe.
Prolapsed rectum.

doo de hatuli.
The 'falling of thunder' [thought to burn trees].

doo de lolomango.
Separated (of crude coconut oil).

doo de ssui.
Still damp (but becoming dry).

doodoo. (R-- DOO$_1$)
v.

doodooanga. (R-1 DOO$_1$)
n.

doodou.
Your [3] one. *pp.*

doo tahulinga.
Bad-mannered.

doo togonogo.
Separation of the tip (caudal vertebrae) of the spine.

doo tuugau.
A dislocation of the *tuugau.*

doo gaiaa.
Attack by surprise or stealth; ambush.

doogonga. (B-1 DOGO$_1$)
—; a clearing through coral beds to allow for canoe passage. *n.*

dookaa. (P-- DOGAA)
a.

dookaanga. (P-1 DOGAA)
n.

dookalala.
Stilts, walk on stilts. *a.*

doo halehale me.
Risky, unreliable.

doohia. (B-2 DOHI)
v.

doohinga. (B-1 DOHI)
n.

doohunga. (B-1 DOHU)
n.

doo i de....
Expulsion or voluntary withdrawal (from a group).

doo i de ubu.
Too big in size (of clothes).

doo i hainga a me.
Wait for a long time (beyond the time expected).

doo lalo.
Unsuccessful.

doo lodolodo.
Risky, unreliable.

doolohi.
Chase, run after. *v.*

doolohinga. (B-1 DOOLOHI)
n.

doolonga. (B-1 DOLO)
—; a track left by a crawling thing. *n.*

dooluu.
Your [2] one. *pp.*

doo ma gu....
Fall into the bad habit of; do something which is difficult to rectify.

doo mai de malino.
Completely calm.

doo me.
Plant things.

doo me (ai).
Make fun of, ridicule.

doo mua.
Very.

doonunga. (B-1 DONU$_{1a}$)
n.

doonga.
Tools, equipment (incl. fishing gear). *n.*

doo ngaage.
South wind.

doonga a lima.
One's own tools, or tools with which one is familiar.

doonga pada.
Heavy-duty equipment or fishing gear; a large penis.

doo ngaiho.
The blowing of the wind from the north.

doonginga. (B-1 DONGI)
n.

doo sala.
Accidentally.

dua$_1$.
Diameter (of rope, etc.). *n.*

dua$_2$.
Away from; in back of; after; back (of the body). *nl.*

duaa dai.
Seasick but unable to throw up.

duaa dodo.
Labor pains (of a woman in childbirth).

dua agau.
Beyond the reef, pertaining to the open sea, — like to fish [ds].

duaahaho. (DUA$_2$, HAHO)
Outside of (e.g., a building). *nl.*

dua alohagi.
Fishing line of a size appropriate for trolling.

duaanui. (DUA$_1$, NUI$_1$)
Coconut palm frond spines. *n.*

dua pada.
To plait with thick strands.

dua daabasi.
The size of fishing line appropriate for tuna fishing.

duadae. (DAE_3, DUA_2)
Gullible, be a sucker. *v.*

dua dama.
The pallor of a female following childbirth.

duadonu. ($DONU_{1a}$, DUA_2)
Luck, good fortune. *a.*

dua duiagi.
Fishing line of the largest size (on which a whole *belubelu* is used as bait).

dua gaahanga.
One of the lines of which *gaahanga* is composed).

duagi.
To clean fish (taking the insides out). *v.*

duagia. (B-2 DUAGI)
v.

dua gi lunga.
Thicker (line or rope, etc.).

dua gina.
Fishing line of a size appropriate for *gina* fishing.

duagina. (B-2 DUAGI)
v.

duaginga. (B-1 DUAGI)
n.

dua haangoda de boo.
Fishing line of a size appropriate for *haangoda de boo.*

dua hagalalo.
Fishing line of a size appropriate for the *hagalalo* method of fishing.

$duai_1$.
Old (in the past). *a.*

$duai_2$.
Stool grater (for grating coconuts). *n.*

duai lalo vae.
A type of coconut grater which is placed under the leg.

dua lele.
To throw one's back out of joint.

dua lligi.
Thin (line or rope, etc.); fine (thread, etc.); tenderly.

dua-nei.
Of or from the Marshall islands [ds].

dua nnui.
Violence; a type of rope (thick, with thick strands).

dua saali.
One of the lines of which *saali* is composed.

duasala. (DUA_2, $SALA_2$)
Hardship, difficulty. *a.*

duasivi. (DUA_2, SIVI)
The back of the spine. *n.*

duba.
Land crab sp. (small). *n.*

dube.
Movements perceived under the covers; the swarming of maggots in meat. *a.*

dubea. (B-2 DUBE)
v.

dubedube. (R-- DUBE)
a.

dubedubea. (R-2 DUBE)
v.

dubedubenga. (R-1 DUBE)
n.

dubenga. (B-1 DUBE)
n.

dubu.
Exceed (the amount required), too — (e.g., many). *a.*

dubua. (B-2 DUBU)
—; a person of extraordinary ability. *v.*

dubuanga. (B-1 DUBU)
n.

dubudubu. (R-- DUBU)
a.

dubudubua. (R-2 DUBU)
v.

dubudubuanga. (R-1 DUBU)
n.

dubudubulia. (R-2 DUBU)
v.

dubulia. (B-2 DUBU)
v.

dubuna.
Grandparent, ancestor. *n.*

dudu.
Set fire to, burn. *v.*

dudu de niho.
A method of treating toothaches in which a burning root (of the *aoa* tree) is applied to the tooth (which later disintegrates).

dutudu. (R-- DUDU)
Play with fire. *v.*

dutuduanga. (R-1 DUDU)
n.

duge.
Either side of a recession in the top of a *duludulu*. *n.*

dugi₁.
Punch, hit, strike; bump into; pound —, pound on. *d.*

dugi₂.
Scare away, chase away. *v.*

dugia. (B-2 DUGI₂)
v.

dugi de lodo.
To fish in various places (in the lagoon) in order to catch as many fish (of any kind) as possible.

dugidugi₁. (R-- DUGI₁)
v.

dugidugi₂. (R-- DUGI₂)
v.

dugidugia₁. (R-2 DUGI₁)
v.

dugidugia₂. (R-2 DUGI₂)
v.

dugidugina. (R-2 DUGI₂)
v.

dugiduginga₁. (R-1 DUGI₁)
n.

dugiduginga₂. (R-1 DUGI₂)
n.

dugi gee.
Chase away (in a certain direction).

dugilima. (DUGI₁, LIMA)
Elbow. *n.*

dugina. (B-2 DUGI₂)
v.

duginga. (B-1 DUGI₂)
n.

dugu.
Put, place [verb]; leave (put down). *v.*

dugua. (B-2 DUGU)
v.

duguagi. (B-- DUGUa)
Be suspicious of (someone). *v.*

duguaginga. (B-1 DUGUa)
n.

dugu dagidahi.
Place (or leave off) one at a time.

dugu dahi.
Accomplish or complete something in a single effort; fishing with a single line.

dugu de gubenga.
Set a *gubenga* net.

dugu de gumigumi.
Allow one's beard to grow, unshaven.

dugu de laa.
Lower sail.

dugu de uinga.
To lay down a new cover of palm fronds on *uinga*.

dugudugu. (R-- DUGU)
v.

dugudugua. (R-2 DUGU)
v.

duguduguagi. (R-- DUGUa)
v.

duguduguaginga. (R-1 DUGUa)
n.

dugudugu iho.
A technique of massage.

dugudugulia. (R-2 DUGU)
v.

dugudugunga. (R-1 DUGU)
n.

dugu gee.
Put aside, set aside; treat (a person) differently from others.

dugulia. (B-2 DUGU)
v.

duha.
Divide among, division (in arithmetic). *v.*

duhaduha. (R-- DUHA)
v.

duhaduhanga. (R-1 DUHA)
n.

duhalia. (B-2 DUHA)
v.

dui.
Stab with a sharp object, pierce with a sharp object, sew, string (flowers or fish, etc.); straight course (of a canoe). *v.*

duia. (B-2 DUI)
v.

duiaanga. (B-3 DUI)
The way in which something is stuck by a sharp object. *n.*

duiagi. (B-- DUI_a)
Fishing using a whole fish as bait. *v.*

duiagina. (B-2 DUI_a)
v.

duiaginga. (B-1 DUI_a)
n.

duidui. (R-- DUI)
v.

duiduia. (R-2 DUI)
—; covered with sharp spines, etc. *v.*

duiduinga. (R-1 DUI)
n.

duilaa.
To be unable to attract members of the opposite sex. *v.*

duilaa gee.
To be exceedingly unsuccessful with members of the opposite sex.

duilaanga. (B-1 DUILAA)
n.

dui mamu.
A string of fish.

dui manu.
A line of flying birds.

dui moni.
A fleet of canoes (in line).

duinga. (B-1 DUI)
—; seam (in clothes). *n.*

dulagi.
Appearance, example, situation. *n.*

dulagi ange.
Look like.

dulagi be --.
It seems that —.

dulagi daudahi.
Alike (in appearance).

dulagi sala.
Bad situation; presenting a poor appearance (esp. when ill).

$duli_1$. (B-- $DULI_3$)
Bird sp.: golden plover (*Plurialis dominica*). *n.*

$duli_2$.
Knee. *n.*

duliduli. (R-- $DULI_1$)
Hurting of one's ears from high-pitched noises. *v.*

dulidulia. (R-2 $DULI_1$)
v.

duliduli nga. (R-1 $DULI_1$)
n.

dulivai. ($DULI_3$, VAI)
A type of coconut (reddish in color). *n.*

duludulu. (R-- DULU)
Ooze. *d.*

duluduluanga. (R-1 DULU)
n.

dumanu.
Appearance, situation. *n.*

dumanu sala.
Bad situation; poor in appearance.

dumuagi.
Top of the head, bare hilltop. *n.*

Dumulu. (B-- DUMULU)
July. *n.*

duna.
Larvae (of mosquito, etc.) found in water. *n.*

$dunu_1$.
Cook, heat up; boil (water). *v.*

$dunu_2$.
A hole in the base of a coconut tree trunk (which collects water for drinking). *n.*

dunudunu. (R-- DUNU$_1$)
v.

dunu madamada.
Rare (not cooked thoroughly).

dungadungagi. (R-- DUNGAGI)
v.

dungadungaginga. (R-1 DUNGAGI)
n.

dungagi.
Nod (one's head). *v.*

dungagi ange.
Nod one's head toward (to beckon or indicate agreement, etc.).

dungaginga. (B-1 DUNGAGI)
n.

dungu.
Smell (something). *v.*

dungua. (B-2 DUNGU)
v.

dunguanga. (B-1 DUNGU)
n.

dungudungu. (R-- DUNGU)
Have a good sense of smell. *v.*

dungudungua. (R-2 DUNGU)
Repeatedly smell (something). *v.*

dungudunguanga. (R-1 DUNGU)
n.

dungudungulia. (R-2 DUNGU)
v.

dungu iho.
Smell oneself.

dungulia. (B-2 DUNGU)
v.

duoi.
Parasites (intestinal) of fish. *n.*

duosi.
Servant. *a.*

duu$_1$.
d.

duu$_2$.
Stand, situated; married. *v.*

duu$_3$. (B-- DUU$_{1a}$)
Half (of something like a coconut). *n.*

duua. (B-2 DUU$_2$)
v.

duuaa.
To be in trouble. *v.*

duuaanga. (B-1 DUUAA)
n.

duuanga. (B-1 DUU$_2$)
n.

duu ange.
Wait for; resemble someone (owing to a consanguineal relationship).

duu baeao.
Piece of coconut husk.

duu-baeao.
Fish sp.: filefish.

duu baebae.
To appear in the distance as a row of small objects (like adjacent islets on the atoll).

duu bale.
Not quite vertical.

duu beleala. (ALA$_2$, BELE, DUU$_{1a}$)
Immature coconut apple. *n.*

duu biho.
Haircut; cut hair.

duubulei. (BULE, DUU$_2$)
Head of the penis. *n.*

duubunga. (B-1 DUBU)
n.

duu podo.
Do something at short intervals; often, frequently.

duudae. (XCO DAE$_3$)
Feces. *n.*

duudae baa.
The dust produced by working pearl shell to make a hook.

duudae goede.
The inky excretion of the octopus.

duudae maadau.
[= *duudae baa*, q.v.].

duudae nguu.
The inky excretion of the squid.

duudagi.
Connect up, join up, continue upon. *v.*

duudagina. (B-2 DUUDAGI)
v.

duudaginga. (B-1 DUUDAGI)
n.

duu dalo.
Piece of soft taro.

duudane. (XCO $DANE_2$)
Buttock. *n.*

duudanga. (B-1 DUU_1)
—; (a big) piece of; verse (of a song). *n.*

duudanga aheahe.
Refrain (of song).

duudangaa solo.
A package of *solo* (food) wrapped in coconut leaves and heated; flashlight battery.

duudanga daahili.
Verse of a song.

duu de --$_1$.
Having plenty of.

duu de --$_2$.
Make a string figure.

duu de gona.
Umbilical hernia.

duu de ogaanga.
Having husked many coconuts (as evidenced by the many husks lying about).

duu de umada.
A rainbow appearing in the sky.

duudia. (B-2 DUU_1)
v.

duu donu.
Vertical.

duudua.
Taro plot. *n.*

duudua-a-de-honu.
Seaweed sp.

duuduagi. (R-- DUAGI)
v.

duuduagia. (R-2 DUAGI)
v.

duuduagina. (R-2 DUAGI)
v.

duuduaginga. (R-1 DUAGI)
n.

duu duli.
Kneel.

duudunga. (B-1 DUDU)
n.

duuduu$_1$. (R-- DUU_1)
v.

duuduu$_2$. (R-- DUU_2)
Stand around (idly); defecate [baby talk]; hillock, high. *v.*

duuduua. (R-2 DUU_2)
—; taro plot. *v.*

duuduuanga. (R-1 DUU_2)
n.

duuduudagi. (R-- DUUDAGI)
v.

duuduudagina. (R-2 DUUDAGI)
v.

duuduudaginga. (R-1 DUUDAGI)
n.

duuduudanga. (R-1 DUU_1)
n.

duuduudia. (R-2 DUU_1)
v.

duuduu lagi.
A diving platform (made from a tree stuck in a coral head).

duuduulagi. (R-- DUU_{2C})
v.

duuduulagia. (R-2 DUU_{2C})
v.

duuduulagina. (R-2 DUU_{2C})
v.

duuduulaginga. (R-1 DUU_{2C})
n.

duuduuli. (R-- DUULI)
v.

duuduulia$_1$. (R-2 DUU_2)
v.

duuduulia$_2$. (R-2 DUULI)
v.

duuduulinga. (R-1 DUULI)
n.

duuduu manu.
A diving platform (made from a tree stuck in a coral head).

duu taelodo.
Obtain one's quota.

duu taua.
Outbreak of war.

duu gaha.
A large piece of *gaha* (used for *mili gaadinga*), or from which sennit fibers are obtained).

duu galeve.
To collect the sap of a coconut tree (from its inflorescence).

duu gaso.
Vertical, straight up and down.

duugau. (GAU_{1b}, DUU_2)
Legs at the base of the canoe mast. *n.*

duu gee.
Out of alignment.

duugia. (B-2 $DUGI_1$)
—; tired of. *v.*

duugia i de gai.
Be tired of eating a particular kind of food.

duu gili somo.
The coconut meat remaining in a germinated coconut after the coconut apple has been removed.

duuginga. (B-1 $DUGI_1$)
n.

duugiva.
Rough texture, of a plaited object (such as a mat). *a.*

duugivaanga. (B-1 DUUGIVA)
n.

duugunga. (B-1 DUGU)
n.

duugunga o de henua.
Customs of the island (Nukuoro).

duu keli.
Firmly in place, earnestly.

duu kolu.
Stand bracing oneself.

duuhaa. (B-2 DUHA)
v.

duu hagasabasaba.
To stand in a place from which one is liable to fall.

duu hakaa.
A piece of coconut husk.

duu-hakaa.
Fish sp. (var. of *duubaeao*).

duuhanga. (B-1 DUHA)
n.

duuhia. (E-2 DUHI)
v.

duuhia ange.
Praised (by others).

duuhinga. (E-1 DUHI)
n.

duuhua. (DUU_{2a}, HUA_1)
Single, unmarried. *a.*

duuhuli.
A type of wave [must be followed either by *ina*, or by another base]. *v.*

duu i de liiliagi.
Equal in status [owing to having the same skills and being of common descent].

duu inai.
A type of mat [a half *inai*].

duula. (B-- DUU_{2b})
The direction from which the wind blows. *n.*

duulagi. (B-- DUU_{2c})
To sail crosswind (for maximum speed). *v.*

duulagia. (B-2 DUU_{2c})
v.

duulagina. (B-2 DUU_{2c})
v.

duulaginga. (B-1 DUU_{2c})
n.

duulale.
A type of game. *n.*

$duulanga_1$. (B-1 DUU_{2b})
The sector from which the wind blows. *n.*

$duulanga_2$. (B-1 DUU_2)
The place of, the track of (something). *n.*

duu-lellele.
Apodous sea cucumber.

duuli.
Surround. *v.*

duulia₁. (B-2 DUU₂)
v.

duulia₂. (B-2 DUULI)
v.

duuli lua.
A method of throwing one's opponent in wrestling.

duulinga. (B-1 DUULI)
n.

duu lua.
To have the strength or capacity of two persons; to take on two persons in a fight.

duulua. (DUU₂, LUA)
Fish sp.: jack (= large *alaala*). *n.*

duumaa. (DUU₂d, MAA₄)
Remainder (less than the preceding number); about, approximately. *u.*

duumaa de gelegele.
Trillion (a million million).

duu malaelae.
An open field (having no trees).

duu midomido.
An abrupt stop of a trajectory (because one end of the missile has dug into the ground, etc.).

duu-mmea.
Sea cucumber sp.

duu modu.
Vertical cut.

duu molomolo.
Visible clearly.

duumono. (DUU₂, MONO)
A type of prepared food (made from taro). *n.*

duu mugamuga.
Half of an unripe coconut; buttock.

duu munimuni.
Hide and seek (a game).

duunaa. (B-2 DUNU₁)
v.

duunanga. (B-1 DUNU₁)
—; that which has been cooked. *n.*

duu nui.
To lower a bunch of cut coconuts from a coconut tree with a rope.

duunga gima.
Half of a clam shell.

duu ngavesi.
A cover of a box.

duungia. (B-2 DUDU)
v.

duu-o-de-hine.
Anything sticky which pulls apart like jelly (applied to certain kinds of sea cucumbers, etc.).

duu saba.
Unstable, poorly balanced.

duusaba.
A type of musical instrument (a stretched palm leaf jiggled while blown against). *n.*

duu ubu haohao.
A piece of taro cooked in a coconut shell with coconut oil.

duu-uli.
Sea cucumber sp.

taa. (E-- DAA₁)
daa at one time; make a sharp turn [pl.]. *v.*

taa de lui.
To bail water from a canoe.

taadeu.
Our [incl. 3] one. *pp.*

taa hagabiibii.
To bail a canoe rapidly.

taane sauaa.
Shark (euphemism).

taanginga. (P-1 DANGI)
n.

taau.
Our [incl. 2] one. *pp.*

taba. (P-- DABA)
A flashing of several lights, a blink of the eyes. *v.*

tabaanga. (P-1 DABA)
n.

tae. (P-- DAE₂)
a.

taenga. (P-1 DAE$_2$)
n.

tagi. (E-- DAGI$_1$)
Tow, drag; suspend from. *v.*

tagi ange.
Contribute (material things) to.

tagi gee.
Tow away.

tagudai. (DAGU$_2$, DAI$_1$)
Coast, shoreline. *nl.*

taha. (E-- DAHA)
A certain string in string figures. *n.*

tahi$_1$. (E-- DAHI$_1$)
First, best. *u.*

tahi$_2$. (E-- DAHI$_2$)
Clean off. *v.*

tahi i tanuaa.
Best of all.

Tahi-laangi. (DAHI$_1$, LAANGI)
Monday ('first day'). *nt.*

Tahi-malama. (DAHI$_1$, MALAMA)
January ('first month'). *nt.*

tai. (E-- DAI$_2$)
[Var. of *dai$_2$*]. *mt.*

taiao daiao.
Tomorrow morning.

taiao danuaa.
Good morning!

tala$_1$. (E-- DALA$_1$)
v.

tala$_2$. (P-- DALA$_2$)
a.

tala$_3$. (E-- DALA$_3$)
v.

tala$_4$. (E-- DALA$_{4b}$)
Rough in texture (as perceived at one time). *a.*

tala baubau.
Confess wrongs.

tala hai sala.
Confess one's sins or errors.

tale. (E-- DALE)
Touch quickly. *v.*

tale age.
Light a match in the dark.

tale ange.
Sharpen (knife).

tale taane.
A tough man.

tali. (E-- DALI$_1$)
Hope for, expectant, waiting; going along with. *v.*

tali hagalodolodo.
Hopeful expectation.

tamaa gauligi.
Baby.

tama e manege.
A person who is capable at almost anything.

tama hagaai.
Poor fellow!

tama legalega.
Infant.

tama legalega eidu.
Pupil of the eye; a cry of a bird or human that sounds like the cry of a baby; the name of a ghost.

tama nei.
[An exclamation, about = Wow!; or, no kidding!; or, watch it!].

tama ulungi.
Coxswain of a canoe rigged for the pole fishing of tuna [he also handles the pole].

tanu. (P-- DANU)
a.

tanuanga. (P-1 DANU)
n.

tanga. (P-- DANGA)
Loose (not tight) [pl.]. *a.*

tangada abasasa.
A European person (or an American).

tangada adi longo.
Gossipy person, tattletale.

tangada aduhale.
The sort of person who feels at home everywhere and is continually visiting [considered uncouth].

tangada dee doo gi de me.
Uncouth person.

tangada hagaai.
Poor fellow!

tangada hai me dabu.
Cult priest.

tangada hai sauaa.
Magician, sorcerer.

tangada maagaga.
Industrious person.

tangada made.
Now you've done it!

tangada sisi.
Secretary.

tangada ssele.
Stupid ass!

tanga gee.
Separated from.

tangi. (P-- DANGI)
Make noise (as an individual). *a.*

tangi gi de me.
All of a sudden (an action not violent).

tao. (E-- DAO_1)
Soak (in water). *v.*

taoa. (E-2 DAO_1)
v.

tao tangada.
To immerse a person in medication.

taonga. (E-1 DAO_1)
n.

tao o de moso.
A coconut frond spine which has fallen and stuck upright in the ground.

tau. (P-- DAU_3)
a.

tau ange.
Cause to be absorbed by.

tau ange luu mada.
Have noticed.

tau ono pagola.
Punished for his bad deeds.

tea. (E-- DEA)
White. *a.*

tea age langi.
The light before daybreak.

teaanga. (E-1 DEA)
n.

tea gee.
Pallor.

tea ma agiagi.
Dead white (whitest hue imaginable).

tee.
NEGATIVE DECISIVE ASPECT MARKER. *mt.*

tee aamia donu.
Not enough.

teeginga. (E-1 $DEGI_2$)
n.

teevenga. (E-1 DEVE)
n.

$tegi_1$. (E-- $DEGI_2$)
Aroused (sexually); tickled (esp. sexually). *a.*

$tegi_2$. (P-- $DEGI_3$)
a.

tegi kano.
Tickled.

tele. (P-- DELE)
v.

teungaalodo. ($LODO_1$, UNGAA)
Middle (of something round); center. *nl.*

teve. (E-- DEVE)
Hair (or feathers) standing on end. *a.*

teve de biho.
To have the hair (of one's head) standing on end.

teve de gili.
Gooseflesh.

tiba. (P-- $DIBA_1$)
a.

tibaanga. (P-1 $DIBA_1$)
n.

tibalia. (P-2 $DIBA_1$)
v.

tige. (P-- DIGE)
a.

tigelia. (P-2 DIGE)
v.

tigi.
Not yet —. *mt.*

tigi ai.
Not yet.

tigiai donu.
None (at least up to now).

tigi galania.
Far from finished.

tigi velo ono aga.
Not firmly situated or settled, unsettled conditions.

tigo.
Defecate. *a.*

tiigenga. (P-1 DIGE)
n.

tiigonga. (B-1 TIGO)
n.

tiinonga o tangada.
Undesirable personal characteristics.

tili. (E-- DILI)
dili at one time. *v.*

tili aalanga.
Exhausted (physically or mentally); discouraged; completely relaxed.

tili de galauna.
Set *galauna.*

tili de maalama.
Shoot out a light into the distance.

tili gee.
Throw away.

tili mada.
Go at top speed.

tili moumou.
Waste (by not using).

tilo. (E-- $DILO_1$)
[Imperative form of *dilo*]. *v.*

tilo danuaa.
Good-looking, handsome; beautiful (esp. owing to having a graceful manner).

tilo gauligi.
To regard something from the perspective of a child.

tilo iho.
To consider one's own situation.

tilo mahamaha.
Having a good appearance.

tino boo.
Full moon (a period comprising two nights).

toga. (P-- $DOGA_1$)
a.

togaanga. (P-1 $DOGA_1$)
n.

togalia. (P-2 $DOGA_1$)
v.

togo. (E-- $DOGO_1$)
To propel (once) by means of a punt pole. *v.*

togoa. (E-2 $DOGO_1$)
v.

togolia. (E-2 $DOGO_1$)
v.

tohi. (E-- DOHI)
Make into strips. *v.*

tola. (P-- DOLA)
a.

tolaanga. (P-1 DOLA)
n.

tolo. (E-- DOLO)
Crawl. *a.*

tolo i de baeao.
Elderly and infirm.

Tolu-laangi. (DOLU, LAANGI)
Wednesday ('third day'). *nt.*

Tolu-malama. (DOLU, MALAMA)
March. *nt.*

tonu. (P-- $DONU_{1a}$)
a.

too. (P-- DOO_1)
—; be the loser (because of someone's actions). *a.*

tooanga. (P-1 DOO_1)
n.

too donu.
Certain, sure, graceful, definitely.

too gee.
Clumsy, unskillful, awkward (not dexterous).

too geegee.
Happening at different times or places.

too gili.
Wrinkled skin (from age).

toogonga. (E-1 $DOGO_1$)
n.

too luu bakau.
Extremely tired.

too madaaua.
Drip, fall drop by drop.

tua de baba.
Lower back (of a human).

tua de beau.
Beyond the seaward reef.

tubu. (P-- DUBU)
a.

tugi. (E-- $DUGI_1$)
v.

tugi ange --.
Contradict by —.

tugi dua.
Go backwards.

tugi taaea.
A fishing method (using hermit crabs for bait).

tugolo.
Information (by definition, true) acquired from one's parents. *n.*

tugu. (E-- DUGU)
Crouch. *a.*

tugunga. (E-1 DUGU)
n.

tuhi. (E-- DUHI)
Praise (someone), honor. *v.*

tuhi hagadegi.
Praise with all one's heart (esp. God).

tuhi iho.
Praise oneself.

tulu. (E-- DULU)
Ooze a lot at one time. *a.*

tuluanga. (E-1 DULU)
n.

tuu_1. (E-- DUU_1)
Cut (something). *v.*

tuu_2. (P-- DUU_2)
v.

tuu daga holiage.
Circumcise.

tuu de biigi.
To castrate a pig.

tuu de galeve.
Make palm toddy.

tuu dege.
Having corners, square, rectangular.

tuu taalonga.
To escape (of fish, after having been speared).

tuu todo.
Stop bleeding.

tuugau i daha.
Clitoris.

tuugau i lodo.
Cervix.

tuu gili.
Gooseflesh, disgusted, horror-fascination.

tuugiva. (P-- DUUGIVA)
a.

tuugivaanga. (P-1 DUUGIVA)
n.

tuu hagalele.
Stop suddenly; cut suddenly.

tuu mai.
Limit, discontinue, shorten (by cutting off one end).

tuu uaua.
Dilated veins.

e_1.
By. *mp.*

e_2.
GENERAL ASPECT MARKER. *mt.*

ea.
To surface (while swimming); to be on the surface of the water; stop swimming. *a.*

ea age.
Stop swimming (and come up on land).

eaanga. (B-1 EA)
n.

eaea. (R-- EA)
a.

eaeaanga. (R-1 EA)
n.

ea gi lunga.
To ride high in the water (e.g., of a canoe).

e aha goe.
How about?

eba.
A sleeping mat (child's). *n.*

ebuebu. (R-- EBU)
Foam, bubbles. *v.*

ebuebua. (R-2 EBU)
Covered with *ebuebu.* *v.*

ebuebunga. (R-1 EBU)
n.

e dee daadaaia.
To be in no hurry.

e dee haalo.
Refuse to accept (something).

ee.
VOCATIVE PARTICLE. *mp.*

ee laa.
So!

ega.
A sound indicating surprise. *i.*

e galemu.
It's alright!

ege.
Raise up (so that higher). *v.*

egea. (B-2 EGE)
v.

ege age.
Raise up (something) from its previous trajectory.

ege ange.
Move (something) over.

egeege. (R-- EGE)
v.

egeegea. (R-2 EGE)
v.

egeegelia. (R-2 EGE)
v.

egeegenga. (R-1 EGE)
n.

ege iho.
Lower (something).

egelia. (B-2 EGE)
v.

egenga. (B-1 EGE)
n.

e hanuhanu i de +PRONOUN.
Know something about.

e hia?.
How many?

eidu.
Ghost, spirit, god. *n.*

eidu ai.
Treat as a totem, worship, treat as a supernatural being.

elaa.
A sound indicating surprise. *a.*

elaaelaa. (R-- ELAA)
A sound indicating surprise. *a.*

eleele. (R-- ELE)
Fish sp.: shark sp.? *n.*

eligi.
Chief of the island (?) [archaic]; captain of a modern ship. *a.*

e lodo goe.
Watch out!

elunga. (B-- $LUNGA_a$)
Top of, the position over (something). *n.*

eoo.
A sound indicating agreement. *i.*

eu.
Shoulder (top of). *n.*

eu doo.
A dislocation of the shoulder joint.

eu sege.
A dislocation of the shoulder joint.

ga.
INCEPTIVE ASPECT MARKER; if, and (esp. in enumeration), and then. *mt.*

gaa_1.
[Var. of *ga*]. *mt.*

gaa_2.
To catch fire, aflame. *a.*

gaabea. (B-2 GABE)
v.

gaabenga. (B-1 GABE)
n.

gaabinga. (B-1 GABI)
n.

gaadanga. (B-1 $GADA_1$)
n.

gaa de malala.
There is sufficient [a conventional

expression]; an argumentative and stubborn person; argumentative.

gaadia. (B-2 GADI)
v.

gaadinga. (B-1 $GADI_a$)
Fully mature coconut meat; the final stage of development of the coconut, after *gaadinga gaha dea*; copra. *n.*

gaadinga gaha paa.
A coconut with an unusually small-sized kernel.

gaadinga gaha dea.
A coconut which is nearly mature; the stage of development of the coconut between *modomodo madagii* and *gaadinga.*

gaadinga hagaangiangi.
Copra dried in the wind (not in the sun or in an oven).

gaadinga hai ngadi ubu.
Coconut with a shell of a size appropriate for use as a cooking vessel.

gaadinga lamallie.
A coconut with an unusually large-sized kernel.

gaadinga osi.
A coconut selected as a seedling.

$gaagaa_1$. (B-- GAAGAA)
Baby, infant. *a.*

$gaagaa_2$. (R-- GAA_2)
Easily ignited. *a.*

gaagaanga. (R-1 GAA_2)
n.

gaagaasia. (S-2 $GASI_2$)
Rubbed against (of lines only). *v.*

gaagaasiaanga. (S-3 $GASI_2$)
n.

$gaagaaui_1$*. (R-- $GAAUI_1$)
v.

$gaagaaui_2$. (R-- $GAAUI_2$)
v.

$gaagaauia_1$*. (R-2 $GAAUI_1$)
v.

$gaagaauia_2$. (R-2 $GAAUI_2$)
v.

$gaagaauinga_1$*. (R-1 $GAAUI_1$)
n.

$gaagaauinga_2$. (R-1 $GAAUI_2$)
n.

gaagea. (B-2 GAGE)
v.

gaa gee de nnamu.
Having a strong odor.

gaagenga. (B-1 GAGE)
—; ladder, stairway. *n.*

gaagose.
Sea cucumber sp. *n.*

ga aha.
And then did what?

gaahagi.
The useless tuber-like growths on the *bie* plant. *a.*

ga aha laa.
What's the matter with you?

gaahanga.
A rope used to assist in climbing. *n.*

gaainga. (B-1 GAI_2)
—; temporary dwelling. *n.*

gaalau.
Bird sp.: brown booby? *n.*

gaalau-ango.
Plant sp.: tumeric plant (*Curcuma* sp.).

gaa lava.
And then.

gaalinga. (B-1 GALI)
—; an indentation (like that resulting from being wound tightly with string). *n.*

gaaloa. (B-2 $GALO_3$)
v.

$gaalonga_1$. (B-1 $GALO_1$)
n.

$gaalonga_2$. (B-1 $GALO_2$)
n.

$gaalonga_3$. (B-1 $GALO_3$)
n.

gaamunga. (B-1 $GAMU_2$)
n.

gaanoni*.
An omen of death [exact nature not known]. *n.*

gaanuunu. (B-- GAANUNU)
Breast. *n.*

gaanga. (B-1 GAA$_2$)
n.

gaasia.
Coral sp.: (looks like a flower). *n.*

gaasinga. (B-1 GASI$_1$)
n.

gaaui$_1$*.
Take (someone) along (with one) (esp. carrying, etc.). *v.*

gaaui$_2$.
A line (for retrieving) attached to a spear; assemble (something from parts) by fastening together; strap, harness. *v.*

gaauia$_1$*. (B-2 GAAUI$_1$)
v.

gaauia$_2$. (B-2 GAAUI$_2$)
v.

gaaui i tao.
A line (for retrieving) which is attached to a spear.

gaauinga$_1$*. (B-1 GAAUI$_1$)
n.

gaauinga$_2$. (B-1 GAAUI$_2$)
n.

gaavee. (B-2 GAVE$_1$)
v.

gaavenga. (B-1 GAVE$_1$)
n.

gaba$_1$.
The part toward (something else); edge (of shore); hip; beginning of (a season, day, etc.). *nl.*

gaba$_2$.
Flap (as wings). *a.*

gaba aasanga.
The sides of the watercourses between islets on the atoll.

gabaanga. (B-1 GABA$_2$)
n.

gaba de aasanga.
A side of the watercourses between islets on the atoll.

gaba de ahiahi.
Early evening, late in the afternoon.

gabaduu.
To sail a canoe against the wind; paddle or pole a canoe against the current. *v.*

gabaduunga. (B-1 GABADUU)
n.

gaba taiao.
Early morning.

gabaea.
To hang oneself (suicide). *v.*

gabaea mai.
Found hanged (suicide).

gabaeanga. (B-1 GABAEA)
n.

gabagaba. (R-- GABA$_2$)
—; aerial roots of the breadfruit tree. *a.*

gabagabanga. (R-1 GABA$_2$)
n.

gaba-moe.
Fish sp.: cardinal fish.

gabanibaonga. (BANI, BAO)
Room (of a house). *n.*

gabe.
Gouge out. *v.*

gabea.
(In angling) the failure of a bait bundle to come untied and release the bait. *v.*

gabeaanga. (B-1 GABEA)
n.

gabetili*. (?)
Parent-in-law. *n.*

gabegabe. (R-- GABE)
—; to paddle (a canoe). *v.*

gabegabea. (R-2 GABE)
v.

gabegabelia. (R-2 GABE)
v.

gabegabenga. (R-1 GABE)
n.

gabe manava.
Eat sparingly (just enough to maintain one's strength), have a snack.

gabi.
Hold something between two (or more) other things; grab (between other things, e.g., fingers). *v.*

gabia. (B-2 GABI)
Held firmly (under the arm or between the fingers, etc.). *v.*

gabidia. (B-2 GABI)
Held firmly (by something not part of the human body). *v.*

gabigabi. (R-- GABI)
—; jellyfish sp. [N]. *v.*

gabigabia. (R-2 GABI)
Repeatedly grubbing. *v.*

gabigabidia. (R-2 GABI)
Repeatedly held. *v.*

gabigabinga. (R-1 GABI)
n.

gabinivali. (?)
A kind of ancient song. *n.*

gabinivalianga. (B-1 GABINIVALI)
n.

gabi saele.
Carry around holding.

gabogabola. (R-- GABOLA)
v.

gabogabolaanga. (R-1 GABOLA)
n.

gabola.
Flatten out something mushy. *v.*

gabolaanga. (B-1 GABOLA)
n.

gabou.
Fish sp.: scad? *n.*

gabugabu. (R-- GABU)
Shore. *nl.*

gabuibui. (?)
A type of prepared food (made with dried taro). *n.*

gapese.
A method of pole fishing at night (on the seaward reef). *v.*

gapeseanga. (B-1 GAPESE)
n.

gapua.
Large fissures or depressions in the reef (incomplete channels). *v.*

gada$_1$.
Laugh. *a.*

gada$_2$.
Fish sp.: jack. *n.*

gada-ahai.
Fish sp.: jack? (an oceanic fish).

gada-alaala.
Fish sp.: jack? (like *alaala*).

ga dae ai.
Until.

ga dae laa huu.
Very, too much.

gadagada. (R-- GADA$_1$)
Laugh (more than a single laugh). *a.*

gadagada-a-vaga. (?)
A very small tuna. *n.*

gadagada doo me.
Laugh at.

gada gimoo.
Smile (esp. for no good reason or when embarrassed).

gadaha.
Bird sp.: great frigate bird (*Fregata minor*). *n.*

gada-laagau-ngaadai.
Fish sp.

gada-laagau-ngauda.
Fish sp.: rudderfish.

gada-moana.
Fish sp.: jack? (an oceanic fish).

gadea.
The side of the canoe away from the outrigger float. *n.*

gadebega.
A type of basket. *n.*

gadi.
Bite. *v.*

gadigadi. (R-- GADI)
—; itch. *v.*

gadigadia. (R-2 GADI)
v.

gadigadi gauvae.
Chattering of teeth (from cold).

gadigadinga. (R-1 GADI)
n.

gadinibidi.
A type of fishhook (made from pearl shell). *n.*

gadoa.
To be overdue for parturition. *v.*

gadoaanga. (B-1 GADOA)
n.

gadoi. (XCO DOI_a)
A type of coconut with an edible husk [the juice of which stains clothes]. *v.*

gadunga.
Fire-plow. *n.*

gatae.
Fishing net (attached to a frame or handle). *n.*

gaegaehala. (R-- GAEHALA)
A growth of still immature breadfruit on trees. *a.*

gaehala.
Immature breadfruit; an aerial root of a pandanus tree which is used as a jump rope. *a.*

$gaga_1$.
The fibrous sheathing (at the base of the petiole sheath of the flower) on the coconut tree. *n.*

$gaga_2$.
Bird sp. *n.*

gagai. (T-- GAI_2)
Propensity of fish to bite (one at a time). *v.*

gage.
Climb; climb up on. *v.*

gage de henua.
Invade.

gage gaahanga.
To climb a coconut tree, using *gaahanga.*

gagelia. (B-2 GAGE)
v.

gage saali.
To climb a breadfruit tree using *saali.*

gagu.
Well-mannered. *a.*

gakage. (R-- GAGE)
v.

gakagelia. (R-2 GAGE)
v.

gaha.
The portion of the coconut husk from which long fibers are obtained. *n.*

gahaalava.
Orange-colored (like a certain variety of coconut). *a.*

gaha biigi.
A rope for tying pigs.

gaha paa.
A coconut with a small kernel.

gaha dea.
Having almost ripe coconuts (whose husk fibers are white).

gaha mea.
Having orange coconuts (of a coconut tree).

gaha nuui.
Having green coconuts (of a coconut tree).

gahao.
Plant sp.: tree sp.: ochrosia tree (*Ochrosia oppositifolia* (Lam.) K. Sch.). *n.*

gaha uli.
Having brown (ripe) coconuts (of a coconut tree).

ga hia?.
How many will it be?

gahu.
Put on, wear, cover up (the body). *a.*

gahuanga. (B-1 GAHU)
n.

ga-hudi.
Plant sp.: tree sp.: banana tree; banana (fruit).

gahuduna.
Ridge pole cover. *n.*

gahugahu. (R-- GAHU)
a.

gahugahuanga. (R-1 GAHU)
n.

gai_1.
Trust, believe in. *a.*

gai_2.
Eat; food. *v.*

gai_3.
But, and, then, so. *mi.*

gaiaa.
Steal, dishonest, cheat; to ask or accept too readily. *v.*

gaiaa dau bodu.
Commit adultery.

gaiaadia. (B-2 GAIAA)
Stolen. *v.*

gaiaanga. (B-1 GAIAA)
n.

gai aha.
And then what?

gai ange nei.
A misfortune owing to —.

gai baalau.
Eat messily (getting food on one's face); make a mess (esp. involving liquid or organic material).

gaibea.
Crab sp.: shore crab, land crab, grapsid crab, ghost crab. *n.*

gaibea-lausedi.
Trapezeid crab.

gai boo.
Eat early in the morning.

gai busibusi.
Take the bait tentatively (of fish).

gai dagidagi.
Eat while walking; food for sale which is carried on the road.

gai de baibu.
Smoke cigarettes.

gai de henua.
Native food (not imported).

gai ga aha.
Too bad!

gaigai. (R-- GAI_2)
—; humans taken as food by ghosts. *v.*

gaigai a usu.
Flatus.

gaigaina. (R-2 GAI_2)
v.

gai gi de mahi.
Eat as much as possible.

gai ginigini.
Eat sparingly (esp. fish — in order not to use up).

gai hagadoedoe.
Eat sparingly (to save for later).

gai hagalongolongo.
Eat sparingly (to save some for others).

gai hagalulu.
Habituated to taking bait (fish); feed on bait.

gai haganamunamu.
Eat sparingly (in order to save some food for later).

gai hagassii.
Eat messily (letting the food fall from one's hands and mouth).

gai hilihili.
Eat only certain foods prepared in certain ways by certain people; fussy (about food).

gai holoholo.
Eat fast.

gailalopoli. (BOLI, GAI_2, LALO)
Stingy. *a.*

gai lima dahi.
To eat taro without fish (or fish without taro).

gai lima lua.
Eat greedily (with both hands).

gailingalinga. (GAI_2, LINGA)
Continually wanting to eat. *a.*

gailulu.
Bird sp.: booby?

gaimalie. (GAI_2, MALIE)
Good at food preparation (not wasteful). *a.*

gai mamu dua nnui.
To eat fish up (not saving any for later).

gai me.
Eat food.

gai me hagadau doa.
Eat as though competing against other eaters in a test of manliness (e.g., to eat fish with the scales and all).

gai modo.
Eat when still unripe.

gai moumou.
Wasteful of food.

gaina. (B-2 GAI_2)
v.

gainanga.
A person having special powers (occult

powers, strength, status, or knowledge). *v.*

gaini.
Any lattice-like arrangement. *n.*

gai niivoi.
To eat food without washing one's hands after having prepared a corpse for burial [a traditional sign of manliness].

gai nnao$_1$.
Eat messily.

gai nnao$_2$.
Exaggerate (esp. in storytelling).

gainga.
Trash, garbage; braided dead coconut fronds used in buttressing the sides of *uinga*. *v.*

gai ngaadahi.
A distribution of fish to the whole island population.

gai ngaadai.
[= *gai ngaadahi*].

gainga o de moana.
Fish (when abundant in the ocean nearby).

gai ngole.
Wasteful, improvident.

gaisaa. (GAI$_2$, SAA$_1$)
Wasteful in preparing food, uneconomical. *v.*

gai salusalu.
Prepare food wastefully (too much must be thrown away).

gai samusamu.
Eat left-overs (that most people would throw out).

gai valaai.
Take medicine.

galaahuu.
Cheek, sides of the canoe prow. *n.*

galaanga*.
To look for members of the opposite sex by walking around at night. *v.*

galaanganga*. (B-1 GALAANGA)
n.

galababa. (?)
A type of prepared food (made from breadfruit skin). *n.*

galabe.
Sea cucumber sp. (several spp.). *n.*

galabe-duiduia.
Sea cucumber sp.

galagala. (R-- GALA)
Sponge sp. (several spp.). *n.*

galagalaanga*. (R-- GALAANGA)
v.

galagalaanganga*.
(R-1 GALAANGA) *n*

galagalani. (R-- GALANI)
Come close to the end of. *a.*

galagalania. (R-2 GALANI)
a.

galagalanianga. (R-1 GALANI)
n.

galagalasi. (R-- GALASI)
v.

galagalasia. (R-2 GALASI)
v.

galagalasinga. (R-1 GALASI)
n.

galani.
Almost finished, nearly finished; [from the Ponapean *karenieng*?]. *a.*

galania. (B-2 GALANI)
a.

galanianga. (B-1 GALANI)
n.

galasi.
Steal [a less pejorative word than *gaiaa*]. *v.*

galasia. (B-2 GALASI)
v.

galasinga. (B-1 GALASI)
n.

galauna.
A big net for fishing, requiring several persons to manipulate. *v.*

galavagu.
Sponge sp.

galavalava. (R-- GALAVA)
The grains in the trunk wood of the coconut tree which are hard, dark, and sharp. *n.*

galegale.
White matter (the sediment in palm toddy, or the powder-like substance on a pandanus key). *v.*

galegalea. (B-2 GALEGALE)
v.

galegaleanga. (B-1 GALEGALE)
n.

galele.
A method of fishing (casting with a pole)for tuna). *v.*

galemu.
[Preceded always by *e* or *dee*]. *u.*

galeu.
A change of wind direction. *a.*

galeua. (B-2 GALEU)
v.

galeunga. (B-1 GALEU)
n.

galeva.
Fish sp.: shark sp.? *n.*

galevaleva. (R-- GALEVA)
Bird sp. *n.*

galeve.
The sap of the coconut tree (taken from the inflorescence). *n.*

galeve maimai.
Fresh (unfermented) *galeve.*

galeve sali.
A coconut tree which produces much *galeve.*

galeve vii.
Fermented *galeve*, palm toddy.

gali.
Wound around; tied or fastened tightly. *v.*

galia. (B-2 GALI)
v.

gali ange.
Wound around or tied or fastened very tightly.

galigali. (R-- GALI)
v.

galigi.
Covered all over with. *a.*

galigianga. (B-1 GALIGI)
n.

galisi.
Lizard sp. *n.*

galo$_1$.
Look at, stare. *a.*

galo$_2$.
To show signs of being pregnant; a color change of fruit indicating ripening. *a.*

galo$_3$.
Stir. *v.*

galo$_4$.
Fish sp.: goatfish (= small *vede*). *n.*

galoa. (B-2 GALO$_1$)
Attractive to members of the opposite sex. *v.*

galo ahi.
Sparks.

galo de laa.
The reddish sky at sunset.

galogalo$_1$. (R-- GALO$_1$)
Look around (with one's eyes only). *a.*

galogalo$_2$. (R-- GALO$_3$)
v.

galogalo malama.
The last quarter of the moon (rising in the east just before sunrise).

galogalonga$_1$. (R-1 GALO$_1$)
n.

galo-gila.
Fish sp.: goatfish.

galo hagalegunga.
To look at a member of the opposite sex in a presumptuous way.

galohia. (B-2 GALO$_1$)
Attractive to members of the opposite sex. *v.*

galo hilo.
Not cooked completely.

galoi.
Having soft thighs [a term of endearment used by a man to a woman]. *n.*

galo saele.
Look around (moving one's body about).

galo sugi mada.
Glimpse.

galu.
Viscous sputum. *n.*

galua. (B-2 GALU)
Having viscous sputum. *v.*

galubu.
A type of toy. *n.*

galugalu. (R-- GALU)
Any jelly-like substance; jellyfish sp. [N]. *v.*

gamagama. (R-- GAMA)
Seaweed sp. *n.*

gamai.
Bring to me, carry to me [see *gavange*]. *a.*

gamalie. (B-- $MALIE_b$)
Do attentively. *a.*

gamedi. (C-- GUMEDI)
[Var. of *gumedi*]. *n.*

gamedi vai salo.
A type of bowl.

gammenge-baabaa.
Mollusk sp.: *Bursidae* spp.

gammenge-gabe-de-liidogi.
Mollusk sp.: murex shell.

gammenge-hai-gili-dabeo.
Mollusk sp.: *Thais luteostoma.*

gammenge-maimai.
Mollusk sp.: *Vasum turbinellus.*

gammenge-olomanga.
Mollusk sp.: *Thais armigera.*

$gamu_1$.
Coral (any kind). *v.*

$gamu_2$.
Cut (something). *v.*

$gamua_1$. (B-2 $GAMU_1$)
Covered with *gamu.* *v.*

$gamua_2$. (B-2 $GAMU_2$)
v.

$gamugamu_1$. (R-- $GAMU_1$)
Coral sp. *v.*

$gamugamu_2$. (R-- $GAMU_2$)
v.

$gamugamua_1$. (R-2 $GAMU_1$)
Covered all over (or here and there) with *gamu.* *v.*

$gamugamua_2$. (R-2 $GAMU_2$)
v.

gamugamunga. (R-1 $GAMU_2$)
n.

gana.
Bad person. *n.*

ganabu.
The base of a coconut tree trunk. *n.*

ganae.
Fish sp.: mullet. *n.*

ganae-oo.
Fish sp.: threadfin.

ganaudogo.
An abundance of fish, birds, or other animals which are good to eat [an omen of death]. *n.*

ganava.
Plant sp.: tree sp.: cordia tree (*Cordia subcordata* Lam.). *n.*

ganimago.
Mollusk sp.: *Malea pomum.* *n.*

ganimua. (GANO, MUA)
The eldest child of a couple. *n.*

ganimuli. (GANO, $MULI_1$)
The second child of a couple. *n.*

ganimuumuni. (?)
A type of string figure. *n.*

gannui. ($GANO_a$, NUI_1)
The gelatinous layer in the kernel of the immature coconut. *a.*

gannui koi.
gannui which has been scraped out of the shell to be eaten.

gannui ina.
White (of the portion of a woman's thighs hidden under her sarong).

gannui mada balabala.
gannui which is soft and mushy.

gannui mada makaga.
gannui which is firm.

gannui ngadaa.
A coconut which has less *gannui* than would be expected at its stage of maturity.

gano.
Flesh of, meat of. *n.*

gano agau.
Reef (including land thereon).

ganoango. (ANGO, GANO)
Yellow. *a.*

gano dae.
The net of a hand net (not including the net's handle).

gano dea.
The soft wood just under the bark of a tree.

ga noho.
After a time.

ganomada. ($GANO_b$, $MADA_3$)
Eye. *n.*

gano moana.
Open sea, far away from any land.

gano niho.
Gums (of mouth).

gano siga.
Strands (of cloth).

gango.
Burned (overcooked food). *a.*

gaogao. (R-- GAO)
Side of; the part surrounding; environs of; sides of the abdomen. *nl.*

gasa.
Run aground. *a.*

gasaanga. (B-1 GASA)
n.

gasagasa. (R-- GASA)
a.

$gasi_1$.
Jump up (with both feet leaving the ground). *a.*

$gasi_2$. (B-- $GASI_3$)
Mollusk sp.: *Asaphis dichotoma.* *n.*

gasia.
Worthwhile, important, valuable. *v.*

gasiaanga. (B-1 GASIA)
n.

gasigasi. (R-- $GASI_1$)
v.

$gasigasia_1$. (R-- GASIA)
v.

$gasigasia_2$. (R-2 $GASI_2$)
Rubbed against, scratched. *v.*

gasigasiaanga. (R-3 $GASI_2$)
n.

gasigasinga. (R-1 $GASI_1$)
n.

gasigi.
Plant sp.: hemp-leaved vitex shrub (*Vitex negundo* var. *bicolor* (Willd.) Lam.). *n.*

gaso. (B-- $GASO_2$)
Roof thatch rafters (of pandanus slats). *n.*

gasogaso. (R-- $GASO_1$)
Narrow [sing.]. *a.*

gasogasoanga. (R-1 $GASO_1$)
n.

gasogo.
To have sexual pleasure (of males only) either by intercourse, or by regarding a naked woman. *v.*

gasogoanga. (B-1 GASOGO)
n.

gau_1.
Handle, appendage. *n.*

gau_2. (B-- GAU_3)
Grouping (of people). *n.*

gau_3. (B-- GAU_{1a})
Lymph nodes (enlarged). *v.*

gaua. (B-2 GAU_{1a})
To have enlarged lymph nodes. *v.*

gauanga. ($ANGA_3$, GAU_{1d})
Thigh. *n.*

gauanga mahagi.
Dislocated thigh bone.

gauasa. (B-- GAU_{1f})
The pectoral fin of a fish and the surrounding flesh. *n.*

gau bini.
A tool used in braiding rope.

gau bini baalanga.
An iron rod.

gau dagodo.
The boom of a sail.

gau dahi.
A method of fishing for tuna (angling with a single baited hook?).

gau de henua.
Natives.

gauea.
Bird sp.: white-rumped swift (*Apus pacificus*) (The native term applies possibly to several spp.). *n.*

gaugau₁. (R-- GAU1a)
Be disposed to have enlarged lymph nodes. *v.*

gaugau₂. (R-- GAU2)
To bathe (including swimming for the purpose of bathing). *v.*

gaugaua. (R-2 GAU1a)
v.

gaugau dalinga.
Exterior of the ear; a loop-like handle.

gaugauna. (R-- GAUNA)
v.

gaugaunanga. (R-1 GAUNA)
n.

gaugaunga. (R-1 GAU2)
n.

gau hadu.
The board to which the metal grater for grating taro is attached.

gau henua gee.
Foreigners (lit., 'people from other lands').

gau ivi.
Skinny.

gau laagau.
The shaft of a spear.

gau lama.
Rachis of the coconut leaf.

gauligi.
Child, young person. *a.*

gauligi ange.
Younger than.

gauligi daane.
Male child, boy.

gauligi hahine.
Female child, girl.

gauligi iho.
Next younger than.

gauligi mai ange.
The one next younger still.

gau looloa gaadinga.
A bunch of fully mature coconuts.

gau mai moni.
Foreigners (lit., 'people who came in canoes').

gau mai vaga.
[= *gau mai moni*].

gau-me.
Gill (of a fish).

gauna.
Invite. *v.*

gaunanga. (B-1 GAUNA)
n.

gaunga.
The partially burned wood or coconut husk which is left over after a fire. *n.*

gauvae. (XCO GAU1c)
Jaw; a set of false teeth. *n.*

gava₁.
Cut open. *v.*

gava₂.
Bird sp.: reef heron (*Demiegretta sacra*). *n.*

ga vaa laa dangada.
Oh dear (that's not good)!

gavaanga. (B-1 GAVA1)
n.

gavaausu. (?)
Plant sp.: tree sp.: Barringtonia tree (*Barringtonia asiatica* (L.) Kurz). *n.*

gavada.
A type of basket [used for scooping up fish which have been caught in a net]. *n.*

gava-dea.
Reef heron — white phase.

gavadu.
Give or carry (something) to you [see *gave*]. *a.*

gavagava. (R-- GAVA3)
Weather-hardened black driftwood. *n.*

gavage.
Give or bring up [see *gave*]. *a.*

gavaligi.
Fish sp.

gavange.
Give or bring to (someone) [see *gave*]. *a.*

gava-uli.
Reef heron — grey phase.

$gave_1$.
d.

$gave_2$.
The name of a name-group. *n.*

gaveaa. (B-2 $GAVE_1$)
Taken; [not the imperative forms; c.f. *gaavee*]. *v.*

gave ala.
A method of plaiting mats.

gave bae.
A row of stones piled on top of each other.

gavegave. (R-- $GAVE_1$)
—; rays of the sun. *v.*

gave hua podo.
Sprint (footrace of short distance).

gave hua loa.
[Var. of *gave ua loa*].

gave lodo.
Attract attention.

gave ua podo.
[Var. of *gave hua podo*].

gave ua loa.
A long-distance footrace.

gavia.
Crazy person; insane person. *n.*

gavidi.
A type of fishhook (made from turtle shell). *n.*

gea.
Hawksbill turtle. *n.*

geao.
Plant sp.: plant-shrub sp. (*Sida fallax* Walp.). *n.*

gede.
Basket (the generic term). *n.*

gede aola.
A type of basket.

gede dua dahi.
A type of basket.

gede gabi de husi.
A type of basket [carried to the taro patch].

gede hadu.
A type of basket [used for hauling stones for the earth oven].

gede hangaabo.
A type of basket [having a cover].

gede maduu.
A type of basket.

gee.
Differently, of a different sort; away from; strange. *mv.*

geegee. (R-- GEE)
Completely differently. *mv.*

geelinga. (B-1 GELI)
—; a hole (which has been dug). *n.*

geelonga. (B-1 GELO)
A depression (in the reef, or ground, etc.). *n.*

geenunga. (B-1 GENU)
n.

geesaa.
Mollusk sp.: *Fimbria soverbii.* *n.*

geesaama. (B-- GEESAMA)
Outrigger cross boom (of a canoe). *n.*

geevee.
Bird sp.: eastern whimbrel (*Numenius phaeopus).* *n.*

gegeli. (T-- GELI)
Struggle. *a.*

gegelianga. (T-1 GELI)
n.

gegeno.
Alligator, crocodile. *n.*

gelegele. (R-- GELE)
Sand, soil, dirty. *a.*

gelegeleanga. (R-1 GELE)
n.

gelegele dea.
Sand.

gelegele gumi hue.
Fine-grained sand.

gelegele malama.
Sand with disk-like particles.

gelegele uli.
Black soil [soil with high organic content].

gelemea.
A by-product of the tumeric-making process.

geli.
Dig. *v.*

gelia. (B-2 GELI)
v.

geligeli. (R-- GELI)
v.

geligelia. (R-2 GELI)
v.

geligelinga. (R-1 GELI)
n.

gelo.
Deep. *a.*

gelogelo. (R-- GELO)
Having many depressions (e.g., a corrugated surface). *v.*

gelogelonga. (R-1 GELO)
—; depressions (in the reef, or ground, etc.). *n.*

gelu-agau.
Fish sp.: tang.

gelu-hai-usu.
Fish sp.: unicorn fish.

gelu-hai-vaelo.
Fish sp.: tang.

gelu-uliuli.
Fish sp.: tang?

gemo.
Fast, swift. *a.*

gemoanga. (B-1 GEMO)
n.

gemo ange huu de --.
Rapidly becoming —.

gemogemo. (R-- GEMO)
a.

gemogemoanga. (R-1 GEMO)
n.

genu.
A movement of the hips, as in the act of sexual intercourse. *v.*

genua. (B-2 GENU)
v.

genugenu. (R-- GENU)
v.

genugenua. (R-2 GENU)
v.

genugenunga. (B-1 GENU)
n.

geu.
Shake one's head (once) to one side. *v.*

geua. (B-2 GEU)
v.

geu de madangi.
A change of wind direction.

geu gee.
To jerk one's head away from something.

geugeu. (R-- GEU)
Shake one's head back and forth; [a sign interpreted as meaning 'that's not right!']. *v.*

geugeua. (R-2 GEU)
v.

geugeunga. (R-1 GEU)
n.

geunga. (B-1 GEU)
—; behavior (of a person); the manner (of a person). *n.*

gi$_1$.
Toward, to, in order to. *mp.*

gi$_2$.
DESIDERATIVE ASPECT MARKER. *mt.*

giado.
Outrigger boom. *n.*

giado taelodo.
The outrigger booms toward the center of the canoe.

giado madua.
Main outrigger booms.

giado manu.
The smaller outrigger booms at the ends of the canoe.

gi-ange muhuu.
I hope that —.

giba.
Swelling of the testicles. *v.*

gibaanga. (B-1 GIBA)
n.

gida.
Each one. *pi.*

gidaadeu.
We [incl.]. *pi.*

gidaau.
We two [incl.]. *pi.*

gi daha.
To the outside; in the environs of.

gida ma gida.
Each individual...

gide.
See. *v.*

gideanga. (B-1 GIDE)
n.

gidee. (B-2 GIDE)
Seen. *a.*

gidee (laa) goe.
See what I mean!

gide eidu.
To see a vision, hallucinate.

gide eidu ina.
To see a vision, hallucinate.

gidee iho.
Be aware of oneself.

gidee mai.
Found out (or be found out).

gide gauligi.
To see from the perspective of a small child.

gidegide. (R-- GIDE)
v.

gidegideanga. (R-1 GIDE)
n.

gide malie.
Get in the habit of.

gide sala.
Misidentify.

gideu.
Plant sp.: fern sp. *n.*

gidigidi. (R-- GIDI)
Short. *v.*

gidigidianga. (R-1 GIDI)
n.

gidigidi laa lalo.
A very short person, midget; miniature, diminutive.

giebu.
Plant sp.: spider lily (*Hymenocallis littoralis* (Jacq.) Salisb.). *n.*

gieuli.
Lizard sp. *n.*

gi hanu donu huu.
Any kind whatsoever.

gii.
A high-pitched sound, soft, high-pitched crying (as by children). *a.*

gii age.
Cry out softly.

giianga. (B-1 GII)
n.

giidada.
Misfortune which will occur in the future (as ascertained through divination). *v.*

giidagi.
Relish (meat or fish, or something substituting for meat or fish, eaten with taro, etc.). *v.*

giidagi ange gi --.
Eat a side dish with —.

giidaginga. (B-1 GIIDAGI)
n.

gii talinga.
Tinnitus.

giigii$_1$. (R-- GII)
—; laugh. *a.*

giigii$_2$. (R-- GII)
Fish sp.: squirrelfish (= small *malaugulu*? *n.*

giigiianga. (R-1 GII)
n.

giigii saele.
Giggle.

giinia. (B-2 GINI)
v.

giininga. (B-1 GINI)
n.

giivada.
Good fortune in the future, as revealed by divination. *a.*

giivia.
To have something in one's eye. *v.*

giiviaanga. (B-1 GIIVIA)
n.

gilaadeu.
They. *pi.*

gilaau.
They two. *pi.*

gili.
Skin. *v.*

gili agau.
A moss-like covering of the reef; fish which live on the reef.

gili belu.
Dead epidermis (can be peeled without pain).

gili dabeo.
A fungus infection of the skin, ringworm.

gili dalo.
Hillock.

gili dama.
Soft-skinned.

giligili. (R-- GILI)
Coral rubble; (human) skin in an unhealthy condition. *v.*

giligili tai.
Horizon.

giligilisau. (R-- $GILI_b$)
Go around habitually without clothes. *a.*

giligilisaunga. (R-1 $GILI_b$)
n.

gili hano.
Separation of the hard interior parts of the tree trunk [a condition which spoils the tree for making a canoe].

gili hau.
The inner bark of the hibiscus.

gili iga.
A type of high cloud.

gili laa.
Suntanned.

gili langi.
A type of cloud (not associated with rain).

gili maalama.
Light-skinned.

gili malali.
Clean [adj.]; neat.

gili malanga.
A type of skin disease.

gilisau. (B-- $GILI_b$)
Naked. *a.*

gilisaunga. (B-1 $GILI_b$)
n.

gili solasola.
Leathery black skin (of humans).

gili somo.
The coconut meat of a germinating coconut (after the coconut apple has been removed).

gili ulunga.
Pillowcase.

gima.
Mollusk sp.: horse hoof clam (*Hippopus hippopus*). *n.*

gimaadeu.
We [excl.]. *pi.*

gimaau.
We two [excl.]. *pi.*

$gimoo_1$.
Rat. *n.*

$gimoo_2$.
Fish sp.: silversides (The native term is applied to several spp.). *n.*

gina.
Fish sp.: rainbow runner. *n.*

ginadoa.
A boil on the body that is hard and painful, and which will not come to a head. *v.*

ginadoaanga. (B-1 GINADOA)
n.

gini.
Pick with one's fingers; to pinch off, or pinch and pull at the same time. *v.*

ginigini$_1$. (R-- GINI)
v.

ginigini$_2$. (R-- GINI)
Mollusk sp.: *Tellinidae* spp.; *Pharonella* spp.). *n.*

giniginia. (R-2 GINI)
v.

ginigini looloa.
A game played by children.

ginigininga. (R-1 GINI)
n.

gini hua o hegau.
To receive the rewards of work well done (or punishment for evil deeds).

gini manu.
Pick flowers.

ginogino. (R-- KINO)
Inclined not to enjoy something (esp. food) by being overly sensitive to filth. *a.*

ginuede. (?)
Bird sp.: [Ponapean? — see *manu kono*]. *n.*

gio.
Mollusk sp.: *Charonia* spp. *n.*

givigivi. (R-- GIVI)
Bird sp.: ruddy turnstone (*Arenaria interpres*). *n.*

go.
"It is...". *mp.*

go hee.
Where exactly?

goa.
Termite. *n.*

goai.
Who? *b.*

goai de +PRONOUN.
Which of — (you, etc.)?

goai ne siilia.
Who asked you? [an expression of recent invention].

gobagoba. (R-- GOBA)
Bushy (of hair). *v.*

gobagobaanga. (R-1 GOBA)
n.

gobegobe. (R-- GOBE)
Cough (repeatedly). *a.*

gobegobeanga. (R-1 GOBE)
n.

gobugobu. (R-- GOBU)
Splash (or make noise like splashing) repeatedly. *a.*

gobugobuanga. (R-1 GOBU)
n.

godi.
To trim. *v.*

godia. (B-2 GODI)
v.

godigodi. (R-- GODI)
v.

godigodia. (R-2 GODI)
v.

godigodinga. (R-1 GODI)
n.

godi mai.
A certain type of manipulation in playing with string figures.

godinga. (B-1 GODI)
n.

goe. (B-- GOE$_1$)
You [1]. *pi.*

goede.
Octopus. *n.*

goehau.
Plant sp.: tree sp.: hibiscus tree (*Hibiscus tiliaceus* L.).

goe iloo.
It's up to you!

gogo.
Bent slightly (like a round-shouldered person). *a.*

gogoanga. (B-1 GOGO)
n.

gogo dua.
Bent backwards.

gogo gi mua.
Bent forward.

gogono. (T-- GONO)
Moan. *a.*

gogonoanga. (T-1 GONO)
n.

gogoo. (T-- GOO_1)
[Pl. of *googoo*]. *a.*

gogooanga. (T-1 GOO_1)
n.

gohu.
Dark (absence of light). *a.*

gohu boo dangodango.
A pitch-black night.

gohu de lodo.
Ignorant.

gohu de me.
Become dark (with no natural light).

gohugohu. (R-- GOHU)
Becoming very dark (decreasing in natural light). *a.*

gohugohulia. (R-2 GOHU)
a.

gohugohunga. (R-1 GOHU)
n.

gohulia. (B-2 GOHU)
a.

goi_1.
Still (as in 'he is still coming'). *mt.*

goi_2.
Scrape —. *d.*

goia. (B-2 GOI_2)
v.

$goigoi_1$. (R-- GOI_2)
v.

$goigoi_2$. (R-- GOI_2)
Bird sp.: Polynesian tattler (*Heteroscelus brevipes*). *n.*

goigoia. (R-2 GOI_2)
v.

goigoinga. (R-1 GOI_2)
n.

$goinga_1$. (B-- GOINGA)
A boundary marker (of stone). *n.*

$goinga_2$. (B-1 GOI_2)
n.

goinga o tai.
High-water mark.

golee.
Seed, testicles. *n.*

goli.
Scrape off —. *d.*

goligoli. (R-- GOLI)
—; whorls in the hair of the head. *v.*

goligolia. (R-2 GOLI)
v.

goligolinga. (R-1 GOLI)
n.

goli manu.
Pick flowers.

golo.
Remember an incident with a view toward revenge. *v.*

$goloa_1$. (B-2 GOLO)
v.

$goloa_2$. (B-- GOLOA)
Gear, tools, goods, supplies (but not food). *a.*

goloa abasasa.
European goods or tools.

goloa baalanga.
Metal-working tools.

goloa de henua.
Gear of local manufacture.

goloa duu biho.
Barber's tools.

golo age.
Continually *golo* voluntarily.

goloa haangoda.
Fishing gear.

goloa hagadaahao.
Recreational equipment.

goloa hai hegau.
Tools (for work).

goloa hai umu.
Implements and supplies needed in connection with use of the earth oven.

goloa hebagi.
Arms (tools of war).

goloa hesuihagi.
Goods which are bartered.

goloa labagau.
Carpenter's tools.

goloa lalo.
Gear obtained from foreign lands.

goloa o de hine.
Female genitalia.

goloa o taane.
Male genitalia.

gologolo. (R-- GOLO)
v.

gologoloa. (R-2 GOLO)
v.

golomagi. (B-- GOLO$_a$)
Patient, (not impetuous); restrained (not prone to act on impulse). *v.*

golomagia. (B-2 GOLO$_a$)
v.

golomagi iho.
To exercise great patience or restraint for one's own benefit.

golomagi lodo.
Self-controlled.

golomagina. (B-2 GOLO$_a$)
v.

golomaginga. (B-1 GOLO$_a$)
n.

golo me.
Unforgiving.

golu.
Pray for the welfare of —. *d.*

golugolu. (R-- GOLU)
v.

golugolua. (R-2 GOLU)
v.

golugolunga. (R-1 GOLU)
n.

gona$_1$.
Very —. *d.*

gona$_2$.
Navel. *n.*

gona odi.
Too much.

gonogono. (R-- GONO)
Grunt (like a pig) repeatedly. *a.*

gonogonoanga. (R-1 GONO)
n.

goo$_1$.
A sound made to indicate one's presence (in response to being called from afar); an owl-like hoot (of birds). *a.*

goo$_2$.
Taro spade. *n.*

gooanga. (B-1 GOO$_1$)
n.

goobai.
Hat. *a.*

goobai dada.
Umbrella.

goobai lau.
A hat made from pandanus leaves.

goobainga. (B-1 GOOBAI)
n.

goobai-o-lillo.
Mollusk sp.: trochus.

goodo.
To have just. *mt.*

goodou.
You [3]. *pi.*

googoo$_1$. (R-- GOO$_1$)
— [sing.]. *a.*

googoo$_2$. (R-- GOO$_1$)
Bird sp.: Japanese snipe (*Capella hardwickii*). *n.*

googooanga. (R-1 GOO$_1$)
n.

goohunga. (B-1 GOHU)
Dark images, shadows in the darkness. *n.*

goolia. (B-2 GOLI)
v.

goolinga. (B-1 GOLI)
n.

goolua. (B-2 GOLU)
v.

goolunga. (B-1 GOLU)
n.

gooluu.
You two. *pi.*

goonanga. (B-1 GONA$_1$)
A record set by an individual (or team). *n.*

goononga$_1$. (B-1 GONO)
n.

goononga$_2$. (B-- GOONONGA)
A record (set in competitive sports). *n.*

goononga gee.
To set a record.

goosia. (E-2 GOSI$_1$)
v.

goosinga. (E-1 GOSI$_1$)
n.

goosuu.
Fish sp.: jack. *n.*

gosigosi. (R-- GOSI$_1$)
To scratch (slightly) repeatedly. *v.*

gosigosia. (R-2 GOSI$_1$)
Scratched (of something solid only). *v.*

gosigosinga. (R-1 GOSI$_1$)
n.

goso.
Bothered, annoyed. *a.*

gosoanga. (B-1 GOSO)
n.

gosolia. (B-2 GOSO)
a.

gu.
DECISIVE ASPECT MARKER. *mt.*

gu aha.
Why?

guani.
A type of fish trap (with net sides). *n.*

guanga.
A type of basket. *n.*

guao.
The hard sap of a non-native tree which is occasionally washed up on shore [used for making perfume]. *n.*

guba.
Fish sp.: cardinal fish (The native term is applied to several spp.). *n.*

guba-baabaa.
Fish sp.: cardinal fish.

guba-dee-gaina.
Fish sp.

gubenga.
A large net for fishing. *v.*

gubo.
Work with concentration in the midst of a group. *v.*

guboa. (B-2 GUBO)
Being used in connection with group activity. *v.*

guboanga. (B-1 GUBO)
n.

gubogubo. (R-- GUBO)
v.

guboguboa. (R-2 GUBO)
v.

guboguboanga. (R-1 GUBO)
n.

gubu.
Joint (of the hand or foot); verse (of a song). *n.*

gubu daahili.
Verse of a song.

gubu dae.
Intestines which appear to have segmentation.

gubu dao.
A join of the spear shaft which is made of two pieces of wood.

gubu dolo.
A joint of the sugarcane.

gubu lima.
Hand, wrist.

gubu madila.
A joint of bamboo.

gubu vae.
Foot, ankle.

gu dee galemu.
Recovering from an illness (getting better).

gudu.
Louse (head), or similar exoparasite of plants or animals (e.g., bird lice, scale insects, sap-feeding beetles, darkling beetles, etc.). *n.*

gudua. (B-2 GUDU)
Abounding in lice. *v.*

guduaanga. (B-3 GUDU)
Abounding in lice. *n.*

gu gide huu.
Spoiled (having acquired a bad habit).

gugu.
To have the capacity (or size or strength) for; suited to. *a.*

guguanga. (B-1 GUGU)
n.

gugu ange.
Able to look after others; able to withstand.

gugu iho.
Useless (person) in anything involving others (capable only of taking care of oneself).

gu hagaola loo.
Just missed catching.

gu hia?.
How many was it?

gulabe.
Rectum. *n.*

gulu.
Plant sp.: tree sp.: breadfruit. *n.*

gulu bala.
Tree-ripened breadfruit.

gulu daladala.
Breadfruit with rough skin.

gulu koi.
A type of prepared food (breadfruit which has been cooked over hot coals with the skin on).

gulu maimai.
A type of prepared food (ripe breadfruit which has been cooked in an *umu*).

gulu malali.
Breadfruit with smooth skin.

gulunieli. (?)
Plant sp. *n.*

gu malaia donu.
To have been lucky.

gumedi.
Bowl (wooden). *n.*

gumedi de henua.
A type of bowl.

gumedi hadu.
A bowl (pottery) [not indigenous].

gumedi vai solo.
A type of bowl.

gumi$_1$.
d.

gumi$_2$.
Calculate —, figure out —. *d.*

gumi$_3$.
A measurement: by tens of fathoms. *n.*

gumidia$_1$. (B-2 GUMI$_1$)
v.

gumidia$_2$. (B-2 GUMI$_2$)
v.

gumigumi$_1$. (R-- GUMI$_1$)
v.

gumigumi$_2$. (R-- GUMI$_2$)
v.

gumigumi$_3$. (R-- GUMI$_{1a}$)
Chin, beard. *n.*

gumigumia$_1$. (R-2 GUMI$_1$)
v.

gumigumia$_2$. (R-2 GUMI$_2$)
v.

gumigumidia$_1$. (R-2 GUMI$_1$)
v.

gumigumidia$_2$. (R-2 GUMI$_2$)
v.

gumiguminga. (R-1 GUMI$_1$)
n.

gumigumi-o-sogo.
Plant sp.: epiphytic fern (*Vittaria incurvata* Cav.).

gu odi ange ona.
He has done all he could.

gu odi mai ogu.
I have done all I could!

gu oo ina mai.
Shout to announce important news (e.g., to announce the arrival of a ship).

gu soe donu.
Unmistakably, for certain.

guuduma.
A (dry) elevation in the taro bog; hillock (in the taro bog only). *n.*

guumanga. (B-1 GUMI$_2$)
Calculation, arithmetic. *n.*

guumia$_1$. (B-2 GUMI$_1$)
v.

guumia$_2$. (B-2 GUMI$_2$)
v.

guuminga. (B-1 GUMI$_1$)
n.

kaa$_1$.
A type of sound, made to attract birds. *a.*

kaa$_2$. (P-- GAA$_2$)
a.

kaa$_3$. (E-- GAA$_3$)
Mangrove crab. *n.*

kaadanga. (P-1 GADA$_1$)
n.

kaakaa. (R-- KAA$_1$)
a.

kaakaanga. (R-1 KAA$_1$)
n.

kaalonga. (P-1 GALO$_2$)
n.

kaanga. (B-1 KAA$_1$)
n.

kaba$_1$. (E-- GABA$_4$)
Wait! *i.*

kaba$_2$. (P-- GABA$_2$)
a.

kaba$_3$. (E-- GABA$_3$)
Do prematurely. *a.*

kaba ai loo.
Wait until — !

kaba donu.
Wait!

kaba kaba.
Wait! Wait!

kaba muhuu.
Please wait!

kabe. (E-- GABE)
v.

kabi. (E-- GABI)
Tight (of clothes), stuffed. *v.*

kabianga. (E-1 GABI)
n.

kada. (P-- GADA$_1$)
a.

kadi. (E-- GADI)
Bite hard; tightly packed; jammed up. *v.*

kadi ange.
Fastened on to (by being stuck in).

kadi gauvae.
To clench one's teeth (from cold).

kage. (P-- GAGE)
v.

kahu. (P-- GAHU)
a.

kahuanga. (P-1 GAHU)
n.

kai$_1$. (P-- GAI$_1$)
a.

kai$_2$. (P-- GAI$_2$)
Propensity of fish to bite (a whole school at once). *v.*

kai$_3$. (B-- KAI$_1$)
Boiling. *a.*

kai$_4$. (B-- KAI$_2$)
Legend, story. *n.*

kaianeane. (XCO KAI$_2$)
Show-off. *a.*

kaikai. (R-- KAI$_1$)
a.

kai laanui.
Show-off; a legend concerning the founding of Nukuoro.

kala$_1$.
Smarting of skin which has been cut, or of an abrasion, when in contact with seawater, etc. *a.*

kala$_2$.
Fragrance (esp. of food). *a.*

kalaanga$_1$. (B-1 KALA$_1$)
n.

kalaanga$_2$. (B-1 KALA$_2$)
n.

kali. (P-- GALI)
v.

kalo$_1$. (P-- GALO$_1$)
a.

kalo$_2$. (P-- GALO$_2$)
a.

kalo$_3$. (E-- GALO$_3$)
Stir up. *v.*

kalo$_4$. (B-- KALO)
Sharp (as a knife); a sharp pointed canoe (designed to ride easily in rough seas). *a.*

kaloanga. (B-1 KALO)
n.

kalo talinga.
Clean out, or scratch, inside the ear.

kalo gee.
Strabismus (esp. the form in which one eye is turned outward from the nose); cross-eyed.

kana.
WARNING ASPECT MARKER; don't ever —!; be careful!; lest. *mt.*

kana adu.
Perhaps; Watch yourself!

kana mai.
Watch your step around me!

kanamalie. (KANA, MALIE)
Tasty (especially of taro). *a.*

kano. (E-- GANO)
Penis, meat, flesh. *n.*

kano avaavaa.
Porous.

kano de langi.
A blue and cloudless sky.

kano maailaba.
The wood next to the core of a tree.

kano maalama.
A phosphorescent flash in the water.

kano made.
Slightly aged meat.

kano malie.
A tasty tuber of good quality.

kano mouli.
Fresh meat (including fish).

kano mugamuga.
A crunching noise made when masticating certain foods (like cucumbers).

kanosaa. (GANO, SAA_1)
A tasteless tuber of poor quality. *a.*

kano siabo.
The meat on the side of the fish's head.

kangi.
Sharp (as a knife), pointed. *a.*

kangi baasi lua.
Double-edged.

kangi de hagasaele.
A quick-witted person (who realizes his goals fast).

kangi de maanadu.
A quick-witted person (who realizes his goals fast).

kangi odi.
Too sharp.

kasa. (P-- GASA)
a.

kasi. (P-- $GASI_1$)
v.

kaso. (P-- $GASO_1$)
Narrow [pl.]. *a.*

kasoanga. (P-1 $GASO_1$)
n.

kau_1. (E-- GAU_4)
Fish sp.: (any small jack-like fish). *n.*

kau_2. (E-- GAU_2)
To swim (or make motions of swimming, as babies do). *v.*

kau donu.
Used to, easy to.

kau gee.
Not used to; hard to.

kaunga. (E-1 GAU_2)
n.

kava.
To feel uncomfortably warm. *a.*

kavaanga. (B-1 KAVA)
n.

kave. (E-- $GAVE_1$)
Take. *v.*

kave dagi de momo.
Take a little (or few) at a time.

kave dahi.
Do at one time.

kave e hakide.
Take someone in order to train or teach him.

kave gi de mahi.
Obtain by force.

kave houhou.
Race to take.

kave huaame.
Take the whole thing.

keeligi.
Put away against a contingency; take precautions. *v.*

keeligianga. (B-1 KEELIGI)
n.

keli. (E-- GELI)
Root around (disturbing the coral layer of a yard by shuffling, or by pawing the ground). *a.*

kelo. (P-- GELO)
a.

kemo. (P-- GEMO)
a.

keomanga. (P-1 GEMO)
n.

kena.
Pale; whitish-yellow. *a.*

kenaanga. (B-1 KENA)
n.

keu. (P-- GEU)
v.

kide. (P-- GIDE)
a.

kideanga. (P-1 GIDE)
n.

kii$_1$.
Win, overcome. *a.*

kii$_2$.
Move away. *v.*

kii$_3$. (P-- GII)
a.

kiia. (B-2 KII$_2$)
v.

kii adu.
Get out!

kii age.
Move upward; reach a certain age.

kiianga$_1$. (B-1 KII$_1$)
n.

kiianga$_2$. (B-1 KII$_2$)
n.

kiianga$_3$. (P-1 GII)
n.

kii ange.
Increase.

kii gee.
Move away from.

kii iho.
Smaller, lesser (in rank, importance, strength, development, etc.).

kii mai.
Decreasing.

kilaa. (B-- LAA$_{1c}$)
There in the distance. *b.*

kinaa. (B-- NAA$_{1c}$)
There near you. *b.*

kinei. (B-- NEI$_c$)
Here in this place. *b.*

kini$_1$. (E-- GINI)
Pick at one time, pinch at one time. *v.*

kini$_2$. (E-- GINI)
Plant sp.: tree sp.: Terminalia tree (*Terminalia samoensis* Tech.). *n.*

kino.
Hate. *a.*

kino made.
Hate vehemently, completely disgusted.

kivi.
Thin (bony). *a.*

kobe. (E-- GOBE)
Cough (a single time). *a.*

kobeanga. (E-1 GOBE)
n.

kobu. (E-- GOBU)
Splash (once). *a.*

kobuanga. (E-1 GOBU)
n.

kobu dango.
The splash of a small object (like a *dango*) hitting the water at high velocity.

koe. (E-- GOE$_1$)
[Var. of *goe*]. *pi.*

koe se aha.
Who do you think you are?

kohu. (P-- GOHU)
—; very dark in color. *a.*

koi. (E-- GOI$_2$)
Scrape (a single act), scraper. *v.*

koli. (E-- GOLI)
Scrape off (with one's finger), scratch up. *v.*

kolili.
I'm only kidding! *i.*

kolu. (E-- GOLU)
Pray for the welfare of—; do earnestly. *v.*

kolu de henua.
Pray for the welfare of the whole island (and its population).

kona. (E-- $GONA_1$)
Very, too much. *a.*

kona ange.
Become much worse.

kona iho.
Be too much for one.

kona loo.
Too much!

kona odi.
Too much.

kono. (E-- GONO)
Grunt (once). *a.*

koo. (P-- GOO_1)
a.

kooanga. (P-1 GOO_1)
n.

$kosi_1$. (E-- $GOSI_1$)
To scratch (once). *v.*

$kosi_2$. (E-- $GOSI_2$)
Mollusk sp.: *Cardium* sp. *n.*

kosi-honga-agau.
Mollusk sp.: *Trachycardium orbita*

koso. (P-- GOSO)
a.

kosoanga. (P-1 GOSO)
n.

kosolia. (P-2 GOSO)
a.

$kumi_1$. (E-- $GUMI_1$)
To squeeze by grabbing. *v.*

$kumi_2$. (E-- $GUMI_2$)
Calculate (do arithmetic), figure out. *v.*

kumi tangi.
To control one's crying.

haa_1.
Bear — (as a tree). *d.*

haa_2. (B-- HAA_{1a})
Coconut palm frond. *n.*

haa_3.
Four. *an.*

haa-alaala.
The fourth number of a counting game played to determine who is "it".

haa daha.
The outer coconut palm frond.

haadia. (B-2 HADI)
v.

haadinga. (B-1 HADI)
—; curve (e.g., of a road). *n.*

haadinga haiava.
Bend in a path.

haadodo.
The connecting pegs of the outrigger float. *n.*

haa-dolo.
Fish sp.: squirrelfish.

haadua. (E-2 $HADU_1$)
v.

haadunga. (E-1 $HADU_1$)
n.

haagia. (B-2 HAGI)
v.

haagina. (B-2 HAGI)
v.

haaginga. (B-1 HAGI)
n.

$haahaa_1$. (R-- HAA_1)
v.

$haahaa_2$. (R-- HAA_2)
To search for in the dark; to seek blindly using only one's hands to locate something; similarly, any action that is tentative. *v.*

haahaagia. (R-2 HAA_2)
v.

haahaaligi. (R-- HAALIGI)
v.

haahaaligia. (R-2 HAALIGI)
v.

haahaaligidia. (R-2 HAALIGI)
v.

haahaaliginga. (R-1 HAALIGI)
n.

haahaalo. (R-- HAALO)
v.

haahaaloa. (R-2 HAALO)
v.

haahaalonga. (R-1 HAALO)
n.

haahaanau. (R-- HAANAU)
a.

haahaanialo. (R-- HAANIALO)
To put *haanialo* on in several places. *v.*

haahaanialoanga. (R-1 HAANIALO)
n.

haahaanga$_1$. (R-1 HAA$_1$)
n.

haahaanga$_2$. (R-1 HAA$_2$)
n.

haahaango. (T-- HANGO)
Wake up (someone) insistently. *v.*

haahaangoa. (T-2 HANGO)
v.

haahangoda. (R-- HAANGODA)
To fish first in one place, then in another. *v.*

haahaangodaanga.
(R-1 HAANGODA) *n*

haahaangoda ange.
Prowl around (to attack).

haahaangodalia. (R-2 HAANGODA)
A place which has been fished in over and over. *v.*

haahaangona. (S-2 HANGO)
v.

haahaangonga. (T-1 HANGO)
n.

haahaa saele.
Search here and there.

haahaau. (R-- HAAU)
v.

haahaaunga. (R-1 HAAU)
n.

haahadi. (T-- HADI)
[Pl. of *hadi*]. *v.*

haahadia. (T-2 HADI)
v.

haahadinga. (T-1 HADI)
n.

haahaula. (R-- ULA$_{1b}$)
v.

haahaula age de me.
Become bright (with morning sunlight).

haahaulanga. (R-1 ULA$_{1b}$)
n.

haahaulasia. (R-2 ULA$_{1b}$)
v.

haahine. (P-- HAHINE)
Women. *n.*

haaide.
Measure (exactly). *v.*

haaidea. (B-2 HAAIDE)
v.

haaidenga. (B-1 HAAIDE)
n.

haaina.
Stare at. *v.*

haaina dangada.
Stare at people indiscreetly (esp. strangers).

haainanga. (B-1 HAAINA)
n.

haainasia. (B-2 HAAINA)
v.

Haa-laangi. (HAA$_3$, LAANGI)
Thursday [lit., the 'fourth day']. *nt.*

haalala.
Stand leaning. *v.*

haa leu.
A leaf which has turned yellowish-brown.

haalia. (B-2 HALI)
v.

haaligi.
Wrap from under, wrap around; to line something (e.g., a box, with paper). *v.*

haaligia. (B-2 HAALIGI)
v.

haaligidia. (B-2 HAALIGI)
v.

haaliginga. (B-1 HAALIGI)
n.

haalinga. (B-1 HALI)
n.

haalo.
Extend one's hand, reach out; to expect

things from others, and accept too readily. *v.*

haaloa. (B-2 HAALO)
v.

haa lodo.
The inner coconut palm frond.

haalonga. (B-1 HAALO)
n.

Haa-malama. (HAA_3, MALAMA)
April [lit., the 'fourth month']. *nt.*

haa manu.
The young (of an animal) born at the same time (e.g., a litter, etc.); the offspring of (sharing the characteristics of).

haanau.
Born; delivery (of a baby); give birth to. *a.*

haanaunga. (B-1 HAANAU)
n.

haanau ssene.
Yield interest.

haanialo.
A bracing cross-beam [?]. *v.*

haanialoanga. (B-1 HAANIALO)
n.

haanoa. (B-2 HHANO)
Wash someone's hands (or mouth). *v.*

haanonga. (B-1 HHANO)
n.

haangaa. (E-2 HANGA)
v.

haangaa lodo i de gai.
Be continually hungry, owing to having a distended stomach from regularly eating too much.

haangai.
To feed (someone). *v.*

haangoa. (B-2 HANGO)
v.

haangoda.
Fishing. *v.*

haangodaanga. (B-1 HAANGODA)
n.

haangoda de agau.
A method of fishing (with a line on the reef).

haangoda de boo.
A method of fishing (at night, beyond the reef).

haangoda de lodo.
To fish in the lagoon.

haangoda dua agau.
Fishing beyond the reef (on the seaward side of the atoll).

haangoda dua beau.
A fishing method (used on the seaward reef during the day) employing a line, with hermit crabs for bait).

haangoda dugidugi.
A method of fishing (night fishing outside the reef, using hermit crabs for bait).

haangoda ina.
[= *haangodalia*].

haangodalia. (B-2 HAANGODA)
A suitable (place) for fishing. *v.*

haangoda mada aasanga.
To fish for *labelabe*.

haangona. (B-2 HANGO)
v.

haangonga. (B-1 HANGO)
n.

haaoa. (B-2 HAO_2)
v.

haaonga. (B-1 HAO_2)
n.

haasinga. (B-1 HASI)
n.

haau.
Suckle (at the breast). *v.*

$haaua_1$. (B-2 HAU)
v.

$haaua_2$. (B-2 HAAU)
v.

$haaunga_1$. (E-1 HAU)
n.

$haaunga_2$. (B-1 HAAU)
n.

haau unuunu.
Breast-feed.

hada.
Shelf, platform, raft, floor (of planks); car; a clam nursery, men's house [archaic]. *n.*

hadahada. (R-- HADA)
Chest. *n.*

hadahada ama.
The platform fastened on top of the outrigger booms of a canoe.

hadi.
Broken (as a stick), bent up. *a.*

hadi aho.
[Var. of *hadi haho*].

hadi bala.
To rely on others for the things one should provide for oneself.

hadi bodo.
Breaking of waves at short intervals.

hadi de uga.
The curvature of a fish line when angling (due to underwater currents).

hadihadi. (R-- HADI)
Break many times or in many places. *v.*

hadihadia. (R-2 HADI)
v.

hadihadinga. (R-1 HADI)
n.

hadi haho.
Steep (inclination).

hadi modu.
Sheer drop-off (as at the edge of a cliff).

hadinga. (B-1 HADI)
Joint (of an arm or leg). *n.*

hadiugu. (HADI, UGU)
A unit of linear measure (from the end of an outstretched hand to the bent elbow of the other arm). *v.*

hadu$_1$.
Invented —, made-up —; layout of (preliminary work on) plaiting. *v.*

hadu$_2$.
Stone, rock, a piece of weathered coral. *n.*

hadua. (B-2 HADU$_1$)
v.

hadu alo.
The bottom portion of a fish.

hadu-bunga.
Mollusk sp.: *Chama iostoma.*

hadu daahili.
To make up a song.

hadu de gaanunu.
Nipple of breast.

hadu de moana.
A type of string figure.

hadu-gamugamu.
Coral sp.

hadu goinga.
Boundary stone.

hadugolaa. (GOLAA, HADU$_2$)
Any stone of volcanic origin [imported from volcanic islands]. *n.*

haduhadu$_1$. (R-- HADU$_1$)
v.

haduhadu$_2$. (R-- HADU$_2$)
Thick (not watery). *v.*

haduhadua$_1$. (R-2 HADU$_1$)
v.

haduhadua$_2$. (R-2 HADU$_2$)
Rocky (full of stones). *v.*

haduhadunga$_1$. (R-1 HADU$_1$)
n.

haduhadunga$_2$. (R-1 HADU$_2$)
n.

hadu hagamogomogo.
Gem.

hadu-i-de-ssala.
Coral sp.: red organ-pipe coral [used for making necklaces].

hadu lalo.
A stone on which hermit crabs are crushed (to use for bait).

Hadu-lehu. (HADU$_2$, LEHU)
The name of a ghost in Nukuoro legend. *nn.*

hadu lunga.
A stone used to crush hermit crabs (for bait).

hadu-maadau.
Coral sp. [used for polishing pearl shell fish hooks].

hadu mada.
Eyeball.

hadu-mada-pula.
Coral sp.: (several spp. — poisonous).

hadu manava.
Heart.

hadu-mangeo.
Cushion starfish.

hadu me llanga.
Lay out plaited work.

hadu muna.
Lie (tell a falsehood).

hadunga. (B-1 HADU$_1$)
n.

hadu o de mamu.
The hard stomach-like organ of certain fish.

hadu solo bulaga*.
A taro grater made from a certain type of coral.

hadu-uaua.
Mollusk sp.: *Spondylus* sp.

hadu-uli.
Coral sp.: blue coral.

hatuli.
Thunder. *v.*

haehaele. (R-- HAELE)
v.

haehaelea. (R-2 HAELE)
v.

haehaelenga. (R-1 HAELE)
n.

haele.
Bring up (children), discipline (children). *v.*

haelea. (B-2 HAELE)
v.

haelenga. (B-1 HAELE)
n.

haele sala.
Spoil (children), bring up (children) badly.

haelu.
Var. of *hailu*. *v.*

haga-.
CAUSATIVE PREFIX; cause to (be, become, have, know) —. *mf.*

hagaabasasa. (BE- ABASASA)
Act like or emulate Europeans. *v.*

hagaabiabi. (RE ABI$_1$)
v.

hagaabiabia. (RE2 ABI$_1$)
v.

hagaabiabinga. (RE1 ABI$_1$)
n.

hagaabida. (BE- AABIDA)
v.

hagaabidanga. (BE1 AABIDA)
n.

hagaabo. (BE- ABO)
v.

hagaaboabo. (RE- ABO)
v.

hagaaboabolia. (RE2 ABO)
v.

hagaaboabonga. (RE1 ABO)
n.

hagaaboabongi. (RE- ABONGI)
v.

hagaabolia. (BE2 ABO)
v.

hagaabonga. (BE1 ABO)
n.

hagaabongi. (BE- ABONGI)
v.

hagaabulu. (BE- ABULU)
v.

hagaabuluanga. (BE1 ABULU)
n.

hagaapulu. (PE- ABULU)
v.

hagaapuluanga. (PE1 ABULU)
n.

hagaada$_1$. (BE- ADA$_1$)
Give a picture to. *v.*

hagaada$_2$. (BE- AADA)
v.

hagaadaada. (RE- ADA$_1$)
Getting to be near daybreak. *v.*

hagaadaadamai. (RE- ADA$_{1a}$)
v.

hagaadaadamaia. (RE2 ADA$_{1a}$)
v.

hagaadaadamainga. (RE1 ADA_{1a})
n.

hagaadalia. (BE2 AADA)
v.

hagaadamai. (BE- ADA_{1a})
v.

hagaadamaia. (BE2 ADA_{1a})
v.

hagaadamainga. (BE1 ADA_{1a})
n.

hagaadanga. (BE1 AADA)
n.

hagaadiidii. (BE- DII_a)
v.

hagaadiidiia. (BE2 DII_a)
v.

hagaadiidiinga. (BE1 DII_a)
n.

hagaaduadu. (RE- ADU_1)
Say bad things about people. *v.*

hagaaduadu dangada.
Critical of others.

hagaaduadu iho.
Self-criticism.

hagaaduadulia. (RE2 ADU_1)
v.

hagaaduadunga. (RE1 ADU_1)
n.

hagaadugau. (BE- ADU_{4a})
Arrange things in a row or line. *v.*

hagaadugaua. (BE2 ADU_{4a})
v.

hagaadugauanga. (BE1 ADU_{4a})
n.

hagaadugaulia. (BE2 ADU_{4a})
v.

hagaaduisiisi. (BE- ADUISIISI)
To treat someone as a first husband or wife. *v.*

hagaadumua. (BE- ADUMUA)
v.

hagaadumuaanga. (BE1 ADUMUA)
n.

hagaagahi. (R-- HAGAHI)
Call (someone). *v.*

hagaagahia. (R-2 HAGAHI)
v.

hagaagahinga. (R-1 HAGAHI)
n.

hagaagahi sseeloo.
To call out "sail ho!".

hagaagai. (BE- GAI_{2a})
v.

hagaagainga. (BE1 GAI_{2a})
n.

hagaageageli. (RE- AGELI)
v.

hagaageagelia. (RE2 AGELI)
v.

hagaageagelinga. (RE1 AGELI)
n.

hagaageli. (BE- AGELI)
v.

hagaagelia. (BE2 AGELI)
v.

hagaagelinga. (BE1 AGELI)
n.

hagaagiagilau. (RE- AGILAU)
v.

hagaagiagilaua. (RE2 AGILAU)
v.

hagaagiagilaunga. (RE1 AGILAU)
n.

hagaagilau. (BE- AGILAU)
v.

hagaagilaua. (BE2 AGILAU)
v.

hagaagilaunga. (BE1 AGILAU)
n.

hagaago. (BE- AGO_1)
Imitate; show, teach; to urge. *v.*

hagaagoa. (BE2 AGO_1)
v.

$hagaagoago_1$. (RE- AGO_1)
Lesson, make learn, cause to teach. *v.*

$hagaagoago_2$. (RE- AGO_2)
Cause taro to be fibrous (e.g., by the planting method employed). *v.*

hagaagoagoa. (RE2 AGO_1)
v.

hagaagoagona. (RE2 AGO_1)
v.

hagaagoagonga. (RE1 AGO_1)
n.

hagaagona. (BE2 AGO_1)
v.

hagaagonga. (BE1 AGO_1)
n.

hagaagu. (BE- AGU)
v.

hagaagua. (BE2 AGU)
v.

hagaaguagu. (RE- AGU)
v.

hagaaguagua. (RE2 AGU)
v.

hagaaguagule. (RE- AGULE)
v.

hagaaguagulea. (RE2 AGULE)
v.

hagaaguagulenga. (RE1 AGULE)
n.

hagaaguagulia. (RE2 AGU)
v.

hagaaguagunga. (RE1 AGU)
n.

hagaagule. (BE- AGULE)
v.

hagaagulea. (BE2 AGULE)
v.

hagaagulenga. (BE1 AGULE)
n.

hagaagulia. (BE2 AGU)
v.

hagaagunga. (BE1 AGU)
n.

hagaaha. (BE- AHA_1)
Cause to do what? *v.*

hagaahea. (BE2 AHE)
v.

hagaaheahe. (RE- AHE)
v.

hagaaheahea. (RE2 AHE)
v.

hagaaheahelia. (RE2 AHE)
v.

hagaaheahenga. (RE1 AHE)
n.

hagaahee. (BE- HEE_{2a})
When? (near future). *a.*

hagaahelia. (BE2 AHE)
v.

hagaahe mai.
Return to the fold.

hagaahenga. (BE1 AHE)
n.

hagaahi. (BE- AHI_1)
Provide fire to or for; hungry; eat something. *v.*

hagaahiahi. (RE- AHI_1)
Wait until nearly sunset (to do something). *a.*

hagaahu. (BE- AAHU)
v.

hagaahulu. (BE- AAHULU)
v.

hagaahunga. (BE1 AAHU)
n.

hagaai.
Be in a serious situation. *a.*

hagaaigoli. (GOLI, HAGAAI)
A food tree on another's land. *n.*

hagaala₁. (BE- ALA_1)
Make mat sections. *v.*

hagaala₂. (BE- ALA_2)
v.

hagaalaala. (RE- ALA_2)
—; defecate. *v.*

hagaalaaladi. (RE- $LADI_a$)
v.

hagaalaaladia. (RE2 $LADI_a$)
v.

hagaalaaladinga. (RE1 $LADI_a$)
n.

hagaalaalanga. (RE1 ALA_2)
n.

hagaalaange. (BE- ALA_{2a})
v.

hagaaladi. (BE- $LADI_a$)
v.

hagaaladia. (BE2 LADI$_a$)
v.

hagaaladinga. (BE1 LADI$_a$)
n.

hagaalahage. (BE- ALA$_{2b}$)
a.

hagaalahenua. (BE- HENUA$_a$)
Provide land for. *v.*

hagaalali. (BE- AALALI)
v.

hagaali. (BE- ALI)
To mention or expose something just enough so that the remainder is obvious. *v.*

hagaalia. (BE2 ALI)
v.

hagaaliali$_1$. (RE- ALI)
To attempt to attract a member of the opposite sex through exhibitionism. *v.*

hagaaliali$_2$. (RE- ALI)
v.

hagaalialia. (RE2 ALI)
v.

hagaalialinga$_1$. (RE1 ALI)
n.

hagaalialinga$_2$. (RE1 ALI)
n.

hagaaligi. (BE- ALIGI)
Install as a priest (of a cult). *v.*

hagaalinga$_1$. (BE1 ALI)
n.

hagaalinga$_2$. (BE- AALINGA)
n.

hagaalingaanga. (BE1 AALINGA)
n.

hagaalo$_1$. (BE- ALO$_1$)
v.

hagaalo--$_2$. (BE- ALO$_2$)
v.

hagaaloa. (BE2 ALO$_1$)
v.

hagaaloalo$_1$. (RE- ALO$_1$)
v.

hagaaloalo--$_2$. (RE- ALO$_2$)
v.

hagaaloaloa. (RE2 ALO$_1$)
v.

hagaaloalo-mea. (ALO$_2$, MEA)
Cause to become red (of fully mature coconut meat). *v.*

hagaaloalonga. (RE1 ALO$_1$)
n.

hagaaloalo-uli. (ALO$_2$, ULI$_1$)
Cause to become dark (of fully mature coconut meat). *v.*

hagaaloha. (BE- ALOHA)
Piteous, pitiful. *a.*

hagaalo-malie. (ALO$_2$, MALIE)
Cause to become *alomalie*. *v.*

hagaalomasige. (BE- ALOMASIGE)
v.

hagaalomasigeanga.
(BE1 ALOMASIGE) *n.*

hagaalo-mea. (ALO$_2$, MEA)
Cause to be red (of fully mature coconut meat). *v.*

hagaalonga. (BE1 ALO$_1$)
n.

hagaalo-uli. (ALO$_2$, ULI$_1$)
Cause to be dark (of fully mature coconut meat). *v.*

hagaalualu. (RE- ALU)
v.

hagaalualukaba. (RE- ALU$_a$)
v.

hagaalualukabaanga. (RE1 ALU$_a$)
n.

hagaalukaba. (BE- ALU$_a$)
Cause to leave quickly, force out. *v.*

hagaalukabaanga. (BE1 ALU$_a$)
n.

hagaamia. (BE- AAMIA)
v.

hagaamo. (BE- AMO)
v.

hagaamoa. (BE2 AMO)
v.

hagaamoaa. (BE2 AMO)
v.

hagaamoaanga. (BE3 AMO)
n.

hagaamoamo. (RE- AMO)
v.

hagaamoamoa. (RE2 AMO)
v.

hagaamoamoaa. (RE2 AMO)
v.

hagaamoamoaanga. (RE3 AMO)
n.

hagaamoamoanga. (RE1 AMO)
n.

hagaamoamoea. (RE2 AMO)
v.

hagaamoamoenga. (RE3 AMO)
n.

hagaamoamonga. (RE1 AMO)
n.

hagaamoanga. (BE1 AMO)
n.

hagaamoea. (BE2 AMO)
v.

hagaamoeanga. (BE3 AMO)
n.

hagaamonga. (BE1 AMO)
n.

hagaamu$_1$. (BE- AMU)
v.

hagaamu$_2$. (U-- MUA$_a$)
Pay respect to, honor (someone). *v.*

hagaamua$_1$. (BE2 AMU)
v.

hagaamua$_2$. (BE- MUA$_a$)
Accord honor to. *v.*

hagaamuaanga. (BE1 MUA$_a$)
n.

hagaamuamu. (RE- AMU)
v.

hagaamuamuia. (RE2 AMU)
v.

hagaamuamulia. (RE2 AMU)
v.

hagaamuamunga. (RE1 AMU)
n.

hagaamuanga. (BE1 AMU)
n.

hagaamuia. (BE2 AMU)
v.

hagaamuli. (BE- MULI$_{1a}$)
Treat as junior. *v.*

hagaamulia. (BE2 MULI$_{1a}$)
v.

hagaamunga. (BE1 AMU)
n.

hagaaneane. (RE- ANE)
Console; excite sexually. *v.*

hagaaneanea. (RE2 ANE)
v.

hagaaneanenga. (RE1 ANE)
n.

hagaanu. (BE- ANU)
Cause to dance or sway. *v.*

hagaanua. (BE2 ANU)
v.

hagaanuanu. (RE- ANU)
v.

hagaanuanua. (RE2 ANU)
v.

hagaanuanumanga. (RE1 ANU)
n.

hagaanuanumia. (RE2 ANU)
v.

hagaanuanunga. (RE1 ANU)
n.

hagaanumanga. (BE1 ANU)
n.

hagaanumia. (BE2 ANU)
v.

hagaanunga. (BE1 ANU)
n.

hagaanga$_1$. (BE- ANGA$_1$)
v.

hagaanga$_2$. (PE- ANGA$_1$)
v.

hagaanga$_3$. (BE- ANGA$_2$)
v.

hagaangaa. (BE2 ANGA$_2$)
v.

hagaangaanga$_1$. (RE- ANGA$_1$)
v.

hagaangaanga$_2$. (RE- ANGA$_2$)
v.

hagaangaangaa. (RE2 ANGA$_2$)
v.

hagaangaangahia. (RE2 ANGA$_1$)
v.

hagaangahia$_1$. (BE2 ANGA$_1$)
v.

hagaangahia$_2$. (PE2 ANGA$_1$)
v.

hagaangi. (BE- ANGI)
v.

hagaangia. (BE2 ANGI)
v.

hagaangiangi. (RE- ANGI)
—; expose to a breeze. *v.*

hagaangiangia. (RE2 ANGI)
v.

hagaangiangina. (RE2 ANGI)
v.

hagaangianginga. (RE1 ANGI)
n.

hagaangina. (BE2 ANGI)
v.

hagaanginga. (BE1 ANGI)
v.

hagaao$_1$. (BE- AO$_1$)
Intend to stay up until daybreak. *v.*

hagaao$_2$. (BE- AO$_2$)
Cause to be sufficient. *v.*

hagaaoa$_1$. (BE2 AO$_1$)
To have purposely stayed up until daybreak. *v.*

hagaaoa$_2$. (BE2 AO$_2$)
Cause to have been sufficient, relieve. *v.*

hagaaoa$_3$. (BE- AOA$_2$)
Cause to bear misshapen fruit (e.g., by not picking in bunches). *v.*

hagaaoanga. (BE1 AOA$_2$)
n.

hagaaoao$_1$. (RE- AO$_1$)
Habitually and purposely remain up until daybreak. *v.*

hagaaoao$_2$. (RE- AO$_2$)
v.

hagaaoaoa$_1$. (RE2 AO$_1$)
Have purposely and habitually remained up until daybreak. *v.*

hagaaoaoa$_2$. (RE2 AO$_2$)
Cause to have been continuously sufficient; aid (by giving something); help (with provisions). *v.*

hagaaoaonga$_1$. (RE1 AO$_1$)
Way of having purposely stayed up until daybreak (once). *n.*

hagaaoaonga$_2$. (RE1 AO$_2$)
n.

hagaaonga$_1$. (BE1 AO$_1$)
Way of staying up until daybreak. *n.*

hagaaonga$_2$. (BE1 AO$_2$)
n.

hagaasanga. (BE- SANGA$_a$)
To create *aasanga*. *v.*

hagaasasi. (BE- AASASI)
v.

hagaasasia. (BE2 AASASI)
v.

hagaasasinga. (BE1 AASASI)
n.

hagaasoaso. (RE- ASO$_2$)
Spouse. *n.*

hagaasu. (BE- ASU)
v.

hagaasua. (BE2 ASU)
v.

hagaasunga. (BE1 ASU)
n.

hagaau$_1$. (BE- AU$_1$)
To create an ocean current. *v.*

hagaau$_2$. (BE- AAU)
v.

hagaaua. (BE2 AAU)
v.

hagaauaau. (RE- AAU)
v.

hagaauaaua. (RE2 AAU)
v.

hagaauaaunga. (RE1 AAU)
n.

hagaau aloha.
Poor (not rich).

hagaaugau. (BE- AUGAU)
Cause infection. *v.*

hagaaugaua. (BE2 AUGAU)
Cause to be infected. *v.*

hagaaugaunga. (BE1 AUGAU)
State of becoming infected. *n.*

hagaau gee.
Bashful, shy (timid about attending social affairs), timid.

hagaaunga. (BE1 AAU)
n.

hagaausa. (BE- AAUSA)
Cause to leave a wake. *v.*

hagaausanga. (BE1 AAUSA)
n.

hagaava₁. (BE- AVA_1)
Make a channel. *v.*

hagaava₂. (BE- AVA_2)
Relieve. *v.*

hagaava age.
Be relieved for a short time.

hagaavaanga₁. (BE1 AVA_1)
n.

hagaavaanga₂. (BE1 AVA_2)
n.

hagaava ange.
Lean on someone for support.

hagaavaava₁. (RE- AVA_1)
v.

hagaavaava₂. (RE- AVA_2)
Provide or receive support continually. *v.*

hagaavaavaanga₁. (RE1 AVA_1)
n.

hagaavaavaanga₂. (RE1 AVA_2)
n.

hagabaa₁. (BE- BAA_1)
Cause to come into contact with; chase by trying to head off. *v.*

hagabaa₂. (BE- BAA_2)
To crack (as a nut). *v.*

hagabaabaa₁. (RE- BAA_1)
v.

hagabaabaa₂. (TE- BAA_2)
v.

hagabaabaa₃. (RE- BAA_4)
v.

hagabaabaagia. (RE2 BAA_5)
Make no headway and be carried sideways (by a current or the wind) against a reef, etc. *v.*

hagabaabaanga₁. (TE1 BAA_2)
n.

hagabaabaanga₂. (RE1 BAA_4)
n.

hagabaabaasi. (RE- BAASI)
v.

hagabaabaasianga. (RE1 BAASI)
n.

hagabaabanga. (BE1 BAA_4)
n.

hagabaabaoa. (RE- BAOA)
v.

hagabaabaoanga. (RE1 BAOA)
n.

hagabaabunga. (BE1 BABU)
n.

hagabaabuu. (BE- BAABUU)
v.

hagabaabuua. (BE2 BAABUU)
v.

hagabaabuunga. (BE1 BAABUU)
n.

hagabaadunga. (BE1 BADU)
n.

hagabaatai. (PE- BADAI)
v.

hagabaataianga. (PE1 BADAI)
n.

hagabaagava. (XE- BAA_5)
To threaten violence. *v.*

hagabaageaa. (BE- BAAGEAA)
v.

hagabaageaanga. (BE1 BAAGEAA)
n.

hagabaagia. (BE2 BAA_5)
v.

hagabaakuu. (PE- BAGUU)
v.

hagabaakuua. (PE2 BAGUU)
v.

hagabaakuulia. (PE2 BAGUU)
v.

hagabaakuunga. (PE1 BAGUU)
n.

hagabaalasa. (BE- BAALASA)
v.

hagabaalasaanga. (BE1 BAALASA)
n.

hagabaalasi. (BE- BAALASI)
v.

hagabaalau. (BE- BAALAU)
v.

hagabaalaua. (BE2 BAALAU)
v.

hagabaalaunga. (BE1 BAALAU)
n.

hagabaalunga. (BE1 $BALU_1$)
n.

hagabaani. (BE- BAANI)
v.

hagabaania. (BE2 BAANI)
v.

hagabaaninga. (BE1 BAANI)
n.

hagabaanga. (BE1 BAA_2)
n.

hagabaanginga. (BE1 $BANGI_1$)
n.

hagabaangoa. (PE- BANGOA)
Causing prostration. *v.*

hagabaangoaanga. (PE1 BANGOA)
n.

hagabaasanga. (BE1 $BASA_1$)
n.

hagabaasi. (BE- BAASI)
Do toward one side. *v.*

hagababa. (BE- BAA_4)
Become engaged to marry; make level, make flat; prepare for, make ready. *v.*

hagababaa. (TE- BAA_2)
v.

hagababaanga. (RE1 BAA_2)
n.

hagababaiangi. (BE- BABAIANGI)
v.

hagababalia. (BE2 BAA_4)
v.

hagababu. (BE- BABU)
v.

hagababulia. (BE2 BABU)
v.

hagabapaba. (RE- BAA_4)
v.

hagabapabaanga. (RE1 BAA_4)
n.

hagabapabalia. (RE2 BAA_4)
v.

hagabapabu. (RE- BABU)
v.

hagabapabuanga. (RE1 BABU)
n.

hagabapabulia. (RE2 BABU)
v.

hagabadabaatai. (U-- BADAI)
[The causative form of *badabaatai*]. *v.*

hagabadabaataianga. (U-- BADAI)
[The nominal form of *hagabadabaatai*]. *n.*

hagabadabadai. (RE- BADAI)
v.

hagabadabadaianga. (RE1 BADAI)
n.

hagabadai. (BE- BADAI)
v.

hagabadaianga. (BE1 BADAI)
n.

hagabadioda. (BE- BADIODA)
v.

hagabadiodaanga. (BE1 BADIODA)
n.

hagabadodi. (BE- $DODI_a$)
v.

hagabadodia. (BE2 $DODI_a$)
v.

hagabadodinga. (BE1 $DODI_a$)
n.

hagabadotodi. (RE- $DODI_a$)
v.

hagabadotodia. (RE2 $DODI_a$)
v.

hagabadotodinga. (RE1 DODIa)
n.

hagabadu. (BE- BADU)
v.

hagabadua. (BE2 BADU)
v.

hagabadubadu. (RE- BADU)
v.

hagabadubadua. (RE2 BADU)
v.

hagabadubadulia. (RE2 BADU)
v.

hagabadubadunga. (RE1 BADU)
n.

hagabadulia. (BE2 BADU)
v.

hagabae. (BE- BAE)
v.

hagabaea. (BE2 BAE)
—; to hang oneself (suicide). *v.*

hagabaebae. (RE- BAE)
v.

hagabaebaea. (RE2 BAE)
v.

hagabaebaenga. (RE1 BAE)
n.

hagabaenga. (BE1 BAE)
n.

hagabagekege. (BE- BAGEKEGE)
v.

hagabagekegeanga.
(BE1 BAGEKEGE) *n.*

hagabagekegelia.
(BE2 BAGEKEGE) *v.*

hagabagia. (BE2 BAGI)
v.

hagabagiaanga. (BE1 BAGI)
n.

hagabagibagia. (RE2 BAGI)
v.

hagabagibagianga. (RE1 BAGI)
n.

hagabagobago. (RE- BAGO)
v.

hagabagobagoanga. (RE1 BAGO)
n.

hagabagobagolia. (RE2 BAGO)
v.

hagabaguu. (BE- BAGUU)
v.

hagabaguua. (BE2 BAGUU)
v.

hagabaguu ange.
Move against something so fast that it appears to be coming at one.

hagabaguulia. (BE2 BAGUU)
v.

hagabaguunga. (BE1 BAGUU)
n.

hagabahhaa. (BE- BAHHAA)
To exhale suddenly; making exhalation noises. *v.*

hagabahhaanga. (BE1 BAAHAA)
n.

hagabala. (BE- BALA)
Allow to become soft; prostrate oneself (esp. to hide). *v.*

hagabalaagula. (PE- BALAGULA)
v.

hagabalaagulaanga.
(PE1 BALAGULA) *n.*

hagabalaavini. (PE- BALAVINI)
v.

hagabalabala. (RE- BALA)
Make loose; make soft; be a defeatist. *v.*

hagabalabalaanga. (RE1 BALA)
n.

hagabalabalagula.
(RE- BALAGULA) *v.*

hagabalabalagulaanga.
(RE1 BALAGULA) *n.*

hagabalabalasi. (RE- BAALASI)
v.

hagabalabalasia. (RE2 BAALASI)
v.

hagabalabalasinga. (RE1 BAALASI)
n.

hagabalabalavini. (RE- BALAVINI)
v.

hagabalagelage. (BE- BALAGELAGE)
To have come to be unable to walk. *n.*

hagabalagelageanga. (BE1 BALAGELAGE) *n.*

hagabalaginagina. (BE- BALAa) *v.*

hagabalagula. (BE- BALAGULA) *v.*

hagabalagulaanga. (BE1 BALAGULA) *n.*

hagabalala. (BE- BALALA) *v.*

hagabalalaanga. (BE1 BALALA) *n.*

hagabalasia. (BE2 BAALASI) *v.*

hagabalasinga. (BE1 BAALASI) *n.*

hagabalaulau. (BE- BALAULAU) *v.*

hagabalaulaua. (BE2 BALAULAU) *v.*

hagabalaulaunga. (BE1 BALAULAU) *n.*

hagabalavini. (BE- BALAVINI) *v.*

hagabaledilo. (BE- BALEDILO) *v.*

hagabalia. (BE- BALIA) *v.*

hagabaliaanga. (BE1 BALIA) *n.*

hagabalu. (BE- BALU$_1$) *v.*

hagabalua. (BE2 BALU$_1$) *v.*

hagabalubalu. (RE- BALU$_1$) *v.*

hagabalubalua. (RE2 BALU$_1$) *v.*

hagabalubalunga. (RE1 BALU$_1$) *n.*

hagabangabanga. (RE- BANGA$_1$) *v.*

hagabangabangalia. (RE2 BANGA$_1$) *v.*

hagabangi. (BE- BANGI$_1$) *v.*

hagabangia. (BE2 BANGI$_1$) *v.*

hagabangibangi. (RE- BANGI$_1$) *v.*

hagabangibangia. (RE2 BANGI$_1$) *v.*

hagabangibanginga. (RE1 BANGI$_1$) *n.*

hagabangoa. (BE- BANGOA)
—; give in to exhaustion. *v.*

hagabangoaanga. (BE1 BANGOA) *n.*

hagabangobangoa. (RE- BANGOA)
—; given to prostration. *v.*

hagabangobangoaanga. (RE1 BANGOA) *n.*

hagabaoa. (BE- BAOA) *v.*

hagabaoanga. (BE1 BAOA) *n.*

hagabasa. (BE- BASA$_1$)
Cause someone to speak; convince. *v.*

hagabasaa. (BE2 BASA$_1$)
Be talked into. *v.*

hagabasabasa. (RE- BASA$_1$) *v.*

hagabasabasaanga. (RE1 BASA$_1$) *n.*

hagabasabasalia$_1$. (RE2 BASA$_1$)
Cause to be convinced. *v.*

hagabasabasalia$_2$. (RE- BASALIA) *v.*

hagabasabasaliaanga. (RE1 BASALIA) *n.*

hagabasalia$_1$. (BE2 BASA$_1$)
Convince someone completely. *v.*

hagabasalia$_2$. (BE- BASALIA) *v.*

hagabasaliaanga. (BE1 BASALIA) *n.*

hagabau. (BE- BAU$_1$)
Measure, calculate, estimate. *v.*

hagabaua. (BE2 BAU$_1$)
Figure out, determine. *v.*

hagabauanga. (BE1 BAU$_1$)
n.

hagabaubau. (RE- BAU$_2$)
Criticize; cause bad feelings; scrape taro inadequately. *v.*

hagabaubaua. (RE2 BAU$_2$)
v.

hagabaubauanga. (RE3 BAU$_2$)
To have been criticized. *a.*

hagabaubaulia. (RE2 BAU$_2$)
v.

hagabaubaunga. (RE1 BAU$_2$)
n.

hagabaulia. (BE2 BAU$_1$)
Figure out, determine. *v.*

hagabaunga. (BE1 BAU$_1$)
n.

hagabeabeau. (RE- BEAU)
v.

hagabeabeaua. (RE2 BEAU)
v.

hagabeabeaunga. (RE1 BEAU)
n.

hagabebe. (BE- BEBE$_1$)
v.

hagabebea. (BE2 BEBE$_1$)
v.

hagabebeanga. (BE1 BEBE$_1$)
n.

hagabebee. (TE- BEE)
v.

hagabebeeanga. (TE1 BEE)
n.

hagabebela. (BE- BEBELA)
v.

hagabebelia. (BE2 BEBE$_1$)
v.

hagabedage. (BE- BEDAGE)
v.

hagabedageanga. (BE1 BEDAGE)
n.

hagabedi. (BE- BEDI)
v.

hagabedia. (BE2 BEDI)
v.

hagabedianga. (BE1 BEDI)
n.

hagabedibedi. (RE- BEDI)
v.

hagabedibedia. (RE2 BEDI)
v.

hagabedibedianga. (RE1 BEDI)
n.

hagabei. (BE- BEI)
v.

hagabeibei. (RE- BEI)
v.

hagabela. (BE- BELA)
Provide *bela* for. *v.*

hagabelabela. (RE- BELA)
v.

hagabelabelaanga. (RE1 BELA)
v.

hagabibi. (BE- BIBI$_2$)
To cook food in an earth oven for a short time (just to heat it up). *v.*

hagabibianga. (BE1 BIBI$_2$)
n.

hagabido. (BE- BIDO)
Carrying (two persons), with each person carrying an end [dp]. *v.*

hagabidoa. (BE2 BIDO)
Be the last. *v.*

hagabigi$_1$. (BE- BIGI$_1$)
v.

hagabigi$_2$. (BE- BIGI$_2$)
Strive to be like. *v.*

hagabigia. (BE2 BIGI$_1$)
v.

hagabigianga. (BE1 BIGI$_1$)
n.

hagabigibigi$_1$. (RE- BIGI$_1$)
v.

hagabigibigi$_2$. (RE- BIGI$_2$)
v.

hagabigibigia. (RE2 BIGI$_1$)
—; make covered with something sticky. *v.*

hagabigibigilia. (RE2 BIGI$_1$)
v.

hagabigibiginga. (RE1 BIGI$_1$)
n.

hagabigilia. (BE2 BIGI$_1$)
v.

hagabigo. (BE- BIGO)
v.

hagabigobigo. (RE- BIGO)
Wiggle. *v.*

hagabigobigolia. (RE2 BIGO)
v.

hagabigobigonga. (RE1 BIGO)
n.

hagabigo de ngago.
Fool (someone), deceive.

hagabigolia. (BE2 BIGO)
v.

hagabiho. (BE- BIHO)
Cause to become a leader. *v.*

hagabii. (BE- BII)
v.

hagabiia. (BE2 BII)
v.

hagabiianga. (BE1 BII)
n.

hagabiibii. (RE- BII)
v.

hagabiibiia. (RE2 BII)
v.

hagabiibiianga. (RE1 BII)
n.

hagabiigia. (BE2 BIGI$_1$)
To make sticky. *v.*

hagabiiginga. (BE1 BIGI$_1$)
Way of making sticky. *n.*

hagabiigonga. (BE1 BIGO)
n.

hagabiihingi. (BE- BIIHINGI)
v.

hagabiilinga. (BE1 BILI$_1$)
n.

hagabili. (BE- BILI$_1$)
v.

hagabilia. (BE2 BILI$_1$)
v.

hagabilibili. (RE- BILI$_1$)
v.

hagabilibilia. (RE2 BILI$_1$)
v.

hagabilibilinga. (RE1 BILI$_1$)
n.

hagabinaaina. (BE- BINAAINA)
a.

hagabinabinaaina.
(RE- BINAAINA) *a.*

hagabini$_1$. (BE- BINI)
Plant sp.: tree sp. (*Soulamea amara* Lam.). *n.*

hagabini$_2$. (BE- BINI)
Insect sp.: cockroach. *n.*

hagabinga. (BE- BINGA)
Name (something). *v.*

hagabinga ange.
Be known as, called by the name —.

hagabingabinga. (RE- BINGA)
v.

hagabingabingalia. (RE2 BINGA)
v.

hagabingalia. (BE2 BINGA)
v.

hagaboaa. (BE- BOAA)
v.

hagaboaanga. (BE1 BOAA)
n.

hagabobo. (BE- BOBO)
v.

hagaboboanga. (BE1 BOBO)
n.

hagabobolia. (BE2 BOBO)
v.

hagabopobo. (RE- BOBO)
v.

hagabopoboanga. (RE1 BOBO)
n.

hagabopobolia. (RE2 BOBO)
v.

hagaboda. (BE- BODA)
v.

hagabodaanga. (BE1 BODA)
n.

hagabodalia. (BE2 BODA)
v.

hagabodobodo. (RE- BODO)
v.

hagabodobodoanga. (RE1 BODO)
n.

hagabodobodolia. (RE2 BODO)
v.

hagabodubodu. (RE- $BODU_2$)
v.

hagaboduboduanga. (RE1 $BODU_2$)
n.

hagabogi. (BE- BOGI)
v.

hagabogia. (BE2 BOGI)
v.

hagabogibogi. (RE- BOGI)
v.

hagabogibogia. (RE2 BOGI)
v.

hagabogiboginga. (RE1 BOGI)
n.

hagabogobogo. (RE- $BOGO_2$)
v.

hagabogobogoanga. (RE1 $BOGO_2$)
n.

hagabogobogolia. (RE2 $BOGO_2$)
v.

hagaboi. (BE- BOI)
v.

hagaboia. (BE2 BOI)
v.

hagaboiboi. (RE- BOI)
v.

hagaboiboia. (RE2 BOI)
v.

hagaboiboinga. (RE1 BOI)
n.

hagaboinga. (BE1 BOI)
n.

hagabole. (BE- BOLE)
v.

hagabolea. (BE2 BOLE)
v.

hagabolebole. (RE- BOLE)
v.

hagabolebolea. (RE2 BOLE)
v.

hagabolebolenga. (RE1 BOLE)
n.

hagabolebolengia. (RE2 BOLE)
v.

hagabolengia. (BE2 BOLE)
v.

hagabolo. (BE- $BOLO_2$)
To include in one's will. *v.*

hagaboloa. (BE2 $BOLO_2$)
v.

hagabolobolo. (RE- $BOLO_2$)
v.

hagaboloboloa. (RE2 $BOLO_2$)
v.

hagabolobolonga. (RE1 $BOLO_2$)
n.

hagabona. (BE- BONA)
v.

hagabonaanga. (BE1 BONA)
n.

hagabonabona. (RE- BONA)
v.

hagabonabonaanga. (RE1 BONA)
n.

hagabonabonalia. (RE2 BONA)
v.

hagabonalia. (BE2 BONA)
v.

hagabonga. (BE- BONGA)
v.

hagabongabonga. (RE- BONGA)
v.

hagabongabongalia. (RE2 BONGA)
v.

hagabongalia. (BE2 BONGA)
v.

hagaboo$_1$. (BE- BOO$_1$)
a.

hagaboo$_2$. (BE- BOO$_2$)
Greet; take leave of. *a.*

hagaboo$_3$. (BE- BOO$_3$)
v.

hagabooanga$_1$. (BE1 BOO$_1$)
n.

hagabooanga$_2$. (BE1 BOO$_3$)
n.

hagaboobodo. (TE- BODO)
v.

hagaboobodoanga. (TE1 BODO)
n.

hagaboobodolia. (TE2 BODO)
v.

hagabooboo$_1$. (RE- BOO$_1$)
a.

hagabooboo$_2$. (RE- BOO$_3$)
v.

hagaboobooanga$_1$. (RE1 BOO$_1$)
n.

hagaboobooanga$_2$. (RE1 BOO$_3$)
n.

hagaboobooogia. (RE2 BOO$_1$)
v.

hagaboobosu. (TE- BOSU)
v.

hagaboobosuanga. (TE1 BOSU)
n.

hagaboobosulia. (TE2 BOSU)
v.

hagaboogia. (BE2 BOO$_1$)
v.

hagabooginga. (BE1 BOGI)
n.

hagabooiaa. (BE- BOI$_a$)
v.

hagaboolenga. (BE1 BOLE)
n.

hagaboolonga. (BE1 BOLO$_2$)
n.

hagaboongia. (BE2 BOO$_2$)
Remain somewhere until dark. *v.*

hagabosu. (BE- BOSU)
v.

hagabosuanga. (BE1 BOSU)
n.

hagabosulia. (BE2 BOSU)
v.

hagabouli. (BE- BOULI)
v.

hagaboulianga. (BE1 BOULI)
n.

hagabuaalali. (BE- BUAALALI)
v.

hagabubu. (BE- BUBU)
v.

hagabubuanga. (BE1 BUBU)
n.

hagabubulia. (BE2 BUBU)
v.

hagabupubu. (RE- BUBU)
v.

hagabupubuanga. (RE1 BUBU)
n.

hagabupubulia. (RE2 BUBU)
v.

hagabudu. (BE- BUDU)
Collect in one place together, accumulate. *v.*

hagabudua. (BE2 BUDU)
v.

hagabudubudu. (RE- BUDU)
Accumulate repeatedly. *v.*

hagabudubudua. (RE2 BUDU)
v.

hagabudubudulia. (RE2 BUDU)
v.

hagabudubudunga. (RE1 BUDU)
n.

hagabudulia. (BE2 BUDU)
v.

hagabudu me.
Selfish.

hagabuge. (BE- BUGE)
v.

hagabugubugu. (RE- BUGU)
v.

hagabugubugua. (RE2 BUGU)
v.

hagabugubuguhia. (RE2 BUGU)
v.

hagabula. (BE- BULA)
v.

hagabulaanga. (BE1 BULA)
n.

hagabulabula. (RE- BULA)
v.

hagabulabulaanga. (RE1 BULA)
n.

hagabuliaamou.
(BE- BULIAAMOU) *v.*

hagabuiliaamoua.
(BE2 BULIAAMOU) *v.*

hagabuliaamounga.
(BE1 BULIAAMOU) *n.*

hagabulibuliaamou.
(RE- BULIAAMOU) *v.*

hagabulibuliaamoua.
(RE2 BULIAAMOU) *v.*

hagabulibuliaamounga.
(RE1 BULIAAMOU) *n.*

hagabulubulu ange.
Make do with.

hagabulumau. (XE- BULU$_a$)
Watch your step climbing! *a.*

hagabunana. (BE- BUNANA)
v.

hagabunehulu. (BE- BUNEHULU)
v.

hagabunehuluanga.
(BE1 BUNEHULU) *n.*

hagabuni. (BE- BUNI)
Gather together (people); have sexual relations. *v.*

hagabunia. (BE2 BUNI)
Close up, bring together. *v.*

hagabunibuni. (RE- BUNI)
Add together from different sources. *v.*

hagabunibunia. (RE2 BUNI)
—; close up many at one time. *v.*

hagabunibunidia. (RE2 BUNI)
v.

hagabunibuninga. (RE1 BUNI)
—; different totals. *n.*

hagabuni de henua.
To call an all-island meeting.

hagabunidia. (BE2 BUNI)
Add up. *v.*

hagabungaadogi.
(PE- BUNGADOGI) *v.*

hagabungaadogianga.
(PE1 BUNGADOGI) *n.*

hagabungaaleu. (PE- BUNGALEU)
v.

hagabungaaleua. (PE2 BUNGALEU)
v.

hagabungaaleua.
(PE2 BUNGALEU) *v.*

hagabungaaleunga.
(PE1 BUNGALEU) *n.*

hagabungabungadogi.
(RE- BUNGADOGI) *v.*

hagabungabungadogianga.
(RE1 BUNGADOGI) *n.*

hagabungadogi.
(BE- BUNGADOGI) *v.*

hagabungadogianga.
(BE1 BUNGADOGI) *n.*

hagabungaleua. (BE2 BUNGALEU)
v.

hagabungaleunga.
(BE1 BUNGALEU) *n.*

hagabungubungu.
(RE- BUNGU) *v.*

hagabungubunguanga.
(RE1 BUNGU) *n.*

hagabungubungulia. (RE2 BUNGU)
Cause to be expanded. *v.*

hagabuu$_1$. (BE- BUU$_3$)
v.

hagabuu$_2$. (BE- BUU$_4$)
—; accuse. *v.*

hagabuua$_1$. (BE2 BUU$_3$)
Crowd away from. *v.*

hagabuua$_2$. (BE2 BUU$_4$)
v.

hagabuuanga$_1$. (BE1 BUU$_3$)
n.

hagabuuanga$_2$. (BE1 BUU$_4$)
n.

hagabuu ange.
Blame (someone), incriminate (someone).

hagabuubudu. (TE- BUDU)
v.

hagabuubudua. (TE2 BUDU)
v.

hagabuubudulia. (TE2 BUDU)
v.

hagabuubudunga. (TE1 BUDU)
n.

hagabuubuu$_1$. (RE- BUU$_3$)
v.

hagabuubuu$_2$. (RE- BUU$_4$)
v.

hagabuubuua$_1$. (RE2 BUU$_3$)
v.

hagabuubuua$_2$. (RE2 BUU$_4$)
v.

hagabuubuuanga$_1$. (RE1 BUU$_3$)
n.

hagabuubuuanga$_2$. (RE1 BUU$_4$)
n.

hagabuubuuia$_1$. (RE2 BUU$_4$)
—; cause to be repeatedly *puu*. *v.*

hagabuubuuia$_2$. (RE2 BUU$_3$)
v.

hagabuubuulia. (RE2 BUU$_4$)
v.

hagabuubuusagi. (RE- BUUSAGI)
v.

hagabuubuusagia. (RE2 BUUSAGI)
v.

hagabuubuusaginga.
(RE1 BUUSAGI) *n.*

hagabuudunga. (BE1 BUDU)
—; a pile of things which have been accumulated. *n.*

hagabuugani. (BE- BUUGANI)
v.

hagabuuganianga. (BE1 BUUGANI)
n.

hagabuuia$_1$. (BE2 BUU$_3$)
v.

hagabuuia$_2$. (BE2 BUU$_4$)
v.

hagabuulei. (BE- BUULEI)
Put a ring on (someone). *v.*

hagabuuleinga. (BE1 BUULEI)
n.

hagabuulia. (BE2 BUU$_4$)
v.

hagabuulinga. (BE1 BULI)
Group of animate things. *n.*

hagabuulunga. (BE1 BUU$_4$)
Accuse (someone) of having had sexual relations with someone else. *v.*

hagabuulunga iho.
To *hagabuulunga* oneself.

hagabuuninga. (BE1 BUNI)
n.

hagabuusagi. (BE- BUUSAGI)
v.

hagabuusagia. (BE2 BUUSAGI)
v.

hagabuusaginga. (BE1 BUUSAGI)
n.

hagabuusagisagi. (SE- BUUSAGI)
v.

hagabuusagisagia. (SE2 BUUSAGI)
v.

hagabuusagisaginga.
(SE1 BUUSAGI) *n.*

hagapaa$_1$. (PE- BAA$_1$)
v.

hagapaa$_2$. (PE- BAA$_2$)
v.

hagapaalanga. (PE1 BALA)
n.

hagapaalenga. (PE1 BALE$_2$)
n.

hagapaanga. (PE1 BAA$_2$)
n.

hagapaasanga. (PE1 BASA$_1$)
n.

hagapaba. (PE- BAA$_4$)
v.

hagapabalia. (PE2 BAA$_4$)
v.

hagapada. (BE- PADA)
v.

hagapadaanga. (BE1 PADA)
n.

hagapadalia. (BE2 PADA)
v.

hagapago. (EE- BAGO)
v.

hagapagoanga. (EE1 BAGO)
n.

hagapago donu.
Fortunate result.

hagapago iho.
To descend suddenly.

hagapago sala.
Unfortunate result.

hagapai. (BE- PAI)
v.

hagapala. (PE- BALA)
v.

hagapale. (PE- BALE$_2$)
Teach to steer, allow to steer, lean against. *v.*

hagapanga. (PE- BANGA$_1$)
v.

hagapangalia. (PE2 BANGA$_1$)
v.

hagapasa. (PE- BASA$_1$)
Cause several people to speak; mediate an argument so that the disputants will speak to each other. *v.*

hagapasalia. (PE2 BASA$_1$)
Convince (several people) completely. *v.*

hagapedi. (PE- BEDI)
v.

hagapedia. (PE2 BEDI)
v.

hagapedianga. (PE1 BEDI)
n.

hagapee. (EE- BEE)
v.

hagapeeanga. (EE1 BEE)
n.

hagapena. (EE- BENA)
v.

hagapenaanga. (EE1 BENA)
n.

hagapigi. (EE- BIGI$_1$)
v.

hagapigi ange.
Stick against (something), go with someone.

hagapigi saele.
Go around with someone constantly.

hagapigo. (PE- BIGO)
v.

hagapigolia. (PE2 BIGO)
v.

hagapii. (EE- BII)
v.

hagapiia. (EE2 BII)
v.

hagapiianga. (EE1 BII)
n.

hagapiigia. (EE2 BIGI$_1$)
Make stuck to. *v.*

hagapiiginga. (EE1 BIGI$_1$)
n.

hagapiigonga. (PE1 BIGO)
n.

hagapili$_1$. (PE- BILI$_1$)
v.

hagapili$_2$. (EE- BILI$_2$)
Boring. *a.*

hagapilo. (EE- BILO)
Let decay; allow to stink. *v.*

hagapiloanga. (EE1 BILO)
n.

hagapobo. (PE- BOBO)
v.

hagapoboanga. (PE1 BOBO)
n.

hagapobolia. (PE2 BOBO)
v.

hagapoda. (PE- BODA)
v.

hagapodaanga. (PE1 BODA)
n.

hagapodalia. (PE2 BODA)
v.

hagapodo. (PE- BODO)
v.

hagapodoanga. (PE1 BODO)
n.

hagapodolia. (PE2 BODO)
v.

hagapogo. (EE- $BOGO_2$)
Fold up (one fold); cause to crumple up. *v.*

hagapogoanga. (EE1 $BOGO_2$)
n.

hagapogolia. (EE2 $BOGO_2$)
v.

hagapoi. (PE- BOI)
v.

hagapoia. (PE2 BOI)
v.

hagapoinga. (PE1 BOI)
n.

hagapole. (PE- BOLE)
v.

hagapolengia. (PE2 BOLE)
v.

hagaponga. (PE- BONGA)
v.

hagapongalia. (PE2 BONGA)
v.

hagapoolea. (PE2 BOLE)
v.

hagapoolenga. (PE1 BOLE)
n.

hagapugu. (PE- BUGU)
v.

hagapugua. (PE2 BUGU)
v.

hagapugulia. (PE2 BUGU)
v.

hagapula. (EE- BULA)
v.

hagapulaanga. (EE1 BULA)
n.

hagapulu. (BE- PULU)
v.

hagapuluanga. (BE1 PULU)
n.

hagapuni. (PE- BUNI)
—; add, total up. *v.*

hagapunidia. (PE2 BUNI)
Add up (many things). *v.*

hagapungu. (PE- BUNGU)
v.

hagapunguanga. (PE1 BUNGU)
n.

hagapungulia. (PE2 BUNGU)
v.

hagapuu. (PE- BUU_4)
v.

hagapuua. (PE2 BUU_4)
v.

hagapuuanga. (PE1 BUU_4)
n.

hagapuugunga. (PE1 BUGU)
n.

hagapuulia. (PE2 BUU_4)
v.

hagapuunia. (PE2 BUNI)
Add up (many things). *v.*

hagapuuninga. (PE1 BUNI)
A total of. *n.*

hagadaa. (BE- DAA_1)
v.

hagadaabasi. (BE- DAABASI)
v.

hagadaabasinga. (BE1 DAABASI)
n.

hagadaabeduge.
(BE- DAABEDUGE) *v.*

hagadaabedugeanga.
(BE1 DAABEDUGE) *n.*

hagadaabui. (BE- BUI_a)
v.

hagadaabuia. (BE2 BUI_a)
v.

hagadaabuinga. (BE1 BUI_a)
n.

hagadaadaa. (RE- DAA$_1$)
v.

hagadaadaabasi. (RE- DAABASI)
v.

hagadaadaabasinga.
(RE1 DAABASI) *n.*

hagadaadaabeduge.
(RE- DAABEDUGE) *v.*

hagadaadaabedugeanga.
(RE1 DAABEDUGE) *n.*

hagadaadaaia. (RE2 DAA$_1$)
v.

hagadaadaaligi. (RE- DAA$_{1a}$)
v.

hagadaadaaligidanga. (RE1 DAA$_{1a}$)
n.

hagadaadaaligidia. (RE2 DAA$_{1a}$)
v.

hagadaadaalo. (RE- DAALO)
v.

hagadaadaaloa. (RE2 DAALO)
v.

hagadaadaalonga. (RE1 DAALO)
n.

hagadaadaanga. (RE1 DAA$_1$)
n.

hagadaadaangia. (RE2 DADA$_1$)
v.

hagadaadaavalo. (RE- VALO$_1$)
v.

hagadaadaavaloanga. (RE1 VALO$_1$)
n.

hagadaadanga. (BE1 DADA$_1$)
n.

hagadaatugu. (BE- DAATUGU)
v.

hagadaatuguanga.
(BE1 DAATUGU) *n.*

hagadaatugulia. (BE2 DAATUGU)
v.

hagadaaganga. (BE- DAAGANGA)
Kind (of), sort (of), variety (of). *n.*

hagadaaginga. (BE1 DAGI$_1$)
n.

hagadaakai. (PE- DAGA$_{1c}$)
v.

hagadaakaia. (·PE2 DAGA$_{1c}$)
v.

hagadaakainga. (PE1 DAGA$_{1c}$)
n.

hagadaakodo. (PE- DAGODO)
v.

hagadaakodoanga. (PE1 DAGODO)
n.

hagadaakodolia. (PE2 DAGODO)
v.

hagadaahaa. (BE- DAAHAA)
v.

hagadaahao. (BE- DAAHAO)
Play (games); game, amusement; amuse oneself. *v.*

hagadaahaoa. (BE2 DAAHAO)
v.

hagadaahao ai.
Do something as though it were a game.

hagadaahaonga. (BE1 DAAHAO)
n.

hagadaahea. (PE- DAHEA)
v.

hagadaaheaanga. (PE1 DAHEA)
n.

hagadaahili. (BE- DAAHILI)
Make someone sing. *v.*

hagadaahilia. (BE2 DAAHILI)
v.

hagadaahilinga. (BE1 DAAHILI)
n.

hagadaahuli. (PE- HULI$_a$)
v.

hagadaahulia. (PE2 HULI$_a$)
v.

hagadaahulianga. (PE1 HULI$_a$)
n.

hagadaahulinga. (PE1 HULI$_a$)
n.

hagadaahunga. (BE1 DAHU)
n.

hagadaaia. (BE2 DAA_1)
v.

hagadaalea$_1$. (BE2 DALE)
v.

hagadaalea$_2$. (PE- DALEA)
[Pl. of *hagadalea*]; tiresome. *v.*

hagadaaleaanga. (PE1 DALEA)
n.

hagadaalenga. (BE1 DALE)
n.

hagadaaligi. (BE- DAA_{1a})
v.

hagadaaligidanga. (BE1 DAA_{1a})
n.

hagadaaligidia. (BE2 DAA_{1a})
v.

hagadaalo. (BE- DAALO)
v.

hagadaaloa. (BE2 DAALO)
v.

hagadaalonga. (BE1 DAALO)
n.

hagadaaminga. (BE1 DAMI)
n.

hagadaane. (BE- DAANE)
To act like a human. *v.*

hagadaaneanga. (BE1 DAANE)
n.

hagadaanga. (BE1 DAA_1)
n.

hagadaangage. (PE- $DANGA_a$)
v.

hagadaangageanga.
(PE1 $DANGA_a$) *n.*

hagadaangenge.
(BE- DAANGENGE) *v.*

hagadaasele. (BE- $SELE_{1a}$)
v.

hagadaaselea. (BE2 $SELE_{1a}$)
v.

hagadaaseleanga. (BE1 $SELE_{1a}$)
n.

hagadaava. (BE- DAAVA)
v.

hagadaavaanga. (BE1 DAAVA)
n.

hagadaavalo. (BE- $VALO_1$)
v.

hagadaavaloanga. (BE1 $VALO_1$)
n.

hagadaba. (BE- DABA)
—; to say that —. *v.*

hagadabaanga. (BE1 DABA)
n.

hagadabadaba. (RE- DABA)
v.

hagadabadabaanga. (RE1 DABA)
n.

hagadabadabalia. (RE2 DABA)
v.

hagadabadaballahi. (RE- $LAHI_a$)
v.

hagadabalia. (BE2 DABA)
v.

hagadaballahi. (BE- $LAHI_a$)
v.

hagadabanimeeli.
(BE- DABANIMEELI)
To make payment for medical treatment. *v.*

hagadabena. (BE- $BENA_a$)
Prepare, make ready. *v.*

hagadabenaanga. (BE1 $BENA_a$)
n.

hagadabena ange.
Prepare for.

hagadabena iho.
Prepare oneself, make oneself ready.

hagadabenalia. (BE2 $BENA_a$)
v.

hagadabeo. (BE- DABEO)
v.

hagadabeoanga. (BE1 DABEO)
n.

hagadabu. (BE- $DABU_1$)
Restrict. *v.*

hagadabua. (BE2 $DABU_1$)
v.

hagadabuanga. (BE1 DABU$_1$)
n.

hagadabudabui. (RE- DABUI)
v.

hagadabudabuia. (RE2 DABUI)
v.

hagadabudabuinga. (RE1 DABUI)
n.

hagadabui. (BE- DABUI)
v.

hagadabuia. (BE2 DABUI)
v.

hagadabuinga. (BE1 DABUI)
n.

hagadabulia. (BE2 DABU$_1$)
v.

hagadada. (BE- DADA$_1$)
v.

hagadadangi. (TE- DANGI)
v.

hagadadanginga. (TE1 DANGI)
n.

hagadadango. (TE- DANGO$_1$)
v.

hagadadangoanga. (TE1 DANGO$_1$)
n.

hagadadangolia. (TE2 DANGO$_1$)
v.

hagadadau. (TE- DAU$_3$)
v.

hagadadaua. (TE2 DAU$_3$)
v.

hagadadaulia. (TE2 DAU$_3$)
v.

hagadadaunga. (TE1 DAU$_3$)
n.

hagadatada. (RE- DADA$_1$)
v.

hagadatadaanga. (RE1 DADA$_1$)
n.

hagadae$_1$. (BE- DAE$_1$)
To give a hand net to. *v.*

hagadae$_2$. (BE- DAE$_2$)
v.

hagadaea. (BE2 DAE$_2$)
v.

hagadaedae$_1$. (RE- DAE$_1$)
—; to instruct in hand net fishing. *v.*

hagadaedae$_2$. (RE- DAE$_2$)
v.

hagadaedaea$_1$. (RE2 DAE$_1$)
v.

hagadaedaea$_2$. (RE2 DAE$_2$)
v.

hagadaedaelia. (RE2 DAE$_2$)
v.

hagadaedaenga$_1$. (RE1 DAE$_1$)
n.

hagadaedaenga$_2$. (RE1 DAE$_2$)
n.

hagadaelia. (BE2 DAE$_2$)
v.

hagadaemaha. (BE- DAEMAHA)
Put weight on, make unhappy. *v.*

hagadaemahaanga.
(BE1 DAEMAHA) *n.*

hagadaemahadia.
(BE2 DAEMAHA)
Put too much weight on. *v.*

hagadaemahalia. (BE2 DAEMAHA)
—; insult (someone). *v.*

hagadaenga. (BE1 DAE$_2$)
n.

hagadaga$_1$. (BE- DAGA$_1$)
Go from one place to another, and another, etc. *v.*

hagadaga$_2$. (BE- DAGA$_2$)
v.

hagadaga age.
Improving.

hagadagaanga$_1$. (BE1 DAGA$_1$)
n.

hagadagaanga$_2$. (BE1 DAGA$_2$)
n.

hagadaga ange.
Increase in.

hagadagabuli. (BE- DAGA$_{1a}$)
v.

hagadagabulianga. (BE1 DAGA$_{1a}$)
n.

hagadagadaga$_1$. (RE- DAGA$_1$)
Go from one place to another, and another, and another, etc. *v.*

hagadagadaga$_2$. (RE- DAGA$_2$)
v.

hagadagadagaanga$_1$. (RE1 DAGA$_1$)
n.

hagadagadagaanga$_2$. (RE1 DAGA$_2$)
n.

hagadagadagabuli. (RE- DAGA$_{1a}$)
v.

hagadagadagabulianga.
(RE1 DAGA$_{1a}$) *n.*

hagadagadagai. (RE- DAGA$_{1c}$)
v.

hagadagadagaia. (RE2 DAGA$_{1c}$)
v.

hagadagadagainga. (RE1 DAGA$_{1c}$)
n.

hagadagadagalia$_1$. (RE2 DAGA$_1$)
v.

hagadagadagalia$_2$. (RE2 DAGA$_2$)
v.

hagadagadagasala. (RE- DAGA$_{1d}$)
v.

hagadagadagasalaanga.
(RE1 DAGA$_{1d}$) *n.*

hagadagai. (BE- DAGA$_{1c}$)
v.

hagadagaia. (BE2 DAGA$_{1c}$)
v.

hagadaga iho.
Worsening.

hagadagainga. (BE1 DAGA$_{1c}$)
n.

hagadagalia$_1$. (BE2 DAGA$_1$)
v.

hagadagalia$_2$. (BE2 DAGA$_2$)
v.

hagadaga mai.
Decrease in —; travel toward speaker.

hagadagasala. (BE- DAGA$_{1d}$)
Blame (someone), accuse. *v.*

hagadagasalaanga. (BE1 DAGA$_{1d}$)
n.

hagadagi. (BE- DAGI$_1$)
v.

hagadagidagi. (RE- DAGI$_1$)
v.

hagadagidagina. (RE2 DAGI$_1$)
v.

hagadagidaginga. (RE1 DAGI$_1$)
n.

hagadagina. (BE2 DAGI$_1$)
v.

hagadagodo. (BE- DAGODO)
Cause to lie down or remain; illustrate by examples. *v.*

hagadagodoanga. (BE1 DAGODO)
n.

hagadagodo gee ina.
Change.

hagadagodolia. (BE2 DAGODO)
v.

hagadagoobala.
(BE- DAGOOBALA) *v.*

hagadagoobalaanga.
(BE1 DAGOOBALA) *n.*

hagadaguu. (BE- DAGUU)
A small axe, hatchet. *n.*

hagadaha. (BE- DAHA)
To stay at a distance; to keep one's distance. *v.*

hagadahadaha. (RE- DAHA)
Keep staying away. *v.*

hagadahadia. (BE2 DAHA)
v.

hagadahea. (BE- DAHEA)
To allow the wind or current to carry the canoe [a method of fishing]. *v.*

hagadaheaanga. (BE1 DAHEA)
n.

hagadahedhea. (RE- DAHEA)
v.

hagadahedaheaanga.
(RE1 DAHEA) *n.*

hagadahi. (BE- DAHI$_1$)
A counting system for days, based on the lunar phases. *v.*

hagadahola. (BE- DAHOLA)
v.

hagadaholaanga. (BE1 DAHOLA)
n.

hagadahu. (BE- DAHU)
v.

hagadahua. (BE2 DAHU)
v.

hagadahudahu. (RE- DAHU)
v.

hagadahudahua. (RE2 DAHU)
v.

hagadahudahulia. (RE2 DAHU)
v.

hagadahudahunga. (RE1 DAHU)
n.

hagadahuli. (BE- $HULI_a$)
v.

hagadahulia. (BE2 $HULI_a$)
v.

hagadahulianga. (BE1 $HULI_a$)
n.

hagadahulihuli. (RE- $HULI_a$)
v.

hagadahulihulia. (RE2 $HULI_a$)
v.

hagadahulihulianga. (RE1 $HULI_a$)
n.

hagadahulinga. (BE1 $HULI_a$)
n.

hagadai. (BE- DAI_1)
Furnish salt to. *v.*

hagadai --. (BE- DAI_2)
u.

hagadaia. (BE2 DAA_1)
v.

hagadaihadu. (BE- $HADU_{2a}$)
v.

hagadaina. (BE- DAINA)
To put (someone) into a sibling or cousin relationship (as by an adoption). *v.*

hagadala. (BE- $DALA_2$)
v.

hagadalaanga. (BE1 $DALA_2$)
n.

hagadalabaimanugadele. (?)
[BE form of *dalabaimanugadele*]. *v.*

$hagadaladala_1$. (RE- $DALA_{4b}$)
v.

$hagadaladala_2$. (RE- $DALA_2$)
v.

$hagadaladalaanga_1$. (RE1 $DALA_{4b}$)
n.

$hagadaladalaanga_2$. (RE1 $DALA_2$)
n.

hagadaladalaehala.
(RE- DALAEHALA) *v.*

hagadaladalaehalaanga.
(RE1 DALAEHALA) *n.*

hagadalaehala.
(BE- DALAEHALA) *v.*

hagadalaehalaanga.
(BE1 DALAEHALA) *n.*

hagadalangasau.
(BE- DALANGASAU) *v.*

hagadalangasaua.
(BE2 DALANGASAU) *v.*

hagadalangasaunga.
(BE1 DALANGASAU) *n.*

hagadale --. (BE- DALE)
Touch —. *v.*

hagadalea. (BE- DALEA)
Make someone tired [sing.]; punish [sing.]. *v.*

hagadaleaanga. (BE1 DALEA)
n.

hagadaleba. (BE- $LEBA_a$)
v.

hagadalebaanga. (BE1 $LEBA_a$)
n.

hagadalebaleba. (RE- $LEBA_a$)
v.

hagadalebalebaanga. (RE1 $LEBA_a$)
n.

hagadalebu. (BE- DALEBU)
v.

hagadalebua. (BE2 DALEBU)
v.

hagadalebuanga. (BE1 DALEBU)
n.

hagadalebulebu. (RE- DALEBU)
v.

hagadalebulebua. (RE2 DALEBU)
v.

hagadalebulebuanga.
(RE1 DALEBU) *n.*

hagadaledale. (RE- DALE)
v.

hagadaledalea. (RE2 DALE)
v.

hagadaledalenga. (RE1 DALE)
n.

hagadali. (BE- $DALI_2$)
Accumulate (bring together); gather up; imprisonment (short term). *v.*

hagadalia. (BE2 $DALI_2$)
v.

hagadalianga. (BE1 $DALI_2$)
n.

hagadalodalo. (RE- $DALO_1$)
v.

hagadalodaloa. (RE2 $DALO_1$)
v.

hagadalodaloanga. (RE1 $DALO_1$)
n.

hagadalodalosia. (RE2 $DALO_1$)
v.

hagadama. (BE- DAMA)
Treat as a child. *v.*

hagadamadama. (RE- DAMA)
Act like a child (as a behavior pattern). *v.*

hagadamadamaanga. (RE1 DAMA)
n.

hagadamana. (BE- DAMANA)
Treat someone as a father or other senior male relative. *v.*

hagadami. (BE- DAMI)
v.

hagadamia. (BE2 DAMI)
v.

hagadamidami. (RE- DAMI)
v.

hagadamidamia. (RE2 DAMI)
v.

hagadamidaminga. (RE1 DAMI)
n.

hagadane. (BE- $DANE_1$)
v.

hagadanea. (BE2 $DANE_1$)
v.

hagadaneaanga. (BE3 $DANE_1$)
n.

hagadanedane. (RE- $DANE_1$)
v.

hagadanedanea. (RE2 $DANE_1$)
v.

hagadanedaneaanga. (RE3 $DANE_1$)
n.

hagadania. (?)
A type of prepared food (made from breadfruit). *n.*

hagadanu. (BE- DANU)
Sink below the horizon, burrow into the sand. *v.*

hagadanuaa. (BE- DANUAA)
Make good, lead a good life [a newly coined expression]. *v.*

hagadanuaa magavaa.
Make peace between people, conciliate.

hagadanuanga. (BE1 DANU)
n.

hagadanudanu. (RE- DANU)
v.

hagadanudanuanga. (RE1 DANU)
n.

hagadanudanumanga. (RE1 DANU)
n.

hagadanudanumia. (RE2 DANU)
v.

hagadanumanga. (BE1 DANU)
n.

hagadanumia. (BE2 DANU)
v.

hagadangada. (BE- DANGADA)
Treat someone as a human being. *v.*

hagadangadanga. (RE- DANGA)
Loosen. *v.*

hagadangadangaanga.
(RE1 DANGA) *n.*

hagadangadangalebu.
(RE- DANGA$_b$) *v.*

hagadangadangalebua.
(RE2 DANGA$_b$) *v.*

hagadangadangalebunga.
(RE1 DANGA$_b$) *n.*

hagadangadangalia. (RE2 DANGA)
v.

hagadangage. (BE- DANGA$_a$)
v.

hagadangageanga. (BE1 DANGA$_a$)
n.

hagadangalebu. (BE- DANGA$_b$)
v.

hagadangalebua. (BE2 DANGA$_b$)
v.

hagadangalebunga. (BE1 DANGA$_b$)
n.

hagadangi. (BE- DANGI)
—; play (a musical instument). *v.*

hagadangia. (BE2 DANGI)
v.

hagadangidangi. (RE- DANGI)
Play music; make someone keep crying. *v.*

hagadangidangia. (RE2 DANGI)
v.

hagadangidanginga. (RE1 DANGI)
n.

hagadanginga. (BE1 DANGI)
n.

hagadango. (BE- DANGO$_1$)
v.

hagadangoa. (BE2 DANGO$_1$)
v.

hagadangoanga. (BE1 DANGO$_1$)
n.

hagadangodango. (RE- DANGO$_1$)
v.

hagadangodangoa. (RE2 DANGO$_1$)
v.

hagadangodangoanga.
(RE1 DANGO$_1$) *n.*

hagadangodangolia. (RE2 DANGO$_1$)
v.

hagadangolia. (BE2 DANGO$_1$)
v.

hagadau$_1$. (BE- DAU$_{1b}$)
—; make well-known, make someone a —. *v.*

hagadau$_2$. (BE- DAU$_2$)
v.

hagadau$_3$. (BE- DAU$_3$)
v.

hagadau$_4$. (BE- DAU$_4$)
Create —. *d.*

hagadaua$_1$. (BE2 DAU$_1$)
v.

hagadaua$_2$. (BE2 DAU$_2$)
v.

hagadaua$_3$. (BE2 DAU$_3$)
—; wage war against. *v.*

hagadauaa. (BE- DAUAA)
v.

hagadauaabulu. (BE- ABULU)
v.

hagadauaadea. (AADEA, DAU$_7$)
To clear out a place. *v.*

hagadau aaloha.
Love each other (esp. of persons of the opposite sex).

hagadauaanga$_1$. (BE3 DAU$_3$)
n.

hagadauaanga$_2$. (BE1 DAUAA)
n.

hagadauagi. (BE- DAU$_{2a}$)
v.

hagadauagia. (BE2 DAU$_{2a}$)
v.

hagadauagina. (BE2 DAU$_{2a}$)
—; expose oneself to the sun. *v.*

hagadauaginga. (BE1 DAU$_{2a}$)
n.

hagadau bale.
Cooperate; help one another.

hagadaubaleanga. (XE- BALE$_1$)
n.

hagadaubodobodo. (BODO, DAU_{1b})
Shorten (time or rope). *v.*

hagadaubulebule. (BE- $BULE_{a}$)
To change coloring (esp. fish in anxiety states). *v.*

hagadaubulebuleanga. (BE1 BULE)
n.

$hagadaudau_{1}$. (RE- DAU_{3})
v.

$hagadaudau_{2}$. (RE- DAU_{2})
—; pass overhead (of clouds); move toward the end of the tether. *v.*

$hagadaudaua_{1}$. (RE2 DAU_{3})
v.

$hagadaudaua_{2}$. (RE2 DAU_{2})
v.

hagadaudauagi. (RE- DAU_{2a})
v.

hagadaudauagia. (RE2 DAU_{2a})
v.

hagadaudauagina. (RE2 DAU_{2a})
v.

hagadaudauaginga. (RE1 DAU_{2a})
n.

$hagadaudaulia_{1}$. (RE2 DAU_{3})
v.

$hagadaudaulia_{2}$. (RE2 DAU_{2})
v.

$hagadaudaunga_{1}$. (RE1 DAU_{3})
n.

$hagadaudaunga_{2}$. (RE1 DAU_{2})
n.

hagadau doa.
To show one's strength by doing something difficult.

hagadau doo.
To transfer a string figure from one person's fingers to another's.

hagadaudoo. (DAU_{1b}, DOO_{1})
Compete to see who is stronger. *a.*

hagadau doolohi.
Chase each other.

hagadau tugi.
Punch each other.

hagadau gaiaa.
Steal from one another.

hagadau gavange.
Compete (between groups).

hagadau kino.
Hate each other.

hagadau hai me ai.
Use jointly or collectively.

hagadaula. (BE- DAULA)
To anchor. *v.*

hagadaulanga. (BE1 DAULA)
n.

$hagadaulia_{1}$. (BE2 DAU_{1})
v.

$hagadaulia_{2}$. (BE2 DAU_{2})
v.

$hagadaulia_{3}$. (BE2 DAU_{3})
v.

hagadaulooloa. (XE- DAU_{1b})
Prolong, extend. *v.*

hagadau-me. (DAU_{1b}, ME)
Enemy; dispute (with someone), argue. *a.*

$hagadaunga_{1}$. (BE1 DAU_{1})
n.

$hagadaunga_{2}$. (BE1 DAU_{2})
n.

$hagadaunga_{3}$. (BE1 DAU_{3})
n.

hagadauulu. (BE- ULU_{2a})
v.

hagadauulua. (BE2 ULU_{2a})
v.

hagadauulunga. (BE1 ULU_{2a})
n.

hagadau vaasuu.
Be attracted to or like each other (of members of the opposite sex).

hagadeadea. (RE- DEA)
v.

hagadeadeaanga. (RE1 DEA)
n.

hagadeai. (BE- DEAI)
Cause to become non-existent. *v.*

hagadeainga. (BE1 DEAI)
n.

hagadebedebe. (RE- DEBE)
v.

hagadeeai. (BE- DEAI$_a$)
Refuse to. *v.*

hagadeehehee. (BE- DEEHEHEE)
v.

hagadeeheheeanga.
(BE1 DEEHEHEE) *n.*

hagadeeheheelia.
(BE2 DEEHEHEE) *v.*

hagadeelenga. (BE1 DELE)
n.

hagadeengaa. (BE- DEENGAA)
Let's — right away and get it over with! *d.*

hagadege. (BE- DEGE)
Cause to wiggle the hips once. *v.*

hagadegea. (BE2 DEGE)
v.

hagadegedege. (RE- DEGE)
v.

hagadegedegea. (RE2 DEGE)
v.

hagadegedegelia. (RE2 DEGE)
v.

hagadegelia. (BE2 DEGE)
[Var. of *hagadegea*]. *v.*

hagadegi$_1$. (BE- DEGI$_1$)
v.

hagadegi$_2$. (BE- DEGI$_3$)
Praise (God only). *v.*

hagadegia. (BE2 DEGI$_1$)
v.

hagadegidegi. (RE- DEGI$_1$)
v.

hagadegidegia. (RE2 DEGI$_1$)
v.

hagadegideginga. (RE1 DEGI$_1$)
n.

hagadeginga. (BE1 DEGI$_1$)
n.

hagadele. (BE- DELE)
v.

hagadelea. (BE2 DELE)
v.

hagadeledele. (RE- DELE)
—; to play with a model canoe in the water (by children). *v.*

hagadeledelea. (RE2 DELE)
v.

hagadeledelenga. (RE1 DELE)
n.

hagadeledelengia. (RE2 DELE)
v.

hagadelengia. (BE2 DELE)
v.

hagademo. (BE- DEMO)
Pout [sing.]. *v.*

hagademoanga. (BE1 DEMO)
n.

hagademodemo. (RE- DEMO)
v.

hagademodemoanga. (RE1 DEMO)
n.

hagademodemolia. (RE2 DEMO)
v.

hagademolia. (BE2 DEMO)
v.

hagadengadenga. (RE- DENGA$_2$)
v.

hagadengadengalia. (RE2 DENGA$_2$)
v.

hagadevedeve. (RE- DEVE)
v.

hagadevedevea. (RE2 DEVE)
v.

hagadevedevelia. (RE2 DEVE)
v.

hagadevedevenga. (RE1 DEVE)
n.

hagadiba. (BE- DIBA$_1$)
Incline to one side. *v.*

hagadibaanga. (BE1 DIBA$_1$)
n.

hagadibadiba. (RE- DIBA$_1$)
Rock back and forth to one side. *v.*

hagadibadibaanga. (RE1 DIBA$_1$)
n.

hagadibadiba de lima.
To wiggle one's hand [a signal that the speaker is lying].

hagadibadibalia. (RE2 DIBA$_1$)
Cause to *hagadibadiba*. *v.*

hagadibalia. (BE2 DIBA$_1$)
Cause to tip to one side. *v.*

hagadidi. (BE- DIDI$_1$)
To put a grass skirt on someone else. *v.*

hagadidianga. (BE1 DIDI$_1$)
n.

hagaditidi. (RE- DIDI$_2$)
To skip a stone across the water. *v.*

hagaditidianga. (RE1 DIDI$_2$)
n.

hagaditidi de hadu.
To skip a stone across the water.

hagaditidilia. (RE2 DIDI$_2$)
v.

hagaditidi mai de moni.
A canoe going so fast it rides high in water (and is planing).

hagaditidi vae dahi.
Hop on one foot.

hagadige. (BE- DIGE)
v.

hagadige de madaangudu.
A prolonged conversation (on subjects of little importance).

hagadigedige. (RE- DIGE)
v.

hagadigedigelia. (RE2 DIGE)
v.

hagadigedigenga. (RE1 DIGE)
n.

hagadigelia. (BE2 DIGE)
v.

hagadii. (BE- DII)
v.

hagadiianga. (BE1 DII)
n.

hagadiidii$_1$. (RE- DII)
v.

hagadiidii$_2$. (BE- DIIDII)
Help to urinate (e.g., by taking a baby outside). *v.*

hagadiidiianga. (RE1 DII)
n.

hagadiidiinei. (RE- DIINEI)
v.

hagadiidiineia. (RE2 DIINEI)
v.

hagadiidiineinga. (RE1 DIINEI)
n.

hagadiidiinga. (BE1 DIIDII)
n.

hagadiidiingia. (RE2 DII)
v.

hagadiigenga. (BE1 DIGE)
n.

hagadiilinga. (BE1 DILI)
—; descendants (in one generation only). *n.*

hagadiinei. (BE- DIINEI)
v.

hagadiineia. (BE2 DIINEI)
v.

hagadiineinga. (BE1 DIINEI)
n.

hagadiinonga. (BE1 DINO$_1$)
—; treat as having supernatural power. *v.*

hagadiingia. (BE2 DII)
v.

hagadiingia saele.
To go about exposing oneself to the sun's rays.

hagadili. (BE- DILI)
Produce offspring. *v.*

hagadilia. (BE2 DILI)
v.

hagadilidili. (RE- DILI)
v.

hagadilidilia. (BE2 DILI)
v.

hagadilidilinga. (RE1 DILI)
n.

hagadilimangali. (XE- DILI)
To teach someone to *dilimangali.* *v.*

hagadinana. (BE- DINANA)
To treat as *dinana.* *v.*

hagadinihu. (BE- DINIHU)
v.

hagadino. (BE- DINO$_1$)
Provide a portion or share. *v.*

hagadinoangahulu. (XE- DINO$_2$)
Make a total of ten people. *v.*

hagadingale. (BE- DINGALE)
v.

hagadoa. (BE- DOA)
Act like a giant. *v.*

hagadoadoa. (BE- DOADOA)
v.

hagadoadoaanga. (BE1 DOADOA)
n.

hagadodi. (BE- DODI)
Walk with a limp (permanently). *v.*

hagadodinga. (BE1 DODI)
n.

hagadodo. (BE- DODO)
v.

hagadotodi. (RE- DODI)
Walk with a limp (temporarily). *v.*

hagadotodianga. (RE1 DODI)
n.

hagadotodo. (RE- DODO)
v.

hagadotodoanga. (RE1 DODO)
n.

hagadotodolia. (RE2 DODO)
v.

hagadoe. (BE- DOE)
Put aside, leave for later, conserve. *v.*

hagadoea. (BE2 DOE)
v.

hagadoedoe. (RE- DOE)
v.

hagadoedoea. (RE2 DOE)
v.

hagadoedoenga. (RE1 DOE)
n.

hagadoenga. (BE1 DOE)
n.

hagadoga. (BE- DOGA$_1$)
v.

hagadogaa. (BE- DOGAA)
—; shameful, to embarrass (someone). *v.*

hagadogaa dangada.
Embarrass people by one's actions.

hagadogaanga$_1$. (BE1 DOGA$_1$)
n.

hagadogaanga$_2$. (BE1 DOGAA)
n.

hagadogadoga. (RE- DOGA$_1$)
v.

hagadogadogaa. (RE- DOGAA)
v.

hagadogadogaanga$_1$. (RE1 DOGA$_1$)
n.

hagadogadogaanga$_2$. (RE1 DOGAA)
n.

hagadogadogalia. (RE2 DOGA$_1$)
v.

hagadogalia. (BE2 DOGA$_1$)
v.

hagadogia. (BE2 DOGI)
v.

hagadogiaanga. (BE3 DOGI)
n.

hagadogo. (BE- DOGO$_1$)
v.

hagadogo +NUMBER. (BE- DOGO$_2$)
To join (to make up a group of a certain number). *v.*

hagadogoa. (BE2 DOGO$_1$)
v.

hagadogodogo. (RE- DOGO$_1$)
v.

hagadogodogoa. (RE2 DOGO$_1$)
v.

hagadogodogoisi. (RE- DOGO$_{2a}$)
v.

hagadogodogolia. (RE2 DOGO$_1$)
v.

hagadogodogona. (RE2 DOGO$_1$)
v.

hagadogodogonga. (RE1 DOGO$_1$)
n.

hagadogoisi. (BE- DOGO$_{2a}$)
Reduce in number, make fewer. *v.*

hagadogolia. (BE2 DOGO$_1$)
v.

hagadogona. (BE2 DOGO$_1$)
v.

hagadoha. (BE- DOHA)
v.

hagadohaa. (BE2 DOHA)
v.

hagadohaanga. (BE1 DOHA)
n.

hagadohadoha. (RE- DOHA)
v.

hagadohadohaa. (RE2 DOHA)
v.

hagadohadohaanga. (RE1 DOHA)
n.

hagadohadohalia. (RE2 DOHA)
v.

hagadohalia. (BE2 DOHA)
v.

hagadohu. (BE- DOHU)
v.

hagadohua. (BE2 DOHU)
v.

hagadohudohu. (RE- DOHU)
v.

hagadohudohua. (RE2 DOHU)
v.

hagadohudohulia. (RE2 DOHU)
v.

hagadohudohunga. (RE1 DOHU)
n.

hagadohulia. (BE2 DOHU)
v.

hagadoi. (BE- DOI)
—; also, = *gadoi.* *v.*

hagadoia. (BE2 DOI)
v.

hagadoidoi. (RE- DOI)
v.

hagadoidoia. (RE2 DOI)
v.

hagadoidoinga. (RE1 DOI)
n.

hagadoinga. (BE1 DOI)
n.

hagadola. (BE- DOLA)
v.

hagadolaanga. (BE1 DOLA)
n.

hagadoladola. (RE- DOLA)
v.

hagadoladolaanga. (RE1 DOLA)
n.

hagadoli. (BE- DOLI)
v.

hagadolia. (BE2 DOLI)
v.

hagadolidoli. (RE- DOLI)
v.

hagadolidolia. (RE2 DOLI)
v.

hagadolidolinga. (RE1 DOLI)
n.

hagadolinga. (BE1 DOLI)
n.

hagadolo. (BE- DOLO)
v.

hagadoloa. (BE2 DOLO)
v.

hagadoloanga. (BE1 DOLO)
n.

hagadolodolo. (RE- DOLO)
v.

hagadolodoloa. (RE2 DOLO)
v.

hagadolodolohi. (RE- DOOLOHI)
v.

hagadolodolohia. (RE2 DOOLOHI)
v.

hagadolodolohinga.
(RE1 DOOLOHI) *n.*

hagadolodolona. (RE2 DOLO)
v.

hagadolodolonga. (RE1 DOLO)
n.

hagadolodolongia. (RE2 DOLO)
Slack off on (a rope) little by little. *v.*

hagadolona. (BE2 DOLO)
v.

hagadolu (ina). (BE- DOLU)
Make a total of three. *v.*

hagadona. (BE- DONA)
v.

hagadonadona. (RE- DONA)
v.

hagadonu. (BE- $DONU_{1a}$)
Trust, believe; interpret; support as a witness. *v.*

hagadonudonu. (RE- $DONU_{1a}$)
v.

hagadonudonuanga.
(RE1 $DONU_{1a}$) *n.*

hagadonudonusia. (RE2 $DONU_{1a}$)
v.

hagadonu muna.
Act as an interpreter.

hagadonusia. (BE2 $DONU_{1a}$)
v.

hagadongi. (BE- DONGI)
v.

hagadongia. (BE2 DONGI)
v.

hagadongidongi. (RE- DONGI)
v.

hagadongidongia. (RE2 DONGI)
v.

hagadongidonginga. (RE1 DONGI)
n.

hagadonginga. (BE1 DONGI)
n.

hagadoo. (BE- DOO_1)
v.

hagadooa. (BE2 DOO_1)
v.

hagadooanga. (BE1 DOO_1)
n.

hagadoopeva. (BE- DOOPEVA)
Play a trick on. *v.*

hagadoo dai.
To fish off the reef for tuna.

hagadoodoo. (RE- DOO_1)
v.

hagadoodooa. (RE2 DOO_1)
v.

hagadoodooanga. (RE1 DOO_1)
n.

hagadoodoo denga muna.
Boast foolishly about one's ability (when it is obvious that one is inept).

hagadoogonga. (BE1 $DOGO_1$)
n.

hagadookaa. (PE- DOGAA)
v.

hagadookaanga. (PE1 DOGAA)
n.

hagadookalala.
(BE- DOOKALALA) *v.*

hagadoohunga. (BE1 DOHU)
n.

hagadoolohi. (BE- DOOLOHI)
v.

hagadoolohia. (BE2 DOOLOHI)
v.

hagadoolohinga. (BE1 DOOLOHI)
n.

hagadoonunga. (BE1 $DONU_{1a}$)
—; meaning. *n.*

hagadua. (BE- DUA_1)
To coil or plait using — [number of] strands; change the size of. *d.*

hagaduagi. (BE- DUAGI)
v.

hagaduagia. (BE2 DUAGI)
v.

hagaduagina. (BE2 DUAGI)
v.

hagaduaginga. (BE1 DUAGI)
n.

hagaduai. (BE- $DUAI_1$)
Cause to be worn out. *v.*

hagaduasala. (XE- DUA_2)
Suffer, punish. *v.*

hagadube. (BE- DUBE)
v.

hagadubea. (BE2 DUBE)
v.

hagadubedube. (RE- DUBE)
v.

hagadubedubea. (RE2 DUBE)
v.

hagadubedubenga. (RE1 DUBE)
n.

hagadubenga. (BE1 DUBE)
n.

hagadubu. (BE- DUBU)
—; respect (someone); make a string figure; transfigure. *v.*

hagadubua. (BE2 DUBU)
v.

hagadubu dinae.
The name of a certain type of string figure.

hagadubudubu. (RE- DUBU)
v.

hagadubudubua. (RE2 DUBU)
v.

hagadubudubuanga. (RE1 DUBU)
n.

hagadubudubulia. (RE2 DUBU)
v.

hagadubu gina.
The name of a certain type of string figure.

hagadubu gi se --.
Transfigure into a —.

hagadubu hue vini.
The name of a certain type of string figure.

hagadubulia. (BE2 DUBU)
v.

hagadubu maduu paa.
The name of a certain type of string figure.

hagadubu manu baabaa.
The name of a certain type of string figure.

hagadubu mangoo.
The name of a certain type of string figure.

hagadubuna. (BE- DUBUNA)
Treat as *dubuna.* *v.*

hagadubu o de adu.
The name of a certain type of string figure.

hagadubu o de ahi.
The name of a certain type of string figure.

hagadubu o de moe.
The name of a certain type of string figure.

hagadubu o madaligi.
The name of a certain type of string figure.

hagadubu o manu.
The name of a certain type of string figure.

hagadugi$_1$. (BE- DUGI$_1$)
v.

hagadugi$_2$. (BE- DUGI$_2$)
v.

hagadugia. (BE2 DUGI$_2$)
v.

hagadugidugi$_1$. (RE- DUGI$_1$)
v.

hagadugidugi$_2$. (RE- DUGI$_2$)
v.

hagadugidugia$_1$. (RE2 DUGI$_1$)
v.

hagadugidugia$_2$. (RE2 DUGI$_2$)
v.

hagadugidugina. (RE2 DUGI$_2$)
v.

hagadugiduginga$_1$. (RE1 DUGI$_1$)
n.

hagadugiduginga$_2$. (RE1 DUGI$_2$)
n.

hagadugina. (BE2 DUGI$_2$)
v.

hagaduginga. (BE1 DUGI$_2$)
n.

hagaduguagi. (BE- DUGU$_a$)
v.

hagaduguaginga. (BE1 DUGU$_a$)
n.

hagadugudugu. (RE- DUGU)
Crouch repeatedly. *v.*

hagaduguduguaginga.
(RE1 DUGU$_a$) *n.*

hagadugu lalo.
Self-deprecatory, downgrade.

hagadui. (BE- DUI)
—; to lean way over in order to observe. *v.*

hagaduia. (BE2 DUI)
v.

hagaduiaanga. (BE3 DUI)
n.

hagaduiagi. (BE- DUI_a)
v.

hagaduiagina. (BE2 DUI_a)
v.

hagaduiaginga. (BE1 DUI_a)
n.

hagaduidui. (RE- DUI)
To move about (leaning way over) in order to observe. *a.*

hagaduiduia. (RE2 DUI)
v.

hagaduiduinga. (RE1 DUI)
n.

hagaduilaa. (BE- DUILAA)
v.

hagaduilaanga. (BE1 DUILAA)
n.

hagaduinga. (BE1 DUI)
n.

hagadulagi. (BE- DULAGI)
Imitate, illustrate, give an example; fashion something to be like something else. *v.*

hagadulagianga. (BE1 DULAGI)
n.

hagaduliduli. (RE- $DULI_1$)
v.

hagadulidulia. (RE2 $DULI_1$
v.

hagaduliduIinga. (RE1 $DULI_1$
n.

hagaduludulu. (RE- DULU)
v.

hagaduluduluanga. (RE1 DULU)
n.

hagadumanu. (BE- DUMANU)
Cause to look like. *v.*

hagadunu. (BE- $DUNU_1$)
v.

hagadungadungagi.
(RE- DUNGAGI) *v.*

hagadungadungaginga.
(RE1 DUNGAGI) *n.*

hagadungagi. (BE- DUNGAGI)
v.

hagadungu. (BE- DUNGU)
Smell something purposively. *v.*

hagadungua. (BE2 DUNGU)
v.

hagadunguanga. (BE1 DUNGU)
n.

hagadungudungu. (RE- DUNGU)
v.

hagadungudungua. (RE2 DUNGU)
v.

hagadungudunguanga.
(RE1 DUNGU) *n.*

hagadungudungulia.
(RE2 DUNGU) *v.*

hagadungulia. (BE2 DUNGU)
v.

hagaduosi. (BE- DUOSI)
v.

hagaduu. (BE- DUU_2)
—; construct, set up, build (something). *v.*

hagaduua. (BE2 DUU_2)
v.

hagaduuaa. (BE- DUUAA)
v.

hagaduuaanga. (BE1 DUUAA)
n.

hagaduuanga. (BE1 DUU_2)
n.

hagaduubunga. (BE1 DUBU)
n.

hagaduudagi. (BE- DUUDAGI)
v.

hagaduudagina. (BE2 DUUDAGI)
v.

hagaduudaginga. (BE1 DUUDAGI)
n.

hagaduu dala.
Angry and ready to fight.

hagaduu de uinga.
To place stakes on the sides of *uinga.*

hagaduuduagi. (RE- DUAGI)
v.

hagaduuduagia. (RE2 DUAGI)
v.

hagaduuduagina. (RE2 DUAGI)
v.

hagaduuduaginga. (RE1 DUAGI)
n.

hagaduuduu. (RE- DUU_2)
—; stand on tiptoes, rise up (as a person does). *v.*

hagaduuduua. (RE2 DUU_2)
v.

hagaduuduuanga. (RE1 DUU_2)
n.

hagaduuduudagi. (RE- DUUDAGI)
v.

hagaduuduudagina.
(RE2 DUUDAGI) *v.*

hagaduuduudaginga.
(RE1 DUUDAGI) *n.*

hagaduuduulagi. (RE- DUU_{2c})
v.

hagaduuduulagia. (RE2 DUU_{2c})
v.

hagaduuduulagina. (RE2 DUU_{2c})
v.

hagaduuduulaginga. (RE1 DUU_{2c})
n.

hagaduuduulanga. (RE1 DUU_2)
A style of construction (consistently followed). *n.*

hagaduuduuli. (RE- DUULI)
v.

hagaduuduulia. (RE2 DUU_2)
v.

hagaduuduulinga. (RE1 DUULI)
n.

hagaduuduulou. (RE- DUULOU)
v.

hagaduuduuloua. (RE2 DUULOU)
v.

hagaduuduulounga.
(RE1 DUULOU) *n.*

hagaduu eidu.
Superstitious; to believe in ghosts.

hagaduu gaiaa.
Suspicious by nature.

hagaduugau. (BE- GAU_{1b})
To make a handle for (e.g., a knife); to fasten with pegs. *v.*

hagaduugaua. (BE2 GAU_{1b})
v.

hagaduugauanga. (BE1 GAU_{1b})
n.

hagaduugaunga. (BE1 GAU_{1b})
n.

hagaduugia. (BE2 $DUGI_1$)
v.

hagaduuginga. (BE1 $DUGI_1$)
n.

hagaduugiva. (BE- DUUGIVA)
v.

hagaduugivaanga.
(BE1 DUUGIVA) *n.*

hagaduuhua. (BE- DUU_{2a})
v.

hagaduuhuli. (BE- DUUHULI)
To create *duuhuli.* *v.*

hagaduu i luu goo.
[An expression equivalent to "damn it"].

hagaduulagi. (BE- DUU_{2c})
v.

hagaduulagia. (BE2 DUU_{2c})
v.

hagaduulagina. (BE2 DUU_{2c})
v.

hagaduulaginga. (BE1 DUU_{2c})
n.

hagaduulanga. (BE1 DUU_2)
Method of construction; appearance (e.g., of a ship, house, or other construction). *n.*

hagaduuli. (BE- DUULI)
v.

hagaduulia. (BE2 DUU_2)
v.

hagaduulinga. (BE1 DUULI)
n.

hagaduulou. (BE- DUULOU)
Eat ravenously. *v.*

hagaduuloua. (BE2 DUULOU)
v.

hagaduulounga. (BE1 DUULOU)
n.

hagaduumaa. (BE- DUU_{2d})
Add a portion. *v.*

hagaduu me.
Miserly.

hagaduu ngae.
Earnestly; to the limits of one's capacity; struggle (e.g., to complete work).

hagaduu ngavesi.
Make boxes.

hagaduu ssaalanga.
Search intently for.

hagataa. (EE- DAA_1)
v.

hagataagina. (EE2 $DAGI_1$)
v.

hagataaginga. (EE1 $DAGI_1$)
n.

hagataalea. (EE2 DALE)
v.

hagataalenga. (EE1 DALE)
n.

hagataanga. (EE1 DAA_1)
n.

hagataanginga. (PE1 DANGI)
n.

hagataba. (PE- DABA)
v.

hagatabaanga. (PE1 DABA)
n.

hagatabalia. (PE2 DABA)
v.

hagatae. (PE- DAE_2)
v.

hagataea. (PE2 DAE_2)
v.

hagataelia. (PE2 DAE_2)
v.

hagataenga. (PE1 DAE_2)
—; one leg of a back-and-forth canoe course. *n.*

hagatagi. (EE- $DAGI_1$)
v.

hagatai --. (EE- DAI_2)
u.

hagatala. (PE- $DALA_2$)
—; fool around, play a joke on. *v.*

hagatalaanga₁. (PE1 $DALA_2$)
n.

hagatalaanga₂. (EE1 $DALA_3$)
n.

hagatala gee.
Wanting always to *hagatala.*

hagatala senga.
Foolishly rough playing or joking.

hagatale. (EE- DALE)
—; try, attempt. *v.*

hagatanu. (PE- DANU)
—; do with a maximum application of effort. *v.*

hagatanuanga. (PE1 DANU)
n.

hagatanu iho.
Take a nap.

hagatanga. (PE- DANGA)
—; move away from. *v.*

hagatangaanga. (PE1 DANGA)
n.

hagatangalia. (PE2 DANGA)
v.

hagatangi. (PE- DANGI)
v.

hagatangia. (PE2 DANGI)
v.

hagatangohi. (BE- TANGOHI)
The fading of light after sunset. *v.*

hagatau₁. (EE- DAU_1)
Arrange (in order), a program; name one after another; refuse to do one's part because of someone else's actions. *v.*

hagatau₂. (PE- DAU_3)
v.

hagataua₁. (EE2 DAU_1)
v.

hagataua₂. (PE2 DAU_3)
v.

hagatauanga. (EE1 DAU_1)
—; row (of things). *n.*

hagataulia₁. (EE2 DAU₁)
v.

hagataulia₂. (PE2 DAU₃)
v.

hagataunga. (PE1 DAU₃)
n.

hagatea. (EE- DEA)
—; become white. *v.*

hagateaanga. (EE1 DEA)
n.

hagateeginga. (EE1 DEGI₂)
n.

hagateelea. (PE2 DELE)
v.

hagateelenga. (PE1 DELE)
n.

hagateevenga. (EE1 DEVE)
n.

hagategi. (EE- DEGI₂)
a.

hagategia. (EE1 DEGI₂)
v.

hagategi kano.
Tickled (not sexually).

hagategilia. (EE1 DEGI₂)
v.

hagatele. (PE- DELE)
v.

hagatelengia. (PE2 DELE)
v.

hagatemo. (PE- DEMO)
v.

hagatemoanga. (PE1 DEMO)
n.

hagatemolia. (PE2 DEMO)
v.

hagateve. (EE- DEVE)
Bristle, ready for a fight (of animals). *v.*

hagatevea. (EE2 DEVE)
[= *hagatevelia*]. *v.*

hagatevelia. (EE2 DEVE)
Cause to bristle. *v.*

hagatiba. (PE- DIBA₁)
v.

hagatibaanga. (PE1 DIBA₁)
n.

hagatibalia. (PE2 DIBA₁)
v.

hagatige. (PE- DIGE)
v.

hagatigelia. (PE2 DIGE)
v.

hagatigo. (BE- TIGO)
v.

hagatigoa. (BE2 TIGO)
v.

hagatigolia. (BE2 TIGO)
v.

hagatiigenga. (PE1 DIGE)
n.

hagatiigonga. (BE1 TIGO)
n.

hagatiilinga. (EE1 DILI)
n.

hagatili. (EE- DILI)
Swoop down, swoop across. *v.*

hagatoga. (PE- DOGA₁)
v.

hagatogaanga. (PE1 DOGA₁)
n.

hagatogalia. (PE2 DOGA₁)
v.

hagatogo. (EE- DOGO₁)
v.

hagatogoa. (EE2 DOGO₁)
v.

hagatogolia. (EE2 DOGO₁)
v.

hagatola. (PE- DOLA)
v.

hagatolaanga. (PE1 DOLA)
n.

hagatolo. (EE- DOLO)
—; slack off on (a rope). *v.*

hagatoloa. (EE2 DOLO)
—; also, = *hagatolongia*. *v.*

hagatolongia. (EE2 DOLO)
Slack off completely on (a rope). *v.*

hagatoo. (PE- DOO$_1$)
v.

hagatooa. (PE2 DOO$_1$)
v.

hagatooanga. (PE1 DOO$_1$)
n.

hagatoo donu.
Promise, contract with; swear to the truth of.

hagatoogonga. (EE1 DOGO$_1$)
n.

hagatoolonga. (EE1 DOLO)
n.

hagatoo mua.
Take every possible precaution, insure.

hagatubu. (PE- DUBU)
—; exaggerate. *v.*

hagatubua. (PE2 DUBU)
v.

hagatubuanga. (PE1 DUBU)
n.

hagatubulia. (PE2 DUBU)
v.

hagatubu me.
Exaggerate matters.

hagatugi. (EE- DUGI$_1$)
v.

hagatugu. (EE- DUGU)
Crouch down. *v.*

hagatuguanga. (EE1 DUGU)
n.

hagatugu tai.
Ebbing of tide.

hagatugulia. (EE2 DUGU)
v.

hagatui. (PE- DUI)
[Pl. of *hagadui* — 'observe' sense only]. *a.*

hagatuia. (PE2 DUI)
v.

hagatuinga. (PE1 DUI)
n.

hagatulu. (EE- DULU)
v.

hagatuluanga. (EE1 DULU)
n.

hagatulu mai.
Ooze out.

hagatuugiva. (PE- DUUGIVA)
v.

hagatuugivaanga. (PE1 DUUGIVA)
n.

hagaea. (BE- EA)
v.

hagaeaanga. (BE1 EA)
n.

hagaeaea. (RE- EA)
—; stutter [lit. 'going and coming']. *v.*

hagaeaeaanga. (RE1 EA)
n.

hagaebuebu. (RE- EBU)
v.

hagaebuebua. (RE2 EBU)
v.

hagaebuebunga. (RE1 EBU)
n.

hagaedeede. (BE- EDEEDE)
Balance precariously. *v.*

hagaedeedea. (BE2 EDEEDE)
v.

hagaedeedenga. (BE1 EDEEDE)
n.

hagaege. (BE- EGE)
v.

hagaegea. (BE2 EGE)
v.

hagaegeege. (RE- EGE)
v.

hagaegeegea. (RE2 EGE)
v.

hagaegeegelia. (RE2 EGE)
v.

hagaegeegenga. (RE1 EGE)
n.

hagaegelia. (BE2 EGE)
v.

hagaeidu. (BE- EIDU)
Treat as an *eidu*. *v.*

hagaeligi. (BE- ELIGI)
Treat as an *eligi*. *v.*

hagaeligianga. (BE1 ELIGI)
n.

hagaeueu. (RE- EU)
A shrugging movement of the shoulders. *v.*

hagagaabea. (BE2 GABE)
v.

hagagaabenga. (BE1 GABE)
n.

hagagaabinga. (BE1 GABI)
n.

hagagaadinga. (BE- GADIa)
v.

hagagaagaa. (BE- GAAGAA)
Behave like a baby. *v.*

hagagaagaasia. (SE2 $GASI_2$)
v.

hagagaagaasiaanga. (SE3 $GASI_2$)
n.

hagagaagaaui. (RE- $GAAUI_2$)
v.

hagagaagaauia. (RE2 $GAAUI_2$)
v.

hagagaagaauinga. (RE1 $GAAUI_2$)
n.

hagagaahagi. (BE- GAAHAGI)
v.

hagagaainga. (BE1 GAI_2)
n.

hagagaalinga. (BE1 GALI)
n.

hagagaaui. (BE- $GAAUI_2$)
v.

hagagaauia. (BE2 $GAAUI_2$)
v.

hagagaauinga. (BE1 $GAAUI_2$)
n.

hagagaba$_1$. (BE- $GABA_1$)
Wait for. *d.*

hagagaba$_2$. (BE- $GABA_2$)
v.

hagagabaanga. (BE1 $GABA_2$)
n.

hagagabaduu. (BE- GABADUU)
v.

hagagabaduunga. (BE1 GABADUU)
n.

hagagabaea. (BE- GABAEA)
— [a var. of *hakabaea* used only occassionally]. *v.*

hagagabaeanga. (BE1 GABAEA)
— [var. of *hakabaeanga*]. *n.*

hagagabagaba. (RE- $GABA_2$)
v.

hagagabagabaanga. (RE1 $GABA_2$)
n.

hagagabe. (BE- GABE)
v.

hagagabegabe. (RE- GABE)
v.

hagagabegabea. (RE2 GABE)
v.

hagagabegabelia. (RE2 GABE)
v.

hagagabegabenga. (RE1 GABE)
n.

hagagabi. (BE- GABI)
v.

hagagabia. (BE2 GABI)
v.

hagagabidia. (BE2 GABI)
v.

hagagabigabi. (RE- GABI)
v.

hagagabigabia. (RE2 GABI)
v.

hagagabigabidia. (RE2 GABI)
v.

hagagabigabinga. (RE1 GABI)
n.

hagagabinivali. (BE- GABINIVALI)
v.

hagagabinivalianga.
(BE1 GABINIVALI) *n.*

hagagabogabola. (RE- GABOLA)
v.

hagagabogabolanga.
(RE1 GABOLA) *n.*

hagagabola. (BE- GABOLA)
v.

hagagabolaanga. (BE1 GABOLA)
n.

hagagabugabu. (RE- GABU)
Create a channel through land (by wind or wave action). *v.*

hagagapua. (BE- GAPUA)
To create *gapua*. *v.*

hagagadi. (BE- GADI)
v.

hagagadigadi. (RE- GADI)
v.

hagagaehala. (BE- GAEHALA)
To cause to have immature breadfruit. *v.*

hagagaehalaanga.
(BE1 GAEHALA) *n.*

hagagahaalava.
(BE- GAHAALAVA) *v.*

hagagai₁. (BE- GAI₁)
v.

hagagai₂. (BE- GAI₂)
v.

hagagaiaadia. (BE2 GAIAA)
v.

hagagaiaanga. (BE1 GAIAA)
n.

hagagaina. (BE2 GAI₂)
v.

hagagainanga. (BE- GAINANGA)
v.

hagagainga. (BE- GAINGA)
Litter up. *v.*

hagagalaanga*. (BE- GALAANGA)
v.

hagagalaanganga*.
(BE1 GALAANGA) *n.*

hagagalagalaanga*.
(RE- GALAANGA) *v.*

hagagalagalaanganga*.
(RE1 GALAANGA) *n.*

hagagalagalani. (RE- GALANI)
v.

hagagalagalania. (RE2 GALANI)
v.

hagagalagalanianga.
(RE1 GALANI) *n.*

hagagalani. (BE- GALANI)
v.

hagagalania. (BE2 GALANI)
v.

hagagalanianga. (BE1 GALANI)
n.

hagagalauna. (BE- GALAUNA)
Teach to use *galauna*. *v.*

hagagalegale. (BE- GALEGALE)
v.

hagagalegalea. (BE2 GALEGALE)
v.

hagagalegaleanga.
(BE1 GALEGALE) *n.*

hagagalele. (BE- GALELE)
Teach to *galale*. *v.*

hagagaleu. (BE- GALEU)
v.

hagagaleua. (BE2 GALEU)
v.

hagagaleunga. (BE1 GALEU)
n.

hagagali. (BE- GALI)
v.

hagagalia. (BE2 GALI)
v.

hagagaligali. (RE- GALI)
v.

hagagaligalia. (RE2 GALI)
v.

hagagaligalinga. (RE1 GALI)
n.

hagagaligi. (BE- GALIGI)
v.

hagagaligianga. (BE1 GALIGI)
n.

hagagalua. (BE2 GALU)
v.

hagagalugalua. (RE2 GALU)
Cause to have more and more *galu*. *v.*

hagagamu. (BE- GAMU₁)
v.

hagagamua. (BE2 GAMU₁)
v.

hagagamugamu. (RE- GAMU$_1$)
v.

hagagamugamua. (RE2 GAMU$_1$)
v.

hagaganabu. (BE- GANABU)
v.

hagaganabuanga. (BE1 GANABU)
n.

hagaganimua. (XE- GANO)
To treat as an eldest child. *v.*

hagaganimuli. (XE- GANO)
To treat as a child younger than the eldest. *v.*

hagaganomada --. (XE- GANO$_b$)
To have a look of — on one's face. *d.*

hagagango. (BE- GANGO)
v.

hagagasia. (BE- GASIA)
v.

hagagasiaanga. (BE1 GASIA)
n.

hagagasigasia. (RE2 GASI$_2$)
v.

hagagasigasiaanga. (RE3 GASI$_2$)
n.

hagagasogo. (BE- GASOGO)
v.

hagagasogoanga. (BE1 GASOGO)
n.

hagagau. (BE- GAU$_{1a}$)
v.

hagagaua. (BE2 GAU$_{1a}$)
v.

hagagaugau. (RE- GAU$_{1a}$)
v.

hagagaugaua. (RE2 GAU$_{1a}$)
v.

hagagaugauna. (RE- GAUNA)
v.

hagagaugaunanga. (RE1 GAUNA)
n.

hagagaugaunga. (RE1 GAU$_{1a}$)
n.

hagagauligi. (BE- GAULIGI)
v.

hagagauligianga. (BE1 GAULIGI)
n.

hagagauna. (BE- GAUNA)
v.

hagagaunanga. (BE1 GAUNA)
n.

hagagaunga. (BE1 GAU$_{1a}$)
n.

hagageelinga. (BE1 GELI)
n.

hagageelonga. (BE1 GELO)
n.

hagageenunga. (BE1 GENU)
n.

hagageli. (BE- GELI)
v.

hagagelia. (BE2 GELI)
v.

hagageligeli. (RE- GELI)
v.

hagageligelia. (RE2 GELI)
v.

hagageligelinga. (RE1 GELI)
n.

hagagelo. (BE- GELO)
v.

hagageloa. (BE2 GELO)
v.

hagagelogelo. (RE- GELO)
v.

hagagelogeloa. (RE2 GELO)
v.

hagagelogelonga. (RE1 GELO)
n.

hagagemogemo. (RE- GEMO)
v.

hagagemogemoanga. (RE1 GEMO)
n.

hagagemogemolia. (RE2 GEMO)
v.

hagagenu. (BE- GENU)
v.

hagagenua. (BE2 GENU)
v.

hagagenugenu. (RE- GENU)
v.

hagagenugenua. (RE2 GENU)
v.

hagagenugenunga. (RE1 GENU)
n.

hagageu. (BE- GEU)
v.

hagageua. (BE2 GEU)
v.

hagageugeu. (RE- GEU)
v.

hagageugeua. (RE2 GEU)
v.

hagageugeunga. (RE1 GEU)
n.

hagageunga. (BE1 GEU)
n.

hagagiba. (BE- GIBA)
v.

hagagibaanga. (BE1 GIBA)
n.

hagagide. (BE- GIDE)
v.

hagagideanga. (BE1 GIDE)
n.

hagagidegide. (RE- GIDE)
v.

hagagidegideanga. (RE1 GIDE)
n.

hagagidegidelia. (RE2 GIDE)
v.

hagagidelia. (BE2 GIDE)
v.

hagagidigidi. (RE- GIDI)
v.

hagagidigidianga. (RE1 GIDI)
n.

hagagii. (BE- GII)
v.

hagagiia. (BE2 GII)
v.

hagagiianga. (BE1 GII)
n.

hagagiidada. (BE- GIIDADA)
v.

hagagiidagi. (BE- GIIDAGI)
v.

hagagiidagina. (BE2 GIIDAGI)
v.

hagagiidaginga. (BE1 GIIDAGI)
n.

hagagiigii. (RE- GII)
v.

hagagiigiia. (RE2 GII)
v.

hagagiigiianga. (RE1 GII)
n.

hagagiininga. (BE1 GINI)
n.

hagagiivada. (BE- GIIVADA)
v.

hagagiivia. (BE- GIIVIA)
v.

hagagiiviaanga. (BE1 GIIVIA)
n.

hagagili. (BE- GILI)
Cause to have skin disease. *v.*

hagagilia. (BE2 GILI)
v.

hagaginadoa. (BE- GINADOA)
v.

hagaginadoaanga.
(BE1 GINADOA) *n.*

hagagini. (BE- GINI)
v.

hagaginia. (BE2 GINI)
v.

hagaginigini. (RE- GINI)
v.

hagaginiginia. (RE2 GINI)
v.

hagaginigininga. (RE1 GINI)
n.

hagaginogino. (RE- KINO)
v.

hagagobagoba. (RE- GOBA)
v.

hagagobagobaanga. (RE1 GOBA)
n.

hagagobegobe. (RE- GOBE)
v.

hagagobegobeanga. (RE1 GOBE)
n.

hagagobegobelia. (RE2 GOBE)
v.

hagagobugobu. (RE- GOBU)
v.

hagagobugobua. (RE2 GOBU)
v.

hagagobugobuanga. (RE1 GOBU)
n.

hagagobugobulia. (RE2 GOBU)
v.

hagagodi. (BE- GODI)
v.

hagagodia. (BE2 GODI)
v.

hagagodigodi. (RE- GODI)
v.

hagagodigodia. (RE2 GODI)
v.

hagagodigodinga. (RE1 GODI)
n.

hagagodinga. (B1 GODI)
n.

hagagogo. (BE- GOGO)
v.

hagagogoa. (BE2 GOGO)
v.

hagagogoanga. (BE1 GOGO)
n.

hagagogono. (TE- GONO)
v.

hagagogonoanga. (TE1 GONO)
n.

hagagogoo. (TE- GOO_1)
v.

hagagogooa. (TE2 GOO_1)
v.

hagagogooanga. (TE1 GOO_1)
n.

hagagogoolia. (TE2 GOO_1)
v.

hagagoli. (BE- GOLI)
v.

hagagoligoli. (RE- GOLI)
v.

hagagoligolia. (RE2 GOLI)
v.

hagagoligolinga. (RE1 GOLI)
n.

hagagolo. (BE- GOLO)
v.

hagagoloa. (BE2 GOLO)
v.

hagagoloanga. (BE1 GOLO)
n.

hagagologolo. (RE- GOLO)
v.

hagagologoloa. (RE2 GOLO)
v.

hagagologoloanga. (RE1 GOLO)
n.

hagagona. (BE- $GONA_1$)
Spend most of one's time —; become (or make) more —. *d.*

hagagonaanga. (BE1 $GONA_1$)
n.

hagagonogono. (RE- GONO)
v.

hagagonogonoanga. (RE1 GONO)
n.

hagagoo. (BE- GOO_1)
v.

hagagooa. (BE2 GOO_1)
v.

hagagooanga. (BE1 GOO_1)
n.

hagagoogoo. (RE- GOO_1)
v.

hagagoogooa. (RE2 GOO_1)
v.

hagagoogooanga. (RE1 GOO_1)
n.

hagagoogoolia. (RE2 GOO_1)
v.

hagagoolia$_1$. (BE2 GOLI)
v.

hagagoolia$_2$. (BE2 GOO_1)
v.

hagagoolinga. (BE1 GOLI)
n.

hagagoosia. (EE2 $GOSI_1$)
v.

hagagoosinga. (EE1 $GOSI_1$)
n.

hagagosigosi. (RE- $GOSI_1$)
v.

hagagosigosia. (RE2 $GOSI_1$)
v.

hagagosigosinga. (RE1 $GOSI_1$)
n.

hagagubenga. (BE- GUBENGA)
To teach someone to use a *gubenga.* *v.*

hagagubo. (BE- GUBO)
v.

hagaguboa. (BE2 GUBO)
v.

hagaguboanga. (BE1 GUBO)
n.

hagagubogubo. (RE- GUBO)
v.

hagaguboguboa. (RE2 GUBO)
v.

hagaguboguboanga. (RE1 GUBO)
n.

hagagudu. (BE- GUDU)
Cause to have lice (by transfer). *v.*

hagagudua. (BE2 GUDU)
v.

hagaguduaanga. (BE3 GUDU)
n.

hagagugu. (BE- GUGU)
v.

hagaguguanga. (BE1 GUGU)
n.

hagagumi. (BE- $GUMI_1$)
v.

hagagumigumi. (RE- $GUMI_1$)
v.

hagagumiguminga. (RE1 $GUMI_1$)
n.

hagaguuminga. (BE1 $GUMI_1$)
n.

hagakaa. (BE- KAA_1)
v.

hagakaakaa. (RE- KAA_1)
v.

hagakaakaanga. (RE1 KAA_1)
n.

hagakaanga. (BE1 KAA_1)
n.

hagakaba. (EE- $GABA_3$)
v.

hagakabe. (EE- GABE)
v.

hagakabi. (EE- GABI)
v.

hagakabianga. (EE1 GABI)
n.

hagakadi. (EE- GADI)
v.

$hagakai_1$. (PE- GAI_1)
v.

$hagakai_2$. (PE- GAI_2)
v.

$hagakai_3$. (BE- KAI_1)
v.

hagakaikai. (RE- KAI_1)
v.

$hagakala_1$. (BE- $KALA_1$)
v.

$hagakala_2$. (BE- $KALA_2$)
v.

$hagakalaanga_1$. (BE1 $KALA_1$)
n.

$hagakalaanga_2$. (BE1 $KALA_2$)
n.

hagakali. (PE- GALI)
v.

hagakalo. (BE- KALO)
v.

hagakaloanga. (BE1 KALO)
n.

hagakaso. (PE- $GASO_1$)
v.

hagakasoanga. (PE1 $GASO_1$)
n.

hagakasolia. (PE2 $GASO_1$)
v.

hagakau. (EE- GAU$_2$)
v.

hagakaua. (EE2 GAU$_2$)
v.

hagakaulia. (EE2 GAU$_2$)
v.

hagakaunga. (EE1 GAU$_2$)
n.

hagakava. (BE- KAVA)
v.

hagakavaanga. (BE1 KAVA)
n.

hagakeeligi. (BE- KEELIGI)
v.

hagakeeligianga. (BE1 KEELIGI)
n.

hagakeelonga. (PE1 GELO)
n.

hagakelo. (PE- GELO)
v.

hagakeloa. (PE2 GELO)
v.

hagakemo. (PE- GEMO)
v.

hagakemoanga. (PE1 GEMO)
n.

hagakemolia. (PE2 GEMO)
v.

hagakena. (BE- KENA)
v.

hagakenaanga. (BE1 KENA)
n.

hagakenalia. (BE2 KENA)
v.

hagakii$_1$. (BE- KII$_1$)
v.

hagakii$_2$. (PE- GII)
v.

hagakiia. (PE2 GII)
v.

hagakiianga$_1$. (BE1 KII$_1$)
n.

hagakiianga$_2$. (PE1 GII)
n.

hagakii dalinga.
Producing a high-pitched noise in the ear; the itch felt in the ear when something very sweet is eaten.

hagakino. (BE- KINO)
v.

hagakivi. (BE- KIVI)
v.

hagakobe. (EE- GOBE)
v.

hagakobeanga. (EE1 GOBE)
n.

hagakobelia. (EE2 GOBE)
v.

hagakobu. (EE- GOBU)
v.

hagakobua. (EE2 GOBU)
v.

hagakobuanga. (EE1 GOBU)
n.

hagakobulia. (EE2 GOBU)
v.

hagakolili. (BE- KOLILI)
To use the word *kolili*. *v.*

hagakona. (EE- GONA$_1$)
Become (or make) much worse. *v.*

hagakonaanga. (EE1 GONA$_1$)
n.

hagakono. (BE- GONO)
v.

hagakonoanga. (BE1 GONO)
n.

hagakoo. (PE- GOO$_1$)
—; cough up. *v.*

hagakooa. (PE2 GOO$_1$)
v.

hagakoolia. (PE2 GOO$_1$)
v.

hagakosi. (EE- GOSI$_1$)
v.

hagakumi. (EE- GUMI$_1$)
v.

hagahaa (ina). (BE- HAA$_3$)
Make a total of four. *v.*

hagahaadinga. (BE1 HADI)
n.

hagahaahaa$_1$. (RE- HAA$_1$)
v.

hagahaahaa$_2$. (RE- HAA$_2$)
v.

hagahaahaagia. (RE2 HAA$_2$)
v.

hagahaahaaligia. (RE2 HAALIGI)
v.

hagahaahaaligidia. (RE2 HAALIGI)
v.

hagahaahaaliginga.
(RE1 HAALIGI) *n.*

hagahaahaalo. (RE- HAALO)
v.

hagahaahaaloa. (RE2 HAALO)
v.

hagahaahaalonga. (RE1 HAALO)
n.

hagahaahaanau. (RE- HAANAU)
To help to deliver children on many occasions. *v.*

hagahaahaanaua. (RE2 HAANAU)
v.

hagahaahaanaunga.
(RE1 HAANAU) *n.*

hagahaahaanialo.
(RE- HAANIALO) *v.*

hagahaahaanialoanga.
(RE1 HAANIALO) *n.*

hagahaahaanga. (RE1 HAA$_1$)
n.

hagahaahaangoda.
(RE- HAANGODA) *v.*

hagahaahaangodaanga.
(RE1 HAANGODA) *n.*

hagahaahaangodalia.
(RE2 HAANGODA) *v.*

hagahaahaau. (RE- HAAU)
v.

hagahaahaaua. (RE2 HAAU)
v.

hagahaahaaunga. (RE1 HAAU)
n.

hagahaahadi. (TE- HADI)
v.

hagahaahadia. (TE2 HADI)
v.

hagahaahadinga. (TE1 HADI)
n.

hagahaahine. (PE- HAHINE)
Treat as women. *a.*

hagahaaide. (BE- HAAIDE)
v.

hagahaaidea. (BE2 HAAIDE)
v.

hagahaaidenga. (BE1 HAAIDE)
n.

hagahaaina. (BE- HAAINA)
v.

hagahaainanga. (BE1 HAAINA)
n.

hagahaainasia. (BE2 HAAINA)
v.

hagahaalala. (BE- HAALALA)
v.

hagahaalia. (BE2 HALI)
v.

hagahaaligi. (BE- HAALIGI)
v.

hagahaaligia. (BE2 HAALIGI)
v.

hagahaaligidia. (BE2 HAALIGI)
v.

hagahaaliginga. (BE1 HAALIGI)
n.

hagahaalinga. (BE1 HALI)

hagahaalo. (BE- HAALO)
—; encourage to *haalo*. *v.*

hagahaaloa. (BE2 HAALO)
v.

hagahaalonga. (BE1 HAALO)
n.

hagahaanau. (BE- HAANAU)
To help to deliver a child (as a midwife does). *v.*

hagahaanaunga. (BE1 HAANAU)
n.

hagahaanialo. (BE- HAANIALO)
v.

hagahaanialoanga.
(BE1 HAANIALO) *n.*

hagahaanoa. (BE2 HHANO)
v.

hagahaanonga. (BE1 HHANO)
n.

hagahaangoda. (BE- HAANGODA)
To teach to fish. *v.*

hagahaangodaanga.
(BE1 HAANGODA) *n.*

hagahaangodalia.
(BE2 HAANGODA) *v.*

hagahaau. (BE- HAAU)
v.

hagahaaua. (BE2 HAAU)
v.

hagahaaunga. (BE1 HAAU)
n.

hagahadi. (BE- HADI)
—; break in (something new). *v.*

hagahadia. (BE2 HADI)
v.

hagahadihadi. (RE- HADI)
v.

hagahadihadia. (RE2 HADI)
v.

hagahadihadinga. (RE1 HADI)
n.

hagahaduhadu. (RE- $HADU_2$)
v.

hagahaduhadua. (RE2 $HADU_2$)
v.

hagahaduhadunga. (RE1 $HADU_2$)
n.

hagahaehaele. (RE- HAELE)
v.

hagahaehaelea. (RE2 HAELE)
v.

hagahaehaelenga. (RE1 HAELE)
n.

hagahaele. (BE- HAELE)
v.

hagahaelea. (BE2 HAELE)
v.

hagahaelenga. (BE1 HAELE)
n.

hagahahaunu. (BE- UNU_{1b})
v.

hagahahaunua. (RE2 UNU_{1b})
v.

hagahahaunumanga. (RE1 UNU_{1b})
n.

hagahahaunumia. (RE2 UNU_{1b})
v.

hagahahaununga. (RE1 UNU_{1b})
n.

hagahahine. (BE- HAHINE)
Treat as a woman. *a.*

hagahai. (BE- HAI_1)
v.

hagahaia. (BE2 HAI_1)
v.

hagahaibodu. (XE- $BODU_1$)
Wedding; perform a wedding. *v.*

hagahaigabungi.
(BE- HAIGABUNGI)
Make shy. *v.*

hagahaigabungianga.
(BE1 HAIGABUNGI) *n.*

hagahaigamaiana.
(BE- HAIGAMAIANA)
Treat as important. *v.*

hagahaihai. (RE- HAI_1)
v.

hagahaihaia. (RE2 HAI_1)
v.

hagahaihainga. (RE1 HAI_1)
n.

hagahailu. (BE- HAILU)
v.

hagahailua. (BE2 HAILU)
v.

hagahailunga. (BE1 HAILU)
n.

hagahainoo. (BE- HAINOO)
v.

hagahainooa. (BE2 HAINOO)
v.

hagahainooanga. (BE1 HAINOO)
n.

hagahainoonga. (BE1 HAINOO)
n.

hagahainga. (BE1 HAI$_1$)
n.

hagahala. (BE- HALA)
A sleeping mat. *n.*

hagahale. (BE- HALE)
Begin to form (of a situation). *v.*

hagahalea. (BE2 HALE)
v.

hagahalehale. (RE- HALE)
v.

hagahalehalea. (RE2 HALE)
v.

hagahalehalenga. (RE1 HALE)
n.

hagahalenga. (BE1 HALE)
n.

hagahali. (BE- HALI)
d.

hagahalihali. (RE- HALI)
v.

hagahalihalia. (RE2 HALI)
v.

hagahalihalinga. (RE1 HALI)
n.

hagahana. (BE- HANA)
Reheat or recook food (to preserve it for a longer time). *v.*

hagahana age.
Recook for several days.

hagahanaanga. (BE1 HANA)
n.

hagahana ange.
Recook for a very little while.

hagahanahana. (RE- HANA)
Recook over and over. *v.*

hagahanahanaanga. (RE1 HANA)
n.

hagahanahanasia. (RE2 HANA)
v.

hagahana iho.
Recook for a little while.

hagahanasia. (BE2 HANA)
v.

hagahanaua. (B2 HAANAU)
v.

hagahano. (BE- HANO)
v.

hagahanohano. (RE- HANO)
v.

hagahanolia. (BE2 HANO)
v.

hagahao. (BE- HAO$_1$)
v.

hagahaoa. (BE2 HAO$_1$)
v.

hagahaohao. (RE- HAO$_1$)
v.

hagahaohaoa. (RE2 HAO$_1$)
v.

hagahaohaoli. (RE- HAOLI)
v.

hagahaohaolia$_1$. (RE2 HAO$_1$)
v.

hagahaohaolia$_2$. (RE2 HAOLI)
v.

hagahaohaolinga. (RE1 HAOLI)
n.

hagahaohaonga. (RE1 HAO$_1$)
n.

hagahaoli. (BE- HAOLI)
v.

hagahaolia$_1$. (BE2 HAO$_1$)
v.

hagahaolia$_2$. (BE2 HAOLI)
v.

hagahaolinga. (BE1 HAOLI)
n.

hagahaonga. (BE1 HAO$_1$)
n.

hagahasi. (BE- HASI)
v.

hagahasia. (BE2 HASI)
v.

hagahasihasi. (RE- HASI)
v.

hagahasihasia. (RE2 HASI)
v.

hagahasihasinga. (RE1 HASI)
n.

hagahasinga. (BE1 HASI)
n.

hagahau. (BE- HAU)
—; put a garland on someone or provide someone with a garland. *v.*

hagahaua. (BE2 HAU)
v.

hagahauhau. (RE- HAU)
v.

hagahauhaunga. (RE1 HAU)
n.

hagahaunu. (BE- UNU_{1b})
Cause to drink alcoholic beverages. *v.*

hagahaunua. (BE2 UNU_{1b})
v.

hagahaunumanga. (BE1 UNU_{1b})
n.

hagahaunumia. (BE2 UNU_{1b})
v.

hagahaununga. (BE1 UNU_{1b})
n.

hagahaunga. (BE1 HAU)
n.

hagahausia. (BE2 HAU)
v.

hagahebaa. (BG- BAA_1)
v.

hagahebaanga. (BG1 BAA_1)
n.

hagahebaa ngudu.
Converse (conversation).

hagahebahebaa. (RG- BAA_1)
v.

hagahebahebaanga. (RG1 BAA_1)
n.

hagahebahebaledage.
(RE- HEBALEDAGE) *n.*

hagahebaledage.
(BE- BEHALEDAGE) *v.*

hagahebaledageanga.
(BE1 HEBALEDAGE) *n.*

hagaheboheboIo. (RE- HEBOLO)
v.

hagaheboheboloanga.
(RE1 HEBOLO) *n.*

hagaheboheboohagi. (RE- BOO_{1b})
v.

hagaheboheboohagia. (RE2 BOO_{1b})
v.

hagaheboheboohaginga.
(RE1 BOO_{1b}) *n.*

hagahebolo. (BE- HEBOLO)
v.

hagaheboloanga. (BE1 HEBOLO)
n.

hagaheboohagi. (BE- BOO_{1b})
v.

hagaheboohagia. (BE2 BOO_{1b})
v.

hagaheboohaginga. (BE1 BOO_{1b})
n.

hagahebuhebuihagi. (RE- BUI_b)
v.

hagahebuhebuihagina. (RE2 BUI_b)
v.

hagahebuhebuihaginga.
(RE1 BUI_b) *n.*

hagahebuihagi. (BE- BUI_b)
v.

hagahebuihagina. (BE2 BUI_b)
v.

hagahebuihaginga. (BE1 BUI_b)
n.

hagahedaadoi. (BE- HEDAADOI)
v.

hagahedaadoia. (BE2 HEDAADOI)
v.

hagahedaadoinga.
(BE1 HEDAADOI) *n.*

hagahedae. (BG- DAE_2)
Make equal; go to meet. *v.*

hagahedaea. (BG2 DAE_2)
v.

hagahedaelia. (BG2 DAE_2)
v.

hagahedaenga. (BG1 DAE_2)
n.

hagahedahedaadoi.
(RE- HEDAADOI) *v.*

hagahedahedaadoia.
(RE2 HEDAADOI) *v.*

hagahedahedaadoinga.
(RE1 HEDAADOI) *n.*

hagahedahedangisi. (RE- $NGISI_a$)
v.

hagahedahedangisia. (RE2 $NGISI_a$)
v.

hagahedahedangisinga.
(RE1 $NGISI_a$) *n.*

hagahedangisi. (BE- $NGISI_a$)
v.

hagahedangisia. (BE2 $NGISI_a$)
v.

hagahedangisinga. (BE1 $NGISI_a$)
n.

hagahedu. (BE- HEDU)
v.

hagahetugi. (EG- $DUGI_1$)
v.

hagahetugianga. (EG1 $DUGI_1$)
n.

hagaheedua. (BE2 HEDU)
v.

hagaheedunga. (BE1 HEDU)
n.

hagaheehee. (RE- HEE_1)
v.

hagaheeheea. (RE2 HEE_1)
v.

hagaheeheenga. (RE1 HEE_1)
n.

hagaheeheui. (RE- HEUI)
v.

hagaheeheuia. (RE2 HEUI)
v.

hagaheeheuinga. (RE1 HEUI)
n.

hagaheelanga*. (BE1 HELA)
n.

hagahegabidi. (BE- $GABI_a$)
v.

hagahegahegabidi. (RE- $GABI_a$)
v.

hagahegahegabidianga.
(RE1 $GABI_a$) *n.*

hagahegai. (BG- GAI_2)
v.

hagahegainga. (BG1 GAI_2)
n.

hagahegide. (BG- GIDE)
v.

hagahegideanga. (BG1 GIDE)
n.

hagahegidelia. (BG2 GIDE)
v.

hagaheiangi. (BE- HEIANGI)
Act smart (openly). *v.*

hagaheiloo. (BG- ILOO)
Make the acquaintance of. *v.*

hagaheiloonga. (BG1 ILOO)
n.

hagahela*. (BE- HELA)
v.

hagahelahela*. (RE- HELA)
v.

hagahelahelaanga*. (RE1 HELA)
n.

hagahelelei. (BE- $LELE_a$)
v.

hagaheleleia. (B-2 $LELE_a$)
v.

hagaheleleinga. (BE1 $LELE_a$)
n.

hagahellumi. (BE- HELLUMI)
v.

hagahellumianga. (BE1 HELLUMI)
n.

hagaheloongoi.
(BE- HELOONGOI)
Compare; act as an intermediary or mediator; get acquainted with. *v.*

hagaheloongoia.
(BE2 HELOONGOI) *v.*

hagaheloongoinga.
(BE1 HELOONGOI) *n.*

hagahelui. (BG- LUI$_1$)
v.

hagaheluia. (BG2 LUI$_1$)
v.

hagaheluinga. (BG1 LUI$_1$)
n.

hagahemuu. (BG- MUU$_1$)
v.

hagahemuua. (BG2 MUU$_1$)
v.

hagahemuumuu. (RG- MUU$_1$)
v.

hagahemuumuua. (RG2 MUU$_1$)
v.

hagahemuumuunga. (RG1 MUU$_1$)
n.

hagahemuunga. (BG1 MUU$_1$)
n.

hagahenua. (BE- HENUA)
Give land to. *v.*

hagahenuu. (BE- HENUU$_1$)
v.

hagahenuua. (BE2 HENUU$_1$)
v.

hagahenuunga. (BE1 HENUU$_1$)
n.

hagaheohi. (BE- HEOHI)
To correct (someone or something). *v.*

hagaheohinga. (BE1 HEOHI)
n.

hagahesilihagi. (BE- SILI$_{3a}$)
v.

hagahesilihaginga. (BE1 SILI$_{3a}$)
n.

hagahesilisilihagi. (RE- SILI$_{3a}$)
n.

hagahesohesongi. (RE- SONGI$_a$)
v.

hagahesohesongia. (RE2 SONGI$_a$)
v.

hagahesohesonginga.
(RE1 SONGI$_a$) *n.*

hagahesongi. (BE- SONGI$_a$)
v.

hagahesongia. (BE2 SONGI$_a$)
v.

hagahesonginga. (BE1 SONGI$_a$)
n.

hagahesuihagi. (BE- SUI$_a$)
v.

hagahesuihagina. (BE2 SUI$_a$)
v.

hagahesuihaginga. (BE1 SUI$_a$)
n.

hagahesuisuihagi. (RE- SUI$_a$)
v.

hagahesuisuihagina. (RE2 SUI$_a$)
v.

hagahesuisuihaginga. (RE1 SUI$_a$)
n.

hagaheui. (BE- HEUI)
v.

hagaheuia. (BE2 HEUI)
v.

hagaheuinga. (BE1 HEUI)
n.

hagahevaalogi. (BE- HEVAALOGI)
v.

hagahevaalogia.
(BE2 HEVAALOGI) *v.*

hagahevaaloginga.
(BE1 HEVAALOGI) *n.*

hagahhaa. (EE- HAA$_1$)
v.

hagahhaanga. (EE1 HAA$_1$)
n.

hagahhali. (EE- HALI)
v.

hagahhano. (BE- HHANO)
Show someone how to wash his hands (or mouth). *v.*

hagahhau. (EE- HAU)
v.

hagahhela°. (EE- HELA)
v.

hagahhelaanga°. (EE1 HELA)
n.

hagahhoda. (EE- HODA$_1$)
v.

hagahhogi. (BE- HHOGI)
v.

hagahhogia. (BE2 HHOGI)
v.

hagahhogilia. (BE2 HHOGI)
v.

hagahhola. (EE- HOLA)
v.

hagahholu. (EE- HOLU)
v.

hagahhou. (EE- HOU)
v.

hagahhoua. (EE2 HOU)
v.

hagahhoulia. (EE2 HOU)
v.

hagahhounga. (EE1 HOU)
n.

hagahhua. (PE- HUA_1)
v.

hagahhuaanga. (PE1 HUA_1)
n.

hagahhuda. (EE- HUDA)
v.

hagahhudaanga. (EE1 HUDA)
n.

hagahhudi. (EE- $HUDI_1$)
v.

hagahhuna. (EE- HUNA)
v.

hagahhunaanga. (EE1 HUNA)
n.

hagahhuu. (BE- HHUU)
v.

hagahhuuhhuu. (RE- HHUU)
v.

hagahhuuhhuunga. (RE1 HHUU)
n.

hagahhuunga. (BE1 HHUU)
n.

hagahi.
Call (someone) once. *v.*

hagahia. (B-2 HAGAHI)
v.

hagahidi. (BE- HIDI)
—; weigh (on a balance). *v.*

hagahidia. (BE2 HIDI)
v.

hagahidihidi. (RE- HIDI)
v.

hagahidihidia. (RE2 HIDI)
v.

hagahidihidinga. (RE1 HIDI)
n.

hagahidi i tege.
To throw a wrestler using one's hip.

hagahidu (ina). (BE- HIDU)
The name of a person in a traditional story. *v.*

hagahiidagi. (BE- HIIDAGI)
v.

hagahiidagina. (BE2 HIIDAGI)
v.

hagahiidaginga. (BE1 HIIDAGI)
n.

hagahiidinga. (BE1 HIDI)
n.

hagahiihidi. (TE- HIDI)
v.

hagahiihidia. (TE2 HIDI)
v.

hagahiihidinga. (TE1 HIDI)
n.

hagahiihiidagi. (RE- HIIDAGI)
v.

hagahiihiidagina. (RE2 HIIDAGI)
v.

hagahiihiidaginga. (RE1 HIIDAGI)
n.

hagahiilonga. (BE1 HILO)
n.

hagahilo. (BE- HILO)
v.

hagahiloa. (BE2 HILO)
v.

hagahilohilo. (RE- HILO)
v.

hagahilohiloa. (RE2 HILO)
v.

hagahilohilonga. (RE1 HILO)
n.

hagahilohilosia. (RE2 HILO)
v.

hagahilosia. (BE2 HILO)
v.

hagahinahinangalosaa.
(RE- $HINA_b$) *v.*

hagahinahinangalosaanga.
(RE1 $HINA_b$) *n.*

hagahinangalomalie*. (BE- $HINA_a$)
n.

hagahinangalosaa. (BE- $HINA_b$)
a.

hagahinangalosaanga. (BE1 $HINA_b$)
n.

hagahinga. (B-1 HAGAHI)
n.

hagahoa. (BE- HOA_1)
—; a boil (on the body), carbuncle. *v.*

hagahobulaa. (BE- HOBULAA)
v.

hagahobulaanga. (BE1 HOBULAA)
n.

hagahoda. (BE- $HODA_2$)
v.

hagahodaanga. (BE1 $HODA_2$)
n.

hagahodahoda. (RE- $HODA_1$)
v.

hagahodahodaanga. (RE1 $HODA_1$)
n.

hagahodalia. (BE2 $HODA_2$)
v.

hagahodooligi. (BE- HODOOLIGI)
To install as chief. *v.*

hagahodu. (BE- HODU)
v.

hagahodua. (BE2 HODU)
v.

hagahoduhodu. (RE- HODU)
v.

hagahoduhodua. (RE2 HODU)
v.

hagahoduhodunga. (RE1 HODU)
n.

hagahodunga. (BE1 HODU)
n.

hagahoe. (BE- HOE_2)
v.

hagahoea. (BE2 HOE_2)
v.

hagahoenga. (BE1 HOE_2)
n.

hagahogihogi. (RE- HHOGI)
v.

hagahogihogia. (RE2 HHOGI)
v.

hagahogihogilia. (RE2 HHOGI)
v.

hagahogihoginga. (RE1 HHOGI)
n.

hagahola. (BE- HOLA)
v.

hagaholahola. (RE- HOLA)
v.

hagaholaholaa. (RE2 HOLA)
v.

hagaholaholanga. (RE1 HOLA)
n.

hagaholaholasia. (RE2 HOLA)
v.

hagaholasia. (BE2 HOLA)
v.

hagaholau. (BE- HOLAU)
Banish from the island (in a canoe with no paddle or food). *v.*

hagaholaua. (BE2 HOLAU)
v.

hagaholaunga. (BE1 HOLAU)
n.

hagaholi. (BE- HOLI)
Begin to form (something). *v.*

hagaholia. (BE2 HOLI)
v.

hagaholiage. (BE- HOLIAGE)
v.

hagaholiagina. (BE2 HOLIAGE)
v.

hagaholiaginga. (BE1 HOLIAGE)
n.

hagaholiholi. (RE- HOLI)
v.

hagaholiholia. (RE2 HOLI)
v.

hagaholiholiage. (RE- HOLIAGE)
v.

hagaholiholiagina.
(RE2 HOLIAGE) *v.*

hagaholiholiaginga.
(RE1 HOLIAGE) *n.*

hagaholiholinga. (RE1 HOLI)
n.

hagaholinga. (BE1 HOLI)
n.

hagaholoholoi.
(BE- HOLOHOLOI)
To use *holoholoi*. *v.*

hagaholoholoia.
(BE2 HOLOHOLOI) *v.*

hagaholoholoinga.
(BE1 HOLOHOLOI) *n.*

hagaholu. (BE- HOLU)
d.

hagaholuholu. (RE- HOLU)
v.

hagaholuholua. (RE2 HOLU)
v.

hagaholuholunga. (RE1 HOLU)
n.

hagahono. (BE- HONO)
v.

hagahonoa. (BE2 HONO)
v.

hagahonohono. (RE- HONO)
v.

hagahonohonoa. (RE2 HONO)
v.

hagahonohononga. (RE1 HONO)
n.

hagahononga. (BE1 HONO)
n.

hagahonu. (BE- $HONU_1$)
Fill up; to fully realize one's potential (for happiness, etc.). *v.*

hagahonua. (BE2 $HONU_1$)
v.

hagahonu age lodo.
Feel uncomfortably sated with food and unable to eat.

hagahonuhonu. (RE- $HONU_1$)
v.

hagahonuhonua. (RE2 $HONU_1$)
v.

hagahonuhonumia. (RE2 $HONU_1$)
v.

hagahonuhonunga. (RE1 $HONU_1$)
n.

hagahonumia. (BE2 $HONU_1$)
v.

hagahongagainga. (BE- $HONGA_a$)
To make a child urinate. *v.*

hagahongagelegele. (BE- $HONGA_b$)
To make a child defecate. *v.*

hagahoodanga. (EE1 $HODA_1$)
n.

hagahooginga. (BE1 HHOGI)
n.

hagahoohanga. (BE- HOOHANGA)
Allow birds to nest, or prepare a place for their nesting. *v.*

hagahoohonu. (TE- $HONU_1$)
v.

hagahoohonua. (TE2 $HONU_1$)
v.

hagahoohonumia. (TE2 $HONU_1$)
v.

hagahoohonunga. (TE1 $HONU_1$)
n.

hagahoohoo. (RE- HOO)
To scare fish, etc. *v.*

hagahoohooanga. (RE1 HOO)
n.

hagahoohooia. (RE2 HOO)
v.

hagahoolaa. (BE2 HOLA)
v.

hagahoolanga. (BE1 HOLA)
n.

hagahoolua. (BE2 HOLU)
v.

hagahoolunga. (BE1 HOLU)
n.

hagahoonunga. (BE1 $HONU_1$)
n.

hagahoou. (BE- HOOU)
Make like new. *v.*

hagahooua. (BE2 HOOU)
v.

hagahooulia. (BE2 HOOU)
v.

hagahoounga. (BE1 HOOU)
n.

hagahouhou. (RE- HOU)
v.

hagahouhoua. (RE2 HOU)
v.

hagahouhoulia. (RE2 HOU)
v.

hagahouhounga. (RE1 HOU)
n.

hagahua. (BE- HUA_1)
—; to shape roughly (as in making a canoe); show-off. *v.*

hagahuaalavao.
(BE- HUAALAVAO) *v.*

hagahuaalavaonga.
(BE1 HUAALAVAO) *n.*

hagahuaanga. (BE1 HUA_1)
n.

hagahuahua. (RE- HUA_1)
v.

hagahuahuaanga. (RE1 HUA_1)
n.

hagahudi --. (BE- $HUDI_1$)
d.

hagahudihudi. (RE- $HUDI_1$)
v.

hagahudihudinga. (RE1 $HUDI_1$)
n.

hagahui --. (BE- HUI_1)
v.

hagahuihui. (RE- HUI_1)
v.

hagahuihuia. (RE2 HUI_1)
v.

hagahuihuinga. (RE1 HUI_1)
n.

hagahula. (BE- HULA)
The sac in a fish which emerges from its mouth when it is brought up from a great depth. *n.*

hagahule. (BE- HULE)
v.

hagahulehule. (RE- HULE)
v.

hagahulehulei. (RE- $HULE_a$)
v.

hagahulehuleia. (RE2 $HULE_a$)
v.

hagahulehuleinga. (RE1 $HULE_a$)
n.

hagahulehulenga. (RE1 HULE)
n.

hagahulei. (BE- $HULE_a$)
v.

hagahuleia. (BE2 $HULE_a$)
v.

hagahuleinga. (BE1 $HULE_a$)
n.

hagahuli. (BE- HULI)
v.

hagahulia. (BE2 HULI)
v.

hagahulihuli. (RE- HULI)
v.

hagahulihulia. (RE2 HULI)
v.

hagahulihulinga. (RE1 HULI)
n.

hagahulihulisia. (RE2 HULI)
v.

hagahulinga. (BE1 HULI)
n.

hagahulisia. (BE2 HULI)
v.

$hagahulu_1$. (BE- $HULU_2$)
v.

$hagahulu_2$. (BE- $HULU_3$)
Make a total of ten. *v.*

hagahulua. (BE2 $HULU_2$)
v.

hagahuluhulu$_1$. (RE- HULU$_1$)
v.

hagahuluhulu$_2$. (RE- HULU$_2$)
v.

hagahuluhulua$_1$. (RE2 HULU$_1$)
v.

hagahuluhulua$_2$. (RE2 HULU$_2$)
v.

hagahuluhulunga$_1$. (RE1 HULU$_1$)
n.

hagahuluhulunga$_2$. (RE1 HULU$_2$)
n.

hagahulunga. (BE1 HULU$_2$)
n.

hagahuna. (BE- HUNA)
v.

hagahunahuna. (RE- HUNA)
v.

hagahunahunaanga. (RE1 HUNA)
n.

hagahunahunalia. (RE2 HUNA)
v.

hagahunalia. (BE2 HUNA)
v.

hagahuubuudoi.
(BE- HUUBUUDOI) *v.*

hagahuubuudoia.
(BE2 HUUBUUDOI) *v.*

hagahuubuudoinga.
(BE1 HUUBUUDOI) *n.*

hagahuudanga$_1$. (BE1 HUA$_1$)
n.

hagahuudanga$_2$. (BE1 HUDI$_1$)
n.

hagahuudia$_1$. (BE2 HUA$_1$)
v.

hagahuudia$_2$. (BE2 HUDI$_1$)
v.

hagahuuhuli. (TE- HULI)
v.

hagahuuhulia. (TE2 HULI)
v.

hagahuuhulinga. (TE1 HULI)
n.

hagahuuhulisia. (TE2 HULI)
v.

hagahuuhuna. (TE- HUNA)
v.

hagahuuhunaanga. (TE1 HUNA)
n.

hagahuuhunalia. (TE2 HUNA)
v.

hagahuuhuu. (BE- HUU$_3$)
v.

hagahuuhuua. (BE2 HUU$_3$)
v.

hagahuuia. (BE2 HUI$_1$)
v.

hagahuuinga. (BE1 HUI$_1$)
n.

hagahuulenga. (BE1 HULE)
n.

hagahuunanga. (BE1 HUNA)
n.

hagaiai. (BE- IAI)
v.

hagaiaianga. (RE- ANGA$_{2a}$)
v.

hagaiaiangaa. (RE2 ANGA$_{2a}$)
v.

hagaianga. (BE- ANGA$_{2a}$)
v.

hagaiangaa. (BE2 ANGA$_{2a}$)
v.

hagaida. (BE- IDA)
To bare one's teeth (by opening the lips). *v.*

hagaida de gauvae.
To bare one's teeth (by opening the lips to expose the whole set of teeth).

hagaidaida. (RE- IDA)
Cry uncontrollably (hysterically); a disturbance of breathing. *v.*

hagaidaidanga. (RE1 IDA)
n.

hagaidanga. (BE1 IDA)
n.

hagaidi. (BE- IDI)
v.

hagaidia. (BE2 IDI)
v.

hagaidihia. (BE2 IDI)
v.

hagaidiidi. (RE- IDI)
v.

hagaidiidia. (RE2 IDI)
v.

hagaidiidihia. (RE2 IDI)
v.

hagaidiidinga. (RE1 IDI)
n.

hagaidinga. (BE1 IDI)
n.

hagaieiangi. (BE- IEIANGI)
—; to cure (someone). *v.*

hagaieianginga. (BE1 IEIANGI)
n.

hagaiho. (BE- IHO)
Show (someone) how to climb down. *v.*

hagaihoanga. (BE1 IHO)
n.

hagaihoiho. (RE- IHO)
v.

hagaihoihoanga. (RE1 IHO)
n.

hagaihoiholia. (RE2 IHO)
v.

hagaiholia. (BE2 IHO)
v.

hagaila. (BE- ILA)
v.

hagailaage. (BE- ILAAGE)
Set free. *v.*

hagailaila. (RE- ILA)
v.

hagailailaage. (RE- ILAAGE)
v.

hagailangi. (HAGAI, LANGI$_2$)
A type of prepared food (made from breadfruit). *n.*

hagailangi-bangi. (XCO BANGI$_2$)
A type of prepared food (*bangi* soaked in coconut milk). *n.*

hagailangi daahaa.
A type of prepared food (like *dalogo*, but without *somo* or *mugamuga*).

hagaili. (BE- ILI)
—; strike (give a blow to). *v.*

hagailia. (BE2 ILI)
—; cause to blow away. *v.*

hagailihia. (BE2 ILI)
—; cause to blow away. *v.*

hagailiili. (RE- ILI)
v.

hagailiilia. (RE2 ILI)
v.

hagailiilihia. (RE2 ILI)
v.

hagailiilinga. (RE1 ILI)
n.

hagailinga. (BE1 ILI)
n.

hagailoha. (BE- ILOHA)
v.

hagailohaanga. (BE1 ILOHA)
n.

hagailonga. (CF ILOO)
v.

hagailonga$_1$. (?)
Sign, mark, signal, omen. *v.*

hagailonga$_2$. (?)
Fish sp.?: damselfish? *n.*

hagailonga ange agina.
Assign (someone) to; use something as a landmark.

hagailoo. (BE- ILOO)
Announce. *v.*

hagailoonga. (BE1 ILOO)
n.

hagailosia. (BE2 ILO)
v.

hagailosiaanga. (BE3 ILO)
n.

hagaina. (BE- INA$_1$)
v.

hagainaanga. (BE1 INA$_1$)
n.

hagainaina. (RE- INA$_1$)
v.

hagainainaanga. (RE1 INA$_1$)
n.

hagainau. (BE- INAU)
v.

hagainaua. (BE2 INAU)
v.

hagainaunga. (BE1 INAU)
n.

hagaino. (BE- INO)
v.

hagainoino. (RE- INO)
v.

hagainoinonga. (RE1 INO)
n.

hagainonga. (BE1 INO)
n.

hagaingoo. (BE- INGOO)
Give a name to, named, called. *v.*

hagaingoo ai.
Called by (named).

hagaingooanga. (BE1 INGOO)
n.

hagaioo. (BE- IOO)
Cause to give. *v.*

hagaiooanga. (BE1 IOO)
n.

hagaisi. (BE- ISI$_1$)
v.

hagaisia. (BE2 ISI$_1$)
v.

hagaisihia. (BE2 ISI$_1$)
v.

hagaisiisi. (RE- ISI$_1$)
v.

hagaisiisia. (RE2 ISI$_1$)
v.

hagaisiisihia. (RE2 ISI$_1$)
v.

hagaisiisinga. (RE1 ISI$_1$)
n.

hagaisinga. (BE1 ISI$_1$)
n.

hagaiviivia. (RE2 IVI)
v.

hagaiviiviaanga. (RE3 IVI)
n.

hagalaabunga. (BE1 LABU)
n.

hagalaaganga. (EE1 LAGA)
n.

hagalaagia. (BE2 LAAGII)
v.

hagalaagii. (BE- LAAGII)
Decorate, adorn; ornament [verb]. *v.*

hagalaaginga. (BE1 LAAGII)
n.

hagalaagua. (BE2 LAGU)
v.

hagalaagunga. (BE1 LAGU)
n.

hagalaalaa. (RE- LAA$_3$)
v.

hagalaalaanui. (RE- LAANUI)
v.

hagalaalaanuia. (RE2 LAANUI)
v.

hagalaalaanuinga. (RE1 LAANUI)
n.

hagalaalaanga. (RE1 LAA$_3$)
n.

hagalaalaangia. (RE2 LALA)
v.

hagalaaladi. (BE- LAALADI)
v.

hagalaaladia. (BE2 LAALADI)
v.

hagalaaladinga. (BE1 LAALADI)
n.

hagalaanui. (BE- LAANUI)
—; enlarge. *v.*

hagalaanuia. (BE2 LAANUI)
v.

hagalaanuinga. (BE1 LAANUI)
n.

hagalaangaa. (BE2 LANGA)
Teach to plait (mats, etc.). *v.*

hagalaangia. (BE2 LALA)
v.

hagalaanginga. (BE1 $LANGI_1$)
n.

hagalaangona. (BE2 $LONGO_1$)
v.

hagalaavea. (BE2 LAVE)
v.

hagalaavenga. (BE1 LAVE)
n.

hagalaba. (BE- $LABA_1$)
v.

hagalabaagau. (PE- LABAGAU)
v.

hagalabaagaua. (PE2 LABAGAU)
v.

hagalabaagaunga. (PE1 LABAGAU)
n.

hagalabaai*. (BE- LABAAI)
v.

hagalabaaia*. (BE2 LABAAI)
v.

hagalabaainga*. (BE1 LABAAI)
n.

hagalabaanga. (BE1 $LABA_1$)
n.

hagalabagau. (BE- LABAGAU)
v.

hagalabagaua. (BE2 LABAGAU)
v.

hagalabagaunga. (BE1 LABAGAU)
n.

hagalabalaba. (RE- $LABA_1$)
v.

hagalabalabaanga. (RE1 $LABA_1$)
n.

hagalabu. (BE- LABU)
v.

hagalabua. (BE2 LABU)
v.

hagalabulabu. (RE- LABU)
v.

hagalabulabua. (RE2 LABU)
v.

hagalabulabunga. (RE1 LABU)
n.

hagalapede. (BE- LAPEDE)
v.

hagalapedea. (BE2 LAPEDE)
v.

hagalapedenga. (BE1 LAPEDE)
n.

hagaladi. (BE- LADI)
v.

hagaladia. (BE2 LADI)
v.

hagaladiladi. (RE- LADI)
v.

hagaladiladia. (RE2 LADI)
v.

hagaladiladinga. (RE1 LADI)
n.

hagaladinga. (BE1 LADI)
n.

hagalaelae. (RE- LAE)
v.

hagalaelaea. (RE2 LAE)
v.

hagalaelaenga. (RE1 LAE)
n.

hagalagalaga. (RE- LAGA)
v.

hagalagalagai. (BE- LAGALAGAI)
v.

hagalagalagaia. (BE2 LAGALAGAI)
v.

hagalagalagainga.
(BE1 LAGALAGAI) *n.*

hagalagalaganga. (RE1 LAGA)
n.

hagalagohia. (BE- $LAGO_2$)
v.

hagalagohiaanga. (BE1 $LAGO_2$)
n.

hagalagolago. (BE- $LAGO_1$)
Cause to increase in numbers, multiply. *v.*

hagalagolagoa. (RE2 $LAGO_1$)
Cause to be numerous. *v.*

hagalagolagoaa. (BE- $LAGO_{2a}$)
v.

hagalagolagoaanga. (BE1 $LAGO_{2a}$)
n.

hagalagolagoanga. (RE1 $LAGO_1$)
n.

hagalagolagohia. (RE- $LAGO_2$)
v.

hagalagolagohiaanga.
(RE1 $LAGO_2$) *n.*

hagalagu --. (BE- LAGU)
d.

hagalagulagu. (RE- LAGU)
v.

hagalagulagua. (RE2 LAGU)
v.

hagalagulagunga. (RE1 LAGU)
n.

hagalahalaha. (RE- LAHA)
v.

hagalahalahaanga. (RE1 LAHA)
n.

hagalahilahi. (RE- LAHI)
v.

hagalahilahia. (BE2 LAHI)
v.

hagalahilahinga. (RE1 LAHI)
n.

hagalahu. (BE- LAHU)
v.

hagalahua. (BE2 LAHU)
v.

hagalahulahu. (RE- LAHU)
v.

hagalahulahua. (RE2 LAHU)
v.

hagalahulahunga. (RE1 LAHU)
n.

hagalahunga. (BE1 LAHU)
n.

hagalala. (BE- LALA)
v.

hagalalaa. (BE2 LALA)
v.

hagalalaanga. (BE1 LALA)
n.

hagalalau. (TE- LAU_1)
v.

hagalalaua. (TE2 LAU_1)
v.

hagalalaunga. (TE1 LAU_1)
n.

hagalallala. (RE- LALA)
v.

hagalalo. (BE- LALO)
Angling (a fishing method). *v.*

hagalamalamallie. (RE- $MALIE_a$)
v.

hagalamallie. (BE- $MALIE_a$)
v.

hagalanea. (BE- LANEA)
Cause to increase in quantity; greedy. *v.*

hagalanibene. (BE- LANIBENE)
v.

hagalanibeneanga.
(BE1 LANIBENE) *n.*

hagalanu. (BE- LANU)
Rinse off salt water from the body (with fresh water). *v.*

hagalanuanga. (BE1 LANU)
n.

hagalanumia. (BE2 LANU)
v.

hagalanga --. (BE- LANGA)
d.

hagalangaa. (BE2 LANGA)
v.

hagalangadia. (BE2 LANGA)
v.

hagalangalanga. (RE- LANGA)
v.

hagalangalangaa. (RE2 LANGA)
v.

hagalangi. (BE- $LANGI_1$)
v.

hagalangia. (BE2 $LANGI_1$)
v.

hagalangilangi. (RE- $LANGI_1$)
v.

hagalangilangia. (RE2 LANGI$_1$)
v.

hagalangilanginga. (RE1 LANGI$_1$)
n.

hagalango. (BE- LANGO$_1$)
v.

hagalangoa. (BE2 LANGO$_1$)
v.

hagalangolango. (RE- LANGO$_1$)
v.

hagalangolangoa. (RE2 LANGO$_1$)
v.

hagalangolangona. (RE2 LANGO$_1$)
v.

hagalangolangonga. (RE1 LANGO$_1$)
n.

hagalangona. (BE2 LANGO$_1$)
v.

hagalangonga. (BE1 LANGO$_1$)
n.

hagalao --. (BE- LAO$_1$)
d.

hagalaoa. (BE2 LAO$_1$)
v.

hagalaohie. (BE- LAOHIE)
v.

hagalaolao. (RE- LAO$_1$)
v.

hagalaolaoa. (RE2 LAO$_1$)
v.

hagalaolaohie. (RE- LAOHIE)
v.

hagalaolaonga. (RE1 LAO$_1$)
n.

hagalaonga. (BE1 LAO$_1$)
n.

hagalau$_1$. (BE- LAU$_1$)
—; able to catch many (esp. fish). *v.*

hagalau--$_2$. (BE- LAU$_2$)
Cause to have leaves which —. *d.*

hagalau$_3$. (BE- LAU$_4$)
Make a total of one hundred. *v.*

hagalaua. (BE2 LAU$_1$)
v.

hagalauali. (BE- LAUALI)
v.

hagalauasaasa. (BE- LAUASAASA)
v.

hagalauasaasaanga.
(BE1 LAUASAASA) *n.*

hagalaudanga. (BE1 LAU$_1$)
— (ex. 'good at fishing' meaning); way of being hooked. *n.*

hagalaudia. (BE2 LAU$_1$)
v.

hagalaudodole. (XE- LAU$_3$)
Cause to grow small. *v.*

hagalaulau$_1$. (RE- LAU$_1$)
v.

hagalaulau$_2$. (RE- LAULAU)
v.

hagalaulau$_3$. (RE- LAU$_4$)
Make many hundreds. *v.*

hagalaulaua$_1$. (RE2 LAU$_1$)
v.

hagalaulaua$_2$. (RE2 LAULAU)
v.

hagalaulaudanga. (RE1 LAU$_1$)
n.

hagalaulaudia. (RE2 LAU$_1$)
v.

hagalaulaunga$_1$. (RE1 LAU$_1$)
n.

hagalaulaunga$_2$. (RE1 LAULAU)
n.

hagalaumalie. (BE- LAU$_{3a}$)
v.

hagalaunga. (BE1 LAU$_1$)
—; way of being hooked. *n.*

hagalava. (BE- LAVA)
v.

hagalavalava. (RE- LAVA)
v.

hagalavalavaanga. (BE1 LAVA)
n.

hagalave. (BE- LAVE)
v.

hagalavelave. (RE- LAVE)
v.

hagalavelavea. (RE2 LAVE)
v.

hagalavelavenga. (RE1 LAVE)
n.

hagalealea. (RE- LEA)
v.

hagalealeaanga. (RE1 LEA)
n.

hagaleba. (BE- LEBA)
v.

hagalebaleba. (RE- LEBA)
v.

hagalebu. (BE- LEBU)
v.

hagalebua. (BE2 LEBU)
v.

hagalebulebu. (RE- LEBU)
v.

hagalebulebua. (RE2 LEBU)
v.

hagalebulebunga. (RE1 LEBU)
n.

hagaleebunga. (BE1 LEBU)
n.

hagaleelenga. (BE1 LELE)
n.

hagaleengia. (BE2 LELE)
v.

hagaleenginga. (BE1 LENGI)
n.

hagalegunga. (BE- LEGUNGA)
Show off (esp. in front of members of the opposite sex). *a.*

hagalehu. (BE- LEHU)
v.

hagalehua. (BE2 LEHU)
v.

hagalehulehu. (RE- LEHU)
v.

hagalehulehua. (RE2 LEHU)
v.

hagalehulehunga. (RE1 LEHU)
n.

hagalehunga. (BE1 LEHU)
n.

hagaleia. (BE2 LELE)
v.

hagalele. (BE- LELE)
—; do suddenly. *v.*

hagalele mouli.
Startle; surprise (someone).

hagalengi. (BE- LENGI)
v.

hagalengia. (BE2 LENGI)
v.

hagalengilengi. (RE- LENGI)
v.

hagalengilengia. (RE2 LENGI)
v.

hagalengilenginga. (RE1 LENGI)
n.

hagaleo. (BE- LEO)
To produce sound. *v.*

hagaleoleo. (RE- LEO)
v.

hagaleu. (BE- LEU)
—; allow to become *leu*, as when fruit is picked and left to ripen. *v.*

hagaleua. (BE2 LEU)
v.

hagaleuleu. (RE- LEU)
v.

hagaleuleua. (RE2 LEU)
v.

hagaleuleunga. (RE1 LEU)
n.

hagaleunga. (BE1 LEU)
n.

hagaleva. (BE- LEVA)
—; to swing. *v.*

hagalevaanga. (BE1 LEVA)
n.

hagalevaleva. (RE- LEVA)
v.

hagalevalevaanga. (RE1 LEVA)
n.

hagalevango. (BE- LEVANGO)
v.

hagaliagi. (BE- LIAGI)
v.

hagaliagina. (BE2 LIAGI)
v.

hagaliaginga. (BE1 LIAGI)
n.

hagalibi. (BE- LIBI)
v.

hagalibia. (BE2 LIBI)
v.

hagalibilibi. (RE- LIBI)
v.

hagalibilibia. (RE2 LIBI)
v.

hagalibilibinga. (RE1 LIBI)
n.

hagalibinga. (BE1 LIBI)
n.

hagalibo. (BE- $LIBO_1$)
v.

hagaliboa. (BE2 $LIBO_1$)
v.

hagalibolibo. (RE- $LIBO_1$)
v.

hagaliboliboa. (RE2 $LIBO_1$)
v.

hagalibolibonga. (RE1 $LIBO_1$)
n.

hagaligiligi. (RE- LIGI)
To speed up (to get over with). *v.*

hagaligiligia. (RE2 LIGI)
v.

hagaliibonga. (BE1 $LIBO_1$)
n.

hagaliiliagi. (RE- LIAGI)
v.

hagaliiliagina. (RE2 LIAGI)
v.

hagaliiliaginga. (RE1 LIAGI)
n.

hagaliilonga. (BE1 LILO)
n.

hagalili₁. (BE- LILI_1)
v.

hagalili₂. (BE- LILI_{1a})
A type of prepared food (like *dalogo* but without the immature coconut meat). *n.*

hagalili₃. (BE- LILI_3)
—; anger (toward someone). *v.*

hagalilia. (BE2 LILI_1)
v.

hagalilianga. (BE1 LILI_3)
n.

hagalilinga. (BE1 LILI_1)
n.

hagalillili₁. (RE- LILI_1)
v.

hagalillili₂. (RE- LILI_3)
v.

hagalillilianga. (RE1 LILI_3)
n.

hagalillilinga. (RE1 LILI_1)
n.

hagalilo. (BE- LILO)
Take shelter, to shelter (something from the elements); block out (from sight). *v.*

hagalilolilo. (RE- LILO)
v.

hagalilolilonga. (RE1 LILO)
n.

hagalilolilongia. (RE2 LILO)
v.

hagalilongia. (BE2 LILO)
v.

hagalima (ina). (BE- $LIMA_a$)
Make a total of five. *v.*

hagalimadi. (BE- LIMADI)
v.

hagalimadia. (BE2 LIMADI)
v.

hagalimadinga. (BE1 LIMADI)
n.

hagalimalima. (RE- LIMA)
v.

hagalimalimaanga. (RE1 LIMA)
n.

hagallabaanga. (PE1 $LABA_1$)
n.

hagallabu. (EE- LABU)
d.

hagallaga. (EE- LAGA)
v.

hagallago. (EE- LAGO$_1$)
v.

hagallagoanga. (EE1 LAGO$_1$)
n.

hagallagu. (EE- LAGU)
v.

hagallaha. (PE- LAHA)
v.

hagallahaanga. (PE1 LAHA)
n.

hagallahi. (BE- LAHI)
v.

hagallahia. (PE2 LAHI)
v.

hagallahinga. (BE1 LAHI)
n.

hagallama. (EE- LAMA)
v.

hagallanga. (EE- LANGA)
v.

hagallau. (PE- LAU$_1$)
v.

hagallaua. (PE2 LAU$_1$)
v.

hagallaudia. (PE2 LAU$_1$)
v.

hagallaunga. (PE1 LAU$_1$)
n.

hagallava. (PE- LAVA)
v.

hagallavaanga. (PE1 LAVA)
n.

hagallea. (EE- LEA)
v.

hagalleaanga. (EE1 LEA)
n.

hagalleba. (PE- LEBA)
v.

hagalleengia. (PE2 LENGI)
v.

hagalleenginga. (PE1 LENGI)
n.

hagallele. (PE- LELE)
v.

hagallengi. (PE- LENGI)
v.

hagalleo. (PE- LEO)
To produce many sounds. *v.*

hagalleu. (PE- LEU)
v.

hagalleua. (PE2 LEU)
v.

hagalleunga. (PE1 LEU)
n.

hagalleva. (PE- LEVA)
v.

hagallevaanga. (PE1 LEVA)
n.

hagallibo. (PE- LIBO$_1$)
v.

hagalliboa. (PE2 LIBO$_1$)
v.

hagallidi. (BE- LLIDI)
v.

hagallidianga. (BE1 LLIDI)
n.

hagalligi. (EE- LIGI)
Make very small. *v.*

hagalliibonga. (PE1 LIBO$_1$)
n.

hagalliilonga. (PE1 LILO)
n.

hagallili. (PE- LILI$_3$)
v.

hagallilianga. (PE1 LILI$_3$)
n.

hagallilo. (PE- LILO)
v.

hagallilongia. (PE2 LILO)
v.

hagalloa. (PE- LOA$_1$)
v.

hagalloaanga. (PE1 LOA$_1$)
n.

hagalloba. (EE- LOBA$_1$)
v.

hagallobaanga. (EE1 LOBA$_1$)
n.

hagalloba ange.
To slacken the boom sheet (of a sailing canoe).

hagallobo. (EE- LOBO)
v.

hagallodo. (PE- $LODO_2$)
d.

hagallogo°. (EE- LOGO)
Chant (in the old religious ceremony). *n.*

hagallogoanga. (EE1 LOGO)
n.

hagallohi. (EE- LOHI)
v.

hagallohia. (EE2 LOHI)
v.

hagallonga. (BE- LLONGA)
v.

hagallongo. (EE- $LONGO_1$)
Listen to, pay attention to; be aware of. *v.*

hagallongo de lau nui.
To obtain oracular information by listening to the sounds made by coconut leaves.

hagallongo i muna.
Obey.

hagallou. (EE- LOU)
v.

hagalloua. (EE2 LOU)
v.

hagallounga. (EE1 LOU)
n.

hagalludu. (EE- LUDU)
v.

hagalludua. (EE2 LUDU)
v.

hagalluhi. (EE- LUHI)
v.

hagalluhia. (EE2 LUHI)
v.

hagalluhianga. (EE1 LUHI)
n.

hagallui. (PE- LUI_1)
—; to flip over (as in diving a sommersault). *v.*

hagalluia. (PE2 LUI_1)
v.

hagalluinga. (PE1 LUI_1)
n.

hagalluu. (BE- LLUU)
v.

hagaloa. (BE- LOA_1)
Groove; a path (lengthwise) in the taro bog. *v.*

hagalobadia. (EE2 $LOBA_1$)
v.

hagalobaloba. (RE- $LOBA_1$)
v.

hagalobalobaanga. (RE1 $LOBA_1$)
n.

hagalobalobadia. (RE2 $LOBA_1$)
v.

hagalobodia. (BE2 LOBO)
v.

hagalobolobo. (RE- LOBO)
v.

hagaloboloboa. (RE2 LOBO)
v.

hagalobolobodia. (RE2 LOBO)
v.

hagalobolobonga. (RE1 LOBO)
n.

hagalodo. (BE- $LODO_2$)
To stimulate a desire for. *v.*

hagalodolodo. (RE- $LODO_2$)
Hope for (want). *v.*

hagalohilohi. (RE- LOHI)
v.

hagalohilohia. (RE2 LOHI)
v.

hagalohilohinga. (RE1 LOHI)
n.

hagalollolo. (RE- LOLO)
Lubricate. *v.*

hagalolloloanga. (RE1 LOLO)
n.

hagalolo. (BE- LOLO)
To add oil (esp. coconut cream) to food. *v.*

hagaloloanga. (BE1 LOLO)
n.

hagaloma. (BE- LOMA)
v.

hagaloma de me.
Calm weather, with no noise.

hagalongaa. (BE- LONGO$_{1a}$) [= *hagalongoaa*]. *a.*

hagalongoaa. (BE- LONGO$_{1a}$) *a.*

hagalongohie. (BE- LONGO$_{2a}$) *v.*

hagalongolongo. (RE- LONGO$_1$) —; do carefully. *v.*

hagalongolongo ngadaa. Slow to respond to suggestions or commands (because resisting).

hagalongosaa. (BE- LONGO$_2$) *v.*

hagalooboa. (BE2 LOBO) *v.*

hagaloobonga. (BE1 LOBO) *n.*

hagaloohinga. (BE1 LOHI) *n.*

hagalooloa. (RE- LOA$_1$) Lengthen, prolong. *v.*

hagalooloaanga. (RE1 LOA$_1$) *n.*

hagaloolonaa. (RE- LOONAA) *v.*

hagaloolonaanga. (RE1 LOONAA) *n.*

hagaloonaa. (BE- LOONAA) *v.*

hagaloonaanga. (BE1 LOONAA) *n.*

hagaloosi. (BE- LOOSI) Guard, watch, keep an eye on. *v.*

hagaloosia. (BE2 LOOSI) *v.*

hagaloosinga. (BE1 LOOSI) *n.*

hagalou. (BE- LOU) *v.*

hagaloua. (BE2 LOU) *v.*

hagaloulou. (RE- LOU) —; constipating. *v.*

hagalouloua. (RE2 LOU) *v.*

hagaloulouaanga. (RE3 LOU) *n.*

hagaloulounga. (RE1 LOU) *n.*

hagalounga. (BE1 LOU) *n.*

hagalua (ina). (BE- LUA) Make a total of two. *v.*

hagaludu. (BE- LUDU) *d.*

hagaluduludu. (RE- LUDU) *v.*

hagaluduludua. (RE2 LUDU) *v.*

hagaluduludunga. (RE1 LUDU) *n.*

hagaluei. (BE- LUEI) *v.*

hagalueia. (BE2 LUEI) Vomit, vomitus. *v.*

hagalueinga. (BE1 LUEI) *n.*

hagaluluei. (RE- LUEI) *v.*

hagaluelueia. (RE2 LUEI) Repeatedly *hagalueia.* *v.*

hagaluelueinga. (RE1 LUEI) *n.*

hagaluhiluhi. (RE- LUHI) *v.*

hagaluhiluhia. (RE2 LUHI) *v.*

hagaluhiluhinga. (RE1 LUHI) *n.*

hagalui. (BE- LUI$_1$) *v.*

hagaluia. (BE2 LUI$_1$) *v.*

hagaluilui. (RE- LUI$_1$) —; to flip over and over (as in diving a sommersault). *v.*

hagaluiluia. (RE2 LUI$_1$) *v.*

hagaluiluinga. (RE1 LUI$_1$) *n.*

hagaluinga. (BE1 LUI_1)
n.

hagalulu. (BE- LULU)
—; to attract fish (or animals) by feeding them; a type of old chant [sung by a priest at daybreak to chase ghosts from the village, and wake up people to work]. *v.*

hagalulua. (BE2 LULU)
v.

hagalulu de langi.
Attract rain (by making certain noises).

hagalulu de madangi.
To attract the wind (by making certain noises).

hagalulunga. (BE1 LULU)
n.

hagalulungia. (BE2 LULU)
v.

hagaluudunga. (BE1 LUDU)
n.

hagaluulunga. (BE1 LULU)
—; a good fishing spot (where fish are accustomed to take the bait). *n.*

hagaluuluu. (TE- LULU)
v.

hagaluuluua. (TE2 LULU)
v.

hagaluuluunga. (TE1 LULU)
—; a place to which fish have been attracted by bait. *n.*

hagaluuluungagi.
(RE- LUUNGAGI) *v.*

hagaluuluungagina.
(RE2 LUUNGAGI) *v.*

hagaluuluungaginga.
(RE1 LUUNGAGI) *n.*

hagaluungagi. (BE- LUUNGAGI)
v.

hagaluungagina.
(BE2 LUUNGAGI) *v.*

hagaluungaginga.
(BE1 LUUNGAGI) *n.*

hagamaa₁. (BE- MAA_1)
To rinse off salt water from the body (with fresh water). *v.*

hagamaa₂. (BE- MAA_2)
To treat (someone) as *maa₂*. *v.*

hagamaabunga. (BE1 MABU)
—; resting place. *n.*

hagamaadai*. (BE- MAADAI)
v.

hagamaadau₁. (BE- MAADAU)
Barb. *n.*

hagamaadau₂. (BE- MADAU)
A current which flows to the right. *n.*

hagamaadenga₁. (BE1 $MADE_1$)
n.

hagamaadenga₂. (BE1 $MADE_2$)
n.

hagamaadinga. (BE1 MADI)
n.

hagamaadoha. (BF- DOHA)
v.

hagamaadohaanga. (PF1 DOHA)
n.

hagamaadohalia. (PF2 DOHA)
v.

hagamaadohi. (PF- DOHI)
v.

hagamaadohinga. (PF1 DOHI)
n.

hagamaadolu. (BE- MAADOLU)
v.

hagamaadua. (PE- MADUA)
Be oldest among. *v.*

hagamaatagu. (PE- MADAGU)
v.

hagamaataguanga. (PE1 MADAGU)
n.

hagamaatagudia. (PE2 MADAGU)
v.

hagamaatagulia. (PE2 MADAGU)
v.

hagamaatala. (PF- $DALA_1$)
v.

hagamaatalaanga. (PF1 $DALA_1$)
n.

hagamaatogo. (BE- MAATOGO)
v.

hagamaatogoanga. (BE1 MAATOGO) *n.*

hagamaatogolia. (BE2 MAATOGO) *v.*

hagamaatua. (PE- MADUA) —; [pl. of *hagamaadua*]. *v.*

hagamaaege. (PF- EGE) *v.*

hagamaaegea. (PF2 EGE) *v.*

hagamaaegeanga. (PF1 EGE) *n.*

hagamaaegelia. (PF2 EGE) *v.*

hagamaagaga. (EE- MAKAGA) *v.*

hagamaagagaanga. (EE1 MAKAGA) *n.*

hagamaagagalia. (EE2 MAKAGA) *v.*

hagamaaganga$_1$. (BE1 MAGA$_1$) *n.*

hagamaaganga$_2$. (BE1 MAGA$_2$) *n.*

hagamaagila. (BE- MAAGILA) *v.*

hagamaagilaanga. (BE1 MAAGILA) *n.*

hagamaagoda. (BE- MAAGODA) *v.*

hagamaagodanga. (BE1 MAAGODA) *n.*

hagamaaguluaa. (BE- MAAGULUAA) *v.*

hagamaaguluaanga. (BE1 MAAGULUAA) *n.*

hagamaakau. (PE- MAGAU) *v.*

hagamaakaua. (PE2 MAGAU) *v.*

hagamaakaulia. (PE2 MAGAU) *v.*

hagamaakaunga. (PE1 MAGAU) *n.*

hagamaakulu. (PE- MAGULU) *v.*

hagamaahagi. (PF- HAGI) *v.*

hagamaahagia. (PF2 HAGI) *v.*

hagamaahagina. (PF2 HAGI) *v.*

hagamaahaginga. (PF1 HAGI) *n.*

hagamaahana. (PF- HANA) *v.*

hagamaahanaanga. (PF1 HANA) *n.*

hagamaahanasia. (PF2 HANA) *v.*

hagamaahanga. (PF- HANGA) *v.*

hagamaahe. (BF- AHE) *v.*

hagamaaheahe. (RF- AHE) *v.*

hagamaaheahenga. (RF1 AHE) *n.*

hagamaahedu. (PF- HEDU) *v.*

hagamaahedua. (PF2 HEDU) *v.*

hagamaahedunga. (PF1 HEDU) *n.*

hagamaahenga. (BF1 AHE) *n.*

hagamaahia. (EF2 MAHI) *v.*

hagamaahiaanga. (EF3 MAHI) *n.*

hagamaahidi. (PF- HIDI) *v.*

hagamaahidia. (PF2 HIDI) *v.*

hagamaahidinga. (PF1 HIDI) *n.*

hagamaahola. (PF- HOLA) *v.*

hagamaaholaanga. (PF1 HOLA)
n.

hagamaaholasia. (PF2 HOLA)
v.

hagamaahole. (PF- HOLE)
v.

hagamaaholea. (PF2 HOLE)
v.

hagamaaholenga. (PF1 HOLE)
n.

hagamaahuge. (PF- HUGE)
v.

hagamaahugea. (PF2 HUGE)
v.

hagamaahugeanga. (PF1 HUGE)
n.

hagamaahugelia. (PF2 HUGE)
v.

hagamaahule. (PF- HULE)
v.

hagamaahulea. (PF2 HULE)
v.

hagamaahulenga. (PF1 HULE)
n.

hagamaahunga. (BE1 MAHU)
n.

hagamaai. (BE- MAAI)
v.

hagamaaia. (BE2 MAAI)
v.

hagamaaileele. (BE- MAAILEELE)
—; commit suicide. *v.*

hagamaaileelenga.
(BE1 MAAILEELE) *n.*

hagamaainga. (BE1 MAAI)
n.

hagamaaiongi. (BE- MAAIONGI)
Depressed (mentally); unable to think, move, or talk (as a result of psychic depression or trauma). *a.*

hagamaaionginga.
(BE1 MAAIONGI) *n.*

hagamaaisi. (PF- ISI_1)
v.

hagamaaisia. (PF2 ISI_1)
v.

hagamaaisihia. (PF2 ISI_1)
v.

hagamaaisinga. (PF1 ISI_1)
n.

hagamaalaia. (PE- MALAIA)
v.

hagamaalaiaanga. (PE1 MALAIA)
n.

hagamaalali. (PE- MALALI)
v.

hagamaalalianga. (PE1 MALALI)
n.

hagamaalama. (BE- MAALAMA)
Brighten, illuminate. *v.*

hagamaalamangia.
(BE2 MAALAMA) *v.*

hagamaalanga. (PF- LANGA)
v.

hagamaalemo. (PE- MALEMO)
v.

hagamaalemoanga.
(PE1 MALEMO) *n.*

hagamaalena. (PF- LENA)
v.

hagamaalenaanga. (PF1 LENA)
n.

hagamaaleva. (PE- MALEVA)
v.

hagamaalibi. (PF- LIBI)
v.

hagamaalibia. (PF2 LIBI)
v.

hagamaalibinga. (PF1 LIBI)
n.

hagamaalili. (PE- $MALILI_1$)
v.

hagamaalilianga. (PE1 $MALILI_1$)
n.

hagamaalino. (PE- MALINO)
v.

hagamaalinoanga. (PE1 MALINO)
n.

hagamaalinongia. (PE2 MALINO)
v.

hagamaalingi. (PF- LINGI)
v.

hagamaalingia. (PF2 LINGI)
v.

hagamaalinginga. (PF1 LINGI)
n.

hagamaalioso. (BE- MAALIOSO)
v.

hagamaalo. (BE- MAALO)
v.

hagamaalogu. (PE- MALOGU)
v.

hagamaalogunga. (PE1 MALOGU)
n.

hagamaalonga. (B1 MAALO)
n.

hagamaaloolo. (RE- MAALO)
v.

hagamaaloolonga. (RE1 MAALO)
n.

hagamaalui. (PF- LUI_1)
v.

hagamaaluinga. (PF1 LUI_1)
n.

hagamaamaa. (RE- MAA_3)
v.

hagamaamaadolu.
(RE- MAADOLU) *v.*

hagamaamaatogo.
(RE- MAATOGO) *v.*

hagamaamaatogoanga.
(RE1 MAATOGO) *n.*

hagamaamaatogolia.
(RE2 MAATOGO) *v.*

hagamaamaagila. (RE- MAAGILA)
v.

hagamaamaagilaanga.
(RE1 MAAGILA) *n.*

hagamaamaagoda.
(RE- MAAGODA) *v.*

hagamaamaagodanga.
(RE1 MAAGODA) *n.*

hagamaamaai. (RE- MAAI)
v.

hagamaamaaia. (RE2 MAAI)
v.

hagamaamaainga. (RE1 MAAI)
n.

hagamaamaaiongi.
(RE- MAAIONGI)
Continually *hagamaaiongi.* *a.*

hagamaamaaionginga.
(RE1 MAAIONGI) *n.*

hagamaamaalama.
(SE- MAALAMA)
Shine on continuously. *v.*

hagamaamaalamangia.
(RE2 MAALAMA) *v.*

hagamaamaalioso.
(RE- MAALIOSO) *v.*

hagamaamaalo. (SE- MAALO)
v.

hagamaamaalonga. (SE1 MAALO)
n.

hagamaamaanadu.
(RE- MAANADU)
Keep reminding or keep remembering. *v.*

hagamaamaanadua.
(RE2 MAANADU) *v.*

hagamaamaanaduanga.
(RE1 MAANADU) *n.*

hagamaamaane. (RE- $MAANE_1$)
Make lighter; choose the easiest work (rather than the more difficult). *v.*

hagamaamaaneanga.
(RE1 $MAANE_1$) *n.*

hagamaamaane de lodo.
Cheer up (someone).

hagamaamaanu. (RE- MAANU)
v.

hagamaamaanunga. (RE1 MAANU)
n.

hagamaamaanga. (RE1 MAA_3)
n.

hagamaamaangalo.
(RE- MAANGALO) *v.*

hagamaamaangaloanga. (RE1 MAANGALO) *n*

hagamaamaangi. (RE- MAANGI) *v.*

hagamaamaangia. (RE2 MAANGI) *v.*

hagamaamaanginga. (RE1 MAANGI) *n.*

hagamaamaasina. (RE- MAASINA) *v.*

hagamaamaasinaanga. (RE1 MAASINA) *n.*

hagamaamaaua. (RE- MAAUA) *v.*

hagamaamaauaanga. (RE1 MAAUA) *n.*

hagamaamaava. (SE- MAAVA) *v.*

hagamaamaavaanga. (SE1 MAAVA) *n.*

hagamaamasa. (E- MASA) *v.*

hagamaamasaanga. (PE1 MASA) *n.*

hagamaamasalia. (PE2 MASA) *v.*

hagamaanadu. (BE- MAANADU) Remember, remind. *v.*

hagamaanaduanga. (BE1 MAANADU) *n.*

hagamaanava. (PE- MANAVA) *v.*

hagamaanavaanga. (PE1 MANAVA) *n.*

hagamaanegabo. (BE- $MAANE_{2a}$) *v.*

hagamaanegaboanga. (BE1 $MAANE_{2a}$) *n.*

hagamaanege. (PF- NEGE) *v.*

hagamaanegea. (PF2 NEGE) *v.*

hagamaanegelia. (PF2 NEGE) *v.*

hagamaanegenga. (PF1 NEGE) *n.*

hagamaaniha. (BE- MAANIHA) *v.*

hagamaanihaanga. (BE1 MAANIHA) *n.*

hagamaanongi. (PE- MANONGI) *v.*

hagamaanu. (BE- MAANU) *v.*

hagamaanu age. Pull oneself up by one's arms.

hagamaanuga. (BE- MAANUGA) *v.*

hagamaanugaanga. (BE1 MAANUGA) *n.*

hagamaanuhi. (PE- MANUHI) *v.*

hagamaanuhianga. (PE1 MANUHI) *n.*

hagamaanunga. (BE1 MAANU) *n.*

hagamaanga. (BE1 MAA_1) *n.*

hagamaangalo. (BE- MAANGALO) *v.*

hagamaangaloanga. (BE1 MAANGALO) *n.*

hagamaangi. (BE- MAANGI) *v.*

hagamaangia. (BE2 MAANGI) *v.*

hagamaanginga. (BE1 MAANGI) *n.*

hagamaangoa. (BE- MAANGOA) *v.*

hagamaangoanga. (BE1 MAANGOA) *n.*

hagamaaoha. (PF- OHA) *v.*

hagamaaohanga. (PF1 OHA) *n.*

hagamaasae. (BE- SAE_{1a}) *v.*

hagamaasaea. (BE2 SAE_{1a})
v.

hagamaasaenga. (BE1 SAE_{1a})
n.

hagamaasanga$_1$. (BE1 MASA)
n.

hagamaasanga$_2$. (PF- SANGA)
v.

hagamaasei. (BE- MAASEI)
—; reduce in size. *v.*

hgamaaseia. (BE2 MAASEI)
v.

hagamaasei ange.
Make smaller (away from one).

hagamaasei mai.
Make smaller (toward one).

hagamaaseinga. (BE1 MAASEI)
n.

hagamaaseu. (PF- SEU)
v.

hagamaaseua. (PF2 SEU)
v.

hagamaaseunga. (PF1 SEU)
n.

hagamaasina. (BE- MAASINA)
v.

hagamaasinaanga.
(BE1 MAASINA) *n.*

hagamaasinga. (BE1 $MASI_1$)
n.

hagamaasole. (PE- MASOLE)
v.

hagamaasoleanga. (PE1 MASOLE)
n.

hagamaasugi. (PF- $SUGI_1$)
v.

hagamaasugia. (PF2 $SUGI_2$)
v.

hagamaasuginga. (PF1 $SUGI_2$)
n.

hagamaasui. (BE- MASUI)
A current which flows to the left. *n.*

hagamaaua. (BE- MAAUA)
v.

hagamaauaanga. (BE1 MAAUA)
n.

hagamaaui. (BE- MAAUI)
v.

hagamaauia. (BE2 MAAUI)
v.

hagamaauinga. (BE1 MAAUI)
n.

hagamaava. (BE- MAAVA)
v.

hagamaavaanga. (BE1 MAAVA)
n.

hagamaavaava. (RE- MAAVA)
v.

hagamaavaavaanga. (RE1 MAAVA)
n.

hagamaavae. (PF- VAE_1)
v.

hagamaavaea. (PF2 VAE_1)
v.

hagamaavaelia. (PF2 VAE_1)
v.

hagamaavaenga. (PF1 VAE_1)
n.

hagamabu. (BE- MABU)
Rest, relax, quit (a job). *v.*

hagamabua. (BE2 MABU)
Cause to *hagamabu*. *v.*

hagamabu age.
Return to land from sea (esp. of birds).

hagamabu iho.
Rest for a short time.

hagamabulia. (BE2 MABU)
Cause to *hagamabu*. *v.*

hagamabumabu. (RE- MABU)
v.

hagamabumabua. (RE2 MABU)
v.

hagamabumabulia. (RE2 MABU)
v.

hagamabumabunga. (RE1 MABU)
n.

hagamada--$_1$. (BE- $MADA_3$)
—; look as though. *d.*

hagamada--$_2$. (BE- MADA$_{3a}$)
Basis (with respect to common ascendents)for a relationship of—. *d.*

hagamada--$_3$. (BE- MADA$_2$)
Make a total of — tens. *d.*

hagamadaagi. (BE- MADAAGI)
To teach someone to *madaagi.* *v.*

hagamadaagianga.
(BE1 MADAAGI) *n.*

hagamadaaginga. (BE1 MADAAGI)
n.

hagamadaala. (BE- MADA$_{3b}$)
v.

hagamadaalanga. (BE1 MADA$_{3b}$)
n.

hagamadaali. (BE- MADAALI)
v.

hagamadaaligi. (PE- MADALIGI$_1$)
v.

hagamadaaligianga.
(PE1 MADALIGI$_1$) *n.*

hagamadabuunou. (BE- MADA$_{3h}$)
v.

hagamadabuunoua. (BE2 MADA$_{3h}$)
v.

hagamadabuunounga.
(BE1 MADA$_{3d}$) *n.*

hagamadagabubu. (BE- GABUBU$_a$)
v.

hagamadagabubua.
(BE2 GABUBU$_a$) *v.*

hagamadagabubuanga.
(BE1 GABUBU$_a$) *n.*

hagamadagabubulia.
(BE2 GABUBU$_a$) *v.*

hagamadagu. (BE- MADAGU)
Scare (someone); frighten (someone). *v.*

hagamadaguanga. (BE1 MADAGU)
n.

hagamadagudagu. (RE- MADAGU)
v.

hagamadagudaguanga.
(RE1 MADAGU) *n.*

hagamadagudagudia.
(RE2 MADAGU) *v.*

hagamadagudagulia.
(RE2 MADAGU) *v.*

hagamadagudia. (BE2 MADAGU)
v.

hagamadagulia. (BE2 MADAGU)
v.

hagamadahuuhua. (BE- MADA$_{3d}$)
Cause to have pimples. *v.*

hagamadahuuhuaanga.
(BE1 MADA$_{3d}$) *n.*

hagamadala. (BF- DALA$_1$)
v.

hagamadalaanga. (BF1 DALA$_1$)
n.

hagamadaladala. (RF- DALA$_1$)
v.

hagamadaladalaanga. (RF1 DALA$_1$)
n.

hagamadaligi. (BE- MADALIGI$_1$)
v.

hagamadaligianga.
(BE1 MADALIGI$_1$) *n.*

hagamadamada. (RE- MADA$_3$)
—; share equally; cause to compete. *v.*

hagamadamadaanga. (RE1 MADA$_3$)
n.

hagamadamada ngaadahi.
Share equally among.

hagamadamataia. (RE- MATAIA)
v.

hagamadamataianga. (RE1 MATAIA)
n.

hagamadaniiga. (BE- MADA$_{3e}$)
v.

hagamadaniigaanga. (BE1 MADA$_{3e}$)
n.

hagamadangi. (BE- MADANGI)
v.

hagamade$_1$. (BE- MADE$_1$)
Do as hard or fast as possible. *v.*

hagamade$_2$. (BE- MADE$_2$)
v.

hagamadea. (BE2 MADE$_1$)
v.

hagamadegi. (BF- DEGI$_1$)
v.

hagamadegidegi. (RF- DEGI$_1$)
v.

hagamadegideginga. (RF1 DEGI$_1$)
n.

hagamadeginga. (BF1 DEGI$_1$)
n.

hagamadelia. (BE2 MADE$_2$)
v.

hagamademade$_1$ --. (RE- MADE$_1$)
Work as little as possible; tarry in order to avoid. *d.*

hagamademade$_2$. (RE- MADE$_2$)
v.

hagamademade gaiaa.
Cringe to deceive one's opponent into thinking one is afraid (when one is not).

hagamademadelia. (RE2 MADE$_2$)
v.

hagamademadenga. (RE1 MADE$_2$)
n.

hagamadi. (BE- MADI)
v.

hagamadia. (BE- MADIA)
Show-off. *a.*

hagamadiaanga. (BE1 MADIA)
n.

hagamadimadi. (RE- MADI)
v.

hagamadimadinga. (RE1′ MADI)
n.

hagamadoha. (BF- DOHA)
v.

hagamadohaanga. (BF1 DOHA)
n.

hagamadohadoha. (RF- DOHA)
v.

hagamadohadohaanga.
(RF1 DOHA) *n.*

hagamadohadohalia. (RF2 DOHA)
v.

hagamadohalia. (BF2 DOHA)
v.

hagamadohi. (BF- DOHI)
v.

hagamadohinga. (BF1 DOHI)
n.

hagamadolidoli. (RF- DOLI)
v.

hagamadolidolia. (RF2 DOLI)
v.

hagamadolidolinga. (RF1 DOLI)
n.

hagamadua. (BE- MADUA)
Act like a grown-up (when still a child). *v.*

hagamadumadua. (RE- MADUA)
To act as though very old. *v.*

hagamataia. (BE- MATAIA)
v.

hagamataianga. (BE1 MATAIA)
n.

hagamatili. (EF- DILI)
v.

hagamatilianga. (EF1 DILI)
n.

hagamae. (BE- MAE)
v.

hagamaege. (BF- EGE)
v.

hagamaegea. (BF2 EGE)
v.

hagamaegeege. (RF- EGE)
v.

hagamaegeegea. (RF2 EGE)
v.

hagamaegeegelia. (RF2 EGE)
v.

hagamaegeegenga. (RF1 EGE)
n.

hagamaegelia. (BF2 EGE)
v.

hagamaegenga. (BF1 EGE)
n.

hagamaemae. (RE- MAE)
v.

hagamaemaenga. (RE1 MAE)
n.

hagamaenga. (BE1 MAE)
n.

hagamaeva. (BE- MAEVA)
v.

hagamaevaanga. (BE1 MAEVA)
n.

hagamaevaeva. (RE- MAEVA)
v.

hagamaevaevaanga. (RE1 MAEVA)
n.

hagamaga₁. (BE- MAGA₁)
v.

hagamaga₂. (BE- MAGA₂)
v.

hagamagaa. (BE2 MAGA₁)
v.

hagamagaalili. (PE- MAGALILI)
v.

hagamagaalilianga.
(PE1 MAGALILI) *n.*

hagamagakaga. (RE- MAKAGA)
v.

hagamagakagaanga.
(RE1 MAKAGA) *n.*

hagamagakagalia. (RE2 MAKAGA)
v.

hagamagalili. (BE- MAGALILI)
v.

hagamagalilianga.
(BE1 MAGALILI) *n.*

hagamagalillili. (SE- MAGALILI)
v.

hagamagalilllilianga.
(SE1 MAGALILI) *n.*

hagamagamaga. (RE- MAGA₁)
v.

hagamagamagaanga.
(RE1 MAGA₁) *n.*

hagamagamagalili.
(RE- MAGALILI) *v.*

hagamagamagalilianga.
(RE1 MAGALILI) *n.*

hagamagano. (BF- GANO)
v.

hagamaganoanga. (BF1 GANO)
n.

hagamagau. (BE- MAGAU)
—; commit or attempt suicide. *v.*

hagamagaua. (BE2 MAGAU)
v.

hagamagaugau. (RE- MAGAU)
v.

hagamagaugaua. (RE2 MAGAU)
v.

hagamagaugaulia. (RE2 MAGAU)
v.

hagamagaugaunga. (RE1 MAGAU)
n.

hagamagaulia. (BE2 MAGAU)
v.

hagamagaunga. (BE1 MAGAU)
n.

hagamagi. (BE- MAGI)
v.

hagamagiaa. (BE- MAGIAA)
v.

hagamagiaanga. (BE1 MAGIAA)
n.

hagamagianga. (BE1 MAGI)
n.

hagamagilia. (BE2 MAGI)
v.

hagamagimagi. (RE- MAGI)
v.

hagamagimagiaa. (RE- MAGIAA)
v.

hagamagimagiaanga.
(RE1 MAGIAA) *n.*

hagamagimagianga. (RE1 MAGI)
n.

hagamagimagilia. (RE2 MAGI)
v.

hagamagini. (BF- GINI)
v.

hagamaginianga. (BF1 GINI)
n.

hagamaginigini. (RF- GINI)
v.

hagamaginiginianga. (RF1 GINI)
n.

hagamago. (BE- MAGO)
v.

hagamagomago. (RE- MAGO)
v.

hagamagona. (BF- $GONA_1$)
v.

hagamagonaanga. (BF1 $GONA_1$)
n.

hagamagua. (BE- MAGUA)
To cause someone to steal. *v.*

hagamaguaanga. (BE1 MAGUA)
n.

hagamagulu. (BE- MAGULU)
—; reluctant to do or initiate (through fear of failure). *v.*

hagamagulugulu. (RE- MAGULU)
v.

hagamakaga. (BE- MAKAGA)
—; to persist in maintaining the truth of a falsehood. *v.*

hagamakagaanga. (BE1 MAKAGA)
n.

hagamakagalia. (BE2 MAKAGA)
v.

hagamahaa. (BF- HAA_1)
v.

hagamahaahaa. (RF- HAA_1)
v.

hagamahaahaanga. (RF1 HAA_1)
n.

hagamahaanga. (BF1 HAA_1)
n.

hagamahagi. (BF- HAGI)
v.

hagamahagia. (BF2 HAGI)
v.

hagamahagihagi. (RF- HAGI)
v.

hagamahagihagia. (RF2 HAGI)
v.

hagamahagihagina. (RF2 HAGI)
v.

hagamahagihaginga. (RF1 HAGI)
n.

hagamahagina. (BF2 HAGI)
v.

hagamahaginga. (BF1 HAGI)
n.

hagamahamaha. (RE- MAHA)
—; keep silent, pray. *v.*

hagamahamahaanga. (RE1 MAHA)
n.

hagamahamahalia. (RE2 MAHA)
v.

hagamahanga. (BF- HANGA)
v.

hagamahangahanga. (RF- HANGA)
v.

hagamahedu. (BF- HEDU)
v.

hagamahedua. (BF2 HEDU)
v.

hagamaheduhedu. (RF- HEDU)
v.

hagamaheduhedua. (RF2 HEDU)
v.

hagamaheduhedunga. (RF1 HEDU)
n.

hagamahedunga. (BF1 HEDU)
n.

hagamahidi. (BF- HIDI)
v.

hagamahidia. (BF2 HIDI)
v.

hagamahidihidi. (RF- HIDI)
v.

hagamahidihidia. (RF2 HIDI)
v.

hagamahidihidinga. (RF1 HIDI)
n.

hagamahiidinga. (BF1 HIDI)
n.

hagamahimahi. (RE- MAHI)
v.

hagamahimahianga. (RE1 MAHI)
n.

hagamahola. (BF- HOLA)
v.

hagamaholaanga. (BF1 HOLA)
n.

hagamaholadage. (BF- $HOLA_a$)
v.

hagamaholadageanga.
(BF1 $HOLA_a$) *n.*

hagamaholahola. (RF- HOLA)
v.

hagamaholaholaanga. (RF1 HOLA)
n.

hagamaholaholadage. (RF- $HOLA_a$)
n.

hagamaholaholasia. (RF2 HOLA)
v.

hagamaholasia. (BF2 HOLA)
v.

hagamahole. (BF- HOLE)
v.

hagamaholea. (BF2 HOLE)
v.

hagamaholehole. (RF- HOLE)
v.

hagamaholeholea. (RF2 HOLE)
v.

hagamaholehlenga. (BF1 HOLE)
n.

hagamaholenga. (BF1 HOLE)
n.

hagamahu. (BE- MAHU)
v.

hagamahuanga. (BE1 MAHU)
n.

hagamahuda. (BF- HUDA)
v.

hagamahudaanga. (BF1 HUDA)
n.

hagamahuge. (BF- HUGE)
v.

hagamahugea. (BF2 HUGE)
v.

hagamahugeanga. (BF1 HUGE)
n.

hagamahugehuge. (RF- HUGE)
v.

hagamahugehugea. (RF2 HUGE)
v.

hagamahugehugeanga.
(RF1 HUGE) *n.*

hagamahugehugelia. (RF2 HUGE)
v.

hagamahugelia. (BF2 HUGE)
v.

hagamahule. (BF- HULE)
v.

hagamahulea. (BF2 HULE)
v.

hagamahulehule. (RF- HULE)
v.

hagamahulehulea. (RF2 HULE)
v.

hagamahulehulenga. (RF1 HULE)
n.

hagamahulenga. (BF1 HULE)
n.

hagamahulia. (BE2 MAHU)
v.

hagamahumahu. (RE- MAHU)
v.

hagamahumahuanga. (RE1 MAHU)
n.

hagamahumahulia. (RE2 MAHU)
v.

hagamahumahunga. (RE1 MAHU)
n.

hagamaiana.
[Var. of *haigamaiana*]. *a.*

hagamaili. (BF- ILI)
v.

hagamailia. (BF2 ILI)
v.

hagamailiili. (RF- ILI)
v.

hagamailiilia. (RF2 ILI)
v.

hagamailiilinga. (RF1 ILI)
n.

hagamailinga. (BF1 ILI)
n.

hagamaimai. (RE- MAI_2)
Sweeten. *v.*

hagamaimaia. (RE2 MAI_2)
v.

hagamaimainga. (RE1 MAI_2)
n.

hagamaimaingaa. (RE- MAINGAA)
v.

hagamaimaingaanga.
(RE1 MAINGAA) *n.*

hagamainu. (BE- MAINU)
Provide with bait. *v.*

hagamaingaa. (BE- MAINGAA)
Cause one to feel *maingaa.* *v.*

hagamaingaanga. (BE1 MAINGAA)
n.

hagamaisi. (BF- ISI_1)
v.

hagamaisia. (BF2 ISI_1)
v.

hagamaisihia. (BF2 ISI_1)
v.

hagamaisiisi. (RF- ISI_1)
v.

hagamaisiisia. (RF2 ISI_1)
v.

hagamaisiisihia. (RF2 ISI_1)
v.

hagamaisiisinga. (RF1 ISI_1)
n.

hagamaisinga. (BF1 ISI_1)
n.

hagamalaelae. (RF- LAE)
v.

hagamalaelaea. (RF2 LAE)
v.

hagamalaelaenga. (RF1 LAE)
n.

hagamalaia. (BE- MALAIA)
v.

hagamalaiaanga. (BE1 MALAIA)
n.

hagamalali. (BE- MALALI)
v.

hagamalalianga. (BE1 MALALI)
n.

hagamalalidage. (BE- $MALALI_a$)
v.

hagamalalidageanga.
(BE1 $MALALI_a$) *n.*

hagamalamalali. (RE- MALALI)
v.

hagamalamalalianga.
(RE1 MALALI) *n.*

hagamalamalama.
(RE- MAALAMA) Shine. *v.*

hagamalamalau. (RE- $MALAU_1$)
v.

hagamalamalauanga.
(RE1 $MALAU_1$) *n.*

hagamalamalaunga. (RE1 $MALAU_1$)
n.

hagamalanga. (BF- LANGA)
v.

hagamalangalanga. (RF- LANGA)
v.

hagamalangilangi.
(BE- MALANGILANGI)
Please (someone), cheer up (someone); cheerful by nature, joyous. *v.*

hagamalau. (BE- $MALAU_1$)
v.

hagamalauanga. (BE1 $MALAU_1$)
n.

hagamalaunga. (BE1 $MALAU_1$)
n.

hagamalele. (BF- LELE)
Complete (something); kill (someone). *v.*

hagamaleleanga. (BF1 LELE)
n.

hagamalemalemo. (RE- MALEMO)
To swim with one's nose barely out of the water (as do small children). *v.*

hagamalemalemoanga.
(RE1 MALEMO) *n.*

hagamalemo. (BE- MALEMO)
v.

hagamalemoanga. (BE1 MALEMO)
n.

hagamalemolemo. (RE- MALEMO)
[Var. of *hagamalemalemo*]. *v.*

hagamalemolemoanga.
(RE1 MALEMO)
[Var. of *hagamalemalemoanga*]. *n.*

hagamalena. (BF- LENA)
v.

hagamalenaanga. (BF1 LENA)
n.

hagamalenalena. (RF- LENA)
v.

hagamalenalenaanga. (RF1 LENA)
n.

hagamaleva. (BE- MALEVA)
v.

hagamalibi. (BF- LIBI)
Rush, speed up. *v.*

hagamalibia. (BF2 LIBI)
v.

hagamalibilibi. (RF- LIBI)
v.

hagamalibilibia. (RF2 LIBI)
v.

hagamalibilibinga. (RF1 LIBI)
n.

hagamalibinga. (BF1 LIBI)
n.

hagamalili. (BE- $MALILI_1$)
v.

hagamalilianga. (BE1 $MALILI_1$)
n.

hagamalillili. (RE- $MALILI_1$)
v.

hagamalillilianga. (RE1 $MALILI_1$)
n.

hagamalimalino. (RE- MALINO)
v.

hagamalimalinoanga.
(RE1 MALINO) *n.*

hagamalimalinongia.
(RE2 MALINO) *v.*

hagamalino. (BE- MALINO)
—; smooth seas. *v.*

hagamalinoanga. (BE1 MALINO)
n.

hagamalinolino. (SE- MALINO)
v.

hagamalinolinoanga.
(SE1 MALINO) *n.*

hagamalinolinongia.
(SE2 MALINO) *v.*

hagamalinongia. (BE2 MALINO)
v.

hagamalingi. (BF- LINGI)
v.

hagamalingia. (BF2 LINGI)
v.

hagamalingilingi. (RF- LINGI)
v.

hagamalingilingia. (RF2 LINGI)
v.

hagamalingilinginga. (RF1 LINGI)
n.

hagamalinginga. (BF1 LINGI)
n.

hagamalo. (BE- MALO)
Provide clothes for. *v.*

hagamalogu. (BE- MALOGU)
v.

hagamalogulogu. (RE- MALOGU)
v.

hagamalogulogunga.
(RE1 MALOGU) *n.*

hagamalogunga. (BE1 MALOGU)
n.

hagamalu. (BE- MALU)
v.

hagamalui. (BF- LUI_1)
v.

hagamaluia. (BF2 LUI_1)
v.

hagamaluilui. (RF- LUI_1)
v.

hagamaluiluia. (RF2 LUI_1)
v.

hagamaluiluinga. (RF1 LUI_1)
n.

hagamaluinga. (BF1 LUI_1)
n.

hagamalumalu. (RE- MALU)
v.

hagamaluu. (BE- MALUU)
v.

hagamaluulu. (BE- MALUULU)
— ; to water (plants). *v.*

hagamaluulunga.
(BE1 MALUULU) *n.*

hagamaluunga. (BE1 MALUU)
n.

hagamamaeva. (SE- MAEVA)
v.

hagamamaevaanga. (SE1 MAEVA)
n.

hagamami. (BE- MAMI)
—; add flavor to. *v.*

hagamamia. (BE2 MAMI)
v.

hagamaminga. (BE1 MAMI)
n.

hagamammami. (RE- MAMI)
v.

hagamammamianga. (RE1 MAMI)
n.

hagamanadua. (BE2 MAANADU)
v.

hagamanamanadua.
(RE2 MAANADU) *v.*

hagamanamanava. (RE- MANAVA)
v.

hagamanamanavaanga.
(RE1 MANAVA) *n.*

hagamanaunau*.
(BE- MANAUNAU) *v.*

hagamanaunaua*.
(BE2 MANAUNAU) *v.*

hagamanaunaunga*.
(BE1 MANAUNAU) *n.*

hagamanava. (BE- MANAVA)
v.

hagamanavaanga. (BE1 MANAVA)
n.

hagamanavanava. (SE- MANAVA)
v.

hagamanavanavaanga.
(SE1 MANAVA) *n.*

hagamanavasaa. (BE- $MANAVA_a$)
Risky, dangerous. *a.*

hagamanavasaanga.
(BE1 $MANAVA_a$) *n.*

hagamanege. (BF- NEGE)
—; disobedient, stubborn, talk back to. *v.*

hagamanegea. (BF2 NEGE)
v.

hagamanegeanga. (BF1 NEGE)
n.

hagamanegelia. (BF2 NEGE)
v.

hagamanegenege. (RF- NEGE)
v.

hagamanegenegea. (RF2 NEGE)
v.

hagamanegenegelia. (RF2 NEGE)
v.

hagamanegenegenga. (RF1 NEGE)
n.

hagamanida. (BE- MANIDA)
Lift (something) up. *v.*

hagamanidaanga. (BE1 MANIDA)
n.

hagamanigangi. (BE- MANIGANGI)
v.

hagamanigangianga.
(BE1 MANIGANGI) *n.*

hagamanihaniha. (RE- MAANIHA)
v.

hagamanihanihaanga.
(RE1 MAANIHA) *n.*

hagamano. (BE- MANO)
Make a total of one thousand. *v.*

hagamanomano. (RE- MANO)
Make many thousands. *v.*

hagamanongi. (BE- MANONGI)
v.

hagamanu. (BE- MANU)
Cause to have disease. *v.*

hagamanua. (BE2 MANU)
v.

hagamanugia. (BE- MANUGIA)
v.

hagamanugiaanga.
(BE1 MANUGIA) *n.*

hagamanuhi. (BE- MANUHI)
v.

hagamanuhianga. (BE1 MANUHI)
n.

hagamanuia. (BE- MANUIA)
—; bless (someone). *v.*

hagamanuiaanga. (BE1 MANUIA)
n.

hagamanumanu. (RE- MANU)
v.

hagamanumanua. (RE2 MANU)
v.

hagamanumanugia.
(RE- MANUGIA) *v.*

hagamanumanugiaanga.
(RE1 MANUGIA) *n.*

hagamanumanuhi.
(RE- MANUHI) *v.*

hagamanumanuhianga.
(RE1 MANUHI) *n.*

hagamangamanga. (RE- MANGA)
—; to move with the extremities spread out (as in trying to scare a child). *v.*

hagamangamangalia.
(RE2 MANGA) *v.*

hagamangemangeo.
(RE- MANGEO) *v.*

hagamangeo. (BE- MANGEO)
v.

hagamangunngungu.
(RF- NGUNGU) *v.*

hagamangunngunguanga.
(RF1 NGUNGU) *n.*

hagamanguangungulia.
(RF2 NGUNGU) *v.*

hagamao --. (BE- MAO)
d.

hagamaoa. (BE2 MAO)
v.

hagamaoha. (BF- OHA)
v.

hagamaohanga. (BF1 OHA)
n.

hagamaohaoha. (RF- OHA)
v.

hagamaohaohanga. (RF1 OHA)
n.

hagamao lalo.
Humble, modest.

hagamao lunga.
Arrogant, haughty, overbearing, proud.

hagamaomao. (RE- MAO)
v.

hagamaomaoa. (RE2 MAO)
v.

hagamaomaonga. (RE1 MAO)
n.

hagamaonga. (BE1 MAO)
n.

hagamasaagage. (PE- MASAGAGE)
v.

hagamasaagageanga.
(PE1 MASAGAGE) *n.*

hagamasaala. (BE- MASAALA)
v.

hagamasaalanga. (BE1 MASAALA)
n.

hagamasae. (BF- SAE_1)
v.

hagamasaea. (BF2 SAE_1)
v.

hagamasaenga. (BF1 SAE_1)
n.

hagamasaesae. (RF- SAE_1)
v.

hagamasaesaea. (RF2 SAE_1)
v.

hagamasaesaenga. (RF1 SAE_1)
n.

hagamasagage. (BE- MASAGAGE)
v.

hagamasagageanga.
(BE1 MASAGAGE) *n.*

hagamasaia. (BE2 MASA)
v.

hagamasaiaanga. (BE3 MASA)
n.

hagamasalaba. (BE- MASALABA)
v.

hagamasalia. (BE2 MASA)

hagamasamasa. (RE- MASA)
v.

hagamasamasaiaanga. (RE3 MASA)
n.

hagamasamasalia. (RE2 MASA)
v.

hagamasana. (BE- MASANA)
v.

hagamasanaanga. (BE1 MASANA)
n.

hagamasausau. (BE- MASAUSAU)
v.

hagamasausaua. (BE2 MASAUSAU)
v.

hagamasausaunga.
(BE1 MASAUSAU) *n.*

hagamasavavvava. (RE- $VAVA_a$)
v.

hagamasavavvavaanga.
(RE1 $VAVA_a$) *n.*

hagamaselesele. (RF- $SELE_2$)
v.

hagamaseleselea. (RF2 $SELE_2$)
v.

hagamaseleselenga. (RF1 $SELE_2$)
n.

hagamaseu. (BF- SEU)
v.

hagamaseua. (BF2 SEU)
v.

hagamaseunga. (BF1 SEU)
n.

hagamasi. (BE- $MASI_1$)
v.

hagamasia. (BE2 $MASI_1$)
v.

hagamasimasi₁. (RE- $MASI_1$)
v.

hagamasimasi₂. (RE- $MASI_2$)
v.

hagamasimasia. (RE2 $MASI_1$)
v.

hagamasimasinga₁. (RE1 $MASI_1$)
n.

hagamasimasinga₂. (RE1 $MASI_2$)
n.

hagamasoasoa. (BE- MASOASOA)
v.

hagamasoasoaanga.
(BE1 MASOASOA) *n.*

hagamasole. (BE- MASOLE)
v.

hagamasoleanga. (BE1 MASOLE)
n.

hagamasolesole. (RE- MASOLE)
v.

hagamasolesoleanga.
(RE1 MASOLE) *n.*

hagamassaa. (BE- MASSAA)
v.

hagamasagaila.
(BE- MASSAGAILA) *v.*

hagamassagailaanga.
(BE1 MASSAGAILA) *n.*

hagamassagalala.
(BE- MASSAGALALA) *v.*

hagamassagalalaanga.
(BE1 MASSAGALALA) *n.*

hagamassagalalaanga.
(BE1 MASSAGALALA) *n.*

hagamassaganga. (BE- $MASA_a$)
v.

hagamassanganga. (BF1 SANGA)
v.

hagamassogosogo.
(BE- $SOGOSOGO_a$) *v.*

hagamassogosogoanga. (BE1 $SOGOSOGO_a$) *n.*

hagamassogosogolia. (BE2 $SOGOSOGO_a$) *v.*

hagamasugi. (BF- $SUGI_1$) *v.*

hagamasugia. (BF2 $SUGI_1$) *v.*

hagamasuginga. (BF1 $SUGI_1$) *n.*

hagamasugisugi. (RF- $SUGI_1$) *v.*

hagamasugisugia. (RF2 $SUGI_1$) *v.*

hagamasugisuginga. (RF1 $SUGI_1$) *n.*

$hagamau_1$. (BE- MAU_1) *v.*

$hagamau_2$. (BE- MAU_2) To strive to become acquainted with. *v.*

$hagamau_3$. (BE- MAU_3) —; tie up (by winding rope around a pole). *v.*

$hagamaua_1$. (BE2 MAU_1) *v.*

$hagamaua_2$. (BE2 MAU_2) *v.*

$hagamaua_3$. (BE2 MAU_3) *v.*

$hagamaulia_1$. (BE2 MAU_1) *v.*

$hagamaulia_2$. (BE2 MAU_2) *v.*

$hagamaumau_1$. (RE- MAU_1) *v.*

$hagamaumau_2$. (RE- MAU_2) Study, attempt to memorize. *v.*

$hagamaumau_3$. (RE- MAU_3) *v.*

$hagamaumaua_1$. (RE2 MAU_1) *v.*

$hagamaumaua_2$. (RE2 MAU_2) *v.*

$hagamaumaua_3$. (RE2 MAU_3) *v.*

$hagamaumaulia_1$. (RE2 MAU_1) *v.*

$hagamaumaulia_2$. (RE2 MAU_2) *v.*

$hagamaumaunga_1$. (RE1 MAU_1) *n.*

$hagamaumaunga_2$. (RE1 MAU_2) *n.*

$hagamaumaunga_3$. (RE1 MAU_3) *n.*

hagamaunusi. (BF- UNUSI) *v.*

hagamaunusia. (BF2 UNUSI) *v.*

hagamaunusinga. (BF1 UNUSI) *n.*

hagamaunuunusi. (RF- UNUSI) *v.*

hagamaunuunusia. (RF2 UNUSI) *v.*

hagamaunuunusinga. (RF1 UNUSI) *n.*

$hagamaunga_1$. (BE1 MAU_1) *n.*

$hagamaunga_2$. (BE1 MAU_2) *n.*

$hagamaunga_3$. (BE1 MAU_3) *n.*

hagamavaevae. (RF- VAE_1) *v.*

hagamavaevaea. (RF2 VAE_1) *v.*

hagamavaevaelia. (RF2 VAE_1) *v.*

hagamavaevaenga. (RF1 VAE_1) *n.*

hagame (ange). (BE- ME) Move a little way toward —. *a.*

hagameamea. (RE- MEA) *v.*

hagameameaanga. (RE1 MEA) *n.*

hagameanga. (BE1 ME)
n.

hagame ange laa.
A little later.

hagameelenga. (BE1 $MELE_1$)
n.

hagamele. (BE- $MELE_1$)
[Var. of *haigamaiana*]. *v.*

hagamelea. (BE2 $MELE_1$)
v.

hagamelemele. (RE- $MELE_1$)
v.

hagamelemelea. (RE2 $MELE_1$)
v.

hagamelemelenga. (RE1 $MELE_1$)
n.

hagameme (iho). (RE- ME)
Gradually decreasing (in noise level, force of wind, etc.). *a.*

hagamemeanga. (RE1 ME)
n.

hagamenemene. (RE- MENE)
v.

hagamenemeneanga. (RE1 MENE)
n.

hagamenemenelia. (RE2 MENE)
v.

hagamenemenengia. (RE2 MENE)
v.

hagamidi. (BE- $MIDI_1$)
—; appear in a dream. *v.*

hagamidia. (BE2 $MIDI_1$)
v.

$hagamidimidi_1$. (RE- $MIDI_1$)
v.

$hagamidimidi_2$. (RE- $MIDI_2$)
Having a strong undertow. *v.*

$hagamidimidia_1$. (RE2 $MIDI_1$)
v.

$hagamidimidia_2$. (RE2 $MIDI_2$)
v.

$hagamidimidinga_1$. (RE1 $MIDI_1$)
n.

$hagamidimidinga_2$. (RE1 $MIDI_2$)
n.

hagamiidia. (BE2 $MIDI_2$)
v.

$hagamiidinga_1$. (BE1 $MIDI_1$)
n.

$hagamiidinga_2$. (BE1 $MIDI_2$)
n.

hagamiili. (BE- MIILI)
v.

hagamiilia. (BE2 $MILI_1$)
v.

hagamiilinga. (BE1 MIILI)
n.

$hagamiilinga_1$. (BE1 $MILI_1$)
n.

$hagamiilinga_2$. (BE1 $MILI_2$)
n.

hagamiilonga. (BE1 $MILO_1$)
n.

hagamiisinga. (BE1 MISI)
n.

$hagamili_1$. (BE- $MILI_1$)
v.

$hagamili_2$. (BE- $MILI_2$)
v.

hagamilia. (BE2 $MILI_2$)
v.

$hagamilimili_1$. (RE- $MILI_1$)
v.

$hagamilimili_2$. (RE- $MILI_2$)
v.

$hagamilimilia_1$. (RE2 $MILI_1$)
v.

$hagamilimilia_2$. (RE2 $MILI_2$)
v.

$hagamilimilinga_1$. (RE1 $MILI_1$)
n.

$hagamilimilinga_2$. (RE1 $MILI_2$)
n.

hagamilo. (BE- $MILO_1$)
v.

hagamiloa. (BE2 $MILO_1$)
v.

hagamilomilo. (RE- $MILO_1$)
v.

hagamilomiloa. (RE2 MILO$_1$)
v.

hagamilomilonga. (RE1 MILO$_1$)
n.

hagamilomilosanga. (RE1 MILO$_1$)
n.

hagamilomilosia. (RE2 MILO$_1$)
—; to be carried away by a current repeatedly or continually. *v.*

hagamilosanga. (BE1 MILO$_1$)
n.

hagamilosia. (BE2 MILO$_1$)
—; to be carried away by a current. *v.*

hagamimi. (BE- MIMI)
v.

hagamimia. (BE2 MIMI)
v.

hagamimianga. (BE1 MIMI)
n.

hagamimmimi. (RE- MIMI)
v.

hagamimmimia. (RE2 MIMI)
v.

hagamimmimianga. (RE1 MIMI)
n.

hagamisi. (BE- MISI)
v.

hagamisia. (BE2 MISI)
v.

hagamisimisi. (RE- MISI)
v.

hagamisimisia. (RE2 MISI)
v.

hagamisimisinga. (RE1 MISI)
n.

hagammaasinga. (EE1 MASI$_2$)
n.

hagammabu. (PE- MABU)
v.

hagammabua. (PE2 MABU)
v.

hagammabulia. (BE2 MABU)
v.

hagammade. (PE- MADE$_2$)
v.

hagammadelia. (PE2 MADE$_2$)
v.

hagammadenga. (PE1 MADE$_2$)
n.

hagammae. (EE- MAE)
v.

hagammae lodo.
Insult (someone).

hagammae manava.
Tease cruelly.

hagammaenga. (EE1 MAE)
n.

hagammaga. (PE- MAGA$_2$)
v.

hagammagi. (PE- MAGI)
v.

hagammagianga. (PE1 MAGI)
n.

hagammagilia. (PE2 MAGI)
v.

hagammahi. (EE- MAHI)
Persevere, try hard to. *v.*

hagammahianga. (EE1 MAHI)
n.

hagammahu. (PE- MAHU)
v.

hagammahuanga. (PE1 MAHU)
n.

hagammahulia. (PE2 MAHU)
v.

hagammala. (BE- MMALA)
v.

hagammalaanga. (BE1 MMALA)
n.

hagammano. (PE- MANO)
v.

hagammanu. (EE- MANU)
v.

hagammao. (EE- MAO)
v.

hagammaoa. (EE2 MAO)
v.

hagammaonga. (EE1 MAO)
n.

hagammasa. (EE- MASA)
—; dry (something). *v.*

hagammasaanga. (EE1 MASA)
n.

hagammasalia. (EE2 MASA)
v.

hagammasi. (EE- MASI$_2$)
v.

hagammau$_1$. (PE- MAU$_1$)
v.

hagammau$_2$. (EE- MAU$_2$)
Memorize. *v.*

hagammau$_3$. (BE- MMAU)
Poisonous. a.

hagammaua$_1$. (PE2 MAU$_1$)
v.

hagammaua$_2$. (EE2 MAU$_2$)
v.

hagammauanga. (BE1 MMAU)
n.

hagammau de ngudu.
Argumentative in a disrespectful way.

hagammaulia$_1$. (PE2 MAU$_1$)
v.

hagammaulia$_2$. (EE2 MAU$_2$)
v.

hagammaunga$_1$. (PE1 MAU$_1$)
n.

hagammaunga$_2$. (EE1 MAU$_2$)
n.

hagammea. (EE- MEA)
v.

hagammeaanga. (EE1 MEA)
n.

hagammele. (PE- MELE$_1$)
v.

hagammene. (EE- MENE)
v.

hagammeneanga. (EE1 MENE)
n.

hagammene dua.
Go backwards (esp. a canoe).

hagammenelia. (EE2 MENE)
v.

hagammenengia. (EE2 MENE)
v.

hagammidi. (EE- MIDI$_2$)
Suction of a sea current, undertow. *v.*

hagammiilia. (PE2 MILI$_2$)
v.

hagammiilinga. (PE1 MILI$_2$)
n.

hagammiilonga. (PE1 MILO$_1$)
n.

hagammili$_1$. (EE- MILI$_1$)
v.

hagammili$_2$. (PE- MILI$_2$)
v.

hagammilo. (PE- MILO$_1$)
v.

hagammilosanga. (PE1 MILO$_1$)
n.

hagammoa. (EE- MOO$_b$)
v.

hagammoaanga. (EE1 MOO$_b$)
n.

hagammodo. (PE- MODO)
v.

hagammodoanga. (PE1 MODO)
n.

hagammodolia. (PE2 MODO)
v.

hagammoe. (PE- MOE$_2$)
v.

hagammoea$_1$. (PE2 MOE$_1$)
v.

hagammoea$_2$. (PE2 MOE$_2$)
v.

hagammoenga$_1$. (PE1 MOE$_1$)
n.

hagammoenga$_2$. (PE1 MOE$_2$)
n.

hagammogo. (EE- MOGO$_4$)
v.

hagammogoa. (EE2 MOGO$_4$)
v.

hagammogoanga. (EE1 $MOGO_4$)
n.

hagammogolia. (EE2 $MOGO_4$)
v.

hagammoli. (PE- MOLI)
v.

hagammudi. (EE- MMUDI)
v.

hagammudia. (EE2 MMUDI)
v.

hagammuga. (PE- $MUGA_1$)
v.

hagammugaanga. (PE1 $MUGA_1$)
n.

hagammule. (EE- MULE)
v.

hagammulea. (EE2 MULE)
v.

hagammuleanga. (EE1 MULE)
n.

hagammulo. (PE- MULO)
v.

hagammuni. (BE- MMUNI)
Hide (something) from. *v.*

hagammuni iho.
Keep to oneself (what one has done).

hagammusa. (PE- MUSA)
v.

hagammusaanga. (PE1 MUSA)
n.

hagammusalia. (PE2 MUSA)
v.

hagammusu. (PE- MUSU)
v.

hagammuu. (PE- MUU_1)
v.

hagammuua. (PE2 MUU_1)
v.

hagammuudinga. (EE1 MMUDI)
n.

hagammuulia. (PE2 MUU_1)
v.

hagammuuloa. (PE2 MULO)
v.

hagammuulonga. (PE1 MULO)
n.

hagammuunga. (PE1 MUU_1)
n.

hagammuusua. (PE2 MUSU)
v.

hagamodimodi. (RE- MODI)
v.

hagamodimodinga. (RE1 MODI)
n.

hagamodo. (BE- MODO)
v.

hagamodolia. (BE2 MODO)
v.

hagamodomodo. (RE- MODO)
v.

hagamodomodoanga. (RE1 MODO)
n.

hagamodomodolia. (RE2 MODO)
v.

hagamodu. (BE- MODU)
—; decide formally; render a final decision. *v.*

hagamodua. (BE2 MODU)
v.

hagamodulia. (BE2 MODU)
v.

hagamodumodu. (RE- MODU)
v.

hagamodumodua. (RE2 MODU)
v.

hagamodumodulia. (RE2 MODU)
v.

hagamodumodunga. (RE1 MODU)
n.

hagamoe$_1$. (BE- MOE_1)
Put to bed. *v.*

hagamoe$_2$. (BE- MOE_2)
v.

hagamoea$_1$. (BE2 MOE_1)
v.

hagamoea$_2$. (BE2 MOE_2)
v.

hagamoeagi. (BE- MOE_{1a})
v.

hagamoeagina. (BE2 MOE$_{1a}$)
v.

hagamoeaginga. (BE1 MOE$_{1a}$)
n.

hagamoebili. (BE- MOE$_{1b}$)
a.

hagamoebilianga. (BE1 MOE$_{1b}$)
n.

hagamoemoe$_1$. (RE- MOE$_1$)
v.

hagamoemoe$_2$. (RE- MOE$_2$)
v.

hagamoemoea$_1$. (RE2 MOE$_1$)
v.

hagamoemoea$_2$. (RE2 MOE$_2$)
v.

hagamoemoeagi. (RE- MOE$_{1a}$)
v.

hagamoemoeagina. (RE2 MOE$_{1a}$)
v.

hagamoemoeaginga. (RE1 MOE$_{1a}$)
n.

hagamoemoenga$_1$. (RE1 MOE$_1$)
n.

hagamoemoenga$_2$. (RE1 MOE$_2$)
n.

hagamoenga$_1$. (BE1 MOE$_1$)
n.

hagamoenga$_2$. (BE1 MOE$_2$)
n.

hagamogomogo$_1$. (RE- MOGO$_1$)
Take special care of, cherish. *v.*

hagamogomogo$_2$. (RE- MOGO$_2$)
Cause to be muscular. *v.*

hagamogomogoa. (RE2 MOGO$_1$)
v.

hagamogomogoanga$_1$.
(RE1 MOGO$_1$) *n.*

hagamogomogoanga$_2$.
(RE1 MOGO$_2$) *n.*

hagamogomogolia. (RE2 MOGO$_1$)
v.

hagamoli --. (BE- MOLI)
d.

hagamolimoli. (RE- MOLI)
v.

hagamolimolia. (RE2 MOLI)
v.

hagamolimolinga. (RE1 MOLI)
n.

hagamolo. (BE- MOLO$_1$)
v.

hagamoloa. (BE2 MOLO$_1$)
v.

hagamolomolo$_1$. (RE- MOLO$_1$)
v.

hagamolomolo$_2$. (RE- MOLO$_2$)
v.

hagamolomoloa. (RE2 MOLO$_1$)
v.

hagamolomoloanga. (RE1 MOLO$_2$)
n.

hagamolomolonga. (RE1 MOLO$_1$)
n.

hagamommomo. (RE- MOMO)
Reduce a little at a time. *v.*

hagamomo. (BE- MOMO)
Reduce in quantity. *v.*

hagamomoanga. (BE1 MOMO)
n.

hagamomogo. (TE- MOGO$_1$)
v.

hagamomogoanga. (TE1 MOGO$_1$)
n.

hagamomolia. (BE2 MOMO)
v.

hagamoni. (BE- MONI)
Provide a canoe for. *v.*

hagamoodonga. (BE1 MODO)
n.

hagamoodunga. (BE1 MODU)
n.

hagamoolau. (BE- MOOLAU)
Hurry, rush. *v.*

hagamoolaua. (BE2 MOOLAU)
Cause to hurry. *v.*

hagamoolaunga. (BE1 MOOLAU)
n.

hagamoolia. (BE2 MOLI)
v.

hagamoolinga. (BE1 MOLI)
n.

hagamoolonga. (BE1 $MOLO_1$)
n.

hagamoomodu. (TE- MODU)
v.

hagamoomodua. (TE2 MODU)
v.

hagamoomodulia. (TE2 MODU)
v.

hagamoomodunga. (TE1 MODU)
n.

hagamoomoosee. (RE- MOO_d)
v.

hagamoomooseenga. (RE1 MOO_d)
n.

hagamoomoosugia. (RE- MOO_a)
v.

hagamoomoosugiaanga.
(RE1 MOO_a) *n.*

hagamoomuna. (BE- MOO_c)
v.

hagamoosee. (BE- MOO_d)
v.

hagamooseenga. (BE1 MOO_d)
n.

hagamoosugia. (BE- MOO_a)
v.

hagamoosugiaanga. (BE1 MOO_a)
n.

hagamosongenge.
(BE- MOSONGENGE) *v.*

hagamossogosogo.
(CE- $SOGOSOGO_a$) *v.*

hagamossogosogoanga.
(CE1 $SOGOSOGO_a$) *n.*

hagamossogosogolia.
(CE2 $SOGOSOGO_a$) *v.*

hagamou. (BE- MOU)
Include in a *mou*. *v.*

hagamouli. (BE- MOULI)
Give life to, bring back life; food (prepared for a meal). *v.*

hagamoulia. (BE2 MOULI)
v.

hagamoulinga. (BE1 MOULI)
n.

hagamoumou. (BE- MOUMOU)
v.

hagamoumoua. (BE2 MOUMOU)
v.

hagamoumoulia. (BE2 MOUMOU)
v.

hagamoumounga. (BE1 MOUMOU)
n.

hagamoumousia. (RE2 MOUSI)
v.

hagamoumousinga. (RE1 MOUSI)
n.

hagamounu. (BE- MOUNU)
—; separate oneself from. *v.*

hagamounuunga. (BE1 MOUNU)
n.

hagamounuunu. (RE- MOUNU)
v.

hagamounuununga. (RE1 MOUNU)
n.

hagamousi. (BE- MOUSI)
v.

hagamousia. (BE2 MOUSI)
v.

hagamousinga. (BE1 MOUSI)
n.

hagamua. (BE- MUA)
Be first; get closer to. *v.*

hagamuaanga. (BE1 MUA)
n.

hagamudimudi. (RE- MMUDI)
v.

hagamudimudia. (RE2 MMUDI)
v.

hagamudimudinga. (RE1 MMUDI)
n.

hagamudumudu. (RE- $MUDU_1$)
Do slowly, delay. *v.*

hagamudumudua. (RE2 $MUDU_1$)
v.

hagamudumuduanga. (RE1 MUDU$_1$) *n.*

hagamudumudulia. (RE2 MUDU$_1$) *v.*

hagamuga. (BE- MUGA$_1$) *v.*

hagamugaanga. (BE1 MUGA$_1$) *n.*

hagamugalia. (BE2 MUGA$_1$) *v.*

hagamugamuga. (RE- MUGA$_1$) *v.*

hagamugamugaanga. (RE1 MUGA$_1$) *n.*

hagamugamugalia. (RE2 MUGA$_1$) *v.*

hagamui. (BE- MUI) *v.*

hagamuia. (BE2 MUI) *v.*

hagamuimui. (RE- MUI) *v.*

hagamuimuia. (RE2 MUI) *v.*

hagamuimuinga. (RE1 MUI) *n.*

hagamuinga. (BE1 MUI) *n.*

hagamule --. (BE- MULE) *d.*

hagamulegi. (BE- MULEGI) *v.*

hagamulegianga. (BE1 MULEGI) *n.*

hagamulemule. (RE- MULE) *v.*

hagamulemuleanga. (RE1 MULE) *n.*

hagamuli$_1$. (BE- MULI$_1$) Be late, tarry. *v.*

hagamuli$_2$. (BE- MULI$_2$) *v.*

hagamulia. (BE2 MULI$_2$) *v.*

hagamuliagi. (BE- MULI$_{1b}$) Cause to be last. *v.*

hagamuliagina. (BE2 MULI$_{1b}$) *v.*

hagamuliaginga. (BE1 MULI$_{1b}$) *n.*

hagamulimuli$_1$. (RE- MULI$_1$) "This is the end" (of a chant). *v.*

hagamulimuli$_2$. (RE- MULI$_2$) *v.*

hagamulimulia. (RE2 MULI$_2$) *v.*

hagamulo. (BE- MULO) *v.*

hagamuloa. (BE2 MULO) *v.*

hagamulomulo. (RE- MULO) *v.*

hagamulomuloa. (RE2 MULO) *v.*

hagamulomulonga. (RE1 MULO) *n.*

hagamunamuna. (RE- MUNA) *v.*

hagamunimuni. (RE- MMUNI) *v.*

hagamunimunia. (RE2 MMUNI) *v.*

hagamunimuninga. (RE1 MMUNI) *n.*

hagamusa. (BE- MUSA) *v.*

hagamusalia. (BE2 MUSA) *v.*

hagamusamusa. (RE- MUSA) *v.*

hagamusamusaanga. (RE1 MUSA) *n.*

hagamusamusalia. (RE2 MUSA) *v.*

hagamusu. (BE- MUSU) *v.*

hagamusua. (BE2 MUSU) *v.*

hagamusumusu. (RE- MUSU)
v.

hagamusumusua. (RE2 MUSU)
v.

hagamusumusunga. (RE1 MUSU)
n.

hagamuu. (BE- MUU_1)
v.

hagamuua. (BE2 MUU_1)
v.

hagamuulia. (BE2 MUU_1)
v.

hagamuulonga. (BE1 MULO)
n.

hagamuumuu. (RE- MUU_1)
v.

hagamuumuua. (RE2 MUU_1)
v.

hagamuumuulia. (RE2 MUU_1)
v.

hagamuumuunga. (RE1 MUU_1)
n.

hagamuunia. (BE2 MMUNI)
v.

hagamuuninga. (BE1 MMUNI)
n.

hagamuunga. (BE1 MUU_1)
n.

hagamuusanga. (BE1 MUSA)
n.

hagamuusunga. (BE1 MUSU)
n.

haganaa. (BE- NAA_2)
To calm down someone who is excited or unhappy. *v.*

haganaabanga. (BE1 NABA)
n.

haganaabenga. (BE1 NABE)
n.

haganaadia. (BE2 NAA_2)
v.

haganaanga. (BE1 NAA_2)
n.

haganaba. (BE- NABA)
v.

haganabanaba. (RE- NABA)
v.

haganabanabaanga. (RE1 NABA)
n.

haganabe. (BE- NABE)
v.

haganabea. (BE2 NABE)
v.

haganabelia. (BE2 NABE)
v.

haganabenabe. (RE- NABE)
v.

haganabenabea. (RE2 NABE)
v.

haganabenabelia. (RE2 NABE)
v.

haganabenabenga. (RE1 NABE)
n.

haganagonago*. (RE- NAGO)
v.

haganagonagoa*. (RE2 NAGO)
v.

haganagonagolia*. (RE2 NAGO)
v.

haganagonagonga*. (RE1 NAGO)
n.

haganamuaa. (BE- NAMUAA)
v.

haganamuaanga. (BE1 NAMUAA)
n.

haganamunamu. (RE- NNAMU)
v.

haganamunamua. (RE2 NNAMU)
v.

haganamunamuanga.
(RE1 NNAMU) *n.*

haganamunamulia. (RE2 NNAMU)
v.

haganannadu. (RE- NNADU)
v.

haganannaduanga. (RE1 NNADU)
n.

hagaannadulia. (RE2 NNADU)
v.

haganannanu. (RE- NANU)
v.

haganannanua. (RE2 NANU)
v.

haganannanuanga. (RE1 NANU)
n.

haganannanulia. (RE2 NANU)
v.

haganannanumia. (RE2 NANU)
v.

hagananu. (BE- NANU)
v.

hagananua. (BE2 NANU)
v.

hagananuanga. (BE1 NANU)
n.

hagananulia. (BE2 NANU)
v.

hagananumia. (BE2 NANU)
v.

haganao. (BE- NAO)
v.

haganaoa. (BE2 NAO)
v.

haganaolia. (BE2 NAO)
v.

haganaonao. (RE- NAO)
v.

haganaonaoa. (RE2 NAO)
v.

haganaonaolia. (RE2 NAO)
v.

haganaonaonga. (RE1 NAO)
n.

haganaonga. (BE1 NAO)
n.

haganebu. (BE- NEBU)
v.

haganebua. (BE2 NEBU)
v.

haganebunebu. (RE- NEBU)
v.

haganebunebua. (RE2 NEBU)
v.

haganebunebunga. (RE1 NEBU)
n.

haganebunga. (BE1 NEBU)
n.

haganeegenga. (BE1 NEGE)
n.

haganeevenga. (BE1 NEVE)
n.

haganege. (BE- NEGE)
v.

haganegea. (BE2 NEGE)
v.

haganegelia. (BE2 NEGE)
v.

haganegenege. (RE- NEGE)
v.

haganegenegea. (RE2 NEGE)
v.

haganegenegelia. (RE2 NEGE)
v.

haganegenegenga. (RE1 NEGE)
n.

haganehu. (BE- NEHU)
v.

haganehua. (BE2 NEHU)
v.

haganehunehu. (RE- NEHU)
v.

haganehunehua. (RE2 NEHU)
v.

haganehunehunga. (RE1 NEHU)
n.

haganehunga. (BE1 NEHU)
n.

haganengenenge. (RE- NENGE)
v.

haganengenengea. (RE2 NENGE)
v.

haganengenengeanga.
(RE1 NENGE) *n.*

haganengenengelia. (RE2 NENGE)
v.

haganeve. (BE- NEVE)
v.

haganevea. (BE2 NEVE)
v.

haganeveia. (BE2 NEVE)
v.

haganeveinga. (BE1 NEVE)
n.

haganeveneve. (RE- NEVE)
v.

haganevenevea. (RE2 NEVE)
v.

haganeveneveia. (RE2 NEVE)
v.

haganeveneveinga. (RE1 NEVE)
n.

haganevenevenga. (RE1 NEVE)
n.

haganigo. (BE- NIGO)
v.

haganigoa. (BE2 NIGO)
v.

haganigolia. (BE2 NIGO)
v.

haganigonigo. (RE- NIGO)
v.

haganigonigoa. (RE2 NIGO)
v.

haganigonigoi. (RE- $NIGO_a$)
v.

haganigonigoia. (RE2 $NIGO_a$)
v.

haganigonigoinga. (RE1 $NIGO_a$)
n.

haganigonigolia. (RE2 NIGO)
v.

haganigonigonga. (RE1 NIGO)
n.

haganiigoi. (BE- $NIGO_a$)
v.

haganiigoia. (BE2 $NIGO_a$)
v.

haganiigoinga. (BE1 $NIGO_a$)
n.

haganiigonga. (BE1 NIGO)
n.

hagannaba. (PE- NABA)
v.

hagannadu. (BE- NNADU)
v.

hagannaduanga. (BE1 NNADU)
n.

hagannadulia. (BE2 NNADU)
v.

hagannagi. (BE- NNAGI)
Lean against. *v.*

hagannagia. (BE2 NNAGI)
v.

hagannaginga. (BE1 NNAGI)
n.

hagannamu. (BE- NNAMU)
v.

hagannamua. (BE2 NNAMU)
v.

hagannamu age.
Eat a little of.

hagannamuanga. (BE1 NNAMU)
n.

hagannamulia. (BE2 NNAMU)
v.

hagannanu. (PE- NANU)
v.

hagannanua. (PE2 NANU)
v.

hagannanuanga. (PE1 NANU)
n.

hagannanulia. (PE2 NANU)
v.

hagannanumia. (PE2 NANU)
v.

haganneegenga. (PE1 NEGE)
n.

hagannege. (PE- NEGE)
v.

hagannegea. (PE2 NEGE)
v.

hagannegelia. (PE2 NEGE)
v.

hagannigo. (PE- NIGO)
v.

hagannigoa. (PE2 NIGO)
v.

hagannigolia. (PE2 NIGO)
v.

haganniigonga. (PE1 NIGO)
n.

hagannoho. (PE- NOHO)
v.

hagannohoa. (PE2 NOHO)
v.

hagannohoanga. (PE1 NOHO)
n.

hagannoholia. (PE2 NOHO)
v.

hagannoo. (BE- NNOO)
v.

hagannooanga. (BE1 NNOO)
n.

hagannui. (PE- NUI_2)
v.

hagannuia. (PE2 NUI_2)
v.

hagannuinga. (PE1 NUI_2)
n.

haganngali. (EE- NGALI)
v.

haganngana. (EE- NGANA)
v.

hagannganaanga. (EE1 NGANA)
n.

hagannganalia. (EE2 NGANA)
v.

haganngani. (PE- NGANI)
v.

haganngao. (EE- NGAO)
v.

haganngaoa. (EE2 NGAO)
v.

haganngaoanga. (EE1 NGAO)
n.

haganngaolia. (EE2 NGAO)
v.

haganngii. (PE- NGII)
v.

haganngiia. (PE2 NGII)
v.

haganngiianga. (PE1 NGII)
n.

haganngolo. (BE- NNGOLO)
v.

haganngoloa. (BE2 NNGOLO)
v.

haganodi. (BE- NODI)
v.

haganodia. (BE2 NODI)
v.

haganodinodi. (RE- NODI)
v.

haganodinodia. (RE2 NODI)
v.

haganodinodinga. (RE1 NODI)
n.

haganodinga. (BE1 NODI)
n.

haganoganoga. (BE- NOGANOGA)
v.

haganoganogaanga.
(BE1 NOGANOGA) *n.*

haganoho. (BE- NOHO)
—; stop (someone or something). *v.*

haganohoa. (BE2 NOHO)
v.

haganohoanga. (BE1 NOHO)
n.

haganoholia. (BE2 NOHO)
v.

haganohonoho. (RE- NOHO)
v.

haganohonohoa. (RE2 NOHO)
v.

haganohonohoanga. (RE1 NOHO)
n.

haganohonoholia. (RE2 NOHO)
v.

haganoobiho. (BE- NOOBIHO)
v.

haganoobihoanga.
(BE1 NOOBIHO) *n.*

haganoodagi. (BE- NOODAGI) *v.*

haganoodagianga. (BE1 NOODAGI) *n.*

haganoodalo. (BE- NOODALO) *n.*

haganoodaloanga. (BE1 NOODALO) *n.*

haganoogele. (BE- NOOGELE) *v.*

haganoogeleanga. (BE1 NOOGELE) *n.*

haganoomeemea. (BE- NOOMEEMEA) *v.*

haganoomeemeaanga. (BE1 NOOMEEMEA) *n.*

haganoonogia. (BE- NOONOGIA) *v.*

haganoonogiaanga. (BE1 NOONOGIA) *n.*

haganoonoobiho. (RE- NOOBIHO) *v.*

haganoonoobihoanga. (RE1 NOOBIHO) *n.*

haganoonoodagi. (RE- NOODAGI) *v.*

haganoonoodagianga. (RE1 NOODAGI) *n.*

haganoonoodalo. (RE- NOODALO) *v.*

haganoonoodaloanga. (RE1 NOODALO) *n.*

haganoonoogele. (RE- NOOGELE) *v.*

haganoonoogeleanga. (RE1 NOOGELE) *n.*

haganoonounu. (RE- NOUNU) *v.*

haganoonounfunga. (RE1 NOUNU) *n.*

haganounu. (BE- NOUNU) *v.*

haganounga. (BE1 NOUNU) *n.*

haganuui. (BE- NUUI) *v.*

haganuuia. (BE2 NUUI) *v.*

haganuuinga. (BE1 NUUI) *n.*

hagangaadonga. (BE1 NGADO) *n.*

hagangaaheahe. (BE- NGAHEAHE) *v.*

hagangaaheaheanga. (BE1 NGAHEAHE) *n.*

hagangaaholu. (PE- $HOLU_a$) *v.*

hagangaaholua. (PE2 $HOLU_a$) *v.*

hagangaaholunga. (PE1 $HOLU_a$) *n.*

hagangaalia. (BE2 NGALI) *v.*

hagangaalinga. (BE1 NGALI) *n.*

hagangaalogu. (PE- NGALOGU) *v.*

hagangaalogua. (PE2 NGALOGU) *v.*

hagangaalogunga. (PE1 NGALOGU) *n.*

hagangaalonga. (BE1 NGALO) *n.*

hagangaalue. (PE- NGALUE) *v.*

hagangaaluea. (PE2 NGALUE) *v.*

hagangaalueanga. (PE1 NGALUE) *n.*

hagangaalulu. (BE- $LULU_a$) *v.*

hagangaaluluanga. (BE1 $LULU_a$) *n.*

hagangaaninga. (BE1 NGANI) *n.*

hagangaangaa. (BE- NGAANGAA) *v.*

hagangaangaanga.
(BE1 NGAANGAA) *n.*

hagangaangauda.
(RE- NGAUDA) *v.*

hagangaangaudanga.
(RE1 NGAUDA) *n.*

hagangaaobo. (PE- NGAOBO)
v.

hagangaaoboanga. (PE1 NGAOBO)
n.

hagangaaue. (PE- NGAUE)
v.

hagangaauea. (PE2 NGAUE)
v.

hagangaauenga. (PE1 NGAUE)
n.

hagangaavali. (PE- NGAVALI)
v.

hagangaavalianga. (PE1 NGAVALI)
n.

hagangadaa. (BE- NGADAA)
Come with difficulty; a difficult delivery (of a baby). *v.*

hagangadaanga. (BE1 NGADAA)
n.

hagangadi --. (BE- NGADI)
v.

hagangadi me.
Treat as unimportant; to sacrifice (not thinking of oneself).

hagangado. (BE- NGADO)
v.

hagangadoa. (BE2 NGADO)
v.

hagangadolia. (BE2 NGADO)
v.

hagangadolo. (BE- $DOLO_b$)
v.

hagangadoloanga. (BE1 $DOLO_b$)
n.

hagangaholu. (BE- $HOLU_a$)
v.

hagangaholua. (BE2 $HOLU_a$)
v.

hagangaholuholu. (RE- $HOLU_a$)
v.

hagangaholuholua. (RE2 $HOLU_a$)
v.

hagangaholuholunga. (RE1 $HOLU_a$)
n.

hagangaholunga. (BE1 $HOLU_a$)
n.

hagangali --. (BE- NGALI)
d.

hagangalingali. (RE- NGALI)
v.

hagangalingalia. (RE2 NGALI)
v.

hagangalingalinga. (RE1 NGALI)
n.

hagangalo. (BE- NGALO)
Forget purposely. *v.*

hagangaloa. (BE2 NGALO)
v.

hagangalogu. (BE- NGALOGU)
v.

hagangalogua. (BE2 NGALOGU)
v.

hagangalogulogu.
(RE- NGALOGU) *v.*

hagangalogulogua.
(RE2 NGALOGU) *v.*

hagangalogulogunga.
(RE) NGALOGU) *n.*

hagangalogunga. (BE1 NGALOGU)
n.

hagangalongalo. (RE- NGALO)
v.

hagangalongaloa. (RE2 NGALO)
v.

hagangalongalonga. (RE1 NGALO)
n.

hagangalubelube.
(BE- NGALUBELUBE) *v.*

hagangalubelubea.
(BE2 NGALUBELUBE) *v.*

hagangalubelubenga.
(BE1 NGALUBELUBE) *n.*

hagangalue. (BE- NGALUE)
v.

hagangaluea. (BE2 NGALUE)
v.

hagangalueanga. (BE1 NGALUE)
n.

hagangalullulu. (RE- LULUa)
v.

hagangalulluluanga. (RE1 LULUa)
n.

hagangalungalue. (RE- NGALUE)
v.

hagangalungaluea. (RE2 NGALUE)
v.

hagangalungalueang.
(RE1 NGALUE) *an.*

haganganangana. (RE- NGANA)
v.

haganganangananga.
(RE1 NGANA) *n.*

haganganangan alia. (RE2 NGANA)
v.

hagangani. (BE- NGANI)
v.

hagangania. (BE2 NGANI)
v.

haganganingani. (RE- NGANI)
v.

haganganingania. (RE2 NGANI)
v.

haganganinganinga. (RE1 NGANI)
n.

hagangaobo. (BE- NGAOBO)
v.

hagangaoboanga. (BE1 NGAOBO)
n.

hagangaoboobo. (RE- NGAOBO)
v.

hagangaobooboanga.
(RE1 NGAOBO) *n.*

hagangaoheohe.
(BE- NGAOHEOHE) *v.*

hagangaoheoheanga.
(BE1 NGAOHEOHE) *n.*

hagangaoheolhelia.
(BE2 NGAOHEOHE) *v.*

hagangaolo. (BE- NGAOLO)
v.

hagangaoloa. (BE2 NGAOLO)
v.

hagangaolonga. (BE1 NGAOLO)
n.

hagangaongao. (RE- NGAO)
v.

hagangaongaoa. (RE2 NGAO)
v.

hagangaongaoanga. (RE1 NGAO)
n.

hagangaongaolia. (RE2 NGAO)
v.

hagangaongaolo. (RE- NGAOLO)
v.

hagangaongaoloa. (RE2 NGAOLO)
v.

hagangaongaolonga.
(RE1 NGAOLO) *n.*

hagangau. (BE- NGAU)
—; provide food for, share food with. *v.*

hagangaua. (BE2 NGAU)
v.

hagangauda. (BE- NGAUDA)
v.

hagangaudanga. (BE1 NGAUDA)
n.

hagangaue. (BE- NGAUE)
Move (something). *v.*

hagangauea. (RE2 NGAUE)
v.

hagangauenga. (BE1 NGAUE)
n.

hagangaulia. (BE2 NGAU)
v.

hagangaunga. (BE1 NGAU)
n.

hagangaungau. (RE- NGAU)
v.

hagangaungaua. (RE2 NGAU)
v.

hagangaungaue. (RE- NGAUE)
v.

hagangaungauea. (RE2 NGAUE)
v.

hagangaungauenga. (RE1 NGAUE)
n.

hagangaungaulia. (RE2 NGAU)
v.

hagangaungaunga. (RE1 NGAU)
n.

hagangavali. (BE- NGAVALI)
v.

hagangavalianga. (BE1 NGAVALI)
n.

hagangavalivali. (RE- NGAVALI)
v.

hagangavalivalianga.
(RE1 NGAVALI) *n.*

hagangii. (BE- NGII)
v.

hagangiia. (BE2 NGII)
v.

hagangiianga. (BE1 NGII)
n.

hagangiingii. (RE- NGII)
v.

hagangiingiia. (RE2 NGII)
v.

hagangiingiianga. (RE1 NGII)
n.

hagangiisinga. (BE1 NGISI)
n.

hagangisi. (BE- NGISI)
v.

hagangisingisi. (RE- NGISI)
v.

hagangisingisinga. (RE1 NGISI)
n.

hagangole. (BE- NGOLE)
v.

hagangolea. (BE2 NGOLE)
v.

hagangolengole. (RE- NGOLE)
v.

hagangolengolea. (RE2 NGOLE)
v.

hagangolengolenga. (RE1 NGOLE)
n.

hagangolongolo. (RE- NNGOLO)
v.

hagangolongoloa. (RE2 NNGOLO)
v.

hagangolongolonga.
(RE1 NNGOLO) *n.*

hagangoolenga. (BE1 NGOLE)
n.

hagangoolonga. (BE1 NNGOLO)
n.

haganguu. (BE- $NGUU_1$)
—; ask permission. *v.*

haganguua. (BE2 $NGUU_1$)
v.

haganguulia. (BE2 $NGUU_1$)
v.

haganguunguu. (RE- $NGUU_1$)
v.

haganguunguua. (RE2 $NGUU_1$)
v.

haganguunguuanga. (RE1 $NGUU_1$)
n.

haganguunguulia. (RE2 $NGUU_1$)
v.

hagao.
Buy, sell, repay. *v.*

hagaoa. (B-2 HAGAO)
v.

hagaoanga. (B-1 HAGAO)
—; price, wages; prize. *n.*

hagaoanga gi lunga.
Good wages; a good price.

hagao baubau.
Low wages, low-priced.

hagaobe. (BE- OBE)
Cause to have *obe.* *v.*

hagaobea. (BE2 OBE)
v.

hagaobenga. (BE1 OBE)
n.

hagaobeobe. (RE- OBE)
v.

hagaobeobea. (RE2 OBE)
v.

hagaobeobenga. (RE1 OBE)
n.

hagaoda$_1$. (BE- ODA$_1$)
v.

hagaoda$_2$. (BE- ODA$_2$)
A type of prepared food (a kind of *dalogo* made without water). *n.*

hagaodaanga. (BE1 ODA$_1$)
n.

hagaoda tugi.
A type of prepared food (made from mashed taro and grated coconut).

hagaodaia. (BE2 ODA$_1$)
v.

hagaodalia. (BE2 ODA$_1$)
v.

hagaoda-lolo.
Fish sp. (= large *llahi*).

hagaodaoda. (RE- ODA$_1$)
v.

hagaodaodaanga. (RE1 ODA$_1$)
n.

hagaodaodaia. (RE2 ODA$_1$)
v.

hagaodaodalia. (RE2 ODA$_1$)
v.

hagaodea. (BE- ODEA)
The time at which it is midday. *v.*

hagaodi. (BE- ODI)
End of (e.g., time). *v.*

hagaodia. (BE2 ODI)
Finish up, be last. *v.*

hagaodinga. (BE1 ODI)
n.

hagaodiodi. (RE- ODI)
v.

hagaodiodia. (RE2 ODI)
v.

hagaodiodinga. (RE1 ODI)
n.

hagaodo. (BE- ODO$_1$)
v.

hagaodoa. (BE2 ODO$_1$)
v.

hagaodohia. (BE2 ODO$_1$)
v.

hagaodolia. (BE2 ODO$_1$)
v.

hagaodonga. (BE1 ODO$_1$)
n.

hagaodoodo. (RE- ODO$_1$)
v.

hagaodoodoa. (RE2 ODO$_1$)
v.

hagaodoodohia. (RE2 ODO$_1$)
v.

hagaodoodolia. (RE2 ODO$_1$)
v.

hagaodoodonga. (RE1 ODO$_1$)
n.

hagaoga. (BE- OGA)
v.

hagaogaanga. (BE1 OGA)
n.

hagaogahia. (BE2 OGA)
v.

hagaogaoga. (RE- OGA)
v.

hagaogaogaanga. (RE1 OGA)
n.

hagaogaogahia. (RE2 OGA)
v.

hagaogo. (BE- OGO$_1$)
v.

hagaogoa. (BE2 OGO$_1$)
v.

hagaogoanga. (BE1 OGO$_1$)
n.

hagaogohia. (BE2 OGO$_1$)
v.

hagaogolia. (BE2 OGO$_1$)
v.

hagaogonga. (BE1 OGO$_1$)
n.

hagaogoogo. (RE- OGO$_1$)
v.

hagaogoogoa. (RE2 OGO$_1$)
v.

hagaogoogoanga. (RE1 OGO$_1$)
n.

hagaogoogohia. (RE2 OGO$_1$)
v.

hagaogoogolia. (RE2 OGO$_1$)
v.

hagaogoogonga. (RE1 OGO$_1$)
n.

hagaoho. (BE- OHO)
v.

hagaohoanga. (BE1 OHO)
n.

hagaohooho$_1$. (RE- OHO)
v.

hagaohooho$_2$. (BE- OHOOHO)
v.

hagaohoohoanga$_1$. (RE1 OHO)
n.

hagaohoohoanga$_2$. (BE1 OHOOHO)
n.

hagaohu. (BE1 OHU)
v.

hagaohua. (BE2 OHU)
v.

hagaohunga. (BE1 OHU)
n.

hagaohuohu. (RE- OHU)
v.

hagaohuohua. (RE2 OHU)
v.

hagaohuohunga. (RE1 OHU)
n.

hagaoia. (BE- OIA)
v.

hagaola. (BE- OLA)
Save from. *v.*

hagaolaa. (BE- OLAA)
v.

hagaolaanga. (BE1 OLA)
n.

hagaolaaolaa. (RE- OLAA)
v.

hagaolaola. (RE- OLA)
v.

hagaolaolaanga. (RE1 OLA)
n.

hagaolioli. (BE- OLIOLI)
v.

hagaoliolia. (BE2 OLIOLI)
v.

hagaoliolinga. (BE1 OLIOLI)
n.

hagaono (ina). (BE- ONO$_1$)
Make a total of six. *v.*

hagaonoonogia. (RE2 ONO$_2$)
v.

hagaonoonogiaanga. (RE3 ONO$_2$)
n.

hagao ngadaa.
Expensive.

hagao ngaohie.
Inexpensive.

hagaongaonga. (RE- ONGA)
Moving one's head back and forth in time to music. *v.*

hagaonge. (BE- ONGE)
v.

hagaongea. (BE2 ONGE)
v.

hagaongeonge. (RE- ONGE)
v.

hagaongeongea. (RE2 ONGE)
v.

hagaoo$_1$. (BE- OO$_1$)
v.

hagaoo$_2$. (BE- OO$_2$)
v.

hagaooanga. (BE1 OO$_2$)
n.

hagaoohia. (BE2 OO$_2$)
v.

hagaoohiaanga. (BE3 OO$_2$)
n.

hagaoohu. (PE- OHU)
v.

hagaoohua. (PE2 OHU)
v.

hagaoohunga. (PE1 OHU)
n.

hagaooi. (BE- OOI)
v.

hagaooinga. (BE1 OOI)
n.

hagaooiooi. (RE- OOI)
v.

hagaooiooinga. (RE1 OOI)
n.

hagaoomea. (BE- OOMEA)
To wait until *oomea.* *v.*

hagaoomeaanga. (BE1 OOMEA)
n.

hagaoonga. (BE1 OO_1)
n.

hagaoooo. (RE- OO_1)
v.

hagaooonga. (RE1 OO_1)
n.

hagaoosonga. (BE1 OSO)
n.

hagaosi. (BE- OSI)
v.

hagaosia. (BE2 OSI)
v.

hagaosinga. (BE1 OSI)
n.

hagaosiosi. (RE- OSI)
v.

hagaosiosia. (RE2 OSI)
v.

hagaosiosinga. (RE1 OSI)
n.

hagaoso. (BE- OSO)
v.

hagaosoa. (BE2 OSO)
v.

hagaosoanga. (BE1 OSO)
n.

hagaosohia. (BE2 OSO)
v.

hagaosolia. (BE2 OSO)
v.

hagaosongia. (BE2 OSO)
v.

hagaosooso. (RE- OSO)
v.

hagaosoosoa. (RE2 OSO)
v.

hagaosoosoanga. (RE1 OSO)
n.

hagaosoosohia. (RE2 OSO)
v.

hagaosoosolia. (RE2 OSO)
v.

hagaosoosonga. (RE1 OSO)
n.

hagaosoosongia. (RE2 OSO)
v.

hagaovea. (BE- OVEA)
v.

hagaoveaanga. (BE1 OVEA)
n.

hagaoveovea. (RE- OVEA)
v.

hagaoveoveaanga. (RE1 OVEA)
n.

hagasaa. (BE- SAA_1)
Quarrel (like children). *a.*

hagasaabai. (BE- SAABAI)
v.

hagasaabaia. (BE2 SAABAI)
v.

hagasaabainga. (BE1 SAABAI)
n.

hagasaabanga. (BE1 $SABA_2$)
n.

hagasaabonga. (BE1 SABO)
n.

hagasaapala. (PE- SABALA)
v.

hagasaaganga. (BE1 SAGA)
n.

hagasaagonga. (BE1 SAGO)
n.

hagasaagule. (BE- SAAGULE)
Teach how to *saagule*. *v.*

hagasaahea. (BE- SAAHEA)
v.

hagasaaheaanga. (BE1 SAAHEA)
n.

hagasaalani. (PE- SALANI)
v.

hagasaalania. (PE2 SALANI)
v.

hagasaalaninga. (PE1 SALANI)
n.

hagasaaliba. (BE- SAALIBA)
v.

hagasaalibaanga. (BE1 SAALIBA)
n.

hagasaalinga. (BE1 SALI)
n.

hagasaaloa. (BE- SAALOA)
To encounter good (or bad) fortune. *v.*

hagasaaloaanga. (BE1 SAALOA)
n.

hagasaalohia. (BE- SAALOHIA)
v.

hagasaalohiaanga.
(BE1 SAALOHIA) *n.*

hagasaalua. (BE2 SALU)
v.

hagasaalulu. (PE- SALULU)
v.

hagasaaluluanga. (PE1 SALULU)
n.

hagasaalunga. (CF SAA_2)
n.

$hagasaalunga_1$. (BE1 SALU)
n.

$hagasaalunga_2$. (BE- SAALUNGA)
Spirit, soul, name-group. *v.*

hagasaalunga ange.
Call (someone) by the name of his name-group.

hagasaalunga de langi.
A member of the Christian Endeavor Society.

hagasaamumu. (PE- SAMUMU)
v.

hagasaamumuanga.
(PE1 SAMUMU) *n.*

hagasaanga. (BE1 SAA_1)
n.

hagasaangia. (BE2 SAA_1)
To encounter good (or bad) fortune. *v.*

hagasaangiaanga. (BE3 SAA_1)
n.

hagasaasaagule. (SE- SAAGULE)
v.

hagasaasaagulea. (SE2 SAAGULE)
v.

hagasaasaagulenga.
(SE1 SAAGULE) *n.*

hagasaasaalohia.
(RE- SAALOHIA) *v.*

hagasaasaalohiaanga.
(RE1 SAALOHIA) *n.*

hagasaasanga. (BE1 SASA)
n.

hagasaava. (BE- SAAVA)
v.

hagasaavaanga. (BE1 SAAVA)
n.

hagasaavala. (PE- SAVALA)
v.

hagasaavale. (BE- SAAVALE)
v.

hagasaavaleanga. (BE1 SAAVALE)
n.

hagasaavali. (PE- SAVALI)
v.

hagasaavalia. (PE2 SAVALI)
v.

hagasaavalianga. (PE1 SAVALI)
n.

hagasaavini. (PE- SAVINI)
v.

hagasaba₁. (BE- SABA₁)
v.

hagasaba₂. (BE- SABA₂)
v.

hagasabaanga. (BE1 SABA₁)
n.

hagasabaia. (BE2 SAABAI)
v.

hagasabainga. (BE1 SAABAI)
n.

hagasabala. (BE- SABALA)
Talk (someone) into (something). *v.*

hagasabalabala. (RE- SABALA)
v.

hagasabalia₁. (BE2 SABA₁)
v.

hagasabalia₂. (BE2 SABA₂)
v.

hagasabanaana.
(BE- SABANAANA) *v.*

hagasabasaba. (RE- SABA₁)
—; to get into a dangerous position (as children climbing trees). *v.*

hagasabasabaanga. (RE1 SABA₁)
n.

hagasabasabai. (RE- SAABAI)
v.

hagasabasabaia. (RE2 SAABAI)
v.

hagasabasabainga. (RE1 SAABAI)
n.

hagasabasabalia. (RE2 SABA₁)
v.

hagasabeeloi. (BE- SABEELOI)
v.

hagasabeeloinga. (BE1 SABEELOI)
n.

hagasabo. (BE- SABO)
v.

hagasaboa. (BE2 SABO)
v.

hagasabolia. (BE2 SABO)
v.

hagasabosabo. (RE- SABO)
v.

hagasabosaboa. (RE2 SABO)
v.

hagasabosabolia. (RE2 SABO)
v.

hagasabosabonga. (RE1 SABO)
n.

hagasae. (BE- SAE₂)
v.

hagasaea. (BE2 SAE₂)
v.

hagasae gili.
Pierce the skin superficially.

hagasaele. (BE- SAELE)
—; meeting; decide (come to a considered conclusion); thought. *v.*

hagasaelea. (BE2 SAELE)
v.

hagasaele age.
Make up one's mind; lift up (in a steady motion).

hagasaeleanga. (BE1 SAELE)
n.

hagasaelenga. (BE1 SAELE)
n.

hagasaelesaele. (RE- SAELE)
—; to think about something (esp. a problem) for a long time (keep turning it over in one's mind). *v.*

hagasaelesaelea. (RE2 SAELE)
v.

hagasaelesaeleanga. (RE1 SAELE)
n.

hagasaelesaelenga. (RE1 SAELE)
n.

hagasaelia. (BE2 SAE₂)
v.

hagasaenga. (BE1 SAE₂)
n.

hagasaesae. (RE- SAE₂)
v.

hagasaesaele. (SE- SAELE)
v.

hagasaesaelea. (SE2 SAELE)
v.

hagasaesaeleanga. (SE1 SAELE)
n.

hagasaesaelenga. (SE1 SAELE)
n.

hagasaesaenga. (RE1 SAE_2)
n.

hagasaga. (BE- SAGA)
v.

hagasagalia. (BE2 SAGA)
v.

hagasaganaa. (BE- SAGANA)
v.

hagasaganaanga. (BE1 SAGANA)
n.

hagasagasaga. (RE- SAGA)
v.

hagasagasagaanga. (RE1 SAGA)
n.

hagasagasagalia. (RE2 SAGA)
v.

hagasagasagana. (RE- SAGANA)
v.

hagasagasaganaanga.
(RE1 SAGANA) *n.*

hagasagea. (BE- SAGEA)
v.

hagasageaanga. (BE1 SAGEA)
n.

hagasagesagea. (RE- SAGEA)
v.

hagasagesageaanga. (RE1 SAGEA)
n.

hagasagisagili. (BE- SAGISAGILI)
v.

hagasagisagilianga.
(BE1 SAGISAGILI) *n.*

hagasago. (BE- SAGO)
—; pull, move, or raise, gently. *v.*

hagasagolia. (BE2 SAGO)
v.

hagasagosago. (RE- SAGO)
—; take a little from several different sources. *v.*

hagasagosagoanga. (RE1 SAGO)
n.

hagasagosagolia. (RE2 SAGO)
v.

hagasagulea. (BE2 SAAGULE)
v.

hagasagulenga. (BE1 SAAGULE)
n.

hagasagusagule. (RE- SAAGULE)
v.

hagasagusagulea. (RE2 SAAGULE)
v.

hagasagusagulenga.
(RE1 SAAGULE) *n.*

hagasahu. (BE- SAHU)
To catch water (in something). *v.*

hagasahua. (BE2 SAHU)
v.

hagasahuanga. (BE1 SAHU)
n.

hagasahulia. (BE2 SAHU)
v.

hagasahusahu. (RE- SAHU)
v.

hagasahusahua. (RE2 SAHU)
v.

hagasahusahulia. (RE2 SAHU)
v.

hagasaibo. (BE- SAIBO)
v.

hagasaibonga. (BE1 SAIBO)
n.

hagasaidule. (BE- SAIDULE)
v.

hagasaiduleanga. (BE1 SAIDULE)
n.

hagasaisaidule. (RE- SAIDULE)
v.

hagasaisaiduleanga.
(RE1 SAIDULE) *n.*

hagasalani. (BE- SALANI)
v.

hagasalania. (BE2 SALANI)
v.

hagasalaninga. (BE1 SALANI)
n.

hagasalasalani. (RE- SALANI)
v.

hagasalasalania. (RE2 SALANI)
v.

hagasalasalaninga. (RE1 SALANI)
n.

hagasalau. (BE- SALAU)
—; be *salau* with respect to something else. *v.*

hagasalaua. (BE2 SALAU)
v.

hagasalaunga. (BE1 SALAU)
n.

hagasali. (BE- SALI)
v.

hagasalia. (BE2 SALI)
v.

hagasalibaadaa.
(BE- SALIBAADAA) *v.*

hagasalibaadaanga.
(BE1 SALIBAADAA) *n.*

hagasalisali. (RE- SALI)
—; arm-wrestling. *v.*

hagasalisalia. (RE2 SALI)
v.

hagasalisalinga. (RE1 SALI)
n.

hagasalu. (BE- SALU)
—; the shaping (of something) by planing. *v.*

hagasalua. (BE2 SALU)
v.

hagasalulu. (BE- SALULU)
v.

hagasaluluanga. (BE1 SALULU)
n.

hagasalusalu. (RE- SALU)
v.

hagasalusalua. (RE2 SALU)
v.

hagasalusalunga. (RE1 SALU)
n.

hagasamumu. (BE- SAMUMU)
v.

hagasamumuanga.
(BE1 SAMUMU) *n.*

hagasanosano. (RE- SANO)
v.

hagasanosanoanga. (RE1 SANO)
n.

hagasanga. (BE- SANGA)
v.

hagasangaa. (BE2 SANGA)
v.

hagasangalia. (BE2 SANGA)
v.

hagasanganga. (BE1 SANGA)
—; to walk with one's legs apart. *a.*

hagasangasanga. (RE- SANGA)
v.

hagasangasangaa. (RE2 SANGA)
v.

hagasangasangalia. (RE2 SANGA)
v.

hagasangasanganga. (RE1 SANGA)
n.

hagasango. (BE- SANGO)
v.

hagasangoanga. (BE1 SANGO)
n.

hagasangolia. (BE2 SANGO)
v.

hagasangosango. (RE- SANGO)
v.

hagasangosangoanga.
(RE1 SANGO) *n.*

hagasangosangolia. (RE2 SANGO)
v.

hagasao$_1$ --. (BE- SAO$_1$)
d.

hagasao$_2$. (BE- SAO$_2$)
Let out (something), disburse (money). *v.*

hagasaoa. (BE2 SAO$_2$)
v.

hagasaoanga. (BE1 SAO$_1$)
n.

hagasaohia$_1$. (BE2 SAO$_1$)
v.

hagasaohia$_2$. (BE2 SAO$_2$)
Make oneself available. *v.*

hagasaohiaanga. (BE3 SAO_2)
n.

hagasaolia. (BE2 SAO_2)
v.

hagasaonga. (BE1 SAO_2)
n.

hagasaosao$_1$ --. (RE- SAO_1)
d.

hagasaosao$_2$. (RE- SAO_2)
v.

hagasaosaoa. (RE2 SAO_2)
v.

hagasaosaoanga. (RE1 SAO_1)
n.

hagasaosaohia$_1$. (RE2 SAO_1)
v.

hagasaosaohia$_2$. (RE2 SAO_2)
—; [causative form of *saosaohia*$_2$]. *v.*

hagasaosaohiaanga. (RE3 SAO_2)
[BE1 form of *saosaohia*]. *n.*

hagasaosaolia. (RE2 SAO_2)
v.

hagasaosaonga. (RE1 SAO_2)
n.

hagasasa. (BE- SASA)
v.

hagasasalia. (BE2 SASA)
v.

hagasasao. (TE- SAO_2)
v.

hagasasaoa. (TE2 SAO_2)
v.

hagasasaolia. (TE2 SAO_2)
v.

hagasasaonga. (TE1 SAO_2)
n.

hagasassabe. (RE- SSABE)
v.

hagasassabeanga. (RE1 SSABE)
n.

hagasassano. (TE- SANO)
v.

hagasassanoanga. (TE1 SANO)
n.

hagasassasa. (RE- SASA)
v.

hagasassasaanga. (RE1 SASA)
n.

hagasassasalia. (RE2 SASA)
v.

hagasau --. (BE- SAU_1)
d.

hagasauaa. (BE- SAUAA)
—; empower; do (usually bad things) with *sauaa*; approve (as a law by higher authority). *v.*

hagasauaanga. (BE1 SAUAA)
n.

hagasaubaligi. (BE- SAUBALIGI)
v.

hagasaudia. (BE2 SAU_1)
v.

hagasaudiaanga. (BE3 SAU_1)
n.

hagasaugalo. (BE- $GALO_{3a}$)
v.

hagasaugaloa. (BE2 $GALO_{3a}$)
v.

hagasaugalonga. (BE1 $GALO_{3a}$)
n.

hagasaulaba. (BE- SAULABA)
Treat as *saulaba.* *v.*

hagasau madangi.
To be exposed to the wind.

hagasaunga. (BE- SAUNGA)
v.

hagasausau. (RE- SAU_1)
v.

hagasausauaa. (RE- SAUAA)
v.

hagasausauaanga. (RE1 SAUAA)
n.

hagasausaubaligi.
(RE- SAUBALIGI) *v.*

hagasausaudia. (RE2 SAU_1)
v.

hagasausaudiaanga. (RE3 SAU_1)
n.

hagasausaugalo. (RE2 GALO$_{3a}$)
v.

hagasausaugaloa. (RE2 GALO$_{3a}$)
v.

hagasausaugalonga. (RE1 GALO$_{3a}$)
n.

hagasausaunga$_1$. (RE1 SAU$_1$)
n.

hagasausaunga$_2$. (RE- SAUNGA)
n.

hagasauvalovalo. (BE- VALO$_{1a}$)
v.

hagasauvalovalonga. (BE1 VALO$_{1a}$)
n.

hagasavala. (BE- SAVALA)
v.

hagasavali. (BE- SAVALI)
v.

hagasavalia. (BE2 SAVALI)
v.

hagasavalianga. (BE1 SAVALI)
n.

hagasavasavala. (RE- SAVALA)
v.

hagasavasavale. (RE- SAAVALE)
v.

hagasavasavaleanga.
(RE1 SAAVALE) *n.*

hagasavasavali. (RE- SAVALI)
v.

hagasavasavalia. (RE2 SAVALI)
v.

hagasavasavalianga. (RE1 SAVALI)
n.

hagasavini. (BE- SAVINI)
v.

hagasebaga. (?)
Make a total of ten billion. *v.*

hagasebu. (BE- SEBU)
v.

hagasebua. (BE2 SEBU)
v.

hagasebuaanga. (BE3 SEBU)
n.

hagasebugi. (?)
Make a total of one billion. *v.*

hagasebusebu. (RE- SEBU)
v.

hagasebusebua. (RE2 SEBU)
v.

hagasebusebuaanga. (RE3 SEBU)
n.

hagasee$_1$. (BE- SEE$_1$)
—; scold, bawl out, chide. *v.*

hagasee$_2$. (BE- SEE$_2$)
Just barely; [same limitations of distribution as *see*$_2$]. *a.*

hagaseeanga. (BE1 SEE$_1$)
n.

hagaseegenga. (BE1 SEGE)
n.

hagaseegina. (BE2 SEE$_1$)
v.

hagaseeginga. (BE1 SEE$_1$)
n.

hagaseelenga. (BE1 SELE$_1$)
n.

hagaseelunga. (BE1 SELU)
n.

hagaseeninga. (BE1 SENI)
n.

hagaseenga$_1$. (BE1 SEE$_1$)
n.

hagaseenga$_2$. (BE1 SEE$_2$)
Way of just being able to. *n.*

hagaseenganga. (BE1 SENGA)
n.

hagaseesee$_1$. (RE- SEE$_1$)
v.

hagaseesee$_2$. (RE- SEE$_3$)
v.

hagaseeseeanga$_1$. (RE1 SEE$_1$)
n.

hagaseeseeanga$_2$. (RE1 SEE$_3$)
n.

hagaseeseenga$_1$. (RE1 SEE$_1$)
n.

hagaseeseenga$_2$. (RE1 SEE$_3$)
n.

hagaseevoivoi. (BE- SEE$_{1a}$)
v.

hagaseevoivoia. (BE2 SEE$_{1a}$)
v.

hagaseevoivoinga. (BE1 SEE$_{1a}$)
n.

hagasege. (BE- SEGE)
v.

hagasegea. (BE2 SEGE)
Let slip or slide. *v.*

hagasegedia. (BE2 SEGE)
Let slip or slide. *v.*

hagasegelia. (BE2 SEGE)
Let slip or slide. *v.*

hagasegesege. (RE- SEGE)
—; surf-riding (for amusement). *v.*

hagasegesegea. (RE2 SEGE)
v.

hagasegesege ange.
Allow someone to do as he pleases.

hagasegesegedia. (RE2 SEGE)
v.

hagasegesegelia. (RE2 SEGE)
v.

hagasegesegenga. (RE1 SEGE)
n.

hagaseguli. (?)
Make a total of one hundred thousand. *v.*

hagasehua. (BE- SEHUA)
To make a total of 1000 coconuts. *v.*

hagasele. (BE- SELE$_1$)
v.

hagaselea. (BE2 SELE$_1$)
v.

hagaseleia. (BE2 SELE$_2$)
v.

hagaselesele. (RE- SELE$_1$)
v.

hagaseleselea. (RE2 SELE$_1$)
v.

hagaseleseleia. (RE2 SELE$_1$)
v.

hagaseleselenga. (RE1 SELE$_1$)
n.

hagaseloo. (?)
Make a total of one million. *v.*

hagaselu. (BE- SELU)
v.

hagaselua. (BE2 SELU)
v.

hagaselumia. (BE2 SELU)
v.

hagaseluselu. (RE- SELU)
v.

hagaseluselua. (RE2 SELU)
v.

hagaseluselumia. (RE2 SELU)
v.

hagaseluselunga. (RE1 SELU)
n.

hagasemada. (?)
Make a total of ten thousand. *v.*

hagasemuna. (?)
Make a total of one hundred million. *v.*

hagaseni. (BE- SENI)
—; put to bed. *v.*

hagasenia. (BE2 SENI)
v.

hagaseniseni. (RE- SENI)
v.

hagasenisenia. (RE2 SENI)
v.

hagaseniseninga. (RE1 SENI)
n.

hagasenga. (BE- SENGA)
Fool (someone), deceive, trick (someone). *v.*

hagasengaa. (?)
Make a total of ten million. *v.*

hagasengalia. (BE2 SENGA)
v.

hagasengasenga. (RE- SENGA)
—; to speak in parables or riddles. *v.*

hagasengasengaanga. (RE1 SENGA) *n.*

hagasengasengalia. (RE2 SENGA) *v.*

hagasiba. (BE- $SIBA_1$) *v.*

hagasibalia. (BE2 $SIBA_1$) *v.*

hagasibasiba. (RE- $SIBA_1$) *v.*

hagasibasibaanga. (RE1 $SIBA_1$) *n.*

hagasibasibalia. (RE2 $SIBA_1$) *v.*

hagasiga. (BE- SIGA) *v.*

hagasigahia. (BE2 SIGA) *v.*

hagasigale. (BE- SIGALE) *v.*

hagasigaleanga. (BE1 SIGALE) *n.*

hagasigalia. (BE2 SIGA) *v.*

hagasigasiga. (RE- SIGA) *v.*

hagasigasigaanga. (RE1 SIGA) *n.*

hagasigasigahia. (RE2 SIGA) *v.*

hagasigasigale. (RE- SIGALE) *v.*

hagasigasigaleanga. (RE1 SIGALE) *n.*

hagasigasigalia. (RE2 SIGA) *v.*

hagasigi. (BE- SIGI) *v.*

hagasigia. (BE2 SIGI) *v.*

hagasigidia. (BE2 SIGI) *v.*

hagasigilia. (BE2 SIGI) *v.*

hagasigisigi. (RE- SIGI) *v.*

hagasigisigia. (RE2 SIGI) *v.*

hagasigisigidia. (RE2 SIGI) *v.*

hagasigisigilia. (RE2 SIGI) *v.*

hagasigisiginga. (RE1 SIGI) *n.*

hagasigo. (BE- SIGO) *v.*

hagasigoa. (BE2 SIGO) *v.*

hagasigohia. (BE2 SIGO) *v.*

hagasigolia. (BE2 SIGO) *v.*

hagasigosigo. (RE- SIGO) *v.*

hagasigosigoa. (RE2 SIGO) *v.*

hagasigosigohia. (RE2 SIGO) *v.*

hagasigosigolia. (RE2 SIGO) *v.*

hagasigosigonga. (RE1 SIGO) *n.*

hagasii. (BE- SII) —; wheel. *v.*

$hagasiia_1$. (BE2 SII) *v.*

$hagasiia_2$. (BE2 $SISI_1$) *v.*

hagasiibanga. (BE1 $SIBA_1$) *n.*

hagasiiganga. (BE1 SIGA) *n.*

hagasiiginga. (BE1 SIGI) *n.*

hagasiigonga. (BE1 SIGO) *n.*

hagasiilangaa mada. The appearance of fish or edible

animals in great numbers (an omen of death).

hagasiilinga$_1$. (BE1 SILI$_1$)
n.

hagasiilinga$_2$. (BE1 SILI$_3$)
n.

hagasii lolo.
Wheel.

hagasiinga. (BE1 SII)
n.

hagasiinganga. (BE1 SINGA)
n.

hagasiisii$_1$. (RE- SII)
v.

hagasiisii$_2$. (TE- SISI$_1$)
v.

hagasiisiia$_1$. (RE2 SII)
v.

hagasiisiia$_2$. (TE2 SISI$_1$)
v.

hagasiisiianga. (TE1 SISI$_1$)
n.

hagasiisiinga. (RE1 SII)
n.

hagasiiviivii. (BE- VIIVII$_a$)
v.

hagasiiviiviia. (BE2 VIIVII$_a$)
v.

hagasiiviiviinga. (BE1 VIIVII$_a$)
n.

hagasiivinga. (BE1 SIVI)
n.

hagasila. (BE- SILA)
v.

hagasilaanga. (BE1 SILA)
n.

hagasilasila. (RE- SILA)
v.

hagasilasilaanga. (RE1 SILA)
n.

hagasileia. (BE2 SILA)
v.

hagasilesileia. (RE2 SILA)
v.

hagasili$_1$. (BE- SILI$_1$)
v.

hagasili$_2$. (BE- SILI$_2$)
d.

hagasili$_3$. (BE- SILI$_3$)
v.

hagasilia$_1$. (BE2 SILI$_1$)
v.

hagasilia$_2$. (BE2 SILI$_3$)
v.

hagasilisili$_1$. (RE- SILI$_1$)
v.

hagasilisili$_2$. (RE- SILI$_3$)
v.

hagsilisilia$_1$. (RE2 SILI$_1$)
v.

hagasilisilia$_2$. (RE2 SILI$_3$)
v.

hagasilisilinga$_1$. (RE1 SILI$_1$)
n.

hagasilisilinga$_2$. (RE1 SILI$_3$)
n.

hagasilisilivaahea.
(RE- SILIVAAHEA) *v.*

hagasilisilivaahenga.
(RE1 SILIVAAHEA) *n.*

hagasilivaahea.
(BE- SILIVAAHEA) *v.*

hagasilivaahenga.
(BE1 SILIVAAHEA) *n.*

hagasinaa. (BE2 SINA)
v.

hagasinasinaa. (RE2 SINA)
v.

hagasinga. (BE- SINGA)
—; lean over toward. *v.*

hagasingalia. (BE2 SINGA)
v.

hagasingano. (BE- SINGANO)
Cause to bear *singano*. *v.*

hagasingasinga. (RE- SINGA)
v.

hagasingasingaanga. (RE1 SINGA)
n.

hagasingasingalia. (RE2 SINGA)
v.

hagasisi. (BE- $SISI_1$)
v.

hagasissisi. (RE- $SISI_1$)
v.

hagasississianga. (RE1 $SISI_1$)
n.

hagasiva (ina). (BE- SIVA)
Make a total of nine. *v.*

hagasivi. (BE- SIVI)
—; cause to not repeat an action. *v.*

hagasivia. (BE2 SIVI)
v.

hagasivisivi. (RE- SIVI)
v.

hagasivisivia. (RE2 SIVI)
v.

hagasivisivinga. (RE1 SIVI)
n.

hagasoa. (BE- SOA)
Go with someone; cause to increase in number. *v.*

hagasoaanga. (BE1 SOA)
n.

hagasoa ange.
Go along with others, join the crowd.

hagasoasoa. (RE- SOA)
v.

hagasoasoaanga. (RE1 SOA)
n.

hagasobo. (BE- SOBO)
v.

hagasoboa. (BE2 SOBO)
v.

hagasobolia. (BE2 SOBO)
v.

hagasobosobo. (RE- SOBO)
v.

hagasobosoboa. (RE2 SOBO)
v.

hagasobosobolia. (RE2 SOBO)
v.

hagasobosobonga. (RE1 SOBO)
n.

hagasoe. (BE- SOE)
—; go directly, speak directly (without circumlocution). *v.*

hagasoea. (BE2 SOE)
v.

hagasoe ange.
Aim at.

hagasoelia. (BE2 SOE)
v.

hagasoenga. (BE1 SOE)
—; show-off; proud, abrupt in manner. *a.*

hagasoesoe. (RE- SOE)
—; to level off (ground, etc.); to go about one's business without regard to others. *v.*

hagasoesoea. (RE2 SOE)
v.

hagasoesoelia. (RE2 SOE)
v.

hagasoesoenga. (RE1 SOE)
n.

hagasoesoe saele.
To walk about without greeting others.

hagasogoisi. (BE- SOGOISI)
[Var. of *hagadogoisi*]. *v.*

hagasogosogo. (BE- SOGOSOGO)
v.

hagasogosogoisi. (RE- SOGOISI)
[Var. of *hagadogodogoisi*]. *v.*

hagasogosogolia.
(BE2 SOGOSOGO) *v.*

hagasolasola. (RE- SOLA)
v.

hagasolasolaanga. (RE1 SOLA)
n.

hagasolo. (BE- SOLO)
—; take turns. *v.*

hagasoloa. (BE2 SOLO)
v.

hagasolo age.
Keep postponing or delaying.

hagasoloanga. (BE1 SOLO)
n.

hagasolona. (BE2 SOLO)
v.

hagasolonga. (BE1 SOLO)
n.

hagasolosolo. (RE- SOLO)
v.

hagasolosoloa. (RE2 SOLO)
v.

hagasolosoloanga. (RE1 SOLO)
n.

hagasolosolona. (RE2 SOLO)
v.

hagasolosolonga. (RE1 SOLO)
n.

hagasolovaani. (BE- SOLOVAANI)
v.

hagasomo. (BE- $SOMO_1$)
—; bed of sprouting coconuts; to stick out one's tongue. *v.*

hagasomo de alelo.
Stick out one's tongue.

hagasomolia. (BE2 $SOMO_1$)
v.

hagasomosomo. (RE- $SOMO_1$)
v.

hagasomosomolia. (RE2 $SOMO_1$)
v.

hagasomosomonga. (RE1 $SOMO_1$)
n.

hagasoobonga. (BE1 SOBO)
n.

hagasooloa. (EE2 SOLO)
v.

hagasoolona. (EE2 SOLO)
v.

hagasoolonga. (EE1 SOLO)
n.

hagasoomonga. (BE1 $SOMO_1$)
n.

hagasoosoa. (BE- SOOSOA)
To put *soosoa* on a canoe. *v.*

hagasoosoaanga. (BE1 SOOSOA)
v.

hagasoosobo. (TE- SOBO)
v.

hagasoosoboa. (TE2 SOBO)
v.

hagasoosobolia. (TE2 SOBO)
v.

hagasoosobonga. (TE1 SOBO)
n.

hagasou. (BE- SOU)
v.

hagasoua. (BE2 SOU)
v.

hagasounga. (BE1 SOU)
n.

hagassaalia. (PE2 SALI)
v.

hagassaba. (PE- $SABA_2$)
v.

hagassabalia. (PE2 $SABA_2$)
v.

hagassabe. (BE- SSABE)
v.

hagassabeanga. (BE1 SSABE)
n.

hagassabo. (PE- SABO)
v.

hagassaboa. (PE2 SABO)
v.

hagassabolia. (PE2 SABO)
v.

hagassae. (PE- SAE_2)
v.

hagassaea. (PE2 SAE_2)
v.

hagassaelia. (PE2 SAE_2)
v.

hagassaenga. (PE1 SAE_2)
n.

hagassaga. (PE- SAGA)
v.

hagassagalia. (PE2 SAGA)
v.

hagassago. (PE- SAGO)
v.

hagassagoanga. (PE1 SAGO)
n.

hagassagolia. (PE2 SAGO)
v.

hagassahu. (BE- SSAHU)
To try one's best to do something bad or harmful. *v.*

hagassahuanga. (BE1 SSAHU)
n.

hagassali. (PE- SALI)
v.

hagassalu. (EE- SALU)
v.

hagassalua. (EE2 SALU)
v.

hagassalunga. (EE1 SALU)
n.

hagassano. (EE- SANO)
v.

hagassanoanga. (EE1 SANO)
n.

hagassango. (PE- SANGO)
v.

hagassangoanga. (PE1 SANGO)
n.

hagassangolia. (PE2 SANGO)
v.

hagassao$_1$. (EE- SAO$_1$)
v.

hagassao$_2$. (PE- SAO$_2$)
v.

hagassaoanga. (EE1 SAO$_1$)
n.

hagassaolia. (PE2 SAO$_2$)
v.

hagassaonga. (PE1 SAO$_2$)
n.

hagassasa. (PE- SASA)
v.

hagassasalia. (PE2 SASA)
v.

hagassau. (EE- SAU$_1$)
v.

hagassaua. (EE2 SAU$_1$)
v.

hagassaulia. (EE2 SAU$_1$)
v.

hagassaunga. (BE1 SAU$_1$)
n.

hagassee$_1$. (PE- SEE$_1$)
v.

hagassee$_2$. (PE- SEE$_2$)
a.

hagassee$_3$. (EE- SEE$_3$)
—; to act as though innocent (when guilty). *v.*

hagasseeanga. (EE1 SEE$_3$)
n.

hagasseegenga. (PE1 SEGE)
n.

hagasseenia. (PE2 SENI)
v.

hagasseevanga. (BE1 SSEVA)
n.

hagassege. (PE- SEGE)
v.

hagassegea. (PE2 SEGE)
v.

hagassegedia. (PE2 SEGE)
v.

hagassege i hegau.
Procrastinate (about work); refuse to participate in work.

hagassegelia. (PE2 SEGE)
v.

hagasseni. (PE- SENI)
v.

hagassenga. (PE- SENGA)
v.

hagassengalia. (PE2 SENGA)
v.

hagasseva. (BE- SSEVA)
v.

hagassevalia. (BE2 SSEVA)
v.

hagassiba. (PE- SIBA$_1$)
v.

hagassibalia. (PE2 SIBA$_1$)
v.

hagassigo. (EE- SIGO)
v.

hagassigoa. (EE2 SIGO)
v.

hagassigohia. (EE2 SIGO)
v.

hagassigolia. (EE2 SIGO)
v.

hagassii$_1$. (PE- SII)
v.

hagassii$_2$. (BE- SSII)
v.

hagassiia. (PE2 SII)
v.

hagassiigonga. (EE1 SIGO)
n.

hagassiinga$_1$. (PE1 SII)
n.

hagassiinga$_2$. (BE1 SSII)
n.

hagassiisiinga. (RE1 SSII)
n.

hagassiissii. (RE- SSII)
v.

hagassila. (PE- SILA)
v.

hagassilaanga. (PE1 SILA)
n.

hagassili$_1$. (PE- SILI$_1$)
v.

hagassili$_2$. (PE- SILI$_3$)
v.

hagassilia. (PE2 SILI$_1$)
v.

hagassinga. (PE- SINGA)
v.

hagassingaanga. (PE1 SINGA)
n.

hagassingalia. (PE2 SINGA)
v.

hagassivia. (PE2 SIVI)
v.

hagassobo. (PE- SOBO)
v.

hagassoboa. (PE2 SOBO)
v.

hagassobolia. (PE2 SOBO)
v.

hagassoe. (PE- SOE)
Straighten out; decide an issue (by higher authority). *v.*

hagassoea. (PE2 SOE)
v.

hagassoelia. (PE2 SOE)
v.

hagassoenga. (PE1 SOE)
n.

hagassoga. (BE- SSOGA)
[Var. of *hagassogo*]. *v.*

hagassogaanga. (BE1 SSOGA)
[Var. of *hagassogoanga*]. *n.*

hagassogalia. (BE2 SSOGA)
[Var. of *hagassogolia*]. *v.*

hagassogo. (BE- SSOGO)
v.

hagassogoanga. (BE1 SSOGO)
n.

hagassogolia. (BE2 SSOGO)
v.

hagassolo. (EE- SOLO)
—; to scrape slightly in passing. *v.*

hagassomo. (PE- SOMO$_1$)
v.

hagassomolia. (PE2 SOMO$_1$)
v.

hagassongo. (BE- SSONGO)
v.

hagassoomonga. (PE1 SOMO$_1$)
n.

hagassui. (BE- SUU$_1$)
—; urinate. *v.*

hagassuia. (BE2 SUU$_1$)
v.

hagassui age.
Eat or drink just a little bit.

hagassuinga. (BE1 SUU$_1$)
n.

hagassula. (PE- SULA)
v.

hagassulangia. (PE2 SULA)
v.

hagassulu. (PE- SULU)
v.

hagassulumia. (PE2 SULU)
v.

hagassunu. (BE- SSUNU)
—; teach to *sunu*; to give (someone) something to *sunu*. *v.*

hagassunua. (BE2 SSUNU)
v.

hagassunumia. (BE2 SSUNU)
v.

hagassuulanga. (PE1 SULA)
n.

hagassuulua. (PE2 SULU)
v.

hagassuulunga. (PE1 SULU)
n.

hagasua. (BE- SUA)
v.

hagasuaanga. (BE1 SUA)
n.

hagasualia. (BE2 SUA)
v.

hagasuanga. (BE1 SUU_{1a})
v.

hagasuasua. (RE- SUA)
v.

hagasuasuaanga. (RE1 SUA)
n.

hagasuasualia. (RE2 SUA)
v.

hagasugi$_1$. (BE- $SUGI_1$)
v.

hagasugi$_2$. (BE- $SUGI_2$)
Shorten, abbreviate; abbreviation, acronym, nickname. *v.*

hagasugia. (BE2 $SUGI_1$)
v.

hagasugi ange.
To use an abbreviated name or acronym.

hagasugisugi$_1$. (RE- $SUGI_1$)
v.

hagasugisugi$_2$. (RE- $SUGI_2$)
Repeatedly shorten or abbreviate. *v.*

hagasugisugia. (RE2 $SUGI_1$)
v.

hagasugisuginga. (RE1 $SUGI_1$)
n.

hagasuguia. (BE2 SUUGUI)
v.

hagasuguinga. (BE1 SUUGUI)
n.

hagasugusugui. (RE- SUUGUI)
v.

hagasugusuguia. (RE2 SUUGUI)
v.

hagasugusuguinga. (RE1 SUUGUI)
n.

hagasuisui. (RE- SUU_1)
v.

hagasuisuia. (RE2 SUU_1)
v.

hagasuisuinga. (RE1 SUU_1)
n.

hagasula. (BE- SULA)
v.

hagasula tangada.
Successfully promote the candidacy of someone (or elect or appoint him) to a coveted position.

hagasulangia. (BE2 SULA)
v.

hagasulasula. (RE- SULA)
v.

hagasulasulaanga. (RE1 SULA)
n.

hagasulasulangia. (RE2 SULA)
v.

hagasulegi. (BE- SULEGI)
v.

hagasulu. (BE- SULU)
—; annoint (in baptism). *v.*

hagasulua. (BE2 SULU)
v.

hagasulumanga. (BE1 SULU)
n.

hagasulumia. (BE2 SULU)
v.

hagasulusulu. (RE- SULU)
v.

hagasulusulua. (RE2 SULU)
v.

hagasulusulumanga. (RE1 SULU)
n.

hagasulusulumia. (RE2 SULU)
v.

hagasulusulunga. (RE1 SULU)
n.

hagasumu. (BE- $SUMU_1$)
v.

hagasumua. (BE2 $SUMU_1$)
v.

hagasumulia. (BE2 $SUMU_1$)
v.

hagasumusumu. (RE- $SUMU_1$)
v.

hagasumusumua. (RE2 $SUMU_1$)
v.

hagasumusumulia. (RE2 $SUMU_1$)
v.

hagasumusumunga. (RE1 $SUMU_1$)
n.

hagasunusunu₁. (RE- SUNU)
v.

hagasunusunu₂. (RE- SSUNU)
v.

hagasunusunua₁. (RE2 SUNU)
v.

hagasunusunua₂. (RE2 SSUNU)
v.

hagasunusunumia. (RE2 SSUNU)
v.

hagasunusununga₁. (RE1 SUNU)
n.

hagasunusununga₂. (RE1 SSUNU)
n.

hagasuuduuduu. (BE- SUU_{1b})
v.

hagasuuduuduua. (BE2 SUU_{1b})
v.

hagasuuduuduulia. (BE2 SUU_{1b})
v.

hagasuuduuduunga. (BE1 SUU_{1b})
n.

hagasuuginga. (BE1 $SUGI_1$)
n.

hagasuugui. (BE- SUUGUI)
v.

hagasuuguia. (BE2 SUUGUI)
v.

hagasuuguinga. (BE1 SUUGUI)
n.

hagasuulanga. (BE1 SULA)
n.

hagasuulunga. (BE1 SULU)
n.

hagasuumunga. (BE1 $SUMU_1$)
n.

hagasuunugi. (BE- SUUNUGI)
v.

hagasuunugia. (BE2 SUUNUGI)
v.

hagasuunuginga. (BE1 SUUNUGI)
n.

hagasuununga. (BE1 SSUNU)
n.

hagasuungia. (BE2 SUU_1)
v.

hagasuusuunugi. (RE- SUUNUGI)
v.

hagasuusuunugia. (RE2 SUUNUGI)
v.

hagasuusuunuginga.
(RE1 SUUNUGI) *n.*

hagasuusuungia. (RE2 SUU_1)
v.

hagaua₁. (BE- UA_1)
v.

hagaua₂. (BE- UA_2)
v.

hagauaa. (BE- UAA)
v.

hagauaanga₁. (BE1 UA_1)
n.

hagauaanga₂. (BE1 UA_2)
n.

hagauaanga₃. (BE1 UAA)
n.

hagauaauaa. (RE- UAA)
v.

hagauaauaanga. (RE1 UAA)
n.

hagauadanga. (BE1 UA_2)
n.

hagauaua$_1$. (RE- UA_1)
v.

hagauaua$_2$. (RE- UA_2)
v.

hagauaua$_3$. (RE- UA_3)
v.

hagauauaanga$_1$. (RE1 UA_1)
n.

hagauauaanga$_2$. (RE1 UA_2)
n.

hagauauaanga$_3$. (RE1 UA_3)
n.

hagauauadanga. (RE1 UA_2)
n.

hagauba. (BE- UBA)
v.

hagaubaanga. (BE1 UBA)
n.

hagaubauba. (RE- UBA)
v.

hagaubaubaanga. (RE1 UBA)
n.

hagauda. (BE- UDA_1)
—; anoint (in baptism). *v.*

hagauda de hau.
Put on a *hau.*

hagauda de hine.
A certain method of delivering a child.

hagauda i tege.
Carry a basket, etc., on one's hip.

hagaudalia. (BE2 UDA_1)
v.

hagaudanga. (BE1 UDA_1)
—; the load or capacity (of a ship or canoe). *n.*

hagaudua. (BE- UDUA)
v.

hagauduuduhi. (BE- UDUUDUHI)
v.

hagauduuduhia.
(BE2 UDUUDUHI) *v.*

hagauduuduhinga.
(BE1 UDUUDUHI) *n.*

hagaue. (BE- UE)
v.

hagauea. (BE2 UE)
A sleeping mat. *v.*

hagauenga. (BE1 UE)
n.

hagaueue. (RE- UE)
v.

hagaueuea. (RE2 UE)
v.

hagaueuenga. (RE1 UE)
n.

hagaugu. (BE- UGU)
v.

hagaugua. (BE2 UGU)
v.

hagauguanga. (BE1 UGU)
n.

hagauguhia. (BE2 UGU)
v.

hagauguugu. (RE- UGU)
v.

hagauguugua. (RE2 UGU)
v.

hagauguuguanga. (RE1 UGU)
n.

hagauguuguhia. (RE2 UGU)
v.

hagauhe. (BE- UHE)
v.

hagauhea. (BE2 UHE)
v.

hagauheanga. (BE1 UHE)
n.

hagauhenga. (BE1 UHE)
n.

hagauheuhe. (RE- UHE)
v.

hagauheuhea. (RE2 UHE)
v.

hagauheuheanga. (RE1 UHE)
n.

hagauheuhenga. (RE1 UHE)
n.

hagauhi. (BE- UHI)
v.

hagauhia. (BE2 UHI)
v.

hagauhinga. (BE1 UHI)
n.

hagauhiuhi. (RE- UHI)
v.

hagauhiuhia. (RĖ2 UHI)
v.

hagauhiuhinga. (RE1 UHI)
n.

hagaui$_1$. (BE- UI$_1$)
v.

hagaui$_2$. (BE- UI$_2$)
—; remove (clothes, etc.), disrobe, undress; lose contact with. *v.*

hagauia$_1$. (BE2 UI$_1$)
v.

hagauia$_2$. (BE2 UI$_2$)
v.

hagaui gee.
Avoid.

hagauinga$_1$. (BE1 UI$_1$)
n.

hagauinga$_2$. (BE1 UI$_2$)
n.

hagauiui$_1$. (RE- UI$_1$)
v.

hagauiui$_2$. (RE- UI$_2$)
v.

hagauiuia$_1$. (RE2 UI$_1$)
v.

hagauiuia$_2$. (RE2 UI$_2$)
v.

hagauiuinga$_1$. (RE1 UI$_1$)
n.

hagauiuinga$_2$. (RE1 UI$_2$)
n.

hagaula. (BE- ULA$_1$)
v.

hagaulaanga. (BE1 ULA$_1$)
n.

hagaulalo. (BE- ULALO)
v.

hagaulaloanga. (BE1 ULALO)
n.

hagaulaula. (RE- ULA$_1$)
v.

hagaulaulaanga. (RE1 ULA$_1$)
n.

hagaulaulavvaa. (RE- ULA$_{1a}$)
v.

hagaulaulavvaanga. (RE1 ULA$_{1a}$)
n.

hagaulavvaa. (BE- ULA$_{1a}$)
v.

hagaulavvaanga. (BE1 ULA$_{1a}$)
n.

hagauli. (BE- ULI$_1$)
—; become dark (in color). *v.*

hagaulia. (BE2 ULI$_1$)
v.

hagaulianga. (BE1 ULI$_1$)
n.

hagauliuli. (RE- ULI$_1$)
v.

hagauliulia. (RE2 ULI$_1$)
v.

hagauliulianga. (RE1 ULI$_1$)
n.

hagaulu$_1$. (BE- ULU$_1$)
—; to put oneself between others (as children do). *v.*

hagaulu$_2$. (BE- ULU$_1$)
Fish sp.: shark sp. *n.*

hagaulua. (BE2 ULU$_1$)
v.

hagauludino. (BE- ULU$_{1a}$)
v.

hagauludinoanga. (BE1 ULU$_{1a}$)
n.

hagauluhia. (BE2 ULU$_1$)
v.

hagaului. (BE- ULU$_{1b}$)
v.

hagauluia. (BE2 ULU$_{1b}$)
v.

hagauluinga. (BE1 ULU$_{1b}$) *n.*

hagaulumagi. (BE- ULU$_{1c}$) *v.*

hagaulumagia. (BE2 ULU$_{1c}$) *v.*

hagaulumagina. (BE2 ULU$_{1c}$) *v.*

hagaulumaginga. (BE1 ULU$_{1c}$) *n.*

hagaulunga$_1$. (BE1 ULU$_1$) *n.*

hagaulunga$_2$. (BE- ULUNGA) *v.*

hagaulungaanga. (BE1 ULUNGA) *n.*

hagaulungi. (BE- ULUNGI) *v.*

hagaulungia. (BE2 ULUNGI) *v.*

hagaulunginga. (BE1 ULUNGI) *n.*

hagauluulu. (RE- ULU$_1$) *v.*

hagauluulua. (RE2 ULU$_1$) *v.*

hagauluuludino. (RE- ULU$_{1a}$) *v.*

hagauluuludinoanga. (RE1 ULU$_{1a}$) *n.*

hagauluuluhia. (RE2 ULU$_1$) *v.*

hagauluului. (RE- ULU$_{1b}$) *v.*

hagauluuluia. (RE2 ULU$_{1b}$) *v.*

hagauluuluinga. (RE1 ULU$_{1b}$) *n.*

hagauluulumagi. (RE- ULU$_{1c}$) *v.*

hagauluulumagia. (RE2 ULU$_{1c}$) *v.*

hagauluulumagina. (RE2 ULU$_{1c}$) *v.*

hagauluulumaginga. (RE1 ULU$_{1c}$) *n.*

hagauluulunga$_1$. (RE1 ULU$_1$) *n.*

hagauluulunga$_2$. (RE- ULUNGA) *v.*

hagauluulungaanga. (RE1 ULUNGA) *n.*

hagauluulungi. (RE- ULUNGI) *v.*

hagauluulungia. (RE2 ULUNGI) *v.*

hagauluulunginga. (RE1 ULUNGI) *n.*

hagaumalie. (BE- UMALIE) *v.*

hagaumaumalie. (RE- UMALIE) *v.*

hagaumidi. (BE- UMIDI) *v.*

hagaumidianga. (BE1 UMIDI) *n.*

hagaumiumidi. (RE- UMIDI) *v.*

hagaumiumidianga. (RE1 UMIDI) *n.*

hagaunu. (BE- UNU$_1$) *v.*

hagaunumanga. (BE1 UNU$_1$) *n.*

hagaunumia. (BE2 UNU$_1$) *v.*

hagaunusaagi. (BE- UNUSAAGI) *v.*

hagaunusaaginga. (BE1 UNUSAAGI) *n.*

hagaunusi. (BE- UNUSI) *v.*

hagaunusia. (BE2 UNUSI) *v.*

hagaunusinga. (BE1 UNUSI) *n.*

hagaunuunu. (RE- UNU$_1$) *v.*

hagaunuunumanga. (RE1 UNU_1)
— ['drink' meaning only]. *n.*

hagaunuunumia. (RE2 UNU_1)
v.

hagaunuunusaagi.
(RE- UNUSAAGI) *v.*

hagaunuunusaaginga.
(RE1 UNUSAAGI) *n.*

hagaunuunusi. (RE- UNUSI)
v.

hagaunuunusia. (RE2 UNUSI)
v.

hagaunuunusinga. (RE1 UNUSI)
n.

hagausi. (BE- USI)
Darkening of the sky or clouds (a sign of impending rain). *v.*

hagausia. (BE2 USI)
v.

hagausi age.
Appearance of rain clouds on the horizon.

hagausi mai.
The appearance of rain clouds.

hagausinga. (BE1 USI)
Rain cloud (includes all cumulus types). *n.*

hagausiusi. (RE- USI)
Becoming darker (of sky or clouds). *v.*

hagausiusia. (RE2 USI)
v.

hagausiusi de me.
A sky covered with rain clouds.

hagausiusinga. (RE1 USI)
n.

hagausubee. (BE- USU_{3a})
v.

hagausubeeanga. (BE1 USU_{3a})
n.

hagausuusubee. (RE- USU_{3a})
v.

hagausuusubeeanga. (RE1 USU_{3a})
n.

hagauu₁. (BE- UU_1)
v.

hagauu₂. (BE- UU_2)
v.

hagauu₃. (BE- UU_3)
Suckle, nurse (feed milk). *v.*

hagauunga. (BE1 UU_2)
n.

hagauuuu. (RE- UU_2)
v.

hagauuuunga. (RE1 UU_2)
n.

hagavaa. (BE- VAA_1)
v.

hagavaagia. (BE2 VAA_2)
v.

hagavaagina. (BE2 VAA_2)
v.

hagavaaginga. (BE1 VAA_2)
n.

hagavaaligi. (BE- VAA_{3b})
v.

hagavaaligiligi. (RE- VAA_{3b})
v.

hagavaalunga. (BE1 $VALU_1$)
n.

hagavaanga. (BE1 VAA_1)
n.

hagavaassega. (PE- VASEGA)
v.

hagavaassegaanga. (PE1 VASEGA)
n.

hagavaassuu. (PE- VAASUU)
v.

hagavaassuunga. (PE1 VAASUU)
n.

hagavaasuu. (BE- VAASUU)
—; healed, well (after sickness), recuperated; good (not bad, but not the best), OK; appropriate. *v.*

hagavaasuunga. (BE1 VAASUU)
n.

hagavaavaa. (RE- VAA_1)
v.

hagavaavaagia. (RE2 VAA$_2$)
v.

hagavaavaagina. (RE2 VAA$_2$)
v.

hagavaavaaginga. (RE1 VAA$_2$)
n.

hagavaavaanga. (RE1 VAA$_1$)
n.

hagavaavaasuu. (RE- VAASUU)
v.

hagavaavaasuunga.
(RE1 VAASUU) *n.*

hagavae. (BE- VAE$_1$)
v.

hagavaea. (BE2 VAE$_1$)
v.

hagavaenga. (BE1 VAE$_1$)
n.

hagavaevae. (RE- VAE$_1$)
v.

hagavaevaea. (RE2 VAE$_1$)
v.

hagavaevaelia. (RE2 VAE$_1$)
v.

hagavaevaenga. (RE1 VAE$_1$)
n.

hagavagavaga. (RE- VAGA$_2$)
Punishment of a person by confinement (without food or drink) until his death. *v.*

hagavagavagaanga. (RE1 VAGA$_2$)
n.

hagavage. (BE- VAGE$_2$)
v.

hagavagea. (BE2 VAGE$_2$)
v.

hagavagelia. (BE2 VAGE$_2$)
v.

hagavagenga. (BE1 VAGE$_2$)
n.

hagavagevage. (RE- VAGE$_2$)
v.

hagavagevagea. (RE2 VAGE$_2$)
v.

hagavagevagelia. (RE2 VAGE$_2$)
v.

hagavagevagenga. (RE1 VAGE$_2$)
n.

hagavakaa. (BE- VAKAA)
v.

hagavakaanga. (BE1 VAKAA)
n.

hagavaia. (BE2 VAI)
v.

hagavaiaanga. (BE3 VAI)
n.

hagavaiduu. (BE- VAIDUU)
To act as though one were lazy. *v.*

hagavaiduua. (BE2 VAIDUU)
v.

hagavaiduunga. (BE1 VAIDUU)
n.

hagavaivai. (RE- VAI)
Cause to become watery, or less viscous. *v.*

hagavaivaia. (RE2 VAI)
v.

hagavaivainga. (RE1 VAI)
n.

hagavalea. (BE2 VALE)
v.

hagavaleaanga. (BE3 VALE)
n.

hagavalu. (BE- VALU$_1$)
v.

hagavalu (ina). (BE- VALU$_2$)
Make a total of eight. *v.*

hagavalua. (BE2 VALU$_1$)
v.

hagavalusia. (BE2 VALU$_1$)
v.

hagavaluvalu. (RE- VALU$_1$)
v.

hagavaluvalua. (RE2 VALU$_1$)
v.

hagavaluvalunga. (RE1 VALU$_1$)
n.

hagavaluvalusia. (RE2 VALU$_1$)
v.

hagavasega. (BE- VASEGA)
v.

hagavasegaanga. (BE1 VASEGA)
n.

hagavasevasega. (RE- VASEGA)
v.

hagavasevasegaanga.
(RE1 VASEGA) *n.*

hagavasu. (BE- VASU)
v.

hagavasunga. (BE1 VASU)
n.

hagavasuvasu. (RE- VASU)
v.

hagavasuvasunga. (RE1 VASU)
n.

hagavava. (BE- VAVA)
v.

hagavavaanga. (BE1 VAVA)
n.

hagavavvava. (RE- VAVA)
v.

hagavavvavaanga. (RE1 VAVA)
n.

hagavedevede. (RE- $VEDE_1$)
v.

hagavedevedea. (RE2 $VEDE_1$)
v.

hagavedevedenga. (RE1 $VEDE_1$)
n.

hagaveedea. (BE2 $VEDE_1$)
v.

hagaveedenga. (BE1 $VEDE_1$)
n.

hagaveelenga. (BE1 VELE)
n.

hagaveelonga. (BE1 VELO)
n.

hagaveevenga. (BE1 VEVE)
n.

hagavela. (BE- VELA)
v.

hagavelaanga. (BE1 VELA)
n.

hagavelavela. (RE- VELA)
v.

hagavelavelaanga. (RE1 VELA)
n.

hagavele. (BE- VELE)
v.

hagavelea. (BE2 VELE)
v.

hagavelevele. (RE- VELE)
v.

hagavelevelea. (RE2 VELE)
v.

hagavelevelenga. (RE1 VELE)
n.

hagavelo. (BE- VELO)
v.

hagaveloa. (BE2 VELO)
v.

hagavelosia. (BE2 VELO)
v.

hagavelovelo. (RE- VELO)
v.

hagaveloveloa. (RE2 VELO)
v.

hagavelovelonga. (RE1 VELO)
n.

hagavelovelosia. (RE2 VELO)
v.

hagaveve. (BE- VEVE)
v.

hagavevea. (BE2 VEVE)
v.

hagavevelia. (BE2 VEVE)
v.

hagavii. (BE- VII)
v.

hagaviia. (BE2 VII)
v.

hagaviilinga. (BE1 VILI)
n.

hagaviininga. (BE1 VINI)
n.

hagaviinga. (BE1 VII)
n.

hagaviivii. (BE- VIIVII)
v.

hagaviiviia. (BE2 VIIVII)
v.

hagaviiviinga. (BE1 VIIVII)
n.

hagavili. (BE- VILI)
v.

hagavilia. (BE2 VILI)
v.

hagavilivili. (RE- VILI)
v.

hagavilivilia. (RE2 VILI)
v.

hagavilivilinga. (RE1 VILI)
n.

hagavini. (BE- VINI)
v.

hagavinia. (BE2 VINI)
v.

hagavinivini. (RE- VINI)
v.

hagavinivinia. (RE2 VINI)
v.

hagavinivininga. (RE1 VINI)
n.

hagavogi$_1$. (BE- VOGI$_1$)
v.

hagavogi$_2$. (BE- VOGI$_2$)
A whistle (made with the lips). *v.*

hagavogia. (BE2 VOGI$_1$)
v.

hagavoginga. (BE1 VOGI$_1$)
n.

hagavogivogi$_1$. (RE- VOGI$_1$)
v.

hagavogivogi$_2$. (RE- VOGI$_2$)
v.

hagavogivogia. (RE2 VOGI$_1$)
v.

hagavogivoginga$_1$. (RE1 VOGI$_1$)
n.

hagavogivoginga$_2$. (RE1 VOGI$_2$)
n.

hagavooginga. (BE1 VOGI$_2$)
n.

hagavvae. (EE- VAE$_1$)
v.

hagavvaea. (EE2 VAE$_1$)
v.

hagavvaelia. (EE2 VAE$_1$)
v.

hagavvala. (BE- VVALA)
v.

hagavvalaanga. (BE1 VVALA)
n.

hagavvale. (BE- VVALE)
Spirit possession. *v.*

hagavvaleanga. (BE1 VVALE)
n.

hagavvalo. (BE- VVALO)
v.

hagavvasu. (PE- VASU)
v.

hagavvasunga. (PE1 VASU)
n.

hagavvava. (PE- VAVA)
v.

hagavvavaanga. (PE1 VAVA)
n.

hagavvede. (EE- VEDE$_1$)
—; to teach to massage. *v.*

hagavvela. (PE- VELA)
—; hot (of the weather). *v.*

hagavvelaanga. (PE1 VELA)
n.

hagavvini. (PE- VINI)
v.

hagavvogi. (PE- VOGI$_2$)
v.

hagehageli. (R-- HAGELI)
v.

hagehagelia. (R-2 HAGELI)
v.

hagehagelinga. (R-1 HAGELI)
n.

hageli.
A sort of sound in ancient chants. *v.*

hagelia. (B-2 HAGELI)
v.

hagelinga. (B-1 HAGELI)
n.

hagi.
Pick (fruit) by grabbing and twisting off. *v.*

hagi ade.
Insult (someone).

hagihagi. (R-- HAGI)
v.

hagihagia. (R-2 HAGI)
v.

hagihagina. (R-2 HAGI)
v.

hagihaginga. (R-1 HAGI)
n.

hagili. (B-- $GILI_a$)
Speak (or sing) with phelgm in one's throat. *v.*

hagilianga. (B-1 GILI)
n.

hagi me.
Pick coconuts.

hakaa. (BE- GAA_2)
—; sharpen (a knife), rub against; husk of the coconut. *v.*

hakaadia₁. (BE2 GAA_2)
v.

hakaadia₂. (BE2 GADI)
Make tightly packed. *v.*

hakaa tuai.
To sharpen a coconut grater blade.

hakaagaaui*. (RE- $GAAUI_1$)
v.

hakaagaauia°. (RE2 $GAAUI_1$)
v.

hakaagaauinga*. (RE1 $GAAUI_1$)
n.

hakaagea. (BE2 GAGE)
v.

hakaagenga. (BE1 GAGE)
n.

hakaalonga₁. (BE1 $GALO_1$)
n.

hakaalonga₂. (BE1 $GALO_2$)
n.

hakaanga. (BE1 GAA_2)
n.

hakaaui*. (BE- $GAAUI_1$)
v.

hakaauia*. (BE2 $GAAUI_1$)
v.

hakaauinga*. (BE1 $GAAUI_1$)
n.

hakaau unuunu.
To cause an infant to feed at the breast.

hakabaea. (BE- GABAEA)
— [usual form]. *v.*

hakabaeanga. (BE1 GABAEA)
— [usual form]. *n.*

hakabea. (BE- GABEA)
v.

hakabeaanga. (BE1 GABEA)
n.

hakada. (BE- $GADA_1$)
v.

hakadagada. (RE- $GADA_1$)
v.

hakadanga. (BE1 $GADA_1$)
Funny, unserious, jesting, silly. *a.*

hakadigadi. (RE- GADI)
v.

hakadoa. (BE- GADOA)
v.

hakadoaanga. (BE1 GADOA)
n.

hakage. (BE- GAGE)
v.

hakagelia. (BE2 GAGE)
v.

hakagu. (BE- GAGU)
v.

hakagudia. (BE2 GAGU)
v.

hakagulia. (BE2 GAGU)
v.

hakahu. (BE- GAHU)
v.

hakahuanga. (BE1 GAHU)
n.

hakahudia. (BE2 GAHU)
v.

hakahugahu. (RE- GAHU)
v.

hakahugahuanga. (RE1 GAHU)
n.

hakahugahudia. (RE2 GAHU)
v.

hakahugahulia. (RE2 GAHU)
v.

hakahulia. (BE2 GAHU)
v.

hakai. (B-- KAI_{2a})
To put something on one's ear; an earring. *v.*

hakaia. (B-2 KAI_{2a})
v.

hakai-a-bagila.
Mollusk sp.: *Cerithiidae* spp.

hakainga. (B-1 KAI_{2a})
n.

hakaligali. (SE- GALI)
Grooved. *v.*

$hakalo_1$. (BE- $GALO_1$)
v.

$hakalo_2$. (BE- $GALO_2$)
v.

hakaloa. (BE2 $GALO_1$)
v.

hakalogalo. (RE- $GALO_1$)
v.

hakalohia. (BE2 $GALO_1$)
v.

hakangi. (BE- KANGI)
v.

hakaogao. (RE- GAO)
To sit on one buttock. *v.*

hakasa. (BE- GASA)
v.

hakasaanga. (BE1 GASA)
n.

hakasalia. (BE2 GASA)
v.

hakasogaso. (RE- $GASO_1$)
v.

hakasogasoa. (RE2 $GASO_1$)
v.

hakasogasoanga. (RE1 $GASO_1$)
n.

hakasogasolia. (RE2 $GASO_1$)
v.

hakau. (BE- GAU_1)
v.

hakauanga. (XE- GAU_{1d})
A handle of something. *n.*

hakaugau. (RE- GAU_2)
v.

hakaugaua. (RE2 GAU_2)
To bathe (someone). *v.*

hakaugaunga. (RE1 GAU_2)
n.

hakaunuunu. (B-- UNU_{1a})
To nurse (an infant at the breast). *v.*

hakaunuunuanga. (B-1 UNU_{1a})
n.

hakaunuunumia. (B-2 UNU_{1a})
v.

hakeelinga. (EE1 GELI)
n.

hakelegele. (RE- GELE)
—; make certain sounds to attract fish. *v.*

hakelegelea. (RE2 GELE)
v.

hakelegeleanga. (RE1 GELE)
n.

hakeli. (EE- GELI)
v.

hakelia. (EE2 GELI)
v.

hakelogelonga. (RE1 GELO)
n.

hakemo. (BE- GEMO)
v.

hakemoanga. (BE1 GEMO)
n.

hakemolia. (BE2 GEMO)
v.

hakide. (B-- GIDE$_a$)
To reveal oneself to someone (of a ghost); to show (familiarize with). *v.*

hakideanga. (B-1 GIDE$_a$)
n.

hakide gauligi.
Spoil children.

hakide gee.
Spoil (a child).

hakidelia. (B-2 GIDE$_a$)
v.

hakii$_1$. (B-- GII$_a$)
Larynx, epiglottis, trachea. *n.*

hakii$_2$. (BE- KII$_2$)
Move away completely; get out of the way. *v.*

hakiia. (BE2 KII$_2$)
Move (something) away completely. *v.*

hakii adu.
Get out!

hakiianga. (BE1 KII$_2$)
n.

hakii gee.
[= *kii gee*].

hakiigia. (B-- GII$_b$)
To swell up (from being filled with air — like a balloon). *v.*

hakiigiaanga. (B-1 GII$_b$)
n.

hakiinga. (BE1 KII$_2$)
n.

hakiligilisau. (RE- GILI$_b$)
v.

hakiligilisaua. (RE2 GILI$_b$)
v.

hakiligilisaunga. (RE1 GILI$_b$)
n.

hakilisau. (BE- GILI$_b$)
v.

hakilisaua. (BE2 GILI$_b$)
v.

hakilisaunga. (BE1 GILI$_b$)
n.

hakino gee.
Filthy, disgusting.

hakohu. (BE- GOHU)
v.

hakohuanga. (BE1 GOHU)
n.

hakohugohu. (RE- GOHU)
v.

hakohugohuanga. (RE1 GOHU)
n.

hakohugohulia. (RE2 GOHU)
v.

hakohulia. (BE2 GOHU)
v.

hakohu luu mada.
Squint (eyes), frown.

hakoloa. (BE- GOLOA)
Provide *goloa* for; support (someone, with material things). *v.*

hakoloaanga. (BE1 GOLOA)
n.

hakolona. (BE- GOLONA)
Mollusk sp.: auger shell (*Terebridae* sp.). *n.*

hakooanga. (PE1 GOO$_1$)
n.

hakoobai. (BE- GOOBAI)
Put a hat on (someone). *v.*

hakoobaia. (BE2 GOOBAI)
v.

hakoobainga. (BE1 GOOBAI)
n.

hakoso. (BE- GOSO)
v.

hakosoanga. (BE1 GOSO)
n.

hakosolia. (BE2 GOSO)
v.

haha.
Mouth odor. *n.*

hahaunu. (R-- UNU$_{1b}$)
v.

hahaunua. (R-2 UNU$_{1b}$)
v.

hahaunumanga. (R-1 UNU$_{1b}$)
n.

hahaunumia. (R-2 UNU_{1b})
v.

hahaununga. (R-1 UNU_{1b})
n.

hahine.
Woman. *n.*

haho.
Outside of. *nl.*

hai_1.
Do, make, use; have sexual intercourse. *v.*

hai_2.
Be in the relationship of; having a — (as in *hai maalisa*) [from *iai*?]. *d.*

haia. (B-2 HAI_1)
v.

hai aabi.
Having many rooms or sections.

haiadaligi*. (ALIGI, HAI_2)
The eldest child of the eldest child. *n.*

hai aha.
What relationship?

hai ange.
Do to; do for, fix; say to.

hai aoa ina.
Bear misshapen fruit.

haiava. (AVA_1, HAI_{1a})
Road, pathway (for going), track; ocean liner. *n.*

hai baasi.
Take sides against, oppose.

hai bao.
Divided into compartments.

hai be --.
It would seem that —.

hai be se manu.
Promiscuous (especially if indiscreet or known to have sexual relations with one's own relatives).

hai bodu.
Married couple, marry; the relationship between spouses.

hai daadaa.
The relationship between siblings.

hai daahili.
To compose songs.

hai daalanga.
Talkative, chatterbox, talk animatedly.

hai dagelo.
Deep-bottomed.

hai dago.
Ritual observances.

hai dahi doo.
Trick someone.

hai dahi heohi.
Maintain one's position in an argument (against contrary positions).

hai daina.
The relationship between siblings or cousins.

hai dama.
Pregnant.

hai damaahine.
The relationship between parent and daughter.

hai damana.
The relationship between father (or other male elder) and child (or one treated as child).

hai dangada.
The relationship between relatives, related (of persons).

hai dauaa.
Be in a wrinkled condition.

hai de ama.
To have a spouse.

hai de biho.
Act smart (deviously).

hai de boo (o).
Celebrate the birthday (of).

hai de eidu.
One of two children's games [one like hide-and-seek, another like tag].

hai de gubenga.
To use a *gubenga* for fishing.

hai de hagamaanadu.
Remembrance, observance of (e.g., a holiday).

hai de hai.
Stubborn, willful.

hai de hilihili.
Hold an election.

hai de ingoo.
Make a good name for oneself (by one's ingratiating behavior).

hai dinana.
The relationship between mother (or other female elder) and child (or one treated as a child).

hai dodo.
Bleeding profusely.

hai donu.
Do properly by accident; do on purpose [when preceded by *se*].

hai dubuna.
The relationship between grandparent and grandchild.

hai duu.
To carry a baby about.

hai taelodo.
Obtain something in great number.

haitoga. ($DOGA_3$, HAI_1)
An opening for a door or window. *n.*

hai gaavenga.
Restless (of a child).

haigabungi.
Act strangely, act shyly. *a.*

haigabungianga.
(B-1 HAIGABUNGI) *n.*

hai gai.
Prepared food; cook food.

hai gaiaa.
Use without permission.

hai gainga.
Make an area messy by throwing trash around.

hai galauna.
Fish with the *galauna* net.

haigamaiana.
Effective, useful, worthwhile, important. *a.*

hai ganabu.
The stage in the development of a coconut tree in which *ganabu* begins to develop.

hai gauligi.
Each child is somewhat different!

hai gi de mahi.
Do or take by force, rape.

hai goinga.
Aggrandizement of one's land holdings by moving others' *goinga.*

hai kai.
Show-off, proud.

hai hagadubu.
To fashion a string figure.

haihai. (R-- HAI_1)
v.

haihaia. (R-2 HAI_1)
v.

haihai me.
Be doing something suspicious.

haihainga. (R-1 HAI_1)
n.

haihainga a --.
Way of repeatedly —.

hai hegau.
Work [verb].

hai hegau hilo.
Work hypocritically (appearing to follow the rules but secretly violating the prohibitions).

hai huaabodu.
Treat someone (including one's spouse) as a relative by not asking permission to use or borrow property; treat a relative as belonging to another family altogether.

hai huaame.
Punctilious, be particular.

hai hua laa.
Do indifferently.

hai hulu o --.
Act mad like —.

hai huuhuaa me.
Sorcery.

hai lodo.
Resentful.

hailu.
Wipe oneself (after defecating). *v.*

hailua. (B-2 HAILU)
v.

hailunga. (B-1 HAILU)
n.

hai maa.
The relationship of spouse's sibling to sibling's spouse.

hai maadua.
Mention of one's elders by others.

hai maalisa.
Having an overhanging reef shelf.

hai mada dabu.
An avoidance relationship (between kin).

hai madangi.
Pass wind (flatus).

hai mainu.
Collect bait.

hai me.
Industrious.

hai me a gauligi.
A childish act.

hai me a gimoo.
To act insincerely.

hai me a leangi.
Bad-mannered.

hai me balavini.
To conduct oneself clumsily.

hai me daahea.
Search for driftwood or other beached objects.

hai me dagi.
Work slowly.

hai me dogaa.
Behave with embarrassment or shyness.

hai me dua nnui.
Do violently.

hai me gaiaa.
To be reluctant to express oneself openly (esp. to persons in certain types of relationship to one).

hai me galasi.
To steal after having sort of asked for.

hai me gavia.
Do crazy things.

hai me hagamadia.
Behave in a more-or-less show-off manner.

hai me hebagi.
Be on the point of fighting.

hai me hoosenga.
Somewhat *hoosenga.*

hai me ma --.
Sort of —.

hai me madua.
Act grown up.

hai me magua.
Sort of steal.

hai me moolau.
An habitually fast worker.

hai me mudumudu.
A habitually *mudumudu.*

hai me mulegi.
To show off (esp. in front of members of the opposite sex).

hai me mule me.
Habitually slow or late.

hai modo.
Eat (or pick) when still unripe.

hai mogobuna.
The relationship between grandparent and grandchild.

hai mogomogo.
Muscular; daring (show off), bold; strong (person); active physically.

hai moni.
Sailor.

hai moumou.
Use wastefully.

hai muna.
Public meeting.

hai naa hanu me.
Something will happen...

hainamanilaluoo. (?)
Secret friend of the opposite sex. *n.*

hainoo.
Permitted, open to the public, secular [opposite of *dabu*]. *v.*

hainooa. (B-2 HAINOO)
v.

hainooanga. (B-1 HAINOO)
n.

hainoonga. (B-1 HAINOO)
n.

hainga. (B-1 HAI_1)
—; law, procedure, rule. *n.*

hainga a --.
Way of doing —.

haingaa me.
Work requiring a large work force.

hai ngadaa.
Difficult.

hai ngaohie.
Easy.

hainga soe.
A just law.

hai sala.
Mistake, error.

hai samu.
To gossip.

hai saulaba.
The relationship of parent-in-law to child-in-law.

hai soa.
The relationship between friends; friendship.

hai sogosogo.
Masturbate oneself.

hai sseu.
Wasteful.

hai sumu.
Having a diamond-shaped decoration or form, etc.

hai uaua.
Dilated veins.

haiva.
Work, activity, occupation. *n.*

haiva dee agona.
Sexual activity, [lit., 'the activity which is not taught'].

hai vaivai me.
Have sexual relations.

hala.
Plant sp.: tree sp.: pandanus (several varieties). *n.*

hala a buadaia.
A log used as a lever or fulcrum.

halaasola. (CF SOLA)
Mollusk sp.: clam sp. (a type of *baasua*). *n.*

hala dudu.
A noise like that of burning pandanus (loud crackling).

hala goobai.
A wooden form used in making hats.

hala langa goobai.
A form for plaiting hats.

hale.
House, dwelling, building. *n.*

hale baabaa.
Frame house.

hale baalanga.
Frame house.

hale pono.
Prison, jail.

hale daane.
Men's house (modern usage).

hale dabeo*.
Menstrual hut.

hale daumaha.
Church (building).

hale de henua.
A house of indigenous construction (thatch).

hale duu biho.
Barber shop.

hale gaainga.
Hotel.

hale gai.
Restaurant.

hale gaugau.
Bath house.

hale goloa.
Store.

hale haahine.
A house of prostitution.

hale hadu.
A house of brick or cement construction.

hale hagao me.
Store.

hale hai niho.
Dentist's office.

halehale --. (R-- HALE)
Developing (of a situation). *d.*

halehale dagodo.
Guarded condition or prognosis (of a sick person); unsettled (of a situation, the weather, etc.).

halehale dagodo lodo.
Nauseated.

halehale dangada.
A suspicious character.

halehale gaiaa.
Cloying insincere humility.

halehale me.
A developing situation.

halehale me donu huu.
Surprisingly, it turned out to be possible!

hale hongagelegele.
Out house.

hale i lodo.
Rib cage, thoracic cavity.

hale langadala.
Thatch-roofed house (of palm frond thatch).

hale lau.
Thatch-roofed house (of pandanus leaf thatch).

hale maadenga.
Mortuary house.

hale magi.
Hospital, dispensary.

hale neveneve.
Spider web.

hale nnoa.
Prison, jail.

hale o de henua.
Community meeting house.

hale suunugi.
A house with eaves touching the ground [an old style].

hali.
d.

halihali. (R-- HALI)
v.

halihalia. (R-2 HALI)
v.

halihalibaa. (CF HALI)
Fish sp.: flatfish. *n.*

halihalinga. (R-1 HALI)
n.

hallaba. (B-- $LABA_{2b}$)
The base of a palm frond spine; rifle. *n.*

hanange. (ANGE, HANO)
Go to. *a.*

hanaua. (B-2 HAANAU)
v.

hannoo. (E-- HANO)
Go! *i.*

hannoo kaba.
Go now, right away! Beat it!

hano.
Go [sing.]. *a.*

hano ahe.
Echo.

hano ai.
Attend (e.g., church services).

hano ai huu.
Forever.

hano de leebunga.
Run (of a color); fade (of a color).

hano de mama.
Escaping fumes (from a poorly sealed container).

hano gaogao.
Move sideways.

hano gee.
Go away [sing.].

hano gi bouli gee.
To transfigure oneself.

hano gi de maalama.
Transfiguration of ghosts or spirits into human form.

hano gi oona.
Very, exceedingly.

hano goe.
See what I told you!

hano kaba.
Go immediately!

hanohano. (R-- HANO)
Go repeatedly; diarrhea. *a.*

hanohano ai huu.
Go on and on until —.

hanohano dua.
Suffer a setback; almost fall; gorge oneself; stagger backwards (e.g., under load).

hano i luu moana.
Die (a person).

hano laa.
Previous.

hano laa uda.
Go on foot.

hanolia. (B-2 HANO)
Suitable for a trip (e.g., a car, a road, etc.). *v.*

hano mouli.
Disappear alive (esp. into another world).

hano muhuu loo.
Let's see...

hanonga. (B-1 HANO)
Trip, journey. *n.*

hano saele.
Wander around.

hanu$_1$. (B-- HANU)
Some. *ma.*

hanu$_2$. (B-- HANU)
To have. *a.*

hanu age.
Regain.

hanu ange.
Some more.

hanuhanu. (R-- HANU)
Few; gaining in. *a.*

hanu me.
A secret friend of the opposite sex.

hanu momo.
Little bit, few.

hanga.
Horn (of an animal) [N]; a husking stick [N]; move apart [dp]; open up (one's mouth) [dp]; tie coconuts together with strips ripped from the coconut's outer husk [V]. *d.*

hangaa. (B-2 HANGA)
v.

hangaabo. (B-- HANGA$_a$)
The fitting together of the two halves of something, so that it is closed. *v.*

hangaaboa. (B-2 HANGA$_a$)
v.

hangaabolia. (B-2 HANGA$_a$)
v.

hangaabonga. (B-1 HANGA$_a$)
n.

hanga benu.
To extract pandanus seeds by splitting the fruit.

hangahanga. (R-- HANGA)
v.

hangahangaa. (R-2 HANGA)
v.

hangahangaabo. (R-- HANGA$_a$)
v.

hangahangaaboa. (R-2 HANGA$_a$)
v.

hangahangaabolia. (R-2 HANGA$_a$)
v.

hangahangaabonga. (R-1 HANGA$_a$)
n.

hangahangai. (R-- HAANGAI)
v.

hangahangaia. (R-2 HAANGAI)
v.

hangahangaina. (R-2 HAANGAI)
v.

hangahangainga. (R-1 HAANGAI)
n.

hangaia. (B-2 HAANGAI)
v.

hangaina. (B-2 HAANGAI)
v.

hangainga. (B-1 HAANGAI)
n.

hanga-mea.
[Var. of *angamea*]. *n.*

hango.
d.

hangohango. (R-- HANGO)
v.

hangohangoa. (R-2 HANGO)
v.

hangohangona. (R-2 HANGO)
v.

hangohangonga. (R-1 HANGO)
n.

hao$_1$.
Drill through, burrow. *v.*

hao$_2$.
d.

haoa. (B-2 HAO$_1$)
v.

haohao$_1$. (R-- HAO$_1$)
v.

haohao$_2$. (R-- HAO$_2$)
v.

haohaoa$_1$. (R-2 HAO$_1$)
v.

haohaoa$_2$. (R-2 HAO$_2$)
v.

haohaoli. (R-- HAOLI)
v.

haohaolia$_1$. (R-2 HAO$_1$)
v.

haohaolia$_2$. (R-2 HAOLI)
v.

haohaolinga. (R-1 HAOLI)
n.

haohaonga$_1$. (R-1 HAO$_1$)
n.

haohaonga$_2$. (R-1 HAO$_2$)
n.

haoli.
Cover up. *v.*

haolia$_1$. (B-2 HAO$_1$)
v.

haolia$_2$. (B-2 HAOLI)
v.

haolinga. (B-1 HAOLI)
n.

haonga. (B-1 HAO$_1$)
—; a hole (in something). *n.*

hasi.
To cut off a taro corm from its stalk. *v.*

hasia. (B-2 HASI)
v.

hasihasi. (R-- HASI)
v.

hasihasia. (R-2 HASI)
v.

hasihasinga. (R-1 HASI)
n.

hasi made.
To cut a taro corm from its stalk so far up the stalk that it won't grow a new corm when it is planted.

hau.
A garland of flowers (as a headdress or necklace); tie up — [dp], fasten by tying (wrapping) — [dp]. *a.*

hauala.
Seaweed sp.

hau baba.
Tie up temporarily (not as securely as if permanently).

hau bule.
Shell necklace or headdress.

hauhau. (R-- HAU)
v.

hauhaunga. (R-1 HAU)
n.

hauhausanga. (R-1 HAU)
[Pl. of *hausanga*]. *n.*

haula. (B-- ULA$_{1b}$)
Set fire to (causing large flames); light (a lamp). *v.*

haulanga. (B-1 ULA$_{1b}$)
n.

haula ngongo.
To roast *ngongo* (in a fire).

haulasia. (B-2 ULA$_{1b}$)
v.

haulia. (B-2 HAU)
v.

hau manu.
A garland of flowers, headdress, necklace.

haunu. (B-- UNU$_{1b}$)
[= *hagaunu*]. *v.*

haunua. (B-2 UNU$_{1b}$)
v.

haunumanga. (B-1 UNU$_{1b}$)
n.

haunumia. (B-2 UNU_{1b})
v.

haunumga. (B-1 UNU_{1b})
n.

haunga. (B-1 HAU)
Manner of wearing a flower garland. *n.*

hausanga. (B-1 HAU)
A wrapping (of string) around the join of a pole. *n.*

hausia. (B-2 HAU)
—; an ache in a muscle. *v.*

hau singano.
Garland of *singano.*

he-.
RECIPROCAL PREFIX. *mf.*

hebaa. (BD- BAA_1)
Be close. *a.*

hebagi. (BD- BAGI)
Fight. *a.*

hebahebaa. (RD- BAA_1)
Crowded together. *a.*

hebahebaledage.
(R-- HEBALEDAGE) *v.*

hebahebaledageanga.
(R-1 HEBALEDAGE) *n.*

hebaledage.
A confluence of currents (making the water choppy). *v.*

hebaledageanga.
(B-1 HEBALEDAGE) *n.*

hebohebolo. (R-- HEBOLO)
a.

heboheboohagi. (R-- BOO_{1b})
Fight frequently. *a.*

heboheboohaginga. (R-1 BOO_{1b})
n.

hebolo.
A sign made with the eyes. *a.*

heboloanga. (B-1 HEBOLO)
n.

heboohagi. (B-- BOO_{1b})
Fight. *a.*

heboohagi lima.
Fist fight.

heboohagi mai.
Found fighting.

heboohaginga. (B-1 BOO_{1b})
n.

hebuhebuihagi. (R-- BUI_b)
v.

hebuihagi. (B-- BUI_b)
Provide an abundance of bait to keep fish in close. *v.*

hebuihagina. (B-2 BUI_b)
v.

hebuihaginga. (B-1 BUI_b)
n.

hedaadoi.
Collide. *a.*

hedaadoinga. (B-1 HEDAADOI)
n.

hedae. (BD- DAE_2)
Meet up with; be even with each other. *a.*

hedaenga. (BD1 DAE_2)
n.

hedahedaadoi. (R-- HEDAADOI)
a.

hedahedaadoinga. (R-1 HEDAADOI)
n.

hedahedangisi. (R-- $NGISI_a$)
a.

hedahedangisinga. (R-1 $NGISI_a$)
n.

hedangisi. (B-- $NGISI_a$)
To make noise by scraping things together (e.g., the grinding sound of jaws). *a.*

hedangisinga. (B-1 $NGISI_a$)
n.

hedau.
Plant sp.: tree sp.: Alexandrian laurel tree (*Calophyllum inophyllum* L.). *n.*

hedogi. (BD- DOGI)
The sound of tapping. *v.*

hedu.
Fold up —. *d.*

heduge. (CF $DUGI_1$)
Slate-pencil urchin. *n.*

heduhedu. (R-- HEDU)
v.

heduhedua. (R-2 HEDU)
v.

heduhedunga. (R-1 HEDU)
n.

heduu.
Star, planet. *n.*

hetugi. (ED- $DUGI_1$)
Meet by chance, encounter. *a.*

hetugianga. (ED1 $DUGI_1$)
n.

hee. (B-- HEE_2)
Where?, what kind?, which? *mv.*

heedua. (B-2 HEDU)
v.

heedunga. (B-1 HEDU)
n.

heehee. (R-- HEE_1)
Cry out. *a.*

heeheenga. (R-1 HEE_1)
n.

heeheui. (R-- HEUI)
v.

heeheuinga. (R-1 HEUI)
n.

heelanga*. (B-1 HELA)
n.

hegabidi. (B-- $GABI_a$)
Packed closely together; crowded together in a small place. *v.*

hegabidianga. (B-1 $GABI_a$)
n.

hegahega. (R-- HEGA)
Lung. *n.*

hegahegabidi. (R-- $GABI_a$)
v.

hegahegabidianga. (R-1 $GABI_a$)
n.

hegai. (BD- GAI_2)
Eat ravenously. *a.*

hegainga. (BD1 GAI_2)
n.

hegau.
Work, activity, occupation. *n.*

hegau baubau.
Bad deeds.

hege.
The name of a name-group. *n.*

hegide. (BD- GIDE)
See each other; meet up with. *a.*

hegideanga. (BD1 GIDE)
n.

hegide mada.
Early morning, before daybreak (when one can just barely recognize a person).

heiangi.
Smart, intelligent, clever. *a.*

heiloo. (BD- ILOO)
Know each other, understand each other. *a.*

heiloonga. (BD1 ILOO)
n.

hela*.
Spread one's legs (esp. a woman in the act of sexual intercourse). *v.*

helahela*. (R-- HELA)
v.

helahelaanga*. (R-1 HELA)
n.

helahelau. (R-- HELAU)
v.

helahelaua. (R-2 HELAU)
v.

helahelaunga. (R-1 HELAU)
n.

helau.
Sorcery. *v.*

helaua. (B-2 HELAU)
v.

helaunga. (B-1 HELAU)
n.

helelei. (B-- $LELE_a$)
Fly at the same time. *a.*

heleleinga. (B-1 $LELE_a$)
n.

helii.
Plant sp.: grass sp. (*Lepturus repens* (Forst.) R.Br.). *n.*

helii-baalanga.
Plant sp.: grass sp.

helii-lausedi.
Seaweed sp.

hellumi.
Melee. *v.*

hellumianga. (B-1 HELLUMI)
n.

hellumi de henua.
Mass confusion or panic.

heloongoi.
Fit together with (match) each other; have an understanding with one another (e.g., as do lovers); understand one another. *a.*

heloongoinga. (B-1 HELOONGOI)
n.

helui. (BD- LUI_1)
Diminution of. *a.*

heluinga. (BD1 LUI_1)
n.

hemuu. (BD- MUU_1)
Talk to one another. *a.*

hemuumuu. (RD- MUU_1)
a.

hemuumuunga. (RD1 MUU_1)
n.

hemuunga. (BD1 MUU_1)
n.

henua.
A land mass, an island, a country, or any other geopolitical unit. *n.*

henua abasasa.
Land of the Europeans (including America, Japan, etc.).

henua gai dangada.
'land of the cannibals' (esp. New Guinea).

henua gee.
Foreign lands.

henua gelegele.
Atoll [lit., 'land with sandy soil'].

henua i lalo (alodahi).
World (lands other than Nukuoro).

henua mounga.
A land where there are mountains (a high island or a continental land mass).

$henuu_1$.
A method of plaiting. *v.*

$henuu_2$.
Placenta. *n.*

henuua. (B-2 $HENUU_1$)
v.

henuunga. (B-1 $HENUU_1$)
n.

henga.
The name of a name-group. *n.*

heohi.
Correct, right, just, fair, true. *a.*

heohianga. (B-1 HEOHI)
n.

heohi ange.
Suited to, fit (with), appropriate to.

hesilihagi. (B-- $SILI_{3a}$)
To pass each other on intersecting courses; dislocated (joint of the body). *v.*

hesilihagi gee.
To have *hesilihagi* by a considerable distance.

hesilihaginga. (B-1 $SILI_{3a}$)
n.

hesilihaginga haiava.
Intersection.

hesilisilihagi. (R-- $SILI_{3a}$)
Repeatedly *hesilihagi.* *v.*

hesilisilihaginga. (R-1 $SILI_{3a}$)
n.

hesohesongi. (R-- $SONGI_a$)
Repeatedly *hesongi.* *a.*

hesohesonginga. (R-1 $SONGI_a$)
n.

hesongi. (B-- $SONGI_a$)
Kiss (Polynesian style), embrace. *a.*

hesongia. (B-2 $SONGI_a$)
v.

hesonginga. (B-1 $SONGI_a$)
n.

hesuihagi. (B-- SUI_a)
Exchange, trade. *v.*

hesuihagina. (B-2 SUI_a)
v.

hesuihaginga. (B-1 SUI$_a$)
n.

hesuisuihagi. (R-- SUI$_a$)
Repeatedly *hesuihagi.* *v.*

hesuisuihagina. (R-2 SUI$_a$)
v.

hesuisuihaginga. (R-1 SUI$_a$)
n.

heui.
Question (something) carefully. *v.*

heuia. (B-2 HEUI)
v.

heuinga. (B-1 HEUI)
n.

hevaalogi.
The screaming of many people at the same time. *a.*

hevaaloginga. (B-1 HEVAALOGI)
n.

hhaa. (E-- HAA$_1$)
Blossom forth. *v.*

hhaanga. (E-1 HAA$_1$)
n.

hhadi. (E-- HADI)
Snapped off. *v.*

hhadi iho luu vae.
Take a short break (in work involving standing).

hhadu. (E-- HADU$_1$)
Invented, made-up (e.g., a story). *a.*

hhagi. (E-- HAGI)
Make a sharp turn; *hagi* at one time. *v.*

hhagi de baa galele.
Jerking of a fishing lure to attract fish; a method of extracting a lure from the fish's mouth.

hhagi gee.
Turn away from (to avoid), veer.

hhali. (E-- HALI)
Scoop up (of solids only). *v.*

hhali gee.
Scoop out.

hhali lo te laagau.
A depression in a log (an abnormal growth).

hhano.
Wash one's own hands (or mouth). *v.*

hhano gi daha.
To wash one's hands in such a way that the dirty water does not fall back into the basin or well.

hhanga. (E-- HANGA)
Split open, open up, or separate, all at once. *v.*

hhanga dalogo.
To make *dalogo.*

hhanga de ngudu.
Open one's mouth.

hhanga lua.
Split in two.

hhanga luu vae.
Spread one's legs.

hhango. (E-- HANGO)
Wake up (someone). *v.*

hhao. (E-- HAO$_2$)
Fill, stuff (something into or full of). *v.*

hhao tuula.
To sail so as to fill one's sails with wind (sailing crosswind).

hhau. (E-- HAU)
Tie up, fasten by tying (wrapping). *v.*

hhedu. (E-- HEDU)
Fold up (several folds), roll up. *v.*

hhela*. (E-- HELA)
Spread one's legs wide apart at one time. *v.*

hhelaanga*. (E-1 HELA)
n.

hhoa. (E-- HOA$_1$)
Crack open; break into pieces; cut a hole in. *v.*

hhoa de biho.
Fool (someone).

hhoa de lae.
To run into misfortune as a result of one's evil deeds.

hhoa de usu.
To encounter unexpected misfortune as a result of one's evil deeds.

hhoda. (E-- HODA$_1$)
Gasp for breath (once). *a.*

hhoda age.
Suck in air (esp. when asleep or unconscious).

hhogi.
A sharp sound, like the report of a rifle. *a.*

hhola. (E-- HOLA)
hola at one time. *v.*

hhola mai saiolo.
To allow the sail to fill with wind, holding on to the boom sheet (after luffing).

hhole. (E-- HOLE)
Peel (something). *v.*

hholu. (E-- HOLU)
Bend. *v.*

hhou. (E-- HOU)
Insist upon. *v.*

hhoua. (E-2 HOU)
v.

hhounga. (E-1 HOU)
n.

hhua. (P-- HUA_1)
— (ex., 'sing' meaning). *a.*

hhuaanga. (P-1 HUA_1)
n.

hhuda. (E-- HUDA)
Open one's eyes; awaken for a short time. *a.*

hhudaanga. (E-1 HUDA)
n.

hhudi. (E-- $HUDI_1$)
Pull. *v.*

hhuge. (E-- HUGE)
Open (something), uncover. *v.*

hhuge age malo.
Lift up one's skirts (to expose one's genitals).

hhuge iho.
An opening in the clouds.

hhui. (E-- HUI_1)
Wash (hands or feet or dishes, etc. — but not clothes). *v.*

hhui age.
Eat a snack.

hhui mai tai.
Flow of the tide.

hhule. (E-- HULE)
To expose the head of the penis by pulling back the foreskin. *v.*

hhuna. (E-- HUNA)
Hide at one time. *v.*

hhuu.
Chuckle. *a.*

hhuuhhuu. (R-- HHUU)
a.

hhuuhhuunga. (R-1 HHUU)
n.

hhuunga. (B-1 HHUU)
n.

hia.
How many? [in compounds only]. *a.*

hidi.
To topple over [sing.]; stand on one's hands [sing.]; get up (from a sitting position) [sing.]; cause of [when followed by (*mai*) *ai*]. *v.*

hidia. (B-2 HIDI)
v.

hidi bido dane.
Slow-moving or slow-working person.

hidi de honu.
Movement of a turtle (when feeding or submerging).

hidi de mamu dunu.
Curling up of fish (when cooked).

hidi taelodo.
The weight (on a balance) used as a standard measurement.

hidihidi. (R-- HIDI)
—; rock back and forth. *v.*

hidihidia. (R-2 HIDI)
v.

hidihidinga. (R-1 HIDI)
n.

hidinga.
Because of, owing to. *mc.*

hidu.
Seven. *an.*

Hidu-laangi. (HIDU, LAANGI)
Sunday ('seventh day'). *nt.*

hidu-limu.
The seventh number of a counting

game played to determine who is "it".

Hidu-malama. (HIDU, MALAMA)
July ('seventh month'). *nt.*

hiehie. (?)
A type of prepared food (made from breadfruit). *n.*

hieunu. (B-- UNU$_{1c}$)
Thirsty. *a.*

hieununga. (B-1 UNU$_{1c}$)
n.

hii-. (B-- HII$_1$)
Want to. *mf.*

hiidagi.
[Var. of *giidagi*]. *v.*

hiidagina. (B-2 HIIDAGI)
v.

hiidaginga. (B-1 HIIDAGI)
n.

hiidinga$_1$. (B-1 HIDI)
n.

hiidinga$_2$. (C-- HIDINGA)
Because! *b.*

hiihidi. (T-- HIDI)
[Pl. of *hidi*]. *v.*

hiihii. (R-- HII$_2$)
Edge, fringe, rim. *nl.*

hiihiidagi. (R-- HIIDAGI)
v.

hiihiidagina. (R-2 HIIDAGI)
v.

hiihiidaginga. (R-1 HIIDAGI)
n.

hiihii mada.
Eyelashes.

hiilinga. (B-1 HILI)
n.

hiilonga. (B-1 HILO)
n.

hiisoa.
Plant sp.: cassytha vine (*Cassytha filiformis* L.). *n.*

hili$_1$. (B-- HILI)
Pick from among several, choose, elect; particular (choosy) about; make a nest or raft or platform, etc., with sticks. *v.*

hili$_2$. (B-- HILI$_a$)
The name of a name-group. *n.*

hilia. (B-2 HILI)
v.

hili de hau.
Make a *hau.*

hili gee.
Sort out from; set aside (be chosen from a group).

hilihili. (R-- HILI)
Choose carefully from among many, election. *v.*

hilihilia. (R-2 HILI)
v.

hilihilinga. (R-1 HILI)
n.

hilo.
Mix; braid strands of sennit. *v.*

hiloa$_1$. (B-2 HILO)
v.

hiloa$_2$. (B-- HILOA)
Fish sp. *n.*

hilo ange.
Mix with.

hilo hagamaadau.
To braid sennit with the right hand; [the result is considered inferior to sennit made with the left hand].

hilo hagamaasui.
To braid sennit with the left hand; [which is considered to give the best result].

hilohilo. (R-- HILO)
v.

hilohiloa. (R-2 HILO)
v.

hilohilo ma eidu.
A sorcerer able to take human or non-human shapes.

hilohilo me.
Impure.

hilohilonga. (R-1 HILO)
n.

hilohilo senga.
Half-crazy.

hilohilosia. (R-2 HILO)
v.

hilo saele.
Spread venereal disease.

hilosia. (B-2 HILO)
v.

hina.
Ability, capacity (of person), resourcefulness. *n.*

hinahinangalosaa. (R-- $HINA_b$)
a.

hinahinangalosaanga. (R-1 $HINA_b$)
n.

hinangalomalie. (B-- $HINA_a$)
Feel happy or contented or at peace with the world. *a.*

hinangalomalieanga. (B-1 $HINA_a$)
n.

hinangalosaa. (B-- $HINA_b$)
Miss (someone or something); longing (for a person or place). *a.*

hinangalosaa iho.
Self-pity.

hinangalosaanga. (B-1 $HINA_b$)
n.

hine.
Female, woman; [must be preceded by an article]. *n.*

(de) hine dau bodu.
Married woman.

(de) hine duuhua.
Unmarried girl.

(de) hine hai be.
Whore.

(de) hine huuhua.
Pregnant woman.

(de) hine sala daane.
Nymphomaniac.

hoa_1.
d.

hoa_2.
Side (of humans), below the hips. *n.*

hoa lalo.
Anvil; or other hard object (such as a stone) on which something can be struck hard; mortar stone.

hobulaa.
A sound uttered esp. when lifting something. *a.*

hobulaanga. (B-1 HOBULAA)
n.

hoda. (B-- $HODA_2$)
Carve out, drill out; eat out the insides of (as does a rat). *v.*

hodaanga. (B-1 $HODA_2$)
n.

$hodahoda_1$. (R-- $HODA_1$)
Gasp for breath (more than once). *a.*

$hodahoda_2$. (R-- $HODA_2$)
v.

$hodahodaanga_1$. (R-1 $HODA_1$)
n.

$hodahodaanga_2$. (R-1 $HODA_2$)
n.

hodahodaia. (R-2 $HODA_2$)
v.

hodahodalia. (R-2 $HODA_2$)
v.

hodaia. (B-2 $HODA_2$)
v.

hodalia. (B-2 $HODA_2$)
v.

hodo.
The spine of the stingray. *n.*

hodooligi.
Chief (of the island). *a.*

hodu*.
Sighted, appear. *a.*

hodua. (B-2 HODU)
a.

hoduhodu. (R-- HODU)
a.

hoduhodua. (R-2 HODU)
a.

hoduhodunga. (R-1 HODU)
n.

hodunga. (B-1 HODU)
n.

hoe_1.
A canoe paddle. *n.*

hoe$_2$.
Blisters on the skin caused by sunburn. *v.*

hoea. (B-2 HOE$_2$)
Covered with sunburn blisters. *v.*

hoe pale.
A type of canoe paddle designed for steering.

hoe gabegabe.
A canoe paddle (for paddling).

hoenga. (B-1 HOE$_2$)
n.

hogi.
Also. *mv.*

hogihogi. (R-- HHOGI)
a.

hogihoginga. (R-1 HHOGI)
n.

hohhoo. (T-- HOO)
A sound made when surprised. *a.*

hoimanu. (CF MANU)
Fish sp.: eagle ray. *n.*

hola.
To spread out, or lay out flat, something which is folded, piled up, or bent, etc. *v.*

holadage. (B-- HOLA$_a$)
Laid out or spread out all over. *a.*

holadageanga. (B-1 HOLA$_a$)
n.

holahola. (R-- HOLA)
v.

holaholaa. (R-2 HOLA)
v.

holahola aalanga.
Calisthenics, exercises.

holaholanga. (R-1 HOLA)
n.

holaholasia. (R-2 HOLA)
v.

holasa.
A type of mat [made especially for cult houses]. *n.*

holasia. (B-2 HOLA)
v.

holau.
Canoe house. *n.*

hole.
d.

holehole. (R-- HOLE)
Scrape off (with an object or one's finger), to scale (fish). *v.*

holeholea. (R-2 HOLE)
v.

holeholenga. (R-1 HOLE)
n.

holi.
Shape of, form of. *a.*

holia. (B-2 HOLI)
To form (something); make (something) according to some model or plan. *v.*

holiage.
Go about something in a complete circle. *v.*

holiagi. (CF HOLIAGE)
[Var. of *holiage*]. *v.*

holiagina. (B-2 HOLIAGE)
v.

holiaginga. (B-1 HOLIAGE)
n.

holi ange.
Resemble.

holiholi. (R-- HOLI)
Build (of a person); appearance (distinctive of an individual). *n.*

holiholiage. (R-- HOLIAGE)
v.

holiholiagina. (R-2 HOLIAGE)
v.

holiholiaginga. (R-1 HOLIAGE)
n.

holiholinga. (R-1 HOLI)
n.

holinga. (B-1 HOLI)
n.

holo.
Swallow [sing.]. *v.*

hologemo. (XCO HOLO)
[Var. of *hologumu*]. *a.*

holo gumi.
[Var. of *hologumu*]. *a.*

hologumi. (XCO HOLO)
[Var. of *hologumu*]. *a.*

hologumu. (XCO HOLO)
(For a fish) to swallow a hook so that it becomes stuck in the throat. *a.*

holoholo. (R-- HOLO)
v.

holoholoi.
The rope tied to palm fronds in *belubelu* fishing. *v.*

holoholoia. (B-2 HOLOHOLOI)
v.

holoholoinga. (B-1 HOLOHOLOI)
n.

holoholomia. (R-2 HOLO)
v.

holoholonga. (B-1 HOLO)
n.

holomanga. (B-1 HOLO)
Throat (inside). *n.*

holomia. (B-2 HOLO)
v.

holu.
d.

holuholu. (R-- HOLU)
v.

holuholua. (R-2 HOLU)
v.

holuholunga. (R-1 HOLU)
n.

hono.
A patch (on clothes, or a canoe, etc.). *v.*

honoa. (B-2 HONO)
Patched. *v.*

honohono. (R-- HONO)
Having *hono* in several places. *v.*

honohonoa. (R-2 HONO)
v.

honohononga. (R-1 HONO)
n.

hononga. (B-1 HONO)
n.

honu$_1$.
Full [sing.]. *v.*

honu$_2$.
Green turtle (2 varieties). *n.*

honua. (B-2 HONU$_1$)
Filled with. *v.*

honu baabaa.
Fill to the brim.

honu tai.
High tide.

honu tolo.
A turtle of the largest size.

honu kadi.
Filled up completely (with solids); full up (and tightly packed).

honuhonu. (R-- HONU$_1$)
v.

honuhonua. (R-2 HONU$_1$)
v.

honuhonumia. (R-2 HONU$_1$)
v.

honuhonunga. (R-1 HONU$_1$)
n.

honu malingilingi.
Fill to overflowing.

honumia. (B-2 HONU$_1$)
Filled with. *v.*

honu ssele.
Turtle of a size suitable for eating (not quite as big as *honu tolo*).

honu-uda.
Insect sp. (small and turtle-like).

honga.
On top of, on, over, above. *nl.*

honga de masavaa.
At the time of.

honga de mouli.
During the lifetime of.

hongagainga. (B-- HONGA$_a$)
Urinate. *a.*

hongagelegele. (HONGA$_b$, GELE)
Defecate [a euphemism]. *n.*

hongagelegele baalanga.
Rust.

honga iainei.
At this time, these days.

hoo.
A sound made when one is tired, etc. *i.*

hooanga. (B-1 HOA_1)
n.

hoodanga. (E-1 $HODA_1$)
n.

hooginga. (B-1 HHOGI)
n.

hoohanga.
A nest (of birds); pumice stone (found as driftwood). *a.*

hoohoa. (R-- HOA_1)
[Pl. of *hoa*]. *v.*

hoohoa laagau.
Drill wood to make a hole in which to insert the end of a pole (to make a joint).

hoohoanga. (R-1 HOA_1)
n.

hoohoia. (R-2 HOA_1)
v.

hooholo. (T-- HOLO)
[Pl. of *holo*]. *v.*

hoohonu. (T-- $HONU_1$)
[Pl. of *$honu_1$*]. *v.*

hoohonua. (T-2 $HONU_1$)
v.

hoohonumia. (T-2 $HONU_1$)
v.

hoohonunga. (T-1 $HONU_1$)
n.

hoohoo. (R-- HOO)
Repeatedly *hoo*, as when trying to scare something. *a.*

hoohooanga. (R-1 HOO)
n.

hoohooia. (R-2 HOO)
v.

hoohoo ina.
To frighten with sounds.

hooia. (B-2 HOA_1)
v.

hooia donu huu.
At the best possible time or place.

hoolaa. (B-2 HOLA)
v.

hoolanga. (B-1 HOLA)
n.

hoolea. (B-2 HOLE)
v.

hoolenga. (B-1 HOLE)
n.

hoolonga. (B-1 HOLO)
n.

hoolu.
Prow (bottom part). *n.*

hoolua. (B-2 HOLU)
v.

hoolunga. (B-1 HOLU)
n.

hoonunga. (B-1 $HONU_1$)
n.

hoo senga.
Shy (especially in the presence of members of the opposite sex), shamed.

hoosenga. (XCO HOO)
Shy, embarrassed, bashful. *a.*

hoosenga ange.
Embarrassed by.

hoou.
New. *a.*

hoounga. (B-1 HOOU)
n.

hou.
Drill (native bow drill). *v.*

houa. (B-2 HOU)
v.

houhou. (R-- HOU)
—; race. *v.*

houhoua. (R-2 HOU)
v.

houhounga. (R-1 HOU)
n.

hounga. (B-1 HOU)
n.

hua$_1$.
Come out in front; sing (a song); bear (fruit); a swelling (on the skin, or of dough, etc.);a swell (of the sea). *v.*

hua$_2$ +NUMBER. (B-- HUA$_2$)
NUMERAL CLASSIFIER (BY TENS) FOR FRUIT. *mc.*

huaa.
Whole. *d.*

huaabodu. (XCO BODU$_1$)
Family. *n.*

huaaboo. (BOO$_2$, HUAA)
The whole night long. *n.*

huaadangada. (XCO HUAA)
Persons of a certain class or type. *n.*

huaahai. (XCO HUAA)
Expertise. *v.*

huaahenua. (HENUA, HUAA)
Community. *n.*

huaahuu. (AHU, HUA$_1$)
A type of prepared food (made from taro). *n.*

huaahuu daalo.
A type of prepared food (like *huaahuu*, with the addition of bananas or something else sweet).

hua ai.
Be in charge of.

hua-ala.
Flower.

huaalaangi. (HUAA, LAANGI)
Noon; the whole day; a certain day only. *n.*

huaalanga.
A type of coconut tree.

huaalavao.
A strong wind. *v.*

huaalavaonga. (B-1 HUAALAVAO)
n.

huaa me.
A coconut (for drinking); the whole thing.

huaanga. (B-1 HUA$_1$)
n.

huadia.
Fishing pole. *n.*

hua-dolo.
Plant sp.: vine (any sort).

huahua. (R-- HUA$_1$)
v.

huahua ai.
Be in charge of, control, lead.

huahuaa me.
[Var. of *huuhuaa me*].

huahuaanga. (R-1 HUA$_1$)
n.

hua i gadea.
The side of the main body of the canoe away from the outrigger float.

hua-laagau.
Plant sp.: tropical almond (*Terminalia catappa* L.).

hua leu.
Fish eggs (mature—yellowish).

hua ligi.
Having small fruit or nuts (of trees).

hua manu.
Fruit.

hua modo.
Fish eggs (immature).

hua nnui.
Having large fruit or nuts (of trees).

hua o tangada.
Outcome (of individual effort).

huda.
[The generic term for] a verse of an old chant. *n.*

hudaa --. (B-- HUDAA)
Group of things approaching together (e.g., a fleet of canoes). *d.*

hudaa lolo.
Flood-like waves on the reef; tidal wave.

hudaa moni.
A fleet of canoes.

hudi$_1$.
d.

hudi$_2$.
Plant sp.: tree sp.: banana tree. *n.*

hudihudi. (R-- HUDI$_1$)
v.

hudihudia. (R-2 HUDI$_1$)
v.

hudihudinga. (R-1 HUDI$_1$)
n.

hue.
Plant sp.: vine sp. (several spp.). *n.*

huevini. (HUE, VINI)
A type of string figure. *n.*

huga.
Fine threads or strands. *n.*

hugadoo.
All (of things). *u.*

hugahuga. (R-- HUGA)
A type of soft driftwood (used for plugs). *n.*

huge --. (B-- HUGE)
d.

hugehuge. (R-- HUGE)
v.

hugehugea. (R-2 HUGE)
v.

hugehugelia. (R-2 HUGE)
v.

hugehugenga. (R-1 HUGE)
n.

hugelia. (B-2 HUGE)
v.

hui --. (B-- HUI$_1$)
d.

hui hala.
The fruit of the pandanus.

huihui. (R-- HUI$_1$)
v.

huihuia. (R-2 HUI$_1$)
v.

huihuinga. (R-1 HUI$_1$)
n.

hule --. (B-- HULE)
d.

hulehule. (R-- HULE)
—; masturbate. *v.*

hulehulei. (R-- HULE$_a$)
—; masturbate. *v.*

hulehuleia. (R-2 HULE$_a$)
v.

hulehuleinga. (R-1 HULE$_a$)
n.

hulehulenga. (B-1 HULE)
n.

hulei. (B-- HULE$_a$)
To have done the act of *hhule*. *v.*

huleia. (B-2 HULE$_a$)
v.

huleinga. (B-1 HULE$_a$)
n.

huli.
Turn (in place) [sing.]. *v.*

hulia. (B-2 HULI)
v.

hulidonu. (DONU$_{1a}$, HULI)
Right side out (clothes). *a.*

huligee. (GEE, HULI)
Turn away from, turn inside out (of clothes).

hulihuli. (R-- HULI)
v.

hulihulia. (R-2 HULI)
v.

hulihulinga. (R-1 HULI)
n.

hulihulisia. (R-2 HULI)
v.

hulisia. (B-2 HULI)
v.

hulo.
Go [pl.]. *v.*

hulo gee.
Go away [pl.].

hulo gi lunga ma lalo.
Argue heatedly, fight.

hulohulo. (R-- HULO)
v.

hulohulonga. (R-1 HULO)
n.

hulo saele.
Wander around.

hulu$_1$.
Hair (on the body) [rarely heard]. *n.*

hulu$_2$.
Apply liquid on, smear on. *v.*

$hulu_3$.
Ten (in enumeration and compounds only). *a.*

$hulu_4$.
Reactive hostility. *n.*

hulua. (B-2 $HULU_2$)
v.

hulubala. (BALA, $HULU_2$)
Smeared with grease or paint or food, etc. *v.*

$huluhulu_1$. (R-- $HULU_1$)
Hair (on the body). *v.*

$huluhulu_2$. (R-- $HULU_2$)
v.

$huluhulua_1$. (R-2 $HULU_1$)
Hairy. *v.*

$huluhulua_2$. (R-2 $HULU_2$)
v.

huluhulu mada.
Eyebrows.

huluhulu-manenga.
The tenth number of a counting game played to determine who is "it" (= the person who becomes "it").

$huluhulunga_1$. (R-1 $HULU_1$)
n.

$huluhulunga_2$. (R-1 $HULU_2$)
n.

hulu i de lenga.
To paint one's body with tumeric.

hulu made.
The fading of one's hair color (becoming white).

hulu manu.
Feathers.

humai.
Come [sing.]. *a.*

humai nei.
Next —.

huna.
Hide [sing.]; breechclout. *v.*

hunahuna. (R-- HUNA)
v.

hunahunaanga. (R-1 HUNA)
n.

huna me.
A habitual thief.

hune.
Core of the breadfruit; the flower of the breadfruit tree. *n.*

hunehune. (R-- HUNE)
The fibers on the core of the breadfruit. *n.*

hungahunga-a-nui.
The flower of the coconut tree.

hungi.
Tricks of self-defense (some of which are like judo or karate). *v.*

hungia. (B-2 HUNGI)
v.

hungihungi. (R-- HUNGI)
v.

hungihungia. (R-2 HUNGI)
v.

hungihunginga. (R-1 HUNGI)
n.

husi.
Taro bog, swamp. *n.*

huu. (B-- HUU_1)
Occasion when; just like... *mv.*

huubuudoi.
Fat and squat and ugly. *a.*

huubuudoinga. (B-1 HUUBUUDOI)
n.

$huudanga_1$. (B-1 HUA_1)
Way of singing. *n.*

$huudanga_2$. (B-1 $HUDI_1$)
n.

$huudia_1$. (B-2 HUA_1)
v.

$huudia_2$. (B-2 $HUDI_1$)
v.

huugaabungubungu.
(BUNGU, GAA_1, HUA_1)
Very plump.

huugea. (B-2 HUGE)
v.

huugenga. (B-1 HUGE)
n.

huuhua. (S-- HUA_1)
Pregnancy. *a.*

huuhuaa me.
Sorcery (made with chants).

huuhuge. (T-- HUGE)
Open or uncover many things (by several persons). *v.*

huuhugea. (T-2 HUGE)
v.

huuhugelia. (T-2 HUGE)
v.

huuhugenga. (T-1 HUGE)
n.

huuhuli. (T-- HULI)
[Pl. of *huli*]. *v.*

huuhulia. (T-2 HULI)
v.

huuhulinga. (T-1 HULI)
n.

huuhulisia. (T-2 HULI)
v.

huuhuna. (T-- HUNA)
Hide [pl.]. *a.*

huuhunaanga. (T-1 HUNA)
n.

huuhuu$_1$. (B-- HUU$_3$)
To clap one's wet hands together (to dry them). *v.*

huuhuu$_2$. (R-- HUUHUU)
Fish sp.: parrot fish (The native term is applied to many spp.). *n.*

huuhuua. (B-2 HUU$_3$)
v.

huuhuunga. (B-1 HUU$_3$)
n.

huuia. (B-2 HUI$_1$)
v.

huuinga. (B-1 HUI$_1$)
n.

huulenga. (B-1 HULE)
n.

huulinga. (B-1 HULI)
n.

huulonga. (B-1 HULO)
—; a pathway on the open sea. *n.*

huulunga. (B-1 HULU$_2$)
n.

huunanga. (B-1 HUNA)
n.

huunginga. (B-1 HUNGI)
n.

i.
At; with respect to; in; by means of; because of; in spite of; concerning. *mp.*

ia.
He, she, it. *pi.*

iai.
Be (present), have, there is... *a.*

iaianga. (R-- ANGA$_{2a}$)
v.

iai maalie.
Just about right.

iainei. (B-- IAI$_a$)
Now. *b.*

iainei donu.
Right now!

iai sago.
Having special ability (strength, power, etc.) which others do not have, a strong or powerful (person).

ialona. (?)
A type of string figure. *n.*

i ͵ama.
On the same side of a canoe as the outrigger float.

ianga. (B-- ANGA$_{2a}$)
The span between the outstretched thumb and the little finger. *v.*

iangaa. (B-2 ANGA$_{2a}$)
v.

ibu.
[Var. of *ubu*]. *n.*

i dahi me.
Each, apiece.

i dai nei.
Mortlock Islands.

i de baasi.
Concerning; at the behest of; under the auspices of.

i de -- sogosogo.
Apiece, each.

idi.
To husk (a coconut) with one's teeth. *v.*

idia. (B-2 IDI)
v.

idihia. (B-2 IDI)
v.

idiidi$_1$. (R-- IDI)
v.

Idiidi$_2$. (B-- IDIIDI)
April. *n.*

idiidia. (R-2 IDI)
v.

idiidihia. (R-2 IDI)
v.

idiidinga. (R-1 IDI)
n.

idinga. (B-1 IDI)
—; bits of coconut husk which have been removed. *n.*

itebuubuu.
Insect sp.: grasshopper.

ieiange.
[Var. of *ieiangi*]. *a.*

ieiangi.
Recovered from illness. *a.*

ieianginga. (B-1 IEIANGI)
n.

iga*.
Fish (archaic, except in compounds). *n.*

iga-adagahi.
Fish sp.: hawk fish (2 sorts) [so named because it is easy to step on].

iga-ligi.
Fish sp. (a small oceanic school fish slightly larger than *dauoni*).

iga-loa.
Fish sp. (a small flying fish).

iganibongi.
Fish sp.

igauli.
Fish sp.: tang (2 sorts).

igauli-sissisi.
Fish sp.: tang.

igohi.
Fire tongs. *v.*

igohinga. (B-1 IGOHI)
Way of using *igohi*. *n.*

i hee.
Where (in general)?

i hee ai goe.
You lose!

iho.
Get down, climb down; down [MV]. *a.*

iho adu.
You feel like —.

iho age.
Feel like beginning to want —.

ihoanga. (B-1 IHO)
n.

iho ange + PRONOUN.
To have relapsed into (his/her, etc.) —.

iho ange de --.
Feel like (one is) about to —.

iho daahagi.
A calm sea condition, in which the horizon disappears [the horizon being normally marked by surf).

ihoiho. (R-- IHO)
a.

ihoihoanga. (R-1 IHO)
n.

ihoiholia. (R-2 IHO)
Useful for climbing down repeatedly. *v.*

iholia. (B-2 IHO)
Useful for climbing down. *v.*

iho mai.
I feel like —.

iillangi.
Mollusk sp.: *Conus litteratus.*

ila.
A mole (not raised) , or other permanent black spot on the skin. *v.*

ilaage.
Free of (sickness, hardship, etc.). *a.*

ilaage mai.
Free from.

ilaila. (R-- ILA)
Having more than one *ila*. *v.*

ilailaage. (R-- ILAAGE)
a.

ili.
Blow, fan (oneself); inflate (a balloon). *v.*

ilia. (B-2 ILI)
v.

ili taalanga.
Talkative, chatterbox, talk at great length.

ilihia. (B-2 ILI)
—; having one's stomach distended by gas. *v.*

ilihia tinae.
A stomach distended by gas.

ilihia ssave.
The submerging of flying fish below the surface of the water (making them difficult to net).

iliili. (R-- ILI)
v.

iliilia. (R-2 ILI)
v.

iliilihia. (R-2 ILI)
v.

iliilinga. (R-1 ILI)
n.

ili luu bongaa usu.
To dilate one's nostrils [a mannerism which is taken as a sign of emotion].

ilinga. (B-1 ILI)
n.

ilo.
Worm, maggot, intestinal parasites. *v.*

iloha.
Fathom (the span of one's outstretched arms) [var. of *loha*]. *v.*

ilohaanga. (B-1 ILOHA)
n.

iloo.
Know, understand, be intimate with, sure of (and willing to say). *a.*

iloo iho.
Realize, know.

iloo mai.
Know that someone —.

iloo me.
Charlatanism.

iloonga. (B-1 ILOO)
n.

ilosia. (B-2 ILO)
Wormy or maggoty (of something decayed). *v.*

ilosiaanga. (B-3 ILO)
n.

i mua nei.
Beforehand.

imu-mea.
Fish sp.: triggerfish.

imu-uli.
Fish sp.: triggerfish.

ina$_1$.
To light up an area at night (esp. for hunting land crabs). *v.*

ina$_2$.
To it. *mv.*

inaanga. (B-1 INA$_1$)
n.

ina-gi-hale. (HALE, INA$_2$)
A row of thatch. *n.*

inaho.
A school consisting of a certain reef fish sp. (*laumele*). *n.*

inai.
A type of mat. *n.*

inaina. (R-- INA$_1$)
v.

inau.
To look for coconut crabs at night with a light. *v.*

inaunga. (B-1 INAU)
n.

ino.
Bow or nod or genuflect (as a sign of respect). *a.*

ino gi mua.
Bend (one's body) forward.

inoino. (R-- INO)
a.

inoinonga. (R-1 INO)
n.

inonga. (B-1 INO)
n.

ingoo.
Name, a title (used as a name). *n.*

ingooanga. (B-1 INGOO)
n.

io.
A quarter of the body of a tuna when it is cut lengthwise. *n.*

io alo.
Lower *io*, q.v.

io dua.
The upper *io*.

i ono daha.
At his place, with him.

ioo.
To make a sound indicating "take it!" [as an interjection, = "take it!"]. *a.*

ioonga. (B-1 IOO)
Way of giving. *n.*

ise.
Fish sp.: halfbeak. *n.*

ise-ngaio.
Fish sp.: needlefish.

isi. (B-- ISI_1)
To peel off in long thin strips. *v.*

isia. (B-2 ISI_1)
v.

isihia. (B-2 ISI_1)
v.

isiisi. (R-- ISI_1)
v.

isiisia. (R-2 ISI_1)
v.

isiisihia. (R-2 ISI_1)
v.

isiisi luu gauanga.
To tear off (a person's) legs [an expression heard in threats].

isiisi luu gauasa.
To tear from limb to limb.

isiisinga. (R-1 ISI_1)
n.

isinga. (B-1 ISI_1)
n.

ivi.
Bone, needle. *n.*

ivi-a-daea.
Shoulder blade.

ivi-a-duimogo.
Pelvic bone.

ivi de biho.
Skull.

ivi gaogao.
Rib.

iviivia. (R-2 IVI)
Skinny, thin (person), emaciated. *v.*

iviiviaanga. (R-3 IVI)
n.

ivi laanui.
Spine (of the body).

ivi ngongo.
Collar bone.

ivi sulu.
A dislocation of bones such that the ends overlap (corrected by pulling).

laa_1.
There in the distance, then (past). *mv.*

laa_2.
Sun. *n.*

laa_3.
A branch (of a tree). *n.*

laa_4. (B-- LAA_{3b})
A sail. *n.*

laa ange.
And those there.

laabunga. (B-1 LABU)
n.

laa tua.
Besides.

laa tubua.
Daily.

Laaga. (B-- LAAGA)
November. *n.*

laaganga. (E-1 LAGA)
n.

laagau. (B-- LAA$_{3a}$)
Wood, stick (of wood). *n.*

laagau aalo saelenga.
Thatch rafters on the ends of a house.

laagau-bala-uda.
Driftwood sp. (very soft).

laagau-doi.
A driftwood sp., from the sap of which (*doi*) perfume is made.

laagau hagadauaadea.
A cross-beam lashed to a tree to facilitate climbing it.

laagau lui.
A cross (e.g., of wood).

laagei. (CF LAAGII)
[Var. of *laagii*]. *n.*

laagii.
Decoration, ornamentation. *n.*

laagii baubau.
Hideous in appearance (as a ghost).

laaginga. (B-1 LAAGII)
n.

laagua. (B-2 LAGU)
v.

laagunga. (B-1 LAGU)
n.

laa kilaa.
Around there far away.

laa kinaa.
Around there near you.

laa kinei.
Around here.

laaigi.
A driftwood plant sp., with an aromatic sap which is used for perfume. *n.*

laalaa. (R-- LAA$_3$)
Having many branches. *v.*

laalaanui. (R-- LAANUI)
Becoming big. *a.*

laalaanuinga. (R-1 LAANUI)
n.

laalaanga. (R-1 LAA$_3$)
n.

laaladi.
To scratch (an itch). *v.*

laaladia. (B-2 LAALADI)
v.

laaladinga. (B-1 LAALADI)
n.

laalanga$_1$. (B-1 LALA)
n.

laalanga$_2$. (T-- LANGA)
The quality of the weave (of mat plaiting). *n.*

laalangia. (R-2 LALA)
v.

laa magavaa.
In between.

laamaloo.
A divination result indicating bad fortune. *n.*

laamasee.
A divination result indicating good fortune. *n.*

laanui.
Big [sing.]; large [sing.]. *a.*

laanuinga. (B-1 LAANUI)
n.

laangaa. (B-2 LANGA)
To plait completely. *v.*

laangai.
Fishing conditions are —. *d.*

laangai buusagi.
A type of fishing condition in which the sea is boiling with jumping tuna, which are biting at anything.

laangai huli de moana.
A fishing condition in which tuna are jumping (showing their white bellies) and biting.

laangai laamaleu.
A fishing condition in which tuna are jumping but not biting.

laangai milo sanga.
A fishing condition in which fish are not inclined to bite.

laangai ngadi moana.
A fishing condition in which tuna are biting, but do not appear in schools.

laangai sahole.
A fishing condition in which tuna are jumping and biting.

laanganga. (B-1 LANGA)
Way of plaiting. *n.*

laangi.
Day. *n.*

laangia. (B-2 LALA)
—; heat up on an open flame (as in shaping wood). *v.*

laangi dabeo.
A day which is rainy and stormy.

Laangidabu. ($DABU_1$, LAANGI)
Sunday. *nt.*

laangi danuaa.
Hello! Good day!

laangi hagadaahao.
Field day.

Laangihagamouli. (LAANGI, MOULI)
Saturday (the day on which food is prepared for Sunday). *nt.*

laanginga. (B-1 $LANGI_1$)
n.

laavasi.
Meat (or fish, or seafood) which is suitable as food. *n.*

laavea. (B-2 LAVE)
Stumble on. *v.*

laavenga. (B-1 LAVE)
n.

$laba_1$.
Flash (as of lightning). *v.*

$laba_2$.
A dancing paddle. *n.*

labaagau. (P-- LABAGAU)
a.

labaai*.
The confluence, on the reef, of a big wave and the backwash. *v.*

labaaia*. (B-2 LABAAI)
v.

labaainga*. (B-1 LABAAI)
n.

labaanga. (B-1 $LABA_1$)
n.

labagau.
Carpenter; skillful (at a craft); craftsman. *a.*

labagaunga. (B-1 LABAGAU)
n.

labalaba. (R-- $LABA_1$)
—; sparkling. *v.*

labalabaanga. (R-1 $LABA_1$)
n.

laba ngaugau.
A stalk of the elephant-ear plant (*ngaungau*).

labelabe-tea.
Fish sp.

labelabe-uliuli.
Fish sp.: wrasse.

labodo.
Eel, any long worm, snake. *n.*

labodo-daubulebule.
Eel sp.

labodo-tea.
Eel sp.: moray eel.

labodo-sisi.
Eel sp.: snake eel.

labodo-uli.
Eel sp.: moray eel.

labu.
Knead; claw — [dp]. *v.*

labua. (B-2 LABU)
Knead thoroughly. *v.*

labua gee (lodo).
Having an upset stomach; to be on the point of nausea.

labua gee lodo.
To have an upset stomach (being on the point of nausea).

labulabu. (R-- LABU)
v.

labulabua. (R-2 LABU)
v.

labulabunga. (R-1 LABU)
n.

labulabu sala.
Fail to take hold of (or do) properly (leading to an accident, or other unfortunate outcome).

labu manu.
To pet (pets, children, or a member of the opposite sex).

labu ssenga.
To run into trouble (owing to one's misdeeds).

lapede.
Stumble and fall. *v.*

lapedea. (B-2 LAPEDE)
v.

lapedenga. (B-1 LAPEDE)
n.

ladi.
Initiate, begin, start. *v.*

ladia. (B-2 LADI)
v.

ladiladi. (R-- LADI)
v.

ladiladia. (R-2 LADI)
v.

ladiladinga. (R-1 LADI)
n.

ladinga. (B-1 LADI)
n.

latabagea. (XCO GEA)
An ornament made of turtle shell. *n.*

lae.
Forehead. *n.*

laelae (gee). (R-- LAE)
Look (funny). *a.*

laelaenga. (R-1 LAE)
n.

lagalaga. (R-- LAGA)
To put down one foot after the other (as in walking or marching in place). *v.*

lagalagai.
A method of plating coconut palm fronds. *v.*

lagalagaia. (B-2 LAGALAGAI)
v.

lagalagainga. (B-1 LAGALAGAI)
n.

lagalaganga. (R-1 LAGA)
n.

lagi.
Pertaining to the open sea. *n.*

lago. (B-- $LAGO_1$)
About, quite. *d.*

lagohia. (B-- $LAGO_2$)
Wounded. *v.*

lagohiaanga. (B-1 $LAGO_2$)
n.

lagolago. (R-- $LAGO_1$)
Many, plenty, a lot of, much. *a.*

lagolagoaa. (B-- $LAGO_{2a}$)
Destroy or abuse property (for no good reason); vandalism. *v.*

lagolagoaanga. (B-1 $LAGO_{2a}$)
n.

lagolagoanga. (R-1 $LAGO_1$)
Way of being many. *n.*

lagolagohia. (R-- $LAGO_2$)
Wounded in several places or all over. *v.*

lagolagohiaanga. (R-1 $LAGO_2$)
n.

lagu.
d.

lagulagu. (R-- LAGU)
v.

lagulagua. (R-2 LAGU)
v.

lagulagunga. (R-1 LAGU)
n.

lahalaha. (R-- LAHA)
Wide [sing.]; broad [sing.]. *a.*

lahalahaanga. (R-1 LAHA)
n.

lahhie.
Firewood. *n.*

lahilahi. (R-- LAHI)
Fish sp.; tremendous (followed by *ina*). *a.*

lahilahianga. (R-1 LAHI)
n.

laho.
Aerial root of the pandanus tree. *n.*

lahu.
Investigate (to prove one's suspicions). *v.*

lahua. (B-2 LAHU)
v.

lahulahu₁. (R-- LAHU)
v.

lahulahu₂. (R-- LAHU)
Bird sp.: wandering tattler? *Heteroscelus incanus*). *n.*

lahulahua. (R-2 LAHU)
v.

lahulahunga. (R-1 LAHU)
n.

lahu me.
Inclined to be suspicious.

lahunga. (B-1 LAHU)
n.

lailai. (R-- LAI)
Fish sp. (= *lae*?). *n.*

lala.
To roast. *v.*

lalaa. (B-2 LALA)
Sizzling noise (as in frying). *v.*

lala gaadinga.
To heat copra (to dry it).

lalau. (T-- LAU₁)
One after another becoming *lau*₁. *a.*

lalaunga. (T-1 LAU₁)
n.

lale.
Fish sp. (The native term is applied to many spp.). *n.*

lallala. (R-- LALA)
Warm oneself by the fire. *v.*

lalo.
Down, under. *nl.*

lalo ade.
Solar plexus (considered the seat of feeling).

lalo de langi.
Beyond the horizon, far away from the atoll.

lama.
A dry coconut leaf. *n.*

lamalamallie. (R-- MALIEa)
a.

lamallie. (B-- MALIEa)
Bearing big nuts (of coconut trees). *a.*

lamu.
Do some bad deed suddenly or by surprise. *v.*

lamua. (B-2 LAMU)
v.

lamu dada.
A jerk (e.g., of a line).

lamulamu. (R-- LAMU)
v.

lamulamua. (R-2 LAMU)
v.

lamulamunga. (R-1 LAMU)
n.

lamunga. (B-1 LAMU)
n.

lanea.
Much, plenty. *a.*

lanibene.
Separation in coconut oil (when it is aging). *a.*

lanibeneanga. (B-1 LANIBENE)
n.

langa.
Lift, raise up; copy out (by hand); ship from one place to another. *v.*

langaa. (B-2 LANGA)
— (ex. 'plait' meaning). *v.*

langaa lodo.
A sudden access of emotion.

langadala. (DALA₁, LANGAb)
(A piece of) thatch made from coconut palm frond. *n.*

langadala tohi.
A dead coconut leaf torn by the wind [poor for making palm frond thatch].

langa de gauanga.
To lift up the leg of an opponent in wrestling [considered unfair].

langa de gubenga.
To pull up a *gubenga* to store it away.

langa de ivi.
A method of repositioning the bones of the ribcage.

langa de moana.
Becoming stormy (of the sea).

langadia. (B-2 LANGA)
Able to remain afloat with a load. *v.*

langalanga. (R-- LANGA)
v.

langalangaa. (R-2 LANGA)
v.

langi₁.
Start or begin (singing or fighting only). *v.*

langi₂.
Rain, heaven, sky. *n.*

langia. (B-2 LANGI₁)
v.

langi haanau.
A certain kind of rain [an omen of an impending childbirth].

langilangi. (R-- LANGI₁)
v.

langilangia. (R-2 LANGI₁)
v.

langilanginga. (R-1 LANGI₁)
n.

langi maadolu.
Heavy rain.

langi maakau.
The sort of rain which is an omen of death.

langi moni.
The sort of rain which is an omen that a ship will come.

lango₁.
Support (e.g., the weight put upon —). *v.*

lango₂.
Insect sp.: fly, flying ant, wasp; or other similar flying insect. *n.*

langoa. (B-2 LANGO₁)
v.

lango beau.
A method of lashing the outrigger float to the outrigger struts.

langolango. (R-- LANGO₁)
—; inclined to throw one's legs over those sleeping nearby (when sleeping). *v.*

langolangoa. (R-2 LANGO₁)
v.

langolangona₁. (R-2 LANGO₁)
v.

langolangona₂. (R-2 LONGO₁)
Repeatedly heard or felt. *a.*

langolangonga. (R-1 LANGO₁)
n.

langona₁. (B-2 LANGO₁)
v.

langona₂. (B-2 LONGO₁)
Heard, felt. *a.*

langona iho maahana.
Feel punished or victimized.

langonga. (B-1 LANGO₁)
n.

lao₁.
d.

lao₂.
The posterior portion of the coconut crab. *n.*

laoa. (B-2 LAO₁)
—; be stuck in the throat (esp. fish bones). *v.*

lao gau-me.
To grasp a fish by inserting one's fingers in both gills.

laohie.
Dry weather (no rain). *a.*

laohie age.
Improving condition (of weather).

laohie de me.
Good weather (dry).

laolao. (R-- LAO₁)
v.

laolaoa. (R-2 LAO₁)
v.

laolaohie. (R-- LAOHIE)
a.

laolaonga. (R-1 LAO₁)
n.

laonga. (B-1 LAO₁)
n.

laosedi.
Sea water. *n.*

laso.
The posterior portion of the hermit crab. *n.*

laso paava.
Skinny (of people).

la sseioo.
A sound indicating surprise. *i.*

la sseualee.
A sound indicating surprise. *i.*

lau$_1$.
Hooked, caught fast on. *a.*

lau$_2$.
Leaf, or any similar thin, flat thing. *n.*

lau$_3$.
The size of something. *n.*

lau$_4$.
Hundred. *an.*

lauali.
Immature leaves. *v.*

lauasaasa.
Skinny. *v.*

lauasaasaanga. (B-1 LAUASAASA)
n.

laubalabala. (BALA, LAU$_2$)
Slack (of rope); soft (of skin or paper); pliable (of hair); flexible. *a.*

laudanga. (B-1 LAU$_1$)
n.

lau de alelo.
Be unable to speak clearly, owing to a stuttering problem.

lau de ava.
A tuna of large size.

lau de madila.
A tuna of fair size.

laudia. (B-2 LAU$_1$)
v.

laudodole. (DOLE, LAU$_3$)
Smallness. *n.*

lau tulugi.
A tuna of the size next largest to *lau de ava.*

lau-gadaha.
Plant sp.: bird's-nest fern (*Asplenium nidus* L.).

lau kena.
Leaves (or hair) which have lost their natural healthy color.

lau kohu.
Growing well (of plants) [lit., 'having dark green leaves'].

lau hadihadi.
Having wavy hair.

lau henua.
Waves of sufficient size to wash over all land on the atoll; tidal wave.

lau iho laa.
Those of small size.

laulau$_1$. (R-- LAU$_1$)
—; good for hooking. *a.*

laulau$_2$. (R-- LAU$_{2a}$)
A type of basket. *n.*

laulau$_3$. (R-- LAULAU)
Overripe coconut apple. *a.*

laulau$_4$. (R-- LAU$_4$)
Hundreds and hundreds. *an.*

laulaua. (R-2 LAULAU)
a.

laulau a sogo.
A type of basket.

laulaudanga. (R-1 LAU$_1$)
n.

laulau dao gai.
A wrapping (like a basket) for food cooked in the earth oven.

laulaudia. (R-2 LAU$_1$)
v.

laulau gai.
A canoe used to transport food to a feast.

laulau hai daonga.
A type of basket [used for allocating portions at a feast].

laulau hoe.
The blade of the canoe paddle.

laulaunga$_1$. (R-1 LAU$_1$)
Able to be hooked. *n.*

laulaunga$_2$. (R-1 LAULAU)
n.

lau ligi.
Having small leaves.

lau maalie.
Neat-appearing hair or feathers.

lau makaga.
Stiff.

laumalie. (LAU$_{3a}$, MALIE)
Big, great. *a.*

lau manu.
Leaf of a plant.

lau me.
Adjacent (of taro plots only).

laumele.
Fish sp.: tang (2 sorts). *n.*

launga. (B-1 LAU_1)
n.

lau ngago.
The fatty tissue of a fish or animal.

lausamua. (LAU_2, $SAMU_1$)
Untidy in appearance (esp. unshaven, with one's hair in disorder); unkempt. *v.*

lausedi.
[Var. of *laosedi*]. *n.*

laussoe. (LAU_2, SOE)
Having straight hair (not kinky or wavy). *a.*

lauvinivini. (LAU_2, VINI)
Having kinky hair. *v.*

lava.
Finished [sing.]; wealthy [sing.]; wrap—[dp]. *a.*

lava ai donu huu.
Forget it!

lavaanga. (B-1 LAVA)
n.

lava hadu.
Leader (between fishing line and hook).

lava i de goloa.
Having many *goloa.*

lavalava. (R-- LAVA)
Becoming finished or wealthy; keep wrapping; sarong [a recently introduced usage]. *v.*

lavalava lau manu.
A sarong of material with a flowered pattern.

lavasi. (B-- $LAVA_a$)
A leader (between the hook and the fishing line). *n.*

lava sili.
Good enough!; stop!

lave.
Be caught on, stuck on. *a.*

lavelave. (R-- LAVE)
a.

lealea. (R-- LEA)
a.

lealeaanga. (R-1 LEA)
n.

leanga.
Bad person. *n.*

leba.
Flap in the wind (like a flag). *v.*

lebaanga. (B-1 LEBA)
n.

lebaleba. (R-- LEBA)
v.

lebalebaanga. (R-1 LEBA)
n.

lebelebe. (R-- LEBE)
Fish sp.: jack. *n.*

lebidi.
Bird sp.: white tern? *n.*

lebu.
Paint (something); put color on, color (something). *v.*

lebua. (B-2 LEBU)
v.

lebulebu. (R-- LEBU)
v.

lebulebua. (R-2 LEBU)
v.

lebulebunga. (R-1 LEBU)
n.

lede.
Penetrating cold. *n.*

leebunga. (B-1 LEBU)
—; a color (of something). *n.*

leelenga. (B-1 LELE)
n.

leenaa. (B-2 LENA)
v.

leenanga. (B-1 LENA)
n.

leengia. (B-2 LELE)
Jump on; be flown into. *v.*

leenginga. (B-1 LENGI)
n.

leevanga. (B-1 LEVA)
n.

legalega. (R-- LEGA)
Smallness. *n.*

legia.
Bird sp.: white-capped noddy (*Anous minutus*). *n.*

lehu.
Ashes. *v.*

lehua. (B-2 LEHU)
Blurred; covered with ashes. *v.*

lehunga. (B-1 LEHU)
—; way of being blurred. *n.*

leia. (B-2 LELE)
Be jumped upon; be landed upon. *v.*

leia togo mouli.
Hiccough.

lele.
To fly; jump. *v.*

lele age.
Regain consciousness; epilepsy; surfacing (of flying fish).

lele biho.
Dive head first.

lele tua.
To pull a back muscle (or pinch a nerve?) and thus collapse.

lele tuli.
Parturition.

lele mouli.
Surprised [often this expression occurs with a possessive pronoun between the words].

lele sseni.
Insomnia (after sleeping for a short while).

lele vae.
Jump feet first.

lellele. (R-- LELE)
v.

lelleleanga. (R-1 LELE)
n.

lena.
d.

lenalena. (R-- LENA)
v.

lenalenaa. (R-2 LENA)
v.

lenalenaanga. (R-1 LENA)
n.

lenga.
A preparation made from *ango* and *doi doi* (q.v.). *n.*

lengi.
Bloated, inflated, swollen up, bulging. *a.*

lengilengi. (R-- LENGI)
a.

lengilenginga. (R-1 LENGI)
n.

lengisi.
Insect sp.: moth spp. *n.*

leo.
A voice, a sound, an intonational pattern. *n.*

leoleo. (R-- LEO)
The making of sounds repeatedly. *d.*

leu.
The yellow color or softness of fruit (indicating ripeness); ripe. *a.*

leuleu. (R-- LEU)
Becoming *leu*. *a.*

leuleunga. (R-1 LEU)
n.

leunga. (B-1 LEU)
n.

leva.
To sail through the air. *a.*

levaleva. (R-- LEVA)
a.

levalevaanga. (R-1 LEVA)
n.

levango.
Fight. *a.*

leva saele.
Vagrant (having no fixed abode).

liagi.
Dump, throw out (discard). *v.*

liagina. (B-2 LIAGI)
v.

liaginga. (B-1 LIAGI)
n.

libi.
Do rapidly (esp. a repeated action done energetically). *v.*

libia. (B-2 LIBI)
v.

libilibi. (R-- LIBI)
v.

libilibia. (R-2 LIBI)
v.

libilibinga. (R-1 LIBI)
n.

libinga. (B-1 LIBI)
n.

libo$_1$.
Turn end over end; turn in place (of a person). *a.*

libo$_2$.
Fish sp.: jack. *n.*

libo ange de henua.
Feel dizzy or faint, vertigo.

libolibo. (R-- LIBO$_1$)
a.

libolibo ange.
Drunk, dizzy, crazy.

libolibonga. (R-1 LIBO$_1$)
n.

lipaidonga. (?)
Mollusk sp.: *Turbo petholatus.* *n.*

lie.
Lice eggs. *n.*

ligi.
Small — [ds]. *d.*

liholiho. (R-- LIHO)
String twirled from coconut fiber, sennit. *n.*

lii.
Bird sp. (seen only over the ocean). *n.*

liibonga. (B-1 LIBO$_1$)
n.

liiliagi. (R-- LIAGI)
—; a status level [N]; having a close kin relationship [archaic]. *v.*

liiliagi daudahi.
Be of the same status.

liiliagina. (R-2 LIAGI)
v.

liiliaginga. (R-1 LIAGI)
n.

liilonga. (B-1 LILO)
n.

liingia. (B-2 LINGI)
v.

liinginga. (B-1 LINGI)
n.

lili$_1$.
Rippling (of the surface of the sea). *v.*

lili$_2$.
A method of lashing. *v.*

lili$_3$.
Mad at, angry. *a.*

lilia$_1$. (B-2 LILI$_1$)
v.

lilia$_2$. (B-2 LILI$_2$)
v.

lilianga. (B-1 LILI$_3$)
n.

lili baasi gee.
Accuse someone (in an argument, usually between spouses) of taking sides with another family member.

lili mahangahanga.
Mad as the devil.

lilinga$_1$. (B-1 LILI$_1$)
n.

lilinga$_2$. (B-1 LILI$_2$)
n.

lillili$_1$. (R-- LILI$_1$)
v.

lillili$_2$. (R-- LILI$_3$)
Easily angered, short-tempered. *a.*

lillilianga. (R-1 LILI$_3$)
n.

lillilinga. (R-1 LILI$_1$)
n.

lilo.
Disappear, vanish; sheltered (from the elements). *a.*

lilo bule.
Covered up completely.

lilolilo. (R-- LILO)
In a sheltered place. *a.*

lilolilonga. (R-1 LILO)
n.

lilolilongia. (R-2 LILO)
v.

lilongia. (B-2 LILO)
v.

lima₁. (B-- LIMA)
Arm, hand. *n.*

lima₂. (B-- LIMAa)
Five. *án.*

lima-pilo.
The fifth number of a counting game played to determine who is "it".

lima dangada ina.
A patient of one healer who has been treated by another healer.

limadi.
Do fast or quickly. *v.*

limadia. (B-2 LIMADI)
v.

limadinga. (B-1 LIMADI)
n.

Lima-laangi. (LAANGI, LIMAa)
Friday ('fifth day'). *nt.*

lima lele.
Quick to fight, short-tempered.

limalima. (R-- LIMA)
Dexterous (esp. in fighting). *a.*

limalimaanga. (R-1 LIMA)
n.

Lima-malama. (LIMAa, MALAMA)
May ('fifth month'). *nt.*

limamalie. (LIMA, MALIE)
Good at massaging. *a.*

lima ma vae ange.
Work for as a servant.

limilimi. (R-- LIMI)
Coral sp.: brain coral? *n.*

lingi.
d.

lingilingi. (R-- LINGI)
v.

lingilingia. (R-2 LINGI)
Pour little by little. *v.*

lingilinginga. (R-1 LINGI)
n.

llaba. (P-- LABA₁)
v.

llabaanga. (P-1 LABA₁)
n.

llabu. (E-- LABU)
Claw. *v.*

llaga. (E-- LAGA)
Take a single step. *v.*

llago. (E-- LAGO₁)
Mature (of a taro corm which can be used for food). *a.*

llagoanga. (E-1 LAGO₁)
n.

llagu. (E-- LAGU)
Claw. *v.*

llaha. (P-- LAHA)
a.

llahaanga. (P-1 LAHA)
n.

llahi₁. (P-- LAHI)
Thin (pl.). *a.*

llahi₂. (E-- LAHIb)
Fish sp. (= small *hagaudalolo*). *n.*

llahianga. (P-1 LAHI)
n.

llama. (E-- LAMA)
A method of fishing (using torches of *lama* to catch flying fish). *v.*

llanga. (E-- LANGA)
Float (on the surface of the water); plait (mats). *a.*

llao. (E-- LAO₁)
Gouge out (with the hand only); take out of a hole. *v.*

llau₁. (, LAU₁)
—; to have one's forward motion impeded (as when walking through the surf). *a.*

llau₂. (P-- LAU₄)
Hundreds. *a.*

llaunga. (P-1 LAU₁)
n.

llava. (P-- LAVA)
Finished [pl.]; wealthy [pl.]; wrap [independent form]; meat or fish (for a meal). *v.*

llava ai.
Wrapped (tied) around; eat fish or meat with a meal.

llavaanga. (P-1 LAVA)
n.

llave. (P-- LAVE)
a.

llea. (E-- LEA)
Say loudly [with both sing. and pl. subjects]. *a.*

lleaanga. (E-1 LEA)
n.

lleba. (P-- LEBA)
v.

llebaanga. (P-1 LEBA)
n.

lleenginga. (P-1 LENGI)
n.

lleevanga. (P-1 LEVA)
n.

llele. (P-- LELE)
a.

llele age + PRONOUN --.
(My/his, etc.) — has returned.

lleleanga. (P 1 LELE)
n.

llena. (E-- LENA)
Stretch; raise one's eyebrows. *v.*

llena luu mada.
Raise both eyebrows [a sign of assent].

llengi. (P-- LENGI)
a.

lleu. (P-- LEU)
a.

lleu luu mada.
Swelling of the eyes (after crying).

lleu luu malau ngudu.
Swollen lips (from eating spicy foods or foods to which one is allergic).

lleunga. (P-1 LEU)
n.

lleva. (P-- LEVA)
a.

llibo. (P-- $LIBO_1$)
a.

llibo ange luu vae.
Run.

llidi.
Dress up (esp. in new or very fancy clothes). *a.*

llie. (E-- LIE)
The throat of the flying fish net. *n.*

lligi. (E-- LIGI)
Fine (in grain, of hair, etc.); little, small [pl.]. *a.*

lliibonga. (P-1 $LIBO_1$)
n.

lliidinga. (B-1 LLIDI)
n.

lliilonga. (P-1 LILO)
n.

llili. (P-- LILI_3)
a.

llilianga. (P-1 LILI_3)
n.

llilo. (P-- LILO)
Able to be hooked. *a.*

llilo mai.
Decreasing (in number); becoming less.

llilongia. (P-2 LILO)
v.

llimu. (E-- LIMU)
A small *honu*. *n.*

llingi. (E-- LINGI)
Pour out, spill out (sand). *v.*

lloa. (P-- LOA_1)
Long [pl.]. *a.*

lloaanga. (P-1 LOA_1)
n.

lloba. (E-- $LOBA_1$)
Fluttering rapidly (of a sail in the breeze); [also pl. of *lobaloba*]. *a.*

llobaanga. (E-1 $LOBA_1$)
n.

llobo. (E-- LOBO)
To put something in something else. *v.*

llodo. (P-- $LODO_2$)
a.

llohi. (E-- LOHI)
Erosion of sand or soil (esp. of the beach by wave action). *v.*

llohia. (B-2 LOHI)
v.

llonga.
Muscle fatigue. *v.*

llou. (E-- LOU)
Hang down or bent down (of branches, palm fronds, or fishing poles). *v.*

llounga. (E-1 LOU)
n.

lludu. (E-- LUDU)
Take all (of something). *v.*

lludua. (E-2 LUDU)
v.

lluhe. (E-- LUHE)
Plant sp.: sword fern (The native term applies possibly to several spp.). *n.*

lluhi. (E-- LUHI)
An access (of emotion or sensory impression). *a.*

lluhianga. (E-1 LUHI)
n.

llui. (P-- LUI_1)
v.

lluia. (P-2 LUI_1)
v.

lluinga. (P-1 LUI_1)
n.

lluu.
Mad or angry (but not showing it). *a.*

loa₁.
Long — [ds]. *d.*

loa₂.
Ant. *n.*

loada.
Sputum. *n.*

loadu.
Go (toward the hearer) [pl.]. *a.*

loage.
Go (up or toward the village, or land) [pl.]. *a.*

loange.
Go (to the place away from both the speaker and hearer) [pl.]. *a.*

loba. (B-- $LOBA_2$)
A type of mat. *n.*

lobadia. (E-2 $LOBA_1$)
v.

lobadia mai.
To have the sail and mast blown down (because the wind came from the side away from the outrigger).

lobaloba. (R-- $LOBA_1$)
Flapping (of a sail in the breeze) [sing.]. *v.*

lobalobaanga. (R-1 $LOBA_1$)
n.

lobalobadia. (R-2 $LOBA_1$)
v.

lobo.
d.

lobodia. (B-2 LOBO)
v.

lobolobo. (R-- LOBO)
v.

loboloboa. (R-2 LOBO)
v.

lobolobodia. (R-2 LOBO)
v.

lobolobonga. (R-1 LOBO)
n.

lodo₁.
Inside of; lagoon [*te lodo*]. *nl.*

lodo₂.
Want, desire. *a.*

lodo a gauligi.
Immature (in personality); vulnerable to having one's feelings easily hurt.

lodo aheahe.
Unstable temperamentally, inconstant.

lodo baageaa.
Weak-willed, easily tempted; excited easily by the opposite sex.

lodo baba.
Calmness, tranquility, freedom from worries.

lodo bale.
Helpful (sort of person).

lodo basa.
Talkative.

lodo baubau.
Unhappy, upset, sad.

lodo bigede.
Feel cowardly.

lodo daemaha.
Feel unhappy or sad.

lodo dagidahi.
Have differing views (within a group of people).

lodo dama.
Immature in affect.

lodo danuaa.
Contented, happy.

lodo degi.
Having a forgiving nature.

lodo gapua.
Seaward part of a *gapua*.

lodo gaiaa.
Competitive, envious, desirous of retaliating.

lodo gilimalali.
Pureness of heart, innocence.

lodo gi lunga.
Ambitious for a superior position.

lodo gi me.
Acquisitive, covetous.

lodo kabi.
Filled to capacity.

lodo hagamau me.
Selfish with one's possessions, ungiving.

lodo henua.
Inland, bush (uncleared) land, wilderness.

lodo hinangalosaa.
A feeling of *hinangalosaa*; depression (feeling).

lodo laanui.
Large in volume or capacity, spacious inside.

lodo lagolago.
Indecisive, undecided.

lodo $lanea_1$.
Large in volume.

lodo $lanea_2$.
Indecisive, confused.

lodo llidi.
A dandy (always wanting to *llidi*).

lodolodo. (R-- $LODO_2$)
To be desirous continually. *a.*

lodo malangilangi.
Happy.

lodo manege.
Stubborn (esp. in maintaining one's own superiority); be a poor loser.

lodo mao lalo.
Characteristically *hagamao lalo*; self-effacing, meek in spirit.

lodo mao lunga.
Characteristically *hagamao lunga*; egotistical, self-centered, arrogant in spirit.

lodo me muimui.
In the bush (uncleared area).

lodo mmahi.
Persistent, patient, persevering.

lodo senga.
To have unrealistic self-confidence (e.g., in one's capacity to do something impossible); to be foolishly desirous (of the impossible).

lo taane.
Daring, brave, manly.

lo te.
[A contraction of *lodo de...*].

lo te dege.
Inside the corner of.

lo te gelo.
In the deepest part.

lo te hebagi.
During the war.

lo te logunga.
Inside the corner of.

lo te vvela.
The hottest part (of the day, of a fire, etc.).

loeaa.
A type of game. *n.*

lo gunga. (GUNGA, $LODO_1$)
Inside the corner of. *nl.*

$loha_1$. (B-- LOHA)
Fathom (the span of one's outstretched arms). *v.*

loha$_2$. (B-- LOHA$_a$)
Bird sp. (never seen live). *n.*

lohaa. (B-2 LOHA)
v.

lohaanga. (B-1 LOHA)
n.

lohaloha. (R-- LOHA)
Measure off in fathoms. *v.*

lohalohaa. (R-2 LOHA)
v.

lohalohaanga. (R-1 LOHA)
n.

lohi.
d.

lohilohi. (R-- LOHI)
v.

lohilohia. (R-2 LOHI)
v.

lohilohinga. (R-1 LOHI)
n.

loigulu. (GULU, LOI)
A type of prepared food (made from breadfruit). *n.*

loiho.
Go or come down (or toward the lagoon) [pl.]. *a.*

loimada. (LODO$_1$, MADA$_3$)
Tears. *n.*

lollolo. (R-- LOLO)
Oily. *v.*

lolloloanga. (R-1 LOLO)
n.

lolo.
Oil. *n.*

lolo hai haahine.
A love potion (applied to the clothes or body).

lolo manu-de-boo.
A type of medicine (made from coconut oil and centipedes).

lolomango. (LOLO, MANGO)
To clear oil (which is separated from crude coconut oil by heating). *n.*

loma.
Very calm, silent. *a.*

lomolomosi. (R-- LOOMOSI)
Repeatedly or frequently *loomosi.* *v.*

lomolomosia. (R-2 LOOMOSI)
v.

lomolomosinga. (R-1 LOOMOSI)
n.

lomosia. (B-2 LOOMOSI)
v.

longaa. (B-- LONGO$_{1a}$)
Annoyed by noise. *a.*

longo. (B-- LONGO$_1$)
Hear, feel; news. *a.*

longoaa. (B-- LONGO$_{1a}$)
[= *longaa*]. *a.*

longoduli. (XCO LONGO$_1$)
Deaf. *a.*

longohie. (B-- LONGO$_{2a}$)
Big around, fat. *a.*

longo iho.
Be aware of, experience, perceive, feel (in one's mind or body).

longolongo. (R-- LONGO$_1$)
—; acuity of hearing. *a.*

longolongo i adamagi.
To pick up information by asking others, who have lied (so that one's information, therefore, is false).

longolongo iho dalinga.
Pick up information from others' conversation.

longolongo i leaala.
Rumor.

longosaa. (B-- LONGO$_2$)
Small around, thin. *a.*

loo.
About it, concerning it, in it, for it. *mv.*

looboa. (B-2 LOBO)
v.

loobonga. (B-1 LOBO)
n.

loohinga. (B-1 LOHI)
n.

looloa. (R-- LOA$_1$)
Long [sing.]. *a.*

looloaanga. (R-1 LOA_1)
n.

loolodo. (T-- $LODO_1$)
Deep holes in the lagoon reef. *n.*

looloonaa. (R-- LOONAA)
v.

looloonaanga. (R-1 LOONAA)
n.

loomai.
Come or go (toward the speaker) [pl.]. *a.*

loomosi.
Kill someone by holding him under the water until he is drowned. *v.*

loomosinga. (B-1 LOOMOSI)
n.

loonaa.
The sticking of food in the throat (which is cleared by washing it down with liquid). *v.*

loonaanga. (B-1 LOONAA)
n.

loongia. (B-2 LOLO)
To lose one's appetite after eating oily food. *v.*

loselose-ganoanga.
Fish sp.

loselose-uli.
Fish sp.: trumpet fish.

lou.
A pole with a hook at the end, used to pick breadfruit; pick (breadfruit), pull down. *v.*

loua. (B-2 LOU)
v.

lou aama.
The submerging of the outrigger float.

loua ama.
To sail with the outrigger float partially submerged.

lou de gaugau dalinga.
Pull the trigger (of a gun).

lou gulu.
Pick breadfruit.

loulou. (R-- LOU)
To repeatedly use a breadfruit picker; pull (a trigger). *v.*

louloua. (R-2 LOU)
—; constipated. *v.*

loulounga. (R-1 LOU)
n.

lounga. (B-1 LOU)
n.

lua.
Two. *an.*

luaada.
Each person's two. *pta.*

luaadaadeu.
Our [incl. 3] two. *ppa.*

luaadaau.
Our [incl. 2] two. *ppa.*

luaagu.
My two. *ppa.*

luaalaadeu.
Their [3] two. *ppa.*

luaalaau.
Their [2] two. *ppa.*

lua-aligi. (ALIGI, LUA)
Chief mate (of a European ship). *a.*

luaamaadeu.
Our [excl. 3] two. *ppa.*

luaamaau.
Our [excl. 2] two. *ppa.*

luaana.
His two, her two, its two. *ppa.*

luaau.
Your [1] two. *ppa.*

lua-baaua.
The second number of a counting game played to determine who is "it".

Lua-laangi. (LAANGI, LUA)
Tuesday ('second day'). *nt.*

lua lodo.
Undecided.

Lua-malama. (LUA, MALAMA)
February ('second month'). *nt.*

ludu.
d.

luduludu. (R-- LUDU)
Trembling. *v.*

luei.
Spit out (esp. food). *v.*

lueia. (B-2 LUEI)
v.

luei todo.
Cough up blood.

lueinga. (B-1 LUEI)
n.

lueluei. (R-- LUEI)
v.

luelueia. (R-2 LUEI)
v.

luelueinga. (R-1 LUEI)
n.

lugu. (B-- $LUGU_1$)
Take or obtain something by force. *v.*

lugua. (B-2 $LUGU_1$)
v.

lugulugu$_1$. (R-- $LUGU_1$)
v.

lugulugu$_2$. (R-- $LUGU_2$)
Fish sp. *n.*

lugulugua. (R-2 $LUGU_1$)
v.

lugulugunga. (R-1 $LUGU_1$)
n.

lugu me.
Having a tendency to take by force.

lugunga. (B-1 $LUGU_1$)
n.

luhiluhi. (R-- LUHI)
a.

lui$_1$.
Turn (something in direction); change course; reverse, transpose. *v.*

lui$_2$.
The water which has accumulated in a canoe. *n.*

luia. (B-2 LUI_1)
v.

luilui. (R-- LUI_1)
—; turn (something) end over end. *v.*

luiluia. (R-2 LUI_1)
v.

luilui togo.
A measurement of land along the shore [in which the chief had rights] using a punt pole.

luiluinga. (R-1 LUI_1)
n.

luinga. (B-1 LUI_1)
n.

lulu.
To shake (something) rapidly. *v.*

lulua. (B-2 LULU)
v.

lulunga. (B-1 LULU)
n.

lunga.
Up, above, over. *nl.*

lunga age.
Up a little.

lunga ange.
Up more.

luoo.
Your [1] two. *ppo.*

luoodaadeu.
Our [incl. 3] two. *ppo.*

luoodaau.
Our [incl. 2] two. *ppo.*

luoodo.
Each person's two. *pto.*

luoodou.
Your [3] two. *pp.*

luoogu.
My two. *ppo.*

luoolaadeu.
Their [3] two. *ppo.*

luoolaau.
Their [2] two. *ppo.*

luooluu.
Your [2] two. *pp.*

luoomaadeu.
Our [excl. 3] two. *ppo.*

luoomaau.
Our [excl. 2] two. *ppo.*

luoono.
His two, her two, its two. *ppo.*

luu.
The two. *ma.*

luu baasi.
Both sides (of).

luu bido.
Both ends (of).

luu panava.
Scrotum (whole thing).

luu dolodolo.
The phosphorescence on both sides of the atoll channel, marking it at night.

luudunga. (B-1 LUDU)
n.

luu duu.
Covers (of books), two halves.

luu duu de maduu.
Castes (two) of aboriginal Nukuoro society.

luu gili.
Labia minora.

luu hadu a moidigi.
Stone-like organs in the top of the head of flying fish.

luu hua.
Labia majora.

luuluu. (T-- LULU)
To shake (something) back and forth. *v.*

luuluua. (T-2 LULU)
v.

luuluu haha.
Wash one's mouth out, gargle.

luuluuia. (T-2 LULU)
v.

luuluunga. (T-1 LULU)
n.

luuluungagi. (R-- LUUNGAGI)
v.

luuluungagina. (R-2 LUUNGAGI)
v.

luuluungaginga. (R-1 LUUNGAGI)
n.

luu mada.
Face (of a person).

luungagi.
To be in a place protected from the wind, lee. *v.*

luungagina. (B-2 LUUNGAGI)
v.

luungaginga. (B-1 LUUNGAGI)
n.

m-.
For (always followed by *o* or a_1). *mp.*

ma-. (B-- MA_2)
RESULTATIVE PREFIX. *mf.*

ma_1.
And, and so, and thus, and then; with, including. *mi.*

ma_2.
A measure of the quantity of flying fish (*ssave*) caught (by hundreds): e.g., *dolu ma* 'three hundred flying fish'.

maa_1. (B-- MAA_4)
...and the others [after personal names and pronouns]; approximately — [after expressions of quantity]. *u.*

maa_2.
A sibling's souse or spouse' sibling (brother-in-law or sister-in-law) of the same sex. *n.*

$maa\text{-}_3$. (P-- MAA_5)
[Pl. form of *ma-*]. *mf.*

maabunga. (B-1 MABU)
n.

$maada_1$.
For each person's several. *ptma.*

$maada_2$.
For each person's several. *ptmb.*

maadaadeu.
For us [incl. 3]. *pdma.*

maadaau.
For us [incl. 2]. *pdma.*

maadada.
For each person's one. *ptma.*

maadai*.
A cult official (who looked after the cult-house). *n.*

maadau.
Hook, fishhook. *n.*

maadau belubelu.
A type of fishhook (small, for *belubelu* fishing).

maadau daabasi.
A type of fishhook.

maadau dae ssae.
A type of fishhook.

maadau dagi.
A type of fishhook.

maadau daodao.
A type of fishhook (large, for using a piece of fish as bait).

maadau duiagi.
A fishhook of a special type (for *duiagi* fishing).

maadau gina.
A type of fishhook (for *gina* fishing).

maadau hholu.
A fishhook made of wire.

maadau iganibongi.
A type of fishhook (biggest, for *iganibongi* fishing).

maadau mada bodobodo.
A type of fishhook.

maadau mangoo.
A type of fishhook (for sharks).

maadaunga. (B-1 MADAU)
n.

maadegadega. (RC- DEGA)
Bird sp.: a young bird (still unable to fly) of any bird sp. *n.*

maadenga$_1$. (B-1 MADE$_1$)
n.

maadenga$_2$. (B-1 MADE$_2$)
n.

maadinga. (B-1 MADI)
n.

maadodo.
For each person's one. *ptmo.*

maadoha. (PC- DOHA)
a.

maadohaanga. (PC1 DOHA)
n.

maadohi. (PC- DOHI)
a.

maadolu.
Thick (object); heavy or dense (of rain). *a.*

maadoogini. (?)
Harmonica. *n.*

maadua. (P-- MADUA)
Parents, elders. *a.*

maatagu. (P-- MADAGU)
a.

maataguanga. (P-1 MADAGU)
n.

maatala. (PC- DALA$_1$)
a.

maatalaanga. (PC1 DALA$_1$)
n.

maatogo.
Discourage someone (verbally). *v.*

maatogoanga. (B-1 MAATOGO)
n.

maatua. (P-- MADUA)
— (ex. meanings covered by *maadua*). *a.*

maaege. (PC- EGE)
v.

maaegenga. (PC1 EGE)
n.

maagaga. (E-- MAKAGA)
Industrious. *a.*

maagagaanga. (E-1 MAKAGA)
n.

maagaga dua.
To walk with one's shoulders unnaturally thrown back.

maaganga$_1$. (B-1 MAGA$_1$)
n.

maaganga$_2$. (B-1 MAGA$_2$)
n.

maagila.
To appear to be barely separated (as islets on the atoll when seen from a distance); parted slightly. *v.*

maagilaanga. (B-1 MAAGILA)
n.

maagoda.
Jealous (sexual jealousy). *a.*

maagodanga. (B-1 MAAGODA)
n.

maagu.
For me. *pdma.*

maaguluaa.
Dislocated (joint of the body). *a.*

maaguluaanga.
(B-1 MAAGULUAA) *n.*

maakau. (P-- MAGAU)
a.

maakau laa loo dangada.
What a shame!

maakau loo dangada.
Now we're in trouble!

maakaunga. (P-1 MAGAU)
n.

maakulu. (P-- MAGULU)
a.

maahaa. (EC- HAA_1)
Daybreak. *a.*

maahaa ada.
Dawn (first burst of light).

maahagi. (PC- HAGI)
a.

maahana. (PC- HANA)
a.

maahanaanga. (PC1 HANA)
n.

maahanasia. (PC2 HANA)
v.

maahanga. (PC- HANGA)
a.

maahe. (BC- AHE)
Decrease (in strength, rate of growth, etc.). *a.*

maaheahe. (RC- AHE)
Decreasing. *a.*

maaheahenga. (RC1 AHE)
n.

maahedu. (PC- HEDU)
a.

maahedunga. (PC1 HEDU)
n.

maahenga. (BC1 AHE)
n.

maahia. (U-- HII_1)
Want to —. *v.*

maahiaanga. (EC3 MAHI)
n.

maahidi. (PC- HIDI)
a.

maahidinga. (PC1 HIDI)
n.

maahola. (PC- HOLA)
a.

maaholaanga. (PC1 HOLA)
n.

maahole. (PC- HOLE)
a.

maaholenga. (PC1 HOLE)
n.

maahuge. (PC- HUGE)
a.

maahugenga. (PC1 HUGE)
n.

maahule. (PC- HULE)
a.

maahulenga. (PC1 HULE)
n.

maahunga. (B-1 MAHU)
n.

ma ai.
And who?

maai.
Ripen (to become yellow and soft—of breadfruit only). *a.*

maailaba.
Axis (or long thing through the center of something). *n.*

maaileele.
Die, dead (persons or animals). *a.*

maaileelenga. (B-1 MAAILEELE)
n.

maainga. (B-1 MAAI)
n.

maaisi. (PC- ISI_1)
a.

maaisinga. (PC1 ISI_1)
n.

maalaadeu.
For them [3]. *pdma.*

maalaau.
For them [2]. *pdma.*

maalaia. (P-- MALAIA)
a.

maalaiaanga. (P-1 MALAIA)
n.

maalali. (P-- MALALI)
a.

maalalianga. (P-1 MALALI)
n.

maalama.
Light (not dark), bright. *v.*

maalama dua de laa.
The light remaining after sunset.

maalamangia. (B-2 MAALAMA)
Illuminated (by having light shined upon it). *v.*

maalanga. (PC- LANGA)
a.

maalava.
The fatty part of the turtle. *v.*

maalemo. (P-- MALEMO)
a.

maalena. (PC- LENA)
a.

maalenaanga. (PC1 LENA)
n.

maaleva. (P-- MALEVA)
a.

maalibi. (PC- LIBI)
a.

maalibinga. (PC1 LIBI)
n.

maalie.
Exactly; slowly; carefully, gently, softly. *mv.*

maalie ange.
A little later.

maalie loo.
Much later.

maalili. (P-- $MALILI_1$)
a.

maalilianga. (P-1 $MALILI_1$)
n.

maalino. (P-- MALINO)
v.

maalinoanga. (P-1 MALINO)
n.

maalinongia. (P-2 MALINO)
v.

maalingi. (PC- LINGI)
a.

maalinginga. (PC1 LINGI)
n.

maalioso.
Die, dead (persons or animals). *a.*

maalisa.
An overhanging reef shelf. *n.*

maalo.
Energetic, eager, wide-awake; waiting. *a.*

maalo age.
Have become *maalo.*

maaloanga. (B-1 MAALO)
n.

maalogu. (P-- MALOGU)
v.

maalogunga. (P-1 MALOGU)
n.

maaloolo. (R-- MAALO)
Refreshed (e.g., after a rest, or a shower). *a.*

maalooloanga. (R-1 MAALO)
n.

maalui. (PC- LUI_1)
a.

maaluinga. (PC1 LUI_1)
n.

maalunga. (B-1 MALU)
n.

maamaa. (R-- MAA_3)
Chew thoroughly, masticate (soft foods which do not make noise). *v.*

maamaadeu.
For us [excl. 3]. *pdma.*

maamaadolu. (R-- MAADOLU)
Becoming more and more *maadolu.* *a.*

maamaatogo. (R-- MAATOGO)
v.

maamaatogoanga.
(R-1 MAATOGO) *n.*

maamaagila. (R-- MAAGILA)
Becoming slightly parted. *a.*

maamaagilaanga. (R-1 MAAGILA)
n.

maamaagoda. (R-- MAAGODA)
a.

maamaagodanga. (R-1 MAAGODA)
n.

maamaai. (R-- MAAI)
Ripening (of breadfruit only). *a.*

maamaainga. (R-1 MAAI)
n.

maamaalama. (S-- MAALAMA)
v.

maamaalamangia. (S-2 MAALAMA)
Continuously *maalamangia.* *v.*

maamaalia. (R-2 MAA_3)
v.

maamaalioso. (R-- MAALIOSO)
a.

maamaalo. (S-- MAALO)
Becoming more and more *maalo.* *a.*

maamaaloanga. (S-1 MAALO)
n.

maamaanadu. (R-- MAANADU)
Keep thinking about. *v.*

maamaane. (R-- $MAANE_1$)
Light (in weight). *a.*

maamaaneanga. (R-1 $MAANE_1$)
n.

maamaanu. (R-- MAANU)
—; remain stationary in the air (like a bird or a helicopter). *a.*

maamaanunga. (R-1 MAANU)
n.

maamaanga. (R-1 MAA_3)
n.

maamaangalo. (R-- MAANGALO)
Becoming more and more sweet. *v.*

maamaangaloanga.
(R-1 MAANGALO) *n.*

maamaangi. (R-- MAANGI)
Repeatedly or continually *maangi.* *a.*

maamaasina. (R-- MAASINA)
Repeatedly lighted (esp. by moonlight). *v.*

maamaasinaanga. (R-1 MAASINA)
n.

maamaau.
For us [excl. 2]. *pdma.*

maamaaua. (R-- MAAUA)
Frequently *maaua.* *a.*

maamaauaanga. (R-1 MAAUA)
n.

maamaava. (S-- MAAVA)
a.

maamaavaanga. (S-1 MAAVA)
n.

maamasa. (T-- MASA)
[Pl. of *masa*]. *a.*

maana.
For him, for her, for it. *pdma.*

maanadu.
Think, think about; decide; idea, thought. *v.*

maanadu age.
Decide (arrive at a decision), make up one's mind; think up.

maanaduanga. (B-1 MAANADU)
n.

maanadu bodobodo.
Limited in intelligence.

maanadu bolo.
"Assume that —".

maanadu gelo.
Profound thoughts.

maanadu iho.
Think about oneself.

maanetonu.
($DONU_{1a}$, $MAANE_{2b}$, MAANADU)
Act cautiously. *a.*

maanegabo. (B-- $MAANE_{2a}$)
Energetic. *a.*

maanegaboanga. (B-1 $MAANE_{2a}$)
n.

maanege. (PC- NEGE)
a.

maanegenga. (PC1 NEGE)
n.

maanessala.
($MAANE_2$, $SALA_2$, MAANADU)
To mistake something (or someone) for something (or someone) else. *a.*

maaniha.
Strongly desirous of. *a.*

maanihaanga. (B-1 MAANIHA)
n.

maanongi. (P-- MANONGI)
a.

maanu.
To float in place (not drifting) on the surface of the water (with no anchor). *a.*

maanuga.
A wound or large sore (on the body). *v.*

maanugaanga. (B-1 MAANUGA)
n.

maanuhi. (P-- MANUHI)
a.

maanuhianga. (P-1 MANUHI)
n.

maanu iho.
To begin to fish while *maanu.*

maanunga. (B-1 MAANU)
n.

maanga.
Mouthful or spoonful of food. *n.*

maanga booi.
A fingerful of *booi.*

maanga dalogo.
A handful of *dalogo.*

maanga-de-langi.
Worm sp. (makes a spider-like thread).

maangalo.
Sweet. *v.*

maangaloanga. (B-1 MAANGALO)
n.

maangi.
Soar or glide in the air. *a.*

maangoa*.
To be dry. *a.*

maangoaanga. (B-1 MAANGOA)
n.

maaoha. (PC- OHA)
a.

maaohanga. (PC1 OHA)
n.

maasae. (B-- SAE_{1a})
Hatched. *a.*

maasaenga. (B-1 SAE_{1a})
n.

maasanga. (PC- SANGA)
—; twins [triplets, etc., would also be *maasanga*, but no case of such is remembered]. *n.*

maasei.
Small [sing.]. *a.*

maaseinga. (B-1 MAASEI)
n.

maaseu. (PC- SEU)
a.

maaseunga. (PC1 SEU)
n.

maasina.
Moon, light (not darkness). *v.*

maasinaanga. (B-1 MAASINA)
n.

maasinga. (B-1 $MASI_1$)
n.

maasole. (P-- MASOLE)
a.

maasoleanga. (P-1 MASOLE)
n.

maasugi. (PC- $SUGI_1$)
a.

maasuginga. (PC1 $SUGI_1$)
n.

maasuinga. (B-1 MASUI)
n.

maau.
For you [1]. *pdma.*

maaua.
Poisoned (by food). *a.*

maauaanga. (B-1 MAAUA)
n.

maaui.
Give birth to, born. *v.*

maauinga. (B-1 MAAUI)
n.

maava.
Yawn, belch. *a.*

maava age.
Belch.

maavaanga. (B-1 MAAVA)
n.

maavaava. (R-- MAAVA)
a.

maavaavaanga. (R-1 MAAVA)
n.

maavae. (PC- VAE_1)
Separated (two things), divorced. *a.*

maavaenga. (PC1 VAE_1)
n.

mabu.
Rested. *a.*

mabumabu. (R-- MABU)
a.

mabumabunga. (R-1 MABU)
n.

$mada_1$.
Uncooked, raw. *a.*

$mada_2$ +NUMBER. (B-- $MADA_2$)
Tens of. *mc.*

$mada_3$.
Front part of, face, beginning (of a thing); tip (of); point, blade. *nl.*

$mada_4$. (B-- $MADA_{3a}$)
Common ascendents who are *daina* or other connecting links of kin relationship. *n.*

madaa duge.
The tip of a *duge.*

madaa gai.
Firstfruits.

mada agamu.
The essential design features of *tuai.*

madaa gamu.
The measurements and special techniques used in manufacturing *duai.*

mada age (iho).
Take from the bottom (top); take the worst or smallest (best or biggest).

madaagi.
The scout in *belubelu* fishing. *v.*

madaagianga. (B-1 MADAAGI)
n.

madaaginga. (B-1 MADAAGI)
n.

madaa hadu.
Grater (metal) attached to a board for grating taro.

mada ahodo.
Any place where seawater seeps into the taro bog.

$madaala_1$. ($MADA_{3b}$, ALA_1)
Loosely braided; good at twirling sennit. *a.*

$madaala_2$. (ALA_2, $MADA_3$)
Able to remain awake for a long time. *a.*

madaalanga. (B-1 $MADA_{3b}$)
n.

madaali.
Lacking in oil (of a ripe coconut). *a.*

madaaligi. (P-- $MADALIGI_1$)
a.

madaaligianga. (P-1 $MADALIGI_1$)
n.

madaa moni.
Prow of a canoe.

madaangahulu. (XCO $MADA_2$)
Ten (objects). *an.*

Madaangahulu-ma-dahi-malama.
(XCO MALAMA)
November ('eleventh month'). *nt.*

Madaangahulu-ma-lua-malama.
(XCO MALAMA)
December ('twelfth month'). *nt.*

Madaangahulu-malama.
(XCO MALAMA)
October ('tenth month'). *nt.*

madaangudu. ($MADA_3$, NGUDU)
Converse with. *a.*

madaaolo. ($MADA_3$, OLO)
Capital of. *n.*

madaa sele.
Loop of a lasso or noose.

madaa ua.
Drop (of liquid or rain).

mada baabaa.
= *daogili.*

mada baubau.
Flirtatious.

madabiebie. (BIE, $MADA_3$)
Fish sp.: sea bass (2 sorts: 1 large, 1 small). *n.*

madabuunou. (B-- $MADA_{3h}$)
Dull (of an edge or point). *a.*

madabuunoua. (B-2 $MADA_{3h}$)
Become dull. *a.*

madabuunounga. (B-1 $MADA_{3h}$)
n.

madadaagodo. (DAAGODO, $MADA_3$)
Gradual slope or inclination [form *daagodo* only occurs with *mada*]. *a.*

mada dabu.
Affinal relatives who are *maa* or *saulaba* to each other [and therefore between whom respect and avoidance are enjoined]; avoidance relationship.

mada dahi.
Having a single point or blade.

mada dangada ina.
A person of importance (who is liked by the people).

mada dao.
Prow of a fast ship.

mada dotodo.
An abrasion of the skin (red but not bleeding).

mada duulanga.
An important position (spatially).

mada tea gee.
White as a sheet (of a person).

madagabubu. (B-- $GABUBU_a$)
Dull (of an edge, or point). *a.*

madagabubuanga. (B-1 $GABUBU_a$)
n.

madagabubu de maanadu.
Slow-witted.

mada gapua.
Lagoonward part of a *gapua.*

mada-galadi.
Fish sp.: jack.

mada galava.
Spear foreshaft.

mada-galisi. (GALISI, $MADA_3$)
The stem of the coconut. *v.*

madagauhala.
(GAU_{1e}, HALA, $MADA_3$)
The lower abdomen, crotch, pubic area. *n.*

mada gelegele°. Male child.

madagidagi. (RC- $DAGI_1$)
Long ago. *b.*

mada gi daha.
Having the point bent outward (away from its handle).

mada gide.
Sharp-eyed, good at finding things.

mada giivia.
Dim light.

mada gi lodo.
A point which is bent inward (toward its handle).

mada-givi.
Fish sp.

madagu.
Afraid, scared. *a.*

madaguanga. (B-1 MADAGU)
n.

madagudagu. (R-- MADAGU)
Cowardly (concerning others or supernaturals). *a.*

madagudaguanga. (R-1 MADAGU)
n.

madahaa. (XCO $MADA_2$)
Forty. *an.*

madahidu. (XCO $MADA_2$)
Seventy. *an.*

mada hoodanga.
A depression on the windward reef.

mada hoou.
Brand new.

madahuuhua. ($MADA_{3d}$, HUA_1)
Pimple. *v.*

madahuuhuaanga. (B-1 $MADA_{3d}$)
n.

madala. (BC- $DALA_1$)
Be unfastened [sing.]; be untied [sing.]; bloomed [sing.]. *a.*

madalaanga. (BC1 $DALA_1$)
n.

madaladala. (RC- $DALA_1$)
Easily unfastened or untied. *a.*

madaladalaanga. (RC1 $DALA_1$)
n.

madaladala de leo.
A clear and high-pitched singing voice.

mada lahalaha.
Appear to be wide.

madala mai.
Get free, be loose; in bloom.

mada legalega.
A small hole; having small openings.

madali.
With, along with, as well as; at the same time as; in addition to. *mi.*

mada libia.
A very sharp point.

madaligi$_1$.
Skillful at craft work, craftsmanlike; craftsman. *a.*

Madaligi$_2$. (B-- MADALIGI$_2$)
January. *n.*

madaligianga. (B-1 MADALIGI$_1$)
n.

mada ligiligi.
Having small eyes or holes.

madalima. (XCO MADA$_2$)
Fifty. *an.*

mada looloa.
Longer in comparison with; extending farther than appears to be the case.

mada loolodo.
A depression in the reef (where water accumulates).

madalua. (XCO MADA$_2$)
Twenty. *an.*

mada luu mada.
In the presence of someone.

madamada$_1$. (R-- MADA$_1$)
Half-cooked. *a.*

madamada$_2$. (R-- MADA$_3$)
Compete (as between individuals); front of. *v.*

madamada a me.
A miscellaneous assortment.

madamadaanga. (R-1 MADA$_3$)
n.

mada madangi.
Able to point (into the wind) well (of a sailing canoe).

madamada o dangada.
In public.

madamataia. (R-- MATAIA)
Inclined to be (or easily) *mataia*. *v.*

mada mmea.
Dark red.

madaniiga. (B-- MADA$_{3c}$)
Ingrown callus. *v.*

madannia. (B-- MADA$_{3f}$)
Finger. *n.*

madannia i lodo.
Middle finger.

madannia madua.
Thumb.

madannia sisi.
Little finger.

mada nnui.
Having big holes (or entrances, etc.).

mada nuui.
Dark green in color.

madangi.
Wind, gas, flatus. *v.*

madangi danuaa.
Fresh air.

madaoaligi. (CF MADA$_3$)
A type of string figure. *n.*

madaono. (XCO MADA$_2$)
Sixty. *an.*

mada saosao.
Sharp-pointed.

mada sua hadu.
Storm beach (on the seaward reef).

madau.
Right (side). *n.*

madau-dalinga.
Fish sp.: shark sp.?

mada udua.
The point of a promontory or peninsula (esp. if large).

mada-umanga. (MADA$_3$, MANGA, U$_2$)
The bud of a Cyrtosperma taro corm. *n.*

madavaivai. (XCO MADA$_{3g}$)
A type of knot used in net-making. *n.*

madavalu. (XCO MADA$_2$)
Eighty. *an.*

madaviiga. (B-- MADA$_{3i}$)
The needle-like spines on *daudu* fish. *v.*

$made_1$.
Look at in an effort to identify or recognize. *v.*

$made_2$.
Dead (of plants only); numb, paralyzed; go out (of a fire). *a.*

madea. (B-2 $MADE_1$)
Identify, recognize. *v.*

madegi. (BC- $DEGI_1$)
Be jerked. *a.*

madegidegi. (RC- $DEGI_1$)
a.

ma de hia e doe.
A chanted expression, on the last word of which a work group chanting it lifts a heavy object.

$mademade_1$. (R-- $MADE_1$)
v.

$mademade_2$. (R-- $MADE_2$)
a.

mademadea. (R-2 $MADE_1$)
Identify tentatively; to think that one recognizes but not be sure. *v.*

mademadea ange.
Feel sleepy.

mademadenga. (R-1 $MADE_1$)
n.

made sala.
Mistaken (in identifying); mistake someone for another.

madi.
To add organic material to the taro bog. *v.*

madia. (B-2 MADI)
v.

madila.
Bamboo [not native, but drifts ashore]. *n.*

madila diadia.
Bindings wound around a fishing pole to give it extra strength.

madimadi. (R-- MADI)
v.

madimadia. (R-2 MADI)
v.

madimadinga. (R-1 MADI)
n.

madoha. (BC- DOHA)
To be spread out. *a.*

madohaanga. (BC1 DOHA)
n.

madohadoha. (RC- DOHA)
a.

madohadohaanga. (RC1 DOHA)
n.

madohi. (BC- DOHI)
Middle (of something long and thin), halfway; to have gone halfway, to reach the halfway point. *a.*

madohi age.
Reach halfway up.

madohi boo.
Midnight.

madohi iho.
To reach halfway down.

madohi lua.
Middle (of something long and thin), halfway.

madolidoli. (RC- DOLI)
Of unusual age or size. *v.*

madolidolia. (RC2 DOLI)
Very *madolidoli.* *a.*

madolidolinga. (RC1 DOLI)
n.

madua.
Old (persons), mature, full-grown; parent, elder (senior relative). *a.*

maduilau.
Fish sp.: goatfish.

madumadua. (R-- MADUA)
Very old (persons); fully mature and then some. *a.*

maduupaa. (?)
A type of string figure. *n.*

mataia.
Soreness of the eyes after a fishing expedition (from the glare of the sun). *v.*

mataia mai.
Seen being *mataia.*

mataianga. (B-1 MATAIA)
n.

matali. (E-- MADALI)
mi.

mataodao.
Fish sp.: cornetfish.

ma te.
[A contraction of *mada de...*].

ma te duge.
The point of a *madaa duge.*

mateedea. (XCO DEA)
Pustular. *v.*

ma te hakii.
The uvula and the adjacent portions of the oral cavity.

matili. (EC- DILI)
Come up quickly (like fast-sprouting plants or a quickly erupting skin disease). *a.*

matilianga. (EC1 DILI)
n.

matili mai.
Remember vividly (after having forgotten); the sprouting of plants, etc. in great numbers.

matogo +NUMBER.
[The seating capacity of a canoe].

matoloia. (CF DOLO)
A type of prepared food (made from dried breadfruit). *n.*

matolu. (XCO $MADA_2$)
Thirty. *an.*

ma tua.
Besides.

ma tuai.
Coconut grater blade.

mae.
Withered; [also, D form of *$mmae_1$*]. *a.*

maea.
A type of rope (the thickest sort). *n.*

maege. (BC- EGE)
Raised up. *v.*

maegea. (BC2 EGE)
v.

maegeege. (RC- EGE)
v.

maegeegea. (RC2 EGE)
v.

maegeegelia. (RC2 EGE)
v.

maegeegenga. (RC1 EGE)
n.

maegelia. (BC2 EGE)
v.

maegenga. (BC1 EGE)
n.

maemae. (R-- MAE)
—; pain, hurt (children's language). *a.*

maemaenga. (R-1 MAE)
n.

maenga. (B-1 MAE)
n.

maeva.
Move from one place to another. *a.*

maevaanga. (B-1 MAEVA)
n.

maevaeva. (R-- MAEVA)
a.

maevaevaanga. (R-1 MAEVA)
n.

$maga_1$.
Throw; donate (to a collection being made). *v.*

$maga_2$.
Callus. *v.*

magaa. (B-2 $MAGA_1$)
v.

maga ahi.
Glowing embers (without a flame).

magaalili. (P-- MAGALILI)
a.

magaalilianga. (P-1 MAGALILI)
n.

maga de gau dogi.
Masturbate (of males only).

maga de hoe.
To paddle vigorously.

maga tau hoe.
To paddle (a canoe) vigorously.

magakaga. (R-- MAKAGA)
Firmly attached. *a.*

magakagaanga. (R-1 MAKAGA)
n.

magalili.
Feel cold, shivering (from cold); flow (of tide). *a.*

magalilianga. (B-1 MAGALILI)
n.

magalili tai.
Flow (of tide).

magalili mai.
Flow (of tide).

magalillili. (S-- MAGALILI)
Frequently *magalili.* *a.*

magalillilianga. (S-1 MAGALILI)
n.

magamaga. (R-- $MAGA_1$)
v.

magamagaanga. (R-1 $MAGA_1$)
n.

magamagalili. (R-- MAGALILI)
Frequently *magalili.* *a.*

magamagalilianga.
(R-1 MAGALILI) *n.*

magano. (BC- GANO)
Overripe (of pandanus only). *a.*

maganoanga. (BC1 GANO)
n.

magau.
Die, dead, unconscious. *a.*

magau baubau.
Die in agony (owing to having led a bad life).

magau danuaa.
Die peacefully [as shown by a beatific facial expression on the corpse and the calmness of the weather].

magau de laa.
Weakness of the sun's rays (for drying) [usually referring to the late afternoon].

magau de lima.
A paralyzed arm.

magau donu i de lodo.
Want desperately.

magaugau. (R-- MAGAU)
Easily faint or lose consciousness; mortality-prone (e.g., of a family). *a.*

magaugaunga. (R-1 MAGAU)
n.

magau i de hiigai.
Ravenous.

magau i togaa.
Die of shame [figuratively].

magau loo au.
Now I'm really in trouble!

magaunga. (B-1 MAGAU)
n.

magavaa.
Between; the time when; [var. of *masavaa*]. *nl.*

mage.
[Var. of *ma gi*].

ma gi.
In order to.

magi.
Sick, sickness; ill, illness; disease (physical or mental). *a.*

magiaa.
Envious, jealous (non-sexual jealousy). *a.*

magiaanga. (B-1 MAGIAA)
n.

magianga. (B-1 MAGI)
n.

magi dabeo.
Menstruation.

magi dee manava.
Asthma.

magi eaea.
An eruption in a child's mouth, said to result from improper feeding [acute herpes infection?].

magi gobegobe.
Cold (sickness).

magi kino.
Loss of appetite.

magi haahine.
Menstruation.

magi hai dama.
Morning sickness (of pregnancy).

magi hanohano.
Diarrhea.

magi hongagelegele todo.
To have bloody stools [dysentery?].

magi i de malama.
Menstruation.

magi ilihia.
Gastritis (having one's stomach full of gas).

magiininga. (BC1 GINI)
n.

magi iviivi.
Any illness characterized by wasting of the body (esp. t.b.), consumption.

magi labua gee.
Upset stomach (nausea).

magi libolibo.
Dizziness or vertigo (as a chronic condition or illness).

magi luduludu.
The tremor (as though chilled) of a sick person.

magimagi. (R-- MAGI)
Prone to illness. *a.*

magimagiaa. (R-- MAGIAA)
Frequently *magiaa*. *a.*

magimagiaanga. (R-1 MAGIAA)
n.

magimagianga. (R-1 MAGI)
n.

magini. (BC- GINI)
A sudden pain while moving the body (as with a pinched nerve, or a muscle spasm); a sound like that made by snapping one's fingers. *a.*

maginigini. (RC- GINI)
—; *magini* all over. *a.*

maginiginianga. (RC1 GINI)
n.

magi nngahu.
Asthma.

magi nngali.
Any sickness leading to emaciation (e.g., t.b.); a wasting illness (terminal).

magi o de henua.
Cold (sickness), flu.

magi sali usu.
Headcold, runny nose.

magi ssae aalanga.
Sore muscles (not associated with strain).

mago.
Bad weather (high wind or rain, or rough seas). *a.*

mago de henua.
Monsoon winds (from the southwest).

mago de me.
A worsening condition of the weather.

magomago. (R-- MAGO)
a.

magona. (BC- $GONA_1$)
Extraordinary, outstanding, unusual. *a.*

ma gu.
And then.

magua.
Thieving. *a.*

maguaanga. (B-1 MAGUA)
n.

magulu.
Defeated. *a.*

magulugulu. (R-- MAGULU)
To despair (of attaining success). *a.*

magulu mai ange.
Less — than.

makaga.
Hard (solid). *a.*

makagaanga. (B-1 MAKAGA)
n.

makaga lodo.
Stubborn.

mahaa. (BC- HAA_1)
Broken up, cracked, burst. *a.*

mahaa de usu.
To have encountered unexpected misfortune.

mahaahaa. (RC- HAA_1)
[Pl. of *mahaa*]. *a.*

mahagi. (BC- HAGI)
(Fruit) picked off (or caused to fall by wind). *a.*

mahagihagi. (RC- HAGI)
a.

mahagihaginga. (RC1 HAGI)
n.

mahaginga. (BC1 HAGI)
n.

mahamaha. (R-- MAHA)
Pretty, beautiful; look as though appropriate, seemly. *a.*

mahamahaanga. (R-1 MAHA)
n.

mahamaha mai.
To appear beautiful (that thing over there) to me (i.e., from where I am).

mahana. (BC- HANA)
Hot. *a.*

mahana age.
Heartburn [?].

mahanaanga. (BC1 HANA)
v.

mahanahana. (RC- HANA)
Warm. *a.*

mahanahanaanga. (RC1 HANA)
n.

mahanahanasia. (RC2 HANA)
Warmed up. *v.*

mahanasia. (BC2 HANA)
Heated. *v.*

mahanga. (BC- HANGA)
Be split open. *a.*

mahangahanga. (RC- HANGA)
Cracked in many places. *a.*

mahedu. (BC- HEDU)
Folded up, rolled up. *a.*

mahedua.
Sneeze. *n.*

maheduhedu. (RC- HEDU)
a.

maheduhedunga. (RC1 HEDU)
n.

mahedunga. (BC1 HEDU)
n.

ma hee.
Where else?

mahi.
d.

mahianga. (B-1 MAHI)
n.

mahi bodo.
Easily tired.

mahidi. (BC- HIDI)
Separated from and curled up from [like plywood in which the laminations have separated]. *a.*

mahidia. (BC2 HIDI)
v.

mahidihidi. (RC- HIDI)
v.

mahidihidia. (RC2 HIDI)
v.

mahidihidinga. (RC1 HIDI)
n.

mahiidinga. (BC1 HIDI)
n.

mahi loa.
Tireless.

mahimahi. (R-- MAHI)
d.

mahimahianga. (R-1 MAHI)
n.

mahola. (BC- HOLA)
To have been *hola*; plentiful (of food). *a.*

maholaanga. (BC1 HOLA)
n.

maholadage. (BC- $HOLA_a$)
Be *holadage*. *a.*

maholadageanga. (BC1 $HOLA_a$)
n.

mahola gimoo.
To have many dead animals (or fish) lying about.

maholahola. (RC- HOLA)
a.

maholaholaanga. (RC1 HOLA)
n.

maholaholadage. (RC- $HOLA_a$)
Being *holadage* in several places. *a.*

maholahola danuaa age.
Revitalized (by a shower or rest, etc.).

mahole. (BC- HOLE)
Peeled (a great amount having been taken off). *a.*

maholehole. (RC- HOLE)
Scraped, scaled (fish). *a.*

maholeholenga. (RC1 HOLE)
n.

maholenga. (BC1 HOLE)
n.

mahu.
Healed (of a sore). *a.*

mahuanga. (B-1 MAHU)
n.

mahuda. (BC- HUDA)
Be awake for a short time; have one's eyes open. *a.*

mahuda age.
Wake up.

mahudaanga. (BC1 HUDA)
n.

mahuge. (BC- HUGE)
Opened, uncovered. *a.*

mahugehuge. (RC- HUGE)
a.

mahugehugenga. (RC1 HUGE)
n.

mahugenga. (BC1 HUGE)
n.

mahule. (BC- HULE)
a.

mahulehule. (RC- HULE)
a.

mahulehulenga. (RC1 HULE)
n.

mahulenga. (BC1 HULE)
n.

mahulu. (BC- $HULU_4$)
Wakefulness. *n.*

mahumahu. (R-- MAHU)
Becoming *mahu.* *a.*

mahumahuanga. (R-1 MAHU)
n.

mahumahunga. (R-1 MAHU)
n.

mai. (B-- MAI_1)
Toward the speaker; less; nearer. *mv*

mai ange laa.
The next (one) following the one in question.

Maidigi. (B-- MAIDIGI)
August. *n.*

maido.
Fish sp. *n.*

mai i daha.
From outside.

Mailaba. (B-- MAILABA)
September; [uncapitalized] the hollow core of the tree trunk. *n.*

maile.
Plant sp.: maile-scented fern (*Polypodium scolopendria* Burm. F.). *n.*

maili. (BC- ILI)
Fast moving. *a.*

mailiili. (RC- ILI)
Fast moving (over a considerable duration of time). *a.*

mailiilinga. (RC1 ILI)
n.

mailinga. (BC1 ILI)
n.

$maimai_1$. (R-- MAI_2)
Sweet. *a.*

$maimai_2$. (B-- MAIMAI)
To dull a point or sharp edge by striking it against something hard. *a.*

maimaia. (B-2 MAIMAI)
a.

maimai ange.
To have been dulled (from having been struck on a hard object).

maimai de ngudu.
Sweet-talker.

maimai mai.
Become *maimai.*

$maimainga_1$. (R-1 MAI_2)
n.

$maimainga_2$. (B-1 MAIMAI)
n.

maimaingaa. (R-- MAINGAA)
a.

maimaingaanga. (R-1 MAINGAA)
n.

maimai sseni.
To sleep especially well or restfully.

mai moni.
A type of fishhook (made from pearl shell).

mainu.
Bait (on the hook). *n.*

mainu daodao.
Bait for *daodao* fishing [a shiny side

strip of the tuna or *daodao*].

maingaa.
Miss, feel the loss of, or the uselessness of, something of great value. *a.*

maingaa ange nei gi.
To wish one has —.

maingaa ange loo.
Feel really *maingaa* about —.

maingaanga. (B-1 MAINGAA)
n.

maisi. (BC- ISI_1)
Peeled off. *a.*

maisiisi. (RC- ISI_1)
a.

maisiisinga. (RC1 ISI_1)
n.

maisinga. (BC1 ISI_1)
n.

malaangahu*. (AHU, LANGA)
Feast held for a newly launched canoe. *n.*

malaelae. (RC- LAE)
Clear, unobstructed, uncluttered. *a.*

malaelaenga. (RC1 LAE)
n.

malaia.
Have luck which is unexpected (esp. bad, in which case considered retribution for past deeds). *a.*

malaiaanga. (B-1 MALAIA)
n.

malala. (BC- LALA)
Charcoal. *n.*

malali.
Smooth; cleared (of brush or obstructions). *a.*

malalianga. (B-1 MALALI)
n.

malalidage. (B-- $MALALI_a$)
Used up or cleaned out completely. *a.*

malalidageanga. (B-1 $MALALI_a$)
n.

malama.
Month, moon. *n.*

malamala. (R-- MALA)
Small bits of things (e.g., sawdust). *n.*

malamalali. (R-- MALALI)
Becoming more and more *malali*. *a.*

malamalalianga. (R-1 MALALI)
n.

malamalama. (R-- MAALAMA)
Shiny (reflects light). *v.*

malamalau. (R-- $MALAU_1$)
Repeatedly or continuously *malau*$_1$. *a.*

malamalauanga. (R-1 $MALAU_1$)
n.

malamalaunga. (R-1 $MALAU_1$)
n.

malanga. (BC- LANGA)
Lifted up; departed (as a ship); separate from [intrans]; separated from. *a.*

malanga age.
Lifted up from; come up (e.g., weeds).

malangalanga. (RC- LANGA)
Repeatedly (or becoming) *malanga*. *a.*

malangilangi.
Happy, laugh (as a sign of happiness), cheerful. *a.*

malangilangi ai.
Happy with, pleased at; appreciative.

malau$_1$.
Free from (esp. hardship or illness after having had it). *a.*

malau$_2$. (B-- $MALAU_3$)
Fish sp.: squirrelfish (The native term is applied to many spp.). *n.*

malau age.
Free of hardship (after having had it).

malauanga. (B-1 $MALAU_1$)
n.

malaunga. (B-1 $MALAU_1$)
n.

malau ngudu.
Lips.

maleasa.
Fish sp.?: tang? (a kind of *igauli?*). *n.*

malele. (BC- LELE)
Completed. *a.*

maleleanga. (BC1 LELE)
n.

malemale. (R-- MALE)
Areola of the breast; a boil on the body. *n.*

malemalemo. (R-- MALEMO)
[Var. of *malemolemo*]. *a.*

malemo.
Drown. *a.*

malemoanga. (B-1 MALEMO)
n.

malemolemo. (R-- MALEMO)
A careless diver (who is frequently almost drowned). *a.*

malena. (BC- LENA)
Stretched, stretchable. *a.*

malenaanga. (BC1 LENA)
n.

malenalena. (RC- LENA)
—; stretchable. *a.*

malenalenaanga. (RC1 LENA)
n.

maleva.
Present (not absent). *a.*

malianoono. (?)
Fish sp.: lizard fish. *n.*

malibi. (BC- LIBI)
Fast. *a.*

malibilibi. (RC- LIBI)
Crack (of a whip). *a.*

malibilibia. (RC2 LIBI)
Sharp (esp. something which causes sharp pain like a whip). *a.*

malibilibinga. (RC1 LIBI)
n.

malibinga. (BC1 LIBI)
n.

malie.
Good at; good (of food or certain activities only); of exceptional quality. *mv.*

$malili_1$.
Fall out little by little (as hair, or sand when it is poured); powdered (soap, etc.). *a.*

$malili_2$.
Fish sp.: goatfish. *n.*

malilianga. (B-1 $MALILI_1$)
n.

malili gelegele.
Producing hard crumbs when eaten or broken.

malillili. (R-- $MALILI_1$)
Easily made *malili*; to feel the nibbling of fish on a fishing line. *a.*

malillilianga. (R-1 $MALILI_1$)
n.

malimalino. (R-- MALINO)
Becoming more and more *malino*. *v.*

malimalinoanga. (R-1 MALINO)
n.

malimalinongia. (R-2 MALINO)
v.

malino.
Calm (weather), still (wind). *v.*

malinoanga. (B-1 MALINO)
n.

malinolino. (S-- MALINO)
[=*malimalino*]. *v.*

malinolinoanga. (S-1 MALINO)
n.

malinolinongia. (S-2 MALINO)
v.

malinongia. (B-2 MALINO)
Be calmed (e.g., seas). *v.*

malingalinga.
Sideburns (of hair). *n.*

malingi. (BC- LINGI)
Spilled, poured out. *a.*

malingilingi. (RC- LINGI)
Spill out little by little. *a.*

malingilinginga. (RC1 LINGI)
n.

malinginga. (BC1 LINGI)
n.

malo.
Clothes, cloth. *n.*

malo diadia.
Mending holes in clothes by running threads crisscross across the hole.

malo gahu.
Shirt.

malo gahu de boo.
Sheet, blanket.

malogu.
[= *ngalogu*]. *v.*

malogulogu. (R-- MALOGU)
v.

malogulogunga. (R-1 MALOGU)
n.

malo gulu.
Barkcloth [made from the inner skin of the breadfruit].

malogunga. (B-1 MALOGU)
n.

malo haahine.
A dress (female clothing).

malo huna.
Breechclout.

malo lau manu.
Cloth with a flowered pattern.

malo maadolu.
Heavy clothing.

malo-ngiso.
Driftwood sp. [used for making planks].

malo sabo*.
Breechclout.

malu.
Shade (under trees); lee (of wind). *v.*

malua.
Vagina. *n.*

malu gohu.
Becoming darker (as when the sky becomes overcast).

malui. (BC- LUI_1)
Turned (in direction), reversed, transposed. *a.*

maluilui. (RC- LUI_1)
Turned this way and that way, turned over and over. *a.*

maluiluinga. (RC1 LUI_1)
n.

maluinga. (BC1 LUI_1)
n.

malumalu. (R-- MALU)
v.

malumalu de me.
Cloudy day (not bright).

malumalu-tangohi.
(MALU, TANGOHI)
The light after sunset; twilight (in the evening). *a.*

maluu*.
Soft. *v.*

maluulu.
Cool. *a.*

maluulu de me.
The weather is cold!

maluulunga. (B-1 MALUULU)
n.

maluunga. (B-1 MALUU)
n.

mama.
Dust, gas, steam, vapor, fumes, spray (e.g., of waves). *n.*

mamaeva. (S-- MAEVA)
a.

mamaevaanga. (S-1 MAEVA)
n.

mami.
Taste (of something). *v.*

mamia. (B-2 MAMI)
v.

mami age.
Taste (something) a little bit.

mami ange.
Taste (food).

maminga. (B-1 MAMI)
n.

mammami. (R-- MAMI)
Delicious. *a.*

mammamianga. (R-1 MAMI)
n.

mammamu. (R-- MAMU)
Fish (in children's speech only). *n.*

mamu.
Fish (the generic term — cf. Ponapean *mam*). *n.*

mamu de lagi.
The fish which live beyond the outer reef.

mamu-duagaa.
Fish sp.: stingray?

mamu-honga-dai.
Fish sp.: anchovy?, silversides (small)?

mamu-lalo-beau.
Fish sp.: wrasse.

mamu-madohi-lua.
Fish sp.: parrot fish.

mana°.
Supernatural power. *n.*

manadua. (B-2 MAANADU)
--; remembered. *v.*

manamanadua. (R-2 MAANADU)
Keep remembering. *v.*

manamanava. (R-- MANAVA)
[= *manavanava*]. *a.*

manamanavaanga. (R-1 MANAVA)
n.

manaunau°.
Act crazy or insane. *v.*

manaunaua°. (B-2 MANAUNAU)
Crazy, insane. *v.*

manaunaunga°. (B-1 MANAUNAU)
n.

manava.
Breath, breathe; having a good lung capacity (able to remain under water for a long time). *a.*

manavaanga. (B-1 MANAVA)
n.

manava bodo.
Shortness of breath.

manava duuia.
Nervous, apprehensive (suddenly).

manava i lunga.
Sigh (an intake of air) [a sign of emotion].

manavanava. (S-- MANAVA)
Breathing. *a.*

manavanavaanga. (S-1 MANAVA)
n.

manavanava gimoo.
Panting (as when short of breath).

manavasaa. (B-- $MANAVA_a$)
Worried, apprehensive, fearful. *a.*

manavasaanga. (B-1 $MANAVA_a$)
n.

manege. (BC- NEGE)
a.

manege ma de --.
Better than (nothing, etc.).

manegenege. (RC- NEGE)
a.

manegenegenga. (RC1 NEGE)
n.

manegenga. (BC1 NEGE)
n.

manenga.
Fish sp. (= a very large *balagia*, 3-4 feet long). *n.*

manigangi.
Satisfied completely in sexual intercourse. *a.*

manigangianga. (B-1 MANIGANGI)
n.

manihaniha. (R-- MAANIHA)
Inclined to be *maaniha*. *a.*

manihanihaanga. (R-1 MAANIHA)
n.

manini.
Fish sp.: convict tang. *n.*

mano.
Thousand. *an.*

manogo.
Fish sp.: goby. *n.*

manomano. (R-- MANO)
Thousands and thousands. *an.*

manongi.
Fragrant; fragrance (esp. of flowers or perfume). *a.*

$manu_1$. (B-- MANU)
Animal, plant (flora); coral head; throat spacer of a flying fish net. *v.*

$Manu_2$. (B-- $MANU_b$)
March (month of). *n.*

manua. (B-2 MANU)
Diseased. *v.*

manu aabi.
Kite.

manu-a-tababa.
Plant sp.: cycad plant [indigenous?] (*Cycas circinalis* L.).

manu-alioo.
Plant sp.: a variety of taro.

manu-a-luga.
Insect sp.: fruit fly.

manu-a-madaligi.
Bird sp.: short-tailed shearwater (*Puffinus tenirostris*).

manu-daa-uga.
[= *goehau*].

manu dabeo.
Trees and shrubs which grow as weeds.

manu-de-boo.
Centipede.

manu-de-bua.
Bird sp.: sacred kingfisher (*Halcyon sancta*) (The native term applies possibly to several spp.).

manu de gabadanga.
The bird leading a flock (of *ngongo*) to a school of fish [the one fisherman watch].

manu-de-hala.
Insect sp.: walkingstick (a very large grasshopper-like insect).

manu de henua.
Nukuoro varieties of swamp taro (*Cyrtosperma*).

manu-de-laama.
Any of the small flying insects which swarm near a light.

manu dolodolo.
Land animal.

manu dudu dangada.
Insect sp. (= *manu-de-laama*) [poisonous].

manu ea.
Coral head (at or broaching the surface of the water).

manu-gaba-aasanga.
Plant sp.: beach naupaka shrub (*Scaevola taccada* (Gaertnn.) Roxb).

manu-gadi-niho.
Plant sp. [used to make loose teeth firm].

manu gaugau.
Plant sp.: a variety of taro.

manugia.
To appear from time to time on the surface of the water. *a.*

manugiaanga. (B-1 MANUGIA)
n.

manu-gili-maau.
Plant sp.: heliotrope (*Tournefortia argentea* L., = *Messerschmidia argentea* L.).

manu-kono$_1$.
Bird sp. [probably the original Nukuoro name for the *ginuede*].

manu-kono$_2$.
Pigeon [an imported sp.].

manu hagadigedige.
Top (toy).

manu-hagadigedige.
Mollusk sp.: cone shell.

manu-hai-hagahoa.
Millipede.

manu-hai-hau.
Mollusk sp. [a recently coined name, =spp. of *sisi*].

manu hale moni.
A pottery bottle or jar.

manu hao vai.
A bottle (of glass).

manuhi.
Hemorrhage. *a.*

manuhianga. (B-1 MANUHI)
n.

manuia.
Fortunate, lucky, blessed. *a.*

manuiaanga. (B-1 MANUIA)
n.

manu ina.
[= *manua*].

manu-lalo-de-gelegele.
Mantis shrimp.

manu lalo tai.
Sea shell.

manu laosedi.
Sea animal; marine invertebrates.

manu lele.
A bird.

manu-ligi.
Lice (immature); louse (immature).

manumanu. (R-- MANU)
Insect sp. *v.*

manumanugia. (R-- MANUGIA)
v.

manumanugiaanga.
(R-1 MANUGIA) *n.*

manumanuhi. (R-- MANUHI)
Frequently *manuhi.* *a.*

manumanuhianga. (R-1 MANUHI)
n.

manu-manga-lua.
Insect sp.: scorpion.

manu-mangamanga$_1$.
Starfish.

manu-mangamanga$_2$.
Plant sp.: paco fern (*Athyrium* sp.).

manu-mangamanga-i-lote-aasanga.
Serpent cucumber.

manu-mmala.
Plant sp.: glory bower (*Clerodendrum inerme* (L.) Gaertn.).

manu noodagi.
A plant which has been *noodagi.*

manu solo laagau.
File (for filing wood).

manu solo maadau.
File (for filing metal).

manu-solo-maanu.
A jellyfish-like animal in the shape of a flower (burrows into the sand when touched).

manga.
A branch, part of (something having coordinate parts). *n.*

manga lua tae.
Cleft in the buttocks.

mangamanga. (R-- MANGA)
Having many *manga.* *a.*

mangemangeo. (R-- MANGEO)
Covered with *mangeo.* *v.*

mangeo.
A large sore (on the body); a blemish (on the skin). *v.*

mangila.
Plant sp. (a type of *ngaungau*). *n.*

mangoo.
Shark (the generic term). *n.*

mangoo-biho-lua.
Fish sp.: shark sp.

mangoo-dahola.
Fish sp.: blacktip shark.

mangoo-senga.
Fish sp.: shark sp.

mangunngungu. (RC- NGUNGU)
The sound of something being chewed. *a.*

mangunngunguanga.
(RC1 NGUNGU) *n.*

mao.
d.

maoanga. (B-1 MAO)
n.

mao denga ssave.
A scarcity of *ssave.*

maoha. (BC- OHA)
Broken (as a machine), broken down. *a.*

maohanga. (BC1 OHA)
n.

maohaoha. (RC- OHA)
Broken up (into many pieces or groupings). *a.*

maohaohaanga. (RC1 OHA)
n.

maoha saele.
Broken up (into many pieces or groupings).

mao lalo.
Deep, low (in status).

maoli*.
A suspicion which proves to be true. *n.*

mao lunga.
High, high-ranking.

maomao. (R-- MAO)
More and more; diminishing rainfall. *a.*

masa.
Empty, low (tide). *a.*

masaagage. (P-- MASAGAGE)
a.

masaala.
Clear-headed. *v.*

masaalanga. (B-1 MASAALA)
n.

masa bagubagu.
Dry reef (at very low tide).

masa boo.
Mornings following nights during which the tide has gone out (which are good for looking for fish trapped on the reef).

masae. (BC- SAE_1)
Torn, deflowered (of a virgin). *a.*

masaenga. (BC1 SAE_1)
—; a hole (in something torn). *n.*

masaesae. (RC- SAE_1)
a.

masaesaenga. (RC1 SAE_1)
n.

masagage.
Good at fighting. *a.*

masagageanga. (B-1 MASAGAGE)
n.

masagi.
A dance (an ancient type). *n.*

masaia. (B-2 MASA)
Trapped by low water (e.g., canoes, or fish on the reef at low tide). *v.*

masaiaanga. (B-3 MASA)
n.

masalaba.
Clear (not opaque or blurred); shiny (translucent). *a.*

masalabaanga. (B-1 MASALABA)
n.

masalia. (B-2 MASA)
Empty of water. *v.*

masamasa. (R-- MASA)
a.

masamasaiaanga. (R-3 MASA)
n.

masana.
Good (quality). *v.*

masanaanga. (B-1 MASANA)
n.

masausau.
Good at fighting. *v.*

masausaua. (B-2 MASAUSAU)
Be *masausau*. *v.*

masausaunga. (B-1 MASAUSAU)
n.

$masavaa_1$. (BC- SAVAA)
Time when, time of; between, amongst. *n.*

$masavaa_2$. (B-- MASAVAA)
[Var. of *magava*]. *nl.*

masavaa alodahi.
Always.

masavaa danuaa.
A time of peace.

masavaa de gauligi.
Childhood.

masavavvava. (R-- $VAVA_a$)
Having many holes (like a screen). *a.*

masavavvavaanga. (R-1 $VAVA_a$)
n.

maselesele. (RC- $SELE_2$)
Straight-edged. *a.*

maseleselenga. (RC1 $SELE_2$)
n.

maseu. (BC- SEU)
To scatter (when in a group). *a.*

maseunga. (BC1 SEU)
n.

masi. (B-- $MASI_1$)
To scrape or peel breadfruit when the breadfruit is ripe. *v.*

masia. (B-2 $MASI_1$)
v.

$masimasi_1$. (R-- $MASI_2$)
v.

$masimasi_2$. (R-- $MASI_2$)
a.

$masimasi_3$. (R-- $MASI_3$)
Dolphin. *n.*

masimasia. (R-2 $MASI_1$)
v.

masimasinga$_1$. (R-1 MASI$_1$)
n.

masimasinga$_2$. (R-1 MASI$_2$)
n.

masoasoa.
Spacious. *a.*

masoasoaanga. (B-1 MASOASOA)
n.

masole.
Abraded (skin), scratched. *a.*

masoleanga. (B-1 MASOLE)
n.

masole ange.
Barely scratched.

masolesole. (R-- MASOLE)
masole in several places. *a.*

masolesoleanga. (R-1 MASOLE)
n.

massaa (ina). (B-- MASSAA)
Despised by others. *v.*

massaanga. (B-1 MASSAA)
n.

massagaila.
Incompletely cooked. *v.*

massagailaanga.
(B-1 MASSAGAILA) *n.*

massagalala.
Burned (food). *v.*

massagalalaanga.
(B-1 MASSAGALALA) *n.*

massaganga. (B-- MASA$_a$)
To be very dry. *v.*

massanganga. (BC1 SANGA)
Apart, widely spaced. *a.*

massiva. (XCO MADA$_2$)
Ninety. *an.*

massogosogo. (B-- SOGOSOGO$_a$)
Go or do by oneself; a one-man canoe. *a.*

massogosogoanga.
(B-1 SOGOSOGO$_a$) *n.*

massogosogolia. (B-2 SOGOSOGO$_a$)
To have been by oneself. *v.*

masugi. (BC- SUGI$_1$)
Having a hole, pierced. *a.*

masuginga. (BC1 SUGI$_1$)
n.

masugisugi. (RC- SUGI$_1$)
a.

masugisuginga. (RC1 SUGI$_1$)
n.

masui.
Left (side). *n.*

masulu de maasina.
"A person has died.".

mau$_1$.
To finish defecating. *a.*

mau$_2$.
Usual [sing.]; usually [sing.]. *a.*

mau$_3$.
Get, obtain, caught. *a.*

maua. (B-2 MAU$_3$)
Able to, obtained, gotten, caught. *a.*

maua laa.
Never mind!

mau ange huu.
Usually.

mau goloa.
Rich in material possessions.

mau haahine.
Attractive to women (for some inexplicable reason).

maumau$_1$. (R-- MAU$_1$)
a.

maumau$_2$. (R-- MAU$_2$)
a.

maumau$_3$. (R-- MAU$_3$)
a.

maumaunga$_1$. (R-1 MAU$_1$)
n.

maumaunga$_2$. (R-1 MAU$_2$)
n.

maumaunga$_3$. (R-1 MAU$_3$)
n.

mau me.
Successful in obtaining what one wants (things).

maunusi. (BC- UNUSI)
Pulled out, removed (by pulling out). *a.*

maunusinga. (BC1 UNUSI)
n.

maunuunusi. (RC- UNUSI)
[Pl. of *maunusi*]. *a.*

maunuunusinga. (RC1 UNUSI)
n.

maunga$_1$. (B-1 MAU$_1$)
n.

maunga$_2$. (B-1 MAU$_2$)
Way of becoming accustomed to. *n.*

maunga$_3$. (B-1 MAU$_3$)
n.

mavaevae. (RC- VAE$_1$)
Scattered. *a.*

mavaevaenga. (RC1 VAE$_1$)
n.

me.
Thing [a word which can substitute for any nominal, adjectival, or verbal notion]. *v.*

mea.
Red. *d.*

me abadai.
European things (gear, etc.).

me abasasa.
European things (gear, etc.).

me abo (donu).
Truth.

me abo donu.
Real, true.

me aha ai.
What for?

meamea --. (R-- MEA)
Becoming red. *a.*

meameaanga. (R-1 MEA)
n.

me ange laa.
The others.

me balabala.
The soft spot on an infant's head; genitals (of males or females).

me boogia e de eidu.
A black spot on the skin (like a bruise) noticed after sleeping.

me bouli.
The deepest part of the lagoon.

me pasa.
Radio.

me pilo aha.
What's the point of doing this?

me dau.
Thing of importance, worthwhile.

me de lodo.
A fishing place (in the lagoon).

me dili dai.
Any current which flows away from the atoll.

me dili uda.
An ocean current which comes towards the atoll.

me duu.
Clitoris.

me tao.
Dye.

meelenga. (B-1 MELE$_1$)
n.

me-e-ligi.
Taro corm (small).

me gaha dea.
A coconut which is nearly mature.

me gee.
A coconut without any meat.

me gu modu.
Decision.

me hagaahulu.
Prepared food.

me hagadaahao.
Toy.

me hagalolo.
A type of prepared food (made from taro and coconut cream).

me hagaodi.
Last one.

me hagasaga.
A toy (made from a dried breadfruit leaf or a disk of coconut shell) which slides when thrown.

me hagasahu vai.
Gutter (under the eaves of a house).

me hagasengasenga.
Riddle, parable.

me hagasili.
A plant which is allowed to grow extra large (for some reason).

me hakadanga.
Joke, jest; trick (a practical joke).

me hai ada.
Camera.

me hai dago.
Ritual acts, religious acts.

me hai laangi.
Calandar.

me hanga dalogo.
Ingredients of *dalogo.*

me hhadu.
Falsehood, lie.

me hhadu hugadoo.
It's a lie!

me hholu.
Bow (for an arrow).

mele$_1$.
To use a word or expression idiosyncratically in speech. *v.*

mele$_2$.
HYPOTHETICAL ASPECT MARKER; one assumes...; it would appear that... *mt.*

melea. (B-2 MELE$_1$)
v.

melemele. (R-- MELE$_1$)
v.

melemelea. (R-2 MELE$_1$)
v.

melemelenga. (R-1 MELE$_1$)
n.

me maaguluaa.
Dislocated joint (of the body).

me madaali.
A ripe coconut (= *gaadinga*) of poor quality.

me maimai.
Candy.

me mmala.
Bile.

me mmilo.
Current (in the sea).

me naa gi --.
I wish that...

menemene. (R-- MENE)
—; male genital organ, penis. *a.*

menemeneanga. (R-1 MENE)
n.

me ne modu.
Decision.

me osi.
A coconut tree seedling.

mesde-gelee.
Mollusk sp.: olive shell ["Mr. Grey"]. *n.*

me ssalu lau.
A scraper for leaves.

me ssongo aha.
Useless thing.

me vae.
Shoes, slippers.

midi$_1$.
Dream. *v.*

midi$_2$.
d.

midia. (B-2 MIDI$_1$)
Dream about. *v.*

midia ange.
Dream about.

midimidi$_1$. (R-- MIDI$_1$)
v.

midimidi$_2$. (R-- MIDI$_2$)
v.

midimidia. (R-2 MIDI$_2$)
v.

midimidinga$_1$. (R-1 MIDI$_1$)
n.

midimidinga$_2$. (R-1 MIDI$_2$)
n.

midomido. (R-- MIDO)
End of (e.g., a stick). *n.*

miidia. (E-2 MIDI$_2$)
v.

miidinga$_1$. (B-1 MIDI$_1$)
n.

miidinga$_2$. (B-1 MIDI$_2$)
n.

miili.
A type of game [introduced?]. *a.*

miilia. (B-2 $MILI_1$)
v.

miili aheahe.
A version of the game called *miili.*

miilinga$_1$. (B-1 $MILI_1$)
n.

miilinga$_2$. (B-1 $MILI_2$)
n.

miilinga$_3$. (B-1 MIILI)
n.

miilonga. (B-1 $MILO_1$)
n.

miisinga. (B-1 MISI)
n.

mili$_1$ --. (B-- $MILI_1$)
d.

mili$_2$.
Fruitful, fructiferous. *a.*

milimili$_1$. (R-- $MILI_1$)
v.

milimili$_2$. (R-- $MILI_2$)
v.

milimilia. (R-2 $MILI_1$)
v.

milimilinga$_1$. (R-1 $MILI_1$)
n.

milimilinga$_2$. (R-1 $MILI_2$)
n.

milo$_1$.
Twist, turn (something, as a faucet), wind, wring. *v.*

milo$_2$.
Plant sp.: tree sp.: milo tree (*The spesiapopulnea* Sol. ex Correa). *n.*

miloa. (B-2 $MILO_1$)
v.

milo gee.
To turn the opposite way.

milomilo. (R-- $MILO_1$)
—; a whorl in the hair. *v.*

milomilonga. (R-1 $MILO_1$)
n.

milomilosanga. (R-1 $MILO_1$)
The way in which a current moves about. *n.*

milosanga. (B-1 $MILO_1$)
The way in which current flows. *n.*

milosia. (B-2 $MILO_1$)
—; to be taken away by a current. *v.*

mimi.
Urinate. *a.*

mimianga. (B-1 MIMI)
n.

mimmimi. (R-- MIMI)
a.

mimmimianga. (R-1 MIMI)
n.

misi.
A sound made by sucking through pursed lips [like a stage kiss]. *a.*

misimisi. (R-- MISI)
a.

misimisinga. (R-1 MISI)
n.

mmaasinga. (E-1 $MASI_2$)
n.

mmabu. (P-- MABU)
a.

mmade. (P-- $MADE_2$)
a.

mmade aalanga.
Exhausted (physically or mentally).

mmade ange aalanga.
Completely exhausted; completely discouraged.

mmade gimoo.
To die in great numbers.

mmadu. (E-- MADU)
Fish sp.: mojarra fish (= small *sugimanga*). *n.*

mmae. (E-- MAE)
Pain, hurt; withered (of a plant). *a.*

mmae tinae.
Convulsed with laughter.

mmaenga. (E-1 MAE)
n.

mmaga. (P-- $MAGA_2$)
v.

mmagi. (P-- MAGI)
a.

mmagianga. (P-1 MAGI)
n.

mmahi. (E-- MAHI)
Strong, strength, force, power, energy. *a.*

mmahi age de --.
Feel like —.

mmahianga. (E-1 MAHI)
n.

mmahi i de gai.
Eat more than seems appropriate to one's body size.

mmahu. (P-- MAHU)
a.

mmahuanga. (P-1 MAHU)
n.

mmala.
Bitter, sour; unlucky. *a.*

mmalaanga. (B-1 MMALA)
n.

mmala dana (dagu) maanga.
Lose his (my) appetite.

mmala luu mada.
Stinging of one's eyes (e.g., from salt water).

mmano. (P-- MANO)
Thousands. *a.*

mmanu. (E-- MANU)
Do (something). *v.*

mmao. (E-- MAO)
Far, distant. *a.*

mmaoanga. (E-1 MAO)
n.

mmasa. (E-- MASA)
To be dry. *a.*

mmasaanga. (E-1 MASA)
n.

mmasa bagubagu.
Hard and curled up owing to dryness.

mmasalia. (E-2 MASA)
a.

mmasi. (E-- $MASI_2$)
The ripened condition of the fruit of the pandanus (when the keys begin to fall). *a.*

$mmau_1$. (P-- MAU_1)
a.

$mmau_2$. (E-- MAU_2)
Mastered, memorized, known by heart; [pl. of *mau_2*]. *a.*

mmau gava.
Known by heart, memorized, know (how to do something) well.

$mmaunga_1$. (P-1 MAU_1)
n.

$mmaunga_2$. (E-1 MAU_2)
Way of memorizing, (way of having memorized). *n.*

mmea. (E-- MEA)
Red. *a.*

mmeaanga. (E-1 MEA)
n.

mmea be se gaagose.
Red hot (literally).

mmele. (P-- $MELE_1$)
v.

mmene. (E-- MENE)
To contract inside of (like a marine invertebrate inside a shell); detumescence; a sudden loss of desire (e.g., to defecate when people approach). *a.*

mmeneanga. (E-1 MENE)
n.

mmenelia. (E-2 MENE)
v.

mmenengia. (E-2 MENE)
v.

mmenengia mai.
Discourage (someone) about something.

mmene ono me.
To be unable to go to the toilet, owing to the approach of people.

mmidi. (E-- $MIDI_2$)
Suck, suction (e.g., of sea current). *v.*

mmiilinga. (P-1 $MILI_2$)
n.

mmiilonga. (P-1 $MILO_1$)
n.

$mmili_1$. (E-- $MILI_1$)
To crush, to pulverize; rub back and forth in the hands (like a fire drill). *v.*

$mmili_2$. (P-- $MILI_2$)
v.

mmilo. (P-- MILO$_1$)
—; the flow of a current. *v.*

mmilosanga. (P-1 MILO$_1$)
A confluence of currents (from below the surface of the sea). *n.*

mmoa. (E-- MOO$_b$)
Cooked. *a.*

mmoaanga. (E-1 MOO$_b$)
n.

mmoa gango.
Burned food which has been overcooked.

mmodo. (P-- MODO)
a.

mmodoanga. (P-1 MODO)
n.

mmodolia. (P-2 MODO)
v.

mmoe$_1$. (P-- MOE$_1$)
—; to close both eyes. *a.*

mmoe$_2$. (P-- MOE$_2$)
a.

mmoenga$_1$. (P-1 MOE$_1$)
n.

mmoenga$_2$. (P-1 MOE$_2$)
n.

mmogo. (E-- MOGO$_4$)
Insist upon. *v.*

mmogoa. (E-2 MOGO$_4$)
v.

mmogoanga. (E-1 MOGO$_4$)
n.

mmogolia. (E-2 MOGO$_4$)
v.

mmoli. (E-- MOLI)
Haul (all at once or as fast as possible). *v.*

mmoli gee.
Haul away from.

mmolo. (P-- MOLO$_1$)
a.

mmudi. (E-- MMUDI)
Sprinkling (of rain). *a.*

mmuga. (P-- MUGA$_1$)
v.

mmugaanga. (P-1 MUGA$_1$)
n.

mmule. (E-- MULE)
Slow, late. *a.*

mmuleanga. (E-1 MULE)
n.

mmulo. (P-- MULO)
v.

mmulu. (E-- MULU)
Stroke, rub gently. *v.*

mmuni.
Hidden, hide. *a.*

mmusa. (P-- MUSA)
[Pl. of *musa* — considering each as *musa*, rather than the whole group]. *v.*

mmusu. (P-- MUSU)
v.

mmuu. (P-- MUU$_1$)
a.

mmuudinga. (E-1 MMUDI)
n.

mmuulonga. (P-1 MULO)
n.

mmuunga. (P-1 MUU$_1$)
n.

moa$_1$. (B-- MOA)
Bird sp. *n.*

moa$_2$. (B-- MOO)
The blossom of the banana tree. *n.*

moa-a-daila.
Bird sp. (= large *moa*).

moaga.
Fish sp.: goatfish. *n.*

moahulu.
Fish sp.: goatfish. *n.*

moana.
Open sea, the atmosphere. *n.*

moana dabeo.
Rough seas.

moana dugidugi.
Far from any land, in the open sea.

moana magalili.
A cold underwater current.

moana ngaadai.
Far from land (the place from which

the atoll is just barely visible).

modimodi. (R-- MODI)
Walk stealthily in a crouch. *a.*

modimodinga. (R-1 MODI)
n.

modo.
Unripe. *a.*

modolia. (B-2 MODO)
v.

modomodo. (R-- MODO)
A nearly mature coconut; the stage in the development of the coconut between *dahaa madagiigii* and *modomodo madagii.* *a.*

modomodoanga. (R-1 MODO)
n.

modomodo mada gii.
The stage of development of the coconut between *modomodo* and *gaadinga gaha de a.*

modu.
Cut off, disconnected; an islet (on the atoll); to have been decided formally; to have been adjudicated. *a.*

modu taalonga.
To escape (of fish, after having been speared).

modu gee.
Cut away from; separated from.

modu mai (adu, ange).
Become one's (your, their) exclusive possession.

modumodu. (R-- MODU)
Broken in many places (like string), easily broken (e.g., of rope). *a.*

modumodunga. (R-1 MODU)
n.

modu sogosogo.
Separated from others, and by itself.

motogo.
[Var. of *matogo*].

moe$_1$.
Sleep; die; not yet blossomed (of a flower). *a.*

moe$_2$.
Round, spherical, circular ; a loop. *a.*

moea. (B-2 MOE$_1$)
A person who is able to catch many flying fish (because the fish seem not to awaken at his approach). *v.*

moeagi. (B-- MOE$_{1a}$)
Do by stealth. *v.*

moeagina. (B-2 MOE$_{1a}$)
v.

moeaginga. (B-1 MOE$_{1a}$)
n.

moe baubau.
Sleep without regard to remaining decently covered; die in agony [cf. *magau baubau*].

moebili. (B-- MOE$_{1b}$)
To long for another's presence at bedtime. *a.*

moebilianga. (B-1 MOE$_{1b}$)
n.

moe danuaa.
Die in peace.

moe dige.
To roll away from one's bedding while sleeping (on the floor).

moe dolo.
To sneak into another's house at night for the purpose of having sexual relations.

moe tao.
Sleep soundly.

moe iho.
Sleep for a short time, nap; sleep overnight in place other than one's usual sleeping place.

moele.
A lie (an untruth). *n.*

moemoe$_1$. (R-- MOE$_1$)
a.

moemoe$_2$. (R-- MOE$_2$)
Becoming more *moe$_2$*. *a.*

moemoeagi. (R-- MOE$_{1a}$)
v.

moemoeagina. (R-2 MOE$_{1a}$)
v.

moemoeaginga. (R-1 MOE$_{1a}$)
n.

moemoenga$_1$. (R-1 MOE$_1$)
n.

moemoenga$_2$. (R-1 MOE$_2$)
n.

moenga$_1$. (B-1 MOE$_1$)
—; bedclothes, bedding; a place for sleeping. *n.*

moenga$_2$. (B-1 MOE$_2$)
n.

mogo. (B-- MOGO$_3$)
Coconut apple (young and edible).

mogobuna.
Grandchild, descendant of. *n.*

mogomogo. (R-- MOGO$_2$)
Muscles (of the body). *v.*

moomogoanga. (R-1 MOGO$_2$)
n.

mogomogo ina.
Muscular.

moigaga.
Fibers of the coconut husk. *n.*

moli --. (B-- MOLI)
d.

molimoli. (R-- MOLI)
Haul (little by little). *v.*

molimolia. (R-2 MOLI)
v.

molimoli ange.
Take up slack in a line with hitches in order to maintain tension on something being hauled (e.g., a ship stuck on the reef during the moments when it is floated by waves).

molimoli taula.
To take hitches in a rope until it is taut (and continue to take hitches as the rope becomes slack).

molimoli i tuu gaha.
To express coconut oil out of the residue (*oda*) from which some oil has already been expressed.

molimolinga. (R-1 MOLI)
n.

molimoli ngaadai.
A distribution of the catch of a communal fishing expedition.

molo$_1$.
To make a knot of hair. *v.*

molo$_2$. (B-- MOLO$_1$)
A noose for fishing. *n.*

moloa. (B-2 MOLO$_1$)
Knotted (of hair). *v.*

molomolo$_1$. (R-- MOLO$_1$)
v.

molomolo$_2$. (R-- MOLO$_2$)
Round, clear (in outline). *a.*

molomoloa. (R-2 MOLO$_1$)
v.

molomoloanga. (R-1 MOLO$_2$)
n.

molomolo de biho.
Round-headed.

molomolo iho (age).
Appear clearly.

molomolonga. (R-1 MOLO$_1$)
n.

momme.
A place. *n.*

momme aadea.
Clearing (e.g., in the woods).

momme hagadaahao.
Playground.

momme hagassoe.
Court (of law).

momme hai lua.
A fishing spot (beyond the seaward reef) where either reef or ocean fish can be found.

mommomo. (R-- MOMO)
A little at a time. *a.*

mommomoanga. (R-1 MOMO)
n.

momo.
A little, a small amount of. *a.*

momoanga. (B-1 MOMO)
n.

momo dai sii.
A very very little (in quantity).

momogo. (T-- MOGO$_1$)
Want. *d.*

momogoanga. (T-1 MOGO$_1$)
n.

momolia. (B-2 MOMO)
Decrease in quantity. *a.*

momo loo huu.
Just a very little.

moni.
Canoe. *n.*

moni dui.
A canoe rigged for casting for tuna.

moni galele.
A canoe rigged for *galele* fishing.

moni kalo.
A canoe with rounded sides (designed to ride easily in rough seas).

moni hagadeledele.
Model (or toy) canoe.

moni hai gubenga.
A canoe rigged for *gubenga* fishing.

moni lele.
Airplane.

moni sulu.
Submarine.

moni velovelo.
A canoe with men going spear fishing.

moo balabala.
Barely cooked.

mooda.
For each person's several. *ptmp.*

moodaadeu.
For us [incl. 3]. *pdmo.*

moodaau.
For us [incl. 2]. *pdmo.*

moodo.
For each person's several. *ptmo.*

moodonga. (B-1 MODO)
n.

moodou.
For you [3]. *pdm.*

moodunga. (B-1 MODU)
n.

moogu.
For me. *pdmo.*

moolaadeu.
For them [3]. *pdmo.*

moolaau.
For them [2]. *pdmo.*

moolau.
Fast, quick, early. *a.*

moolau huu.
Punctual.

moolau lodo.
Having a short temper.

moolaunga. (B-1 MOOLAU)
n.

moole.
[Var. of *moele*]. *n.*

moolia. (B-2 MOLI)
v.

moolinga. (B-1 MOLI)
n.

moolonga. (B-1 $MOLO_1$)
n.

mooluu.
For you [2]. *pdm.*

moomaadeu.
For us [excl. 3]. *pdmo.*

moomaau.
For us [excl. 2]. *pdmo.*

moomada. ($MADA_1$, MOO_b)
Half-cooked. *a.*

$moomoa_1$. (R-- MOO)
Balls of grated taro (for making *huaahuu*). *n.*

$moomoa_2$. (R-- MOO)
The shoot from a germinating coconut. *n.*

moomoa-ganoango.
Fish sp.: boxfish (yellow).

moomoa-uliuli.
Fish sp.: boxfish (dark blue).

moomodu. (T-- MODU)
[Pl. of *modu*]; collapse completely. *a.*

moomodunga. (T-1 MODU)
n.

moomoosee. (R-- MOO_d)
v.

moomooseenga. (R-1 MOO_d)
n.

moomoosugia. (R-- MOO_a)
v.

moomoosugiaanga. (R-1 MOO_a)
n.

moomuna. (B-- MOO_c)
Fatty. *a.*

moona.
For him, for her, for it. *pdmo.*

moono.
For his, for hers, for its. *pdmo.*

moosee. (MOO_d, SEE_2)
Not quite cooked (of anything but fish). *v.*

mooseenga. (B-1 MOO_d)
n.

moosugia. (B-- MOO_a)
Ripened unevenly (of breadfruit only). *v.*

moosugiaanga. (B-1 MOO_a)
n.

moosugia ange.
Somewhat *moosugia.*

moou.
For you [1]. *pdmo.*

moso.
Bird sp.: starling (*Apolonis opacus*). *n.*

mosongenge.
A name children tease each other with. *n.*

mossogosogo.
(C-- $SOGOSOGO_a$) *a.*

mossogosogoanga.
(C-1 $SOGOSOGO_a$) *n.*

mossogosogolia.
(C-2 $SOGOSOGO_a$) *v.*

mou.
Age grade (those reaching adolescence within a few years of each other); a mnemonic chant enumerating the names of the islets, flora, fauna, chief priests, etc.; [archaic: those born during the tenure of one chief priest]. *n.*

mougu.
Plant sp.: *Fleurya ruderalis* (Forst.f.) Gaud. ex. Wedd. *n.*

mouli.
Living, alive; life; life-style; that on which life seems to depend (e.g., favorite food or activity); life-principle (spirit, soul, etc.). *a.*

mouli age.
Regain consciousness, rise from the dead.

mouli age de --.
Regain feeling in — (part of body which was numb).

mouli danuaa.
Easy living, a good life.

mouli dangada.
Delinquent person (periodically exhibiting bad behavior).

mouli-o-nono. (CF MOULI)
[= *malianoono*]. *n.*

moumou.
Wasteful, waste (something). *v.*

moumoua. (B-2 MOUMOU)
v.

moumoulia. (B-2 MOUMOU)
v.

moumounga. (B-1 MOUMOU)
n.

moumousi. (R-- MOUSI)
Repeatedly being *mousi.* *a.*

moumousinga. (R-1 MOUSI)
n.

mounounga. (R-1 MOUNU)
n.

mounu.
To take a cover (or other thing that fits into or on something) off. *a.*

mounuuga. (B-1 MOUNU)
n.

mounuunu. (R-- MOUNU)
Easily *mounu.* *a.*

mousi.
Defeated, lose (battle, game, etc.). *a.*

mousinga. (B-1 MOUSI)
n.

mua.
Front (position), before, ahead. *nl.*

mua mai (adu, ange).
Next to me (you, him).

muaamoni*. (MONI, MUA)
A song formerly sung while dancing. *n.*

mua iho (age).
Next above (below).

mudimudi. (R-- MMUDI)
a.

mudimudinga. (R-1 MMUDI)
n.

mudumudu₁. (R-- $MUDU_1$)
Slow moving (while working), slow acting, slow thinking. *a.*

mudumudu$_2$. (R-- MUDU$_2$)
Fish sp.: damselfish. *n.*

mudumudua. (R-2 MUDU$_1$)
a.

mudumuduanga. (R-1 MUDU$_1$)
n.

mudumudu-dua-beau.
Fish sp.: damselfish.

mudumudulia. (R-2 MUDU$_1$)
a.

mudumudu-odaoda.
Fish sp.: damselfish.

muga. (B-- MUGA$_1$)
Used (or done, heard, or known) over and over until bored with. *v.*

mugaanga. (B-1 MUGA$_1$)
n.

mugalia. (B-2 MUGA$_1$)
v.

mugamuga$_1$. (R-- MUGA$_1$)
v.

mugamuga$_2$. (R-- MUGA$_2$)
The muscle of a bivalve; the first stage of development of the coconut, before *daahaa; to crackle when chewed* [*of godi* and *madaanui* only]. *v.*

mugamugaanga. (R-1 MUGA$_1$)
n.

muhuu.
Please! [a request]. *mv.*

mui.
Gathered around (something). *v.*

muia. (B-2 MUI)
Be *mui.* *v.*

muimui. (R-- MUI)
Crowded (owing to a disorder of things); dense (underbrush). *v.*

muimuia. (R-2 MUI)
Be *muimui.* *v.*

muimuinga. (R-1 MUI)
n.

muinga. (B-1 MUI)
n.

mule --. (B-- MULE)
d.

mulegi.
Show off (in front of members of the opposite sex). *v.*

mulegianga. (B-1 MULEGI)
n.

mulemule. (R-- MULE)
a.

mulemulenga. (R-1 MULE)
n.

muli$_1$.
After, end (rearward part), later. *nl.*

muli$_2$.
Debt, owe. *a.*

muliagi. (B-- MULI$_{1b}$)
Afterward. *b.*

muliagina. (B-2 MULI$_{1b}$)
Last, final. *a.*

muliaginga. (B-1 MULI$_{1b}$)
n.

muli de huaalaangi.
Afternoon.

muli lele.
The rear tip of the turtle shell.

muli madangi.
Sailing downwind.

muli mai ange.
A little later, by and by.

muli mai loo.
Much later.

muli moni.
Stern.

mulimuli$_1$. (R-- MULI$_1$)
Much later; the very end. *v.*

mulimuli$_2$. (R-- MULI$_2$)
a.

muli sua hadu.
Reefward of the storm beach; beach rock.

mulo.
Roll up. *v.*

muloa. (B-2 MULO)
v.

mulomulo. (R-- MULO)
v.

mulomuloa. (R-2 MULO)
v.

mulomulonga. (R-1 MULO)
n.

mulu --. (B-- MULU)
d.

mulu gudu.
Grab while pulling; destroy by falling on or through; break through any obstacles in one's path.

mulumulu. (R-- MULU)
v.

mulumulua. (R-2 MULU)
v.

mulumulu aamanu.
Moss (on rocks or coral).

mulumulunga. (R-1 MULU)
n.

muna.
Word, language, speech. *n.*

muna abo (donu).
Truth.

muna abo donu.
Truth.

muna pada.
Harsh words.

muna daemaha.
Words which hurt.

muna de henua.
The Nukuoro language.

muna hai alaa.
Oh my goodness!

muna hhadu.
Lie (falsehood).

muna madua.
Words used only by elders (which are not normally part of a child's vocabulary).

muna maimai.
[= *ngudu maimai*].

munamuna. (R-- MUNA)
A short prayer. *a.*

muna o de henua.
A community meeting (for listening to speeches or instructions).

muna o tangada.
Speak of the devil!

munimuni. (R-- MMUNI)
a.

munimuninga. (R-1 MMUNI)
n.

musa.
The sound of many little school fish feeding at the surface of the water. *v.*

musalia. (B-2 MUSA)
a.

musamusa. (R-- MUSA)
v.

musamusaanga. (R-1 MUSA)
n.

musamusalia. (R-2 MUSA)
a.

musu.
Whispering. *v.*

musua. (B-2 MUSU)
v.

musumusu. (R-- MUSU)
Whisper (to someone). *v.*

musumusua. (R-2 MUSU)
v.

musumusu laa lalo.
Whisper softly.

musumusunga. (R-1 MUSU)
n.

muu$_1$.
Utter (words or sounds), reply (to someone). *a.*

muu$_2$.
Fish sp.: snapper (The native term is applied to many spp.). *n.*

muulenga. (B-1 MULE)
n.

muulonga. (B-1 MULO)
n.

muulua. (B-2 MULU)
v.

muulunga. (B-1 MULU)
n.

muu-madagao.
Fish sp.: snapper?

muu-madavai.
Fish sp. (rare).

muumuu. (R-- MUU_1)
a.

muumuu kaiaa.
To remain silent (in order to hide a misdeed of oneself or others).

muumuunga. (R-1 MUU_1)
n.

muuninga. (B-1 MMUNI)
n.

muunga. (B-1 MUU_1)
n.

muusanga. (B-1 MUSA)
n.

muusunga. (B-1 MUSU)
n.

naa. (B-- NAA_1)
There near you; in the future. *mv.*

naabanga. (B-1 NABA)
n.

naabenga. (B-1 NABE)
n.

naa gaalava.
So what?

naa huu.
When, if.

naamulolo. (LOLO, NAAMU)
Ramrod; [the etymology of this word is totally obscure]. *n.*

naanunga. (B-1 NANU)
n.

naba.
A slip of the tongue. *a.*

naba i de muna.
Converse earnestly.

nabanaba. (R-- NABA)
a.

nabanabaanga. (R-1 NABA)
n.

nabe.
To hook under the waistband or belt. *v.*

nabea. (B-2 NABE)
v.

nabelia. (B-2 NABE)
v.

nabenabe. (R-- NABE)
v.

nabenabea. (R-2 NABE)
v.

nabenabelia. (R-2 NABE)
v.

nabenabenga. (R-1 NABE)
n.

nagonago*. (R-- NAGO)
The sound of sloshing water (or of sexual intercourse). *v.*

nagonagoa*. (R-2 NAGO)
v.

nagonagolia*. (R-2 NAGO)
v.

nagonagonga*. (R-1 NAGO)
n.

namanama. (R-- NAMA)
Fish sp. (like *ngaa*, but longer and thinner). *n.*

namu.
Mosquito. *n.*

namuaa.
A sore on the lips (believed to result from missing a meal). *v.*

namuaanga. (B-1 NAMUAA)
n.

namunamu. (R-- NNAMU)
a.

namunamuanga. (R-1 NNAMU)
n.

nannadu. (R-- NNADU)
v.

nannaduanga. (R-1 NNADU)
n.

nannadulia. (R-2 NNADU)
v.

nannanu. (R-- NANU)
a.

nanu.
Grumble, complain. *a.*

nanua. (B-2 NANU)
The object of a complaint. *v.*

nanuanga. (B-1 NANU)
n.

nanulia. (B-2 NANU)
The object of a complaint. *v.*

nanumia. (B-2 NANU)
The object of a complaint. *v.*

nao.
To extract by gouging out with a finger. *v.*

naoa. (B-2 NAO)
v.

nao baasua.
To cllect *baasua.*

nao gasi.
Eat messily (by poking at all of the food instead of touching only the portion to be eaten).

naolia. (B-2 NAO)
v.

naonao. (R-- NAO)
v.

naonaonga. (R-1 NAO)
n.

naonga. (B-1 NAO)
n.

nau*.
Plant sp. (the archaic name of *manu-gaba-aasanga*). *n.*

ne.
PERFECTIVE ASPECT MARKER; if. *mt.*

nebu.
To do something so earnestly that one has no time to talk; be very busy. *v.*

nebua. (B-2 NEBU)
Be *nebu.* *v.*

nebu ange.
To perceive that others are occupied.

nebunebu. (R-- NEBU)
v.

nebunebua. (R-2 NEBU)
Be *nebunebu.* *v.*

nebunebunga. (R-1 NEBU)
n.

nebunga. (B-1 NEBU)
n.

neegenga. (B-1 NEGE)
n.

neevenga. (B-1 NEVE)
n.

nege.
Move (something) a little way over. *v.*

negea. (B-2 NEGE)
v.

negelia. (B-2 NEGE)
v.

negenege. (R-- NEGE)
v.

negenegenga. (R-1 NEGE)
n.

ne hia?.
How many has it been?

nehu.
Clear (in focus). *v.*

nehua. (B-2 NEHU)
v.

nehunehu. (R-- NEHU)
v.

nehunehua. (R-2 NEHU)
v.

nehunehunga. (R-1 NEHU)
n.

nehunga. (B-1 NEHU)
n.

nei.
Here, now. *mv.*

nengenenge. (R-- NENGE)
Tickle; to catch an octupus by tickling it (to dislodge it from its hole). *v.*

nengenengea. (R-2 NENGE)
v.

nengenengeanga. (R-1 NENGE)
n.

nengenengelia. (R-2 NENGE)
v.

neve.
Blurred (out of focus). *v.*

nevea. (B-2 NEVE)
Be *neve.* *v.*

neveia. (B-2 NEVE)
Be *neve.* *v.*

neveinga. (B-1 NEVE)
n.

neveneve. (R-- NEVE)
—; spider. *v.*

neveneveinga. (R-1 NEVE)
n.

nevenevenga. (R-1 NEVE)
n.

ni$_1$.
Belonging to. *mp.*

ni$_2$.
GENERAL ARTICLE (PL.); they (things) are... *ma.*

niaada.
Belonging to each person's several. *ptnb.*

niaai. (AI, NI$_1$)
Whose? *b.*

ni aha.
What are these?

nigo.
Go around in a circle; wind around. *v.*

nigoa. (B-2 NIGO)
v.

nigolia. (B-2 NIGO)
v.

nigonigo. (R-- NIGO)
v.

nigonigoi. (R-- NIGO$_a$)
v.

nigonigoia. (R-2 NIGO$_a$)
v.

nigonigoinga. (R-1 NIGO$_a$)
n.

niho.
Tooth, teeth. *n.*

niho gai.
Permanent teeth (appearing after deciduous teeth).

niho gaina.
Teeth with cavities.

niho hagadolo.
Incisor teeth.

niho ngalo.
Molar teeth, wisdom teeth.

niho vaiuu.
Milk teeth, deciduous teeth.

nii. (C-- NI$_1$)
[Var. of *ni*$_1$]. *mp.*

niiada.
Belonging to each person's several. *ptna.*

niiadaadeu.
Belonging to our [incl. 3]. *pdna.*

niiadaau.
Belonging to our [incl. 2]. *pdna.*

niiagu.
Belonging to my. *pdna.*

niialaadeu.
Belonging to their [3]. *pdna.*

niialaau.
Belonging to their [2]. *pdna.*

niiamaadeu.
Belonging to our [excl. 3]. *pdna.*

niiamaau.
Belonging to our [excl. 2]. *pdna.*

niiana.
Belonging to his (or hers, or its). *pdna.*

niiau.
Belonging to your [1]. *pdna.*

niidada.
Belonging to each person's one. *ptna.*

niidodo.
Belonging to each person's one. *ptno.*

niigoi. (B-- NIGO$_a$)
Wind around (of a rope, etc.). *v.*

niigoia. (B-2 NIGO$_a$)
v.

niigoinga. (B-1 NIGO$_a$)
n.

niigonga. (B-1 NIGO)
n.

niiodaaden.
Belonging to our [inc. 3]. *pdno.*

niiodaau.
Belonging to our [incl. 2]. *pdno.*

niiodo.
Belonging to each person's several. *ptno.*

niiodou.
Belonging to your [3]. *pdn.*

niiogu.
Belonging to my. *pdno.*

niiolaadeu.
Belonging to their [3]. *pdno.*

niiolaau.
Belonging to their [2]. *pdno.*

niioluu.
Belonging to your [2]. *pdn.*

niiomaadeu.
Belonging to our [excl. 3]. *pdno.*

niiomaau.
Belonging to our [excl. 2]. *pdno.*

niiono.
Belonging to his (or hers, or its). *pdno.*

niioo.
Belonging to your [1]. *pdno.*

nioai. (AI, NI_1)
Whose? *b.*

niooda.
Belonging to each person's several. *ptnp.*

nnaba. (P-- NABA)
a.

nnadu.
To receive a shock (as when hit, or by an explosion). *v.*

nnaduanga. (B-1 NNADU)
n.

nnadulia. (B-2 NNADU)
v.

nnamu.
Odor, smell (of something), greasy. *a.*

nnamuanga. (B-1 NNAMU)
n.

nnamu hagaduugia.
Stench.

nnanu. (P-- NANU)
a.

nnege. (P-- NEGE)
v.

nnigo. (P-- NIGO)
v.

nnoa. (E-- NOA)
Tie. *v.*

nnoa nounu.
Tied in such a way that pulling the end of the string will undo it.

nnoho. (P-- NOHO)
v.

nnoo.
Covetous, envious. *a.*

nnooanga. (B-1 NNOO)
n.

nnoo hagamau me.
Insatiably acquisitive.

nnui. (P-- NUI_2)
Large [pl.]; big [pl.]. *a.*

nnuinga. (P-1 NUI_2)
n.

noa.
Tied (as with rope). *v.*

noaanga. (B-1 NOA)
n.

nodi.
To tie a knot in the hair. *v.*

nodia. (B-2 NODI)
v.

nodinodi. (R-- NODI)
v.

nodinodia. (R-2 NODI)
v.

nodinodinga. (R-1 NODI)
n.

nodinga. (B-1 NODI)
n.

noganoga.
A method of plaiting mats. *v.*

noganogaanga. (B-1 NOGANOGA)
n.

nogo.
PAST PROGRESSIVE ASPECT MARKER *mt.*

noho.
Stay, sit, stop; freeze, coagulate; live (at); remain (somewhere); be situated. *v.*

nohoa. (B-2 NOHO)
Occupied. *v.*

noho ai.
Occupy or live in (a place).

nohoanga. (B-1 NOHO)
—; position. *n.*

nohoanga hodooligi.
The place where the chief lives (at the moment).

noho baba.
Live peacefully.

noho dau donu.
Sit quietly.

noho dodo.
Coagulation of blood.

noho donu.
Properly situated or loaded (of a canoe).

noho hagamaaiongi.
To sit as though stunned (i.e., as though *hagamaaiongi*).

noho hagamolomolo.
To sit by oneself (away from the main group).

noho hhanga.
Sit with one's legs spread apart.

noho iho --.
Keep secret.

noho lalo.
Overloaded (almost to the point of sinking).

noholia. (B-2 NOHO)
Occupied. *v.*

noho maadai.
Sit quietly.

noho mai (adu, ange).
Resist me (you, them), oppose me (you, them).

noho moso.
Able to support one's weight (e.g., a branch of a tree).

noho mua.
Overloaded in front (of a canoe).

noho muli.
Overloaded in the stern (of a canoe).

nohonoho. (R-- NOHO)
v.

nohonohoa. (R-2 NOHO)
v.

nohonohoanga. (R-1 NOHO)
n.

nohonoholia. (R-2 NOHO)
v.

noho senga (adu).
Be ignorant (of what is happening).

nohu.
Fish sp.: stone-fish. *n.*

nonnonu. (R-- $NONU_1$)
v.

nonnonua. (R-2 $NONU_1$)
v.

nonnonumanga. (R-1 $NONU_1$)
n.

nonnonumia. (R-2 $NONU_1$)
v.

nonnonunga. (R-1 $NONU_1$)
n.

$nonu_1$.
Filter, sift. *v.*

$nonu_2$*.
Plant sp.: tree sp. (the archaic name of *bugaliaa*). *n.*

nonua. (B-2 $NONU_1$)
v.

nonumanga. (B-1 $NONU_1$)
n.

nonumia. (B-2 $NONU_1$)
v.

noo. (B-- NOO_1)
If. *mi.*

noobiho.
Be enemies (of individuals only). *a.*

noobihoanga. (B-1 NOOBIHO)
n.

noodagi.
Forbidden to use (esp. plants reserved for the owner's use by tying the trunk). *v.*

noodagianga. (B-1 NOODAGI)
n.

noodalo.
Duplicate. *v.*

noodaloanga. (B-1 NOODALO)
n.

noodanga. (B-1 NOA)
Bundle, knot; a set of 12 different fishing lures. *n.*

noodia. (B-2 NOA)
v.

noogele.
To tie a knot so that it is difficult to untie. *v.*

noogeleanga. (B-1 NOOGELE)
n.

nooligi. (LIGI, NOO_3)
A small knife. *n.*

noomeemea.
A wave of sufficient force to wash over normally dry land; tidal wave. *v.*

noomeemeaanga.
(B-1 NOOMEEMEA) *n.*

noonoa. (R-- NOA)
v.

noonogia.
Bloated from ingesting too much fat. *v.*

noonogiaanga. (B-1 NOONOGIA)
n.

noonoobiho. (R-- NOOBIHO)
a.

noonoobihoanga. (R-1 NOOBIHO)
n.

noonoodagi. (R-- NOODAGI)
v.

noonoodagianga. (R-1 NOODAGI)
n.

noonoodalo. (R-- NOODALO)
v.

noonoodaloanga. (R-1 NOODALO)
n.

noonoodanga. (R-1 NOA)
n.

noonoodia. (R-2 NOA)
v.

noonoogele. (R-- NOOGELE)
v.

noonoogeleanga. (R-1 NOOGELE)
n.

noonounu. (R-- NOUNU)
Repeatedly *nounu.* *v.*

noonunga. (B-1 $NONU_1$)
n.

nounu.
To tie a knot so that it is easily undone (by pulling one end of the string). *v.*

noununga. (B-1 NOUNU)
n.

nugu.
Land, islet.

nui. (B-- NUI_1)
Plant sp.: tree sp.: coconut tree. *n.*

nui hoohoa.
A coconut tree trunk incised with steps [to facilitate climbing].

nuinui. (R-- NUI_1)
A sp. of driftwood (resembling *aha-bagua*), the core of which is used for the hoop of the flying fish net. *n.*

nuui.
Green. *a.*

nuuinga. (B-1 NUUI)
n.

ngaa.
Fish sp. *n.*

ngaadahi. (B-- $DAHI_{1a}$)
Both, as one. *n.*

ngaadai. (B-- DAI_1)
Lagoonward. *nl.*

ngaadonga. (B-1 NGADO)
n.

ngaage. (B-- AGE_a)
Downtown. *nl.*

ngaage nei.
Gilbert Islands.

ngaaheahe. (B-- NGAHEAHE)
Taro which is watery or gummy. *v.*

ngaaheaheanga. (B-1 NGAHEAHE)
n.

ngaahee. (B-- HEE_{2e})
Where? *b.*

ngaaholu. (P-- $HOLU_a$)
a.

ngaaholunga. (P-1 $HOLU_a$)
n.

ngaalia. (B-2 NGALI)
v.

ngaalinga. (B-1 NGALI)
n.

ngaalogu. (P-- NGALOGU)
a.

ngaalogua. (P-2 NGALOGU)
v.

ngaalogunga. (P-1 NGALOGU)
n.

ngaalonga. (B-1 NGALO)
n.

ngaalue. (P-- NGALUE)
a.

ngaalueanga. (P-1 NGALUE)
n.

ngaalulu. (B-- $LULU_a$)
A rattling or sloshing around inside (of something shaken). *a.*

ngaaluluanga. (B-1 $LULU_a$)
n.

ngaaninga. (B-1 NGANI)
n.

ngaangaa.
Not sturdy, rickety. *v.*

ngaangaanga. (B-1 NGAANGAA)
n.

ngaangaa-ulu. (XCO $HULU_1$)
Hair of the head [derived from *hulu*?]. *n.*

ngaangaaulu. (CF NGA-)

ngaangauda. (R-- NGAUDA)
Habitually *ngauda.* *v.*

ngaangaudanga. (R-1 NGAUDA)
n.

ngaaobo. (P-- NGAOBO)
v.

ngaaoboanga. (P-1 NGAOBO)
n.

ngaaue. (P-- NGAUE)
a.

ngaauenga. (P-1 NGAUE)
n.

ngaavali. (P-- NGAVALI)
v.

ngaavalianga. (P-1 NGAVALI)
n.

ngadaa.
With difficulty. *mv.*

ngadaa mai.
Difficult for me; difficult to come.

ngadala.
Fish sp.: sea bass (The native term is applied to many spp.). *n.*

ngadau.
Year; age (of a person). *n.*

ngadau age.
Older.

ngadau iho.
Younger.

ngadi--. (B-- NGADI)
Hollow, vacant, empty; nothing, worthless, useless. *mf.*

ngadi basa.
Small talk; idle conversation.

ngadi biho.
Head.

ngadi dangada.
An ordinary person, commoner; a person of slight social value.

ngadi daumaha.
Religions which are not in the Judaeo-Christian tradition, pagan cults.

ngadi diinonga.
Pagan gods, idols.

ngadi duu.
Naked.

ngadi gai.
Eat taro without fish (or fish without taro).

ngadi gavadu.
A gift (to the hearer); a present (to the hearer).

ngadi hai bodu.
Common-law marriage, concubinage.

ngadi hanonga.
A useless journey.

ngadi humai.
Come without bringing anything (such as gifts).

ngadi laangi.
A day other than Sunday; a day on which nothing is accomplished.

ngadi mahamaha --.
Beautiful but otherwise useless.

ngadi me.
Nothing, unimportant, useless, worthless.

ngadi moana.
[= *laangai ngadi moana*].

ngadi ngavesi.
An empty box.

ngadi seesee.
Walk barefoot, stroll.

ngadi uaa.
Assent to insincerely.

ngadi ubu.
An empty coconut shell used as a container.

ngadi vai.
A coconut shell used for water storage (on fishing trips).

ngado.
Come to the end or limit (of something). *a.*

ngadoa. (B-2 NGADO)
To have *ngado*. *v.*

ngadolia. (B-2 NGADO)
To have *ngado*. *v.*

ngadolo. (B-- $DOLO_b$)
A landslide or similar movement of things. *a.*

ngadoloanga. (B-1 DOLO)
n.

$ngae_1$.
Head. *n.*

$ngae_2$.
Mollusk sp.: giant clam sp. *n.*

ngaengae. (R-- $NGAE_1$)
To become dizzy in the water. *v.*

ngago.
Brain; egg. *n.*

ngaholu. (B-- $HOLU_a$)
Bent. *a.*

ngaholuholu. (R-- $HOLU_a$)
a.

ngaholuholunga. (R-1 $HOLU_a$)
n.

ngaholunga. (B-1 $HOLU_a$)
n.

ngahui. (B-- HUI_2)
Tens of coconuts [cf. *dehui*]. *n.*

ngaiho. (B-- IHO_a)
Uptown. *nl.*

ngaio.
Fish sp.: needlefish. *n.*

ngaio-golai.
Fish sp.: needlefish.

ngali --. (B-- NGALI)
d.

ngalingali. (R-- NGALI)
v.

ngalingalia. (R-2 NGALI)
v.

ngalingalinga. (R-1 NGALI)
n.

ngalo.
Forget. *v.*

ngaloa. (B-2 NGALO)
v.

ngalogu.
Push in, crumple up; bend out of shape (temporarily); easily changed in shape (esp. by pushing). *a.*

ngalogua. (B-2 NGALOGU)
v.

ngalogulogu. (R-- NGALOGU)
Easily *ngalogu* in many places. *a.*

ngalogulogua. (R-2 NGALOGU)
v.

ngalogulogunga. (R-1 NGALOGU)
n.

ngalogunga. (B-1 NGALOGU)
n.

ngalongalo. (R-- NGALO)
Forgetful, absent-minded. *a.*

ngalongaloa. (R-2 NGALO)
v.

ngalongalonga. (R-1 NGALO)
n.

ngalubelube.
Tremble or vibrate in the air. *v.*

ngalubelubea.
(B-2 NGALUBELUBE) *v.*

ngalubelubenga.
(B-1 NGALUBELUBE) *n.*

ngalue.
Move slightly, change position. *a.*

ngalue age.
Increased, augmented.

ngalueanga. (B-1 NGALUE)
n.

ngalue ange.
Increase.

ngalue de gauvae.
Dislocated jaw.

ngalue de hakii.
Dislocated larynx.

ngalue iho.
Reduced, decreased.

ngalue mai.
Decrease.

ngalullulu. (R-- $LULU_a$)
Shaky. *a.*

ngalulluluanga. (R-1 $LULU_a$)
n.

ngalungalue. (R-- NGALUE)
a.

ngalungalueanga. (R-1 NGALUE)
n.

nganangana. (R-- NGANA)
Loud (noise) repeatedly. *a.*

ngananganaanga. (R-1 NGANA)
n.

ngananganalia. (R-2 NGANA)
v.

ngani.
Going around in a complete circle (like a belt). *a.*

ngania. (B-2 NGANI)
v.

ngani adu.
ngani toward others; fit around one as a belt etc.

ngani mai.
ngani toward oneself; fit (of clothes).

nganingani. (R-- NGANI)
a.

nganinganinga. (R-1 NGANI)
n.

ngaobo.
Easily bent out of shape. *v.*

ngaoboanga. (B-1 NGAOBO)
n.

ngaoboobo. (R-- NGAOBO)
v.

ngaobooboanga. (R-1 NGAOBO)
n.

ngaoheohe.
Easily bent (impermanently). *v.*

ngaoheoheanga. (B-1 NGAOHEOHE)
n.

ngaohie.
Easily. *mv.*

ngaolo.
To make noise (irregular repeated sounds). *a.*

ngaoloa. (B-2 NGAOLO)
Noisy (irregular repeated sounds). *v.*

ngaolonga. (B-1 NGAOLO)
n.

ngaongao. (R-- NGAO)
v.

ngaongaoa. (R-2 NGAO)
v.

ngaongaoanga. (R-1 NGAO)
n.

ngaongaolia. (R-2 NGAO)
v.

ngaongaolo. (R-- NGAOLO)
v.

ngaongaolonga. (R-1 NGAOLO)
n.

$ngau_1$. (C-- AU_2)
[Var. of au_1]. *pi.*

$ngau_2$. (B-- NGAU)
Chew (e.g., to suck juice out but not swallow it). *v.*

ngaua. (B-2 NGAU)
v.

ngauda. (CF NGA-)

$ngauda_1$. (XCO UDA_2)
Inland of; landlubber. *nl.*

ngauda$_2$. (B-- NGAUDA)
An unenthusiastic fisherman. *a.*

ngaudanga. (B-1 NGAUDA)
n.

ngaue.
Move (oneself), moved. *a.*

ngaue age.
Increase (in rank or price, etc.).

ngaueanga. (B-1 NGAUE)
n.

ngaue ange.
Increase (in price, etc.).

ngaue iho.
Reduce (in rank, price, etc.).

ngaue mai.
To reduce (in price, etc.).

ngau hala.
Bite someone.

ngaunga. (B-1 NGAU)
n.

ngaungau$_1$. (R-- NGAU)
v.

ngaungau$_2$. (R-- NGAU)
Plant sp.: elephant ear (*Alocasia*). *n.*

ngaungaua. (R-2 NGAU)
v.

ngaungaue. (R-- NGAUE)
a.

ngaungauenga. (R-1 NGAUE)
n.

ngaungaunga. (R-1 NGAU)
n.

ngaungau-ulu. (XCO HULU$_1$)
[Var. of *ngaangaaulu*]. *n.*

ngavali.
Bent slightly (not sharply). *a.*

ngavalianga. (B-1 NGAVALI)
n.

ngavalivali. (R-- NGAVALI)
Repeatedly *ngavali* (as a diving board in use). *a.*

ngavalivalianga. (R-1 NGAVALI)
n.

ngavesi.
Box, coffin, crate. *n.*

ngavesi haangoda.
Fishing tackle box.

ngii.
A high-pitched sound. *v.*

ngiianga. (B-1 NGII)
n.

ngiingii. (R-- NGII)
v.

ngiisinga. (B-1 NGISI)
n.

ngisi.
A squeaking sound. *v.*

ngisi$_a$. (CF DANGI)

ngisingisi. (R-- NGISI)
v.

ngole.
Use up, use unwisely (not saving some for later), waste. *v.*

ngolea. (B-2 NGOLE)
v.

ngole age.
Use smallest first.

ngole iho.
To use the biggest first.

ngolengole. (R-- NGOLE)
v.

ngolengolea. (R-2 NGOLE)
v.

ngolengolenga. (R-1 NGOLE)
n.

ngolongolo. (R-- NNGOLO)
a.

ngongo.
Bird sp.: common noddy (*Anous stolidus*). *n.*

ngoolenga. (B-1 NGOLE)
n.

ngoolonga. (B-1 NNGOLO)
n.

ngudu.
Mouth. *n.*

ngudu$_a$. (B-- NGUDU)
Mouth of, rim of. *nl.*

ngudu aahua.
Islet shore (except that facing the lagoon).

ngudu ai.
Act as an interpreter.

ngudu gaiaa.
Charlatan.

ngudula. (?)
Fish sp.: snapper. *n.*

ngudu lagolago.
Lie (tell a falsehood).

ngudu leelee*.
Talkative, loquacious.

ngudu leia.
Be the object of continual gossip; scorned.

ngudu leidi*.
Be the object of continual gossip; scorned.

ngudu maimai.
Flattery or other communication by which one attempts to ingratiate oneself; unctuous, cloying, winsome.

ngudu malie.
Eloquent (of a person).

ngudu-me. (ME, NGUDU)
Boundary of a taro plot. *n.*

ngu te.
[A contraction of *ngudu de...*].

ngu te lodo.
The edge of the lagoon reef.

ngungu.
Chew, masticate (solids which make noise). *v.*

nguu$_1$.
A faint sound, like humming. *a.*

nguu$_2$.
Squid (3 types). *n.*

nguua. (B-2 NGUU$_1$)
Be *nguu.* *v.*

nguuanga. (B-1 NGUU$_1$)
n.

nguudia. (B-2 NGUNGU)
v.

nguulia. (B-2 NGUU$_1$)
Be *nguu.* *v.*

nguunguu. (R-- NGUU$_1$)
a

nguunguuanga. (R-1 NGUU$_1$)
n.

nngahu. (E-- NGAHU)
Fish sp.: damselfish. *n.*

nngali. (E-- NGALI)
To take a bite out of something held in the hand (food only). *v.*

nngana. (E-- NGANA)
Loud (noise). *a.*

nnganaanga. (E-1 NGANA)
n.

nnganalia. (E-2 NGANA)
v.

nngani. (P-- NGANI)
a.

nngao. (E-- NGAO)
Loud (sound). *v.*

nngaoa. (E-2 NGAO)
Noisy (a loud, individually perceived, noise). *v.*

nngaoanga. (E-1 NGAO)
n.

nngao dalinga.
Hurting in the ears from noise.

nngaolia. (E-2 NGAO)
Noise (a loud, individually perceived, noise). *v.*

nngie. (E-- NGIE)
Plant sp.: crepe myrtle shrub (*Pemphis acidula* Forst.). *n.*

nngii. (P-- NGII)
v.

nngisi. (P-- NGISI)
v.

nngolo.
A steady sound (e.g., of a machine, of rain, or of vibration). *a.*

nnguu. (P-- NGUU$_1$)
a.

o.
RELATIONAL PARTICLE I. *mr.*

oa.
Gunwales (at the top of the canoe). *n.*

oaa.
A sound indicating disagreement or displeasure; Oh my gosh! *a.*

obe.
Eye of the taro corm. *n.*

obea. (B-2 OBE)
To have an eye (of a taro corm). *v.*

obenga. (B-1 OBE)
n.

obeobea. (R-2 OBE)
Having many eyes (of the taro corm). *v.*

oda$_1$.
Eat (something) raw. *v.*

oda$_2$.
Grated coconut meat after the oil has been expressed. *n.*

odaadeu.
Our [incl. 3] several. *ppo.*

odaanga. (B-1 ODA$_1$)
n.

odaau.
Our [incl. 2] several. *ppo.*

odaia. (B-2 ODA$_1$)
v.

odalia. (B-2 ODA$_1$)
v.

odaoda$_1$. (R-- ODA$_1$)
v.

odaoda$_2$. (R-- ODA$_3$)
Driftwood (any sort). *n.*

odea.
Noon, midday. *a.*

odi$_a$.
Already; very. *mv.*

odi$_b$. (B-- ODI)
Gone, finished, used up. *a.*

odi ai loo.
That's the end! That's all!

odi ange.
Even (number); complete (none missing); reach the maximum.

odi de masavaa.
Having insufficient time remaining for (something).

odi iho.
Just finished.

odi mai (adu, ange).
All (e.g., have come).

odinga. (B-1 ODI)
n.

odiodi. (R-- ODI)
Long since finished, done, or gone. *a.*

odiodi$_a$. (R-- ODI$_a$)
Long since, a long time ago. *b.*

odi sango.
Completely cleaned up or finished; all gone; each and every one all gone.

odo$_1$.
To roof (a house), to thatch (a house). *v.*

odo$_2$.
Each person's several. *pto.*

odoa. (B-2 ODO$_1$)
v.

odohia. (B-2 ODO$_1$)
v.

odolia. (B-2 ODO$_1$)
v.

odomalie. (XCO ODO$_2$)
Delicious (of coconut apples only). *a.*

odonga. (B-1 ODO$_1$)
—; the string used for securing thatch to the roof frame. *n.*

odoodo. (R-- ODO$_1$)
v.

odoodoa. (R-2 ODO$_1$)
v.

odoodohia. (R-2 ODO$_1$)
v.

odoodonga. (R-1 ODO$_1$)
n.

odou.
[Var. of *oodou*]. *pp.*

oga.
To husk (a coconut) with a sharp stick. *v.*

ogaanga. (B-1 OGA)
—; the husk of a coconut (remaining after husking). *n.*

ogahia. (B-2 OGA)
v.

ogaoga. (R-- OGA)
v.

ogaogaanga. (R-1 OGA)
n.

ogo$_1$.
Pick up one at a time (by hand). *v.*

ogo$_2$.
Purlin. *n.*

ogo$_3$.
The attachment of a clam to the reef. *n.*

ogoa. (B-2 OGO$_1$)
v.

ogoanga. (B-1 OGO$_1$)
n.

ogohia. (B-2 OGO$_1$)
v.

ogolia. (B-2 OGO$_1$)
v.

ogonga. (B-1 OGO$_1$)
n.

ogoogo. (R-- OGO$_1$)
v.

ogoogoa. (R-2 OGO$_1$)
v.

ogoogoanga. (R-1 OGO$_1$)
n.

ogoogohia. (R-2 OGO$_1$)
v.

ogoogolia. (R-2 OGO$_1$)
v.

ogoogonga. (R-1 OGO$_1$)
n.

ogu.
My several. *ppo.*

oha.
Break, break up, destroy; damage, ruin. *v.*

ohaa. (B-2 OHA)
v.

oha de ganomada.
To work on a craft item (e.g., a canoe) with a model in mind of the finished product which is different from that of the person who began the work.

oha de nnoho paba.
Disturb the peace.

ohalia. (B-2 OHA)
v.

ohaoha. (R-- OHA)
v.

ohaohaa. (R-2 OHA)
v.

ohaohaanga. (R-1 OHA)
n.

ohaohalia. (R-2 OHA)
v.

oha valaai.
To disobey the instructions of a healer.

oho.
To do something, or go somewhere, early in the morning. *v.*

oho adu.
Go early.

oho age.
The following morning.

ohoanga. (B-1 OHO)
n.

oho boo.
To *oho* while still dark.

oho iho.
Come ashore early in the morning.

oho mai.
Come early.

ohooho$_1$. (R-- OHO)
v.

ohooho$_2$. (B-- OHOOHO)
Frightened by noise. *v.*

ohoohoanga$_1$. (R-1 OHO)
n.

ohoohoanga$_2$. (B-1 OHOOHO)
n.

ohu.
A depression in a tree trunk. *v.*

ohua. (B-2 OHU)
Characterized by having *ohu*. *v.*

ohuohu. (R-- OHU)
Having many *ohu*. *v.*

ohuohunga. (R-1 OHU)
n.

oia.
A sound used to communicate the tiredness of the speaker, or that the speaker recognizes his mistake. *a.*

ola.
Free, escaped; survive, safe. *a.*

olaa.
A sound expressing surprise or disapproval. *a.*

olaadeu.
Their [3] several. *ppo.*

olaanga. (B-1 OLA)
n.

olaaolaa. (R-- OLAA)
a.

olaau.
Their [2] several. *ppo.*

olaola. (R-- OLA)
a.

olaolaanga. (R-1 OLA)
n.

olioli.
To put an infant to sleep by singing a lullaby. *v.*

oliolia. (B-2 OLIOLI)
v.

oliolinga. (B-1 OLIOLI)
n.

olo.
An area in which sand has accumulated; beach, sand spit. *n.*

olonoa.
Sea cucumber sp. *n.*

olongaa.
Plant sp.: tree sp.: a shrubby tree sp. *Pipturus argenteus* (Forst.f.) Wedd.). *n.*

oluu.
[Var. of *ooluu*]. *pp.*

omaadeu.
Our [excl. 3] several. *ppo.*

omaau.
Our [excl. 2] several. *ppo.*

ona.
His several, her several, its several. *ppo.*

ono_1.
Six. *an.*

ono_2.
Fish sp.: barracuda. *n.*

ono_3.
His several, her several, its several. *ppo.*

onodaa.
Mollusk sp.: *Spondylus* sp. *n.*

Ono-laangi. (LAANGI, ONO_1)
Saturday ('sixth day'). *nt.*

Ono-malama. (MALAMA, ONO_1)
June ('sixth month'). *nt.*

onoonogia. (R-2 ONO_2)
An overindulgence in fatty foods, leading to a loss of appetite. *v.*

onoonogiaanga. (R-3 ONO_2)
n.

ono-samono.
The sixth number of a counting game played to determine who is "it".

onge.
Famine. *v.*

ongea. (B-2 ONGE)
v.

ongeonge. (R-- ONGE)
v.

ongeongea. (R-2 ONGE)
v.

oo.
Your [1] several. *ppo.*

oo_1.
Shout. *a.*

oo_2.
Fit to (or into). *a.*

oo_3*.
A ration of food for a long canoe voyage. *n.*

ooanga. (B-1 OO_2)
n.

ooda.
Each person's several. *pto.*

oodou.
Your [3] several. *pp.*

oo tanga.
Too big (clothes), spacious.

ooha. (P-- OHA)
v.

oohaa. (P-2 OHA)
v.

oohalia. (P-2 OHA)
v.

oohanga. (P-1 OHA)
n.

oohia. (B-2 OO_2)
(For a canoe) to be able to navigate on the reef (i.e., the tide not being so low that it is too shallow). *v.*

oohiaanga. (B-3 OO_2)
n.

oohu. (P-- OHU)
v.

oohua. (P-2 OHU)
v.

oohunga. (B-1 OHU)
n.

ooi.
A sound used in communicating at a distance (= "yes?"). *a.*

oo iho (age).
Able to enter, going up (down).

ooinga. (B-1 OOI)
n.

ooiooi. (R-- OOI)
a.

ooiooinga. (R-1 OOI)
n.

ooluu.
Your [2] several. *pp.*

oomea.
Afternoon (late). *a.*

oomeaanga. (B-1 OOMEA)
n.

oonga. (B-1 OO_1)
n.

oooo. (R-- OO_1)
a.

oosonga. (B-1 OSO)
n.

osi.
A seedling; a shoot (of another plant) set aside for planting a seedling. *v.*

osia. (B-2 OSI)
Taken for planting. *v.*

osinga. (B-1 OSI)
n.

osiosi. (R-- OSI)
v.

osiosia. (R-2 OSI)
v.

osiosinga. (R-1 OSI)
n.

oso.
Smell (something) by sniffing, kiss (Polynesian style). *v.*

osoa. (B-2 OSO)
v.

osoanga. (B-1 OSO)
n.

osohia. (B-2 OSO)
v.

osolia. (B-2 OSO)
v.

osongia. (B-2 OSO)
v.

osooso. (R-- OSO)
v.

osoosoa. (R-2 OSO)
v.

osoosoanga. (R-1 OSO)
n.

osoosohia. (R-2 OSO)
v.

osoosolia. (R-2 OSO)
v.

osoosonga. (R-1 OSO)
n.

osoosongia. (R-2 OSO)
v.

ou.
Yes! *a.*

ouaa. (U-- OU)
Yes! Certainly! *a.*

ouou. (R-- OU)
Yes! Yes! *a.*

ovea.
Disheveled (as the chicken feathers on a much-used trolling lure). *v.*

oveaanga. (B-1 OVEA)
n.

oveovea. (R-- OVEA)
v.

oveoveaanga. (R-1 OVEA)
n.

saa_1.
Bad. *mv.*

saa_2.
A share of food (esp. for children). *n.*

saabai.
Lift up and carry; carry (a burden). *v.*

saabaia. (B-2 SAABAI)
v.

saabai moni doo.
Carry a canoe (over the reef at low tide).

saabainga. (B-1 SAABAI)
n.

saabanga. (B-1 $SABA_2$)
n.

saabini.
Wrap up, tie up. *v.*

saabonga. (B-1 SABO)
n.

saabudu. (CF SAA_1)
Fish sp. (= large *saagahinoa*). *n.*

saapala. (P-- SABALA)
a.

saagahinoa. (CF SAA_1)
Fish sp. (= small *saabudu*). *n.*

saaganga. (B-1 SAGA)
n.

saagonga. (B-1 SAGO)
n.

saagule.
Pick head lice. *v.*

saahea.
Be caught (esp. fish) and secured. *a.*

saaheaanga. (B-1 SAAHEA)
n.

saalaa. (E-2 $SALA_1$)
v.

saalani. (P-- SALANI)
v.

saalaninga. (P-1 SALANI)
n.

saalanga. (E-1 $SALA_1$)
n.

saali.
A type of rope (used for climbing breadfruit trees). *n.*

saaliba.
Rush around (of a group of people). *a.*

saalibaanga. (B-1 SAALIBA)
n.

saalinga. (B-1 SALI)
n.

saalingaa nui.
The rainwater which flows down a bent coconut tree (collected for drinking).

saalohia.
Hungry. *v.*

saalohiaanga. (B-1 SAALOHIA)
n.

saalua. (B-2 SALU)
Scraped (a little taken away), scratched. *v.*

saaluanga. (B-1 SALU)
A scratch (on the skin). *n.*

saalulu. (P-- SALULU)
a.

saaluluanga. (P-1 SALULU)
n.

saalunga. (B-1 SALU)
n.

saaminga. (B-1 SAMI)
n.

saamua. (B-2 $SAMU_1$)
v.

saamumu. (P-- SAMUMU)
a.

saamumuanga. (P-1 SAMUMU)
n.

saamunga. (B-1 $SAMU_1$)
—; food, eat heartily. *a.*

saasaagule. (S-- SAAGULE)
v.

saasaagulea. (S-2 SAAGULE)
v.

saasaagulenga. (S-1 SAAGULE)
n.

saasaalohia. (R-- SAALOHIA)
v.

saasaalohiaanga. (R-1 SAALOHIA)
n.

saasanga. (B-1 SASA)
n.

saava.
Skinny, thin (lacking in flesh). *v.*

saavaanga. (B-1 SAAVA)
n.

saavala. (P-- SAVALA)
a.

saavale.
Spit, drool, sputum. *v.*

saavaleanga. (B-1 SAAVALE)
n.

saavale ina.
Fish or meat which is watery in texture and bad-tasting.

saavali. (P-- SAVALI)
v.

saavini. (P-- SAVINI)
a.

saba$_1$.
Be in a precarious position. *v.*

saba$_2$.
Capable (of a person). *v.*

sabaia. (B-2 SAABAI)
v.

sabainga. (B-1 SAABAI)
n.

sabala.
Willing to. *a.*

sabalabala. (R-- SABALA)
Always agreeing with. *a.*

sabalia$_1$. (B-2 SABA$_1$)
Be in a situation in which *saba*$_1$. *v.*

sabalia$_2$. (B-2 SABA$_2$)
Be *saba*. *v.*

sabanaana.
A phosphorescent flash in the water. *v.*

sabasaba. (R-- SABA$_1$)
Unstably balanced. *v.*

sabasabai. (R-- SAABAI)
v.

sabasabaia. (R-2 SAABAI)
v.

sabasabainga. (R-1 SAABAI)
n.

sabasabalia. (R-2 SABA$_1$)
v.

sabeeloi.
Wrap up (something) hastily [obligatorily followed by *ina* in transitive usage]. *v.*

sabeeloinga. (B-1 SABEELOI)
n.

sabinia. (B-2 SAABINI)
v.

sabininga. (B-1 SAABINI)
—; package, bundle (wrapped up). *n.*

sabisabini. (R-- SAABINI)
Wrap up or tie up over and over. *v.*

sabisabinia. (R-2 SAABINI)
v.

sabisabininga. (R-1 SAABINI)
n.

sabo.
Do slowly. *v.*

saboa. (B-2 SABO)
v.

sabolia. (B-2 SABO)
v.

sabosabo. (R-- SABO)
v.

sabosaboa. (R-2 SABO)
v.

sabosabolia. (R-2 SABO)
v.

sabosabonga. (R-1 SABO)
n.

sada.
Each person's. *ptsa.*

sae$_1$.
d.

sae$_2$.
Suffer, be in pain; crave for, desperate. *a.*

saea. (B-2 SAE$_1$)
v.

sae de hadu.
Make a grater (by punching holes in sheet metal).

sae iho.
Tear from the top down; break through the bush (coming downhill).

saele.
Wander aimlessly, to walk around. *v.*

saelea. (B-2 SAELE)
Walked upon. *v.*

saeleanga. (B-1 SAELE)
n.

saelenga. (B-1 SAELE)
—; road, walkway, path (for walking). *n.*

saelesaele. (R-- SAELE)
To wander around continually (from past time to the present). *v.*

saelesaeleanga. (R-1 SAELE)
n.

saelesaelenga. (R-1 SAELE)
n.

sae mai.
Break through the bush (toward one).

saenga$_1$. (B-1 SAE$_1$)
n.

saenga$_2$. (B-1 SAE$_2$)
n.

saesae$_1$. (R-- SAE$_1$)
v.

saesae$_2$. (R-- SAE$_2$)
a.

saesaea. (R-2 SAE$_1$)
v.

saesaele. (S-- SAELE)
To wander around continually (doing so at present and likely to be doing so in the future). *v.*

saesaelea. (S-2 SAELE)
To be continually walked upon. *v.*

saesaeleanga. (S-1 SAELE)
n.

saesaelenga. (S-1 SAELE)
n.

saesaenga$_1$. (R-1 SAE$_1$)
n.

saesaenga$_2$. (R-1 SAE$_2$)
n.

saga.
Glide (in the air); to overhang (of something flat). *a.*

saga gee.
saga away from; extend out in space.

saga gi daha.
saga away from; extend out in space.

sagana.
Watch carefully, keep an eye on. *v.*

saganaa. (B-2 SAGANA)
v.

saganaa iho goe.
Watch out!

saganaanga. (B-1 SAGANA)
n.

sagasaga. (R-- SAGA)
a.

sagasagaanga. (R-1 SAGA)
n.

sagasagana. (R-- SAGANA)
v.

sagasaganaa. (R-2 SAGANA)
v.

sagasaganaanga. (R-1 SAGANA)
n.

sagea.
To do something without regard for others (because one is excited). *v.*

sageaanga. (B-1 SAGEA)
n.

sagea gee.
Extremely *sagea.*

sagesagea. (R-- SAGEA)
v.

sagesageaanga. (R-1 SAGEA)
n.

sagisagili.
To say dirty words to someone. *v.*

sagisagilianga. (B-1 SAGISAGILI)
n.

sago.
Tough (like meat); stiff (like a heavy fishing pole). *v.*

sagu.
My. *pdsa.*

sagulaa.
Fish sp.: sailfish or marlin [generic name]. *n.*

sagulaa-dagua.
Fish sp.

sagulaa-saamono.
Fish sp.

sagulea. (B-2 SAAGULE)
v.

sagulenga. (B-1 SAAGULE)
n.

sagusagule. (R-- SAAGULE)
v.

sagusagulea. (R-2 SAAGULE)
v.

sagusagulenga. (R-1 SAAGULE)
n.

sahe.
Any material used to absorb a menstrual flow. *n.*

sahole. (B-- $SAHOLE_1$)
Fish sp.: mountain bass. *n.*

sahudu.
Fish sp.: sea bass. *n.*

sai_1.
Wrap, cover up (with several layers). *v.*

sai_2.
Group of (e.g., *agu sai* 'my children'). *n.*

saia. (B-2 SAI_1)
v.

saibo.
Rush around (of a group of people). *a.*

saibonga. (B-1 SAIBO)
n.

saibo saele.
Rush around aimlessly (of a group of people).

saidule.
Wrapped up or covered up completely. *v.*

saiduleanga. (B-1 SAIDULE)
n.

sai moni.
A fleet of canoes.

sainga. (B-1 SAI_1)
n.

saiolo.
A sail [from Eng. "sail"?]. *n.*

saiolo duli magaga.
A type of string figure.

saisai. (R-- SAI_1)
v.

saisaia. (R-2 SAI_1)
v.

saisaidule. (R-- SAIDULE)
v.

saisaiduleanga. (R-1 SAIDULE)
n.

saisainga. (R-1 SAI_1)
n.

sala. (B-- $SALA_2$)
Mistake, error, accident. *n.*

salaa.
Fish sp.: flying fish. *n.*

Salaboli. (B-- SALABOLI)
May. *n.*

salahagi. (B-- $SALA_{1a}$)
An expedition to look for valuable drifting objects, either in the lagoon or in the open sea near the atoll. *v.*

salahaginga. (B-1 $SALA_{1a}$)
n.

salani.
Beginning to ripen (indicated by a yellowish color—of, e.g., bananas and papayas). *v.*

salani ange.
Just a little *salani.*

salaninga. (B-1 SALANI)
n.

salasala. (R-- $SALA_1$)
v.

salasalaa. (R-2 $SALA_1$)
v.

salasalahagi. (R-- $SALA_{1a}$)
Repeatedly *salahagi.* *v.*

salasalahaginga. (R-1 $SALA_{1a}$)
n.

salasalani. (R-- SALANI)
Becoming *salani* in one part, but not yet *salani* all over. *v.*

salasalaninga. (R-1 SALANI)
n.

salasalanga. (R-1 $SALA_1$)
n.

salau.
Inclined, slanting, not straight, not perpendicular to. *a.*

salaunga. (B-1 SALAU)
n.

sali.
Flow, seep. *a.*

salibaadaa.
A type of low cloud. *v.*

salibaadaanga. (B-1 SALIBAADAA)
n.

sali daadaa.
To sweat.

sali de usu.
Runny nose.

sali dodo.
Bleed.

sali tae.
Intractable watery diarrhea.

sali gee.
Flow away.

sali loimada.
To tear (in the eyes because, e.g., of smoke).

salisali. (R-- SALI)
a.

salisalinga. (R-1 SALI)
n.

sali ssaavale.
Salivate.

salu.
Scrape (something), plane (something), scrape off (with an object), peel (with a knife toward one). *v.*

salua. (B-2 SALU)
Scraped (a lot taken away), peeled (a little amount taken off), planed. *v.*

salulu.
The noise of an explosion or loud report (as when two things collide). *a.*

saluluanga. (B-1 SALULU)
n.

salu mai.
Make smaller by planing or scraping.

salusalu. (R-- SALU)
v.

sami.
d.

samisami. (R-- SAMI)
v.

samisaminga. (R-1 SAMI)
n.

samouli.
The spirit of a human being after his death. *n.*

Samouli-daane. (DAANE, SAMOULI)
The name of *Vave* after his death. *nn.*

samu. (B-- $SAMU_2$)
Gossip, slander. *v.*

samua. (B-2 $SAMU_2$)
Slandered; to have been an object of gossip. *v.*

samuanga. (B-1 $SAMU_2$)
n.

samulia. (B-2 $SAMU_1$)
v.

samemu.
The noise of an explosion or collision [= same meaning as *salulu*]. *a.*

samumuanga. (B-1 SAMUMU)
n.

samusamu. (R-- $SAMU_1$)
v.

samusamua. (R-2 $SAMU_1$)
v.

samusamulia. (R-2 $SAMU_1$)
v.

samusamunga. (R-1 $SAMU_1$)
n.

sana.
His, hers, its. *pdsa.*

saniba.
Fish sp.: silversides. *n.*

sanosano. (R-- SANO)
a.

sanosanoanga. (R-1 SANO)
n.

sanga.
Have sexual intercourse, fornicate. *v.*

sangaa. (B-2 SANGA)
v.

sangatai.
Mollusk sp.: *Spondylus* sp. *n.*

sangalia. (B-2 SANGA)
v.

sanganga. (B-1 SANGA)
n.

sangasanga. (R-- SANGA)
v.

sangasangaa. (R-2 SANGA)
v.

sangasangalia. (R-2 SANGA)
v.

sangasanganga. (R-1 SANGA)
n.

sango.
Wild (of animals scared of humans). *a.*

sangoanga. (B-1 SANGO)
n.

sangolia. (B-2 SANGO)
a.

sangosango. (R-- SANGO)
a.

sangosangoanga. (R-1 SANGO)
n.

sangosangolia. (R-2 SANGO)
a.

sao$_1$.
d.

sao$_2$.
Get out from or through, escape. *a.*

saoanga. (B-1 SAO$_1$)
n.

sao de lahalaha.
More wide than long.

sao de leo.
Clear in elocution or in one's singing voice.

sao de looloa.
Rectangular (not square), oval.

sao gainga.
Sweep or clean up trash.

saohia$_1$. (B-2 SAO$_1$)
v.

saohia$_2$. (B-2 SAO$_2$)
Have time for, free, available. *v.*

saohiaanga. (B-3 SAO$_2$)
n.

saonga. (B-1 SAO$_2$)
n.

saosao$_1$. (R-- SAO$_1$)
v.

saosao$_2$. (R-- SAO$_2$)
—; good at penetrating (as a canoe with a narrow prow). *a.*

saosaoanga. (R-1 SAO$_1$)
n.

saosaohia$_1$. (R-2 SAO$_1$)
v.

saosaohia$_2$. (R-2 SAO$_2$)
—; [redup. form of *saohia$_2$*]. *v.*

saosaohiaanga. (R-3 SAO$_2$)
n.

saosaonga. (R-1 SAO$_2$)
n.

sasa.
To talk or move in one's sleep, or when delerious. *a.*

sasaanimadava. (?)
Fish sp.: shark sp.? *n.*

sasae. (T-- SAE$_1$)
—; habitually *ssae$_1$*. *v.*

sasa gee.
Impetuous in act or movement (leading to frequent error).

sasao. (T-- SAO$_2$)
Escape one after the other. *a.*

sasaonga. (T-1 SAO$_2$)
n.

sasau. (T-- SAU$_1$)
Increasing in velocity (of wind). *v.*

sasaudia. (T-2 SAU$_1$)
v.

sasaunga. (T-1 SAU$_1$)
n.

sassabe. (R-- SSABE)
About to leave, prepare to leave. *a.*

sassabeanga. (R-1 SSABE)
n.

sassano. (T-- SANO)
Becoming *ssano*. *a.*

sassanoanga. (T-1 SANO)
n.

sassasa. (R-- SASA)
— ; stammer (from nervousness). *a.*

sassasaanga. (R-1 SASA)
n.

sau$_1$.
d.

sau$_2$.
[An abbreviated form of *saulaba*]. *n.*

sau$_3$.
Your. *pdsa.*

sauaa.
Power (electrical, magical, etc.); powerful (esp. supernaturally); very much [MV]. *a.*

sauaanga. (B-1 SAUAA)
n.

sau aloalo.
Echo.

sau alohenua.
Eddying of the wind (constantly changing direction) close to land.

saubaligi.
Graceful in dancing. *v.*

saudia. (B-2 SAU$_1$)
Be exposed to the wind (not sheltered). *v.*

saudiaanga. (B-3 SAU$_1$)
n.

sauduu.
Mermaid. *n.*

saugalo. (B-- GALO$_{3a}$)
Stir. *v.*

saugaloa. (B-2 GALO$_{3a}$)
v.

saugalonga. (B-1 GALO$_{3a}$)
n.

saugalo saele.
Search for here and there, wander around looking for.

saulaba.
Parent-in-law, child-in-law, mother-in-law, father-in-law, son-in-law, daughter-in-law. *n.*

sauligi.
A type of adze (with a rotatable head). *n.*

saulolua. (?)
Fish sp.: triggerfish. *n.*

sau makaga.
Blow steadily (of wind).

sau makaga de madangi.
The blowing of wind steadily (for a long time) from one direction.

saunoa.
Completely, very. *mv.*

saunga.
Having an unpleasant body odor. *a.*

sausau$_1$. (R-- SAU$_1$)
v.

sausau$_2$. (R-- SAU$_3$)
Fish sp.: lion-fish. *n.*

sausauaa. (R-- SAUAA)
a.

sausauaanga. (R-1 SAUAA)
n.

sausaubaligi. (R-- SAUBALIGI)
Always *saubaligi.* *v.*

sausaudia. (R-2 SAU$_1$)
Continually blown upon (by the wind). *v.*

sausaudiaanga. (R-3 SAU$_1$)
n.

sausaugalo. (R-- GALO$_{3a}$)
v.

sausaugaloa. (R-2 GALO$_{3a}$)
v.

sausaugalonga. (R-1 GALO$_{3a}$)
n.

sausaunga$_1$. (R-1 SAU$_1$)
n.

sausaunga$_2$. (R-- SAUNGA)
Continually *saunga.* *a.*

sauvalovalo. (B-- VALO$_{1a}$)
Echo. *v.*

sauvalovalonga. (B-1 VALO$_{1a}$)
n.

savaa.
Soon (will happen). *a.*

savala.
Interested in, enjoys. *a.*

savali.
Hungry. *v.*

savalinga. (B-1 SAVALI)
n.

savasavaa. (R-- SAVAA)
Getting closer to the time (of happening). *v.*

savasavala. (R-- SAVALA)
Becoming interested in; getting to enjoy. *a.*

savasavale. (R-- SAAVALE)
a.

savasavaleanga. (R-1 SAAVALE)
n.

savasavali. (R-- SAVALI)
Always hungry. *v.*

savasavalinga. (R-1 SAVALI)
n.

savini.
Run, move fast (as fish, or a canoe). *a.*

savini dua.
Run backwards, move backwards fast.

savini gee.
Run away.

se.
GENERAL ARTICLE [SING.]; it is a ... *ma.*

seaamonga. (XCO AAMONGA)
A unit of (twenty) coconuts for making *huaahuu*. *n.*

seada.
Each person's. *ptsa.*

se aha.
What is it?

se aha au naa.
You are wrong! That's not right! I don't agree!

se aha ga hai.
It's not possible! Don't worry about it! (I don't think so.).

se aha goe.
You're a nobody!

sebaga. (?)
Tens of billions. *an.*

se biho.
Clever (scheme or trick).

sebu.
Seen on the surface of the sea from time to time. *a.*

sebua. (B-2 SEBU)
v.

sebuaanga. (B-3 SEBU)
n.

sebugi. (?)
Billions. *an.*

sebusebu. (R-- SEBU)
a.

sebusebua. (R-2 SEBU)
v.

sebusebuaanga. (R-3 SEBU)
n.

sedaadeu.
Our [incl. 3]. *pds.*

sedaau.
Our [incl. 2]. *pds.*

see$_1$.
Cry aloud. *a.*

see$_2$.
Barely, just barely [obligatorily followed by *loo huu*, *donu huu*, or *ma de*]. *a.*

seeanga. (B-1 SEE$_1$)
n.

see boiboi saele.
Stagger about (from a head injury), move as though unconscious.

Seedaa. (B-- SEEDAA)
October. *n.*

seegenga. (B-1 SEGE)
n.

seelea. (E-2 SELE$_2$)
v.

seelenga$_1$. (B-1 SELE$_1$)
n.

seelenga$_2$. (B-1 SELE$_2$)
n.

seelunga. (B-1 SELU)
—; the manner (of an individual) of doing something. *n.*

seeninga. (B-1 SENI)
n.

seenga. (B-1 SEE$_1$)
n.

seenganga. (B-1 SENGA)
n.

seesee$_1$. (R-- SEE$_1$)
a.

seesee$_2$. (R-- SEE$_3$)
Walk, move slowly (as a fish). *v.*

seeseeanga$_1$. (R-1 SEE$_1$)
n.

seeseeanga$_2$. (R-1 SEE$_3$)
n.

seesee haangoda saele.
Look for girls.

seesee hagadaahao.
Walk (for recreation).

seesee hagadibadiba.
Waddle.

seeseenga$_1$. (R-1 SEE$_1$)
n.

seeseenga$_2$. (R-1 SEE$_3$)
n.

seevoivoi. (B-- SEE$_{1a}$)
Cry uncontrollably (hysterically inaccessible). *a.*

seevoivoia. (B-2 SEE$_{1a}$) .
To be in the state of *seevoivoi.* *v.*

seevoivoinga. (B-1 SEE$_{1a}$)
n.

se gainga.
Abundant.

se galubu.
Very fast.

se gava.
Know (how to do something) well.

sege.
Slip, slide, to ride, to surf. *v.*

sege de --.
Plenty of —, a lot of —.

sege de gauanga.
Dislocated thigh bone.

sege gee.
Slip or slide away from.

segesege. (R-- SEGE)
—; slippery. *v.*

segesegenga. (R-1 SEGE)
n.

se goo.
Adept at.

segoodo --. (B-- SEGOODO)
To have just —. *d.*

seguli. (?)
Hundreds of thousands. *an.*

se hagabau.
Do deliberately (esp. something bad); willful, mean.

se hia?.
Just how many?

se hono.
Fit well or properly.

seisei. (R-- SEI)
Fish sp.: pipefish. *n.*

selaadeu.
Their [3]. *pds.*

selaau.
Their [2]. *pds.*

sele$_1$.
Lasso, noose; to catch with a lasso or noose. *v.*

sele$_2$.
To chop down. *v.*

selea$_1$. (B-2 SELE$_1$)
v.

selea$_2$. (B-2 SELE$_2$)
v.

sele gi tonu.
Make sure of.

seleia. (B-2 SELE$_2$)
To cut one's hand by a hand-held fish line, when it is taken by a fish. *v.*

selesele$_1$. (R-- SELE$_1$)
v.

selesele$_2$. (R-- SELE$_2$)
v.

seleselea. (R-2 SELE$_1$)
v.

seleseleia (R-2 SELE$_2$)
v.

seleselenga$_1$. (R-1 SELE$_1$)
n.

seleselenga$_2$. (R-1 SELE$_2$)
n.

seloo. (?)
Millions. *an.*

selu.
To comb (hair). *v.*

selua. (B-2 SELU)
v.

selumia. (B-2 SELU)
v.

seluselu. (R-- SELU)
v.

seluselua. (R-2 SELU)
v.

seluselumia. (R-2 SELU)
v.

seluselunga. (R-1 SELU)
n.

semaadeu.
Our [excl. 3]. *pds.*

semaau.
Our [excl. 2]. *pds.*

semada. (?)
Tens of thousands. *an.*

se me be hee.
Extraordinary or unusual (esp. in size).

se me pilo aha.
Don't bother!

se me gi hee.
In which direction is the current running?

se mouli dangada.
Rascal.

semuna. (?)
Hundreds of millions. *an.*

seni.
Sleep. *a.*

seni ahiahi.
Go to bed early (in the evening).

seni alaala.
Sleep fitfully (esp. because one is thinking about having to arise early); wake up repeatedly owing to anxiety.

seni ange.
Rest up for (e.g., the next day's work).

seni tao.
Sleep soundly.

seni gi de ao.
Sleep late (into daytime).

seni iho.
Take a nap, stay overnight (away from home).

seni magau.
Sleep soundly (owing to exhaustion).

seniseni. (R-- SENI)
—; sleepyhead. *a.*

seniseninga. (R-1 SENI)
n.

senga.
Crazy; dumb, foolish, ignorant; senseless, drunk. *a.*

sengaa. (?)
Tens of millions. *an.*

sengalia. (B-2 SENGA)
Deceived, fooled; made dependent upon (e.g., gifts). *v.*

senga maido.
Stupidly unafraid of danger (like *maido*).

senga manu.
Stupid (like an animal).

sengasenga. (R-- SENGA)
a.

sengasengaanga. (R-1 SENGA)
n.

seoda.
Each person's. *ptso.*

seseu. (T-- SEU)
Push (now and into the future) [pl. only]. *v.*

seseua. (T-2 SEU)
v.

seseunga. (T-1 SEU)
n.

seu.
d.

seua. (B-2 SEU)
v.

seunga. (B-1 SEU)
n.

se ungaa husi gee.
Do something different from that which was intended.

seuseu. (R-- SEU)
v.

seuseua. (R-2 SEU)
v.

seuseunga. (R-1 SEU)
n.

siba$_1$.
Move to one side (involuntarily) while walking. *v.*

siba$_2$.
Fish sp. (small flying fish). *n.*

sibalia. (B-2 SIBA$_1$)
v.

sibasiba. (R-- SIBA$_1$)
Walk off-balance. *v.*

sibasibaanga. (R-1 SIBA$_1$)
n.

sibasibalia. (R-2 SIBA$_1$)
v.

siga.
To make a fire with a fire plow; to make a net with a net needle spool [called *siga*]; to escape (of fish) from a net (through its holes); sew up a hole (in clothing). *v.*

siga de mamu.
An escape of fish from a fishing net (through its holes).

sigahia. (B-2 SIGA)
v.

sigale.
Scull (a boat). *v.*

sigaleanga. (B-1 SIGALE)
n.

sigale saele.
Search for.

sigalia. (B-2 SIGA)
v.

sigasiga. (R-- SIGA)
v.

sigasigaanga. (R-1 SIGA)
n.

sigasigahia. (R-2 SIGA)
v.

sigasigale. (R-- SIGALE)
v.

sigasigaleanga. (R-1 SIGALE)
n.

sigasigalia. (R-2 SIGA)
v.

sigi.
Transfer (from one place to another), transplant; a technique of finishing a mat edge; to assist in the delivery of a baby (by manually extracting it from the birth canal); to tack a canoe (by transferring the mast from one end of the canoe to the other). *v.*

sigia. (B-2 SIGI)
v.

sigidaumaha. (XCO SIGI)
Collection (in church), offering (in church), sacrifice, tithe. *v.*

sigi de hagahala.
A technique of finishing a mat edge.

sigidia. (B-2 SIGI)
v.

sigilia. (B-2 SIGI)
v.

sigi manu.
To transplant a plant.

sigisigi. (R-- SIGI)
v.

sigisigia. (R-2 SIGI)
v.

sigisigidia. (R-2 SIGI)
v.

sigisigilia. (R-2 SIGI)
v.

sigisigi mai (adu, ange).
Say bad things about one to one's face.

sigisiginga. (R-1 SIGI)
n.

sigo.
To catch (e.g., a ball); pull in a line; move a canoe to another spot when fishing (i.e., to pull in one's lines first); to climb a tree without using climbing aids [*gaahanga*]. *v.*

sigoa. (B-2 SIGO)
v.

sigo de muna.
Remember what one has heard.

sigohia. (B-2 SIGO)
v.

sigo ina uavesi.
Don't forget!

sigolia. (B-2 SIGO)
v.

sigosigo. (R-- SIGO)
—; juggle. *v.*

sigosigoa. (R-2 SIGO)
v.

sigosigohia. (R-2 SIGO)
v.

sigosigolia. (R-2 SIGO)
v.

sigosigonga. (R-1 SIGO)
n.

sii.
A stream or jet of water; dysentery. *a.*

siia. (B-2 $SISI_1$)
v.

siia gi moana ngaadai.
Drift downwind, away from land.

$siianga_1$. (B-1 $SISI_1$)
— ; writing (on paper); a letter (of the alphabet); a character (written symbol). *n.*

siibanga. (B-1 $SIBA_1$)
n.

sii bido lua.
Vomiting and having diarrhea at the same time ('flowing from both ends').

sii diidii.
Urinate.

sii tae.
Diarrhea which escapes without one realizing (caused by eating oily fish).

sii talaa umada.
A wash of waves at the prow of a canoe, when it is sailing fast.

siiganga. (B-1 SIGA)
n.

siiginga. (B-1 SIGI)
n.

siigonga. (B-1 SIGO)
—; a coil of rope. *n.*

siili.
A stick used in a children's game. *n.*

siilia. (B-2 $SILI_2$)
v.

$siilinga_1$. (B-1 $SILI_1$)
n.

$siilinga_2$. (B-1 $SILI_2$)
n.

$siilinga_3$. (B-1 $SILI_3$)
n.

siilinga a muna.
Trial or formal inquiry.

sii mada daahaa.
A fine jet of water.

siinga. (B-1 SII)
n.

siinganga. (B-1 SINGA)
n.

$siisii_1$. (R-- SII)
a.

$siisii_2$. (T-- $SISI_1$)
Fishing (with a pole); fishing pole. *v.*

siisiia. (T-2 $SISI_1$)
Fished in (place). *v.*

siisiianga. (T-1 $SISI_1$)
n.

siisiinga. (R-1 SII)
n.

sii valavala.
Spray.

siiviivii. (B-- VIIVII_a)
A way of singing a child to sleep. *v.*

siiviiviia. (B-2 VIIVII_a)
v.

siiviiviinga. (B-1 VIIVII_a)
n.

siivinga. (B-1 SIVI)
n.

sila.
Look for. *v.*

silaanga. (B-1 SILA)
n.

silasila. (R-- SILA)
Look around for. *v.*

silasilaanga. (R-1 SILA)
n.

sileia. (B-2 SILA)
—; look at that! *v.*

sileia doo soa.
Look, your neighbor is competing against you!

silesileia. (R-2 SILA)
v.

sili$_1$.
Stopped, ended. *a.*

sili$_2$.
d.

sili$_3$.
To pass a point (in space) or a stage of development. *a.*

silia. (B-2 SILI$_3$)
a.

sili gee.
Stand out from (others in a group) in distance or height.

sili iho.
Have just stopped; calm down (of a person).

sili muna.
Inquisitive (prone to ask too many questions).

silisili$_1$. (R-- SILI$_1$)
Drawing to an end. *a.*

silisili$_2$. (R-- SILI$_2$)
v.

silisili$_3$. (R-- SILI$_3$)
v.

silisilia$_1$. (R-2 SILI$_2$)
—; ask around. *v.*

silisilia$_2$. (R-2 SILI$_3$)
a.

silisilinga$_1$. (R-1 SILI$_1$)
n.

silisilinga$_2$. (R-1 SILI$_2$)
n.

silisilinga$_3$. (R-1 SILI$_3$)
n.

silisilivaahea. (R-- SILIVAAHEA)
Frequently *silivaahea.* *v.*

silisilivaahenga. (R-1 SILIVAAHEA)
n.

silivaahea.
Wander about with no fixed abode. *v.*

silivaahenga. (B-1 SILIVAAHEA)
n.

sina.
White (or grey) hair (appearing in old age). *n.*

sinaa. (B-2 SINA)
Having white hair. *v.*

sinaanga. (B-3 SINA)
n.

sinasinaa. (R-2 SINA)
White-headed; old (of living things); big (of animals). *v.*

sinasinaanga. (R-1 SINA)
n.

singa.
Overhand. *v.*

singa gee.
Lean away from.

singalia. (B-2 SINGA)
Overhung. *v.*

singa mai (adu, ange).
Come carrying.

singano.
The flower of the pandanus tree. *v.*

singasinga. (R-- SINGA)
To wave back and forth (as a coconut tree in the wind). *v.*

singasingaanga. (R-1 SINGA)
n.

singasingalia. (R-2 SINGA)
v.

singa sogosogo.
Do something (e.g., work) all by oneself.

sio.
Waterspout (esp. the air causing it); whirlwind. *n.*

sisi$_1$.
To move one end of something long and thin by pressure on the other end; to lift a fishing pole; to write (with a pen or pencil); cut copra. *v.*

sisi$_2$.
Mollusk sp.: *Neritidae* spp. *n.*

sisi baalasi.
Printing (block letters).

sisi gaadinga.
To cut copra.

sisi galisi.
Striped (with thin lines).

sisi lima.
Longhand (writing).

sissisi. (R-- SISI$_1$)
Striped (having stripes). *a.*

sissisianga. (R-1 SISI$_1$)
n.

siva.
Nine. *an.*

siva-dahanga.
The ninth number of a counting game played to determine who is "it"

sivi.
Give up. *a.*

sivisivi. (R-- SIVI)
a.

sivisivinga. (R-1 SIVI)
n.

soa.
A friend; many (people). *a.*

soaa lodo.
The paddlers of a canoe which is engaged in catching flying fish.

soaanga. (B-1 SOA)
n.

soa hagaaloha.
A good friend.

soasoa. (R-- SOA)
Increasing in number (people). *a.*

soasoaanga. (R-1 SOA)
n.

sobaga.
Fish sp.: tang. *n.*

sobalo.
Fish sp.: needlefish. *n.*

sobo.
Rise up (as the sun), get up, jump up. *a.*

sobo de laa.
Rising of the sun.

sobolia. (B-2 SOBO)
v.

sobosobo. (R-- SOBO)
a.

sobosobolia. (R-2 SOBO)
v.

sobosobonga. (R-1 SOBO)
n.

sodo.
Each person's. *ptso.*

soe.
Straight, not crooked; level. *a.*

soe age.
Straight up; decide (for oneself).

soe daa dahi.
Straight as can be.

soe iho.
Straight down; decided for one by the will of God.

soe lodo modu.
To remain (or sit, or stand) motionless (as when praying).

soe mai.
Decided for one by the will of God.

soenga. (B-1 SOE)
n.

soesoe. (R-- SOE)
Straight or level all over (as a playing field); somewhat level or straight. *a.*

soesoe gulu.
A young breadfruit tree.

soesoenga. (R-1 SOE)
n.

sogoisi.
[Var. of *dogoisi*]. *a.*

sogoisi loo huu.
[Var. of *dogoisi loo huu*].

sogosogo.
Alone, only, by oneself; each. *v.*

sogosogoisi. (R-- SOGOISI)
[Var. of *dogodogoisi*]. *a.*

sogu.
My. *pdso.*

soi$_1$ (adu, mai, ange). (B-- SOI$_1$)
Assume. *d.*

soi$_2$.
d.

soia. (B-2 SOI$_2$)
v.

soi adu --.
Expect that — but.

soinga. (B-1 SOI$_2$)
n.

soisoi$_1$ (adu, mai, ange). (R-- SOI$_1$)
d.

soisoi$_2$. (R-- SOI$_2$)
v.

soisoia. (R-2 SOI$_2$)
v.

soisoinga. (R-1 SOI$_2$)
n.

solasola. (R-- SOLA)
Not homogenous or smooth (as lumpy dough, or the grated surface of taro). *v.*

solasolaanga. (R-1 SOLA)
n.

solo.
To grate or file (something); to launch or beach a canoe by dragging it along the shore; a type of prepared food (made from grated taro). *v.*

soloa. (B-2 SOLO)
v.

soloanga. (B-1 SOLO)
n.

solona. (B-2 SOLO)
v.

solonga. (B-1 SOLO)
n.

solosolo. (R-- SOLO)
v.

solosoloa. (R-2 SOLO)
v.

solosoloanga. (R-1 SOLO)
n.

solosolona. (R-2 SOLO)
v.

solosolonga. (R-1 SOLO)
n.

solovaani.
Thin and straight (of a person) [e.g., having flat buttocks — considered ugly]. *v.*

somo$_1$.
Grow, develop; coconut apple. *a.*

somo$_2$.
d.

somoanga. (B-1 SOMO$_2$)
n.

somo boi.
Grow abnormally (having defects).

somo dae.
Fully mature coconut apple.

somodia. (B-2 SOMO$_2$)
v.

somo haahine.
A fleshy (non-muscular) man.

somolia. (B-2 SOMO$_2$)
v.

somosomo$_1$. (R-- SOMO$_1$)
Grow fast or well anywhere (e.g., as a weed). *a.*

somosomo$_2$. (R-- SOMO$_2$)
v.

somosomoa. (R-2 SOMO$_2$)
v.

somosomoanga. (R-1 SOMO$_2$)
n.

somosomodia. (R-2 SOMO$_2$)
v.

somosomolia. (R-2 SOMO$_2$)
v.

somosomonga$_1$. (R-1 SOMO$_1$)
n.

somosomonga$_2$. (R-1 SOMO$_2$)
n.

sono.
His, hers, its. *pdso.*

songagi.
A bad sort of person. *n.*

songosongo. (R-- SSONGO)
—; genitals (of males or females). *n.*

soo.
Your [1]. *pdso.*

soobonga. (B-1 SOBO)
—; the direction or spot from which the sun rises; rising (of the sun, etc.). *n.*

soodo.
Lead (metal), bullet; [the etymology of this word is obscure]. *n.*

soodou.
Your [3]. *pds.*

sooloa. (E-2 SOLO)
v.

soolona. (E-2 SOLO)
v.

soolonga. (E-1 SOLO)
—; spouse [rarely heard]. *n.*

sooluu.
Your [2]. *pds.*

soomoa. (B-2 $SOMO_2$)
v.

soomonga$_1$. (B-1 $SOMO_1$)
—; build (of the body). *n.*

soomonga$_2$. (B-1 $SOMO_2$)
n.

soosoa.
Outrigger float lashings (complementary to the connecting pegs). *n.*

soosoaanga. (B-1 SOOSOA)
n.

soosobo. (T-- SOBO)
Get up [pl.], jump up [pl.]. *a.*

soosobolia. (T-2 SOBO)
v.

soosobonga. (T-1 SOBO)
n.

sou.
A gust of wind. *v.*

sou daane.
A sudden strong gust of wind.

sou hahine.
A steady, light gust of wind.

sounga. (B-1 SOU)
n.

ssaba. (P-- $SABA_2$)
v.

ssabe.
Leave, go away. *a.*

ssabe age.
Eat.

ssabeanga. (B-1 SSABE)
n.

ssabo. (P-- SABO)
v.

ssae$_1$. (E-- SAE_1)
Rip, tear, deflower (a virgin). *v.*

ssae$_2$. (P-- SAE_2)
—; the sensation felt in the teeth when eating lemon. *a.*

ssae aalanga.
Sore in the muscles.

ssae de hine.
To deflower a girl.

ssae de leo.
To project one's voice better (e.g., after clearing one's throat).

ssae de manava.
Struggle to breathe.

ssaenga. (P-1 SAE_2)
n.

ssaga. (P-- SAGA)
a.

ssaga bau.
[Var. of *se hagabau*].

ssago. (P-- SAGO)
v.

ssahu.
Inquisitive, mischievous (as a child). *a.*

ssahuanga. (B-1 SSAHU)
n.

ssai. (E-- SAI_1)
Wrap or cover completely. *v.*

ssala$_1$. (E-- $SALA_1$)
Look for, search, hunt for. *v.*

ssala$_2$. (E-- $SALA_2$)
n.

ssali. (P-- SALI)
a.

ssalu. (E-- SALU)
salu at one time or energetically. *v.*

ssami. (E-- SAMI)
Eat. *v.*

ssami age.
Eat a snack.

ssamu. (E-- $SAMU_1$)
Lick. *v.*

ssano. (E-- SANO)
Know about, be acquainted with. *a.*

ssanoanga. (E-1 SANO)
n.

ssano i de ia.
Known by him.

ssanga. (E-- SANGA)
Lower longitudinal tie beam purlin. *n.*

ssango. (P-- SANGO)
a.

ssangoanga. (P-1 SANGO)
n.

ssangolia. (P-2 SANGO)
v.

$ssao_1$. (E-- SAO_1)
Sweep, clean up. *v.*

$ssao_2$. (P-- SAO_2)
a.

$ssaoanga_1$. (E-1 SAO_1)
n.

$ssaonga_2$. (P-1 SAO_2)
n.

ssasa. (P-- SASA)
a.

ssau. (E-- SAU_1)
Blow (of the wind). *v.*

ssaunga. (E-1 SAU_1)
n.

ssave.
Fish sp.: flying fish. *n.*

ssave-a-bao.
Fish sp.: flying fish.

ssave de loolodo.
Flying fish inside the lagoon.

ssave haula.
To roast *ssave* (in the fire of a torch).

$ssee_1$. (P-- SEE_1)
a.

$ssee_2$. (P-- SEE_2)
a.

$ssee_3$. (E-- SEE_3)
To lurch, to move sideways; to wish to be carried (of a baby). *a.*

sseeanga. (E-1 SEE_3)
n.

ssee de hiigai.
Famished, ravenous.

ssee gee.
Veer from an intended trajectory.

sseevanga. (B-1 SSEVA)
n.

ssege. (P-- SEGE)
a.

ssege tama.
Miscarriage, abortion (spontaneous).

ssele. (E-- $SELE_2$)
Cut (something); make an incision. *v.*

ssele i de niho.
Damn it!

ssema. (E-- SEMA)
Jellyfish sp. *n.*

sseni. (P-- SENI)
a.

$ssenga_a$. (P-- SENGA)
a.

$ssenga_b$. (E-- SENGA)
The streamer on a trolling lure. *v.*

sseu. (E-- SEU)
Push violently. *v.*

sseu gee.
Push away, push aside (in one direction).

sseunga. (E-1 SEU)
n.

sseva.
Scarce (applied usually only to *ssave*). *a.*

ssevalia. (B-2 SSEVA)
v.

ssiba. (P-- $SIBA_1$)
v.

ssibalia. (P-2 $SIBA_1$)
v.

ssigo. (E-- SIGO)
Catch on to, understand; clever, a fast learner. *a.*

ssii$_1$. (P-- SII)
—; broken in many pieces (as glass when dropped). *a.*

ssii$_2$. (B-- SSII)
A hissing sound [used to indicate disapproval (esp. to bothersome children, or to chase chickens)]. *a.*

ssiigonga. (E-1 SIGO)
n.

ssii mommomo.
Broken up into small pieces.

ssiinga$_1$. (P-1 SII)
n.

ssiinga$_2$. (B-1 SSII)
n.

ssiinganga. (P-1 SINGA)
n.

ssiisii. (R-- SSII)
a.

ssiisiinga. (R-1 SSII)
n.

ssila. (P-- SILA)
v.

ssilaanga. (P-1 SILA)
n.

ssili$_1$. (P-- SILI$_1$)
a.

ssili$_2$. (E-- SILI$_2$)
Ask. *v.*

ssili$_3$. (P-- SILI$_3$)
a.

ssili age.
Address a question to a group.

ssili mada.
To faint, be unconscious.

ssinga. (P-- SINGA)
v.

ssingalia. (P-2 SINGA)
v.

Ssiva-malama. (MALAMA, SIVA)
September ('ninth month'). *nt.*

ssivi. (P-- SIVI)
a.

ssobo. (E-- SOBO)
Rise (of stars, or of the moon or sun). *a.*

ssoe. (P-- SOE)
a.

ssoenga. (P-1 SOE)
n.

ssoga.
[Var. of *ssogo*]. *v.*

ssogaanga. (B-1 SSOGA)
[Var. of *ssogoanga*]. *n.*

ssogalia. (B-2 SSOGA)
[Var. of *ssogolia*]. *v.*

ssogo.
Grated raw taro which has dried out. *v.*

ssogoanga. (B-1 SSOGO)
n.

ssogolia. (B-2 SSOGO)
To be *ssogo*. *v.*

ssoi. (E-- SOI$_2$)
To foretell a death by words or actions (which cause death). *v.*

ssoia. (E-2 SOI$_2$)
v.

ssoinga. (E-1 SOI$_2$)
n.

ssolo. (E-- SOLO)
Wipe, scrub, clean up (by wiping), erase. *v.*

ssomo$_1$. (P-- SOMO$_1$)
a.

ssomo$_2$. (E-- SOMO$_2$)
Suck one's finger. *v.*

ssongo.
Stink. *v.*

ssuanga. (E-1 SUU$_{1a}$)
Stained in one place. *n.*

ssui. (B-- SUU$_1$)
Wet. *a.*

ssui de maasina.
The rising of the moon after the setting of the sun (i.e., when the moon is still below the water when the sun sets).

ssuilebelebe.
Completely wet all over.

ssuinga. (B-1 SUU$_1$)
n.

ssui o de hine.
Amniotic fluid.

ssula. (P-- SULA)
a.

ssulu. (P-- SULU)
v.

ssunu. (CF UNU$_1$)
v.

ssunu$_1$. (E-- SUNU)
v.

ssunu$_2$. (B-- SSUNU)
Suck, smoke (cigarettes). *v.*

ssunua. (B-2 SSUNU)
v.

ssunumia. (B-2 SSUNU)
v.

ssuonioni.
Sand. *v.*

ssuonioni ina.
Sandy.

ssuulanga. (P-1 SULA)
n.

sua$_1$. (B-- SUA)
Root up (soil); wrestling holds; rowing motion. *v.*

sua$_2$. (B-- SUU$_{1a}$)
Wet and dried [occurs only in compounds]. *d.*

sua aaleloi.
A wrestling maneuver.

sua age.
Dig up soil to uncover (something).

suaanga. (B-1 SUA)
n.

sua bagu.
A stain which has left a dry residue.

sua hadu.
Storm beach.

sua hadu umu.
Stones (dead coral) used in the earth oven.

sua iho.
To dig away soil, letting the soil slide down (e.g., from the side of a hill).

sualia. (B-2 SUA)
v.

suanga. (B-1 SUU$_{1a}$)
A stain (impermanent) left by something wet. *v.*

sua saele.
Search for by rooting around.

suasua. (R-- SUA)
v.

suasuaanga. (R-1 SUA)
n.

suasualia. (R-2 SUA)
v.

suasua mai (adu, ange).
To row a canoe (with a paddle).

suasuanga. (R-1 SUU$_{1a}$)
Stained all over. *v.*

sugi$_1$.
Pierce (slightly), stab (lightly), lance (e.g., a boil). *v.*

sugi$_2$.
Tail. *n.*

sugia. (B-2 SUGI$_1$)
v.

sugi au.
A current of choppy water between other currents.

sugi-daa. (CF SUGI$_2$)
Fish sp.: tang. *n.*

sugi de ngudu.
The corner of the mouth.

sugi talinga.
Piercing of the ear (for insertion of an ornament).

sugi hagabolebole.
The tip of anything slender and long (e.g., the tail of an animal).

sugi-laagoo. (CF SUGI$_2$)
Fish sp.: goatfish. *n.*

sugi lima.
Forearm.

sugimada. (MADA$_3$, SUGI$_2$)
The outer corner of the eye. *n.*

sugimada ina.
Catch a glimpse of.

sugi-manga. (CF $SUGI_2$)
Fish sp. (= large *madu*). *n.*

sugisugi. (R-- $SUGI_1$)
v.

sugisugia. (R-2 $SUGI_1$)
v.

sugisuginga. (R-1 $SUGI_1$)
n.

sugi vae.
Lower leg (between the ankle and the knee).

suguia. (B-2 SUUGUI)
v.

suguinga. (B-1 SUUGUI)
—; joint, connection. *n.*

sugusugui. (R-- SUUGUI)
Connect up or join several things. *v.*

sugusuguia. (R-2 SUUGUI)
v.

sugusuguinga. (R-1 SUUGUI)
n.

sui.
Change, replace. *v.*

suia. (B-2 SUI)
v.

sui ange.
Take revenge, get even; pay back (a debt).

sui de lodo.
Change one's mind.

sui hagahoou.
Change of personality (for the better).

suinga. (B-1 SUI)
n.

suisui$_1$. (R-- SUI)
v.

suisui$_2$. (R-- SUU_1)
—; become wet [followed by *ange*]. *a.*

suisuia. (R-2 SUI)
v.

suisuinga$_1$. (R-1 SUI)
n.

suisuinga$_2$. (R-1 SUU_1)
n.

sula.
Appear (sighted); succeed. *v.*

sula boo.
The appearance in early morning of a ship (or plane).

sula dagidahi --.
Once in a while it happens that—.

sula de hegau.
Successfully completed work.

sula tumuagi.
Bald-headed.

sula gi dahi henua.
To have visited abroad.

sulangia. (B-2 SULA)
To have appeared or succeeded. *v.*

sulasula. (R-- SULA)
v.

sulasulaanga. (R-1 SULA)
n.

sulegi.
Work (in a group) busily. *a.*

sulu.
Dive, fall head first; anoint (hair with oil). *v.*

sulua. (B-2 SULU)
v.

sulu de gelo.
Diving in the area in back of the center of the communal fishing net (the deepest part, in which the fish are trapped).

sulu de laa.
The setting of the sun.

sulu gi mua.
Fall forward.

sulu i hegau.
Busy (with work or obligations).

sulumanga. (B-1 SULU)
n.

sulumanga o de laa.
The direction in which the sun sets.

sulumia. (B-2 SULU)
v.

sulu moso.
Be wet all over (esp. when one's hair is dripping).

sulu saele.
To throw oneself about (as children do when unhappy).

sulusulu. (R-- SULU)
v.

sulusulua. (R-2 SULU)
v.

sulusulumanga. (R-1 SULU)
n.

sulusulumia. (R-2 SULU)
v.

sulusulunga. (R-1 SULU)
n.

sumu$_1$.
A method of lashing (which is diamond-shaped) and of decorating mats (with a diamond-shaped design). *v.*

sumu$_2$.
Fish sp.: triggerfish, filefish (The native term is applied to many spp.). *n.*

sumua. (B-2 SUMU$_1$)
v.

sumu-dea.
Fish sp.

sumu-gaaleva.
Fish sp.: filefish.

sumu ina.
To make diamond-shaped designs in plaiting or lashing.

sumulia. (B-2 SUMU$_1$)
v.

sumusumua. (R-2 SUMU$_1$)
v.

sumusumulia. (R-2 SUMU$_1$)
v.

sumusumunga. (R-1 SUMU$_1$)
n.

sunu.
An oil slick on the water's surface. *n.*

sunusunu$_1$. (R-- SUNU)
Oily. *v.*

sunusunu$_2$. (R-- SSUNU)
v.

sunusunua$_1$. (R-2 SUNU)
Be covered with oil. *v.*

sunusunua$_2$. (R-2 SSUNU)
v.

sunusunumia. (R-2 SSUNU)
v.

sunusununga. (R-1 SSUNU)
n.

sussunubega. (?)
Fish sp.: wrasse. *n.*

suu. (B-- SUU$_2$)
Fishhook keeper. *n.*

suuduuduu. (B-- SUU$_{1b}$)
Defecate [children's language]. *v.*

suuduuduunga. (B-1 SUU$_{1b}$)
n.

suugelegele. (GELE, SUU$_{1a}$)
v.

suuginga. (B-1 SUGI$_1$)
n.

suugui.
Connect, join together. *v.*

suuguia. (B-2 SUUGUI)
v.

suugui ange.
Join to, connect to, connect up with.

suuguinga. (B-1 SUUGUI)
n.

suukaha. (GAHA, SUU$_{1a}$)
The land near shore [on which the chief traditionally had some rights]. *n.*

suulanga. (B-1 SULA)
n.

suulee.
Fish sp. (var. *dabaduu*). *n.*

suulunga. (B-1 SULU)
n.

suumunga. (B-1 SUMU$_1$)
n.

suunibongi. (BONGI, SUU$_{1a}$)
A coral formation (resembling a man) at the bottom of the lagoon; a method of pole fishing at night. *n.*

suunugi.
Skewer, hold something down with the end of a long implement. *v.*

suunugia. (B-2 SUUNUGI)
v.

suunuginga. (B-1 SUUNUGI)
n.

suununga$_1$. (B-1 SUNU)
—; way of sucking. *n.*

suununga$_2$. (B-1 SSUNU)
n.

suungia. (B-2 SUU$_1$)
Damp. *v.*

suusuunugi. (R-- SUUNUGI)
v.

suusuunugia. (R-2 SUUNUGI)
v.

suusuunuginga. (R-1 SUUNUGI)
n.

suusuungia. (R-2 SUU$_1$)
v.

u +NUMBER. (B-- U$_1$)
NUMERAL CLASSIFIER (BY TENS) FOR LONG THIN OBJECTS, ALSO NIGHTS. *mc.*

ua$_1$.
Come in (tide). *v.*

ua$_2$.
Rain [archaic, except in compounds]. *v.*

ua$_3$.
Neck. *n.*

ua$_4$ +NUMBER. (B-- UA$_4$)
NUMERAL CLASSIFIER (BY TENS) FOR PIECES OF THATCH ROOFING. *mc.*

uaa.
Yes!; assent to, agree to. *a.*

uaanga$_1$. (B-1 UA$_1$)
n.

uaanga$_2$. (B-1 UA$_2$)
n.

uaanga$_3$. (B-1 UAA)
n.

uaasei.
A type of small knife. *n.*

uaauaa. (R-- UAA)
a.

uaauaanga. (R-1 UAA)
n.

uadanga. (B-1 UA$_2$)
An intermittent downpour (of rain) [considered an omen of birth, death, or the coming arrival of a ship]. *v.*

ua dea.
Bird sp.: white-throated frigate bird.

ua dodo.
Rain of a reddish color [an omen of death].

uaduu. (DUU$_2$, UA$_2$)
Waterspout (esp. full of water) [meterological condition]. *n.*

ua lolo.
A disturbance in the sea caused by schools of big fish feeding on little fish.

ua mai.
The rising of the tide.

ua-mea.
Bird sp.: red-throated frigate bird.

uasaa. (XCO UA$_3$)
A good time associated with good food. *n.*

uaua$_1$. (R-- UA$_1$)
v.

uaua$_2$. (R-- UA$_2$)
v.

uaua$_3$. (R-- UA$_{3a}$)
Vein, tendon, nerve, plastic filament. *n.*

uaua$_4$ (ange). (R-- UA$_3$)
Crave for (food). *a.*

uauaanga$_1$. (R-1 UA$_1$)
n.

uauaanga$_2$. (R-1 UA$_2$)
n.

uauaanga$_3$. (R-1 UA$_3$)
n.

uauadanga. (R-1 UA$_2$)
v.

uaua mouli.
Veins pulsing.

uba.
Not level. *v.*

ubaanga. (B-1 UBA)
n.

ubauba. (R-- UBA)
v.

ubaubaanga. (R-1 UBA)
n.

ubu.
Kneecap, the shell of the coconut. *n*.

ubu aahao.
[Var. of *ubu haohao*].

ubu haohao.
A type of prepared food (made from taro and coconut cream).

ubu hhoa.
A type of prepared food dish (made from taro cooked in a half coconut shell).

ubu loada.
A coconut shell used for expectoration.

uda$_1$.
To board (a ship or canoe). *v*.

uda$_2$.
Inland. *nl*.

uda henua.
The land above the high-water mark; extensive holdings in land.

udaia. (B-2 UDA$_1$)
To have room for (on a ship or canoe); arrive on time (to board a ship or canoe). *v*.

udo.
The soft wood around the center of a tree trunk. *n*.

udonga. (B-1 UDO)
n.

udongi.
A line holding together the palm fronds used in communal net fishing. *n*.

udoudo. (R-- UDO)
Having soft wood in the interior (of a tree). *v*.

udu.
Fish sp.: snapper. *n*.

udua.
Promontory, peninsula. *n*.

udu-hai-vaelo.
Fish sp.

uduu. (DUU$_{1a}$, U$_2$)
A half shell, a cover (of something). *n*.

uduuduhi.
To do little by little or gradually. *v*.

uduuduhia. (B-2 UDUUDUHI)
v.

uduuduhinga. (B-1 UDUUDUHI)
n.

ue.
Move something from one place to another; to cause to move (as in starting a machine). *v*.

uea. (B-2 UE)
v.

ue age.
Raise or increase (volume of radio or price, etc.).

ueanga. (B-1 UE)
n.

ue ange.
Increase (speed or power, etc.).

ue gee.
Move to another place.

ue iho.
Lower or decrease (the volume of a radio, price, etc.).

uenga. (B-1 UE)
n.

ueue. (R-- UE)
v.

ueuea. (R-2 UE)
v.

ueueanga. (R-1 UE)
n.

ueue ange.
Exaggerate.

ueuenga. (R-1 UE)
n.

uga$_1$.
Fishing line, rope (of a sort suitable for fishing). *n*.

uga$_2$.
A disturbance of water at the mouth of the atoll's channel, due to an outflowing tide. *n*.

uga de henua.
The native variety of fishing line.

uga duiagi.
The fishing line used in *duiagi* fishing.

ugallalo. (XCO UGA$_1$)
Fishing (angling with a line) to an unusual depth. *a.*

ugu.
Rub (with pressure, as in using sandpaper); the skin of the stingray used for sanding). *v.*

ugua. (B-2 UGU)
v.

uguanga. (B-1 UGU)
n.

uguhia. (B-2 UGU)
v.

uguugu. (R-- UGU)
v.

uguugua. (R-2 UGU)
v.

uguuguanga. (R-1 UGU)
n.

uguuguhia. (R-2 UGU)
v.

uhaa. (XCO U$_1$)
Forty, of days + nights. *u.*

uhado.
Worm sp. (large, white). *n.*

uhe.
Wasteful of taro when peeling it (i.e., inclined to peel too much away). *v.*

uhea. (B-2 UHE)
v.

uheanga. (B-1 UHE)
n.

uhenga. (B-1 UHE)
n.

uheuhe. (R-- UHE)
v.

uheuhea. (R-2 UHE)
v.

uheuheanga. (R-1 UHE)
n.

uheuhenga. (R-1 UHE)
n.

uhi.
To replace the ridge pole cover of a thatch house; to cover the sides of a house with plaited green coconut leaves (as protection against ghosts) [archaic]. *v.*

uhia. (B-2 UHI)
v.

uhi daguu.
Turtle ribs (used as knives in rituals).

uhinga. (B-1 UHI)
n.

uhiuhi. (R-- UHI)
v.

uhiuhia. (R-2 UHI)
v.

uhiuhinga. (R-1 UHI)
n.

uhuuhu.
Fish sp. (var. of *huuhuu*). *n.*

ui$_1$.
Pick pandanus (*ui hala*). *v.*

ui$_2$.
To go past a point (in time or place), or past a certain stage. *a.*

uia. (B-2 UI$_1$)
v.

ui age.
Pass over.

ui iho.
Pass under.

uila.
Lightning, electricity. *n.*

ui modo.
To pick pandanus while it is still unripe.

uinga$_1$. (B-1 UI$_1$)
n.

uinga$_2$. (B-1 UI$_2$)
n.

uinga$_3$. (B-- UI$_{2a}$)
Paths in the taro bog, made from dry palm fronds. *n.*

uiui$_1$. (R-- UI$_1$)
v.

uiui$_2$. (R-- UI$_2$)
a.

uiuia. (R-2 UI_1)
v.

uiuinga$_1$. (R-1 UI_1)
n.

uiuinga$_2$. (R-1 UI_2)
n.

ula$_1$.
Flame, aflame, burning. *a.*

ula$_2$.
Lobster spp. *n.*

ula age.
Be on fire.

ulaanga. (B-1 ULA_1)
n.

ula-dai.
Rock lobster sp.: longusta.

ula de gili.
Inflammation; red in the face, flushed; sunburned.

ulahi.
Fish sp.: parrot fish. *n.*

ulalo.
Not level (esp. a person when sleeping). *v.*

ulaloanga. (B-1 ULALO)
n.

ulaula. (R-- ULA_1)
a.

ulaulaanga. (R-1 ULA_1)
n.

ulaulavvaa. (R-- ULA_{1a})
a.

ulaulavvaanga. (R-1 ULA_{1a})
n.

ulavvaa. (B-- ULA_{1a})
Burn with a high flame. *a.*

ulavvaanga. (B-1 ULA_{1a})
n.

uli$_1$.
Dark (in color), blackened; covered with (people, flies, etc.). *a.*

uli$_2$.
A sprout of a plant suitable for planting. *n.*

uli$_3$.
Fish sp. (several spp.). *n.*

ulianga. (B-1 ULI_1)
n.

uli bela.
Jet black.

ulimagallai. (LLAI, $MAGA_2$, ULI_1)
Jet black. *a.*

uliuli. (R-- ULI_1)
Black. *a.*

uliulianga. (R-1 ULI_1)
n.

ulu$_1$.
Enter, join (a group), get in; wounded (by something which has pierced); level (an area); remove all fruit from a coconut tree. *v.*

ulu$_2$.
Topmost part. *nl.*

ulua$_1$. (B-2 ULU_1)
—; entered. *v.*

ulua$_2$. (B-- ULUA)
Fish sp. (resembles *gada*, but bigger). *n.*

ulua-gabugabu-tai.
Fish sp.: round herring?, goby?

ulu age.
Take from the bottom upward.

ulu-davage.
Plant sp.: tree sp.: Indian coral tree (*Erythrina variegata* L.).

ulu de henua.
To cover the land (such as do the branches of breadfruit trees).

uludino. (B-- ULU_{1a})
Shed skin (as does a reptile). *a.*

uludinoanga. (B-1 ULU_{1a})
n.

ulu-dugi.
Fish sp.: hawk fish.

ulu-dugi-lalo-beau.
Fish sp.: hawk fish.

ulu-hai-bogo-lua.
Fish sp. (resembles *hoimanu*, but much bigger).

uluhia. (B-2 ULU_1)
—; a sudden access of hostile feeling; interfered with; entered. *v.*

uluhia e de lede.
Become freezing cold (of a person).

ulu hudi*.
Young girl.

ului. (B-- ULU_{1b})
Turn inside out. *v.*

uluia. (B-2 ULU_{1b})
v.

ulu i daane.
Boy-chaser, boy-crazy.

ulu i haahine.
Ladies' man, girl-crazy.

ulu iho.
Take from the top downward.

ulu i lalo.
Bottom part.

ulu i lunga.
Top part.

uluinga. (B-1 ULU_{1b})
n.

ulu laagau.
Medicine (from a plant).

ulumagi. (B-- ULU_{1c})
Put on (clothes), wear. *v.*

ulumagi age.
Cover or put on from the bottom up.

ulumagi iho.
Cover or put on from the top down.

ulumagina. (B-2 ULU_{1c})
v.

ulumaginga. (B-1 ULU_{1c})
n.

ulu manu.
Coral head (submerged).

ulumonu.
Porpoise. *n.*

ulunga.
Pillow, lie with one's head on a pillow. *v.*

ulungaa iga.
A pair of copulating fish (or turtles, or whales, or stingrays.

ulungaa mamu.
A pair of copulating fish, (or turtles, or whales, or stingrays).

ulungaanga. (B-1 ULUNGA)
n.

ulunga hala.
A pillow made from a pandanus log (having various magical uses).

ulungi.
Steer (a canoe). *v.*

ulungia. (B-2 ULUNGI)
v.

ulunginga. (B-1 ULUNGI)
n.

ulu sele dababa.
[A phrase said aloud to attract sharks].

uluulu. (R-- ULU_1)
v.

uluulua. (R-2 ULU_1)
v.

uluuludino. (R-- ULU_{1a})
a.

uluuludinoanga. (R-1 ULU_{1a})
n.

uluuluhia. (R-2 ULU_1)
v.

uluului. (R-- ULU_{1b})
v.

uluuluia. (R-2 ULU_{1b})
v.

uluuluinga. (R-1 ULU_{1b})
n.

uluulumagi. (R-- ULU_{1c})
v.

uluulumagia. (R-2 ULU_{1c})
v.

uluulumagina. (R-2 ULU_{1c})
v.

uluulumaginga. (R-1 ULU_{1c})
n.

uluulunga$_1$. (R-1 ULU_1)
n.

uluulunga$_2$. (R-- ULUNGA)
Repeatedly *ulunga.* *v.*

uluulungi. (R-- ULUNGI)
v.

uluulungia. (R-2 ULUNGI)
v.

uluulunginga. (R-1 ULUNGI)
n.

uma.
The chestbone of a bird (used as a tool). *n.*

umada.
Rainbow. *n.*

umalei. (?)
Fish sp. (rare). *n.*

umalie.
Delicious (of pandanus only). *a.*

umanga. (MANGA, U_2)
A bunch of *Cyrtosperma* taro corm buds planted together. *n.*

umaumalie. (R-- UMALIE)
Constantly bearing delicious fruit (of a pandanus tree only). *v.*

umidi.
Hungry for fish or meat. *a.*

umidianga. (B-1 UMIDI)
n.

umiumidi. (R-- UMIDI)
Like (someone or something), feel affection for. *a.*

umiumidianga. (R-1 UMIDI)
n.

umolo.
Fish sp. (two kinds). *n.*

umu.
Cook house, earth oven. *n.*

umu lehu.
An earth oven for making coral lime [for masonry] from coral.

una.
The carapace of the hawksbill turtle. *n.*

una dabu.
The part of the turtle shell nearest to the neck.

unahi.
Scale (of a fish). *n.*

unu. (B-- UNU_1)
Drink; pull in the mast stay sheet (on a canoe). *v.*

Unu. (B-- UNU_2)
The name of a star; the name of a folk tale character. *n.*

unudi.
Prow or stern cover (of a canoe). *n.*

unumanga. (B-1 UNU_1)
Drinking party. *n.*

unumia. (B-2 UNU_1)
v.

ununga. (B-1 UNU_1)
n.

unusaagi.
Deception. *v.*

unusaaginga. (B-1 UNUSAAGI)
n.

unusi.
Pull out (e.g., a sword from its scabbard). *v.*

unusia. (B-2 UNUSI)
v.

unusinga. (B-1 UNUSI)
n.

unuunu. (R-- UNU_1)
—; suck on the breast, nurse (at the breast). *v.*

unuunumanga. (R-1 UNU_1)
n.

unuunumia. (R-2 UNU_1)
v.

unuununga. (R-1 UNU_1)
n.

unuunusaagi. (R-- UNUSAAGI)
v.

unuunusaaginga. (R-1 UNUSAAGI)
n.

unuunusi. (R-- UNUSI)
v.

unuunusia. (R-2 UNUSI)
v.

unuunusinga. (R-1 UNUSI)
n.

unga.
Hermit crab (lives on dry land). *n.*

ungaa.
Portion of, group of (fish or animals). *d.*

ungaa husi.
[The generic name for] sections of the taro patch.

ungaa lodo.
Middle part (of something round).

ungaa mamu.
A school of fish.

ungaa me.
A section of the village; village.

unga-goo.
Mollusk sp.: vermetid gastropod sp.

unga-lausedi.
Hermit crab (lives in water).

useahi. (AHI$_1$, USE)
Smoke, steam. *v.*

useahi ina.
To be annoyed by smoke.

useahinga. (X-1 USE)
n.

usegi*.
A type of song [archaic]. *n.*

uso.
Umbilical cord. *n.*

usu$_1$.
(For a bird) to catch with its beak. *v.*

usu$_2$.
Push. *v.*

usu$_3$.
Nose. *n.*

usua$_1$. (B-2 USU$_1$)
v.

usua$_2$. (B-2 USU$_2$)
v.

usubee. (B-- USU$_{3a}$)
Blow one's nose; mucus (blown from the nose). *a.*

usubeeanga. (B-1 USU$_{3a}$)
n.

usubee o unu.
Foam (from the sea) on shore.

usuhia$_1$. (B-2 USU$_1$)
v.

usuhia$_2$. (B-2 USU$_2$)
v.

usulia. (B-2 USU$_2$)
v.

usunga$_1$. (B-1 USU$_1$)
n.

usunga$_2$. (B-1 USU$_2$)
n.

usuusu$_1$. (R-- USU$_1$)
v.

usuusu$_2$. (R-- USU$_2$)
v.

usuusua$_1$. (R-2 USU$_1$)
v.

usuusua$_2$. (R-2 USU$_2$)
v.

usuusu ange.
Encourage, egg on (e.g., to fight); try to talk into.

usuusubee. (R-- USU$_{3a}$)
a.

usuusubeeanga. (R-1 USU$_{3a}$)
n.

usuusuhia$_1$. (R-2 USU$_1$)
v.

usuusuhia$_2$. (R-2 USU$_2$)
v.

usuusulia. (R-2 USU$_2$)
v.

usuusunga$_1$. (R-1 USU$_1$)
n.

usuusunga$_2$. (R-1 USU$_2$)
n.

uu$_1$.
The presentation of a foetus at birth (e.g., head first). *v.*

uu$_2$.
Yes! *a.*

uu$_3$.
Milk. *n.*

uu$_4$.
A fish trap (of wood); a bundle (e.g., of sticks); a cigarette-holder, made from a coconut leaf. *n.*

uuanga. (B-1 UU$_1$)
n.

uubiho. (BIHO, UU$_1$)
Head-first presentation of a foetus at birth. *v.*

uu dogo.
A bundle of sticks.

uu duaa nui.
Broom.

uulunga. (B-1 ULU_1)
n.

uumadua. (MADUA, UU_3)
Desirous of suckling when past nursing age, to breast-feed beyond infancy. *a.*

uumolo. (?)
Fish sp. (rare — like *huhu* — about 2 feet long with dark rust-colored skin). *n.*

uunga. (B-1 UU_2)
n.

uuuu. (R-- UU_2)
a.

uuuunga. (R-1 UU_2)
n.

uuvae. (XCO UU_1)
A feet-first presentation of the foetus in delivery. *a.*

uvada*.
Penis. *n.*

vaa--$_1$. (B-- VAA_3)
Able to. *mf.*

vaa$_2$. (B-- VAA_1)
To make noise (in a group); the sudden jumping of a school of flying fish (when they are scared by the light). *v.*

vaadagidahi. (XCO VAA_{3a})
Scattered (not in a cluster). *v.*

vaagia. (B-2 VAA_2)
Found or caught doing something wrong. *v.*

vaagina. (B-2 VAA_2)
[Var. of *vaagia*]. *v.*

vaaginga. (B-1 VAA_2)
n.

vaalanga. (LANGA, VAA_3)
Made-up (of a story only). *n.*

vaalanga a kai.
A story which is not true, a made-up story.

vaaligi. (B-- VAA_{3b})
Small [pl.]; little [pl.]; immature taro corm. *a.*

vaaligiligi. (R-- VAA_{3b})
Very small [pl.]; very little [pl.]. *a.*

vaalunga. (B-1 $VALU_1$)
n.

vaanga$_1$. (B-1 VAA_1)
n.

vaanga$_2$. (B-1 VAA_3)
Manner of doing things. *n.*

vaassega. (P-- VASEGA)
a.

vaassegaanga. (P-1 VASEGA)
n.

vaassuu. (P-- VAASUU)
a.

vaassuunga. (P-1 VAASUU)
n.

vaasuu.
Like (someone or something), feel affection for. *a.*

vaasuu ai loo.
I like it (or him or her) very much.

vaasuunga. (B-1 VAASUU)
n.

vaavaa. (R-- VAA_1)
v.

vaavaagia. (R-2 VAA_2)
Repeatedly being *vaagia*. *v.*

vaavaagina. (R-2 VAA_2)
[Var. of *vaavaagia*]. *v.*

vaavaaginga. (R-1 VAA_2)
n.

vaavaanga. (R-1 VAA_1)
n.

vaavaasuu. (R-- VAASUU)
Steadily *vaasuu*. *a.*

vaavaasuunga. (R-1 VAASUU)
n.

vaavanga. (B-1 VAVA)
n.

vadu.
Give (to hearer). *a.*

vaduvadu. (R-- VADU)
a.

vae$_1$.
Separate, divide; treat differently, sort out, part (e.g., hair). *v.*

vae$_2$.
Foot (including leg), leg. *n.*

vaea. (B-2 VAE_1)
v.

vaedama. (DAMA, VAE_1)
Play favorites amongst one's children. *a.*

vae hagasii.
Wheel (one only).

vaelia. (B-2 VAE_1)
v.

vaelo.
A long, thin appendage (e.g., barbel or streamer rays of a fish); the alleged cords in the body connected to the genitalia [massaged to alleviate illness]. *n.*

vaenga. (B-1 VAE_1)
—; portion, share, division (e.g., of a tract); district, precinct (electoral); a measure (from the end of the outstretched arm to the center of the chest). *n.*

vaenga o de langi.
Milky Way.

vaeunga. (XCO VAE_1)
A method of lashing. *v.*

vaevae. (R-- VAE_1)
v.

vaevaea. (R-2 VAE_1)
v.

vaevaelia. (R-2 VAE_1)
v.

vaevaenga. (R-1 VAE_1)
n.

vaga*. (B-- $VAGA_1$)
A big ship or canoe. *n.*

vaga loosi*.
A canoe used by the guardians of the island (in olden times) to meet canoes coming to the island.

$vage_1$.
Bring up, put up, take up. *v.*

$vage_2$.
To be aware of vaguely (e.g., the presence of a person when one is almost asleep). *v.*

vagea. (B-2 $VAGE_2$)
v.

vage i de lodo.
To occur to one that someone else is doing something to affect one's mood (favorably or unfavorably).

vagelia. (B-2 $VAGE_2$)
v.

vagenga. (B-1 $VAGE_2$)
n.

vagevage. (R-- $VAGE_2$)
v.

vagevagea. (R-2 $VAGE_2$)
v.

vagevagelia. (R-2 $VAGE_2$)
v.

vagevagenga. (R-1 $VAGE_2$)
n.

vakaa.
Be in trouble, in danger, or in a precarious situation. *v.*

vakaa laa loo.
Too bad for him (I don't care)!

vakaa loo dangada.
See what happened! (the hearer having been forewarned).

vakaanga. (B-1 VAKAA)
n.

vai.
Liquid, water. *n.*

vaia. (B-2 VAI)
Abounding in water. *v.*

vaiaanga. (B-3 VAI)
Way of being watery. *n.*

vai ango.
A yellowish discharge from the genitalia (of either males or females).

vai dea.
A whitish discharge from the genitalia (of either males or females).

vai diadia.
A covered coconut shell which fishermen used to use for a drinking water container and (in emergencies) as a shark foil.

vai doo.
Waterfall.

vaiduu.
Lazy. *a.*

vaiduunga. (B-1 VAIDUU)
n.

vaigelegele. (GELE, VAI)
Filthy, very dirty. *a.*

vai geli.
Well (for water, in the ground).

vai langi.
Rainwater.

vai malo.
Perfume.

vai mea.
A reddish discharge from the genitalia (of either males or females).

vai nui.
Coconut milk.

vai nui hhoa.
Very calm seas.

vai saalia.
A group of drifting objects on the surface of the sea (brought together by the currents).

vai sulu.
Pomade (for hair).

vaiuso. (USO, VAI)
Good-tasting, cooked *Cyrtosperma* taro; the gummy remainder when *dagadaga* is grated. *n.*

vai uu.
Milk.

vaivai. (R-- VAI)
Watery; bad — [when followed by another word]. *a.*

vaivai adamai.
Remember poorly.

vaivai basa.
Dirty or obscene language; foulmouthed, swear.

vaivai daahili.
A dirty song.

vaivaidagodo. (DAGODO, VAI)
Unscrupulous, immoral, evil. *a.*

vaivai hai.
Do badly, abuse.

vaivai hanonga.
An excursion for an evil purpose (esp. involving a sexual quest).

vaivai me.
A disgusting business; genitals (of males or females).

vaivai ngudu.
Evil-tongued, lying (dishonest, foulmouthed.

valaai.
Medicine. *n.*

valaai buliaamou.
Medicine to cure longing (homesickness or longing for a person).

valaai de henua.
Native medicine.

valaai tala hai sala.
Medicine to obviate the effects of *oha valaai.*

valaai tao.
Dye.

valaai kino.
Medicine taken to regain one's appetite.

valaai hagasili lodo.
A medicine taken to reduce one's anger, or any other strong emotion.

valaai hagauseahi.
Medication administered in steam or smoke.

valaai hai haahine.
A love potion (to attract women).

valagei.
Coral sp.: whip black coral. *n.*

vale.
Mold (fungus); any slippery jelly-like substance. *n.*

valea. (B-2 VALE)
Moldy; to have been in a place for a long time. *v.*

valeaanga. (B-3 VALE)
n.

valea i de noho.
Tired of waiting for someone.

valo. (B-- $VALO_2$)
Mollusk sp.: *Pinnidae* spp. *n.*

valovalo. (R-- $VALO_3$)
Plant sp.: tree sp.: a small tree sp. (*Premna obtusifolia* R. Br.). *n.*

$valu_1$.
To grate (esp. coconut) on a stool grater (*duai*). *v.*

$valu_2$.
Eight. *an.*

$valu_3$.
Fish sp. (= large *dangii*). *n.*

valua. (B-2 $VALU_1$)
v.

valu-dangau.
The eighth number of a counting game played to determine who is "it".

Valu-malama. (MALAMA, $VALU_2$)
August ('eighth month'). *nt.*

valusia. (B-2 $VALU_1$)
v.

valuvalu. (R-- $VALU_1$)
v.

valuvalua. (R-2 $VALU_1$)
v.

valuvalunga. (R-1 $VALU_1$)
n.

valuvalusia. (R-2 $VALU_1$)
v.

vanei.
Suspect that — (wouldn't be surprised if)...; I wonder how much...? *mi.*

vanei ai.
(E.g., I) wonder how —?

vanei naa.
(E.g., I) wonder if...?

vangani.
Bad person. *n.*

vange.
Give to (him, her, or them). *a.*

vange gi de hainga.
Sue (in court), complain about (to the authorities).

vangevange. (R-- VANGE)
—; exaggerate; extremely show-off in manner. *a.*

vao.
Wilderness, uninhabited place; the skin of the *ngaungau* plant, which contains an irritating substance. *n.*

vaolia. (B-2 VAO)
Still having some of the irritating substance within (of *ngaungau* skin). *v.*

vasega.
Apprehensive (e.g., about a public appearance); nervous (only in a social context); anxious (in a social situation). *a.*

vasegaanga. (B-1 VASEGA)
n.

vasevasega. (R-- VASEGA)
a.

vasevasegaanga. (R-1 VASEGA)
n.

vasu*.
Timid, shy. *v.*

vasunga. (B-1 VASU)
n.

vasuvasu. (R-- VASU)
v.

vasuvasunga. (R-1 VASU)
n.

vava.
Leaky. *a.*

vava de gede.
Forgetful (esp. with increasing age).

vava de ngudu.
Talkative, indiscreet.

vavvava. (R-- VAVA)
Leaking in many places. *a.*

vavvavaanga. (R-1 VAVA)
n.

$vede_1$.
d.

$vede_2$.
Fish sp.: goatfish. *n.*

vede-mea.
Fish sp.: goatfish.

vedevede. (R-- $VEDE_1$)
v.

vedevedea. (R-2 $VEDE_1$)
v.

vedevedenga. (R-1 $VEDE_1$)
n.

veedea. (B-2 $VEDE_1$)
v.

veedenga. (B-1 $VEDE_1$)
n.

veelenga. (B-1 VELE)
—; a garden. *n.*

veelonga. (B-1 VELO)
n.

veevenga. (B-1 VEVE)
n.

vela.
Burned. *a.*

velaanga. (B-1 VELA)
n.

velavela. (R-- VELA)
a.

velavelaanga. (R-1 VELA)
n.

vele.
To weed (a garden); to clear bush (overgrowth); to pluck (feathers). *v.*

velea. (B-2 VELE)
v.

vele de henua.
Win over all comers (esp. in an athletic contest).

vele duli.
Pull by the hair (in fighting).

vele me.
To weed (a garden).

velevele. (R-- VELE)
—; to clear land (or a path, etc.) of weeds and underbrush. *v.*

velevelea. (R-2 VELE)
v.

velevelenga. (R-1 VELE)
n.

veli.
Sea urchin sp.: *Echinometra* spp. *n.*

veli-daubulebule.
Sea urchin sp.: *Diadema* sp.

veli-tea.
Burrowing heart urchin.

veli-uli.
Sea urchin sp.: *Diadema* sp.

velo.
To spear (someone); stab, pierce; jab, poke; inject, insert. *v.*

veloa. (B-2 VELO)
v.

velo aga.
To sprout roots.

velo age.
Go up straight.

velo daohi.
To spear (something) without releasing the spear.

velo de baledilo.
To sprout (of plants).

velo de hagasii.
A type of game.

velo tili.
Throw a spear; go directly.

velo huu --.
Inclined to do —.

velo iho.
Come down straight.

velo mai (adu, ange).
Come (go) straight.

velosia. (B-2 VELO)
v.

velosia de lodo.
Shocked.

velo ssina.
Beginning to show white hairs on one's head.

velo suunugi.
To spear something and hold it against something solid with the spear.

velovelo. (R-- VELO)
v.

veloveloa. (R-2 VELO)
v.

velovelonga. (R-1 VELO)
n.

velovelosia. (R-2 VELO)
v.

veve.
To line an earth oven (*umu*) with stones, logs, or coconut husks. *v.*

vevea. (B-2 VEVE)
v.

vevelia. (B-2 VEVE)
v.

vii.
Fermented, spoiled (of cooked food left too long). *a.*

viilinga. (B-1 VILI)
n.

viininga. (B-1 VINI)
n.

viinga. (B-1 VII)
n.

viivii.
Put to sleep (esp. a child) by rocking in the arms or singing to. *v.*

viiviia. (B-2 VIIVII)
v.

viiviinga. (B-1 VIIVII)
n.

vili.
Do rapidly. *v.*

vilia. (B-2 VILI)
v.

vilidogi. (DOGI, VILI)
Chatterbox, a person who speaks fast. *v.*

vilivili. (R-- VILI)
v.

vilivilia. (R-2 VILI)
v.

vilivilinga. (R-1 VILI)
n.

vini.
Wound around, tangled up, confused; equal in skill and strength (in a wrestling contest — so no one wins). *v.*

vinia. (B-2 VINI)
v.

vini de ngudu.
A screwed up mouth (as of a child on the point of crying).

vinigoso. (GOSO, VINI)
Entangled in apparent disorder. *v.*

vinivini. (R-- VINI)
Really *vini*; kinky (of hair); wrinkled (of skin or clothes). *v.*

vinivinia. (R-2 VINI)
v.

vinivininga. (R-1 VINI)
n.

$vogi_1$.
To shame (someone) by teasing or insulting him. *v.*

$vogi_2$.
Whistling (with the lips). *a.*

vogia. (B-2 $VOGI_1$)
v.

voginga. (B-1 $VOGI_1$)
n.

$vogivogi_1$. (R-- $VOGI_1$)
v.

$vogivogi_2$. (R-- $VOGI_2$)
a.

vogivogia. (R-2 $VOGI_1$)
v.

$vogivoginga_1$. (R-1 $VOGI_1$)
n.

$vogivoginga_2$. (R-1 $VOGI_2$)
n.

voi.
Plant sp.: tree sp. (*Mammea odorata* (Raf.) Kost.). *n.*

vooginga. (B-1 $VOGI_2$)
n.

vvaalanga. (B-1 VVALA)
n.

vvaalonga. (B-1 VVALO)
n.

vvae. (E-- VAE_1)
v.

vvae ange.
Divide into portions.

vvae de biho.
Part one's hair.

vvae gee.
Isolate, separate from, set aside (from a group).

vvala.
A piercingly bright light; the cutting of a fast canoe through water. *a.*

vvalo.
The noise of, e.g., a sail flapping, or the vibration of an airplane propeller, or the splashing of a canoe cutting through the water. *v.*

vvasu. (P-- VASU)
v.

vvasunga. (P-1 VASU)
n.

vvava. (P-- VAVA)
a.

vvavaanga. (P-1 VAVA)
n.

vvede. (E-- $VEDE_1$)
To massage. *v.*

vvela. (P-- VELA)
—; hot (of an object). *a.*

vvelaanga. (P-1 VELA)
n.

vvela de aloha.
Feel very sorry for.

vvela mai (adu, ange).
I (you, he, or she) want to — very badly.

vvini. (P-- VINI)
v.

ENGLISH-NUKUORO

a
One, a: *dahi*$_1$.

abbreviate
Shorten, abbreviate: *hagasugi*$_2$.

abbreviation
Abbreviation, acronym, nickname: *hagasugi*$_2$.

abdomen
The lower abdomen, crotch, pubic area: *madagauhala.*

ability
Ability, capacity (of person), resourcefulness: *hina.*

able
Able to: *vaa—*$_1$.
Able to, obtained, gotten, caught: *maua.*

abnormal
Abnormal: *boi.*
Temporarily abnormal: *boi a eidu.*

abortion
Miscarriage, abortion (spontaneous): *ssege tama.*

about
About how much?: *aahee maa.*
About it, concerning it, in it, for it: *loo.*
About this, much more...: *denei ange naa.*
About to (in time): *bigi*$_2$.
About when? (future): *aahee maa.*
About, approximately: *duumaa.*
About, quite: *lago.*

above
On top of, on, over, above: *honga.*
Up, above, over: *lunga.*

abraded
Abraded (skin), scratched: *masole.*

abrasion
An abrasion of the skin (red but not bleeding): *mada dotodo.*

absent
Not present, absent: *dee maeva.*

absent-minded
Forgetful, absent-minded: *dee anga; ngalongalo.*

abundant
Abundant: *se gainga.*

abuse
Do badly, abuse: *vaivai hai.*

access
A sudden access of emotion: *langaa lodo.*
A sudden access of hostile feeling: *uluhia.*
An access (of emotion or sensory impression): *lluhi.*

accident
Mistake, error, accident: *sala.*

accidentally
Accidentally: *doo sala.*

accord
Accord honor to: *hagaamua*$_2$.

according to
According to —: *ange gi; bolo*$_1$.

accumulate
Accumulate (bring together): *hagadali.*
Collect in one place together, accumulate: *hagabudu.*

accuse
Accuse (someone) of having had sexual relations with someone else: *hagabuulunga.*
Accuse: *hagabuu*$_2$.
Accuse someone (in an argument, usually between spouses) of taking sides with another family member: *lili baasi gee.*
Blame (someone), accuse: *hagadagasala.*

accustomed
Become accustomed to: *aboabo.*

acquaintance
Make the acquaintance of: *hagaheiloo.*

acquainted
Know about, be acquainted with: *ssano.*
To strive to become acquainted with: *hagamau*$_2$.

acquisitive
Acquisitive (and acting on acquisitive impulses): *boo gi me.*
Acquisitive, covetous: *lodo gi me.*
Insatiably acquisitive: *nnoo hagamau me.*

acreage
Plot of (bush) land, acreage: *alahenua.*

acronym
Abbreviation, acronym, nickname: *hagasugi*$_2$.

act
Act cautiously: *maanetonu.*
Act like a child (as a behavior pattern): *hagadamadama.*
Act mad like —: *hai hulu o —.*
Act smart (deviously): *hai de biho.*
Act smart (openly): *hagaheiangi.*
To act like a human: *hagadaane.*

active
Active physically: *hai mogomogo.*

activity
Sexual activity: *haiva dee agona.*
Work, activity, occupation: *haiva; hegau.*

acuity
Acuity of hearing: *longolongo.*

add
Add a portion:*hagaduumaa.*
Add together from different sources: *hagabunibuni.*
Add up (many things): *hagapunidia; hagapuunia.*
Add up: *hagabunidia.*
Add, total up: *hagapuni.*

adept
Adept at: *se goo.*

adjacent
Adjacent (of taro plots only): *lau me.*

adjudicated
To have been adjudicated: *modu.*

adopted
An adopted child: *dama daohi; dama ssala.*

adorn
Decorate, adorn: *hagalaagii.*

adult
Old person, adult: *dangada madua.*

adultery
Commit adultery: *gaiaa dau bodu.*

adze
A type of adze (heavy — for hollowing out logs, etc.): *dogi hoda.*
A type of adze (with a curved blade of *Terebra* shell): *dogi hakolona.*
A type of adze (with a rotatable head): *sauligi.*
A type of adze (with a small blade, for light chipping): *dogi daadaa.*
Adze: *dogi.*

affection
Compassion, affection: *aloha.*
Like (someone or something), feel affection for: *umiumidi.*
Profound affection: *aloha gelo.*

affinal
Affinal relatives who are *maa* or *saulaba* to each other: *mada dabu.*

aflame
Flame, aflame, burning: *ula*$_1$.
To catch fire, aflame: *gaa*$_2$.

afraid
Afraid to assert oneself: *binaaina.*
Afraid, scared: *madagu.*

after
After: *dua*$_2$.
After, end (rearward part), later: *muli*$_1$.

afternoon
Afternoon (late): *oomea.*
Afternoon: *muli de huaalaangi.*
Early evening, late in the afternoon: *gaba de ahiahi.*
Late afternoon and early evening: *ahiahi.*

afterward
Afterward: *muliagi.*

again
Again: *ange; angeange.*

age
Age (of a person): *ngadau.*

age grade
Age grade (those reaching adolescence within a few years of each other): *mou*

age set
Generation, age set: *atangada.*

aggrandizement
Aggrandizement of one's land holdings by moving others' *goinga*: *hai goinga.*

agree
Agree with: *buni ange.*
Assent to, agree to: *uaa.*

aground
Run aground: *gasa.*

ahead
Front (position), before, ahead: *mua.*

aid
Aid (by giving something): *hagaaoaoa*$_2$.
Help, assist, aid (with effort or advice, etc.): *bale*$_1$.

aim
Aim at: *hagasoe ange.*

airplane
Airplane: *moni lele.*

alert
Aware, alert: *angaanga*$_1$.

Alexandrian laurel tree
Plant sp.: tree sp.: Alexandrian laurel tree (*Calophyllum inophyllum* L.): *hedau.*

alignment
Out of alignment: *dùu gee.*

alike
Alike (in appearance): *dulagi daudahi.*
Having the same characteristics, be alike: *dagodo daudahi.*
More-or-less alike: *beibei.*

alive
Living, alive: *mouli.*

all
All (e.g., have come): *odi mai (adu, ange).*
All (of things): *hugadoo.*
All: *alodahi.*

alligator
Alligator, crocodile: *gegeno.*

Allophylus
Plant sp.: tree sp. (*Allophylus timorensis* (DC.) BL.): *dalahalu.*

allotment
A share of, allotment, portion: *dino*$_1$.

allowed
Allowed to, permissible: *alaange.*

almond
Plant sp.: tropical almond (*Terminalia catappa* L.): *hua-laagau.*

almost
Almost (finished or done, etc.): *dai bigi.*
Almost: *adigai.*
Almost none: *dai deeai.*
Almost none at all: *dai deeai donu.*
Almost, nearly: *dai*$_2$.

Alocasia
Plant sp.: elephant ear (*Alocasia*): *ngaungau*$_2$.

alone
Alone, only, by oneself: *sogosogo.*
Only, alone (just one): *daudahi.*

along
Wait for, along with: *dali*$_1$.
With, along with, as well as: *madali.*

already
Already: *odi*$_a$.

also
Also: *hogi.*

always
Always: *masavaa alodahi.*

ambitious
Ambitious for a superior position: *lodo gi lunga.*

ambush
Ambush: *doo gaiaa.*

amniotic fluid
Amniotic fluid: *ssui o de hine.*

amongst
Between, amongst: *masavaa*$_1$.

amuse
Amuse oneself: *hagadaahao.*

amusement
Game, amusement: *hagadaahao.*

ancestor
Grandparent, ancestor: *dubuna.*

anchor
Anchor rope: *ataula.*
To anchor: *hagadaula.*

anchored
Anchored (of ship): *daula.*

anchovy
Fish sp.: anchovy?, silversides (small)?: *mamu-honga-dai.*

and
And then: *gaa lava; ma gu.*
And then, finally...: *agai.*
And, among other things,...: *ama*$_2$.
And, and so, and thus, and then: *ma*$_1$.
But, and, then, so: *gai*$_3$.

anger
Anger (toward someone): *hagalili*$_3$.

angling
Angling (a fishing method): *hagalalo.*
Angling for tuna: *daabasi.*

angry
Angry and ready to fight: *hagaduu dala.*
Bawl out, be angry: *bole.*
Mad at, angry: *lili*$_3$.
Mad or angry (but not showing it): *lluu.*

animal
Animal, plant (flora): *manu*$_1$.
Land animal: *manu dolodolo.*
Sea animal: *manu laosedi.*

ankle
Foot, ankle: *gubu vae.*

annoint
Annoint (in baptism): *hagasulu.*

announce
Announce: *hagailoo.*

annoyed
Annoyed by noise: *longaa.*
Bothered, annoyed: *goso.*

anoint
Anoint (hair with oil): *sulu.*
Anoint (in baptism): *hagauda.*

another
Another thing altogether: *dagodo gee (ma).*

Anous
Bird sp.: common noddy (*Anous stolidus*): *ngongo.*
Bird sp.: white-capped noddy (*Anous minutus*): *legia.*

answer
Answer, reply: *basa ange.*

ant
Ant: *loa*$_2$.
Insect sp.: fly, flying ant, wasp: *lango*$_2$.

anvil
Anvil: *hoa lalo.*

anxiety
Acute anxiety attack: *buni ange lodo.*
Anxiety state (psychological condition): *bebe de lodo.*

anxious
Anxious (in a social situation): *vasega.*
Be very nervous, be very anxious: *bebea; bebelia.*
Nervous, anxious (for reasons not connected with other people): *bebe*$_1$.

apart
Apart, widely spaced: *massanganga.*

apiece
Apiece, each: *i de — sogosogo.*
Each, apiece: *i dahi me.*

apodous sea cucumber
Apodous sea cucumber: *duu-lellele.*

apologize
Ask permission of, apologize to: *dangidangi ange.*
Beg, apologize: *dangidangi.*
Beg, apologize, or ask permission in an insistent manner: *dangidangi keli.*

Apolonis
Bird sp.: starling (*Apolonis opacus*): *moso.*

appear
Appear (sighted): *sula.*
Appear clearly: *molomolo iho (age).*
Appear from yonder: *dagodo mai.*
Appear there (from here): *dagodo adu.*
Sighted, appear: *hodu*.*

appearance
Appearance (distinctive of an individual): *holiholi.*
Appearance (e.g., of a ship, house, or other construction): *hagaduulanga.*
Appearance, example, situation: *dulagi.*
Appearance, situation: *dumanu.*
Having a good appearance: *tilo mahamaha.*

appeared
To have appeared or succeeded: *sulangia.*

appendage
Appendage, fin, spine (extending from a fish, etc.): *dala*$_4$.
Handle, appendage: *gau*$_1$.

appetite
Lose his (my) appetite: *mmala dana (dagu) maanga.*

apply
Apply liquid on, smear on: *hulu*$_2$.

appoint
Appoint: *dongi ange.*

apportioned
Equally apportioned: *dau ngaadahi*$_1$.

appreciative
Appreciative: *malangilangi ai.*

apprehensive
Apprehensive (e.g., about a public appearance): *vasega.*
Nervous, apprehensive (suddenly): *manava duuia.*
Worried, apprehensive, fearful: *manavasaa.*

appropriate
Appropriate: *hagavaasuu.*
Look as though appropriate, seemly: *mahamaha.*
Suited to, fit (with), appropriate to: *heohi ange.*

approve
Approve (as a law by higher authority): *hagasauaa.*

approximately
About, approximately: *duumaa.*
Approximately —: *maa_1.*

April
April: *Haa-malama; $Idiidi_2$.*

Apus
Bird sp.: white-rumped swift (*Apus pacificus*) (The native term applies possibly to several spp.): *gauea.*

archipelago
Archipelago: *aduhenua.*

Arcophagia
Mollusk sp.: *Arcophagia scobinata*: *bibi-maadau.*

Arenaria
Bird sp.: ruddy turnstone (*Arenaria interpres*): *givigivi.*

areola
Areola of the breast: *malemale.*

argue
Argue against: *daohi ange dahi hai.*
Argue heatedly, fight: *hulo gi lunga ma lalo.*
Dispute (with someone), argue: *hagadau-me.*

argumentative
An argumentative and stubborn person: *gaa de malala.*
Argumentative: *gaa de malala.*
Argumentative in a disrespectful way: *hagammau de ngudu.*

arithmetic
Calculation, arithmetic: *guumanga.*

arm
Arm, hand: *$lima_1$.*
Upper arm: *dahido lima.*

arm-wrestling
Arm-wrestling: *hagasalisali.*

armpit
Armpit: *ahinga.*

arms
Arms (tools of war): *goloa hebagi.*

around
Outside, away, around: *daha.*

aroused
Aroused (sexually): *$tegi_1$.*

arrange
Arrange (in order), a program: *$hagatau_1$.*
Arrange things in a row or line: *hagaadugau.*

arrangement
Arrangement of things into a straight row: *adugau.*

arrive
Arrive at: *dae_2.*
Arrive on time (to board a ship or canoe): *udaia.*
To beach (a canoe), arrive at: *dau_3.*

arrived
To have arrived at: *daea.*

arrogant
Arrogant, haughty, overbearing, proud: *hagamao lunga.*
Egotistical, self-centered, arrogant in spirit: *lodo mao lunga.*

arrow
Arrow (for a bow): *dao me hholu.*

arrowroot
Plant sp.: Polynesian arrowroot (*Tacca leontopetaloides* (L.) O.K.): *bie.*

Asaphis
Mollusk sp.: *Asaphis dichotoma*: *$gasi_2$.*

ashamed
Bashful, ashamed, shy, embarrassed: *dogaa.*

ashes
Ashes: *lehu.*

ask
Ask: *$ssili_2$.*
Ask around: *$silisilia_1$.*

ask permission
Ask permission of, apologize to: *dangidangi ange.*

Asplenium
Plant sp.: bird's-nest fern (*Asplenium nidus* L.): *lau-gadaha.*

assent
Assent to insincerely: *ngadi uaa.*
Assent to, agree to: *uaa.*

assign
Assign (someone) to: *hagailonga ange agina.*

assist
Help, assist, aid (with effort or advice, etc.): *bale*$_1$.

assume
Assume: *soi*$_1$ (*adu, mai, ange*).

asthma
Asthma: *magi dee manava; magi nngahu.*

at
At: *i.*
At his place, with him: *i ono daha.*
At the time of: *honga de masavaa.*
At this time, these days: *honga iainei.*

Athyrium
Plant sp.: paco fern (*Athyrium* sp.): *manu-mangamanga*$_2$.

atoll
Atoll (collection of islets): *adumodu.*
Atoll: *henua gelegele.*

atolls
Group of islands or atolls: *aduhenua.*

attached
Firmly attached: *magakaga.*

attachment
The attachment of a clam to the reef: *ogo*$_3$.

attack
Attack by surprise or stealth: *doo gaiaa.*

attempt
Try, attempt: *hagatale.*

attend
Attend (e.g., church services): *hano ai.*

attention
Attract attention: *gave lodo.*
Pay attention to (notice), be aware of: *anga*$_1$.

attentively
Do attentively: *gamalie.*

attract
Attract attention: *gave lodo.*

attracted
Attracted to: *baageaa ange.*
Be attracted to or like each other (of members of the opposite sex): *hagadau vaasuu.*

attractive
Attractive to members of the opposite sex: *galoa; galohia.*
Attractive to women (for some inexplicable reason): *mau haahine.*

auger shell
Mollusk sp.: auger shell (*Terebridae* sp.): *hakolona.*

augmented
Increased, augmented: *ngalue age.*

August
August ('eighth month'): *Valu-malama.*
August: *Maidigi.*

aunt
Mother, aunt: *dinana.*

auspices
Under the auspices of: *i de baasi.*

available
Have time for, free, available: *saohia*$_2$.
Make oneself available: *hagasaohia*$_2$.

avoid
Avoid: *hagaui gee.*

avoidance relationship
Avoidance relationship: *mada dabu.*

awake
Able to remain awake for a long time: *madaala*$_2$.
Be awake for a short time: *mahuda.*
Be awake, be open: *ala*$_2$.

awaken
Awaken for a short time: *hhuda.*

aware
Aware, alert: *angaanga*$_1$.
Be aware of: *hagallongo.*
Be aware of oneself: *gidee iho.*
Be aware of, experience, perceive, feel (in one's mind or body): *longo iho.*
Pay attention to (notice), be aware of: *anga*$_1$.

awareness
Self-awareness: *anga iho.*

away
Away from: *dua*$_2$*; gee.*
Away from both the speaker and hearer: *ange.*
Outside, away, around: *daha.*

awesome
Forbidden, awesome: *dabu.*

awful
Ugly, awful: *dee vaagidee.*

awkward
Awkward by nature: *balabalavini.*
Clumsy, awkward (e.g., in carriage): *balavini.*
Clumsy, unskillful, awkward (not dexterous): *too gee.*

axe
A small axe, hatchet: *hagadaguu.*
Axe: *daguu.*

axis
Axis (or long thing through the center of something): *maailaba.*

baby
Baby: *tamaa gauligi.*
Baby, infant: *dama legalega*; gaagaa*$_1$.

baby talk
Baby talk: *basa gauligi.*

back
Back (of the body): *dua*$_2$.
In back of: *dua*$_2$.
The back of a human: *baba*$_1$.

backwards
Bent backwards: *gogo dua.*
Go backwards (esp. a canoe): *hagammene dua.*
Go backwards: *tugi dua.*
Run backwards, move backwards fast: *savini dua.*

bad
A bad sort of person: *songagi.*
Bad —: *vaivai.*
Bad: *baubau*$_2$*; saa*$_1$.
Bad character (of a person): *diinonga.*
Bad deeds: *hegau baubau.*
Bad person: *gana; leanga; vangani.*
Bad situation: *dulagi sala; dumanu sala.*
Bad weather: *dangalebu de me.*
Very bad: *dee adahaia.*

bad-mannered
Bad-mannered: *doo tahulinga; hai me a leangi.*

bail
To bail (a canoe): *daa*$_1$.
To bail a canoe rapidly: *taa hagabiibii.*
To bail water from a canoe: *taa de lui.*

bait
Bait (on the hook): *mainu.*
Collect bait: *hai mainu.*

bake
Bake: *dao*$_1$.

balance
Balance precariously: *hagaedeede.*

balanced
Unstable, poorly balanced: *duu saba.*
Unstably balanced: *sabasaba.*

bald-headed
Bald-headed: *sula tumuagi.*

ball
Bladder, balloon, ball: *buu*$_1$.

ballast
Ballast for an outrigger: *baalasa.*

balloon
Bladder, balloon, ball: *buu*$_1$.

ballooning
Ballooning of a sail: *dinae o de laa.*

bamboo
Bamboo: *madila.*

banana
Banana (fruit): *ga-hudi.*

banana tree
Banana tree fibers (for making cloth): *bulada.*
Plant sp.: tree sp.: banana tree: *ga-hudi; hudi*$_2$.

banish
Banish from the island (in a canoe with no paddle or food): *hagaholau.*

banyan tree
Plant sp.: tree sp.: banyan tree (*Ficus prolixa* Forst.): *aoa*$_1$.

barb
Barb: *hagamaadau*$_1$.

barber shop
Barber shop: *hale duu biho.*

bare
To bare one's teeth (by opening the lips to expose the whole set of teeth): *hagaida de gauvae.*

To bare one's teeth (by opening the lips): *hagaida.*
Top of the head, bare hilltop: *dumuagi.*

barely
Barely, just barely: *see*$_2$.
Just barely: *hagasee*$_2$.

barkcloth
Barkcloth: *malo gulu.*

barracuda
Fish sp.: barracuda: *ono*$_2$.

Barringtonia
Plant sp.: tree sp.: Barringtonia tree (*Barringtonia asiatica* (L.) Kurz): *gavaausu.*

Barringtonia tree
Plant sp.: tree sp.: Barringtonia tree (*Barringtonia asiatica* (L.) Kurz): *gavaausu.*

bartered
Goods which are bartered: *goloa hesuihagi.*

base
Stem, base, foot (e.g., of a hill), stump: *dahido.*

bashful
Bashful, ashamed, shy, embarrassed: *dogaa.*
Bashful, shy (timid about attending social affairs), timid: *hagaau gee.*
Shy, embarrassed, bashful: *hoosenga.*

basket
A type of basket: *banuunu; bolobolo a Sogo; bolobolo*$_1$*; dangaligi; gadebega; gavada; gede aola; gede dua dahi; gede gabi de husi; gede hadu; gede hangaabo; gede maduu; guanga; laula a sogo; laula hai doanga; laulau*$_2$.
A wrapping (like a basket) for food cooked in the earth oven: *lalau dao gai.*

basket
(the generic term): *gede.*

bass
Fish sp.: mountain bass: *sahole.*
Fish sp.: sea bass (The native term is applied to many spp.): *ngadala.*
Fish sp.: sea bass (small): *donu*$_3$.
Fish sp.: sea bass (2 sorts: 1 large, 1 small): *madabiebie.*
Fish sp.: sea bass: *hangadala; sahudu.*

bat
To bat around: *daabeduge saele.*

batfish
Fish sp.: batfish?: *bunei.*

bath house
bath house: *hale gaugau.*

bathe
To bathe (including swimming for the purpose of bathing: *gaugau*$_2$.
To bathe (someone): *hakaugaua.*

battle
War, battle: *daua*$_3$.

bawl out
bawl out (speak harshly to): *degideig*$_1$.
bawl out, be angry: *bole.*
scold, bawl out, chide: *hagasee*$_1$.

be
be (present), have, there is...: *iai.*
Be included: *dau*$_1$.
Be situated: *noho.*

beach
Beach, sand spit: *olo.*
Storm beach (on the seaward reef): *mada sua hadu.*
Storm beach: *sua hadu.*
To beach (a canoe) on land: *dau age.*
To beach (a canoe), arrive at: *dau*$_3$.
To beach a canoe without using runners: *dada moni.*
To launch or beach a canoe by dragging it along the shore: *solo.*

beach naupaka shrub
Plant sp.: beach naupaka shrub (*Scaevola taccada* (Gaertn.) Roxb.): *manu-gaba-aasanga.*

bear
Bear (fruit): *hua*$_1$.
Bear — (as a tree): *haa*$_1$.
Bear misshapen fruit: *hai aoa ina.*

beard
Chin, beard: *gumigumi*$_3$.

beat
Beat unmercifully: *daa hatau.*
Hit, strike, beat: *daa*$_1$.

beating
Steady beating (as of a heart): *dili.*

beautiful
Beautiful (esp. owing to having a graceful manner): *tilo danuaa.*

Beautiful but otherwise useless: *ngadi mahamaha —*.
Pretty, beautiful: *mahamaha*.

because
Because of: *i*.
Because of, owing to: *hidinga*.

because!
Because!: *hiidinga*$_2$.

bedclothes
Bedclothes, bedding: *moenga*$_1$.

bedding
Bedclothes, bedding: *moenga*$_1$.

bedridden
Bedridden with illness: *bigo*.

before
Front (position), before, ahead: *mua*.

beforehand
Beforehand: *i mua nei*.

beg
Beg, apologize: *dangidangi*.
Beg, apologize, or ask permission in an insistent manner: *dangidangi keli*.

begin
Initiate, begin: *aladi*.
Initiate, begin, start: *ladi*.
Start or begin (singing or fighting only): *langi*$_1$.

beginning
Beginning of (a season, day, etc.): *gaba*$_1$.
Front part of, face, beginning (of a thing): *mada*$_3$.
The beginning (of an event): *daamada*.
The beginning of a fire: *adilo*.

begun
To have begun it: *damadaa*.

behave
Behave like a baby: *hagagaagaa*.
Behave with embarrassment or shyness: *hai me dogaa*.

behavior
Behavior (of a person): *geunga*.

belch
Belch: *maava age*.
Yawn, belch: *maava*.

believe
To believe in ghosts: *hagaduu eidu*.
Trust, believe: *hagadonu*.
Trust, believe in: *gai*$_1$.

belly
Belly: *dinae*.

belonging
Belonging to: *ni*$_1$.
Belonging to each person's one: *niidada; niidodo*.
Belonging to each person's several: *niaada; niiada; niiodo; niooda*.
Belonging to his (or hers, or its): *niiana; niiono*.
Belonging to my: *niiagu; niiogu*.
Belonging to our: *niiadaadeu; niiadaau; niiamaadeu; niiamaau; niiodaadeu; niiodaau; niiomaadeu; niiomaau*.
Belonging to their: *niialaadeu; niialaau; niiolaadeu; niiolaau*.
Belonging to your: *niiau; niiodou; niioluu; niioo*.

bend
Bend (one's body) forward: *ino gi mua*.
Bend: *hholu*.
Bend in a path: *haadinga haiava*.
Bend one's head backwards: *dangage dua*.
Bend out of shape (temporarily): *ngalogu*.

bent
Bent: *bigo; ngaholu*.
Bent forward: *gogo gi mua*.
Bent slightly (like a round-shouldered person): *gogo*.
Bent slightly (not sharply): *ngavali*.
Bent up (having several bends): *bigobigo*.
Bent up: *bongabonga*.
Bent, curved, defective (of fruit): *bonga*.
Broken (as a stick), bent up: *hadi*.
Hang down or bent down (of branches, palm fronds, or fishing poles): *llou*.

bequeath
Bequeath: *bolo ange*.

beseech
Beseech: *dangidangi keli*.

besides
Besides: *laa tua; ma tua*.

best
Best of all: *tahi i tanuaa*.
First, best: *tahi*$_1$.

better
Better than (nothing, etc.): *manege ma de —*.

Good for, better than: *danuaa ange.*
Improved, better: *danuaa age.*

between
Between: *magavaa.*
Between, amongst: *masavaa*$_1$.

big
Big (and therefore good), strong, tremendous: *dee lahilahia.*
Big (of animals): *sinasinaa.*
Big: *laanui; nnui.*
Big around, fat: *longohie.*
Big, great: *laumalie.*
Too big (clothes), spacious: *oo tanga.*
Too big in size (of clothes): *doo i de ubu.*

bile
Bile: *me mmala.*

billions
Billions: *sebugi.*
Tens of billions: *sebaga.*

bird
A bird: *manu lele.*
A young bird (of any sp. suitable for being raised as a pet): *bunua.*

bird sp.
Bird sp. (= large *moa*): *moa-a-daila.*
Bird sp. (never seen live): *loha*$_2$.
Bird sp. (seen only over the ocean): *lii.*
Bird sp.: *gaga*$_2$*; galevaleva; manu-kono*$_1$*; moa*$_1$.
Bird sp.:: *ginuede.*
Bird sp.: Japanese snipe (*Capella hardwickii*): *googoo*$_2$.
Bird sp.: Polynesian tattler (*Heteroscelus brevipes*): *goigoi*$_2$.
Bird sp.: Polynesian tattler? (*Heteroscelus brevipes*): *dilidili-dogi.*
Bird sp.: a young bird (still unable to fly) of any bird sp.: *maadegadega.*
Bird sp.: booby?: *gailulu.*
Bird sp.: brown booby?: *gaalau.*
Bird sp.: common noddy (*Anous Stolidus*): *ngongo.*
Bird sp.: eastern whimbrel (*Numenius phaeopus*): *geevee.*
Bird sp.: fairy tern (*Gygis alba*): *agiagi.*
Bird sp.: golden plover (*Plurialis dominica*): *duli*$_1$.
Bird sp.: great frigate bird (*Fregata minor*): *gadaha.*
Bird sp.: reef heron (*Demiegretta sacra*): *gava*$_2$.
Bird sp.: ruddy turnstone (*Arenaria interpres*): *givigivi.*
Bird sp.: sacred kingfisher (*Halcyon sancta*) (The native term applies possibly to several spp.): *manu-de-bua.*
Bird sp.: sharp-tailed sandpiper (*Erolia acuminata*): *damaa-manu.*
Bird sp.: short-tailed shearwater (*Puffinus tenuirostris*): *manu-a-madaligi.*
Bird sp.: starling (*Apolonis opacus*): *moso.*
Bird sp.: tern? (a vagrant sp., rarely seen): *dala-hagalulu-madangi; dala-moana; dala*$_5$.
Bird sp.: wandering tattler? (*Heteroscelus incanus*): *lahulahu*$_2$.
Bird sp.: white tern?: *lebidi.*
Bird sp.: white-capped noddy (*Anous minutus*): *legia.*
Bird sp.: white-rumped swift (*Apus pacificus*) (The native term applies possibly to several spp.): *gauea.*
Bird sp.: white-tailed tropic bird (*Phaethon lepturus*): *davage.*

bird's-nest fern
Plant sp.: bird's-nest fern (*Asplenium nidus* L.): *lau-gadaha.*

birth
Give birth to: *haanau.*
Give birth to, born: *maaui.*

birthday
Birthday: *boo*$_2$.

bit
Bit (of something): *bido.*

bite
Bite: *gadi.*
Bite hard: *kadi.*
Bite someone: *ngau hala.*

bitter
Bitter, sour: *mmala.*

black
A pitch-black night: *gohu boo dangodango.*
Black: *uliuli.*
Jet black: *uli bela; ulimagallai.*

black coral
Gorgonian (Coelenterate), false black coral: *aoa-laosedi.*

blackened
Dark (in color), blackened: *uli*$_1$.

blacktip shark
Fish sp.: blacktip shark: *mangoo-dahola.*

bladder
Bladder, balloon, ball: *buu*$_1$.

blade
Point, blade: *mada*$_3$.
The blade of the canoe paddle: *laulau hoe.*

blame
Blame (for something): *dagasala.*
Blame (someone), accuse: *hagadagasala.*
Blame (someone), incriminate (someone): *hagabuu ange.*

blamed
Be always blamed for: *dagadagasala.*

blanket
Sheet, blanket: *malo gahu de boo.*

bleed
Bleed: *sali dodo.*

bleeding
Bleeding profusely: *hai dodo.*
Stop bleding: *tuu todo.*

blemish
A blemish (on the skin): *mangeo.*

blenny
Fish sp.: blenny: *dauleelage.*

bless
Bless (someone): *hagamanuia.*

blessed
Fortunate, lucky, blessed: *manuia.*

blind
Blind: *dee gide.*

blink
A flash of light, a blink of an eye: *daba.*
A flashing of several lights, a blink of the eyes: *taba.*

blisters
Blisters on the skin caused by sunburn: *hoe*$_2$.

bloated
Bloated, inflated, swollen up, bulging: *lengi.*

block
To block (the way): *bono; pono.*

block out
Block out (from sight): *hagalilo.*

blood
Blood: *dodo*$_1$.

bloody
Bloody (of a person): *dotodo.*
Bloody: *dodo ina.*
To have bloody stools: *magi hongagelegele todo.*

bloom
Bloom (of flowers): *ala*$_2$.
In bloom: *madala mai.*

bloomed
Bloomed: *madala.*

blossom
Blossom forth: *hhaa.*

blow
Blow (of the wind): *ssau.*
Blow (with the mouth): *busi.*
Blow away, cause to move (in the water): *angia.*
Blow continuously (wind): *angiangi.*
Blow gently (of wind): *angi.*
Blow one's nose: *usubee.*
Blow steadily (of wind): *sau makaga.*
Blow with increasing force (wind): *angiangi.*
Blow, fan (oneself): *ili.*

blurred
Blurred (out of focus): *neve.*
Blurred: *buu useahi; lehua.*

board
To board (a ship or canoe): *uda*$_1$.

board$_1$
flat, board: *baabaa*$_2$.

boast
Boast foolishly about one's ability (when it is obvious that one is inept): *hagadoodoo denga muna.*

bobbing
Bobbing in the water: *anumia.*

body
Body: *angaanga*$_3$.

body odor
Having an unpleasant body odor: *saunga.*

bodyguard
Bodyguard, soldier: *daagami**.

boggy
Plot of taro bog, boggy soil: *bela*.

boil
A boil (on the body), carbuncle: *hagahoa*.
A boil on the body: *malemale*.
A boil on the body that is hard and painful, and which will not come to a head: *ginadoa*.

boil$_1$
boil (water): *dunu*$_1$.

boiling
Boiling: *kai*$_3$.

bold
Daring (show off), bold: *hai mogomogo*.

bone
Bone, needle: *ivi*.

bonito
Fish sp.: bonito: *adu-balebale-i-dua*.

booby
Bird sp.: booby?: *gailulu*.
Bird sp.: brown booby?: *gaalau*.

boom
Outrigger boom: *giado*.

bored
Be bored: *pili*$_2$.

boring
Boring: *hagapili*$_2$.

born
Born: *haanau*.
Give birth to, born: *maaui*.

both
Both sides (of): *luu baasi*.
Both, as one: *ngaadahi*.

bothered
Bothered, annoyed: *goso*.

bottle
A bottle (of glass): *manu hao vai*.
A pottery botle or jar: *manu hale moni*.

bottom
Bottom part: *ulu i lalo*.
Bottom, foundation: *dagelo*.

boundary
Boundary of a taro plot: *ngudu-me*.

boundary stone
Boundary stone: *hadu goinga*.

bow
Bow (for an arrow): *me hholu*.
Bow or nod or genuflect (as a sign of respect): *ino*.

bowl
A bowl (pottery): *gumedi hadu*.
A type of bowl: *gamedi vai salo; gumedi de henua; gumedi vai solo*.
Bowl (wooden): *gumedi*.

box
Box, coffin, crate: *ngavesi*.

boxfish
Fish sp.: boxfish (dark blue): *moomoa-uliuli*.
Fish sp.: boxfish (yellow): *moomoa-ganoango*.

boy
Boy, young man: *dama daane*.
Male child, boy: *gauligi daane*.

boy-chaser
Boy-chaser, boy-crazy: *ulu i daane*.

boy-crazy
Boy-chaser, boy-crazy: *ulu i daane*.

boyfriend
Boyfriend, girlfriend: *dau soa*.

brackish
Brackish (water): *daava*.

braid
Braid (rope or hair, etc.), wrap with rope: *bini*.
Braid strands of sennit: *hilo*.

braided
Loosely braided: *madaala*$_1$.

brain
Brain: *ngago*.

branch
A branch (of a tree): *laa*$_3$.
A branch, part of (something having coordinate parts): *manga*.
A spear, branch of (part of): *dao*$_2$.

brand
Brand new: *mada hoou*.

brass
Copper or brass or other reddish metal: *baalanga mmea*.

brave
Daring, brave, manly: *lo taane*.

bravest
Bravest in war: *daane mada daua.*

breadfruit
A young breadfruit tree: *soesoe gulu.*
Breadfruit season: *dau gulu.*
Breadfruit with rough skin: *gulu daladala.*
Breadfruit with smooth skin: *gulu malali.*
Immature breadfruit: *gaehala.*
Plant sp.: tree sp.: breadfruit: *gulu.*
Tree-ripened breadfruit: *gulu bala.*

break
Break into pieces: *hhoa.*
Break many times or in many places: *hadihadi.*
Break through any obstacles in one's path: *mulu gudu.*
Break, break up, destroy: *oha.*
Take a short break (in work involving standing): *hhadi iho luu vae.*

break in
Break in (something new): *hagahadi.*

breast
Breast: *gaanuunu.*

breast-feed
Breast-feed: *haau unuunu.*

breath
Breath, breathe: *manava.*
Shortness of breath: *manava bodo.*

breathe
Be unable to breathe: *pono age de manava.*
Breath, breathe: *manava.*

breathing
Breathing: *manavanava.*

breechclout
Breechclout: *huna; malo huna; malo sabo*.*

bright
A piercingly bright light: *vvala.*
Light (not dark), bright: *maalama.*

brighten
Brighten, illuminate: *hagamaalama.*

bring
Bring a lot of: *daabeduge mai.*
Bring up, put up, take up: *vage*$_1$.
Give or bring to (someone): *gavange.*
Give or bring up: *gavage.*

bring together
Close up, bring together: *hagabunia.*

bring up
Bring up (children), discipline (children): *haele.*
Spoil (children), bring up (children) badly: *haele sala.*

bristle
Bristle, ready for a fight (of animals): *hagateve.*

broad
Broad: *lahalaha.*

broad-chested
Broad-chested: *baa lahalaha.*

broken
Broken (as a machine), broken down: *maoha.*
Broken (as a stick), bent up: *hadi.*
Broken in many pieces (as glass when dropped): *ssii*$_1$.
Broken in many places (like string), easily broken (e.g., of rope): *modumodu.*
Broken into small pieces: *dagaligiligi.*
Broken up (into many pieces or groupings): *maoha saele; maohaoha.*
Broken up into small pieces: *ssii mommomo.*
Broken up, cracked, burst: *mahaa.*

broom
Broom: *uu duaa nui.*

brother
Brother, male cousin: *daina daane.*
Brother, sister, sibling, cousin: *daina.*

brother-in-law
A sibling's spouse or spouse's sibling (brother-in-law or sister-in-law) of the same sex: *maa*$_2$.

brown booby
Bird sp.: brown booby?: *gaalau.*

Bruguiera
Plant sp.: oriental mangrove (*Bruguiera gymnorhiza* (L.) Lam.): *donga.*

brush
Shave, sweep, brush off (once): *dahi*$_2$.

bubbles
Foam, bubbles: *ebuebu.*

build
Build (of a person): *holiholi.*

Build (of the body): *soomonga*$_1$.
Build a fire: *dahu*.
Construct, set up, build (something): *hagaduu*.

building
House, dwelling, building: *hale*.

bulging
Bloated, inflated, swollen up, bulging: *lengi*.

bullet
Lead (metal), bullet: *soodo*.

bump
A bump on a tree trunk: *buge*.
Bump into: *dugi*$_1$.

bunch
A bunch: *daa*$_2$.
A bunch of fully mature coconuts: *gau looloa gaadinga*.

bundle
A bundle (e.g. of sticks): *uu*$_4$.
A bundle of sticks: *uu dogo*.
Bundle, knot: *noodanga*.
Package, bundle (wrapped up): *sabininga*.

buried
Buried: *danu*.

burn
Burn with a high flame: *ulavvaa*.
Set fire to, burn: *dudu*.

burned
Burned (food): *massagalala*.
Burned (overcooked food): *gango*.
Burned: *vela*.

burning
Flame, aflame, burning: *ula*$_1$.

burrow
Drill through, burrow: *hao*$_1$.
Sink below the horizon, burrow into the sand: *hagadanu*.

burrowing heart urchin
Burrowing heart urchin: *veli-tea*.

Bursa
Mollusk sp.: *Cymatiidae* spp., also *Bursa bubo*: *buu-kangi-de-muli*.

Bursidae
Mollusk sp.: *Bursidae* spp.: *gammenge-baabaa*.

burst
Broken up, cracked, burst: *mahaa*.
Explode, burst: *paa*$_2$.

bush
In the bush (uncleared area): *lodo me muimui*.
Inland, bush (uncleared) land, wilderness: *lodo henua*.

bushy
Bushy (of hair): *gobagoba*.

busy
Be very busy: *nebu*.
Busy (with work or obligations): *sulu i hegau*.

but
But, and, then, so: *gai*$_3$.

butterfly
Butterfly: *bebe*$_2$.

butterfly fish
Fish sp.: butterfly fish (The native term is applied to many spp.): *dihidihi*.

buttock
Buttock: *duu mugamuga; duudane*.

buttocks
Buttocks: *dae*$_3$.
Having flat buttocks, ugly (because not plump): *biihingi*.

button
Button: *bule dango*.

buy
Buy, sell, repay: *hagao*.

by
By: *e*$_1$.

by and by
A little later, by and by: *muli mai ange*.

cable
Cable, wire (heavy): *daula baalanga*.

calandar
Calandar: *me hai laangi*.

calculate
Calculate (do arithmetic), figure out: *kumi*$_2$.
Measure, calculate, estimate: *hagabau*.

calculation
Calculation, arithmetic: *guumanga*.

calisthenics
Calisthenics, exercises: *holahola aalanga*.

call
Call (someone): *hagaagahi.*
Call (someone) by the name of his name-group: *hagasaalunga ange.*
Call (someone) once: *hagahi.*

called
Be known as, called by the name —: *hagabinga ange.*
Be named, be called: *binga.*
Called by (named): *hagaingoo ai.*
Give a name to, named, called: *hagaingoo.*

callus
Callus: *$maga_2$.*
Ingrown callus: *madaniiga.*

calm
Calm (weather), still (wind): *malino.*
Calm weather, with no noise: *hagaloma de me.*
Completely calm: *doo mai de malino.*
Very calm seas: *vai nui hhoa.*
Very calm, silent: *loma.*

calm down
Calm down (of a person): *sili iho.*
To calm down someone who is excited or unhappy: *haganaa.*

calmed
Be calmed (e.g., seas): *malinongia.*

calmer
Become calmer (after being angry): *diinei de lodo.*

calmness
Calmness, tranqulity, freedom from worries: *lodo baba.*

Calophyllum
Plant sp.: tree sp.: Alexandrian laurel tree (*Calophyllum inophyllum* L.): *hedau.*

camera
Camera: *me hai ada.*

candy
Candy: *me maimai.*

cannibal
Cannibal: *dangada gai dangada.*

canoe
A big ship or canoe: *vaga*.*
Canoe: *moni.*
Model (or toy) canoe: *moni hagadeledele.*

canoe house
Canoe house: *holau.*

canoe paddle
A canoe paddle: *hoe_1.*

capable
A person who is capable at almost anything: *daane e manege; tama e manege.*
Be capable at: *$baubau_1$.*
Capable (of a person): *$saba_2$.*
Capable: *abo.*
Capable of, be the equal of: *bau ange.*
Capable only of looking after oneself (not others): *bau iho.*

capacity
Ability, capacity (of person), resourcefulness: *hina.*
The load or capacity (of a ship or canoe): *hagaudanga.*

Capella
Bird sp.: Japanese snipe (*Capella hardwickii*): *$googoo_2$.*

capital
Capital of: *madaaolo.*

capsize
Capsize: *abongi.*

captain
Captain of a modern ship: *eligi.*

capture
Capture: *boo_1.*

car
Car: *hada.*

carapace
The carapace of the hawksbill turtle: *ango*; una.*

carbuncle
A boil (on the body), carbuncle: *hagahoa.*

cardinal fish
Fish sp.: cardinal fish (The native term is applied to several spp.): *guba.*
Fish sp.: cardinal fish: *gaba-moe; guba-baabaa.*

Cardium
Mollusk sp.: *Cardium* sp.: *$kosi_2$.*

careful!
Be careful!: *kana.*

carefully
Carefully, gently, softly: *maalie.*
Do carefully: *hagalongolongo.*

carom
Carom off: *baa sege.*
Carom off violently: *baa ssalu.*

carpenter
Carpenter: *labagau.*

carry
Bring to me, carry to me: *gamai.*
Carry (a burden): *saabai.*
Carry a basket, etc., on one's hip: *hagauda i tege.*
Carry a canoe (over the reef at low tide): *saabai moni doo.*
Carry a canoe in shallow water: *abaabai.*
Carry around holding: *gabi saele.*
Carry half lifting: *abaabai.*
Carry in one's hands: *dagidagi.*
Give or carry (something) to you: *gavadu.*

carve
Carve out, drill out: *hoda.*

cassytha vine
Plant sp.: cassytha vine (*Cassytha filiformis* L.): *hiisoa.*

castes
Castes (two) of aboriginal Nukuoro society: *luu duu de maduu.*

castrate
To castrate a pig: *tuu de biigi.*

cat's-eye
Cat's-eye (of a shell): *dango*$_2$.

catch
(For a bird) to catch with its beak: *usu*$_1$.
Grab or catch in a single act: *poo.*
To catch (e.g., a ball): *sigo.*
To catch by scooping up (e.g., with a net or basket): *buulou.*
To catch fire, aflame: *gaa*$_2$.
To catch flying fish: *dilimangali.*
To catch water (in something): *hagasahu.*
To catch with a lasso or noose: *sele*$_1$.

catch on to
Catch on to, unerstand: *ssigo.*

caudal vertebrae
Tip of the spine (caudal vertebrae): *dogonogo.*

caught
Able to, obtained, gotten, caught: *maua.*
Be caught (esp. fish) and secured: *saahea.*
Be caught between two or more other things: *bigi*$_1$.
Be caught doing something wrong: *boogia mai.*
Be caught in a storm: *boaa.*
Be caught in strong wind or heavy rain: *boaa ina.*
Be caught on, stuck on: *lave.*
Be caught or hung up on something so as unable to fall (as a felled tree): *bili.*
Found or caught doing something wrong: *vaagia.*
Get, obtain, caught: *mau*$_3$.
Hooked, caught fast on: *lau*$_1$.

cause
Cause to (be, become, have, know) —: *haga-.*

celebrate
Celebrate: *dao de laangi.*
Celebrate the birthday (of): *hai de boo (o).*

center
Center: *teungaalodo.*

centipede
Centipede: *manu-de-boo.*

Cerithiidae
Mollusk sp.: *Cerithiidae* spp.: *hakai-a-bagila.*
Mollusk sp.: *Cerithiidae*: *anga-dogi.*

certain
Certain, sure, graceful, definitely: *too donu.*
Unmistakably, for certain: *gu soe donu.*

cervix
Cervix: *tuugau i lodo.*

Chama
Mollusk sp.: *Chama iostoma*: *hadu-bunga.*

change
A change of wind direction: *dahuli de madangi; geu de madangi.*
Change: *hagadagodo gee ina.*
Change clothes: *dala malo.*
Change course: *lui*$_1$.
Change of heart, change one's mind, repent: *dahuli de lodo.*

Change of personality (for the better): *sui hagahoou.*
Change one's mind: *dahuli; sui de lodo.*
Change, replace: *sui.*
Move slightly, change position: *ngalue.*

channel
Passage, channel: *ava*$_1$.

chant
Chant (ancient): *dau*$_5$.
Chant (in the old religious ceremony): *hagallogo**.

chanting
Chanting (of old chants): *daa (dau).*

character
A character (written symbol): *siianga*$_1$.

charcoal
Charcoal from the coconut shell: *dalaa ubu.*

charge
Be in charge of, control, lead: *huahua ai.*

charlatan
Charlatan: *ngudu gaiaa.*

charlatanism
Charlatanism: *iloo me.*

Charonia
Mollusk sp.: *Charonia* spp.: *gio.*

chase
Chase away (in a certain direction): *dugi gee.*
Chase by trying to head off: *hagabaa*$_1$.
Chase, run after: *doolohi.*
Scare away, chase away: *dugi*$_2$.

chatterbox
Chatterbox, a person who speaks fast: *vilidogi.*
Talkative, chatterbox, talk animatedly: *hai daalanga.*
Talkative, chatterbox, talk at great length: *ili taalanga.*

chattering
Chattering of teeth (from cold): *gadigadi gauvae.*

cheat
Steal, dishonest, cheat: *gaiaa.*

cheek
Cheek, sides of the canoe prow: *galaahuu.*

cheer
Cheer up (someone): *hagamaamaane de lodo.*
Please (someone), cheer up (someone): *hagamalangilangi.*

cheerful
Cheerful by nature, joyous: *hagamalangilangi.*
Happy, laugh (as a sign of happiness), cheerful: *malangilangi.*

cherish
Take special care of, cherish: *hagamogomogo*$_1$.

chest
Chest: *hadahada.*
Chest, front (opposite of back — e.g.,lagoon shore as opposed to seaward reef shore): *aloalo*$_3$.

chew
Chew (e.g., to suck juice out but not swallow it): *ngau*$_2$.
Chew thoroughly, masticate (soft foods which do not make noise): *maamaa.*
Chew, masticate (solids which make noise): *ngungu.*

chide
Scold, bawl out, chide: *hagasee*$_1$.

chief
Chief (of the island): *hodooligi.*
Chief of the island (?): *eligi.*

chief mate
Chief mate (of a European ship): *lua-aligi.*

child
A natural child: *dama donu.*
An adopted child: *dama daohi; dama ssala.*
Child: *dama.*
Child, young person: *gauligi.*
Eldest child: *dama madua.*

child-in-law
Parent-in-law, child-in-law, mother-in-law, father-in-law, son-in-law, daughter-in-law: *saulaba.*

childhood
Childhood: *masavaa de gauligi.*

childish
A childish act: *hai me a gauligi.*

chin
Chin, beard: *gumigumi*$_3$.

Chlamys
Mollusk sp.: *Chlamys schmeltzi*: *dalia-dodo.*

choose
Choose carefully from among many, election: *hilihili.*
Pick from among several, choose, elect: *hili*$_1$.

chop
To chop down: *sele*$_2$.

choppy
Rough or choppy sea condition: *dangalebu.*
Rough or choppy seas: *dangalebu de moana.*

chuckle
Chuckle: *hhuu.*

church
Church (building): *hale daumaha.*
Church (services): *daumaha.*

cigarette-holder
A cigarette-holder, made from a coconut leaf: *uu*$_4$.

circular
Round, spherical, circular: *moe*$_2$.

circumcise
Circumcise: *tuu daga holiage.*

circumference
Waist, circumference: *daogubu.*

circumstance
Situation, circumstance: *dagodo.*

clam
A clam nursery: *hada.*
Mollusk sp.: clam sp. (a type of *baasua*): *aasolo; halaasola.*
Mollusk sp.: clam sp.: *baieu.*
Mollusk sp.: giant clam (*Tridacna squammosa*): *dange.*
Mollusk sp.: giant clam sp.: *ngae*$_2$.
Mollusk sp.: horse hoof clam (*Hippopus hippopus*): *gima.*

clap
Clap hands: *baabaa luu lima.*
To clap one's wet hands together (to dry them): *huuhuu*$_1$.

class
Social class of chiefs and priests: *aagonga i lunga*.*
Social class of those who know the black arts: *aagonga i lalo*.*

claw
Claw: *llabu; llagu.*

clean
Clean: *gili malali.*
To clean fish (taking the insides out): *duagi.*

clean off
Clean off: *daahia; tahi*$_2$.

clean up
Sweep or clean up trash: *sao gainga.*
Sweep, clean up: *ssao*$_1$.
Wipe, scrub, clean up (by wiping), erase: *ssolo.*

cleaned
Completely cleaned up or finished: *odi sango.*
Used up or cleaned out completely: *malalidage.*

clear
Clear (easily seen), unobscured: *aadea.*
Clear (in focus): *nehu.*
Clear (not opaque or blurred): *masalaba.*
Clear (with nothing in the way): *dauaadea.*
Clear, unobstructed, uncluttered: *malaelae.*
Round, clear (in outline): *molomolo*$_2$.
To clear bush (overgrowth): *vele.*
To clear land (or a path, etc.) of weeds and underbrush: *velevele.*
To clear oil (which is separated from crude coconut oil by heating): *lolomango.*
To clear out a place: *hagadauaadea.*

clear-headed
Clear-headed: *masaala.*

cleared
Cleared (of brush or obstructions): *malali.*
Cleared (of obstructions): *dauaadea.*

clearing
Clearing (e.g., in the woods): *momme aadea.*

clench
To clench one's teeth (from cold): *kadi gauvae.*

Clerodendrum
Plant sp.: glory bower (*Clerodendrum inerme* (L.) Gaertn.): *manu-mmala.*

clever
Clever (scheme or trick): *se biho.*
Clever person: *dangada ssigo.*
Clever, a fast learner: *ssigo.*
Smart, intelligent, clever: *heiangi.*

climb
Climb: *gage.*
Climb up on: *gage.*
Get down, climb down: *iho.*
To climb a coconut tree without using a rope (on one's hands or feet) for assistance: *dolo bala.*

clitoris
Clitoris: *me duu; tuugau i daha.*

close
Be close: *hebaa.*
Close to (in meaning): *bigi*$_2$.
Close to, near to: *baa ange.*
Close up to: *buni ange.*
More-or-less close to: *bigibigi*$_2$.

close$_1$
close one's jaws: *dami.*
To close (something): *bono.*
To close both eyes: *mmoe*$_1$.

close up
Close up, bring together: *hagabunia.*
Join, close up (something,e.g., a hole): *buni ange.*

closed up
Closed up, be together (three or more things): *puni.*
Closed up, be together (in a group, or of two individuals): *buni.*

closer
Get closer to: *hagamúa.*

clot
A clot of blood: *dibaa dodo.*

cloth
Clothes, cloth: *malo.*

clothes
Clothes, cloth: *malo.*

cloud
A type of a cloud formation: *dao o gasoni.*
A type of cloud (not associated with rain): *gili langi.*
A type of cloud formation (dark but not threatening rain): *babaiangi.*
A type of cloud formation like *babaiangi*: *pai.*
A type of high cloud: *gili iga.*
A type of low cloud: *salibaadaa.*
Rain cloud (includes all cumulus types): *hagausinga.*

cloudy
Cloudy day (not bright): *malumalu de me.*

cloying
Cloying insincere humility: *halehale gaiaa.*
Unctuous, cloying, winsome: *ngudu maimai.*

club
Fish club (priest): *adu*$_3$.

cluck
Cluck one's tongue: *daa de alelo.*

clumsily
To conduct oneself clumsily: *hai me balavini.*

clumsy
Be clumsy (in physical contest): *baa sala.*
Clumsy: *balagula.*
Clumsy by nature: *balabalavini.*
Clumsy, awkward (e.g., in carriage): *balavini.*
Clumsy, unskillful, awkward (not dexterous): *too gee.*
Habitually clumsy: *balabalagula.*

coagulation
Coagulation of blood: *noho dodo.*

coarse
Be coarse in texture, grain, weave, etc.: *pada.*

coast
Coast, shoreline: *tagudai.*

cockroach
Insect sp.: cockroach: *hagabini*$_2$.
Insect sp.: cockroach sp. (black — foul smelling): *de-hine-aligi*$_1$.

coconut
A coconut (for drinking): *huaa me.*
A coconut which is nearly mature: *gaadinga gaha dea; me gaha dea.*
A coconut with a small kernel: *gaha paa.*

A coconut with an unusually small-sized kernel: *gaadinga gaha paa.*
A drinking coconut: *daahaa.*
A nearly mature coconut: *modomodo.*
A ripe coconut (= *gaadinga*) of poor quality: *me madaali.*
A type of coconut (reddish in color): *dulivai.*
A type of coconut with an edible husk: *gadoi.*
Husk of the coconut: *hakaa.*

coconut apple
Coconut apple (young and edible): *mogo.*
Coconut apple: *somo*$_1$.
Fully mature coconut apple: *somo dae.*
Immature coconut apple: *duu beleala.*
Overripe coconut apple: *laulau*$_3$.

coconut crab
Coconut crab: *baluu.*

coconut meat
Coconut meat (fully mature) of good quality for eating: *alo-malie.*
Coconut meat which has formed in the nut with no sap: *daga*$_2$.

coconut milk
Coconut milk: *vai nui.*

coconut tree
A coconut tree seedling: *me osi.*
A type of coconut tree: *daogave; huaalanga.*
Plant sp.: tree sp.: coconut tree: *nui.*

coffin
Box, coffin, crate: *ngavesi.*

coil
A coil of rope: *siigonga.*

cold
Become freezing cold (of a person): *uluhia e de lede.*
Cold (sickness): *magi gobegobe.*
Cold (sickness), flu: *magi o de henua.*
Feel cold, shivering (from cold): *magalili.*
Penetrating cold: *lede.*

collapse
Collapse (of persons): *dili bala.*
Collapse completely: *moomodu.*

collar bone
Collar bone: *ivi ngongo.*

collect
Collect in one place together, accumulate: *hagabudu.*
To collect *baasua*: *nao baasua.*

collection
Collection (in church), offering (in church), sacrifice, tithe: *sigidaumaha.*

collide
Collide: *hedaadoi.*

Colocasia
Plant sp.: taro (*Colocasia esculenta*), also the corm of this plant: *dalo.*

color
A color (of something): *leebunga.*
Put color on, color (something): *lebu.*

comb
To comb (hair): *selu.*

come
Come (go) straight: *velo mai (adu, ange).*
Come: *humai.*
Come early: *oho mai.*
Come in (tide): *ua*$_1$.
Come or go (toward the speaker): *loomai.*
Come out from (like smoke or pus): *buu*$_2$.
Come out in front: *hua*$_1$.
Come up (e.g., weeds): *malanga age.*
Come with difficulty: *hagangadaa.*
Come without bringing anything (such as gifts): *ngadi humai.*
Difficult to come: *ngadaa mai.*
Go or come down (or toward the lagoon): *loiho.*
Hasten to go or come: *alomasige.*

comfortable
Feel comfortable: *abo.*

common noddy
Bird sp.: common noddy (*Anous stolidus*): *ngongo.*

commoner
An ordinary person, commoner: *ngadi dangada.*

community
Community: *huaahenua.*

companions
Companions or friends who share the

same interests, and who get along well: *dangada ulu.*

compare
Compare: *hagaheloongoi.*

compartment
Room, compartment: *bao.*

compassion
Compassion, affection: *aloha.*

compete
Compete (as between individuals): *madamada*$_2$.
Compete (between groups): *hagadau gavange.*
Compete hard against (as in team sports): *baalasi ange.*
Compete to see who is stronger: *hagadaudoo.*

competitive
Competitive, envious, desirous of retaliating: *lodo gaiaa.*

complain
Grumble, complain: *nanu.*
Sue (in court), complain about (to the authorities): *vange gi de hainga.*

complaint
The object of a complaint: *nanua; nanulia; nanumia.*

complete
Accomplish or complete something in a single effort: *dugu dahi.*
Complete (none missing): *odi ange.*
Complete (something): *hagamalele.*
To complete an act later: *bido.*

completed
Completed: *malele.*

completely
Completely, very: *saunoa.*

compose
To compose songs: *hai daahili.*

compound
Village, compound (aggregation of houses): *aduhale.*

concerning
About it, concerning it, in it, for it: *loo.*
Concerning: *i; i de baasi.*

conch
A conch shell trumpet: *buu*$_1$.
Mollusk sp.: spider conch: *anga-baabaa.*

conciliate
Make peace between people, conciliate: *hagadanuaa magavaa.*

concubinage
Common-law marriage, concubinage: *ngadi hai bodu.*

cone shell
Mollusk sp.: cone shell: *manu-hagadigedige.*

confess
Confess one's sins or errors: *tala hai sala.*
Confess wrongs: *tala baubau.*

confluence
A confluence of currents (making the water choppy): *hebaledage.*
A confluence of ocean currents (on the surface only): *au hebaledage.*
A confluence of ocean currents, or a circular current in which drifting objects remain stationary: *au doga.*

confused
Indecisive, confused: *lodo lanea*$_2$.
Wound around, tangled up, confused: *vini.*

conglomerate
Conglomerate, islet: *adu*$_4$.

conjunctivitis
Conjunctivitis: *bunana.*

connect
Connect up or join several things: *sugusugui.*
Connect up, join up, continue upon: *duudagi.*
Connect, join together: *suugui.*
Join to, connect to, connect up with: *suugui ange.*

connection
Joint, connection: *suguinga.*

consciousness
Regain consciousness: *lele age.*
Regain consciousness, rise from the dead: *mouli age.*

conserve
Put aside, leave for later, conserve: *hagadoe.*

consider
To consider one's own situation: *tilo iho.*

considerate
Considerate, kind, generous: *abo donu.*

console
Console: *hagaaneane.*

constipated
Constipated: *louloua.*

constipating
Constipating: *hagaloulou.*

construct
Construct, set up, build (something): *hagaduu.*

consumption
Any illness characterized by wasting of the body (esp. t.b.), consumption: *magi iviivi.*

contact
Cause to come into contact with: *hagabaa*$_1$.
Make contact with while not aligned: *baa hagasalau.*
Touch (two or more things), be in contact, make contact with uniformly: *baa*$_1$.

contented
Contented, happy: *lodo danuaa.*
Feel happy or contented or at peace with the world: *hinangalomalie.*

continually
Continually: *dee modu.*

continue
Connect up, join up, continue upon: *duudagi.*

contract
To contract inside of (like a marine invertebrate inside a shell): *mmene.*

contract$_1$
promise, contract with: *hagatoo donu.*

contradict
Contradict: *diha.*
Contradict by —: *tugi ange —.*

contribute
Contribute (material things) to: *tagi ange.*
Donate, contribute: *daohi age.*

control
Be in charge of, control, lead: *huahua ai.*
To control one's crying: *kimi tangi.*

Conus
Mollusk sp.: *Conus chaldaeus*: *anengenenge.*
Mollusk sp.: *Conus litteratus*: *iillangi.*

conversation
Idle conversation: *ngadi basa.*

converse
Converse (conversation): *hagahebaa ngudu.*
Converse earnestly: *naba i de muna.*
Converse with: *madaangudu.*

convict tang
Fish sp.: convict tang: *manini.*

convince
Convince (several people) completely: *hagapasalia.*
Convince: *hagabasa.*
Convince someone completely: *hagabasalia*$_1$.

convinced
Cause to be convinced: *hagabasabasalia*$_1$.

convulsed
Convulsed with laughter: *mmae tinae.*

cook
Cook food: *hai gai.*
Cook, heat up: *dunu*$_1$.
To cook food in an earth oven for a short time (just to heat it up): *hagabibi.*

cook house
Cook house, earth oven: *umu.*

cooked
Barely cooked: *moo balabala.*
Cooked: *mmoa.*
Not cooked completely: *galo hilo.*

cool
Cool: *maluulu.*

cooperate
Cooperate: *hagadau bale.*

copper
Copper or brass or other reddish metal: *baalanga mmea.*

copra
Copra: *gaadinga.*
Cut copra: *sisi*$_1$.

copy
Copy out (by hand): *langa.*
Copy, imitate: *ago i me.*

coral
A (live) coral formation: *doga*$_2$*.
Coral (any kind): *gamu*$_1$.
Coral (growing live on the reef): *aamanu.*
Coral rubble: *gi̍ligili.*
Gorgonian (Coelenterate), false black coral: *aoa-laosedi.*

coral head
Coral head (at or broaching the surface of the water): *manu ea.*
Coral head (submerged): *ulu manu.*
Coral head: *aamanu; manu*$_1$.

coral sp.
Coral sp.: *gamugamu*$_1$*; hadu-gamugamu; hadu-maadau.*
Coral sp.: (looks like a flower): *gaasia.*
Coral sp.: (several spp. — poisonous): *hadu-mada-pula.*
Coral sp.: a type of coral which grows on the lagoon bottom: *aalali.*
Coral sp.: blue coral: *hadu-uli.*
Coral sp.: brain coral?: *limilimi.*
Coral sp.: faviid coral: *bugolo.*
Coral sp.: red organ-pipe coral: *hadu-i-de-ssala.*
Coral sp.: whip black coral: *valagei.*

coral tree
Plant sp.: tree sp.: Indian coral tree (*Erythrina variegata* L.): *ulu-davage.*

cordia tree
Plant sp.: tree sp.: cordia tree (*Cordia subcordata* Lam.): *ganava.*

core
Core of the breadfruit: *hune.*
The core of a body boil: *adilo.*

corm
Immature taro corm: *vaaligi.*
Plant sp.: swamp taro (*Cyrtosperma chamissonis*), also the corm of this plant: *daogoli.*
Plant sp.: taro (*Colocasia esculenta*), also the corm of this plant: *dalo.*
Taro corm (small): *me-e-ligi.*

corner
Corner: *dege.*

corners
Having corners, square, rectangular: *tuu dege.*

cornetfish
Fish sp.: cornetfish: *mataodao.*

correct
Correct (suitable), true: *abo.*
Correct, right, just, fair, true: *heohi.*
To correct (someone or something): *hagaheohi.*
Truth, right, correct: *donu*$_2$.

cough
Cough (a single time): *kobe.*
Cough (repeatedly): *gobegobe.*
Cough up: *hagakoo.*
Cough up blood: *luei todo.*

council
A council (of ten) formerly having broad legislative and judicial powers on the atoll: *dinoanga hulu**.

count
Count, read: *dau*$_1$.

country
A land mass, an island, a country, or any other geopolitical unit: *henua.*

couple
Couple (not married): *dau soa.*
Married couple, marry: *hai bodu.*

court
Court (of law): *momme hagassoe.*

cousin
Brother, sister, sibling, cousin: *daina.*

cover
A cover (which closes): *pono.*
A cover for an earth oven: *dau (umu).*
A cover of a box: *duu ngavesi.*
A half shell, a cover (of something): *uduu.*
Cover (something, e.g., to protect it from the elements): *abaaba.*
Cover up (by putting on layer after layer): *dao hadu.*
Cover up (by wrapping up with one layer): *buulou.*
Cover up: *haoli.*
Put a cover on: *pono iho.*

Put on, wear, cover up (the body): *gahu.*
To cover something (e.g., a pot): *bono.*
To cover the land (such as do the branches of breadfruit trees): *ulu de henua.*
Wrap or cover completely: *ssai.*
Wrap, cover up (with several layers): sai_1.

covered
Covered (all over the body) with —: *dohu de angaanga.*
Covered all over (skin) with: *dohu de gili.*
Covered all over with: *galigi.*
Covered up completely: *lilo bule.*
Covered with (people, flies, etc.): uli_1.
Covered with — (of skin only): *bala i de —.*
Covered with *ebuebu*: *ebuebua.*
Wrapped up or covered up completely: *saidule.*

covers
Covers (of books), two halves: *luu duu.*

covetous
Acquisitive, covetous: *lodo gi me.*
Covetous, envious: *nnoo.*

cowardly
Cowardly (concerning others or supernaturals): *madagudagu.*
Cowardly (owing to weak-mindedness): *binaaina.*

cowry shell
Mollusk sp.: cowry shell (many spp.): *bule.*

crab
Coconut crab: *baluu.*
Crab sp.: shore crab, land crab, grapsid crab, ghost crab: *gaibea.*
Hermit crab (lives in water): *unga-lausedi.*
Hermit crab (lives on dry land): *unga.*
Land crab sp. (small): *duba.*
Mangrove crab: kaa_3.
Trapezeid crab: *gaibea-lausedi.*

crack
Crack (of a whip): *malibilibi.*
Crack open: *hhoa.*
Starting to crack: *dele de mahaa.*
To crack (as a nut): $hagabaa_2$.

cracked
Broken up, cracked, burst: *mahaa.*
Cracked in many places: *mahangahanga.*

crackle
To crackle when chewed: $mugamuga_2$.

craftsman
Craftsman: *labagau;* $madaligi_1$.

craftsmanlike
Skillful at craft work, craftsmanlike: $madaligi_1$.

crate
Box, coffin, crate: *ngavesi.*

crave
Crave for (food): $uaua_4$ (ange).
Crave for, desperate: sae_2.

crawl
Crawl: *tolo.*

crazy
Act crazy or insane: *manaunau**.
Crazy: *senga.*
Crazy person: *gavia.*
Crazy, insane: *manaunaua**.
Drunk, dizzy, crazy: *libolibo ange.*

create
Create —: $hagadau_4$.

creep
Creep (a very slow movement over the ground): $dolo_1$.

crepe myrtle shrub
Plant sp.: crepe myrtle shrub (*Pemphis acidula* Forst.): *nngie.*

crime
Fault, crime: *dagasala.*

crippled
Crippled and unable to walk: *balagelage.*
Severely crippled: *balagelage gee.*

critical
Critical of others: *hagaaduadu dangada.*

criticism
Self-criticism: *hagaaduadu iho.*

criticize
Criticize: *hagabaubau.*

criticized
To have been criticized: *hagabaubauanga.*

criticizing
Always criticizing (someone) to (his) face: *dauhuli (ange).*

crocodile
Alligator, crocodile: *gegeno.*

cross
A cross (e.g., of wood): *laagau lui.*

cross-eyed
Cross-eyed: *kalo gee.*

crotch
The lower abdomen, crotch, pubic area: *madagauhala.*

crouch
Crouch: *tugu.*
Crouch down: *hagatugu.*
Crouch on all fours: *dogoduli.*
Crouch repeatedly: *hagadugudugu.*

crowded
Crowded (owing to a disorder of things): *muimui.*
Crowded together: *budubudu; hebahebaa.*
Crowded together closely: *buubudu.*
Crowded together in a small place: *hegabidi.*

crumple
Cause to crumple up: *hagapogo.*
Push in, crumple up: *ngalogu.*

crumpled
Crumpled up: *pogo.*
Pushed out of shape (as a tin can), rumpled, crumpled: *bogobogo*$_2$.

crush
To crush, to pulverize: *mmili*$_1$.

crushed
Be crushed: *balasia.*

crust
Scab, crust: *bagu.*

cry
A cry of a bird or human that sounds like the cry of a baby: *tama legalega eidu.*
Cry: *dangi.*
Cry a lot: *dangidangi.*
Cry aloud: *see*$_1$.
Cry aloud for a long time, wail: *dangi see.*
Cry for effect: *dangi hhadu*$_1$.
Cry out: *heehee.*
Cry out softly: *gii age.*
Cry to oneself: *dangi iho.*
Cry uncontrollably (for a long time): *dangi daudau.*
Cry uncontrollably (hysterically inaccessible): *seevoivoi.*
Cry uncontrollably (hysterically): *hagaidaida.*

cucumber
Apodous sea cucumber: *duu-lellele.*
Sea cucumber sp.: *duu-mmea; duu-uli; gaagose.*
Serpent cucumber: *manu-mangamanga-i-lote-aasanga.*

cults
Religions which are not in the Judaeo-Christian tradition, pagan cults: *ngadi daumaha.*

Curcuma
Plant sp.: tumeric plant (*Curcuma* sp.): *gaalau-ango.*

cure
To cure (someone): *hagaieiangi.*

current
A cold underwater current: *moana magalili.*
A confluence of ocean currents, or a circular current in which drifting objects remain stationary: *au doga.*
A current of choppy water between other currents: *sugi au.*
A strong current in the channel: *dada de ava.*
A type of ocean current far from land in which drifting objects collect: *au madua.*
An ocean current flowing away from land: *au dili dai.*
An ocean current flowing toward land: *au dili uda.*
An ocean current which comes towards the atoll: *me dili uda.*
An ocean current which comes towards the shore (and carries in driftwood, etc.): *dili uda.*
An ocean current which turns away from the reef: *au hagi.*
Any current which flows away from the atoll: *me dili dai.*
Current (in the sea): *me mmilo.*
Upward current: *denga hhuge —.*

currents
(The generic term for the major types of) currents in the open sea: *au*$_1$.

curse
To curse (someone): *basa hagamalaia; daatugu.*

curve
A curve, way of being bent: *biigonga.*
Curve (e.g., of a road): *haadinga.*

curved
Bent, curved, defective (of fruit): *bonga.*

cushion starfish
Cushion starfish: *hadu-mangeo.*

custom
Custom, habit: *dahulinga.*

customs
Customs of the island (Nukuoro): *duugunga o de henua.*

cut
Cut (something): *gamu$_2$; ssele; tuu$_1$.*
Cut a hole in: *hhoa.*
Cut away from: *modu gee.*
Cut copra: *sisi$_1$.*
Cut hair: *duu biho.*
Cut off, disconnected: *modu.*
Cut open: *gava$_1$.*
Cut suddenly: *tuu hagalele.*
To cut one's hand by a hand-held fish line, when it is taken by a fish: *seleia.*
To cut or make a ring around: *daga holiage.*

cutting
The cutting of a fast canoe through water: *vvala.*

cycad plant
Plant sp.: cycad plant (*Cycas circinalis* L.): *manu-a-tababa.*

Cyclotinella
Mollusk sp.: *Cyclotinella remies*, also *Tellinidae* spp.: *bibi.*

Cymatiidae
Mollusk sp.: *Cymatiidae* spp., also *Bursa bubo*: *buu-kangi-de-muli.*

Cyrtosperma
Plant sp.: swamp taro (*Cyrtosperma chamissonis*): *bulaga**.

daily
Daily: *laa tubua.*

damage
Damage, ruin: *oha.*

damn
Damn it!: *ssele i de niho.*

damp
Damp: *suungia.*

damselfish
Fish sp.? damselfish?: *boonei.*
Fish sp.?: damselfish?: *hagailonga$_2$.*
Fish sp.: (The native term is applied to many spp.): damselfish, snapper: *dagugu.*
Fish sp.: damselfish: *mudumudu-dua-beau; mudumudu-odaoda; mudumudu$_2$; nngahu.*

dance
A dance (an ancient type): *masagi.*
To dance: *anu.*

dancing paddle
A dancing paddle: *laba$_2$.*

dandy
A dandy (always wanting to *llidi*): *lodo llidi.*

danger
Be in trouble, in danger, or in a precarious situation: *vakaa.*

dangerous
Risky, dangerous: *hagamanavasaa.*

daring
Daring (show off), bold: *hai mogomogo.*
Daring, brave, manly: *lo taane.*

dark
Become dark (in color): *hagauli.*
Become dark (with no natural light): *gohu de me.*
Becoming very dark (decreasing in natural light): *gohugohu.*
Dark (absence of light): *gohu.*
Dark (in color), blackened: *uli$_1$.*
Dark green in color: *mada nuui.*
Dark images, shadows in the darkness: *goohunga.*
Dark red: *mada mmea.*
Very dark in color: *kohu.*

darkling beetles
Louse (head), or similar exoparasite of plants or animals (e.g., bird lice, scale insects, sap-feeding beetles, darkling beetles, etc.): *gudu.*

darkness
Darkness (of or pertaining to): *bouli.*

daughter
Girl, young woman, daughter: *damaa hine.*

daughter-in-law
Parent-in-law, child-in-law, mother-in-law, father-in-law, son-in-law, daughter-in-law: *saulaba.*

dawn
Dawn (first burst of light): *maahaa ada.*
Dawn (first light): *adaada; dele de ada.*

day
Day: *laangi.*
The whole day: *huaalaangi.*

daybreak
Daybreak (become daylight): *ao age.*
Daybreak: *dele de boialiali; dele de maahaa; maahaa.*
Sort or degree of daybreak: *aonga.*
The light before daybreak: *tea age langi.*
The light just before daybreak: *boialiali.*

daylight
Becoming daylight: *aoao*$_1$.
Daylight: *ao*$_1$.

daytime
Daytime: *ao de me.*

dead
Dead (of plants only): *made*$_2$.
Die, dead (persons or animals): *maaileele; maalioso.*
Die, dead, unconscious: *magau.*
To have been dead for a long time: *buni ange gi de gelegele.*

deaf
Deaf: *longoduli.*

death
Death, die (of a person): *dagosala.*

debt
Debt, owe: *muli*$_2$.

decay
Let decay: *hagapilo.*

deceitful
A talkative, deceitful person: *dama naale.*

deceive
Fool (someone), deceive: *daahanga; hagabigo de ngago.*
Fool (someone), deceive, trick (someone): *hagasenga.*

deceived
Deceived, fooled: *sengalia.*

December
December ('twelfth month'): *Madaangahulu-ma-lua-malama.*
December: *Daholaa*$_a$.

deception
Deception: *unusaagi.*

decide
Decide (arrive at a decision), make up one's mind: *maanadu age.*
Decide (come to a considered conclusion): *hagasaele.*
Decide (for oneself): *soe age.*
Decide: *maanadu.*
Decide an issue (by higher authority): *hagassoe.*
Decide formally: *hagamodu.*

decided
Be decided about: *baba age.*
Decided for one by the will of God: *soe mai.*
To have been decided formally: *modu.*

deciduous teeth
Milk teeth, deciduous teeth: *niho vaiuu.*

decision
Decision: *me gu modu; me ne modu.*

decorate
Decorate, adorn: *hagalaagii.*

decoration
Decoration, ornamentation: *laagii.*

decrease
Decrease (in strength, rate of growth, etc.): *maahe.*
Decrease: *diinei mai; ngalue mai.*
Decrease in —: *hagadaga mai.*
Decrease in quantity: *momolia.*
Lower or decrease (the volume of a radio, price, etc.): *ue iho.*

decreased
Reduced, decreased: *ngalue iho.*

decreasing
Decreasing (in number): *dogoisi mai; llilo mai.*
Decreasing: *kii mai; maaheahe.*

deep
Deep: *gelo.*
Deep, low (in status): *mao lalo.*

deep-bottomed
Deep-bottomed: *hai dagelo.*

defeat
To defeat all comers: *doli de henua.*

defeated
Always fail or be defeated: *dee sao age.*
Defeated: *magulu.*
Defeated, lose (battle, game, etc.): *mousi.*

defeatist
Be a defeatist: *hagabalabala.*

defecate
Defecate: *duuduu*$_2$*; hagaalaala; hongagelegele; suuduuduu; tigo.*

defective
Bent, curved, defective (of fruit): *bonga.*

definitely
Certain, sure, graceful, definitely: *too donu.*

deflower
Rip, tear, deflower (a virgin): *ssae*$_1$.

deflowered
Torn, deflowered (of a virgin): *masae.*

delay
Do slowly, delay: *hagamudumudu.*

delaying
Keep postponing or delaying: *hagasolo age.*

deliberately
Do deliberately (esp. something bad): *se hagabau.*

delicious
Delicious (of coconut apples only): *odomalie.*
Delicious (of pandanus only): *umalie.*
Delicious: *mammami.*

delinquent
Delinquent person (periodically exhibiting bad behavior): *mouli dangada.*

delivery
Delivery (of a baby): *haanau.*

Demiegretta
Bird sp.: reef heron (*Demiegretta sacra*): *gava*$_2$.

dense
Dense (underbrush): *muimui.*
Heavy or dense (of rain): *maadolu.*

departed
Departed (as a ship): *malanga.*

depend
Depend on (e.g., to come), rely on: *dahi tali.*
Depend upon (e.g., for sustenance): *dau ange.*

depressed
Depressed (mentally): *hagamaaiongi.*

depression
A depression (in the reef, or ground, etc.): *geelonga.*
A depression in a tree trunk: *ohu.*

depression$_1$
depression (feeling): *lodo hinangalosaa.*

descend
To descend suddenly: *hagapago iho.*

descendant
Grandchild, descendant of: *mogobuna.*

descendants
Descendants (in all inferior generations): *aamuli.*
Descendants (in one generation only): *hagadiilinga.*

desire
To desire physically a member of the opposite sex: *aneane.*
To stimulate a desire for: *hagalodo.*
Want, desire: *lodo*$_2$.

desirous
Strongly desirous of: *maaniha.*
To be desirous continually: *lodolodo.*

despair
To despair (of attaining success): *magulugulu.*

desperate
Crave for, desperate: *sae*$_2$.

despised
Despised by others: *massaa (ina).*

destroy
Break, break up, destroy: *oha.*
Destroy or abuse property (for no good reason): *lagolagoaa.*

deteriorated
Deteriorated: *bopobo.*

determine
Figure out, determine: *baua; baulia; hagabaua; hagabaulia.*

detumescence
Detumescence: *mmene.*

develop
Grow, develop: *somo*$_1$.

developing
Developing (of a situation): *halehale* —.

dexterous
Dexterous (esp. in fighting): *limalima.*

Diadema
Sea urchin sp.: *Diadema* sp.: *veli-daubulebule; veli-uli.*

dialect
Manner of speaking, idiolect, dialect: *baasanga.*

diameter
Diameter (of rope, etc.): *dua*$_1$.

diamond-shaped
Having a diamond-shaped decoration or form, etc.: *hai sumu.*

diarrhea
Diarrhea: *hanohano; magi hanohano.*
Diarrhea which escapes without one realizing (caused by eating oily fish): *sii tae.*
Intractable watery diarrhea: *sali tae.*

die
Death, die (of a person): *dagosala.*
Die (a person): *hano i luu moana.*
Die: *moe*$_1$.
Die in agony (owing to having led a bad life): *magau baubau.*
Die in agony: *moe baubau.*
Die in peace: *moe danuaa.*
Die of shame: *magau i togaa.*
Die peacefully: *magau danuaa.*
Die, dead (persons or animals): *maaileele; maalioso.*
Die, dead, unconscious: *magau.*
To die in great numbers: *mmade gimoo.*

different
Different (from): *dagodo gee (ma).*

differently
Completely differently: *geegee.*
Differently, of a different sort: *gee.*

difficult
Difficult: *hai ngadaa.*
Difficult for me: *ngadaa mai.*
Difficult to come: *ngadaa mai.*

difficulty
Hardship, difficulty: *duasala.*

dig
Dig: *geli.*
Dig up soil to uncover (something): *sua age.*

dilate
To dilate one's nostrils: *ili luu bongaa usu.*

dilated
Dilated veins: *tuu uaua.*

dim
Dim light: *mada giivia.*

diminish
Diminish (in intensity): *ahe iho.*

diminution
Diminution of: *helui.*

diminutive
Miniature, diminutive: *gidigidi laa lalo.*

directly
Go directly, speak directly (without circumlocution): *hagasoe.*

dirty
A dirty song: *vaivai daahili.*
Dirty (like *bela*): *belabela.*
Filthy, very dirty: *vaigelegele.*

disappear
Disappear, vanish: *lilo.*

disappointing
Extremely disappointing: *dee vaagidee.*

disburse
Let out (something), disburse (money): *hagasao*$_2$.

discharge
A reddish discharge from the genitalia (of either males or females): *vai mea.*
A whitish discharge from the genitalia (of either males or females): *vai dea.*
A yellowish discharge from the genitalia (of either males or females): *vai ango.*

discipline
Bring up (children), discipline (children): *haele.*

disconnected
Cut off, disconnected: *modu.*

discontinue
Limit, discontinue, shorten (by cutting off one end): *tuu mai.*

discourage
Discourage (someone) about something: *mmenengia mai.*
Discourage someone (verbally): *maatogo.*

discouraged
Completely discouraged: *mmade ange aalanga.*
Discouraged: *tili aalanga.*

disease
Disease (physical or mental): *magi.*

diseased
Diseased: *manua.*

disgusted
Gooseflesh, disgusted, horror-fascination: *tuu gili.*
Hate vehemently, completely disgusted: *kino made.*

disgusting
A disgusting business: *vaivai me.*
Filthy, disgusting: *hakino gee.*

disheveled
Disheveled (as the chicken feathers on a much-used trolling lure): *ovea.*

dishonest
Steal, dishonest, cheat: *gaiaa.*

dislocated
Dislocated (joint of the body): *hesilihagi; maaguluaa.*
Dislocated ankle: *dahuli de vae.*
Dislocated jaw: *ngalue de gauvae.*
Dislocated joint (of the body): *me maaguluaa.*
Dislocated larynx: *ngalue de hakii.*
Dislocated thigh bone: *doo de gauanga; gauanga mahagi; sege de gauanga.*

dislocation
A dislocation of bones such that the ends overlap (corrected by pulling): *ivi sulu.*
A dislocation of the *tuugau*: *doo tuugau.*
A dislocation of the shoulder joint: *bakau doo; eu doo; eu sege.*

disobedient
Disobedient, stubborn, talk back to: *hagamanege.*

disobey
To disobey the instructions of a healer: *oha valaai.*

dispensary
Hospital, dispensary: *hale magi.*

dispute
Dispute (with someone), argue: *hagadau-me.*

disregard
Disregard: *dili.*

disrobe
Remove (clothes, etc.), disrobe, undress: *hagaui*$_2$.

disseminate
Disseminate information: *adi saele.*

distant
Far, distant: *mmao.*

distended
Having one's stomach distended by gas: *ilihia.*

district
District, precinct (electoral): *vaenga.*

disturb
Disturb the peace: *oha de nnoho paba.*

dive
Dive head first: *lele biho.*
Dive, fall head first: *sulu.*

divide
Divide among, division (in arithmetic): *duha.*
Divide into portions: *vvae ange.*
Divide up: *dohidohi.*
Separate, divide: *vae*$_1$.

divination
Divination: *buubuu*$_1$.

divine
To divine (for omens): *buubuua; buubuulia.*

division
Divide among, division (in arithmetic): *duha.*
Portion, share, division (e.g., of a tract): *vaenga.*

divorced
Separated (two things), divorced: *maavae.*

dizziness
Dizziness or vertigo (as a chronic condition or illness): *magi libolibo.*

dizzy
Dizzy: *boiboi.*

Drunk, dizzy, crazy: *libolibo ange.*
Feel dizzy or faint, vertigo: *libo ange de henua.*

do
Do (something): *mmanu.*
Do at one time: *aalo dahi; kave dahi.*
Do attentively: *gamalie.*
Do by stealth: *moeagi.*
Do carefully: *hagalongolongo.*
Do earnestly: *dee manava age; kolu.*
Do fast or quickly: *limadi.*
Do for, fix: *hai ange.*
Do indifferently: *hai hua laa.*
Do on purpose: *hai donu.*
Do or take by force, rape: *hai gi de mahi.*
Do rapidly (esp. a repeated action done energetically): *libi.*
Do rapidly: *vili.*
Do slowly: *sabo.*
Do slowly, delay: *hagamudumudu.*
Do something (e.g., work) all by oneself: *singa sogosogo.*
Do something at short intervals: *duu podo.*
Do something shameful (for shame!): *booiaa (!).*
Do suddenly: *hagalele.*
Do to: *hai ange.*
Do unhesitatingly: *deai me hagalongolongo.*
Do very attentively: *dee gamalie.*
Do violently: *hai me dua nnui.*
Do with a maximum application of effort: *hagatanu.*
Do, make, use: *hai*$_1$.
Go or do by oneself: *massogosogo.*

dolphin
Dolphin: *masimasi*$_3$.

don't
Don't ever —!: *kana.*
Don't tell me!: *dee tala mai!.*

donate
Donate (to a collection being made): *maga*$_1$.
Donate, contribute: *daohi age.*

done
Long since finished, done, or gone: *odiodi.*

door
Door: *abaaba.*

double-edged
Double-edged: *kangi baasi lua.*

doubt
I doubt it!: *deai loo me.*

down
Down: *iho.*
Down, under: *lalo.*

downgrade
Self-deprecatory, downgrade: *hagadugu lalo.*

downpour
An intermittent downpour (of rain): *uadanga.*
Downpour (of rain): *dango de langi.*

downtown
Downtown: *ngaage.*

drag
Tow, drag: *tagi.*

dragging
Dragging: *daagina.*

dragonfly
Dragonfly: *boobua.*

drawing
Drawing to an end: *silisili*$_1$.

dream
Dream: *midi*$_1$.
Dream about: *midia; midia ange.*

drenched
Drenched: *balapigi.*

dress
A dress (female clothing): *malo haahine.*

dress up
Dress up (esp. in new or very fancy clothes): *llidi.*

drift
Drift: *dahea.*
Drift aimlessly: *dahedahea.*
Drift away: *dahea gee.*
Drift downwind, away from land: *siia gi moana ngaadai.*
Drift toward place where speaker is: *dahea age.*
Drift toward the place where the speaker is not: *dahea iho.*

driftwood
Driftwood (any sort): *odaoda*$_2$.
Weather-hardened black driftwood: *gavagava.*

driftwood sp.
Driftwood sp. (resembles *bagua*): *aha-bagua.*
Driftwood sp. (very soft): *laagau-bala-uda.*
Driftwood sp. (white in the center): *aha-dea.*
Driftwood sp.: *malo-ngiso.*

drill
Carve out, drill out: *hoda.*
Drill (native bow drill): *hou.*
Drill through, burrow: *hao*$_1$.
Drill wood to make a hole in which to insert the end of a pole (to make a joint): *hoohoa laagau.*

drink
Drink: *unu.*
Eat or drink just a little bit: *hagassui age.*

drip
Drip, fall drop by drop: *too madaaua.*

drizzle
Drizzle: *amuamu iho.*

drool
Spit, drool, sputum: *saavale.*

drop
Drop (of liquid or rain): *madaa ua.*
Drop down: *doo*$_1$.

drown
Drown: *malemo.*

drum
Drum (native): *aasii.*

drunk
Drunk, dizzy, crazy: *libolibo ange.*
Senseless, drunk: *senga.*

dry
Dry (something): *hagammasa.*
Dry (something) by artificial heat: *aadiidii.*
Dry in the sun: *dauagi.*
Dry out (fish or food to preserve it): *dao bagu.*
Dry season: *dau laohie.*
To be dry: *maangoa**; *mmasa.*
To be dry and smooth: *pulu.*
To be very dry: *massaganga.*

dull
Dull (of an edge or point): *madabuunou.*
Dull (of an edge, or point): *madagabubu.*

dulled
To have been dulled (from having been struck on a hard object): *maimai ange.*

dumb
Dumb, foolish, ignorant: *senga.*

dump
Dump, throw out (discard): *liagi.*

duplicate
Duplicate: *noodalo.*

during
During the lifetime of: *honga de mouli.*

dust
Dust, gas, steam, vapor, fumes, spray (e.g., of waves): *mama.*

dwelling
House, dwelling, building: *hale.*
Temporary dwelling: *gaainga.*

dye
Dye: *me tao; valaai tao.*

dysentery
Dysentery: *sii.*

each
Apiece, each: *i de — sogosogo.*
Each: *sogosogo.*
Each and every: *alodahi hugadoo.*
Each individual: *dahi ma dahi.*
Each individual...: *gida ma gida.*
Each of —: *denga*$_1$.
Each of — I have in mind: *dengaa.*
Each one: *gida.*
Each, apiece: *i dahi me.*

each person's
Each person's: *sada; seada; seoda; sodo.*
Each person's one: *dada*$_3$*; dodo*$_2$.
Each person's several: *ada*$_3$*; odo*$_2$*; ooda.*
Each person's two: *luaada; luoodo.*

eager
Energetic, eager, wide-awake: *maalo.*

eagle ray
Fish sp.: eagle ray: *hoimanu.*

ear
Ear: *dalinga*$_1$.

early
Fast, quick, early: *moolau.*

earnestly
Earnestly: *hagaduu ngae.*
Firmly in place, earnestly: *duu keli.*

earring
An earring: *hakai.*

earth oven
Cook house, earth oven: *umu.*

earthworm
Earthworm: *dangaloa*$_2$.

easily
Easily: *dee kona; ngaohie.*

eastern whimbrel
Bird sp.: eastern whimbrel (*Numenius phaeopus*): *geevee.*

easy
Easy: *hai ngaohie.*
Easy living, a good life: *mouli danuaa.*
Used to, easy to: *kau donu.*

eat
Eat (something) raw: *oda*$_1$.
Eat: *gai*$_2$*; ssabe age; ssami.*
Eat a little of: *hagannamu age.*
Eat a side dish with —: *giidagi ange gi —.*
Eat a snack: *hhui age; ssami age.*
Eat as much as possible: *gai gi de mahi.*
Eat early in the morning: *gai boo.*
Eat fast: *gai holoholo.*
Eat fish or meat with a meal: *llava ai.*
Eat food: *gai me.*
Eat greedily (with both hands): *gai lima lua.*
Eat left-overs (that most people would throw out): *gai samusamu.*
Eat messily (by poking at all of the food instead of touching only the portion to be eaten): *nao gasi.*
Eat messily (getting food on one's face): *gai baalau.*
Eat messily (letting the food fall from one's hands and mouth): *gai hagassii.*
Eat messily: *gai nnao*$_1$.
Eat more than seems appropriate to one's body size: *mmahi i de gai.*
Eat only certain foods prepared in certain ways by certain people: *gai hilihili.*
Eat or drink just a little bit: *hagassui age.*
Eat ravenously: *bole gi de gai; hagaduulou; hegai.*
Eat something: *hagaahi.*
Eat sparingly (esp. fish — in order not to use up): *gai ginigini.*
Eat sparingly (in order to save some food for later): *gai haganamunamu.*
Eat sparingly (just enough to maintain one's strength), have a snack: *gabe manava.*
Eat sparingly (to save for later): *gai hagadoedoe.*
Eat sparingly (to save some for others): *gai hagalongolongo.*
Eat taro without fish (or fish without taro): *ngadi gai.*
Food, eat heartily: *saamunga.*

eave
Eave (of a house): *abitala.*

ebbing
Ebbing of tide: *hagatugu tai.*

Echinometra
Sea urchin sp.: *Echinometra* spp.: *veli.*

echo
Echo: *hano ahe; sau aloalo; sauvalovalo.*

eddy
An eddy caused by a current: *buusagi.*
An eddy left by a paddle stroke: *bunaa hoe.*

eddying
Eddying of the wind (constantly changing direction) close to land: *sau alohenua.*

edge
Edge (of shore): *gaba*$_1$.
Edge, fringe, rim: *hiihii.*

edged
Double-edged: *kangi baasi lua.*

eel
Eel, any long worm, snake: *labodo.*

eel sp.
Eel sp.: *labodo-daubulebule.*
Eel sp.: moray eel: *labodo-tea; labodo-uli.*
Eel sp.: snake eel: *labodo-sisi.*

effective
Effective, useful, worthwhile, important: *haigamaiana.*

egg
Egg: *ngago.*

egg on
Encourage, egg on (e.g., to fight): *usuusu ange.*

eggs
Fish eggs (immature): *hua modo.*
Fish eggs (mature—yellowish): *hua leu.*

egotistical
Egotistical, self-centered, arrogant in spirit: *lodo mao lunga.*

eight
Eight: *valu*$_2$.

eighty
Eighty: *madavalu.*

either
Or, either: *be.*

either...or
Either...or: *be...be.*

ejaculate
Semen, ejaculate: *bii.*

elbow
Elbow: *dugilima.*

elder
Father, uncle, senior male relative, male elder, person in a fatherly relationship: *damana.*
Parent, elder (senior relative): *madua.*

elderly
Elderly and infirm: *tolo i de baeao.*

elders
Parents, elders: *maadua.*

eldest
Eldest child: *dama madua.*
The eldest child of a couple: *ganimua.*

elect
Pick from among several, choose, elect: *hili*$_1$.

election
Choose carefully from among many, election: *hilihili.*

electricity
Lightning, electricity: *uila.*

elephant ear
Plant sp.: elephant ear (*Alocasia*): *ngaungau*$_2$.

eloquent
Eloquent (of a person): *ngudu malie.*

emaciated
Skinny, thin (person), emaciated: *iviivia.*

embankment
An embankment around a taro plot: *dahadaha.*

embarrass
Shameful, to embarrass (someone): *hagadogaa.*

embarrassed
Bashful, ashamed, shy, embarrassed: *dogaa.*
Embarrassed by: *hoosenga ange.*
Shy, embarrassed, bashful: *hoosenga.*

embarrassment
Behave with embarrassment or shyness: *hai me dogaa.*

embers
Glowing embers (without a flame): *maga ahi.*

embrace
Kiss (Polynesian style), embrace: *hesongi.*

empower
Empower: *hagasauaa.*

empty
Empty of water: *masalia.*
Empty, low (tide): *masa.*
Hollow, vacant, empty: *ngadi—.*

enclose
Enclose: *daabui.*

encounter
Meet by chance, encounter: *hetugi.*
To encounter good (or bad) fortune: *hagasaaloa.*

encourage
Encourage, egg on (e.g., to fight): *usuusu ange.*

end
After, end (rearward part), later: *muli*$_1$.
End (extremity): *bido.*
End of (e.g., a stick): *midomido.*
End of (e.g., time): *hagaodi.*
The very end: *mulimuli*$_1$.

ended
Stopped, ended: *sili*$_1$.

enemies
Be enemies (of individuals only): *noobiho.*

enemy
Enemy: *hagadau-me.*

energetic
Energetic: *maanegabo.*
Energetic, eager, wide-awake: *maalo.*

energy
Strong, strength, force, power, energy: *mmahi.*

engaged
Become engaged to marry: *hagababa.*

enjoys
Interested in, enjoys: *savala.*

enlarge
Enlarge: *hagalaanui.*

enough
Not enough: *tee aamia donu.*
Sufficient, enough: *dohu.*

entangled
Entangled in apparent disorder: *vinigoso.*

enter
Enter, join (a group), get in: *ulu*$_1$.

entered
Entered: *ulua*$_1$*; uluhia.*

envious
Competitive, envious, desirous of retaliating: *lodo gaiaa.*
Covetous, envious: *nnoo.*
Envious, jealous (non-sexual jealousy): *magiaa.*

epidemic
Epidemic: *dau magi.*

epidermis
Dead epidermis (can be peeled without pain): *gili belu.*

epiglottis
Larynx, epiglottis, trachea: *hakii*$_1$.

epilepsy
Epilepsy: *lele age.*

epiphytic fern
Plant sp.: epiphytic fern (*Vittaria incurvata* Cav.): *gumigumi-o-sogo.*

equal
Capable of, be the equal of: *bau ange.*
Equal in skill and strength (in a wrestling contest — so no one wins): *vini.*
Equal in status: *duu i de liiliagi.*
Make equal: *hagahedae.*

equipment
Recreational equipment: *goloa hagadaahao.*
Tools, equipment (incl. fishing gear): *doonga.*

erase
Wipe, scrub, clean up (by wiping), erase: *ssolo.*

erection
Erection (of penis): *dola.*

Erolia
Bird sp.: sharp-tailed sandpiper (*Erolia acuminata*): *damaa-manu.*

erosion
Erosion of sand or soil (esp. of the beach by wave action): *llohi.*

error
Mistake, error: *hai sala.*
Mistake, error, accident: *sala.*

eruptions
Eruptions on the skin (e.g., hives, insect bites, etc.): *dala hhua.*

Erythrina
Plant sp.: tree sp.: Indian coral tree (*Erythrina variegata* L.): *ulu-davage.*

escape
Escape one after the other: *sasao.*
Get out from or through, escape: *sao*$_2$.
To escape (of fish) from a net (through its holes): *siga.*
To escape (of fish, after having been speared): *modu taalonga; tuu taalonga.*

escaped
Free, escaped: *ola.*

estimate
Measure, calculate, estimate: *hagabau.*

eternally
Forever, eternally: *dee ngado mai.*

European
European: *abadai; abasasa.*
European goods or tools: *goloa abasasa.*
European in manner or appearance: *abasasa huu.*
European persons (including Americans): *dangada abadai; dangada abasasa.*
European things (gear, etc.): *me abadai; me abasasa.*

even
Be even with each other: *hedae.*
Even (number): *odi ange.*

even number
Even number: *daelodo odi ange.*

evening
Early evening, late in the afternoon: *gaba de ahiahi.*
Late afternoon and early evening: *ahiahi.*

evensong
Evensong (last service of the day): *daumaha hagalava.*

everybody
Everything, everybody: *alodahi hugadoo.*

everything
Everything, everybody: *alodahi hugadoo.*

evil
Unscrupulous, immoral, evil: *vaivaidagodo.*

evil-tongued
Evil-tongued, lying (dishonest, foulmouthed: *vaivai ngudu.*

exactly
Exactly: *maalie.*

exaggerate
Exaggerate (esp. in storytelling): *gai nnao$_2$.*
Exaggerate: *hagatubu; ueue ange; vangevange.*
Exaggerate matters: *hagatubu me.*

example
Appearance, example, situation: *dulagi.*

exceed
Exceed (the amount required), too — (e.g., many): *dubu.*

exceedingly
Very, exceedingly: *hano gi oona.*

exchange
Exchange, trade: *hesuihagi.*

excite
Excite sexually: *hagaaneane.*

excited
Excited easily by the opposite sex: *lodo baageaa.*
Excited with joy: *pula luu mada.*

excursion
An excursion for an evil purpose (esp. involving a sexual quest): *vaivai hanonga.*

exercises
Calisthenics, exercises: *holahola aalanga.*

exhalation
Exhalation of air under water (forming bubbles): *dili ebuebu.*

exhale
To exhale suddenly: *hagabahhaa.*

exhausted
Completely exhausted: *mmade ange aalanga.*
Exhausted (physically or mentally): *dili aalanga; mmade aalanga; tili aalanga.*
Slow down, be exhausted (physically), feel unenergetic: *bangoa.*

exhaustion
Give in to exhaustion: *hagabangoa.*

exoparasite
Louse (head), or similar exoparasite of plants or animals (e.g., bird lice, scale insects, sap-feeding beetles, darkling beetles, etc.): *gudu.*

expanded
Cause to be expanded: *hagabungubungulia.*

expect
Expect that — but: *soi adu —.*
To expect things from others, and accept too readily: *haalo.*

expectant
Hope for, expectant, waiting: *tali.*

expectation
Hopeful expectation: *tali hagalodolodo.*

expedition
An expedition to look for valuable drifting objects, either in the lagoon or in the open sea near the atoll: *salahagi.*

expensive
Expensive: *hagao ngadaa.*

experience
Be aware of, experience, perceive, feel (in one's mind or body): *longo iho.*

expertise
Expertise: *huaahai.*

explode
Explode, burst: *paa$_2$.*

expose
Expose oneself to the sun: *dagodoanga; hagadauagina.*
Expose to a breeze: *hagaangiangi.*

exposed
Be exposed to the wind (not sheltered): *saudia.*

express
To express coconut oil out of the

residue (*oda*) from which some oil has already been expressed: *molimoli i tuu gaha.*

expulsion
Expulsion or voluntary withdrawal (from a group): *doo i de....*

extend
Extend one's hand, reach out: *haalo.*
Extend out in space: *saga gee; saga gi daha.*
Extend to: *dagi*$_1$.
Prolong, extend: *hagadaulooloa.*

extinguish
To extinguish (e.g., a fire, or the life of a plant, or the heat of the sun — as by clouds): *diinei.*

extract
To extract by gouging out with a finger: *nao.*
To extract pandanus seeds by splitting the fruit: *hanga benu.*

extraordinary
Extraordinary or unusual (esp. in size): *se me be hee.*
Extraordinary, outstanding, unusual: *magona.*

eye
Eye: *ganomada.*
Eye of the taro corm: *obe.*

eyeball
Eyeball: *hadu mada.*

eyebrows
Eyebrows: *huluhulu mada.*

eyelashes
Eyelashes: *hiihii mada.*

face
Face (of a person): *luu mada.*
Front part of, face, beginning (of a thing): *mada*$_3$.

fade
Fade (of a color): *hano de leebunga.*

fail
Always fail or be defeated: *dee sao age.*

faint
Feel dizzy or faint, vertigo: *libo ange de henua.*
To faint, be unconscious: *ssili mada.*

fair
Correct, right, just, fair, true: *heohi.*

fairy tern
Bird sp.: fairy tern (*Gygis alba*): *agiagi.*

fall
Almost fall: *hanohano dua.*
Dive, fall head first: *sulu.*
Fall: *doo*$_1$.
Fall forward: *sulu gi mua.*
Fall out little by little (as hair, or sand when it is poured): *malili*$_1$.
Fall over (as a felled tree): *baguu.*
Grab (in order to restrain, e.g., a person), fall upon: *dango*$_1$.

fallen
Grabbed, fallen upon: *dangoa; dangolia.*

fallopian tubes
Ovaries and fallopian tubes: *bualeu.*

falsehood
Falsehood, lie: *me hhadu.*

familiarize
To show (familiarize with): *hakide.*

family
Family: *huaabodu.*

famine
Famine: *onge.*

famished
Famished, ravenous: *ssee de hiigai.*

famous
Well-known, famous: *daudau*$_1$.

fan
Blow, fan (oneself): *ili.*
Fan: *angiangi.*

far
Beyond the horizon, far away from the atoll: *lalo de langi.*
Far from any land, in the open sea: *moana dugidugi.*
Far from land (the place from which the atoll is just barely visible): *moana ngaadai.*
Far, distant: *mmao.*

farther
More, farther: *ange.*

fashion
Fashion something to be like something else: *hagadulagi.*

fast
Do fast or quickly: *limadi.*

Fast: *malibi.*
Fast moving (over a considerable duration of time): *mailiili.*
Fast moving: *maili.*
Fast, quick, early: *moolau.*
Fast, swift: *gemo.*
Very fast: *se galubu.*

fasten
Tie up, fasten by tying (wrapping): *hhau.*
To fasten (a rope, etc.) between two points: *dau*$_2$.

fastened
Fastened on to (by being stuck in): *kadi ange.*
Tied or fastened tightly: *gali.*
Wound around or tied or fastened very tightly: *gali ange.*

fat
Big around, fat: *longohie.*
Fat (of, e.g., a person): *bedi.*
Fat and squat and ugly: *huubuudoi.*
Getting fat: *bedibedi.*

father
Father, uncle, senior male relative, male elder, person in a fatherly relationship: *damana.*

father-in-law
Parent-in-law, child-in-law, mother-in-law, father-in-law, son-in-law, daughter-in-law: *saulaba.*

fathom
Fathom (the span of one's outstretched arms): *iloha; loha*$_1$.

fatigue
Muscle fatigue: *llonga.*

fatty
Fatty: *moomuna.*
The fatty tissue of a fish or animal: *lau ngago.*

fault
Fault, crime: *dagasala.*

faviid coral
Coral sp.: faviid coral: *bugolo.*

favorites
Play favorites amongst one's children: *vaedama.*

fear
Fear (as perceived somatically): *bonabona.*

fearful
Become fearful: *bonabona age.*
Feel fearful: *bonabona age lodo.*
Worried, apprehensive, fearful: *manavasaa.*

fearless
Fearless (socially): *dee vasu.*

feast
Feast: *daonga.*
Feast held for a newly launched canoe: *malaangahu*.*

feathers
Feathers: *hulu manu.*
Feathers of a rooster standing out on its neck (when angry): *dauaahe.*

February
February ('second month'): *Lua-malama.*
February: *Daagelo.*

feces
Feces: *duudae.*

feed
To feed (someone): *haangai.*

feel
Be aware of, experience, perceive, feel (in one's mind or body): *longo iho.*
Feel cold, shivering (from cold): *magalili.*
Feel comfortable: *abo.*
Feel cowardly: *lodo bigede.*
Feel dizzy or faint, vertigo: *libo ange de henua.*
Feel happy or contented or at peace with the world: *hinangalomalie.*
Feel like (one is) about to —: *iho ange de —.*
Feel like —: *mmahi age de —.*
Feel shy in the presence of: *dogaa ange.*
Feel sleepy: *mademadea ange.*
Feel sorry for or sympathetic toward: *aloha ai.*
Feel uncomfortably sated with food and unable to eat: *hagahonu age lodo.*
Feel very sorry for: *vvela de aloha.*
Hear, feel: *longo.*
I feel like —: *iho mai.*
Like (someone or something), feel affection for: *umiumidi; vaasuu.*
Slow down, be exhausted (physically), feel unenergetic: *bangoa.*
You feel like —: *iho adu.*

feeling
A sudden access of hostile feeling: *uluhia.*

felt
Heard, felt: *langona*$_2$.

female
Female child, girl: *gauligi hahine.*
Female, woman: *hine.*

fermented
Fermented *galeve*, palm toddy: *galeve vii.*
Fermented, spoiled (of cooked food left too long): *vii.*

fern
Plant sp.: bird's-nest fern (*Asplenium nidus* L.): *lau-gadaha.*
Plant sp.: epiphytic fern (*Vittaria incurvata* Cav.): *gumigumi-o-sogo.*
Plant sp.: fern sp.: *gideu.*
Plant sp.: maile-scented fern (*Polypodium scolopendria* Burm. F.): *maile.*
Plant sp.: paco fern (*Athyrium* sp.): *manu-mangamanga*$_2$.
Plant sp.: sword fern (The native term applies possibly to several spp.): *lluhe.*

festooned
Festooned with (e.g., flags): *dauaahe.*

few
Few: *dogoisi; hanuhanu.*
Little bit, few: *hanu momo.*
Very few: *dogoisi loo huu.*

fewer
Becoming fewer and fewer: *dogodogoisi.*

fibers
Banana tree fibers (for making cloth): *bulada.*
Fibers for the manufacture of rope or cloth, etc.: *amu.*
Fibers of the coconut husk: *moigaga.*
Fine threads or hairs or fibers (in feather or leaf, etc.): *amu ligi.*
Taro fibers: *agoago*$_2$.
The fibers on the core of the breadfruit: *hunehune.*
The short fibers of the mature coconut husk: *bulu.*

Ficus
Plant sp.: tree sp.: banyan tree (*Ficus prolixa* Forst.): *aoa*$_1$.

field day
Field day: *laangi hagadaahao.*

fifty
Fifty: *madalima.*

-fight
Argue heatedly, fight: *hulo gi lunga ma lalo.*
Fight: *hebagi; heboohagi; levango.*
Fight frequently: *heboheboohagi.*
Fight hand-to-hand: *dalepagi.*
Fist fight: *heboohagi lima.*

fighting
Be on the point of fighting: *hai me hebagi.*

figure
Calculate (do arithmetic), figure out: *kumi*$_2$.
Number, figure: *daelodo.*

figure out
Calculate —, figure out —: *gumi*$_2$.
Figure out, determine: *baua; baulia; hagabaua; hagabaulia.*

filament
Vein, tendon, nerve, plastic filament: *uaua*$_3$.

file
File (for filing metal): *manu solo maadau.*
File (for filing wood): *manu solo laagau.*
To grate or file (something): *solo.*

filefish
Fish sp.: filefish: *duu-baeao; sumu-gaaleva.*
Fish sp.: triggerfish, filefish (The native term is applied to many spp.): *sumu*$_2$.

fill
Fill to overflowing: *honu malingilingi.*
Fill to the brim: *honu baabaa.*
Fill up: *hagahonu.*
Fill, stuff (something into or full of): *hhao.*

filled
Filled to capacity: *lodo kabi.*
Filled up completely (with solids): *honu kadi.*
Filled with: *honua; honumia.*

filter
Filter, sift: *nonu*$_1$.

filthy
Filthy, disgusting: *hakino gee.*
Filthy, very dirty: *vaigelegele.*

Fimbria
Mollusk sp.: *Fimbria soverbii*: *geesaa.*

fin
Appendage, fin, spine (extending from a fish, etc.): *dala*$_4$.

final
Last, final: *muliagina.*

fine
Fine (in grain, of hair, etc.): *lligi.*
Fine (thread, etc.): *dua lligi.*

fine-feathered
Fine-feathered: *amu ligi.*

finger
Finger: *madannia.*
Little finger: *madannia sisi.*
Middle finger: *madannia i lodo.*

fingernail
Fingernail: *angaanga madannia.*

finish
Finish up, be last: *hagaodia.*

finished
Almost finished, nearly finished: *galani.*
Becoming finished or wealthy: *lavalava.*
Completely cleaned up or finished: *odi sango.*
Finished: *lava.*
Gone, finished, used up: *odi*$_b$.
Long since finished, done, or gone: *odiodi.*

fire
Be on fire: *ula age.*
Fire: *ahi.*

fire tongs
Fire tongs: *igohi.*

fire-plow
Fire-plow: *gadunga.*

firewood
Firewood: *lahhie.*

firmly
Firmly in place, earnestly: *duu keli.*

first
Be first: *hagamua.*
First, best: *tahi*$_1$.

firstfruits
Firstfruits: *madaa gai.*

fish
Fish (archaic, except in compounds): *iga**.
Fish (in children's speech only): *mammamu.*
Fish (the generic term — cf. Ponapean *mam*): *mamu.*
Fish (when abundant in the ocean nearby): *gainga o de moana.*
Fish which live on the reef: *gili agau.*
The fish which live beyond the outer reef: *mamu de lagi.*

fish club
Fish club (priest): *adu*$_3$.

fish eggs
Fish eggs (immature): *hua modo.*
Fish eggs (mature—yellowish): *hua leu.*

fish sp.
Fish sp. (*Trachinotus bailloni*): *bilibili-hadu.*
Fish sp. (The native term is applied to many spp.): *lale.*
Fish sp. (= *lae*?): *lailai.*
Fish sp. (= a very large *balagia*, 3-4 feet long): *manenga.*
Fish sp. (= large *dada*): *anga-mea.*
Fish sp. (= large *datada*, also = small *angamea*): *dada*$_2$.
Fish sp. (= large *llahi*): *hagaoda-lolo.*
Fish sp. (= large *madu*): *sugi-manga.*
Fish sp. (= large *saagahinoa*): *saabudu.*
Fish sp. (= large *tonu*, also = large *hagaodalolo*): *ava*$_3$.
Fish sp. (= small *hagaudalolo*): *llahi*$_2$.
Fish sp. (= small *saabudu*): *saagahinoa.*
Fish sp. (= small *valu*): *dangii.*
Fish sp. (a rare school fish which looks like *saniba*): *dauoni-baabaa.*
Fish sp. (a small flying fish): *iga-loa.*
Fish sp. (a small oceanic school fish slightly larger than *dauoni*): *iga-ligi.*
Fish sp. (a sort which burrows in the sand): *datanu.*
Fish sp. (like *ngaa*, but longer and thinner): *namanama.*
Fish sp. (rare — like *huhu* — about 2 feet long with dark rust-colored skin): *uumolo.*
Fish sp. (rare): *bani-magevageva; muu-madavai; umalei.*

Fish sp. (resembles *gada*, but bigger): *ulua*$_2$.
Fish sp. (resembles *hoimanu*, but much bigger): *ulu-hai-bogo-lua.*
Fish sp. (several spp.): *uli*$_3$.
Fish sp. (small flying fish): *siba*$_2$.
Fish sp. (two kinds): *umolo.*
Fish sp. (var. *dabaduu*): *suulee.*
Fish sp. (var. of *duubaeao*): *duu-hakaa.*
Fish sp. (var. of *huuhuu*): *uhuuhu.*
Fish sp.? damselfish?: *boonei.*
Fish sp.?: damselfish?: *hagailonga*$_2$.
Fish sp.?: tang? (a kind of *igauli?)*: *maleasa.*
Fish sp.: *adu-balebale-i-dai; balagia; balu-daaea; balu-malau;balu*$_2$*; bangabanga*$_2$*; buu-ili; datane-uli; dauoni; diinonga-o-salo; gada-laagau-ngaadai; gavaligi; guba-dee-gaina; hiloa*$_2$*; iganibongi; hiloa*$_2$*; iganibongi; labelabe-tea; lahilahi; loselose-ganoanga; lugulugu*$_2$*; mada-givi; maido; ngaa; sagulaa-saamono; sumu-dea; udu-hai-vaelo.*
Fish sp.: (The native term is applied to many spp.): damselfish, snapper: *dagugu.*
Fish Sp.: (a small *suulee* or a var. of *suulee*): *dabaduu.*
Fish Sp.: (any small jack-like fish): *kau*$_1$.
Fish sp.: anchovy?, silversides (small?): *manu-honga-dai.*
Fish sp.: barracuda: *ono*$_2$.
Fish sp.: batfish?: *bunei.*
Fish sp.: blacktip shark: *mangoo-dahola.*
Fish sp.: blenny: *dauleelage.*
Fish sp.: bonito: *adu-balebale-i-dua.*
Fish sp.: boxfish (dark blue): *mooma-uliuli.*
Fish sp.: boxfish (yellow): *mooma-ganoango.*
Fish sp.: butterfly fish (The native term is applied to many spp.): *dihidihi.*
Fish sp.: cardinal fish (The native term is applied to several spp.): *guba.*
Fish sp.: cardinal fish: *gaba-moe; guba-baabaa.*
Fish sp.: convict tang: *manini.*
Fish sp.: cornetfish: *mantoadao.*
Fish sp.: damselfish: *mudumudu-dua-beau; mudumudu-odaoda; mudumudu*$_2$*; nngahu.*
Fish sp.: eagle ray: *hoimanu.*
Fish sp.: filefish: *duu-baeao; sumu-gaaleva.*
Fish sp.: flatfish: *halihalibaa.*
Fish sp.: flying fish: *salaa; ssave; ssave-a-bao.*
Fish sp.: goat fish (= *madulilau sisisi*): *ahulu.*
Fish sp.: goatfish (= small *vede*): *galo*$_4$.
Fish sp.: goatfish: *galo-gila; maduilau; malili*$_2$*; moaga; moahulu; sugi-laagoo; vede-mea; vede*$_2$.
Fish sp.: goby?, sleeper?: *dama-a-de-galabe.*
Fish sp.: goby: *dotonogaa; manogo.*
Fish sp.: halfbeak: *ise.*
Fish sp.: hawk fish (2 sorts): *iga-adagahi.*
Fish sp.: hawk fish: *ulu-dugi; ulu-dugi-lalo-beau.*
Fish sp.: jack (= large *alaala*): *duulua.*
Fish sp.: jack (2 sorts) (= small *tulua*): *alaala*$_1$.
Fish sp.: jack? (an oceanic fish): *gada-ahai; gada-moana.*
Fish sp.: jack? (like *alaala*): *gada-alaala.*
Fish sp.: jack: *gada*$_2$*; goosuu; lebelebe; libo*$_2$*; mada-galadi.*
Fish sp.: lion-fish: *sausau*$_2$.
Fish sp.: lizard fish?: *dababa-gabugabu-tai.*
Fish sp.: lizard fish: *malianoono.*
Fish sp.: milkfish: *baleao.*
Fish sp.: mojarra fish (= small *sugimanga*): *mmadu.*
Fish sp.: mountain bass: *sahole.*
Fish sp.: mullet: *dalinga*$_2$*; ganae.*
Fish sp.: needlefish: *ise-ngaio; ngaio; ngaio-golai; sobalo.*
Fish sp.: parrot fish (The native term is applied to many spp.): *huuhuu*$_2$.
Fish sp.: parrot fish: *balagia-a-de-gaga; mamu-madohi-lua; ulahi.*
Fish sp.: pipefish: *seisei.*
Fish sp.: puffer: *dala-galoi.*
Fish sp.: rabbitfish: *baaua; bangongo.*
Fish sp.: rainbow runner: *gina.*
Fish sp.: round herring?, goby?: *ulua-gabugabu-tai.*
Fish sp.: rudderfish: *gada-laagau-ngauda.*
Fish sp.: scad?: *badii; belubelu; gabou.*
Fish sp.: sea bass (The native term is applied to many spp.): *ngadala.*
Fish sp.: sea bass (= small *ava*): *donu*$_3$.

Fish sp.: sea bass (2 sorts: 1 large, 1 small): *madabiebie.*
Fish sp.: sea bass: *bangadala; sahudu.*
Fish sp.: shark sp.: *dababa; hagaulu*$_2$*; mangoo-biho-lua; mangoo-senga.*
Fish sp.: shark sp.?: *alava; eleele; galeva; madau-dalinga; pula-laalaa; sasaanimadava.*
Fish sp.: silversides (The native term is applied to several spp.): *gimoo*$_2$.
Fish sp.: silversides: *saniba.*
Fish sp.: skipjack tuna: *adu*$_2$.
Fish sp.: snapper (The native term is applied to many spp.): *muu*$_2$.
Fish sp.: snapper (= large *babudaea*): *daaea.*
Fish sp.: snapper (= small *dada*): *datada*$_2$.
Fish sp.: snapper (= small *daea*): *babu-daaea.*
Fish sp.: snapper?: *muu-madagao.*
Fish sp.: snapper: *balu-udu; dagabe; dangau-daa-sissisi; dangau-dongi; dangau-laha; dangau-paava; ngudula; udu.*
Fish sp.: spiny puffer: *daudu.*
Fish sp.: squirrelfish (The native term is applied to many spp.): *malau*$_2$.
Fish sp.: squirrelfish (= small *malaugulu*?: *giigii*$_2$.
Fish sp.: squirrelfish: *baba*$_2$*; daa*$_3$*; dala-loa; daladala*$_4$*; haa-dolo.*
Fish sp.: stingray?: *mamu-duagaa.*
Fish sp.: stone-fish: *nohu.*
Fish sp.: tang (2 sorts): *igauli; laumele.*
Fish sp.: tang?: *gelu-uliuli.*
Fish sp.: tang: *abi; balangi; bulaga-a-leo; gelu-agau; gelu-hai-vaelo; igauli-sissisi; sobaga; sugi-daa.*
Fish sp.: threadfin: *ganae-oo.*
Fish sp.: triggerfish: *imu-mea; imu-uli; saulolua.*
Fish sp.: triggerfish, filefish (The native term is applied to many spp.): *sumu*$_2$.
Fish sp.: trumpet fish: *loselose-uli.*
Fish sp.: tuna sp.: *dagua-bodo.*
Fish sp.: unicorn fish: *gelu-hai-usu.*
Fish sp.: wahoo: *daodao*$_2$.
Fish sp.: white-tip shark: *aso.*
Fish sp.: wrasse (2 sorts: 1 white, 1 red): *babu-honga-agau.*
Fish sp.: wrasse: *banganga; labelabe-uliuli; mamu-lalo-beau; sussunubega.*
Fish sp.: yellow fin tuna (3 sorts?): *dagua*$_2$.

fish trap
A fish trap (of wood): *uu*$_4$.

fish weir
Fish weir: *bae mamu.*

fished
Fished in (place): *siisiia.*

fisherman
An avid fisherman: *dangada duaagau.*
An unenthusiastic fisherman: *ngauda*$_2$.
Fisherman: *dangada haangoda.*
Skillful fisherman: *daudai.*

fishhook
A type of fishhook (made from pearl shell): *gadinibidi; mai moni.*
A type of fishhook (made from turtle shell): *gavidi.*
Hook, fishhook: *maadau.*

fishhook keeper
Fishhook keeper: *suu.*

fishing
Fishing (angling with a line) to an unusual depth: *ugallalo.*
Fishing (with a pole): *siisii*$_2$.
Fishing: *haangoda.*
Fishing beyond the reef (on the seaward side of the atoll): *haangoda dua agau.*
Fishing using a whole fish as bait: *duiagi.*
Fishing with a single line: *dugu dahi.*

fishing gear
Fishing gear: *goloa haangoda.*

fishing line
Fishing line of a size appropriate for *gina* fishing: *dua gina.*
Fishing line of a size appropriate for *haangoda de boo*: *dua haangoda de boo.*
Fishing line of a size appropriate for the *hagalalo* method of fishing: *dua hagalalo.*
Fishing line of a size appropriate for trolling: *dua alohagi.*
Fishing line of the largest size (on which a whole *belubelu* is used as bait): *dua duiagi.*
Fishing line of the sort used for *adu fishing*: *aho.*
Fishing line, rope (of a sort suitable for fishing): *uga*$_1$.

fishing net
Fishing net (attached to a frame or handle): *gatae.*

fishing pole
Fishing pole: *huadia; siisii*$_2$.

fit
Fit (of clothes): *ngani mai.*
Fit around one as a belt etc.: *ngani adu.*
Fit to (or into): *oo*$_2$.
Fit together with (match) each other: *heloongoi.*
Fit well or properly: *se hono.*
Not fit: *dee heloongoi.*
Suited to, fit (with), appropriate to: *heohi ange.*

five
Five: *lima*$_2$.

fix
Do for, fix: *hai ange.*

flail
Move jerkily, flail (one's legs), flounder about: *dagai.*

flame
Flame, aflame, burning: *ula*$_1$.

flap
Flap (as wings): *gaba*$_2$.
Flap briskly in the wind: *daleba.*
Flap in the wind (like a flag): *leba.*

flapping
Flapping (of a sail in the breeze): *lobaloba.*
To bring one's hands and arms (or wings) down or back once (as in waving, swimming, or the flapping of a bird's wings): *balu*$_1$.

flash
A flash (e.g., of light): *bula.*
A flash of light, a blink of an eye: *daba.*
Flash (as of lightning): *laba*$_1$.

flashing
A flashing of several lights, a blink of the eyes: *taba.*
Twinkling, flashing, winking: *dabadaba*$_1$.

flashlight battery
Flashlight battery: *duudangaa solo.*

flat
Flat, board: *baabaa*$_2$.
Make level, make flat: *hagababa.*

flatfish
Fish sp.: flatfish: *halihalibaa.*

flatten
Flatten out something mushy: *gabola.*

flattery
Flattery or other communication by which one attempts to ingratiate oneself: *ngudu maimai.*

flatulence
Flatus, the sound of flatulence: *bee.*

flatulent
Be flatulent: *bebee.*

flatus
Flatus: *gaigai a usu.*
Flatus, the sound of flatulence: *bee.*
Wind, gas, flatus: *madangi.*

flee
Flee (of a small school of fish): *aasasi.*

fleet
A fleet of canoes (in line): *dui moni.*
A fleet of canoes: *hudaa moni; sai moni.*

flesh
Flesh of, meat of: *gano.*
Penis, meat, flesh: *kano.*

fleshy
A fleshy (non-muscular) man: *somo haahine.*

Fleurya
Plant sp.: *Fleurya ruderalis* (Forst.f.) Gaud. ex. Wedd.: *mougu.*

flexible
Flexible: *laubalabala.*

flip
To flip over (as in diving a sommersault): *hagallui.*

flirtatious
Flirtatious: *mada baubau.*

float
Float (on the surface of the water): *llanga.*
Outrigger float: *ama*$_1$.
To float in place (not drifting) on the surface of the water (with no anchor): *maanu.*

flock
Flock of birds (feeding on a school of fish): *dau manu.*

flooded
Flooded, washed out: *dolona.*

floor
Shelf, platform, raft, floor (of planks): *hada.*

flounder
Move jerkily, flail (one's legs), flounder about: *dagai.*

flow
Flow (of tide): *magalili; magalili mai; magalili tai.*
Flow away: *sali gee.*
Flow, seep: *sali.*
The flow of a current: *mmilo.*

flower
Flower: *hua-ala.*
The flower of the breadfruit tree: *hune.*
The flower of the coconut tree: *hungahunga-a-nui.*

flu
Cold (sickness), flu: *magi o de henua.*

flushed
Red in the face, flushed: *ula de gili.*

flutter
Flutter against (as a hooked fish): *bapaba.*

fluttering
Fluttering rapidly (of a sail in the breeze): *lloba.*

fly
Insect sp.: fly, flying ant, wasp: *lango*$_2$.
Insect sp.: fruit fly: *manu-a-luga.*
To fly: *lele.*

flying ant
Insect sp.: fly, flying ant, wasp: *lango*$_2$.

flying fish
Fish sp.: flying fish: *salaa; ssave; ssave-a-bao.*

foam
Foam (from the sea) on shore: *usubee o unu.*
Foam, bubbles: *ebuebu.*

foetus
A foetus which has been aborted: *dama doo; dama ssege.*
Deformed foetus: *dama de bialodo.*

fold
Fold up (one fold): *hagapogo.*
Fold up (several folds), roll up: *hhedu.*

folded
Folded up, rolled up: *mahedu.*

folds
The folds of skin around the waist: *debedebe.*

follow
Follow (someone): *daudali.*
Follow another's will: *daudali i lodo.*
Follow in order to spy on: *bido dagi.*

food
Food (prepared for a meal): *hagamouli.*
Food: *gai*$_2$.
Food, eat heartily: *saamunga.*
Prepared food: *hai gai; me hagaahulu.*

fool
Fool (someone): *hhoa de biho.*
Fool (someone), deceive: *daahanga; hagabigo de ngago.*
Fool (someone), deceive, trick (someone): *hagasenga.*

fool around
Fool around, play a joke on: *hagatala.*

fooled
Be a sucker, be fooled easily: *dau duadae.*
Deceived, fooled: *sengalia.*

foolish
Dumb, foolish, ignorant: *senga.*

foot
Foot (including leg), leg: *vae*$_2$.
Foot, ankle: *gubu vae.*
Stem, base, foot (e.g., of a hill), stump: *dahido.*

footprint
Toe, footprint: *dabuvae.*

for
About it, concerning it, in it, for it: *loo.*
For (always followed by *o* or *a*$_1$): *m-.*
For each person's one: *maadada; maadodo.*
For each person's several: *maada*$_1$*; maada*$_2$*; mooda; moodo.*
For him, for her, for it: *maana; maana; moona.*
For his, for hers, for its: *moono; moono.*
For me: *maagu; moogu.*
For them: *maalaadeu; maalaau; moolaadeu; moolaau.*
For us: *maadaadeu; maadaau; maamaadeu; maamaau; moodaadeu; moodaau; moomaadeu; moomaau.*
For you: *maau; moodou; mooluu; moou.*
To it, for it: *agina.*

for example
For instance, for example: *bei tagodo.*

for instance
For instance, for example: *bei tagodo.*

forbidden
Forbidden to use (esp. plants reserved for the owner's use by tying the trunk): *noodagi.*
Forbidden, awesome: *dabu.*

force
Strong, strength, force, power, energy: *mmahi.*

forced out
Be forced out of: *buu*$_2$.

forearm
Forearm: *sugi lima.*

forehead
Forehead: *lae.*

foreign
Foreign lands: *henua gee.*

foreigners
Foreigners (lit., 'people from other lands'): *gau henua gee.*
Foreigners (lit., 'people who came in canoes'): *gau mai moni.*
Foreigners, strangers: *dangada henua gee.*

forenoon
Forenoon (from dawn to noon): *baasi gi taiao.*

forever
Forever: *hano ai huu.*
Forever, eternally: *dee ngado mai.*

forget
Forget: *ngalo.*
Forget it!: *lava ai donu huu.*
Forget purposely: *hagangalo.*

forgetful
Forgetful (esp. with increasing age): *vava de gede.*
Forgetful, absent-minded: *dee anga; ngalongalo.*

forgive
Forgive (someone), pardon (someone): *degi ange.*

forgiving
Having a forgiving nature: *lodo degi.*
Kind, generous, forgiving: *degi*$_2$.

form
Shape of, form of: *holi.*
To form (something): *holia.*

fornicate
Have sexual intercourse, fornicate: *sanga.*

fornication
Fornication: *dagodo hai sala.*

fortunate
Fortunate result: *hagapago donu.*
Fortunate, lucky, blessed: *manuia.*

fortunately
Fortunately, luckily —: *adigai huu.*
Fortunately, luckily: *de eidu pale.*

fortune
Luck, good fortune: *duadonu.*

forty
Forty: *madahaa.*
Forty, of days + nights: *uhaa.*

foulmouthed
Evil-tongued, lying (dishonest, foulmouthed: *vaivai ngudu.*
Foulmouthed, swear: *vaivai basa.*

found
Found or caught doing something wrong: *vaagia.*
Found out (or be found out): *gidee mai.*

foundation
Bottom, foundation: *dagelo.*

four
Four: *haa*$_3$.

fraction
Fraction (in arithmetic): *diba*$_2$.

fragrance
Fragrance (esp. of flowers or perfume): *manongi.*
Fragrance (esp. of food): *kala*$_2$.

fragrant
Fragrant: *manongi.*

free
Free from (esp. hardship or illness after having had it): *malau*$_1$.
Free from: *ilaage mai.*
Free, escaped: *ola.*
Get free, be loose: *madala mai.*
Have time for, free, available: *saohia*$_2$.
Set free: *hagailaage.*

freedom
Calmness, tranquility, freedom from worries: *lodo baba.*

freeze
Freeze, coagulate: *noho.*

Fregata
Bird sp.: great frigate bird (*Fregata minor*): *gadaha.*

frequently
Often, frequently: *duu podo.*

fresh
Fresh air: *madangi danuaa.*

Friday
Friday ('fifth day'): *Lima-laangi.*

friend
A friend: *soa.*
A good friend: *soa hagaaloha.*
A secret friend of the opposite sex: *hanu me.*

friends
Companions or friends who share the same interests, and who get along well: *dangada ulu.*
The relationship between friends: *hai soa.*

friendship
Friendship: *hai soa.*

frigate bird
Bird sp.: great frigate bird (*Fregata minor*): *gadaha.*
Bird sp.: red-throated frigate bird: *ua-mea.*
Bird sp.: white-throated frigate bird: *ua dea.*

frighten
Frighten (someone): *hagamadagu.*
To frighten with sounds: *hoohoo ina.*

frightened
Frightened by noise: *ohooho*$_2$.

fringe
Edge, fringe, rim: *hiihii.*

frond
Coconut palm frond: *haa*$_2$.
The inner coconut palm frond: *haa lodo.*
The outer coconut palm frond: *haa daha.*

front
Chest, front (opposite of back — e.g.,lagoon shore as opposed to seaward reef shore): *aloalo*$_3$.
Front (position), before, ahead: *mua.*
Front of: *madamada*$_2$.
Front part of, face, beginning (of a thing): *mada*$_3$.

frown
Squint (eyes), frown: *hakohu luu mada.*

fructiferous
Fruitful, fructiferous: *mili*$_2$.

fruit
Fruit: *hua manu.*
Misshapen fruit: *aoa*$_2$.

fruit fly
Insect sp.: fruit fly: *manu-a-luga.*

fruitful
Fruitful, fructiferous: *mili*$_2$.

fulcrum
A log used as a lever or fulcrum: *hala a buadaia.*

full
Full: *honu*$_1$.
Full to capacity: *dohu lodo.*
Full up (and tightly packed): *honu kadi.*

full moon
Full moon (a period comprising two nights): *tino boo.*

full-grown
Old (persons), mature, full-grown: *madua.*

fumes
Dust, gas, steam, vapor, fumes, spray (e.g., of waves): *mama.*

fungus
A fungus infection of the skin (consisting of superficial white spots): *dane.*
A fungus infection of the skin, ringworm: *gili dabeo.*

funny
Funny, unserious, jesting, silly: *hakadanga.*

fussy
Fussy (about food): *gai hilihili.*

gaining
Gaining in: *hanuhanu.*

game
A type of game: *loeaa.*
Game, amusement: *hagadaahao.*

garbage
Trash, garbage: *gainga.*

garden
A garden: *veelenga.*

gargle
Wash one's mouth out, gargle: *luuluu haha.*

garland
A garland of flowers (as a headdress or necklace): *hau.*
A garland of flowers, headdress, necklace: *hau manu.*

gas
Dust, gas, steam, vapor, fumes, spray (e.g., of waves): *mama.*
Wind, gas, flatus: *madangi.*

gasp
Gasp for breath (more than once): *hodahoda*$_1$.
Gasp for breath (once): *hhoda.*

gastritis
Gastritis (having one's stomach full of gas): *magi ilihia.*

gastropod
Mollusk sp.: vermetid gastropod sp.: *unga-goo.*

gather
Gather or pleat in material: *dauaahe.*
Gather together (people): *hagabuni.*
Gather together in a group: *dagabuli.*
Gather up: *hagadali.*

gathered
Gathered around (something): *mui.*

gear
Gear obtained from foreign lands: *goloa lalo.*
Gear of local manufacture: *goloa de henua.*
Gear, tools, goods, supplies (but not food): *goloa*$_2$.

gem
Gem: *hadu hagamogomogo.*

generation
Generation, age set: *atangada.*

generous
Considerate, kind, generous: *abo donu.*
Having a kind or generous nature: *degidegi*$_3$.
Kind, generous, forgiving: *degi*$_2$.

genital
Male genital organ, penis: *menemene.*

genitalia
Female genitalia: *goloa o de hine.*
Male genitalia: *goloa o taane.*

genitals
Genitals (of males or females): *me balabala; songosongo; vaivai me.*

gentle
Gentle, mild-mannered, soft-spoken: *daudonu.*

gentleman
Gentleman, person who is good: *daane abo donu.*

gently
Carefully, gently, softly: *maalie.*
Slowly, gently, skillfully, etc.: *damaa.*

genuflect
Bow or nod or genuflect (as a sign of respect): *ino.*

get
Enter, join (a group), get in: *ulu*$_1$.
Get down, climb down: *iho.*
Get down, get off: *doo*$_1$.
Get out from or through, escape: *sao*$_2$.
Get out!: *hakii adu; kii adu.*
Get something quickly: *degi*$_1$.
Get up, jump up: *soosobo.*
Get, obtain, caught: *mau*$_3$.
Rise up (as the sun), get up, jump up: *sobo.*

get even
Take revenge, get even: *sui ange.*

get up
Get up (from a sitting position): *hidi.*

getting
Getting closer to the time (of happening): *savasavaa.*

ghost
Ghost (children's language): *baabaoa.*
Ghost, spirit, god: *eidu.*

ghost crab
Crab sp.: shore crab, land crab, grapsid crab, ghost crab: *gaibea.*

giant
Giant: *doa.*
Very big giant: *doa agalala.*

giant clam
Mollusk sp.: giant clam (*Tridacna squammosa*): *dange.*
Mollusk sp.: giant clam sp.: *ngae*$_2$.

gift
A gift (to the hearer): *ngadi gavadu.*

giggle
Giggle: *giigii saele.*

Gilbertese
Gilbertese people: *de gau duuli sou.*

gill
Gill (of a fish): *gau-me.*

girl
Female child, girl: *gauligi hahine.*
Girl, young woman, daughter: *damaa hine.*
Immature girl: *bua moe.*
Unmarried girl: *(de) hine duuhua.*
Young girl: *ulu hudi*.*

girl-crazy
Ladies' man, girl-crazy: *ulu i haahine.*

girlfriend
Boyfriend, girlfriend: *dau soa.*

give
Give (to hearer): *vadu.*
Give or bring to (someone): *gavange.*
Give or bring up: *gavage.*
Give or carry (something) to you: *gavadu.*
Give to (him, her, or them): *vange.*

give birth
Give birth to: *haanau.*
Give birth to, born: *maaui.*

give up
Give up: *sivi.*

glide
Glide (in the air): *saga.*
Soar or glide in the air: *maangi.*

glimpse
Glimpse: *galo sugi mada.*

glory bower
Plant sp.: glory bower (*Clerodendrum inerme* (L.) Gaertn.): *manu-mmala.*

gluttonous
Gluttonous: *dee haaoa i de gai.*

go
Come (go) straight: *velo mai (adu, ange).*
Come or go (toward the speaker): *loomai.*
Go (to the place away from both the speaker and hearer): *loange.*
Go (toward the hearer): *loadu.*
Go (up or toward the village, or land): *loage.*
Go: *hano; hulo.*
Go along with others, join the crowd: *hagasoa ange.*
Go around in a circle: *nigo.*
Go at top speed: *tili mada.*
Go away: *hano gee; hulo gee.*
Go backwards (esp. a canoe): *hagammene dua.*
Go directly: *velo tili.*
Go early: *oho adu.*
Go from house to house: *aduhale.*
Go from one place to another in a group: *daga*$_1$.
Go from one place to another, and another, etc.: *hagadaga*$_1$.
Go immediately!: *hano kaba.*
Go on and on until —: *hanohano ai huu.*
Go on foot: *hano laa uda.*
Go or come down (or toward the lagoon): *loiho.*
Go or do by oneself: *massogosogo.*
Go out (of a fire): *made*$_2$.
Go to: *hanange.*
Go toward land (from the lagoon): *daa age.*
Go toward the lagoon (from land): *daa iho.*
Go up straight: *velo age.*
Go!: *hannoo.*
Hasten to go or come: *alomasige.*
Leave, go away: *ssabe.*
Return, go back: *ahe.*
Stick against (something), go with someone: *hagapigi ange.*

goat
Fish sp.: goat fish (=*madulilau sisisi*): *ahulu.*

goatfish
Fish sp.: goatfish (= small *vede*): *galo*$_4$.
Fish sp.: goatfish: *galo-gila; maduilau; malili*$_2$*; moaga; moahulu; sugi-laagoo; vede-mea; vede*$_2$.

goby
Fish sp.: goby?, sleeper?: *dama-a-de-galabe.*
Fish sp.: goby: *dotonogaa; manogo.*
Fish sp.: round herring?, goby?: *ulua-gabugabu-tai.*

god
Ghost, spirit, god: *eidu.*

going
Going along with: *tali.*

Going steady (of an unmarried couple): *dau soa.*

golden plover
Bird sp.: golden plover (*Plurialis dominica*): *duli*$_1$.

gone
Gone, finished, used up: *odi*$_b$.
Long since finished, done, or gone: *odiodi.*

good
Easy living, a good life: *mouli danuaa.*
Good (not bad, but not the best), OK: *hagavaasuu.*
Good (not evil or false): *abo donu.*
Good (of food or certain activities only): *malie.*
Good (quality): *masana.*
Good ! Hello! Good-bye!: *danuaa.*
Good enough!: *danuaa sili.*
Good one: *daane masana.*

good at
Good at: *abo ange; malie.*
Good at fighting: *masausau.*
Good at food preparation (not wasteful): *gaimalie.*
Sharp-eyed, good at finding things: *mada gide.*

good for
Good for, better than: *danuaa ange.*

Good-bye!
Good ! Hello! Good-bye!: *danuaa.*

good-looking
Good-looking, handsome: *tilo danuaa.*

goods
Gear, tools, goods, supplies (but not food): *goloa*$_2$.

gooseflesh
Gooseflesh: *teve de gili.*
Gooseflesh, disgusted, horror-fascination: *tuu gili.*

gorge
Gorge oneself: *hanohano dua.*

gorgonian
Gorgonian (Coelenterate), false black coral: *aoa-laosedi.*

gossip
Gossip, slander: *samu.*
To gossip: *hai samu.*

gossipy
Gossipy person, tattletale: *tangada adi longo.*

gotten
Able to, obtained, gotten, caught: *maua.*

gouge
Gouge out (with the hand only): *llao.*
Gouge out: *gabe.*

gouging
To extract by gouging out with a finger: *nao.*

grab
Grab (between other things, e.g., fingers): *gabi.*
Grab (in order to restrain, e.g., a person), fall upon: *dango*$_1$.
Grab (with one's hand): *boo*$_1$.
Grab or catch in a single act: *poo.*
Grab up: *buli.*
Grab up all at once: *puli.*
Grab up one thing after another: *bulibuli.*
Grab while pulling: *mulu gudu.*

grabbed
Grabbed, fallen upon: *dangoa; dangolia.*

graceful
Certain, sure, graceful, definitely: *too donu.*
Graceful in dancing: *saubaligi.*

grandchild
Grandchild, descendant of: *mogobuna.*

grandfather
Grandfather: *dahidonga.*

grandparent
Grandparent, ancestor: *dubuna.*

grapsid crab
Crab sp.: shore crab, land crab, grapsid crab, ghost crab: *gaibea.*

grass skirt
Grass skirt (of hibiscus fiber or palm leaf): *didi.*

grass sp.
Plant sp.: grass sp. (*Lepturus repens* (Forst.) R.Br.): *helii.*
Plant sp.: grass sp.: *helii-baalanga.*

grasshopper
Insect sp.: grasshopper: *itebuubuu.*

grate
To grate (esp. coconut) on a stool grater (*duai*): *valu*$_1$.
To grate or file (something): *solo.*

grater
A type of coconut grater which is placed under the leg: *duai lalo vae.*
Grater (metal) attached to a board for grating taro: *madaa hadu.*
Stool grater (for grating coconuts): *duai*$_2$.

grave
Grave (for burial): *daanunga.*

greasy
Be greasy: *buu*$_3$.
Odor, smell (of something), greasy: *nnamu.*
Sticky, greasy: *baalau.*

great
Big, great: *laumalie.*

greedy
Greedy: *hagalanea.*

green
Dark green in color: *mada nuui.*
Green: *nuui.*

green turtle
Green turtle (2 varieties): *honu*$_2$.

greet
Greet: *hagaboo*$_2$.

groove
Groove: *hagaloa.*

grooved
Grooved: *hakaligali.*

group
Group of (e.g., *agu sai* 'my children'): *sai*$_2$.
Group of animate things: *hagabuulinga.*
Group of islands or atolls: *aduhenua.*
Group of islets: *adumodu.*
Group of things approaching together (e.g., a fleet of canoes): *hudaa —.*
Pile of, group of: *buudunga.*
Portion of, group of (fish or animals): *ungaa.*

grouping
Grouping (of people): *gau*$_2$.

grow
Grow abnormally (having defects): *somo boi.*
Grow fast or well anywhere (e.g., as a weed): *somosomo*$_1$.
Grow, develop: *somo*$_1$.

grumble
Grumble, complain: *nanu.*

grunt
Grunt (once): *kono.*

guard
Guard, watch, keep an eye on: *hagaloosi.*

guarded
Guarded condition or prognosis (of a sick person): *halehale dagodo.*

Guettarda
Plant sp.: tree sp. (*Guettarda speciosa* L.): *bua.*

guilt
Guilt: *dagasala.*

gullible
Gullible, be a sucker: *duadae.*

gum
Gum (to chew), sap (of trees): *bigibigi*$_1$.

gums
Gums (of mouth): *gano niho.*

gun
Gun or any weapon of similar nature: *bagi.*
Machine gun: *bagi mada lagolago.*

gunwales
Gunwales (at the top of the canoe): *oa.*

gust
A gust of wind: *sou.*

guts
Guts, intestines: *dae*$_3$.

gutter
Gutter (under the eaves of a house): *me hagasahu vai.*

Gygis
Bird sp.: fairy tern (*Gygis alba*): *agiagi.*

habit
Custom, habit: *dahulinga.*

hair
Hair (on the body): *hulu*$_1$; *huluhulu*$_1$.
Hair of the head: *ngaangaa-ulu.*
Having kinky hair: *lauvinivini.*
Having straight hair (not kinky or wavy): *laussoe.*
Having wavy hair: *lau hadihadi.*

Having white hair: *sinaa.*
To have the hair (of one's head) standing on end: *teve de biho.*
White (or grey) hair (appearing in old age): *sina.*

haircut
Haircut: *duu biho.*

hairs
Fine threads or hairs or fibers (in feather or leaf, etc.): *amu ligi.*

hairy
Hairy: *huluhulua*$_1$.

Halcyon
Bird sp.: sacred kingfisher (*Halcyon sancta*) (The native term applies possibly to several spp.): *manu-de-bua.*

half
A half shell, a cover (of something): *uduu.*
Half (of something like a coconut): *duu*$_3$.
Half of a clam shell: *duunga gima.*
Half of an unripe coconut: *duu mugamuga.*
Side, half: *baasi.*

half-cooked
Half-cooked: *madamada*$_1$; *moomada.*

half-crazy
Half-crazy: *hilohilo senga.*

halfbeak
Fish sp.: halfbeak: *ise.*

halfway
Middle (of something long and thin), halfway: *madohi; madohi lua.*

hallucinate
To see a vision, hallucinate: *gide eidu; gide eidu ina.*

hand
Arm, hand: *lima*$_1$.
Hand, wrist: *gubu lima.*

hand net
Hand net: *dae*$_1$.

handful
A handful of *dalogo*: *maanga dalogo.*

handle
A handle of something: *hakauanga.*
Handle, appendage: *gau*$_1$.

handsome
Good-looking, handsome: *tilo danuaa.*

hang
Hang down or bent down (of branches, palm fronds, or fishing poles): *llou.*
To hang oneself (suicide): *gabaea; hagabaea.*

hang around
To hang around someone's house in the expectation of being served food: *dama gaiaa.*

happen
Soon (will happen): *savaa.*

happening
Happening continually but one at a time: *dili dagidahi.*

happy
Contented, happy: *lodo danuaa.*
Feel happy or contented or at peace with the world: *hinangalomalie.*
Happy (lot., 'to slap one's sides'): *paa de hoa.*
Happy: *lodo malangilangi.*
Happy with, pleased at: *malangilangi ai.*
Happy, laugh (as a sign of happiness), cheerful: *malangilangi.*

harbor
Harbor (place where boats anchor): *daulanga.*

hard
Hard (solid): *makaga.*
Hard and curled up owing to dryness: *mmasa bagubagu.*
Hard to: *kau gee.*

hardly
Hardly any: *dai deai.*

hardship
Hardship, difficulty: *duasala.*

hardwood
Hardwood in the tree trunk: *daihadu.*

hardworking
Industrious, hardworking: *dinihu.*

harmonica
Harmonica: *maadoogini.*

harness
Strap, harness: *gaaui*$_2$.

harpoon
A spear or harpoon to which a line is attached: *dao tili.*

harsh
Harsh words: *muna pada.*

hasten
Hasten to go or come: *alomasige.*

hat
Hat: *goobai.*

hatched
Hatched: *maasae.*

hatchet
A small axe, hatchet: *hagadagu u.*

hate
Hate: *kino.*
Hate each other: *hagadau kino.*
Hate vehemently, completely disgusted: *kino made.*

haughty
Arrogant, haughty, overbearing, proud: *hagamao lunga.*

haul
Haul (all at once or as fast as possible): *mmoli.*
Haul (little by little): *molimoli.*
Haul away from: *mmoli gee.*

have
Be (present), have, there is...: *iai.*
To have: *hanu*$_2$.

hawk fish
Fish sp.: hawk fish (2 sorts): *iga-adagahi.*
Fish sp.: hawk fish: *ulu-dugi; ulu-dugi-lalo-beau.*

hawksbill turtle
Hawksbill turtle: *gea.*
The carapace of the hawksbill turtle: *ango*.*

he
He, she, it: *ia.*

head
Head: *biho; ngadi biho; ngae*$_1$.
Head of the penis: *duubulei.*

headache
Headache: *biho ngaalulu.*

headcold
Headcold, runny nose: *magi sali usu.*

headdress
A garland of flowers (as a headdress or necklace): *hau.*
A garland of flowers, headdress, necklace: *hau manu.*
Shell necklace or headdress: *hau bule.*

healed
Healed (of a sore): *mahu.*
Healed, well (after sickness), recuperated: *hagavaasuu.*

hear
Hear, feel: *longo.*

heard
Heard, felt: *langona*$_2$.

heart
Heart: *hadu manava.*

heartburn
Heartburn: *mahana age.*

heat
Cook, heat up: *dunu*$_1$.
Heat up on an open flame (as in shaping wood): *laangia.*

heated
Heated: *mahanasia.*

heaven
Rain, heaven, sky: *langi*$_2$.

heaviness
Heaviness, sadness, unhappiness: *daemahaanga.*

heavy
Heavy or dense (of rain): *maadolu.*
Heavy, oppressive, hard to take: *daemaha; daemahadia; daemahalia.*

heavy-duty
Heavy-duty equipment or fishing gear: *doonga pada.*

held
Held firmly (by something not part of the human body): *gabidia.*
Held firmly (under the arm or between the fingers, etc.): *gabia.*

heliotrope
Plant sp.: heliotrope (*Tournefortia argentea* L., = *Messerschmidia argentea* L.): *manu-gili-maau.*

Hello!
Good ! Hello! Good-bye!: *danuaa.*
Hello! Good day!: *laangi danuaa.*

help
Help (with provisions): *hagaaoaoa*$_2$.
Help one another: *hagadau bale*.
Help to urinate (e.g., by taking a baby outside): *hagadiidii*$_2$.
Help, assist, aid (with effort or advice, etc.): *bale*$_1$.

helpful
Helpful (sort of person): *lodo bale*.
Helpful toward: *aloha ina*.

hemorrhage
Hemorrhage: *manuhi*.

hemp-leaved vitex shrub
Plant sp.: hemp-leaved vitex shrub (*Vitex negundo* var. *bicolor* (Willd.) Lam.): *gasigi*.

her
His one, her one, its one: *dana; dono*.
His several, her several, its several: *ana*$_3$*; ona; ono*$_3$.
His two, her two, its two: *luaana; luoono*.

here
Here in this place: *kinei*.
Here, now: *nei*.

hermit crab
Hermit crab (lives in water): *unga-lausedi*.
Hermit crab (lives on dry land): *unga*.

Hernandia tree
Plant sp.: tree sp.: Hernandia tree (*Hernandia sonora* L.): *bingibingi*.

hernia
Umbilical hernia: *duu de gona*.

heron
Bird sp.: reef heron (*Demiegretta sacra*): *gava*$_2$.
Reef heron — grey phase: *gava-uli*.
Reef heron — white phase: *gava-dea*.

herring
Fish sp.: round herring?, goby?: *ulua-gabugabu-tai*.

hers
His, hers, its: *sana; sono*.

Heteroscelus
Bird sp.: Polynesian tattler (*Heteroscelus brevipes*): *goigoi*$_2$.
Bird sp.: Polynesian tattler? (*Heteroscelus brevipes*): *dilidili-dogi*.
Bird sp.: wandering tattler? (*Heteroscelus incanus*): *lahulahu*$_2$.

hibiscus tree
Plant sp.: tree sp.: hibiscus tree (*Hibiscus tiliaceus* L.): *goehau*.

hiccough
Hiccough: *leia togo mouli*.

hidden
Hidden, hide: *mmuni*.

hide
Hidden, hide: *mmuni*.
Hide (something) from: *hagammuni*.
Hide: *huna; huuhuna*.
Hide at one time: *hhuna*.

hide and seek
Hide and seek (a game): *duu munimuni*.

hideous
Hideous in appearance (as a ghost): *laagii baubau*.

high
High, high-ranking: *mao lunga*.
Hillock, high: *duuduu*$_2$.

high-ranking
High-ranking: *aamua*.
High, high-ranking: *mao lunga*.

high-water mark
High-water mark: *daungaangalu; goinga o tai*.

higher
Higher: *aamua ange*.

hillock
Hillock (in the taro bog only): *guuduma*.
Hillock: *gili dalo*.
Hillock, high: *duuduu*$_2$.

hip
Hip: *gaba*$_1$.

Hippopus
Mollusk sp.: horse hoof clam (*Hippopus hippopus*): *gima*.

his
His one, her one, its one: *dana; dono*.
His several, her several, its several: *ana*$_3$*; ona; ono*$_3$.
His two, her two, its two: *luaana; luoono*.
His, hers, its: *sana; sono*.

hissing
A hissing sound: *ssii*$_2$.

hit
Be hit (by wind, bullet, spear, etc.): *bagia.*
Be hit (usually forcefully) by wind: *baa i de madangi.*
Be hit: *dau*$_3$.
Be hit by (usually a strong) wind: *dau de madangi.*
Hit and run: *dale gaiaa.*
Hit or tap with the hand or foot: *badu.*
Hit repeatedly (on one occasion): *dadau.*
Hit, strike, beat: *daa*$_1$.
Punch, hit, strike: *dugi*$_1$.

hives
Eruptions on the skin (e.g., hives, insect bites, etc.): *dala hhua.*

hoist
To hoist a sail: *dada saiolo.*

hold
Hold (in one's hand): *boo*$_1$.
Hold an election: *hai de hilihili.*
Hold hands: *bigi lima.*
Hold something between two (or more) other things: *gabi.*
Hold, restrain, keep (from): *daohi.*
Lift or hold one end of something: *bidoa.*
Skewer, hold something down with the end of a long implement: *suunugi.*

hole
A hole (in something torn): *masaenga.*
A hole (in something): *haonga.*
A hole (which has been dug): *geelinga.*
A small hole: *mada legalega.*
Having a hole, pierced: *masugi.*

hollow
Hollow, vacant, empty: *ngadi*—.

homesick
Long for, homesick: *buliaamou.*

honor
Pay respect to, honor (someone): *hagaamu*$_2$.
Praise (someone), honor: *tuhi.*

hook
Hook, fishhook: *maadau.*
To hook under the waistband or belt: *nabe.*

hooked
Hooked, caught fast on: *lau*$_1$.

hop
Hop on one foot: *hagaditidi vae dahi.*

hope
Hope for (want): *hagalodolodo.*
Hope for, expectant, waiting: *tali.*

hopeful
Hopeful expectation: *tali hagalodolodo.*

horizon
Horizon: *giligili tai.*

horn
Horn (of an animal): *hanga.*

horror-fascination
Gooseflesh, disgusted, horror-fascination: *tuu gili.*

horse hoof clam
Mollusk sp.: horse hoof clam (*Hippopus hippopus*): *gima.*

hospital
Hospital, dispensary: *hale magi.*

hostile
A sudden access of hostile feeling: *uluhia.*

hostility
Reactive hostility: *hulu*$_4$.

hot
Hot (of an object): *vvela.*
Hot (of the weather): *hagavvela.*
Hot: *mahana.*
Red hot (literally): *mmea be se gaagose.*

hotel
Hotel: *hale gaainga.*

hottest
The hottest part (of the day, of a fire, etc.): *lo te vvela.*

house
A house of brick or cement construction: *hale hadu.*
A house of indigenous construction (thatch): *hale de henua.*
A house of prostitution: *hale haahine.*
Bath house: *hale gaugau.*
Canoe house: *holau.*
Cook house, earth oven: *umu.*
Frame house: *hale baabaa; hale baalanga.*

House, dwelling, building: *hale.*
Men's house (modern usage): *hale daane.*
Out house: *hale hongagelegele.*
Thatch-roofed house (of palm frond thatch): *hale langadala.*
Thatch-roofed house (of pandanus leaf thatch): *hale lau.*

hug
Hug: *buuludi.*

human
Person, human being, relative: *dangada.*

humble
Humble, modest: *hagamao lalo.*

hump
A hump on a tree trunk (where a branch failed to flower): *denga*$_2$.

hundred
Hundred: *lau*$_4$.

hundreds
Hundreds: *llau*$_2$.
Hundreds and hundreds: *laulau*$_4$.

hung
Hung up, suspended from: *dau*$_2$.

hungry
Always hungry: *savasavali.*
Hungry: *dai hiigai; hagaahi; saalohia; savali.*
Hungry for fish or meat: *umidi.*

hunt for
Look for, search, hunt for: *ssala*$_1$.

hurry
Be in a hurry to: *daadaaia ange.*
Hurry, rush: *hagamoolau.*

hurt
Pain, hurt (children's language): *maemae.*
Pain, hurt: *mmae.*

hurting
Hurting in the ears from noise: *nngao dalinga.*
Hurting of one's ears from high-pitched noises: *duliduli.*

husk
Husk of the coconut: *hakaa.*
Husk of the mature coconut: *baeao.*
Piece of coconut husk: *duu baeao.*
The husk of a coconut (remaining after husking): *ogaanga.*
To husk (a coconut) with a sharp stick: *oga.*
To husk (a coconut) with one's teeth: *idi.*

husking stick
A husking stick: *hanga.*

Hymenocallis
Plant sp.: spider lily (*Hymenocallis littoralis* (Jacq.) Salisb.): *giebu.*

I
I: *au*$_2$.

idea
Idea, thought: *maanadu.*
Incomplete idea: *bulubulu maanadu.*

identify
Identify tentatively: *mademadea.*
Identify, recognize: *madea.*

idiolect
Manner of speaking, idiolect, dialect: *baasanga.*

idiot
Idiot: *boi dugidugi.*

idol
An idol representing a spirit: *diinonga eidu.*

idols
Pagan gods, idols: *ngadi diinonga.*

if
If: *ne; noo.*
If ever: *be aha naa huu.*
If, in the case that: *daudonu.*
When, if: *naa huu.*

ignite
Ignite a fire by making sparks with a stone: *ahi tugi.*

ignorant
Be ignorant (of what is happening): *noho senga (adu).*
Dumb, foolish, ignorant: *senga.*
Ignorant: *gohu de lodo.*
Ignorant person: *dangada gohu.*

ill
Ill, illness: *magi.*
Incurably ill: *dee ahe mai.*
Seriously ill and not improving: *dagodo lalo.*

To be in a serious condition, critically ill or injured: *beaha.*

illness
Ill, illness: *magi.*

illuminate
Brighten, illuminate: *hagamaalama.*

illuminated
Illuminated (by having light shined upon it): *maalamangia.*

illustrate
Illustrate by examples: *hagadagodo.*
Imitate, illustrate, give an example: *hagadulagi.*

image
Picture, image, reflection, shadow: *ada*$_1$.

imitate
Copy, imitate: *ago i me.*
Imitate: *hagaago.*
Imitate, illustrate, give an example: *hagadulagi.*

immature
Immature (in personality): *lodo a gauligi.*
Immature in affect: *lodo dama.*

immoral
Unscrupulous, immoral, evil: *vaivaidagodo.*

impeded
To have one's forward motion impeded (as when walking through the surf): *llau*$_1$.

impetuous
Impetuous in act or movement (leading to frequent error): *sasa gee.*

importance
Of importance: *dau*$_1$.

important
Effective, useful, worthwhile, important: *haigamaiana.*
Special one, important one: *daane ssili dala.*
Worthwhile, important, valuable: *gasia.*

impression
An impression left by a hard object pressing on a soft one: *baabanga.*

imprisonment
Imprisonment (short term): *hagadali.*

improved
Improved, better: *danuaa age.*

improvident
Wasteful, improvident: *gai ngole.*

improving
Improving: *hagadaga age.*

impure
Impure: *hilohilo me.*

in
About it, concerning it, in it, for it: *loo.*
In: *i.*

in addition to
In addition to: *madali.*

in charge of
Be in charge of: *hua ai.*

in order to
Toward, to, in order to: *gi*$_1$.

in spite of
In spite of: *i.*

incision
Make an incision: *ssele.*

incisor
Incisor teeth: *niho hagadolo.*

inclination
Gradual slope or inclination: *madadaagodo.*

incline
Incline to one side: *hagadiba.*

inclined
Inclined to do —: *velo huu —.*
Inclined, slanting, not straight, not perpendicular to: *salau.*

included
Be included: *dau*$_1$.

including
With, including: *ma*$_1$.

incomplete
Incomplete idea: *bulubulu maanadu.*

inconsiderate
Inconsiderate: *dee vasu.*

inconstant
Unstable temperamentally, inconstant: *lodo aheahe.*

increase
Increase (in price, etc.): *ngaue ange.*

Increase (in rank or price, etc.): *ngaue age.*
Increase (speed or power, etc.): *ue ange.*
Increase: *kii ange; ngalue ange.*
Increase in: *hagadaga ange.*
Raise or increase (volume of radio or price, etc.): *ue age.*

increased
Increased, augmented: *ngalue age.*

incriminate
Blame (someone), incriminate (someone): *hagabuu ange.*

incubation
Incubation of eggs (by a hen): *baalasi ngago.*

incurably
Incurably ill: *dee ahe mai.*

indecisive
Indecisive, confused: *lodo lanea*$_2$.
Indecisive, undecided: *lodo lagolago.*

Indian coral tree
Plant sp.: tree sp.: Indian coral tree (*Erythrina variegata* L.): *ulu-davage.*

Indian mulberry tree
Plant sp.: tree sp.: Indian mulberry tree (*Morinda citrifolia* L.): *bugaliaa.*

indifferent
Indifferent: *dee hilihili.*

indiscreet
Talkative, indiscreet: *vava de ngudu.*

industrious
Industrious: *hai me; maagaga.*
Industrious person: *tangada maagaga.*
Industrious, hardworking: *dinihu.*

inexpensive
Inexpensive: *hagao ngaohie.*

infant
Baby, infant: *dama legalega**; *gaagaa*$_1$.
Infant: *dibo; tama legalega.*

infected
Cause to be infected: *hagaaugaua.*
Infected: *augaua.*
State of becoming infected: *hagaaugaunga.*

infection
Cause infection: *hagaaugau.*

infirm
Elderly and infirm: *tolo i de baeao.*

inflammation
Inflammation: *ula de gili.*
Redness or inflammation of the skin (e.g., a welt): *dala mmea.*

inflate
Inflate (a balloon): *ili.*

inflated
Bloated, inflated, swollen up, bulging: *lengi.*

information
Information (by definition, true) acquired from one's parents: *tugolo.*

ingredients
Ingredients of *dalogo*: *me hanga dalogo.*

initiate
Initiate, begin: *aladi.*
Initiate, begin, start: *ladi.*

injured
To be in a serious condition, critically ill or injured: *beaha.*

inland
Inland: *uda*$_2$.
Inland of: *ngauda*$_1$.
Inland, bush (uncleared) land, wilderness: *lodo henua.*

innocence
Pureness of heart, innocence: *lodo gilimalali.*

inquiry
Trial or formal inquiry: *siilinga a muna.*

inquisitive
Inquisitive (prone to ask too many questions): *sili muna.*
Inquisitive, mischievous (as a child): *ssahu.*

insane
Act crazy or insane: *manaunau**.
Crazy, insane: *manaunaua**.
Insane person: *gavia.*

insect bites
Eruptions on the skin (e.g., hives, insect bites, etc.): *dala hhua.*

insect sp.
Insect sp. (= *manu-de-laama*): *manu dudu dangada.*
Insect sp. (small and turtle-like): *honu-uda.*

Insect sp.: *bodubodu-o-uda; boobua; manumanu.*
Insect sp.: a phosphorescent insect: *pula.*
Insect sp.: cockroach: *hagabini*$_2$.
Insect sp.: cockroach sp. (black — foul smelling): *de-hine-aligi*$_1$.
Insect sp.: fly, flying ant, wasp: *lango*$_2$.
Insect sp.: fruit fly: *manu-a-luga.*
Insect sp.: grasshopper: *itebuubuu.*
Insect sp.: moth spp.: *lengisi.*
Insect sp.: scorpion: *manu-manga-lua.*
Insect sp.: walkingstick (a very large grasshopper-like insect): *manu-de-hala.*

insert
Inject, insert: *velo.*

inside
Inside of: *lodo*$_1$.
Inside the corner of: *lo te dege.*

insincerely
To act insincerely: *hai me a gimoo.*

insist
Insist upon: *hhou; mmogo.*

insomnia
Insomnia (after sleeping for a short while): *lele sseni.*

instantaneous
Instantaneous, in the blinking of an eye: *daba de ganomada.*

insult
Insult (someone): *hagadaemahalia; hagammae lodo; hagi ade.*

insure
Take every possible precaution, insure: *hagatoo mua.*

intelligent
Smart, intelligent, clever: *heiangi.*

intercept
Intercept: *aalu.*

interested
Becoming interested in: *savasavala.*
Interested in, enjoys: *savala.*

interfered
Interfered with: *uluhia.*

interpret
Interpret: *hagadonu.*

interpreter
Act as an interpreter: *hagadonu muna; ngudu ai.*

intersection
Intersection: *hesilihaginga haiava.*

intestines
Guts, intestines: *dae*$_3$.

intimate
Know, understand, be intimate with, sure of (and willing to say): *iloo.*

invade
Invade: *gage de henua.*

invented
Invented, made-up (e.g., a story): *hhadu.*

invertebrates
Marine invertebrates: *manu laosedi.*

investigate
Investigate (to prove one's suspicions): *lahu.*

invite
Invite: *gauna.*

iron
Cast iron: *baalanga uli.*
Iron (a piece of): *aladoidoi.*

island
A land mass, an island, a country, or any other geopolitical unit: *henua.*

islands
Group of islands or atolls: *aduhenua.*

islet
An islet (on the atoll): *modu.*
Conglomerate, islet: *adu*$_4$.
Islet: *ahu.*
Land, islet: *nugu.*

islets
Group of islets: *adumodu.*

isolate
Isolate, separate from, set aside (from a group): *vvae gee.*

it
He, she, it: *ia.*
It is a...: *se.*
The, thing, it: *de ia.*

itch
Itch: *gadigadi.*

its
His one, her one, its one: *dana; dono.*
His several, her several, its several: *ana*$_3$*; ona; ono*$_3$.

His two, her two, its two: *luaana; luoono.*
His, hers, its: *sana; sono.*

jab
Jab, poke: *velo.*

jack
Fish sp.: jack (= large *alaala*): *duulua.*
Fish sp.: jack (2 sorts) (= small *tulua*): *alaala*$_1$.
Fish sp.: jack? (an oceanic fish): *gada-ahai; gada-moana.*
Fish sp.: jack? (like *alaala*): *gada-alaala.*
Fish sp.: jack: *gada*$_2$*; goosuu; lebelebe; libo*$_2$*; mada-galadi.*

jail
Prison, jail: *hale nnoa; hale pono.*

jammed up
Jammed up: *kadi.*

January
January ('first month'): *Tahi-Malama.*
January: *Madaligi*$_2$.

Japanese snipe
Bird sp.: Japanese snipe (*Capella hardwickii*): *googoo*$_2$.

jar
A pottery bottle or jar: *manu hale moni.*

jaw
Jaw: *gauvae.*

jealous
Envious, jealous (non-sexual jealousy): *magiaa.*
Jealous (sexual jealousy): *maagoda.*

jelly-like
Any jelly-like substance: *galugalu.*

jellyfish sp.
Jellyfish sp.: *galugalu; ssema.*

jerk
A jerk (e.g., of a line): *lamu dada.*
To jerk: *degi*$_1$.
To jerk one's head away from something: *geu gee.*
To jerk repeatedly: *datada*$_1$*; degidegi*$_1$.
To jerk to a stop (as at the end of a tether): *badodi.*
To jerk violently: *badodi gee.*

jerked
Be jerked: *madegi.*

jerking
Jerking of a fishing lure to attract fish: *hhagi de baa galele.*
Jerking of the tail: *daasugi.*

jest
Joke, jest: *me hakadanga.*

jesting
Funny, unserious, jesting, silly: *hakadanga.*

jet
A fine jet of water: *sii mada daahaa.*
A stream or jet of water: *sii.*

jet black
Jet black: *uli bela; ulimagallai.*

join
Connect up or join several things: *sugusugui.*
Connect up, join up, continue upon: *duudagi.*
Connect, join together: *suugui.*
Enter, join (a group), get in: *ulu*$_1$.
Go along with others, join the crowd: *hagasoa ange.*
Join to, connect to, connect up with: *suugui ange.*
Join, close up (something,e.g., a hole): *buni ange.*
To join (to make up a group of a certain number): *hagadogo* + NUMBER.

joint
A joint of bamboo: *gubu madila.*
Joint (of an arm or leg): *hadinga.*
Joint (of the hand or foot): *gubu.*
Joint, connection: *suguinga.*

joke
Joke, jest: *me hakadanga.*

joking
Foolishly rough playing or joking: *hagatala senga.*

journey
Trip, journey: *hanonga.*

joy
Excited with joy: *pula luu mada.*

joyous
Cheerful by nature, joyous: *hagamalangilangi.*

juggle
Juggle: *sigosigo.*

July
July ('seventh month'): *Hidu-malama.*
July: *Dumulu.*

jump
Get up, jump up: *soosobo.*
Jump: *lele.*
Jump feet first: *lele vae.*
Jump on: *leengia.*
Jump up (with both feet leaving the ground): *gasi*$_1$.
Rise up (as the sun), get up, jump up: *sobo.*

June
June ('sixth month'): *Ono-malama.*
June: *Alamooi.*

junior
Treat as junior: *hagaamuli.*

just
Barely, just barely: *see*$_2$.
Correct, right, just, fair, true: *heohi.*
Just a little *salani*: *salani ange.*
Just about right: *iai maalie.*
Just like...: *huu.*
Only, just (no more than): *donu huu.*

keep
Hold, restrain, keep (from): *daohi.*
Keep to oneself (what one has done): *hagammuni iho.*

keep in
Keep in (e.g., pigs): *buibui.*

keep out
Keep out (e.g., wind): *buibui.*

kick
Kick: *badu.*
Step on, kick with one's heel: *dagahi.*

kill
Kill (someone): *hagamalele.*
Kill someone by holding him under the water until he is drowned: *loomosi.*
To kill: *daa*$_1$.

kind
Considerate, kind, generous: *abo donu.*
Having a kind or generous nature: *degidegi*$_3$.
Kind, generous, forgiving: *degi*$_2$.

kind$_1$
kind (of), sort (of), variety (of): *daaganga*$_3$*; hagadaaganga.*

kingfisher
Bird sp.: sacred kingfisher (*Halcyon sancta*) (The native term applies possibly to several spp.): *manu-de-bua.*

kinky
Having kinky hair: *lauvinivini.*
Kinky (of hair): *vinivini.*

kiss
Kiss (Polynesian style), embrace: *hesongi.*
Smell (something) by sniffing, kiss (Polynesian style): *oso.*

kite
Kite: *manu aabi.*

knead
Knead: *labu.*
Knead thoroughly: *labua.*

knee
Knee: *duli*$_2$.

kneecap
Kneecap, the shell of the coconut: *ubu.*

kneel
Kneel: *duu duli.*

knife
A type of small knife: *uaasei.*

knot
A knot tied at the end of a rope or a string to prevent its unravelling: *bona.*
Bundle, knot: *noodanga.*
To make a knot of hair: *molo*$_1$.
To tie a knot in the hair: *nodi.*

knotted
Knotted (of hair): *moloa.*

know
Know (how to do something) well: *se gava.*
Know about, be acquainted with: *ssano.*
Know each other, understand each other: *heiloo.*
Know something about: *e hanuhanu i de* + PRONOUN.
Know that someone —: *iloo mai.*
Know, understand, be intimate with, sure of (and willing to say): *iloo.*
Known by heart, memorized, know (how to do something) well: *mmau gava.*
Realize, know: *iloo iho.*

known
Be known as, called by the name —: *hagabinga ange.*
Known by heart, memorized, know (how to do something) well: *mmau gava.*
Mastered, memorized, known by heart: *mmau*$_2$.

labia majora
Labia majora: *luu hua.*

labia minora
Labia minora: *luu gili.*

labor
Labor pains (of a woman in childbirth): *duaa dodo.*

ladder
Ladder, stairway: *gaagenga.*

ladies' man
Ladies' man, girl-crazy: *ulu i haahine.*

lagoon
Lagoon: *ahangi; lodo*$_1$.
Lagoon, sea, salt: *dai*$_1$.
The deepest part of the lagoon: *me bouli.*

lagoonward
Lagoonward: *ngaadai.*
Lagoonward of the islets of the atoll: *aalohi modu.*

laid
Laid out or spread out all over: *holadage.*

lance
Pierce (slightly), stab (lightly), lance (e.g., a boil): *sugi*$_1$.

land
Land, islet: *nugu.*
Plot of (bush) land, acreage: *alahenua.*

land crab
Crab sp.: shore crab, land crab, grapsid crab, ghost crab: *gaibea.*

land mass
A land mass, an island, a country, or any other geopolitical unit: *henua.*

land on
Land on (as a bird lands on the branch of a tree): *doga*$_1$.

landlubber
A person who rarely goes fishing, landlubber: *dangada ngauda.*
Landlubber: *ngauda*$_1$.

landmark
Use something as a landmark: *hagailonga ange agina.*

landslide
A landslide or similar movement of things: *ngadolo.*

language
Word, language, speech: *muna.*

large
Large: *laanui; nnui.*
Large in volume: *lodo lanea*$_1$.
Large in volume or capacity, spacious inside: *lodo laanui.*

larvae
Larvae (of mosquito, etc.) found in water: *duna.*

larynx
Larynx, epiglottis, trachea: *hakii*$_1$.

lasso
Lasso, noose: *sele*$_1$.

last
Be the last: *hagabidoa.*
Finish up, be last: *hagaodia.*
Last one: *me hagaodi.*
Last, final: *muliagina.*

late
Be late, tarry: *hagamuli*$_1$.
Slow, late: *mmule.*

later
A little later: *hagame ange laa; maalie ange.*
A little later, by and by: *muli mai ange.*
After, end (rearward part), later: *muli*$_1$.
Much later: *maalie loo; muli mai loo; mulimuli*$_1$.

lattice-like
Any lattice-like arrangement: *gaini.*

laugh
Happy, laugh (as a sign of happiness), cheerful: *malangilangi.*
Laugh (more than a single laugh): *gadagada.*
Laugh: *gada*$_1$*; giigii*$_1$.
Laugh abnormally: *boi malangilangi.*
Laugh all the time at nothing: *boi gadagada.*
Laugh at: *gadagada doo me.*

launch
To launch or beach a canoe by dragging it along the shore: *solo.*

law
Law, procedure, rule: *hainga.*

lay out
To spread out, or lay out flat, something which is folded, piled up, or bent, etc.: *hola.*

layout
Layout of (preliminary work on) plaiting: *hadu*$_1$.

lazy
Lazy: *vaiduu.*
To act as though one were lazy: *hagavaiduu.*

lead
Be in charge of, control, lead: *huahua ai.*
Lead away from: *dagi gee.*
Lead, show the way, leader (of a group): *dagi*$_1$.
Make good, lead a good life: *hagadanuaa.*

lead$_1$
lead (metal), bullet: *soodo.*

leader
A leader (between the hook and the fishing line): *lavasi.*
A leader (for a fishline, made of *olonga*): *dagaa.*
Lead, show the way, leader (of a group): *dagi*$_1$.
Leader (between fishing line and hook): *lava hadu.*

leaf
Leaf of a plant: *lau manu.*
Leaf, or any similar thin, flat thing: *lau*$_2$.
The immature leaf of any plant, except of the coconut: *dilo*$_2$.

leaking
Leaking in many places: *vavvava.*

leaky
Leaky: *vava.*

lean
Lean (in one direction): *bagau.*
Lean against: *hagannagi.*
Lean away from: *singa gee.*
Lean on someone for support: *hagaava ange.*
Lean over toward: *hagasinga.*
Teach to steer, allow to steer, lean against: *hagapale.*

learn
Learn by heart: *ago i ıua; daohi i tua.*
Learn, teach: *ago.*

learning
Learning, teaching: *agoago*$_1$.

leave
About to leave, prepare to leave: *sassabe.*
Leave (put down): *dugu.*
Leave quickly (usually under duress): *alukaba.*
Leave, go away: *ssabe.*
Place (or leave off) one at a time: *dugu dagidahi.*
Put aside, leave for later, conserve: *hagadoe.*

lee
Lee (of wind): *malu.*
To be in a place protected from the wind, lee: *luungagi.*

left
Left (side): *masui.*
Left side, left-handed: *baasi masui.*

left over
Left over, remain: *doe.*
Still remaining, still left over: *doedoe.*

left-handed
Left side, left-handed: *baasi masui.*

leftovers
Small and useless particles, leftovers: *amuamu.*

leg
Foot (including leg), leg: *vae*$_2$.
Lower leg (between the ankle and the knee): *sugi vae.*

legend
Legend, story: *daalanga*$_3$*; kai*$_4$.

lengthen
Lengthen, prolong: *hagalooloa.*

Lepturus
Plant sp.: grass sp. (*Lepturus repens* (Forst.) R.Br.): *helii.*

less
Becoming less: *llilo mai.*
Less — than: *magulu mai ange.*
Less: *mai.*

lesser
Smaller, lesser (in rank, importance, strength, development, etc.): *kii iho.*

lesson
Lesson, make learn, cause to teach: *hagaagoago*$_1$.

lest
Lest: *kana.*

let go
Let go, throw away, lose something: *dili.*

let out
Let out (something), disburse (money): *hagasao*$_2$.

let's
Let's (later): *aha naa.*
Let's (now): *aha nei.*
Let's —: *daa de —.*
Let's — right away!: *deengaa.*

letter
A letter (of the alphabet): *siianga*$_1$.

level
Level (an area): *ulu*$_1$.
Level (not bumpy): *baba*$_1$.
Level: *soe.*
Not level (esp. a person when sleeping): *ulalo.*
Not level: *uba.*
Not level, tipped to one side: *diba*$_1$.
Somewhat level or straight: *soesoe.*
Straight or level all over (as a playing field): *soesoe.*
To level off (ground, etc.): *hagasoesoe.*

lever
A log used as a lever or fulcrum: *hala a buadaia.*

lice
Abounding in lice: *gudua; guduaanga.*
Lice (immature): *manu-ligi.*
Lice eggs: *lie.*
Pick head lice: *ageli; agule.*

lick
Lick: *ssamu.*

lie
A lie (an untruth): *moele.*
Falsehood, lie: *me hhadu.*
Lie (falsehood): *muna hhadu.*
Lie (tell a falsehood): *hadu muna; ngudu lagolago.*

lie$_1$
pillow, lie with one's head on a pillow: *ulunga.*

lie down
Lie down: *baabuu; baani; daakodo; dagodo.*

life
Life: *mouli.*

life-principle
Life-principle (spirit, soul, etc.): *mouli.*

life-style
Life-style: *mouli.*

lift
Lift (something) up: *hagamanida.*
Lift or hold one end of something: *bidoa.*
Lift up (in a steady motion): *hagasaele age.*
Lift up: *amo.*
Lift up and carry: *saabai.*
Lift, raise up: *langa.*
To lift a fishing pole: *sisi*$_1$.

lifted
Lifted up: *malanga.*
Lifted up from: *malanga age.*

light
Dim light: *mada giivia.*
Light (a lamp): *haula.*
Light (not dark), bright: *maalama.*
Light a match in the dark: *tale age.*
Moon, light (not darkness): *maasina.*
The light after sunset: *malumalu-tangohi.*
The light before daybreak: *tea age langi.*
To light (a torch): *bula.*

light$_1$
light (in weight): *maamaane.*

light up
To light up suddenly: *pula.*

light-skinned
Light-skinned: *gili maalama.*

lighter
Becoming lighter in color: *deadea.*

lightning
Lightning, electricity: *uila.*

like
Be attracted to or like each other (of

members of the opposite sex): *hagadau vaasuu.*
Be like, be the same as: *bei.*
Just like: *baa huu i —.*
Like (someone or something), feel affection for: *umiumidi; vaasuu.*
Strive to be like: *hagabigi*$_2$.

lily
Plant sp.: spider lily (*Hymenocallis littoralis* (Jacq.) Salisb.): *giebu.*

limit
Limit, discontinue, shorten (by cutting off one end): *tuu mai.*

limited
Limited in intelligence: *maanadu bodobodo.*

limp
Have a limp (physical condition): *dodi.*

limping
Limping (as an action): *dotodi.*

line
A line of flying birds: *dui manu.*
Arrange things in a row or line: *hagaadugau.*

line$_1$
to line something (e.g., a box, with paper): *haaligi.*

lion-fish
Fish sp.: lion-fish: *sausau*$_2$.

lips
Lips: *malau ngudu.*

liquid
Liquid, water: *vai.*

listen
Listen to, pay attention to: *hagallongo.*

litter
Litter up: *hagagainga.*

little
A little, a small amount of: *momo.*
A very very little (in quantity): *momo dai sii.*
Little: *damaa me; vaaligi.*
Little bit, few: *hanu momo.*
Little, small: *lligi.*
Very little: *vaaligiligi.*

little finger
Little finger: *madannia sisi.*

live
Live (at): *noho.*
Live peacefully: *noho baba.*
Occupy or live in (a place): *noho ai.*

liver
Liver: *ade.*

living
Living, alive: *mouli.*

lizard fish
Fish sp.: lizard fish?: *dababa-gabugabu-tai.*
Fish sp.: lizard fish: *malianoono.*

lizard sp.
Lizard sp.: *belu; dabula; galisi; gieuli.*

load
The load or capacity (of a ship or canoe): *hagaudanga.*

loaded
Properly situated or loaded (of a canoe): *noho donu.*

lobster
Lobster spp.: *ula*$_2$.
Rock lobster sp.: longusta: *ula-dai.*
Slipper lobster: *dabadaba*$_2$.

long
Long: *lloa; looloa.*

long for
Long for, homesick: *buliaamou.*

longhand
Longhand (writing): *sisi lima.*

longing
Longing (for a person or place): *hinangalosaa.*

longusta
Rock lobster sp.: longusta: *ula-dai.*

look
Look (funny): *laelae (gee).*
Look after: *diiloo.*
Look around (moving one's body about): *galo saele.*
Look around (with one's eyes only): *galogalo*$_1$.
Look around for: *silasila.*
Look as though: *hagamada—*$_1$.
Look at (inspect): *dilo*$_1$.
Look at attentively: *diiloo.*
Look at in an effort to identify or recognize: *made*$_1$.

Look at, stare: *galo*$_1$.
Look for: *sila.*
Look for, search, hunt for: *ssala*$_1$.
Look here and there: *bulabula.*
Look like: *dulagi ange.*

lookout
Watchful, be on the lookout, keep an eye on: *dagitilo.*

loop
A loop: *moe*$_2$.
Loop of a lasso or noose: *madaa sele.*

loose
Get free, be loose: *madala mai.*
Loose (not tight): *dangadanga; tanga.*
Make loose: *hagabalabala.*

loosen
Loosen: *hagadangadanga.*

loquacious
Talkative, loquacious: *ngudu leelee**.

lose
Defeated, lose (battle, game, etc.): *mousi.*
Let go, throw away, lose something: *dili.*
Lose contact with: *hagaui*$_2$.
Lose his (my) appetite: *mmala dana (dagu) maanga.*
Lose one's voice (from straining one's vocal cords): *dee masae de leo.*

loser
Be a poor loser: *lodo manege.*
Be the loser (because of someone's actions): *too.*

lot
Many, plenty, a lot of, much: *lagolago.*
Plenty of —, a lot of —: *sege de —.*

loud
Loud (noise): *nngana.*
Loud (sound): *nngao.*

louse
Louse (head), or similar exoparasite of plants or animals (e.g., bird lice, scale insects, sap-feeding beetles, darkling beetles, etc.): *gudu.*
Louse (immature): *manu-ligi.*

love
Love: *bili makaga.*
Love each other (esp. of persons of the opposite sex): *hagadau aaloha.*
Self-love: *aloha iho.*

love potion
A love potion (applied to the clothes or body): *lolo hai haahine.*
A love potion (to attract women): *valaai hai haahine.*

love song
A love song: *daahili dau soa.*

low
Deep, low (in status): *mao lalo.*
Empty, low (tide): *masa.*
Low (in altitude): *baa iho.*

low-priced
Low wages, low-priced: *hagao baubau.*

lower
Lower (something): *ege iho.*
Lower *io*, q.v.: *io alo.*
Lower or decrease (the volume of a radio, price, etc.): *ue iho.*
Lower sail: *dugu de laa.*

lubricate
Lubricate: *hagalollolo.*

luck
Bad luck: *pagola.*
Luck, good fortune: *duadonu.*

luckily
Fortunately, luckily —: *adigai huu.*
Fortunately, luckily: *de eidu pale.*

lucky
Fortunate, lucky, blessed: *manuia.*
To have been lucky: *gu malaia donu.*

lung
Lung: *hegahega.*

lurch
To lurch, to move sideways: *ssee*$_3$.

lure
Fishing lure of pearl shell, used in *galele* fishing: *baa galele.*

Lycopodium
Plant sp.: *Lycopodium phlegmaria* L.: *dala-dalaa-moa.*

lying
Evil-tongued, lying (dishonest, foulmouthed: *vaivai ngudu.*

lymph nodes
Lymph nodes (enlarged): *gau*$_3$.

mad
Be mad (as indicated by one's movements): *bole.*

Get mad: *bula de ganomada.*
Mad as the devil: *lili mahangahanga.*
Mad at, angry: $lili_3$.
Mad or angry (but not showing it): *lluu.*

made-up
Invented —, made-up —: $hadu_1$.
Invented, made-up (e.g., a story): *hhadu.*
Made-up (of a story only): *vaalanga.*

maggot
Worm, maggot, intestinal parasites: *ilo.*

magician
Magician, sorcerer: *tangada hai sauaa.*

magnet
Magnet: *baalanga sauaa.*

maile-scented fern
Plant sp.: maile-scented fern (*Polypodium scolopendria* Burm. F.): *maile.*

make
Do, make, use: hai_1.
Make (something) according to some model or plan: *holia.*
Make a string figure: *duu de* $—_2$; *hagadubu.*
Make boxes: *hagaduu ngavesi.*
Make into strips: *tohi.*
Make palm toddy: *tuu de galeve.*
Make soft: *hagabalabala.*
Make someone tired: *hagadalea.*

make noise
To make noise (in a group): vaa_2.

male
Brother, male cousin: *daina daane.*
Father, uncle, senior male relative, male elder, person in a fatherly relationship: *damana.*
Male child: *mada gelegele**.
Male child, boy: *gauligi daane.*
Man, male: *daane.*

Malea
Mollusk sp.: *Malea pomum*: *ganimago.*

Mammea
Plant sp.: tree sp. (*Mammea odorata* (Raf.) Kost.): *voi.*

man
Boy, young man: *dama daane.*
Man, male: *daane.*
Married man or woman: *dau bodu.*

mangrove
Plant sp.: oriental mangrove (*Bruguiera gymnorhiza* (L.) Lam.): *donga.*

mangrove crab
Mangrove crab: kaa_3.

manly
Daring, brave, manly: *lo taane.*

manner
Manner of doing things: $vaanga_2$.
The manner (of a person): *geunga.*
The manner (of an individual) of doing something: *seelunga.*

mantis shrimp
Mantis shrimp: *manu-lalo-de-gelegele.*

many
A great many: *daubasa; dee adagaigaina.*
Many (people): *soa.*
Many, plenty, a lot of, much: *lagolago.*
Very many —: $basa_2$ —.

March
March (month of): $Manu_2$.
March: *Tolu-malama.*

marine invertebrates
Marine invertebrates: *manu laosedi.*

mark
Sign, mark, signal, omen: $hagailonga_1$.

marlin
Fish sp.: sailfish or marlin: *sagulaa.*

marriage
Common-law marriage, concubinage: *ngadi hai bodu.*

married
Married: duu_2.
Married couple, marry: *hai bodu.*
Married man or woman: *dau bodu.*
Married woman: *(de) hine dau bodu.*

marry
Married couple, marry: *hai bodu.*

Marshall islands
Of or from the Marshall islands: *Dua-nei.*

massage
Massage (as a medical treatment): *booboo me.*
To massage: *vvede.*

mast
Mast (of a canoe): *bou.*

mastered
Mastered, memorized, known by heart: *mmau₂*.

masticate
Chew thoroughly, masticate (soft foods which do not make noise): *maamaa*.
Chew, masticate (solids which make noise): *ngungu*.

masturbate
Masturbate (of males only): *maga de gau dogi*.
Masturbate: *hulehule; hulehulei*.
Masturbate oneself: *hai sogosogo*.

mat
A sleeping mat (child's): *eba*.
A sleeping mat: *hagahala; hagauea*.
A type of floor mat: *dabagau*.
A type of mat: *holasa; inai; loba*.

match
Fit together with (match) each other: *heloongoi*.

mate
Chief mate (of a European ship): *lua-aligi*.

mature
Mature (of a taro corm which can be used for food): *llago*.
Old (persons), mature, full-grown: *madua*.

maximum
Reach the maximum: *odi ange*.

May
May ('fifth month'): *Lima-malama*.
May: *Salaboli*.

maybe
Perhaps, maybe: *agu made; dagu made*.

mean
Mean (by nature), unkind: *abo sala*.
Willful, mean: *se hagabau*.

meaning
Meaning: *hagadoonunga*.

measure
Measure (exactly): *haaide*.
Measure by spans (*anga*): *angaanga₂*.
Measure off in fathoms: *lohaloha*.
Measure, calculate, estimate: *hagabau*.

meat
Flesh of, meat of: *gano*.
Fresh meat (including fish): *kano mouli*.
Meat (or fish, or seafood) which is suitable as food: *laavasi*.
Meat or fish (for a meal): *llava*.
Penis, meat, flesh: *kano*.

meaty
Meaty (not having much fat): *daangenge*.

meddle
Meddle in others' affairs: *badai*.

meddlesome
Extremely meddlesome: *badai gee*.

mediate
Mediate an argument so that the disputants will speak to each other: *hagapasa*.

medicine
Medicine (from a plant): *ulu laagau*.
Medicine: *valaai*.
Medicine to cure longing (homesickness or longing for a person): *valaai buliaamou*.
Native medicine: *valaai de henua*.
Take medicine: *gai valaai*.

meek
Self-effacing, meek in spirit: *lodo mao lalo*.

meet
Go to meet: *hagahedae*.
Meet by chance, encounter: *hetugi*.
Meet up with: *hedae; hegide*.

meeting
A community meeting (for listening to speeches or instructions): *muna o de henua*.
Meeting: *hagasaele*.
Public meeting: *hai muna*.

melee
Melee: *hellumi*.

member
Member (of the body, a house, etc.): *aalanga*.

memorize
Memorize: *dau i tua; hagammau₂*.
Study, attempt to memorize: *hagamaumau₂*.

memorized
Known by heart, memorized, know (how to do something) well: *mmau gava*.
Mastered, memorized, known by heart: *mmau₂*.

men's house
Men's house (modern usage): *hale daane.*
Men's house: *hada.*

mend
To mend (clothes): *bono.*

menstrual hut
Menstrual hut: *hale dabeo*.*

menstruation
Menstruation: *magi dabeo; magi haahine; magi i de malama.*

mermaid
Mermaid: *sauduu.*

mess
Make a mess (esp. involving liquid or organic material): *gai baalau.*

Messerschmidia
Plant sp.: heliotrope (*Tournefortia argentea* L., = *Messerschmidia argentea* L.): *manu-gili-maau.*

messy
Ugly-looking, messy, sloppy: *balaulau.*

metal
Metal (any kind): *baalanga*$_2$*.*

methinks
Methinks: *agu bau; dagu bau.*

method
Method of construction: *hagaduulanga.*

midday
Noon, midday: *odea.*

middle
Middle (of something long and thin), halfway: *madohi; madohi lua.*
Middle (of something round): *teungaalodo.*
Middle part (of something round): *ungaa lodo.*

midget
A very short person, midget: *gidigidi laa lalo.*

midnight
Midnight: *madohi boo.*

midwife
Midwife: *de hine hagahaanau.*

mild-mannered
Gentle, mild-mannered, soft-spoken: *daudonu.*

milk
Milk: *uu*$_3$*; vai uu.*

milk teeth
Milk teeth, deciduous teeth: *niho vaiuu.*

milkfish
Fish sp.: milkfish: *baleao.*

Milky Way
Milky Way: *vaenga o de langi.*

millions
Hundreds of millions: *semuna.*
Millions: *seloo.*
Tens of millions: *sengaa.*

millipede
Millipede: *manu-hai-hagahoa.*

milo tree
Plant sp.: tree sp.: milo tree (*The spesiapopulnea* Sol. ex Correa): *milo*$_2$*.*

miniature
Miniature, diminutive: *gidigidi laa lalo.*

miscarriage
Miscarriage, abortion (spontaneous): *ssege tama.*

miscellaneous
A miscellaneous assortment: *madamada a me.*

mischievous
Inquisitive, mischievous (as a child): *ssahu.*

miserly
Miserly: *hagaduu me.*

misidentify
Misidentify: *gide sala.*

misjudge
Underestimate, misjudge: *dee hagabaulia.*

mismated
Mismated (not matched properly): *dee heloongoi.*

miss
Miss (someone or something): *hinangalosaa.*
Miss, feel the loss of, or the uselessness of, something of great value: *maingaa.*

mistake
Mistake someone for another: *made sala.*

Mistake, error: *hai sala.*
Mistake, error, accident: *sala.*
To mistake something (or someone) for something (or someone) else: *maanessala.*

mistaken
Mistaken (in identifying): *made sala.*

misunderstand
Misunderstand: *donu gee; donu sala.*
Misunderstand one another: *dee heloongoi.*

Mitra
Mollusk sp.: *Mitra mitra*: *dalia-mea.*

mix
Mix: *hilo.*
Mix with: *hilo ange.*

mnemonic
A mnemonic chant enumerating the names of the islets, flora, fauna, chief priests, etc.: *mou.*

moan
Moan: *gogono.*

model
Model (or toy) canoe: *moni hagadeledele.*
Prototype, model (something from which a copy can be made): *$anga_3$* —.

modest
Humble, modest: *hagamao lalo.*

mojarra fish
Fish sp.: mojarra fish (= small *sugimanga*): *mmadu.*

molar teeth
Molar teeth, wisdom teeth: *niho ngalo.*

mold
Mold (fungus): *vale.*

moldy
Moldy: *valea.*

mole
A mole (not raised), or other permanent black spot on the skin: *ila.*
Wart, mole (raised): *dona.*

mollusk sp
Mollusk sp: a bivalve sp.: *dohe.*

mollusk sp.
Mollusk sp.: *buu hale moni; manu-hai-hau.*
Mollusk sp.: *Arcophagia scobinata*: *bibi-maadau.*
Mollusk sp.: *Asaphis dichotoma*: *$gasi_2$.*
Mollusk sp.: *Bursidae* spp.: *gammenge-baabaa.*
Mollusk sp.: *Cardium* sp.: *$kosi_2$.*
Mollusk sp.: *Cerithiidae* spp.: *hakai-a-bagila.*
Mollusk sp.: *Cerithiidae*: *anga-dogi.*
Mollusk sp.: *Chama iostoma*: *hadu-bunga.*
Mollusk sp.: *Charonia* spp.: *gio.*
Mollusk sp.: *Chlamys schmeltzi*: *dalia-dodo.*
Mollusk sp.: *Conus chaldaeus*: *anengenenge.*
Mollusk sp.: *Conus litteratus*: *iillangi.*
Mollusk sp.: *Cyclotinella remies*, also *Tellinidae* spp.: *bibi.*
Mollusk sp.: *Cymatiidae* spp., also *Bursa bubo*: *buu-kangi-de-muli.*
Mollusk sp.: *Fimbria soverbii*: *geesaa.*
Mollusk sp.: *Malea pomum*: *ganimago.*
Mollusk sp.: *Mitra mitra*: *dalia-mea.*
Mollusk sp.: *Neritidae* spp.: *$sisi_2$.*
Mollusk sp.: *Pinnidae* spp.: *valo.*
Mollusk sp.: *Spondylus* sp.: *hadu-uaua; onodaa; sangatai.*
Mollusk sp.: *Tellinidae* spp.: *$ginigini_2$.*
Mollusk sp.: *Thais armigera*: *gammenge-olomanga.*
Mollusk sp.: *Thais luteostoma*: *gammenge-hai-gili-dabeo.*
Mollusk sp.: *Trachycardium orbita*: *kosi-honga-agau.*
Mollusk sp.: *Tridacna maxima*: *baasua*
Mollusk sp.: *Turbo argyrostoma*: *alili.*
Mollusk sp.: *Turbo petholatus*: *lipaidonga.*
Mollusk sp.: *Vasum turbinellus*: *gammenge-maimai.*
Mollusk sp.: a bivalve: *bibi-gabugabu-tai.*
Mollusk sp.: auger shell (*Terebridae* sp.): *hakolona.*
Mollusk sp.: clam sp. (a type of *baasua*): *aasolo; halaasola.*
Mollusk sp.: cone shell: *manu-hagadigedige.*
Mollusk sp.: cowry shell (many spp.): *bule.*
Mollusk sp.: giant clam (*Tridacna squammosa*): *dange.*
Mollusk sp.: giant clam sp.: *$ngae_2$.*

Mollusk sp.: horse hoof clam (*Hippopus hippopus*): *gima.*
Mollusk sp.: murex shell: *gammenge-gabe-de-liidogi.*
Mollusk sp.: olive shell: *mesde-gelee.*
Mollusk sp.: pearl oyster: *baa*$_2$.
Mollusk sp.: pearly nautilus shell: *alelo-hatuli.*
Mollusk sp.: spider conch: *anga-baabaa.*
Mollusk sp.: vermetid gastropod sp.: *unga-goo.*

Monday
Monday ('first day'): *Tahi-laangi.*

mons veneris
Mons veneris: *bugu.*

monsoon
Monsoon winds (from the southwest): *mago de henua.*

month
Month, moon: *malama.*

moon
Full moon (a period comprising two nights): *tino boo.*
Month, moon: *malama.*
Moon, light (not darkness): *maasina.*

moray eel
Eel sp.: moray eel: *labodo-tea; labodo-uli.*

more
More and more: *maomao.*
More, farther: *ange.*
Some more: *hanu ange.*

Morinda
Plant sp.: tree sp.: Indian mulberry tree (*Morinda citrifolia* L.): *bugaliaa.*

morning
Early morning, before daybreak (when one can just barely recognize a person): *hegide mada.*
Morning, tomorrow: *daiao.*

morning sickness
Morning sickness (of pregnancy): *magi hai dama.*

morning star
Morning star: *de heduu o taiao.*

mortality-prone
Mortality-prone (e.g., of a family): *magaugau.*

mortar
Mortar stone: *hoa lalo.*

Mortlock Islands
Mortlock Islands: *i dai nei.*

mortuary
Mortuary house: *hale maadenga.*

mosquito
Mosquito: *namu.*

mosquito net
Mosquito net: *dau namu.*

moss
Moss (on rocks or coral): *mulumulu aamanu.*

moth
Insect sp.: moth spp.: *lengisi.*

mother
Mother, aunt: *dinana.*
Natural mother: *dinana donu.*

mother-in-law
Parent-in-law, child-in-law, mother-in-law, father-in-law, son-in-law, daughter-in-law: *saulaba.*

mountain bass
Fish sp.: mountain bass: *sahole.*

mouth
Mouth: *ngudu.*
Mouth of, rim of: *ngudu*$_a$.

mouth odor
Mouth odor: *haha.*

mouthful
Mouthful or spoonful of food: *maanga.*

move
Move (oneself), moved: *ngaue.*
Move (something): *hagangaue.*
Move (something) a little way over: *nege.*
Move (something) away completely: *hakiia.*
Move (something) over: *ege ange.*
Move a canoe to another spot when fishing (i.e., to pull in one's lines first): *sigo.*
Move about: *bubu.*
Move apart: *hanga.*
Move away: *kii*$_2$.
Move away completely: *hakii*$_2$.
Move away from: *hagatanga; kii gee.*
Move from one place to another: *dele; maeva.*

Move jerkily (as when stumbling): *bagekege.*
Move jerkily: *badotodi.*
Move jerkily, flail (one's legs), flounder about: *dagai.*
Move sideways: *hano gaogao.*
Move sideways while moving forward (as a canoe slipping in the water): *baagia.*
Move skillfully: *bubu donu.*
Move slightly, change position: *ngalue.*
Move something by using a lever (esp. a pole) on a fulcrum: *diha.*
Move something from one place to another: *ue.*
Move swiftly: *deledele.*
Move to another place: *ue gee.*
Move toward the end of the tether: *hagadaudau*$_2$.
Move unskillfully: *bubu sala.*
Move upward: *kii age.*
Pull, move, or raise, gently: *hagasago.*
Run, move fast (as fish, or a canoe): *savini.*
Stagger about (from a head injury), move as though unconscious: *see boiboi saele.*
To lurch, to move sideways: *ssee*$_3$.
Walk, move slowly (as a fish): *seesee*$_2$.

moved
Be moved about: *daaligi.*
Move (oneself), moved: *ngaue.*
To have been moved about by the wind: *daaligidia.*

movement
A jerky movement, caused by the wind (e.g., the flapping of a sail): *daaligi.*

moving
Slow moving (while working), slow acting, slow thinking: *mudumudu*$_1$.

much
Many, plenty, a lot of, much: *lagolago.*
Much later: *muli mai loo.*
Much, plenty: *lanea.*
Too much: *gona odi.*
Very, too much: *kona.*

mucus
Mucus (blown from the nose): *usubee.*

mulberry tree
Plant sp.: tree sp.: Indian mulberry tree (*Morinda citrifolia* L.): *bugaliaa.*

mullet
Fish sp.: mullet: *dalinga*$_2$*; ganae.*

multiply
Cause to increase in numbers, multiply: *hagalagolago.*

murder
To murder someone so that others don't see: *daa gaiaa.*

murex shell
Mollusk sp.: murex shell: *gammenge-gabe-de-liidogi.*

muscle
The muscle of a bivalve: *mugamuga*$_2$.

muscles
Muscles (of the body): *mogomogo.*

muscular
Muscular: *hai mogomogo; mogomogo ina.*

mushy
Soft, mushy, offering no resistance: *bala.*

musty
Musty smell: *pilo bopobo.*

my
My: *sagu; sogu.*
My one: *dagu*$_2$*; dogu.*
My several: *agu*$_2$*; ogu.*
My two: *luaagu; luoogu.*

nail
Nail (of metal): *baalanga tugi.*

naked
Naked: *gilisau; ngadi duu.*

name
Name (something): *hagabinga.*
Name one after another: *hagatau*$_1$.
Name, a title (used as a name): *ingoo.*

name-group
Spirit, soul, name-group: *hagasaalunga*$_2$.
The name of a name-group: *ala*$_3$*; dolo*$_3$*; doloa; gave*$_2$*; hege; hili*$_2$.

named
Be named, be called: *binga.*
Called by (named): *hagaingoo ai.*
Give a name to, named, called: *hagaingoo.*

nap
Sleep for a short time, nap: *moe iho.*

Take a nap: *hagatanu iho.*
Take a nap, stay overnight (away from home): *seni iho.*

narrow
Narrow: *gasogaso; kaso.*

natives
Natives: *gau de henua.*
Natives of Nukuoro: *dangada de henua.*

natural
A natural child: *dama donu.*

naupaka shrub
Plant sp.: beach naupaka shrub (*Scaevola taccada* (Gaertn.) Roxb.): *manu-gaba-aasanga.*

nauseated
Nauseated: *halehale dagodo lodo.*

nautilus
Mollusk sp.: pearly nautilus shell: *alelo-hatuli.*

navel
Navel: *gona*$_2$.

navigator
Master navigator (having also the ability to forecast the weather): *balia.*

near
Close to, near to: *baa ange.*

nearer
Nearer: *mai.*

nearly
Almost, nearly: *dai*$_2$.

neat
Neat: *gili malali.*

neck
Neck: *ua*$_3$.

necklace
A garland of flowers (as a headdress or necklace): *hau.*
A garland of flowers, headdress, necklace: *hau manu.*
Shell necklace or headdress: *hau bule.*

needle
Bone, needle: *ivi.*

needlefish
Fish sp.: needlefish: *ise-ngaio; ngaio; ngaio-golai; sobalo.*

Neritidae
Mollusk sp.: *Neritidae* spp.: *sisi*$_2$.

nerve
Vein, tendon, nerve, plastic filament: *uaua*$_3$.

nervous
Be very nervous, be very anxious: *bebea; bebelia.*
Nervous (only in a social context): *vasega.*
Nervous, anxious (for reasons not connected with other people): *bebe*$_1$.
Nervous, apprehensive (suddenly): *manava duuia.*

nest
A nest (of birds): *hoohanga.*

net
A big net for fishing, requiring several persons to manipulate: *galauna.*
A large net for fishing: *gubenga.*
A net on a long handle: *buu*$_1$.
Fishing net (attached to a frame or handle): *gatae.*
Hand net: *dae*$_1$.
Mosquito net: *dau namu.*
The net of a hand net (not including the net's handle): *gano dae.*
To net flying fish: *bulobulou.*

never mind!
Never mind!: *maua laa.*

new
Brand new: *mada hoou.*
New: *hoou.*

news
News: *longo.*
Spread news or rumors: *dele de longo.*

next
After tomorrow, the one after the next one: *adu laa.*
Next —: *humai nei.*
Next above (below): *mua iho (age).*
Next to me (you, him): *mua mai (adu, ange).*
The next (one) following the one in question: *mai ange laa.*

nice
Nice, pleasing: *dagodo mahamaha.*

nickname
Abbreviation, acronym, nickname: *hagasugi*$_2$.

night
A pitch black night: *buni lunga ma lalo.*

Night: *boo*$_2$.
The following night: *boo iho*.
The whole night long: *huaaboo*.

nights
Nights (2) when the full moon appears just after sunset: *dino boo*.

nine
Nine: *siva*.

ninety
Ninety: *massiva*.

nipple
Nipple of breast: *hadu de gaanunu*.

no
No more, no other: *deai ange*.
None, no —, nothing: *deai*.

no!
Positively no!: *deeai donu*.

nod
Bow or nod or genuflect (as a sign of respect): *ino*.
Nod (one's head): *dungagi*.
Nod one's head toward (to beckon or indicate agreement, etc.): *dungagi ange*.

noddy
Bird sp.: common noddy (*Anous stolidus*): *ngongo*.
Bird sp.: white-capped noddy (*Anous minutus*): *legia*.

noise
Make a great deal of noise (vocal): *daavalo*.
Make noise (as an individual): *tangi*.
Make noise repeatedly: *dadangi*.
Noise (a loud, individually perceived, noise): *nngaolia*.

noisy
Noisy (a loud, individually perceived, noise): *nngaoa*.
Noisy (irregular repeated sounds): *ngaoloa*.

none
Almost none: *dai deeai*.
Almost none at all: *dai deeai donu*.
None (at least up to now): *tigiai donu*.
None at all: *deai donu*.
None, no —, nothing: *deai*.

noon
Noon: *huaalaangi*.
Noon, midday: *odea*.
Past noon: *baguu de laa*.

noose
A noose for fishing: *molo*$_2$.
Lasso, noose: *sele*$_1$.

nose
Nose: *usu*$_3$.

nostril
Nostril: *bongaa usu*.

not yet
Not yet —: *tigi*.
Not yet: *tigi ai*.

nothing
None, no —, nothing: *deai*.
Nothing at all: *deai donu angaanga*.
Nothing, unimportant, useless, worthless: *ngadi me*.

nothingness
Nothingness: *deainga*.

noticed
Have noticed: *tau ange luu mada*.

November
November ('eleventh month'): *Madaangahulu-ma-dahi-malama*.
November: *Laaga*.

now
Here, now: *nei*.
Now: *iainei*.
Now you've done it!: *tangada made*.
Right now!: *iainei donu*.

numb
Numb, paralyzed: *made*$_2$.

number
Number, figure: *daelodo*.

Numenius
Bird sp.: eastern whimbrel (*Numenius phaeopus*): *geevee*.

nurse
Suck on the breast, nurse (at the breast): *unuunu*.
Suckle, nurse (feed milk): *hagauu*$_3$.
To nurse (an infant at the breast): *hakaunuunu*.

nymphomaniac
Nymphomaniac: *(de) hine sala daane*.

OK
Good (not bad, but not the best), OK: *hagavaasuu*.

OK!
OK! (good): *danuaa loo.*

obey
Obey: *hagallongo i muna.*

observance
Remembrance, observance of (e.g., a holiday): *hai de hagamaanadu.*

observe
Stare at, observe closely: *daumada.*

obtain
Get, obtain, caught: *mau*$_3$.
Obtain by force: *kave gi de mahi.*
Obtain the smallest first: *doli age.*
Take or obtain something by force: *lugu.*
To obtain the biggest first: *doli iho.*

obtained
Able to, obtained, gotten, caught: *maua.*

occupation
Work, activity, occupation: *haiva; hegau.*

occupied
Occupied: *nohoa; noholia.*

occupy
Occupy or live in (a place): *noho ai.*

occurring
Occurring in great numbers: *dau*$_4$.

ocean liner
Ocean liner: *haiava.*

ochrosia tree
Plant sp.: tree sp.: ochrosia tree (*Ochrosia oppositifolia* (Lam.) K. Sch.): *gahao.*

October
October ('tenth month'): *Madaangahulu-malama.*
October: *Seedaa.*

octopus
Octopus: *goede.*

odd number
Odd number: *daelodo dee odi ange.*

odor
Having an unpleasant body odor: *saunga.*
Odor, smell (of something), greasy: *nnamu.*

offering
Collection (in church), offering (in church), sacrifice, tithe: *sigidaumaha.*

offspring
Produce offspring: *hagadili.*
The offspring of (sharing the characteristics of): *haa manu.*

often
Often, frequently: *duu podo.*

oil
Oil: *lolo.*

oily
Oily: *lollolo; sunusunu*$_1$.

old
Old (in the past): *duai*$_1$.
Old (of living things): *sinasinaa.*
Old (persons), mature, full-grown: *madua.*
Old person, adult: *dangada madua.*
Very old (persons): *madumadua.*

older
Older: *ngadau age.*

oldest
Be oldest among: *hagamaadua.*

olive shell
Mollusk sp.: olive shell: *mesde-gelee.*

omen
Sign, mark, signal, omen: *hagailonga*$_1$.

on
On top of, on, over, above: *honga.*

one
One, a: *dahi*$_1$.

one-man
A one-man canoe: *massogosogo.*

only
Alone, only, by oneself: *sogosogo.*
Only, alone (just one): *daudahi.*
Only, just (no more than): *donu huu.*
The only child of a couple: *dama dagidahi.*

ooze
Ooze: *duludulu.*
Ooze out: *hagatulu mai.*

open
An open field (having no trees): *duu malaelae.*
Be awake, be open: *ala*$_2$.

Open (something), uncover: *hhuge.*
Open one's eyes: *hhuda.*
Open one's eyes widely: *pula.*
Open one's mouth: *hhanga de ngudu.*
Open or uncover many things (by several persons): *huuhuge.*
Open up (one's mouth): *hanga.*
Permitted, open to the public, secular: *hainoo.*
Split open, open up, or separate, all at once: *hhanga.*

opened
Opened, uncovered: *mahuge.*

opening
An opening for a door or window: *haitoga.*
An opening in the clouds: *hhuge iho.*

operculum
Operculum of a gastropod: *dango*$_2$.

oppose
Resist me (you, them), oppose me (you, them): *noho mai (adu, ange).*
Take sides against, oppose: *hai baasi.*

opposing
The opposing side: *de baasi gee.*

oppressive
Heavy, oppressive, hard to take: *daemaha; daemahadia; daemahalia.*

or
Or, either: *be.*

orange-colored
Orange-colored (like a certain variety of coconut): *gahaalava.*

ordinary
An ordinary person, commoner: *ngadi dangada.*

organ-pipe coral
Coral sp.: red organ-pipe coral: *hadu-i-de-ssala.*

oriental mangrove
Plant sp.: oriental mangrove (*Bruguiera gymnorhiza* (L.) Lam.): *donga.*

origin
Origin, source: *damadanga.*

ornament
Ornament: *hagalaagii.*

ornamentation
Decoration, ornamentation: *laagii.*

others
The others: *me ange laa.*

our
Our: *sedaadeu; sedaau; semaadeu; semaau.*
Our one: *demaadeu; demaau; taadeu; taau.*
Our several: *adaadeu; adaau; amaadeu; amaau; odaadeu; odaau; omaadeu; omaau.*
Our two: *luaadaadeu; luaadaau; luaamaadeu; luaamaau; luoodaadeu; luoodaau; luoomaadeu; luoomaau.*

out house
Out house: *hale hongagelegele.*

outbreak
Outbreak of war: *duu taua.*

outcome
Outcome (of individual effort): *hua o tangada.*

outrigger boom
Outrigger boom: *giado.*

outrigger float
Outrigger float: *ama*$_1$.

outside
Outside of (e.g., a building): *duaahaho.*
Outside of: *haho.*
Outside, away, around: *daha.*

outstanding
Extraordinary, outstanding, unusual: *magona.*

oval
Rectangular (not square), oval: *sao de looloa.*

ovaries
Ovaries and fallopian tubes: *bualeu.*

oven
Cook house, earth oven: *umu.*

over
On top of, on, over, above: *honga.*
Up, above, over: *lunga.*

overbearing
Arrogant, haughty, overbearing, proud: *hagamao lunga.*

overcome
Win, overcome: *kii*$_1$.

overhand
Overhand: *singa.*

overhang
To overhang (of something flat): *saga.*

overhung
Overhung: *singalia.*

overloaded
Overloaded (almost to the point of sinking): *noho lalo.*

overripe
Overripe (of pandanus only): *magano.*

overworked
Overworked: *daia e de hegau.*

owe
Debt, owe: *$muli_2$.*

oyster
Mollusk sp.: pearl oyster: *baa_2.*

package
Package, bundle (wrapped up): *sabininga.*

packed
Packed closely together: *hegabidi.*
Tightly packed: *kadi.*

paco fern
Plant sp.: paco fern (*Athyrium* sp.): *$manu\text{-}mangamanga_2$.*

paddle
A canoe paddle (for paddling): *hoe gabegabe.*
A canoe paddle: *hoe_1.*
A dancing paddle: *$laba_2$.*
A type of canoe paddle designed for steering: *hoe pale.*
To paddle (a canoe): *$aloalo_1$; gabegabe.*
To paddle (a canoe) vigorously: *maga tau hoe.*
To paddle vigorously: *maga de hoe.*

pagan
Pagan gods, idols: *ngadi diinonga.*
Religions which are not in the Judaeo-Christian tradition, pagan cults: *ngadi daumaha.*

pain
Pain, hurt (children's language): *maemae.*
Pain, hurt: *mmae.*
Suffer, be in pain: *sae_2.*

paint
Paint (something): *lebu.*
To paint one's body with tumeric: *hulu i de lenga.*

pair
A pair of copulating fish, (or turtles, or whales, or stingrays): *ulungaa mamu.*

pale
Pale: *kena.*

pallor
Pallor: *tea gee.*
The pallor of a female following childbirth: *dua dama.*

palm
Palm (of the hand): *alohi lima.*

palm toddy
Fermented *galeve*, palm toddy: *galeve vii.*

pandan tree
Plant sp.: tree sp.: pandan tree (*Pandanus dubius* Spreng.): *bagua.*

Pandanus
Plant sp.: tree sp.: pandan tree (*Pandanus dubius* Spreng.): *bagua.*

pandanus
Plant sp.: tree sp.: pandanus (several varieties): *hala.*

pandanus plug
A pandanus plug after it has been chewed: *benu.*

panting
Panting (as when short of breath): *manavanava gimoo.*

parable
Riddle, parable: *me hagasengasenga.*

paralyzed
A paralyzed arm: *magau de lima.*
Numb, paralyzed: *$made_2$.*
Paralyzed by fear: *buni ange lodo.*

parasites
Parasites (intestinal) of fish: *duoi.*
Worm, maggot, intestinal parasites: *ilo.*

pardon
Forgive (someone), pardon (someone): *degi ange.*

parent
Parent, elder (senior relative): *madua.*

parent-in-law
Parent-in-law: *gabetili**.*
Parent-in-law, child-in-law,

mother-in-law, father-in-law, son-in-law, daughter-in-law: *saulaba.*

parents
Parents, elders: *maadua.*

parrot fish
Fish sp.: parrot fish (The native term is applied to many spp.): *huuhuu*$_2$.
Fish sp.: parrot fish: *balagia-a-de-gaga; mamu-madohi-lua; ulahi.*

part
(Small) piece of, part of: *dalaa.*
A branch, part of (something having coordinate parts): *manga.*
Part (of something): *diba*$_2$.
Part one's hair: *vvae de biho.*
Treat differently, sort out, part (e.g., hair): *vae*$_1$.

parted
Parted slightly: *maagila.*

particles
Particles of rotting wood or thatch, etc.: *bodubodu.*

particular
Particular (choosy) about: *hili*$_1$.
Punctilious, be particular: *hai huaame.*

parturition
Parturition: *lele tuli.*

party
Dancing party: *anumanga.*
Drinking party: *unumanga.*

pass
Pass over: *ui age.*
Pass overhead (of clouds): *hagadaudau*$_2$.
Pass under: *ui iho.*
To pass a point (in space) or a stage of development: *sili*$_3$.
To pass each other on intersecting courses: *hesilihagi.*

pass wind
Pass wind (flatus): *hai madangi.*

passage
Passage, channel: *ava*$_1$.

pat
Continuously touch or slap lightly, pat: *baabaa*$_1$.

patch
A patch (on clothes, or a canoe, etc.): *hono.*

patched
Patched: *honoa.*

path
A path (lengthwise) in the taro bog: *hagaloa.*
Path (a minor, not major, thoroughfare): *dao haiava.*
Path, route: *dagalonga*; dagamanga*.*
Road, walkway, path (for walking): *saelenga.*

paths
Paths in the taro bog, made from dry palm fronds: *uinga*$_3$.

pathway
A pathway on the open sea: *huulonga.*
Road, pathway (for going), track: *haiava.*

patient
Patient, (not impetuous): *golomagi.*
Persistent, patient, persevering: *lodo mmahi.*

pay
Pay back (a debt): *sui ange.*
Pay respect to, honor (someone): *hagaamu*$_2$.

pay attention
Listen to, pay attention to: *hagallongo.*
Pay attention to (notice), be aware of: *anga*$_1$.

payment
Payment for medical treatment: *dabanimeeli.*

peace
Disturb the peace: *oha de nnoho paba.*
Make peace between people, conciliate: *hagadanuaa magavaa.*

pearl
Pearl: *ango*.*

pearl oyster
Mollusk sp.: pearl oyster: *baa*$_2$.

pearly nautilus
Mollusk sp.: pearly nautilus shell: *alelo-hatuli.*

peck
Peck at: *dongi.*

peel
Peel (something): *hhole.*
Scrape (something), plane (something), scrape off (with an

object), peel (with a knife toward one): *salu.*

peeled
Peeled (a great amount having been taken off): *mahole.*
Peeled off: *maisi.*
Scraped (a lot taken away), peeled (a little amount taken off), planed: *salua.*

pelvic bone
Pelvic bone: *ivi-a-duimogo.*

Pemphis
Plant sp.: crepe myrtle shrub (*Pemphis acidula* Forst.): *nngie.*

peninsula
Promontory, peninsula: *udua.*

penis
A large penis: *doonga pada.*
Male genital organ, penis: *menemene.*
Penis: *diidii$_2$; uvada**.*
Penis, meat, flesh: *kano.*

perceive
Be aware of, experience, perceive, feel (in one's mind or body): *longo iho.*

perform
Perform a wedding: *hagahaibodu.*

perfume
Perfume: *vai malo.*

perhaps
Perhaps: *dee galo; dee kasi; kana adu.*
Perhaps, maybe: *agu made; dagu made.*

permissible
Allowed to, permissible: *alaange.*

permission
Ask permission: *haganguu.*
Beg, apologize, or ask permission in an insistent manner: *dangidangi keli.*

permitted
Permitted, open to the public, secular: *hainoo.*

perpendicular
Inclined, slanting, not straight, not perpendicular to: *salau.*

persevere
Persevere, try hard to: *hagammahi.*

persevering
Persistent, patient, persevering: *lodo mmahi.*

persistent
Persistent, patient, persevering: *lodo mmahi.*

person
Gentleman, person who is good: *daane abo donu.*
Person, human being, relative: *dangada.*
Unimportant person: *bulubulu dangada.*

persons
Persons of a certain class or type: *huaadangada.*

perspiration
Sweat, perspiration: *daadaa$_2$.*

pet
To pet (pets, children, or a member of the opposite sex): *labu manu.*

Phaethon
Bird sp.: white-tailed tropic bird (*Phaethon lepturus*): *davage.*

Pharonella
Pharonella spp.): *ginigini$_2$.*

phrase
Word, phrase: *dalaa muna.*

pick
Pick (breadfruit), pull down: *lou.*
Pick (fruit) by grabbing and twisting off: *hagi.*
Pick at one time, pinch at one time: *kini$_1$.*
Pick breadfruit: *lou gulu.*
Pick coconuts: *hagi me.*
Pick flowers: *gini manu; goli manu.*
Pick from among several, choose, elect: *hili$_1$.*
Pick head lice: *ageli; agule.*
Pick pandanus (*ui hala*): *ui$_1$.*
Pick up one at a time (by hand): *ogo$_1$.*
Pick with one's fingers: *gini.*

picked
(Fruit) picked off (or caused to fall by wind): *mahagi.*

picture
Picture, image, reflection, shadow: *ada$_1$.*

piece
(A big) piece of: *duudanga.*
(Small) piece of, part of: *dalaa.*
A piece of coconut husk: *duu hakaa.*

pieces
Useless pieces: *bidobido.*

pierce
Pierce (slightly), stab (lightly), lance (e.g., a boil): *sugi*$_1$.
Pierce the skin superficially: *hagasae gili.*
Stab with a sharp object, pierce with a sharp object, sew, string (flowers or fish, etc.): *dui.*
Stab, pierce: *velo.*

pierced
Having a hole, pierced: *masugi.*

piercing
Piercing of the ear (for insertion of an ornament): *sugi talinga.*

pigeon
Pigeon: *manu-kono*$_2$.

pile
A pile of things which have been accumulated: *hagabuudunga.*
Pile of, group of: *buudunga.*

pillow
A pillow made from a pandanus log (having various magical uses): *ulunga hala.*
Pillow, lie with one's head on a pillow: *ulunga.*

pillowcase
Pillowcase: *gili ulunga.*

pimple
Pimple: *madahuuhua.*

pinch
Pick at one time, pinch at one time: *kini*$_1$.
Pinch (with the fingers): *bangi*$_1$.
To pinch off, or pinch and pull at the same time: *gini.*

Pinnidae
Mollusk sp.: *Pinnidae* spp.: *valo.*

pipefish
Fish sp.: pipefish: *seisei.*

Pipturus
Plant sp.: tree sp.: a shrubby tree sp. (*Pipturus argenteus* (Forst.f.) Wedd.): *olongaa.*

Pisonia
Plant sp.: tree sp. (*Pisonia grandis* R.B.): *buga.*

piteous
Piteous, pitiful: *hagaaloha.*

pitiful
Piteous, pitiful: *hagaaloha.*

place
A place: *momme.*
At his place, with him: *i ono daha.*
Place (or leave off) one at a time: *dugu dagidahi.*
Put, place: *dugu.*
The place of, the track of (something): *duulanga*$_2$.

placenta
Placenta: *henuu*$_2$.

plait
Plait (mats): *llanga.*
To plait with thick strands: *dua pada.*

plane
Scrape (something), plane (something), scrape off (with an object), peel (with a knife toward one): *salu.*

planed
Scraped (a lot taken away), peeled (a little amount taken off), planed: *salua.*

planet
Star, planet: *heduu.*

planing
A canoe going so fast it rides high in water (and is planing): *hagaditidi mai de moni.*

plant
Animal, plant (flora): *manu*$_1$.
Plant (something): *doo*$_1$.
Plant things: *doo me.*
To plant taro slips: *bogi.*

plant sp.
Plant sp. (a type of *ngaungau*): *mangila.*
Plant sp. (not native — drifts ashore — used for making perfume): *adidi.*
Plant sp. (the archaic name of *manu-gaba-aasanga*): *nau*.*
Plant sp.: *dalia; dogodoganga*; gulunieli; manu-gadi-niho.*
Plant sp.: *Fleurya ruderalis* (Forst.f.) Gaud. ex. Wedd.: *mougu.*
Plant sp.: *Lycopodium phlegmaria* L.: *dala-dalaa-moa.*
Plant sp.: Polynesian arrowroot (*Tacca leontopetaloides* (L.) O.K.): *bie.*
Plant sp.: a variety of taro: *manu-alioo.*
Plant sp.: beach naupaka shrub (*Scaevola taccada* (Gaertn.) Roxb.):

manu-gaba-aasanga.
Plant sp.: bird's-nest fern (*Asplenium nidus* L.): *lau-gadaha.*
Plant sp.: cassytha vine (*Cassytha filiformis* L.): *hiisoa.*
Plant sp.: crepe myrtle shrub (*Pemphis acidula* Forst.): *nngie.*
Plant sp.: cycad plant (*Cycas circinalis* L.): *manu-a-tababa.*
Plant sp.: elephant ear (*Alocasia*): *ngaungau*$_2$.
Plant sp.: epiphytic fern (*Vittaria incurvata* Cav.): *gumigumi-o-sogo.*
Plant sp.: fern sp.: *gideu.*
Plant sp.: glory bower (*Clerodendrum inerme* (L.) Gaertn.): *manu-mmala.*
Plant sp.: grass sp. (*Lepturus repens* (Forst.) R.Br.): *helii.*
Plant sp.: grass sp.: *helii-baalanga.*
Plant sp.: heliotrope (*Tournefortia argentea* L., = *Messerschmidia argentea* L.): *manu-gili-maau.*
Plant sp.: hemp-leaved vitex shrub (*Vitex negundo* var. *bicolor* (Willd.) Lam.): *gasigi.*
Plant sp.: maile-scented fern (*Polypodium scolopendria* Burm. F.): *maile.*
Plant sp.: oriental mangrove (*Bruguiera gymnorhiza* (L.) Lam.): *donga.*
Plant sp.: paco fern (*Athyrium* sp.): *manu-mangamanga*$_2$.
Plant sp.: plant-shrub sp. (*Sida fallax* Walp.): *geao.*
Plant sp.: shrub sp. (*Ximenia americana* L.): *dala*$_6$.
Plant sp.: silver bush (*Sophora tormentosa* L.): *dangaloa*$_1$.
Plant sp.: spider lily (*Hymenocallis littoralis* (Jacq.) Salisb.): *giebu.*
Plant sp.: sugarcane: *dolo*$_2$.
Plant sp.: swamp taro (*Cyrtosperma chamissonis*): *bulaga**.
Plant sp.: swamp taro (*Cyrtosperma chamissonis*), also the corm of this plant: *daogoli.*
Plant sp.: sword fern (The native term applies possibly to several spp.): *lluhe.*
Plant sp.: taro (*Colocasia esculenta*), also the corm of this plant: *dalo.*
Plant sp.: tree sp. (*Allophylus timorensis* (DC.) Bl.): *dalahalu.*
Plant sp.: tree sp. (*Guettarda speciosa* L.): *bua.*
Plant sp.: tree sp. (*Mammea odorata* (Raf.) Kost.): *voi.*
Plant sp.: tree sp. (*Pisonia grandis* R.B.): *buga.*
Plant sp.: tree sp. (*Soulamea amara* Lam.): *hagabini*$_1$.
Plant sp.: tree sp. (the archaic name of *bugaliaa*): *nonu*$_2$*.
Plant sp.: tree sp.: Alexandrian laurel tree (*Calophyllum inophyllum* L.): *hedau.*
Plant sp.: tree sp.: Barringtonia tree (*Barringtonia asiatica* (L.) Kurz): *gavaausu.*
Plant sp.: tree sp.: Hernandia tree (*Hernandia sonora* L.): *bingibingi.*
Plant sp.: tree sp.: Indian coral tree (*Erythrina variegata* L.): *ulu-davage.*
Plant sp.: tree sp.: Indian mulberry tree (*Morinda citrifolia* L.): *bugaliaa.*
Plant sp.: tree sp.: Terminalia tree (*Terminalia samoensis* Rech.): *kini*$_2$.
Plant sp.: tree sp.: a shrubby tree sp. (*Pipturus argenteus* (Forst.f.) Wedd.): *olongaa.*
Plant sp.: tree sp.: a small tree sp. (*Premna obtusifolia* R.Br.): *valovalo.*
Plant sp.: tree sp.: banana tree: *ga-hudi.*
Plant sp.: tree sp.: banyan tree (*Ficus prolixa* Forst.): *aoa*$_1$.
Plant sp.: tree sp.: breadfruit: *gulu.*
Plant sp.: tree sp.: coconut tree: *nui.*
Plant sp.: tree sp.: cordia tree (*Cordia subcordata* Lam.): *ganava.*
Plant sp.: tree sp.: hibiscus tree (*Hibiscus tiliaceus* L.): *goehau.*
Plant sp.: tree sp.: milo tree (*Thespesiapopulnea* Sol. ex Correa): *milo*$_2$.
Plant sp.: tree sp.: ochrosia tree (*Ochrosia oppositifolia* (Lam.) K. Sch.): *gahao.*
Plant sp.: tree sp.: pandan tree (*Pandanus dubius* Spreng.): *bagua.*
Plant sp.: tree sp.: pandanus (several varieties): *hala.*
Plant sp.: tropical almond (*Terminalia catappa* L.): *hua-laagau.*
Plant sp.: tumeric plant (*Curcuma* sp.): *gaalau-ango.*
Plant sp.: vine sp. (several spp.): *hue.*
Plant sp.: wedelia creeper (*Wedelia biflora* (L.) DC.): *aigimea.*

planted
Planted: *dooa.*

platform
Shelf, platform, raft, floor (of planks): *hada.*

play
Play (a musical instument): *hagadangi.*
Play (games): *hagadaahao.*
Play music: *hagadangidangi.*
To play with a model canoe in the water (by children): *hagadeledele.*

play a joke on
Fool around, play a joke on: *hagatala.*

play a trick on
Play a trick on: *hagadoopeva.*

play favorites
Play favorites amongst one's children: *vaedama.*

playground
Playground: *momme hagadaahao.*

playing
Foolishly rough playing or joking: *hagatala senga.*

please
Please wait!: *kaba muhuu.*

please$_1$
please (someone), cheer up (someone): *hagamalangilangi.*

please!
Please!: *muhuu.*

pleased
Happy with, pleased at: *malangilangi ai.*

pleasing
Nice, pleasing: *dagodo mahamaha.*

pleat
Gather or pleat in material: *dauaahe.*

plentiful
Plentiful (of food): *mahola.*

plenty
Having plenty of: *duu de —$_1$.*
Many, plenty, a lot of, much: *lagolago.*
Much, plenty: *lanea.*
Plenty of —, a lot of —: *sege de —.*

pliable
Pliable (of hair): *laubalabala.*

plot
Plot of (bush) land, acreage: *alahenua.*
Plot of taro bog, boggy soil: *bela.*
Taro plot: *duudua; duuduua.*

plover
Bird sp.: golden plover (*Plurialis dominica*): *duli$_1$.*

pluck
To pluck (feathers): *vele.*

plump
Plump (tending toward fat): *bedi.*
Plump: *bungubungu; pungu.*
Very plump: *huugaabungubungu.*

Plurialis
Bird sp.: golden plover (*Plurialis dominica*): *duli$_1$.*

point
Able to point (into the wind) well (of a sailing canoe): *mada madangi.*
Point at: *dongi.*
Point, blade: *mada$_3$.*
The point of a promontory or peninsula (esp. if large): *mada udua.*

pointed
Sharp (as a knife), pointed: *kangi.*

poisoned
Poisoned (by food): *maaua.*

poisonous
Poisonous: *hagammau$_3$.*

poke
Jab, poke: *velo.*

pole
A pole with a hook at the end, used to pick breadfruit: *lou.*
Fishing pole: *huadia; siisii$_2$.*
Ridge pole (lower): *dao dahuuhuu.*
Ridge pole (upper): *dao badu.*

Polynesian arrowroot
Plant sp.: Polynesian arrowroot (*Tacca leontopetaloides* (L.) O.K.): *bie.*

Polynesian tattler
Bird sp.: Polynesian tattler (*Heteroscelus brevipes*): *goigoi$_2$.*
Bird sp.: Polynesian tattler? (*Heteroscelus brevipes*): *dilidili-dogi.*

Polypodium
Plant sp.: maile-scented fern (*Polypodium scolopendria* Burm. F.): *maile.*

pomade
Pomade (for hair): *vai sulu.*

poor
Poor (not rich): *hagaau aloha.*
Poor fellow!: *tama hagaai; tangada hagaai.*
Poor in appearance: *dumanu sala.*

popular
Popular: *daulia*$_1$.
Very popular: *dahi i daho dangada.*

porous
Porous: *kano avaavaa.*

porpoise
Porpoise: *ulumonu.*

port
Port (for ships): *daulanga.*

portion
A share of, allotment, portion: *dino*$_1$.
Portion of, group of (fish or animals): *ungaa.*
Portion, share (of something): *diba*$_2$.
Portion, share, division (e.g., of a tract): *vaenga.*

position
Move slightly, change position: *ngalue.*
Position: *nohoanga.*

postponing
Keep postponing or delaying: *hagasolo age.*

potion
A love potion (applied to the clothes or body): *lolo hai haahine.*
A love potion (to attract women): *valaai hai haahine.*

pottery
A bowl (pottery): *gumedi hadu.*
A pottery bottle or jar: *manu hale moni.*

pound
Pound —, pound on: *dugi*$_1$.

pour
Pour little by little: *lingilingia.*
Pour out, spill out (sand): *llingi.*

poured
Spilled, poured out: *malingi.*

pout
Pout: *hagademo.*

powdered
Powdered (soap, etc.): *malili*$_1$.

power
Power (electrical, magical, etc.): *sauaa.*
Strong, strength, force, power, energy: *mmahi.*
Supernatural power: *mana*.*

powerful
Having special ability (strength, power, etc.) which others do not have, a strong or powerful (person): *iai sago.*
Powerful (esp. supernaturally): *sauaa.*

praise
Praise (God only): *hagadegi*$_2$.
Praise (someone), honor: *tuhi.*
Praise oneself: *tuhi iho.*
Praise with all one's heart (esp. God): *tuhi hagadegi.*

praised
Praised (by others): *duuhia ange.*

prank
Trick, prank: *doopeva*.*

pray
Keep silent, pray: *hagamahamaha.*
Pray: *dalodalo.*
Pray earnestly: *dalodalo keli.*
Pray fervently: *dangidangi keli.*
Pray for: *dalodaloa; dalodalosia.*
Pray for the welfare of —: *golu; kolu.*
Pray for the welfare of the whole island(and its population): *kolu de henua.*
Pray silently: *dalodalo i de lodo.*

prayer
A short prayer: *munamuna.*

preacher
Teacher, preacher: *dangada agoago.*

precarious
Be in a precarious position: *saba*$_1$.
Be in trouble, in danger, or in a precarious situation: *vakaa.*

precautions
Take precautions: *pena.*

precinct
District, precinct (electoral): *vaenga.*

pregnancy
Pregnancy: *huuhua.*

pregnant
Pregnant: *hai dama.*
Pregnant and almost ready to deliver: *adumua.*
Pregnant woman: *(de) hine huuhua.*

Premna
Plant sp.: tree sp.: a small tree sp. (*Premna obtusifolia* R.Br.): *valovalo.*

prepare
Prepare food wastefully (too much must be thrown away): *gai salusalu.*
Prepare for: *hagadabena ange.*

Prepare for, make ready: *hagababa.*
Prepare oneself, make oneself ready: *hagadabena iho.*
Prepare, make ready: *hagadabena.*

presence
In the presence of someone: *mada luu mada.*

present
A present (to the hearer): *ngadi gavadu.*

present$_1$
present (not absent): *maleva.*

press
Press down or against: *baalasi.*

pretty
Pretty, beautiful: *mahamaha.*

previous
Previous: *hano laa.*

price
Price, wages: *hagaoanga.*

pricked
Pricked: *dalaehala.*

priest
Cult priest: *tangada hai me dabu.*
Priest (of a cult): *aligi.*

printing
Printing (block letters): *sisi baalasi.*

prison
Prison, jail: *hale nnoa; hale pono.*

prize
Prize: *hagaoanga.*

procedure
Law, procedure, rule: *hainga.*

procrastinate
Procrastinate (about work): *hagassege i hegau.*

productive
Productive, yield a great amount of: *daua*$_1$.

profound
Profound thoughts: *maanadu gelo.*

program
Arrange (in order), a program: *hagatau*$_1$.

prolapsed
Prolapsed rectum: *doo de gulabe.*

prolong
Lengthen, prolong: *hagalooloa.*
Prolong, extend: *hagadaulooloa.*

promiscuous
Promiscuous (especially if indiscreet or known to have sexual relations with one's own relatives): *hai be se manu.*

promise
Promise, contract with: *hagatoo donu.*

promontory
Promontory, peninsula: *udua.*

pronounce
Speak, pronounce, utter (words): *dagu*$_1$.

prostrate
Prostrate oneself (esp. to hide): *hagabala.*

prostration
Causing prostration: *hagabaangoa.*
Given to prostration: *hagabangobangoa.*

prototype
Prototype, model (something from which a copy can be made): *anga*$_3$ —.

proud
Arrogant, haughty, overbearing, proud: *hagamao lunga.*
Proud, abrupt in manner: *hagasoenga.*
Show-off, proud: *hai kai.*

provide
Provide a portion or share: *hagadino.*

prow
Prow (bottom part): *hoolu.*
Prow of a canoe: *madaa moni.*
Prow of a fast ship: *mada dao.*

prowl
Prowl around (to attack): *haahaangoda ange.*

prowler
Prowler: *bebela.*

pubic
The lower abdomen, crotch, pubic area: *madagauhala.*

puffer
Fish sp.: puffer: *dala-galoi.*
Fish sp.: spiny puffer: *daudu.*

Puffinus
Bird sp.: short-tailed shearwater (*Puffinus tenuirostris*): *manu-a-madaligi.*

pugnacious
Extremely pugnacious: *agilau gee.*
Pugnacious: *agilau.*

pull
Pick (breadfruit), pull down: *lou.*
Pull (a trigger): *loulou.*
Pull: *dada*$_1$; *hhudi.*
Pull continuously: *daadaangia.*
Pull in a line: *sigo.*
Pull oneself up by one's arms: *hagamaanu age.*
Pull out (e.g., a sword from its scabbard): *unusi.*
Pull up slowly or gently with one's fingers: *abiabi.*
Pull, move, or raise, gently: *hagasago.*

pulled
Pulled out, removed (by pulling out): *maunusi.*

pulling
Grab while pulling: *mulu gudu.*

pulverize
To crush, to pulverize: *mmili*$_1$.

pumice
Pumice stone (found as driftwood): *hoohanga.*

punch
Punch, hit, strike: *dugi*$_1$.

punctilious
Punctilious, be particular: *hai huaame.*

punctual
Punctual: *moolau huu.*

punish
Punish: *hagadalea.*
Suffer, punish: *hagaduasala.*

punished
Feel punished or victimized: *langona iho maahana.*
Punished for his bad deeds: *paa ono pagola.*

punishment
Punishment: *baadunga; pagola.*
Punishment of a person by confinement (without food or drink) until his death: *hagavagavaga.*
Receive one's punishment, suffer: *paa ono maahana.*

punt
To punt (propel a canoe by poling): *dogo*$_1$.
To punt while standing up on the stern gunwales of a canoe: *dogo duu.*

punt pole
Punt pole: *dogo*$_1$.

pupil
Pupil of the eye: *tama legalega eidu.*

pureness
Pureness of heart, innocence: *lodo gilimalali.*

purlin
Purlin: *ogo*$_2$.

pus
Pus: *augau.*

push
Push (now and into the future): *seseu.*
Push: *usu*$_2$.
Push aside (in all directions): *bae.*
Push away, push aside (in one direction): *sseu gee.*
Push in, crumple up: *ngalogu.*
Push violently: *sseu.*

pushed
Pushed out of shape (as a tin can), rumpled, crumpled: *bogobogo*$_2$.

pustular
Pustular: *mateedea.*

put
Bring up, put up, take up: *vage*$_1$.
Put a ring on (someone): *hagabuulei.*
Put aside, leave for later, conserve: *hagadoe.*
Put aside, set aside: *dugu gee.*
Put away against a contingency: *keeligi.*
Put on (clothes), wear: *ulumagi.*
Put on, wear, cover up (the body): *gahu.*
Put to bed: *hagaseni.*
Put to sleep (esp. a child) by rocking in the arms or singing to: *viivii.*
Put, place: *dugu.*

quadrants
The four quadrants of the sky: *baasi e haa o de langi.*

quality
Of exceptional quality: *malie.*

quarrel
Quarrel (like children): *hagasaa.*

question
Question (something) carefully: *heui.*

quick
Fast, quick, early: *moolau.*
Quick to fight, short-tempered: *lima lele.*

quick-witted
A quick-witted person (who realizes his goals fast): *kangi de hagasaele; kangi de maanadu.*
Be quick-witted in an emergency: *dalangasau.*

quickly
Do fast or quickly: *limadi.*

quit
Rest, relax, quit (a job): *hagamabu.*

quite
About, quite: *lago.*

quota
Obtain one's quota: *duu taelodo.*

rabbitfish
Fish sp.: rabbitfish: *baaua; bangongo.*

race
Race: *houhou.*
Race to take: *kave houhou.*

rachis
Rachis of the coconut leaf: *gau lama.*

radio
Radio: *me pasa.*

raft
Shelf, platform, raft, floor (of planks): *hada.*

rag
Rag: *bulubulu malo.*

rain
Rain: *bala langi; ua*$_2$.
Rain of a reddish color: *ua dodo.*
Rain, heaven, sky: *langi*$_2$.

rain cloud
A rain cloud (dropping its rain) seen in the distance: *dama de gaehala.*
Rain cloud (includes all cumulus types): *hagausinga.*

rainbow
Rainbow: *umada.*

rainbow runner
Fish sp.: rainbow runner: *gina.*

raining
Raining without let-up: *dee madaladala de langi.*

rainwater
Rainwater: *vai langi.*

rainy
Rainy season: *dau langi.*

raise
Lift, raise up: *langa.*
Pull, move, or raise, gently: *hagasago.*
Raise both eyebrows: *llena luu mada.*
Raise one's eyebrows: *llena.*
Raise one's head up or back: *dangage.*
Raise or increase (volume of radio or price, etc.): *ue age.*
Raise up (so that higher): *ege.*
Raise up (something) from its previous trajectory: *ege age.*

raised
Raised up: *maege.*

ramrod
Ramrod: *naamulolo.*

rape
Do or take by force, rape: *hai gi de mahi.*

rare
Rare (not cooked thoroughly): *dunu madamada.*

rascal
Rascal: *se mouli dangada.*

rat
Rat: *gimoo*$_1$.

rattling
A rattling or sloshing around inside (of something shaken): *ngaalulu.*

ravenous
Famished, ravenous: *ssee de hiigai.*
Ravenous: *magau i de hiigai.*

raw
Eat (something) raw: *oda*$_1$.
Uncooked, raw: *mada*$_1$.

ray
Fish sp.: eagle ray: *hoimanu.*

rays
Rays of the sun: *gavegave.*

reach
Extend one's hand, reach out: *haalo.*
Reach a certain age: *kii age.*
Reach halfway up: *madohi age.*
Reach land: *dau age.*

read
Count, read: *dau*$_1$.

ready
Prepare for, make ready: *hagababa.*
Prepare oneself, make oneself ready: *hagadabena iho.*
Prepare, make ready: *hagadabena.*
Ready for: *baba ange.*
To be ready: *baba*$_1$.

real
Real, really: *donu*$_1$.
Real, true: *abo donu; me abo donu.*

realize
Realize, know: *iloo iho.*
Realize, understand: *donu iho.*
To fully realize one's potential (for happiness, etc.): *hagahonu.*

really
Real, really: *donu*$_1$.

recall
Recall slightly: *adaadamai.*
Recollect or recall past events or persons, etc.: *adamai.*

recognize
Identify, recognize: *madea.*

recollect
Recollect or recall past events or persons, etc.: *adamai.*

recook
Recook for a very little while: *hagahana ange.*
Recook for several days: *hagahana age.*
Reheat or recook food (to preserve it for a longer time): *hagahana.*

record
A record (set in competitive sports): *goononga*$_2$.
A record set by an individual (or team): *goonanga.*
Keep a record of: *daohi taelodi.*

recovered
Recovered from illness: *ieiangi.*

recovering
Recovering from an illness (getting better): *gu dee galemu.*

rectangular
Having corners, square, rectangular: *tuu dege.*
Rectangular (not square), oval: *sao de looloa.*

rectum
Rectum: *gulabe.*

recuperated
Healed, well (after sickness), recuperated: *hagavaasuu.*

recuperating
Recuperating (after an illness): *dagodo gee (ma).*

red
Dark red: *mada mmea.*
Red: *mea; mmea.*
Red in the face, flushed: *ula de gili.*

red hot
Red hot (literally): *mmea be se gaagose.*

reduce
Reduce (in rank, price, etc.): *ngaue iho.*
Reduce in number, make fewer: *hagadogoisi.*
Reduce in quantity: *hagamomo.*
Reduce in size: *hagamaasei.*
To reduce (in price, etc.): *ngaue mai.*

reduced
Reduced, decreased: *ngalue iho.*

reef
Reef (including land thereon): *gano agau.*
Reef (the portion which is sometimes under water): *agau.*

reef heron
Bird sp.: reef heron (*Demiegretta sacra*): *gava*$_2$.
Reef heron — grey phase: *gava-uli.*
Reef heron — white phase: *gava-dea.*

reflection
Picture, image, reflection, shadow: *ada*$_1$.

refrain
Refrain (of song): *duudanga aheahe.*

refreshed
Refreshed (e.g., after a rest, or a shower): *maaloolo.*

refuse
Refuse to: *hagadeeai.*
Refuse to accept (something): *e dee haalo.*
Refuse to do one's part because of someone else's actions: *hagatau*$_1$.
Refuse to participate in work: *hagassege i hegau.*

regain
Regain: *hanu age.*

reheat
Reheat or recook food (to preserve it for a longer time): *hagahana.*

relapsed
To have relapsed into (his/her, etc.) —: *iho ange* + PRONOUN—.

relate
Relate news or gossip: *adi.*
Relate repeatedly: *adiadi.*
Tell, say to, relate: *dala*$_3$.

related
The relationship between relatives, related (of persons): *hai dangada.*

relationship
An avoidance relationship (between kin): *hai mada dabu.*
Be in the relationship of: *hai*$_2$.
Having a close kin relationship: *liiliagi.*
The relationship between father (or other male elder) and child (or one treated as child): *hai damana.*
The relationship between friends: *hai soa.*
The relationship between grandparent and grandchild: *hai dubuna; hai mogobuna.*
The relationship between mother (or other female elder) and child (or one treated as a child): *hai dinana.*
The relationship between parent and daughter: *hai damaahine.*
The relationship between relatives, related (of persons): *hai dangada.*
The relationship between siblings: *hai daadaa.*
The relationship between siblings or cousins: *hai daina.*
The relationship between spouses: *hai bodu.*
The relationship of parent-in-law to child-in-law: *hai saulaba.*
What relationship?: *hai aha.*

relative
Person, human being, relative: *dangada.*

relatives
Relatives by marriage or adoption, etc.: *dangada mai i daha.*

relax
Rest, relax, quit (a job): *hagamabu.*

relaxed
Completely relaxed: *tili aalanga.*

release
Release one at a time or intermittently or sporadically: *dili dagidahi age.*

relief
Relief, be relieved: *ava*$_2$.

relieve
Cause to have been sufficient, relieve: *hagaaoa*$_2$.
Relieve: *hagaava*$_2$.

relieved
Relief, be relieved: *ava*$_2$.

religion
Religion: *daumaha.*

religious
Religious observance: *daumaha.*
Ritual activities, religious activities: *dago.*
Ritual acts, religious acts: *me hai dago.*

relish
Relish (meat or fish, or something substituting for meat or fish, eaten with taro, etc.): *giidagi.*

reluctant
Reluctant to do or initiate (through fear of failure): *hagamagulu.*

rely
Depend on (e.g., to come), rely on: *dahi tali.*
To rely on others for the things one should provide for oneself: *hadi bala.*

remain
Left over, remain: *doe.*
Remain (somewhere): *noho.*

remainder
Remainder (less than the preceding number): *duumaa.*

remember
Remember an incident with a view toward revenge: *golo.*
Remember childhood experiences: *adamai gauligi.*
Remember poorly: *vaivai adamai.*
Remember vividly (after having forgotten): *matili mai.*
Remember what one has heard: *sigo de muna.*
Remember, remind: *hagamaanadu.*

remembered
Remembered: *manadua.*

remembrance
Remembrance, observance of (e.g., a holiday): *hai de hagamaanadu.*

remind
Remember, remind: *hagamaanadu.*

remove
Remove (clothes, etc.), disrobe, undress: *hagaui$_2$.*
Remove: *aau.*
Remove all fruit from a coconut tree: *ulu$_1$.*

removed
Pulled out, removed (by pulling out): *maunusi.*

render
Render a final decision: *hagamodu.*

reoccur
Start again, reoccur: *ahe age.*

repay
Buy, sell, repay: *hagao.*

repent
Change of heart, change one's mind, repent: *dahuli de lodo.*

replace
Change, replace: *sui.*

reply
Answer, reply: *basa ange.*
Utter (words or sounds), reply (to someone): *muu$_1$.*

resemble
Resemble: *holi ange.*
Resemble closely: *delaa tee madea.*
Resemble someone (owing to a consanguineal relationship): *duu ange.*

resentful
Resentful: *hai lodo.*

resist
Resist me (you, them), oppose me (you, them): *noho mai (adu, ange).*

resistance
Soft, mushy, offering no resistance: *bala.*

resourcefulness
Ability, capacity (of person), resourcefulness: *hina.*

respect
Respect (someone): *hagadubu.*

rest
Rest for a short time: *hagamabu iho.*
Rest up for (e.g., the next day's work): *seni ange.*
Rest, relax, quit (a job): *hagamabu.*

restaurant
Restaurant: *hale gai.*

rested
Rested: *mabu.*

resting
Resting place: *hagamaabunga.*

restless
Restless (of a child): *hai gaavenga.*

restrain
Hold, restrain, keep (from): *daohi.*

restrained
Restrained (not prone to act on impulse): *golomagi.*

restrict
Restrict: *hagadabu.*

result
Fortunate result: *hagapago donu.*
Unfortunate result: *hagapago sala.*

return
Return to land from sea (esp. of birds): *hagamabu age.*
Return to the fold: *hagaahe mai.*
Return, go back: *ahe.*

returning
Keep returning: *aheahe.*

reveal
To reveal oneself to someone (of a ghost): *hakide.*

revenge
Take revenge, get even: *sui ange.*

reverse
Reverse, transpose: *lui$_1$.*

reversed
Turned (in direction), reversed, transposed: *malui.*

revitalized
Revitalized (by a shower or rest, etc.): *maholahola danuaa age.*

revolve
Roll over or about, turn (as of a wheel), spin, revolve, rotate: *dige.*

rib
Rib: *ivi gaogao.*

rib cage
Rib cage, thoracic cavity: *hale i lodo.*

rich
Rich in material possessions: *mau goloa.*

rickety
Not sturdy, rickety: *ngaangaa.*

riddle
Riddle, parable: *me hagasengasenga.*

ride
Slip, slide, to ride, to surf: *sege.*
To ride high in the water (e.g., of a canoe): *ea gi lunga.*

ridge pole
Ridge pole (lower): *dao dahuuhuu.*
Ridge pole (upper): *dao badu.*
Ridge pole cover: *gahuduna.*
Ridge pole support (end): *dao bou.*

ridicule
Make fun of, ridicule: *doo me (ai).*

rifle
Rifle: *hallaba.*

right
Correct, right, just, fair, true: *heohi.*
Just about right: *iai maalie.*
Right (side): *madau.*
Right side, right-handed: *baasi madau.*
Truth, right, correct: *donu*$_2$.

right side out
Right side out (clothes): *hulidonu.*

right-handed
Right side, right-handed: *baasi madau.*

rim
Edge, fringe, rim: *hiihii.*
Mouth of, rim of: *ngudu*$_a$.

ring
Ring (for a finger): *buulei.*
Ring the bell: *daa de baalanga.*

ringing
Tinnitus, a ringing sound in the ear: *dangi talinga.*

ringworm
A fungus infection of the skin, ringworm: *gili dabeo.*

rinse
Rinse off salt water from the body (with fresh water): *hagalanu.*
To rinse off salt water from the body (with fresh water): *hagamaa*$_1$.

rip
Rip, tear, deflower (a virgin): *ssae*$_1$.

ripe
Ripe: *leu.*

ripen
Beginning to ripen (indicated by a yellowish color—of, e.g., bananas and papayas): *salani.*
Ripen (to become yellow and soft—of breadfruit only): *maai.*

ripening
Ripening (of breadfruit only): *maamaai.*

rise
Regain consciousness, rise from the dead: *mouli age.*
Rise (of stars, or of the moon or sun): *ssobo.*
Rise up (as the sun), get up, jump up: *sobo.*
Stand on tiptoes, rise up (as a person does): *hagaduuduu.*

rising
Rising (of the sun, etc.): *soobonga.*
Rising of the sun: *sobo de laa.*

risky
Risky, dangerous: *hagamanavasaa.*
Risky, unreliable: *doo halehale me; doo lodolodo.*

ritual
Ritual activities, religious activities: *dago.*
Ritual acts, religious acts: *me hai dago.*
Ritual observances: *hai dago.*

road
Road, pathway (for going), track: *haiava.*
Road, walkway, path (for walking): *saelenga.*

roast
To roast *ngongo* (in a fire): *haula ngongo.*
To roast: *lala.*

rock
Rock back and forth: *hidihidi.*
Rock back and forth to one side: *hagadibadiba.*
Stone, rock, a piece of weathered coral: *hadu*$_2$.

rock lobster
Rock lobster sp.: longusta: *ula-dai.*

rocky
Rocky (full of stones): *haduhadua*$_2$.

rod
An iron rod: *gau bini baalanga.*

roll
Fold up (several folds), roll up: *hhedu.*

roll over
Roll over or about, turn (as of a wheel), spin, revolve, rotate: *dige.*

roll up
Roll up: *mulo.*

rolled
Folded up, rolled up: *mahedu.*

rolling
Rolling of thunder: *paa de hatuli.*

roof
To roof (a house), to thatch (a house): *odo*$_1$.

roofing
Metal roofing: *baalanga dua hale.*

room
Room (of a house): *aabi; gabanibaonga.*
Room, compartment: *bao.*
To have room for (on a ship or canoe): *udaia.*

root
Aerial root of the pandanus tree: *laho.*
Root (of a tree or plant): *aga.*
Root around (disturbing the coral layer of a yard by shuffling, or by pawing the ground): *keli.*
Root up (soil): *sua*$_1$.

rope
A rope for tying palm fronds together to make a *belubelu* seine: *daula mada lau nui.*
A rope used to assist the climber of a breadfruit tree: *daula gage.*
A rope used to lower a bunch of coconuts to the ground: *daula duu nui.*
A rope used to pull a coconut tree in the desired direction when felling it: *daula sele nui.*
A type of rope (thick, with thick strands): *dua nnui.*
A type of rope (used for climbing breadfruit trees): *saali.*
Anchor rope: *ataula.*
Fishing line, rope (of a sort suitable for fishing): *uga*$_1$.
Rope (heavy): *daula.*

rotate
Roll over or about, turn (as of a wheel), spin, revolve, rotate: *dige.*

rotten
Rotten: *bobo.*

rough
Rough in texture (as perceived at one time): *tala*$_4$.
Rough in texture (as perceived over time): *daladala*$_4$.
Rough or choppy sea condition: *dangalebu.*
Rough or choppy seas: *dangalebu de moana.*

round
Round, clear (in outline): *molomolo*$_2$.
Round, spherical, circular: *moe*$_2$.
To round off a sharp edge: *diinei mai dege.*

round herring
Fish sp.: round herring?, goby?: *ulua-gabugabu-tai.*

round-headed
Round-headed: *molomolo de biho.*

route
Path, route: *dagalonga**; dagamanga*.*

row
Arrange things in a row or line: *hagaadugau.*
Arrangement of things into a straight row: *adugau.*
Row (of things): *hagatauanga.*
Row of plants: *dooanga.*

row$_1$
to row a canoe (with a paddle): *suasua mai (adu, ange).*

rowing
Rowing motion: *sua*$_1$.

rub
Rub (with pressure, as in using sandpaper): *ugu.*
Rub back and forth in the hands (like a fire drill): *mmili*$_1$.
Sharpen (a knife), rub against: *hakaa.*
Stroke, rub gently: *mmulu.*

rubbed
Rubbed against (of lines only): *gaagaasia.*
Rubbed against, scratched: *gasigasia*$_2$.

rubble
Coral rubble: *giligili.*

rudderfish
Fish sp.: rudderfish: *gada-laagau-ngauda.*

ruddy turnstone
Bird sp.: ruddy turnstone (*Arenaria interpres*): *givigivi.*

ruin
Damage, ruin: *oha.*

rule
Law, procedure, rule: *hainga.*

rumor
Rumor: *longolongo i leaala.*

rumors
Spread news or rumors: *dele de longo.*

rumpled
Pushed out of shape (as a tin can), rumpled, crumpled: *bogobogo*$_2$.

run
Chase, run after: *doolohi.*
Run (of a color): *hano de leebunga.*
Run: *llibo ange luu vae.*
Run aground: *gasa.*
Run away: *savini gee.*
Run, move fast (as fish, or a canoe): *savini.*

runny
Headcold, runny nose: *magi sali usu.*
Runny nose: *sali de usu.*

rush
Hurry, rush: *hagamoolau.*
Rush (usually preceded by *dee*): *daadaaia.*
Rush around (of a group of people): *saaliba; saibo.*
Rush around aimlessly (of a group of people): *saibo saele.*
Rush because of an emergency: *deledele hainga a me.*
Rush, speed up: *hagamalibi.*

rust
Rust: *hongagelegele baalanga.*

sacred kingfisher
Bird sp.: sacred kingfisher (*Halcyon sancta*) (The native term applies possibly to several spp.): *manu-de-bua.*

sacrifice
Collection (in church), offering (in church), sacrifice, tithe: *sigidaumaha.*
To sacrifice (not thinking of oneself): *hagangadi me.*

sad
Feel unhappy or sad: *lodo daemaha.*
Unhappy, upset, sad: *lodo baubau.*

sadness
Heaviness, sadness, unhappiness: *daemahaanga.*

safe
Survive, safe: *ola.*

sail
A sail: *laa*$_4$*; saiolo.*
To sail (a canoe): *dele.*
To sail crosswind (for maximum speed): *duulagi.*
To sail so as to fill one's sails with wind (sailing crosswind): *hhao tuula.*
To sail through the air: *leva.*

sailfish
Fish sp.: sailfish or marlin: *sagulaa.*

sailor
Sailor: *hai moni.*
Sailor, seaman: *daane hai moni.*

salivate
Salivate: *sali ssaavale.*

salt
Lagoon, sea, salt: *dai*$_1$.

same
Be like, be the same as: *bei.*
Having the same characteristics, be alike: *dagodo daudahi.*

sand
Fine-grained sand: *gelegele gumi hue.*
Sand: *gelegele dea; ssuonioni.*
Sand with disk-like particles: *gelegele malama.*
Sand, soil, dirty: *gelegele.*

sand spit
A lagoonward sand spit next to a channel between islets on the atoll: *alobagi.*
Beach, sand spit: *olo.*
Sand spit: *adudau.*

sandpiper
Bird sp.: sharp-tailed sandpiper (*Erolia acuminata*): *damaa-manu.*

sandy
Sandy: *ssuonioni ina.*

sap
Gum (to chew), sap (of trees): *bigibigi*$_1$
The sap of a hardwood sp. which drifts ashore (used for making perfume): *doi-avaava.*
The sap of the coconut tree (taken from the inflorescence): *galeve.*

sap-feeding beetles
Louse (head), or similar exoparasite of plants or animals (e.g., bird lice, scale insects, sap-feeding beetles, darkling beetles, etc.): *gudu.*

sarong
Sarong: *lavalava.*

satiated
Be satiated with food: *bosu.*
Satiated: *pulu.*

satisfied
Be satisfied completely: *dae de lodo.*
Satisfied completely in sexual intercourse: *manigangi.*

Saturday
Saturday ('sixth day'): *Ono-laangi.*
Saturday (the day on which food is prepared for Sunday): *Laangihagamouli.*

save
Save from: *hagaola.*

say
Say bad things about people: *hagaaduadu.*
Say loudly: *llea.*
Say or tell (esp. in confidence): *agu*$_1$.
Say out loud: *agu age; dagu age.*
Say to: *hai ange.*
Say to oneself: *agu iho.*
Say what is on one's mind: *basa soe.*
Speak, talk, say: *basa*$_1$.
Tell, say to, relate: *dala*$_3$.
To say that —: *hagadaba.*

saying
Saying: *basabasa.*

scab
Scab, crust: *bagu.*

scad
Fish sp.: scad?: *badii; belubelu; gabou.*

Scaevola
Plant sp.: beach naupaka shrub (*Scaevola taccada* (Gaertn.) Roxb.): *manu-gaba-aasanga.*

scale
Scale (of a fish): *unahi.*
Scrape off (with an object or one's finger), to scale (fish): *holehole.*

scale insects
Louse (head), or similar exoparasite of plants or animals (e.g., bird lice, scale insects, sap-feeding beetles, darkling beetles, etc.): *gudu.*

scaled
Scraped, scaled (fish): *maholehole.*

scarce
Scarce (applied usually only to *ssave*): *sseva.*

scare
Scare (someone): *hagamadagu.*
Scare away, chase away: *dugi*$_2$.
To scare fish, etc.: *hagahoohoo.*

scared
Afraid, scared: *madagu.*

scatter
To scatter (when in a group): *maseu.*

scattered
Scattered (not in a cluster): *vaadagidahi.*
Scattered: *mavaevae.*

scheme
An evil scheme: *doo*$_2$.

school
A school of fish: *ungaa mamu.*

scold
Scold, bawl out, chide: *hagasee*$_1$.

scoop
Scoop out: *hhali gee.*
Scoop out by inserting a knife between the meat and the shell (e.g., in cutting copra): *dagasisi.*
Scoop up (liquids only), spoon: *asu.*
Scoop up (liquids or solids): *daa*$_1$.
Scoop up (of solids only): *hhali.*

scorned
Scorned: *ngudu leia; ngudu leidi**.

scorpion
Insect sp.: scorpion: *manu-manga-lua.*

scrape
Scrape (a single act), scrapr: *koi.*
Scrape (something), plane (something), scrape off (with an object), peel (with a knife toward one): *salu.*

Scrape —: *goi*$_2$.
Scrape off (with an object or one's finger), to scale (fish): *holehole.*
Scrape off (with one's finger), scratch up: *koli.*

scraped
Scraped (a little taken away), scratched: *saalua.*
Scraped (a lot taken away), peeled (a little amount taken off), planed: *salua.*
Scraped, scaled (fish): *maholehole.*

scraper
A scraper for leaves: *me ssalu lau.*
Scrape (a single act), scraper: *koi.*

scratch
A scratch (on the skin): *saaluanga.*
Scrape off (with one's finger), scratch up: *koli.*
To scratch (an itch): *laaladi.*
To scratch (once): *kosi*$_1$.
To scratch (slightly) repeatedly: *gosigosi.*

scratched
Abraded (skin), scratched: *masole.*
Barely scratched: *masole ange.*
Rubbed against, scratched: *gasigasia*$_2$.
Scraped (a little taken away), scratched: *saalua.*
Scratched (of something solid only): *gosigosia.*

screaming
The screaming of many people at the same time: *hevaalogi.*

scrotum
Scrotum (one side only): *panava.*
Scrotum (whole thing): *luu panava.*

scrub
Wipe, scrub, clean up (by wiping), erase: *ssolo.*

scull
Scull (a boat): *sigale.*

sea
Lagoon, sea, salt: *dai*$_1$.
Open sea, far away from any land: *gano moana.*
Open sea, the atmosphere: *moana.*

sea animal
Sea animal: *manu laosedi.*

sea bass
Fish sp.: sea bass (The native term is applied to many spp.): *ngadala.*
Fish sp.: sea bass (= small *ava*): *donu*$_3$.
Fish sp.: sea bass (2 sorts: 1 large, 1 small): *madabiebie.*
Fish sp.: sea bass: *bangadala; sahudu.*

sea cucumber
Apodous sea cucumber: *duu-lellele.*
Sea cucumber (many spp.): *banibani.*
Sea cucumber sp. (several spp.): *galabe.*
Sea cucumber sp.: *duu-mmea; duu-uli; gaagose; galabe-duiduia; olonoa.*

sea shell
Sea shell: *manu lalo tai.*

sea urchin
Sea urchin sp.: *Diadema* sp.: *veli-daubulebule; veli-uli.*
Sea urchin sp.: *Echinometra* spp.: *veli.*

sea water
Sea water: *laosedi.*

seam
Seam (in clothes): *duinga.*

seaman
Sailor, seaman: *daane hai moni.*

search
Look for, search, hunt for: *ssala*$_1$.
Search for: *sigale saele.*
Search for driftwood or other beached objects: *hai me daahea.*
Search for here and there, wander around looking for: *saugalo saele.*
Search here and there: *haahaa saele.*
Search intently for: *hagaduu ssaalanga.*

seasick
Seasick: *daia e tuaadai.*
Seasick but unable to throw up: *duaa dai.*

season
Breadfruit season: *dau gulu.*
Dry season: *dau laohie.*
Rainy season: *dau langi.*
The season during which flies are most numerous: *dau lango.*
The season in which fish are abundant: *dau mamu.*
The season in which seasonally available food is abundant: *dau gai.*

seaweed sp.
Seaweed sp.: *duudua-a-de-honu; gamagama; hauala; helii-lausedi.*

second
The second child of a couple: *ganimuli.*

secret
Keep secret: *noho iho* —.

secretary
Secretary: *tangada sisi.*

secretion
Secretion of the genitalia (male or female): *dingale.*

sector
The sector from which the wind blows: *duulanga*$_1$.

secular
Permitted, open to the public, secular: *hainoo.*

see
See: *gide.*
See each other: *hegide.*
See what happened! (the hearer having been forewarned): *vakaa loo dangada.*

seed
Seed of the pandanus: *benu.*
Seed, testicles: *golee.*

seedling
A coconut tree seedling: *me osi.*
A seedling: *osi.*
A shoot (of another plant) set aside for planting a seedling: *osi.*

seen
Seen: *gidee.*

seep
Flow, seep: *sali.*
Seep (of water): *basalia*$_2$

self-awareness
Self-awareness: *anga iho.*

self-love
Self-love: *aloha iho.*

self-centered
Egotistical, self-centered, arrogant in spirit: *lodo mao lunga.*

self-controlled
Self-controlled: *golomagi lodo.*

self-deprecatory
Self-deprecatory, downgrade: *hagadugu lalo.*

self-effacing
Self-effacing, meek in spirit: *lodo mao lalo.*

self-pity
Self-pity: *hinangalosaa iho.*

selfish
Selfish: *hagabudu me.*
Selfish with one's possessions, ungiving: *lodo hagamau me.*

sell
Buy, sell, repay: *hagao.*

semen
Semen, ejaculate: *bii.*

send away
Send away: *alualumia.*

send for
Send for: *aalu.*

sennit
String twirled from coconut fiber, sennit: *liholiho.*

senseless
Senseless, drunk: *senga.*

separate
Isolate, separate from, set aside (from a group): *vvae gee.*
Separate from: *malanga.*
Separate oneself from: *hagamounu.*
Separate, divide: *vae*$_1$.
Split open, open up, or separate, all at once: *hhanga.*

separated
Separated (of crude coconut oil): *doo de lolomango.*
Separated (two things), divorced: *maavae.*
Separated from: *malanga; modu gee; tanga gee.*
Separated from and curled up from: *mahidi.*
Separated from others, and by itself: *modu sogosogo.*

separation
Separation in coconut oil (when it is aging): *lanibene.*

September
September ('ninth month'): *Ssiva-malama.*
September: *Mailaba.*

serious
Serious: *dee adagaigaina.*

serpent cucumber
Serpent cucumber: *manu-mangamanga-i-lote-aasanga.*

servant
Servant: *duosi.*

set
Set *galauna*: *tili de galauna.*

set a record
To set a record: *goononga gee.*

set aside
Isolate, separate from, set aside (from a group): *vvae gee.*
Put aside, set aside: *dugu gee.*
Set aside (be chosen from a group): *hili gee.*

set fire to
Set fire to (causing large flames): *haula.*
Set fire to, burn: *dudu.*

set free
Set free: *hagailaage.*

set up
Construct, set up, build (something): *hagaduu.*

setback
Suffer a setback: *hanohano dua.*

setting
The setting of the moon: *danu de maasina.*
The setting of the sun: *danu de laa; sulu de laa.*

settled
Properly settled: *baba donu.*
Recently settled: *baba iho.*
To have been settled for some time: *baba odi.*

seven
Seven: *hidu.*

seventy
Seventy: *madahidu.*

sew
Sew up a hole (in clothing): *siga.*
Stab with a sharp object, pierce with a sharp object, sew, string (flowers or fish, etc.): *dui.*

sexual
Have sexual intercourse: *hai*$_1$.
Have sexual intercourse, fornicate: *sanga.*
Have sexual relations: *hagabuni; hai vaivai me.*
Sexual activity: *haiva dee agona.*

shade
Shade (under trees): *malu.*

shadow
Picture, image, reflection, shadow: *ada*$_1$.

shadows
Dark images, shadows in the darkness: *goohunga.*

shaft
The shaft of a spear: *gau laagau.*

shake
Shake one's head (once) to one side: *geu.*
Shake one's head back and forth: *geugeu.*
To shake (something) back and forth: *luuluu.*
To shake (something) rapidly: *lulu.*

shaking
Shaking: *bolebole; pole.*

shaky
Shaky: *ngalullulu.*

shallow
Shallow (bowl, basket, etc.): *bedage.*
Shallow (e.g., waters): *baa age.*

shame
To shame (someone) by teasing or insulting him: *vogi*$_1$.

shamed
Shy (especially in the presence of members of the opposite sex), shamed: *hoo senga.*

shameful
Shameful, to embarrass (someone): *hagadogaa.*

shape
Shape of, form of: *holi.*
To shape roughly (as in making a canoe): *hagahua.*

shaping
The shaping (of something) by planing: *hagasalu.*

share
A share of food (esp. for children): *saa*$_2$.
A share of, allotment, portion: *dino*$_1$.
Portion, share (of something): *diba*$_2$.
Portion, share, division (e.g., of a tract): *vaenga.*

Provide food for, share food with: *hagangau.*
Share equally: *hagamadamada.*
Share equally among: *hagamadamada ngaadahi.*

shark
Fish sp.: blacktip shark: *mangoo-dahola.*
Fish sp.: shark sp.: *dababa; hagaulu$_2$; mangoo-biho-lua; mangoo-senga.*
Fish sp.: shark sp.?: *alava; eleele; galeva; madau-dalinga; pula-laalaa.*
Fish sp.: white-tip shark: *aso.*
Shark (euphemism): *daane sauaa; taane sauaa.*
Shark (the generic term): *mangoo.*

sharp
A very sharp point: *mada libia.*
Sharp (as a knife): *dalabaimanugadele; kalo$_4$.*
Sharp (as a knife), pointed: *kangi.*
Sharp (esp. something which causes sharp pain like a whip): *malibilibia.*

sharp-eyed
Sharp-eyed, good at finding things: *mada gide.*

sharp-tailed sandpiper
Bird sp.: sharp-tailed sandpiper (*Erolia acuminata*): *damaa-manu.*

sharpen
Sharpen (a knife), rub against: *hakaa.*
Sharpen (knife): *tale ange.*

sharpshooter
Sharpshooter: *damaa tili.*

shave
Shave: *dahia.*
Shave one's beard: *dahi de gumigumi.*
Shave, sweep, brush off (once): *dahi$_2$.*

she
He, she, it: *ia.*

shearwater
Bird sp.: short-tailed shearwater (*Puffinus tenuirostris*): *manu-a-madaligi.*

shed
Shed skin (as does a reptile): *uludino.*

sheer
Sheer drop-off (as at the edge of a cliff): *hadi modu.*

sheet
Sheet, blanket: *malo gahu de boo.*

shelf
Shelf, platform, raft, floor (of planks): *hada.*

shell
Kneecap, the shell of the coconut: *ubu.*
Sea shell: *manu lalo tai.*
The shell of a turtle, crab, etc.: *baba$_1$.*

shelter
Take shelter, to shelter (something from the elements): *hagalilo.*

sheltered
Sheltered (from the elements): *lilo.*

shine
Shine (e.g., a flashlight) on: *dili.*
Shine (sun): *dii.*
Shine: *hagamalamalama.*
Shine a flashlight indiscriminately on people: *baalasi saele.*
Shine a flashlight toward me (you): *baalasi mai (adu).*

shining
The shining of the sun: *dii de laa.*

shiny
Shiny (reflects light): *malamalama.*
Shiny (translucent): *masalaba.*

ship
A big ship or canoe: *vaga*.*
Ship from one place to another: *langa.*

shirt
Shirt: *malo gahu.*

shivering
Feel cold, shivering (from cold): *magalili.*

shocked
Shocked: *velosia de lodo.*

shoes
Shoes, slippers: *me vae.*

shoot
A shoot (of another plant) set aside for planting a seedling: *osi.*
Shoot at: *dili.*
Shoot out a light into the distance: *tili de maalama.*

shooting star
Shooting star: *dangaloa$_3$.*

shore
Islet shore (except that facing the lagoon): *ngudu aahua.*
Shore: *gabugabu.*

shore crab
Crab sp.: shore crab, land crab, grapsid crab, ghost crab: *gaibea.*

shoreline
Coast, shoreline: *tagudai.*

short
A very short person, midget: *gidigidi laa lalo.*
Short (in duration): *daubodobodo.*
Short: *bodobodo; gidigidi.*
Uselessly short: *bido gamu.*

short temper
Having a short temper: *moolau lodo.*

short-tailed shearwater
Bird sp.: short-tailed shearwater (*Puffinus tenuirostris*): *manu-a-madaligi.*

short-tempered
Easily angered, short-tempered: *lillili*$_2$.
Quick to fight, short-tempered: *lima lele.*

shorten
Limit, discontinue, shorten (by cutting off one end): *tuu mai.*
Shorten (time or rope): *hagadaubodobodo.*
Shorten, abbreviate: *hagasugi*$_2$.

shortness
Shortness of breath: *manava bodo.*

shoulder
Shoulder (the whole joint), wing: *bakau.*
Shoulder (top of): *eu.*

shoulder blade
Shoulder blade: *ivi-a-daea.*

shout
Shout: *oo*$_1$.
Shout to announce important news (e.g., to announce the arrival of a ship): *gu oo ina mai.*

show
Lead, show the way, leader (of a group): *dagi*$_1$.
Show, teach: *hagaago.*
To show (familiarize with): *hakide.*

show off
Show off (esp. in front of members of the opposite sex): *hagalegunga.*
Show off (in front of members of the opposite sex): *mulegi.*

show-off
Extremely show-off in manner: *vangevange.*
Show-off: *hagahua; hagamadia; hagasoenga; kai laanui; kaianeane.*
Show-off, proud: *hai kai.*

shrimp
Mantis shrimp: *manu-lalo-de-gelegele.*

shrub
Plant sp.: beach naupaka shrub (*Scaevola taccada* (Gaertn.) Roxb.): *manu-gaba-aasanga.*
Plant sp.: crepe myrtle shrub (*Pemphis acidula* Forst.): *nngie.*
Plant sp.: hemp-leaved vitex shrub (*Vitex negundo* var. *bicolor* (Willd.) Lam.): *gasigi.*
Plant sp.: shrub sp. (*Ximenia americana* L.): *dala*$_6$.

shrugging
A shrugging movement of the shoulders: *hagaeueu.*

shrunken
Become skinny, become shrunken: *bangabanga mai.*
Skinny, shrunken: *bangabanga*$_1$.

shy
Bashful, ashamed, shy, embarrassed: *dogaa.*
Bashful, shy (timid about attending social affairs), timid: *hagaau gee.*
Feel shy in the presence of: *dogaa ange.*
Shy (especially in the presence of members of the opposite sex), shamed: *hoo senga.*
Shy, embarrassed, bashful: *hoosenga.*
Timid, shy: *vasu**.

shyness
Behave with embarrassment or shyness: *hai me dogaa.*

sibling
Brother, sister, sibling, cousin: *daina.*
Sibling (mostly children's talk): *daadaa*$_3$.

sick
Sick, sickness: *magi.*

sickness
Sick, sickness: *magi.*

Sida
Plant sp.: plant-shrub sp. (*Sida fallax* Walp.): *geao.*

side
Left side, left-handed: *baasi masui.*
Right side, right-handed: *baasi madau.*
Side (of humans), below the hips: *hoa*$_2$.
Side of (part away from), with: *daho.*
Side of: *gaogao.*
Side, half: *baasi.*
The opposing side: *de baasi gee.*

sideburns
Sideburns (of hair): *malingalinga.*

sides
Both sides (of): *luu baasi.*
Take sides against, oppose: *hai baasi.*

sieve
Sieve: *dangadanga.*

sift
Filter, sift: *nonu*$_1$.

sigh
Sigh (an intake of air): *manava i lunga.*

sighted
Sighted, appear: *hodu**.

sign
Sign, mark, signal, omen: *hagailonga*$_1$.

signal
Sign, mark, signal, omen: *hagailonga*$_1$.

silent
Keep silent, pray: *hagamahamaha.*
Very calm, silent: *loma.*

silly
Funny, unserious, jesting, silly: *hakadanga.*

silver bush
Plant sp.: silver bush (*Sophora tormentosa* L.): *dangaloa*$_1$.

silversides
Fish sp.: anchovy?, silversides (small)?: *mamu-honga-dai.*
Fish sp.: silversides (The native term is applied to several spp.): *gimoo*$_2$.
Fish sp.: silversides: *saniba.*

sing
Sing (a song): *hua*$_1$.
Sing: *daahili.*
Sing a melody: *daa taahili.*
Sing off-key: *daa gee taahili.*
Sing on-key: *daa donu taahili.*

single
Single, unmarried: *duuhua.*

sink
Sink (completely): *dahea gi lalo.*
Sink (until submerged): *abulu.*
Sink all at once: *aapulu.*

sinkable
Easily sinkable: *abuabulu.*

sister
Brother, sister, sibling, cousin: *daina.*
Sister, female cousin: *daina hahine.*

sister-in-law
A sibling's spouse or spouse's sibling (brother-in-law or sister-in-law) of the same sex: *maa*$_2$.

sit
Sit on (as chicken hatching eggs): *baalasi.*
Sit quietly: *noho dau donu; noho maadai.*
Sit with one's legs spread apart: *noho hhanga.*
Stay, sit, stop: *noho.*

situated
Be situated: *noho.*
Properly situated or loaded (of a canoe): *noho donu.*
Stand, situated: *duu*$_2$.

situation
Appearance, example, situation: *dulagi.*
Appearance, situation: *dumanu.*
Situation, circumstance: *dagodo.*

six
Six: *ono*$_1$.

sixty
Sixty: *madaono.*

size
The size of something: *lau*$_3$.

sizzling
Sizzling noise (as in frying): *lalaa.*

skewer
Skewer, hold something down with the end of a long implement: *suunugi.*
Stab, skewer: *daalo.*

skillful
Skillful (at a craft): *labagau.*
Skillful at craft work, craftsmanlike: *madaligi*$_1$.
Skillful at fighting (opp. of *baa sala*): *baa donu.*
Skillful fisherman: *daudai.*

Skillful in the use of an adze: *damaa dogi.*

skillfully
Slowly, gently, skillfully, etc.: *damaa.*

skin
Skin: *gili.*

skinny
Become skinny, become shrunken: *bangabanga mai.*
Skinny (of people): *laso paava.*
Skinny: *gau ivi; lauasaasa.*
Skinny, shrunken: *bangabanga*$_1$.
Skinny, thin (lacking in flesh): *saava.*
Skinny, thin (person), emaciated: *iviivia.*

skip
To skip a stone across the water: *hagaditidi; hagaditidi de hadu.*

skipjack tuna
Fish sp.: skipjack tuna: *adu*$_2$.

skirt
Grass skirt (of hibiscus fiber or palm leaf): *didi.*

skittish
Easily startled, skittish, wild (of animals): *aada.*

skull
Skull: *ivi de biho.*

sky
A blue and cloudless sky: *kano de langi.*
Rain, heaven, sky: *langi*$_2$.

slack
Slack (of rope): *dau balabala; laubalabala.*
Slack off on (a rope): *hagatolo.*

slacken
To slacken the boom sheet (of a sailing canoe): *hagalloba ange.*

slander
Gossip, slander: *samu.*

slandered
Slandered: *samua.*

slanting
Inclined, slanting, not straight, not perpendicular to: *salau.*

slap
Continuously touch or slap lightly, pat: *baabaa*$_1$.
Slap: *baagia.*

slate-pencil urchin
Slate-pencil urchin: *heduge.*

sleep
Sleep: *moe*$_1$*; seni.*
Sleep fitfully (esp. because one is thinking about having to arise early): *seni alaala.*
Sleep fitfully: *alaala*$_2$.
Sleep for a short time, nap: *moe iho.*
Sleep late (into daytime): *seni gi de ao.*
Sleep soundly (owing to exhaustion): *seni magau.*
Sleep soundly: *moe tao; seni tao.*
Sleep without regard to remaining decently covered: *moe baubau.*
To sleep especially well or restfully: *maimai sseni.*

sleeper
Fish sp.: goby?, sleeper?: *dama-a-de-galabe.*

sleepy
Feel sleepy: *mademadea ange.*
Sleepy: *dai seni.*
Very sleepy: *daia e sseni.*

sleepyhead
Sleepyhead: *seniseni.*

slide
Slip or slide away from: *sege gee.*
Slip, slide, to ride, to surf: *sege.*

sling
Sling: *buada.*

slip
A slip of the tongue: *naba.*
Slip or slide away from: *sege gee.*
Slip out of one's hands (e.g., a line on which a big fish has been caught): *dele.*
Slip, slide, to ride, to surf: *sege.*

slipper lobster
Slipper lobster: *dabadaba*$_2$.

slippers
Shoes, slippers: *me vae.*

slippery
Slippery: *segesege.*

slope
Gradual slope or inclination: *madadaagodo.*
The slope of a canoe's keel: *daaligidanga.*

sloppy
Ugly-looking, messy, sloppy: *balaulau.*

sloshing
A rattling or sloshing around inside (of something shaken): *ngaalulu.*

slow
Slow down, be exhausted (physically), feel unenergetic: *bangoa.*
Slow in running or walking: *bunehulu.*
Slow to respond to suggestions or commands (because resisting): *hagalongolongo ngadaa.*
Slow, late: *mmule.*

slow moving
Slow moving (while working), slow acting, slow thinking: *mudumudu*$_1$.

slow-moving
Be (in fact) slow-moving (while attempting to hurry): *buugani.*
Slow-moving or slow-working person: *hidi bido dane.*

slow-witted
Slow-witted: *madagabubu de maanadu.*

slowly
Do slowly: *sabo.*
Slowly: *maalie.*
Slowly, gently, skillfully, etc.: *damaa.*

small
Little, small: *lligi.*
Small: *damaa me; maasei; vaaligi.*
Small around, thin: *longosaa.*
Very small: *vaaligiligi.*

smaller
Make smaller: *diinei mai.*
Smaller, lesser (in rank, importance, strength, development, etc.): *kii iho.*

smallness
Smallness: *laudodole; legalega.*

smart
Smart, intelligent, clever: *heiangi.*

smarting
Smarting of skin which has been cut, or of an abrasion, when in contact with seawater, etc.: *kala*$_1$.

smear
Apply liquid on, smear on: *hulu*$_2$.

smeared
Smeared with grease or paint or food, etc.: *hulubala.*

smell
Odor, smell (of something), greasy: *nnamu.*
Smell (something): *dungu.*
Smell (something) by sniffing, kiss (Polynesian style): *oso.*

smile
Smile (esp. for no good reason or when embarrassed): *gada gimoo.*
Smile: *dele de gada.*

smoke
Smoke cigarettes: *gai de baibu.*
Smoke, steam: *useahi.*
Suck, smoke (cigarettes): *ssunu*$_2$.

smooth
Smooth: *malali.*
Smooth seas: *hagamalino.*
To be dry and smooth: *pulu.*
To smooth rough edges: *diinei.*

snake
Eel, any long worm, snake: *labodo.*

snake eel
Eel sp.: snake eel: *labodo-sisi.*

snapped
Snapped off: *hhadi.*

snapper
Fish sp.: (The native term is applied to many spp.): damselfish, snapper: *dagugu.*
Fish sp.: snapper (The native term is applied to many spp.): *muu*$_2$.
Fish sp.: snapper (= large *babudaea*): *daaea.*
Fish sp.: snapper (= small *dada*): *datada*$_2$.
Fish sp.: snapper (= small *daea*): *babu-daaea.*
Fish sp.: snapper?: *muu-madagao.*
Fish sp.: snapper: *balu-udu; dagabe; dangau-daa-sissisi; dangau-dongi; dangau-laha; dangau-paava; ngudula; udu.*

snare
To snare birds (with a loop on the end of a pole): *dada manu.*

sneak
Sneak a look: *dili gaiaa; dilo gaiaa.*
To sneak into another's house at night for the purpose of having sexual relations: *moe dolo.*

sneeze
Sneeze: *mahedua.*
Sneeze loudly: *paa de mahedua.*

snipe
Bird sp.: Japanese snipe (*Capella hardwickii*): *googoo*$_2$.

so
But, and, then, so: *gai*$_3$.

so!
So!: *ee laa.*

soak
Soak (in water): *buibui; tao.*

soar
Soar or glide in the air: *maangi.*

soft
Allow to become soft: *hagabala.*
Make soft: *hagabalabala.*
Soft (of skin or paper): *laubalabala.*
Soft: *maluu*.*
Soft, mushy, offering no resistance: *bala.*
Very soft or weak (of things only): *balabala.*

soft-skinned
Soft-skinned: *gili dama.*

soft-spoken
Gentle, mild-mannered, soft-spoken: *daudonu.*

softly
Carefully, gently, softly: *maalie.*

soil
Black soil: *gelegele uli.*
Sand, soil, dirty: *gelegele.*

solar plexus
Solar plexus (considered the seat of feeling): *lalo ade.*

soldier
Bodyguard, soldier: *daagami*.*
Soldier: *daane hebagi.*

sole
Sole (of the foot): *alohi vae.*

some
Some: *hanu*$_1$.
Some more: *hanu ange.*

somewhat
Somewhat *moosugia*: *moosugia ange.*

son-in-law
Parent-in-law, child-in-law, mother-in-law, father-in-law, son-in-law, daughter-in-law: *saulaba.*

song
A church song: *daahili daumaha.*
A dirty song: *vaivai daahili.*
A love song: *daahili dau soa.*
A popular (secular) song: *daahili lo te gohu.*
A song formerly sung while dancing: *muaamoni*.*
A song which is for amusement only (one which is not 'serious', i.e., not religious): *daahili hagadaahao.*
Song: *daahili.*
Song service (in church): *daumaha daahili.*

soon
Soon (will happen): *savaa.*
Soon —: *dee savaa (naa) de —.*

Sophora
Plant sp.: silver bush (*Sophora tormentosa* L.): *dangaloa*$_1$.

sorcerer
A sorcerer able to take human or non-human shapes: *hilohilo ma eidu.*
Magician, sorcerer: *tangada hai sauaa.*

sorcery
Sorcery (made with chants): *huuhuaa me.*
Sorcery: *hai huuhuaa me; helau.*

sore
A large sore (on the body): *mangeo.*
A sore on the lips (believed to result from missing a meal): *namuaa.*
A wound or large sore (on the body): *maanuga.*
Sore in the muscles: *ssae aalanga.*

soreness
Soreness of the eyes after a fishing expedition (from the glare of the sun): *mataia.*

sorry
Feel very sorry for: *vvela de aloha.*

sort
Kind (of), sort (of), variety (of): *daaganga*$_3$*; hagadaaganga.*

sort of
Sort of —: *hai me ma —.*

sort out
Sort out from: *hili gee.*
Treat differently, sort out, part (e.g., hair): *vae*$_1$.

soul
Spirit, soul, name-group: *hagasaalunga*$_2$.

Soulamea
Plant sp.: tree sp. (*Soulamea amara* Lam.): *hagabini*$_1$.

sound
A squeaking sound: *ngisi.*
A voice, a sound, an intonational pattern: *leo.*

sour
Bitter, sour: *mmala.*

source
Origin, source: *damadanga.*

spaced
Apart, widely spaced: *massanganga.*

spacious
Large in volume or capacity, spacious inside: *lodo laanui.*
Spacious: *masoasoa.*
Too big (clothes), spacious: *oo tanga.*

spade
Taro spade: *goo*$_2$.

span
The span between the outstretched thumb and the little finger: *ianga.*

sparkling
Sparkling: *labalaba.*

sparks
Sparks: *galo ahi.*

speak
Cause someone to speak: *hagabasa.*
Speak (or express oneself) strangely: *basa gee.*
Speak (or sing) with phelgm in one's throat: *hagili.*
Speak arrogantly: *basa hagamao lunga.*
Speak as an elder (treating the hearer as a child): *basa madua.*
Speak badly of someone: *basa baubau.*
Speak directly (so that one's meaning is clear): *basa soe.*
Speak disconnectedly with rage: *basa degidegi.*
Speak harshly: *basa pada.*
Speak humbly: *basa hagamao lalo.*
Speak in riddles or aphoristically or in parables: *basa hagasengasenga.*
Speak indirectly (so that the meaning is vague): *basa lilo.*
Speak loudly: *basa gi lunga.*
Speak moderately: *basa dau donu; basa maalie.*
Speak sagely: *basa gelo.*
Speak senselessly: *basa senga.*
Speak so as to change the impression one's previous words have made: *basa hagassee.*
Speak undiplomatically: *basa dua nnui.*
Speak ungrammatically: *basa too gee.*
Speak, pronounce, utter (words): *dagu*$_1$.
Speak, talk, say: *basa*$_1$.

speaking
Manner of speaking, idiolect, dialect: *baasanga.*

spear
A spear or harpoon to which a line is attached: *dao tili.*
A spear with a barb: *dao hagamaadau.*
A spear with a hinged barb: *dao malui.*
A spear, branch of (part of): *dao*$_2$.
To spear (someone): *velo.*
To spear (something) without releasing the spear: *velo daohi.*
To spear something and hold it against something solid with the spear: *velo suunugi.*

special
Special one, important one: *daane ssili dala.*

speech
Word, language, speech: *muna.*

speed
Rush, speed up: *hagamalibi.*
To speed up (to get over with): *hagaligiligi.*

spherical
Round, spherical, circular: *moe*$_2$.

spider
Spider: *neveneve.*

spider conch
Mollusk sp.: spider conch: *anga-baabaa.*

spider lily
Plant sp.: spider lily (*Hymenocallis littoralis* (Jacq.) Salisb.): *giebu.*

spider web
Spider web: *hale neveneve.*

spill
Pour out, spill out (sand): *llingi.*
Spill out little by little: *malingilingi.*

spilled
Spilled, poured out: *malingi.*

spin
Roll over or about, turn (as of a wheel), spin, revolve, rotate: *dige.*

spine
Appendage, fin, spine (extending from a fish, etc.): *dala*$_4$.
Spine (of the body): *ivi laanui.*

spiny puffer
Fish sp.: spiny puffer: *daudu.*

spiny starfish
Spiny starfish: *dolo-mea.*

spirit
A spirit which is worshipped: *diinonga.*
Ghost, spirit, god: *eidu.*
Spirit, soul, name-group: *hagasaalunga*$_2$.
The spirit of a human being after his death: *samouli.*

spirit possession
Spirit possession: *hagavvale.*

spit
Spit out (esp. food): *luei.*
Spit, drool, sputum: *saavale.*

splash
Splash (once): *kobu.*
Splash (or make noise like splashing) repeatedly: *gobugobu.*
The splash of a small object (like a *dango*) hitting the water at high velocity: *kobu dango.*
To splash water on something with the hand: *dabui.*

splashed
Splashed, sprinkled: *pii.*

split
Be split open: *mahanga.*
Split in two: *hhanga lua.*
Split open, open up, or separate, all at once: *hhanga.*

spoil
Spoil (a child): *hakide gee.*
Spoil (children), bring up (children) badly: *haele sala.*
Spoil children: *hakide gauligi.*

spoiled
Fermented, spoiled (of cooked food left too long): *vii.*
Spoiled (having acquired a bad habit): *gu gide huu.*

Spondylus
Mollusk sp.: *Spondylus* sp.: *hadu-uaua; onodaa; sangatai.*

sponge sp.
Sponge sp. (several spp.): *galagala.*
Sponge sp.: *galavagu.*

spoon
Scoop up (liquids only), spoon: *asu.*

spoonful
Mouthful or spoonful of food: *maanga.*

spot
A spot (e.g., on the skin): *dongi.*

spotted
Spotted (covered with spots): *daubulebule.*

spouse
One's first spouse: *aduisiisi.*
Spouse: *bodu; hagaasoaso; soolonga.*
To have a spouse: *hai de ama.*

spray
Dust, gas, steam, vapor, fumes, spray (e.g., of waves): *mama.*
Spray: *sii valavala.*

spread
Spread news or rumors: *dele de longo.*
Spread one's legs (esp. a woman in the act of sexual intercourse): *hela**.
Spread one's legs: *hhanga luu vae.*
Spread one's legs wide apart at one time: *hhela**.
Spread venereal disease: *hilo saele.*

spread out
Laid out or spread out all over: *holadage.*
To be spread out: *madoha.*
To spread out (something): *doha.*
To spread out, or lay out flat, something which is folded, piled up, or bent, etc.: *hola.*

sprinkled
Splashed, sprinkled: *pii.*

sprinkling
Sprinkling (of rain): *mmudi.*

sprint
Sprint (footrace of short distance): *gave hua podo.*

sprout
A sprout of a plant suitable for planting: *uli*$_2$.
To sprout (of plants): *velo de baledilo.*
To sprout roots: *velo aga.*

sprouting
The sprouting of plants, etc., in great numbers: *matili mai.*

sputum
Spit, drool, sputum: *saavale.*
Sputum: *loada.*
Viscous sputum: *galu.*

square
Having corners, square, rectangular: *tuu dege.*

squashed
Be squashed: *balaginagina.*

squat
Fat and squat and ugly: *huubuudoi.*

squeaking
A squeaking sound: *ngisi.*

squeeze
To squeeze by grabbing: *kumi*$_1$.

squid
Squid (3 types): *nguu*$_2$.

squint
Squint (eyes), frown: *hakohu luu mada.*

squirrelfish
Fish sp.: squirrelfish (The native term is applied to many spp.): *malau*$_2$.
Fish sp.: squirrelfish (= small *malaugulu*?: *giigii*$_2$.
Fish sp.: squirrelfish: *baba*$_2$; *daa*$_3$; *dala-loa; daladala*$_4$; *haa-dolo.*

stab
Pierce (slightly), stab (lightly), lance (e.g., a boil): *sugi*$_1$.
Stab with a sharp object, pierce with a sharp object, sew, string (flowers or fish, etc.): *dui.*
Stab, pierce: *velo.*
Stab, skewer: *daalo.*

stabbed
To have been stabbed (esp. accidentally by *hanga*): *daaloa.*

staccato
The staccato sound of one hard object being struck against another: *bapabu.*

stagger
Stagger about (from a head injury), move as though unconscious: *see boiboi saele.*
Stagger backwards (e.g., under load): *hanohano dua.*

stain
A stain (impermanent) left by something wet: *suanga.*
A stain which has left a dry residue: *sua bagu.*
Stain (permanent): *doi.*

stained
Stained all over: *suasuanga.*
Stained in one place: *ssuanga.*

stairway
Ladder, stairway: *gaagenga.*

stalk
A stalk of the elephant-ear plant (*ngaungau*): *laba ngaugau.*

stammer
Stammer (from nervousness): *sassasa.*

stand
Stand around (idly): *duuduu*$_2$.
Stand leaning: *haalala.*
Stand on one's hands: *hidi.*
Stand on tiptoes, rise up (as a person does): *hagaduuduu.*
Stand, situated: *duu*$_2$.

stand out
Stand out from (others in a group) in distance or height: *sili gee.*

standing
Standing out all over (of feathers, etc.): *devedeve.*

star
Morning star: *de heduu o taiao.*
Shooting star: *dangaloa*$_3$.
Star, planet: *heduu.*

stare
Look at, stare: *galo*$_1$.
Stare at: *haaina.*
Stare at people indiscreetly (esp. strangers): *haaina dangada.*
Stare at, observe closely: *daumada.*

starfish
Cushion starfish: *hadu-mangeo.*

Spiny starfish: *dolo-mea.*
Starfish: *manu-mangamanga*$_1$.

starling
Bird sp.: starling (*Apolonis opacus*): *moso.*

start
Initiate, begin, start: *ladi.*
Start: *daamada.*
Start a fire (or an engine): *dahu.*
Start again: *daamada age.*
Start again, reoccur: *ahe age.*
Start or begin (singing or fighting only): *langi*$_1$.

started
To have started it: *damadaa.*

startle
Startle: *hagalele mouli.*

startled
Easily startled, skittish, wild (of animals): *aada.*

status
A status level: *liiliagi.*

stay
Stay for only a short time: *dee mahana tae.*
Stay for only a very short time: *dee baa tae.*
Stay, sit, stop: *noho.*
Take a nap, stay overnight (away from home): *seni iho.*

steal
Steal: *galasi.*
Steal, dishonest, cheat: *gaiaa.*
Take something, steal something: *bogo.*
To steal after having sort of asked for: *hai me galasi.*

steam
Dust, gas, steam, vapor, fumes, spray (e.g., of waves): *mama.*
Smoke, steam: *useahi.*

steel
Stainless steel: *baalanga tea.*

steep
Steep (inclination): *hadi haho.*

steer
Steer (a canoe): *ulungi.*
Steer (e.g., a canoe): *bale*$_2$.
Steer toward (away from) land: *pale age (iho).*
To steer a canoe to the side away from its outrigger (opp. of *baabaa ama*): *baabaa gadea.*

stem
Stem, base, foot (e.g., of a hill), stump: *dahido.*
The stem of the coconut: *mada-galisi.*

stench
Stench: *nnamu hagaduugia.*

step
Step on, kick with one's heel: *dagahi.*

stepfather
Stepfather: *damana mai i daha.*

stepmother
Stepmother: *dinana mai i daha.*

stern
Stern: *muli moni.*

stick
Wood, stick (of wood): *laagau.*

stick$_1$
stick against (something), go with someone: *hagapigi ange.*

stick out
Stick out one's tongue: *hagasomo de alelo.*
To stick out one's tongue: *hagasomo.*

sticky
Sticky, greasy: *baalau.*
To make sticky: *hagabiigia.*
Way of making sticky: *hagabiiginga.*

stiff
Stiff (like a heavy fishing pole): *sago.*
Stiff: *lau makaga.*

still
Calm (weather), still (wind): *malino.*

still$_1$
still (as in 'he is still coming'): *goi*$_1$.

stilts
Stilts, walk on stilts: *dookalala.*

stimulate
To stimulate a desire for: *hagalodo.*

stinging
Stinging of one's eyes (e.g., from salt water): *mmala luu mada.*

stingray
Fish sp.: stingray?: *mamu-duagaa.*

stingy
Stingy: *gailalopoli.*

stink
Allow to stink: *hagapilo.*
Stink: *pilo; ssongo.*

stir
Stir: *galo$_3$; saugalo.*
Stir up: *kalo$_3$.*

stolen
Stolen: *gaiaadia.*

stomach
Stomach: *danngaho.*

stone
Any stone of volcanic origin: *hadugolaa.*
Stone, rock, a piece of weathered coral: *hadu$_2$.*

stone-fish
Fish sp.: stone-fish: *nohu.*

stools
To have bloody stools: *magi hongagelegele todo.*

stop
Stay, sit, stop: *noho.*
Stop (someone or something): *haganoho.*
Stop bleeding: *tuu todo.*
Stop suddenly: *tuu hagalele.*
Stop swimming (and come up on land): *ea age.*
Stop swimming: *ea.*

stop!
Stop!: *lava sili.*

stopped
Stopped, ended: *sili$_1$.*

store
Store: *hale goloa; hale hagao me.*

storekeeper
Storekeeper: *dangada hagao me.*

storm
An electrical storm: *dada de uila.*

storm beach
Storm beach (on the seaward reef): *mada sua hadu.*
Storm beach: *sua hadu.*

stormy
Becoming stormy (of the sea): *langa de moana.*

story
A story which is not true: *dalanga a kai.*
A story which is not true, a made-up story: *vaalanga a kai.*
Legend, story: *daalanga$_3$; kai$_4$.*

strabismus
Strabismus (esp. the form in which one eye is turned outward from the nose): *kalo gee.*

straggly
Straggly (hair or feathers): *boda.*

straight
Having straight hair (not kinky or wavy): *laussoe.*
Inclined, slanting, not straight, not perpendicular to: *salau.*
Somewhat level or straight: *soesoe.*
Straight as can be: *soe daa dahi.*
Straight course (of a canoe): *dui.*
Straight or level all over (as a playing field): *soesoe.*
Straight up: *soe age.*
Straight, not crooked: *soe.*
Vertical, straight up and down: *duu gaso.*

straight-edged
Straight-edged: *maselesele.*

straighten
Straighten out: *hagassoe.*

strands
Fine threads or strands: *huga.*
Strands (of cloth): *gano siga.*

strange
Strange: *gee.*

strangers
Foreigners, strangers: *dangada henua gee.*

strap
Strap, harness: *gaaui$_2$.*

stream
A stream or jet of water: *sii.*

strength
Strong, strength, force, power, energy: *mmahi.*

stretch
Stretch: *llena.*

stretchable
Stretchable: *malenalena.*
Stretched, stretchable: *malena.*

stretched
Equally stretched (of two or more ropes): *dau ngaadahi*$_2$.
Stretched, stretchable: *malena.*
Tightly stretched (not slack): *dau makaga.*

strike
Hit, strike, beat: *daa*$_1$.
Punch, hit, strike: *dugi*$_1$.
Strike (a match): *dale.*
Strike (give a blow to): *hagaili.*

string
A string of fish: *dui mamu.*
Stab with a sharp object, pierce with a sharp object, sew, string (flowers or fish, etc.): *dui.*
String twirled from coconut fiber, sennit: *liholiho.*

striped
Striped (having stripes): *sissisi.*
Striped (with stripes): *daasissisi.*
Striped (with thin lines): *sisi galisi.*

stroke
A steady stroke (as of an adze): *dili.*
Stroke, rub gently: *mmulu.*

stroll
Walk barefoot, stroll: *ngadi seesee.*

strong
Big (and therefore good), strong, tremendous: *dee lahilahia.*
Having special ability (strength, power, etc.) which others do not have, a strong or powerful (person): *iai sago.*
Strong (person): *hai mogomogo.*
Strong, strength, force, power, energy: *mmahi.*

struggle
Struggle (e.g., to complete work): *hagaduu ngae.*
Struggle: *gegeli.*
Struggle to get free: *daasugi.*

strut
Walk proudly, strut: *deledele kau.*

stubborn
An argumentative and stubborn person: *gaa de malala.*
Disobedient, stubborn, talk back to: *hagamanege.*
Stubborn (esp. in maintaining one's own superiority): *lodo manege.*
Stubborn: *makaga lodo.*
Stubborn, willful: *hai de hai.*

stuck
Be caught on, stuck on: *lave.*
Be stuck: *pigi.*
Be stuck in the throat (esp. fish bones): *laoa.*
Be stuck to completely: *biigia.*
Make stuck to: *hagapiigia.*

study
Study, attempt to memorize: *hagamaumau*$_2$.

stuff
Fill, stuff (something into or full of): *hhao.*

stuffed
Tight (of clothes), stuffed: *kabi.*

stumble
Stumble and fall: *lapede.*
Stumble on: *laavea.*
Stumble, trip (fall): *badodi.*

stump
Stem, base, foot (e.g., of a hill), stump: *dahido.*

stupid
Stupid (like an animal): *senga manu.*
Stupid ass!: *tangada ssele.*

sturdy
Not sturdy, rickety: *ngaangaa.*

stutter
Stutter: *basa hagaeaea; hagaeaea.*

style
A style of construction (consistently followed): *hagaduuduulanga.*

submarine
Submarine: *moni sulu.*

succeed
Succeed: *sula.*

succeeded
To have appeared or succeeded: *sulangia.*

successful
Successful in obtaining what one wants (things): *mau me.*

suck
Suck in air (esp. when asleep or unconscious): *hhoda age.*
Suck on the breast, nurse (at the breast): *unuunu.*
Suck one's finger: *ssomo*$_2$.
Suck, smoke (cigarettes): *ssunu*$_2$.

Suck, suction (e.g., of sea current): *mmidi.*

sucker

A sucker (a person who is easily fooled): *dangada dau duadae.*
Be a sucker, be fooled easily: *dau duadae.*
Gullible, be a sucker: *duadae.*

suckle

Suckle (at the breast): *haau.*
Suckle, nurse (feed milk): *hagauu*$_3$.

suction

Suck, suction (e.g., of sea current): *mmidi.*
Suction of a sea current, undertow: *hagammidi.*

sue

Sue (in court), complain about (to the authorities): *vange gi de hainga.*

suffer

Receive one's punishment, suffer: *paa ono maahana.*
Suffer a setback: *hanohano dua.*
Suffer, be in pain: *sae*$_2$.
Suffer, punish: *hagaduasala.*

sufficient

Sufficient: *ao*$_2$.
Sufficient for: *dohu ange.*
Sufficient for the purpose or need: *aamia.*
Sufficient, enough: *dohu.*

sugarcane

Plant sp.: sugarcane: *dolo*$_2$.

suicide

Commit or attempt suicide: *hagamagau.*
Commit suicide: *hagamaaileele.*

suited

Suited to: *gugu.*
Suited to, fit (with), appropriate to: *heohi ange.*

sun

Sun: *laa*$_2$.

sunburned

Sunburned: *ula de gili.*

Sunday

Sunday ('seventh day'): *Hidu-laangi.*
Sunday: *Laangidabu.*

sunk

Nearly sunk: *dauaabulu.*

suntanned

Suntanned: *gili laa.*

supernatural

Supernatural power: *mana*.*
Treat as a totem, worship, treat as a supernatural being: *eidu ai.*

superstitious

Superstitious: *hagaduu eidu.*

supplies

Gear, tools, goods, supplies (but not food): *goloa*$_2$.

support

Support (e.g., the weight put upon —): *lango*$_1$.
Support (someone, with material things): *hakoloa.*

sure

Certain, sure, graceful, definitely: *too donu.*
Know, understand, be intimate with, sure of (and willing to say): *iloo.*

surf

A wave, the surf: *beau.*
Slip, slide, to ride, to surf: *sege.*

surf-riding

Surf-riding (for amusement): *hagasegesege.*

surface

To surface (while swimming): *ea.*

surfacing

Surfacing (of flying fish): *lele age.*

surprise

Surprise (someone): *hagalele mouli.*

surprised

Surprised: *lele mouli.*

surround

Surround: *duuli.*

survive

Survive, safe: *ola.*

suspect

Suspect that — (wouldn't be surprised if)...: *vanei.*

suspend

Suspend from: *tagi.*

suspended

Hung up, suspended from: *dau*$_2$.

suspicion

A suspicion which proves to be true: *maoli°.*

suspicious
A suspicious character: *halehale dangada.*
Be suspicious of (someone): *duguagi.*
Suspicious by nature: *hagaduu gaiaa.*

swallow
Swallow: *holo.*

swamp
Taro bog, swamp: *husi.*

swamp taro
Plant sp.: swamp taro (*Cyrtosperma chamissonis*): *bulaga**.
Plant sp.: swamp taro (*Cyrtosperma chamissonis*), also the corm of this plant: *daogoli.*

sway
Cause to dance or sway: *hagaanu.*

swear
Foulmouthed, swear: *vaivai basa.*
Swear to the truth of: *hagatoo donu.*

sweat
Sweat, perspiration: *daadaa*$_2$.
To sweat: *sali daadaa.*

sweep
Shave, sweep, brush off (once): *dahi*$_2$.
Sweep or clean up trash: *sao gainga.*
Sweep, clean up: *ssao*$_1$.

sweet
Sweet: *maangalo; maimai*$_1$.

sweet-talker
Sweet-talker: *maimai de ngudu.*

sweeten
Sweeten: *hagamaimai.*

swell
A swell (of the sea): *hua*$_1$.

swell up
To swell up (from being filled with air — like a balloon): *hakiigia.*

swelling
A swelling (on the skin, or of dough, etc.): *hua*$_1$.
Swelling of the eyes (after crying): *lleu luu mada.*
Swelling of the testicles: *giba.*

swift
Fast, swift: *gemo.*

swift$_1$
bird sp.: white-rumped swift (*Apus pacificus*) (The native term applies possibly to several spp.): *gauea.*

swim
To swim (or make motions of swimming, as babies do): *kau*$_2$.

swing
A swing (made of rope): *daula hagalevaleva.*
To swing: *hagaleva.*
To swing one's arms (when walking): *dili de lima.*

swollen
Bloated, inflated, swollen up, bulging: *lengi.*
Swollen: *bugubugu; pugu.*
Swollen lips (from eating spicy foods or foods to which one is allergic): *lleu luu malau ngudu.*

swoop
Swoop down, swoop across: *hagatili.*

sword fern
Plant sp.: sword fern (The native term applies possibly to several spp.): *lluhe.*

sympathetic
Feel sorry for or sympathetic toward: *aloha ai.*

Tacca
Plant sp.: Polynesian arrowroot (*Tacca leontopetaloides* (L.) O.K.): *bie.*

tack
To tack a canoe (by transferring the mast from one end of the canoe to the other): *sigi.*

tackle box
Fishing tackle box: *ngavesi haangoda.*

tail
Tail: *sugi*$_2$.

take
Bring up, put up, take up: *vage*$_1$.
Do or take by force, rape: *hai gi de mahi.*
Take (someone) along (with one) (esp. carrying, etc.): *gaaui*$_1$*.
Take: *kave.*
Take a little (or few) at a time: *kave dagi de momo.*
Take a lot of: *daabeduge adu ange.*
Take all (of something): *lludu.*
Take from the bottom (top): *mada age (iho).*
Take from the bottom upward: *ulu age.*

Take medicine: *gai valaai.*
Take or obtain something by force: *lugu.*
Take precautions: *keeligi.*
Take sides against, oppose: *hai baasi.*
Take something, steal something: *bogo.*
Take the bait tentatively (of fish): *gai busibusi.*
Take the worst or smallest (best or biggest): *mada age (iho).*
Take turns: *hagasolo.*
Take up a string figure (from another's hands): *doo*$_1$.

talk
Disobedient, stubborn, talk back to: *hagamanege.*
Small talk: *ngadi basa.*
Speak, talk, say: *basa*$_1$.
Talk (someone) into (something): *hagasabala.*
Talk back: *baasanga tugi ange muna.*
Talk to one another: *hemuu.*
Talkative, chatterbox, talk animatedly: *hai daalanga.*
Talkative, chatterbox, talk at great length: *ili taalanga.*
Try to talk into: *usuusu ange.*

talkative
A talkative, deceitful person: *dama naale.*
Talkative: *lodo basa.*
Talkative, chatterbox, talk animatedly: *hai daalanga.*
Talkative, chatterbox, talk at great length: *ili taalanga.*
Talkative, indiscreet: *vava de ngudu.*
Talkative, loquacious: *ngudu leelee*.*

tame
Tame: *dala*$_2$.

tang
Fish sp.?: tang? (a kind of *igauli?*): *maleasa.*
Fish sp.: convict tang: *manini.*
Fish sp.: tang (2 sorts): *igauli; laumele.*
Fish sp.: tang?: *gelu-uliuli.*
Fish sp.: tang: *abi; balangi; bulaga-a-leo; gelu-agau; gelu-hai-vaelo; igauli-sissisi; sobaga; sugi-daa.*

tangled
Wound around, tangled up, confused: *vini.*

tap
Hit or tap with the hand or foot: *badu.*

taro
Plant sp.: a variety of taro: *manu-alioo.*
Plant sp.: swamp taro (*Cyrtosperma chamissonis*): *bulaga*.*
Plant sp.: swamp taro (*Cyrtosperma chamissonis*), also the corm of this plant: *daogoli.*
Plant sp.: taro (*Colocasia esculenta*), also the corm of this plant: *dalo.*

taro bog
Plot of taro bog, boggy soil: *bela.*
Taro bog, swamp: *husi.*

taro fibers
Taro fibers: *agoago*$_2$.

taro spade
Taro spade: *goo*$_2$.

tarry
Be late, tarry: *hagamuli*$_1$.
Tarry in order to avoid: *hagamademade*$_1$ —.

taste
Taste (food): *mami ange.*
Taste (of something): *mami.*
Taste (something) a little bit: *mami age.*
Taste strange (of liquid): *daava.*

tasty
Tasty (especially of taro): *kanamalie.*

tattle
To tattle: *adi longo.*

tattler
Bird sp.: Polynesian tattler (*Heteroscelus brevipes*): *goigoi*$_2$.
Bird sp.: Polynesian tattler? (*Heteroscelus brevipes*): *dilidili-dogi.*
Bird sp.: wandering tattler? (*Heteroscelus incanus*): *lahulahu*$_2$.

tattletale
Gossipy person, tattletale: *tangada adi longo.*

tattoo
To tattoo: *daa*$_1$.

teach
Learn, teach: *ago.*
Show, teach: *hagaago.*

teacher
Teacher, preacher: *dangada agoago.*

teaching
Learning, teaching: *agoago*$_1$.

tear
Rip, tear, deflower (a virgin): *ssae*$_1$.

tear$_1$
to tear (in the eyes because, e.g., of smoke): *sali loimada.*

tears
Tears: *loimada.*

tease
Tease cruelly: *'hagammae manava.*

teeth
Incisor teeth: *niho hagadolo.*
Permanent teeth (appearing after deciduous teeth): *niho gai.*
Teeth with cavities: *niho gaina.*
Tooth, teeth: *niho.*

tell
Say or tell (esp. in confidence): *agu*$_1$.
Tell, say to, relate: *dala*$_3$.

tell apart
Hard to tell apart from: *delaa tee madea.*

Tellinidae
Mollusk sp.: *Tellinidae* spp.: *ginigini*$_2$.

tempted
Weak-willed, easily tempted: *lodo baageaa.*

ten
Ten (in enumeration and compounds only): *hulu*$_3$.
Ten (objects): *madaangahulu.*

tenderly
Tenderly: *dua lligi.*

tendon
Vein, tendon, nerve, plastic filament: *uaua*$_3$.

Terebridae
Mollusk sp.: auger shell (*Terebridae* sp.): *hakolona.*

Terminalia
Plant sp.: tree sp.: Terminalia tree (*Terminalia samoensis* Rech.): *kini*$_2$.
Plant sp.: tropical almond (*Terminalia catappa* L.): *hua-laagau.*

Terminalia tree
Plant sp.: tree sp.: Terminalia tree (*Terminalia samoensis* Rech.): *kini*$_2$.

termite
Termite: *goa.*

tern
Bird sp.: fairy tern (*Gygis alba*): *agiagi.*
Bird sp.: tern? (a vagrant sp., rarely seen): *dala-hagalulu-madangi; dala-moana; dala*$_5$.
Bird sp.: white tern?: *lebidi.*

testament
Testament: *boolonga.*

testicles
Seed, testicles: *golee.*
Testicles: *bulabula.*

Thais
Mollusk sp.: *Thais armigera*: *gammenge-olomanga.*
Mollusk sp.: *Thais luteostoma*: *gammenge-hai-gili-dabeo.*

that
That one (near you): *denaa.*
That one (over there): *delaa.*

thatch
(A piece of) thatch made from coconut palm frond: *langadala.*
To roof (a house), to thatch (a house): *odo*$_1$.

thatch-roofed
Thatch-roofed house (of palm frond thatch): *hale langadala.*
Thatch-roofed house (of pandanus leaf thatch): *hale lau.*

The
Plant sp.: tree sp.: milo tree (*The spesiapopulnea* Sol. ex Correa): *milo*$_2$.

the
The (several): *denga*$_1$.
The (several) I have in mind: *dengaa.*
The one: *de.*
The two: *luu.*
The, thing, it: *de ia.*

their
Their: *selaadeu; selaau.*
Their one: *delaadeu; delaau.*
Their several: *alaadeu; alaau; olaadeu; olaau.*
Their two: *luaalaadeu; luaalaau; luoolaadeu; luoolaau.*

then
But, and, then, so: *gai*$_3$.

Then what? (distant future): *aahee naa.*
Then what? (immediate future): *aahee nei.*
Then which?: *aahee huu.*
There in the distance, then (past): *laa*$_1$.

there
Be (present), have, there is...: *iai.*
There in the distance: *kilaa.*
There in the distance, then (past): *laa*$_1$.
There near you: *kinaa; naa.*

therefore
Therefore (with respect to that there): *delaa ai.*
Therefore (with respect to this here): *denei ai.*
Therefore (with respect to this, there near you, or concerning, you): *denaa ai.*

these
At this time, these days: *honga iainei.*
These: *anei.*
These now: *anei nei.*

they
They (things) are...: *ni*$_2$.
They: *gilaadeu.*
They two: *gilaau.*

thick
Thick (not watery): *haduhadu*$_2$.
Thick (object): *maadolu.*

thicker
Thicker (line or rope, etc.): *dua gi lunga.*

thief
A habitual thief: *huna me.*
Thief: *dangada gaiaa.*

thieving
Thieving: *magua.*

thigh
The back of the thigh: *dahido vae.*
Thigh: *gauanga.*

thigh bone
Dislocated thigh bone: *gauanga mahagi; sege de gauanga.*

thin
Skinny, thin (lacking in flesh): *saava.*
Skinny, thin (person), emaciated: *iviivia.*
Small around, thin: *longosaa.*
Thin (bony): *kivi.*
Thin (line or rope, etc.): *dua lligi.*
Thin (of long flat object): *daballahi.*
Thin (pl.): *llahi*$_1$.
Thin and straight (of a person): *solovaani.*

thing
The, thing, it: *de ia.*
Thing: *daane; me.*
Thing of importance, worthwhile: *me dau.*
Useless thing: *me ssongo aha.*

think
Think about oneself: *maanadu iho.*
Think up: *maanadu age.*
Think, think about: *maanadu.*

thirsty
Thirsty: *dai hieunu; hieunu.*
To be very thirsty: *buni de ua.*

thirty
Thirty: *matolu.*

this
This is another one!: *denei ange.*
This is exactly right!: *denei ange maalie.*
This one (near you): *denaa.*
This one: *denei.*

thoracic cavity
Rib cage, thoracic cavity: *hale i lodo.*

thoroughfare
Thoroughfare: *dagalia*$_1$.

those
Those (away from the speaker): *anaa.*
Those over there: *alaa.*

thought
Idea, thought: *maanadu.*
Thought: *hagasaele.*

thousand
Thousand: *mano.*

thousands
Hundreds of thousands: *seguli.*
Tens of thousands: *semada.*
Thousands: *mmano.*
Thousands and thousands: *manomano.*

threadfin
Fish sp.: threadfin: *ganae-oo.*

threads
Fine threads or hairs or fibers (in feather or leaf, etc.): *amu ligi.*

Fine threads or strands: *huga.*

threaten
To threaten violence: *hagabaagava.*

three
Three: *dolu.*

throat
Throat (inside): *holomanga.*
Throat (of fish only): *alohaha.*

throw
Throw: *maga*$_1$.
Throw a spear: *velo tili.*
To throw a wrestler using one's hip: *hagahidi i tege.*

throw away
Let go, throw away, lose something: *dili.*
Throw away: *tili gee.*

throw out
Dump, throw out (discard): *liagi.*

thumb
Thumb: *madannia madua.*

thunder
Rolling of thunder: *paa de hatuli.*
Thunder: *hatuli.*

Thursday
Thursday: *Haa-laangi.*

tickle
Tickle: *nengenenge.*

tickled
Tickled (esp. sexually): *tegi*$_1$.
Tickled (not sexually): *hagategi kano.*
Tickled: *tegi kano.*

ticklish
Ticklish: *degidegi*$_2$.

tidal wave
Tidal wave: *hudaa lolo; lau henua; noomeemea.*

tide
Flood tide: *buaalali.*
Flow of the tide: *hhui mai tai.*
High tide: *honu tai.*
The rsing of the tide: *ua mai.*

tie
Tie: *nnoa.*
Tie up (by winding a rope around a pole): *hagamau*$_3$.
Tie up temporarily (not as securely as if permanently): *hau baba.*
Tie up, fasten by tying (wrapping): *hhau.*
Wrap up, tie up: *saabini.*

tied
Be tied (e.g., in a footrace): *dee hai gee.*
Tied (as with rope): *noa.*
Tied or fastened tightly: *gali.*
Wound around or tied or fastened very tightly: *gali ange.*
Wrapped (tied) around: *llava ai.*

tight
Tight (of clothes), stuffed: *kabi.*

time
Time when, time of: *masavaa*$_1$.

timid
Bashful, shy (timid about attending social affairs), timid: *hagaau gee.*
Timid, shy: *vasu**.

tinnitus
Tinnitus: *gii talinga.*
Tinnitus, a ringing sound in the ear: *dangi talinga.*

tiny
Tiny: *damaa me.*

tip
The tip of anything slender and long (e.g., the tail of an animal): *sugi hagabolebole.*
Tip (of): *mada*$_3$.

tipped
Not level, tipped to one side: *diba*$_1$.

tired
Be tired of eating a particular kind of food: *duugia i de gai.*
Easily tired: *mahi bodo.*
Extremely tired: *too luu bakau.*
Tired: *daalea*$_2$*; dalea.*
Tired of: *duugia.*
Tired of waiting for someone: *valea i de noho.*

tireless
Tireless: *mahi loa.*

tiresome
Tiresome: *hagadaalea*$_2$.

tithe
Collection (in church), offering (in church), sacrifice, tithe: *sigidaumaha.*

title
Name, a title (used as a name): *ingoo.*

to
To it: *ina*$_2$.
To it, for it: *agina.*
Toward, to, in order to: *gi*$_1$.

today
Today (in the past): *anailaa (nei).*
Today (sometime): *ailaa.*

toddy
Fermented *galeve*, palm toddy: *galeve vii.*

toe
Big toe: *dabuvae madua.*
Little toe: *dabuvae sisi.*
Toe, footprint: *dabuvae.*

toenail
Toenail: *angaanga dabuvae.*

together
Be more-or-less together: *bunibuni.*
Closed up, be together (three or more things): *puni.*
Closed up, be together (in a group, or of two individuals): *buni.*

tomorrow
Morning, tomorrow: *daiao.*

tomorrow morning
Tomorrow morning: *taiao daiao.*

tomorrow night
Tomorrow night: *boo aleduu.*

tongs
Fire tongs: *igohi.*

tongue
Tongue: *alelo.*

tonight
Tonight (future): *aboo nei.*
Tonight (past): *anaboo nei.*
Tonight: *aboo.*

too
Exceed (the amount required), too — (e.g., many): *dubu.*
Too much: *gona odi.*
Very, too much: *ga dae laa huu; kona.*

tools
Barber's tools: *goloa duu biho.*
Gear, tools, goods, supplies (but not food): *goloa*$_2$.
Metal-working tools: *goloa baalanga.*
Tools (for work): *goloa hai hegau.*
Tools, equipment (incl. fishing gear): *doonga.*

tooth
Tooth, teeth: *niho.*

top
On top of, on, over, above: *honga.*
Top (toy): *manu hagadigedige.*
Top of the head, bare hilltop: *dumuagi.*
Top of, the position over (something): *elunga.*
Top part: *ulu i lunga.*

topmost
Topmost mast: *ulu*$_2$.
Topmost part of any standing object: *de ulu hagabolehole.*

topple
To topple over: *hidi.*

torn
Torn, deflowered (of a virgin): *masae.*

total
A total of: *hagapuuninga.*

totem
Treat as a totem, worship, treat as a supernatural being: *eidu ai.*

touch
Continuously touch or slap lightly, pat: *baabaa*$_1$.
Touch (someone or something with the hand): *poo ange.*
Touch (two or more things being in contact): *dale.*
Touch (two or more things), be in contact, make contact with uniformly: *baa*$_1$.
Touch —: *hagadale —.*
Touch quickly: *tale.*

tough
A tough man: *tale taane.*
Tough (like meat): *sago.*

Tournefortia
Plant sp.: heliotrope (*Tournefortia argentea* L., = *Messerschmidia argentea* L.): *manu-gili-maau.*

tow
Tow away: *tagi gee.*
Tow, drag: *tagi.*

toward
Toward, to, in order to: *gi*$_1$.

towing
Towing: *daagina.*

toy
Model (or toy) canoe: *moni hagadeledele.*
Toy: *me hagadaahao.*

trachea
Larynx, epiglottis, trachea: *hakii*$_1$.

Trachinotus
Fish sp. (*Trachinotus bailloni*): *bilibili-hadu.*

Trachycardium
Mollusk sp.: *Trachycardium orbita*: *kosi-honga-agau.*

track
A track left by a crawling thing: *doolonga.*
Road, pathway (for going), track: *haiava.*
The place of, the track of (something): *duulanga*$_2$.

trade
Exchange, trade: *hesuihagi.*

trampled
Trampled down (from people walking on): *dagalia*$_1$.

tranquility
Calmness, tranquility, freedom from worries: *lodo baba.*

transfer
Transfer (from one place to another), transplant: *sigi.*
Transfer of a string figure from hand to hand: *doo de —.*

transfiguration
Transfiguration of ghosts or spirits into human form: *hano gi de maalama.*

transfigure
Transfigure: *hagadubu.*
Transfigure into a —: *hagadubu gi se —.*

transmitted
Be transmitted: *dele.*

transplant
To transplant a plant: *sigi manu.*
Transfer (from one place to another), transplant: *sigi.*

transpose
Reverse, transpose: *lui*$_1$.

transposed
Turned (in direction), reversed, transposed: *malui.*

trapezeid crab
Trapezeid crab: *gaibea-lausedi.*

trash
Trash, garbage: *gainga.*

travelled
Heavily travelled: *dagadagalia*$_1$.

treat
Treat (a person) differently from others: *dugu gee.*
Treat as a child: *hagadama.*
Treat as a woman: *hagahahine.*
Treat as an *eidu*: *hagaeidu.*
Treat as having supernatural power: *hagadiinonga.*
Treat differently, sort out, part (e.g., hair): *vae*$_1$.

tree
A food tree on another's land: *hagaaigoli.*
Plant sp.: tree sp.: Alexandrian laurel tree (*Calophyllum inophyllum* L.): *hedau.*

tree sp.
Plant sp.: tree sp. (*Allophylus timorensis* (DC.) Bl.): *dalahalu.*
Plant sp.: tree sp. (*Guettarda speciosa* L.): *bua.*
Plant sp.: tree sp. (*Mammea odorata* (Raf.) Kost.): *voi.*
Plant sp.: tree sp. (*Pisonia grandis* R.B.): *buga.*
Plant sp.: tree sp. (*Soulamea amara* Lam.): *hagabini*$_1$.
Plant sp.: tree sp.: Alexandrian laurel tree (*Calophyllum inophyllum* L.): *hedau.*
Plant sp.: tree sp.: Barringtonia tree (*Barringtonia asiatica* (L.) Kurz): *gavaausu.*
Plant sp.: tree sp.: Hernandia tree (*Hernandia sonora* L.): *bingibingi.*
Plant sp.: tree sp.: Indian coral tree (*Erythrina variegata* L.): *ulu-davage.*
Plant sp.: tree sp.: Indian mulberry tree (*Morinda citrifolia* L.): *bugaliaa.*
Plant sp.: tree sp.: Terminalia tree (*Terminalia samoensis* Rech.): *kini*$_2$.
Plant sp.: tree sp.: a shrubby tree sp. (*Pipturus argenteus* (Forst.f.) Wedd.): *olongaa.*
Plant sp.: tree sp.: a small tree sp. (*Premna obtusifolia* R.Br.): *valovalo.*

Plant sp.: tree sp.: banana tree: *ga-hudi; hudi*$_2$.
Plant sp.: tree sp.: banyan tree (*Ficus prolixa* Forst.): *aoa*$_1$.
Plant sp.: tree sp.: breadfruit: *gulu.*
Plant sp.: tree sp.: coconut tree: *nui.*
Plant sp.: tree sp.: cordia tree (*Cordia subcordata* Lam.): *ganava.*
Plant sp.: tree sp.: hibiscus tree (*Hibiscus tiliaceus* L.): *goehau.*
Plant sp.: tree sp.: milo tree (*The spesiapopulnea* Sol. ex Correa): milo$_2$.
Plant sp.: tree sp.: ochrosia tree (*Ochrosia oppositifolia* (Lam.) K. Sch.): *gahao.*
Plant sp.: tree sp.: pandan tree (*Pandanus dubius* Spreng.): *bagua.*
Plant sp.: tree sp.: pandanus (several varieties): *hala.*

tremble
Tremble or vibrate in the air: *ngalubelube.*

trembling
Trembling: *bolebole; luduludu; pole.*
Trembling of legs: *balu gauanga.*

tremendous
Big (and therefore good), strong, tremendous: *dee lahilahia.*

tremor
The tremor (as though chilled) of a sick person: *magi luduludu.*

trial
Trial or formal inquiry: *siilinga a muna.*

trick
Fool (someone), deceive, trick (someone): *hagasenga.*
Trick (a practical joke): *me hakadanga.*
Trick someone: *hai dahi doo.*
Trick, prank: *doopeva*.*

tricks
Tricks of self-defense (some of which are like judo or karate): *hungi.*

Tridacna
Mollusk sp.: *Tridacna maxima*: *baasua.*
Mollusk sp.: giant clam (*Tridacna squammosa*): *dange.*

triggerfish
Fish sp.: triggerfish: *imu-mea; imu-uli; saulolua.*
Fish sp.: triggerfish, filefish (The native term is applied to many spp.): *sumu*$_2$.

trillion
Trillion (a million million): *duumaa de gelegele.*

trim
To trim: *godi.*

trip
Stumble, trip (fall): *badodi.*

trip$_1$
trip, journey: *hanonga.*

trochus
Mollusk sp.: trochus: *goobai-o-lillo.*

trolling
Trolling: *dada alohagi.*

tropic bird
Bird sp.: white-tailed tropic bird (*Phaethon lepturus*): *davage.*

tropical almond
Plant sp.: tropical almond (*Terminalia catappa* L.): *hua-laagau.*

trouble
Be in trouble, in danger, or in a precarious situation: *vakaa.*
To be in trouble: *duuaa.*

true
Correct (suitable), true: *abo.*
Correct, right, just, fair, true: *heohi.*
Real, true: *abo donu; me abo donu.*

trumpet
A conch shell trumpet: *buu*$_1$.

trumpet fish
Fish sp.: trumpet fish: *loselose-uli.*

trust
Trust, believe: *hagadonu.*
Trust, believe in: *gai*$_1$.

truth
Truth: *me abo (donu); muna abo (donu).*
Truth, right, correct: *donu*$_2$.

try
Try, attempt: *hagatale.*

Tuesday
Tuesday ('second day'): *Lua-laangi.*

tumeric
Plant sp.: tumeric plant (*Curcuma* sp.): *gaalau-ango.*

tuna
A tuna of fair size: *lau de madila.*
A tuna of large size: *lau de ava.*
A tuna of the size next largest to *lau de*

ava: *lau tulugi*.
A very small tuna: *gadagada-a-vaga*.
Fish sp.: skipjack tuna: adu_2.
Fish sp.: tuna sp.: *dagua-bodo; dagua-loa*.
Fish sp.: yellow fin tuna (3 sorts?): $dagua_2$.
The largest sort of tuna: *davaia**.

Turbo
Mollusk sp.: *Turbo petholatus; lipaidonga*.

turbulent
Turbulent (air or seas): *dalebu*.

turn
Roll over or about, turn (as of a wheel), spin, revolve, rotate: *dige*.
To make a sharp turn: daa_1.
To turn the opposite way: *milo gee*.
Turn (in place): *huli*.
Turn (something in direction): lui_1.
Turn (something) end over end: *luilui*.
Turn away from (to avoid), veer: *hhagi gee*.
Turn away from, turn inside out (of clothes): *huligee; huligee*.
Turn back: *dahuli*.
Turn end over end: $libo_1$.
Turn in place (of a person): $libo_1$.
Turn inside out: *ului*.
Twist, turn (something, as a faucet), wind, wring: $milo_1$.

turned
Turned (in direction), reversed, transposed: *malui*.
Turned this way and that way, turned over and over: *maluilui*.

turnstone
Bird sp.: ruddy turnstone (*Arenaria interpres*): *givigivi*.

turtle
A turtle of the largest size: *honu tolo*.
Green turtle (2 varieties): $honu_2$.
Hawksbill turtle: *gea*.
Turtle of a size suitable for eating (not quite as big as *honu tolo*): *honu ssele*.
Turtle ribs (used as knives in rituals): *uhi daguu*.

twenty
Twenty: *madalua*.

twilight
Twilight (in the evening): *malumalu-tangohi*.

twinkling
Twinkling (of many stars or phosphorescent insects, etc.): *bulabula*.
Twinkling, flashing, winking: $dabadaba_1$.

twins
Twins: *maasanga*.

twist
Twist, turn (something, as a faucet), wind, wring: $milo_1$.

twitching
Twitching of an eye: *datada de galomada*.

two
The two: *luu*.
Two: *lua*.

ugly
A foetus which has been aborted, ugly; *dama pala*.
Fat and squat and ugly: *huubuudoi*.
Having flat buttocks, ugly (because not plump): *biihingi*.
Ugly, awful: *dee vaagidee*.

ugly-looking
Ugly-looking: *daadaanga sala*.
Ugly-looking, messy, sloppy: *balaulau*.

umbilical cord
Umbilical cord: *uso*.

umbrella
Umbrella: *goobai dada*.

unafraid
Stupidly unafraid of danger (like *maido*): *senga maido*.

uncle
Father, uncle, senior male relative, male elder, person in a fatherly relationship: *damana*.

unclean
Unclean, unkempt: *dabeo*.

uncluttered
Clear, unobstructed, uncluttered: *malaelae*.

uncomfortable
Uncomfortable (esp. socially): *dee abo*.

unconscious
Die, dead, unconscious: *magau*.
To faint, be unconscious: *ssili mada*.

uncooked
Uncooked, raw: $mada_1$.

uncouth
Uncouth: *dee gagu.*
Uncouth person: *tangada dee doo gi de me.*

uncover
Open (something), uncover: *hhuge.*

uncovered
Opened, uncovered: *mahuge.*

unctuous
Unctuous, cloying, winsome: *ngudu maimai.*

undecided
Indecisive, undecided: *lodo lagolago.*
Undecided: *lua lodo.*

under
Down, under: *lalo.*

underestimate
Underestimate, misjudge: *dee hagabaulia.*

understand
Catch on to, understand: *ssigo.*
Know each other, understand each other: *heiloo.*
Know, understand, be intimate with, sure of (and willing to say): *iloo.*
Realize, understand: *donu iho.*
Understand (someone or something): *donu ange.*
Understand: *donu*$_2$.
Understand one another: *heloongoi.*
Understand somewhat: *donudonu.*

undertow
Suction of a sea current, undertow: *hagammidi.*

undo
Unfasten, undo, untie: *dala*$_1$.

undress
Remove (clothes, etc.), disrobe, undress: *hagaui*$_2$.

uneconomical
Wasteful in preparing food, uneconomical: *gaisaa.*

unenergetic
Slow down, be exhausted (physically), feel unenergetic: *bangoa.*
Unenergetic: *bangobangoa.*

unenlightened
Unenlightened person: *dangada lo te gohu.*

unfasten
Unfasten, undo, untie: *dala*$_1$.

unfastened
Be unfastened: *madala.*

unforgiving
Unforgiving: *golo me.*

unforgotten
Unforgotten: *bili i de lodo.*

unfortunate
Unfortunate result: *hagapago sala.*

ungiving
Selfish with one's possessions, ungiving: *lodo hagamau me.*

unhappiness
Heaviness, sadness, unhappiness: *daemahaanga.*

unhappy
Feel unhappy or sad: *lodo daemaha.*
Put weight on, make unhappy: *hagadaemaha.*
Unhappy, upset, sad: *lodo baubau.*

unicorn fish
Fish sp.: unicorn fish: *gelu-hai-usu.*

unimportant
Nothing, unimportant, useless, worthless: *ngadi me.*
Treat as unimportant: *hagangadi me.*
Unimportant person: *bulubulu dangada.*
Unimportant work: *bulubulu hegau.*

uninhabited
Wilderness, uninhabited place: *vao.*

uninterested
Uninterested in: *dee savala.*

unkempt
Unclean, unkempt: *dabeo.*
Unkempt: *lausamua.*

unkind
Mean (by nature), unkind: *abo sala.*

unlucky
Unlucky: *mmala.*

unmarried
Single, unmarried: *duuhua.*

unmistakably
Unmistakably, for certain: *gu soe donu.*

unobscured
Clear (easily seen), unobscured: *aadea.*

unobstructed
Clear, unobstructed, uncluttered: *malaelae.*
Unobstructed: *aadea moana; dauaadea.*

unplanned
Unscheduled, unplanned: *daa hagalele.*

unreliable
Risky, unreliable: *doo halehale me; doo lodolodo.*

unripe
Unripe: *modo.*

unscheduled
Unscheduled, unplanned: *daa hagalele.*

unscrupulous
Unscrupulous, immoral, evil: *vaivaidagodo.*

unserious
Funny, unserious, jesting, silly: *hakadanga.*

unsettled
Not firmly situated or settled, unsettled conditions: *tigi velo ono aga.*
Unsettled (of a situation, the weather, etc.): *halehale dagodo.*

unskillful
Clumsy, unskillful, awkward (not dexterous): *too gee.*
Unskillful (at difficult activities): *bungadogi; bungaleu.*

unstable
Unstable temperamentally, inconstant: *lodo aheahe.*
Unstable, poorly balanced: *duu saba.*

unsteady
Unsteady (as a ship on the sea): *dibadiba.*

unsuccessful
Unsuccessful: *doo lalo.*

untidy
Untidy in appearance (esp. unshaven, with one's hair in disorder): *lausamua.*

untie
Unfasten, undo, untie: *dala*$_1$.

untied
Be untied: *madala.*

until
Until: *ga dae ai.*

unusual
Extraordinary or unusual (esp. in size): *se me be hee.*
Extraordinary, outstanding, unusual: *magona.*

up
Up: *age.*
Up a little: *lunga age.*
Up more: *lunga ange.*
Up, above, over: *lunga.*

upset
To have an upset stomach (being on the point of nausea): *labua gee lodo.*
Unhappy, upset, sad: *lodo baubau.*
Upset stomach (nausea): *magi labua gee.*

uptown
Uptown: *ngaiho.*

urchin
Burrowing heart urchin: *veli-tea.*
Sea urchin sp.: *Diadema* sp.: *veli-daubulebule; veli-uli.*
Sea urchin sp.: *Echinometra* spp.: *veli.*
Slate-pencil urchin: *heduge.*

urge
To urge: *hagaago.*

urinate
Urinate: *diidii*$_2$; *hagassui; hongagainga; mimi; sii diidii.*

use
Do, make, use: *hai*$_1$.
Use jointly or collectively: *hagadau hai me ai.*
Use up, use unwisely (not saving some for later), waste: *ngole.*
Use without permission: *hai gaiaa.*

used to
Not used to: *kau gee.*
Used to, easy to: *kau donu.*

used up
Gone, finished, used up: *odi*$_b$.
Used up or cleaned out completely: *malalidage.*

useful
Effective, useful, worthwhile, important: *haigamaiana.*

useless
Nothing, unimportant, useless, worthless: *ngadi me.*
Useless (things or matters): *bulubulu.*
Useless: *deai me ao ai.*
Useless pieces: *bidobido.*
Worthless or useless: *buu goede.*

usual
Usual: *mau*$_2$.

usually
Usually: *mau ange huu; mau*$_2$.

utter
Speak, pronounce, utter (words): *dagu*$_1$.
Utter (words or sounds), reply (to someone): *muu*$_1$.

uvula
The uvula and the adjacent portions of the oral cavity: *ma te hakii.*

vacant
Hollow, vacant, empty: *ngadi—.*

vagina
Vagina: *malua.*

vagrant
Vagrant (having no fixed abode): *leva saele.*

valuable
Worthwhile, important, valuable: *gasia.*

value
Worth, value: *bauanga; baunga.*

vandalism
Vandalism: *lagolagoaa.*

vanish
Disappear, vanish: *lilo.*

vapor
Dust, gas, steam, vapor, fumes, spray (e.g., of waves): *mama.*

variety
Kind (of), sort (of), variety (of): *daaganga*$_3$; *hagadaaganga.*

Vasum
Mollusk sp.: *Vasum turbinellus*: *gammenge-maimai.*

veer
Turn away from (to avoid), veer: *hhagi gee.*
Veer from an intended trajectory: *ssee gee.*

vein
Vein, tendon, nerve, plastic filament: **uaua**$_3$.

verdant
Verdant (indicating growing well): *dauulu.*

vermetid gastropod
Mollusk sp.: vermetid gastropod sp.: *unga-goo.*

verse
Verse (of a song): *duudanga, gubu.*
Verse of a song: *duudanga daahili; gubu daahili.*

vertebra
Vertebra: *bule.*

vertebrae
Tip of the spine (caudal vertebrae): *dogonogo.*

vertical
Vertical: *duu donu.*
Vertical, straight up and down: *duu gaso.*

vertigo
Dizziness or vertigo (as a chronic condition or illness): *magi libolibo.*
Feel dizzy or faint, vertigo: *libo ange de henua.*

very
Completely, very: *saunoa.*
Very —: *gona*$_1$.
Very: *dee adahaia; doo mua; odi*$_a$.
Very few: *dogoisi loo huu.*
Very much: *sauaa.*
Very, exceedingly: *hano gi oona.*
Very, too much: *ga dae laa huu; kona.*

vibrate
Tremble or vibrate in the air: *ngalubelube.*

vicious
Vicious: *alasala.*

victimized
Feel punished or victimized: *langona iho maahana.*

village
Village: *ungaa me.*
Village, compound (aggregation of houses): *aduhale.*

vine
Plant sp.: cassytha vine (*Cassytha filiformis* L.): *hiisoa.*
Plant sp.: vine (any sort): *hua-dolo.*
Plant sp.: vine sp. (several spp.): *hue.*

violence
Violence: *dua nnui.*

violent
Violent in word or action: *baagava.*

visible
Visible clearly: *duu molomolo.*

vision
To see a vision, hallucinate: *gide eidu; gide eidu ina.*

Vitex
Plant sp.: hemp-leaved vitex shrub (*Vitex negundo* var. *bicolor* (Willd.) Lam.): *gasigi.*

Vittaria
Plant sp.: epiphytic fern (*Vittaria incurvata* Cav.): *gumigumi-o-sogo.*

voice
A voice, a sound, an intonational pattern: *leo.*

vomit
Vomit, vomitus: *hagalueia.*

vomitus
Vomit, vomitus: *hagalueia.*

voyeurism
Voyeurism: *dilongaagau.*

waddle
Waddle: *seesee hagadibadiba.*

wage
Wage war against: *hagadaua*$_3$.

wages
Price, wages: *hagaoanga.*

wahoo
Fish sp.: wahoo: *daodao*$_2$.

wail
Cry aloud for a long time, wail: *dangi see.*
Wail (when crying): *dangi hagaeaea.*
Wail loudly (when crying): *dangi hagahadihadi.*

waist
Waist, circumference: *daogubu.*

wait
Hardly able to wait for: *dee vaaseegina.*
Wait for: *duu ange; hagagaba*$_1$.
Wait for, along with: *dali*$_1$.
Wait until — !: *kaba ai loo.*
Wait until nearly sunset (to do something): *hagaahiahi.*
Wait!: *kaba*$_1$.

wait!
Please wait!: *kaba muhuu.*
Wait!: *kaba donu.*

waiting
Hope for, expectant, waiting: *tali.*

wake
Wake (of a ship): *aausa.*

wake up
Wake up (from sleep): *alahage.*
Wake up (someone): *hhango.*
Wake up (someone) insistently: *haahaango.*
Wake up: *mahuda age.*
Wake up repeatedly owing to anxiety: *seni alaala.*

wakefulness
Wakefulness: *mahulu.*

walk
Stilts, walk on stilts: *dookalala.*
Walk (for recreation): *seesee hagadaahao.*
Walk around aimlessly: *deledele saele.*
Walk barefoot, stroll: *ngadi seesee.*
Walk off-balance: *sibasiba.*
Walk proudly, strut: *deledele kau.*
Walk stealthily in a crouch: *modimodi.*
Walk with a limp (permanently): *hagadodi.*
Walk with a limp (temporarily): *hagadotodi.*
Walk, move slowly (as a fish): *seesee*$_2$.
Wander aimlessly, to walk around: *saele.*

walked upon
Walked upon: *saelea.*

walkingstick
Insect sp.: walkingstick (a very large grasshopper-like insect): *manu-de-hala.*

walkway
Road, walkway, path (for walking): *saelenga.*

wall
Roof support (top) poles, wall plates: *dao ssanga.*

wander
Search for here and there, wander around looking for: *saugalo saele.*
Wander about with no fixed abode: *silivaahea.*
Wander aimlessly, to walk around: *saele.*
Wander around: *hano saele; hulo saele.*

wandering tattler
Bird sp.: wandering tattler? (*Heteroscelus incanus*): *lahulahu*$_2$.

want
Want: *momogo.*
Want desperately: *magau donu i de lodo.*
Want to —: *maahia.*
Want to: *hii-.*
Want, desire: *lodo*$_2$.

war
War, battle: *daua*$_3$.

warm
To feel uncomfortably warm: *kava.*
Warm: *mahanahana.*
Warm oneself by the fire: *lallala.*

warmed
Warmed up: *mahanahanasia.*

wart
Wart, mole (raised): *dona.*

wash
Wash (hands or feet or dishes, etc. — but not clothes): *hhui.*
Wash one's mouth out, gargle: *luuluu haha.*
Wash one's own hands (or mouth): *hhano.*
Wash someone's hands (or mouth): *haanoa.*

wash up
Wash up on shore: *baoa.*
Wash up on shore and beach thereon. *baoa age.*
Wash up on shore continually: *baabaoa.*

washed out
Flooded, washed out: *dolona.*

wasp
Insect sp.: fly, flying ant, wasp: *lango*$_2$.

waste
Use up, use unwisely (not saving some for later), waste: *ngole.*
Waste (by not using): *tili moumou.*
Wasteful, waste (something): *moumou.*

wasteful
Wasteful: *hai sseu.*
Wasteful in preparing food, uneconomical: *gaisaa.*
Wasteful of food: *gai moumou.*
Wasteful of taro when peeling it (i.e., inclined to peel too much away): *uhe.*
Wasteful, improvident: *gai ngole.*
Wasteful, waste (something): *moumou.*

watch
Guard, watch, keep an eye on: *hagaloosi.*
Watch carefully, keep an eye on: *sagana.*

watch out!
Watch out!: *dai sagana iho goe; e lodo goe; saganaa iho goe.*

watchful
Watchful, be on the lookout, keep an eye on: *dagitilo.*

water
Liquid, water: *vai.*
Sea water: *laosedi.*
To water (plants): *hagamaluulu.*

water bug
Insect sp.: water bug: *daamadaa-sele.*

watercourse
A watercourse between islets on the atoll: *aasanga.*

waterfall
Waterfall: *vai doo.*

waterspout
Waterspout (esp. full of water): *uaduu.*
Waterspout (esp. the air causing it): *sio.*

watery
Watery (of prepared food): *boibala.*
Watery: *vaivai.*

wave
A wave, the surf: *beau.*
To wave back and forth (as a coconut tree in the wind): *singasinga.*

waving
To bring one's hands and arms (or wings) down or back once (as in waving, swimming, or the flapping of a bird's wings): *balu*$_1$.

wavy
Having wavy hair: *lau hadihadi.*

we
We: *gidaadeu; gimaadeu.*
We two: *gidaau; gimaau.*

weak
Very soft or weak (of things only): *balabala.*
Weak (of a person): *baageaa.*

weak-willed
Weak-willed, easily tempted: *lodo baageaa.*

weakening
Weakening (becoming weaker): *baạgeaa iho.*

wealthy
Becoming finished or wealthy: *lavalava.*
Wealthy: *lava; llava.*

wear
Put on (clothes), wear: *ulumagi.*
Put on, wear, cover up (the body): *gahu.*

weather
Bad weather: *dangalebu de me.*

web
Spider web: *hale neveneve.*

wedding
Wedding: *hagahaibodu.*

wedelia
Plant sp.: wedelia creeper (*Wedelia biflora* (L.) DC.): *aigimea.*

Wednesday
Wednesday ('third day'): *Tolu-laangi.*

weed
To weed (a garden): *boo manu; vele; vele me.*

weigh
Weigh (on a balance): *hagahidi.*

weight
The weight (on a balance) used as a standard measurement: *hidi taelodo.*

weir
Fish weir: *bae mamu.*

well
Healed, well (after sickness), recuperated: *hagavaasuu.*
Well (for water, in the ground): *vai geli.*
Well (not sick): *abo donu.*

well-known
Well-known, famous: *daudau*$_1$.

well-mannered
Well-mannered: *gagu.*

welt
Redness or inflammation of the skin (e.g., a welt): *dala mmea.*

wet
Be wet all over (esp. when one's hair is dripping): *sulu moso.*
Be wet from the rain: *dogia.*
Become wet: *suisui*$_2$.
Completely wet all over: *ssuilebelebe.*
Get wet: *biia.*
Wet: *ssui.*
Wet and dried: *sua*$_2$.

whale
Whale: *daholaa.*

what for?
What for?: *aha ai.*

what next?
What next?: *aha goi.*

what?
What?: *aha.*

whatever
Whatever: *be aha naa huu.*

wheel
Wheel (one only): *vae hagasii.*
Wheel: *hagasii; hagasii lolo.*

when
When, if: *naa huu.*

when?
When? (distant future): *aahee loo.*
When? (indefinite future): *aahee.*
When? (near future): *hagaahee.*
When? (past time): *anahee.*

where
Where (in general)?: *i hee.*
Where else?: *ma hee.*
Where exactly?: *go hee.*
Where?: *ngaahee.*
Where?, what kind?, which?: *hee.*

which
Where?, what kind?, which?: *hee.*
Which is it?: *de aha.*
Which of — (you, etc.)?: *goai de* + PRONOUN.
Which were those?: *aahee laa.*
Which?: *ahee; dehee.*

whimbrel
Bird sp.: eastern whimbrel (*Numenius phaeopus*): *geevee.*

whip black coral
Coral sp.: whip black coral: *valagei.*

whirlwind
Whirlwind: *sio.*

whisper
Whisper (to someone): *musumusu.*
Whisper softly: *musumusu laa lalo.*

whispering
Whispering: *musu.*

whistle
A whistle (made with the lips): *hagavogi*$_2$.

whistling
Whistling (with the lips): *vogi*$_2$.

white
Become white: *hagatea.*
Dead white (whitest hue imaginable): *tea ma agiagi.*
Having white hair: *sinaa.*
The white excretion of the *banibani*: *dae banibani.*
White (of the portion of a woman's thighs hidden under her sarong): *gannui ina.*
White (or grey) hair (appearing in old age): *sina.*
White: *tea.*
White as a sheet (of a person): *mada tea gee.*

white tern
Bird sp.: white tern?: *lebidi.*

white-capped noddy
Bird sp.: white-capped noddy (*Anous minutus*): *legia.*

white-headed
White-headed: *sinasinaa.*

white-rumped swift$_1$
Bird sp.: white-rumped swift (*Apus pacificus*) (The native term applies possibly to several spp.): *gauea.*

white-tailed tropic bird
Bird sp.: white-tailed tropic bird (*Phaethon lepturus*): *davage.*

white-throated frigate bird
Bird sp.: white-throated frigate bird: *ua dea.*

white-tip shark
Fish sp.: white-tip shark: *aso.*

who?
Who?: *goai.*

whoever
Whoever: *be goai (naa huu).*

whole
The whole thing: *huaa me.*
Whole: *huaa.*

whore
Whore: *(de) hine hai be.*

whorl
A whorl in the hair: *milomilo.*

whorls
Whorls in the hair of the head: *goligoli.*

whose?
Whose?: *niaai; nioai.*

why?
Why?: *gu aha.*

wide
Wide: *lahalaha.*

wide-awake
Energetic, eager, wide-awake: *maalo.*

wiggle
To wiggle one's hand: *hagadibadiba de lima.*
Wiggle: *hagabigobigo.*

wild
Wild (of animals scared of humans): *sango.*

wilderness
Inland, bush (uncleared) land, wilderness: *lodo henua.*
Wilderness, uninhabited place: *vao.*

will
Make a will (for oneself or others): *bolo*$_2$.

willful
Stubborn, willful: *hai de hai.*
Willful, mean: *se hagabau.*

willing
Willing to: *sabala.*

win
Win over all comers (esp. in an athletic contest): *vele de henua.*
Win, overcome: *kii*$_1$.

wind
A strong wind: *huaalavao.*
Twist, turn (something, as a faucet), wind, wring: *milo*$_1$.
Wind around (of a rope, etc.): *niigoi.*
Wind around: *nigo.*
Wind, gas, flatus: *madangi.*

wing
Shoulder (the whole joint), wing: *bakau.*

winking
Twinkling, flashing, winking: *dabadaba*$_1$.

winsome
Unctuous, cloying, winsome: *ngudu maimai.*

wipe
Wipe oneself (after defecating): *hailu.*
Wipe, scrub, clean up (by wiping), erase: *ssolo.*

wire
Cable, wire (heavy): *daula baalanga.*

wisdom teeth
Molar teeth, wisdom teeth: *niho ngalo.*

wish
I wish that...: *me naa gi* —.
To wish one has —: *maingaa ange nei gi.*

with
At his place, with him: *i ono daha.*
Side of (part away from), with: *daho.*
With, along with, as well as: *madali.*
With, including: *ma*$_1$.

withdrawal
Expulsion or voluntary withdrawal (from a group): *doo i de....*

withered
Withered (of a plant): *mmae.*
Withered: *mae.*

withstand
Be able to withstand: *pula.*

woman
Female, woman: *hine.*
Girl, young woman, daughter: *damaa hine.*
Married man or woman: *dau bodu.*
Married woman: *(de) hine dau bodu.*
Woman: *hahine.*

women
Women: *haahine.*

wonder
(E.g., I) wonder how —?: *vanei ai.*
(E.g., I) wonder if...?: *vanei naa.*

wood
The soft wood around the center of a tree trunk: *udo.*
The soft wood just under the bark of a tree: *gano dea.*
The wood next to the core of a tree: *kano maailaba.*
Wood, stick (of wood): *laagau.*

word
Word: *alaa muna.*
Word, language, speech: *muna.*
Word, phrase: *dalaa muna.*

work
Unimportant work: *bulubulu hegau.*
Work (in a group) busily: *sulegi.*
Work: *hai hegau.*
Work as little as possible: *hagamademade*$_1$ —.
Work beyond one's endurance: *pala ivi.*
Work for as a servant: *lima ma vae ange.*
Work hypocritically (appearing to follow the rules but secretly violating the prohibitions): *hai hegau hilo.*
Work seriously: *daabeduge; daaligi.*
Work slowly: *hai me dagi.*
Work with concentration in the midst of a group: *gubo.*
Work, activity, occupation: *haiva; hegau.*

world
World (lands other than Nukuoro): *henua i lalo (alodahi).*

worm
Eel, any long worm, snake: *labodo.*
Worm, maggot, intestinal parasites: *ilo.*

worm sp.
Worm sp. (large, white): *uhado.*
Worm sp. (makes a spider-like thread): *maanga-de-langi.*

wormy
Wormy or maggoty (of something decayed): *ilosia.*

worried
Worried, apprehensive, fearful: *manavasaa.*

worse
Become (or make) much worse: *hagakona.*
Become much worse: *kona ange.*

worsening
Worsening: *hagadaga iho.*

worship
Treat as a totem, worship, treat as a supernatural being: *eidu ai.*

worth
To be worth it: *bau.*
Worth, value: *bauanga; baunga.*

worthless
Nothing, unimportant, useless, worthless: *ngadi me.*
Worthless or useless: *buu goede.*

worthwhile
Effective, useful, worthwhile, important: *haigamaiana.*
Thing of importance, worthwhile: *me dau.*
Worthwhile person: *dangada haigamaiana.*
Worthwhile, important, valuable: *gasia.*

wound
Wound around: *gali.*
Wound around or tied or fastened very tightly: *gali ange.*
Wound around, tangled up, confused: *vini.*

wound$_1$
a wound (on the body, from a spear, etc.): *daalonga.*
A wound or large sore (on the body): *maanuga.*

wounded
Wounded (by something which has pierced): *ulu*$_1$.
Wounded: *lagohia.*
Wounded in several places or all over: *lagolagohia.*

wrap
Braid (rope or hair, etc.), wrap with rope: *bini.*
Wrap: *llava.*
Wrap from under, wrap around: *haaligi.*
Wrap or cover completely: *ssai.*
Wrap up (something) hastily: *sabeeloi.*
Wrap up, tie up: *saabini.*
Wrap, cover up (with several layers): *sai*$_1$.

wrapped
Wrapped (tied) around: *llava ai.*
Wrapped up or covered up completely: *saidule.*

wrapping
A wrapping (of string) around the join of a pole: *hausanga.*

wrasse
Fish sp.: wrasse (2 sorts: 1 white, 1 red): *babu-honga-agau.*
Fish sp.: wrasse: *banganga; labelabe-uliuli; mamu-lalo-beau; sussunubega.*

wrestle
Wrestle: *daudau*$_3$.

wrestling
Wrestling holds: *sua*$_1$.

wring
Twist, turn (something, as a faucet), wind, wring: *milo*$_1$.

wrinkled
Be in a wrinkled condition: *hai dauaa.*
Wrinkled (of skin or clothes): *vinivini.*
Wrinkled: *dauaa.*
Wrinkled skin (from age): *too gili.*

wrist
Hand, wrist: *gubu lima.*

write
To write (with a pen or pencil): *sisi*$_1$.

writing
Writing (on paper): *siianga*$_1$.

Ximenia
Plant sp.: shrub sp. (*Ximenia americana* L.): *dala*$_6$.

yawn
Yawn, belch: *maava.*

year
Year: *ngadau.*

yellow
Whitish-yellow: *kena.*
Yellow: *ganoango.*

yellow fin tuna
Fish sp.: yellow fin tuna (3 sorts?): *dagua*$_2$.

yes!
Yes!: *ou; uaa; uu*$_2$.
Yes! Certainly!: *ouaa.*
Yes! Yes!: *ouou.*

yesterday
Yesterday: *anaahi.*

yield
Productive, yield a great amount of: *daua*$_1$.
Yield interest: *haanau ssene.*

you
You: *goe; goodou.*
You two: *gooluu.*

young
Boy, young man: *dama daane.*
Child, young person: *gauligi.*
Girl, young woman, daughter: *damaa hine.*
Young girl: *ulu hudi**.

younger
Younger: *ngadau iho.*
Younger than: *gauligi ange.*

youngest
The youngest child of a couple: *dibononi.*

your
Your: *sau_3; soo; soodou; sooluu.*
Your one: *dau_6; doo_3; doodou; dooluu.*
Your several: *au_3; oo; oodou; ooluu.*
Your two: *luaau; luoo; luoodou; luooluu.*

ROOT LIST

A_1

B — a_1. *mr.* RELATIONAL PARTICLE 2.

ID — **dangi a beini.** To have smelled ripe pandanus.

ID — **gaigai a usu.** Flatus.

A_2

B — a_2. *ma.* PERSONAL ARTICLE.

A_3

B — **a-**$_3$. *mf.* PLURAL PREFIX.

XCO — **ahee.** *b.* Which?

XCO — **alaa.** *b.* Those over there.

XCO — **anaa.** *b.* Those (away from the speaker).

XCO — **anei.** *b.* These.

CF — **aamanu.** Coral (growing live on the reef); coral head.

A_4

CF — **ailaa.** Today (sometime).

AA_1

B — **aa**$_1$. *i.* The sound of hesitation noise.

AA_2

B — **aa-**$_2$. *mf.* FUTURE TIME PREFIX.

CF — **aagai.** Continually wanting to eat.

CF — **aahee.** When? (indefinite future).

AA_3

CF — **aasanga.** A watercourse between islets on the atoll.

AABI

B — **aabi.** *n.* Room (of a house).

ID — **hai aabi.** Having many rooms or sections.

ID — **manu aabi.** Kite.

AABIDA

B — **aabida.** *v.* Make a coil of dried pandanus leaves.

B 1 — **aabidanga.** *n.* —.

BE — **hagaabida.** *v.* —.

BE1 — **hagaabidanga.** *n.* —.

AADA

B — **aada.** *a.* Easily startled, skittish, wild (of animals).

BE — **hagaada**$_2$. *v.* —.

BE1 — **hagaadanga.** *n.* —.

BE2 — **hagaadalia.** *v.* —.

AADEA

B — **aadea.** *v.* Clear (easily seen), unobscured.

XCO — **dauaadea.** *v.* Clear (with nothing in the way); unobstructed; cleared (of obstructions).

XE — **hagadauaadea.** *v.* To clear out a place.

ID — **aadea moana.** Unobstructed.

ID — **laagau hagadauaadea.** A cross-beam lashed to a tree to facilitate climbing it.

ID — **momme aadea.** Clearing (e.g., in the woods).

AAHAO

ID — **ubu aahao.** [var. of *ubu haohao*].

AAHU

B — **aahu.** *a.* The intense pain resulting from having one's skin punctured by a poisonous fish.

B 1 — **aahunga.** *n.* —.

BE — **hagaahu.** *v.* —.

BE1 — **hagaahunga.** *n.* —.

AAHULU

B — **aahulu.** *v.* To leave food cooking overnight.

BE — **hagaahulu.** *v.* —.

ID — **me hagaahulu.** Prepared food.

AALALI

B — **aalali.** *v.* Coral sp.: a type of coral which grows on the lagoon bottom.

BE — **hagaalali.** *v.* —.

AALELOI

ID — **sua aaleloi.** A wrestling maneuver.

AALINGA

B — **aalinga.** *a.* Moving around just under the water.

B 1 **aalingaanga.** *n.* —.
BE **hagaalinga$_2$.** *n.* —.
BE1 **hagaalingaanga.** *n.* —.

AALO
ID **aalo dahi.** Do at one time.
ID **laagau aalo saelenga.** Thatch rafters on the ends of a house.

AAMIA
B **aamia.** *v.* Sufficient for the purpose or need.
BE **hagaamia.** *v.* —.
ID **tee aamia donu.** Not enough.

AAMONGA
XCO **deaamonga.** *n.* [var. of *seaamonga*].
XCO **seaamonga.** *n.* A unit of (twenty) coconuts for making *huaahuu.*

AASASI
B **aasasi.** *a.* Flee (of a small school of fish).
B 1 **aasasinga.** *n.* —.
BE **hagaasasi.** *v.* —.
BE1 **hagaasasinga.** *n.* —.
BE2 **hagaasasia.** *v.* —.

AASII
B **aasii.** *n.* Drum (native).

AAU
B **aau.** *v.* Remove.
B 1 **aaunga.** *n.* —; the incompletely burned earth oven fuel remaining when the oven is uncovered.
B 2 **aaua.** *v.* —.
BE **hagaau$_2$.** *v.* —.
BE1 **hagaaunga.** *n.* —.
BE2 **hagaaua.** *v.* —.
R **aauaau.** *v.* —.
R 1 **aauaaunga.** *n.* —.
R 2 **aauaaua.** *v.* —.
RE **hagaauaau.** *v.* —.
RE1 **hagaauaaunga.** *n.* —.
RE2 **hagaauaaua.** *v.* —.
ID **aau ai naa.** More so.
ID **hagaau aloha.** Poor (not rich).
ID **hagaau gee.** Bashful, shy (timid about attending social affairs), timid.

AAUSA
B **aausa.** *v.* Wake (of a ship).
B 1 **aausanga.** *n.* Way of leaving a wake.
BE **hagaausa.** *v.* Cause to leave a wake.
BE1 **hagaausanga.** *n.* —.
ID **aausa ina.** A sea condition resembling that resulting from a ship leaving a wake.

ABA
CF **abadai.** European [adj.].
CF **abasasa.** European.

ABAABAI
B **abaabai.** *v.* Carry a canoe in shallow water; carry half lifting.
B 1 **abaabainga.** *n.* —.
B 2 **abaabaia.** *v.* —.
CF **saabai.** Lift up and carry; carry (a burden).

ABADAI
B **abadai.** *na.* European [adj.].
ID **dangada abadai.** European persons (including Americans).
ID **me abadai.** European things (gear, etc.).

ABASASA
B **abasasa.** *na.* European.
BE **hagaabasasa.** *v.* Act like or emulate Europeans.
ID **abasasa huu.** European in manner or appearance.
ID **dangada abasasa.** European persons (including Americans).
ID **tangada abasasa.** A European person (or an American).
ID **goloa abasasa.** European goods or tools.
ID **henua abasasa.** Land of the Europeans (including America, Japan, etc.).
ID **me abasasa.** European things (gear, etc.).

ABI$_1$

R **abiabi.** *v*. Pull up slowly or gently with one's fingers.
R 1 **abiabinga.** *n*. —.
R 2 **abiabia.** *v*. —.
RE **hagaabiabi.** *v*. —.
RE1 **hagaabiabinga.** *n*. —.
RE2 **hagaabiabia.** *v*. —.

ABI$_2$

B **abi.** *n*. Fish sp.: tang.

ABITALA

B **abitala.** *n*. Eave (of a house).

ABO

B **abo.** *a*. Capable; correct (suitable), true; feel comfortable.
B 1 **aabonga.** *n*. —.
BE **hagaabo.** *v*. —.
BE1 **hagaabonga.** *n*. —.
BE2 **hagaabolia.** *v*. —.
P **aabo.** *a*. —.
R **aboabo.** *a*. Become accustomed to.
RE **hagaaboabo.** *v*. —.
RE1 **hagaaboabonga.** *n*. —.
RE2 **hagaaboabolia.** *v*. —.
ID **abo ange.** Good at.
ID **abo donu.** Good (not evil or false); real, true; well (not sick); considerate, kind, generous.
ID **abo manu.** To correct someone without justification.
ID **abo sala.** Mean (by nature), unkind.
ID **daane abo donu.** Gentleman; person who is good.
ID **dee abo.** Uncomfortable (esp. socially).
ID **me abo (donu).** Truth.
ID **me abo donu.** Real, true.
ID **muna abo (donu).** Truth.

ABONGI

B **abongi.** *a*. Capsize.
BE **hagaabongi.** *v*. —.
P **aabongi.** *a*. —.
R **aboabongi.** *a*. Easily capsizable.
RE **hagaaboabongi.** *v*. —.
ID **abongi baasi.** Capsize sideways.
ID **bido abongi.** Capsize eventually.

ABULU

B **abulu.** *a*. Sink (until submerged).
B 1 **abuluanga.** *n*. —.
BE **hagaabulu.** *v*. —.
BE **hagadauaabulu.** *v*. —.
BE1 **hagaabuluanga.** *n*. —.
E **aapulu.** *a*. Sink all at once.
E 1 **aapuluanga.** *n*. —.
P **aabulu.** *a*. —.
P 1 **aabuluanga.** *n*. —.
PE **hagaapulu.** *v*. —.
PE1 **hagaapuluanga.** *n*. —.
R **abuabulu.** *a*. Easily sinkable.
XCO **dauaabulu.** *v*. Nearly sunk.

ADA$_1$

B **ada$_1$.** *n*. Picture, image, reflection, shadow.
BE **hagaada$_1$.** *v*. Give a picture to.
R **adaada.** *a*. Dawn (first light).
RE **hagaadaada.** *v*. Getting to be near daybreak.
ID **adaada age.** The first light of the moon.
ID **baalasi de ada.** To take a picture.
ID **dele de ada.** Dawn (first light).
ID **maahaa ada.** Dawn (first burst of light).
ID **me hai ada.** Camera.
CF **aadea.** Clear (easily seen), unobscured.

ADA$_{1a}$

B **adamai.** *v*. Recollect or recall past events or persons, etc.
B 1 **adamainga.** *n*. —.
B 2 **adamaia.** *v*. —.
BE **hagaadamai.** *v*. —.
BE1 **hagaadamainga.** *n*. —.
BE2 **hagaadamaia.** *v*. —.
R **adaadamai.** *a*. Recall slightly.
R 1 **adaadamainga.** *n*. —.

R 2 **adaadamaia.** *v.* —.
RE **hagaadaadamai.** *v.* —.
RE1 **hagaadaadamainga.** *n.* —.
RE2 **hagaadaadamaia.** *v.* —.
ID **adamai gauligi.** Remember childhood experiences.
ID **vaivai adamai.** Remember poorly.

ADA$_2$
B **ada$_2$.** *mf.* CONJECTURAL PREFIX.

ADE
B **ade.** *n.* Liver.
ID **doo ade.** [a joking expression: lit., 'your liver'!].
ID **hagi ade.** Insult (someone).
ID **lalo ade.** Solar plexus (considered the seat of feeling).

ADI
B **adi.** *v.* Relate news or gossip.
B 1 **adinga.** *n.* —.
B 2 **adia.** *v.* —.
R **adiadi.** *v.* Relate repeatedly.
R 1 **adiadinga.** *n.* —.
R 2 **adiadia.** *v.* —.
ID **adi longo.** To tattle.
ID **adi saele.** Disseminate information.
ID **tangada adi longo.** Gossipy person, tattletale.
CF **adigai.** Luckily did not —, fortunately it did not —; if more; almost.

ADIDI
B **adidi.** *n.* Plant sp. (not native — drifts ashore — used for making perfume).

ADIGAI
B **adigai.** *mi.* Luckily did not —, fortunately it did not —; if more; almost.
ID **adigai huu.** Were it not for; fortunately, luckily —.

ADU$_1$
B **adu$_1$.** *mv.* Toward hearer.
RE **hagaaduadu.** *v.* Say bad things about people.
RE1 **hagaaduadunga.** *n.* —.
RE2 **hagaaduadulia.** *v.* —.
ID **adu ange laa.** The one following the one in question.
ID **adu laa.** After tomorrow, the one after the next one.
ID **boo adu laa.** Day after tomorrow at night.
ID **daabeduge adu ange.** Take a lot of.
ID **dagodo adu.** Appear there (from here).
ID **kii adu.** Get out!
ID **hagaaduadu dangada.** Critical of others.
ID **hagaaduadu iho.** Self-criticism.
ID **hakii adu.** Get out!
ID **iho adu.** You feel like —.
ID **noho mai (adu, ange).** Resist me (you, them), oppose me (you, them).
ID **ngani adu.** *ngani* toward others; fit around one as a belt etc.
ID **oho adu.** Go early.
ID **soi adu —.** Expect that — but.
CF **loadu.** Go (toward the hearer) [pl.].

ADU$_2$
B **adu$_2$.** *n.* Fish sp.: skipjack tuna.
XFL **adu-balebale-i-dai.** *n.* Fish sp.
XFL **adu-balebale-i-dua.** *n.* Fish sp.: bonito.
ID **hagadubu o de adu.** The name of a certain type of string figure.

ADU$_3$
B **adu$_3$.** *n.* Fish club (priest).

ADU$_4$
B **adu$_4$.** *n.* Conglomerate, islet.
XCO **adudai.** *n.* "Islands to the west of Nukuoro" (the Mortlocks?).
XCO **adudau.** *n.* Sand spit.
XCO **aduhale.** *a.* Village, compound (aggregation of houses); go from

house to house.

XCO **aduhenua.** *n.* Group of islands or atolls; archipelago.

XCO **adumodu.** *n.* Group of islets; atoll (collection of islets).

ID **tangada aduhale.** The sort of person who feels at home everywhere and is continually visiting [considered uncouth].

ADU 4a

B **adugau.** *v.* Arrangement of things into a straight row.

B 1 **adugauanga.** *n.* —.

B 2 **adugaua.** *v.* —.

B 2 **adugaulia.** *v.* —.

BE **hagaadugau.** *v.* Arrange things in a row or line.

BE1 **hagaadugauanga.** *n.* —.

BE2 **hagaadugaua.** *v.* —.

BE2 **hagaadugaulia.** *v.* —.

ID **adugau daane.** Part of the plug of the pandanus.

ADUISIISI

BE **hagaaduisiisi.** *v.* To treat someone as a first husband or wife.

ADUMUA

B **adumua.** *v.* Pregnant and almost ready to deliver; first among a group of pregnant women to deliver.

BE **hagaadumua.** *v.* —.

BE1 **hagaadumuaanga.** *n.* —.

AGA

B **aga.** *n.* Root (of a tree or plant).

R **agaaga.** *n.* Having lots of roots.

ID **tigi velo ono aga.** Not firmly situated or settled, unsettled conditions.

ID **velo aga.** To sprout roots.

AGALALA

ID **doa agalala.** Very big giant.

AGAU

B **agau.** *n.* Reef (the portion which is sometimes under water).

ID **dagahia de agau.** Reef which has been trampled previously by lobster hunters (and therefore is poor for lobstering).

ID **dua agau.** Beyond the reef, pertaining to the open sea, — like to fish [ds].

ID **gano agau.** Reef (including land thereon).

ID **gili agau.** A moss-like covering of the reef; fish which live on the reef.

ID **haangoda de agau.** A method of fishing (with a line on the reef).

ID **haangoda dua agau.** Fishing beyond the reef (on the seaward side of the atoll).

AGE

B **age.** *mv.* Up.

ID **adaada age.** The first light of the moon.

ID **agu age.** Say out loud.

ID **ahe age.** Start again, reoccur.

ID **anu age.** To dance below people.

ID **ao age.** Daybreak (become daylight).

ID **baa age.** Shallow (e.g., waters).

ID **baba age.** Be decided about.

ID **baoa age.** Wash up on shore and beach thereon.

ID **bonabona age.** Become fearful.

ID **bonabona age lodo.** Feel fearful.

ID **paa age.** Explode from below.

ID **pale age (iho).** Steer toward (away from) land.

ID **daa age.** Go toward land (from the lagoon).

ID **daamada age.** Start again.

ID **dahea age.** Drift toward place where speaker is.

ID **daiao age.** The following morning.

ID **danuaa age.** Improved, better.

ID **dangage age.** Raise up one's

head from a lowered position.

ID **daohi age.** Donate, contribute.

ID **dau age.** To beach (a canoe) on land; reach land.

ID **dau age de inai.** Be in the lee of the atoll while fishing (i.e., in a place protected from the wind).

ID **dee manava age.** Do earnestly.

ID **dee sao age.** Always fail or be defeated.

ID **dili dagidahi age.** Release one at a time or intermittently or sporadically.

ID **doli age.** Obtain the smallest first.

ID **tea age langi.** The light before daybreak.

ID **ea age.** Stop swimming (and come up on land).

ID **ege age.** Raise up (something) from its previous trajectory.

ID **gii age.** Cry out softly.

ID **golo age.** Continually *golo* voluntarily.

ID **kii age.** Move upward; reach a certain age.

ID **haahaula age de me.** Become bright (with morning sunlight).

ID **hagaava age.** Be relieved for a short time.

ID **hagadaga age.** Improving.

ID **hagahana age.** Recook for several days.

ID **hagahonu age lodo.** Feel uncomfortably sated with food and unable to eat.

ID **hagamaanu age.** Pull oneself up by one's arms.

ID **hagamabu age.** Return to land from sea (esp. of birds).

ID **hagannamu age.** Eat a little of.

ID **hagasaele age.** Make up one's mind; lift up (in a steady motion).

ID **hagasolo age.** Keep postponing or delaying.

ID **hagassui age.** Eat or drink just a little bit.

ID **hagausi age.** Appearance of rain clouds on the horizon.

ID **hanu age.** Regain.

ID **hhoda age.** Suck in air (esp. when asleep or unconscious).

ID **hhuge age malo.** Lift up one's skirts (to expose one's genitals).

ID **hhui age.** Eat a snack.

ID **iho age.** Feel like beginning to want —.

ID **laohie age.** Improving condition (of weather).

ID **lele age.** Regain consciousness; epilepsy; surfacing (of flying fish).

ID **llele age** + PRONOUN—. (My/his, etc.) — has returned.

ID **maalo age.** Have become *maalo.*

ID **maanadu age.** Decide (arrive at a decision), make up one's mind; think up.

ID **maava age.** Belch.

ID **madohi age.** Reach halfway up.

ID **mahana age.** Heartburn [?].

ID **maholahola danuaa age.** Revitalized (by a shower or rest, etc.).

ID **mahuda age.** Wake up.

ID **malanga age.** Lifted up from; come up (e.g., weeds).

ID **malau age.** Free of hardship (after having had it).

ID **mami age.** Taste (something) a little bit.

ID **mmahi age de —.** Feel like —.

ID **mouli age.** Regain consciousness, rise from the dead.

ID **mouli age de —.** Regain feeling in — (part of body which was numb).

ID **ngadau age.** Older.

ID **ngalue age.** Increased, augmented.

ID **ngaue age.** Increase (in

rank or price, etc.).
ID **ngole age.** Use smallest first.
ID **oho age.** The following morning.
ID **soe age.** Straight up; decide (for oneself).
ID **ssabe age.** Eat.
ID **ssami age.** Eat a snack.
ID **ssili age.** Address a question to a group.
ID **sua age.** Dig up soil to uncover (something).
ID **ue age.** Raise or increase (volume of radio or price, etc.).
ID **ui age.** Pass over.
ID **ula age.** Be on fire.
ID **ulu age.** Take from the bottom upward.
ID **velo age.** Go up straight.
CF **loage.** Go (up or toward the village, or land) [pl.].

AGE$_a$
B **ngaage.** *nl.* Downtown.
ID **doo ngaage.** South wind.
ID **ngaage nei.** Gilbert Islands.

AGELI
B **ageli.** *v.* Pick head lice.
B 1 **agelinga.** *n.* —.
B 2 **agelia.** *v.* —.
BE **hagaageli.** *v.* —.
BE1 **hagaagelinga.** *n.* —.
BE2 **hagaagelia.** *v.* —.
R **ageageli.** *v.* —.
R 1 **ageagelinga.** *n.* —.
R 2 **ageagelia.** *v.* —.
RE **hagaageageli.** *v.* —.
RE1 **hagaageagelinga.** *n.* —.
RE2 **hagaageagelia.** *v.* —.
CF **agule.** Pick head lice.

AGI
R **agiagi.** *n.* Bird sp.: fairy tern (*Gygis alba*).
ID **tea ma agiagi.** Dead white (whitest hue imaginable).
CF **madaagi.** The scout in *belubelu* fishing.

AGILAU
B **agilau.** *v.* Pugnacious.
B 1 **agilaunga.** *n.* —.
B 2 **agilaua.** *v.* —.
BE **hagaagilau.** *v.* —.
BE1 **hagaagilaunga.** *n.* —.
BE2 **hagaagilaua.** *v.* —.
R **agiagilau.** *v.* —.
R 1 **agiagilaunga.** *n.* —.
R 2 **agiagilaua.** *v.* —.
RE **hagaagiagilau.** *v.* —.
RE1 **hagaagiagilaunga.** *n.* —.
RE2 **hagaagiagilaua.** *v.* —.

AGINA
B **agina.** *mv.* To it, for it.
ID **hagailonga ange agina.** Assign (someone) to; use something as a landmark.

AGO$_1$
B **ago.** *v.* Learn, teach.
B 1 **agonga.** *n.* —.
B 2 **agoa.** *v.* —.
B 2 **agona.** *v.* —.
BE **hagaago.** *v.* Imitate; show, teach; to urge.
BE1 **hagaagonga.** *n.* —.
BE2 **hagaagoa.** *v.* —.
BE2 **hagaagona.** *v.* —.
P **aago.** *v.* —.
P 1 **aagonga.** *n.* —.
P 2 **aagoa.** *v.* —.
P 2 **aagona.** *v.* —.
R **agoago$_1$.** *v.* Learning, teaching.
R 1 **agoagonga.** *n.* —.
R 2 **agoagoa.** *v.* —.
R 2 **agoagona.** *v.* —.
RE **hagaagoago$_1$.** *v.* Lesson, make learn, cause to teach.
RE1 **hagaagoagonga.** *n.* —.
RE2 **hagaagoagoa.** *v.* —.
RE2 **hagaagoagona.** *v.* —.
ID **aagonga i lalo.** Social class of those who know the black arts.
ID **aagonga i lunga.** Social class of chiefs and priests.
ID **ago i tua.** Learn by heart.
ID **ago i me.** Copy, imitate.
ID **biho o de agoago.** Topic of a sermon.
ID **dangada agoago.** Teacher, preacher.
ID **haiva dee agona.** Sexual

activity, [lit., 'the activity which is not taught'].

AGO$_2$

R **agoago$_2$.** *v.* Taro fibers.
RE **hagaagoago$_2$.** *v.* Cause taro to be fibrous (e.g., by the planting method employed).

AGU

B 1 **aagunga.** *n.* —.
B 2 **agua.** *v.* —.
B 2 **agulia.** *v.* —.
BE **hagaagu.** *v.* —.
BE1 **hagaagunga.** *n.* —.
BE2 **hagaagua.** *v.* —.
BE2 **hagaagulia.** *v.* —.
R **aguagu.** *v.* —.
R 1 **aguagunga.** *n.* —.
R 2 **aguagua.** *v.* —.
R 2 **aguagulia.** *v.* —.
RE **hagaaguagu.** *v.* —.
RE1 **hagaaguagunga.** *n.* —.
RE2 **hagaaguagua.** *v.* —.
RE2 **hagaaguagulia.** *v.* —.
ID **agu age.** Say out loud.
ID **agu iho.** Say to oneself.
CF **dagu$_1$.** Speak, pronounce, utter (words).

AGU$_1$

B **agu$_1$.** *v.* Say or tell (esp. in confidence).

AGULE

B **agule.** *v.* Pick head lice.
B 1 **agulenga.** *n.* —.
B 2 **agulea.** *v.* —.
BE **hagaagule.** *v.* —.
BE1 **hagaagulenga.** *n.* —.
BE2 **hagaagulea.** *v.* —.
R **aguagule.** *v.* —.
R 1 **aguagulenga.** *n.* —.
R 2 **aguagulea.** *v.* —.
RE **hagaaguagule.** *v.* —.
RE1 **hagaaguagulenga.** *n.* —.
RE2 **hagaaguagulea.** *v.* —.
CF **ageli.** Pick head lice.

AHA$_1$

B **aha.** *v.* What?
BE **hagaaha.** *v.* Cause to do what?
XCO **beaha.** *a.* To be in a serious condition, critically ill or injured.
ID **aha ai.** What for?
ID **aha goi.** What next?
ID **aha goi delaa.** What was I going to say?
ID **aha laa.** I wonder why?
ID **aha naa.** Let's (later).
ID **aha nei.** Let's (now).
ID **be aha naa huu.** Whatever; if ever.
ID **de aha.** Which is it?
ID **e aha goe.** How about?
ID **ga aha.** And then did what?
ID **ga aha laa.** What's the matter with you?
ID **gai aha.** And then what?
ID **gai ga aha.** Too bad!
ID **gu aha.** Why?
ID **koe se aha.** Who do you think you are?
ID **hai aha.** What relationship?
ID **me aha ai.** What for?
ID **me pilo aha.** What's the point of doing this?
ID **me ssongo aha.** Useless thing.
ID **ni aha.** What are these?
ID **se aha.** What is it?
ID **se aha au naa.** You are wrong! That's not right! I don't agree!
ID **se aha ga hai.** It's not possible! Don't worry about it! (I don't think so.).
ID **se aha goe.** You're a nobody!

AHA$_2$

XFL **aha-bagua.** *n.* Driftwood sp. (resembles *bagua*).
XFL **aha-dea.** *n.* Driftwood sp. (white in the center).

AHANGI

B **ahangi.** *n.* Lagoon.

AHE

B **ahe.** *v.* Return, go back.
B 1 **ahenga.** *n.* —.
B 2 **ahelia.** *v.* —.
BC **maahe.** *a.* Decrease (in strength, rate of growth, etc.).
BC1 **maahenga.** *n.* —.

BE1 **hagaahenga.** *n.* —.
BE2 **hagaahea.** *v.* —.
BE2 **hagaahelia.** *v.* —.
BF **hagamaahe.** *v.* —.
BF1 **hagamaahenga.** *n.* —.
P **aahe.** *v.* —.
P 1 **aahenga.** *n.* —.
R **aheahe.** *v.* Keep returning.
R 1 **aheahenga.** *n.* —.
R 2 **aheahelia.** *v.* —.
RC **maaheahe.** *a.* Decreasing.
RC1 **maaheahenga.** *n.* —.
RE **hagaaheahe.** *v.* —.
RE1 **hagaaheahenga.** *n.* —.
RE2 **hagaaheahea.** *v.* —.
RE2 **hagaaheahelia.** *v.* —.
RF **hagamaaheahe.** *v.* —.
RF1 **hagamaaheahenga.** *n.* —.
XCO **dauaahe.** *a.* Gather or pleat in material; feathers of a rooster standing out on its neck (when angry); festooned with (e.g., flags).
ID **ahe age.** Start again, reoccur.
ID **ahe iho.** Diminish (in intensity).
ID **ahe ina.** Wind around completely once.
ID **dee ahe mai.** Incurably ill.
ID **duudanga aheahe.** Refrain (of song).
ID **hagaahe mai.** Return to the fold.
ID **hano ahe.** Echo.
ID **lodo aheahe.** Unstable temperamentally, inconstant.
ID **miili aheahe.** A version of the game called *miili.*

AHI_1
B **ahi.** *n.* Fire.
BE **hagaahi.** *v.* Provide fire to or for; hungry; eat something.
RE **hagaahiahi.** *a.* Wait until nearly sunset (to do something).
XCO **useahi.** *v.* Smoke, steam.
ID **ahi tugi.** Ignite a fire by making sparks with a stone.
ID **galo ahi.** Sparks.
ID **hagadubu o de ahi.** The name of a certain type of string figure.
ID **maga ahi.** Glowing embers (without a flame).
CF **lahhie.** Firewood.

AHI_{1a}
B **ahiahi.** *a.* Late afternoon and early evening.
ID **ahiahi danuaa.** Good afternoon! Good evening!
ID **gaba de ahiahi.** Early evening, late in the afternoon.
ID **seni ahiahi.** Go to bed early (in the evening).

AHI_{1b}
B **anaahi.** *b.* Yesterday.

AHI_2
ID **ahi dangada.** A (mat) wrapping for dead persons who are disposed of in the sea [a precontact custom].
ID **ahi malo.** A mat wrapping for clothes.

AHINGA
B **ahinga.** *n.* Armpit.

AHO
B **aho.** *n.* Fishing line of the sort used for *adu fishing.*
CF **hadi aho.** [var. of *hadi haho*].
CF **oho.** To do something, or go somewhere, early in the morning.

AHU
B **ahu.** *n.* Islet.
XCO **malaangahu.** *n.* Feast held for a newly launched canoe.
ID **ngudu aahua.** Islet shore (except that facing the lagoon).
CF **aahulu.** To leave food cooking overnight.
CF **huaahuu.** A type of prepared food (made from taro).

AHULU

B **ahulu.** *n.* Fish sp.: goat fish (= *madulilau sisisi*).

AI

B **ai.** *mv.* PREDICATE COMPLEMENT.

XCO **niaai.** *b.* Whose?

XCO **nioai.** *b.* Whose?

ID **aahee ai.** Then which?

ID **aha ai.** What for?

ID **alaa ai.** Those only.

ID **alaa ai huu.** Those there only then.

ID **alaa ai laa.** Those there then were.

ID **alaa ai loo.** Those there then are.

ID **aloha ai.** Feel sorry for or sympathetic toward.

ID **anaa ai.** These (there) only.

ID **anaa ai huu.** Those only then.

ID **anaa ai laa.** Those then were those.

ID **anaa ai loo.** Those then are.

ID **anei ai.** These (here) only.

ID **anei ai huu.** These only then.

ID **anei ai laa.** These then were those.

ID **anei ai loo.** These then are.

ID **danuaa ai loo.** Well, OK! (this time, but next time watch it!).

ID **delaa ai.** Therefore (with respect to that there).

ID **delaa ai huu.** That was it (as before)!

ID **delaa ai laa.** That there was it!

ID **delaa ai loo.** That was it at last!

ID **denaa ai.** Therefore (with respect to this, there near you, or concerning, you).

ID **denaa ai huu.** That is it then!

ID **denaa ai laa.** That was it!

ID **denaa ai loo.** That is it (which has been decided upon).

ID **denei ai.** Therefore (with respect to this here).

ID **denei ai huu.** This is it still.

ID **denei ai laa.** This is that then.

ID **denei ai loo.** This then is —.

ID **tigi ai.** Not yet.

ID **eidu ai.** Treat as a totem, worship, treat as a supernatural being.

ID **kaba ai loo.** Wait until — !

ID **hagadaahao ai.** Do something as though it were a game.

ID **hagadau hai me ai.** Use jointly or collectively.

ID **hagaingoo ai.** Called by (named).

ID **hano ai.** Attend (e.g., church services).

ID **hano ai huu.** Forever.

ID **hanohano ai huu.** Go on and on until —.

ID **hua ai.** Be in charge of.

ID **llava ai.** Wrapped (tied) around; eat fish or meat with a meal.

ID **malangilangi ai.** Happy with, pleased at; appreciative.

ID **me aha ai.** What for?

ID **noho ai.** Occupy or live in (a place).

ID **ngudu ai.** Act as an interpreter.

ID **odi ai loo.** That's the end! That's all!

ID **vaasuu ai loo.** I like it (or him or her) very much.

ID **vanei ai.** (E.g., I) wonder how —?

CF **deeai.** [an emphatic form of *deai*].

CF **goai.** Who?

AILAA

B **ailaa.** *b.* Today (sometime).

XCO **anailaa (nei).** *b.* Today (in the past).

XCO **anailaa laa.** It was today that.

ALA$_1$

B **ala$_1$.** *v.* A section of a mat.

BE **hagaala$_1$.** *v.* Make mat sections.

XCO **madaala$_1$.** *a.* Loosely

braided; good at twirling sennit.
ID **ala galigi.** A method of mat making.
ID **gave ala.** A method of plaiting mats.
CF **alahenua.** Plot of (bush) land, acreage.

ALA_2
B **ala_2.** *a.* Be awake, be open; bloom (of flowers).
BE **$hagaala_2$.** *v.* —.
P **aala.** *a.* —.
R **$alaala_2$.** *a.* Sleep fitfully.
RE **hagaalaala.** *v.* —; defecate.
RE1 **hagaalaalanga.** *n.* —.
XCO **alasala.** *a.* Vicious.
XCO **$madaala_2$.** *a.* Able to remain awake for a long time.
XFL **hauala.** *n.* Seaweed sp.
XFL **hua-ala.** *n.* Flower.
ID **alaala dangada.** False labor pains (of a pregnant woman).
ID **dagi ala.** Go around aimlessly.
ID **seni alaala.** Sleep fitfully (esp. because one is thinking about having to arise early); wake up repeatedly owing to anxiety.
CF **duu beleala.** Immature coconut apple.
CF **huaalavao.** A strong wind.

ALA_{2a}
B **alaange.** *a.* Allowed to, permissible.
BE **hagaalaange.** *v.* —.

ALA_{2b}
B **alahage.** *a.* Wake up (from sleep).
BE **hagaalahage.** *a.* —.

ALA_3
B **ala_3.** *n.* The name of a name-group.

ALAALA
B **$alaala_1$.** *n.* Fish sp.: jack (2 sorts) (= small *tulua*).
XFL **gada-alaala.** *n.* Fish sp.: jack? (like *alaala*).
ID **haa-alaala.** The fourth number of a counting game played to determine who is "it".

ALADOIDOI
B **aladoidoi.** *n.* Iron (a piece of).

ALAMOOI
B **Alamooi.** *n.* June.

ALAVA
B **alava.** *n.* Fish sp.: shark sp.?

ALEDUU
ID **boo aleduu.** Tomorrow night.

ALELO
B **alelo.** *n.* Tongue.
XFL **alelo-hatuli.** *n.* Mollusk sp.: pearly nautilus shell.
ID **daa de alelo.** Cluck one's tongue.
ID **hagasomo de alelo.** Stick out one's tongue.
ID **lau de alelo.** Be unable to speak clearly, owing to a stuttering problem.
CF **sua aaleloi.** A wrestling maneuver.

ALI
BE **hagaali.** *v.* To mention or expose something just enough so that the remainder is obvious.
BE1 **$hagaalinga_1$.** *n.* —.
BE2 **hagaalia.** *v.* —.
R **aliali.** *v.* The barely formed gelatinous layer inside the immature coconut.
R 1 **alialinga.** *n.* —.
RE **$hagaaliali_1$.** *v.* To attempt to attract a member of the opposite sex through exhibitionism.
RE **$hagaaliali_2$.** *v.* —.
RE1 **$hagaalialinga_1$.** *n.* —.
RE1 **$hagaalialinga_2$.** *n.* —.
RE2 **hagaalialia.** *v.* —.
XCO **boialiali.** *n.* The light just before daybreak.

CF **lauali.** Immature leaves.
CF **madaali.** Lacking in oil (of a ripe coconut).

ALIGI
B **aligi.** *a.* Priest (of a cult).
BE **hagaaligi.** *v.* Install as a priest (of a cult).
XCO **De-hine-aligi$_2$.** *nn.* The chief female spirit on Nukuoro (in legendary times).
XCO **haiadaligi.** *n.* The eldest child of the eldest child.
XCO **lua-aligi.** *a.* Chief mate (of a European ship).

ALILI
B **alili.** *n.* Mollusk sp.: *Turbo argyrostoma.*

ALIOO
XFL **manu-alioo.** *n.* Plant sp.: a variety of taro.

ALO$_1$
B 1 **aalonga.** *n.* —.
B 1 **alohanga.** *n.* A streak of smooth water in the sea.
B 2 **aaloa.** *v.* —.
BE **hagaalo$_1$.** *v.* —.
BE1 **hagaalonga.** *n.* —.
BE2 **hagaaloa.** *v.* —.
E **aalo.** *v.* Come by paddling.
R **aloalo$_1$.** *v.* To paddle (a canoe).
R 1 **aloalonga.** *n.* —.
R 2 **aloaloa.** *v.* —.
RE **hagaaloalo$_1$.** *v.* —.
RE1 **hagaaloalonga.** *n.* —.
RE2 **hagaaloaloa.** *v.* —.
XCO **dauaalo.** *v.* Steady paddling.
ID **aalo lo te moana.** A disturbance (local) of air.
ID **aloalo me.** The current nearest to the (seaward) outer reef of the atoll.
ID **sau aloalo.** Echo.

ALO$_{1a}$
ID **dada alohagi.** Trolling.
ID **dua alohagi.** Fishing line of a size appropriate for trolling.

ALO$_2$
B **alo-.** *d.* Coloring of coconut meat.
BE **hagaalo—$_2$.** *v.* —.
R **aloalo$_2$.** *d.* Becoming colored (of coconut meat only).
RE **hagaaloalo—$_2$.** *v.* —.
XCO **aloalo-mea.** *a.* Becoming red (of fully mature coconut meat).
XCO **aloalo-uli.** *a.* Becoming dark (of fully mature coconut meat).
XCO **alo-malie.** *a.* Coconut meat (fully mature) of good quality for eating.
XCO **alo-mea.** *a.* Reddish color (of fully mature coconut meat).
XCO **alo-uli.** *a.* Dark color (of fully mature coconut meat).
XE **hagaaloalo-mea.** *v.* Cause to become red (of fully mature coconut meat).
XE **hagaaloalo-uli.** *v.* Cause to become dark (of fully mature coconut meat).
XE **hagaalo-malie.** *v.* Cause to become *alomalie.*
XE **hagaalo-mea.** *v.* Cause to be red (of fully mature coconut meat).
XE **hagaalo-uli.** *v.* Cause to be dark (of fully mature coconutmeat).
ID **aloalo gaadinga.** The part of a coconut's meat next to the sap.

ALO$_3$
R **aloalo$_3$.** *n.* Chest, front (opposite of back — e.g.,lagoon shore as opposed to seaward reef shore).
XCO **alobagi.** *v.* A lagoonward sand spit next to a channel between islets on the atoll.
XCO **alohaha.** *n.* Throat (of fish only).
ID **hadu alo.** The bottom portion of a fish.
ID **io alo.** Lower *io*, q.v.

CF maalo. Energetic, eager, wide-awake; waiting.

ALO3a

B **alohi.** *n.* Anything forming a semi-circle.

P **aalohi.** *n.* The portion of the atoll lagoon just lagoonward of the fringing reef.

ID **aalohi modu.** Lagoonward of the islets of the atoll.

ID **alohi lima.** Palm (of the hand).

ID **alohi vae.** Sole (of the foot).

ALODAHI

B **alodahi.** *n.* All.

ID **alodahi hugadoo.** Everything, everybody; each and every.

ALOHA

B **aloha.** *a.* Compassion, affection.

BE **hagaaloha.** *a.* Piteous, pitiful.

P **aaloha.** *a.* —.

ID **aloha ai.** Feel sorry for or sympathetic toward.

ID **aloha gelo.** Profound affection.

ID **aloha iho.** Self-love.

ID **aloha ina.** Helpful toward.

ID **hagaau aloha.** Poor (not rich).

ID **hagadau aaloha.** Love each other (esp. of persons of the opposite sex).

ID **soa hagaaloha.** A good friend.

ID **vvela de aloha.** Feel very sorry for.

ALOMASIGE

B **alomasige.** *a.* Hasten to go or come.

B 1 **alomasigeanga.** *n.* —.

BE **hagaalomasige.** *v.* —.

BE1 **hagaalomasigeanga.** *n.* —.

ALOO

ID **aloo anahee.** For how long has this been going on?

ALU

B 1 **alumanga.** *n.* —.

B 2 **alumia.** *v.* —.

E **aalu.** *v.* Intercept; send for.

E 1 **aalunga.** *n.* —.

E 2 **aalua.** *v.* —.

R **alualu.** *v.* — (ex. 'intercept' meanings) .

R 1 **alualumanga.** *n.* —.

R 1 **alualunga.** *n.* —.

R 2 **alualua.** *v.* —.

R 2 **alualumia.** *v.* Send away [no meaning 'intercept' as *alualua*].

RE **hagaalualu.** *v.* —.

XCO **dauaalu.** *v.* Always borrowing or begging.

ALUa

B **alukaba.** *v.* Leave quickly (usually under duress).

B 1 **alukabaanga.** *n.* —.

BE **hagaalukaba.** *v.* Cause to leave quickly, force out.

BE1 **hagaalukabaanga.** *n.* —.

P **aalukaba.** *v.* —.

R **alualukaba.** *v.* —.

RE **hagaalualukaba.** *v.* —.

RE1 **hagaalualukabaanga.** *n.* —.

AMA

B **ama1.** *n.* Outrigger float.

ID **baabaa ama.** To steer a canoe to its outrigger side (opp. of *baabaa gadea*).

ID **dau ama.** The mast stay tied to the outrigger boom.

ID **hadahada ama.** The platform fastened on top of the outrigger booms of a canoe.

ID **hai de ama.** To have a spouse.

ID **i ama.** On the same side of a canoe as the outrigger float.

ID **loua ama.** To sail with the outrigger float partially submerged.

AMO

B **amo.** *v.* Lift up.

B 1 **amoanga.** *n.* —.

B 1 **amonga.** *n.* —.

B 2 **amoa.** *v.* —.
B 2 **amoaa.** *v.* —.
B 2 **amoea.** *v.* —.
B 3 **amoaanga.** *n.* —.
B 3 **amoeanga.** *n.* —.
BE **hagaamo.** *v.* —.
BE1 **hagaamoanga.** *n.* —.
BE1 **hagaamonga.** *n.* —.
BE2 **hagaamoa.** *v.* —.
BE2 **hagaamoaa.** *v.* —.
BE2 **hagaamoea.** *v.* —.
BE3 **hagaamoaanga.** *n.* —.
BE3 **hagaamoeanga.** *n.* —.
R **amoamo.** *v.* Keep lifting one thing after another.
R 1 **amoamoanga.** *n.* —.
R 1 **amoamonga.** *n.* —.
R 2 **amoamoa.** *v.* —.
R 2 **amoamoaa.** *v.* —.
R 2 **amoamoea.** *v.* —.
R 3 **amoamoaanga.** *n.* —.
R 3 **amoamoeanga.** *n.* —.
RE **hagaamoamo.** *v.* —.
RE1 **hagaamoamoanga.** *n.* —.
RE1 **hagaamoamonga.** *n.* —.
RE2 **hagaamoamoa.** *v.* —.
RE2 **hagaamoamoaa.** *v.* —.
RE2 **hagaamoamoea.** *v.* —.
RE3 **hagaamoamoaanga.** *n.* —.
RE3 **hagaamoamoenga.** *n.* —.

AMU
B **amu.** *v.* Twirl fibers (with *ina*); fibers for the manufacture of rope or cloth, etc.
B 1 **aamunga.** *n.* —.
B 2 **amuia.** *v.* —.
B 2 **amulia.** *v.* —.
BE **hagaamu$_1$.** *v.* —.
BE1 **hagaamuanga.** *n.* —.
BE1 **hagaamunga.** *n.* —.
BE2 **hagaamua$_1$.** *v.* —.
BE2 **hagaamuia.** *v.* —.
R **amuamu.** *v.* —; small and useless particles, leftovers.
R 1 **amuamunga.** *n.* —.
R 2 **amuamuia.** *v.* —.
R 2 **amuamulia.** *v.* —.
RE **hagaamuamu.** *v.* —.
RE1 **hagaamuamunga.** *n.* —.
RE2 **hagaamuamuia.** *v.* —.
RE2 **hagaamuamulia.** *v.* —.
ID **amuamu iho.** Drizzle.
ID **amu ligi.** Fine threads or hairs or fibers (in feather or leaf, etc.); fine-feathered.

ANA$_1$
B **ana-$_1$.** *mf.* PAST TIME PREFIX.
XCO **anaahi.** *b.* Yesterday.
XCO **anataiao.** This morning.
XCO **anahee.** *b.* When? (past time).
XCO **anailaa (nei).** *b.* Today (in the past).
XCO **anailaa laa.** It was today that.
ID **aloo anahee.** For how long has this been going on?
ID **anaange laa hanu.** A little while ago.

ANA$_2$
B **ana$_2$.** *mt.* [var. of *kana*].

ANE
R **aneane.** *n.* To desire physically a member of the opposite sex.
R 1 **aneanenga.** *n.* —.
R 2 **aneanea.** *v.* —.
RE **hagaaneane.** *v.* Console; excite sexually.
RE1 **hagaaneanenga.** *n.* —.
RE2 **hagaaneanea.** *v.* —.

ANU
B **anu.** *v.* To dance.
B 1 **aanunga.** *n.* —.
B 1 **anumanga.** *n.* —; dancing party.
B 2 **anumia.** *v.* Bobbing in the water.
BE **hagaanu.** *v.* Cause to dance or sway.
BE1 **hagaanumanga.** *n.* —.
BE1 **hagaanunga.** *n.* —.
BE2 **hagaanua.** *v.* —.
BE2 **hagaanumia.** *v.* —.
P **aanu.** *v.* —.
P 1 **aanumanga.** *n.* —.
R **anuanu.** *v.* —.
R 1 **anuanumanga.** *n.* —.
R 1 **anuanunga.** *n.* —.
R 2 **anuanumia.** *v.* —.
RE **hagaanuanu.** *v.* —.

RE1 **hagaanuanumanga.** *n.* —.
RE1 **hagaanuanunga.** *n.* —.
RE2 **hagaanuanua.** *v.* —.
RE2 **hagaanuanumia.** *v.* —.
ID **anu age.** To dance below people.
ID **anuanumia age.** Visibly bobbing up and down in the sea.

ANGA$_1$

B **anga$_1$.** *a.* Pay attention to (notice), be aware of.
B 2 **angahia.** *v.* —.
BE **hagaanga$_1$.** *v.* —.
BE2 **hagaangahia$_1$.** *v.* —.
P **aanga.** *a.* —.
P 2 **aangahia.** *v.* —.
PE **hagaanga$_2$.** *v.* —.
PE2 **hagaangahia$_2$.** *v.* —.
R **angaanga$_1$.** *a.* Aware, alert.
R 2 **angaangahia.** *v.* —.
RE **hagaangaanga$_1$.** *v.* —.
RE2 **hagaangaangahia.** *v.* —.
ID **anga gee.** Turn one's attention away from.
ID **anga iho.** Self-awareness.
ID **dee anga.** Forgetful, absent-minded.

ANGA$_2$

B **anga$_2$.** *v.* The span of the outstretched thumb and little finger; a measurement of one span.
B 2 **angaa.** *v.* —.
BE **hagaanga$_3$.** *v.* —.
BE2 **hagaangaa.** *v.* —.
R **angaanga$_2$.** *a.* Measure by spans (*anga*).
RE **hagaangaanga$_2$.** *v.* —.
RE2 **hagaangaangaa.** *v.* —.
XFL **anga-baabaa.** *n.* Mollusk sp.: spider conch.
XFL **anga-dogi.** *n.* Mollusk sp.: *Cerithiidae.*
XFL **anga-mea.** *n.* Fish sp. (= large *dada*).

ANGA$_{2a}$

B **ianga.** *v.* The span between the outstretched thumb and the little finger.
B 2 **iangaa.** *v.* —.
BE **hagaianga.** *v.* —.
BE2 **hagaiangaa.** *v.* —.
R **iaianga.** *v.* —.
RE **hagaiaianga.** *v.* —.
RE2 **hagaiaiangaa.** *v.* —.

ANGA$_3$

B **anga$_3$ —.** *d.* Prototype, model (something from which a copy can be made).
R **angaanga$_3$.** *n.* Body.
XCO **gauanga.** *n.* Thigh.
ID **angaanga dabuvae.** Toenail.
ID **angaanga madannia.** Fingernail.
ID **anga dua.** An adze blade which is set at a right angle to its handle.
ID **anga gi lodo.** An adze blade which is set at less than a right angle to its handle.
ID **deai donu angaanga.** Nothing at all.
ID **dohu de angaanga.** Covered (all over the body) with —.

ANGE

B **ange.** *mv.* Away from both the speaker and hearer; more, farther; again.
R **angeange.** *mv.* Again.
XCO **hanange.** *a.* Go to.
ID **aahee ange.** What else?
ID **aamua ange.** Higher.
ID **abo ange.** Good at.
ID **adu ange laa.** The one following the one in question.
ID **alaa ange huu.** That there [pl.] much more only.
ID **alaa ange maalie.** Those there are exactly right.
ID **alaa ange naa.** About that [pl.] (over there) much more.
ID **anaa ange.** And these (there).
ID **anaa ange huu.** That [pl.] much more only.
ID **anaa ange maalie.** Those are exactly right.
ID **anaa ange naa.** About that [pl.] (here) much more.
ID **anaange laa hanu.** A little

while ago.

ID **anei ange.** And these (here).

ID **anei ange huu.** This [pl.] much more only.

ID **anei ange maalie.** These are exactly right.

ID **anei ange naa.** About this [pl.] much more.

ID **angeange laa.** The one following the one in question.

ID **ange gi.** According to —.

ID **ange laa.** The next but one.

ID **baa ange.** Close to, near to.

ID **baageaa ange.** Attracted to.

ID **baalasi ange.** Compete hard against (as in team sports).

ID **baasanga tugi ange muna.** Talk back.

ID **baba ange.** Ready for.

ID **basa ange.** Answer, reply.

ID **bau ange.** Capable of, be the equal of.

ID **bigi ange.** Just about like —.

ID **bolo ange.** Bequeath.

ID **boolaa ange.** Say *boolaa* to.

ID **boo mai ange laa.** The second night following.

ID **buni ange.** Agree with; join, close up (something,e.g., a hole); close up to.

ID **poo ange.** Touch (someone or something with the hand).

ID **daadaaia ange.** Be in a hurry to.

ID **daahanga ange.** Give pleasure to someone by giving him something.

ID **daelodo dee odi ange.** Odd number.

ID **daelodo odi ange.** Even number.

ID **danuaa ange.** Good for, better than.

ID **dangidangi ange.** Ask permission of, apologize to.

ID **daohi ange dahi hai.** Argue against.

ID **dau ange.** Depend upon (e.g., for sustenance).

ID **deai ange loo soo savaa.** Now I've got you!

ID **delaa ange.** That there is another one!

ID **delaa ange maalie.** That there is exactly right!

ID **delaa ange naa.** About that [sing.] (over there), much more.

ID **denaa ange.** This there is another one!

ID **denaa ange maalie.** That is exactly right!

ID **denaa ange naa.** About that [sing.] (here), much more.

ID **denei ange.** This is another one!

ID **denei ange maalie.** This is exactly right!

ID **denei ange naa.** About this [sing.], much more...

ID **dii ange.** A method of fishing in which the lure at the end of the pole is jerked to attract fish.

ID **diidii ange.** Urinate against.

ID **dilia ange.** Give fish to.

ID **dogaa ange.** Feel shy in the presence of.

ID **dohu ange.** Sufficient for.

ID **donu ange.** Understand (someone or something).

ID **dongi ange.** Appoint.

ID **dulagi ange.** Look like.

ID **dungagi ange.** Nod one's head toward (to beckon or indicate agreement, etc.).

ID **duu ange.** Wait for; resemble someone (owing to a consanguineal relationship).

ID **duuhia ange.** Praised (by others).

ID **tagi ange.** Contribute (material things) to.

ID **tale ange.** Sharpen (knife).

ID **tau ange.** Cause to be absorbed by.

ID **tau ange luu mada.** Have noticed.

ID **tugi ange —.** Contradict by —.

ID **ege ange.** Move

(something) over.
ID **gali ange.** Wound around or tied or fastened very tightly.
ID **gauligi ange.** Younger than.
ID **gauligi mai ange.** The one next younger still.
ID **gemo ange huu de —.** Rapidly becoming —.
ID **giidagi ange gi —.** Eat a side dish with —.
ID **gugu ange.** Able to look after others; able to withstand.
ID **gu odi ange ona.** He has done all he could.
ID **kadi ange.** Fastened on to (by being stuck in).
ID **kii ange.** Increase.
ID **kona ange.** Become much worse.
ID **haahaangoda ange.** Prowl around (to attack).
ID **hagabaguu ange.** Move against something so fast that it appears to be coming at one.
ID **hagabinga ange.** Be known as, called by the name —.
ID **hagabuu ange.** Blame (someone), incriminate (someone).
ID **hagapigi ange.** Stick against (something), go with someone.
ID **hagadabena ange.** Prepare for.
ID **hagadaga ange.** Increase in.
ID **hagahana ange.** Recook for a very little while.
ID **hagailonga ange agina.** Assign (someone) to; use something as a landmark.
ID **hagalloba ange.** To slacken the boom sheet (of a sailing canoe).
ID **hagamaasei ange.** Make smaller (away from one).
ID **hagame ange laa.** A little later.
ID **hagasaalunga ange.** Call (someone) by the name of his name-group.
ID **hagasegesege ange.** Allow someone to do as he pleases.
ID **hagasoa ange.** Go along with others, join the crowd.
ID **hagasoe ange.** Aim at.
ID **hai ange.** Do to; do for, fix; say to.
ID **hanu ange.** Some more.
ID **heohi ange.** Suited to, fit (with), appropriate to.
ID **hilo ange.** Mix with.
ID **holi ange.** Resemble.
ID **hoosenga ange.** Embarrassed by.
ID **iho ange** + PRONOUN—. To have relapsed into (his/her, etc.) —.
ID **iho ange de —.** Feel like (one is) about to —.
ID **laa ange.** And those there.
ID **libo ange de henua.** Feel dizzy or faint, vertigo.
ID **libolibo ange.** Drunk, dizzy, crazy.
ID **llibo ange luu vae.** Run.
ID **mademadea ange.** Feel sleepy.
ID **magulu mai ange.** Less — than.
ID **mai ange laa.** The next (one) following the one in question.
ID **maimai ange.** To have been dulled (from having been struck on a hard object).
ID **maingaa ange nei gi.** To wish one has —.
ID **maingaa ange loo.** Feel really *maingaa* about —.
ID **mami ange.** Taste (food).
ID **masole ange.** Barely scratched.
ID **mau ange huu.** Usually.
ID **me ange laa.** The others.
ID **midia ange.** Dream about.
ID **molimoli ange.** Take up slack in a line with hitches in order to maintain tension on something being hauled (e.g., a ship stuck on the reef during the moments when it is floated by waves).

ID **moosugia ange.** Somewhat *moosugia*.

ID **muli mai ange.** A little later, by and by.

ID **noho mai (adu, ange).** Resist me (you, them), oppose me (you, them).

ID **ngalue ange.** Increase.

ID **ngaue ange.** Increase (in price, etc.).

ID **odi ange.** Even (number); complete (none missing); reach the maximum.

ID **salani ange.** Just a little *salani*.

ID **seni ange.** Rest up for (e.g., the next day's work).

ID **sui ange.** Take revenge, get even; pay back (a debt).

ID **suugui ange.** Join to, connect to, connect up with.

ID **ue ange.** Increase (speed or power, etc.).

ID **ueue ange.** Exaggerate.

ID **usuusu ange.** Encourage, egg on (e.g., to fight); try to talk into.

ID **vvae ange.** Divide into portions.

CF **loange.** Go (to the place away from both the speaker and hearer) [pl.].

ANGI

B **angi.** *v.* Blow gently (of wind); a disturbance (of the water).

B 1 **anginga.** *n.* —.

B 2 **angia.** *v.* Blow away, cause tomove (in the water).

B 2 **angina.** *v.* —.

BE **hagaangi.** *v.* —.

BE1 **hagaanginga.** *v.* —.

BE2 **hagaangia.** *v.* —.

BE2 **hagaangina.** *v.* —.

R **angiangi.** *v.* Blow with increasing force (wind); blow continuously (wind); fan.

R 1 **angianginga.** *n.* —.

R 2 **angiangia.** *v.* —.

R 2 **angiangina.** *v.* —.

RE **hagaangiangi.** *v.* —; expose to a breeze.

RE1 **hagaangianginga.** *n.* —.

RE2 **hagaangiangia.** *v.* —.

RE2 **hagaangiangina.** *v.* —.

ID **gaadinga hagaangiangi.** Copra dried in the wind (not in the sun or in an oven).

ANGO

B **ango.** *n.* The carapace of the hawksbill turtle; pearl.

XCO **ganoango.** *a.* Yellow.

XFL **gaalau-ango.** *n.* Plant sp.: tumeric plant (*Curcuma* sp.).

ID **vai ango.** A yellowish discharge from the genitalia (of either males or females).

AO$_1$

B **ao$_1$.** *v.* Daylight.

B 1 **aonga.** *n.* Sort or degree of daybreak.

B 2 **aoa$_3$.** *v.* To inadvertently remain up until daybreak.

BE **hagaao$_1$.** *v.* Intend to stay up until daybreak.

BE1 **hagaaonga$_1$.** *n.* Way of staying up until daybreak.

BE2 **hagaaoa$_1$.** *v.* To have purposely stayed up until daybreak.

R **aoao$_1$.** *v.* Becoming daylight.

R 1 **aoaonga.** *n.* Way of staying up until daybreak.

R 2 **aoaoa.** *v.* Habitually remain up until daybreak.

RE **hagaaoao$_1$.** *v.* Habitually and purposely remain up until daybreak.

RE1 **hagaaoaonga$_1$.** *n.* Way of having purposely stayed up until daybreak (once).

RE2 **hagaaoaoa$_1$.** *v.* Have purposely and habitually remained up until daybreak.

ID **ao age.** Daybreak (become daylight).

ID **ao de me.** Daytime.

ID **ao ina.** Inadvertently

	remain up until daybreak (= *aoa*).
ID	**seni gi de ao.** Sleep late (into daytime).
CF	**daiao.** Morning, tomorrow.
CF	**oomea.** Afternoon (late).

AO_2

B	**ao_2.** *a.* Sufficient.
BE	**$hagaao_2$.** *v.* Cause to be sufficient.
BE1	**$hagaaonga_2$.** *n.* —.
BE2	**$hagaaóa_2$.** *v.* Cause to have been sufficient, relieve.
R	**$aoao_2$.** *a.* Continuously sufficient.
RE	**$hagaaoao_2$.** *v.* —.
RE1	**$hagaaoaonga_2$.** *n.* —.
RE2	**$hagaaoaoa_2$.** *v.* Cause to have been continuously sufficient; aid (by giving something); help (with provisions).
ID	**deai me ao ai.** Useless.
CF	**hagao.** Buy, sell, repay.

AOA_1

B	**aoa_1.** *n.* Plant sp.: tree sp.: banyan tree (*Ficus prolixa* Forst.).
XFL	**aoa-laosedi.** *n.* Gorgonian (Coelenterate), false black coral.

AOA_2

B	**aoa_2.** *v.* Misshapen fruit.
BE	**$hagaaoa_3$.** *v.* Cause to bear misshapen fruit (e.g., by not picking in bunches).
BE1	**hagaaoanga.** *n.* —.
ID	**hai aoa ina.** Bear misshapen fruit.

AOO

B	**aoo.** *i.* A kind of sound, indicating surprise.

ASA

CF	**aasasi.** Flee (of a small school of fish).
CF	**gauasa.** The pectoral fin of a fish and the surrounding flesh.
CF	**lauasaasa.** Skinny.

ASO_1

B	**aso.** *n.* Fish sp.: white-tip shark.

ASO_2

RE	**hagaasoaso.** *n.* Spouse.

ASU

B	**asu.** *v.* Scoop up (liquids only), spoon.
B 1	**aasunga.** *n.* —.
B 2	**asua.** *v.* —.
B 2	**asulia.** *v.* —.
BE	**hagaasu.** *v.* —.
BE1	**hagaasunga.** *n.* —.
BE2	**hagaasua.** *v.* —.
R	**asuasu.** *v.* —.
R 1	**asuasunga.** *n.* —.
R 2	**asuasua.** *v.* —.
R 2	**asuasulia.** *v.* —.

AU_1

B	**au_1.** *v.* (The generic term for the major types of) currents in the open sea.
BE	**$hagaau_1$.** *v.* To create an ocean current.
ID	**au dili dai.** An ocean current flowing away from land.
ID	**au dili uda.** An ocean current flowing toward land.
ID	**au doga.** A confluence of ocean currents, or a circular current in which drifting objects remain stationary.
ID	**au hagi.** An ocean current which turns away from the reef.
ID	**au hebaledage.** A confluence of ocean currents (on the surface only).
ID	**au madua.** A type of ocean current far from land in which drifting objects collect.
ID	**sugi au.** A current of choppy water between other currents.
CF	**beau.** A wave, the surf.

AU_2

B	**au_2.** *pi.* I.
C	**$ngau_1$.** *pi.* [var. of *au_1*].
ID	**au e dee gai naa loo.** I'll bet you can't!
ID	**au ga sano.** I give up!
ID	**denei au.** It is I!

ID **magau loo au.** Now I'm really in trouble!

AU$_3$

B **au$_3$.** *ppa.* Your several.

AUDE

B **aude.** *mt.* NEGATIVE PRESCRIPTIVE ASPECT MARKER.

C **audee.** *mt.* [var. of *aude*].

ID **aude haia.** No kidding?

ID **aude vaavaa.** Don't talk about this to anyone!

ID **au taadaaia.** Don't rush! Take it easy!

AUGAU

B **augau.** *v.* Pus.

B 1 **augaunga.** *n.* The appearance of an infected area.

B 2 **augaua.** *v.* Infected.

BE **hagaaugau.** *v.* Cause infection.

BE1 **hagaaugaunga.** *n.* State of becoming infected.

BE2 **hagaaugaua.** *v.* Cause to be infected.

AVA$_1$

B **ava$_1$.** *v.* Passage, channel.

BE **hagaava$_1$.** *v.* Make a channel.

BE1 **hagaavaanga$_1$.** *n.* —.

R **avaava.** *v.* Full of holes.

R 1 **avaavaanga.** *n.* —.

RE **hagaavaava$_1$.** *v.* —.

RE1 **hagaavaavaanga$_1$.** *n.* —.

XCO **haiava.** *n.* Road, pathway (for going), track; ocean liner.

XFL **doi-avaava.** *n.* The sap of a hardwood sp. which drifts ashore (used for making perfume).

ID **dada de ava.** A strong current in the channel.

ID **dao haiava.** Path (a minor, not major, thoroughfare).

ID **lau de ava.** A tuna of large size.

AVA$_2$

B **ava$_2$.** *a.* Relief, be relieved.

BE **hagaava$_2$.** *v.* Relieve.

BE1 **hagaavaanga$_2$.** *n.* —.

RE **hagaavaava$_2$.** *v.* Provide or receive support continually.

RE1 **hagaavaavaanga$_2$.** *n.* —.

ID **hagaava age.** Be relieved for a short time.

ID **hagaava ange.** Lean on someone for support.

AVA$_3$

B **ava$_3$.** *n.* Fish sp. (= large *tonu*, also = large *hagaodalolo*).

BAA$_1$

B **baa$_1$.** *a.* Touch (two or more things), be in contact, make contact with uniformly.

BD **hebaa.** *a.* Be close.

BE **hagabaa$_1$.** *v.* Cause to come into contact with; chase by trying to head off.

BG **hagahebaa.** *v.* —.

BG1 **hagahebaanga.** *n.* —.

P **paa$_1$.** *a.* —.

PE **hagapaa$_1$.** *v.* —.

R **baabaa$_1$.** *a.* Continuously touch or slap lightly, pat.

RD **hebahebaa.** *a.* Crowded together.

RE **hagabaabaa$_1$.** *v.* —.

RG **hagahebahebaa.** *v.* —.

RG1 **hagahebahebaanga.** *n.* —.

ID **baa age.** Shallow (e.g., waters).

ID **baa ange.** Close to, near to.

ID **baabaa luu lima.** Clap hands.

ID **baa hagasalau.** Make contact with while not aligned.

ID **baa huu i —.** Just like.

ID **baa i de madangi.** Be hit (usually forcefully) by wind.

ID **baa iho.** Low (in altitude).

ID **paa i daalinga.** Move in closely (of birds) to *daalinga*.

ID **paa ono pagola.** Punished for his bad deeds.

ID **paa ono maahana.** Receive one's punishment, suffer.

ID **dee baa tae.** Stay for only a very short time.

ID gaadinga gaha paa. A coconut with an unusually small-sized kernel.
ID gaha paa. A coconut with a small kernel.
ID hagahebaa ngudu. Converse (conversation).
CF baalau. Sticky, greasy.

BAA_2

BE **$hagabaa_2$.** *v.* To crack (as a nut).
BE1 **hagabaanga.** *n.* —.
P **paa_2.** *a.* Explode, burst.
PE **$hagapaa_2$.** *v.* —.
PE1 **hagapaanga.** *n.* —.
RE1 **hagababaanga.** *n.* —.
T **babaa.** *a.* A crackling sound, the sound of continuous explosions.
TE **$hagabaabaa_2$.** *v.* —.
TE **hagababaa.** *v.* —.
TE1 **$hagabaabaanga_1$.** *n.* —.
ID **paa age.** Explode from below.
ID **paa de hatuli.** Rolling of thunder.
ID **paa de hoa.** Happy (lit., 'to slap one's sides').
ID **paa de mahedua.** Sneeze loudly.
ID **paa iho.** Explode from above.

BAA_3

B **baa_2.** *n.* Mollusk sp.: pearl oyster.
ID **baa galele.** Fishing lure of pearl shell, used in *galele* fishing.
ID **duudae baa.** The dust produced by working pearl shell to make a hook.
ID **hhagi de baa galele.** Jerking of a fishing lure to attract fish; a method of extracting a lure from the fish's mouth.

BAA_4

B **$baba_1$.** *a.* Level (not bumpy); (any sort of) flat base (esp. the board on which mats are plaited), the consolidated reef under water or sand; the back of a human; the shell of a turtle, crab, etc.; to be ready.
B **$baba_2$.** *n.* Fish sp.: squirrelfish.
B 1 **baabanga.** *n.* —; an impression left by a hard object pressing on a soft one.
B 2 **babalia.** *a.* —.
BE **hagababa.** *v.* Become engaged to marry; make level, make flat; prepare for, make ready.
BE1 **hagabaabanga.** *n.* —.
BE2 **hagababalia.** *v.* —.
P **paba.** *a.* —.
PE **hagapaba.** *v.* —.
PE2 **hagapabalia.** *v.* —.
R **$baabaa_2$.** *a.* Flat, board.
R **bapaba.** *a.* Flutter against (as a hooked fish).
R 1 **baabaanga.** *n.* —.
R 1 **bapabaanga.** *n.* —.
RE **$hagabaabaa_3$.** *v.* —.
RE **hagabapaba.** *v.* —.
RE1 **$hagabaabaanga_2$.** *n.* —.
RE1 **hagabapabaanga.** *n.* —.
RE2 **hagabapabalia.** *v.* —.
XFL **anga-baabaa.** *n.* Mollusk sp.: spider conch.
ID **baa lahalaha.** Broad-chested.
ID **baba age.** Be decided about.
ID **baba ange.** Ready for.
ID **baba donu.** Properly settled.
ID **baba iho.** Recently settled.
ID **baba odi.** To have been settled for some time.
ID **paa i tua tinae.** Have an empty stomach.
ID **tua de baba.** Lower back (of a human).
ID **hagadubu manu baabaa.** The name of a certain type of string figure.
ID **hale baabaa.** Frame house.
ID **hau baba.** Tie up temporarily (not as securely as if permanently).
ID **honu baabaa.** Fill to the brim.
ID **lodo baba.** Calmness,

tranquility, freedom from worries.
ID **mada baabaa.** = *daogili.*
ID **noho baba.** Live peacefully.
ID **oha de nnoho paba.** Disturb the peace.

BAA$_{4a}$
B **abaaba.** *v.* Door; cover (something, e.g., to protect it from the elements).

BAA$_5$
B 2 **baagia.** *v.* Move sideways while moving forward (as a canoe slipping in the water); slap.
BE2 **hagabaagia.** *v.* —.
RE2 **hagabaabaagia.** *v.* Make no headway and be carried sideways (by a current or the wind) against a reef, etc.
XCO **baagava.** *n.* Violent in word or action.
XE **hagabaagava.** *v.* To threaten violence.
ID **baabaa ama.** To steer a canoe to its outrigger side (opp. of *baabaa gadea*).
ID **baabaa gadea.** To steer a canoe to the side away from its outrigger (opp. of *baabaa ama*).
ID **baa donu.** Skillful at fighting (opp. of *baa sala*).
ID **baagia age.** To be carried to the shore (of a canoe) by a current or the wind.
ID **baa sala.** Be clumsy (in physical contest).
ID **baa sege.** Carom off.
ID **baa ssalu.** Carom off violently.

BAABUU
B **baabuu.** *a.* Lie down [baby talk].
B 1 **baabuunga.** *n.* —.
BE **hagabaabuu.** *v.* —.
BE1 **hagabaabuunga.** *n.* —.
BE2 **hagabaabuua.** *v.* —.

BAAGEAA
B **baageaa.** *a.* Weak (of a person).
B 1 **baageaanga.** *n.* —.
BE **hagabaageaa.** *v.* —.
BE1 **hagabaageaanga.** *n.* —.
ID **baageaa ange.** Attracted to.
ID **baageaa iho.** Weakening (becoming weaker).
ID **lodo baageaa.** Weak-willed, easily tempted; excited easily by the opposite sex.

BAAHAA
BE1 **hagabahhaanga.** *n.* —.

BAALANGA
B **baalanga$_2$.** *n.* Metal (any kind) [from Trade Malay?].
XFL **helii-baalanga.** *n.* Plant sp.: grass sp.
ID **baalanga dua hale.** Metal roofing.
ID **baalanga tea.** Stainless steel.
ID **baalanga tugi.** Nail (of metal).
ID **baalanga mmea.** Copper or brass or other reddish metal.
ID **baalanga sauaa.** Magnet.
ID **baalanga uli.** Cast iron.
ID **daa de baalanga.** Ring the bell.
ID **daula baalanga.** Cable, wire (heavy).
ID **gau bini baalanga.** An iron rod.
ID **goloa baalanga.** Metal-working tools.
ID **hale baalanga.** Frame house.
ID **hongagelegele baalanga.** Rust.

BAALASA
B **baalasa.** *v.* Ballast for an outrigger [from Eng. 'ballast'?].
B 1 **baalasaanga.** *n.* —.
BE **hagabaalasa.** *v.* —.
BE1 **hagabaalasaanga.** *n.* —.

BAALASI

B	**baalasi.** *v.* Press down or against; sit on (as chicken hatching eggs).
B 1	**baalasinga.** *n.* —.
B 2	**balasia.** *v.* —; be crushed.
BE	**hagabaalasi.** *v.* —.
BE1	**hagabalasinga.** *n.* —.
BE2	**hagabalasia.** *v.* —.
R	**balabalasi.** *v.* —.
R 1	**balabalasinga.** *n.* —.
R 2	**balabalasia.** *v.* —.
RE	**hagabalabalasi.** *v.* —.
RE1	**hagabalabalasinga.** *n.* —.
RE2	**hagabalabalasia.** *v.* —.
ID	**baalasi ange.** Compete hard against (as in team sports).
ID	**baalasi de ada.** To take a picture.
ID	**baalasi mai (adu).** Shine a flashlight toward me (you).
ID	**baalasi ngago.** Incubation of eggs (by a hen).
ID	**baalasi saele.** Shine a flashlight indiscriminately on people.
ID	**sisi baalasi.** Printing (block letters).
CF	**baa$_1$.** Touch (two or more things), be in contact, make contact with uniformly.
CF	**bala.** Soft, mushy, offering no resistance.

BAALAU

B	**baalau.** *a.* Sticky, greasy.
B 1	**baalaunga.** *n.* —.
BE	**hagabaalau.** *v.* —.
BE1	**hagabaalaunga.** *n.* —.
BE2	**hagabaalaua.** *v.* —.
ID	**gai baalau.** Eat messily (getting food on one's face); make a mess (esp. involving liquid or organic material).
CF	**balaulau.** Ugly-looking, messy, sloppy.

BAANI

B	**baani.** *a.* Lie down.
B 1	**baaninga.** *n.* —.
BE	**hagabaani.** *v.* —.
BE1	**hagabaaninga.** *n.* —.
BE2	**hagabaania.** *v.* —.
CF	**bani.** —.

BAASI

B	**baasi.** *nl.* Side, half.
BE	**hagabaasi.** *v.* Do toward one side.
R	**baabaasi.** *v.* A fishing method (angling with the side of a flying fish as bait).
R 1	**baabaasianga.** *n.* —.
RE	**hagabaabaasi.** *v.* —.
RE1	**hagabaabaasianga.** *n.* —.
ID	**abongi baasi.** Capsize sideways.
ID	**baasi e haa o de langi.** The four quadrants of the sky.
ID	**baasi gi taiao.** Forenoon (from dawn to noon).
ID	**baasi lua.** Having two useful sides.
ID	**baasi madau.** Right side, right-handed.
ID	**baasi masui.** Left side, left-handed.
ID	**de baasi gee.** The opposing side.
ID	**kangi baasi lua.** Double-edged.
ID	**hai baasi.** Take sides against, oppose.
ID	**i de baasi.** Concerning; at the behest of; under the auspices of.
ID	**lili baasi gee.** Accuse someone (in an argument, usually between spouses) of taking sides with another family member.
ID	**luu baasi.** Both sides (of).

BAASUA

B	**baasua.** *n.* Mollusk sp.: *Tridacna maxima.*
ID	**nao baasua.** To collect *baasua.*

BAAUA

B	**baaua.** *n.* Fish sp.: rabbitfish.

ID **lua-baaua.** The second number of a counting game played to determine who is "it".

BAAVA

ID **laso paava.** Skinny (of people).

BABAIANGI

B **babaiangi.** *v.* A type of cloud formation (dark but not threatening rain).
BE **hagababaiangi.** *v.* —.
ID **babaiangi ina.** Cloudy, with clouds of the *babaiangi* type.

BABU

B **babu.** *a.* The noise of one hard object struck against another (as the snapping of fingers).
B 1 **baabunga.** *n.* —.
B 2 **babulia.** *v.* —.
BE **hagababu.** *v.* —.
BE1 **hagabaabunga.** *n.* —.
BE2 **hagababulia.** *v.* —.
R **bapabu.** *a.* The staccato sound of one hard object being struck against another.
R 1 **bapabuanga.** *n.* —.
RE **hagabapabu.** *v.* —.
RE1 **hagabapabuanga.** *n.* —.
RE2 **hagabapabulia.** *v.* —.
XFL **babu-daaea.** *n.* Fish sp.: snapper (= small *daea*).
XFL **babu-honga-agau.** *n.* Fish sp.: wrasse (2 sorts: 1 white, 1 red).

BADAI

B **badai.** *a.* Meddle in others' affairs.
B 1 **badaianga.** *n.* —.
BE **hagabadai.** *v.* —.
BE1 **hagabadaianga.** *n.* —.
P **baatai.** *a.* —.
P 1 **baataianga.** *n.* —.
PE **hagabaatai.** *v.* —.
PE1 **hagabaataianga.** *n.* —.
R **badabadai.** *a.* Having a tendency to meddle in others' affairs.
R 1 **badabadaianga.** *n.* —.
RE **hagabadabadai.** *v.* —.
RE1 **hagabadabadaianga.** *n.* —.
U **badabaatai.** *a.* [pl. form of *badabadai*].
U **badabaataianga.** *n.* [the nominal form of *badabaatai*].
U **hagabadabaatai.** *v.* [the causative form of *badabaatai*].
U **hagabadabaataianga.** *n.* [the nominal form of *hagabadabaatai*].
ID **badai gee.** Extremely meddlesome.

BADI

CF **badioda.** The residue remaining after coconut oil has been heated; the residue remaining after arrowroot starch-making.

BADII

B **badii.** *n.* Fish sp.: scad?

BADIODA

B **badioda.** *v.* The residue remaining after coconut oil has been heated; the residue remaining after arrowroot starch-making.
B 1 **badiodaanga.** *n.* —.
BE **hagabadioda.** *v.* —.
BE1 **hagabadiodaanga.** *n.* —.

BADU

B **badu.** *v.* Hit or tap with the hand or foot; kick.
B 1 **baadunga.** *n.* —; punishment.
B 2 **badua.** *v.* —.
B 2 **badulia.** *v.* —.
BE **hagabadu.** *v.* —.
BE1 **hagabaadunga.** *n.* —.
BE2 **hagabadua.** *v.* —.
BE2 **hagabadulia.** *v.* —.
R **badubadu.** *v.* —.
R 1 **badubadunga.** *n.* —.
RE **hagabadubadu.** *v.* —.
RE1 **hagabadubadunga.** *n.* —.
RE2 **hagabadubadua.** *v.* —.
RE2 **hagabadubadulia.** *v.* —.
ID **dao badu.** Ridge pole (upper).

BAE

B	**bae.** *v.* An arrangement of rocks to make a retaining wall or pier, etc.; push aside (in all directions).
B 1	**baenga.** *n.* —.
B 2	**baea.** *v.* —.
B 2	**baelia.** *v.* —.
BE	**hagabae.** *v.* —.
BE1	**hagabaenga.** *n.* —.
BE2	**hagabaea.** *v.* —; to hang oneself (suicide).
R	**baebae.** *v.* —; a row of stones.
R 1	**baebaenga.** *n.* —.
R 2	**baebaea.** *v.* —.
RE	**hagabaebae.** *v.* —.
RE1	**hagabaebaenga.** *n.* —.
RE2	**hagabaebaea.** *v.* —.
ID	**bae mamu.** Fish weir.
ID	**duu baebae.** To appear in the distance as a row of small objects (like adjacent islets on the atoll).
ID	**gave bae.** A row of stones piled on top of each other.

BAEAO

B	**baeao.** *n.* Husk of the mature coconut.
ID	**duu baeao.** Piece of coconut husk.
ID	**tolo i de baeao.** Elderly and infirm.

BAGEKEGE

B	**bagekege.** *v.* Move jerkily (as when stumbling).
B 1	**bagekegeanga.** *n.* —.
B 2	**bagekegelia.** *v.* —.
BE	**hagabagekege.** *v.* —.
BE1	**hagabagekegeanga.** *n.* —.
BE2	**hagabagekegelia.** *v.* —.

BAGI

B	**bagi.** *n.* Gun or any weapon of similar nature.
B 2	**bagia.** *v.* Be hit (by wind, bullet, spear, etc.).
B 3	**bagiaanga.** *n.* —.
BD	**hebagi.** *a.* Fight.
BE1	**hagabagiaanga.** *n.* —.
BE2	**hagabagia.** *v.* —.
E	**pagi.** *d.* [occurs only in phrases].
R	**bagibagi.** *n.* [occurs only in phrases].
R 1	**bagibagiaanga.** *n.* —.
R 2	**bagibagia.** *v.* —.
RE1	**hagabagibagianga.** *n.* —.
RE2	**hagabagibagia.** *v.* —.
XCO	**dalepagi.** *a.* Fight hand-to-hand.
ID	**bagibagi de me.** All of a sudden (violent actions).
ID	**bagi mada lagolago.** Machine gun.
ID	**daane hebagi.** Soldier.
ID	**goloa hebagi.** Arms (tools of war).
ID	**hai me hebagi.** Be on the point of fighting.
ID	**lo te hebagi.** During the war.
CF	**heboohagi.** Fight.

BAGO

E	**pago.** *a.* The sound of any sudden violent contact; the sound of an explosion.
E 2	**pagolia.** *v.* —.
EE	**hagapago.** *v.* —.
EE1	**hagapagoanga.** *n.* —.
R	**bagobago.** *a.* —.
RE	**hagabagobago.** *v.* —.
RE1	**hagabagobagoanga.** *n.* —.
RE2	**hagabagobagolia.** *v.* —.
ID	**hagapago iho.** To descend suddenly.

BAGOLA

E	**pagola.** *n.* Bad luck; punishment.
ID	**paa ono pagola.** Punished for his bad deeds.
ID	**tau ono pagola.** Punished for his bad deeds.
ID	**hagapago donu.** Fortunate result.
ID	**hagapago sala.** Unfortunate result.

BAGU

B	**bagu.** *n.* Scab, crust.
ID	**dao bagu.** Dry out (fish or food to preserve it).
ID	**masa bagubagu.** Dry reef (at very low tide).

ID mmasa bagubagu. Hard and curled up owing to dryness.
ID sua bagu. A stain which has left a dry residue.

BAGUA
B **bagua.** *n.* Plant sp.: tree sp.: pandan tree (*Pandanus dubius* Spreng.).
XFL **aha-bagua.** *n.* Driftwood sp. (resembles *bagua*).

BAGUU
B **baguu.** *a.* Fall over (as a felled tree); tip over; lean (in one direction).
B 1 **baguunga.** *n.* —.
BE **hagabaguu.** *v.* —.
BE1 **hagabaguunga.** *n.* —.
BE2 **hagabaguua.** *v.* —.
BE2 **hagabaguulia.** *v.* —.
P **baakuu.** *a.* —.
P 1 **baakuunga.** *n.* —.
PE **hagabaakuu.** *v.* —.
PE1 **hagabaakuunga.** *n.* —.
PE2 **hagabaakuua.** *v.* —.
PE2 **hagabaakuulia.** *v.* —.
ID **baguu de laa.** Past noon.
ID **hagabaguu ange.** Move against something so fast that it appears to be coming at one.

BAKAU
B **bakau.** *n.* Shoulder (the whole joint), wing.
ID **bakau dahi de manu.** Not to go fishing when other groups are going.
ID **bakau doo.** A dislocation of the shoulder joint.
ID **too luu bakau.** Extremely tired.

BAHHAA
B **bahhaa.** *a.* To make a sound, like that of a turtle gasping for breath; the sound of air exhaled suddenly.
B 1 **bahhaanga.** *n.* —.
BE **hagabahhaa.** *v.* To exhale suddenly; making exhalation noises.

BAI
CF **dalabaimanugadele.** Sharp (as a knife).

BAIEU
B **baieu.** *n.* Mollusk sp.: clam sp.

BALA
B **bala.** *a.* Soft, mushy, offering no resistance.
B 1 **baalanga$_1$.** *n.* —.
BE **hagabala.** *v.* Allow to become soft; prostrate oneself (esp. to hide).
P **pala.** *a.* —.
P 1 **paalanga.** *n.* —.
PE **hagapala.** *v.* —.
PE1 **hagapaalanga.** *n.* —.
R **balabala.** *a.* Very soft or weak (of things only).
RE **hagabalabala.** *v.* Make loose; make soft; be a defeatist.
RE1 **hagabalabalaanga.** *n.* —.
XCO **balapigi.** *v.* Drenched.
XCO **boibala.** *a.* Watery (of prepared food).
XCO **hulubala.** *v.* Smeared with grease or paint or food, etc.
XCO **laubalabala.** *a.* Slack (of rope); soft (of skin or paper); pliable (of hair); flexible.
XFL **laagau-bala-uda.** *n.* Driftwood sp. (very soft).
ID **bala i de —.** Covered with — (of skin only).
ID **bala langi.** Rain.
ID **pala boo maasina.** The time of the month when rain is most likely to occur (1st quarter).
ID **pala de langi.** It's raining!
ID **pala ivi.** Work beyond one's endurance.
ID **daahaa mada balabala.** The stage of development of the coconut between *mugamuga* and *daahaa*.
ID **dama pala.** A foetus which has been aborted, ugly [said jokingly].
ID **dili bala.** Collapse (of persons).

ID	**dolo bala.** To climb a coconut tree without using a rope (on one's hands or feet) for assistance.
ID	**gannui mada balabala.** *gannui* which is soft and mushy.
ID	**hadi bala.** To rely on others for the things one should provide for oneself.
ID	**me balabala.** The soft spot on an infant's head; genitals (of males or females).
ID	**moo balabala.** Barely cooked.
CF	**baalasi.** Press down or against; sit on (as chicken hatching eggs).
CF	**balagelage.** Crippled and unable to walk.
CF	**balagula.** Clumsy.
CF	**balavini.** Clumsy, awkward (e.g., in carriage).

BALA$_a$

B	**balaginagina.** *a.* Be squashed.
BE	**hagabalaginagina.** *v.* —.

BALAGELAGE

B	**balagelage.** *a.* Crippled and unable to walk.
B 1	**balagelageanga.** *n.* —.
BE	**hagabalagelage.** *v.* To have come to be unable to walk.
BE1	**hagabalagelageanga.** *n.* —.
ID	**balagelage gee.** Severely crippled.

BALAGIA

XFL	**balagia.** *n.* Fish sp.
XFL	**balagia-a-de-gaga.** *n.* Fish sp.: parrot fish.

BALAGULA

B	**balagula.** *a.* Clumsy.
B 1	**balagulaanga.** *n.* —.
BE	**hagabalagula.** *v.* —.
BE1	**hagabalagulaanga.** *n.* —.
P	**balaagula.** *a.* —.
P 1	**balaagulaanga.** *n.* —.
PE	**hagabalaagula.** *v.* —.
PE1	**hagabalaagulaanga.** *n.* —.
R	**balabalagula.** *a.* Habitually clumsy.
R 1	**balabalagulaanga.** *n.* —.
RE	**hagabalabalagula.** *v.* —.
RE1	**hagabalabalagulaanga.** *n.* —.
CF	**balavini.** Clumsy, awkward (e.g., in carriage).

BALALA

B	**balala.** *v.* The sound of sucking liquid; the sound of coitus.
B 1	**balalaanga.** *n.* —.
BE	**hagabalala.** *v.* —.
BE1	**hagabalalaanga.** *n.* —.

BALANGI

B	**balangi.** *n.* Fish sp.: tang.

BALAULAU

B	**balaulau.** *a.* Ugly-looking, messy, sloppy.
B 1	**balaulaunga.** *n.* —.
BE	**hagabalaulau.** *v.* —.
BE1	**hagabalaulaunga.** *n.* —.
BE2	**hagabalaulaua.** *v.* —.
CF	**baalau.** Sticky, greasy.

BALAVINI

B	**balavini.** *a.* Clumsy, awkward (e.g., in carriage).
BE	**hagabalavini.** *v.* —.
P	**balaavini.** *a.* —.
PE	**hagabalaavini.** *v.* —.
R	**balabalavini.** *a.* Clumsy by nature; awkward by nature.
RE	**hagabalabalavini.** *v.* —.
ID	**hai me balavini.** To conduct oneself clumsily.

BALE$_1$

B	**bale$_1$.** *v.* Help, assist, aid (with effort or advice, etc.).
B 1	**baalenga$_1$.** *n.* —.
B 2	**balea.** *v.* —.
R	**balebale$_1$.** *v.* —.
R 1	**balebalenga$_1$.** *n.* —.
R 2	**balebalea$_1$.** *v.* —.
XE	**hagadaubaleanga.** *n.* —.
ID	**de eidu pale.** Fortunately, luckily.

ID hagadau bale. Cooperate; help one another.

ID lodo bale. Helpful (sort of person).

BALE$_2$

B **bale$_2$.** *v.* Steer (e.g., a canoe).

B 1 **baalenga$_2$.** *n.* —.

B 2 **baalea.** *v.* —.

P **pale.** *v.* —.

PE **hagapale.** *v.* Teach to steer, allow to steer, lean against.

PE1 **hagapaalenga.** *n.* —.

R **balebale$_2$.** *v.* —.

R 1 **balebalenga$_2$.** *n.* —.

R 2 **balebalea$_2$.** *v.* —.

XFL **bale-masevaseva.** *n.* [var. of *bani-magevageva*].

XG **hoe pale.** A type of canoe paddle designed for steering.

ID **pale age (iho).** Steer toward (away from) land.

ID **duu bale.** Not quite vertical.

CF **hebaledage.** A confluence of currents (making the water choppy).

BALEAO

B **baleao.** *n.* Fish sp.: milkfish.

BALEDILO

B **baledilo.** *v.* The stage of plant growth at which immature leaves appear.

BE **hagabaledilo.** *v.* —.

ID **velo de baledilo.** To sprout (of plants).

BALI

B **bali.** *n.* Immature coconut palm leaves.

CF **baledilo.** The stage of plant growth at which immature leaves appear.

BALIA

B **balia.** *a.* Master navigator (having also the ability to forecast the weather).

B 1 **baliaanga.** *n.* —.

BE **hagabalia.** *v.* —.

BE1 **hagabaliaanga.** *n.* —.

BALO

E **palo.** *n.* A watery area extending into a land area (e.g., a bay).

BALU$_1$

B **balu$_1$.** *v.* To bring one's hands and arms (or wings) down or back once (as in waving, swimming, or the flapping of a bird's wings).

B 1 **baalunga.** *n.* —.

B 2 **balua.** *v.* —.

BE **hagabalu.** *v.* —.

BE1 **hagabaalunga.** *n.* —.

BE2 **hagabalua.** *v.* —.

R **balubalu.** *v.* —.

R 1 **balubalunga.** *n.* —.

RE **hagabalubalu.** *v.* —.

RE1 **hagabalubalunga.** *n.* —.

RE2 **hagabalubalua.** *v.* —.

ID **balu gauanga.** Trembling of legs.

ID **balu moso.** Constant movement of the hands and feet, as when struggling (resembling the movements of a young starling).

BALU$_2$

B **balu$_2$.** *n.* Fish sp.

XFL **balu-daaea.** *n.* Fish sp.

XFL **balu-malau.** *n.* Fish sp.

XFL **balu-udu.** *n.* Fish sp.: snapper.

BALUU

B **baluu.** *n.* Coconut crab.

BANE

B **bane.** *n.* The flat top of the shark's snout.

BANI

R **banibani.** *n.* Sea cucumber (many spp.).

XCO **gabanibaonga.** *n.* Room (of a house).

XFL **bani-gegeva.** *n.* [var. of *bani-magevageva*].

XFL **bani-magevageva.** *n.* Fish sp. (rare).

ID **dae banibani.** The white

excretion of the *banibani.*
CF **baani.** Lie down.

BANUUNU
B **banuunu.** *n.* A type of basket.

BANGA$_1$
P **panga.** *a.* [pl. form of *bangabanga*].
PE **hagapanga.** *v.* —.
PE2 **hagapangalia.** *v.* —.
R **bangabanga**$_1$**.** *a.* Skinny, shrunken.
RE **hagabangabanga.** *v.* —.
RE2 **hagabangabangalia.** *v.* —.
ID **bangabanga mai.** Become skinny, become shrunken.

BANGA$_2$
banganga. *n.* Fish sp.: wrasse.
R **bangabanga**$_2$**.** *n.* Fish sp.
CF **bangadala.** Fish sp.: sea bass.

BANGI$_1$
B **bangi**$_1$**.** *v.* Pinch (with the fingers).
B 1 **baanginga.** *n.* —.
B 2 **bangia.** *v.* —.
BE **hagabangi.** *v.* —.
BE1 **hagabaanginga.** *n.* —.
BE2 **hagabangia.** *v.* —.
R **bangibangi.** *v.* —.
R 1 **bangibanginga.** *n.* —.
R 2 **bangibangia.** *v.* —.
RE **hagabangibangi.** *v.* —.
RE1 **hagabangibanginga.** *n.* —.
RE2 **hagabangibangia.** *v.* —.
ID **bangi dua beau.** A certain way of pinching with the fingers.
ID **bangi mada aasanga.** A certain way of pinching with the fingers.

BANGI$_2$
B **bangi**$_2$**.** *n.* A type of prepared food (made from dried breadfruit).
XCO **hagailangi-bangi.** *n.* A type of prepared food (*bangi* soaked in coconut milk).

BANGOA
B **bangoa.** *a.* Slow down, be exhausted (physically), feel unenergetic.
B 1 **bangoaanga.** *n.* —.
BE **hagabangoa.** *v.* —; give in to exhaustion.
BE1 **hagabangoaanga.** *n.* —.
P **baangoa.** *a.* —.
P 1 **baangoaanga.** *n.* —.
PE **hagabaangoa.** *v.* Causing prostration.
PE1 **hagabaangoaanga.** *n.* —.
R **bangobangoa.** *a.* —; unenergetic.
R 1 **bangobangoaanga.** *n.* —.
RE **hagabangobangoa.** *v.* —; given to prostration.
RE1 **hagabangobangoaanga.** *n.* —.

BANGONGO
B **bangongo.** *n.* Fish sp.: rabbitfish.

BANGULU
B **bangulu.** *n.* A part of the traditional loom.

BAO
B **bao.** *n.* Room, compartment.
XCO **gabanibaonga.** *n.* Room (of a house).
ID **hai bao.** Divided into compartments.

BAOA
B **baoa.** *v.* Wash up on shore.
B 1 **baoanga.** *n.* —.
BE **hagabaoa.** *v.* —.
BE1 **hagabaoanga.** *n.* —.
R **baabaoa.** *v.* Wash up on shore continually; ghost (children's language).
R 1 **baabaoanga.** *n.* —.
RE **hagabaabaoa.** *v.* —.
RE1 **hagabaabaoanga.** *n.* —.
ID **baoa age.** Wash up on shore and beach thereon.
ID **dangada baoa.** Dead person buried at sea who washes back up on shore.

BASA$_1$
B **basa**$_1$**.** *v.* Speak, talk, say.

B 1	**baasanga.** *n.* Manner of speaking, idiolect, dialect.
B 2	**basaa.** *v.* Be talked into.
B 2	**basalia**$_1$**.** *v.* Be talked about (one person or thing only).
BE	**hagabasa.** *v.* Cause someone to speak; convince.
BE1	**hagabaasanga.** *n.* —.
BE2	**hagabasaa.** *v.* Be talked into.
BE2	**hagabasalia**$_1$**.** *v.* Convince someone completely.
P	**pasa.** *v.* —.
P 2	**pasalia.** *v.* Be talked about (many persons or things).
PE	**hagapasa.** *v.* Cause several people to speak; mediate an argument so that the disputants will speak to each other.
PE1	**hagapaasanga.** *n.* —.
PE2	**hagapasalia.** *v.* Convince (several people) completely.
R	**basabasa.** *v.* —; saying.
R 1	**basabasaanga.** *n.* —.
R 2	**basabasalia**$_1$**.** *v.* Be talked about frequently.
RE	**hagabasabasa.** *v.* —.
RE1	**hagabasabasaanga.** *n.* —.
RE2	**hagabasabasalia**$_1$**.** *v.* Cause to be convinced.
ID	**baasanga tugi ange muna.** Talk back.
ID	**basa ange.** Answer, reply.
ID	**basa baubau.** Speak badly of someone.
ID	**basa pada.** Speak harshly.
ID	**basa dau donu.** Speak moderately.
ID	**basa degidegi.** Speak disconnectedly with rage.
ID	**basa dua nnui.** Speak undiplomatically.
ID	**basa too gee.** Speak ungrammatically.
ID	**basa gauligi.** To imitate a child's manner of talking; baby talk.
ID	**basa gee.** Speak (or express oneself) strangely.
ID	**basa gelo.** Speak sagely.
ID	**basa gi lunga.** Speak loudly.
ID	**basa hagaeaea.** Stutter.
ID	**basa hagamalaia.** To curse (someone).
ID	**basa hagamao lalo.** Speak humbly.
ID	**basa hagamao lunga.** Speak arrogantly.
ID	**basa hagasengasenga.** Speak in riddles or aphoristically or in parables.
ID	**basa hagassee.** Speak so as to change the impression one's previous words have made.
ID	**basa lilo.** Speak indirectly (so that the meaning is vague).
ID	**basa maalie.** Speak moderately.
ID	**basa madua.** Speak as an elder (treating the hearer as a child).
ID	**basa senga.** Speak senselessly.
ID	**basa soe.** Say what is on one's mind; speak directly (so that one's meaning is clear).
ID	**lodo basa.** Talkative.
ID	**me pasa.** Radio.
ID	**ngadi basa.** Small talk; idle conversation.
ID	**vaivai basa.** Dirty or obscene language; foulmouthed, swear.

BASA$_2$

B	**basa**$_2$ **—.** *d.* Very many —.
XCO	**daubasa.** *na.* A great many.

BASALIA

B	**basalia**$_2$**.** *v.* Seep (of water).
B 1	**basaliaanga.** *n.* —.
BE	**hagabasalia**$_2$**.** *v.* —.
BE1	**hagabasaliaanga.** *n.* —.
R	**basabasalia**$_2$**.** *v.* —.
R 1	**basabasaliaanga.** *n.* —.
RE	**hagabasabasalia**$_2$**.** *v.* —.
RE1	**hagabasabasaliaanga.** *n.* —.

BAU$_1$

B	**bau.** *a.* To be worth it.
B 1	**bauanga.** *n.* Worth, value.
B 1	**baunga.** *n.* Worth, value.
B 2	**baua.** *v.* Figure out, determine.

B 2 **baulia.** *v.* Figure out, determine.

BE **hagabau.** *v.* Measure, calculate, estimate.

BE1 **hagabauanga.** *n.* —.

BE1 **hagabaunga.** *n.* —.

BE2 **hagabaua.** *v.* Figure out, determine.

BE2 **hagabaulia.** *v.* Figure out, determine.

P **pau.** *a.* —.

R **baubau$_1$.** *a.* Be capable at.

ID **agu bau.** Methinks.

ID **bau ange.** Capable of, be the equal of.

ID **bau iho.** Capable only of looking after oneself (not others).

ID **dagu bau.** Methinks.

ID **dee hagabaulia.** Underestimate, misjudge.

ID **se hagabau.** Do deliberately (esp. something bad); willful, mean.

ID **ssaga bau.** [var. of *se hagabau*].

BAU$_2$

R **baubau$_2$.** *a.* Bad.

RE **hagabaubau.** *v.* Criticize; cause bad feelings; scrape taro inadequately.

RE1 **hagabaubaunga.** *n.* —.

RE2 **hagabaubaua.** *v.* —.

RE2 **hagabaubaulia.** *v.* —.

RE3 **hagabaubauanga.** *a.* To have been criticized.

ID **basa baubau.** Speak badly of someone.

ID **tala baubau.** Confess wrongs.

ID **hagao baubáu.** Low wages, low-priced.

ID **hegau baubau.** Bad deeds.

ID **laagii baubau.** Hideous in appearance (as a ghost).

ID **lodo baubau.** Unhappy, upset, sad.

ID **mada baubau.** Flirtatious.

ID **magau baubau.** Die in agony (owing to having led a bad life).

ID **moe baubau.** Sleep without regard to remaining decently covered; die in agony [cf. *magau baubau*].

BE

B **be.** *mi.* Or, either.

XCO **beaha.** *a.* To be in a serious condition, critically ill or injured.

ID **be...be.** Either...or.

ID **be goai (naa huu).** Whoever.

ID **behee.** Like what?

ID **be ne.** If there might be —.

ID **dee beaha.** All right! It's nothing!

ID **dulagi be —.** It seems that —.

ID **hai be —.** It would seem that —.

ID **hai be se manu.** Promiscuous (especially if indiscreet or known to have sexual relations with one's own relatives).

ID **se me be hee.** Extraordinary or unusual (esp. in size).

BE$_a$

B **abe.** *mi.* "Or, to cite just one more example...".

BEAU

B **beau.** *v.* A wave, the surf.

R **beabeau.** *v.* Choppy seas.

R 1 **beabeaunga.** *n.* —.

R 2 **beabeaua.** *v.* —.

RE **hagabeabeau.** *v.* —.

RE1 **hagabeabeaunga.** *n.* —.

RE2 **hagabeabeaua.** *v.* —.

ID **bangi dua beau.** A certain way of pinching with the fingers.

HAVE **dai beau.** Rough seas at a certain time. seaward reef. hi

ID **tua de beau.** Beyond the seaward reef.

ID **haangoda dua beau.** A fishing method (used on the seaward reef during the day) employing a line, with hermit crabs for bait).

ID **lango beau.** A method of lashing the outrigger float to the outrigger struts.

BEBE$_1$

B **bebe$_1$.** *v.* Nervous, anxious

	(for reasons not connected with other people).
B 1	**bebeanga.** *n.* —.
B 2	**bebea.** *v.* Be very nervous, be very anxious.
B 2	**bebelia.** *v.* Be very nervous, be very anxious.
BE	**hagabebe.** *v.* —.
BE1	**hagabebeanga.** *n.* —.
BE2	**hagabebea.** *v.* —.
BE2	**hagabebelia.** *v.* —.
ID	**bebe de lodo.** Anxiety state (psychological condition).

BEBE₂

B	**bebe₂.** *n.* Butterfly.

BEBELA

B	**bebela.** *n.* Prowler.
BE	**hagabebela.** *v.* —.

BEDAGE

B	**bedage.** *v.* Shallow (bowl, basket, etc.).
B 1	**bedageanga.** *n.* —.
BE	**hagabedage.** *v.* —.
BE1	**hagabedageanga.** *n.* —.
ID	**bedage ina.** Shallow on the inside.

BEDI

B	**bedi.** *a.* Fat (of, e.g., a person); plump (tending toward fat).
B 1	**bedianga.** *n.* —.
BE	**hagabedi.** *v.* —.
BE1	**hagabedianga.** *n.* —.
BE2	**hagabedia.** *v.* —.
P	**pedi.** *a.* —.
P 1	**pedianga.** *n.* —.
PE	**hagapedi.** *v.* —.
PE1	**hagapedianga.** *n.* —.
PE2	**hagapedia.** *v.* —.
R	**bedibedi.** *a.* Getting fat.
R 1	**bedibedianga.** *n.* —.
RE	**hagabedibedi.** *v.* —.
RE1	**hagabedibedianga.** *n.* —.
RE2	**hagabedibedia.** *v.* —.

BEE

B	**bee.** *n.* Flatus, the sound of flatulence.
E	**pee.** *a.* Pass wind (flatus).
E 1	**peeanga.** *n.* —.
EE	**hagapee.** *v.* —.
EE1	**hagapeeanga.** *n.* —.
T	**bebee.** *a.* Be flatulent.
T 1	**bebeeanga.** *n.* —.
TE	**hagabebee.** *v.* —.
TE1	**hagabebeeanga.** *n.* —.
ID	**dama muli bee.** The twelfth child born to a couple.

BEGA

B	**bega.** *i.* A sound indicating surprise.

BEI

B	**bei.** *a.* Be like, be the same as.
BE	**hagabei.** *v.* —.
R	**beibei.** *a.* More-or-less alike.
RE	**hagabeibei.** *v.* —.
ID	**bei tagodo.** For instance, for example; just like —.
ID	**(de) hine hai be.** Whore.

BELA

B	**bela.** *n.* Plot of taro bog, boggy soil.
BE	**hagabela.** *v.* Provide *bela* for.
R	**belabela.** *v.* Dirty (like *bela*).
R 1	**belabelaanga.** *n.* —.
RE	**hagabelabela.** *v.* —.
RE1	**hagabelabelaanga.** *n.* —.
ID	**danu bela.** Spade in organic matter (to enrich taro plantings).
ID	**danu de bela.** Spade up taro plots, adding mulch.
ID	**uli bela.** Jet black.

BELE

CF	**duu beleala.** Immature coconut apple.

BELU

B	**belu.** *n.* Lizard sp.
R	**belubelu.** *n.* Fish sp.: scad?
ID	**dige de belubelu.** A circuit made by a school of *belubelu*.
ID	**gili belu.** Dead epidermis (can be peeled without pain).

BENA

E	**pena.** *v.* Take precautions.
E 1	**penaanga.** *n.* —.

EE	**hagapena.** *v.* —.
EE1	**hagapenaanga.** *n.* —.

BENA$_a$

BE	**hagadabena.** *v.* Prepare, make ready.
BE1	**hagadabenaanga.** *n.* —.
BE2	**hagadabenalia.** *v.* —.
ID	**hagadabena ange.** Prepare for.
ID	**hagadabena iho.** Prepare oneself, make oneself ready.

BENU

B	**benu.** *n.* A pandanus plug after it has been chewed; seed of the pandanus.
ID	**hanga benu.** To extract pandanus seeds by splitting the fruit.

BESE

B	**bese.** *n.* One of the harmony parts in old chants.

BIALODO

ID	**dama de bialodo.** Deformed foetus [lit., 'looking like an animal'].

BIBI$_1$

B	**bibi.** *n.* Mollusk sp.: *Cyclotinella remies*, also *Tellinidae* spp.
XFL	**bibi-gabugabu-tai.** *n.* Mollusk sp.: a bivalve.
XFL	**bibi-maadau.** *n.* Mollusk sp.: *Arcophagia scobinata.*

BIBI$_2$

BE	**hagabibi.** *v.* To cook food in an earth oven for a short time (just to heat it up).
BE1	**hagabibianga.** *n.* —.

BIDO

B	**bido.** *nl.* End (extremity); bit (of something); to complete an act later [dp].
B 2	**bidoa.** *v.* Lift or hold one end of something.
BE	**hagabido.** *v.* Carrying (two persons), with each person carrying an end [dp].
BE2	**hagabidoa.** *v.* Be the last.
R	**bidobido.** *d.* Useless pieces.
ID	**bido abongi.** Capsize eventually.
ID	**bido dagi.** Follow in order to spy on.
ID	**bido gamu.** Uselessly short.
ID	**hidi bido dane.** Slow-moving or slow-working person.
ID	**luu bido.** Both ends (of).
ID	**sii bido lua.** Vomiting and having diarrhea at the same time ('flowing from both ends').

BIE

B	**bie.** *n.* Plant sp.: Polynesian arrowroot (*Tacca leontopetaloides* (L.) O.K.).
CF	**madabiebie.** Fish sp.: sea bass (2 sorts: 1 large, 1 small).

BIGE

B	**bige.** *n.* A strip of land extending into the sea or a swamp.

BIGEDE

ID	**lodo bigede.** Feel cowardly.

BIGI$_1$

B	**bigi$_1$.** *a.* Be caught between two or more other things.
B 1	**biginga.** *n.* —.
BE	**hagabigi$_1$.** *v.* —.
BE1	**hagabigianga.** *n.* —.
BE1	**hagabiiginga.** *n.* Way of making sticky.
BE2	**hagabigia.** *v.* —.
BE2	**hagabigilia.** *v.* —.
BE2	**hagabiigia.** *v.* To make sticky.
E	**pigi.** *a.* Be stuck.
E 1	**biiginga.** *n.* —.
E 2	**biigia.** *v.* Be stuck to completely.
EE	**hagapigi.** *v.* —.
EE1	**hagapiiginga.** *n.* —.
EE2	**hagapiigia.** *v.* Make stuck to.
R	**bigibigi$_1$.** *v.* —; gum (to chew), sap (of trees).
R 1	**bigibiginga.** *n.* —.
R 2	**bigibigia.** *v.* Covered with

	something sticky.
RE	**hagabigibigi$_1$.** *v.* —.
RE1	**hagabigibiginga.** *n.* —.
RE2	**hagabigibigia.** *v.* —; make covered with something sticky.
RE2	**hagabigibigilia.** *v.* —.
XCO	**balapigi.** *v.* Drenched.
ID	**bigi lima.** Hold hands.
ID	**hagapigi ange.** Stick against (something), go with someone.
ID	**hagapigi saele.** Go around with someone constantly.

BIGI$_2$

B	**bigi$_2$.** *a.* Close to (in meaning); about to (in time).
BE	**hagabigi$_2$.** *v.* Strive to be like.
R	**bigibigi$_2$.** *a.* More-or-less close to.
RE	**hagabigibigi$_2$.** *v.* —.
ID	**bigi ange.** Just about like —.
ID	**dai bigi.** Almost (finished or done, etc.); just about.

BIGO

B	**bigo.** *a.* Bent; bedridden with illness.
B 1	**biigonga.** *n.* A curve, way of being bent.
BE	**hagabigo.** *v.* —.
BE1	**hagabiigonga.** *n.* —.
BE2	**hagabigolia.** *v.* —.
P	**pigo.** *a.* —.
P 1	**piigonga.** *n.* —.
PE	**hagapigo.** *v.* —.
PE1	**hagapiigonga.** *n.* —.
PE2	**hagapigolia.** *v.* —.
R	**bigobigo.** *a.* Bent up (having several bends).
R 1	**bigobigonga.** *n.* —.
RE	**hagabigobigo.** *v.* Wiggle.
RE1	**hagabigobigonga.** *n.* —.
RE2	**hagabigobigolia.** *v.* —.
ID	**hagabigo de ngago.** Fool (someone), deceive.

BIHO

B	**biho.** *n.* Head; body of a trolling lure.
BE	**hagabiho.** *v.* Cause to become a leader.
XCO	**uubiho.** *v.* Head-first presentation of a foetus at birth.
ID	**biho ngaalulu.** Headache.
ID	**biho o de agoago.** Topic of a sermon.
ID	**duu biho.** Haircut; cut hair.
ID	**teve de biho.** To have the hair (of one's head) standing on end.
ID	**goloa duu biho.** Barber's tools.
ID	**hai de biho.** Act smart (deviously).
ID	**hale duu biho.** Barber shop.
ID	**hhoa de biho.** Fool (someone).
ID	**ivi de biho.** Skull.
ID	**lele biho.** Dive head first.
ID	**molomolo de biho.** Round-headed.
ID	**ngadi biho.** Head.
ID	**se biho.** Clever (scheme or trick).
ID	**vvae de biho.** Part one's hair.

BII

B	**bii.** *a.* Semen, ejaculate.
B 1	**biianga.** *n.* —.
B 2	**biia.** *v.* Get wet.
BE	**hagabii.** *v.* —.
BE1	**hagabiianga.** *n.* —.
BE2	**hagabiia.** *v.* —.
E	**pii.** *a.* Splashed, sprinkled.
E 1	**piianga.** *n.* —.
EE	**hagapii.** *v.* —.
EE1	**hagapiianga.** *n.* —.
EE2	**hagapiia.** *v.* —.
R	**biibii.** *a.* Ejaculate repeatedly.
R 1	**biibiianga.** *n.* —.
RE	**hagabiibii.** *v.* —.
RE1	**hagabiibiianga.** *n.* —.
RE2	**hagabiibiia.** *v.* —.
ID	**bii o madahasi.** A certain kind of phosphorescence in seawater at night.
ID	**taa hagabiibii.** To bail a canoe rapidly.

BIIHINGI

B	**biihingi.** *v.* Having flat

buttocks, ugly (because not plump).
BE **hagabiihingi.** *v.* —.

$BILI_1$
B **bili.** *a.* Be caught or hung up on something so as unable to fall (as a felled tree).
BE **hagabili.** *v.* —.
BE1 **hagabiilinga.** *n.* —.
BE2 **hagabilia.** *v.* —.
P **$pili_1$.** *a.* —.
PE **$hagapili_1$.** *v.* —.
R **bilibili.** *v.* Having a tendency to be *bili.*
RE **hagabilibili.** *v.* —.
RE1 **hagabilibilinga.** *n.* —.
RE2 **hagabilibilia.** *v.* —.
ID **bili i de lodo.** Unforgotten.
ID **bili makaga.** Love.
CF **bilibili-hadu.** Fish sp. (*Trachinotus bailloni*).

$BILI_2$
E **$pili_2$.** *a.* Be bored.
EE **$hagapili_2$.** *a.* Boring.

BILO
E **pilo.** *a.* Stink.
EE **hagapilo.** *v.* Let decay; allow to stink.
EE1 **hagapiloanga.** *n.* —.
ID **pilo bopobo.** Musty smell.
ID **dale pilo.** A game (like tag), to leave something unfinished after having tried only slightly.
ID **lima-pilo.** The fifth number of a counting game played to determine who is "it".
ID **me pilo aha.** What's the point of doing this?
ID **se me pilo aha.** Don't bother!

BINAAINA
B **binaaina.** *a.* Cowardly (owing to weak-mindedness); afraid to assert oneself; not live up to one's obligations.
BE **hagabinaaina.** *a.* —.
R **binabinaaina.** *a.* —.
RE **hagabinabinaaina.** *a.* —.

BINI
B **bini.** *v.* Braid (rope or hair, etc.), wrap with rope.
B 1 **biininga.** *n.* —.
B 2 **binia.** *v.* —.
BE **$hagabini_1$.** *n.* Plant sp.: tree sp. (*Soulamea amara* Lam.).
BE **$hagabini_2$.** *n.* Insect sp.: cockroach.
R **binibini.** *v.* —.
R 1 **binibininga.** *n.* —.
R 2 **binibinia.** *v.* —.
ID **bini dali gadaha.** A method of braiding *dali* into string to make a bird snare; six-ply braiding (of rope).
ID **bini daubeemala.** A method of making flower headdresses.
ID **bini gaahanga.** Three-ply braiding (of rope).
ID **gau bini.** A tool used in braiding rope.
ID **gau bini baalanga.** An iron rod.

BINGA
B **binga.** *a.* Be named, be called; regarded as.
BE **hagabinga.** *v.* Name (something).
BE2 **hagabingalia.** *v.* —.
R **bingabinga.** *a.* The repeated use of a term or name in conversation.
RE **hagabingabinga.** *v.* —.
RE2 **hagabingabingalia.** *v.* —.
ID **hagabinga ange.** Be known as, called by the name —.

BINGI
R **bingibingi.** *n.* Plant sp.: tree sp.: Hernandia tree (*Hernandia sonora* L.).

BOA
B **boa.** *n.* Record catch (of fish) by an individual during his lifetime on

any one fishing expedition.

BOAA

B **boaa.** *v.* Be caught in a storm.
B 1 **boaanga$_2$.** *n.* —.
BE **hagaboaa.** *v.* —.
BE1 **hagaboaanga.** *n.* —.
ID **boaa ina.** Be caught in strong wind or heavy rain.
ID **boaa ina mai.** Prevented from coming by being caught in a storm.

BOBO

B **bobo.** *a.* Rotten.
B 1 **boboanga.** *n.* —.
BE **hagabobo.** *v.* —.
BE1 **hagaboboanga.** *n.* —.
BE2 **hagabobolia.** *v.* —.
P **pobo.** *a.* —.
P 1 **poboanga.** *n.* —.
PE **hagapobo.** *v.* —.
PE1 **hagapoboanga.** *n.* —.
PE2 **hagapobolia.** *v.* —.
R **bopobo.** *a.* Deteriorated.
R 1 **bopoboanga.** *n.* —.
RE **hagabopobo.** *v.* —.
RE1 **hagabopoboanga.** *n.* —.
RE2 **hagabopobolia.** *v.* —.
ID **pilo bopobo.** Musty smell.
ID **dalinga bobo.** Having a runny ear (with pus).

BODA

B **boda.** *v.* Straggly (hair or feathers).
B 1 **bodaanga.** *n.* —.
BE **hagaboda.** *v.* —.
BE1 **hagabodaanga.** *n.* —.
BE2 **hagabodalia.** *v.* —.
P **poda.** *v.* —.
PE **hagapoda.** *v.* —.
PE1 **hagapodaanga.** *n.* —.
PE2 **hagapodalia.** *v.* —.

BODO

P **podo.** *a.* —.
P 1 **podoanga.** *n.* —.
PE **hagapodo.** *v.* —.
PE1 **hagapodoanga.** *n.* —.
PE2 **hagapodolia.** *v.* —.
R **bodobodo.** *a.* Short [sing.].
R 1 **bodobodoanga.** *n.* —.
RE **hagabodobodo.** *v.* —.
RE1 **hagabodobodoanga.** *n.* —.
RE2 **hagabodobodolia.** *v.* —.
T **boobodo.** *a.* Occurring at short intervals.
T 1 **boobodoanga.** *n.* —.
TE **hagaboobodo.** *v.* —.
TE1 **hagaboobodoanga.** *n.* —.
TE2 **hagaboobodolia.** *v.* —.
XCO **daubodobodo.** *a.* Short (in duration).
XE **hagadaubodobodo.** *v.* Shorten (time or rope).
XFL **dagua-bodo.** *n.* Fish sp.: tuna sp.
ID **daa hagabodobodo.** Make a quick trip.
ID **daa hagapodo.** [pl. of *daa haga bodobodo*].
ID **duu podo.** Do something at short intervals; often, frequently.
ID **gave hua podo.** Sprint (footrace of short distance).
ID **gave ua podo.** [var. of *gave hua podo*].
ID **hadi bodo.** Breaking of waves at short intervals.
ID **maanadu bodobodo.** Limited in intelligence.
ID **mahi bodo.** Easily tired.
ID **manava bodo.** Shortness of breath.

BODU$_1$

B **bodu.** *n.* Spouse.
XCO **huaabodu.** *n.* Family.
XE **hagahaibodu.** *v.* Wedding; perform a wedding.
ID **dau bodu.** Married man or woman.
ID **gaiaa dau bodu.** Commit adultery.
ID **hai bodu.** Married couple, marry; the relationship between spouses.
ID **hai huaabodu.** Treat someone (including one's spouse) as a relative by not asking permission to use or borrow property; treat a relative as belonging to another family altogether.

ID **(de) hine dau bodu.** Married woman.

ID **ngadi hai bodu.** Common-law marriage, concubinage.

BODU$_2$

R **bodubodu.** *v.* Particles of rotting wood or thatch, etc.

R 1 **boduboduanga.** *n.* —.

RE **hagabodubodu.** *v.* —.

RE1 **hagaboduboduanga.** *n.* —.

XFL **bodubodu-o-uda.** *n.* Insect sp.

BOGI

B **bogi.** *v.* To plant taro slips.

B 1 **booginga.** *n.* —.

B 2 **bogia.** *v.* —.

BE **hagabogi.** *v.* —.

BE1 **hagabooginga.** *n.* —.

BE2 **hagabogia.** *v.* —.

R **bogibogi.** *v.* —.

R 1 **bogiboginga.** *n.* —.

R 2 **bogibogia.** *v.* —.

RE **hagabogibogi.** *v.* —.

RE1 **hagabogiboginga.** *n.* —.

RE2 **hagabogibogia.** *v.* —.

BOGO$_1$

B **bogo.** *v.* Take something, steal something.

B 1 **bogoanga.** *n.* —.

B 2 **bogoa.** *v.* —.

B 2 **bogolia.** *v.* —.

R **bogobogo$_1$.** *v.* —.

R 1 **bogobogoanga$_1$.** *n.* —.

R 2 **bogobogoa.** *v.* —.

R 2 **bogobogolia.** *v.* —.

BOGO$_2$

E **pogo.** *v.* Crumpled up.

E 1 **pogoanga.** *n.* —.

EE **hagapogo.** *v.* Fold up (one fold); cause to crumple up.

EE1 **hagapogoanga.** *n.* —.

EE2 **hagapogolia.** *v.* —.

R **bogobogo$_2$.** *v.* Pushed out of shape (as a tin can), rumpled, crumpled.

R 1 **bogobogoanga$_2$.** *n.* —.

RE **hagabogobogo.** *v.* —.

RE1 **hagabogobogoanga.** *n.* —.

RE2 **hagabogobogolia.** *v.* —.

BOI

B **boi.** *a.* Abnormal [sing.].

B 1 **boinga.** *n.* —.

BE **hagaboi.** *v.* —.

BE1 **hagaboinga.** *n.* —.

BE2 **hagaboia.** *v.* —.

P **poi.** *a.* —.

P 1 **poinga.** *n.* —.

PE **hagapoi.** *v.* —.

PE1 **hagapoinga.** *n.* —.

PE2 **hagapoia.** *v.* —.

R **boiboi.** *a.* Repeatedly displaying signs of abnormality; dizzy.

R 1 **boiboinga.** *n.* —.

RE **hagaboiboi.** *v.* —.

RE1 **hagaboiboinga.** *n.* —.

RE2 **hagaboiboia.** *v.* —.

XCO **boibala.** *a.* Watery (of prepared food).

ID **boi a eidu.** Temporarily abnormal.

ID **boi dugidugi.** Idiot.

ID **boi gadagada.** Laugh all the time at nothing.

ID **boi malangilangi.** Laugh abnormally.

ID **see boiboi saele.** Stagger about (from a head injury), move as though unconscious.

ID **somo boi.** Grow abnormally (having defects).

BOIa

B **booiaa** (!). *a.* Do something shameful (for shame!).

BE **hagabooiaa.** *v.* —.

BOLE

B **bole.** *a.* Bawl out, be angry; be mad (as indicated by one's movements).

B 1 **boolenga.** *n.* —.

B 2 **bolengia.** *v.* Do something without reflection.

BE **hagabole.** *v.* —.

BE1 **hagaboolenga.** *n.* —.

BE2 **hagabolea.** *v.* —.

BE2 **hagabolengia.** *v.* —.

P **pole.** *a.* —; shaking [pl.]; trembling [pl.].

P 1 **poolenga.** *n.* —.

PE **hagapole.** *v.* —.
PE1 **hagapoolenga.** *n.* —.
PE2 **hagapolengia.** *v.* —.
PE2 **hagapoolea.** *v.* —.
R **bolebole.** *a.* Trembling [sing.]; shaking [sing.]; inclined to bawl out.
R 1 **bolebolenga.** *n.* —.
RE **hagabolebole.** *v.* —.
RE1 **hagabolebolenga.** *n.* —.
RE2 **hagabolebolea.** *v.* —.
RE2 **hagabolebolengia.** *v.* —.
ID **bole gi de gai.** Eat ravenously.
ID **de ulu hagabolebole.** Topmost part of any standing object.
ID **sugi hagabolebole.** The tip of anything slender and long (e.g., the tail of an animal).

BOLI

B **boli.** *v.* Take special care of.
B 1 **boolinga.** *n.* —.
B 2 **bolia.** *v.* —.
R **boliboli.** *v.* —.
R 1 **bolibolinga.** *n.* —.
XCO **gailalopoli.** *a.* Stingy.

BOLO$_1$

B **bolo$_1$.** *mi.* According to —.
ID **au e hai bolo.** "I thought that —".
ID **dagu hai bolo.** "One would have thought that —".
ID **maanadu bolo.** "Assume that —".

BOLO$_2$

B **bolo$_2$.** *v.* Make a will (for oneself or others).
B 1 **boolonga.** *n.* Testament.
B 2 **boloa.** *v.* —.
BE **hagabolo.** *v.* To include in one's will.
BE1 **hagaboolonga.** *n.* —.
BE2 **hagaboloa.** *v.* —.
R **bolobolo$_2$.** *v.* —.
R 1 **bolobolonga.** *n.* —.
R 2 **boloboloa.** *v.* —.
RE **hagabolobolo.** *v.* —.
RE1 **hagabolobolonga.** *n.* —.
RE2 **hagaboloboloa.** *v.* —.
ID **bolo ange.** Bequeath.
ID **bolo iho.** To make oneself the beneficiary of a will which one has made for another.

BOLOBOLO

B **bolobolo$_1$.** *n.* A type of basket.
XG **bolobolo a Sogo.** A type of basket.

BONA

B **bona.** *n.* A knot tied at the end of a rope or a string to prevent its unravelling.
BE **hagabona.** *v.* —.
BE1 **hagabonaanga.** *n.* —.
BE2 **hagabonalia.** *v.* —.
R **bonabona.** *a.* Fear (as perceived somatically); having many *bona.*
R 1 **bonabonaanga.** *n.* —.
RE **hagabonabona.** *v.* —.
RE1 **hagabonabonaanga.** *n.* —.
RE2 **hagabonabonalia.** *v.* —.
ID **bonaa ua.** The sheath of the turtle's neck.
ID **bonabona age.** Become fearful.
ID **bonabona age lodo.** Feel fearful.

BONO

B **bono.** *d.* To close (something); to mend (clothes); to cover something (e.g., a pot); to block (the way).
B 1 **boononga.** *n.* —.
B 2 **bonodia.** *v.* —.
E **pono.** *v.* —; a cover (which closes); to block (the way) [as a single act].
R **bonobono.** *v.* —.
R 1 **bonobononga.** *n.* —.
R 2 **bonobonodia.** *v.* —.
XCO **Pono-haanau.** *nn.* The name of a spirit.
ID **bono aasanga.** A method of fishing (by blocking the channel at high tide).
ID **pono age de manava.** Be unable to breathe.
ID **pono iho.** Put a cover on.
ID **hale pono.** Prison, jail.

BONGA

B **bonga.** *a.* Bent, curved, defective (of fruit).
BE **hagabonga.** *v.* —.
BE2 **hagabongalia.** *v.* —.
P **ponga.** *a.* —.
PE **hagaponga.** *v.* —.
PE2 **hagapongalia.** *v.* —.
R **bongabonga.** *a.* Bent up.
RE **hagabongabonga.** *v.* —.
RE2 **hagabongabongalia.** *v.* —.

BONGA$_a$

B **bongaa —.** *d.* That which is hollow.
ID **bongaa hala.** Any long and hollow object (e.g., a pipe or a hose).
ID **bongaa manu.** Large, exposed roots (e.g., of the breadfruit tree).
ID **bongaa usu.** Nostril.
ID **ili luu bongaa usu.** To dilate one's nostrils [a mannerism which is taken as a sign of emotion].

BONGI

XCO **suunibongi.** *n.* A coral formation (resembling a man) at the bottom of the lagoon; a method of pole fishing at night.

BOO$_1$

B **boo$_1$.** *d.* Grab (with one's hand); hold (in one's hand); capture.
B 1 **boaanga$_1$.** *n.* A period (of time) during which many people require massage (for fractures).
B 1 **booanga$_1$.** *n.* —.
B 2 **boogia.** *v.* —.
BE **hagaboo$_1$.** *a.* —.
BE1 **hagabooanga$_1$.** *n.* —.
BE2 **hagaboogia.** *v.* —.
E **poo.** *a.* Grab or catch in a single act.
E 1 **pooanga.** *n.* —.
R **booboo$_1$.** *a.* —.
R 1 **boobooanga.** *n.* —.
R 2 **booboogia.** *v.* —.
RE **hagabooboo$_1$.** *a.* —.
RE1 **hagaboobooanga$_1$.** *n.* —.
RE2 **hagabooboogia.** *v.* —.
ID **booboo me.** Massage (as a medical treatment).
ID **boogia mai.** Be caught doing something wrong.
ID **boo gi de gai.** Continually wanting to eat.
ID **boo gi me.** Acquisitive (and acting on acquisitive impulses).
ID **boo manu.** To weed (a garden).
ID **poo ange.** Touch (someone or something with the hand).
ID **poo mai.** A unit of measurement (from the end of the extended thumb to the other side of the clenched fist).
ID **me boogia e de eidu.** A black spot on the skin (like a bruise) noticed after sleeping.

BOO$_{1a}$

B **booi.** *n.* A type of prepared food (made from mashed taro and coconut juice).
R **booboo$_2$.** *n.* A type of prepared food (made from taro or breadfruit).
ID **maanga booi.** A fingerful of *booi.*
CF **boibala.** Watery (of prepared food).

BOO$_{1b}$

B **heboohagi.** *a.* Fight.
B 1 **heboohaginga.** *n.* —.
BE **hagaheboohagi.** *v.* —.
BE1 **hagaheboohaginga.** *n.* —.
BE2 **hagaheboohagia.** *v.* —.
R **heboheboohagi.** *a.* Fight frequently.
R 1 **heboheboohaginga.** *n.* —.
RE **hagaheboheboohagi.** *v.* —.
RE1 **hagaheboheboohaginga.** *n.* —.
RE2 **hagaheboheboohagia.** *v.* —.
ID **heboohagi lima.** Fist fight.
ID **heboohagi mai.** Found fighting.

BOO$_2$

B **boo$_2$.** *a.* Night; birthday.

B 2 **boongia.** *v.* Be caught by darkness unexpectedly.
BE **hagaboo$_2$.** *a.* Greet; take leave of.
BE2 **hagaboongia.** *v.* Remain somewhere until dark.
XCO **boialiali.** *n.* The light just before daybreak.
XCO **huaaboo.** *n.* The whole night long.
XFL **manu-de-boo.** *n.* Centipede.
ID **boo adu laa.** Day after tomorrow at night.
ID **boo aleduu.** Tomorrow night.
ID **boo dabeo.** A night which is rainy and stormy.
ID **boo danuaa.** Good night! Good evening!
ID **boo dolu de gulu.** The third day after breadfruit has been picked (after which it is not good to eat).
ID **boo taiao.** Early morning.
ID **boo gi dai.** The period when the quarter moon appears in the west just after sunset.
ID **boo gi dua.** The period when the quarter moon appears in the east just before sunrise.
ID **boo hagalele mouli.** A night on which the making of noise is permitted (i.e., on certain holidays).
ID **boo iho.** The following night.
ID **boo i lalo o tangada.** The last days of a person's life.
ID **boo mai ange laa.** The second night following.
ID **boo seniseni.** A type of children's game (played in the water, like tag).
ID **pala boo maasina.** The time of the month when rain is most likely to occur (1st quarter).
ID **daula de boo.** A rope carried in the canoe (esp. at night) for anchoring or tying canoes together in case of strong wind.
ID **dele de boialiali.** Daybreak.
ID **dino boo.** Nights (2) when the full moon appears just after sunset.
ID **dua haangoda de boo.** Fishing line of a size appropriate for *haangoda de boo.*
ID **tino boo.** Full moon (a period comprising two nights).
ID **gai boo.** Eat early in the morning.
ID **gohu boo dangodango.** A pitch-black night.
ID **haangoda de boo.** A method of fishing (at night, beyond the reef).
ID **hai de boo (o).** Celebrate the birthday (of).
ID **madohi boo.** Midnight.
ID **malo gahu de boo.** Sheet, blanket.
ID **masa boo.** Mornings following nights during which the tide has gone out (which are good for looking for fish trapped on the reef).
ID **oho boo.** To *oho* while still dark.
ID **sula boo.** The appearance in early morning of a ship (or plane).

BOO$_{2a}$
B **aboo.** *b.* Tonight.
ID **aboo nei.** Tonight (future).

BOO$_{2b}$
B **anaboo.** *b.* Last night.
ID **anaboo taiao.** Early this morning.
ID **anaboo nei.** Tonight (past).

BOO$_3$
B **boo$_3$.** *a.* A type of sound, indicating surprise.
B 1 **booanga$_2$.** *n.* —.
BE **hagaboo$_3$.** *v.* —.
BE1 **hagabooanga$_2$.** *n.* —.
RE **hagabooboo$_2$.** *v.* —.
RE1 **hagaboobooanga$_2$.** *n.* —.
XCO **boolaa.** *a.* A type of sound, indicating surprise.
XCO **boolleiee.** *a.* A type of sound, made to frighten someone.

ID	**boo ga dae laa.** My goodness!
ID	**boolaa ange.** Say *boolaa* to.

BOOBUA

B	**boobua.** *n.* Insect sp.; dragonfly.

BOONEI

B	**boonei.** *n.* Fish sp.? : damselfish?

BOSU

B	**bosu.** *a.* Be satiated with food [sing.].
B 1	**bosuanga.** *n.* —.
BE	**hagabosu.** *v.* —.
BE1	**hagabosuanga.** *n.* —.
BE2	**hagabosulia.** *v.* —.
T	**boobosu.** *a.* [pl. of *bosu*].
TE	**hagaboobosu.** *v.* —.
TE1	**hagaboobosuanga.** *n.* —.
TE2	**hagaboobosulia.** *v.* —.

BOU

B	**bou.** *n.* Mast (of a canoe).
ID	**dao bou.** Ridge pole support (end).

BOULI

B	**bouli.** *a.* Darkness (of or pertaining to).
B 1	**boulianga.** *n.* —.
BE	**hagabouli.** *v.* —.
BE1	**hagaboulianga.** *n.* —.
ID	**bouli gee.** An alternative mode of existence (such as the world of ghosts).
ID	**hano gi bouli gee.** To transfigure oneself.
ID	**me bouli.** The deepest part of the lagoon.

BUA

B	**bua.** *n* Plant sp.: tree sp. (*Guettarda speciosa* L.).
XFL	**manu-de-bua.** *n.* Bird sp.: sacred kingfisher (*Halcyon sancta*) (The native term applies possibly to several spp.).

BUA$_a$

XCO	**bualeu.** *n.* Ovaries and fallopian tubes.
ID	**bua moe.** Immature girl.

BUAALALI

B	**buaalali.** *v.* Flood tide.
B 1	**buaalalianga.** *n.* —.
BE	**hagabuaalali.** *v.* —.

BUADA

B	**buada.** *v.* Sling.
B 1	**buadaanga.** *n.* —.
B 2	**buadalia.** *v.* Cast with a sling.
ID	**dangi buada.** The noise made by a fast-moving projectile.

BUBU

B	**bubu.** *a.* Move about.
B 1	**bubuanga.** *n.* —.
BE	**hagabubu.** *v.* —.
BE1	**hagabubuanga.** *n.* —.
BE2	**hagabubulia.** *v.* —.
R	**bupubu.** *a.* Make a lot of noise (not vocal).
R 1	**bupubuanga.** *n.* —.
RE	**hagabupubu.** *v.* —.
RE1	**hagabupubuanga.** *n.* —.
RE2	**hagabupubulia.** *v.* —.
ID	**bubu donu.** Move skillfully.
ID	**bubu sala.** Move unskillfully.

BUDU

B	**budu.** *n.* The appearance of many fish (or birds, or animals which are good to eat) after a death.
B 1	**buudunga.** *n.* Pile of, group of.
BE	**hagabudu.** *v.* Collect in one place together, accumulate.
BE1	**hagabuudunga.** *n.* —; a pile of things which have been accumulated.
BE2	**hagabudua.** *v.* —.
BE2	**hagabudulia.** *v.* —.
R	**budubudu.** *a.* Crowded together.
R 1	**budubudunga.** *n.* —.
RE	**hagabudubudu.** *v.* Accumulate repeatedly.
RE1	**hagabudubudunga.** *n.* —.
RE2	**hagabudubudua.** *v.* —.
RE2	**hagabudubudulia.** *v.* —.
T	**buubudu.** *a.* Crowded together closely.

T 1 **buubudunga.** *n.* —.
TE **hagabuubudu.** *v.* —.
TE1 **hagabuubudunga.** *n.* —.
TE2 **hagabuubudua.** *v.* —.
TE2 **hagabuubudulia.** *v.* —.
ID **hagabudu me.** Selfish.

BUGA
B **buga.** *n.* Plant sp.: tree sp. (*Pisonia grandis* R.B.).
XFL **bugaliaa.** *n.* Plant sp.: tree sp.: Indian mulberry tree (*Morinda citrifolia* L.).

BUGE
B **buge.** *n.* A bump on a tree trunk.
BE **hagabuge.** *v.* —.

BUGOLO
B **bugolo.** *n.* Coral sp.: faviid coral.

BUGU
B **bugu.** *n.* Mons veneris.
B 1 **buugunga.** *n.* Conformation of a *bugu*.
P **pugu.** *a.* Swollen [pl.].
P 1 **puugunga.** *n.* The slopes of swellings or protuberances.
PE **hagapugu.** *v.* —.
PE1 **hagapuugunga.** *n.* —.
PE2 **hagapugua.** *v.* —.
PE2 **hagapugulia.** *v.* —.
R **bugubugu.** *a.* Swollen [sing.].
R 1 **bugubugunga.** *n.* The slope of a swelling or protuberance.
RE **hagabugubugu.** *v.* —.
RE2 **hagabugubugua.** *v.* —.
RE2 **hagabugubuguhia.** *v.* —.

BUI
R **buibui.** *v.* Keep in (e.g., pigs); keep out (e.g., wind); soak (in water).
R 1 **buibuinga.** *n.* —.
R 2 **buibuia.** *v.* —.

BUI$_a$
B **daabui.** *v.* Enclose.
B 1 **daabuinga.** *n.* —.
B 2 **daabuia.** *v.* —.
BE **hagadaabui.** *v.* —.
BE1 **hagadaabuinga.** *n.* —.
BE2 **hagadaabuia.** *v.* —.

BUI$_b$
B **hebuihagi.** *v.* Provide an abundance of bait to keep fish in close.
B 1 **hebuihaginga.** *n.* —.
B 2 **hebuihagina.** *v.* —.
BE **hagahebuihagi.** *v.* —.
BE1 **hagahebuihaginga.** *n.* —.
BE2 **hagahebuihagina.** *v.* —.
R **hebuhebuihagi.** *v.* —.
RE **hagahebuhebuihagi.** *v.* —.
RE1 **hagahebuhebuihaginga.** *n.* —.
RE2 **hagahebuhebuihagina.** *v.* —.

BULA
B **bula.** *a.* A flash (e.g., of light); a quick glance; to light (a torch).
B 1 **bulaanga.** *n.* —.
BE **hagabula.** *v.* —.
BE1 **hagabulaanga.** *n.* —.
E **pula.** *a.* Open one's eyes widely; to light up suddenly; insect sp.: a phosphorescent insect.
E 1 **pulaanga.** *n.* —.
EE **hagapula.** *v.* —.
EE1 **hagapulaanga.** *n.* —.
R **bulabula.** *a.* Testicles; look here and there; to have a lot of spots; twinkling (of many stars or phosphorescent insects, etc.).
R 1 **bulabulaanga.** *n.* —.
RE **hagabulabula.** *v.* —.
RE1 **hagabulabulaanga.** *n.* —.
XFL **hadu-mada-pula.** *n.* Coral sp.: (several spp. — poisonous).
ID **bula de ganomada.** Get mad.
ID **pula luu mada.** Excited with joy.

BULADA
B **bulada.** *n.* Banana tree fibers (for making cloth).

BULAGA
B **bulaga.** *n.* Plant sp.: swamp taro (*Cyrtosperma chamissonis*).
ID **hadu solo bulaga.** A taro grater made from a certain type of coral.
CF **bulaga-a-leo.** Fish sp.: tang.

BULE
B **bule.** *n.* Vertebra; mollusk sp.: cowry shell (many spp.).
BE1 **hagadaubulebuleanga.** *n.* —.
XCO **duubulei.** *n.* Head of the penis.
ID **bule dango.** Button.
ID **hau bule.** Shell necklace or headdress.
ID **lilo bule.** Covered up completely.

BULE$_a$
B **daubulebule.** *a.* Spotted (covered with spots).
B 1 **daubulebuleanga.** *n.* —.
BE **hagadaubulebule.** *v.* To change coloring (esp. fish in anxiety states).

BULI
B **buli.** *v.* Grab up.
B 1 **buulinga.** *n.* —.
B 2 **buulia.** *v.* —.
BE1 **hagabuulinga.** *n.* Group of animate things.
E **puli.** *v.* Grab up all at once.
R **bulibuli.** *v.* Grab up one thing after another.
R 1 **bulibulinga.** *n.* —.
R 2 **bulibulia.** *v.* —.
XCO **dagabuli.** *v.* Gather together in a group.

BULIAAMOU
B **buliaamou.** *a.* Long for, homesick.
B 1 **buliaamounga.** *n.* —.
BE **hagabuliaamou.** *v.* —.
BE1 **hagabuliaamounga.** *n.* —.
BE2 **hagabuliaamoua.** *v.* —.
R **bulibuliaamou.** *a.* Prone to long for.
R 1 **bulibuliaamounga.** *n.* —.
RE **hagabulibuliaamou.** *v.* —.
RE1 **hagabulibuliaamounga.** *n.* —.
RE2 **hagabulibuliaamoua.** *v.* —.
ID **valaai buliaamou.** Medicine to cure longing (homesickness or longing for a person).

BULU
B **bulu.** *n.* The short fibers of the mature coconut husk.
R **bulubulu.** *d.* Useless (things or matters).
ID **bulubulu dangada.** Unimportant person.
ID **bulubulu hegau.** Unimportant work.
ID **bulubulu maanadu.** Incomplete idea.
ID **bulubulu malo.** Rag.
ID **bulu giidagi.** A type of caulking compound, made from *bulu* and sap.
ID **hagabulubulu ange.** Make do with.

BULU$_a$
XE **hagabulumau.** *a.* Watch your step climbing!

BUNAA
B **bunaa.** *n.* The trail left behind a canoe paddle in the water (or a similar disturbance of the water).
ID **bunaa hoe.** An eddy left by a paddle stroke.

BUNANA
B **bunana.** *a.* Conjunctivitis.
BE **hagabunana.** *v.* —.

BUNEHULU
B **bunehulu.** *a.* Slow in running or walking.
B 1 **bunehuluanga.** *n.* —.
BE **hagabunehulu.** *v.* —.
BE1 **hagabunehuluanga.** *n.* —.

BUNEI
B **bunei.** *n.* Fish sp.: batfish?

BUNI
B **buni.** *a.* Closed up, be

together (in a group, or of two individuals).

B 1 **buuninga.** *n.* —.

BE **hagabuni.** *v.* Gather together (people); have sexual relations.

BE1 **hagabuuninga.** *n.* —.

BE2 **hagabunia.** *v.* Close up, bring together.

BE2 **hagabunidia.** *v.* Add up.

P **puni.** *a.* Closed up [pl.], be together (three or more things).

PE **hagapuni.** *v.* —; add, total up.

PE1 **hagapuuninga.** *n.* A total of.

PE2 **hagapunidia.** *v.* Add up (many things).

PE2 **hagapuunia.** *v.* Add up (many things).

R **bunibuni.** *a.* Be more-or-less together.

RE **hagabunibuni.** *v.* Add together from different sources.

RE1 **hagabunibuninga.** *n.* —; different totals.

RE2 **hagabunibunia.** *v.* —; close up many at one time.

RE2 **hagabunibunidia.** *v.* —.

ID **buni ange.** Agree with; join, close up (something,e.g., a hole); close up to.

ID **buni ange gi de gelegele.** To have been dead for a long time.

ID **buni ange lodo.** Paralyzed by fear; acute anxiety attack.

ID **buni de ua.** To be very thirsty.

ID **buni lunga ma lalo.** A pitch black night.

ID **hagabuni de henua.** To call an all-island meeting.

BUNUA

B **bunua.** *n.* A young bird (of any sp. suitable for being raised as a pet).

BUNGA

XFL **hadu-bunga.** *n.* Mollusk sp.: *Chama iostoma.*

CF **bungadogi.** Unskillful (at difficult activities).

CF **bungaleu.** Unskillful (at difficult activities).

BUNGADOGI

B **bungadogi.** *a.* Unskillful (at difficult activities).

B 1 **bungadogianga.** *n.* —.

BE **hagabungadogi.** *v.* —.

BE1 **hagabungadogianga.** *n.* —.

P **bungaadogi.** *a.* —.

P 1 **bungaadogianga.** *n.* —.

PE **hagabungaadogi.** *v.* —.

PE1 **hagabungaadogianga.** *n.* —.

R **bungabungadogi.** *a.* —.

R 1 **bungabungadogianga.** *n.* —.

RE **hagabungabungadogi.** *v.* —.

RE1 **hagabungabungadogianga.** *n.* —.

BUNGALEU

B **bungaleu.** *a.* Unskillful (at difficult activities).

B 1 **bungaleunga.** *n.* —.

BE **hagabungaleu.** *v.* —.

BE1 **hagabungaleunga.** *n.* —.

BE2 **hagabungaleua.** *v.* —.

P **bungaaleu.** *a.* —.

P 1 **bungaaleunga.** *n.* —.

PE **hagabungaaleu.** *v.* —.

PE1 **hagabungaaleunga.** *n.* —.

PE2 **hagabungaaleua.** *v.* —.

BUNGU

P **pungu.** *a.* Plump [pl.].

P 1 **punguanga.** *n.* —.

PE **hagapungu.** *v.* —.

PE1 **hagapunguanga.** *n.* —.

PE2 **hagapungulia.** *v.* —.

R **bungubungu.** *a.* Plump [sing.].

R 1 **bungubunguanga.** *n.* —.

RE **hagabungubungu.** *v.* —.

RE1 **hagabungubunguanga.** *n.* —.

RE2 **hagabungubungulia.** *v.* Cause to be expanded.

XCO **huugaabungubungu.** Very plump.

BUSI

B **busi.** *v.* Blow (with the mouth).

B 1 **buusinga.** *n.* —.

B 2 **busia.** *v.* —.

R busibusi. *v.* —.
R 1 busibusinga. *n.* —.
R 2 busibusia. *v.* —.
ID gai busibusi. Take the bait tentatively (of fish).
CF buusagi. An eddy caused by a current.

BUU_1
B **buu₁**. *n.* Bladder, balloon, ball; the head of the octopus; a net on a long handle; a conch shell trumpet; or any other round, hollow, inflatable object.
XFL **buu-kangi-de-muli.** *n.* Mollusk sp.: *Cymatiidae* spp., also *Bursa bubo.*
XFL **buu-ili.** *n.* Fish sp.
ID **buu goede.** Worthless or useless ['like an octopus without a head'].
ID **buu hale moni.** Mollusk sp.
ID **buu unga.** An empty seashell; one of (a pair of) diving goggles.

BUU_2
R **$buubuu_1$**. *v.* Divination.
R 1 **buubuuanga.** *n.* —.
R 1 **buubuunga.** *n.* —.
R 2 **buubuua.** *v.* To divine (for omens).
R 2 **buubuulia.** *v.* To divine (for omens).
XFL **itebuubuu.** *n.* Insect sp.: grasshopper.
ID **buubuu a lada.** A type of puzzle.
ID **buu tangada.** An omen of death (when a certain kind or size of fish is caught).

BUU_3
B **buu_3**. *a.* Be greasy.
B 1 **$buuanga_1$**. *n.* —.
BE **$hagabuu_1$**. *v.* —.
BE1 **$hagabuuanga_1$**. *n.* —.
BE2 **$hagabuua_1$**. *v.* Crowd away from.
BE2 **$hagabuuia_1$**. *v.* —.
R **$buubuu_2$**. *a.* —.
RE **$hagabuubuu_1$**. *v.* —.
RE1 **$hagabuubuuanga_1$**. *n.* —.
RE2 **$hagabuubuua_1$**. *v.* —.
RE2 **$hagabuubuuia_2$**. *v.* —.

BUU_4
B **buu_2**. *a.* Come out from (like smoke or pus); be forced out of.
B 1 **$buuanga_2$**. *n.* —.
B 2 **buuia.** *v.* Be struck with something shot out from something else.
BE **$hagabuu_2$**. *v.* —; accuse.
BE1 **$hagabuuanga_2$**. *n.* —.
BE1 **hagabuulunga.** *v.* Accuse (someone) of having had sexual relations with someone else.
BE2 **$hagabuua_2$**. *v.* —.
BE2 **$hagabuuia_2$**. *v.* —.
BE2 **hagabuulia.** *v.* —.
P **puu.** *a.* — forced out.
PE **hagapuu.** *v.* —.
PE1 **hagapuuanga.** *n.* —.
PE2 **hagapuua.** *v.* —.
PE2 **hagapuulia.** *v.* —.
R **$buubuu_3$**. *a.* —.
RE **$hagabuubuu_2$**. *v.* —.
RE1 **$hagabuubuuanga_2$**. *n.* —.
RE2 **$hagabuubuua_2$**. *v.* —.
RE2 **$hagabuubuuia_1$**. *v.* —; cause to be repeatedly *puu.*
RE2 **hagabuubuulia.** *v.* —.
ID **buu de mama.** Air filled with *mama.*
ID **buu useahi.** Blurred.
ID **hagabuu ange.** Blame (someone), incriminate (someone).
ID **hagabuulunga iho.** To *hagabuulunga* oneself.
CF **buusagi.** An eddy caused by a current.

BUUGANI
B **buugani.** *a.* Be (in fact) slow-moving (while attempting to hurry).
B 1 **buuganianga.** *n.* —.
BE **hagabuugani.** *v.* —.
BE1 **hagabuuganianga.** *n.* —.

BUUGANGA
B **buuganga.** *n.* A trip for a festive or recreational purpose.

BUULEI
B **buulei.** *a.* Ring (for a finger).
BE **hagabuulei.** *v.* Put a ring on (someone).
BE1 **hagabuuleinga.** *n.* —.

BUULOU
B **buulou.** *v.* Cover up (by wrapping up with one layer); to catch by scooping up (e.g., with a net or basket).
B 1 **buulounga.** *n.* —.
B 2 **buuloua.** *v.* —.
R **bulobulou.** *v.* To net flying fish.
R 1 **bulobulounga.** *n.* —.
R 2 **bulobuloua.** *v.* —.

BUULUDI
B **buuludi.** *v.* Hug.
B 1 **buuludinga.** *n.* —.
B 2 **buludia.** *v.* —.
R **bulubuludi.** *v.* Keep hugging.
R 1 **bulubuludinga.** *n.* —.
R 2 **bulubuludia.** *v.* —.

BUUNOU
CF **madabuunou.** Dull (of an edge or point).

BUUSAGI
B **buusagi.** *v.* An eddy caused by a current.
B 1 **buusaginga.** *n.* —.
BE **hagabuusagi.** *v.* —.
BE1 **hagabuusaginga.** *n.* —.
BE2 **hagabuusagia.** *v.* —.
R **buubuusagi.** *v.* —.
R 1 **buubuusaginga.** *n.* —.
RE **hagabuubuusagi.** *v.* —.
RE1 **hagabuubuusaginga.** *n.* —.
RE2 **hagabuubuusagia.** *v.* —.
S **buusagisagi.** *a.* To be laden with scent (of air).
SE **hagabuusagisagi.** *v.* —.
SE1 **hagabuusagisaginga.** *n.* —.
SE2 **hagabuusagisagia.** *v.* —.
ID **laangai buusagi.** A type of fishing condition in which the sea is boiling with jumping tuna, which are biting at anything.

PADA
B **pada.** *a.* Be coarse in texture, grain, weave, etc.
B 1 **padaanga.** *n.* —.
BE **hagapada.** *v.* —.
BE1 **hagapadaanga.** *n.* —.
BE2 **hagapadalia.** *v.* —.
ID **basa pada.** Speak harshly.
ID **doonga pada.** Heavy-duty equipment or fishing gear; a large penis.
ID **dua pada.** To plait with thick strands.
ID **muna pada.** Harsh words.

PAI
B **pai.** *v.* A type of cloud formation like *babaiangi.*
BE **hagapai.** *v.* —.
CF **babaiangi.** A type of cloud formation (dark but not threatening rain).

PANAVA
B **panava.** *n.* Scrotum (one side only).
ID **luu panava.** Scrotum (whole thing).

PULU
B **pulu.** *v.* To be dry and smooth; satiated; be able to withstand.
B 1 **puluanga.** *n.* —.
BE **hagapulu.** *v.* —.
BE1 **hagapuluanga.** *n.* —.

DAA$_1$
B **daa$_1$.** *v.* To make a sharp turn [sing.]; a back-handed slap or jerking of anything which moves (e. g., a hand, foot, tail, tongue, etc.); to tattoo; hit, strike, beat; to kill; to wash clothes; scoop up (liquids or solids); to bail (a canoe).
B 1 **daanga.** *n.* —.
B 2 **daaia.** *v.* Wash clothes completely; scoop up completely.
B 2 **daia.** *v.* To *daa* completely (excepting meanings 'make a sharp turn', 'wash clothes', 'scoop up', 'bail').

BE hagadaa. *v.* — .
BE1 hagadaanga. *n.* — .
BE2 hagadaaia. *v.* — .
BE2 hagadaia. *v.* — .
E taa. *v.* *daa* at one time; make a sharp turn [pl.].
EE hagataa. *v.* — .
EE1 hagataanga. *n.* — .
R daadaa$_1$. *v.* — .
R 1 daadaanga. . — ; appearance of (i.e. 'way in which made').
R 2 daadaaia. *v.* — ; rush (usually preceded by *dee*).
RE hagadaadaa. *v.* — .
RE1 hagadaadaanga. *n.* — .
RE2 hagadaadaaia. *v.* — .
XCO daasississi. *v.* Striped (with stripes).
XCO daasugi. *v.* Struggle to get free; jerking of the tail.
XFL manu-daa-uga. *n.* [*goehau*].
ID au taadaaia. Don't rush! Take it easy!
ID daadaaia ange. Be in a hurry to.
ID daadaanga sala. Ugly-looking.
ID daa de + NUMBER. It is — o'clock.
ID daa de alelo. Cluck one's tongue.
ID daa de baalanga. Ring the bell.
ID daa de gaehala. To swing a jump rope made of *gaehala*.
ID daa de hia?. What time is it?
ID daa de masavaa. Time's up! It's time for...
ID daa gaiaa. To murder someone so that others don't see.
ID daa hatau. Beat unmercifully.
ID daa hagasaalei. Make a striped design in tatooing.
ID daa hhali. An adze stroke, used to chip out the interior of a bowl, canoe, etc.
ID daa mouli. Take life away from.
ID daa sseu. A way of forming the body of a canoe.
ID daia e de hegau. Overworked.
ID daia e tuaadai. Seasick.
ID daia e tulidaa. Urgency in micturation.
ID daia e sseni. Very sleepy.
ID dogi daadaa. A type of adze (with a small blade, for light chipping).
ID taa de lui. To bail water from a canoe.
ID taa hagabiibii. To bail a canoe rapidly.
ID e dee daadaaia. To be in no hurry.
ID soe daa dahi. Straight as can be.
CF daatugu. To curse (someone).
CF daagami. Bodyguard, soldier.
CF daalo. Stab, skewer.
CF daasele. To swing a rope (in a jump rope game) so as to cause the jumper to trip.
CF daavalo. Make a great deal of noise (vocal).
CF hedaadoi. Collide.

DAA$_{1a}$

B daaligi. *v.* Do something seriously; be moved about; a jerky movement, caused by the wind (e.g., the flapping of a sail); work seriously.
B 1 daaligidanga. *n.* The slope of a canoe's keel.
B 2 daaligidia. *v.* To have been moved about by the wind.
BE hagadaaligi. *v.* —.
BE1 hagadaaligidanga. *n.* —.
BE2 hagadaaligidia. *v.* —.
R daadaaligi. *v.* —.
R 1 daadaaligidanga. *n.* The way of being moved about in the air.
R 2 daadaaligidia. *v.* —.
RE hagadaadaaligi. *v.* —.
RE1 hagadaadaaligidanga. *n.* —.
RE2 hagadaadaaligidia. *v.* —.

DAA$_2$

R daadaa$_2$. *n.* Sweat [noun], perspiration.
ID daa (dau). Chanting (of old chants).

ID **daa de hagallogo.** Perform certain old religious ceremonies or chants.
ID **daa donu taahili.** Sing on-key.
ID **daa taahili.** Sing a melody.
ID **daa gee taahili.** Sing off-key.
ID **sali daadaa.** To sweat.

DAA3
B **daa2.** *n.* A bunch.

DAA4
B **daa3.** *n.* Fish sp.: squirrelfish.

DAA5
ID **daa age.** Go toward land (from the lagoon).
ID **daa de —.** Let's —.
ID **daa hagabodobodo.** Make a quick trip.
ID **daa hagapodo.** [pl. of *daa haga bodobodo*].
ID **daa hagalele.** Unscheduled, unplanned.
ID **daa iho.** Go toward the lagoon (from land).

DAABASI
B **daabasi.** *v.* Angling for tuna.
B 1 **daabasinga.** *n.* —.
BE **hagadaabasi.** *v.* —.
BE1 **hagadaabasinga.** *n.* —.
R **daadaabasi.** *v.* —.
R 1 **daadaabasinga.** *n.* —.
RE **hagadaadaabasi.** *v.* —.
RE1 **hagadaadaabasinga.** *n.* —.
ID **dua daabasi.** The size of fishing line appropriate for tuna fishing.

DAABEDUGE
B **daabeduge.** *v.* Work seriously.
B 1 **daabedugeanga.** *n.* —.
BE **hagadaabeduge.** *v.* —.
BE1 **hagadaabedugeanga.** *n.* —.
R **daadaabeduge.** *v.* —.
R 1 **daadaabedugeanga.** *n.* —.
RE **hagadaadaabeduge.** *v.* —.
RE1 **hagadaadaabedugeanga.** *n.* —.
ID **daabeduge adu ange.** Take a lot of.
ID **daabeduge mai.** Bring a lot of.
ID **daabeduge saele.** To bat around.

DAADAA
B **daadaa3.** *n.* Sibling (mostly children's talk).
ID **hai daadaa.** The relationship between siblings.

DAATUGU
B **daatugu.** *v.* To curse (someone).
B 1 **daatuguanga.** *n.* —.
B 2 **daatugulia.** *v.* —.
BE **hagadaatugu.** *v.* —.
BE1 **hagadaatuguanga.** *n.* —.
BE2 **hagadaatugulia.** *v.* —.

DAAEA
B **daaea.** *n.* Fish sp.: snapper (= large *babudaea*).
XFL **babu-daaea.** *n.* Fish sp.: snapper (= small *daea*).
XFL **balu-daaea.** *n.* Fish sp.
ID **tugi taaea.** A fishing method (using hermit crabs for bait).

DAAGAMI
B **daagami.** *n.* Bodyguard, soldier.

DAAGANGA
B **daaganga3.** *n.* Kind (of), sort (of), variety (of).
BE **hagadaaganga.** *n.* Kind (of), sort (of), variety (of).

DAAGELO
B **Daagelo.** *n.* February.

DAAGODO
XCO **madadaagodo.** *a.* Gradual slope or inclination [form *daagodo* only occurs with *mada*].

DAAHAA
B **daahaa.** *a.* A drinking coconut; to have drinking coconuts (of a tree); the stage of development of the coconut between *dahaa mada balabala* and *dahaa*

mada makaga.

BE **hagadaahaa.** *v.* —.

ID **daahaa mada balabala.** The stage of development of the coconut between *mugamuga* and *daahaa.*

ID **daahaa mada giigii.** The stage of development of the coconut between *daahaa mada makaga* and *modomodo.*

ID **daahaa mada makaga.** The stage of development of the coconut between *daahaa* and *daahaa mada giigii.*

ID **hagailangi daahaa.** A type of prepared food (like *dalogo,* but without *somo* or *mugamuga*).

ID **sii mada daahaa.** A fine jet of water.

DAAHAGI

ID **iho daahagi.** A calm sea condition, in which the horizon disappears [the horizon being normally marked by surf).

DAAHANGA

B **daahanga.** *v.* Fool (someone), deceive.

B 2 **daahangadia.** *v.* —.

B 2 **daahangalia.** *v.* —.

ID **daahanga ange.** Give pleasure to someone by giving him something.

DAAHAO

BE **hagadaahao.** *v.* Play (games); game, amusement; amuse oneself.

BE1 **hagadaahaonga.** *n.* —.

BE2 **hagadaahaoa.** *v.* —.

ID **daahili hagadaahao.** A song which is for amusement only (one which is not 'serious', i.e., not religious).

ID **daumaha hagadaahao.** Social activities which are held in the church under church auspices.

ID **goloa hagadaahao.** Recreational equipment.

ID **hagadaahao ai.** Do something as though it were a game.

ID **laangi hagadaahao.** Field day.

ID **me hagadaahao.** Toy.

ID **momme hagadaahao.** Playground.

ID **seesee hagadaahao.** Walk (for recreation).

DAAHILI

B **daahili.** *v.* Song; sing.

BE **hagadaahili.** *v.* Make someone sing.

BE1 **hagadaahilinga.** *n.* —.

BE2 **hagadaahilia.** *v.* —.

ID **daa donu taahili.** Sing on-key.

ID **daa taahili.** Sing a melody.

ID **daa gee taahili.** Sing off-key.

ID **daahili daumaha.** A church song.

ID **daahili dau soa.** A love song.

ID **daahili hagadaahao.** A song which is for amusement only (one which is not 'serious', i.e., not religious).

ID **daahili lo te gohu.** A popular (secular) song.

ID **daumaha daahili.** Song service (in church).

ID **duudanga daahili.** Verse of a song.

ID **gubu daahili.** Verse of a song.

ID **hadu daahili.** To make up a song.

ID **hai daahili.** To compose songs.

ID **vaivai daahili.** A dirty song.

DAALINGA

B **daalinga₂.** *n.* An area near the flowering part of the coconut tree (where birds perch).

ID **paa i daalinga.** Move in closely (of birds) to *daalinga.*

DAALO

B **daalo.** *v.* Stab, skewer.

B 1 **daalonga.** *n.* —; a wound (on the body, from a

spear, etc.).
B 2 **daaloa.** *v.* To have been stabbed (esp. accidentally by *hanga*).
BE **hagadaalo.** *v.* —.
BE1 **hagadaalonga.** *n.* —.
BE2 **hagadaaloa.** *v.* —.
R **daadaalo.** *v.* —.
R 1 **daadaalonga.** *n.* —.
R 2 **daadaaloa.** *v.* —.
RE **hagadaadaalo.** *v.* —.
RE1 **hagadaadaalonga.** *n.* —.
RE2 **hagadaadaaloa.** *v.* —.
ID **tuu taalonga.** To escape (of fish, after having been speared).
ID **huaahuu daalo.** A type of prepared food (like *huaahuu*, with the addition of bananas or something else sweet).
ID **modu taalonga.** To escape (of fish, after having been speared).

DAAMADA
B **daamada.** *v.* Start; the beginning (of an event).
B 1 **damadanga.** *n.* —; origin, source.
B 2 **damadaa.** *v.* To have started it; to have begun it.
ID **daamada age.** Start again.
ID **daumaha daamada.** The morning prayer service (before the major church service).

DAANE
B **daane.** *n.* Man, male; thing [in some contexts only].
BE **hagadaane.** *v.* To act like a human.
BE1 **hagadaaneanga.** *n.* —.
XCO **Samouli-daane.** *nn.* The name of *Vave* after his death.
ID **adugau daane.** Part of the plug of the pandanus.
ID **daane abo donu.** Gentleman, person who is good.
ID **daane dagidahi.** A person having unique skills or traits of personality.
ID **daane dau.** A person of importance (specially accomplished).
ID **daane dee lahilahia.** A very special one (rarely seen).
ID **daane e manege.** A person who is capable at almost anything.
ID **daane gasia.** A person who is useful to others.
ID **daane hai moni.** Sailor, seaman.
ID **daane honu.** A person of many accomplishments.
ID **daane i lalo.** A person who fails at everything he tries.
ID **daane mada daua.** Bravest in war.
ID **daane mada duulanga.** A person able to do things others cannot.
ID **daane masana.** Good one.
ID **daane sauaa.** A person of extraordinary ability; shark (euphemism).
ID **daane ssili dala.** Special one, important one.
ID **daina daane.** Brother, male cousin.
ID **dama daane.** Boy, young man.
ID **taane sauaa.** Shark (euphemism).
ID **tale taane.** A tough man.
ID **gauligi daane.** Male child, boy.
ID **goloa o taane.** Male genitalia.
ID **hale daane.** Men's house (modern usage).
ID **(de) hine sala daane.** Nymphomaniac.
ID **lo taane.** Daring, brave, manly.
ID **sou daane.** A sudden strong gust of wind.
ID **ulu i daane.** Boy-chaser, boy-crazy.

DAANGENGE
B **daangenge.** *v.* Meaty (not having much fat).
BE **hagadaangenge.** *v.* —.

DAAVA
B **daava.** *v.* Brackish (water); taste strange (of liquid).

B 1 **daavaanga.** *n.* —.
BE **hagadaava.** *v.* —.
BE1 **hagadaavaanga.** *n.* —.

DABA
B **daba.** *a.* A flash of light, a blink of an eye.
B 1 **dabaanga.** *n.* —.
BE **hagadaba.** *v.* —; to say that —.
BE1 **hagadabaanga.** *n.* —.
BE2 **hagadabalia.** *v.* —.
P **taba.** *v.* A flashing of several lights, a blink of the eyes.
P 1 **tabaanga.** *n.* —.
PE **hagataba.** *v.* —.
PE1 **hagatabaanga.** *n.* —.
PE2 **hagatabalia.** *v.* —.
R **dabadaba$_1$.** *v.* Twinkling, flashing, winking.
R **dabadaba$_2$.** *n.* Slipper lobster.
R 1 **dabadabaanga.** *n.* —.
RE **hagadabadaba.** *v.* —.
RE1 **hagadabadabaanga.** *n.* —.
RE2 **hagadabadabalia.** *v.* —.
XFL **dabaduu.** *n.* Fish sp.: (a small *suulee* or a var. of *suulee*).
ID **daba de ganomada.** Instantaneous, in the blinking of an eye.
CF **dabagau.** A type of floor mat.
CF **latabagea.** An ornament made of turtle shell.

DABABA
B **dababa.** *n.* Fish sp.: shark sp.
XFL **dababa-gabugabu-tai.** *n.* Fish sp.: lizard fish?
ID **ulu sele dababa.** [a phrase said aloud to attract sharks].

DABAGAU
B **dabagau.** *n.* A type of floor mat.

DABANIMEELI
B **dabanimeeli.** *a.* Payment for medical treatment.
BE **hagadabanimeeli.** *v.* To make payment for medical treatment.

DABEO
B **dabeo.** *v.* Unclean, unkempt.
B 1 **dabeoanga.** *n.* —.
BE **hagadabeo.** *v.* —.
BE1 **hagadabeoanga.** *n.* —.
ID **boo dabeo.** A night which is rainy and stormy.
ID **de hine dabeo.** A menstruating woman.
ID **gili dabeo.** A fungus infection of the skin, ringworm.
ID **hale dabeo.** Menstrual hut.
ID **laangi dabeo.** A day which is rainy and stormy.
ID **magi dabeo.** Menstruation.
ID **manu dabeo.** Trees and shrubs which grow as weeds.
ID **moana dabeo.** Rough seas.

DABU$_1$
B **dabu.** *a.* Forbidden, awesome.
B 1 **dabuanga.** *n.* —.
BE **hagadabu.** *v.* Restrict.
BE1 **hagadabuanga.** *n.* —.
BE2 **hagadabua.** *v.* —.
BE2 **hagadabulia.** *v.* —.
XCO **Laangidabu.** *nt.* Sunday.
ID **dabu de —?.** Why not —?
ID **tangada hai me dabu.** Cult priest.
ID **hai mada dabu.** An avoidance relationship (between kin).
ID **mada dabu.** Affinal relatives who are *maa* or *saulaba* to each other [and therefore between whom respect and avoidance are enjoined]; avoidance relationship.
ID **una dabu.** The part of the turtle shell nearest to the neck.

DABU$_2$
XCO **dabuvae.** *n.* Toe, footprint.
ID **dabuvae madua.** Big toe.
ID **dabuvae sisi.** Little toe.

DABUI
B **dabui.** *v.* To splash water on something with the hand.
B 1 **dabuinga.** *n.* —.

B 2 **dabuia.** *v.* To *dabui* at one time.
BE **hagadabui.** *v.* —.
BE1 **hagadabuinga.** *n.* —.
BE2 **hagadabuia.** *v.* —.
R **dabudabui.** *v.* —.
R 1 **dabudabuinga.** *n.* —.
R 2 **dabudabuia.** *v.* —.
RE **hagadabudabui.** *v.* —.
RE1 **hagadabudabuinga.** *n.* —.
RE2 **hagadabudabuia.** *v.* —.

DABULA
B **dabula.** *n.* Lizard sp.

DABUNA
B **dabuna.** *n.* Part of the female genitalia.

DADA$_1$
B **dada$_1$.** *v.* Pull.
B 1 **daadanga.** *n.* —.
B 2 **daangia.** *v.* —.
BE **hagadada.** *v.* —.
BE1 **hagadaadanga.** *n.* —.
R **datada$_1$.** *v.* To jerk repeatedly; an intermittent sharp pain.
R 1 **datadaanga.** *n.* —.
R 2 **daadaangia.** *v.* Pull continuously.
RE **hagadatada.** *v.* —.
RE1 **hagadatadaanga.** *n.* —.
RE2 **hagadaadaangia.** *v.* —.
ID **dada alohagi.** Trolling.
ID **dada de ava.** A strong current in the channel.
ID **dada de uila.** An electrical storm.
ID **dada gaehala.** Picking even small breadfruit (to avoid having to change one's position, which would be necessary in order to pick breadfruit of the proper size).
ID **dada mamu.** An impatient fisherman.
ID **dada manu.** To snare birds (with a loop on the end of a pole).
ID **dada me.** To obtain taro (by pulling up the tubers).
ID **dada moni.** To beach a canoe without using runners [considered bad practice].
ID **dada saele.** Always being borrowed.
ID **dada saiolo.** To hoist a sail.
ID **dada soosoa.** To put *soosoa* on the canoe.
ID **datada de galomada.** Twitching of an eye.
ID **goobai dada.** Umbrella.
ID **lamu dada.** A jerk (e.g., of a line).
CF **giidada.** Misfortune which will occur in the future (as ascertained through divination).

DADA$_2$
B **dada$_2$.** *n.* Fish sp. (= large *datada*, also = small *angamea*).
R **datada$_2$.** *n.* Fish sp.: snapper (= small *dada*).

DATANE
XFL **datane-uli.** *n.* Fish sp.

DAE$_1$
B **dae$_1$.** *n.* Hand net.
BE **hagadae$_1$.** *v.* To give a hand net to.
R **daedae$_1$.** *v.* To catch continuously with a hand net.
R 1 **daedaenga$_1$.** *n.* —.
R 2 **daedaea$_1$.** *v.* —.
RE **hagadaedae$_1$.** *v.* —; to instruct in hand net fishing.
RE1 **hagadaedaenga$_1$.** *n.* —.
RE2 **hagadaedaea$_1$.** *v.* —.
ID **dae maduu.** A method of pulling flying fish into the canoe with a hand net.
ID **damaa dae.** Skillful at catching flying fish.
ID **gano dae.** The net of a hand net (not including the net's handle).
CF **gatae.** Fishing net (attached to a frame or handle).

DAE$_2$
B **dae$_2$.** *a.* Arrive at.
B 1 **daenga.** *n.* —.
B 2 **daea.** *a.* To have arrived at.

BD **hedae.** *a.* Meet up with; be even with each other.
BD1 **hedaenga.** *n.* —.
BE **hagadae$_2$.** *v.* —.
BE1 **hagadaenga.** *n.* —.
BE2 **hagadaea.** *v.* —.
BE2 **hagadaelia.** *v.* —.
BG **hagahedae.** *v.* Make equal; go to meet.
BG1 **hagahedaenga.** *n.* —.
BG2 **hagahedaea.** *v.* —.
BG2 **hagahedaelia.** *v.* —.
P **tae.** *a.* —.
P 1 **taenga.** *n.* —.
PE **hagatae.** *v.* —.
PE1 **hagataenga.** *n.* —; one leg of a back-and-forth canoe course.
PE2 **hagataea.** *v.* —.
PE2 **hagataelia.** *v.* —.
R **daedae$_2$.** *a.* To reach many places.
R 1 **daedaenga$_2$.** *n.* —.
R 2 **daedaea$_2$.** *a.* Have reached many places.
RE **hagadaedae$_2$.** *v.* —.
RE1 **hagadaedaenga$_2$.** *n.* —.
RE2 **hagadaedaea$_2$.** *v.* —.
RE2 **hagadaedaelia.** *v.* —.
ID **boo ga dae laa.** My goodness!
ID **dae de lodo.** Be satisfied completely.
ID **dae de ua.** Have a good time.
ID **dae gi oona.** Be tops.
ID **dee daea donu.** Unexpectedly.
ID **dee lago dae.** Not really good or sufficient, etc.
ID **ga dae ai.** Until.
ID **ga dae laa huu.** Very, too much.
ID **ivi-a-daea.** Shoulder blade.
ID **somo dae.** Fully mature coconut apple.
CF **daelodo.** Number, figure; the outrigger boom between the *giado madua* and the *giado manu.*

DAE$_3$

B **dae$_3$.** *n.* Guts, intestines; buttocks.
XCO **daegalala.** *n.* — internal organ of fish (long and dark).
XCO **duadae.** *v.* Gullible, be a sucker.
XCO **duudae.** *n.* Feces.
ID **dae banibani.** The white excretion of the *banibani.*
ID **dangada dau duadae.** A sucker (a person who is easily fooled).
ID **dau duadae.** Be a sucker, be fooled easily.
ID **dee baa tae.** Stay for only a very short time.
ID **dee mahana tae.** Stay for only a short time.
ID **duudae baa.** The dust produced by working pearl shell to make a hook.
ID **duudae goede.** The inky excretion of the octopus.
ID **duudae maadau.** [= *duudae baa,* q.v.].
ID **duudae nguu.** The inky excretion of the squid.
ID **gubu dae.** Intestines which appear to have segmentation.
ID **manga lua tae.** Cleft in the buttocks.
ID **sali tae.** Intractable watery diarrhea.
ID **sii tae.** Diarrhea which escapes without one realizing (caused by eating oily fish).

DAELODO

B **daelodo.** *n.* Number, figure; the outrigger boom between the *giado madua* and the *giado manu.*
ID **daelodo dau.** A large enough number to "count".
ID **daelodo dee odi ange.** Odd number.
ID **daelodo gi lunga.** A large number of.
ID **daelodo odi ange.** Even number.
ID **daohi taelodi.** Keep a record of.
ID **duu taelodo.** Obtain one's quota.
ID **giado taelodo.** The

outrigger booms toward the center of the canoe.

ID **hai taelodo.** Obtain something in great number.

ID **hidi taelodo.** The weight (on a balance) used as a standard measurement.

DAEMAHA

B **daemaha.** *a.* Heavy, oppressive, hard to take.

B 1 **daemahaanga.** *n.* Heaviness, sadness, unhappiness.

daemahadia. *v.* Heavy, oppressive, hard to take.

B 2 **daemahalia.** *v.* Heavy, oppressive, hard to take.

BE **hagadaemaha.** *v.* Put weight on, make unhappy.

BE1 **hagadaemahaanga.** *n.* —.

BE2 **hagadaemahadia.** *v.* Put too much weight on.

BE2 **hagadaemahalia.** *v.* —; insult (someone).

ID **lodo daemaha.** Feel unhappy or sad.

ID **muna daemaha.** Words which hurt.

DAGA$_1$

B **daga$_1$.** *v.* Go from one place to another in a group.

B 1 **daaganga$_1$.** *n.* Way of travelling.

B 1 **dagalonga.** *n.* Path, route.

B 1 **dagamanga.** *n.* Path, route.

B 2 **dagalia$_1$.** *v.* Trampled down (from people walking on); thoroughfare.

BE **hagadaga$_1$.** *v.* Go from one place to another, and another, etc.

BE1 **hagadagaanga$_1$.** *n.* —.

BE2 **hagadagalia$_1$.** *v.* —.

R **dagadaga$_1$.** *v.* —.

R 1 **dagadagaanga$_1$.** *n.* —.

R 2 **dagadagalia$_1$.** *v.* Heavily travelled.

RE **hagadagadaga$_1$.** *v.* Go from one place to another, and another, and another, etc.

RE1 **hagadagadagaanga$_1$.** *n.* —.

RE2 **hagadagadagalia$_1$.** *v.* —.

ID **daga holiage.** Surrounding area; to cut or make a ring around.

ID **daga ula.** Go lobster catching.

ID **tuu daga holiage.** Circumcise.

ID **hagadaga age.** Improving.

ID **hagadaga ange.** Increase in.

ID **hagadaga iho.** Worsening.

ID **hagadaga mai.** Decrease in —; travel toward speaker.

DAGA$_{1a}$

B **dagabuli.** *v.* Gather together in a group.

B 1 **dagabulianga.** *n.* —.

BE **hagadagabuli.** *v.* —.

BE1 **hagadagabulianga.** *n.* —.

R **dagadagabuli.** *v.* —.

R 1 **dagadagabulianga.** *n.* —.

RE **hagadagadagabuli.** *v.* —.

RE1 **hagadagadagabulianga.** *n.* —.

DAGA$_{1b}$

B **dagaa.** *v.* A leader (for a fishline, made of *olonga*).

B 1 **dagaanga.** *n.* Way of tying the leader to a fish hook.

ID **dagaa de maadau.** To tie a leader to a fish hook.

DAGA$_{1c}$

B **dagai.** *a.* Move jerkily, flail (one's legs), flounder about.

B 1 **dagainga.** *n.* —.

BE **hagadagaia.** *v.* —.

BE1 **hagadagainga.** *n.* —.

BE2 **hagadagai.** *v.* —.

P **daakai.** *a.* —.

P 1 **daakainga.** *n.* —.

PE **hagadaakai.** *v.* —.

PE1 **hagadaakainga.** *n.* —.

PE2 **hagadaakaia.** *v.* —.

R **dagadagai.** *a.* Tending to *dagai.*

R 1 **dagadagainga.** *n.* —.

RE **hagadagadagai.** *v.* —.

RE1 **hagadagadagainga.** *n.* —.

RE2 **hagadagadagaia.** *v.* —.

DAGA$_{1d}$

B **dagasala.** *n.* Blame (for something); guilt; fault, crime.

B 1 **dagasalaanga.** *n.* —.
BE **hagadagasala.** *v.* Blame (someone), accuse.
BE1 **hagadagasalaanga.** *n.* —.
R **dagadagasala.** *v.* Be always blamed for.
R 1 **dagadagasalaanga.** *n.* —.
RE **hagadagadagasala.** *v.* —.
RE1 **hagadagadagasalaanga.** *n.* —.

DAGA$_{1e}$
B **dagahi.** *v.* Step on, kick with one's heel.
B 1 **dagahinga.** *n.* —.
B 2 **dagahia.** *v.* —.
R **dagadagahi.** *v.* —.
R 1 **dagadagahinga.** *n.* —.
R 2 **dagadagahia.** *v.* —.
XFL **iga-adagahi.** *n.* Fish sp.: hawk fish (2 sorts) [so named because it is easy to step on].
ID **dagahia de agau.** Reef which has been trampled previously by lobster hunters (and therefore is poor for lobstering).
ID **dagahi ange gi de —.** Serve as a side dish for.

DAGA$_2$
B **daga$_2$.** *v.* Loosely clinging to a surface (outer or inner); coconut meat which has formed in the nut with no sap.
B 1 **daaganga$_2$.** *n.* —.
B 2 **dagalia$_2$.** *v.* —.
BE **hagadaga$_2$.** *v.* —.
BE1 **hagadagaanga$_2$.** *n.* —.
BE2 **hagadagalia$_2$.** *v.* —.
R **dagadaga$_2$.** *v.* —.
R 1 **dagadagaanga$_2$.** *n.* —.
R 2 **dagadagalia$_2$.** *v.* —.
RE **hagadagadaga$_2$.** *v.* —.
RE1 **hagadagadagaanga$_2$.** *n.* —.
RE2 **hagadagadagalia$_2$.** *v.* —.
XCO **dagaligiligi.** *a.* Broken into small pieces.
XCO **dagasisi.** *v.* Scoop out by inserting a knife between the meat and the shell (e.g., in cutting copra).

DAGABE
B **dagabe.** *n.* Fish sp.: snapper.

DAGI$_1$
B **dagi$_1$.** *v.* Lead, show the way, leader (of a group); extend to.
B 1 **daginga.** *n.* —.
B 2 **dagia.** *v.* —.
B 2 **dagina.** *v.* —.
BE **hagadagi.** *v.* —.
BE1 **hagadaaginga.** *n.* —.
BE2 **hagadagina.** *v.* —.
E **tagi.** *v.* Tow, drag; suspend from.
E 2 **daagina.** *v.* Towing; dragging.
EE **hagatagi.** *v.* —.
EE1 **hagataaginga.** *n.* —.
EE2 **hagataagina.** *v.* —.
R **dagidagi.** *v.* —; carry in one's hands.
R 1 **dagidaginga.** *n.* —.
R 2 **dagidagina.** *v.* —.
RC **madagidagi.** *b.* Long ago.
RE **hagadagidagi.** *v.* —.
RE1 **hagadagidaginga.** *n.* —.
RE2 **hagadagidagina.** *v.* —.
XCO **dagitilo.** *v.* Watchful, be on the lookout, keep an eye on.
ID **bido dagi.** Follow in order to spy on.
ID **dagi ala.** Go around aimlessly.
ID **dagi gee.** Lead away from.
ID **tagi ange.** Contribute (material things) to.
ID **tagi gee.** Tow away.
ID **gai dagidagi.** Eat while walking; food for sale which is carried on the road.
ID **hai me dagi.** Work slowly.

DAGI$_2$
B **dagi$_2$ + NUMBER.** *mc.* — each.
XCO **dagidogoisi.** *a.* Very few for each one.
XCO **dagihia.** How many for each?
XCO **dagilagolago.** *a.* Many for each.
XCO **dagilanea.** *a.* Each having a lot.
XCO **dagimomo.** *a.* Few for each one.
XCO **dagisoa.** *a.* Many (people)

at each (time or place, etc.).
ID **daane dagidahi.** A person having unique skills or traits of personality.
ID **dama dagidahi.** The only child of a couple.
ID **dili dagidahi.** Happening continually but one at a time.
ID **dugu dagidahi.** Place (or leave off) one at a time.
ID **kave dagi de momo.** Take a little (or few) at a time.
ID **lodo dagidahi.** Have differing views (within a group of people).
ID **sula dagidahi —.** Once in a while it happens that —.

DAGO
B **dago.** *n.* Ritual activities, religious activities.
R 1 **dagodagonga.** *n.* —.
XCO **dagosala.** *v.* Death, die (of a person).
ID **dee ni dago.** Never mind!
ID **hai dago.** Ritual observances.
ID **me hai dago.** Ritual acts, religious acts.

DAGODO
B **dagodo.** *a.* Situation, circumstance; lie down [sing.]; be in place [sing.].
B 1 **dagodoanga.** *n.* —; expose oneself to the sun.
B 2 **dagodolia.** *v.* Be slept upon for a long time [sing.]; be in place for a long time [sing.].
BE **hagadagodo.** *v.* Cause to lie down or remain; illustrate by examples.
BE1 **hagadagodoanga.** *n.* —.
BE2 **hagadagodolia.** *v.* —.
P **daakodo.** *a.* Be in place [pl.]; lie down [pl.].
P 1 **daakodoanga.** *n.* —.
P 2 **daakodolia.** *v.* Be slept upon for a long time [pl.], be in place for a long time [pl.].
PE **hagadaakodo.** *v.* —.
PE1 **hagadaakodoanga.** *n.* —.
PE2 **hagadaakodolia.** *v.* —.
XCO **vaivaidagodo.** *a.* Unscrupulous, immoral, evil.
ID **ahee oo dagodo?.** How are you?
ID **alaa dagodo.** Those there are the circumstances...
ID **anaa dagodo.** Those are the circumstances...
ID **anei dagodo.** These are the circumstances...
ID **bei tagodo.** For instance, for example; just like —.
ID **dagodo adu.** Appear there (from here).
ID **dagodo be —.** It seems that...
ID **dagodo daudahi.** Having the same characteristics, be alike.
ID **dagodo gee (ma).** Another thing altogether; different (from); recuperating (after an illness).
ID **dagodo hai sala.** Fornication.
ID **dagodo lalo.** Seriously ill and not improving.
ID **dagodo mahamaha.** Nice, pleasing.
ID **dagodo mai.** Appear from yonder.
ID **delaa tagodo.** That there is the situation...
ID **denaa tagodo.** That is the situation...
ID **denei tagodo.** This is the situation...
ID **gau dagodo.** The boom of a sail.
ID **hagadagodo gee ina.** Change.
ID **halehale dagodo.** Guarded condition or prognosis (of a sick person); unsettled (of a situation, the weather, etc.).
ID **halehale dagodo lodo.** Nauseated.

DAGOOBALA
B **dagoobala.** *v.* Fall on something and smash it.
B 1 **dagoobalaanga.** *n.* —.
BE **hagadagoobala.** *v.* —.

BE1 **hagadagoobalaanga.** *n.* —.

$DAGU_1$

B **$dagu_1$.** *v.* Speak, pronounce, utter (words).
B 1 **daagunga.** *n.* —.
B 2 **$dagua_1$.** *v.* —.
B 2 **dagulia.** *v.* —.
B 2 **daguna.** *v.* —.
R **dagudagu.** *v.* —; give commands.
R 1 **dagudagunga.** *n.* —.
R 2 **dagudagua.** *v.* —.
R 2 **dagudagulia.** *v.* —.
R 2 **dagudaguna.** *v.* —.
ID **dagua de —.** Not only the —, but think also of the —!
ID **dagu age.** Say out loud.
ID **dee dagua —.** It goes without saying that — is better!
CF **agu_1.** Say or tell (esp. in confidence).

$DAGU_2$

XCO **tagudai.** *nl.* Coast, shoreline.

DAGUA

B **$dagua_2$.** *n.* Fish sp.: yellow fin tuna (3 sorts?).
XFL **dagua-bodo.** *n.* Fish sp.: tuna sp.
XFL **dagua-loa.** *n.* Fish sp.: tuna sp.

DAGUGU

B **dagugu.** *n.* Fish sp.: (The native term is applied to many spp.): damselfish, snapper.

DAGUU

B **daguu.** *n.* Axe.
BE **hagadaguu.** *n.* A small axe, hatchet.
ID **daguu kalo.** A thin straight-bladed (easily sharpened)axe blade.
ID **uhi daguu.** Turtle ribs (used as knives in rituals).

DAHA

B **daha.** *nl.* Outside, away, around.
BE **hagadaha.** *v.* To stay at a distance; to keep one's distance.
BE2 **hagadahadia.** *v.* —.
E **taha.** *n.* A certain string in string figures.
R **dahadaha.** *v.* An embankment around a taro plot.
RE **hagadahadaha.** *v.* Keep staying away.
ID **daha de hia maa.** About what time is it?
ID **damana mai i daha.** Stepfather.
ID **dangada mai i daha.** Relatives by marriage or adoption, etc.
ID **gi daha.** To the outside; in the environs of.
ID **haa daha.** The outer coconut palm frond.
ID **hhano gi daha.** To wash one's hands in such a way that the dirty water does not fall back into the basin or well.
ID **i ono daha.** At his place, with him.
ID **mada gi daha.** Having the point bent outward (away from its handle).
ID **mai i daha.** From outside.
ID **saga gi daha.** *saga* away from; extend out in space.

DAHANGA

ID **siva-dahanga.** The ninth number of a counting game played to determine who is "it".

DAHEA

B **dahea.** *a.* Drift [sing.].
BE **hagadahea.** *v.* To allow the wind or current to carry the canoe [a method of fishing].
BE1 **hagadaheaanga.** *n.* —.
P **daahea.** *a.* —.
P 1 **daaheaanga.** *n.* —.
PE **hagadaahea.** *v.* —.
PE1 **hagadaaheaanga.** *n.* —.
R **dahedahea.** *a.* Drift aimlessly.
R 1 **dahedaheaanga.** *n.* —.

RE hagadahedahea. *v.* —.
RE1 hagadahedaheaanga. *n.* –
ID **dahea age.** Drift toward place where speaker is.
ID **dahea gee.** Drift away.
ID **dahea gi lalo.** Sink (completely).
ID **dahea iho.** Drift toward the place where the speaker is not.
ID **hai me daahea.** Search for driftwood or other beached objects.

DAHI₁

B **dahi₁.** *an.* One, a.
BE **hagadahi.** *v.* A counting system for days, based on the lunar phases.
E **tahi₁.** *u.* First, best.
XCO **daudahi.** *a.* Only, alone (just one).
XCO **Diba-dahi.** *nn.* The name of a person in a traditional story.
XCO **Tahi-laangi.** *nt.* Monday ('first day').
XCO **Tahi-malama.** *nt.* January ('first month').
ID **aalo dahi.** Do at one time.
ID **dahi tali.** Depend on (e.g., to come), rely on.
ID **dahi i daho dangada.** Very popular.
ID **dahi ma dahi.** Each individual.
ID **dahi-malali.** The first number of a counting game played to determine who is "it".
ID **daohi ange dahi hai.** Argue against.
ID **deai ma gi dahi.** None at all as you should very well know! [prob. = *deai maua gi dahi*].
ID **dugu dahi.** Accomplish or complete something in a single effort; fishing with a single line.
ID **tahi i tanuaa.** Best of all.
ID **gai lima dahi.** To eat taro without fish (or fish without taro).
ID **gau dahi.** A method of fishing for tuna (angling with a single baited hook?).
ID **kave dahi.** Do at one time.
ID **hagaditidi vae dahi.** Hop on one foot.
ID **hai dahi doo.** Trick someone.
ID **hai dahi heohi.** Maintain one's position in an argument (against contrary positions).
ID **i dahi me.** Each, apiece.
ID **mada dahi.** Having a single point or blade.
ID **soe daa dahi.** Straight as can be.
CF **vaadagidahi.** Scattered (not in a cluster).

DAHI₁a

B **ngaadahi.** *n.* Both, as one.
ID **gai ngaadahi.** A distribution of fish to the whole island population.
ID **gai ngaadai.** [= *gai ngaadahi*].
ID **hagamadamada ngaadahi.** Share equally among.
ID **molimoli ngaadai.** A distribution of the catch of a communal fishing expedition.

DAHI₁b

ID **dagodo daudahi.** Having the same characteristics, be alike.
ID **dulagi daudahi.** Alike (in appearance).
ID **liiliagi daudahi.** Be of the same status.

DAHI₂

B **dahi₂.** *v.* A stroking motion with something in the hand; shave, sweep, brush off (once).
B 1 **daahinga.** *n.* Way of brushing off or sweeping.
B 1 **dahinga.** *n.* Way of shaving.
B 2 **dahia.** *v.* Shave [trans.].
E **tahi₂.** *v.* Clean off.
E 2 **daahia.** *v.* Clean off.
R **dahidahi.** *v.* —.
R 1 **dahidahinga.** *n.* —.
R 2 **dahidahia.** *v.* —.

ID	**dahi de gumigumi.** Shave one's beard.

DAHIDO

B	**dahido.** *nl.* Stem, base, foot (e.g., of a hill), stump.
P	**daahido.** *n.* —.
ID	**dahido lima.** Upper arm.
ID	**dahido mada.** Inner corner of the eye.
CF	**dahidonga.** Grandfather.

DAHO

B	**daho.** *nl.* Side of (part away from), with.
ID	**dahi i daho dangada.** Very popular.

DAHOLA

B	**dahola.** *v.* A method of fishing (night fishing on the reef with torches).
B 1	**daholaanga.** *n.* —.
BE	**hagadahola.** *v.* —.
BE1	**hagadaholaanga.** *n.* —.
XFL	**mangoo-dahola.** *n.* Fish sp.: blacktip shark.

DAHOLAA

B	**daholaa.** *n.* Whale.

DAHOLAA$_a$

B	**Daholaa$_a$.** *n.* December.

DAHU

B	**dahu.** *v.* Start a fire (or an engine); build a fire.
B 1	**daahunga.** *n.* —.
B 2	**dahua.** *v.* —.
B 2	**dahulia.** *v.* —.
BE	**hagadahu.** *v.* —.
BE1	**hagadaahunga.** *n.* —.
BE2	**hagadahua.** *v.* —.
R	**dahudahu.** *v.* —.
R 1	**dahudahunga.** *n.* —.
R 2	**dahudahua.** *v.* —.
R 2	**dahudahulia.** *v.* —.
RE	**hagadahudahu.** *v.* —.
RE1	**hagadahudahunga.** *n.* —.
RE2	**hagadahudahua.** *v.* —.
RE2	**hagadahudahulia.** *v.* —.

DAHUUHUU

B	**dahuuhuu.** *n.* The topmost part of the house.
ID	**dao dahuuhuu.** Ridge pole (lower).

DAI$_1$

B	**dai$_1$.** *nl.* Lagoon, sea, salt.
B	**ngaadai.** *nl.* Lagoonward.
BE	**hagadai.** *v.* Furnish salt to.
XCO	**adudai.** *n.* "Islands to the west of Nukuoro" (the Mortlocks?).
XCO	**Dai-nei.** *np.* "Islands to the west" (the Mortlocks?).
XCO	**daudai.** *a.* Skillful fisherman.
XCO	**tagudai.** *nl.* Coast, shoreline.
ID	**au dili dai.** An ocean current flowing away from land.
ID	**boo gi dai.** The period when the quarter moon appears in the west just after sunset.
ID	**dai beau.** Rough seas at a certain time.
ID	**dili dai.** Any current flowing away from the atoll.
ID	**doo dai.** Appearing from lagoonward; to come from lagoonward; wind direction from the west.
ID	**duaa dai.** Seasick but unable to throw up.
ID	**giligili tai.** Horizon.
ID	**goinga o tai.** High-water mark.
ID	**hagadoo dai.** To fish off the reef for tuna.
ID	**hagatugu tai.** Ebbing of tide.
ID	**honu tai.** High tide.
ID	**i dai nei.** Mortlock Islands.
ID	**magalili tai.** Flow (of tide).
ID	**manu lalo tai.** Sea shell.
ID	**me dili dai.** Any current which flows away from the atoll.
ID	**moana ngaadai.** Far from land (the place from which the atoll is just barely visible).
ID	**siia gi moana ngaadai.** Drift downwind, away from land.
CF	**abadai.** European [adj.].

CF **mataia.** Soreness of the eyes after a fishing expedition (from the glare of the sun).

DAI$_2$

B **dai$_2$.** *mt.* Almost, nearly.
BE **hagadai —.** *u.* —.
C **dahi$_3$.** *mt.* [var. of *dai$_1$* — only recently used].
E **tai.** *mt.* [var. of *dai$_2$*].
EE **hagatai —.** *u.* —.
ID **dai (tigi) lago —.** Becoming more — (but not quite).
ID **dai bigi.** Almost (finished or done, etc.); just about.
ID **dai deai.** Hardly any.
ID **dai hieunu.** Thirsty.
ID **dai hiigai.** Hungry.
ID **dai sagana iho goe.** Watch out!
ID **dai seni.** Sleepy.
CF **daiao.** Morning, tomorrow.
CF **daihadu.** Hardwood in the tree trunk.

DAIAO

B **daiao.** *n.* Morning, tomorrow.
XCO **anataiao.** This morning.
ID **anaboo taiao.** Early this morning.
ID **baasi gi taiao.** Forenoon (from dawn to noon).
ID **boo taiao.** Early morning.
ID **daiao age.** The following morning.
ID **de heduu o taiao.** Morning star.
ID **taiao daiao.** Tomorrow morning.
ID **taiao danuaa.** Good morning!
ID **gaba taiao.** Early morning.

DAINA

B **daina.** *n.* Brother, sister, sibling, cousin.
BE **hagadaina.** *v.* To put (someone) into a sibling or cousin relationship (as by an adoption).
ID **daina daane.** Brother, male cousin.
ID **daina hahine.** Sister, female cousin.
ID **hai daina.** The relationship between siblings or cousins.

DALA$_1$

B **dala$_1$.** *v.* Unfasten, undo, untie.
B 1 **daalanga$_1$.** *n.* —.
B 2 **daalaa$_1$.** *v.* —.
BC **madala.** *a.* Be unfastened [sing.]; be untied [sing.]; bloomed [sing.].
BC1 **madalaanga.** *n.* —.
BF **hagamadala.** *v.* —.
BF1 **hagamadalaanga.** *n.* —.
E **tala$_1$.** *v.* —.
PC **maatala.** *a.* —.
PC1 **maatalaanga.** *n.* —.
PF **hagamaatala.** *v.* —.
PF1 **hagamaatalaanga.** *n.* —.
R **daladala$_1$.** *v.* —.
R 1 **daladalaanga$_1$.** *n.* —.
R 2 **daladalaa$_1$.** *v.* —.
RC **madaladala.** *a.* Easily unfastened or untied.
RC1 **madaladalaanga.** *n.* —.
RF **hagamadaladala.** *v.* —.
RF1 **hagamadaladalaanga.** *n.* —.
XCO **langadala.** *n.* (A piece of) thatch made from coconut palm frond.
ID **dala malo.** Change clothes.
ID **dee madaladala de langi.** Raining without let-up.
ID **madaladala de leo.** A clear and high-pitched singing voice.
ID **madala mai.** Get free, be loose; in bloom.
ID **valaai tala hai sala.** Medicine to obviate the effects of *oha valaai.*

DALA$_2$

B **dala$_2$.** *a.* Tame [sing.]; not be timid or uneasy in another's presence [sing.].
B 1 **daalanga$_2$.** *n.* —.
BE **hagadala.** *v.* —.
BE1 **hagadalaanga.** *n.* —.
P **tala$_2$.** *a.* —.
PE **hagatala.** *v.* —; fool around, play a joke on.

PE1 **hagatalaanga**$_1$. *n.* —.
R **daladala**$_2$. *a.* —.
R 1 **daladalaanga**$_2$. *n.* —.
RE **hagadaladala**$_2$. *v.* —.
RE1 **hagadaladalaanga**$_2$. *n.* —.
ID **hagatala gee.** Wanting always to *hagatala.*
ID **hagatala senga.** Foolishly rough playing or joking.

DALA$_3$

B **dala**$_3$. *v.* Tell, say to, relate.
B 1 **daalanga**$_3$. *n.* Way of telling; legend, story.
B 2 **daalaa**$_2$. *v.* —.
E **tala**$_3$. *v.* —.
EE1 **hagatalaanga**$_2$. *n.* —.
R **daladala**$_3$. *v.* Say again and again.
R 1 **daladalaanga**$_3$. *n.* —.
R 2 **daladalaa**$_2$. *v.* —.
ID **dalanga a kai.** A story which is not true.
ID **dee tala mai!.** Don't tell me!
ID **tala baubau.** Confess wrongs.
ID **tala hai sala.** Confess one's sins or errors.
ID **hagaduu dala.** Angry and ready to fight.
ID **hai daalanga.** Talkative, chatterbox, talk animatedly.
ID **ili taalanga.** Talkative, chatterbox, talk at great length.

DALA$_4$

B **dala**$_4$. *n.* Appendage, fin, spine (extending from a fish, etc.).
XFL **dala-galoi.** *n.* Fish sp.: puffer.
XFL **dala-loa.** *n.* Fish sp.: squirrelfish.
ID **daane ssili dala.** Special one, important one.
ID **dala gaogao.** The part of the human body between the hip and the ribs.
CF **dalaehala.** Pricked.
CF **ngadala.** Fish sp.: sea bass (The native term is applied to many spp.).

DALA$_{4a}$

B **dalaa.** *n.* (Small) piece of, part of.
ID **alaa muna.** Word [= *dalaa muna*].
ID **dalaa mada.** [= *dalaa umada*].
ID **dalaa manu.** Piece of broken glass.
ID **dalaa muna.** Word, phrase.
ID **dalaa ubu.** Charcoal from the coconut shell.
ID **dalaa umada.** Prow spray of a ship.
ID **sii talaa umada.** A wash of waves at the prow of a canoe, when it is sailing fast.
CF **dalabaimanugadele.** Sharp (as a knife).

DALA$_{4b}$

E **tala**$_4$. *a.* Rough in texture (as perceived at one time).
R **daladala**$_4$. *a.* Rough in texture (as perceived over time); fish sp.: squirrelfish.
RE **hagadaladala**$_1$. *v.* —.
RE1 **hagadaladalaanga**$_1$. *n.* —.
ID **dala hhua.** Eruptions on the skin (e.g., hives, insect bites, etc.).
ID **dala mmea.** Redness or inflammation of the skin (e.g., a welt).
ID **gulu daladala.** Breadfruit with rough skin.

DALA$_5$

B **dala**$_5$. *n.* Bird sp.: tern? (a vagrant sp., rarely seen).
XFL **dala-hagalulu-madangi.** *n.* Bird sp.: tern? (a vagrant sp., rarely seen).
XFL **dala-moana.** *n.* Bird sp.: tern? (a vagrant sp., rarely seen).

DALA$_6$

B **dala**$_6$. *n.* Plant sp.: shrub sp. (*Ximenia americana* L.).
XFL **dala-dalaa-moa.** *n.* Plant sp.: *Lycopodium phlegmaria* L.

CF	**dalahalu.** Plant sp.: tree sp. (*Allophylus timorensis* (DC.) Bl.).

DALABAI

CF	**dalabaimanugadele.** Sharp (as a knife).

DALAEHALA

B	**dalaehala.** *v.* Pricked.
B 1	**dalaehalaanga.** *n.* —.
BE	**hagadalaehala.** *v.* —.
BE1	**hagadalaehalaanga.** *n.* —.
R	**daladalaehala.** *v.* —.
R 1	**daladalaehalaanga.** *n.* —.
RE	**hagadaladalaehala.** *v.* —.
RE1	**hagadaladalaehalaanga.** *n.* —.

DALAHALU

B	**dalahalu.** *n.* Plant sp.: tree sp. (*Allophylus timorensis* (DC.) Bl.).

DALANGASAU

B	**dalangasau.** *v.* Be quick-witted in an emergency.
B 1	**dalangasauanga.** *n.* —.
BE	**hagadalangasau.** *v.* —.
BE1	**hagadalangasaunga.** *n.* —.
BE2	**hagadalangasaua.** *v.* —.

DALE

B	**dale.** *v.* Touch (two or more things being in contact); strike (a match).
B 1	**daalenga.** *n.* —.
B 2	**daalea$_1$.** *v.* —.
BE	**hagadale —.** *v.* Touch —.
BE1	**hagadaalenga.** *n.* —.
BE2	**hagadaalea$_1$.** *v.* —.
E	**tale.** *v.* Touch quickly.
EE	**hagatale.** *v.* —; try, attempt.
EE1	**hagataalenga.** *n.* —.
EE2	**hagataalea.** *v.* —.
R	**daledale.** *v.* Repeatedly touch lightly.
R 1	**daledalenga.** *n.* —.
RE	**hagadaledale.** *v.* —.
RE1	**hagadaledalenga.** *n.* —.
RE2	**hagadaledalea.** *v.* —.
XCO	**dalepagi.** *a.* Fight hand-to-hand.
ID	**dale pilo.** A game (like tag), to leave something unfinished after having tried only slightly.
ID	**dale gaiaa.** Provoke a fight by banging against someone (as children do); hit and run.
ID	**tale age.** Light a match in the dark.

DALEA

B	**dalea.** *a.* Tired [sing.].
B 1	**daleaanga.** *n.* —.
BE	**hagadalea.** *v.* Make someone tired [sing.]; punish [sing.].
BE1	**hagadaleaanga.** *n.* —.
P	**daalea$_2$.** *a.* Tired [pl.].
P 1	**daaleaanga.** *n.* —.
PE	**hagadaalea$_2$.** *v.* [pl. of *hagadalea*]; tiresome.
PE1	**hagadaaleaanga.** *n.* —.

DALEBU

B	**dalebu.** *v.* Turbulent (air or seas).
B 1	**dalebuanga.** *n.* —.
B 2	**dalebua.** *v.* —.
BE	**hagadalebu.** *v.* —.
BE1	**hagadalebuanga.** *n.* —.
BE2	**hagadalebua.** *v.* —.
R	**dalebulebu.** *v.* —.
R 1	**dalebulebuanga.** *n.* —.
R 2	**dalebulebua.** *v.* —.
RE	**hagadalebulebu.** *v.* —.
RE1	**hagadalebulebuanga.** *n.* —.
RE2	**hagadalebulebua.** *v.* —.

DALI$_1$

B	**dali$_1$.** *v.* Wait for, along with.
B 1	**daalinga$_1$.** *n.* —.
B 2	**daalia.** *v.* —.
E	**tali.** *v.* Hope for, expectant, waiting; going along with.
R	**dalidali.** *v.* —.
R 1	**dalidalinga.** *n.* —.
R 2	**dalidalia.** *v.* —.
ID	**dahi tali.** Depend on (e.g., to come), rely on.
ID	**dali hagavagavaga.** [= *hagavagavaga*].
ID	**tali hagalodolodo.** Hopeful expectation.

CF madali. With, along with, as well as; at the same time as; in addition to.

DALI$_{1a}$

XCO **daudali.** *a.* Follow (someone).

ID **daudali i lodo.** Follow another's will.

DALI$_2$

B **dali$_2$.** *n.* Fibers of the cocónut leaf rachi.

BE **hagadali.** *v.* Accumulate (bring together); gather up; imprisonment (short term).

BE1 **hagadalianga.** *n.* —.

BE2 **hagadalia.** *v.* —.

XCO **dalimasanga.** *v.* Way of tying (rope, etc.).

ID **bini dali gadaha.** A method of braiding *dali* into string to make a bird snare; six-ply braiding (of rope).

DALIA

B **dalia.** *n.* Plant sp.

XFL **dalia-dodo.** *n.* Mollusk sp.: *Chlamys schmeltzi.*

XFL **dalia-mea.** *n.* Mollusk sp.: *Mitra mitra.*

DALINGA$_1$

B **dalinga$_1$.** *n.* Ear.

ID **dalinga bobo.** Having a runny ear (with pus).

ID **dangi talinga.** Tinnitus, a ringing sound in the ear [an omen].

ID **gaugau dalinga.** Exterior of the ear; a loop-like handle.

ID **gii talinga.** Tinnitus.

ID **kalo talinga.** Clean out, or scratch, inside the ear.

ID **hagakii dalinga.** Producing a high-pitched noise in the ear; the itch felt in the ear when something very sweet is eaten.

ID **longolongo iho dalinga.** Pick up information from others' conversation.

ID **lou de gaugau dalinga.** Pull the trigger (of a gun).

ID **nngao dalinga.** Hurting in the ears from noise.

ID **sugi talinga.** Piercing of the ear (for insertion of an ornament).

DALINGA$_2$

B **dalinga$_2$.** *n.* Fish sp.: mullet.

XFL **madau-dalinga.** *n.* Fish sp.: shark sp.?

DALO$_1$

R **dalodalo.** *v.* Pray.

R 1 **dalodaloanga.** *n.* —.

R 2 **dalodaloa.** *v.* Pray for.

R 2 **dalodalosia.** *v.* Pray for.

RE **hagadalodalo.** *v.* —.

RE1 **hagadalodaloanga.** *n.* —.

RE2 **hagadalodaloa.** *v.* —.

RE2 **hagadalodalosia.** *v.* —.

ID **dalodalo keli.** Pray earnestly.

ID **dalodalo i de lodo.** Pray silently.

ID **daumaha dalodalo.** Prayer service (church).

DALO$_2$

B **dalo.** *n.* Plant sp.: taro (*Colocasia esculenta*), also the corm of this plant.

ID **duu dalo.** Piece of soft taro.

ID **gili dalo.** Hillock.

DALOGO

B **dalogo.** *n.* A type of prepared food (prepared from grated coconut, coconut apple, and coconut juice).

ID **hhanga dalogo.** To make *dalogo.*

ID **maanga dalogo.** A handful of *dalogo.*

ID **me hanga dalogo.** Ingredients of *dalogo.*

DAMA

B **dama.** *n.* Child.

BE **hagadama.** *v.* Treat as a child.

RE **hagadamadama.** *v.* Act like

a child (as a behavior pattern).

RE1 **hagadamadamaanga.** *n.* —.

XCO **vaedama.** *a.* Play favorites amongst one's children.

XFL **dama-a-de-galabe.** *n.* Fish sp.: goby?, sleeper?

ID **dama adu hale.** A child who wanders around to the homes of others.

ID **dama pala.** A foetus which has been aborted, ugly [said jokingly].

ID **dama daane.** Boy, young man.

ID **dama dagidahi.** The only child of a couple.

ID **dama daohi.** An adopted child.

ID **dama de bialodo.** Deformed foetus [lit., 'looking like an animal'].

ID **dama de gaehala.** A rain cloud (dropping its rain) seen in the distance.

ID **dama doe.** The fourth child born to a couple.

ID **dama donu.** A natural child.

ID **dama doo.** A foetus which has been aborted.

ID **dama gaiaa.** To hang around someone's house in the expectation of being served food [considered bad manners].

ID **dama hodooligi.** Children of the chief [and of the chief's relatives?].

ID **dama iai.** A person who has done something praiseworthy.

ID **dama lalo.** A person who has visited other far-away lands.

ID **dama legalega.** Baby, infant.

ID **dama madua.** Eldest child.

ID **dama moemoe sala.** A fetus out of the proper position (in the womb) for delivery.

ID **dama muli bee.** The twelfth child born to a couple.

ID **dama naale.** A talkative, deceitful person.

ID **dama ssala.** An adopted child.

ID **dama ssege.** A foetus which has been aborted.

ID **dama ulungi.** A man good at catching tuna with a fishing pole.

ID **dua dama.** The pallor of a female following childbirth.

ID **tamaa gauligi.** Baby.

ID **tama e manege.** A person who is capable at almost anything.

ID **tama hagaai.** Poor fellow!

ID **tama legalega.** Infant.

ID **tama legalega eidu.** Pupil of the eye; a cry of a bird or human that sounds like the cry of a baby; the name of a ghost.

ID **tama nei.** [an exclamation, about = Wow!; or, no kidding!; or, watch it!].

ID **tama ulungi.** Coxswain of a canoe rigged for the pole fishing of tuna [he also handles the pole].

ID **gili dama.** Soft-skinned.

ID **hai dama.** Pregnant.

ID **lodo dama.** Immature in affect.

ID **magi hai dama.** Morning sickness (of pregnancy).

ID **ssege tama.** Miscarriage, abortion (spontaneous).

DAMA$_a$

B **damaa.** *d.* DIMINUATIVE PREFIX; slowly, gently, skillfully, etc.

XFL **damaa-manu.** *n.* Bird sp.: sharp-tailed sandpiper (*Erolia acuminata*).

ID **damaa dae.** Skillful at catching flying fish.

ID **damaa dogi.** Skillful in the use of an adze.

ID **damaa tili.** Sharpshooter.

ID **damaa hine.** Girl, young woman, daughter.

ID **damaa hungi.** Skillful at *hungi*.

ID **damaa me.** Small [sing.]; little; tiny.

ID **damaa velo.** Good at spearing fish.

DAMANA
B **damana.** *n.* Father, uncle, senior male relative, male elder, person in a fatherly relationship.
BE **hagadamana.** *v.* Treat someone as a father or other senior male relative.
ID **damana mai i daha.** Stepfather.
ID **hai damana.** The relationship between father (or other male elder) and child (or one treated as child).

DAMI
B **dami.** *v.* Close one's jaws; closing of the two halves of a clam shell.
B 1 **daaminga.** *n.* —.
B 2 **damia.** *v.* —.
BE **hagadami.** *v.* —.
BE1 **hagadaaminga.** *n.* —.
BE2 **hagadamia.** *v.* —.
R **damidami.** *v.* —.
R 1 **damidaminga.** *n.* —.
R 2 **damidamia.** *v.* —.
RE **hagadamidami.** *v.* —.
RE1 **hagadamidaminga.** *n.* —.
RE2 **hagadamidamia.** *v.* —.

DANE$_1$
B **dane.** *v.* A fungus infection of the skin (consisting of superficial white spots).
B 2 **danea.** *v.* To have *dane.*
B 3 **daneaanga.** *n.* —.
BE **hagadane.** *v.* —.
BE2 **hagadanea.** *v.* —.
BE3 **hagadaneaanga.** *n.* —.
R **danedane.** *v.* An extensive infection of *dane.*
R 2 **danedanea.** *v.* Be covered with *dane.*
R 3 **danedaneaanga.** *n.* —.
RE **hagadanedane.** *v.* —.
RE2 **hagadanedanea.** *v.* —.
RE3 **hagadanedaneaanga.** *n.* —.
ID **hidi bido dane.** Slow-moving or slow-working person.

DANE$_2$
XCO **duudane.** *n.* Buttock.

DANNGAHO
B **danngaho.** *n.* Stomach.

DANU
B **danu.** *v.* Buried [sing.]; sunken from view [sing.].
B 1 **daanunga.** *n.* —; grave (for burial).
B 1 **danumanga.** *n.* —.
B 2 **danumia.** *v.* —.
BE **hagadanu.** *v.* Sink below the horizon, burrow into the sand.
BE1 **hagadanuanga.** *n.* —.
BE1 **hagadanumanga.** *n.* —.
BE2 **hagadanumia.** *v.* —.
P **tanu.** *a.* —.
P 1 **tanuanga.** *n.* —.
PE **hagatanu.** *v.* —; do with a maximum application of effort.
PE1 **hagatanuanga.** *n.* —.
R **danudanu.** *v.* To bury a great many, to keep going down (so that it becomes hidden from view).
R 1 **danudanumanga.** *n.* —.
R 2 **danudanumia.** *v.* —.
RE **hagadanudanu.** *v.* —.
RE1 **hagadanudanuanga.** *n.* —.
RE1 **hagadanudanumanga.** *n.* —.
RE2 **hagadanudanumia.** *v.* —.
T **datanu.** *n.* Fish sp. (a sort which burrows in the sand).
ID **boo hagadanu malama.** The nights on which the quarter moon is obscured by rain.
ID **danu bela.** Spade in organic matter (to enrich taro plantings).
ID **danu de laa.** The setting of the sun.
ID **danu de maasina.** The setting of the moon.
ID **hagatanu iho.** Take a nap.

DANUAA
B **danuaa.** *a.* Good ! Hello! Good-bye!
BE **hagadanuaa.** *v.* Make good, lead a good life [a newly

coined expression].
ID **ahiahi danuaa.** Good afternoon! Good evening!
ID **boo danuaa.** Good night! Good evening!
ID **danuaa age.** Improved, better.
ID **danuaa ai loo.** Well, OK! (this time, but next time watch it!).
ID **danuaa ange.** Good for, better than.
ID **danuaa huu.** It's still OK! No wonder!
ID **danuaa loo.** OK! (good).
ID **danuaa mai i hee.** Good according to whom?
ID **danuaa sili.** Good enough!
ID **tahi i tanuaa.** Best of all.
ID **taiao danuaa.** Good morning!
ID **tilo danuaa.** Good-looking, handsome; beautiful (esp. owing to having a graceful manner).
ID **hagadanuaa magavaa.** Make peace between people, conciliate.
ID **laangi danuaa.** Hello! Good day!
ID **lodo danuaa.** Contented, happy.
ID **madangi danuaa.** Fresh air.
ID **magau danuaa.** Die peacefully [as shown by a beatific facial expression on the corpse and the calmness of the weather].
ID **maholahola danuaa age.** Revitalized (by a shower or rest, etc.).
ID **masavaa danuaa.** A time of peace.
ID **moe danuaa.** Die in peace.
ID **mouli danuaa.** Easy living, a good life.

DANGA
P **tanga.** *a.* Loose (not tight) [pl.].
PE **hagatanga.** *v.* —; move away from.
PE1 **hagatangaanga.** *n.* —.
PE2 **hagatangalia.** *v.* —.
R **dangadanga.** *a.* Loose (not tight) [sing.]; sieve [which is shaken to make *bie*].
RE **hagadangadanga.** *v.* Loosen.
RE1 **hagadangadangaanga.** *n.* —.
RE2 **hagadangadangalia.** *v.* —.
XFL **dangaloa₁.** *n.* Plant sp.: silver bush (*Sophora tormentosa* L.).
XFL **dangaloa₂.** *n.* Earthworm.
ID **tanga gee.** Separated from.
ID **oo tanga.** Too big (clothes), spacious.

DANGAa
B **dangage.** *v.* Raise one's head up or back.
B 1 **dangageanga.** *n.* —.
BE **hagadangage.** *v.* —.
BE1 **hagadangageanga.** *n.* —.
P **daangage.** *v.* —.
P 1 **daangageanga.** *n.* —.
PE **hagadaangage.** *v.* —.
PE1 **hagadaangageanga.** *n.* —.
ID **dangage age.** Raise up one's head from a lowered position.
ID **dangage dua.** Bend one's head backwards.

DANGAb
B **dangalebu.** *v.* Rough or choppy sea condition.
B 1 **dangalebunga.** *n.* —.
B 2 **dangalebua.** *v.* —.
BE **hagadangalebu.** *v.* —.
BE1 **hagadangalebunga.** *n.* —.
BE2 **hagadangalebua.** *v.* —.
R **dangadangalebu.** *v.* Becoming rougher (of seas).
R 1 **dangadangalebunga.** *n.* —.
R 2 **dangadangalebua.** *v.* —.
RE **hagadangadangalebu.** *v.* —.
RE1 **hagadangadangalebunga.** *n.* —.
RE2 **hagadangadangalebua.** *v.* —.
ID **dangalebu de me.** Bad weather.
ID **dangalebu de moana.** Rough or choppy seas.

DANGAc

B **dangaligi.** *n.* A type of basket.

DANGAd

B **dangaloa3.** *n.* Shooting star.

DANGADA

B **dangada.** *n.* Person, human being, relative [when preceeded by a possessive pronoun].

BE **hagadangada.** *v.* Treat someone as a human being.

ID **ahi dangada.** A (mat) wrapping for dead persons who are disposed of in the sea [a precontact custom].

ID **alaala dangada.** False labor pains (of a pregnant woman).

ID **boo i lalo o tangada.** The last days of a person's life.

ID **bulubulu dangada.** Unimportant person.

ID **buu tangada.** An omen of death (when a certain kind or size of fish is caught).

ID **dahi i daho dangada.** Very popular.

ID **dangada abadai.** European persons (including Americans).

ID **dangada abasasa.** European persons (including Americans).

ID **dangada agoago.** Teacher, preacher.

ID **dangada baoa.** Dead person buried at sea who washes back up on shore.

ID **dangada dau duadae.** A sucker (a person who is easily fooled).

ID **dangada de henua.** Natives of Nukuoro.

ID **dangada duaagau.** An avid fisherman.

ID **dangada gaiaa.** Thief.

ID **dangada gai dangada.** Cannibal.

ID **dangada gohu.** Ignorant person.

ID **dangada haangoda.** Fisherman.

ID **dangada hagao me.** Storekeeper.

ID **dangada haigamaiana.** Worthwhile person.

ID **dangada henua gee.** Foreigners, strangers.

ID **dangada lo te gohu.** Unenlightened person.

ID **dangada madua.** Old person, adult.

ID **dangada mai i daha.** Relatives by marriage or adoption, etc.

ID **dangada ngauda.** A person who rarely goes fishing, landlubber.

ID **dangada ssigo.** Clever person.

ID **dangada ulu.** Companions or friends who share the same interests, and who get along well.

ID **dangada vai gelegele.** A person of filthy appearance or habits.

ID **dee kai laa dangada.** So, it's not so after all (just as we believed at first)! No wonder!

ID **dili dangada.** To fail to discharge one's obligations to help (esp. one's kin).

ID **tangada abasasa.** A European person (or an American).

ID **tangada adi longo.** Gossipy person, tattletale.

ID **tangada aduhale.** The sort of person who feels at home everywhere and is continually visiting [considered uncouth].

ID **tangada dee doo gi de me.** Uncouth person.

ID **tangada hagaai.** Poor fellow!

ID **tangada hai me dabu.** Cult priest.

ID **tangada hai sauaa.** Magician, sorcerer.

ID **tangada maagaga.** Industrious person.

ID **tangada made.** Now you've done it!

ID **tangada sisi.** Secretary.
ID **tangada ssele.** Stupid ass!
ID **tao tangada.** To immerse a person in medication.
ID **tiinonga o tangada.** Undesirable personal characteristics.
ID **ga vaa laa dangada.** Oh dear (that's not good)!
ID **haaina dangada.** Stare at people indiscreetly (esp. strangers).
ID **hagaaduadu dangada.** Critical of others.
ID **hagadogaa dangada.** Embarrass people by one's actions.
ID **hagasula tangada.** Successfully promote the candidacy of someone (or elect or appoint him) to a coveted position.
ID **hai dangada.** The relationship between relatives, related (of persons).
ID **halehale dangada.** A suspicious character.
ID **henua gai dangada.** 'land of the cannibals' (esp. New Guinea).
ID **hua o tangada.** Outcome (of individual effort).
ID **lima dangada ina.** A patient of one healer who has been treated by another healer.
ID **maakau laa loo dangada.** What a shame!
ID **maakau loo dangada.** Now we're in trouble!
ID **mada dangada ina.** A person of importance (who is liked by the people).
ID **manu dudu dangada.** Insect sp. (= *manu-de-laama*) [poisonous].
ID **mouli dangada.** Delinquent person (periodically exhibiting bad behavior).
ID **muna o tangada.** Speak of the devil!
ID **ngadi dangada.** An ordinary person, commoner; a person of slight social value.
ID **se mouli dangada.** Rascal.
ID **vakaa loo dangada.** See what happened! (the hearer having been forewarned).

DANGADA$_a$
B **atangada.** *n.* Generation, age set.

DANGAU
XFL **dangau-paava.** *n.* Fish sp.: snapper.
XFL **dangau-daa-sissisi.** *n.* Fish sp.: snapper.
XFL **dangau-dongi.** *n.* Fish sp.: snapper.
XFL **dangau-laha.** *n.* Fish sp.: snapper.
XFL **dangau-ngudu-aahua.** *n.* [var. of *dangau dongi*].
XFL **dangau-sissisi.** *n.* [var. of *dangaudaasisisi*].
ID **valu-dangau.** The eighth number of a counting game played to determine who is "it".

DANGE
B **dange.** *n.* Mollusk sp.: giant clam (*Tridacna squammosa*).

DANGI
B **dangi.** *a.* Cry.
B 1 **daanginga.** *n.* —.
BE **hagadangi.** *v.* —; play (a musical instrument).
BE1 **hagadanginga.** *n.* —.
BE2 **hagadangia.** *v.* —.
P **tangi.** *a.* Make noise (as an individual).
P 1 **taanginga.** *n.* —.
PE **hagatangi.** *v.* —.
PE1 **hagataanginga.** *n.* —.
PE2 **hagatangia.** *v.* —.
R **dangidangi.** *a.* Cry a lot; beg, apologize; a type of aboriginal chant.
R 1 **dangidanginga.** *n.* —.
RE **hagadangidangi.** *v.* Play music; make someone keep crying.
RE1 **hagadangidanginga.** *n.* —.
RE2 **hagadangidangia.** *v.* —.
T **dadangi.** *a.* Make noise repeatedly.

TE **hagadadangi.** *v.* —.
TE1 **hagadadanginga.** *n.* —.
ID **dangi a beini.** To have smelled ripe pandanus.
ID **dangi buada.** The noise made by a fast-moving projectile.
ID **dangidangi ange.** Ask permission of, apologize to.
ID **dangidangi keli.** Beg, apologize, or ask permission in an insistent manner; pray fervently; beseech.
ID **dangi daudau.** Cry uncontrollably (for a long time).
ID **dangi de musu.** Hear whispering (of others).
ID **dangi talinga.** Tinnitus, a ringing sound in the ear [an omen].
ID **dangi hagaeaea.** Wail (when crying).
ID **dangi hagahadihadi.** Wail loudly (when crying).
ID **dangi hhadu$_1$.** Cry for effect.
ID **dangi iho.** Cry to oneself.
ID **dangi see.** Cry aloud for a long time, wail.
ID **tangi gi de me.** All of a sudden (an action not violent).
ID **kumi tangi.** To control one's crying.
CF **ngisi$_a$.** —.

DANGII
B **dangii.** *n.* Fish sp. (= small *valu*).

DANGO$_1$
B **dango$_1$.** *v.* Grab (in order to restrain, e.g., a person), fall upon.
B 1 **dangoanga.** *n.* —.
B 2 **dangoa.** *v.* Grabbed, fallen upon.
B 2 **dangolia.** *v.* Grabbed, fallen upon.
BE **hagadango.** *v.* —.
BE1 **hagadangoanga.** *n.* —.
BE2 **hagadangoa.** *v.* —.
BE2 **hagadangolia.** *v.* —.
R **dangodango.** *v.* Repeatedly grab.
R 1 **dangodangoanga.** *n.* —.
R 2 **dangodangoa.** *v.* —.
R 2 **dangodangolia.** *v.* —.
RE **hagadangodango.** *v.* —.
RE1 **hagadangodangoanga.** *n.* —.
RE2 **hagadangodangoa.** *v.* —.
RE2 **hagadangodangolia.** *v.* —.
T **dadango.** *v.* Repeatedly fall upon.
T 2 **dadangolia.** *v.* —.
TE **hagadadango.** *v.* —.
TE1 **hagadadangoanga.** *n.* —.
TE2 **hagadadangolia.** *v.* —.
ID **dango de langi.** Downpour (of rain).
ID **gohu boo dangodango.** A pitch-black night.
CF **hagatangohi.** The fading of light after sunset.

DANGO$_2$
B **dango$_2$.** *n.* Cat's-eye (of a shell); operculum of a gastropod.
ID **bule dango.** Button.
ID **kobu dango.** The splash of a small object (like a *dango*) hitting the water at high velocity.

DAO$_1$
B **dao$_1$.** *v.* Bake.
B 1 **daonga.** *n.* —; feast.
B 2 **daoa.** *v.* —.
B 2 **daolia.** *v.* —.
E **tao.** *v.* Soak (in water).
E 1 **taonga.** *n.* —.
E 2 **taoa.** *v.* —.
R **daodao$_1$.** *v.* —.
R 1 **daodaonga.** *n.* —.
R 2 **daodaoa.** *v.* —.
R 2 **daodaolia.** *v.* —.
XFL **daogili.** *n.* [var. of *daogoli*].
XFL **daogoli.** *n.* Plant sp.: swamp taro (*Cyrtosperma chamissonis*), also the corm of this plant.
XG **laulau hai daonga.** A type of basket [used for allocating portions at a feast].
ID **dao bagu.** Dry out (fish or food to preserve it).

ID dao de laangi. Celebrate.
ID **dao hadu.** Cover up (by putting on layer after layer); give too much (e.g., work) to.
ID **dao hagaahulu.** To leave an earth oven covered, even after the food is cooked.
ID **dao huge.** To open an earth oven as soon as the food is cooked.
ID **tao tangada.** To immerse a person in medication.
ID **me tao.** Dye.
ID **moe tao.** Sleep soundly.
ID **seni tao.** Sleep soundly.
ID **valaai tao.** Dye.

DAO$_2$
B **dao$_2$.** *n.* A spear, branch of (part of).
R **daodao$_2$.** *n.* Fish sp.: wahoo.
XFL **mataodao.** *n.* Fish sp.: cornetfish.
ID **dao tili.** A spear or harpoon to which a line is attached.
ID **dao hagamaadau.** A spear with a barb.
ID **dao haiava.** Path (a minor, not major, thoroughfare).
ID **dao malui.** A spear with a hinged barb.
ID **dao me hholu.** Arrow (for a bow).
ID **dao o gasoni.** A type of a cloud formation [indicates that a storm is imminent].
ID **tao o de moso.** A coconut frond spine which has fallen and stuck upright in the ground.
ID **gaaui i tao.** A line (for retrieving) which is attached to a spear.
ID **gubu dao.** A join of the spear shaft which is made of two pieces of wood.
ID **mada dao.** Prow of a fast ship.
ID **mainu daodao.** Bait for *daodao* fishing [a shiny side strip of the tuna or *daodao*].

DAO$_3$
B **dao$_3$.** *n.* A method of calculating the relative maturity of coconuts by comparing the size of the upper (immature) ones on the tree with the lower (mature) ones; the second of a pair (e.g., *dao dogai*).
XCO **daogave.** *n.* A type of coconut tree [bears seasonally].
XCO **daogubu.** *n.* Waist, circumference.
ID **dao badu.** Ridge pole (upper).
ID **dao beau.** The wave following the highest one.
ID **dao bou.** Ridge pole support (end).
ID **dao dahuuhuu.** Ridge pole (lower).
ID **dao o de nui.** (Topmost) roof support poles, wall plates(from the size of which one can estimate the maturity of those below).
ID **dao ssanga.** Roof support (top) poles, wall plates.

DAOHI
B **daohi.** *v.* Hold, restrain, keep (from).
B 1 **daohinga.** *n.* —.
B 2 **daohia.** *v.* —.
R **daadaohi.** *v.* —.
R 1 **daadaohinga.** *n.* —.
R 2 **daadaohia.** *v.* —.
ID **dama daohi.** An adopted child.
ID **daohi age.** Donate, contribute.
ID **daohi ange dahi hai.** Argue against.
ID **daohi taelodi.** Keep a record of.
ID **daohi i tua.** Learn by heart.
ID **velo daohi.** To spear (something) without releasing the spear.

DAU$_1$
B **dau$_1$.** *v.* Count, read; be included; of importance.

B 1 **daunga$_1$.** *n.* —.
B 2 **daua$_1$.** *v.* — ['count' and 'read' meanings only]; productive, yield a great amount of.
B 2 **daulia$_1$.** *v.* —; popular.
B 3 **dauaanga$_1$.** *n.* —.
BE1 **hagadaunga$_1$.** *n.* —.
BE2 **hagadaua$_1$.** *v.* —.
BE2 **hagadaulia$_1$.** *v.* —.
EE **hagatau$_1$.** *v.* Arrange (in order), a program; name one after another; refuse to do one's part because of someone else's actions.
EE1 **hagatauanga.** *n.* —; row (of things).
EE2 **hagataua$_1$.** *v.* —.
EE2 **hagataulia$_1$.** *v.* —.
R **daudau$_1$.** *v.* —; well-known, famous.
R 1 **daudaunga$_1$.** *n.* —.
R 2 **daudaua$_1$.** *v.* —.
R 2 **daudaulia$_1$.** *v.* —.
XCO **dauaalo.** *v.* Steady paddling.
XCO **daubodobodo.** *a.* Short (in duration).
XCO **daudahi.** *a.* Only, alone (just one).
XCO **daudonu.** *a.* If, in the case that; gentle, mild-mannered, soft-spoken.
XCO **daulooloa.** *a.* Long time.
XCO **daumada.** *v.* Stare at, observe closely.
ID **daane dau.** A person of importance (specially accomplished).
ID **daelodo dau.** A large enough number to "count".
ID **dau ange.** Depend upon (e.g., for sustenance).
ID **dau i tua.** Memorize.
ID **dau ngaadahi$_1$.** Equally apportioned.
ID **dee dau ia.** It's OK!
ID **tau ange luu mada.** Have noticed.
ID **tau ono pagola.** Punished for his bad deeds.
ID **liiliagi daudahi.** Be of the same status.
ID **maga tau hoe.** To paddle (a canoe) vigorously.
ID **me dau.** Thing of importance, worthwhile.
CF **madau.** Right (side).
CF **ngadau.** Year; age (of a person).

DAU$_{1b}$

BE **hagadau$_1$.** *v.* —; make well-known, make someone a —.
XCO **hagadaudoo.** *a.* Compete to see who is stronger.
XCO **hagadau-me.** *a.* Enemy; dispute (with someone), argue.
XE **hagadaubodobodo.** *v.* Shorten (time or rope).
XE **hagadaulooloa.** *v.* Prolong, extend.
ID **gai me hagadau doa.** Eat as though competing against other eaters in a test of manliness (e.g., to eat fish with the scales and all).
ID **hagadau aaloha.** Love each other (esp. of persons of the opposite sex).
ID **hagadau bale.** Cooperate; help one another.
ID **hagadau doa.** To show one's strength by doing something difficult.
ID **hagadau doo.** To transfer a string figure from one person's fingers to another's.
ID **hagadau doolohi.** Chase each other.
ID **hagadau tugi.** Punch each other.
ID **hagadau gaiaa.** Steal from one another.
ID **hagadau gavange.** Compete (between groups).
ID **hagadau kino.** Hate each other.
ID **hagadau hai me ai.** Use jointly or collectively.
ID **hagadau vaasuu.** Be attracted to or like each other (of members of the opposite sex).

DAU$_{1c}$

B **daumaha.** *v.* Church (services); religious observance; religion.

ID **daahili daumaha.** A church song.
ID **daumaha daahili.** Song service (in church).
ID **daumaha daamada.** The morning prayer service (before the major church service).
ID **daumaha dalodalo.** Prayer service (church).
ID **daumaha de manu.** Christmas Eve fete in the church at which "Santa Claus" appears.
ID **daumaha haangoda.** Prayer service held while visiting others' houses [in the hope of getting converts].
ID **daumaha hagadaahao.** Social activities which are held in the church under church auspices.
ID **daumaha hagatoo donu.** Church service of dedication (in which the members renew their vows).
ID **daumaha hagalava.** Evensong (last service of the day).
ID **daumaha hagasaele.** A meeting of church members for business.
ID **daumaha hagaulu.** The church service at which new members are accepted.
ID **daumaha laanui.** The main Sunday religious observance in the church.
ID **hale daumaha.** Church (building).
ID **ngadi daumaha.** Religions which are not in the Judaeo-Christian tradition, pagan cults.
CF **sigidaumaha.** Collection (in church), offering (in church), sacrifice, tithe.

DAU$_2$

B **dau$_2$.** *v.* To fasten (a rope, etc.) between two points; hung up, suspended from.
B 1 **daunga$_2$.** *n.* —.
B 2 **daua$_2$.** *v.* —.
B 2 **daulia$_2$.** *v.* —.
BE **hagadau$_2$.** *v.* —.
BE1 **hagadaunga$_2$.** *n.* —.
BE2 **hagadaua$_2$.** *v.* —.
BE2 **hagadaulia$_2$.** *v.* —.
R **daudau$_2$.** *v.* —.
R 1 **daudaunga$_2$.** *n.* —.
R 2 **daudaua$_2$.** *v.* —.
R 2 **daudaulia$_2$.** *v.* —.
RE **hagadaudau$_2$.** *v.* —; pass overhead (of clouds); move toward the end of the tether.
RE1 **hagadaudaunga$_2$.** *n.* —.
RE2 **hagadaudaua$_2$.** *v.* —.
RE2 **hagadaudaulia$_2$.** *v.* —.
XCO **dauaahe.** *a.* Gather or pleat in material; feathers of a rooster standing out on its neck (when angry); festooned with (e.g., flags).
ID **dau age de inai.** Be in the lee of the atoll while fishing (i.e., in a place protected from the wind).
ID **dau ama.** The mast stay tied to the outrigger boom.
ID **dau balabala.** Slack (of rope).
ID **dau bodobodo.** To tie at the end of a short tether.
ID **dau gadea.** Boom lanyard (of a canoe).
ID **dau laagii.** To put on an ornament for a special purpose.
ID **dau looloa.** To tie at the end of a long tether.
ID **dau makaga.** Tightly stretched (not slack).
ID **dau namu.** Mosquito net.
ID **dau ngaadahi$_2$.** Equally stretched (of two or more ropes).
CF **daula.** Rope (heavy); anchored (of ship).

DAU$_{2a}$

B **dauagi.** *v.* Dry in the sun.
B 1 **dauaginga.** *n.* —.
B 2 **dauagia.** *v.* —.
B 2 **dauagina.** *v.* —.
BE **hagadauagi.** *v.* —.

BE1	**hagadauaginga.** *n.* —.
BE2	**hagadauagia.** *v.* —.
BE2	**hagadauagina.** *v.* —; expose oneself to the sun.
R	**daudauagi.** *v.* —.
R 1	**daudauaginga.** *n.* —.
R 2	**daudauagia.** *v.* —.
R 2	**daudauagina.** *v.* —.
RE	**hagadaudauagi.** *v.* —.
RE1	**hagadaudauaginga.** *n.* —.
RE2	**hagadaudauagia.** *v.* —.
RE2	**hagadaudauagina.** *v.* —.

DAU_3

B	**dau_3.** *a.* Be hit; to beach (a canoe), arrive at.
B 1	**$daunga_3$.** *n.* —.
B 2	**$daua_3$.** *v.* War, battle.
BE	**$hagadau_3$.** *v.* —.
BE1	**$hagadaunga_3$.** *n.* —.
BE2	**$hagadaua_3$.** *v.* —; wage war against.
BE2	**$hagadaulia_3$.** *v.* —.
BE3	**$hagadauaanga_1$.** *n.* —.
P	**tau.** *a.* —.
PE	**$hagatau_2$.** *v.* —.
PE1	**hagataunga.** *n.* —.
PE2	**$hagataua_2$.** *v.* —.
PE2	**$hagataulia_2$.** *v.* —.
R	**$daudau_3$.** *a.* —; wrestle.
R 1	**$daudaunga_3$.** *n.* —.
RE	**$hagadaudau_1$.** *v.* —
RE1	**$hagadaudaunga_1$.** *n.* —.
RE2	**$hagadaudaua_1$.** *v.* —.
RE2	**$hagadaudaulia_1$.** *v.* —.
T	**dadau.** *a.* Hit repeatedly (on one occasion).
T 1	**dadaunga.** *n.* —.
TE	**hagadadau.** *v.* —.
TE1	**hagadadaunga.** *n.* —.
TE2	**hagadadaua.** *v.* —.
TE2	**hagadadaulia.** *v.* —.
XCO	**adudau.** *n.* Sand spit.
XCO	**dauhuli (ange).** *n.* Always criticizing (someone) to (his) face.
XCO	**daungaangalu.** *n.* High-water mark.
ID	**daa hatau.** Beat unmercifully.
ID	**daane mada daua.** Bravest in war.
ID	**dangi daudau.** Cry uncontrollably (for a long time).
ID	**dau age.** To beach (a canoe) on land; reach land.
ID	**dau de madangi.** Be hit by (usually a strong) wind.
ID	**duu taua.** Outbreak of war.
ID	**tau ange.** Cause to be absorbed by.
CF	**madau-dalinga.** Fish sp.: shark sp.?

DAU_4

B	**dau_4.** *d.* Occurring in great numbers.
BE	**$hagadau_4$.** *d.* Create —.
XCO	**dauaalu.** *v.* Always borrowing or begging.
XCO	**daubasa.** *na.* A great many.
ID	**dau dinae.** A period during which many women are pregnant at the same time.
ID	**dau gai.** The season in which seasonally available food is abundant.
ID	**dau gulu.** Breadfruit season.
ID	**dau haanau.** A period during which many children are born.
ID	**dau hala.** The season during which pandanus fruit of the same type matures.
ID	**dau honu.** The season during which tides are highest.
ID	**dau hoohanga.** The season during which birds lay eggs.
ID	**dau langi.** Rainy season.
ID	**dau lango.** The season during which flies are most numerous [coincides with the breadfruit season].
ID	**dau laohie.** Dry season.
ID	**dau maagau.** A period during which many people die.
ID	**dau magi.** Epidemic.
ID	**dau malino.** An area of the sea which is dead calm.
ID	**dau mamu.** The season in which fish are abundant.

ID **dau manu.** Flock of birds (feeding on a school of fish).
ID **dau masa.** The season during which tides are lowest.
ID **dau me.** The sheath of the flower of the coconut tree.
CF **maadau.** Hook, fishhook.

DAU$_5$
B **dau$_5$.** *n.* Chant (ancient).
ID **daa (dau).** Chanting (of old chants).

DAU$_6$
B **dau (umu).** *n.* A cover for an earth oven.

DAU$_7$
XCO **dauaabulu.** *v.* Nearly sunk.
XCO **dauaadea.** *v.* Clear (with nothing in the way); unobstructed; cleared (of obstructions).
XCO **daudai.** *a.* Skillful fisherman.
XE **hagadauaadea.** *v.* To clear out a place.
ID **basa dau donu.** Speak moderately.
ID **dangada dau duadae.** A sucker (a person who is easily fooled).
ID **dau soa.** Boyfriend, girlfriend; couple (not married); going steady (of an unmarried couple).
ID **(de) hine dau bodu.** Married woman.
ID **noho dau donu.** Sit quietly.
CF **daungaangalu.** High-water mark.

DAUAA
B **dauaa.** *v.* Wrinkled.
B 1 **dauaanga$_2$.** *n.* —.
BE **hagadauaa.** *v.* —.
BE1 **hagadauaanga$_2$.** *n.* —.
ID **hai dauaa.** Be in a wrinkled condition.

DAUBEEMALA
ID **bini daubeemala.** A method of making flower headdresses.

DAUDU
B **daudu.** *n.* Fish sp.: spiny puffer.

DAULA
B **daula.** *v.* Rope (heavy); anchored (of ship).
B 1 **daulanga.** *n.* Port (for ships); harbor (place where boats anchor).
BE **hagadaula.** *v.* To anchor.
BE1 **hagadaulanga.** *n.* —.
ID **daula baalanga.** Cable, wire (heavy).
ID **daula de boo.** A rope carried in the canoe (esp. at night) for anchoring or tying canoes together in case of strong wind.
ID **daula de gona.** A cord between the naval and the genitals [according to Nukuoro anatomical lore].
ID **daula duu nui.** A rope used to lower a bunch of coconuts to the ground.
ID **daula gage.** A rope used to assist the climber of a breadfruit tree.
ID **daula hagalevaleva.** A swing (made of rope).
ID **daula luu hadu.** Testicle cords.
ID **daula mada lau nui.** A rope for tying palm fronds together to make a *belubelu* seine.
ID **daula sele nui.** A rope used to pull a coconut tree in the desired direction when felling it.
ID **molimoli taula.** To take hitches in a rope until it is taut (and continue to take hitches as the rope becomes slack).

DAULA$_a$
B **ataula.** *n.* Anchor rope.

DAUNADI
B **daunadi.** *u.* Would it be better if (implying disagreement)?...

DAUONI
B **dauoni.** *n.* Fish sp.

XFL **dauoni-baabaa.** *n.* Fish sp. (a rare school fish which looks like *saniba*).

DAVAGE

B **davage.** *n.* Bird sp.: White-tailed tropic bird (*Phaethon lepturus*).

XFL **ulu-davage.** *n.* Plant sp.: tree sp.: Indian coral tree (*Erythrina variegata* L.).

DAVAIA

B **davaia.** *n.* The largest sort of tuna.

DE

B **de.** *ma.* The one.

ID **de ia.** The, thing, it.

ID **lo te.** [a contraction of *lodo de...*].

ID **ma te.** [a contraction of *mada de...*].

ID **ngu te.** [a contraction of *ngudu de...*].

DEA

B **dea.** *d.* —.

E **tea.** *a.* White.

E 1 **teaanga.** *n.* —.

EE **hagatea.** *v.* —; become white.

EE1 **hagateaanga.** *n.* —.

R **deadea.** *a.* Becoming lighter in color.

R 1 **deadeaanga.** *n.* —.

RE **hagadeadea.** *v.* —.

RE1 **hagadeadeaanga.** *n.* —.

XCO **mateedea.** *v.* Pustular.

XFL **aha-dea.** *n.* Driftwood sp. (white in the center).

XFL **sumu-dea.** *n.* Fish sp.

ID **baalanga tea.** Stainless steel.

ID **tea age langi.** The light before daybreak.

ID **tea gee.** Pallor.

ID **tea ma agiagi.** Dead white (whitest hue imaginable).

ID **gaadinga gaha dea.** A coconut which is nearly mature; the stage of development of the coconut between *modomodo madagii* and *gaadinga*.

ID **gaha dea.** Having almost ripe coconuts (whose husk fibers are white).

ID **gano dea.** The soft wood just under the bark of a tree.

ID **gelegele dea.** Sand.

ID **mada tea gee.** White as a sheet (of a person).

ID **me gaha dea.** A coconut which is nearly mature.

ID **ua dea.** Bird sp.: white-throated frigate bird.

ID **vai dea.** A whitish discharge from the genitalia (of either males or females).

DEAI

B **deai.** *a.* None, no —, nothing.

B 1 **deainga.** *n.* Nothingness.

BE **hagadeai.** *v.* Cause to become non-existent.

BE1 **hagadeainga.** *n.* —.

ID **dai deai.** Hardly any.

ID **deai ange.** No more, no other.

ID **deai ange loo soo savaa.** Now i've got you!

ID **deai donu.** None at all.

ID **deai donu angaanga.** Nothing at all.

ID **deai loo me.** I doubt it!

ID **deai ma gi dahi.** None at all as you should very well know! [prob. = *deai maua gi dahi*].

ID **deai me hagalongolongo.** Do unhesitatingly.

DEAI$_a$

BE **hagadeeai.** *v.* Refuse to.

E **deeai.** *a.* [an emphatic form of *deai*].

ID **dai deeai.** Almost none.

ID **dai deeai donu.** Almost none at all.

ID **deeai donu.** Positively no!

DEBE

R **debedebe.** *v.* The folds of skin around the waist.

R 1 **debedebenga.** *n.* —.

RE **hagadebedebe.** *v.* —.

DEE

B **dee.** *mt.* NEGATIVE ASPECT MARKER.

ID **au e dee gai naa loo.** I'll bet you can't!

ID **dee abo.** Uncomfortable (esp. socially).

ID **dee adagaigaina.** A great many; serious.

ID **dee ahe mai.** Incurably ill.

ID **dee anga.** Forgetful, absent-minded.

ID **dee dau ia.** It's OK!

ID **dee dolia.** Impossible to find the equal of (*dehors concours*).

ID **dee gagu.** Uncouth.

ID **dee galemu.** Never mind!, Don't bother!

ID **dee galo.** Perhaps.

ID **dee gamalie.** Do very attentively.

ID **dee gide.** Blind.

ID **dee kasi.** Perhaps.

ID **dee kona.** Easily.

ID **dee hagabaulia.** Underestimate, misjudge.

ID **dee hanga.** Don't move away from the reef! [an instruction heard when fishing for flying fish].

ID **dee heloongoi.** Misunderstand one another; mismated (not matched properly); not fit; not able to get along with.

ID **dee hilihili.** Indifferent.

ID **dee lahilahia.** Big (and therefore good), strong, tremendous.

ID **dee manava age.** Do earnestly.

ID **dee masae de leo.** Lose one's voice (from straining one's vocal cords).

ID **dee modu.** Continually.

ID **dee savaa (naa) de —.** Soon —.

ID **dee vaagidee.** Ugly, awful; extremely disappointing.

ID **dee vaaseegina.** Hardly able to wait for.

ID **delaa tee madea.** Hard to tell apart from; resemble closely.

ID **gu dee galemu.** Recovering from an illness (getting better).

CF **tee.** NEGATIVE DECISIVE ASPECT MARKER.

DEEHEHEE

B **deehehee.** *v.* To make a certain pattern of sounds to call attention to oneself.

B 1 **deeheheeanga.** *n.* —.

BE **hagadeehehee.** *v.* —.

BE1 **hagadeeheheeanga.** *n.* —.

BE2 **hagadeeheheelia.** *v.* —.

DEENGAA

B **deengaa.** *d.* Let's — right away!

BE **hagadeengaa.** *d.* Let's — right away and get it over with!

ID **deengaa gamalie.** Let's do it attentively!

DEGA

RC **maadegadega.** *n.* Bird sp.: a young bird (still unable to fly) of any bird sp.

DEGANOE

B **deganoe.** *n.* A part of the female genitalia.

DEGE

B **dege.** *nl.* Corner.

BE **hagadege.** *v.* Cause to wiggle the hips once.

BE2 **hagadegea.** *v.* —.

BE2 **hagadegelia.** *v.* [var. of *hagadegea*].

R **degedege.** *v.* To wiggle the hips repeatedly.

RE **hagadegedege.** *v.* —.

RE2 **hagadegedegea.** *v.* —.

RE2 **hagadegedegelia.** *v.* —.

ID **diinei mai dege.** To round off a sharp edge.

ID **tuu dege.** Having corners, square, rectangular.

ID **hagahidi i tege.** To throw a wrestler using one's hip.

ID **hagauda i tege.** Carry a basket, etc., on one's hip.

ID **lo te dege.** Inside the corner of.

DEGI$_1$

B **degi$_1$.** *v.* To jerk; get something quickly.
B 1 **deeginga$_1$.** *n.* —.
B 2 **degia.** *v.* —.
BC **madegi.** *a.* Be jerked.
BE **hagadegi$_1$.** *v.* —.
BE1 **hagadeginga.** *n.* —.
BE2 **hagadegia.** *v.* —.
BF **hagamadegi.** *v.* —.
BF1 **hagamadeginga.** *n.* —.
R **degidegi$_1$.** *v.* To jerk repeatedly; bawl out (speak harshly to).
R 1 **degideginga$_1$.** *n.* —.
R 2 **degidegia.** *v.* —.
RC **madegidegi.** *a.* —.
RE **hagadegidegi.** *v.* —.
RE1 **hagadegideginga.** *n.* —.
RE2 **hagadegidegia.** *v.* —.
RF **hagamadegidegi.** *v.* —.
RF1 **hagamadegideginga.** *n.* —.
ID **basa degidegi.** Speak disconnectedly with rage.

DEGI$_2$

E **tegi$_1$.** *a.* Aroused (sexually); tickled (esp. sexually).
E 1 **teeginga.** *n.* —.
EE **hagategi.** *a.* —.
EE1 **hagateeginga.** *n.* —.
EE1 **hagategia.** *v.* —.
EE1 **hagategilia.** *v.* —.
R **degidegi$_2$.** *a.* Ticklish.
R 1 **degideginga$_2$.** *n.* —.
ID **tegi kano.** Tickled.
ID **hagategi kano.** Tickled (not sexually).

DEGI$_3$

B **degi$_2$.** *a.* Kind, generous, forgiving.
B 1 **deeginga$_2$.** *n.* —.
BE **hagadegi$_2$.** *v.* Praise (God only).
P **tegi$_2$.** *a.* —.
R **degidegi$_3$.** *a.* Having a kind or generous nature.
ID **degi ange.** Forgive (someone), pardon (someone).
ID **tuhi hagadegi.** Praise with all one's heart (esp. God).
ID **lodo degi.** Having a forgiving nature.

DELE

B **dele.** *v.* Move from one place to another; to sail (a canoe); be transmitted; slip out of one's hands (e.g., a line on which a big fish has been caught).
B 1 **deelenga.** *n.* —.
B 2 **delea.** *v.* —.
B 2 **delengia.** *v.* —.
BE **hagadele.** *v.* —.
BE1 **hagadeelenga.** *n.* —.
BE2 **hagadelea.** *v.* —.
BE2 **hagadelengia.** *v.* —.
P **tele.** *v.* —.
PE **hagatele.** *v.* —.
PE1 **hagateelenga.** *n.* —.
PE2 **hagateelea.** *v.* —.
PE2 **hagatelengia.** *v.* —.
R **deledele.** *v.* —; move swiftly.
R 1 **deledelenga.** *n.* —.
RE **hagadeledele.** *v.* —; to play with a model canoe in the water (by children).
RE1 **hagadeledelenga.** *n.* —.
RE2 **hagadeledelea.** *v.* —.
RE2 **hagadeledelengia.** *v.* —.
XCO **deleulu.** *v.* Good at catching tuna.
ID **dele de ada.** Dawn (first light).
ID **dele de boialiali.** Daybreak.
ID **dele de gada.** Smile.
ID **deledele kau.** Walk proudly [culturally disapproved], strut.
ID **deledele hainga a me.** Rush because of an emergency.
ID **deledele saele.** Walk around aimlessly; be spread all over (of news).
ID **dele de longo.** Spread news or rumors.
ID **dele de maahaa.** Daybreak.
ID **dele de mahaa.** Starting to crack.
ID **moni hagadeledele.** Model (or toy) canoe.
CF **dalabaimanugadele.** Sharp (as a knife).

DEMO

BE **hagademo.** *v.* Pout [sing.].

BE1 **hagademoanga.** *n.* —.
BE2 **hagademolia.** *v.* —.
PE **hagatemo.** *v.* —.
PE1 **hagatemoanga.** *n.* —.
PE2 **hagatemolia.** *v.* —.
RE **hagademodemo.** *v.* —.
RE1 **hagademodemoanga.** *n.* —.
RE2 **hagademodemolia.** *v.* —.

DENGA$_1$
B **denga$_1$.** *ma.* The (several); each of—.

DENGA$_{1a}$
B **dengaa.** *ma.* The (several) I have in mind; each of— I have in mind.

DENGA$_2$
B **denga$_2$.** *n.* A hump on a tree trunk (where a branch failed to flower).
R **dengadenga.** *v.* Having many *denga.*
RE **hagadengadenga.** *v.* —.
RE2 **hagadengadengalia.** *v.* —.
ID **denga hhuge —.** Upward current.

DEVE
E **teve.** *a.* Hair (or feathers) standing on end.
E 1 **teevenga.** *n.* —.
EE **hagateve.** *v.* Bristle, ready for a fight (of animals).
EE1 **hagateevenga.** *n.* —.
EE2 **hagatevea.** *v.* [= *hagatevelia*].
EE2 **hagatevelia.** *v.* Cause to bristle.
R **devedeve.** *a.* Standing out all over (of feathers, etc.).
R 1 **devedevenga.** *n.* —.
RE **hagadevedeve.** *v.* —.
RE1 **hagadevedevenga.** *n.* —.
RE2 **hagadevedevea.** *v.* —.
RE2 **hagadevedevelia.** *v.* —.
ID **teve de biho.** To have the hair (of one's head) standing on end.
ID **teve de gili.** Gooseflesh.

DIA
R **diadia.** *v.* To make a cover for something (e.g., a coconut shell) by plaiting or lashing around it.
R 1 **diadiaanga.** *n.* —.
R 2 **diadialia.** *v.* —.
ID **madila diadia.** Bindings wound around a fishing pole to give it extra strength.
ID **malo diadia.** Mending holes in clothes by running threads crisscross across the hole.
ID **vai diadia.** A covered coconut shell which fishermen used to use for a drinking water container and (in emergencies) as a shark foil.

DIBA$_1$
B **diba$_1$.** *a.* Not level, tipped to one side.
B 1 **diibanga.** *n.* —.
B 2 **dibalia.** *v.* —.
BE **hagadiba.** *v.* Incline to one side.
BE1 **hagadibaanga.** *n.* —.
BE2 **hagadibalia.** *v.* Cause to tip to one side.
P **tiba.** *a.* —.
P 1 **tibaanga.** *n.* —.
P 2 **tibalia.** *v.* —.
PE **hagatiba.** *v.* —.
PE1 **hagatibaanga.** *n.* —.
PE2 **hagatibalia.** *v.* —.
R **dibadiba.** *a.* Unsteady (as a ship on the sea).
R 1 **dibadibaanga.** *n.* —.
R 2 **dibadibalia.** *v.* —.
RE **hagadibadiba.** *v.* Rock back and forth to one side.
RE1 **hagadibadibaanga.** *n.* —.
RE2 **hagadibadibalia.** *v.* Cause to *hagadibadiba.*
ID **diba iho.** To tip down; go away from the atoll.
ID **diibanga goo dii.** A game played by children (to determine who is "it").
ID **diibanga o de henua.** The categories of ancient custom.
ID **hagadibadiba de lima.** To wiggle one's hand [a signal that the speaker is lying].

ID seesee hagadibadiba. Waddle.

DIBA$_2$

B **diba$_2$.** *n.* Portion, share (of something); part (of something); fraction (in arithmetic).

ID **dibaa dodo.** A clot of blood.

DIBI

R **dibidibi.** *n.* A square ball (for tossing about) plaited of pandanus leaves.

DIBO

B **dibo.** *n.* Infant.

XCO **dibononi.** *n.* The youngest child of a couple.

DIDI$_1$

B **didi.** *a.* Grass skirt (of hibiscus fiber or palm leaf); to wear a grass skirt.

B 1 **didianga.** *n.* The manner of wearing one's *didi.*

BE **hagadidi.** *v.* To put a grass skirt on someone else.

BE1 **hagadidianga.** *n.* —.

DIDI$_2$

R **ditidi.** *a.* To skim across the surface of land or water.

R 1 **ditidianga.** *n.* —.

RE **hagaditidi.** *v.* To skip a stone across the water.

RE1 **hagaditidianga.** *n.* —.

RE2 **hagaditidilia.** *v.* —.

ID **hagaditidi de hadu.** To skip a stone across the water.

ID **hagaditidi mai de moni.** A canoe going so fast it rides high in water (and is planing).

ID **hagaditidi vae dahi.** Hop on one foot.

DIGE

B **dige.** *a.* Roll over or about, turn (as of a wheel), spin, revolve, rotate.

B 1 **diigenga.** *n.* —.

B 2 **digelia.** *v.* —.

BE **hagadige.** *v.* —.

BE1 **hagadiigenga.** *n.* —.

BE2 **hagadigelia.** *v.* —.

P **tige.** *a.* —.

P 1 **tiigenga.** *n.* —.

P 2 **tigelia.** *v.* —.

PE **hagatige.** *v.* —.

PE1 **hagatiigenga.** *n.* —.

PE2 **hagatigelia.** *v.* —.

R **digedige.** *a.* —.

R 1 **digedigenga.** *n.* —.

R 2 **digedigelia.** *v.* —.

RE **hagadigedige.** *v.* —.

RE1 **hagadigedigenga.** *n.* —.

RE2 **hagadigedigelia.** *v.* —.

XFL **manu-hagadigedige.** *n.* Mollusk sp.: cone shell.

ID **dige de belubelu.** A circuit made by a school of *belubelu.*

ID **hagadige de madaangudu.** A prolonged conversation (on subjects of little importance).

ID **manu hagadigedige.** Top (toy).

ID **moe dige.** To roll away from one's bedding while sleeping (on the floor).

DIHA

B **diha.** *v.* Move something by using a lever (esp. a pole) on a fulcrum; contradict.

B 1 **dihaanga.** *n.* —.

R **dihadiha.** *v.* —.

R 1 **dihadihaanga.** *n.* —.

DIHI

R **dihidihi.** *n.* Fish sp.: butterfly fish (The native term is applied to many spp.).

DII

B **dii.** *v.* Shine (sun).

B 1 **diianga.** *n.* —.

B 2 **diingia.** *v.* To be exposed to the sun's rays.

BE **hagadii.** *v.* —.

BE1 **hagadiianga.** *n.* —.

BE2 **hagadiingia.** *v.* —.

R **diidii$_1$.** *v.* —.

R 1 **diidiianga.** *n.* —.

R 2 **diidiingia.** *v.* Be frequently exposed to the sun's rays.

RE **hagadiidii$_1$.** *v.* —.

RE1 **hagadiidiianga.** *n.* —.
RE2 **hagadiidiingia.** *v.* —.
ID **dii ange.** A method of fishing in which the lure at the end of the pole is jerked to attract fish.
ID **diibanga goo dii.** A game played by children (to determine who is "it").
ID **dii de laa.** The shining of the sun.
ID **hagadiingia saele.** To go about exposing oneself to the sun's rays.
CF **diidegaehala.** The sixth child of a couple.
CF **diihagaai.** The eighth child of a couple.
CF **diilaulauhai.** The seventh child of a couple.
CF **diilevalevanoa.** The fifth child of a couple.
CF **diimadamadanoa.** The ninth child of a couple.
CF **diimolalaaidu.** The tenth child of a couple.

DII$_a$
B **aadiidii.** *v.* Dry (something) by artificial heat.
B 1 **aadiidiinga.** *n.* —.
B 2 **aadiidiia.** *v.* —.
BE **hagaadiidii.** *v.* —.
BE1 **hagaadiidiinga.** *n.* —.
BE2 **hagaadiidiia.** *v.* —.

DIIBULI
B **diibuli.** *n.* A doll representing a spirit (from the story of *duudebaabaa*).

DIIDII
B **diidii**$_2$. *a.* Penis; urinate.
B 1 **diidiinga.** *n.* Manner of urinating.
BE **hagadiidii**$_2$. *v.* Help to urinate (e.g., by taking a baby outside).
BE1 **hagadiidiinga.** *n.* —.
ID **diidii ange.** Urinate against.
ID **sii diidii.** Urinate.

DIINEI
B **diinei.** *v.* To extinguish (e.g., a fire, or the life of a plant, or the heat of the sun — as by clouds); to smooth rough edges.
B 1 **diineinga.** *n.* —.
B 2 **diineia.** *v.* —.
BE **hagadiinei.** *v.* —.
BE1 **hagadiineinga.** *n.* —.
BE2 **hagadiineia.** *v.* —.
R **diidiinei.** *v.* —.
R 1 **diidiineinga.** *n.* —.
R 2 **diidiineia.** *v.* —.
RE **hagadiidiinei.** *v.* —.
RE1 **hagadiidiineinga.** *n.* —.
RE2 **hagadiidiineia.** *v.* —.
ID **diinei de lodo.** Become calmer (after being angry).
ID **diinei de madangi.** A decrease of wind velocity.
ID **diinei de manu.** To kill off plants.
ID **diinei mai.** Make smaller; decrease.
ID **diinei mai dege.** To round off a sharp edge.

DILI
B **dili.** *v.* Shoot at; shine (e.g., a flashlight) on; let go, throw away, lose something; disregard; steady beating (as of a heart); a steady stroke (as of an adze).
B 1 **diilinga.** *n.* —.
B 2 **dilia.** *v.* —.
BE **hagadili.** *v.* Produce offspring.
BE1 **hagadiilinga.** *n.* —; descendants (in one generation only).
BE2 **hagadilia.** *v.* —.
BE2 **hagadilidilia.** *v.* —.
E **tili.** *v.* *dili* at one time.
EC **matili.** *a.* Come up quickly (like fast-sprouting plants or a quickly erupting skin disease).
EC1 **matilianga.** *n.* —.
EE **hagatili.** *v.* Swoop down, swoop across.
EE1 **hagatiilinga.** *n.* —.
EF **hagamatili.** *v.* —.
EF1 **hagamatilianga.** *n.* —.
R **dilidili.** *v.* —.
R 1 **dilidilinga.** *n.* —.
R 2 **dilidilia.** *v.* —.

RE hagadilididili. *v.* —.
RE1 hagadilididilinga. *n.* —.
XCO **dilimangali.** *v.* To catch flying fish [from the Ponapean *indilmenger*?].
XE **hagadilimangali.** *v.* To teach someone to *dilimangali.*
XFL **dilidili-dogi.** *n.* Bird sp.: Polynesian tattler? (*Heteroscelus brevipes*).
ID **au dili dai.** An ocean current flowing away from land.
ID **au dili uda.** An ocean current flowing toward land.
ID **dao tili.** A spear or harpoon to which a line is attached.
ID **dili aalanga.** Exhausted (physically or mentally).
ID **dilia ange.** Give fish to.
ID **dili bala.** Collapse (of persons).
ID **dili dagidahi.** Happening continually but one at a time.
ID **dili dagidahi age.** Release one at a time or intermittently or sporadically.
ID **dili dai.** Any current flowing away from the atoll.
ID **dili dangada.** To fail to discharge one's obligations to help (esp. one's kin).
ID **dili de lima.** To swing one's arms (when walking).
ID **dili ebuebu.** Exhalation of air under water (forming bubbles).
ID **dili uda.** An ocean current which comes towards the shore (and carries in driftwood, etc.).
ID **tili de galauna.** Set *galauna.*
ID **tili de maalama.** Shoot out a light into the distance.
ID **tili gee.** Throw away.
ID **tili mada.** Go at top speed.
ID **tili moumou.** Waste (by not using).
ID **matili mai.** Remember vividly (after having forgotten); the sprouting of plants, etc., in great numbers.
ID **me dili dai.** Any current which flows away from the atoll.
ID **me dili uda.** An ocean current which comes towards the atoll.
ID **velo tili.** Throw a spear; go directly.

DILO$_1$

B **dilo$_1$.** *v.* Look at (inspect).
B 1 **diilonga.** *n.* —.
E **diiloo.** *v.* Look after; look at attentively.
E **tilo.** *v.* [imperative form of *dilo*].
R **dilodilo.** *v.* —.
R 1 **dilodilonga.** *n.* The manner in which one looks at one's reflection or appearance.
XCO **dagitilo.** *v.* Watchful, be on the lookout, keep an eye on.
XCO **dilongaagau.** *v.* Voyeurism.
ID **dili gaiaa.** Sneak a look.
ID **tilo danuaa.** Good-looking, handsome; beautiful (esp. owing to having a graceful manner).
ID **tilo gauligi.** To regard something from the perspective of a child.
ID **tilo iho.** To consider one's own situation.
ID **tilo mahamaha.** Having a good appearance.

DILO$_2$

B **dilo$_2$.** *n.* The immature leaf of any plant, except of the coconut; a coconut leaflet midrib after scraping, soaking and drying.
ID **dohi dilo.** To strip *dilo* (to make plaited hats, etc.).
CF **baledilo.** The stage of plant growth at which immature leaves appear.

DILO$_{2a}$

B **adilo.** *n.* The core of a body boil; the beginning of a fire.

DINAE

B **dinae.** *n.* Belly; the edible white part of clam meat.

ID **paa i tua tinae.** Have an empty stomach.

ID **dau dinae.** A period during which many women are pregnant at the same time.

ID **dinae o de laa.** Ballooning of a sail.

ID **dinae o ssaiolo.** [= *dinae o de laa*].

ID **hagadubu dinae.** The name of a certain type of string figure.

ID **ilihia tinae.** A stomach distended by gas.

ID **mmae tinae.** Convulsed with laughter.

DINANA

B **dinana.** *n.* Mother, aunt; senior female relative, person in a mothering, or motherly, relationship.

BE **hagadinana.** *v.* To treat as *dinana.*

ID **dinana donu.** Natural mother.

ID **dinana mai i daha.** Stepmother.

ID **hai dinana.** The relationship between mother (or other female elder) and child (or one treated as a child).

DINIHU

B **dinihu.** *v.* Industrious, hardworking.

BE **hagadinihu.** *v.* —.

DINO$_1$

B **dino$_1$.** *a.* A share of, allotment, portion.

B 1 **diinonga.** *a.* A spirit which is worshipped; bad character (of a person).

BE **hagadino.** *v.* Provide a portion or share.

BE1 **hagadiinonga.** *v.* —; treat as having supernatural power.

XFL **diinonga-o-salo.** *n.* Fish sp.

ID **diinonga eidu.** An idol representing a spirit.

ID **dinoanga hulu.** A council (of ten) formerly having broad legislative and judicial powers on the atoll.

ID **dino boo.** Nights (2) when the full moon appears just after sunset.

ID **tiinonga o tangada.** Undesirable personal characteristics.

ID **ngadi diinonga.** Pagan gods, idols.

CF **uludino.** Shed skin (as does a reptile).

DINO$_2$

B **dino$_2$ + NUMBER.** *mc.* NUMERAL CLASSIFIER (BY TENS(FOR PERSONS.

XE **hagadinoangahulu.** *v.* Make a total of ten people.

DINGALE

B **dingale.** *n.* Secretion of the genitalia (male or female); the milky sap on some pandanus plugs.

BE **hagadingale.** *v.* —.

DOA

B **doa.** *n.* Giant.

BE **hagadoa.** *v.* Act like a giant.

ID **doa agalala.** Very big giant.

ID **gai me hagadau doa.** Eat as though competing against other eaters in a test of manliness (e.g., to eat fish with the scales and all).

ID **hagadau doa.** To show one's strength by doing something difficult.

CF **ginadoa.** A boil on the body that is hard and painful, and which will not come to a head.

DOADOA

B **doadoa.** *v.* The sound made to attract chickens.

B 1 **doadoaanga.** *n.* —.

BE **hagadoadoa.** *v.* —.

BE1 **hagadoadoaanga.** *n.* —.

DODI

B **dodi.** *a.* Have a limp (physical condition).

B 1 **dodinga.** *n.* —.
BE **hagadodi.** *v.* Walk with a limp (permanently).
BE1 **hagadodinga.** *n.* —.
R **dotodi.** *a.* Limping (as an action).
R 1 **dotodinga.** *n.* —.
RE **hagadotodi.** *v.* Walk with a limp (temporarily).
RE1 **hagadotodianga.** *n.* —.

DODI$_a$
B **badodi.** *v.* To jerk to a stop (as at the end of a tether); stumble, trip (fall).
B 1 **badodinga.** *n.* —.
B 2 **badodia.** *v.* —.
BE **hagabadodi.** *v.* —.
BE1 **hagabadodinga.** *n.* —.
BE2 **hagabadodia.** *v.* —.
R **badotodi.** *v.* Move jerkily.
R 1 **badotodianga.** *n.* —.
RE **hagabadotodi.** *v.* —.
RE1 **hagabadotodinga.** *n.* —.
RE2 **hagabadotodia.** *v.* —.
ID **badodi gee.** To jerk violently.

DODO
B **dodo$_1$.** *v.* Blood.
BE **hagadodo.** *v.* —.
R **dotodo.** *v.* Bloody (of a person).
R 1 **dotodoanga.** *n.* —.
R 2 **dotodolia.** *v.* —.
RE **hagadotodo.** *v.* —.
RE1 **hagadotodoanga.** *n.* —.
RE2 **hagadotodolia.** *v.* —.
XFL **dalia-dodo.** *n.* Mollusk sp.: *Chlamys schmeltzi.*
ID **dibaa dodo.** A clot of blood.
ID **dodo ina.** Bloody [of garments, etc.].
ID **duaa dodo.** Labor pains (of a woman in childbirth).
ID **tuu todo.** Stop bleeding.
ID **hai dodo.** Bleeding profusely.
ID **luei todo.** Cough up blood.
ID **mada dotodo.** An abrasion of the skin (red but not bleeding).
ID **magi hongagelegele todo.** To have bloody stools [dysentery?].
ID **noho dodo.** Coagulation of blood.
ID **sali dodo.** Bleed.
ID **ua dodo.** Rain of a reddish color [an omen of death].

DOE
B **doe.** *a.* Left over, remain.
B 1 **doenga.** *n.* —.
B 2 **doea.** *a.* —.
BE **hagadoe.** *v.* Put aside, leave for later, conserve.
BE1 **hagadoenga.** *n.* —.
BE2 **hagadoea.** *v.* —.
R **doedoe.** *a.* Still remaining, still left over.
R 1 **doedoenga.** *n.* —.
R 2 **doedoea.** *a.* —.
RE **hagadoedoe.** *v.* —.
RE1 **hagadoedoenga.** *n.* —.
RE2 **hagadoedoea.** *v.* —.
ID **dama doe.** The fourth child born to a couple.
ID **gai hagadoedoe.** Eat sparingly (to save for later).
ID **ma de hia e doe.** A chanted expression, on the last word of which a work group chanting it lifts a heavy object.

DOGA$_1$
B **doga$_1$.** *a.* Land on (as a bird lands on the branch of a tree).
B 1 **dogaanga$_1$.** *n.* —.
B 2 **dogalia.** *v.* —.
BE **hagadoga.** *v.* —.
BE1 **hagadogaanga$_1$.** *n.* —.
BE2 **hagadogalia.** *v.* —.
P **toga.** *a.* —.
P 1 **togaanga.** *n.* —.
P 2 **togalia.** *v.* —.
PE **hagatoga.** *v.* —.
PE1 **hagatogaanga.** *n.* —.
PE2 **hagatogalia.** *v.* —.
R **dogadoga.** *a.* —.
R 1 **dogadogaanga$_1$.** *n.* —.
R 2 **dogadogalia.** *v.* —.
RE **hagadogadoga.** *v.* —.
RE1 **hagadogadogaanga$_1$.** *n.* —.
RE2 **hagadogadogalia.** *v.* —.
ID **au doga.** A confluence of ocean currents, or a

circular current in which drifting objects remain stationary.
ID **doga de manu.** Nesting of *gadada*, or *gaalau*, or *gailulu*.

DOGA$_2$
B **doga$_2$.** *n.* A (live) coral formation.

DOGA$_3$
XCO **haitoga.** *n.* An opening for a door or window.

DOGAA
B **dogaa.** *a.* Bashful, ashamed, shy, embarrassed.
B 1 **dogaanga$_2$.** *n.* —.
BE **hagadogaa.** *v.* —; shameful, to embarrass (someone).
BE1 **hagadogaanga$_2$.** *n.* —.
P **dookaa.** *a.* —.
P 1 **dookaanga.** *n.* —.
PE **hagadookaa.** *v.* —.
PE1 **hagadookaanga.** *n.* —.
R **dogadogaa.** *a.* Having a tendency to be *dogaa.*
R 1 **dogadogaanga$_2$.** *n.* —.
RE **hagadogadogaa.** *v.* —.
RE1 **hagadogadogaanga$_2$.** *n.* —.
ID **dogaa ange.** Feel shy in the presence of.
ID **hagadogaa dangada.** Embarrass people by one's actions.
ID **hai me dogaa.** Behave with embarrassment or shyness.
ID **magau i togaa.** Die of shame [figuratively].

DOGAI
B **dogai.** *n.* Transverse tie beam [rests on *ssanga*].

DOGI
B **dogi.** *n.* Adze; a tapping movement.
B 2 **dogia.** *v.* Be wet from the rain.
B 3 **dogiaanga.** *n.* —.
BD **hedogi.** *v.* The sound of tapping.
BE2 **hagadogia.** *v.* —.
BE3 **hagadogiaanga.** *n.* —.
XCO **vilidogi.** *v.* Chatterbox, a person who speaks fast.
XFL **anga-dogi.** *n.* Mollusk sp.: *Cerithiidae.*
XFL **dilididili-dogi.** *n.* Bird sp.: Polynesian tattler? (*Heteroscelus brevipes*).
ID **damaa dogi.** Skillful in the use of an adze.
ID **dogi daadaa.** A type of adze (with a small blade, for light chipping).
ID **dogi hakolona.** A type of adze (with a curved blade of *Terebra* shell).
ID **dogi hoda.** A type of adze (heavy — for hollowing out logs, etc.).
ID **dogi hulihuli.** [= *sauligi*].
ID **maga de gau dogi.** Masturbate (of males only).
CF **bungadogi.** Unskillful (at difficult activities).

DOGO$_1$
B **dogo$_1$.** *v.* To punt (propel a canoe by poling); punt pole.
B 1 **doogonga.** *n.* —; a clearing through coral beds to allow for canoe passage.
B 2 **dogoa.** *v.* —.
B 2 **dogolia.** *v.* —.
B 2 **dogona.** *v.* —.
BE **hagadogo.** *v.* —.
BE1 **hagadoogonga.** *n.* —.
BE2 **hagadogoa.** *v.* —.
BE2 **hagadogolia.** *v.* —.
BE2 **hagadogona.** *v.* —.
E **togo.** *v.* To propel (once) by means of a punt pole.
E 1 **toogonga.** *n.* —.
E 2 **togoa.** *v.* —.
E 2 **togolia.** *v.* —.
EE **hagatogo.** *v.* —.
EE1 **hagatoogonga.** *n.* —.
EE2 **hagatogoa.** *v.* —.
EE2 **hagatogolia.** *v.* —.
R **dogodogo.** *v.* —.
R 1 **dogodoganga.** *n.* Plant sp. [archaic name of *manugilimaau*].
R 1 **dogodogonga.** *n.* —.
R 2 **dogodogoa.** *v.* —.
R 2 **dogodogolia.** *v.* —.

R 2 **dogodogona.** *v.* —.
RE **hagadogodogo.** *v.* —.
RE1 **hagadogodogonga.** *n.* —.
RE2 **hagadogodogoa.** *v.* —.
RE2 **hagadogodogolia.** *v.* —.
RE2 **hagadogodogona.** *v.* —.
XCO **dogoduli.** *a.* Crouch on all fours.
ID **dogo duu.** To punt while standing up on the stern gunwales of a canoe.
ID **dogo huadia.** A way of punting a canoe.
ID **luilui togo.** A measurement of land along the shore [in which the chief had rights] using a punt pole.

$DOGO_2$

B **$dogo_2$ + NUMBER.** *mc.* NUMERAL CLASSIFIER FOR PERSONS (by ones).
BE **hagadogo + NUMBER.** *v.* To join (to make up a group of a certain number).
ID **matogo + NUMBER.** [the seating capacity of a canoe].
ID **motogo.** [var. of *matogo*].

$DOGO_{2a}$

B **dogoisi.** *a.* Few.
BE **hagadogoisi.** *v.* Reduce in number, make fewer.
R **dogodogoisi.** *a.* Becoming fewer and fewer.
RE **hagadogodogoisi.** *v.* —.
XCO **dagidogoisi.** *a.* Very few for each one.
ID **dogoisi loo huu.** Very few.
ID **dogoisi mai.** Decreasing (in number).

DOGONOGO

B **dogonogo.** *n.* Tip of the spine (caudal vertebrae).
ID **doo togonogo.** Separation of the tip (caudal vertebrae) of the spine.

DOHA

B **doha.** *v.* To spread out (something).
B 1 **dohaanga.** *n.* —.
B 2 **dohaa.** *v.* —.
B 2 **dohalia.** *v.* —.
BC **madoha.** *a.* To be spread out.
BC1 **madohaanga.** *n.* —.
BE **hagadoha.** *v.* —.
BE1 **hagadohaanga.** *n.* —.
BE2 **hagadohaa.** *v.* —.
BE2 **hagadohalia.** *v.* —.
BF **hagamaadoha.** *v.* —.
BF **hagamadoha.** *v.* —.
BF1 **hagamadohaanga.** *n.* —.
BF2 **hagamadohalia.** *v.* —.
PC **maadoha.** *a.* —.
PC1 **maadohaanga.** *n.* —.
PF1 **hagamaadohaanga.** *n.* —.
PF2 **hagamaadohalia.** *v.* —.
R **dohadoha.** *v.* —.
R 1 **dohadohaanga.** *n.* —.
R 2 **dohadohaa.** *v.* —.
R 2 **dohadohalia.** *v.* —.
RC **madohadoha.** *a.* —.
RC1 **madohadohaanga.** *n.* —.
RE **hagadohadoha.** *v.* —.
RE1 **hagadohadohaanga.** *n.* —.
RE2 **hagadohadohaa.** *v.* —.
RE2 **hagadohadohalia.** *v.* —.
RF **hagamadohadoha.** *v.* —.
RF1 **hagamadohadohaanga.** *n.* —.
RF2 **hagamadohadohalia.** *v.* —.

DOHE

B **dohe.** *n.* Mollusk sp: a bivalve sp.

DOHI

B **dohi.** *d.* —.
B 1 **dòohinga.** *n.* —.
B 2 **doohia.** *v.* —.
BC **madohi.** *a.* Middle (of something long and thin), halfway; to have gone halfway, to reach the halfway point.
BF **hagamadohi.** *v.* —.
BF1 **hagamadohinga.** *n.* —.
E **tohi.** *v.* Make into strips.
PC **maadohi.** *a.* —.
PF **hagamaadohi.** *v.* —.
PF1 **hagamaadohinga.** *n.* —.
R **dohidohi.** *v.* —; divide up.
R 1 **dohidohinga.** *n.* —.
R 2 **dohidohia.** *v.* —.
ID **dohi dilo.** To strip *dilo* (to make plaited hats, etc.).
ID **dohi lau.** To strip pandanus

leaves (to make mats, etc.).
ID **langadala tohi.** A dead coconut leaf torn by the wind [poor for making palm frond thatch].
ID **madohi age.** Reach halfway up.
ID **madohi boo.** Midnight.
ID **madohi iho.** To reach halfway down.
ID **madohi lua.** Middle (of something long and thin), halfway.

DOHU
B **dohu.** *a.* Sufficient, enough; able to cover a given area.
B 1 **doohunga.** *n.* —.
B 2 **dohulia.** *v.* —.
BE **hagadohu.** *v.* —.
BE1 **hagadoohunga.** *n.* —.
BE2 **hagadohua.** *v.* —.
BE2 **hagadohulia.** *v.* —.
R **dohudohu.** *a.* —.
R 1 **dohudohunga.** *n.* —.
RE **hagadohudohu.** *v.* —.
RE1 **hagadohudohunga.** *n.* —.
RE2 **hagadohudohua.** *v.* —.
RE2 **hagadohudohulia.** *v.* —.
ID **dohu ange.** Sufficient for.
ID **dohu de angaanga.** Covered (all over the body) with —.
ID **dohu de gili.** Covered all over (skin) with.
ID **dohu lodo.** Full to capacity.

DOI
B **doi.** *v.* Stain (permanent); any of a number of hardwood saps [found in driftwood] from which perfume is made.
B 1 **doinga.** *n.* —.
BE **hagadoi.** *v.* —; also, = *gadoi.*
BE1 **hagadoinga.** *n.* —.
BE2 **hagadoia.** *v.* —.
R **doidoi.** *v.* —.
R 1 **doidoinga.** *n.* —.
RE **hagadoidoi.** *v.* —.
RE1 **hagadoidoinga.** *n.* —.
RE2 **hagadoidoia.** *v.* —.
XFL **doi-avaava.** *n.* The sap of a hardwood sp. which drifts ashore (used for making perfume).
XFL **doi-giva.** *n.* The sap of a hardwood sp. which drifts ashore [used for making perfume].
XFL **doi-lesi.** *n.* The sap of a hardwood sp. which drifts ashore [used for making perfume].
XFL **laagau-doi.** *n.* A driftwood sp., from the sap of which (*doi*) perfume is made.
CF **hedaadoi.** Collide.

DOI$_a$
XCO **gadoi.** *v.* A type of coconut with an edible husk [the juice of which stains clothes].

DOLA
B **dola.** *a.* Erection (of penis).
B 1 **dolaanga.** *n.* —.
BE **hagadola.** *v.* —.
BE1 **hagadolaanga.** *n.* —.
P **tola.** *a.* —.
P 1 **tolaanga.** *n.* —.
PE **hagatola.** *v.* —.
PE1 **hagatolaanga.** *n.* —.
R **doladola.** *v.* —.
R 1 **doladolaanga.** *n.* —.
RE **hagadoladola.** *v.* —.
RE1 **hagadoladolaanga.** *n.* —.

DOLE
XCO **laudodole.** *n.* Smallness.

DOLI
B **doli.** *v.* To obtain as many as one can; to defeat all comers.
B 1 **dolinga.** *n.* —.
B 2 **dolia.** *v.* —.
BE **hagadoli.** *v.* —.
BE1 **hagadolinga.** *n.* —.
BE2 **hagadolia.** *v.* —.
R **dolidoli.** *v.* —.
R 1 **dolidolinga.** *n.* —.
R 2 **dolidolia.** *v.* —.
RC **madolidoli.** *v.* Of unusual age or size.
RC1 **madolidolinga.** *n.* —.
RC2 **madolidolia.** *a.* Very *madolidoli.*

RE **hagadolidoli.** *v.* —.
RE1 **hagadolidolinga.** *n.* —.
RE2 **hagadolidolia.** *v.* —.
RF **hagamadolidoli.** *v.* —.
RF1 **hagamadolidolinga.** *n.* —.
RF2 **hagamadolidolia.** *v.* —.
ID **dee dolia.** Impossible to find the equal of (*dehors concours*).
ID **doli age.** Obtain the smallest first.
ID **doli de henua.** To defeat all comers.
ID **doli iho.** To obtain the biggest first.

DOLO

B **dolo$_1$.** *a.* Creep (a very slow movement over the ground).
B **dolo$_2$.** *n.* Plant sp.: sugarcane [several varieties].
B 1 **doolonga.** *n.* —; a track left by a crawling thing.
B 1 **ngadoloanga.** *n.* —.
B 2 **dolona.** *v.* Flooded, washed out.
BE **hagadolo.** *v.* —.
BE1 **hagadoloanga.** *n.* —.
BE2 **hagadoloa.** *v.* —.
BE2 **hagadolona.** *v.* —.
E **tolo.** *a.* Crawl.
EE **hagatolo.** *v.* —; slack off on (a rope).
EE1 **hagatoolonga.** *n.* —.
EE2 **hagatoloa.** *v.* —; also, = *hagatolongia.*
EE2 **hagatolongia.** *v.* Slack off completely on (a rope).
R **dolodolo.** *a.* —; logs on the sides of the house floor (to retain gravel); the bulge on the side of a knife blade.
R 1 **dolodolonga.** *n.* —.
R 2 **dolodolona.** *v.* Often flooded.
RE **hagadolodolo.** *v.* —.
RE1 **hagadolodolonga.** *n.* —.
RE2 **hagadolodoloa.** *v.* —.
RE2 **hagadolodolona.** *v.* —.
RE2 **hagadolodolongia.** *v.* Slack off on (a rope) little by little.
XCO **doloinui.** *a.* A hard lump inside a female's stomach [tumor?]; a coconut of the youngest stage of development.
XFL **dolo-mea.** *n.* Spiny starfish.
XFL **haa-dolo.** *n.* Fish sp.: squirrelfish.
XFL **hua-dolo.** *n.* Plant sp.: vine (any sort).
ID **dolo bala.** To climb a coconut tree without using a rope (on one's hands or feet) for assistance.
ID **dolodolo manu ligi.** The physical sensation (like bugs crawling on one) after one's leg, etc., has been asleep.
ID **dolodolo o de ava.** [= *luu dolodolo*].
ID **honu tolo.** A turtle of the largest size.
ID **luu dolodolo.** The phosphorescence on both sides of the atoll channel, marking it at night.
ID **manu dolodolo.** Land animal.
ID **moe dolo.** To sneak into another's house at night for the purpose of having sexual relations.
ID **niho hagadolo.** Incisor teeth.
CF **doolohi.** Chase, run after.
CF **matoloia.** A type of prepared food (made from dried breadfruit).

DOLO$_a$

B **dolo$_3$.** *n.* The name of a name-group.
ID **gubu dolo.** A joint of the sugarcane.

DOLO$_b$

B **ngadolo.** *a.* A landslide or similar movement of things.
BE **hagangadolo.** *v.* —.
BE1 **hagangadoloanga.** *n.* —.

DOLOA

B **doloa.** *n.* The name of a name-group.

DOLU

B **dolu.** *an.* Three.
BE **hagadolu (ina).** *v.* Make a total of three.
XCO **Diba-dolu.** *nn.* The name of a person in a traditional story.
XCO **Tolu-laangi.** *nt.* Wednesday ('third day').
XCO **Tolu-malama.** *nt.* March.
ID **boo dolu de gulu.** The third day after breadfruit has been picked (after which it is not good to eat).
ID **dolu-inoha.** The third number of a counting game played to determine who is "it".

DONA

B **dona.** *v.* Wart, mole (raised).
BE **hagadona.** *v.* —.
R **donadona.** *v.* Covered with *dona.*
RE **hagadonadona.** *v.* —.

DONU$_{1}$

B **donu$_{1}$.** *mv.* Real, really.
XCO **daudonu.** *a.* If, in the case that; gentle, mild-mannered, soft-spoken.
ID **aahee donu.** Exactly which?
ID **abo donu.** Good (not evil or false); real, true; well (not sick); considerate, kind, generous.
ID **alaa donu.** Those there only.
ID **anaa donu.** Those only.
ID **anei donu.** Only these are the ones.
ID **baa donu.** Skillful at fighting (opp. of *baa sala*).
ID **baba donu.** Properly settled.
ID **basa dau donu.** Speak moderately.
ID **bubu donu.** Move skillfully.
ID **daa donu taahili.** Sing on-key.
ID **daane abo donu.** Gentleman, person who is good.
ID **dahulihuli donu.** Be careful! [said to someone going fishing].
ID **dama donu.** A natural child.
ID **daumaha hagatoo donu.** Church service of dedication (in which the members renew their vows).
ID **deai donu.** None at all.
ID **dee daea donu.** Unexpectedly.
ID **dee haihai donu.** That's for sure!
ID **delaa donu.** That there is it for sure!
ID **denaa donu.** That is it for sure!
ID **denei donu.** This is it for sure!
ID **dinana donu.** Natural mother.
ID **donu huu.** Only, just (no more than).
ID **duu donu.** Vertical.
ID **too donu.** Certain, sure, graceful, definitely.
ID **gi hanu donu huu.** Any kind whatsoever.
ID **gu soe donu.** Unmistakably, for certain.
ID **kaba donu.** Wait!
ID **kau donu.** Used to, easy to.
ID **hagapago donu.** Fortunate result.
ID **hagatoo donu.** Promise, contract with; swear to the truth of.
ID **hai donu.** Do properly by accident; do on purpose [when precededed by *se*].
ID **hooia donu huu.** At the best possible time or place.
ID **iainei donu.** Right now!
ID **me abo donu.** Real, true.
ID **muna abo donu.** Truth.
ID **noho dau donu.** Sit quietly.
ID **noho donu.** Properly situated or loaded (of a canoe).

DONU$_{1a}$

B **donu$_{2}$.** *a.* Understand; truth, right, correct.
B 1 **doonunga.** *n.* —.
BE **hagadonu.** *v.* Trust,

believe; interpret; support as a witness.
BE1 **hagadoonunga.** *n.* —; meaning.
BE2 **hagadonusia.** *v.* —.
P **tonu.** *a.* —.
R **donudonu.** *a.* Understand somewhat.
R 1 **donudonuanga.** *n.* —.
RE **hagadonudonu.** *v.* —.
RE1 **hagadonudonuanga.** *n.* —.
RE2 **hagadonudonusia.** *v.* —.
XCO **duadonu.** *a.* Luck, good fortune.
XCO **hulidonu.** *a.* Right side out (clothes).
XCO **maanetonu.** *a.* Act cautiously.
ID **donu ange.** Understand (someone or something).
ID **donu gee.** Misunderstand.
ID **donu iho.** Realize, understand.
ID **donu sala.** Misunderstand.
ID **hagadonu muna.** Act as an interpreter.
ID **sele gi tonu.** Make sure of.

DONU$_2$
B **donu$_3$.** *n.* Fish sp.: sea bass (= small *ava*).

DONGA
B **donga.** *n.* Plant sp.: oriental mangrove (*Bruguiera gymnorhiza* (L.) Lam.).

DONGI
B **dongi.** *v.* A spot (e.g., on the skin); point at; peck at; a method of fishing for flying fish in which torches are extinguished on alternate legs of the canoe track.
B 1 **doonginga.** *n.* —.
B 2 **dongia.** *v.* —.
BE **hagadongi.** *v.* —.
BE1 **hagadonginga.** *n.* —.
BE2 **hagadongia.** *v.* —.
R **dongidongi.** *v.* Spotted (covered with spots); to keep pointing at or peeking at.
R 1 **dongidonginga.** *n.* —.
R 2 **dongidongia.** *v.* —.
RE **hagadongidongi.** *v.* —.
RE1 **hagadongidonginga.** *n.* —.
RE2 **hagadongidongia.** *v.* —.
ID **dongi ange.** Appoint.
ID **dongi de gelegele.** To peck at the sand (as do some kinds of fish when they are searching for food).
ID **dongi de lae.** A spot on the forehead [worn in ancient religious ceremonies].

DOO$_1$
B **doo$_1$.** *v.* Get down, get off; take up a string figure (from another's hands); fall; plant (something); drop down.
B 1 **dooanga.** *n.* —; row of plants.
B 2 **dooa.** *v.* Planted.
BE **hagadoo.** *v.* —.
BE1 **hagadooanga.** *n.* —.
BE2 **hagadooa.** *v.* —.
P **too.** *a.* —; be the loser (because of someone's actions).
P 1 **tooanga.** *n.* —.
PE **hagatoo.** *v.* —.
PE1 **hagatooanga.** *n.* —.
PE2 **hagatooa.** *v.* —.
R **doodoo.** *v.* —.
R 1 **doodooanga.** *n.* —.
RE **hagadoodoo.** *v.* —.
RE1 **hagadoodooanga.** *n.* —.
RE2 **hagadoodooa.** *v.* —.
XCO **hagadaudoo.** *a.* Compete to see who is stronger.
ID **bakau doo.** A dislocation of the shoulder joint.
ID **basa too gee.** Speak ungrammatically.
ID **dama doo.** A foetus which has been aborted.
ID **daumaha hagatoo donu.** Church service of dedication (in which the members renew their vows).
ID **doo dai.** Appearing from lagoonward; to come from lagoonward; wind direction from the west.
ID **doo de —.** Transfer of a string figure from hand to hand.
ID **doo de gai me.** Miss a meal

or meals (leading to nausea when eating is resumed).
ID **doo de gauanga.** Dislocated thigh bone.
ID **doo de gulabe.** Prolapsed rectum.
ID **doo de hatuli.** The 'falling of thunder' [thought to burn trees].
ID **doo de ssui.** Still damp (but becoming dry).
ID **doo togonogo.** Separation of the tip (caudal vertebrae) of the spine.
ID **doo tuugau.** A dislocation of the *tuugau*.
ID **doo gaiaa.** Atack by surprise or stealth; ambush.
ID **doo halehale me.** Risky, unreliable.
ID **doo i de....** Expulsion or voluntary withdrawal (from a group).
ID **doo i de ubu.** Too big in size (of clothes).
ID **doo i hainga a me.** Wait for a long time (beyond the time expected).
ID **doo lalo.** Unsuccessful.
ID **doo lodolodo.** Risky, unreliable.
ID **doo ma gu....** Fall into the bad habit of; do something which is difficult to rectify.
ID **doo mai de malino.** Completely calm.
ID **doo me.** Plant things.
ID **doo mua.** Very.
ID **doo ngaage.** South wind.
ID **doo ngaiho.** The blowing of the wind from the north.
ID **doo sala.** Accidentally.
ID **tangada dee doo gi de me.** Uncouth person.
ID **too donu.** Certain, sure, graceful, definitely.
ID **too gee.** Clumsy, unskillful, awkward (not dexterous).
ID **too geegee.** Happening at different times or places.
ID **too gili.** Wrinkled skin (from age).
ID **too luu bakau.** Extremely tired.
ID **eu doo.** A dislocation of the shoulder joint.
ID **hagadau doo.** To transfer a string figure from one person's fingers to another's.
ID **hagadoo dai.** To fish off the reef for tuna.
ID **hagadoodoo denga muna.** Boast foolishly about one's ability (when it is obvious that one is inept).
ID **hagatoo donu.** Promise, contract with; swear to the truth of.
ID **hagatoo mua.** Take every possible precaution, insure.
ID **saabai moni doo.** Carry a canoe (over the reef at low tide).
ID **vai doo.** Waterfall.
CF **doonga.** Tools, equipment (incl. fishing gear).

DOO$_2$

B **doo$_2$.** *n.* An evil scheme.
ID **doo ai me.** [= *doo me ai*].
ID **doo tahulinga.** Bad-mannered.
ID **doo me (ai).** Make fun of, ridicule.
ID **gadagada doo me.** Laugh at.
ID **hai dahi doo.** Trick someone.

DOOPEVA

B **doopeva.** *v.* Trick, prank.
BE **hagadoopeva.** *v.* Play a trick on.

DOOKALALA

B **dookalala.** *a.* Stilts, walk on stilts.
BE **hagadookalala.** *v.* —.

DOOLOHI

B **doolohi.** *v.* Chase, run after.
B 1 **doolohinga.** *n.* —.
B 2 **dolohia.** *v.* —.
BE **hagadoolohi.** *v.* —.
BE1 **hagadoolohinga.** *n.* —.

BE2 **hagadoolohia.** *v.* —.
R **dolodolohi.** *v.* —.
R 1 **dolodolohinga.** *n.* —.
R 2 **dolodolohia.** *v.* —.
RE **hagadolodolohi.** *v.* —.
RE1 **hagadolodolohinga.** *n.* —.
RE2 **hagadolodolohia.** *v.* —.
ID **hagadau doolohi.** Chase each other.

DOONGA

B **doonga.** *n.* Tools, equipment (incl. fishing gear).
ID **doonga a lima.** One's own tools, or tools with which one is familiar.
ID **doonga pada.** Heavy-duty equipment or fishing gear; a large penis.

DUA$_1$

B **dua$_1$.** *n.* Diameter (of rope, etc.).
BE **hagadua.** *d.* To coil or plait using — [number of] strands; change the size of.
XCO **duaanui.** *n.* Coconut palm frond spines.
XG **gede dua dahi.** A type of basket.
ID **basa dua nnui.** Speak undiplomatically.
ID **daia e tuaadai.** Seasick.
ID **dua alohagi.** Fishing line of a size appropriate for trolling.
ID **dua pada.** To plait with thick strands.
ID **dua daabasi.** The size of fishing line appropriate for tuna fishing.
ID **dua duiagi.** Fishing line of the largest size (on which a whole *belubelu* is used as bait).
ID **dua gaahanga.** One of the lines of which *gaahanga* is composed).
ID **dua gi lunga.** Thicker (line or rope, etc.).
ID **dua gina.** Fishing line of a size appropriate for *gina* fishing.
ID **dua haangoda de boo.** Fishing line of a size appropriate for *haangoda de boo.*
ID **dua hagalalo.** Fishing line of a size appropriate for the *hagalalo* method of fishing.
ID **dua lligi.** Thin (line or rope, etc.); fine (thread, etc.); tenderly.
ID **dua nnui.** Violence; a type of rope (thick, with thick strands).
ID **dua saali.** One of the lines of which *saali* is composed.
ID **gai mamu dua nnui.** To eat fish up (not saving any for later).
ID **hai me dua nnui.** Do violently.

DUA$_2$

B **dua$_2$.** *nl.* Away from; in back of; after; back (of the body).
XCO **duaahaho.** *nl.* Outside of (e.g., a building).
XCO **duadae.** *v.* Gullible, be a sucker.
XCO **duadonu.** *a.* Luck, good fortune.
XCO **duasala.** *a.* Hardship, difficulty.
XCO **duasivi.** *n.* The back of the spine.
XE **hagaduasala.** *v.* Suffer, punish.
ID **ago i tua.** Learn by heart.
ID **anga dua.** An adze blade which is set at a right angle to its handle.
ID **bangi dua beau.** A certain way of pinching with the fingers.
ID **boo gi dua.** The period when the quarter moon appears in the east just before sunrise.
ID **dangada duaagau.** An avid fisherman.
ID **dangage dua.** Bend one's head backwards.
ID **daohi i tua.** Learn by heart.
ID **dau duadae.** Be a sucker, be fooled easily.
ID **dau i tua.** Memorize.
ID **duaa dai.** Seasick but

unable to throw up.

ID **duaa dodo.** Labor pains (of a woman in childbirth).

ID **dua agau.** Beyond the reef, pertaining to the open sea, — like to fish [ds].

ID **dua dama.** The pallor of a female following childbirth.

ID **dua lele.** To throw one's back out of joint.

ID **Dua-nei.** Of or from the Marshall islands [ds].

ID **tua de baba.** Lower back (of a human).

ID **tugi dua.** Go backwards.

ID **gogo dua.** Bent backwards.

ID **haangoda dua agau.** Fishing beyond the reef (on the seaward side of the atoll).

ID **haangoda dua beau.** A fishing method (used on the seaward reef during the day) employing a line, with hermit crabs for bait).

ID **hagammene dua.** Go backwards (esp. a canoe).

ID **hanohano dua.** Suffer a setback; almost fall; gorge oneself; stagger backwards (e.g., under load).

ID **io dua.** The upper *io*.

ID **laa tua.** Besides.

ID **lele tua.** To pull a back muscle (or pinch a nerve?) and thus collapse.

ID **maagaga dua.** To walk with one's shoulders unnaturally thrown back.

ID **maalama dua de laa.** The light remaining after sunset.

ID **ma tua.** Besides.

ID **savini dua.** Run backwards, move backwards fast.

DUAGI

B **duagi.** *v.* To clean fish (taking the insides out).

B 1 **duaginga.** *n.* —.

B 2 **duagia.** *v.* —.

B 2 **duagina.** *v.* —.

BE **hagaduagi.** *v.* —.

BE1 **hagaduaginga.** *n.* —.

BE2 **hagaduagia.** *v.* —.

BE2 **hagaduagina.** *v.* —.

R **duuduagi.** *v.* —.

R 1 **duuduaginga.** *n.* —.

R 2 **duuduagia.** *v.* —.

R 2 **duuduagina.** *v.* —.

RE **hagaduuduagi.** *v.* —.

RE1 **hagaduuduaginga.** *n.* —.

RE2 **hagaduuduagia.** *v.* —.

RE2 **hagaduuduagina.** *v.* —.

DUAI$_1$

B **duai$_1$.** *a.* Old (in the past).

BE **hagaduai.** *v.* Cause to be worn out.

DUAI$_2$

B **duai$_2$.** *n.* Stool grater (for grating coconuts).

XG **duai lalo vae.** A type of coconut grater which is placed under the leg.

ID **hakaa tuai.** To sharpen a coconut grater blade.

ID **ma tuai.** Coconut grater blade.

DUBA

B **duba.** *n.* Land crab sp. (small).

DUBE

B **dube.** *a.* Movements perceived under the covers; the swarming of maggots in meat.

B 1 **dubenga.** *n.* —.

B 2 **dubea.** *v.* —.

BE **hagadube.** *v.* —.

BE1 **hagadubenga.** *n.* —.

BE2 **hagadubea.** *v.* —.

R **dubedube.** *a.* —.

R 1 **dubedubenga.** *n.* —.

R 2 **dubedubea.** *v.* —.

RE **hagadubedube.** *v.* —.

RE1 **hagadubedubenga.** *n.* —.

RE2 **hagadubedubea.** *v.* —.

DUBU

B **dubu.** *a.* Exceed (the amount required), too — (e.g., many).

B 1 **dubuanga.** *n.* —.
B 1 **duubunga.** *n.* —.
B 2 **dubua.** *v.* —; a person of extraordinary ability.
B 2 **dubulia.** *v.* —.
BE **hagadubu.** *v.* —; respect (someone); make a string figure; transfigure.
BE1 **hagaduubunga.** *n.* —.
BE2 **hagadubua.** *v.* —.
BE2 **hagadubulia.** *v.* —.
P **tubu.** *a.* —.
PE **hagatubu.** *v.* —; exaggerate.
PE1 **hagatubuanga.** *n.* —.
PE2 **hagatubua.** *v.* —.
PE2 **hagatubulia.** *v.* —.
R **dubudubu.** *a.* —.
R 1 **dubudubuanga.** *n.* —.
R 2 **dubudubua.** *v.* —.
R 2 **dubudubulia.** *v.* —.
RE **hagadubudubu.** *v.* —.
RE1 **hagadubudubuanga.** *n.* —.
RE2 **hagadubudubua.** *v.* —.
RE2 **hagadubudubulia.** *v.* —.
ID **hagadubu dinae.** The name of a certain type of string figure.
ID **hagadubu gina.** The name of a certain type of string figure.
ID **hagadubu gi se —.** Transfigure into a —.
ID **hagadubu hue vini.** The name of a certain type of string figure.
ID **hagadubu maduu paa.** The name of a certain type of string figure.
ID **hagadubu manu baabaa.** The name of a certain type of string figure.
ID **hagadubu mangoo.** The name of a certain type of string figure.
ID **hagadubu o de adu.** The name of a certain type of string figure.
ID **hagadubu o de ahi.** The name of a certain type of string figure.
ID **hagadubu o de moe.** The name of a certain type of string figure.
ID **hagadubu o madaligi.** The name of a certain type of string figure.
ID **hagadubu o manu.** The name of a certain type of string figure.
ID **hagatubu me.** Exaggerate matters.
ID **hai hagadubu.** To fashion a string figure.

DUBUNA
B **dubuna.** *n.* Grandparent, ancestor.
BE **hagadubuna.** *v.* Treat as *dubuna.*
ID **hai dubuna.** The relationship between grandparent and grandchild.

DUDU
B **dudu.** *v.* Set fire to, burn.
B 1 **duudunga.** *n.* —.
B 2 **duungia.** *v.* —.
R **dutudu.** *v.* Play with fire.
R 1 **dutuduanga.** *n.* —.
ID **dudu de niho.** A method of treating toothaches in which a burning root (of the *aoa* tree) is applied to the tooth (which later disintegrates).
ID **hala dudu.** A noise like that of burning pandanus (loud crackling).
ID **manu dudu dangada.** Insect sp. (= *manu-de-laama*) [poisonous].

DUGE
B **duge.** *n.* Either side of a recession in the top of a *duludulu.*
ID **madaa duge.** The tip of a *duge.*
ID **ma te duge.** The point of a *madaa duge.*

DUGI$_1$
B **dugi$_1$.** *d.* Punch, hit, strike; bump into; pound —, pound on.
B 1 **duuginga.** *n.* —.
B 2 **duugia.** *v.* —; tired of.
BE **hagadugi$_1$.** *v.* —.

BE1 **hagaduuginga.** *n.* —.
BE2 **hagaduugia.** *v.* —.
E **tugi.** *v.* .
ED **hetugi.** *a.* Meet by chance, encounter.
ED1 **hetugianga.** *n.* —.
EE **hagatugi.** *v.* —.
EG **hagahetugi.** *v.* —.
EG1 **hagahetugianga.** *n.* —.
R **dugidugi$_1$.** *v.* —.
R 1 **dugiduginga$_1$.** *n.* —.
R 2 **dugidugia$_1$.** *v.* —.
RE **hagadugidugi$_1$.** *v.* —.
RE1 **hagadugiduginga$_1$.** *n.* —.
RE2 **hagadugidugia$_1$.** *v.* —.
XCO **dugilima.** *n.* Elbow.
XFL **ulu-dugi.** *n.* Fish sp.: hawk fish.
ID **ahi tugi.** Ignite a fire by making sparks with a stone.
ID **baalanga tugi.** Nail (of metal).
ID **baasanga tugi ange muna.** Talk back.
ID **boi dugidugi.** Idiot.
ID **dugi de lodo.** To fish in various places (in the lagoon) in order to catch as many fish (of any kind) as possible.
ID **duugia i de gai.** Be tired of eating a particular kind of food.
ID **tugi ange —.** Contradict by —.
ID **tugi dua.** Go backwards.
ID **tugi taaea.** A fishing method (using hermit crabs for bait).
ID **haangoda dugidugi.** A method of fishing (night fishing outside the reef, using hermit crabs for bait).
ID **hagadau tugi.** Punch each other.
ID **hagaoda tugi.** A type of prepared food (made from mashed taro and grated coconut).
ID **moana dugidugi.** Far from any land, in the open sea.
ID **nnamu hagaduugia.** Stench.
CF **heduge.** Slate-pencil urchin.

DUGI$_2$

B **dugi$_2$.** *v.* Scare away, chase away.
B 1 **duginga.** *n.* —.
B 2 **dugia.** *v.* —.
B 2 **dugina.** *v.* —.
BE **hagadugi$_2$.** *v.* —.
BE1 **hagaduginga.** *n.* —.
BE2 **hagadugia.** *v.* —.
BE2 **hagadugina.** *v.* —.
R **dugidugi$_2$.** *v.* —.
R 1 **dugiduginga$_2$.** *n.* —.
R 2 **dugidugia$_2$.** *v.* —.
R 2 **dugidugina.** *v.* —.
RE **hagadugidugi$_2$.** *v.* —.
RE1 **hagadugiduginga$_2$.** *n.* —.
RE2 **hagadugidugia$_2$.** *v.* —.
RE2 **hagadugidugina.** *v.* —.
ID **dugi gee.** Chase away (in a certain direction).

DUGU

B **dugu.** *v.* Put, place [verb]; leave (put down).
B 1 **duugunga.** *n.* —.
B 2 **dugua.** *v.* —.
B 2 **dugulia.** *v.* —.
E **tugu.** *a.* Crouch.
E 1 **tugunga.** *n.* —.
EE **hagatugu.** *v.* Crouch down.
EE1 **hagatuguanga.** *n.* —.
EE2 **hagatugulia.** *v.* —.
R **dugudugu.** *v.* —.
R 1 **dugudugunga.** *n.* —.
R 2 **dugudugua.** *v.* —.
R 2 **dugudugulia.** *v.* —.
RE **hagadugudugu.** *v.* Crouch repeatedly.
ID **dugu dagidahi.** Place (or leave off) one at a time.
ID **dugu dahi.** Accomplish or complete something in a single effort; fishing with a single line.
ID **dugu de gubenga.** Set a *gubenga* net.
ID **dugu de gumigumi.** Allow one's beard to grow, unshaven.
ID **dugu de laa.** Lower sail.
ID **dugu de uinga.** To lay down a new cover of palm fronds on *uinga.*
ID **dugudugu iho.** A technique of massage.

ID **dugu gee.** Put aside, set aside; treat (a person) differently from others.

ID **duugunga o de henua.** Customs of the island (Nukuoro).

ID **hagadugu lalo.** Self-deprecatory, downgrade.

ID **hagatugu tai.** Ebbing of tide.

DUGU$_a$

B **duguagi.** *v.* Be suspicious of (someone).

B 1 **duguaginga.** *n.* —.

BE **hagaduguagi.** *v.* —.

BE1 **hagaduguaginga.** *n.* —.

R **duguduguagi.** *v.* —.

R 1 **duguduguaginga.** *n.* —.

RE1 **hagaduguduguaginga.** *n.* —.

DUHA

B **duha.** *v.* Divide among, division (in arithmetic).

B 1 **duuhanga.** *n.* —.

B 2 **duhalia.** *v.* —.

B 2 **duuhaa.** *v.* —.

R **duhaduha.** *v.* —.

R 1 **duhaduhanga.** *n.* —.

DUHI

E **tuhi.** *v.* Praise (someone), honor.

E 1 **duuhinga.** *n.* —.

E 2 **duuhia.** *v.* —.

ID **duuhia ange.** Praised (by others).

ID **tuhi hagadegi.** Praise with all one's heart (esp. God).

ID **tuhi iho.** Praise oneself.

DUI

B **dui.** *v.* Stab with a sharp object, pierce with a sharp object, sew, string (flowers or fish, etc.); straight course (of a canoe).

B 1 **duinga.** *n.* —; seam (in clothes).

B 2 **duia.** *v.* —.

B 3 **duiaanga.** *n.* The way in which something is stuck by a sharp object.

BE **hagadui.** *v.* —; to lean way over in order to observe.

BE1 **hagaduinga.** *n.* —.

BE2 **hagaduia.** *v.* —.

BE3 **hagaduiaanga.** *n.* —.

PE **hagatui.** *a.* [pl. of *hagadui* — 'observe' sense only].

PE1 **hagatuinga.** *n.* —.

PE2 **hagatuia.** *v.* —.

R **duidui.** *v.* —.

R 1 **duiduinga.** *n.* —.

R 2 **duiduia.** *v.* —; covered with sharp spines, etc.

RE **hagaduidui.** *a.* To move about (leaning way over) in order to observe.

RE1 **hagaduiduinga.** *n.* —.

RE2 **hagaduiduia.** *v.* —.

ID **dui mamu.** A string of fish.

ID **dui manu.** A line of flying birds.

ID **dui moni.** A fleet of canoes (in line).

ID **manava duuia.** Nervous, apprehensive (suddenly).

ID **moni dui.** A canoe rigged for casting for tuna.

DUI$_a$

B **duiagi.** *v.* Fishing using a whole fish as bait.

B 1 **duiaginga.** *n.* —.

B 2 **duiagina.** *v.* —.

BE **hagaduiagi.** *v.* —.

BE1 **hagaduiaginga.** *n.* —.

BE2 **hagaduiagina.** *v.* —.

XG **maadau duiagi.** A fishhook of a special type (for *duiagi* fishing).

ID **dua duiagi.** Fishing line of the largest size (on which a whole *belubelu* is used as bait).

ID **uga duiagi.** The fishing line used in *duiagi* fishing.

DUILAA

B **duilaa.** *v.* To be unable to attract members of the opposite sex.

B 1 **duilaanga.** *n.* —.

BE **hagaduilaa.** *v.* —.

BE1 **hagaduilaanga.** *n.* —.

ID **duilaa gee.** To be

exceedingly unsuccessful with members of the opposite sex.

DULAGI

B **dulagi.** *n.* Appearance, example, situation.
BE **hagadulagi.** *v.* Imitate, illustrate, give an example; fashion something to be like something else.
BE1 **hagadulagianga.** *n.* —.
ID **dulagi ange.** Look like.
ID **dulagi be —.** It seems that —.
ID **dulagi daudahi.** Alike (in appearance).
ID **dulagi sala.** Bad situation; presenting a poor appearance (esp. when ill).

DULI$_1$

R **duliduli.** *v.* Hurting of one's ears from high-pitched noises.
R 1 **duliduliNga.** *n.* —.
R 2 **dulidulia.** *v.* —.
RE **hagaduliduli.** *v.* —.
RE1 **hagaduliduliNga.** *n.* —.
RE2 **hagadulidulia.** *v.* —.

DULI$_2$

B **duli$_2$.** *n.* Knee.
XCO **dogoduli.** *a.* Crouch on all fours.
ID **duu duli.** Kneel.
ID **lele tuli.** Parturition.

DULI$_3$

B **duli$_1$.** *n.* Bird sp.: golden plover (*Plurialis dominica*).
XCO **dulivai.** *n.* A type of coconut (reddish in color).
ID **vele duli.** Pull by the hair (in fighting).

DULU

E **tulu.** *a.* Ooze a lot at one time.
E 1 **tuluanga.** *n.* —.
EE **hagatulu.** *v.* —.
EE1 **hagatuluanga.** *n.* —.
R **duludulu.** *d.* Ooze.
R 1 **duluduluanga.** *n.* —.
RE **hagadulududulu.** *v.* —.
RE1 **hagaduluduluanga.** *n.* —.
ID **hagatulu mai.** Ooze out.

DUMANU

B **dumanu.** *n.* Appearance, situation.
BE **hagadumanu.** *v.* Cause to look like.
ID **dumanu sala.** Bad situation; poor in appearance.

DUMUAGI

B **dumuagi.** *n.* Top of the head, bare hilltop.
ID **sula tumuagi.** Bald-headed.

DUMULU

B **Dumulu.** *n.* July.

DUNA

B **duna.** *n.* Larvae (of mosquito, etc.) found in water.

DUNU$_1$

B **dunu$_1$.** *v.* Cook, heat up; boil (water).
B 1 **duunanga.** *n.* —; that which has been cooked.
B 2 **duunaa.** *v.* —.
BE **hagadunu.** *v.* —.
R **dunudunu.** *v.* —.
ID **dunu madamada.** Rare (not cooked thoroughly).
ID **hidi de mamu dunu.** Curling up of fish (when cooked).

DUNU$_2$

B **dunu$_2$.** *n.* A hole in the base of a coconut tree trunk (which collects water for drinking).

DUNGAGI

B **dungagi.** *v.* Nod (one's head).
B 1 **dungaginga.** *n.* —.
BE **hagadungagi.** *v.* —.
R **dungadungagi.** *v.* —.
R 1 **dungadungaginga.** *n.* —.
RE **hagadungadungagi.** *v.* —.
RE1 **hagadungadungaginga.** *n.* —.
ID **dungagi ange.** Nod one's

head toward (to beckon or indicate agreement, etc.).

DUNGU

B **dungu.** *v.* Smell (something).
B 1 **dunguanga.** *n.* —.
B 2 **dungua.** *v.* —.
B 2 **dungulia.** *v.* —.
BE **hagadungu.** *v.* Smell something purposively.
BE1 **hagadunguanga.** *n.* —.
BE2 **hagadungua.** *v.* —.
BE2 **hagadungulia.** *v.* —.
R **dungudungu.** *v.* Have a good sense of smell.
R 1 **dungudunguanga.** *n.* —.
R 2 **dungudungua.** *v.* Repeatedly smell (something).
R 2 **dungudungulia.** *v.* —.
RE **hagadungudungu.** *v.* —.
RE1 **hagadungudunguanga.** *n.* —.
RE2 **hagadungudungua.** *v.* —.
RE2 **hagadungudungulia.** *v.* —.
ID **dungu iho.** Smell oneself.

DUOI

B **duoi.** *n.* Parasites (intestinal) of fish.

DUOSI

B **duosi.** *a.* Servant.
BE **hagaduosi.** *v.* —.

DUU$_1$

B **duu$_1$.** *d.* —.
B 1 **duudanga.** *n.* —; (a big) piece of; verse (of a song).
B 2 **duudia.** *v.* —.
E **tuu$_1$.** *v.* Cut (something).
R **duuduu$_1$.** *v.* —.
R 1 **duuduudanga.** *n.* —.
R 2 **duuduudia.** *v.* —.
ID **daula duu nui.** A rope used to lower a bunch of coconuts to the ground.
ID **duu biho.** Haircut; cut hair.
ID **duudanga aheahe.** Refrain (of song).
ID **duudangaa solo.** A package of *solo* (food) wrapped in coconut leaves and heated; flashlight battery.
ID **duudanga daahili.** Verse of a song.
ID **duu de —$_1$.** Having plenty of.
ID **duu de ogaanga.** Having husked many coconuts (as evidenced by the many husks lying about).
ID **duu taelodo.** Obtain one's quota.
ID **duu gaha.** A large piece of *gaha* (used for *mili gaadinga*), or from which sennit fibers are obtained).
ID **duu galeve.** To collect the sap of a coconut tree (from its inflorescence).
ID **duu modu.** Vertical cut.
ID **duu nui.** To lower a bunch of cut coconuts from a coconut tree with a rope.
ID **tuu daga holiage.** Circumcise.
ID **tuu de biigi.** To castrate a pig.
ID **tuu de galeve.** Make palm toddy.
ID **tuu dege.** Having corners, square, rectangular.
ID **tuu taalonga.** To escape (of fish, after having been speared).
ID **tuu todo.** Stop bleeding.
ID **tuu hagalele.** Stop suddenly; cut suddenly.
ID **tuu mai.** Limit, discontinue, shorten (by cutting off one end).
ID **goloa duu biho.** Barber's tools.
ID **hale duu biho.** Barber shop.
ID **molimoli i tuu gaha.** To express coconut oil out of the residue (*oda*) from which some oil has already been expressed.

DUU$_{1a}$

B **duu$_3$.** *n.* Half (of something like a coconut).
XCO **uduu.** *n.* A half shell, a cover (of something).
XG **gede maduu.** A type of basket.

ID **duu baeao.** Piece of coconut husk.
ID **duu dalo.** Piece of soft taro.
ID **duu hakaa.** A piece of coconut husk.
ID **duu inai.** A type of mat [a half *inai*].
ID **duu mugamuga.** Half of an unripe coconut; buttock.
ID **duunga gima.** Half of a clam shell.
ID **duu ngavesi.** A cover of a box.
ID **duu ubu haohao.** A piece of taro cooked in a coconut shell with coconut oil.
ID **luu duu.** Covers (of books), two halves.
ID **luu duu de maduu.** Castes (two) of aboriginal Nukuoro society.
CF **duu beleala.** Immature coconut apple.

DUU$_2$
B **duu$_2$.** *v.* Stand, situated; married.
B 1 **duuanga.** *n.* —.
B 1 **duulanga$_2$.** *n.* The place of, the track of (something).
B 2 **duua.** *v.* —.
B 2 **duulia$_1$.** *v.* —.
BE **hagaduu.** *v.* —; construct, set up, build (something).
BE1 **hagaduuanga.** *n.* —.
BE1 **hagaduulanga.** *n.* Method of construction; appearance (e.g., of a ship, house, or other construction).
BE2 **hagaduua.** *v.* —.
BE2 **hagaduulia.** *v.* —.
P **tuu$_2$.** *v.* —.
R **duuduu$_2$.** *v.* Stand around (idly); defecate [baby talk]; hillock, high.
R 1 **duuduuanga.** *n.* —.
R 2 **duuduua.** *v.* —; taro plot.
R 2 **duuduulia$_1$.** *v.* —.
RE **hagaduuduu.** *v.* —; stand on tiptoes, rise up (as a person does).
RE1 **hagaduuduuanga.** *n.* —.
RE1 **hagaduuduulanga.** *n.* A style of construction (consistently followed).
RE2 **hagaduuduua.** *v.* —.
RE2 **hagaduuduulia.** *v.* —.
XCO **duubulei.** *n.* Head of the penis.
XCO **duugau.** *n.* Legs at the base of the canoe mast.
XCO **uaduu.** *n.* Waterspout (esp. full of water) [meterological condition].
XFL **dabaduu.** *n.* Fish sp.: (a small *suulee* or a var. of *suulee*).
XFL **duu-baeao.** *n.* Fish sp.: filefish.
XFL **duudua-a-de-honu.** *n.* Seaweed sp.
XFL **duu-hakaa.** *n.* Fish sp. (var. of *duubaeao*).
XFL **duu-lellele.** *n.* Apodous sea cucumber.
XFL **duu-mmea.** *n.* Sea cucumber sp.
XFL **duu-uli.** *n.* Sea cucumber sp.
ID **daane mada duulanga.** A person able to do things others cannot.
ID **dogo duu.** To punt while standing up on the stern gunwales of a canoe.
ID **duu ange.** Wait for; resemble someone (owing to a consanguineal relationship).
ID **duu baebae.** To appear in the distance as a row of small objects (like adjacent islets on the atoll).
ID **duu bale.** Not quite vertical.
ID **duu podo.** Do something at short intervals; often, frequently.
ID **duu de —$_2$.** Make a string figure.
ID **duu de gona.** Umbilical hernia.
ID **duu de umada.** A rainbow appearing in the sky.
ID **duu donu.** Vertical.
ID **duu duli.** Kneel.
ID **duuduu lagi.** A diving platform (made from a tree stuck in a coral head).

ID duuduu manu. A diving platform (made from a tree stuck in a coral head).
ID duu taua. Outbreak of war.
ID duu gaso. Vertical, straight up and down.
ID duu gee. Out of alignment.
ID duu gili somo. The coconut meat remaining in a germinated coconut after the coconut apple has been removed.
ID duu keli. Firmly in place, earnestly.
ID duu kolu. Stand bracing oneself.
ID duu hagasabasaba. To stand in a place from which one is liable to fall.
ID duu i de liiliagi. Equal in status [owing to having the same skills and being of common descent].
ID duu lua. To have the strength or capacity of two persons; to take on two persons in a fight.
ID duu malaelae. An open field (having no trees).
ID duu midomido. An abrupt stop of a trajectory (because one end of the missile has dug into the ground, etc.).
ID duu molomolo. Visible clearly.
ID duu munimuni. Hide and seek (a game).
ID duu-o-de-hine. Anything sticky which pulls apart like jelly (applied to certain kinds of sea cucumbers, etc.).
ID duu saba. Unstable, poorly balanced.
ID tuugau i daha. Clitoris.
ID tuugau i lodo. Cervix.
ID tuu gili. Gooseflesh, disgusted, horror-fascination.
ID tuu uaua. Dilated veins.
ID hagaduu dala. Angry and ready to fight.
ID hagaduu de uinga. To place stakes on the sides of *uinga*.
ID hagaduu eidu. Superstitious; to believe in ghosts.
ID hagaduu gaiaa. Suspicious by nature.
ID hagaduu me. Miserly.
ID hagaduu ngae. Earnestly; to the limits of one's capacity; struggle (e.g., to complete work).
ID hagaduu ngavesi. Make boxes.
ID hagaduu ssaalanga. Search intently for.
ID hai duu. To carry a baby about.
ID mada duulanga. An important position (spatially).
ID me duu. Clitoris.
ID ngadi duu. Naked.
CF duudane. Buttock.
CF duudua. Taro plot.
CF duugiva. Rough texture, of a plaited object (such as a mat).
CF duuhuli. A type of wave [must be followed either by *ina*, or by another base].
CF duulale. A type of game.
CF duulua. Fish sp.: jack (= large *alaala*).
CF duumono. A type of prepared food (made from taro).
CF duusaba. A type of musical instrument (a stretched palm leaf jiggled while blown against).
CF gabaduu. To sail a canoe against the wind; paddle or pole a canoe against the current.
CF heduu. Star, planet.
CF suuduuduu. Defecate [children's language].

DUU2a
B duuhua. *a.* Single, unmarried.
BE hagaduuhua. *v.* —.
ID (de) hine duuhua. Unmarried girl.

DUU2b
B duula. *n.* The direction

from which the wind blows.

B 1 **duulanga₁.** *n.* The sector from which the wind blows.

ID **hhao tuula.** To sail so as to fill one's sails with wind (sailing crosswind).

DUU$_{2c}$

B **duulagi.** *v.* To sail crosswind (for maximum speed).

B 1 **duulaginga.** *n.* —.

B 2 **duulagia.** *v.* —.

B 2 **duulagina.** *v.* —.

BE **hagaduulagi.** *v.* —.

BE1 **hagaduulaginga.** *n.* —.

BE2 **hagaduulagia.** *v.* —.

BE2 **hagaduulagina.** *v.* —.

R **duuduulagi.** *v.* —.

R 1 **duuduulaginga.** *n.* —.

R 2 **duuduulagia.** *v.* —.

R 2 **duuduulagina.** *v.* —.

RE **hagaduuduulagi.** *v.* —.

RE1 **hagaduuduulaginga.** *n.* —.

RE2 **hagaduuduulagia.** *v.* —.

RE2 **hagaduuduulagina.** *v.* —.

DUU$_{2d}$

B **duumaa.** *u.* Remainder (less than the preceding number); about, approximately.

BE **hagaduumaa.** *v.* Add a portion.

ID **duumaa de gelegele.** Trillion (a million million).

DUUAA

B **duuaa.** *v.* To be in trouble.

B 1 **duuaanga.** *n.* —.

BE **hagaduuaa.** *v.* —.

BE1 **hagaduuaanga.** *n.* —.

DUUDAGI

B **duudagi.** *v.* Connect up, join up, continue upon.

B 1 **duudaginga.** *n.* —.

B 2 **duudagina.** *v.* —.

BE **hagaduudagi.** *v.* —.

BE1 **hagaduudaginga.** *n.* —.

BE2 **hagaduudagina.** *v.* —.

R **duuduudagi.** *v.* —.

R 1 **duuduudaginga.** *n.* —.

R 2 **duuduudagina.** *v.* —.

RE **hagaduuduudagi.** *v.* —.

RE1 **hagaduuduudaginga.** *n.* —.

RE2 **hagaduuduudagina.** *v.* —.

DUUDUA

B **duudua.** *n.* Taro plot.

DUUGIVA

B **duugiva.** *a.* Rough texture, of a plaited object (such as a mat).

B 1 **duugivaanga.** *n.* —.

BE **hagaduugiva.** *v.* —.

BE1 **hagaduugivaanga.** *n.* —.

P **tuugiva.** *a.* —.

P 1 **tuugivaanga.** *n.* —.

PE **hagatuugiva.** *v.* —.

PE1 **hagatuugivaanga.** *n.* —.

DUUHULI

B **duuhuli.** *v.* A type of wave [must be followed either by *ina*, or by another base].

BE **hagaduuhuli.** *v.* To create *duuhuli.*

DUULALE

B **duulale.** *n.* A type of game.

DUULI

B **duuli.** *v.* Surround.

B 1 **duulinga.** *n.* —.

B 2 **duulia₂.** *v.* —.

BE **hagaduuli.** *v.* —.

BE1 **hagaduulinga.** *n.* —.

R **duuduuli.** *v.* —.

R 1 **duuduulinga.** *n.* —.

R 2 **duuduulia₂.** *v.* —.

RE **hagaduuduuli.** *v.* —.

RE1 **hagaduuduulinga.** *n.* —.

ID **de gau duuli sou.** Gilbertese people.

ID **duuli lua.** A method of throwing one's opponent in wrestling.

DUULOU

BE **hagaduulou.** *v.* Eat ravenously.

BE1 **hagaduulounga.** *n.* —.

BE2 **hagaduuloua.** *v.* —.

RE **hagaduuduulou.** *v.* —.

RE1 **hagaduuduulounga.** *n.* —.

RE2 **hagaduuduuloua.** *v.* —.

DUUSABA

B **duusaba.** *n.* A type of musical instrument (a stretched palm leaf jiggled while blown against).

TALE

ID **tale ange.** Sharpen (knife).

ID **tale taane.** A tough man.

TANGOHI

BE **hagatangohi.** *v.* The fading of light after sunset.

XCO **malumalu-tangohi.** *a.* The light after sunset; twilight (in the evening).

TEE

B **tee.** *mt.* NEGATIVE DECISIVE ASPECT MARKER.

CF **dee.** NEGATIVE ASPECT MARKER.

TIGI

B **tigi.** *mt.* Not yet —.

ID **tigi ai.** Not yet.

ID **tigiai donu.** None (at least up to now).

ID **tigi galania.** Far from finished.

TIGO

B **tigo.** *a.* Defecate.

B 1 **tiigonga.** *n.* —.

BE **hagatigo.** *v.* —.

BE1 **hagatiigonga.** *n.* —.

BE2 **hagatigoa.** *v.* —.

BE2 **hagatigolia.** *v.* —.

TILI

ID **damaa tili.** Sharpshooter.

TUBUA

ID **laa tubua.** Daily.

TUGOLO

B **tugolo.** *n.* Information (by definition, true) acquired from one's parents.

TUGU

CF **daatugu.** To curse (someone).

TULIDAA

ID **daia e tulidaa.** Urgency in micturation.

E_1

B **e_1.** *mp.* By.

E_2

B **e_2.** *mt.* GENERAL ASPECT MARKER.

EA

B **ea.** *a.* To surface (while swimming); to be on the surface of the water; stop swimming.

B 1 **eaanga.** *n.* —.

BE **hagaea.** *v.* —.

BE1 **hagaeaanga.** *n.* —.

R **eaea.** *a.* —.

R 1 **eaeaanga.** *n.* —.

RE **hagaeaea.** *v.* —; stutter [lit. 'going and coming'].

RE1 **hagaeaeaanga.** *n.* —.

ID **basa hagaeaea.** Stutter.

ID **dangi hagaeaea.** Wail (when crying).

ID **ea age.** Stop swimming (and come up on land).

ID **ea gi lunga.** To ride high in the water (e.g., of a canoe).

ID **magi eaea.** An eruption in a child's mouth, said to result from improper feeding [acute herpes infection?].

ID **manu ea.** Coral head (at or broaching the surface of the water).

EBA

B **eba.** *n.* A sleeping mat (child's).

EBU

R **ebuebu.** *v.* Foam, bubbles.

R 1 **ebuebunga.** *n.* —.

R 2 **ebuebua.** *v.* Covered with *ebuebu.*

RE **hagaebuebu.** *v.* —.

RE1 **hagaebuebunga.** *n.* —.

RE2 **hagaebuebua.** *v.* —.

ID **dili ebuebu.** Exhalation of air under water (forming bubbles).

EDEEDE

BE **hagaedeede.** *v.* Balance precariously.

BE1 **hagaedeedenga.** *n.* —.

BE2 **hagaedeedea.** *v.* —.

EE
B **ee.** *mp.* VOCATIVE PARTICLE.
ID **ee laa.** So!

EGA
B **ega.** *i.* A sound indicating surprise.

EGE
B **ege.** *v.* Raise up (so that higher).
B 1 **egenga.** *n.* —.
B 2 **egea.** *v.* —.
B 2 **egelia.** *v.* —.
BC **maege.** *v.* Raised up.
BC1 **maegenga.** *n.* —.
BC2 **maegea.** *v.* —.
BC2 **maegelia.** *v.* —.
BE **hagaege.** *v.* —.
BE2 **hagaegea.** *v.* —.
BE2 **hagaegelia.** *v.* —.
BF **hagamaege.** *v.* —.
BF1 **hagamaegenga.** *n.* —.
BF2 **hagamaegea.** *v.* —.
BF2 **hagamaegelia.** *v.* —.
PC **maaege.** *v.* —.
PC1 **maaegenga.** *n.* —.
PF **hagamaaege.** *v.* —.
PF1 **hagamaaegeanga.** *n.* —.
PF2 **hagamaaegea.** *v.* —.
PF2 **hagamaaegelia.** *v.* —.
R **egeege.** *v.* —.
R 1 **egeegenga.** *n.* —.
R 2 **egeegea.** *v.* —.
R 2 **egeegelia.** *v.* —.
RC **maegeege.** *v.* —.
RC1 **maegeegenga.** *n.* —.
RC2 **maegeegea.** *v.* —.
RC2 **maegeegelia.** *v.* —.
RE **hagaegeege.** *v.* —.
RE1 **hagaegeegenga.** *n.* —.
RE2 **hagaegeegea.** *v.* —.
RE2 **hagaegeegelia.** *v.* —.
RF **hagamaegeege.** *v.* —.
RF1 **hagamaegeegenga.** *n.* —.
RF2 **hagamaegeegea.** *v.* —.
RF2 **hagamaegeegelia.** *v.* —.
ID **ege age.** Raise up (something) from its previous trajectory.
ID **ege ange.** Move (something) over.
ID **ege iho.** Lower (something).

EIDU
B **eidu.** *n.* Ghost, spirit, god.
BE **hagaeidu.** *v.* Treat as an *eidu.*
ID **boi a eidu.** Temporarily abnormal.
ID **de eidu pale.** Fortunately, luckily.
ID **diinonga eidu.** An idol representing a spirit.
ID **tama legalega eidu.** Pupil of the eye; a cry of a bird or human that sounds like the cry of a baby; the name of a ghost.
ID **eidu ai.** Treat as a totem, worship, treat as a supernatural being.
ID **gide eidu.** To see a vision, hallucinate.
ID **gide eidu ina.** To see a vision, hallucinate.
ID **hagaduu eidu.** Superstitious; to believe in ghosts.
ID **hai de eidu.** One of two children's games [one like hide-and-seek, another like tag].
ID **hilohilo ma eidu.** A sorcerer able to take human or non-human shapes.
ID **me boogia e de eidu.** A black spot on the skin (like a bruise) noticed after sleeping.

ELAA
B **elaa.** *a.* A sound indicating surprise.
R **elaaelaa.** *a.* A sound indicating surprise.

ELE
R **eleele.** *n.* Fish sp.: shark sp.?

ELIGI
B **eligi.** *a.* Chief of the island (?) [archaic]; captain of a modern ship.
BE **hagaeligi.** *v.* Treat as an *eligi.*
BE1 **hagaeligianga.** *n.* —.

EOO

B **eoo.** *i.* A sound indicating agreement.

EU

B **eu.** *n.* Shoulder (top of).

RE **hagaeueu.** *v.* A shrugging movement of the shoulders.

ID **eu doo.** A dislocation of the shoulder joint.

ID **eu sege.** A dislocation of the shoulder joint.

GA

B **ga.** *mt.* INCEPTIVE ASPECT MARKER; if, and (esp. in enumeration), and then.

ID **ga noho.** After a time.

GAA$_1$

B **gaa$_1$.** *mt.* [var. of *ga*].

XCO **huugaabungubungu.** Very plump.

ID **dua gaahanga.** One of the lines of which *gaahanga* is composed).

ID **gaa lava.** And then.

ID **naa gaalava.** So what?

GAA$_2$

B **gaa$_2$.** *a.* To catch fire, aflame.

B 1 **gaanga.** *n.* —.

BE **hakaa.** *v.* —; sharpen (a knife), rub against; husk of the coconut.

BE1 **hakaanga.** *n.* —.

BE2 **hakaadia$_1$.** *v.* —.

P **kaa$_2$.** *a.* —.

R **gaagaa$_2$.** *a.* Easily ignited.

R 1 **gaagaanga.** *n.* —.

ID **duu hakaa.** A piece of coconut husk.

ID **gaa de malala.** There is sufficient [a conventional expression]; an argumentative and stubborn person; argumentative.

ID **gaa gee de nnamu.** Having a strong odor.

ID **hakaa tuai.** To sharpen a coconut grater blade.

GAA$_3$

E **kaa$_3$.** *n.* Mangrove crab.

GAAGAA

B **gaagaa$_1$.** *a.* Baby, infant.

BE **hagagaagaa.** *v.* Behave like a baby.

GAAGOSE

B **gaagose.** *n.* Sea cucumber sp.

ID **mmea be se gaagose.** Red hot (literally).

GAAHAGI

B **gaahagi.** *a.* The useless tuber-like growths on the *bie* plant.

BE **hagagaahagi.** *v.* —.

GAAHANGA

B **gaahanga.** *n.* A rope used to assist in climbing.

ID **bini gaahanga.** Three-ply braiding (of rope).

ID **gage gaahanga.** To climb a coconut tree, using *gaahanga*.

GAALAU

B **gaalau.** *n.* Bird sp.: brown booby?

GAANONI

B **gaanoni.** *n.* An omen of death [exact nature not known].

GAANUNU

B **gaanuunu.** *n.* Breast.

ID **hadu de gaanunu.** Nipple of breast.

GAASIA

B **gaasia.** *n.* Coral sp.: (looks like a flower).

GAAUI$_1$

B **gaaui$_1$.** *v.* Take (someone) along (with one) (esp. carrying, etc.).

B 1 **gaauinga$_1$.** *n.* —.

B 2 **gaauia$_1$.** *v.* —.

BE **hakaaui.** *v.* —.

BE1 **hakaauinga.** *n.* —.

BE2 **hakaauia.** *v.* —.

R gaagaaui$_1$. *v.* —.
R 1 gaagaauinga$_1$. *n.* —.
R 2 gaagaauia$_1$. *v.* —.
RE hakaagaaui. *v.* —.
RE1 hakaagaauinga. *n.* —.
RE2 hakaagaauia. *v.* —.

GAAUI$_2$
B **gaaui$_2$.** *v.* A line (for retrieving) attached to a spear; assemble (something from parts) by fastening together; strap, harness.
B 1 **gaauinga$_2$.** *n.* —.
B 2 **gaauia$_2$.** *v.* —.
BE **hagagaaui.** *v.* —.
BE1 **hagagaauinga.** *n.* —.
BE2 **hagagaauia.** *v.* —.
R **gaagaaui$_2$.** *v.* —.
R 1 **gaagaauinga$_2$.** *n.* —.
R 2 **gaagaauia$_2$.** *v.* —.
RE **hagagaagaaui.** *v.* —.
RE1 **hagagaagaauinga.** *n.* —.
RE2 **hagagaagaauia.** *v.* —.
ID **gaaui i tao.** A line (for retrieving) which is attached to a spear.

GABA$_1$
B **gaba$_1$.** *nl.* The part toward (something else); edge (of shore); hip; beginning of (a season, day, etc.).
BE **hagagaba$_1$.** *d.* Wait for.
XFL **manu-gaba-aasanga.** *n.* Plant sp.: beach naupaka shrub (*Scaevola taccada* (Gaertn.) Roxb.).
ID **gaba aasanga.** The sides of the watercourses between islets on the atoll.
ID **gaba de aasanga.** A side of the watercourses between islets on the atoll.
ID **gaba de ahiahi.** Early evening, late in the afternoon.
ID **gaba taiao.** Early morning.
ID **manu de gabadanga.** The bird leading a flock (of *ngongo*) to a school of fish [the one fisherman watch].

GABA$_2$
B **gaba$_2$.** *a.* Flap (as wings).
B 1 **gabaanga.** *n.* —.
BE **hagagaba$_2$.** *v.* —.
BE1 **hagagabaanga.** *n.* —.
P **kaba$_2$.** *a.* —.
R **gabagaba.** *a.* —; aerial roots of the breadfruit tree.
R 1 **gabagabanga.** *n.* —.
RE **hagagabagaba.** *v.* —.
RE1 **hagagabagabaanga.** *n.* —.
CF **gabaduu.** To sail a canoe against the wind; paddle or pole a canoe against the current.

GABA$_3$
E **kaba$_3$.** *a.* Do prematurely.
EE **hagakaba.** *v.* —.
ID **hannoo kaba.** Go now, right away! Beat it!
ID **hano kaba.** Go immediately!
CF **alu$_a$.** —.

GABA$_4$
E **kaba$_1$.** *i.* Wait!
ID **kaba ai loo.** Wait until — !
ID **kaba donu.** Wait!
ID **kaba kaba.** Wait! Wait!
ID **kaba muhuu.** Please wait!

GABA$_5$
XFL **gaba-moe.** *n.* Fish sp.: cardinal fish.

GABADUU
B **gabaduu.** *v.* To sail a canoe against the wind; paddle or pole a canoe against the current.
B 1 **gabaduunga.** *n.* —.
BE **hagagabaduu.** *v.* —.
BE1 **hagagabaduunga.** *n.* —.

GABAEA
B **gabaea.** *v.* To hang oneself (suicide).
B 1 **gabaeanga.** *n.* —.
BE **hagagabaea.** *v.* — [a var. of *hakabaea* used only occassionally].
BE **hakabaea.** *v.* — [usual form].

BE1 **hagagabaeanga.** *n.* — [var. of *hakabaeanga*].
BE1 **hakabaeanga.** *n.* — [usual form].
ID **gabaea mai.** Found hanged (suicide).
CF **hagabaea.** —; to hang oneself (suicide).

GABE
B **gabe.** *v.* Gouge out.
B 1 **gaabenga.** *n.* —.
B 2 **gaabea.** *v.* —.
BE **hagagabe.** *v.* —.
BE1 **hagagaabenga.** *n.* —.
BE2 **hagagaabea.** *v.* —.
E **kabe.** *v.* —.
EE **hagakabe.** *v.* —.
R **gabegabe.** *v.* —; to paddle (a canoe).
R 1 **gabegabenga.** *n.* —.
R 2 **gabegabea.** *v.* —.
R 2 **gabegabelia.** *v.* —.
RE **hagagabegabe.** *v.* —.
RE1 **hagagabegabenga.** *n.* —.
RE2 **hagagabegabea.** *v.* —.
RE2 **hagagabegabelia.** *v.* —.
XG **hoe gabegabe.** A canoe paddle (for paddling).
ID **gabe manava.** Eat sparingly (just enough to maintain one's strength), have a snack.

GABEA
B **gabea.** *v.* (In angling) the failure of a bait bundle to come untied and release the bait.
B 1 **gabeaanga.** *n.* —.
BE **hakabea.** *v.* —.
BE1 **hakabeaanga.** *n.* —.

GABI
B **gabi.** *v.* Hold something between two (or more) other things; grab (between other things, e.g., fingers).
B 1 **gaabinga.** *n.* —.
B 2 **gabia.** *v.* Held firmly (under the arm or between the fingers, etc.).
B 2 **gabidia.** *v.* Held firmly (by something not part of the human body).
BE **hagagabi.** *v.* —.
BE1 **hagagaabinga.** *n.* —.
BE2 **hagagabia.** *v.* —.
BE2 **hagagabidia.** *v.* —.
E **kabi.** *v.* Tight (of clothes), stuffed.
E 1 **kabianga.** *n.* —.
EE **hagakabi.** *v.* —.
EE1 **hagakabianga.** *n.* —.
R **gabigabi.** *v.* —; jellyfish sp. [N].
R 1 **gabigabinga.** *n.* —.
R 2 **gabigabia.** *v.* Repeatedly grubbing.
R 2 **gabigabidia.** *v.* Repeatedly held.
RE **hagagabigabi.** *v.* —.
RE1 **hagagabigabinga.** *n.* —.
RE2 **hagagabigabia.** *v.* —.
RE2 **hagagabigabidia.** *v.* —.
ID **gabi saele.** Carry around holding.
ID **lodo kabi.** Filled to capacity.

GABIa
B **hegabidi.** *v.* Packed closely together; crowded together in a small place.
B 1 **hegabidianga.** *n.* —.
BE **hagahegabidi.** *v.* —.
R **hegahegabidi.** *v.* —.
R 1 **hegahegabidianga.** *n.* —.
RE **hagahegahegabidi.** *v.* —.
RE1 **hagahegahegabidianga.** *n.* —.

GABINIVALI
B 1 **gabinivalianga.** *n.* —.
BE **hagagabinivali.** *v.* —.
BE1 **hagagabinivalianga.** *n.* —.

GABOLA
B **gabola.** *v.* Flatten out something mushy.
B 1 **gabolaanga.** *n.* —.
BE **hagagabola.** *v.* —.
BE1 **hagagabolaanga.** *n.* —.
R **gabogabola.** *v.* —.
R 1 **gabogabolaanga.** *n.* —.
RE **hagagabogabola.** *v.* —.
RE1 **hagagabogabolaanga.** *n.* —.

GABOU
B gabou. *n.* Fish sp.: scad?

GABU
R **gabugabu.** *nl.* Shore.
RE **hagagabugabu.** *v.* Create a channel through land (by wind or wave action).

GABUBU$_a$
B **madagabubu.** *a.* Dull (of an edge, or point).
B 1 **madagabubuanga.** *n.* —.
BE **hagamadagabubu.** *v.* —.
BE1 **hagamadagabubuanga.** *n.* —.
BE2 **hagamadagabubua.** *v.* —.
BE2 **hagamadagabubulia.** *v.* —.
ID **madagabubu de maanadu.** Slow-witted.

GABUNGI
CF **haigabungi.** Act strangely, act shyly.

GAPESE
B **gapese.** *v* A method of pole fishing at night (on the seaward reef).
B 1 **gapeseanga.** *n.* —.

GAPUA
B **gapua.** *v.* Large fissures or depressions in the reef (incomplete channels).
BE **hagagapua.** *v.* To create *gapua.*
ID **lodo gapua.** Seaward part of a *gapua.*
ID **mada gapua.** Lagoonward part of a *gapua.*

GADA$_1$
B **gada$_1$.** *a.* Laugh.
B 1 **gaadanga.** *n.* —.
BE **hakada.** *v.* —.
BE1 **hakadanga.** *a.* Funny, unserious, jesting, silly.
P **kada.** *a.* —.
P 1 **kaadanga.** *n.* —.
R **gadagada.** *a.* Laugh (more than a single laugh).
RE **hakadagada.** *v.* —.
ID **boi gadagada.** Laugh all the time at nothing.
ID **dele de gada.** Smile.
ID **gadagada doo me.** Laugh at.
ID **gada gimoo.** Smile (esp. for no good reason or when embarrassed).
ID **me hakadanga.** Joke, jest; trick (a practical joke).

GADA$_2$
B **gada$_2$.** *n.* Fish sp.: jack.
XFL **gada-ahai.** *n.* Fish sp.: jack? (an oceanic fish).
XFL **gada-alaala.** *n.* Fish sp.: jack? (like *alaala*).
XFL **gada-laagau-ngaadai.** *n.* Fish sp.
XFL **gada-laagau-ngauda.** *n.* Fish sp.: rudderfish.
XFL **gada-moana.** *n.* Fish sp.: jack? (an oceanic fish).

GADAHA
B **gadaha.** *n.* Bird sp.: great frigate bird (*Fregata minor*).
XFL **lau-gadaha.** *n.* Plant sp.: bird's-nest fern ((*Asplenium nidus* L.).
ID **bini dali gadaha.** A method of braiding *dali* into string to make a bird snare; six-ply braiding (of rope).

GADEA
B **gadea.** *n.* The side of the canoe away from the outrigger float.
ID **baabaa gadea.** To steer a canoe to the side away from its outrigger (opp. of *baabaa ama*).
ID **dau gadea.** Boom lanyard (of a canoe).
ID **hua i gadea.** The side of the main body of the canoe away from the outrigger float.

GADEBEGA
B **gadebega.** *n.* A type of basket.

GADI
B **gadi.** *v.* Bite.
B 2 **gaadia.** *v.* —.
BE **hagagadi.** *v.* —.

BE2 **hakaadia$_2$.** *v.* Make tightly packed.
E **kadi.** *v.* Bite hard; tightly packed; jammed up.
EE **hagakadi.** *v.* —.
R **gadigadi.** *v.* —; itch.
R 1 **gadigadinga.** *n.* —.
R 2 **gadigadia.** *v.* —.
RE **hagagadigadi.** *v.* —.
RE **hakadigadi.** *v.* —.
XFL **manu-gadi-niho.** *n.* Plant sp. [used to make loose teeth firm].
ID **gadigadi gauvae.** Chattering of teeth (from cold).
ID **kadi ange.** Fastened on to (by being stuck in).
ID **kadi gauvae.** To clench one's teeth (from cold).
ID **honu kadi.** Filled up completely (with solids); full up (and tightly packed).

GADI$_a$

B 1 **gaadinga.** *n.* Fully mature coconut meat; the final stage of development of the coconut, after *gaadinga gaha dea*; copra.
BE **hagagaadinga.** *v.* —.
ID **aloalo gaadinga.** The part of a coconut's meat next to the sap.
ID **gaadinga gaha paa.** A coconut with an unusually small-sized kernel.
ID **gaadinga gaha dea.** A coconut which is nearly mature; the stage of development of the coconut between *modomodo madagii* and *gaadinga.*
ID **gaadinga hagaangiangi.** Copra dried in the wind (not in the sun or in an oven).
ID **gaadinga hai ngadi ubu.** Coconut with a shell of a size appropriate for use as a cooking vessel.
ID **gaadinga lamallie.** A coconut with an unusually large-sized kernel.
ID **gaadinga osi.** A coconut selected as a seedling.
ID **gau looloa gaadinga.** A bunch of fully mature coconuts.
ID **lala gaadinga.** To heat copra (to dry it).
ID **sisi gaadinga.** To cut copra.

GADINIBIDI

B **gadinibidi.** *n.* A type of fishhook (made from pearl shell).

GADOA

B **gadoa.** *v.* To be overdue for parturition.
B 1 **gadoaanga.** *n.* —.
BE **hakadoa.** *v.* —.
BE1 **hakadoaanga.** *n.* —.

GADUNGA

B **gadunga.** *n.* Fire-plow.

GATAE

B **gatae.** *n.* Fishing net (attached to a frame or handle).

GAEHALA

B **gaehala.** *a.* Immature breadfruit; an aerial root of a pandanus tree which is used as a jump rope.
BE **hagagaehala.** *v.* To cause to have immature breadfruit.
BE1 **hagagaehalaanga.** *n.* —.
R **gaegaehala.** *a.* A growth of still immature breadfruit on trees.
ID **daa de gaehala.** To swing a jump rope made of *gaehala.*
ID **dada gaehala.** Picking even small breadfruit (to avoid having to change one's position, which would be necessary in order to pick breadfruit of the proper size).
ID **dama de gaehala.** A rain cloud (dropping its rain) seen in the distance.

GAGA$_1$

B **gaga$_1$.** *n.* The fibrous

sheathing (at the base of the petiole sheath of the flower) on the coconut tree.

CF **moigaga.** Fibers of the coconut husk.

GAGA$_2$

B **gaga$_2$.** *n.* Bird sp.

GAGE

B **gage.** *v.* Climb; climb up on.

B 1 **gaagenga.** *n.* —; ladder, stairway.

B 2 **gaagea.** *v.* —.

B 2 **gagelia.** *v.* —.

BE **hakage.** *v.* —.

BE1 **hakaagenga.** *n.* —.

BE2 **hakaagea.** *v.* —.

BE2 **hakagelia.** *v.* —.

P **kage.** *v.* —.

R **gakage.** *v.* —.

R 2 **gakagelia.** *v.* —.

ID **daula gage.** A rope used to assist the climber of a breadfruit tree.

ID **gage de henua.** Invade.

ID **gage gaahanga.** To climb a coconut tree, using *gaahanga.*

ID **gage saali.** To climb a breadfruit tree using *saali.*

GAGU

B **gagu.** *a.* Well-mannered.

BE **hakagu.** *v.* —.

BE2 **hakagudia.** *v.* —.

BE2 **hakagulia.** *v.* —.

ID **dee gagu.** Uncouth.

GAHA

B **gaha.** *n.* The portion of the coconut husk from which long fibers are obtained.

XCO **suukaha.** *n.* The land near shore [on which the chief traditionally had some rights].

ID **duu gaha.** A large piece of *gaha* (used for *mili gaadinga*), or from which sennit fibers are obtained).

ID **gaadinga gaha paa.** A coconut with an unusually small-sized kernel.

ID **gaadinga gaha dea.** A coconut which is nearly mature; the stage of development of the coconut between *modomodo madagii* and *gaadinga.*

ID **gaha biigi.** A rope for tying pigs.

ID **gaha paa.** A coconut with a small kernel.

ID **gaha dea.** Having almost ripe coconuts (whose husk fibers are white).

ID **gaha mea.** Having orange coconuts (of a coconut tree).

ID **gaha nuui.** Having green coconuts (of a coconut tree).

ID **gaha uli.** Having brown (ripe) coconuts (of a coconut tree).

ID **me gaha dea.** A coconut which is nearly mature.

ID **molimoli i tuu gaha.** To express coconut oil out of the residue (*oda*) from which some oil has already been expressed.

CF **gaahanga.** A rope used to assist in climbing.

GAHAALAVA

B **gahaalava.** *a.* Orange-colored (like a certain variety of coconut).

BE **hagagahaalava.** *v.* —.

GAHAO

B **gahao.** *n.* Plant sp.: tree sp.: ochrosia tree (*Ochrosia oppositifolia* (Lam.) K. Sch.).

GAHU

B **gahu.** *a.* Put on, wear, cover up (the body).

B 1 **gahuanga.** *n.* —.

BE **hakahu.** *v.* —.

BE1 **hakahuanga.** *n.* —.

BE2 **hakahudia.** *v.* —.

BE2 **hakahulia.** *v.* —.

P **kahu.** *a.* —.

P 1 **kahuanga.** *n.* —.

R **gahugahu.** *a.* —.
R 1 **gahugahuanga.** *n.* —.
RE **hakahugahu.** *v.* —.
RE1 **hakahugahuanga.** *n.* —.
RE2 **hakahugahudia.** *v.* —.
RE2 **hakahugahulia.** *v.* —.
ID **malo gahu.** Shirt.
ID **malo gahu de boo.** Sheet, blanket.
CF **gahuduna.** Ridge pole cover.

GAHUDUNA

B **gahuduna.** *n.* Ridge pole cover.

GAI$_1$

B **gai$_1$.** *a.* Trust, believe in.
BE **hagagai$_1$.** *v.* —.
P **kai$_1$.** *a.* —.
PE **hagakai$_1$.** *v.* —.
ID **au e dee gai naa loo.** I'll bet you can't!
ID **dee kai laa dangada.** So, it's not so after all (just as we believed at first)! No wonder!

GAI$_2$

B **gai$_2$.** *v.* Eat; food.
B 1 **gaainga.** *n.* —; temporary dwelling.
B 2 **gaina.** *v.* —.
BD **hegai.** *a.* Eat ravenously.
BD1 **hegainga.** *n.* —.
BE **hagagai$_2$.** *v.* —.
BE1 **hagagaainga.** *n.* —.
BE2 **hagagaina.** *v.* —.
BG **hagahegai.** *v.* —.
BG1 **hagahegainga.** *n.* —.
P **kai$_2$.** *v.* Propensity of fish to bite (a whole school at once).
PE **hagakai$_2$.** *v.* —.
R **gaigai.** *v.* —; humans taken as food by ghosts.
R 2 **gaigaina.** *v.* —.
T **gagai.** *v.* Propensity of fish to bite (one at a time).
XCO **gailalopoli.** *a.* Stingy.
XCO **gailingalinga.** *a.* Continually wanting to eat.
XCO **gaimalie.** *a.* Good at food preparation (not wasteful).
XCO **gaisaa.** *v.* Wasteful in preparing food, uneconomical.
XFL **gailulu.** *n.* Bird sp.: booby?
ID **bole gi de gai.** Eat ravenously.
ID **boo gi de gai.** Continually wanting to eat.
ID **dai hiigai.** Hungry.
ID **dangada gai dangada.** Cannibal.
ID **dau gai.** The season in which seasonally available food is abundant.
ID **dee adagaigaina.** A great many; serious.
ID **dee haaoa i de gai.** Gluttonous.
ID **de gai i mua.** Favorite food.
ID **doo de gai me.** Miss a meal or meals (leading to nausea when eating is resumed).
ID **duugia i de gai.** Be tired of eating a particular kind of food.
ID **gai baalau.** Eat messily (getting food on one's face); make a mess (esp. involving liquid or organic material).
ID **gai boo.** Eat early in the morning.
ID **gai busibusi.** Take the bait tentatively (of fish).
ID **gai dagidagi.** Eat while walking; food for sale which is carried on the road.
ID **gai de baibu.** Smoke cigarettes.
ID **gai de henua.** Native food (not imported).
ID **gaigai a usu.** Flatus.
ID **gai gi de mahi.** Eat as much as possible.
ID **gai ginigini.** Eat sparingly (esp. fish — in order not to use up).
ID **gai hagadoedoe.** Eat sparingly (to save for later).
ID **gai hagalongolongo.** Eat sparingly (to save some for others).
ID **gai hagalulu.** Habituated to

taking bait (fish); feed on bait.
ID **gai haganamunamu.** Eat sparingly (in order to save some food for later).
ID **gai hagassii.** Eat messily (letting the food fall from one's hands and mouth).
ID **gai hilihili.** Eat only certain foods prepared in certain ways by certain people; fussy (about food).
ID **gai holoholo.** Eat fast.
ID **gai lima dahi.** To eat taro without fish (or fish without taro).
ID **gai lima lua.** Eat greedily (with both hands).
ID **gai mamu dua nnui.** To eat fish up (not saving any for later).
ID **gai me.** Eat food.
ID **gai me hagadau doa.** Eat as though competing against other eaters in a test of manliness (e.g., to eat fish with the scales and all).
ID **gai modo.** Eat when still unripe.
ID **gai moumou.** Wasteful of food.
ID **gai niivoi.** To eat food without washing one's hands after having prepared a corpse for burial [a traditional sign of manliness].
ID **gai nnao$_1$.** Eat messily.
ID **gai ngaadahi.** A distribution of fish to the whole island population.
ID **gai ngaadai.** [= *gai ngaadahi*].
ID **gai ngole.** Wasteful, improvident.
ID **gai salusalu.** Prepare food wastefully (too much must be thrown away).
ID **gai samusamu.** Eat left-overs (that most people would throw out).
ID **gai valaai.** Take medicine.
ID **haangaa lodo i de gai.** Be continually hungry, owing to having a distended stomach from regularly eating too much.
ID **hai gai.** Prepared food; cook food.
ID **hale gaainga.** Hotel.
ID **hale gai.** Restaurant.
ID **henua gai dangada.** 'land of the cannibals' (esp. New Guinea).
ID **laulau gai.** A canoe used to transport food to a feast.
ID **madaa gai.** Firstfruits.
ID **magau i de hiigai.** Ravenous.
ID **mmahi i de gai.** Eat more than seems appropriate to one's body size.
ID **niho gai.** Permanent teeth (appearing after deciduous teeth).
ID **niho gaina.** Teeth with cavities.
ID **ngadi gai.** Eat taro without fish (or fish without taro).
ID **ssee de hiigai.** Famished, ravenous.
CF **massagaila.** Incompletely cooked.

GAI$_{2a}$
B **aagai.** *a.* Continually wanting to eat.
B 1 **aagainga.** *n.* —.
BE **hagaagai.** *v.* —.
BE1 **hagaagainga.** *n.* —.

GAI$_3$
B **gai$_3$.** *mi.* But, and, then, so.
ID **gai aha.** And then what?
ID **gai ange nei.** A misfortune owing to —.
ID **gai ga aha.** Too bad!
CF **adigai.** Luckily did not —, fortunately it did not —; if more; almost.

GAI$_{3a}$
B **agai.** *mi.* And then, finally...

GAIAA
B **gaiaa.** *v.* Steal, dishonest, cheat; to ask or accept too readily.
B 1 **gaiaanga.** *n.* —.
B 2 **gaiaadia.** *v.* Stolen.
BE1 **hagagaiaanga.** *n.* —.

BE2 **hagagaiaadia.** *v.* —.
ID **daa gaiaa.** To murder someone so that others don't see.
ID **dale gaiaa.** Provoke a fight by banging against someone (as children do); hit and run.
ID **dama gaiaa.** To hang around someone's house in the expectation of being served food [considered bad manners].
ID **dangada gaiaa.** Thief.
ID **dilo gaiaa.** Sneak a look.
ID **doo gaiaa.** Attack by surprise or stealth; ambush.
ID **gaiaa dau bodu.** Commit adultery.
ID **hagadau gaiaa.** Steal from one another.
ID **hagamademade gaiaa.** Cringe to deceive one's opponent into thinking one is afraid (when one is not).
ID **hai gaiaa.** Use without permission.
ID **hai me gaiaa.** To be reluctant to express oneself openly (esp. to persons in certain types of relationship to one).
ID **halehale gaiaa.** Cloying insincere humility.
ID **lodo gaiaa.** Competitive, envious, desirous of retaliating.
ID **muumuu kaiaa.** To remain silent (in order to hide a misdeed of oneself or others).
ID **ngudu gaiaa.** Charlatan.

GAIBEA
B **gaibea.** *n.* Crab sp.: shore crab, land crab, grapsid crab, ghost crab.
XFL **gaibea-lausedi.** *n.* Trapezeid crab.

GAINANGA
B **gainanga.** *v.* A person having special powers (occult powers, strength, status, or knowledge).
BE **hagagainanga.** *v.* —.

GAINI
B **gaini.** *n.* Any lattice-like arrangement.

GAINGA
B **gainga.** *v.* Trash, garbage; braided dead coconut fronds used in buttressing the sides of *uinga.*
BE **hagagainga.** *v.* Litter up.
ID **gainga o de moana.** Fish (when abundant in the ocean nearby).
ID **hai gainga.** Make an area messy by throwing trash around.
ID **sao gainga.** Sweep or clean up trash.
ID **se gainga.** Abundant.

GALA
R **galagala.** *n.* Sponge sp. (several spp.).
XFL **galavagu.** *n.* Sponge sp.

GALAAHUU
B **galaahuu.** *n.* Cheek, sides of the canoe prow.

GALAANGA
B **galaanga.** *v.* To look for members of the opposite sex by walking around at night.
B 1 **galaanganga.** *n.* —.
BE **hagagalaanga.** *v.* —.
BE1 **hagagalaanganga.** *n.* —.
R **galagalaanga.** *v.* —.
R 1 **galagalaanganga.** *n.* —.
RE **hagagalagalaanga.** *v.* —.
RE1 **hagagalagalaanganga.** *n.* —.

GALABE
B **galabe.** *n.* Sea cucumber sp. (several spp.).
XFL **galabe-duiduia.** *n.* Sea cucumber sp.

GALADI
XFL **mada-galadi.** *n.* Fish sp.: jack.

GALANI
B **galani.** *a.* Almost finished,

nearly finished; [from the Ponapean *karenieng*?].
B 1 **galanianga.** *n.* —.
B 2 **galania.** *a.* —.
BE **hagagalani.** *v.* —.
BE1 **hagagalanianga.** *n.* —.
BE2 **hagagalania.** *v.* —.
R **galagalani.** *a.* Come close to the end of.
R 1 **galagalanianga.** *n.* —.
R 2 **galagalania.** *a.* —.
RE **hagagalagalani.** *v.* —.
RE1 **hagagalagalanianga.** *n.* —.
RE2 **hagagalagalania.** *v.* —.
ID **tigi galania.** Far from finished.

GALASI
B **galasi.** *v.* Steal [a less pejorative word than *gaiaa*].
B 1 **galasinga.** *n.* —.
B 2 **galasia.** *v.* —.
R **galagalasi.** *v.* —.
R 1 **galagalasinga.** *n.* —.
R 2 **galagalasia.** *v.* —.
ID **hai me galasi.** To steal after having sort of asked for.

GALAUNA
B **galauna.** *v.* A big net for fishing, requiring several persons to manipulate.
BE **hagagalauna.** *v.* Teach to use *galauna.*
ID **tili de galauna.** Set *galauna.*
ID **hai galauna.** Fish with the *galauna* net.

GALAVA
R **galavalava.** *n.* The grains in the trunk wood of the coconut tree which are hard, dark, and sharp.
ID **mada galava.** Spear foreshaft.

GALEGALE
B **galegale.** *v.* White matter (the sediment in palm toddy, or the powder-like substance on a pandanus key).
B 1 **galegaleanga.** *n.* —.
B 2 **galegalea.** *v.* —.
BE **hagagalegale.** *v.* —.
BE1 **hagagalegaleanga.** *n.* —.
BE2 **hagagalegalea.** *v.* —.

GALELE
B **galele.** *v.* A method of fishing (casting with a pole)for tuna).
BE **hagagalele.** *v.* Teach to *galale.*
ID **baa galele.** Fishing lure of pearl shell, used in *galele* fishing.
ID **hhagi de baa galele.** Jerking of a fishing lure to attract fish; a method of extracting a lure from the fish's mouth.
ID **moni galele.** A canoe rigged for *galele* fishing.

GALEMU
B **galemu.** *u.* [preceded always by *e* or *dee*].
ID **dee galemu.** Never mind!, Don't bother!
ID **e galemu.** It's alright!
ID **gu dee galemu.** Recovering from an illness (getting better).

GALEU
B **galeu.** *a.* A change of wind direction.
B 1 **galeunga.** *n.* —.
B 2 **galeua.** *v.* —.
BE **hagagaleu.** *v.* —.
BE1 **hagagaleunga.** *n.* —.
BE2 **hagagaleua.** *v.* —.

GALEVA
B **galeva.** *n.* Fish sp.: shark sp.?
R **galevaleva.** *n.* Bird sp.

GALEVE
B **galeve.** *n.* The sap of the coconut tree (taken from the inflorescence).
ID **duu galeve.** To collect the sap of a coconut tree (from its inflorescence).
ID **tuu de galeve.** Make palm toddy.
ID **galeve maimai.** Fresh (unfermented) *galeve.*
ID **galeve sali.** A coconut tree which produces much *galeve.*

ID **galeve vii.** Fermented *galeve*, palm toddy.

GALI

B **gali.** *v.* Wound around; tied or fastened tightly.
B 1 **gaalinga.** *n.* —; an indentation (like that resulting from being wound tightly with string).
B 2 **galia.** *v.* —.
BE **hagagali.** *v.* —.
BE1 **hagagaalinga.** *n.* —.
BE2 **hagagalia.** *v.* —.
P **kali.** *v.* —.
PE **hagakali.** *v.* —.
R **galigali.** *v.* —.
RE **hagagaligali.** *v.* —.
RE1 **hagagaligalinga.** *n.* —.
RE2 **hagagaligalia.** *v.* —.
SE **hakaligali.** *v.* Grooved.
ID **gali ange.** Wound around or tied or fastened very tightly.

GALIGI

B **galigi.** *a.* Covered all over with.
B 1 **galigianga.** *n.* —.
BE **hagagaligi.** *v.* —.
BE1 **hagagaligianga.** *n.* —.
ID **ala galigi.** A method of mat making.

GALISI

B **galisi.** *n.* Lizard sp.
XCO **mada-galisi.** *v.* The stem of the coconut.
ID **sisi galisi.** Striped (with thin lines).

GALO$_1$

B **galo$_1$.** *a.* Look at, stare.
B 1 **gaalonga$_1$.** *n.* —.
B 2 **galoa.** *v.* Attractive to members of the opposite sex.
B 2 **galohia.** *v.* Attractive to members of the opposite sex.
BE **hakalo$_1$.** *v.* —.
BE1 **hakaalonga$_1$.** *n.* —.
BE2 **hakaloa.** *v.* —.
BE2 **hakalohia.** *v.* —.
P **kalo$_1$.** *a.* —.
R **galogalo$_1$.** *a.* Look around (with one's eyes only).
R 1 **galogalonga$_1$.** *n.* —.
RE **hakalogalo.** *v.* —.
ID **dee galo.** Perhaps.
ID **galo hagalegunga.** To look at a member of the opposite sex in a presumptuous way.
ID **galo saele.** Look around (moving one's body about).
ID **galo sugi mada.** Glimpse.
ID **kalo gee.** Strabismus (esp. the form in which one eye is turned outward from the nose); cross-eyed.

GALO$_2$

B **galo$_2$.** *a.* To show signs of being pregnant; a color change of fruit indicating ripening.
B 1 **gaalonga$_2$.** *n.* —.
BE **hakalo$_2$.** *v.* —.
BE1 **hakaalonga$_2$.** *n.* —.
P **kalo$_2$.** *a.* —.
P 1 **kaalonga.** *n.* —.
ID **galo ahi.** Sparks.
ID **galo de laa.** The reddish sky at sunset.
ID **galogalo malama.** The last quarter of the moon (rising in the east just before sunrise).

GALO$_3$

B **galo$_3$.** *v.* Stir.
B 1 **gaalonga$_3$.** *n.* —.
B 2 **gaaloa.** *v.* —.
E **kalo$_3$.** *v.* Stir up.
R **galogalo$_2$.** *v.* —.
ID **galo hilo.** Not cooked completely.
ID **kalo talinga.** Clean out, or scratch, inside the ear.

GALO$_{3a}$

B **saugalo.** *v.* Stir.
B 1 **saugalonga.** *n.* —.
B 2 **saugaloa.** *v.* —.
BE **hagasaugalo.** *v.* —.
BE1 **hagasaugalonga.** *n.* —.
BE2 **hagasaugaloa.** *v.* —.
R **sausaugalo.** *v.* —.

R 1 **sausaugalonga.** *n.* —.
R 2 **sausaugaloa.** *v.* —.
RE **hagasausaugalo.** *v.* —.
RE1 **hagasausaugalonga.** *n.* —.
RE2 **hagasausaugaloa.** *v.* —.
ID **saugalo saele.** Search for here and there, wander around looking for.

GALO$_4$
B **galo**$_4$. *n.* Fish sp.: goatfish (= small *vede*).
XFL **galo-gila.** *n.* Fish sp.: goatfish.

GALOI
B **galoi.** *n.* Having soft thighs [a term of endearment used by a man to a woman].

GALU
B **galu.** *n.* Viscous sputum.
B 2 **galua.** *v.* Having viscous sputum.
BE2 **hagagalua.** *v.* —.
R **galugalu.** *v.* Any jelly-like substance; jellyfish sp. [N].
RE2 **hagagalugalua.** *v.* Cause to have more and more *galu*.

GALUBU
B **galubu.** *n.* A type of toy.
ID **se galubu.** Very fast.

GAMA
R **gamagama.** *n.* Seaweed sp.

GAMAI
B **gamai.** *a.* Bring to me, carry to me [see *gavange*].

GAMMENGE
XFL **gammenge-baabaa.** *n.* Mollusk sp.: *Bursidae* spp.
XFL **gammenge-gabe-de-liidogi.** *n.* Mollusk sp.: murex shell.
XFL **gammenge-maimai.** *n.* Mollusk sp.: *Vasum turbinellus.*
XFL **gammenge-olomanga.** *n.* Mollusk sp.: *Thais armigera.*

GAMU$_1$
B **gamu**$_1$. *v.* Coral (any kind).
B 2 **gamua**$_1$. *v.* Covered with *gamu.*
BE **hagagamu.** *v.* —.
BE2 **hagagamua.** *v.* —.
R **gamugamu**$_1$. *v.* Coral sp.
R 2 **gamugamua**$_1$. *v.* Covered all over (or here and there) with *gamu.*
RE **hagagamugamu.** *v.* —.
RE2 **hagagamugamua.** *v.* —.
XFL **hadu-gamugamu.** *n.* Coral sp.

GAMU$_2$
B **gamu**$_2$. *v.* Cut (something).
B 1 **gaamunga.** *n.* —.
B 2 **gamua**$_2$. *v.* —.
R **gamugamu**$_2$. *v.* —.
R 1 **gamugamunga.** *n.* —.
R 2 **gamugamua**$_2$. *v.* —.
ID **bido gamu.** Uselessly short.
ID **madaa gamu.** The measurements and special techniques used in manufacturing *duai.*

GANA
B **gana.** *n.* Bad person.

GANABU
B **ganabu.** *n.* The base of a coconut tree trunk.
BE **hagaganabu.** *v.* —.
BE1 **hagaganabuanga.** *n.* —.
ID **hai ganabu.** The stage in the development of a coconut tree in which *ganabu* begins to develop.

GANAE
B **ganae.** *n.* Fish sp.: mullet.
XFL **ganae-oo.** *n.* Fish sp.: threadfin.

GANAUDOGO
B **ganaudogo.** *n.* An abundance of fish, birds, or other animals which are good to eat [an omen of death].

GANAVA
B **ganava.** *n.* Plant sp.: tree sp.: cordia tree (*Cordia subcordata* Lam.).

GANIMAGO

B **ganimago.** *n.* Mollusk sp.: *Malea pomum.*

GANO

B **gano.** *n.* Flesh of, meat of.
BC **magano.** *a.* Overripe (of pandanus only).
BC1 **maganoanga.** *n.* —.
BF **hagamagano.** *v.* —.
BF1 **hagamaganoanga.** *n.* —.
E **kano.** *n.* Penis, meat, flesh.
XCO **ganimua.** *n.* The eldest child of a couple.
XCO **ganimuli.** *n.* The second child of a couple.
XCO **ganoango.** *a.* Yellow.
XCO **kanosaa.** *a.* A taseless tuber of poor quality.
XE **hagaganimua.** *v.* To treat as an eldest child.
XE **hagaganimuli.** *v.* To treat as a child younger than the eldest.
ID **tegi kano.** Tickled.
ID **gano dea.** The soft wood just under the bark of a tree.
ID **gano moana.** Open sea, far away from any land.
ID **gano niho.** Gums (of mouth).
ID **gano siga.** Strands (of cloth).
ID **kano avaavaa.** Porous.
ID **kano de langi.** A blue and cloudless sky.
ID **kano maailaba.** The wood next to the core of a tree.
ID **kano maalama.** A phosphorescent flash in the water.
ID **kano made.** Slightly aged meat.
ID **kano malie.** A tasty tuber of good quality.
ID **kano mouli.** Fresh meat (including fish).
ID **kano mugamuga.** A crunching noise made when masticating certain foods (like cucumbers).
ID **kano siabo.** The meat on the side of the fish's head.
ID **hagategi kano.** Tickled (not sexually).

GANO$_a$

B **gannui.** *a.* The gelatinous layer in the kernel of the immature coconut.
ID **gannui koi.** *gannui* which has been scraped out of the shell to be eaten.
ID **gannui ina.** White (of the portion of a woman's thighs hidden under her sarong).
ID **gannui mada balabala.** *gannui* which is soft and mushy.
ID **gannui mada makaga.** *gannui* which is firm.
ID **gannui ngadaa.** A coconut which has less *gannui* than would be expected at its stage of maturity.

GANO$_b$

XCO **ganomada.** *n.* Eye.
XE **hagaganomada —.** *d.* To have a look of — on one's face.
ID **bula de ganomada.** Get mad.
ID **daba de ganomada.** Instantaneous, in the blinking of an eye.
ID **datada de galomada.** Twitching of an eye.
ID **oha de ganomada.** To work on a craft item (e.g., a canoe) with a model in mind of the finished product which is different from that of the person who began the work.

GANGO

B **gango.** *a.* Burned (overcooked food).
BE **hagagango.** *v.* —.
ID **mmoa gango.** Burned food which has been overcooked.

GAO

R **gaogao.** *nl.* Side of; the part surrounding; environs of; sides of the abdomen.
RE **hakaogao.** *v.* To sit on one buttock.
ID **dala gaogao.** The part of the human body between

the hip and the ribs.
ID **hano gaogao.** Move sideways.
ID **ivi gaogao.** Rib.

GASA
B **gasa.** *a.* Run aground.
B 1 **gasaanga.** *n.* —.
BE **hakasa.** *v.* —.
BE1 **hakasaanga.** *n.* —.
BE2 **hakasalia.** *v.* —.
P **kasa.** *a.* —.
R **gasagasa.** *a.* —.

GASI$_1$
B **gasi$_1$.** *a.* Jump up (with both feet leaving the ground).
B 1 **gaasinga.** *n.* —.
P **kasi.** *v.* —.
R **gasigasi.** *v.* —.
R 1 **gasigasinga.** *n.* —.

GASI$_2$
R 2 **gasigasia$_2$.** *v.* Rubbed against, scratched.
R 3 **gasigasiaanga.** *n.* —.
RE2 **hagagasigasia.** *v.* —.
RE3 **hagagasigasiaanga.** *n.* —.
S 2 **gaagaasia.** *v.* Rubbed against (of lines only).
S 3 **gaagaasiaanga.** *n.* —.
SE2 **hagagaagaasia.** *v.* —.
SE3 **hagagaagaasiaanga.** *n.* —.
ID **dee kasi.** Perhaps.
CF **gosigosi.** To scratch (slightly) repeatedly.

GASI$_3$
B **gasi$_2$.** *n.* Mollusk sp.: *Asaphis dichotoma.*
ID **nao gasi.** Eat messily (by poking at all of the food instead of touching only the portion to be eaten).
CF **kosi$_2$.** Mollusk sp.: *Cardium* sp.

GASIA
B **gasia.** *v.* Worthwhile, important, valuable.
B 1 **gasiaanga.** *n.* —.
BE **hagagasia.** *v.* —.
BE1 **hagagasiaanga.** *n.* —.
R **gasigasia$_1$.** *v.* —.
ID **daane gasia.** A person who is useful to others.

GASIGI
B **gasigi.** *n.* Plant sp.: hemp-leaved vitex shrub (*Vitex negundo* var. *bicolor* (Willd.) Lam.).

GASO$_1$
P **kaso.** *a.* Narrow [pl.].
P 1 **kasoanga.** *n.* —.
PE **hagakaso.** *v.* —.
PE1 **hagakasoanga.** *n.* —.
PE2 **hagakasolia.** *v.* —.
R **gasogaso.** *a.* Narrow [sing.].
R 1 **gasogasoanga.** *n.* —.
RE **hakasogaso.** *v.* —.
RE1 **hakasogasoanga.** *n.* —.
RE2 **hakasogasoa.** *v.* —.
RE2 **hakasogasolia.** *v.* —.
ID **duu gaso.** Vertical, straight up and down.

GASO$_2$
B **gaso.** *n.* Roof thatch rafters (of pandanus slats).

GASOGO
B **gasogo.** *v.* To have sexual pleasure (of males only) either by intercourse, or by regarding a naked woman.
B 1 **gasogoanga.** *n.* —.
BE **hagagasogo.** *v.* —.
BE1 **hagagasogoanga.** *n.* —.

GAU$_1$
B **gau$_1$.** *n.* Handle, appendage.
BE **hakau.** *v.* —.
XCO **adugau.** *v.* Arrangement of things into a straight row.
XFL **ga-hudi.** *n.* Plant sp.: tree sp.: banana tree; banana (fruit).
XFL **gau-me.** *n.* Gill (of a fish).
ID **gau bini.** A tool used in braiding rope.
ID **gau bini baalanga.** An iron rod.
ID **gau dagodo.** The boom of a sail.
ID **gau dahi.** A method of fishing for tuna (angling

with a single baited hook?).
ID **gaugau dalinga.** Exterior of the ear; a loop-like handle.
ID **gau hadu.** The board to which the metal grater for grating taro is attached.
ID **gau ivi.** Skinny.
ID **gau laagau.** The shaft of a spear.
ID **gau lama.** Rachis of the coconut leaf.
ID **gau looloa gaadinga.** A bunch of fully mature coconuts.
ID **lou de gaugau dalinga.** Pull the trigger (of a gun).
ID **maga de gau dogi.** Masturbate (of males only).
CF **dabagau.** A type of floor mat.
CF **laagau.** Wood, stick (of wood).

GAU$_{1a}$
B **gau$_3$.** *v.* Lymph nodes (enlarged).
B 2 **gaua.** *v.* To have enlarged lymph nodes.
BE **hagagau.** *v.* —.
BE1 **hagagaunga.** *n.* —.
BE2 **hagagaua.** *v.* —.
R **gaugau$_1$.** *v.* Be disposed to have enlarged lymph nodes.
R 2 **gaugaua.** *v.* —.
RE **hagagaugau.** *v.* —.
RE1 **hagagaugaunga.** *n.* —.
RE2 **hagagaugaua.** *v.* —.

GAU$_{1b}$
B **duugau.** *n.* Legs at the base of the canoe mast.
BE **hagaduugau.** *v.* To make a handle for (e.g., a knife); to fasten with pegs.
BE1 **hagaduugauanga.** *n.* —.
BE1 **hagaduugaunga.** *n.* —.
BE2 **hagaduugaua.** *v.* —.
ID **doo tuugau.** A dislocation of the *tuugau.*
ID **tuugau i daha.** Clitoris.
ID **tuugau i lodo.** Cervix.

GAU$_{1c}$
XCO **gauvae.** *n.* Jaw; a set of false teeth.
ID **gadigadi gauvae.** Chattering of teeth (from cold).
ID **kadi gauvae.** To clench one's teeth (from cold).
ID **hagaida de gauvae.** To bare one's teeth (by opening the lips to expose the whole set of teeth).
ID **ngalue de gauvae.** Dislocated jaw.

GAU$_{1d}$
XCO **dilongaagau.** *v.* Voyeurism.
XCO **gauanga.** *n.* Thigh.
XE **hakauanga.** *n.* A handle of something.
ID **balu gauanga.** Trembling of legs.
ID **doo de gauanga.** Dislocated thigh bone.
ID **gauanga mahagi.** Dislocated thigh bone.
ID **isiisi luu gauanga.** To tear off (a person's) legs [an expression heard in threats].
ID **langa de gauanga.** To lift up the leg of an opponent in wrestling [considered unfair].
ID **sege de gauanga.** Dislocated thigh bone.

GAU$_{1e}$
XCO **madagauhala.** *n.* The lower abdomen, crotch, pubic area.

GAU$_{1f}$
B **gauasa.** *n.* The pectoral fin of a fish and the surrounding flesh.
ID **isiisi luu gauasa.** To tear from limb to limb.

GAU$_2$
E **kau$_2$.** *v.* To swim (or make motions of swimming, as babies do).
E 1 **kaunga.** *n.* —.
EE **hagakau.** *v.* —.
EE1 **hagakaunga.** *n.* —.
EE2 **hagakaua.** *v.* —.
EE2 **hagakaulia.** *v.* —.

R	**gaugau$_2$.** *v.* To bathe (including swimming for the purpose of bathing).
R 1	**gaugaunga.** *n.* —.
RE	**hakaugau.** *v.* —.
RE1	**hakaugaunga.** *n.* —.
RE2	**hakaugaua.** *v.* To bathe (someone).
ID	**kau donu.** Used to, easy to.
ID	**kau gee.** Not used to; hard to.
ID	**hale gaugau.** Bath house.
ID	**manu gaugau.** Plant sp.: a variety of taro.
CF	**magau.** Die, dead, unconscious.

GAU$_3$

B	**gau$_2$.** *n.* Grouping (of people).
ID	**de gau duuli sou.** Gilbertese people.
ID	**gau de henua.** Natives.
ID	**gau henua gee.** Foreigners (lit., 'people from other lands').
ID	**gau mai moni.** Foreigners (lit., 'people who came in canoes').
ID	**gau mai vaga.** [= *gau mai moni*].

GAU$_4$

E	**kau$_1$.** *n.* Fish sp.: (any small jack-like fish).
ID	**deledele kau.** Walk proudly [culturally disapproved], strut.

GAUEA

B	**gauea.** *n.* Bird sp.: white-rumped swift (*Apus pacificus*) (The native term applies possibly to several spp.).

GAULIGI

B	**gauligi.** *a.* Child, young person.
BE	**hagagauligi.** *v.* —.
BE1	**hagagauligianga.** *n.* —.
ID	**adamai gauligi.** Remember childhood experiences.
ID	**basa gauligi.** To imitate a child's manner of talking; baby talk.
ID	**tamaa gauligi.** Baby.
ID	**tilo gauligi.** To regard something from the perspective of a child.
ID	**gauligi ange.** Younger than.
ID	**gauligi daane.** Male child, boy.
ID	**gauligi hahine.** Female child, girl.
ID	**gauligi iho.** Next younger than.
ID	**gauligi mai ange.** The one next younger still.
ID	**gide gauligi.** To see from the perspective of a small child.
ID	**hakide gauligi.** Spoil children.
ID	**hai gauligi.** Each child is somewhat different!
ID	**hai me a gauligi.** A childish act.
ID	**lodo a gauligi.** Immature (in personality); vulnerable to having one's feelings easily hurt.
ID	**masavaa de gauligi.** Childhood.

GAUNA

B	**gauna.** *v.* Invite.
B 1	**gaunanga.** *n.* —.
BE	**hagagauna.** *v.* —.
BE1	**hagagaunanga.** *n.* —.
R	**gaugauna.** *v.* —.
R 1	**gaugaunanga.** *n.* —.
RE	**hagagaugauna.** *v.* —.
RE1	**hagagaugaunanga.** *n.* —.

GAUNGA

B	**gaunga.** *n.* The partially burned wood or coconut husk which is left over after a fire.

GAVA$_1$

B	**gava$_1$.** *v.* Cut open.
B 1	**gavaanga.** *n.* —.
ID	**mmau gava.** Known by heart, memorized, know (how to do something) well.
ID	**se gava.** Know (how to do something) well.

GAVA$_2$

B	**gava$_2$.** *n.* Bird sp.: reef heron (*Demiegretta sacra*).

XFL **gava-dea.** *n.* Reef heron — white phase.

XFL **gava-uli.** *n.* Reef heron — grey phase.

$GAVA_3$

R **gavagava.** *n.* Weather-hardened black driftwood.

$GAVA_4$

XFL **gavaligi.** *n.* Fish sp.

GAVADA

B **gavada.** *n.* A type of basket [used for scooping up fish which have been caught in a net].

GAVADU

B **gavadu.** *a.* Give or carry (something) to you [see *gave*].

ID **ngadi gavadu.** A gift (to the hearer); a present (to the hearer).

CF **vadu.** Give (to hearer).

GAVAGE

B **gavage.** *a.* Give or bring up [see *gave*].

CF **$vage_1$.** Bring up, put up, take up.

GAVANGE

B **gavange.** *a.* Give or bring to (someone) [see *gave*].

ID **hagadau gavange.** Compete (between groups).

CF **vange.** Give to (him, her, or them).

$GAVE_1$

B **$gave_1$.** *d.* —.

B 1 **gaavenga.** *n.* —.

B 2 **gaavee.** *v.* —.

B 2 **gaveaa.** *v.* Taken; [not the imperative forms; c.f. *gaavee*].

E **kave.** *v.* Take.

R **gavegave.** *v.* —; rays of the sun.

ID **gave ala.** A method of plaiting mats.

ID **gave bae.** A row of stones piled on top of each other.

ID **gave hua podo.** Sprint (footrace of short distance).

ID **gave hua loa.** [var. of *gave ua loa*].

ID **gave lodo.** Attract attention.

ID **gave ua podo.** [var. of *gave hua podo*].

ID **gave ua loa.** A long-distance footrace.

ID **kave dagi de momo.** Take a little (or few) at a time.

ID **kave dahi.** Do at one time.

ID **kave e hakide.** Take someone in order to train or teach him.

ID **kave gi de mahi.** Obtain by force.

ID **kave houhou.** Race to take.

ID **kave huaame.** Take the whole thing.

ID **hai gaavenga.** Restless (of a child).

CF **daogave.** A type of coconut tree [bears seasonally].

CF **gamai.** Bring to me, carry to me [see *gavange*].

CF **gavadu.** Give or carry (something) to you [see *gave*].

CF **gavage.** Give or bring up [see *gave*].

CF **gavange.** Give or bring to (someone) [see *gave*].

$GAVE_2$

B **$gave_2$.** *n.* The name of a name-group.

GAVIA

B **gavia.** *n.* Crazy person; insane person.

ID **hai me gavia.** Do crazy things.

GAVIDI

B **gavidi.** *n.* A type of fishhook (made from turtle shell).

GEA

B **gea.** *n.* Hawksbill turtle.

XCO **latabagea.** *n.* An ornament made of turtle shell.

GEAO

B **geao.** *n.* Plant sp.: plant-shrub sp. (*Sida fallax* Walp.).

GEDE

B **gede.** *n.* Basket (the generic

term).

XG **gede aola.** A type of basket.

XG **gede dua dahi.** A type of basket.

XG **gede gabi de husi.** A type of basket [carried to the taro patch].

XG **gede hadu.** A type of basket [used for hauling stones for the earth oven].

XG **gede hangaabo.** A type of basket [having a cover].

XG **gede maduu.** A type of basket.

ID **vava de gede.** Forgetful (esp. with increasing age).

GEE

B **gee.** *mv*. Differently, of a different sort; away from; strange.

R **geegee.** *mv*. Completely differently.

XCO **huligee.** Turn away from, turn inside out (of clothes).

ID **agilau gee.** Extremely pugnacious.

ID **anga gee.** Turn one's attention away from.

ID **badai gee.** Extremely meddlesome.

ID **badodi gee.** To jerk violently.

ID **balagelage gee.** Severely crippled.

ID **basa too gee.** Speak ungrammatically.

ID **basa gee.** Speak (or express oneself) strangely.

ID **bouli gee.** An alternative mode of existence (such as the world of ghosts).

ID **daa gee taahili.** Sing off-key.

ID **dagi gee.** Lead away from.

ID **dagodo gee (ma).** Another thing altogether; different (from); recuperating (after an illness).

ID **dahea gee.** Drift away.

ID **dangada henua gee.** Foreigners, strangers.

ID **dee hai gee.** Be tied (e.g., in a footrace).

ID **donu gee.** Misunderstand.

ID **dugi gee.** Chase away (in a certain direction).

ID **dugu gee.** Put aside, set aside; treat (a person) differently from others.

ID **duilaa gee.** To be exceedingly unsuccessful with members of the opposite sex.

ID **duu gee.** Out of alignment.

ID **tagi gee.** Tow away.

ID **tanga gee.** Separated from.

ID **tea gee.** Pallor.

ID **tili gee.** Throw away.

ID **too gee.** Clumsy, unskillful, awkward (not dexterous).

ID **too geegee.** Happening at different times or places.

ID **gaa gee de nnamu.** Having a strong odor.

ID **gau henua gee.** Foreigners (lit.,'people from other lands').

ID **geu gee.** To jerk one's head away from something.

ID **goononga gee.** To set a record.

ID **kalo gee.** Strabismus (esp. the form in which one eye is turned outward from the nose); cross-eyed.

ID **kau gee.** Not used to; hard to.

ID **kii gee.** Move away from.

ID **hagaau gee.** Bashful, shy (timid about attending social affairs), timid.

ID **hagadagodo gee ina.** Change.

ID **hagatala gee.** Wanting always to *hagatala*.

ID **hagaui gee.** Avoid.

ID **hakide gee.** Spoil (a child).

ID **hakino gee.** Filthy, disgusting.

ID **hano gee.** Go away [sing.].

ID **hano gi bouli gee.** To transfigure oneself.

ID **henua gee.** Foreign lands.

ID **hesilihagi gee.** To have

hesilihagi by a considerable distance.

ID **hhagi gee.** Turn away from (to avoid), veer.

ID **hhali gee.** Scoop out.

ID **hili gee.** Sort out from; set aside (be chosen from a group).

ID **hulo gee.** Go away [pl.].

ID **labua gee (lodo).** Having an upset stomach; to be on the point of nausea.

ID **lili baasi gee.** Accuse someone (in an argument, usually between spouses) of taking sides with another family member.

ID **mada tea gee.** White as a sheet (of a person).

ID **me gee.** A coconut without any meat.

ID **milo gee.** To turn the opposite way.

ID **mmoli gee.** Haul away from.

ID **modu gee.** Cut away from; separated from.

ID **saga gee.** *saga* away from; extend out in space.

ID **sagea gee.** Extremely *sagea.*

ID **sali gee.** Flow away.

ID **sasa gee.** Impetuous in act or movement (leading to frequent error).

ID **savini gee.** Run away.

ID **sege gee.** Slip or slide away from.

ID **sili gee.** Stand out from (others in a group) in distance or height.

ID **singa gee.** Lean away from.

ID **ssee gee.** Veer from an intended trajectory.

ID **sseu gee.** Push away, push aside (in one direction).

ID **ue gee.** Move to another place.

ID **vvae gee.** Isolate, separate from, set aside (from a group).

GEESAA

B **geesaa.** *n.* Mollusk sp.: *Fimbria soverbii.*

GEESAMA

B **geesaama.** *n.* Outrigger cross boom (of a canoe).

GEEVEE

B **geevee.** *n.* Bird sp.: eastern whimbrel (*Numenius phaeopus).*

GEGENO

B **gegeno.** *n.* Alligator, crocodile.

GELE

R **gelegele.** *a.* Sand, soil, dirty.

R 1 **gelegeleanga.** *n.* —.

RE **hakelegele.** *v.* —; make certain sounds to attract fish.

RE1 **hakelegeleanga.** *n.* —.

RE2 **hakelegelea.** *v.* —.

XCO **hongagelegele.** *n.* Defecate [a euphemism].

XCO **suugelegele.** *v.* —.

XCO **vaigelegele.** *a.* Filthy, very dirty.

XFL **gelemea.** *n.* A by-product of the tumeric-making process.

ID **buni ange gi de gelegele.** To have been dead for a long time.

ID **dangada vai gelegele.** A person of filthy appearance or habits.

ID **duumaa de gelegele.** Trillion (a million million).

ID **gelegele dea.** Sand.

ID **gelegele gumi hue.** Fine-grained sand.

ID **gelegele malama.** Sand with disk-like particles.

ID **gelegele uli.** Black soil [soil with high organic content].

ID **hale hongagelegele.** Out house.

ID **henua gelegele.** Atoll [lit., 'land with sandy soil'].

ID **hongagelegele baalanga.** Rust.

ID **mada gelegele.** Male child.

ID **magi hongagelegele todo.** To have bloody stools [dysentery?].

ID	**malili gelegele.** Producing hard crumbs when eaten or broken.

GELI

B	**geli.** *v.* Dig.
B 1	**geelinga.** *n.* —; a hole (which has been dug).
B 2	**gelia.** *v.* —.
BE	**hagageli.** *v.* —.
BE1	**hagageelinga.** *n.* —.
BE2	**hagagelia.** *v.* —.
E	**keli.** *a.* Root around (disturbing the coral layer of a yard by shuffling, or by pawing the ground).
EE	**hakeli.** *v.* —.
EE1	**hakeelinga.** *n.* —.
EE2	**hakelia.** *v.* —.
R	**geligeli.** *v.* —.
R 1	**geligelinga.** *n.* —.
R 2	**geligelia.** *v.* —.
RE	**hagageligeli.** *v.* —.
RE1	**hagageligelinga.** *n.* —.
RE2	**hagageligelia.** *v.* —.
T	**gegeli.** *a.* Struggle.
T 1	**gegelianga.** *n.* —.
XFL	**daogoli.** *n.* Plant sp.: swamp taro (*Cyrtosperma chamissonis*), also the corm of this plant.
ID	**dalodalo keli.** Pray earnestly.
ID	**dangidangi keli.** Beg, apologize, or ask permission in an insistent manner; pray fervently; beseech.
ID	**duu keli.** Firmly in place, earnestly.
ID	**vai geli.** Well (for water, in the ground).

GELO

B	**gelo.** *a.* Deep.
B 1	**geelonga.** *n.* A depression (in the reef, or ground, etc.).
BE	**hagagelo.** *v.* —.
BE1	**hagageelonga.** *n.* —.
BE2	**hagageloa.** *v.* —.
P	**kelo.** *a.* —.
PE	**hagakelo.** *v.* —.
PE1	**hagakeelonga.** *n.* —.
PE2	**hagakeloa.** *v.* —.
R	**gelogelo.** *v.* Having many depressions (e.g., a corrugated surface).
R 1	**gelogelonga.** *n.* —; depressions (in the reef, or ground, etc.).
RE	**hagagelogelo.** *v.* —.
RE1	**hagagelogelonga.** *n.* —.
RE1	**hakelogelonga.** *n.* —.
RE2	**hagagelogeloa.** *v.* —.
ID	**aloha gelo.** Profound affection.
ID	**basa gelo.** Speak sagely.
ID	**lo te gelo.** In the deepest part.
ID	**maanadu gelo.** Profound thoughts.
ID	**sulu de gelo.** Diving in the area in back of the center of the communal fishing net (the deepest part, in which the fish are trapped).

GELO$_a$

B	**dagelo.** *n.* Bottom, foundation.
ID	**hai dagelo.** Deep-bottomed.

GELU

XFL	**gelu-agau.** *n.* Fish sp.: tang.
XFL	**gelu-hai-usu.** *n.* Fish sp.: unicorn fish.
XFL	**gelu-hai-vaelo.** *n.* Fish sp.: tang.
XFL	**gelu-uliuli.** *n.* Fish sp.: tang?

GEMO

B	**gemo.** *a.* Fast, swift.
B 1	**gemoanga.** *n.* —.
BE	**hakemo.** *v.* —.
BE1	**hakemoanga.** *n.* —.
BE2	**hakemolia.** *v.* —.
P	**kemo.** *a.* —.
P 1	**kemoanga.** *n.* —.
PE	**hagakemo.** *v.* —.
PE1	**hagakemoanga.** *n.* —.
PE2	**hagakemolia.** *v.* —.
R	**gemogemo.** *a.* —.
R 1	**gemogemoanga.** *n.* —.
RE	**hagagemogemo.** *v.* —.
RE1	**hagagemogemoanga.** *n.* —.
RE2	**hagagemogemolia.** *v.* —.
ID	**gemo ange huu de —.** Rapidly becoming —.

CF hologemo. [var. of *hologumu*].

GENU

B **genu.** *v.* A movement of the hips, as in the act of sexual intercourse.
B 1 **geenunga.** *n.* —.
B 2 **genua.** *v.* —.
BE **hagagenu.** *v.* —.
BE1 **hagageenunga.** *n.* —.
BE2 **hagagenua.** *v.* —.
R **genugénu.** *v.* —.
R 1 **genugenunga.** *n.* —.
R 2 **genugenua.** *v.* —.
RE **hagagenugenu.** *v.* —.
RE1 **hagagenugenunga.** *n.* —.
RE2 **hagagenugenua.** *v.* —.

GEU

B **geu.** *v.* Shake one's head (once) to one side.
B 1 **geunga.** *n.* —; behavior (of a person); the manner (of a person).
B 2 **geua.** *v.* —.
BE **hagageu.** *v.* —.
BE1 **hagageunga.** *n.* —.
BE2 **hagageua.** *v.* —.
P **keu.** *v.* —.
R **geugeu.** *v.* Shake one's head back and forth; [a sign interpreted as meaning 'that's not right!'].
R 1 **geugeunga.** *n.* —.
R 2 **geugeua.** *v.* —.
RE **hagageugeu.** *v.* —.
RE1 **hagageugeunga.** *n.* —.
RE2 **hagageugeua.** *v.* —.
ID **geu de madangi.** A change of wind direction.
ID **geu gee.** To jerk one's head away from something.

GEVA

XFL **bani-gegeva.** *n.* [var. of *bani-magevageva*].
XFL **bani-magevageva.** *n.* Fish sp. (rare).
CF **bale-masevaseva.** [var. of *bani-magevageva*].

GI_1

B **gi_1.** *mp.* Toward, to, in order to.
ID **ange gi.** According to —.
ID **basa gi lunga.** Speak loudly.
ID **boo gi me.** Acquisitive (and acting on acquisitive impulses).
ID **gai gi de mahi.** Eat as much as possible.
ID **kave gi de mahi.** Obtain by force.
ID **maingaa ange nei gi.** To wish one has —.
ID **me naa gi —.** I wish that...
ID **se me gi hee.** In which direction is the current running?
ID **siia gi moana ngaadai.** Drift downwind, away from land.
ID **sulu gi mua.** Fall forward.
CF **kilaa.** There in the distance.
CF **kinaa.** There near you.
CF **kinei.** Here in this place.

GI_2

B **gi_2.** *mt.* DESIDERATIVE ASPECT MARKER.

GIADO

B **giado.** *n.* Outrigger boom.
ID **giado taelodo.** The outrigger booms toward the center of the canoe.
ID **giado madua.** Main outrigger booms.
ID **giado manu.** The smaller outrigger booms at the ends of the canoe.

GIBA

B **giba.** *v.* Swelling of the testicles.
B 1 **gibaanga.** *n.* —.
BE **hagagiba.** *v.* —.
BE1 **hagagibaanga.** *n.* —.

GIDA

B **gida.** *pi.* Each one.
ID **gida ma gida.** Each individual...

GIDE

B **gide.** *v.* See.
B 1 **gideanga.** *n.* —.
B 2 **gidee.** *a.* Seen.
BD **hegide.** *a.* See each other; meet up with.

BD1 **hegideanga.** *n.* —.
BE **hagagide.** *v.* —.
BE1 **hagagideanga.** *n.* —.
BE2 **hagagidelia.** *v.* —.
BG **hagahegide.** *v.* —.
BG1 **hagahegideanga.** *n.* —.
BG2 **hagahegidelia.** *v.* —.
P **kide.** *a.* —.
P 1 **kideanga.** *n.* —.
R **gidegide.** *v.* —.
R 1 **gidegideanga.** *n.* —.
RE **hagagidegide.** *v.* —.
RE1 **hagagidegideanga.** *n.* —.
RE2 **hagagidegidelia.** *v.* —.
ID **dee gide.** Blind.
ID **dee vaagidee.** Ugly, awful; extremely disappointing.
ID **gidee (laa) goe.** See what I mean!
ID **gide eidu.** To see a vision, hallucinate.
ID **gide eidu ina.** To see a vision, hallucinate.
ID **gidee iho.** Be aware of oneself.
ID **gidee mai.** Found out (or be found out).
ID **gide gauligi.** To see from the perspective of a small child.
ID **gide malie.** Get in the habit of.
ID **gide sala.** Misidentify.
ID **gu gide huu.** Spoiled (having acquired a bad habit).
ID **hegide mada.** Early morning, before daybreak (when one can just barely recognize a person).
ID **mada gide.** Sharp-eyed, good at finding things.

GIDE$_a$

B **hakide.** *v.* To reveal oneself to someone (of a ghost); to show (familiarize with).
B 1 **hakideanga.** *n.* —.
B 2 **hakidelia.** *v.* —.
ID **kave e hakide.** Take someone in order to train or teach him.
ID **hakide gauligi.** Spoil children.
ID **hakide gee.** Spoil (a child).

GIDEU

B **gideu.** *n.* Plant sp.: fern sp.

GIDI

R **gidigidi.** *v.* Short.
R 1 **gidigidianga.** *n.* —.
RE **hagagidigidi.** *v.* —.
RE1 **hagagidigidianga.** *n.* —.
ID **gidigidi laa lalo.** A very short person, midget; miniature, diminutive.

GIEBU

B **giebu.** *n.* Plant sp.: spider lily (*Hymenocallis littoralis* (Jacq.) Salisb.).

GIEULI

B **gieuli.** *n.* Lizard sp.

GII

B **gii.** *a.* A high-pitched sound, soft, high-pitched crying (as by children).
B 1 **giianga.** *n.* —.
BE **hagagii.** *v.* —.
BE1 **hagagiianga.** *n.* —.
BE2 **hagagiia.** *v.* —.
P **kii**$_3$. *a.* —.
P 1 **kiianga**$_3$. *n.* —.
PE **hagakii**$_2$. *v.* —.
PE1 **hagakiianga**$_2$. *n.* —.
PE2 **hagakiia.** *v.* —.
R **giigii**$_1$. *a.* —; laugh.
R **giigii**$_2$. *n.* Fish sp.: squirrelfish (= small *malaugulu*?
R 1 **giigiianga.** *n.* —.
RE **hagagiigii.** *v.* —.
RE1 **hagagiigiianga.** *n.* —.
RE2 **hagagiigiia.** *v.* —.
ID **gii age.** Cry out softly.
ID **gii talinga.** Tinnitus.
ID **giigii saele.** Giggle.
ID **hagakii dalinga.** Producing a high-pitched noise in the ear; the itch felt in the ear when something very sweet is eaten.

GII$_a$

B **hakii**$_1$. *n.* Larynx, epiglottis, trachea.
ID **ma te hakii.** The uvula and

the adjacent portions of the oral cavity.
ID **ngalue de hakii.** Dislocated larynx.

GII$_b$
B **hakiigia.** *v.* To swell up (from being filled with air — like a balloon).
B 1 **hakiigiaanga.** *n.* —.

GII$_c$
ID **daahaa mada giigii.** The stage of development of the coconut between *daahaa mada makaga* and *modomodo.*
ID **modomodo mada gii.** The stage of development of the coconut between *modomodo* and *gaadinga gaha de a.*

GIIDADA
B **giidada.** *v.* Misfortune which will occur in the future (as ascertained through divination).
BE **hagagiidada.** *v.* —.

GIIDAGI
B **giidagi.** *v.* Relish (meat or fish, or something substituting for meat or fish, eaten with taro, etc.).
B 1 **giidaginga.** *n.* —.
BE **hagagiidagi.** *v.* —.
BE1 **hagagiidaginga.** *n.* —.
BE2 **hagagiidagina.** *v.* —.
ID **bulu giidagi.** A type of caulking compound, made from *bulu* and sap.
ID **giidagi ange gi —.** Eat a side dish with —.
CF **hiidagi.** [var. of *giidagi*].

GIIVADA
B **giivada.** *a.* Good fortune in the future, as revealed by divination.
BE **hagagiivada.** *v.* —.

GIIVIA
B **giivia.** *v.* To have something in one's eye.
B 1 **giiviaanga.** *n.* —.
BE **hagagiivia.** *v.* —.
BE1 **hagagiiviaanga.** *n.* —.
ID **mada giivia.** Dim light.

GILI
B **gili.** *v.* Skin.
B 1 **hagilianga.** *n.* —.
BE **hagagili.** *v.* Cause to have skin disease.
BE2 **hagagilia.** *v.* —.
R **giligili.** *v.* Coral rubble; (human) skin in an unhealthy condition.
XFL **daogili.** *n.* [var. of *daogoli*].
XFL **manu-gili-maau.** *n.* Plant sp.: heliotrope (*Tournefortia argentea* L., = *Messerschmidia argentea* L.).
ID **dohu de gili.** Covered all over (skin) with.
ID **teve de gili.** Gooseflesh.
ID **too gili.** Wrinkled skin (from age).
ID **tuu gili.** Gooseflesh, disgusted, horror-fascination.
ID **gili agau.** A moss-like covering of the reef; fish which live on the reef.
ID **gili belu.** Dead epidermis (can be peeled without pain).
ID **gili dabeo.** A fungus infection of the skin, ringworm.
ID **gili dalo.** Hillock.
ID **gili dama.** Soft-skinned.
ID **giligili tai.** Horizon.
ID **gili hano.** Separation of the hard interior parts of the tree trunk [a condition which spoils the tree for making a canoe].
ID **gili hau.** The inner bark of the hibiscus.
ID **gili iga.** A type of high cloud.
ID **gili laa.** Suntanned.
ID **gili langi.** A type of cloud (not associated with rain).
ID **gili maalama.** Light-skinned.
ID **gili malali.** Clean [adj.]; neat.

ID **gili malanga.** A type of skin disease.
ID **gili solasola.** Leathery black skin (of humans).
ID **gili somo.** The coconut meat of a germinating coconut (after the coconut apple has been removed).
ID **gili ulunga.** Pillowcase.
ID **hagasae gili.** Pierce the skin superficially.
ID **lodo gilimalali.** Pureness of heart, innocence.
ID **luu gili.** Labia minora.
ID **ula de gili.** Inflammation; red in the face, flushed; sunburned.

GILI$_a$
B **hagili.** *v.* Speak (or sing) with phelgm in one's throat.

GILI$_b$
B **gilisau.** *a.* Naked.
B 1 **gilisaunga.** *n.* —.
BE **hakilisau.** *v.* —.
BE1 **hakilisaunga.** *n.* —.
BE2 **hakilisaua.** *v.* —.
R **giligilisau.** *a.* Go around habitually without clothes.
R 1 **giligilisaunga.** *n.* —.
RE **hakiligilisau.** *v.* —.
RE1 **hakiligilisaunga.** *n.* —.
RE2 **hakiligilisaua.** *v.* —.

GIMA
B **gima.** *n.* Mollusk sp.: horse hoof clam (*Hippopus hippopus*).
ID **duunga gima.** Half of a clam shell.

GIMOO$_1$
B **gimoo$_1$.** *n.* Rat.
ID **gada gimoo.** Smile (esp. for no good reason or when embarrassed).
ID **hai me a gimoo.** To act insincerely.
ID **mahola gimoo.** To have many dead animals (or fish) lying about.
ID **manavanava gimoo.** Panting (as when short of breath).
ID **mmade gimoo.** To die in great numbers.

GIMOO$_2$
B **gimoo$_2$.** *n.* Fish sp.: silversides (The native term is applied to several spp.).

GINA
B **gina.** *n.* Fish sp.: rainbow runner.
ID **dua gina.** Fishing line of a size appropriate for *gina* fishing.
ID **hagadubu gina.** The name of a certain type of string figure.

GINADOA
B **ginadoa.** *v.* A boil on the body that is hard and painful, and which will not come to a head.
B 1 **ginadoaanga.** *n.* —.
BE **hagaginadoa.** *v.* —.
BE1 **hagaginadoaanga.** *n.* —.

GINI
B **gini.** *v.* Pick with one's fingers; to pinch off, or pinch and pull at the same time.
B 1 **giininga.** *n.* —.
B 2 **giinia.** *v.* —.
BC **magini.** *a.* A sudden pain while moving the body (as with a pinched nerve, or a muscle spasm); a sound like that made by snapping one's fingers.
BC1 **magiininga.** *n.* —.
BE **hagagini.** *v.* —.
BE1 **hagagiininga.** *n.* —.
BE2 **hagaginia.** *v.* —.
BF **hagamagini.** *v.* —.
BF1 **hagamaginianga.** *n.* —.
E **kini$_1$.** *v.* Pick at one time, pinch at one time.
E **kini$_2$.** *n.* Plant sp.: tree sp.: Terminalia tree *(Terminalia samoensis* Rech.).

R **ginigini$_1$.** *v.* —.
R **ginigini$_2$.** *n.* Mollusk sp.: *Tellinidae* spp.; *Pharonella* spp.).
R 1 **ginigininga.** *n.* —.
R 2 **giniginia.** *v.* —.
RC **maginigini.** *a.* —; *magini* all over.
RC1 **maginiginianga.** *n.* —.
RE **hagaginigini.** *v.* —.
RE1 **hagaginigininga.** *n.* —.
RE2 **hagaginiginia.** *v.* —.
RF **hagamaginigini.** *v.* —.
RF1 **hagamaginiginianga.** *n.* —.
ID **gai ginigini.** Eat sparingly (esp. fish — in order not to use up).
ID **ginigini looloa.** A game played by children.
ID **gini hua o hegau.** To receive the rewards of work well done (or punishment for evil deeds).
ID **gini manu.** Pick flowers.

GIO
B **gio.** *n.* Mollusk sp.: *Charonia* spp.

GIVI
R **givigivi.** *n.* Bird sp.: ruddy turnstone (*Arenaria interpres*).
XFL **mada-givi.** *n.* Fish sp.

GO
B **go.** *mp.* "It is...".
CF **go hee.** Where exactly?

GOA
B **goa.** *n.* Termite.

GOAI
B **goai.** *b.* Who?
ID **be goai (naa huu).** Whoever.
ID **goai de** + PRONOUN. Which of — (you, etc.)?
ID **goai ne siilia.** Who asked you? [an expression of recent invention].

GOBA
R **gobagoba.** *v.* Bushy (of hair).
R 1 **gobagobaanga.** *n.* —.
RE **hagagobagoba.** *v.* —.
RE1 **hagagobagobaanga.** *n.* —.

GOBE
E **kobe.** *a.* Cough (a single time).
E 1 **kobeanga.** *n.* —.
EE **hagakobe.** *v.* —.
EE1 **hagakobeanga.** *n.* —.
EE2 **hagakobelia.** *v.* —.
R **gobegobe.** *a.* Cough (repeatedly).
R 1 **gobegobeanga.** *n.* —.
RE **hagagobegobe.** *v.* —.
RE1 **hagagobegobeanga.** *n.* —.
RE2 **hagagobegobelia.** *v.* —.
ID **magi gobegobe.** Cold (sickness).

GOBU
E **kobu.** *a.* Splash (once).
E 1 **kobuanga.** *n.* —.
EE **hagakobu.** *v.* —.
EE1 **hagakobuanga.** *n.* —.
EE2 **hagakobua.** *v.* —.
EE2 **hagakobulia.** *v.* —.
R **gobugobu.** *a.* Splash (or make noise like splashing) repeatedly.
R 1 **gobugobuanga.** *n.* —.
RE **hagagobugobu.** *v.* —.
RE1 **hagagobugobuanga.** *n.* —.
RE2 **hagagobugobua.** *v.* —.
RE2 **hagagobugobulia.** *v.* —.
ID **kobu dango.** The splash of a small object (like a *dango*) hitting the water at high velocity.

GODI
B **godi.** *v.* To trim.
B 1 **godinga.** *n.* —.
B 2 **godia.** *v.* —.
BE **hagagodi.** *v.* —.
BE1 **hagagodinga.** *n.* —.
BE2 **hagagodia.** *v.* —.
R **godigodi.** *v.* —.
R 1 **godigodinga.** *n.* —.
R 2 **godigodia.** *v.* —.
RE **hagagodigodi.** *v.* —.
RE1 **hagagodigodinga.** *n.* —.
RE2 **hagagodigodia.** *v.* —.
ID **godi mai.** A certain type of

manipulation in playing with string figures.

GOE$_1$

B **goe.** *pi.* You [1].
E **koe.** *pi.* [var. of *goe*].
ID **dai sagana iho goe.** Watch out!
ID **goe iloo.** It's up to you!
ID **koe se aha.** Who do you think you are?
ID **hano goe.** See what I told you!
ID **i hee ai goe.** You lose!
ID **saganaa iho goe.** Watch out!

GOE$_2$

XFL **goehau.** *n.* Plant sp.: tree sp.: hibiscus tree (*Hibiscus tiliaceus* L.).

GOEDE

B **goede.** *n.* Octopus.
ID **buu goede.** Worthless or useless ['like an octopus without a head'].
ID **duudae goede.** The inky excretion of the octopus.

GOGO

B **gogo.** *a.* Bent slightly (like a round-shouldered person).
B 1 **gogoanga.** *n.* —.
BE **hagagogo.** *v.* —.
BE1 **hagagogoanga.** *n.* —.
BE2 **hagagogoa.** *v.* —.
ID **gogo dua.** Bent backwards.
ID **gogo gi mua.** Bent forward.

GOHU

B **gohu.** *a.* Dark (absence of light).
B 1 **goohunga.** *n.* Dark images, shadows in the darkness.
B 2 **gohulia.** *a.* —.
BE **hakohu.** *v.* —.
BE1 **hakohuanga.** *n.* —.
BE2 **hakohulia.** *v.* —.
P **kohu.** *a.* —; very dark in color.
R **gohugohu.** *a.* Becoming very dark (decreasing in natural light).
R 1 **gohugohunga.** *n.* —.
R 2 **gohugohulia.** *a.* —.
RE **hakohugohu.** *v.* —.
RE1 **hakohugohuanga.** *n.* —.
RE2 **hakohugohulia.** *v.* —.
ID **daahili lo te gohu.** A popular (secular) song.
ID **dangada gohu.** Ignorant person.
ID **dangada lo te gohu.** Unenlightened person.
ID **gohu boo dangodango.** A pitch-black night.
ID **gohu de lodo.** Ignorant.
ID **gohu de me.** Become dark (with no natural light).
ID **hakohu luu mada.** Squint (eyes), frown.
ID **lau kohu.** Growing well (of plants) [lit., 'having dark green leaves'].
ID **malu gohu.** Becoming darker (as when the sky becomes overcast).

GOI$_1$

B **goi$_1$.** *mt.* Still (as in 'he is still coming').
ID **aha goi.** What next?
ID **aha goi delaa.** What was I going to say?

GOI$_2$

B **goi$_2$.** *d.* Scrape —.
B 1 **goinga$_2$.** *n.* —.
B 2 **goia.** *v.* —.
E **koi.** *v.* Scrape (a single act), scraper.
R **goigoi$_1$.** *v.* —.
R **goigoi$_2$.** *n.* Bird sp.: Polynesian tattler (*Heteroscelus brevipes*).
R 1 **goigoinga.** *n.* —.
R 2 **goigoia.** *v.* —.
ID **gannui koi.** *gannui* which has been scraped out of the shell to be eaten.
ID **gulu koi.** A type of prepared food (breadfruit which has been cooked over hot coals with the skin on).

GOINGA

B **goinga$_1$.** *n.* A boundary marker (of stone).
ID **goinga o tai.** High-water mark.

ID **hadu goinga.** Boundary stone.

ID **hai goinga.** Aggrandizement of one's land holdings by moving others' *goinga.*

GOLAA

XCO **hadugolaa.** *n.* Any stone of volcanic origin [imported from volcanic islands].

GOLEE

B **golee.** *n.* Seed, testicles.

GOLI

B **goli.** *d.* Scrape off —.

B 1 **goolinga.** *n.* —.

B 2 **goolia.** *v.* —.

BE **hagagoli.** *v.* —.

BE1 **hagagoolinga.** *n.* —.

BE2 **hagagoolia$_1$.** *v.* —.

E **koli.** *v.* Scrape off (with one's finger), scratch up.

R **goligoli.** *v.* —; whorls in the hair of the head.

R 1 **goligolinga.** *n.* —.

R 2 **goligolia.** *v.* —.

RE **hagagoligoli.** *v.* —.

RE1 **hagagoligolinga.** *n.* —.

RE2 **hagagoligolia.** *v.* —.

XCO **hagaaigoli.** *n.* A food tree on another's land.

ID **goli manu.** Pick flowers.

GOLO

B **golo.** *v.* Remember an incident with a view toward revenge.

B 2 **goloa$_1$.** *v.* —.

BE **hagagolo.** *v.* —.

BE1 **hagagoloanga.** *n.* —.

BE2 **hagagoloa.** *v.* —.

R **gologolo.** *v.* —.

R 2 **gologoloa.** *v.* —.

RE **hagagologolo.** *v.* —.

RE1 **hagagologoloanga.** *n.* —.

RE2 **hagagologoloa.** *v.* —.

ID **golo age.** Continually *golo* voluntarily.

ID **golo me.** Unforgiving.

GOLO$_a$

B **golomagi.** *v.* Patient, (not impetuous); restrained (not prone to act on impulse).

B 1 **golomaginga.** *n.* —.

B 2 **golomagia.** *v.* —.

B 2 **golomagina.** *v.* —.

ID **golomagi iho.** To exercise great patience or restraint for one's own benefit.

ID **golomagi lodo.** Self-controlled.

GOLOA

B **goloa$_2$.** *a.* Gear, tools, goods, supplies (but not food).

BE **hakoloa.** *v.* Provide *goloa* for; support (someone, with material things).

BE1 **hakoloaanga.** *n.* —.

ID **goloa abasasa.** European goods or tools.

ID **goloa baalanga.** Metal-working tools.

ID **goloa de henua.** Gear of local manufacture.

ID **goloa duu biho.** Barber's tools.

ID **goloa haangoda.** Fishing gear.

ID **goloa hagadaahao.** Recreational equipment.

ID **goloa hai hegau.** Tools (for work).

ID **goloa hai umu.** Implements and supplies needed in connection with use of the earth oven.

ID **goloa hebagi.** Arms (tools of war).

ID **goloa hesuihagi.** Goods which are bartered.

ID **goloa labagau.** Carpenter's tools.

ID **goloa lalo.** Gear obtained from foreign lands.

ID **goloa o de hine.** Female genitalia.

ID **goloa o taane.** Male genitalia.

ID **hale goloa.** Store.

ID **lava i de goloa.** Having many *goloa.*

ID **mau goloa.** Rich in material possessions.

GOLONA

BE **hakolona.** *n.* Mollusk sp.: auger shell (*Terebridae* sp.).

ID **dogi hakolona.** A type of adze (with a curved blade of *Terebra* shell).

GOLU

B **golu.** *d.* Pray for the welfare of—.

B 1 **goolunga.** *n.* —.

B 2 **goolua.** *v.* —.

E **kolu.** *v.* Pray for the welfare of—; do earnestly.

R **golugolu.** *v.* —.

R 1 **golugolunga.** *n.* —.

R 2 **golugolua.** *v.* —.

ID **duu kolu.** Stand bracing oneself.

ID **kolu de henua.** Pray for the welfare of the whole island(and its population).

GONA$_1$

B **gona$_1$.** *d.* Very —.

B 1 **goonanga.** *n.* A record set by an individual (or team).

BC **magona.** *a.* Extraordinary, outstanding, unusual.

BE **hagagona.** *d.* Spend most of one's time —; become (or make) more —.

BE1 **hagagonaanga.** *n.* —.

BF **hagamagona.** *v.* —.

BF1 **hagamagonaanga.** *n.* —.

E **kona.** *a.* Very, too much.

EE **hagakona.** *v.* Become (or make) much worse.

EE1 **hagakonaanga.** *n.* —.

ID **dee kona.** Easily.

ID **gona odi.** Too much.

ID **kona ange.** Become much worse.

ID **kona iho.** Be too much for one.

ID **kona loo.** Too much!

ID **kona odi.** Too much.

GONA$_2$

B **gona$_2$.** *n.* Navel.

ID **daula de gona.** A cord between the naval and the genitals [according to Nukuoro anatomical lore].

ID **duu de gona.** Umbilical hernia.

CF **goononga$_2$.** A record (set in competitive sports).

GONO

B 1 **goononga$_1$.** *n.* —.

BE **hagakono.** *v.* —.

BE1 **hagakonoanga.** *n.* —.

E **kono.** *a.* Grunt (once).

R **gonogono.** *a.* Grunt (like a pig) repeatedly.

R 1 **gonogonoanga.** *n.* —.

RE **hagagonogono.** *v.* —.

RE1 **hagagonogonoanga.** *n.* —.

T **gogono.** *a.* Moan.

T 1 **gogonoanga.** *n.* —.

TE **hagagogono.** *v.* —.

TE1 **hagagogonoanga.** *n.* —.

XFL **manu-kono$_1$.** *n.* Bird sp. [probably the original Nukuoro name for the *ginuede*].

XFL **manu-kono$_2$.** *n.* Pigeon [an imported sp.].

GOO$_1$

B **goo$_1$.** *a.* A sound made to indicate one's presence (in response to being called from afar); an owl-like hoot (of birds).

B 1 **gooanga.** *n.* —.

BE **hagagoo.** *v.* —.

BE1 **hagagooanga.** *n.* —.

BE2 **hagagooa.** *v.* —.

BE2 **hagagoolia$_2$.** *v.* —.

P **koo.** *a.* —.

P 1 **kooanga.** *n.* —.

PE **hagakoo.** *v.* —; cough up.

PE1 **hakooanga.** *n.* —.

PE2 **hagakooa.** *v.* —.

PE2 **hagakoolia.** *v.* —.

R **googoo$_1$.** *a.* — [sing.].

R **googoo$_2$.** *n.* Bird sp.: Japanese snipe (*Capella hardwickii*).

R 1 **googooanga.** *n.* —.

RE **hagagoogoo.** *v.* —.

RE1 **hagagoogooanga.** *n.* —.

RE2 **hagagoogooa.** *v.* —.

RE2 **hagagoogoolia.** *v.* —.

T **gogoo.** *a.* [pl. of *googoo*].

T 1 **gogooanga.** *n.* —.
TE **hagagogoo.** *v.* —.
TE1 **hagagogooanga.** *n.* —.
TE2 **hagagogooa.** *v.* —.
TE2 **hagagogoolia.** *v.* —.
ID **se goo.** Adept at.

GOO$_2$
B **goo$_2$.** *n.* Taro spade.
XFL **unga-goo.** *n.* Mollusk sp.: vermetid gastropod sp.
ID **hagaduu i luu goo.** [an expression equivalent to "damn it"].

GOOBAI
B **goobai.** *a.* Hat.
B 1 **goobainga.** *n.* —.
BE **hakoobai.** *v.* Put a hat on (someone).
BE1 **hakoobainga.** *n.* —.
BE2 **hakoobaia.** *v.* —.
XFL **goobai-o-lillo.** *n.* Mollusk sp.: trochus.
ID **goobai dada.** Umbrella.
ID **goobai lau.** A hat made from pandanus leaves.
ID **hala goobai.** A wooden form used in making hats.
ID **hala langa goobai.** A form for plaiting hats.

GOODO
B **goodo.** *mt.* To have just.

GOONONGA
B **goononga$_2$.** *n.* A record (set in competitive sports).
ID **goononga gee.** To set a record.
CF **goonanga.** A record set by an individual (or team).

GOOSUU
B **goosuu.** *n.* Fish sp.: jack.

GOSI$_2$
E **kosi$_1$.** *v.* To scratch (once).
E 1 **goosinga.** *n.* —.
E 2 **goosia.** *v.* —.
EE **hagakosi.** *v.* —.
EE1 **hagagoosinga.** *n.* —.
EE2 **hagagoosia.** *v.* —.
R **gosigosi.** *v.* To scratch (slightly) repeatedly.
R 1 **gosigosinga.** *n.* —.
R 2 **gosigosia.** *v.* Scratched (of something solid only).
RE **hagagosigosi.** *v.* —.
RE1 **hagagosigosinga.** *n.* —.
RE2 **hagagosigosia.** *v.* —.
CF **gasigasia$_2$.** Rubbed against, scratched.

GOSI$_2$
E **kosi$_2$.** *n.* Mollusk sp.: *Cardium* sp.
XFL **kosi-honga-agau.** *n.* Mollusk sp.: *Trachycardium orbita.*
CF **gasi$_2$.** Mollusk sp.: *Asaphis dichotoma.*

GOSO
B **goso.** *a.* Bothered, annoyed.
B 1 **gosoanga.** *n.* —.
B 2 **gosolia.** *a.* —.
BE **hakoso.** *v.* —.
BE1 **hakosoanga.** *n.* —.
BE2 **hakosolia.** *v.* —.
P **koso.** *a.* —.
P 1 **kosoanga.** *n.* —.
P 2 **kosolia.** *a.* —.
XCO **vinigoso.** *v.* Entangled in apparent disorder.

GU
B **gu.** *mt.* DECISIVE ASPECT MARKER.
ID **doo ma gu....** Fall into the bad habit of; do something which is difficult to rectify.
ID **gu aha.** Why?

GUANI
B **guani.** *n.* A type of fish trap (with net sides).

GUANGA
B **guanga.** *n.* A type of basket.

GUAO
B **guao.** *n.* The hard sap of a non-native tree which is occasionally washed up on shore [used for making perfume].

GUBA
B **guba.** *n.* Fish sp.: cardinal fish (The native term is applied to several spp.).

XFL **guba-baabaa.** *n.* Fish sp.: cardinal fish.
XFL **guba-dee-gaina.** *n.* Fish sp.

GUBENGA
B **gubenga.** *v.* A large net for fishing.
BE **hagagubenga.** *v.* To teach someone to use a *gubenga.*
ID **dugu de gubenga.** Set a *gubenga* net.
ID **hai de gubenga.** To use a *gubenga* for fishing.
ID **langa de gubenga.** To pull up a *gubenga* to store it away.
ID **moni hai gubenga.** A canoe rigged for *gubenga* fishing.

GUBO
B **gubo.** *v.* Work with concentration in the midst of a group.
B 1 **guboanga.** *n.* —.
B 2 **guboa.** *v.* Being used in connection with group activity.
BE **hagagubo.** *v.* —.
BE1 **hagaguboanga.** *n.* —.
BE2 **hagaguboa.** *v.* —.
R **gubogubo.** *v.* —.
R 1 **guboguboanga.** *n.* —.
R 2 **guboguboa.** *v.* —.
RE **hagagubogubo.** *v.* —.
RE1 **hagaguboguboanga.** *n.* —.
RE2 **hagaguboguboa.** *v.* —.

GUBU
B **gubu.** *n.* Joint (of the hand or foot); verse (of a song).
XCO **daogubu.** *n.* Waist, circumference.
ID **gubu daahili.** Verse of a song.
ID **gubu dae.** Intestines which appear to have segmentation.
ID **gubu dao.** A join of the spear shaft which is made of two pieces of wood.
ID **gubu dolo.** A joint of the sugarcane.
ID **gubu lima.** Hand, wrist.
ID **gubu madila.** A joint of bamboo.
ID **gubu vae.** Foot, ankle.

GUDU
B **gudu.** *n.* Louse (head), or similar exoparasite of plants or animals (e.g., bird lice, scale insects, sap-feeding beetles, darkling beetles, etc.).
B 2 **gudua.** *v.* Abounding in lice.
B 3 **guduaanga.** *n.* Abounding in lice.
BE **hagagudu.** *v.* Cause to have lice (by transfer).
BE2 **hagagudua.** *v.* —.
BE3 **hagaguduaanga.** *n.* —.
ID **mulu gudu.** Grab while pulling; destroy by falling on or through; break through any obstacles in one's path.

GUGU
B **gugu.** *a.* To have the capacity (or size or strength) for; suited to.
B 1 **guguanga.** *n.* —.
BE **hagagugu.** *v.* —.
BE1 **hagaguguanga.** *n.* —.
ID **gugu ange.** Able to look after others; able to withstand.
ID **gugu iho.** Useless (person) in anything involving others (capable only of taking care of oneself).

GULABE
B **gulabe.** *n.* Rectum.
ID **doo de gulabe.** Prolapsed rectum.

GULU
B **gulu.** *n.* Plant sp.: tree sp.: breadfruit.
XCO **loigulu.** *n.* A type of prepared food (made from breadfruit).
ID **boo dolu de gulu.** The third day after breadfruit has been picked (after which it is not good to eat).

ID dau gulu. Breadfruit season.
ID gulu bala. Tree-ripened breadfruit.
ID gulu daladala. Breadfruit with rough skin.
ID gulu koi. A type of prepared food (breadfruit which has been cooked over hot coals with the skin on).
ID gulu maimai. A type of prepared food (ripe breadfruit which has been cooked in an *umu*).
ID gulu malali. Breadfruit with smooth skin.
ID lou gulu. Pick breadfruit.
ID malo gulu. Barkcloth [made from the inner skin of the breadfruit].
ID soesoe gulu. A young breadfruit tree.

GUMEDI

B	**gumedi.** *n.* Bowl (wooden).
C	**gamedi.** *n.* [var. of *gumedi*].
XG	**gamedi vai salo.** A type of bowl.
XG	**gumedi de henua.** A type of bowl.
XG	**gumedi hadu.** A bowl (pottery) [not indigenous].
XG	**gumedi vai solo.** A type of bowl.

GUMI$_1$

B	**gumi$_1$.** *d.* —.
B 1	**guuminga.** *n.* —.
B 2	**gumidia$_1$.** *v.* —.
B 2	**guumia$_1$.** *v.* —.
BE	**hagagumi.** *v.* —.
BE1	**hagaguuminga.** *n.* —.
E	**kumi$_1$.** *v.* To squeeze by grabbing.
EE	**hagakumi.** *v.* —.
R	**gumigumi$_1$.** *v.* —.
R 1	**gumiguminga.** *n.* —.
R 2	**gumigumia$_1$.** *v.* —.
R 2	**gumigumidia$_1$.** *v.* —.
RE	**hagagumigumi.** *v.* —.
RE1	**hagagumiguminga.** *n.* —.
ID	**gelegele gumi hue.** Fine-grained sand.
ID	**kumi tangi.** To control one's crying.

GUMI$_{1a}$

R	**gumigumi$_3$.** *n.* Chin, beard.
XFL	**gumigumi-o-sogo.** *n.* Plant sp.: epiphytic fern (*Vittaria incurvata* Cav.).
ID	**dahi de gumigumi.** Shave one's beard.
ID	**dugu de gumigumi.** Allow one's beard to grow, unshaven.

GUMI$_2$

B	**gumi$_2$.** *d.* Calculate —, figure out —.
B 1	**guumanga.** *n.* Calculation, arithmetic.
B 2	**gumidia$_2$.** *v.* —.
B 2	**guumia$_2$.** *v.* —.
E	**kumi$_2$.** *v.* Calculate (do arithmetic), figure out.
R	**gumigumi$_2$.** *v.* —.
R 2	**gumigumia$_2$.** *v.* —.
R 2	**gumigumidia$_2$.** *v.* —.

GUMI$_3$

B	**gumi$_3$.** *n.* A measurement: by tens of fathoms.

GUMU

CF	**hologumu.** (For a fish) to swallow a hook so that it becomes stuck in the throat.

GUNGA

CF	**lo gunga.** Inside the corner of.

GUUDUMA

B	**guuduma.** *n.* A (dry) elevation in the taro bog; hillock (in the taro bog only).

KAA$_1$

B	**kaa$_1$.** *a.* A type of sound, made to attract birds.
B 1	**kaanga.** *n.* —.
BE	**hagakaa.** *v.* —.
BE1	**hagakaanga.** *n.* —.
R	**kaakaa.** *a.* —.
R 1	**kaakaanga.** *n.* —.

RE **hagakaakaa.** *v.* —.
RE1 **hagakaakaanga.** *n.* —.

KAI$_1$

B **kai**$_3$. *a.* Boiling.
BE **hagakai**$_3$. *v.* —.
R **kaikai.** *a.* —.
RE **hagakaikai.** *v.* —.
ID **gai nnao**$_2$. Exaggerate (esp. in storytelling).

KAI$_2$

B **kai**$_4$. *n.* Legend, story.
XCO **kaianeane.** *a.* Show-off.
ID **dalanga a kai.** A story which is not true.
ID **kai laanui.** Show-off; a legend concerning the founding of Nukuoro.
ID **hai kai.** Show-off, proud.
ID **vaalanga a kai.** A story which is not true, a made-up story.

KAI$_{2a}$

B **hakai.** *v.* To put something on one's ear; an earring.
B 1 **hakainga.** *n.* —.
B 2 **hakaia.** *v.* —.
XFL **hakai-a-bagila.** *n.* Mollusk sp.: *Cerithiidae* spp.

KALA$_1$

B **kala**$_1$. *a.* Smarting of skin which has been cut, or of an abrasion, when in contact with seawater, etc.
B 1 **kalaanga**$_1$. *n.* —.
BE **hagakala**$_1$. *v.* —.
BE1 **hagakalaanga**$_1$. *n.* —.

KALA$_2$

B **kala**$_2$. *a.* Fragrance (esp. of food).
B 1 **kalaanga**$_2$. *n.* —.
BE **hagakala**$_2$. *v.* —.
BE1 **hagakalaanga**$_2$. *n.* —.

KALO

B **kalo**$_4$. *a.* Sharp (as a knife); a sharp pointed canoe (designed to ride easily in rough seas).
B 1 **kaloanga.** *n.* —.
BE **hagakalo.** *v.* —.
BE1 **hagakaloanga.** *n.* —.
ID **daguu kalo.** A thin straight-bladed (easily sharpened)axe blade.
ID **moni kalo.** A canoe with rounded sides (designed to ride easily in rough seas).

KANA

B **kana.** *mt.* WARNING ASPECT MARKER; don't ever —!; Be careful!; lest.
XCO **kanamalie.** *a.* Tasty (especially of taro).
ID **kana adu.** Perhaps; Watch yourself!
ID **kana mai.** Watch your step around me!

KANGI

B **kangi.** *a.* Sharp (as a knife), pointed.
BE **hakangi.** *v.* —.
ID **kangi baasi lua.** Double-edged.
ID **kangi de hagasaele.** A quick-witted person (who realizes his goals fast).
ID **kangi de maanadu.** A quick-witted person (who realizes his goals fast).
ID **kangi odi.** Too sharp.

KAVA

B **kava.** *a.* To feel uncomfortably warm.
B 1 **kavaanga.** *n.* —.
BE **hagakava.** *v.* —.
BE1 **hagakavaanga.** *n.* —.

KEELIGI

B **keeligi.** *v.* Put away against a contingency; take precautions.
B 1 **keeligianga.** *n.* —.
BE **hagakeeligi.** *v.* —.
BE1 **hagakeeligianga.** *n.* —.

KENA

B **kena.** *a.* Pale; whitish-yellow.
B 1 **kenaanga.** *n.* —.
BE **hagakena.** *v.* —.
BE1 **hagakenaanga.** *n.* —.
BE2 **hagakenalia.** *v.* —.

ID **lau kena.** Leaves (or hair) which have lost their natural healthy color.

KII$_1$

B **kii$_1$.** *a.* Win, overcome.
B 1 **kiianga$_1$.** *n.* —.
BE **hagakii$_1$.** *v.* —.
BE1 **hagakiianga$_1$.** *n.* —.

KII$_2$

B **kii$_2$.** *v.* Move away.
B 1 **kiianga$_2$.** *n.* —.
B 2 **kiia.** *v.* —.
BE **hakii$_2$.** *v.* Move away completely; get out of the way.
BE1 **hakiianga.** *n.* —.
BE1 **hakiinga.** *n.* —.
BE2 **hakiia.** *v.* Move (something) away completely.
ID **kii adu.** Get out!
ID **kii age.** Move upward; reach a certain age.
ID **kii ange.** Increase.
ID **kii gee.** Move away from.
ID **kii iho.** Smaller, lesser (in rank, importance, strength, development, etc.).
ID **kii mai.** Decreasing.
ID **hakii adu.** Get out!
ID **hakii gee.** [= *kii gee*].
CF **giidada.** Misfortune which will occur in the future (as ascertained through divination).

KINO

B **kino.** *a.* Hate.
BE **hagakino.** *v.* —.
R **ginogino.** *a.* Inclined not to enjoy something (esp. food) by being overly sensitive to filth.
RE **hagaginogino.** *v.* —.
ID **kino made.** Hate vehemently, completely disgusted.
ID **hagadau kino.** Hate each other.
ID **hakino gee.** Filthy, disgusting.
ID **magi kino.** Loss of appetite.
ID **valaai kino.** Medicine taken to regain one's appetite.

KIVI

B **kivi.** *a.* Thin (bony).
BE **hagakivi.** *v.* —.

KOLILI

B **kolili.** *i.* I'm only kidding!
BE **hagakolili.** *v.* To use the word *kolili*.

HAA$_1$

B **haa$_1$.** *d.* Bear — (as a tree).
BC **mahaa.** *a.* Broken up, cracked, burst.
BF **hagamahaa.** *v.* —.
BF1 **hagamahaanga.** *n.* —.
E **hhaa.** *v.* Blossom forth.
E 1 **hhaanga.** *n.* —.
EC **maahaa.** *a.* Daybreak.
EE **hagahhaa.** *v.* —.
EE1 **hagahhaanga.** *n.* —.
R **haahaa$_1$.** *v.* —.
R 1 **haahaanga$_1$.** *n.* —.
RC **mahaahaa.** *a.* [pl. of *mahaa*].
RE **hagahaahaa$_1$.** *v.* —.
RE1 **hagahaahaanga.** *n.* —.
RF **hagamahaahaa.** *v.* —.
RF1 **hagamahaahaanga.** *n.* —.
ID **dele de maahaa.** Daybreak.
ID **dele de mahaa.** Starting to crack.
ID **haa manu.** The young (of an animal) born at the same time (e.g., a litter, etc.); the offspring of (sharing the characteristics of).
ID **maahaa ada.** Dawn (first burst of light).
ID **mahaa de usu.** To have encountered unexpected misfortune.

HAA$_{1a}$

B **haa$_2$.** *n.* Coconut palm frond.
ID **haa daha.** The outer coconut palm frond.
ID **haa leu.** A leaf which has turned yellowish-brown.
ID **haa lodo.** The inner coconut palm frond.

HAA$_2$

R **haahaa$_2$.** *v.* To search for in the dark; to seek blindly using only one's hands to locate something; similarly, any action that is tentative.

R 1 **haahaanga$_2$.** *n.* —.
R 2 **haahaagia.** *v.* —.
RE **hagahaahaa$_2$.** *v.* —.
RE2 **hagahaahaagia.** *v.* —.
ID **haahaa saele.** Search here and there.

HAA$_3$
B **haa$_3$.** *an.* Four.
BE **hagahaa (ina).** *v.* Make a total of four.
XCO **Diba-haa.** *nn.* The name of a person in a traditional story.
XCO **Haa-laangi.** *nt.* Thursday [lit., the 'fourth day'].
XCO **Haa-malama.** *nt.* April [lit., the 'fourth month'].
ID **baasi e haa o de langi.** The four quadrants of the sky.
ID **haa-alaala.** The fourth number of a counting game played to determine who is "it".

HAA$_4$
XFL **haa-dolo.** *n.* Fish sp.: squirrelfish.

HAADODO
B **haadodo.** *n.* The connecting pegs of the outrigger float.

HAAIDE
B **haaide.** *v.* Measure (exactly).
B 1 **haaidenga.** *n.* —.
B 2 **haaidea.** *v.* —.
BE **hagahaaide.** *v.* —.
BE1 **hagahaaidenga.** *n.* —.
BE2 **hagahaaidea.** *v.* —.

HAAINA
B **haaina.** *v.* Stare at.
B 1 **haainanga.** *n.* —.
B 2 **haainasia.** *v.* —.
BE **hagahaaina.** *v.* —.
BE1 **hagahaainanga.** *n.* —.
BE2 **hagahaainasia.** *v.* —.
ID **haaina dangada.** Stare at people indiscreetly (esp. strangers).

HAALALA
B **haalala.** *v.* Stand leaning.
BE **hagahaalala.** *v.* —.

HAALIGI
B **haaligi.** *v.* Wrap from under, wrap around; to line something (e.g., a box, with paper).
B 1 **haaliginga.** *n.* —.
B 2 **haaligia.** *v.* —.
B 2 **haaligidia.** *v.* —.
BE **hagahaaligi.** *v.* —.
BE1 **hagahaaliginga.** *n.* —.
BE2 **hagahaaligia.** *v.* —.
BE2 **hagahaaligidia.** *v.* —.
R **haahaaligi.** *v.* —.
R 1 **haahaaliginga.** *n.* —.
R 2 **haahaaligia.** *v.* —.
R 2 **haahaaligidia.** *v.* —.
RE1 **hagahaahaaliginga.** *n.* —.
RE2 **hagahaahaaligia.** *v.* —.
RE2 **hagahaahaaligidia.** *v.* —.

HAALO
B **haalo.** *v.* Extend one's hand, reach out; to expect things from others, and accept too readily.
B 1 **haalonga.** *n.* —.
B 2 **haaloa.** *v.* —.
BE **hagahaalo.** *v.* —; encourage to *haalo*.
BE1 **hagahaalonga.** *n.* —.
BE2 **hagahaaloa.** *v.* —.
R **haahaalo.** *v.* —.
R 1 **haahaalonga.** *n.* —.
R 2 **haahaaloa.** *v.* —.
RE **hagahaahaalo.** *v.* —.
RE1 **hagahaahaalonga.** *n.* —.
RE2 **hagahaahaaloa.** *v.* —.
ID **e dee haalo.** Refuse to accept (something).

HAANAU
B **haanau.** *a.* Born; delivery (of a baby); give birth to.
B 1 **haanaunga.** *n.* —.
B 2 **hanaua.** *v.* —.

BE **hagahaanau.** *v.* To help to deliver a child (as a midwife does).
BE1 **hagahaanaunga.** *n.* —.
BE2 **hagahanaua.** *v.* —.
R **haahaanau.** *a.* —.
RE **hagahaahaanau.** *v.* To help to deliver children on many occasions.
RE1 **hagahaahaanaunga.** *n.* —.
RE2 **hagahaahaanaua.** *v.* —.
XCO **Pono-haanau.** *nn.* The name of a spirit.
ID **dau haanau.** A period during which many children are born.
ID **de hine hagahaanau.** Midwife.
ID **haanau ssene.** Yield interest.
ID **langi haanau.** A certain kind of rain [an omen of an impending childbirth].

HAANIALO
B **haanialo.** *v.* A bracing cross-beam [?].
B 1 **haanialoanga.** *n.* —.
BE **hagahaanialo.** *v.* —.
BE1 **hagahaanialoanga.** *n.* —.
R **haahaanialo.** *v.* To put *haanialo* on in several places.
R 1 **haahaanialoanga.** *n.* —.
RE **hagahaahaanialo.** *v.* —.
RE1 **hagahaahaanialoanga.** *n.* —.

HAANGAI
B **haangai.** *v.* To feed (someone).
B 1 **hangainga.** *n.* —.
B 2 **hangaia.** *v.* —.
B 2 **hangaina.** *v.* —.
R **hangahangai.** *v.* —.
R 1 **hangahangainga.** *n.* —.
R 2 **hangahangaia.** *v.* —.
R 2 **hangahangaina.** *v.* —.

HAANGODA
B **haangoda.** *v.* Fishing.
B 1 **haangodaanga.** *n.* —.
B 2 **haangodalia.** *v.* A suitable (place) for fishing.
BE **hagahaangoda.** *v.* To teach to fish.
BE1 **hagahaangodaanga.** *n.* —.
BE2 **hagahaangodalia.** *v.* —.
R **haahaangoda.** *v.* To fish first in one place, then in another.
R 1 **haahaangodaanga.** *n.* —.
R 2 **haahaangodalia.** *v.* A place which has been fished in over and over.
RE **hagahaahaangoda.** *v.* —.
RE1 **hagahaahaangodaanga.** *n.* —.
RE2 **hagahaahaangodalia.** *v.* —.
XG **ngavesi haangoda.** Fishing tackle box.
ID **dangada haangoda.** Fisherman.
ID **daumaha haangoda.** Prayer service held while visiting others' houses [in the hope of getting converts].
ID **dua haangoda de boo.** Fishing line of a size appropriate for *haangoda de boo.*
ID **goloa haangoda.** Fishing gear.
ID **haahaangoda ange.** Prowl around (to attack).
ID **haangoda de agau.** A method of fishing (with a line on the reef).
ID **haangoda de boo.** A method of fishing (at night, beyond the reef).
ID **haangoda de lodo.** To fish in the lagoon.
ID **haangoda dua agau.** Fishing beyond the reef (on the seaward side of the atoll).
ID **haangoda dua beau.** A fishing method (used on the seaward reef during the day) employing a line, with hermit crabs for bait).
ID **haangoda dugidugi.** A method of fishing (night fishing outside the reef, using hermit crabs for bait).

ID **haangoda ina.** [= *haangodalia*].

ID **haangoda mada aasanga.** To fish for *labelabe*.

ID **seesee haangoda saele.** Look for girls.

HAAU

B **haau.** *v.* Suckle (at the breast).

B 1 **haaunga$_2$.** *n.* —.

B 2 **haaua$_2$.** *v.* —.

BE **hagahaau.** *v.* —.

BE1 **hagahaaunga.** *n.* —.

BE2 **hagahaaua.** *v.* —.

R **haahaau.** *v.* —.

R 1 **haahaaunga.** *n.* —.

RE **hagahaahaau.** *v.* —.

RE1 **hagahaahaaunga.** *n.* —.

RE2 **hagahaahaaua.** *v.* —.

ID **haau unuunu.** Breast-feed.

ID **hakaau unuunu.** To cause an infant to feed at the breast.

HADA

B **hada.** *n.* Shelf, platform, raft, floor (of planks); car; a clam nursery; men's house [archaic].

R **hadahada.** *n.* Chest.

ID **hadahada ama.** The platform fastened on top of the outrigger booms of a canoe.

HADI

B **hadi.** *a.* Broken (as a stick), bent up.

B 1 **haadinga.** *n.* —; curve (e.g., of a road).

B 1 **hadinga.** *n.* Joint (of an arm or leg).

B 2 **haadia.** *v.* —.

BE **hagahadi.** *v.* —; break in (something new).

BE1 **hagahaadinga.** *n.* —.

BE2 **hagahadia.** *v.* —.

E **hhadi.** *v.* Snapped off.

R **hadihadi.** *v.* Break many times or in many places.

R 1 **hadihadinga.** *n.* —.

R 2 **hadihadia.** *v.* —.

RE **hagahadihadi.** *v.* —.

RE1 **hagahadihadinga.** *n.* —.

RE2 **hagahadihadia.** *v.* —.

T **haahadi.** *v.* [pl. of *hadi*].

T 1 **haahadinga.** *n.* —.

T 2 **haahadia.** *v.* —.

TE **hagahaahadi.** *v.* —.

TE1 **hagahaahadinga.** *n.* —.

TE2 **hagahaahadia.** *v.* —.

XCO **hadiugu.** *v.* A unit of linear measure (from the end of an outstretched hand to the bent elbow of the other arm).

ID **dangi hagahadihadi.** Wail loudly (when crying).

ID **haadinga haiava.** Bend in a path.

ID **hadi aho.** [var. of *hadi haho*].

ID **hadi bala.** To rely on others for the things one should provide for oneself.

ID **hadi bodo.** Breaking of waves at short intervals.

ID **hadi de uga.** The curvature of a fish line when angling (due to underwater currents).

ID **hadi haho.** Steep (inclination).

ID **hadi modu.** Sheer drop-off (as at the edge of a cliff).

ID **hhadi iho luu vae.** Take a short break (in work involving standing).

ID **lau hadihadi.** Having wavy hair.

HADU$_1$

B **hadu$_1$.** *v.* Invented —, made-up —; layout of (preliminary work on) plaiting.

B 1 **hadunga.** *n.* —.

B 2 **hadua.** *v.* —.

E **hhadu.** *a.* Invented, made-up (e.g., a story).

E 1 **haadunga.** *n.* —.

E 2 **haadua.** *v.* —.

R **haduhadu$_1$.** *v.* —.

R 1 **haduhadunga$_1$.** *n.* —.

R 2 **haduhadua$_1$.** *v.* —.

ID **dangi hhadu$_1$.** Cry for effect.

ID **hadu daahili.** To make up a song.

ID **hadu me llanga.** Lay out plaited work.

ID **hadu muna.** Lie (tell a falsehood).

ID **me hhadu.** Falsehood, lie.

ID **me hhadu hugadoo.** It's a lie!

ID **muna hhadu.** Lie (falsehood).

HADU$_2$

B **hadu$_2$.** *n.* Stone, rock, a piecé of weathered coral.

R **haduhadu$_2$.** *v.* Thick (not watery).

R 1 **haduhadunga$_2$.** *n.* —.

R 2 **haduhadua$_2$.** *v.* Rocky (full of stones).

RE **hagahaduhadu.** *v.* —.

RE1 **hagahaduhadunga.** *n.* —.

RE2 **hagahaduhadua.** *v.* —.

XCO **hadugolaa.** *n.* Any stone of volcanic origin [imported from volcanic islands].

XCO **Hadu-lehu.** *nn.* The name of a ghost in Nukuoro legend.

XFL **hadu-bunga.** *n.* Mollusk sp.: *Chama iostoma.*

XFL **hadu-gamugamu.** *n.* Coral sp.

XFL **hadu-i-de-ssala.** *n.* Coral sp.: red organ-pipe coral [used for making necklaces].

XFL **hadu-maadau.** *n.* Coral sp. [used for polishing pearl shell fish hooks].

XFL **hadu-mada-pula.** *n.* Coral sp.: (several spp. — poisonous)..

XFL **hadu-mangeo.** *n.* Cushion starfish.

XFL **hadu-uaua.** *n.* Mollusk sp.: *Spondylus* sp.

XFL **hadu-uli.** *n.* Coral sp.: blue coral.

XG **gede hadu.** A type of basket [used for hauling stones for the earth oven].

XG **gumedi hadu.** A bowl (pottery) [not indigenous].

ID **dao hadu.** Cover up (by putting on layer after layer); give too much (e.g., work) to.

ID **daula luu hadu.** Testicle cords.

ID **gau hadu.** The board to which the metal grater for grating taro is attached.

ID **hadu alo.** The bottom portion of a fish.

ID **hadu de gaanunu.** Nipple of breast.

ID **hadu de moana.** A type of string figure.

ID **hadu goinga.** Boundary stone.

ID **hadu hagamogomogo.** Gem.

ID **hadu lalo.** A stone on which hermit crabs are crushed (to use for bait).

ID **hadu lunga.** A stone used to crush hermit crabs (for bait).

ID **hadu mada.** Eyeball.

ID **hadu manava.** Heart.

ID **hadu o de mamu.** The hard stomach-like organ of certain fish.

ID **hadu solo bulaga.** A taro grater made from a certain type of coral.

ID **hagaditidi de hadu.** To skip a stone across the water.

ID **hale hadu.** A house of brick or cement construction.

ID **lava hadu.** Leader (between fishing line and hook).

ID **luu hadu a moidigi.** Stone-like organs in the top of the head of flying fish.

ID **madaa hadu.** Grater (metal) attached to a board for grating taro.

ID **mada sua hadu.** Storm beach (on the seaward reef).

ID **muli sua hadu.** Reefward of the storm beach; beach rock.

ID **sae de hadu.** Make a grater (by punching holes in sheet metal).

ID **sua hadu umu.** Stones (dead coral) used in the

	earth oven.
CF	**bilibili-hadu.** Fish sp. (*Trachinotus bailloni*).

HADU$_{2a}$

B	**daihadu.** *v.* Hardwood in the tree trunk.
BE	**hagadaihadu.** *v.* —.

HATULI

B	**hatuli.** *v.* Thunder.
XFL	**alelo-hatuli.** *n.* Mollusk sp.: pearly nautilus shell.
ID	**paa de hatuli.** Rolling of thunder.
ID	**doo de hatuli.** The 'falling of thunder' [thought to burn trees].

HAELE

B	**haele.** *v.* Bring up (children), discipline (children).
B 1	**haelenga.** *n.* —.
B 2	**haelea.** *v.* —.
BE	**hagahaele.** *v.* —.
BE1	**hagahaelenga.** *n.* —.
BE2	**hagahaelea.** *v.* —.
R	**haehaele.** *v.* —.
R 1	**haehaelenga.** *n.* —.
R 2	**haehaelea.** *v.* —.
RE	**hagahaehaele.** *v.* —.
RE1	**hagahaehaelenga.** *n.* —.
RE2	**hagahaehaelea.** *v.* —.
ID	**haele sala.** Spoil (children), bring up (children) badly.

HAELU

B	**haelu.** *v.* Var. of *hailu.*

HAGA-

B	**haga-.** *mf.* CAUSATIVE PREFIX; cause to (be, become, have, know) —.

HAGAAHULU

ID	**dao hagaahulu.** To leave an earth oven covered, even after the food is cooked.

HAGAAI

B	**hagaai.** *a.* Be in a serious situation.
XCO	**hagaaigoli.** *n.* A food tree on another's land.
ID	**tama hagaai.** Poor fellow!
ID	**tangada hagaai.** Poor fellow!

HAGAHI

B	**hagahi.** *v.* Call (someone) once.
B 1	**hagahinga.** *n.* —.
B 2	**hagahia.** *v.* —.
R	**hagaagahi.** *v.* Call (someone).
R 1	**hagaagahinga.** *n.* —.
R 2	**hagaagahia.** *v.* —.
ID	**hagaagahi sseeloo.** To call out "sail ho!".

HAGAI

CF	**hagailangi.** A type of prepared food (made from breadfruit).
CF	**hagailangi-bangi.** A type of prepared food (*bangi* soaked in coconut milk).

HAGAO

B	**hagao.** *v.* Buy, sell, repay.
B 1	**hagaoanga.** *n.* —; price, wages; prize.
B 2	**hagaoa.** *v.* —.
ID	**dangada hagao me.** Storekeeper.
ID	**hagaoanga gi lunga.** Good wages; a good price.
ID	**hagao baubau.** Low wages, low-priced.
ID	**hagao ngadaa.** Expensive.
ID	**hagao ngaohie.** Inexpensive.
ID	**hale hagao me.** Store.

HAGASAALEI

ID	**daa hagasaalei.** Make a striped design in tatooing.

HAGELI

B	**hageli.** *v.* A sort of sound in ancient chants.
B 1	**hagelinga.** *n.* —.
B 2	**hagelia.** *v.* —.
R	**hagehageli.** *v.* —.
R 1	**hagehagelinga.** *n.* —.
R 2	**hagehagelia.** *v.* —.

HAGI

B	**hagi.** *v.* Pick (fruit) by

	grabbing and twisting off.
B 1	**haaginga.** *n.* —.
B 2	**haagia.** *v.* —.
B 2	**haagina.** *v.* —.
BC	**mahagi.** *a.* (Fruit) picked off (or caused to fall by wind).
BC1	**mahaginga.** *n.* —.
BF	**hagamahagi.** *v.* —.
BF1	**hagamahaginga.** *n.* —.
BF2	**hagamahagia.** *v.* —.
BF2	**hagamahagina.** *v.* —.
E	**hhagi.** *v.* Make a sharp turn; *hagi* at one time.
PC	**maahagi.** *a.* —.
PF	**hagamaahagi.** *v.* —.
PF1	**hagamaahaginga.** *n.* —.
PF2	**hagamaahagia.** *v.* —.
PF2	**hagamaahagina.** *v.* —.
R	**hagihagi.** *v.* —.
R 1	**hagihaginga.** *n.* —.
R 2	**hagihagia.** *v.* —.
R 2	**hagihagina.** *v.* —.
RC	**mahagihagi.** *a.* —.
RC1	**mahagihaginga.** *n.* —.
RF	**hagamahagihagi.** *v.* —.
RF1	**hagamahagihaginga.** *n.* —.
RF2	**hagamahagihagia.** *v.* —.
RF2	**hagamahagihagina.** *v.* —.
ID	**au hagi.** An ocean current which turns away from the reef.
ID	**gauanga mahagi.** Dislocated thigh bone.
ID	**hagi ade.** Insult (someone).
ID	**hagi me.** Pick coconuts.
ID	**hhagi de baa galele.** Jerking of a fishing lure to attract fish; a method of extracting a lure from the fish's mouth.
ID	**hhagi gee.** Turn away from (to avoid), veer.

HAHA

B	**haha.** *n.* Mouth odor.
ID	**luuluu haha.** Wash one's mouth out, gargle.
CF	**alohaha.** Throat (of fish only).

HAHINE

B	**hahine.** *n.* Woman.
BE	**hagahahine.** *a.* Treat as a woman.
P	**haahine.** *n.* Women.
PE	**hagahaahine.** *a.* Treat as women.
ID	**dagu hahine.** My "daughter" or "mother" (not one's natural mother).
ID	**daina hahine.** Sister, female cousin.
ID	**gauligi hahine.** Female child, girl.
ID	**hale haahine.** A house of prostitution.
ID	**lolo hai haahine.** A love potion (applied to the clothes or body).
ID	**magi haahine.** Menstruation.
ID	**malo haahine.** A dress (female clothing).
ID	**mau haahine.** Attractive to women (for some inexplicable reason).
ID	**somo haahine.** A fleshy (non-muscular) man.
ID	**sou hahine.** A steady, light gust of wind.
ID	**ulu i haahine.** Ladies' man, girl-crazy.
ID	**valaai hai haahine.** A love potion (to attract women).
CF	**hine.** Female, woman; [must be preceded by an article].

HAHO

B	**haho.** *nl.* Outside of.
XCO	**duaahaho.** *nl.* Outside of (e.g., a building).
ID	**hadi haho.** Steep (inclination).

HAI$_1$

B	**hai$_1$.** *v.* Do, make, use; have sexual intercourse.
B 1	**hainga.** *n.* —; law, procedure, rule.
B 2	**haia.** *v.* —.
BE	**hagahai.** *v.* —.
BE1	**hagahainga.** *n.* —.
BE2	**hagahaia.** *v.* —.
R	**haihai.** *v.* —.
R 1	**haihainga.** *n.* —.
R 2	**haihaia.** *v.* —.

RE hagahaihai. *v.* —.
RE1 hagahaihainga. *n.* —.
RE2 hagahaihaia. *v.* —.
XCO **haitoga.** *n.* An opening for a door or window.
XFL **gammenge-hai-gili-dabeo.** *n.* Mollusk sp.: *Thais luteostoma.*
XFL **manu-hai-hau.** *n.* Mollusk sp. [a recently coined name, = spp. of *sisi*].
XG **laulau hai daonga.** A type of basket [used for allocating portions at a feast].
ID **aude haia.** No kidding?
ID **au e hai bolo.** "I thought that —".
ID **daane hai moni.** Sailor, seaman.
ID **dagodo hai sala.** Fornication.
ID **dagu hai bolo.** "One would have thought that —".
ID **daohi ange dahi hai.** Argue against.
ID **dee adahaia.** Very; very bad.
ID **dee hai gee.** Be tied (e.g., in a footrace).
ID **dee haihai donu.** That's for sure!
ID **deledele hainga a me.** Rush because of an emergency.
ID **doo i hainga a me.** Wait for a long time (beyond the time expected).
ID **tala hai sala.** Confess one's sins or errors.
ID **tangada hai me dabu.** Cult priest.
ID **tangada hai sauaa.** Magician, sorcerer.
ID **gaadinga hai ngadi ubu.** Coconut with a shell of a size appropriate for use as a cooking vessel.
ID **goloa hai hegau.** Tools (for work).
ID **goloa hai umu.** Implements and supplies needed in connection with use of the earth oven.
ID **hagadau hai me ai.** Use jointly or collectively.
ID **hai aabi.** Having many rooms or sections.
ID **hai ange.** Do to; do for, fix; say to.
ID **hai aoa ina.** Bear misshapen fruit.
ID **hai baasi.** Take sides against, oppose.
ID **hai bao.** Divided into compartments.
ID **hai be —.** It would seem that —.
ID **hai be se manu.** Promiscuous (especially if indiscreet or known to have sexual relations with one's own relatives).
ID **hai daahili.** To compose songs.
ID **hai daalanga.** Talkative, chatterbox, talk animatedly.
ID **hai dagelo.** Deep-bottomed.
ID **hai dago.** Ritual observances.
ID **hai dahi doo.** Trick someone.
ID **hai dahi heohi.** Maintain one's position in an argument (against contrary positions).
ID **hai dama.** Pregnant.
ID **hai dauaa.** Be in a wrinkled condition.
ID **hai de biho.** Act smart (deviously).
ID **hai de boo (o).** Celebrate the birthday (of).
ID **hai de eidu.** One of two children's games [one like hide-and-seek, another like tag].
ID **hai de gubenga.** To use a *gubenga* for fishing.
ID **hai de hagamaanadu.** Remembrance, observance of (e.g., a holiday).
ID **hai de hai.** Stubborn, willful.
ID **hai de hilihili.** Hold an election.
ID **hai de ingoo.** Make a good name for oneself (by one's ingratiating behavior).
ID **hai dodo.** Bleeding profusely.
ID **hai donu.** Do properly by

accident; do on purpose [when precededed by *se*].

ID **hai duu.** To carry a baby about.

ID **hai taelodo.** Obtain something in great number.

ID **hai gaavenga.** Restless (of a child).

ID **hai gai.** Prepared food; cook food.

ID **hai gaiaa.** Use without permission.

ID **hai gainga.** Make an area messy by throwing trash around.

ID **hai galauna.** Fish with the *galauna* net.

ID **hai ganabu.** The stage in the development of a coconut tree in which *ganabu* begins to develop.

ID **hai gauligi.** Each child is somewhat different!

ID **hai gi de mahi.** Do or take by force, rape.

ID **hai goinga.** Aggrandizement of one's land holdings by moving others' *goinga.*

ID **hai kai.** Show-off, proud.

ID **hai hagadubu.** To fashion a string figure.

ID **haihai me.** Be doing something suspicious.

ID **haihainga a —.** Way of repeatedly —.

ID **hai hegau.** Work [verb].

ID **hai hegau hilo.** Work hypocritically (appearing to follow the rules but secretly violating the prohibitions).

ID **hai huaabodu.** Treat someone (including one's spouse) as a relative by not asking permission to use or borrow property; treat a relative as belonging to another family altogether.

ID **hai huaame.** Punctilious, be particular.

ID **hai hua laa.** Do indifferently.

ID **hai hulu o —.** Act mad like —.

ID **hai huuhuaa me.** Sorcery.

ID **hai lodo.** Resentful.

ID **hai madangi.** Pass wind (flatus).

ID **hai mainu.** Collect bait.

ID **hai me.** Industrious.

ID **hai me a gauligi.** A childish act.

ID **hai me a gimoo.** To act insincerely.

ID **hai me a leangi.** Bad-mannered.

ID **hai me balavini.** To conduct oneself clumsily.

ID **hai me daahea.** Search for driftwood or other beached objects.

ID **hai me dagi.** Work slowly.

ID **hai me dogaa.** Behave with embarrassment or shyness.

ID **hai me dua nnui.** Do violently.

ID **hai me gaiaa.** To be reluctant to express oneself openly (esp. to persons in certain types of relationship to one).

ID **hai me galasi.** To steal after having sort of asked for.

ID **hai me gavia.** Do crazy things.

ID **hai me hagamadia.** Behave in a more-or-less show-off manner.

ID **hai me hebagi.** Be on the point of fighting.

ID **hai me hoosenga.** Somewhat *hoosenga.*

ID **hai me ma —.** Sort of —.

ID **hai me madua.** Act grown up.

ID **hai me magua.** Sort of steal.

ID **hai me moolau.** An habitually fast worker.

ID **hai me mudumudu.** A habitually *mudumudu.*

ID **hai me mulegi.** To show off (esp. in front of members of the opposite sex).

ID **hai me mule me.** Habitually slow or late.

ID **hai modo.** Eat (or pick) when still unripe.

ID **hai mogomogo.** Muscular; daring (show off), bold;

strong (person); active physically.
ID **hai moni.** Sailor.
ID **hai moumou.** Use wastefully.
ID **hai muna.** Public meeting.
ID **hai naa hanu me.** Something will happen...
ID **hainga a —.** Way of doing —.
ID **haingaa me.** Work requiring a large work force.
ID **hai ngadaa.** Difficult.
ID **hai ngaohie.** Easy.
ID **hainga soe.** A just law.
ID **hai sala.** Mistake, error.
ID **hai samu.** To gossip.
ID **hai saulaba.** The relationship of parent-in-law to child-in-law.
ID **hai sogosogo.** Masturbate oneself.
ID **hai sseu.** Wasteful.
ID **hai sumu.** Having a diamond-shaped decoration or form, etc.
ID **hai uaua.** Dilated veins.
ID **hai vaivai me.** Have sexual relations.
ID **hale hai niho.** Dentist's office.
ID **(de) hine hai be.** Whore.
ID **magi hai dama.** Morning sickness (of pregnancy).
ID **me hai ada.** Camera.
ID **me hai dago.** Ritual acts, religious acts.
ID **me hai laangi.** Calandar.
ID **momme hai lua.** A fishing spot (beyond the seaward reef) where either reef or ocean fish can be found.
ID **moni hai gubenga.** A canoe rigged for *gubenga* fishing.
ID **muna hai alaa.** Oh my goodness!
ID **vaivai hai.** Do badly, abuse.
ID **vange gi de hainga.** Sue (in court), complain about (to the authorities).

HAI$_{1a}$

XCO **haiava.** *n.* Road, pathway (for going), track; ocean liner.
ID **dao haiava.** Path (a minor, not major, thoroughfare).
ID **haadinga haiava.** Bend in a path.
ID **hesilihaginga haiava.** Intersection.

HAI$_2$

B **hai$_2$.** *d.* Be in the relationship of; having a — (as in *hai maalisa*) [from *iai*?].
XCO **haiadaligi.** *n.* The eldest child of the eldest child.
ID **hai aha.** What relationship?
ID **hai bodu.** Married couple, marry; the relationship between spouses.
ID **hai daina.** The relationship between siblings or cousins.
ID **hai damaahine.** The relationship between parent and daughter.
ID **hai damana.** The relationship between father (or other male elder) and child (or one treated as child).
ID **hai dangada.** The relationship between relatives, related (of persons).
ID **hai dinana.** The relationship between mother (or other female elder) and child (or one treated as a child).
ID **hai dubuna.** The relationship between grandparent and grandchild.
ID **hai maa.** The relationship of spouse's sibling to sibling's spouse.
ID **hai maadua.** Mention of one's elders by others.
ID **hai maalisa.** Having an overhanging reef shelf.
ID **hai mada dabu.** An avoidance relationship (between kin).
ID **hai mogobuna.** The relationship between

grandparent and grandchild.
ID **hai soa.** The relationship between friends; friendship.
ID **ngadi hai bodu.** Common-law marriage, concubinage.

HAIGA
CF **haigabungi.** Act strangely, act shyly.

HAIGABUNGI
B **haigabungi.** *a.* Act strangely, act shyly.
B 1 **haigabungianga.** *n.* —.
BE **hagahaigabungi.** *v.* Make shy.
BE1 **hagahaigabungianga.** *n.* —.

HAIGAMAIANA
B **haigamaiana.** *a.* Effective, useful, worthwhile, important.
BE **hagahaigamaiana.** *v.* Treat as important.
ID **dangada haigamaiana.** Worthwhile person.

HAILU
B **hailu.** *v.* Wipe oneself (after defecating).
B 1 **hailunga.** *n.* —.
B 2 **hailua.** *v.* —.
BE **hagahailu.** *v.* —.
BE1 **hagahailunga.** *n.* —.
BE2 **hagahailua.** *v.* —.

HAINOO
B **hainoo.** *v.* Permitted, open to the public, secular [opposite of *dabu*].
B 1 **hainooanga.** *n.* —.
B 1 **hainoonga.** *n.* —.
B 2 **hainooa.** *v.* —.
BE **hagahainoo.** *v.* —.
BE1 **hagahainooanga.** *n.* —.
BE1 **hagahainoonga.** *n.* —.
BE2 **hagahainooa.** *v.* —.

HAIVA
B **haiva.** *n.* Work, activity, occupation.
ID **haiva dee agona.** Sexual activity, [lit., 'the activity which is not taught'].

HALA
B **hala.** *n.* Plant sp.: tree sp.: pandanus (several varieties).
BE **hagahala.** *n.* A sleeping mat.
XCO **madagauhala.** *n.* The lower abdomen, crotch, pubic area.
XFL **manu-de-hala.** *n.* Insect sp.: walkingstick (a very large grasshopper-like insect).
ID **bongaa hala.** Any long and hollow object (e.g., a pipe or a hose).
ID **dau hala.** The season during which pandanus fruit of the same type matures.
ID **hala a buadaia.** A log used as a lever or fulcrum.
ID **hala dudu.** A noise like that of burning pandanus (loud crackling).
ID **hala goobai.** A wooden form used in making hats.
ID **hala langa goobai.** A form for plaiting hats.
ID **hui hala.** The fruit of the pandanus.
ID **ngau hala.** Bite someone.
ID **ulunga hala.** A pillow made from a pandanus log (having various magical uses).

HALE
B **hale.** *n.* House, dwelling, building.
BE **hagahale.** *v.* Begin to form (of a situation).
BE1 **hagahalenga.** *n.* —.
BE2 **hagahalea.** *v.* —.
R **halehale —.** *d.* Developing (of a situation).
RE **hagahalehale.** *v.* —.
RE1 **hagahalehalenga.** *n.* —.
RE2 **hagahalehalea.** *v.* —.
XCO **aduhale.** *a.* Village, compound (aggregation of houses); go from house to house.
ID **baalanga dua hale.** Metal roofing.
ID **buu hale moni.** Mollusk sp.
ID **dama adu hale.** A child who

wanders around to the homes of others.
ID **doo halehale me.** Risky, unreliable.
ID **tangada aduhale.** The sort of person who feels at home everywhere and is continually visiting [considered uncouth].
ID **hale baabaa.** Frame house.
ID **hale baalanga.** Frame house.
ID **hale pono.** Prison, jail.
ID **hale daane.** Men's house (modern usage).
ID **hale dabeo.** Menstrual hut.
ID **hale daumaha.** Church (building).
ID **hale de henua.** A house of indigenous construction (thatch).
ID **hale duu biho.** Barber shop.
ID **hale gaainga.** Hotel.
ID **hale gai.** Restaurant.
ID **hale gaugau.** Bath house.
ID **hale goloa.** Store.
ID **hale haahine.** A house of prostitution.
ID **hale hadu.** A house of brick or cement construction.
ID **hale hagao me.** Store.
ID **hale hai niho.** Dentist's office.
ID **halehale dagodo.** Guarded condition or prognosis (of a sick person); unsettled (of a situation, the weather, etc.).
ID **halehale dagodo lodo.** Nauseated.
ID **halehale dangada.** A suspicious character.
ID **halehale gaiaa.** Cloying insincere humility.
ID **halehale me.** A developing situation.
ID **halehale me donu huu.** Surprisingly, it turned out to be possible!
ID **hale hongagelegele.** Out house.
ID **hale i lodo.** Rib cage, thoracic cavity.
ID **hale langadala.** Thatch-roofed house (of palm frond thatch).
ID **hale lau.** Thatch-roofed house (of pandanus leaf thatch).
ID **hale maadenga.** Mortuary house.
ID **hale magi.** Hospital, dispensary.
ID **hale neveneve.** Spider web.
ID **hale nnoa.** Prison, jail.
ID **hale o de henua.** Community meeting house.
ID **hale suunugi.** A house with eaves touching the ground [an old style].
ID **manu hale moni.** A pottery bottle or jar.
CF **ina-gi-hale.** A row of thatch.

HALI
B **hali.** *d.* —.
B 1 **haalinga.** *n.* —.
B 2 **haalia.** *v.* —.
BE **hagahali.** *d.* —.
BE1 **hagahaalinga.** *n.* —.
BE2 **hagahaalia.** *v.* —.
E **hhali.** *v.* Scoop up (of solids only).
EE **hagahhali.** *v.* —.
R **halihali.** *v.* —.
R 1 **halihalinga.** *n.* —.
R 2 **halihalia.** *v.* —.
RE **hagahalihali.** *v.* —.
RE1 **hagahalihalinga.** *n.* —.
RE2 **hagahalihalia.** *v.* —.
ID **daa hhali.** An adze stroke, used to chip out the interior of a bowl, canoe, etc.
ID **hhali gee.** Scoop out.
ID **hhali lo te laagau.** A depression in a log (an abnormal growth).
CF **halihalibaa.** Fish sp.: flatfish.

HALU
CF **dalahalu.** Plant sp.: tree sp. (*Allophylus timorensis* (DC.) Bl.).

HANA
BC **mahana.** *a.* Hot.
BC1 **mahanaanga.** *n.* —.
BC2 **mahanasia.** *v.* Heated.
BE **hagahana.** *v.* Reheat or

recook food (to preserve it for a longer time).
BE1 **hagahanaanga.** *n.* —.
BE2 **hagahanasia.** *v.* —.
PC **maahana.** *a.* —.
PC1 **maahanaanga.** *n.* —.
PC2 **maahanasia.** *v.* —.
PF **hagamaahana.** *v.* —.
PF1 **hagamaahanaanga.** *n.* —.
PF2 **hagamaahanasia.** *v.* —.
RC **mahanahana.** *a.* Warm.
RC1 **mahanahanaanga.** *n.* —.
RC2 **mahanahanasia.** *v.* Warmed up.
RE **hagahanahana.** *v.* Recook over and over.
RE1 **hagahanahanaanga.** *n.* —.
RE2 **hagahanahanasia.** *v.* —.
ID **paa ono maahana.** Receive one's punishment, suffer.
ID **dee mahana tae.** Stay for only a short time.
ID **hagahana age.** Recook for several days.
ID **hagahana ange.** Recook for a very little while.
ID **hagahana iho.** Recook for a little while.
ID **langona iho maahana.** Feel punished or victimized.
ID **mahana age.** Heartburn [?].

HANO
B **hano.** *a.* Go [sing.].
B 1 **hanonga.** *n.* Trip, journey.
B 2 **hanolia.** *v.* Suitable for a trip (e.g., a car, a road, etc.).
BE **hagahano.** *v.* —.
BE2 **hagahanolia.** *v.* —.
E **hannoo.** *i.* Gó!
R **hanohano.** *a.* Go repeatedly; diarrhea.
RE **hagahanohano.** *v.* —.
XCO **hanange.** *a.* Go to.
ID **gili hano.** Separation of the hard interior parts of the tree trunk [a condition which spoils the tree for making a canoe].
ID **hannoo kaba.** Go now, right away! Beat it!
ID **hano ahe.** Echo.
ID **hano ai.** Attend (e.g., church services).
ID **hano ai huu.** Forever.
ID **hano de leebunga.** Run (of a color); fade (of a color).
ID **hano de mama.** Escaping fumes (from a poorly sealed container).
ID **hano gaogao.** Move sideways.
ID **hano gee.** Go away [sing.].
ID **hano gi bouli gee.** To transfigure oneself.
ID **hano gi de maalama.** Transfiguration of ghosts or spirits into human form.
ID **hano gi oona.** Very, exceedingly.
ID **hano goe.** See what I told you!
ID **hano kaba.** Go immediately!
ID **hanohano ai huu.** Go on and on until —.
ID **hanohano dua.** Suffer a setback; almost fall; gorge oneself; stagger backwards (e.g., under load).
ID **hano i luu moana.** Die (a person).
ID **hano laa.** Previous.
ID **hano laa uda.** Go on foot.
ID **hano mouli.** Disappear alive (esp. into another world).
ID **hano muhuu loo.** Let's see...
ID **hano saele.** Wander around.
ID **magi hanohano.** Diarrhea.
ID **ngadi hanonga.** A useless journey.
ID **vaivai hanonga.** An excursion for an evil purpose (esp. involving a sexual quest).

HANU
B **hanu₁.** *ma.* Some.
B **hanu₂.** *a.* To have.
R **hanuhanu.** *a.* Few; gaining in.
ID **anaange laa hanu.** A little while ago.
ID **e hanuhanu i de +**

PRONOUN. Know something about.

ID **gi hanu donu huu.** Any kind whatsoever.

ID **hai naa hanu me.** Something will happen...

ID **hanu age.** Regain.

ID **hanu ange.** Some more.

ID **hanu me.** A secret friend of the opposite sex.

ID **hanu momo.** Little bit, few.

HANGA

B **hanga.** *d.* Horn (of an animal) [N]; a husking stick [N]; move apart [dp]; open up (one's mouth) [dp]; tie coconuts together with strips ripped from the coconut's outer husk [V].

B 2 **hangaa.** *v.* —.

BC **mahanga.** *a.* Be split open.

BF **hagamahanga.** *v.* —.

E **hhanga.** *v.* Split open, open up, or separate, all at once.

E 2 **haangaa.** *v.* —.

PC **maahanga.** *a.* —.

PF **hagamaahanga.** *v.* —.

R **hangahanga.** *v.* —.

R 2 **hangahangaa.** *v.* —.

RC **mahangahanga.** *a.* Cracked in many places.

RF **hagamahangahanga.** *v.* —.

ID **dee hanga.** Don't move away from the reef! [an instruction heard when fishing for flying fish].

ID **haangaa lodo i de gai.** Be continually hungry, owing to having a distended stomach from regularly eating too much.

ID **hanga benu.** To extract pandanus seeds by splitting the fruit.

ID **hhanga dalogo.** To make *dalogo.*

ID **hhanga de ngudu.** Open one's mouth.

ID **hhanga lua.** Split in two.

ID **hhanga luu vae.** Spread one's legs.

ID **lili mahangahanga.** Mad as the devil.

ID **me hanga dalogo.** Ingredients of *dalogo.*

ID **noho hhanga.** Sit with one's legs spread apart.

CF **daahanga.** Fool (someone), deceive.

CF **gaahanga.** A rope used to assist in climbing.

HANGA$_a$

B **hangaabo.** *v.* The fitting together of the two halves of something, so that it is closed.

B 1 **hangaabonga.** *n.* —.

B 2 **hangaaboa.** *v.* —.

B 2 **hangaabolia.** *v.* —.

R **hangahangaabo.** *v.* —.

R 1 **hangahangaabonga.** *n.* —.

R 2 **hangahangaaboa.** *v.* —.

R 2 **hangahangaabolia.** *v.* —.

HANGO

B **hango.** *d.* —.

B 1 **haangonga.** *n.* —.

B 2 **haangoa.** *v.* —.

B 2 **haangona.** *v.* —.

E **hhango.** *v.* Wake up (someone).

R **hangohango.** *v.* —.

R 1 **hangohangonga.** *n.* —.

R 2 **hangohangoa.** *v.* —.

R 2 **hangohangona.** *v.* —.

S 2 **haahaangona.** *v.* —.

T **haahaango.** *v.* Wake up (someone) insistently.

T 1 **haahaangonga.** *n.* —.

T 2 **haahaangoa.** *v.* —.

HAO$_1$

B **hao$_1$.** *v.* Drill through, burrow.

B 1 **haonga.** *n.* —; a hole (in something).

B 2 **haoa.** *v.* —.

B 2 **haolia$_1$.** *v.* —.

BE **hagahao.** *v.* —.

BE1 **hagahaonga.** *n.* —.

BE2 **hagahaoa.** *v.* —.

BE2 **hagahaolia$_1$.** *v.* —.

R **haohao$_1$.** *v.* —.

R 1 **haohaonga$_1$.** *n.* —.

R 2 **haohaoa$_1$.** *v.* —.

R 2 **haohaolia₁.** *v.* —.
RE **hagahaohao.** *v.* —.
RE1 **hagahaohaonga.** *n.* —.
RE2 **hagahaohaoa.** *v.* —.
RE2 **hagahaohaolia₁.** *v.* —.

HAO_2
B **hao_2.** *d.* —.
B 1 **haaonga.** *n.* —.
B 2 **haaoa.** *v.* —.
E **hhao.** *v.* Fill, stuff (something into or full of).
R **$haohao_2$.** *v.* —.
R 1 **$haohaonga_2$.** *n.* —.
R 2 **$haohaoa_2$.** *v.* —.
ID **dee haaoa i de gai.** Gluttonous.
ID **duu ubu haohao.** A piece of taro cooked in a coconut shell with coconut oil.
ID **hhao tuula.** To sail so as to fill one's sails with wind (sailing crosswind).
ID **manu hao vai.** A bottle (of glass).
ID **ubu haohao.** A type of prepared food (made from taro and coconut cream).
CF **haoli.** Cover up.

HAOLI
B **haoli.** *v.* Cover up.
B 1 **haolinga.** *n.* —.
B 2 **$haolia_2$.** *v.* —.
BE **hagahaoli.** *v.* —.
BE1 **hagahaolinga.** *n.* —.
BE2 **$hagahaolia_2$.** *v.* —.
R **haohaoli.** *v.* —.
R 1 **haohaolinga.** *n.* —.
R 2 **$haohaolia_2$.** *v.* —.
RE **hagahaohaoli.** *v.* —.
RE1 **hagahaohaolinga.** *n.* —.
RE2 **$hagahaohaolia_2$.** *v.* —.

HASI
B **hasi.** *v.* To cut off a taro corm from its stalk.
B 1 **haasinga.** *n.* —.
B 2 **hasia.** *v.* —.
BE **hagahasi.** *v.* —.
BE1 **hagahasinga.** *n.* —.
BE2 **hagahasia.** *v.* —.
R **hasihasi.** *v.* —.
R 1 **hasihasinga.** *n.* —.
R 2 **hasihasia.** *v.* —.
RE **hagahasihasi.** *v.* —.
RE1 **hagahasihasinga.** *n.* —.
RE2 **hagahasihasia.** *v.* —.
ID **hasi made.** To cut a taro corm from its stalk so far up the stalk that it won't grow a new corm when it is planted.

HAU
B **hau.** *a.* A garland of flowers (as a headdress or necklace); tie up — [dp], fasten by tying (wrapping) — [dp].
B 1 **haunga.** *n.* Manner of wearing a flower garland.
B 1 **hausanga.** *n.* A wrapping (of string) around the join of a pole.
B 2 **$haaua_1$.** *v.* —.
B 2 **haulia.** *v.* —.
B 2 **hausia.** *v.* —; an ache in a muscle.
BE **hagahau.** *v.* —; put a garland on someone or provide someone with a garland.
BE1 **hagahaunga.** *n.* —.
BE2 **hagahaua.** *v.* —.
BE2 **hagahausia.** *v.* —.
E **hhau.** *v.* Tie up, fasten by tying (wrapping).
E 1 **$haaunga_1$.** *n.* —.
EE **hagahhau.** *v.* —.
R **hauhau.** *v.* —.
R 1 **hauhaunga.** *n.* —.
R 1 **hauhausanga.** *n.* [pl. of *hausanga*].
RE **hagahauhau.** *v.* —.
RE1 **hagahauhaunga.** *n.* —.
XFL **goehau.** *n.* Plant sp.: tree sp.: hibiscus tree (*Hibiscus tiliaceus* L.).
XFL **hauala.** *n.* Seaweed sp.
XFL **manu-hai-hau.** *n.* Mollusk sp. [a recently coined name, = spp. of *sisi*].
ID **gili hau.** The inner bark of the hibiscus.
ID **hagauda de hau.** Put on a *hau.*
ID **hau baba.** Tie up temporarily (not as

	securely as if permanently).
ID	**hau bule.** Shell necklace or headdress.
ID	**hau manu.** A garland of flowers, headdress, necklace.
ID	**hau singano.** Garland of *singano.*
ID	**hili de hau.** Make a *hau.*

HE-

B	**he-.** *mf.* RECIPROCAL PREFIX.

HEBALEDAGE

B	**hebaledage.** *v.* A confluence of currents (making the water choppy).
B 1	**hebaledageanga.** *n.* —.
BE	**hagahebaledage.** *v.* —.
BE1	**hagahebaledageanga.** *n.* —.
R	**hebahebaledage.** *v.* —.
R 1	**hebahebaledageanga.** *n.* —.
RE	**hagahebahebaledage.** *n.* ——.
ID	**au hebaledage.** A confluence of ocean currents (on the surface only).

HEBOLO

B	**hebolo.** *a.* A sign made with the eyes.
B 1	**heboloanga.** *n.* —.
BE	**hagahebolo.** *v.* —.
BE1	**hagaheboloanga.** *n.* —.
R	**hebohebolo.** *a.* —.
RE	**hagahebohebolo.** *v.* —.
RE1	**hagaheboheboloanga.** *n.* —.

HEDAADOI

B	**hedaadoi.** *a.* Collide.
B 1	**hedaadoinga.** *n.* —.
BE	**hagahedaadoi.** *v.* —.
BE1	**hagahedaadoinga.** *n.* —.
BE2	**hagahedaadoia.** *v.* —.
R	**hedahedaadoi.** *a.* —.
R 1	**hedahedaadoinga.** *n.* —.
RE	**hagahedahedaadoi.** *v.* —.
RE1	**hagahedahedaadoinga.** *n.* —.
RE2	**hagahedahedaadoia.** *v.* —.
CF	**hedae.** Meet up with; be even with each other.

HEDAU

B	**hedau.** *n.* Plant sp.: tree sp.: Alexandrian laurel tree (*Calophyllum inophyllum* L.).

HEDU

B	**hedu.** *d.* Fold up —.
B 1	**heedunga.** *n.* —.
B 2	**heedua.** *v.* —.
BC	**mahedu.** *a.* Folded up, rolled up.
BC1	**mahedunga.** *n.* —.
BE	**hagahedu.** *v.* —.
BE1	**hagaheedunga.** *n.* —.
BE2	**hagaheedua.** *v.* —.
BF	**hagamahedu.** *v.* —.
BF1	**hagamahedunga.** *n.* —.
BF2	**hagamahedua.** *v.* —.
E	**hhedu.** *v.* Fold up (several folds), roll up.
PC	**maahedu.** *a.* —.
PC1	**maahedunga.** *n.* —.
PF	**hagamaahedu.** *v.* —.
PF1	**hagamaahedunga.** *n.* —.
PF2	**hagamaahedua.** *v.* —.
R	**heduhedu.** *v.* —.
R 1	**heduhedunga.** *n.* —.
R 2	**heduhedua.** *v.* —.
RC	**maheduhedu.** *a.* —.
RC1	**maheduhedunga.** *n.* —.
RF	**hagamaheduhedu.** *v.* —.
RF1	**hagamaheduhedunga.** *n.* —.
RF2	**hagamaheduhedua.** *v.* —.

HEDUU

B	**heduu.** *n.* Star, planet.
ID	**de heduu o taiao.** Morning star.

HEE$_1$

R	**heehee.** *a.* Cry out.
R 1	**heeheenga.** *n.* —.
RE	**hagaheehee.** *v.* —.
RE1	**hagaheeheenga.** *n.* —.
RE2	**hagaheeheea.** *v.* —.
CF	**deehehee.** To make a certain pattern of sounds to call attention to oneself.

HEE$_2$

B	**hee.** *mv.* Where?, what kind?, which?
ID	**behee.** Like what?
ID	**danuaa mai i hee.** Good according to whom?

ID go hee. Where exactly?
ID i hee. Where (in general)?
ID ma hee. Where else?
ID se me be hee. Extraordinary or unusual (esp. in size).
ID se me gi hee. In which direction is the current running?

HEE$_{2a}$

B **aahee.** *b.* When? (indefinite future).
BE **hagaahee.** *a.* When? (near future).
ID **aahee ai.** Then which?
ID **aahee ange.** What else?
ID **aahee donu.** Exactly which?
ID **aahee huu.** Then which?
ID **aahee laa.** Which were those?
ID **aahee loo.** When? (distant future).
ID **aahee maa.** About when? (future); about how much?
ID **aahee naa.** Then what? (distant future).
ID **aahee nei.** Then what? (immediate future).

HEE$_{2b}$

B **ahee.** *b.* Which?
ID **ahee oo dagodo?.** How are you?

HEE$_{2c}$

B **anahee.** *b.* When? (past time).
ID **aloo anahee.** For how long has this been going on?

HEE$_{2d}$

B **dehee.** *b.* Which?

HEE$_{2e}$

B **ngaahee.** *b.* Where?

HEGA

R **hegahega.** *n.* Lung.

HEGAU

B **hegau.** *n.* Work, activity, occupation.
ID **bulubulu hegau.** Unimportant work.
ID **daia e de hegau.** Overworked.
ID **gini hua o hegau.** To receive the rewards of work well done (or punishment for evil deeds).
ID **goloa hai hegau.** Tools (for work).
ID **hagassege i hegau.** Procrastinate (about work); refuse to participate in work.
ID **hai hegau.** Work [verb].
ID **hai hegau hilo.** Work hypocritically (appearing to follow the rules but secretly violating the prohibitions).
ID **hegau baubau.** Bad deeds.
ID **sula de hegau.** Successfully completed work.
ID **sulu i hegau.** Busy (with work or obligations).

HEGE

B **hege.** *n.* The name of a name-group.

HEIANGI

B **heiangi.** *a.* Smart, intelligent, clever.
BE **hagaheiangi.** *v.* Act smart (openly).

HELA

B **hela.** *v.* Spread one's legs (esp. a woman in the act of sexual intercourse).
B 1 **heelanga.** *n.* —.
BE **hagahela.** *v.* —.
BE1 **hagaheelanga.** *n.* —.
E **hhela.** *v.* Spread one's legs wide apart at one time.
E 1 **hhelaanga.** *n.* —.
EE **hagahhela.** *v.* —.
EE1 **hagahhelaanga.** *n.* —.
R **helahela.** *v.* —.
R 1 **helahelaanga.** *n.* —.
RE **hagahelahela.** *v.* —.
RE1 **hagahelahelaanga.** *n.* —.

HELAU

B **helau.** *v.* Sorcery.
B 1 **helaunga.** *n.* —.
B 2 **helaua.** *v.* —.
R **helahelau.** *v.* —.
R 1 **helahelaunga.** *n.* —.
R 2 **helahelaua.** *v.* —.

HELII

B **helii.** *n.* Plant sp.: grass sp. (*Lepturus repens* (Forst.) R.Br.).

XFL **helii-baalanga.** *n.* Plant sp.: grass sp.

XFL **helii-lausedi.** *n.* Seaweed sp.

HELLUMI

B **hellumi.** *v.* Melee.

B 1 **hellumianga.** *n.* —.

BE **hagahellumi.** *v.* —.

BE1 **hagahellumianga.** *n.* —.

ID **hellumi de henua.** Mass confusion or panic.

HELOONGOI

B **heloongoi.** *a.* Fit together with (match) each other; have an understanding with one another (e.g., as do lovers); understand one another.

B 1 **heloongoinga.** *n.* —.

BE **hagaheloongoi.** *v.* Compare; act as an intermediary or mediator; get acquainted with.

BE1 **hagaheloongoinga.** *n.* —.

BE2 **hagaheloongoia.** *v.* —.

ID **dee heloongoi.** Misunderstand one another; mismated (not matched properly); not fit; not able to get along with.

HENUA

B **henua.** *n.* A land mass, an island, a country, or any other geopolitical unit.

BE **hagahenua.** *v.* Give land to.

XCO **aduhenua.** *n.* Group of islands or atolls; archipelago.

XCO **huaahenua.** *n.* Community.

XG **gumedi de henua.** A type of bowl.

ID **dangada de henua.** Natives of Nukuoro.

ID **dangada henua gee.** Foreigners, strangers.

ID **de huu de henua.** The layer of consolidated sand (without coral rubble) next to the reef base under the island.

ID **diibanga o de henua.** The categories of ancient custom.

ID **doli de henua.** To defeat all comers.

ID **duugunga o de henua.** Customs of the island (Nukuoro).

ID **gage de henua.** Invade.

ID **gai de henua.** Native food (not imported).

ID **gau de henua.** Natives.

ID **gau henua gee.** Foreigners (lit., 'people from other lands').

ID **goloa de henua.** Gear of local manufacture.

ID **kolu de henua.** Pray for the welfare of the whole island(and its population).

ID **hagabuni de henua.** To call an all-island meeting.

ID **hale de henua.** A house of indigenous construction (thatch).

ID **hale o de henua.** Community meeting house.

ID **hellumi de henua.** Mass confusion or panic.

ID **henua abasasa.** Land of the Europeans (including America, Japan, etc.).

ID **henua gai dangada.** 'land of the cannibals' (esp. New Guinea).

ID **henua gee.** Foreign lands.

ID **henua gelegele.** Atoll [lit., 'land with sandy soil'].

ID **henua i lalo (alodahi).** World (lands other than Nukuoro).

ID **henua mounga.** A land where there are mountains (a high island or a continental land mass).

ID **lau henua.** Waves of sufficient size to wash over all land on the atoll; tidal wave.

ID **libo ange de henua.** Feel

dizzy or faint, vertigo.

ID **lodo henua.** Inland, bush (uncleared) land, wilderness.

ID **magi o de henua.** Cold (sickness), flu.

ID **mago de henua.** Monsoon winds (from the southwest).

ID **manu de henua.** Nukuoro varieties of swamp taro (*Cyrtosperma*).

ID **muna de henua.** The Nukuoro language.

ID **muna o de henua.** A community meeting (for listening to speeches or instructions).

ID **sau alohenua.** Eddying of the wind (constantly changing direction) close to land.

ID **sula gi dahi henua.** To have visited abroad.

ID **uda henua.** The land above the high-water mark; extensive holdings in land.

ID **uga de henua.** The native variety of fishing line.

ID **ulu de henua.** To cover the land (such as do the branches of breadfruit trees).

ID **valaai de henua.** Native medicine.

ID **vele de henua.** Win over all comers (esp. in an athletic contest).

HENUA$_a$

B **alahenua.** *n.* Plot of (bush) land, acreage.

BE **hagaalahenua.** *v.* Provide land for.

HENUU$_1$

B **henuu$_1$.** *v.* A method of plaiting.

B 1 **henuunga.** *n.* —.

B 2 **henuua.** *v.* —.

BE **hagahenuu.** *v.* —.

BE1 **hagahenuunga.** *n.* —.

BE2 **hagahenuua.** *v.* —.

HENUU$_2$

B **henuu$_2$.** *n.* Placenta.

HENGA

B **henga.** *n.* The name of a name-group.

HEOHI

B **heohi.** *a.* Correct, right, just, fair, true.

B 1 **heohianga.** *n.* —.

BE **hagaheohi.** *v.* To correct (someone or something).

BE1 **hagaheohinga.** *n.* —.

ID **hai dahi heohi.** Maintain one's position in an argument (against contrary positions).

ID **heohi ange.** Suited to, fit (with), appropriate to.

HEUI

B **heui.** *v.* Question (something) carefully.

B 1 **heuinga.** *n.* —.

B 2 **heuia.** *v.* —.

BE **hagaheui.** *v.* —.

BE1 **hagaheuinga.** *n.* —.

BE2 **hagaheuia.** *v.* —.

R **heeheui.** *v.* —.

R 1 **heeheuinga.** *n.* —.

RE **hagaheeheui.** *v.* —.

RE1 **hagaheeheuinga.** *n.* —.

RE2 **hagaheeheuia.** *v.* —.

HEVAALOGI

B **hevaalogi.** *a.* The screaming of many people at the same time.

B 1 **hevaaloginga.** *n.* —.

BE **hagahevaalogi.** *v.* —.

BE1 **hagahevaaloginga.** *n.* —.

BE2 **hagahevaalogia.** *v.* —.

HHANO

B **hhano.** *v.* Wash one's own hands (or mouth).

B 1 **haanonga.** *n.* —.

B 2 **haanoa.** *v.* Wash someone's hands (or mouth).

BE **hagahhano.** *v.* Show someone how to wash his hands (or mouth).

BE1 **hagahaanonga.** *n.* —.

BE2 **hagahaanoa.** *v.* —.

ID **hhano gi daha.** To wash one's hands in such a way that the dirty water does not fall back into the basin or well.

HHOGI

B **hhogi.** *a.* A sharp sound, like the report of a rifle.
B 1 **hooginga.** *n.* —.
BE **hagahhogi.** *v.* —.
BE1 **hagahooginga.** *n.* —.
BE2 **hagahhogia.** *v.* —.
BE2 **hagahhogilia.** *v.* —.
R **hogihogi.** *a.* —.
R 1 **hogihoginga.** *n.* —.
RE **hagahogihogi.** *v.* —.
RE1 **hagahogihoginga.** *n.* —.
RE2 **hagahogihogia.** *v.* —.
RE2 **hagahogihogilia.** *v.* —.

HHUU

B **hhuu.** *a.* Chuckle.
B 1 **hhuunga.** *n.* —.
BE **hagahhuu.** *v.* —.
BE1 **hagahhuunga.** *n.* —.
R **hhuuhhuu.** *a.* —.
R 1 **hhuuhhuunga.** *n.* —.
RE **hagahhuuhhuu.** *v.* —.
RE1 **hagahhuuhhuunga.** *n.* —.

HIA

B **hia.** *a.* How many? [in compounds only].
XCO **dagihia.** How many for each?
ID **be hia.** How many (according to someone)?
ID **daa de hia?.** What time is it?
ID **daha de hia maa.** About what time is it?
ID **de hia.** Which number?
ID **e hia?.** How many?
ID **ga hia?.** How many will it be?
ID **gu hia?.** How many was it?
ID **ma de hia e doe.** A chanted expression, on the last word of which a work group chanting it lifts a heavy object.
ID **ne hia?.** How many has it been?
ID **se hia?.** Just how many?

HIDI

B **hidi.** *v.* To topple over [sing.]; stand on one's hands [sing.]; get up (from a sitting position) [sing.]; cause of [when followed by (*mai*) *ai*].
B 1 **hiidinga**$_1$. *n.* —.
B 2 **hidia.** *v.* —.
BC **mahidi.** *a.* Separated from and curled up from [like plywood in which the laminations have separated].
BC1 **mahiidinga.** *n.* —.
BC2 **mahidia.** *v.* —.
BE **hagahidi.** *v.* —; weigh (on a balance).
BE1 **hagahiidinga.** *n.* —.
BE2 **hagahidia.** *v.* —.
BF **hagamahidi.** *v.* —.
BF1 **hagamahiidinga.** *n.* —.
BF2 **hagamahidia.** *v.* —.
PC **maahidi.** *a.* —.
PC1 **maahidinga.** *n.* —.
PF **hagamaahidi.** *v.* —.
PF1 **hagamaahidinga.** *n.* —.
PF2 **hagamaahidia.** *v.* —.
R **hidihidi.** *v.* —; rock back and forth.
R 1 **hidihidinga.** *n.* —.
R 2 **hidihidia.** *v.* —.
RC **mahidihidi.** *v.* —.
RC1 **mahidihidinga.** *n.* —.
RC2 **mahidihidia.** *v.* —.
RE **hagahidihidi.** *v.* —.
RE1 **hagahidihidinga.** *n.* —.
RE2 **hagahidihidia.** *v.* —.
RF **hagamahidihidi.** *v.* —.
RF1 **hagamahidihidinga.** *n.* —.
RF2 **hagamahidihidia.** *v.* —.
T **hiihidi.** *v.* [pl. of *hidi*].
TE **hagahiihidi.** *v.* —.
TE1 **hagahiihidinga.** *n.* —.
TE2 **hagahiihidia.** *v.* —.
ID **hagahidi i tege.** To throw a wrestler using one's hip.
ID **hidi bido dane.** Slow-moving or slow-working person.
ID **hidi de honu.** Movement of a turtle (when feeding or submerging).
ID **hidi de mamu dunu.** Curling up of fish (when cooked).
ID **hidi taelodo.** The weight

(on a balance) used as a standard measurement.

HIDINGA

B **hidinga.** *mc.* Because of, owing to.

C **hiidinga**$_2$. *b.* Because!

HIDU

B **hidu.** *an.* Seven.

BE **hagahidu (ina).** *v.* The name of a person in a traditional story.

XCO **Diba-hidu.** *nn.* The name of a person in a traditional story.

XCO **Hidu-laangi.** *nt.* Sunday ('seventh day').

XCO **Hidu-malama.** *nt.* July ('seventh month').

ID **hidu-limu.** The seventh number of a counting game played to determine who is "it".

HIE

CF **longohie.** Big around, fat.

HII$_1$

B **hii-.** *mf.* Want to.

U **maahia.** *v.* Want to —.

ID **dai hieunu.** Thirsty.

ID **dai hiigai.** Hungry.

CF **giidagi.** Relish (meat or fish, or something substituting for meat or fish, eaten with taro, etc.).

CF **hiidagi.** [var. of *giidagi*].

HII$_2$

R **hiihii.** *nl.* Edge, fringe, rim.

ID **hiihii mada.** Eyelashes.

HIIDAGI

B **hiidagi.** *v.* [var. of *giidagi*].

B 1 **hiidaginga.** *n.* —.

B 2 **hiidagina.** *v.* —.

BE **hagahiidagi.** *v.* —.

BE1 **hagahiidaginga.** *n.* —.

BE2 **hagahiidagina.** *v.* —.

R **hiihiidagi.** *v.* —.

R 1 **hiihiidaginga.** *n.* —.

R 2 **hiihiidagina.** *v.* —.

RE **hagahiihiidagi.** *v.* —.

RE1 **hagahiihiidaginga.** *n.* —.

RE2 **hagahiihiidagina.** *v.* —.

CF **giidagi.** Relish (meat or fish, or something substituting for meat or fish, eaten with taro, etc.).

HIISOA

B **hiisoa.** *n.* Plant sp.: cassytha vine (*Cassytha filiformis* L.).

HILI

B **hili**$_1$. *v.* Pick from among several, choose, elect; particular (choosy) about; make a nest or raft or platform, etc., with sticks.

B 1 **hiilinga.** *n.* —.

B 2 **hilia.** *v.* —.

R **hilihili.** *v.* Choose carefully from among many, election.

R 1 **hilihilinga.** *n.* —.

R 2 **hilihilia.** *v.* —.

ID **dee hilihili.** Indifferent.

ID **gai hilihili.** Eat only certain foods prepared in certain ways by certain people; fussy (about food).

ID **hai de hilihili.** Hold an election.

ID **hili de hau.** Make a *hau.*

ID **hili gee.** Sort out from; set aside (be chosen from a group).

HILI$_a$

B **hili**$_2$. *n.* The name of a name-group.

HILO

B **hilo.** *v.* Mix; braid strands of sennit.

B 1 **hiilonga.** *n.* —.

B 2 **hiloa**$_1$. *v.* —.

B 2 **hilosia.** *v.* —.

BE **hagahilo.** *v.* —.

BE1 **hagahiilonga.** *n.* —.

BE2 **hagahiloa.** *v.* —.

BE2 **hagahilosia.** *v.* —.

R **hilohilo.** *v.* —.

R 1 **hilohilonga.** *n.* —.

R 2 **hilohiloa.** *v.* —.

R 2 **hilohilosia.** *v.* —.

RE **hagahilohilo.** *v.* —.
RE1 **hagahilohilonga.** *n.* —.
RE2 **hagahilohiloa.** *v.* —.
RE2 **hagahilohilosia.** *v.* —.
ID **galo hilo.** Not cooked completely.
ID **hai hegau hilo.** Work hypocritically (appearing to follow the rules but secretly violating the prohibitions).
ID **hilo ange.** Mix with.
ID **hilo hagamaadau.** To braid sennit with the right hand; [the result is considered inferior to sennit made with the left hand].
ID **hilo hagamaasui.** To braid sennit with the left hand; [which is considered to give the best result].
ID **hilohilo ma eidu.** A sorcerer able to take human or non-human shapes.
ID **hilohilo me.** Impure.
ID **hilohilo senga.** Half-crazy.
ID **hilo saele.** Spread venereal disease.

HILOA
B **hiloa$_2$.** *n.* Fish sp.

HINA
B **hina.** *n.* Ability, capacity (of person), resourcefulness.

HINA$_a$
B **hinangalomalie.** *a.* Feel happy or contented or at peace with the world.
B 1 **hinangalomalieanga.** *n.* —.
BE **hagahinangalomalie.** *n.* ——.

HINA$_b$
B **hinangalosaa.** *a.* Miss (someone or something); longing (for a person or place).
B 1 **hinangalosaanga.** *n.* —.
BE **hagahinangalosaa.** *a.* —.
BE1 **hagahinangalosaanga.** *n.* —.
R **hinahinangalosaa.** *a.* —.
R 1 **hinahinangalosaanga.** *n.* —.
RE **hagahinahinangalosaa.** *v.* —.
RE1 **hagahinahinangalosaanga.** *n.* —.
ID **hinangalosaa iho.** Self-pity.
ID **lodo hinangalosaa.** A feeling of *hinangalosaa*; depression (feeling).

HINE
B **hine.** *n.* Female, woman; [must be preceded by an article].
XCO **De-hine-aligi$_2$.** *nn.* The chief female spirit on Nukuoro (in legendary times).
ID **damaa hine.** Girl, young woman, daughter.
ID **de hine dabeo.** A menstruating woman.
ID **de hine hagahaanau.** Midwife.
ID **duu-o-de-hine.** Anything sticky which pulls apart like jelly (applied to certain kinds of sea cucumbers, etc.).
ID **goloa o de hine.** Female genitalia.
ID **hagauda de hine.** A certain method of delivering a child.
ID **hai damaahine.** The relationship between parent and daughter.
ID **(de) hine dau bodu.** Married woman.
ID **(de) hine duuhua.** Unmarried girl.
ID **(de) hine hai be.** Whore.
ID **(de) hine huuhua.** Pregnant woman.
ID **(de) hine sala daane.** Nymphomaniac.
ID **ssae de hine.** To deflower a girl.
ID **ssui o de hine.** Amniotic fluid.
CF **hahine.** Woman.

HOA$_1$
B **hoa$_1$.** *d.* —.
B 1 **hooanga.** *n.* —.
B 2 **hooia.** *v.* —.
BE **hagahoa.** *v.* —; a boil (on the body), carbuncle.

E **hhoa.** *v.* Crack open; break into pieces; cut a hole in.
R **hoohoa.** *v.* [pl. of *hoa*].
R 1 **hoohoanga.** *n.* —.
R 2 **hoohoia.** *v.* —.
XFL **manu-hai-hagahoa.** *n.* Millipede.
ID **hhoa de biho.** Fool (someone).
ID **hhoa de lae.** To run into misfortune as a result of one's evil deeds.
ID **hhoa de usu.** To encounter unexpected misfortune as a result of one's evil deeds.
ID **hoa lalo.** Anvil; or other hard object (such as a stone) on which something can be struck hard; mortar stone.
ID **hoohoa laagau.** Drill wood to make a hole in which to insert the end of a pole (to make a joint).
ID **hooia donu huu.** At the best possible time or place.
ID **nui hoohoa.** A coconut tree trunk incised with steps [to facilitate climbing].
ID **ubu hhoa.** A type of prepared food dish (made from taro cooked in a half coconut shell).
ID **vai nui hhoa.** Very calm seas.

HOA$_2$
B **hoa$_2$.** *n.* Side (of humans), below the hips.
ID **paa de hoa.** Happy (lit., 'to slap one's sides').

HOBULAA
B **hobulaa.** *a.* A sound uttered esp. when lifting something.
B 1 **hobulaanga.** *n.* —.
BE **hagahobulaa.** *v.* —.
BE1 **hagahobulaanga.** *n.* —.

HODA$_1$
E **hhoda.** *a.* Gasp for breath (once).
E 1 **hoodanga.** *n.* —.
EE **hagahhoda.** *v.* —.
EE1 **hagahoodanga.** *n.* —.
R **hodahoda$_1$.** *a.* Gasp for breath (more than once).
R 1 **hodahodaanga$_1$.** *n.* —.
RE **hagahodahoda.** *v.* —.
RE1 **hagahodahodaanga.** *n.* —.
ID **hhoda age.** Suck in air (esp. when asleep or unconscious).

HODA$_2$
B **hoda.** *v.* Carve out, drill out; eat out the insides of (as does a rat).
B 1 **hodaanga.** *n.* —.
B 2 **hodaia.** *v.* —.
B 2 **hodalia.** *v.* —.
BE **hagahoda.** *v.* —.
BE1 **hagahodaanga.** *n.* —.
BE2 **hagahodalia.** *v.* —.
R **hodahoda$_2$.** *v.* —.
R 1 **hodahodaanga$_2$.** *n.* —.
R 2 **hodahodaia.** *v.* —.
R 2 **hodahodalia.** *v.* —.
ID **dogi hoda.** A type of adze (heavy — for hollowing out logs, etc.).
ID **mada hoodanga.** A depression on the windward reef.

HODO
B **hodo.** *n.* The spine of the stingray.
ID **mada ahodo.** Any place where seawater seeps into the taro bog.

HODOOLIGI
B **hodooligi.** *a.* Chief (of the island).
BE **hagahodooligi.** *v.* To install as chief.
ID **dama hodooligi.** Children of the chief [and of the chief's relatives?].
ID **nohoanga hodooligi.** The place where the chief lives (at the moment).

HODU
B **hodu.** *a.* Sighted, appear.
B 1 **hodunga.** *n.* —.
B 2 **hodua.** *a.* —.
BE **hagahodu.** *v.* —.
BE1 **hagahodunga.** *n.* —.
BE2 **hagahodua.** *v.* —.

R **hoduhodu.** *a.* —.
R 1 **hoduhodunga.** *n.* —.
R 2 **hoduhodua.** *a.* —.
RE **hagahoduhodu.** *v.* —.
RE1 **hagahoduhodunga.** *n.* —.
RE2 **hagahoduhodua.** *v.* —.

HOE$_1$
B **hoe$_1$.** *n.* A canoe paddle.
XG **hoe pale.** A type of canoe paddle designed for steering.
XG **hoe gabegabe.** A canoe paddle (for paddling).
ID **bunaa hoe.** An eddy left by a paddle stroke.
ID **laulau hoe.** The blade of the canoe paddle.
ID **maga de hoe.** To paddle vigorously.
ID **maga tau hoe.** To paddle (a canoe) vigorously.

HOE$_2$
B **hoe$_2$.** *v.* Blisters on the skin caused by sunburn.
B 1 **hoenga.** *n.* —.
B 2 **hoea.** *v.* Covered with sunburn blisters.
BE **hagahoe.** *v.* —.
BE1 **hagahoenga.** *n.* —.
BE2 **hagahoea.** *v.* —.

HOGI
B **hogi.** *mv.* Also.

HOLA
B **hola.** *v.* To spread out, or lay out flat, something which is folded, piled up, or bent, etc.
B 2 **holasia.** *v.* —.
B 2 **hoolaa.** *v.* —.
BC **mahola.** *a.* To have been *hola*; plentiful (of food).
BC1 **maholaanga.** *n.* —.
BE **hagahola.** *v.* —.
BE1 **hagahoolanga.** *n.* —.
BE2 **hagaholasia.** *v.* —.
BE2 **hagahoolaa.** *v.* —.
BF **hagamahola.** *v.* —.
BF1 **hagamaholaanga.** *n.* —.
BF2 **hagamaholasia.** *v.* —.
E **hhola.** *v.* *hola* at one time.
EE **hagahhola.** *v.* —.
PC **maahola.** *a.* —.
PC1 **maaholaanga.** *n.* —.
PF **hagamaahola.** *v.* —.
PF1 **hagamaaholaanga.** *n.* —.
PF2 **hagamaaholasia.** *v.* —.
R **holahola.** *v.* —.
R 1 **holaholanga.** *n.* —.
R 2 **holaholaa.** *v.* —.
R 2 **holaholasia.** *v.* —.
RC **maholahola.** *a.* —.
RC1 **maholaholaanga.** *n.* —.
RE **hagaholahola.** *v.* —.
RE1 **hagaholaholanga.** *n.* —.
RE2 **hagaholaholaa.** *v.* —.
RE2 **hagaholaholasia.** *v.* —.
RF **hagamaholahola.** *v.* —.
RF1 **hagamaholaholaanga.** *n.* —.
RF2 **hagamaholaholasia.** *v.* —.
ID **hhola mai saiolo.** To allow the sail to fill with wind, holding on to the boom sheet (after luffing).
ID **holahola aalanga.** Calisthenics, exercises.
ID **mahola gimoo.** To have many dead animals (or fish) lying about.
ID **maholahola danuaa age.** Revitalized (by a shower or rest, etc.).

HOLA$_a$
B **holadage.** *a.* Laid out or spread out all over.
B 1 **holadageanga.** *n.* —.
BC **maholadage.** *a.* Be *holadage.*
BC1 **maholadageanga.** *n.* —.
BF **hagamaholadage.** *v.* —.
BF1 **hagamaholadageanga.** *n.* —.
RC **maholaholadage.** *a.* Being *holadage* in several places.
RF **hagamaholaholadage.** *n.* ——.

HOLASA
B **holasa.** *n.* A type of mat [made especially for cult houses].

HOLAU
B **holau.** *n.* Canoe house.

BE	**hagaholau.** *v.* Banish from the island (in a canoe with no paddle or food).
BE1	**hagaholaunga.** *n.* —.
BE2	**hagaholaua.** *v.* —.

HOLE

B	**hole.** *d.* —.
B 1	**hoolenga.** *n.* —.
B 2	**hoolea.** *v.* —.
BC	**mahole.** *a.* Peeled (a great amount having been taken off).
BC1	**maholenga.** *n.* —.
BF	**hagamahole.** *v.* —.
BF1	**hagamaholenga.** *n.* —.
BF2	**hagamaholea.** *v.* —.
E	**hhole.** *v.* Peel (something).
PC	**maahole.** *a.* —.
PC1	**maaholenga.** *n.* —.
PF	**hagamaahole.** *v.* —.
PF1	**hagamaaholenga.** *n.* —.
PF2	**hagamaaholea.** *v.* —.
R	**holehole.** *v.* Scrape off (with an object or one's finger), to scale (fish).
R 1	**holeholenga.** *n.* —.
R 2	**holeholea.** *v.* —.
RC	**maholehole.** *a.* Scraped, scaled (fish).
RC1	**maholeholenga.** *n.* —.
RF	**hagamaholehole.** *v.* —.
RF1	**hagamaholeholenga.** *n.* —.
RF2	**hagamaholeholea.** *v.* —.

HOLI

B	**holi.** *a.* Shape of, form of.
B 1	**holinga.** *n.* —.
B 2	**holia.** *v.* To form (something); make (something) according to some model or plan.
BE	**hagaholi.** *v.* Begin to form (something).
BE1	**hagaholinga.** *n.* —.
BE2	**hagaholia.** *v.* —.
R	**holiholi.** *n.* Build (of a person); appearance (distinctive of an individual).
R 1	**holiholinga.** *n.* —.
RE	**hagaholiholi.** *v.* —.
RE1	**hagaholiholinga.** *n.* —.
RE2	**tagaholiholia.** *v.* —.
4ID	**holi ange.** Resemble.

HOLIAGE

B	**holiage.** *v.* Go about something in a complete circle.
B 1	**holiaginga.** *n.* —.
B 2	**holiagina.** *v.* —.
BE	**hagaholiage.** *v.* —.
BE1	**hagaholiaginga.** *n.* —.
BE2	**hagaholiagina.** *v.* —.
R	**holiholiage.** *v.* —.
R 1	**holiholiaginga.** *n.* —.
R 2	**holiholiagina.** *v.* —.
RE	**hagaholiholiage.** *v.* —.
RE1	**hagaholiholiaginga.** *n.* —.
RE2	**hagaholiholiagina.** *v.* —.
ID	**daga holiage.** Surrounding area; to cut or make a ring around.
ID	**tuu daga holiage.** Circumcise.
CF	**holiagi.** [var. of *holiage*].

HOLO

B	**holo.** *v.* Swallow [sing.].
B 1	**holomanga.** *n.* Throat (inside).
B 1	**hoolonga.** *n.* —.
B 2	**holomia.** *v.* —.
R	**holoholo.** *v.* —.
R 1	**holoholonga.** *n.* —.
R 2	**holoholomia.** *v.* —.
T	**hooholo.** *v.* [pl. of *holo*].
XCO	**hologemo.** *a.* [var. of *hologumu*].
XCO	**hologumi.** *a.* [var. of *hologumu*].
XCO	**hologumu.** *a.* (For a fish) to swallow a hook so that it becomes stuck in the throat.
ID	**gai holoholo.** Eat fast.

HOLOHOLOI

B	**holoholoi.** *v.* The rope tied to palm fronds in *belubelu* fishing.
B 1	**holoholoinga.** *n.* —.
B 2	**holoholoia.** *v.* —.
BE	**hagaholoholoi.** *v.* To use *holoholoi.*
BE1	**hagaholoholoinga.** *n.* —.
BE2	**hagaholoholoia.** *v.* —.

HOLU

B	**holu.** *d.* —.

B 1 **hoolunga.** *n.* —.
B 2 **hoolua.** *v.* —.
BE **hagaholu.** *d.* —.
BE1 **hagahoolunga.** *n.* —.
BE2 **hagahoolua.** *v.* —.
E **hholu.** *v.* Bend.
EE **hagahholu.** *v.* —.
R **holuholu.** *v.* —.
R 1 **holuholunga.** *n.* —.
R 2 **holuholua.** *v.* —.
RE **hagaholuholu.** *v.* —.
RE1 **hagaholuholunga.** *n.* —.
RE2 **hagaholuholua.** *v.* —.
XG **maadau hholu.** A fishhook made of wire.
ID **dao me hholu.** Arrow (for a bow).
ID **me hholu.** Bow (for an arrow).

HOLU$_a$

B **ngaholu.** *a.* Bent.
B 1 **ngaholunga.** *n.* —.
BE **hagangaholu.** *v.* —.
BE1 **hagangaholunga.** *n.* —.
BE2 **hagangaholua.** *v.* —.
P **ngaaholu.** *a.* —.
P 1 **ngaaholunga.** *n.* —.
PE **hagangaaholu.** *v.* —.
PE1 **hagangaaholunga.** *n.* —.
PE2 **hagangaaholua.** *v.* —.
R **ngaholuholu.** *a.* —.
R 1 **ngaholuholunga.** *n.* —.
RE **hagangaholuholu.** *v.* —.
RE1 **hagangaholuholunga.** *n.* —.
RE2 **hagangaholuholua.** *v.* —.

HONO

B **hono.** *v.* A patch (on clothes, or a canoe, etc.).
B 1 **hononga.** *n.* —.
B 2 **honoa.** *v.* Patched.
BE **hagahono.** *v.* —.
BE1 **hagahononga.** *n.* —.
BE2 **hagahonoa.** *v.* —.
R **honohono.** *v.* Having *hono* in several places.
R 1 **honohononga.** *n.* —.
R 2 **honohonoa.** *v.* —.
RE **hagahonohono.** *v.* —.
RE1 **hagahonohononga.** *n.* —.
RE2 **hagahonohonoa.** *v.* —.
ID **se hono.** Fit well or properly.

HONU$_1$

B **honu$_1$.** *v.* Full [sing.].
B 1 **hoonunga.** *n.* —.
B 2 **honua.** *v.* Filled with.
B 2 **honumia.** *v.* Filled with.
BE **hagahonu.** *v.* Fill up; to fully realize one's potential (for happiness, etc.).
BE1 **hagahoonunga.** *n.* —.
BE2 **hagahonua.** *v.* —.
BE2 **hagahonumia.** *v.* —.
R **honuhonu.** *v.* —.
R 1 **honuhonunga.** *n.* —.
R 2 **honuhonua.** *v.* —.
R 2 **honuhonumia.** *v.* —.
RE **hagahonuhonu.** *v.* —.
RE1 **hagahonuhonunga.** *n.* —.
RE2 **hagahonuhonua.** *v.* —.
RE2 **hagahonuhonumia.** *v.* —.
T **hoohonu.** *v.* [pl. of *honu$_1$*].
T 1 **hoohonunga.** *n.* —.
T 2 **hoohonua.** *v.* —.
T 2 **hoohonumia.** *v.* —.
TE **hagahoohonu.** *v.* —.
TE1 **hagahoohonunga.** *n.* —.
TE2 **hagahoohonua.** *v.* —.
TE2 **hagahoohonumia.** *v.* —.
ID **daane honu.** A person of many accomplishments.
ID **dau honu.** The season during which tides are highest.
ID **hagahonu age lodo.** Feel uncomfortably sated with food and unable to eat.
ID **honu baabaa.** Fill to the brim.
ID **honu tai.** High tide.
ID **honu kadi.** Filled up completely (with solids); full up (and tightly packed).
ID **honu malingilingi.** Fill to overflowing.

HONU$_2$

B **honu$_2$.** *n.* Green turtle (2 varieties).
XFL **honu-uda.** *n.* Insect sp. (small and turtle-like).
ID **hidi de honu.** Movement of a turtle (when feeding or submerging).

ID	**honu tolo.** A turtle of the largest size.
ID	**honu ssele.** Turtle of a size suitable for eating (not quite as big as *honu tolo*).

HONGA

B	**honga.** *nl.* On top of, on, over, above.
ID	**honga de masavaa.** At the time of.
ID	**honga de mouli.** During the lifetime of.
ID	**honga iainei.** At this time, these days.

HONGA$_a$

B	**hongagainga.** *a.* Urinate.
BE	**hagahongagainga.** *v.* To make a child urinate.

HONGA$_b$

B	**hongagelegele.** *n.* Defecate [a euphemism].
BE	**hagahongagelegele.** *v.* To make a child defecate.
ID	**hale hongagelegele.** Out house.
ID	**hongagelegele baalanga.** Rust.
ID	**magi hongagelegele todo.** To have bloody stools [dysentery?].

HOO

B	**hoo.** *i.* A sound made when one is tired, etc.
R	**hoohoo.** *a.* Repeatedly *hoo*, as when trying to scare something.
R 1	**hoohooanga.** *n.* —.
R 2	**hoohooia.** *v.* —.
RE	**hagahoohoo.** *v.* To scare fish, etc.
RE1	**hagahoohooanga.** *n.* —.
RE2	**hagahoohooia.** *v.* —.
T	**hohhoo.** *a.* A sound made when surprised.
XCO	**hoosenga.** *a.* Shy, embarrassed, bashful.
ID	**hai me hoosenga.** Somewhat *hoosenga*.
ID	**hoohoo ina.** To frighten with sounds.
ID	**hoo senga.** Shy (especially in the presence of members of the opposite sex), shamed.
ID	**hoosenga ange.** Embarrassed by.

HOOHANGA

B	**hoohanga.** *a.* A nest (of birds); pumice stone (found as driftwood).
BE	**hagahoohanga.** *v.* Allow birds to nest, or prepare a place for their nesting.
ID	**dau hoohanga.** The season during which birds lay eggs.

HOOLU

B	**hoolu.** *n.* Prow (bottom part).

HOOU

B	**hoou.** *a.* New.
B 1	**hoounga.** *n.* —.
BE	**hagahoou.** *v.* Make like new.
BE1	**hagahoounga.** *n.* —.
BE2	**hagahooua.** *v.* —.
BE2	**hagahooulia.** *v.* —.
ID	**mada hoou.** Brand new.
ID	**sui hagahoou.** Change of personality (for the better).

HOU

B	**hou.** *v.* Drill (native bow drill).
B 1	**hounga.** *n.* —.
B 2	**houa.** *v.* —.
E	**hhou.** *v.* Insist upon.
E 1	**hhounga.** *n.* —.
E 2	**hhoua.** *v.* —.
EE	**hagahhou.** *v.* —.
EE1	**hagahhounga.** *n.* —.
EE2	**hagahhoua.** *v.* —.
EE2	**hagahhoulia.** *v.* —.
R	**houhou.** *v.* —; race.
R 1	**houhounga.** *n.* —.
R 2	**houhoua.** *v.* —.
RE	**hagahouhou.** *v.* —.
RE1	**hagahouhounga.** *n.* —.
RE2	**hagahouhoua.** *v.* —.
RE2	**hagahouhoulia.** *v.* —.
ID	**kave houhou.** Race to take.

HUA$_1$

B **hua**$_1$. *v.* Come out in front; sing (a song); bear (fruit); a swelling (on the skin, or of dough, etc.);a swell (of the sea).

B. 1 **huaanga.** *n.* —.

B 1 **huudanga**$_1$. *n.* Way of singing.

B 2 **huudia**$_1$. *v.* —.

BE **hagahua.** *v.* —; to shape roughly (as in making a canoe); show-off.

BE1 **hagahuaanga.** *n.* —.

BE1 **hagahuudanga**$_1$. *n.* —.

BE2 **hagahuudia**$_1$. *v.* —.

P **hhua.** *a.* — (ex., 'sing' meaning).

P 1 **hhuaanga.** *n.* —.

PE **hagahhua.** *v.* —.

PE1 **hagahhuaanga.** *n.* —.

R **huahua.** *v.* —.

R 1 **huahuaanga.** *n.* —.

RE **hagahuahua.** *v.* —.

RE1 **hagahuahuaanga.** *n.* —.

S **huuhua.** *a.* Pregnancy.

XCO **duuhua.** *a.* Single, unmarried.

XCO **huugaabungubungu.** Very plump.

XCO **madahuuhua.** *v.* Pimple.

XFL **hua-ala.** *n.* Flower.

XFL **hua-laagau.** *n.* Plant sp.: tropical almond (*Terminalia catappa* L.).

ID **dala hhua.** Eruptions on the skin (e.g., hives, insect bites, etc.).

ID **de hua nei.** This size.

ID **gave hua podo.** Sprint (footrace of short distance).

ID **gave hua loa.** [var. of *gave ua loa*].

ID **gini hua o hegau.** To receive the rewards of work well done (or punishment for evil deeds).

ID **hai hua laa.** Do indifferently.

ID **hai huuhuaa me.** Sorcery.

ID **(de) hine huuhua.** Pregnant woman.

ID **hua ai.** Be in charge of.

ID **huahua ai.** Be in charge of, control, lead.

ID **huahuaa me.** [var. of *huuhuaa me*].

ID **hua i gadea.** The side of the main body of the canoe away from the outrigger float.

ID **hua leu.** Fish eggs (mature—yellowish).

ID **hua ligi.** Having small fruit or nuts (of trees).

ID **hua manu.** Fruit.

ID **hua modo.** Fish eggs (immature).

ID **hua nnui.** Having large fruit or nuts (of trees).

ID **hua o tangada.** Outcome (of individual effort).

ID **huuhuaa me.** Sorcery (made with chants).

ID **luu hua.** Labia majora.

CF **huaahuu.** A type of prepared food (made from taro).

CF **huaalavao.** A strong wind.

HUA$_2$

B **hua**$_2$ + NUMBER. *mc.* NUMERAL CLASSIFIER (BY TENS) FOR FRUIT.

HUAA

B **huaa.** *d.* Whole.

XCO **huaaboo.** *n.* The whole night long.

XCO **huaadangada.** *n.* Persons of a certain class or type.

XCO **huaahai.** *v.* Expertise.

XCO **huaahenua.** *n.* Community.

XCO **huaalaangi.** *n.* Noon; the whole day; a certain day only.

XFL **huaalanga.** *n.* A type of coconut tree.

ID **kave huaame.** Take the whole thing.

ID **hai huaabodu.** Treat someone (including one's spouse) as a relative by not asking permission to use or borrow property; treat a relative as belonging to another family altogether.

ID **hai huaame.** Punctilious, be particular.

ID **huaa me.** A coconut (for drinking); the whole thing.

HUAALAVAO

B **huaalavao.** *v.* A strong wind.
B 1 **huaalavaonga.** *n.* —.
BE **hagahuaalavao.** *v.* —.
BE1 **hagahuaalavaonga.** *n.* —.

HUADIA

B **huadia.** *n.* Fishing pole.
ID **dogo huadia.** A way of punting a canoe.

HUDA

B **huda.** *n.* [the generic term for] a verse of an old chant.
BC **mahuda.** *a.* Be awake for a short time; have one's eyes open.
BC1 **mahudaanga.** *n.* —.
BF **hagamahuda.** *v.* —.
BF1 **hagamahudaanga.** *n.* —.
E **hhuda.** *a.* Open one's eyes; awaken for a short time.
E 1 **hhudaanga.** *n.* —.
EE **hagahhuda.** *v.* —.
EE1 **hagahhudaanga.** *n.* —.
ID **mahuda age.** Wake up.

HUDAA

B **hudaa —.** *d.* Group of things approaching together (e.g., a fleet of canoes).
ID **hudaa lolo.** Flood-like waves on the reef; tidal wave.
ID **hudaa moni.** A fleet of canoes.

HUDI$_1$

B **hudi$_1$.** *d.* —.
B 1 **huudanga$_2$.** *n.* —.
B 2 **huudia$_2$.** *v.* —.
BE **hagahudi —.** *d.* —.
BE1 **hagahuudanga$_2$.** *n.* —.
BE2 **hagahuudia$_2$.** *v.* —.
E **hhudi.** *v.* Pull.
EE **hagahhudi.** *v.* —.
R **hudihudi.** *v.* —.
R 1 **hudihudinga.** *n.* —.
R 2 **hudihudia.** *v.* —.
RE **hagahudihudi.** *v.* —.
RE1 **hagahudihudinga.** *n.* —.

HUDI$_2$

B **hudi$_2$.** *n.* Plant sp.: tree sp.: banana tree.
XFL **ga-hudi.** *n.* Plant sp.: tree sp.: banana tree; banana (fruit).
ID **ulu hudi.** Young girl.

HUE

B **hue.** *n.* Plant sp.: vine sp. (several spp.).
XCO **huevini.** *n.* A type of string figure.
XFL **hua-dolo.** *n.* Plant sp.: vine (any sort).
ID **gelegele gumi hue.** Fine-grained sand.
ID **hagadubu hue vini.** The name of a certain type of string figure.

HUGA

B **huga.** *n.* Fine threads or strands.
R **hugahuga.** *n.* A type of soft driftwood (used for plugs).

HUGADOO

B **hugadoo.** *u.* All (of things).
ID **alodahi hugadoo.** Everything, everybody; each and every.
ID **me hhadu hugadoo.** It's a lie!

HUGE

B **huge —.** *d.* —.
B 1 **huugenga.** *n.* —.
B 2 **hugelia.** *v.* —.
B 2 **huugea.** *v.* —.
BC **mahuge.** *a.* Opened, uncovered.
BC1 **mahugenga.** *n.* —.
BF **hagamahuge.** *v.* —.
BF1 **hagamahugeanga.** *n.* —.
BF2 **hagamahugea.** *v.* —.
BF2 **hagamahugelia.** *v.* —.
E **hhuge.** *v.* Open (something), uncover.
PC **maahuge.** *a.* —.
PC1 **maahugenga.** *n.* —.

PF hagamaahuge. *v.* —.
PF1 hagamaahugeanga. *n.* —.
PF2 hagamaahugea. *v.* —.
PF2 hagamaahugelia. *v.* —.
R hugehuge. *v.* —.
R 1 hugehugenga. *n.* —.
R 2 hugehugea. *v.* —.
R 2 hugehugelia. *v.* —.
RC mahugehuge. *a.* —.
RC1 mahugehugenga. *n.* —.
RF hagamahugehuge. *v.* —.
RF1 hagamahugehugeanga. *n.* —.
RF2 hagamahugehugea. *v.* —.
RF2 hagamahugehugelia. *v.* —.
T **huuhuge.** *v.* Open or uncover many things (by several persons).
T 1 huuhugenga. *n.* —.
T 2 huuhugea. *v.* —.
T 2 huuhugelia. *v.* —.
ID **dao huge.** To open an earth oven as soon as the food is cooked.
ID **denga hhuge —.** Upward current.
ID **hhuge age malo.** Lift up one's skirts (to expose one's genitals).
ID **hhuge iho.** An opening in the clouds.

HUI₁
B **hui —.** *d.* —.
B 1 **huuinga.** *n.* —.
B 2 **huuia.** *v.* —.
BE **hagahui —.** *v.* —.
BE1 **hagahuuinga.** *n.* —.
BE2 **hagahuuia.** *v.* —.
E **hhui.** *v.* Wash (hands or feet or dishes, etc. — but not clothes).
R **huihui.** *v.* —.
R 1 **huihuinga.** *n.* —.
R 2 **huihuia.** *v.* —.
RE **hagahuihui.** *v.* —.
RE1 **hagahuihuinga.** *n.* —.
RE2 **hagahuihuia.** *v.* —.
ID **hhui age.** Eat a snack.
ID **hhui mai tai.** Flow of the tide.

HUI₂
B **dehui.** *n.* Tens of coconuts [cf. *ngahui*].
B **ngahui.** *n.* Tens of coconuts [cf. *dehui*].
ID **hui hala.** The fruit of the pandanus.

HULA
BE **hagahula.** *n.* The sac in a fish which emerges from its mouth when it is brought up from a great depth.

HULE
B **hule —.** *d.* —.
B 1 **huulenga.** *n.* —.
BC **mahule.** *a.* —.
BC1 **mahulenga.** *n.* —.
BE **hagahule.** *v.* —.
BE1 **hagahuulenga.** *n.* —.
BF **hagamahule.** *v.* —.
BF1 **hagamahulenga.** *n.* —.
BF2 **hagamahulea.** *v.* —.
E **hhule.** *v.* To expose the head of the penis by pulling back the foreskin.
PC **maahule.** *a.* —.
PC1 **maahulenga.** *n.* —.
PF **hagamaahule.** *v.* —.
PF1 **hagamaahulenga.** *n.* —.
PF2 **hagamaahulea.** *v.* —.
R **hulehule.** *v.* —; masturbate.
R 1 **hulehulenga.** *n.* —.
RC **mahulehule.** *a.* —.
RC1 **mahulehulenga.** *n.* —.
RE **hagahuiehule.** *v.* —.
RE1 **hagahulehulenga.** *n.* —.
RF **hagamahulehule.** *v.* —.
RF1 **hagamahulehulenga.** *n.* —.
RF2 **hagamahulehulea.** *v.* —.

HULEa
B **hulei.** *v.* To have done the act of *hhule*.
B 1 **huleinga.** *n.* —.
B 2 **huleia.** *v.* —.
BE **hagahulei.** *v.* —.
BE1 **hagahuleinga.** *n.* —.
BE2 **hagahuleia.** *v.* —.
R **hulehulei.** *v.* —; masturbate.
R 1 **hulehuleinga.** *n.* —.
R 2 **hulehuleia.** *v.* —.
RE **hagahulehulei.** *v.* —.

RE1 **hagahulehuleinga.** *n.* —.
RE2 **hagahulehuleia.** *v.* —.

HULI

B **huli.** *v.* Turn (in place) [sing.].
B 1 **huulinga.** *n.* —.
B 2 **hulia.** *v.* —.
B 2 **hulisia.** *v.* —.
BE **hagahuli.** *v.* —.
BE1 **hagahulinga.** *n.* —.
BE2 **hagahulia.** *v.* —.
BE2 **hagahulisia.** *v.* —.
R **hulihuli.** *v.* —.
R 1 **hulihulinga.** *n.* —.
R 2 **hulihulia.** *v.* —.
R 2 **hulihulisia.** *v.* —.
RE **hagahulihuli.** *v.* —.
RE1 **hagahulihulinga.** *n.* —.
RE2 **hagahulihulia.** *v.* —.
RE2 **hagahulihulisia.** *v.* —.
T **huuhuli.** *v.* [pl. of *huli*].
T 1 **huuhulinga.** *n.* —.
T 2 **huuhulia.** *v.* —.
T 2 **huuhulisia.** *v.* —.
TE **hagahuuhuli.** *v.* —.
TE1 **hagahuuhulinga.** *n.* —.
TE2 **hagahuuhulia.** *v.* —.
TE2 **hagahuuhulisia.** *v.* —.
XCO **hulidonu.** *a.* Right side out (clothes).
XCO **huligee.** Turn away from, turn inside out (of clothes).
ID **dogi hulihuli.** [= *sauligi*].
ID **laangai huli de moana.** A fishing condition in which tuna are jumping (showing their white bellies) and biting.

HULI$_a$

B **dahuli.** *a.* Turn back; change one's mind.
B 1 **dahulianga.** *n.* —.
B 1 **dahulinga.** *n.* Custom, habit.
BE **hagadahuli.** *v.* —.
BE1 **hagadahulianga.** *n.* —.
BE1 **hagadahulinga.** *n.* —.
BE2 **hagadahulia.** *v.* —.
P **daahuli.** *a.* —.
P 1 **daahulianga.** *n.* —.
P 1 **daahulinga.** *n.* —.
PE **hagadaahuli.** *v.* —.
PE1 **hagadaahulianga.** *n.* —.
PE1 **hagadaahulinga.** *n.* —.
PE2 **hagadaahulia.** *v.* —.
R **dahulihuli.** *a.* Keep shifting direction.
R 1 **dahulihulianga.** *n.* —.
R 1 **dahulihulinga.** *n.* —.
RE **hagadahulihuli.** *v.* —.
RE1 **hagadahulihulianga.** *n.* —.
RE2 **hagadahulihulia.** *v.* —.
ID **dahuli de lodo.** Change of heart, change one's mind, repent.
ID **dahuli de madangi.** A change of wind direction.
ID **dahuli de vae.** Dislocated ankle.
ID **dahulihuli donu.** Be careful! [said to someone going fishing].
ID **dahuli sabonealo.** The odor of overripe breadfruit.
ID **doo tahulinga.** Bad-mannered.

HULI$_b$

B **dauhuli (ange).** *n.* Always criticizing (someone) to (his) face.

HULO

B **hulo.** *v.* Go [pl.].
B 1 **huulonga.** *n.* —; a pathway on the open sea.
R **hulohulo.** *v.* —.
R 1 **hulohulonga.** *n.* —.
ID **hulo gee.** Go away [pl.].
ID **hulo gi lunga ma lalo.** Argue heatedly, fight.
ID **hulo saele.** Wander around.
CF **loadu.** Go (toward the hearer) [pl.].
CF **loage.** Go (up or toward the village, or land) [pl.].
CF **loange.** Go (to the place away from both the speaker and hearer) [pl.].
CF **loiho.** Go or come down (or toward the lagoon) [pl.].
CF **loomai.** Come or go (toward the speaker) [pl.].

HULU$_1$

B **hulu$_1$.** *n.* Hair (on the body) [rarely heard].

R **huluhulu$_1$.** *v.* Hair (on the body).
R 1 **huluhulunga$_1$.** *n.* —.
R 2 **huluhulua$_1$.** *v.* Hairy.
RE **hagahuluhulu$_1$.** *v.* —.
RE1 **hagahuluhulunga$_1$.** *n.* —.
RE2 **hagahuluhulua$_1$.** *v.* —.
XCO **ngaangaa-ulu.** *n.* Hair of the head [derived from *hulu*?].
XCO **ngaungau-ulu.** *n.* [var. of *ngaangaaulu*].
ID **huluhulu mada.** Eyebrows.
ID **hulu made.** The fading of one's hair color (becoming white).
ID **hulu manu.** Feathers.

HULU$_2$
B **hulu$_2$.** *v.* Apply liquid on, smear on.
B 1 **huulunga.** *n.* —.
B 2 **hulua.** *v.* —.
BE **hagahulu$_1$.** *v.* —.
BE1 **hagahulunga.** *n.* —.
BE2 **hagahulua.** *v.* —.
R **huluhulu$_2$.** *v.* —.
R 1 **huluhulunga$_2$.** *n.* —.
R 2 **huluhulua$_2$.** *v.* —.
RE **hagahuluhulu$_2$.** *v.* —.
RE1 **hagahuluhulunga$_2$.** *n.* —.
RE2 **hagahuluhulua$_2$.** *v.* —.
XCO **hulubala.** *v.* Smeared with grease or paint or food, etc.
ID **hulu i de lenga.** To paint one's body with tumeric.
CF **aahulu.** To leave food cooking overnight.

HULU$_3$
B **hulu$_3$.** *a.* Ten (in enumeration and compounds only).
BE **hagahulu$_2$.** *v.* Make a total of ten.
XCO **Diba-madaangahulu.** *nn.* The name of a person in a traditional story.
ID **dinoanga hulu.** A council (of ten) formerly having broad legislative and judicial powers on the atoll.
ID **huluhulu-manenga.** The tenth number of a counting game played to determine who is "it" (= the person who becomes "it").

HULU$_4$
B **hulu$_4$.** *n.* Reactive hostility.
BC **mahulu.** *n.* Wakefulness.
ID **hai hulu o —.** Act mad like —.

HUMAI
B **humai.** *a.* Come [sing.].
ID **au ga humai nei.** "I'm going on my way now...".
ID **humai nei.** Next —.
ID **ngadaa mai.** Difficult for me; difficult to come.
ID **ngadi humai.** Come without bringing anything (such as gifts).

HUNA
B **huna.** *v.* Hide [sing.]; breechclout.
B 1 **huunanga.** *n.* —.
BE **hagahuna.** *v.* —.
BE1 **hagahuunanga.** *n.* —.
BE2 **hagahunalia.** *v.* —.
E **hhuna.** *v.* Hide at one time.
EE **hagahhuna.** *v.* —.
EE1 **hagahhunaanga.** *n.* —.
R **hunahuna.** *v.* —.
R 1 **hunahunaanga.** *n.* —.
RE **hagahunahuna.** *v.* —.
RE1 **hagahunahunaanga.** *n.* —.
RE2 **hagahunahunalia.** *v.* —.
T **huuhuna.** *a.* Hide [pl.].
T 1 **huuhunaanga.** *n.* —.
TE **hagahuuhuna.** *v.* —.
TE1 **hagahuuhunaanga.** *n.* —.
TE2 **hagahuuhunalia.** *v.* —.
ID **huna me.** A habitual thief.
ID **malo huna.** Breechclout.

HUNE
B **hune.** *n.* Core of the breadfruit; the flower of the breadfruit tree.
R **hunehune.** *n.* The fibers on the core of the breadfruit.

HUNGA
XFL **hungahunga-a-nui.** *n.* The flower of the coconut tree.

HUNGI

B **hungi.** *v.* Tricks of self-defense (some of which are like judo or karate).
B 1 **huunginga.** *n.* —.
B 2 **hungia.** *v.* —.
R **hungihungi.** *v.* —.
R 1 **hungihunginga.** *n.* —.
R 2 **hungihungia.** *v.* —.
ID **damaa hungi.** Skillful at *hungi.*

HUSI

B **husi.** *n.* Taro bog, swamp.
ID **se ungaa husi gee.** Do something different from that which was intended.
ID **ungaa husi.** [the generic name for] sections of the taro patch.

HUU$_1$

B **huu.** *mv.* Occasion when; just like...
ID **aahee huu.** Then which?
ID **abasasa huu.** European in manner or appearance.
ID **adigai huu.** Were it not for; fortunately, luckily —.
ID **alaa ai huu.** Those there only then.
ID **alaa ange huu.** That there [pl.] much more only.
ID **alaa huu.** Those (there) only are the ones.
ID **anaa ai huu.** Those only then.
ID **anaa ange huu.** That [pl.] much more only.
ID **anaa huu.** Those only are the ones.
ID **anei ai huu.** These only then.
ID **anei ange huu.** This [pl.] much more only.
ID **anei huu.** These (here) only are the ones.
ID **baa huu i —.** Just like.
ID **be aha naa huu.** Whatever; if ever.
ID **danuaa huu.** It's still OK! No wonder!
ID **delaa ai huu.** That was it (as before)!
ID **delaa huu.** That was it just as before.
ID **denaa ai huu.** That is it then!
ID **denaa huu.** That is it still.
ID **denei ai huu.** This is it still.
ID **denei huu.** This is it still.
ID **dogoisi loo huu.** Very few.
ID **donu huu.** Only, just (no more than).
ID **ga dae laa huu.** Very, too much.
ID **gemo ange huu de —.** Rapidly becoming —.
ID **gi hanu donu huu.** Any kind whatsoever.
ID **gu gide huu.** Spoiled (having acquired a bad habit).
ID **hano ai huu.** Forever.
ID **hanohano ai huu.** Go on and on until —.
ID **hooia donu huu.** At the best possible time or place.
ID **mau ange huu.** Usually.
ID **momo loo huu.** Just a very little.
ID **moolau huu.** Punctual.
ID **naa huu.** When, if.
ID **sogoisi loo huu.** [var. of *dogoisi loo huu*].
ID **velo huu —.** Inclined to do —.

HUU$_2$

ID **de huu de henua.** The layer of consolidated sand (without coral rubble) next to the reef base under the island.

HUU$_3$

B **huuhuu$_1$.** *v.* To clap one's wet hands together (to dry them).
B 1 **huuhuunga.** *n.* —.
B 2 **huuhuua.** *v.* —.
BE **hagahuuhuu.** *v.* —.
BE2 **hagahuuhuua.** *v.* —.

HUUBUUDOI

B **huubuudoi.** *a.* Fat and squat and ugly.
B 1 **huubuudoinga.** *n.* —.
BE **hagahuubuudoi.** *v.* —.
BE1 **hagahuubuudoinga.** *n.* —.
BE2 **hagahuubuudoia.** *v.* —.

HUUHUU

R **huuhuu$_2$.** *n.* Fish sp.:

parrot fish (The native term is applied to many spp.).

I
B **i.** *mp.* At; with respect to; in; by means of; because of; in spite of; concerning.
ID **ago i tua.** Learn by heart.
ID **ago i me.** Copy, imitate.
ID **bili i de lodo.** Unforgotten.
ID **danuaa mai i hee.** Good according to whom?
ID **i de — sogosogo.** Apiece, each.
ID **i hee.** Where (in general)?
ID **manava i lunga.** Sigh (an intake of air) [a sign of emotion].
ID **ssano i de ia.** Known by him.
ID **sulu i hegau.** Busy (with work or obligations).
ID **ulu i daane.** Boy-chaser, boy-crazy.
CF **boibala.** Watery (of prepared food).

IA
B **ia.** *pi.* He, she, it.
ID **dee dau ia.** It's OK!
ID **de ia.** The, thing, it.
ID **ssano i de ia.** Known by him.

IAI
B **iai.** *a.* Be (present), have, there is...
BE **hagaiai.** *v.* —.
ID **dama iai.** A person who has done something praiseworthy.
ID **iai maalie.** Just about right.
ID **iai sago.** Having special ability (strength, power, etc.) which others do not have, a strong or powerful (person).
CF **iainei.** Now.

IAI$_a$
B **iainei.** *b.* Now.
ID **honga iainei.** At this time, these days.
ID **iainei donu.** Right now!

IBU
B **ibu.** *n.* [var. of *ubu*].

IDA
BE **hagaida.** *v.* To bare one's teeth (by opening the lips).
BE1 **hagaidanga.** *n.* —.
RE **hagaidaida.** *v.* Cry uncontrollably (hysterically); a disturbance of breathing.
RE1 **hagaidaidanga.** *n.* —.
ID **hagaida de gauvae.** To bare one's teeth (by opening the lips to expose the whole set of teeth).

IDI
B **idi.** *v.* To husk (a coconut) with one's teeth.
B 1 **idinga.** *n.* —; bits of coconut husk which have been removed.
B 2 **idia.** *v.* —.
B 2 **idihia.** *v.* —.
BE **hagaidi.** *v.* —.
BE1 **hagaidinga.** *n.* —.
BE2 **hagaidia.** *v.* —.
BE2 **hagaidihia.** *v.* —.
R **idiidi$_1$.** *v.* —.
R 1 **idiidinga.** *n.* —.
R 2 **idiidia.** *v.* —.
R 2 **idiidihia.** *v.* —.
RE **hagaidiidi.** *v.* —.
RE1 **hagaidiidinga.** *n.* —.
RE2 **hagaidiidia.** *v.* —.
RE2 **hagaidiidihia.** *v.* —.

IDIIDI
B **Idiidi$_2$.** *n.* April.

IEIANGE
B **ieiange.** *a.* [var. of *ieiangi*].

IEIANGI
B **ieiangi.** *a.* Recovered from illness.
B 1 **ieianginga.** *n.* —.
BE **hagaieiangi.** *v.* —; to cure (someone).
BE1 **hagaieianginga.** *n.* —.

IGA
B **iga.** *n.* Fish (archaic, except in compounds).

XFL **iga-adagahi.** *n.* Fish sp.: hawk fish (2 sorts) [so named because it is easy to step on].
XFL **iga-ligi.** *n.* Fish sp. (a small oceanic school fish slightly larger than *dauoni*).
XFL **iga-loa.** *n.* Fish sp. (a small flying fish).
XFL **iganibongi.** *n.* Fish sp.
XFL **igauli.** *n.* Fish sp.: tang (2 sorts).
XFL **igauli-sissisi.** *n.* Fish sp.: tang.
ID **gili iga.** A type of high cloud.
ID **ulungaa iga.** A pair of copulating fish (or turtles, or whales, or stingrays.
CF **madaviiga.** The needle-like spines on *daudu* fish.

IGOHI
B **igohi.** *v.* Fire tongs.
B 1 **igohinga.** *n.* Way of using *igohi.*

IHO
B **iho.** *a.* Get down, climb down; down [MV].
B 1 **ihoanga.** *n.* —.
B 2 **iholia.** *v.* Useful for climbing down.
BE **hagaiho.** *v.* Show (someone) how to climb down.
BE1 **hagaihoanga.** *n.* —.
BE2 **hagaiholia.** *v.* —.
R **ihoiho.** *a.* —.
R 1 **ihoihoanga.** *n.* —.
R 2 **ihoiholia.** *v.* Useful for climbing down repeatedly.
RE **hagaihoiho.** *v.* —.
RE1 **hagaihoihoanga.** *n.* —.
RE2 **hagaihoiholia.** *v.* —.
ID **agu iho.** Say to oneself.
ID **ahe iho.** Diminish (in intensity).
ID **aloha iho.** Self-love.
ID **amuamu iho.** Drizzle.
ID **anga iho.** Self-awareness.
ID **baageaa iho.** Weakening (becoming weaker).
ID **baa iho.** Low (in altitude).
ID **baba iho.** Recently settled.
ID **bau iho.** Capable only of looking after oneself (not others).
ID **bolo iho.** To make oneself the beneficiary of a will which one has made for another.
ID **paa iho.** Explode from above.
ID **pale age (iho).** Steer toward (away from) land.
ID **pono iho.** Put a cover on.
ID **daa iho.** Go toward the lagoon (from land).
ID **dahea iho.** Drift toward the place where the speaker is not.
ID **dai sagana iho goe.** Watch out!
ID **dangi iho.** Cry to oneself.
ID **diba iho.** To tip down; go away from the atoll.
ID **doli iho.** To obtain the biggest first.
ID **donu iho.** Realize, understand.
ID **dugudugu iho.** A technique of massage.
ID **dungu iho.** Smell oneself.
ID **tilo iho.** To consider one's own situation.
ID **ege iho.** Lower (something).
ID **gauligi iho.** Next younger than.
ID **gidee iho.** Be aware of oneself.
ID **golomagi iho.** To exercise great patience or restraint for one's own benefit.
ID **gugu iho.** Useless (person) in anything involving others (capable only of taking care of oneself).
ID **kii iho.** Smaller, lesser (in rank, importance, strength, development, etc.).
ID **kona iho.** Be too much for one.
ID **hagaaduadu iho.** Self-criticism.
ID **hagabuulunga iho.** To

hagabuulunga oneself.
ID **hagapago iho.** To descend suddenly.
ID **hagadabena iho.** Prepare oneself, make oneself ready.
ID **hagadaga iho.** Worsening.
ID **hagatanu iho.** Take a nap.
ID **hagahana iho.** Recook for a little while.
ID **hagamabu iho.** Rest for a short time.
ID **hagammuni iho.** Keep to oneself (what one has done).
ID **hhadi iho luu vae.** Take a short break (in work involving standing).
ID **hhuge iho.** An opening in the clouds.
ID **iho adu.** You feel like —.
ID **iho age.** Feel like beginning to want —.
ID **iho ange** + PRONOUN**—.** To have relapsed into (his/her, etc.) —.
ID **iho ange de —.** Feel like (one is) about to —.
ID **iho daahagi.** A calm sea condition, in which the horizon disappears [the horizon being normally marked by surf].
ID **iho mai.** I feel like —.
ID **iloo iho.** Realize, know.
ID **lau iho laa.** Those of small size.
ID **longo iho.** Be aware of, experience, perceive, feel (in one's mind or body).
ID **longolongo iho dalinga.** Pick up information from others' conversation.
ID **maanadu iho.** Think about oneself.
ID **maanu iho.** To begin to fish while *maanu*.
ID **madohi iho.** To reach halfway down.
ID **moe iho.** Sleep for a short time, nap; sleep overnight in place other than one's usual sleeping place.
ID **molomolo iho (age).** Appear clearly.
ID **noho iho —.** Keep secret.
ID **ngadau iho.** Younger.
ID **ngalue iho.** Reduced, decreased.
ID **ngaue iho.** Reduce (in rank, price, etc.).
ID **ngole iho.** To use the biggest first.
ID **odi iho.** Just finished.
ID **oho iho.** Come ashore early in the morning.
ID **oo iho (age).** Able to enter, going up (down).
ID **sae iho.** Tear from the top down; break through the bush (coming downhill).
ID **saganaa iho goe.** Watch out!
ID **seni iho.** Take a nap, stay overnight (away from home).
ID **sili iho.** Have just stopped; calm down (of a person).
ID **soe iho.** Straight down; decided for one by the will of God.
ID **sua iho.** To dig away soil, letting the soil slide down (e.g., from the side of a hill).
ID **ue iho.** Lower or decrease (the volume of a radio, price, etc.).
ID **ui iho.** Pass under.
ID **ulu iho.** Take from the top downward.
ID **ulumagi iho.** Cover or put on from the top down.
ID **velo iho.** Come down straight.
CF **loiho.** Go or come down (or toward the lagoon) [pl.].

IHOa
B **ngaiho.** *nl.* Uptown.
ID **doo ngaiho.** The blowing of the wind from the north.

ILA
B **ila.** *v.* A mole (not raised), or other permanent black spot on the skin.
BE **hagaila.** *v.* —.

R ilaila. v. Having more than one *ila*.
RE hagailaila. v. —.

ILAAGE
B **ilaage.** *a.* Free of (sickness, hardship, etc.).
BE **hagailaage.** *v.* Set free.
R **ilailaage.** *a.* —.
RE **hagailailaage.** *v.* —.
ID **ilaage mai.** Free from.

ILI
B **ili.** *v.* Blow, fan (oneself); inflate (a balloon).
B 1 **ilinga.** *n.* —.
B 2 **ilia.** *v.* —.
B 2 **ilihia.** *v.* —; having one's stomach distended by gas.
BC **maili.** *a.* Fast moving.
BC1 **mailinga.** *n.* —.
BE **hagaili.** *v.* —; strike (give a blow to).
BE1 **hagailinga.** *n.* —.
BE2 **hagailia.** *v.* —; cause to blow away.
BE2 **hagailihia.** *v.* —; cause to blow away.
BF **hagamaili.** *v.* —.
BF1 **hagamailinga.** *n.* —.
BF2 **hagamailia.** *v.* —.
R **iliili.** *v.* —.
R 1 **iliilinga.** *n.* —.
R 2 **iliilia.** *v.* —.
R 2 **iliilihia.** *v.* —.
RC **mailiili.** *a.* Fast moving (over a considerable duration of time).
RC1 **mailiilinga.** *n.* —.
RE **hagailiili.** *v.* —.
RE1 **hagailiilinga.** *n.* —.
RE2 **hagailiilia.** *v.* —.
RE2 **hagailiilihia.** *v.* —.
RF **hagamailiili.** *v.* —.
RF1 **hagamailiilinga.** *n.* —.
RF2 **hagamailiilia.** *v.* —.
XFL **buu-ili.** *n.* Fish sp.
ID **ili taalanga.** Talkative, chatterbox, talk at great length.
ID **ilihia tinae.** A stomach distended by gas.
ID **ilihia ssave.** The submerging of flying fish below the surface of the water (making them difficult to net).
ID **ili luu bongaa usu.** To dilate one's nostrils [a mannerism which is taken as a sign of emotion].
ID **magi ilihia.** Gastritis (having one's stomach full of gas).

ILO
B **ilo.** *v.* Worm, maggot, intestinal parasites.
B 2 **ilosia.** *v.* Wormy or maggoty (of something decayed).
B 3 **ilosiaanga.** *n.* —.
BE2 **hagailosia.** *v.* —.
BE3 **hagailosiaanga.** *n.* —.

ILOHA
B **iloha.** *v.* Fathom (the span of one's outstretched arms) [var. of *loha*].
B 1 **ilohaanga.** *n.* —.
BE **hagailoha.** *v.* —.
BE1 **hagailohaanga.** *n.* —.

ILOO
B **iloo.** *a.* Know, understand, be intimate with, sure of (and willing to say).
B 1 **iloonga.** *n.* —.
BD **heiloo.** *a.* Know each other, understand each other.
BD1 **heiloonga.** *n.* —.
BE **hagailoo.** *v.* Announce.
BE1 **hagailoonga.** *n.* —.
BG **hagaheiloo.** *v.* Make the acquaintance of.
BG1 **hagaheiloonga.** *n.* —.
ID **goe iloo.** It's up to you!
ID **hagailonga ange agina.** Assign (someone) to; use something as a landmark.
ID **iloo iho.** Realize, know.
ID **iloo mai.** Know that someone —.
ID **iloo me.** Charlatanism.
CF **hagailonga.** —.

IMU
XFL **imu-mea.** *n.* Fish sp.: triggerfish.
XFL **imu-uli.** *n.* Fish sp.: triggerfish.

INA
ID **dodo ina.** Bloody [of garments, etc.].

INA$_1$
B **ina$_1$.** *v.* To light up an area at night (esp. for hunting land crabs).
B 1 **inaanga.** *n.* —.
BE **hagaina.** *v.* —.
BE1 **hagainaanga.** *n.* —.
R **inaina.** *v.* —.
RE **hagainaina.** *v.* —.
RE1 **hagainainaanga.** *n.* —.

INA$_2$
B **ina$_2$.** *mv.* To it.
ID **aausa ina.** A sea condition resembling that resulting from a ship leaving a wake.
ID **ahe ina.** Wind around completely once.
ID **aloha ina.** Helpful toward.
ID **ao ina.** Inadvertently remain up until daybreak (= *aoa*).
ID **babaiangi ina.** Cloudy, with clouds of the *babaiangi* type.
ID **bedage ina.** Shallow on the inside.
ID **boaa ina mai.** Prevented from coming by being caught in a storm.
ID **gannui ina.** White (of the portion of a woman's thighs hidden under her sarong).
ID **gu oo ina mai.** Shout to announce important news (e.g., to announce the arrival of a ship).
ID **haangoda ina.** [= *haangodalia*].
ID **hagadagodo gee ina.** Change.
ID **hai aoa ina.** Bear misshapen fruit.
ID **manu ina.** [= *manua*].
ID **saavale ina.** Fish or meat which is watery in texture and bad-tasting.
ID **ssuonioni ina.** Sandy.
ID **sumu ina.** To make diamond-shaped designs in plaiting or lashing.
ID **useahi ina.** To be annoyed by smoke.
CF **ina-gi-hale.** A row of thatch.

INAHO
B **inaho.** *n.* A school consisting of a certain reef fish sp. (*laumele*).

INAI
B **inai.** *n.* A type of mat.
ID **dau age de inai.** Be in the lee of the atoll while fishing (i.e., in a place protected from the wind).
ID **duu inai.** A type of mat [a half *inai*].

INAU
B **inau.** *v.* To look for coconut crabs at night with a light.
B 1 **inaunga.** *n.* —.
BE **hagainau.** *v.* —.
BE1 **hagainaunga.** *n.* —.
BE2 **hagainaua.** *v.* —.

INO
B **ino.** *a.* Bow or nod or genuflect (as a sign of respect).
B 1 **inonga.** *n.* —.
BE **hagaino.** *v.* —.
BE1 **hagainonga.** *n.* —.
R **inoino.** *a.* —.
R 1 **inoinonga.** *n.* —.
RE **hagainoino.** *v.* —.
RE1 **hagainoinonga.** *n.* —.
ID **ino gi mua.** Bend (one's body) forward.

INOHA
ID **dolu-inoha.** The third number of a counting game played to determine who is "it".

INGOO
B **ingoo.** *n.* Name, a title

(used as a name).
B 1 **ingooanga.** *n.* —.
BE **hagaingoo.** *v.* Give a name to, named, called.
BE1 **hagaingooanga.** *n.* —.
ID **hagaingoo ai.** Called by (named).
ID **hai de ingoo.** Make a good name for oneself (by one's ingratiating behavior).

IO
B **io.** *n.* A quarter of the body of a tuna when it is cut lengthwise.
ID **io alo.** Lower *io*, q.v.
ID **io dua.** The upper *io*.

IOO
B **ioo.** *a.* To make a sound indicating "take it!" [as an interjection, = "take it!"].
B 1 **ioonga.** *n.* Way of giving.
BE **hagaioo.** *v.* Cause to give.
BE1 **hagaiooanga.** *n.* —.

ISE
B **ise.** *n.* Fish sp.: halfbeak.
XFL **ise-ngaio.** *n.* Fish sp.: needlefish.

ISI$_1$
B **isi.** *v.* To peel off in long thin strips.
B 1 **isinga.** *n.* —.
B 2 **isia.** *v.* —.
B 2 **isihia.** *v.* —.
BC **maisi.** *a.* Peeled off.
BC1 **maisinga.** *n.* —.
BE **hagaisi.** *v.* —.
BE1 **hagaisinga.** *n.* —.
BE2 **hagaisia.** *v.* —.
BE2 **hagaisihia.** *v.* —.
BF **hagamaisi.** *v.* —.
BF1 **hagamaisinga.** *n.* —.
BF2 **hagamaisia.** *v.* —.
BF2 **hagamaisihia.** *v.* —.
PC **maaisi.** *a.* —.
PC1 **maaisinga.** *n.* —.
PF **hagamaaisi.** *v.* —.
PF1 **hagamaaisinga.** *n.* —.
PF2 **hagamaaisia.** *v.* —.
PF2 **hagamaaisihia.** *v.* —.
R **isiisi.** *v.* —.
R 1 **isiisinga.** *n.* —.
R 2 **isiisia.** *v.* —.
R 2 **isiisihia.** *v.* —.
RC **maisiisi.** *a.* —.
RC1 **maisiisinga.** *n.* —.
RE **hagaisiisi.** *v.* —.
RE1 **hagaisiisinga.** *n.* —.
RE2 **hagaisiisia.** *v.* —.
RE2 **hagaisiisihia.** *v.* —.
RF **hagamaisiisi.** *v.* —.
RF1 **hagamaisiisinga.** *n.* —.
RF2 **hagamaisiisia.** *v.* —.
RF2 **hagamaisiisihia.** *v.* —.
ID **isiisi luu gauanga.** To tear off (a person's) legs [an expression heard in threats].
ID **isiisi luu gauasa.** To tear from limb to limb.

ISI$_2$
CF **dogoisi.** Few.
CF **sogoisi.** [var. of *dogoisi*].

IVI
B **ivi.** *n.* Bone, needle.
R 2 **iviivia.** *v.* Skinny, thin (person), emaciated.
R 3 **iviiviaanga.** *n.* —.
RE2 **hagaiviivia.** *v.* —.
RE3 **hagaiviiviaanga.** *n.* —.
ID **pala ivi.** Work beyond one's endurance.
ID **gau ivi.** Skinny.
ID **ivi-a-daea.** Shoulder blade.
ID **ivi-a-duimogo.** Pelvic bone.
ID **ivi de biho.** Skull.
ID **ivi gaogao.** Rib.
ID **ivi laanui.** Spine (of the body).
ID **ivi ngongo.** Collar bone.
ID **ivi sulu.** A dislocation of bones such that the ends overlap (corrected by pulling).
ID **langa de ivi.** A method of repositioning the bones of the ribcage.
ID **magi iviivi.** Any illness characterized by wasting of the body (esp. t.b.), consumption.
CF **madaviiga.** The needle-like spines on *daudu* fish.

LAA$_1$

B **laa$_1$.** *mv*. There in the distance, then (past).

ID **aahee laa.** Which were those?

ID **adu ange laa.** The one following the one in question.

ID **adu laa.** After tomorrow, the one after the next one.

ID **aha laa.** I wonder why?

ID **alaa ai laa.** Those there then were.

ID **alaa laa.** Those (there) which were there.

ID **anaa ai laa.** Those then were those.

ID **anaa laa.** These (there) which were there.

ID **anaange laa hanu.** A little while ago.

ID **anei ai laa.** These then were those.

ID **anei laa.** These (here) which were there.

ID **angeange laa.** The one following the one in question.

ID **ange laa.** The next but one.

ID **boo adu laa.** Day after tomorrow at night.

ID **boo ga dae laa.** My goodness!

ID **boo mai ange laa.** The second night following.

ID **delaa ai laa.** That there was it!

ID **delaa laa** (?). That there was it (was that it?).

ID **denaa ai laa.** That was it!

ID **denaa laa** (?). That is it there (is that it there?).

ID **denei ai laa.** This is that then.

ID **denei laa** (?). This is that (is this that?).

ID **ga dae laa huu.** Very, too much.

ID **hagame ange laa.** A little later.

ID **hai hua laa.** Do indifferently.

ID **hano laa.** Previous.

ID **laa tua.** Besides.

ID **maakau laa loo dangada.** What a shame!

ID **mai ange laa.** The next (one) following the one in question.

ID **maua laa.** Never mind!

ID **me ange laa.** The others.

ID **vakaa laa loo.** Too bad for him (I don't care)!

LAA$_{1a}$

B **alaa.** *b*. Those over there.

ID **alaa ai.** Those only.

ID **alaa ai huu.** Those there only then.

ID **alaa ai laa.** Those there then were.

ID **alaa ai loo.** Those there then are.

ID **alaa ange.** And those there.

ID **alaa ange huu.** That there [pl.] much more only.

ID **alaa ange maalie.** Those there are exactly right.

ID **alaa ange naa.** About that [pl.] (over there) much more.

ID **alaa dagodo.** Those there are the circumstances...

ID **alaa donu.** Those there only.

ID **alaa huu.** Those (there) only are the ones.

ID **alaa laa.** Those (there) which were there.

ID **alaa loo.** Those (there) were the ones.

ID **alaa maa.** Those there were about (approximately).

ID **alaa muhuu.** How about those there?

ID **alaa muna.** Word [= *dalaa muna*].

ID **alaa naa.** Those only?

ID **alaa naa loo.** Those there seem to be.

ID **alaa nei.** Those now.

ID **alaa sili.** Those there were enough.

ID **muna hai alaa.** Oh my goodness!

LAA$_{1b}$

ID **gidigidi laa lalo.** A very short person, midget; miniature, diminutive.

ID **hano laa uda.** Go on foot.

ID **laa kilaa.** Around there far away.

ID **laa kinaa.** Around there near you.
ID **laa kinei.** Around here.
ID **laa magavaa.** In between.
ID **musumusu laa lalo.** Whisper softly.

LAA1c
B **kilaa.** *b.* There in the distance.
ID **laa kilaa.** Around there far away.

LAA1d
B **delaa.** *b.* That one (over there).
ID **aha goi delaa.** What was I going to say?
ID **delaa ai.** Therefore (with respect to that there).
ID **delaa ai huu.** That was it (as before)!
ID **delaa ai laa.** That there was it!
ID **delaa ai loo.** That was it at last!
ID **delaa ange.** That there is another one!
ID **delaa ange maalie.** That there is exactly right!
ID **delaa ange naa.** About that [sing.] (over there), much more.
ID **delaa donu.** That there is it for sure!
ID **delaa tagodo.** That there is the situation...
ID **delaa tee madea.** Hard to tell apart from; resemble closely.
ID **delaa huu.** That was it just as before.
ID **delaa laa** (?). That there was it (was that it?).
ID **delaa loo.** That was it.
ID **delaa maa.** That there was about (approximately).
ID **delaa muhuu.** How about that one there?
ID **delaa naa** (?). That there will be it (will that be it?).
ID **delaa naa loo.** That there could be it.
ID **delaa nei** (?). That there is it (is that there it?).
ID **delaa sili.** That there is enough.

LAA2
B **laa2.** *n.* Sun.
ID **anailaa laa.** It was today that.
ID **baguu de laa.** Past noon.
ID **danu de laa.** The setting of the sun.
ID **dii de laa.** The shining of the sun.
ID **galo de laa.** The reddish sky at sunset.
ID **gili laa.** Suntanned.
ID **laa tubua.** Daily.
ID **maalama dua de laa.** The light remaining after sunset.
ID **magau de laa.** Weakness of the sun's rays (for drying) [usually referring to the late afternoon].
ID **sobo de laa.** Rising of the sun.
ID **sulu de laa.** The setting of the sun.
ID **sulumanga o de laa.** The direction in which the sun sets.
CF **ailaa.** Today (sometime).

LAA3
B **laa3.** *n.* A branch (of a tree).
R **laalaa.** *v.* Having many branches.
R 1 **laalaanga.** *n.* —.
RE **hagalaalaa.** *v.* —.
RE1 **hagalaalaanga.** *n.* —.
ID **dinae o de laa.** Ballooning of a sail.
ID **dugu de laa.** Lower sail.
CF **laaigi.** A driftwood plant sp., with an aromatic sap which is used for perfume.

LAA3a
B **laagau.** *n.* Wood, stick (of wood).
XFL **hua-laagau.** *n.* Plant sp.: tropical almond (*Terminalia catappa* L.).
XFL **laagau-bala-uda.** *n.* Driftwood sp. (very soft).

XFL	**laagau-doi.** *n.* A driftwood sp., from the sap of which (*doi*) perfume is made.
XG	**manu solo laagau.** File (for filing wood).
ID	**gau laagau.** The shaft of a spear.
ID	**hhali lo te laagau.** A depression in a log (an abnormal growth).
ID	**hoohoa laagau.** Drill wood to make a hole in which to insert the end of a pole (to make a joint).
ID	**laagau aalo saelenga.** Thatch rafters on the ends of a house.
ID	**laagau hagadauaadea.** A cross-beam lashed to a tree to facilitate climbing it.
ID	**laagau lui.** A cross (e.g., of wood).
ID	**ulu laagau.** Medicine (from a plant).

LAA_{3b}

B	**laa_4.** *n.* A sail.

LAAGA

B	**Laaga.** *n.* November.

LAAGII

B	**laagii.** *n.* Decoration, ornamentation.
B 1	**laaginga.** *n.* —.
BE	**hagalaagii.** *v.* Decorate, adorn; ornament [verb].
BE1	**hagalaaginga.** *n.* —.
BE2	**hagalaagia.** *v.* —.
ID	**dau laagii.** To put on an ornament for a special purpose.
ID	**laagii baubau.** Hideous in appearance (as a ghost).
CF	**laagei.** [var. of *laagii*].
CF	**latabagea.** An ornament made of turtle shell.

LAAIGI

B	**laaigi.** *n.* A driftwood plant sp., with an aromatic sap which is used for perfume.

LAALADI

B	**laaladi.** *v.* To scratch (an itch).
B 1	**laaladinga.** *n.* —.
B 2	**laaladia.** *v.* —.
BE	**hagalaaladi.** *v.* —.
BE1	**hagalaaladinga.** *n.* —.
BE2	**hagalaaladia.** *v.* —.

LAAMALEU

ID	**laangai laamaleu.** A fishing condition in which tuna are jumping but not biting.

LAAMALOO

B	**laamaloo.** *n.* A divination result indicating bad fortune.

LAAMASEE

B	**laamasee.** *n.* A divination result indicating good fortune.

LAANUI

B	**laanui.** *a.* Big [sing.]; large [sing.].
B 1	**laanuinga.** *n.* —.
BE	**hagalaanui.** *v.* —; enlarge.
BE1	**hagalaanuinga.** *n.* —.
BE2	**hagalaanuia.** *v.* —.
R	**laalaanui.** *a.* Becoming big.
R 1	**laalaanuinga.** *n.* —.
RE	**hagalaalaanui.** *v.* —.
RE1	**hagalaalaanuinga.** *n.* —.
RE2	**hagalaalaanuia.** *v.* —.
ID	**daumaha laanui.** The main Sunday religious observance in the church.
ID	**kai laanui.** Show-off; a legend concerning the founding of Nukuoro.
ID	**ivi laanui.** Spine (of the body).
ID	**lodo laanui.** Large in volume or capacity, spacious inside.

LAANGAI

B	**laangai.** *d.* Fishing conditions are —.
ID	**laangai buusagi.** A type of fishing condition in

which the sea is boiling with jumping tuna, which are biting at anything.

ID laangai huli de moana. A fishing condition in which tuna are jumping (showing their white bellies) and biting.

ID laangai laamaleu. A fishing condition in which tuna are jumping but not biting.

ID laangai milo sanga. A fishing condition in which fish are not inclined to bite.

ID laangai ngadi moana. A fishing condition in which tuna are biting, but do not appear in schools.

ID laangai sahole. A fishing condition in which tuna are jumping and biting.

LAANGI

B laangi. *n.* Day.

XCO Tahi-laangi. *nt.* Monday ('first day').

XCO Tolu-laangi. *nt.* Wednesday ('third day').

XCO Haa-laangi. *nt.* Thursday [lit., the 'fourth day'].

XCO Hidu-laangi. *nt.* Sunday ('seventh day').

XCO huaalaangi. *n.* Noon; the whole day; a certain day only.

XCO Laangidabu. *nt.* Sunday.

XCO Laangihagamouli. *nt.* Saturday (the day on which food is prepared for Sunday).

XCO Lima-laangi. *nt.* Friday ('fifth day').

XCO Lua-laangi. *nt.* Tuesday ('second day').

XCO Ono-laangi. *nt.* Saturday ('sixth day').

ID dao de laangi. Celebrate.

ID deai ange soo laangi. I'll get you!

ID laangi dabeo. A day which is rainy and stormy.

ID laangi danuaa. Hello! Good day!

ID laangi hagadaahao. Field day.

ID me hai laangi. Calandar.

ID ngadi laangi. A day other than Sunday; a day on which nothing is accomplished.

LAAVASI

B laavasi. *n.* Meat (or fish, or seafood) which is suitable as food.

CF lava. Finished [sing.]; wealthy [sing.]; wrap— [dp].

LABA$_1$

B laba$_1$. *v.* Flash (as of lightning).

B 1 labaanga. *n.* —.

BE hagalaba. *v.* —.

BE1 hagalabaanga. *n.* —.

P llaba. *v.* —.

P 1 llabaanga. *n.* —.

PE1 hagallabaanga. *n.* —.

R labalaba. *v.* —; sparkling.

R 1 labalabaanga. *n.* —.

RE hagalabalaba. *v.* —.

RE1 hagalabalabaanga. *n.* —.

LABA$_2$

B laba$_2$. *n.* A dancing paddle.

LABA$_{2a}$

ID laba ngaugau. A stalk of the elephant-ear plant (*ngaungau*).

LABA$_{2b}$

B hallaba. *n.* The base of a palm frond spine; rifle.

LABAAI

B labaai. *v.* The confluence, on the reef, of a big wave and the backwash.

B 1 labaainga. *n.* —.

B 2 labaaia. *v.* —.

BE hagalabaai. *v.* —.

BE1 hagalabaainga. *n.* —.

BE2 hagalabaaia. *v.* —.

LABAGAU

B labagau. *a.* Carpenter;

skillful (at a craft); craftsman.
B 1 **labagaunga.** *n.* —.
BE **hagalabagau.** *v.* —.
BE1 **hagalabagaunga.** *n.* —.
BE2 **hagalabagaua.** *v.* —.
P **labaagau.** *a.* —.
PE **hagalabaagau.** *v.* —.
PE1 **hagalabaagaunga.** *n.* —.
PE2 **hagalabaagaua.** *v.* —.
ID **goloa labagau.** Carpenter's tools.

LABE
XFL **labelabe-tea.** *n.* Fish sp.
XFL **labelabe-uliuli.** *n.* Fish sp.: wrasse.

LABODO
B **labodo.** *n.* Eel, any long worm, snake.
XFL **labodo-daubulebule.** *n.* Eel sp.
XFL **labodo-tea.** *n.* Eel sp.: moray eel.
XFL **labodo-sisi.** *n.* Eel sp.: snake eel.
XFL **labodo-uli.** *n.* Eel sp.: moray eel.

LABU
B **labu.** *v.* Knead; claw — [dp].
B 1 **laabunga.** *n.* —.
B 2 **labua.** *v.* Knead thoroughly.
BE **hagalabu.** *v.* —.
BE1 **hagalaabunga.** *n.* —.
BE2 **hagalabua.** *v.* —.
E **llabu.** *v.* Claw.
EE **hagallabu.** *d.* —.
R **labulabu.** *v.* —.
R 1 **labulabunga.** *n.* —.
R 2 **labulabua.** *v.* —.
RE **hagalabulabu.** *v.* —.
RE1 **hagalabulabunga.** *n.* —.
RE2 **hagalabulabua.** *v.* —.
ID **labua gee (lodo).** Having an upset stomach; to be on the point of nausea.
ID **labulabu sala.** Fail to take hold of (or do) properly (leading to an accident, or other unfortunate outcome).
ID **labu manu.** To pet (pets, children, or a member of the opposite sex).
ID **labu ssenga.** To run into trouble (owing to one's misdeeds).
ID **magi labua gee.** Upset stomach (nausea).
CF **lagu.** —.

LAPEDE
B **lapede.** *v.* Stumble and fall.
B 1 **lapedenga.** *n.* —.
B 2 **lapedea.** *v.* —.
BE **hagalapede.** *v.* —.
BE1 **hagalapedenga.** *n.* —.
BE2 **hagalapedea.** *v.* —.

LADA
ID **buubuu a lada.** A type of puzzle.

LADI
B **ladi.** *v.* Initiate, begin, start.
B 1 **ladinga.** *n.* —.
B 2 **ladia.** *v.* —.
BE **hagaladi.** *v.* —.
BE1 **hagaladinga.** *n.* —.
BE2 **hagaladia.** *v.* —.
R **ladiladi.** *v.* —.
R 1 **ladiladinga.** *n.* —.
R 2 **ladiladia.** *v.* —.
RE **hagaladiladi.** *v.* —.
RE1 **hagaladiladinga.** *n.* —.
RE2 **hagaladiladia.** *v.* —.

LADI$_a$
B **aladi.** *v.* Initiate, begin.
B 1 **aladinga.** *n.* —.
B 2 **aladia.** *v.* —.
BE **hagaaladi.** *v.* —.
BE1 **hagaaladinga.** *n.* —.
BE2 **hagaaladia.** *v.* —.
R **alaaladi.** *v.* —.
R 1 **alaaladinga.** *n.* —.
R 2 **alaaladia.** *v.* —.
RE **hagaalaaladi.** *v.* —.
RE1 **hagaalaaladinga.** *n.* —.
RE2 **hagaalaaladia.** *v.* —.

LAE
B **lae.** *n.* Forehead.
R **laelae (gee).** *a.* Look (funny).
R 1 **laelaenga.** *n.* —.
RC **malaelae.** *a.* Clear, unobstructed, uncluttered.

RC1 **malaelaenga.** *n.* —.
RE **hagalaelae.** *v.* —.
RE1 **hagalaelaenga.** *n.* —.
RE2 **hagalaelaea.** *v.* —.
RF **hagamalaelae.** *v.* —.
RF1 **hagamalaelaenga.** *n.* —.
RF2 **hagamalaelaea.** *v.* —.
ID **dongi de lae.** A spot on the forehead [worn in ancient religious ceremonies].
ID **duu malaelae.** An open field (having no trees).
ID **hhoa de lae.** To run into misfortune as a result of one's evil deeds.

LAGA
E **llaga.** *v.* Take a single step.
E 1 **laaganga.** *n.* —.
EE **hagallaga.** *v.* —.
EE1 **hagalaaganga.** *n.* —.
R **lagalaga.** *v.* To put down one foot after the other (as in walking or marching in place).
R 1 **lagalaganga.** *n.* —.
RE **hagalagalaga.** *v.* —.
RE1 **hagalagalaganga.** *n.* —.

LAGALAGAI
B **lagalagai.** *v.* A method of plating coconut palm fronds.
B 1 **lagalagainga.** *n.* —.
B 2 **lagalagaia.** *v.* —.
BE **hagalagalagai.** *v.* —.
BE1 **hagalagalagainga.** *n.* —.
BE2 **hagalagalagaia.** *v.* —.

LAGI
B **lagi.** *n.* Pertaining to the open sea.
ID **duuduu lagi.** A diving platform (made from a tree stuck in a coral head).
ID **mamu de lagi.** The fish which live beyond the outer reef.

LAGO$_1$
B **lago.** *d.* About, quite.
BE **hagalagolago.** *v.* Cause to increase in numbers, multiply.
E **llago.** *a.* Mature (of a taro corm which can be used for food).
E 1 **llagoanga.** *n.* —.
EE **hagallago.** *v.* —.
EE1 **hagallagoanga.** *n.* —.
R **lagolago.** *a.* Many, plenty, a lot of, much.
R 1 **lagolagoanga.** *n.* Way of being many.
RE1 **hagalagolagoanga.** *n.* —.
RE2 **hagalagolagoa.** *v.* Cause to be numerous.
XCO **dagilagolago.** *a.* Many for each.
ID **bagi mada lagolago.** Machine gun.
ID **dai (tigi) lago —.** Becoming more — (but not quite).
ID **dee lago —.** Not quite —.
ID **dee lago dae.** Not really good or sufficient, etc.
ID **lodo lagolago.** Indecisive, undecided.
ID **ngudu lagolago.** Lie (tell a falsehood).

LAGO$_2$
B **lagohia.** *v.* Wounded.
B 1 **lagohiaanga.** *n.* —.
BE **hagalagohia.** *v.* —.
BE1 **hagalagohiaanga.** *n.* —.
R **lagolagohia.** *v.* Wounded in several places or all over.
R 1 **lagolagohiaanga.** *n.* —.
RE **hagalagolagohia.** *v.* —.
RE1 **hagalagolagohiaanga.** *n.* —.

LAGO$_{2a}$
B **lagolagoaa.** *v.* Destroy or abuse property (for no good reason); vandalism.
B 1 **lagolagoaanga.** *n.* —.
BE **hagalagolagoaa.** *v.* —.
BE1 **hagalagolagoaanga.** *n.* —.

LAGU
B **lagu.** *d.* —.
B 1 **laagunga.** *n.* —.
B 2 **laagua.** *v.* —.
BE **hagalagu —.** *d.* —.
BE1 **hagalaagunga.** *n.* —.
BE2 **hagalaagua.** *v.* —.
E **llagu.** *v.* Claw.
EE **hagallagu.** *v.* —.
R **lagulagu.** *v.* —.

R 1 **lagulagunga.** *n.* —.
R 2 **lagulagua.** *v.* —.
RE **hagalagulagu.** *v.* —.
RE1 **hagalagulagunga.** *n.* —.
RE2 **hagalagulagua.** *v.* —.
CF **labu.** Knead; claw — [dp].

LAHA
P **llaha.** *a.* —.
P 1 **llahaanga.** *n.* —.
PE **hagallaha.** *v.* —.
PE1 **hagallahaanga.** *n.* —.
R **lahalaha.** *a.* Wide [sing.]; broad [sing.].
R 1 **lahalahaanga.** *n.* —.
RE **hagalahalaha.** *v.* —.
RE1 **hagalahalahaanga.** *n.* —.
ID **baa lahalaha.** Broad-chested.
ID **mada lahalaha.** Appear to be wide.
ID **sao de lahalaha.** More wide than long.

LAHHIE
B **lahhie.** *n.* Firewood.

LAHI
BE **hagallahi.** *v.* —.
BE1 **hagallahinga.** *n.* —.
BE2 **hagalahilahia.** *v.* —.
P **llahi$_1$.** *a.* Thin (pl.).
P 1 **llahianga.** *n.* —.
PE2 **hagallahia.** *v.* —.
R **lahilahi.** *a.* Fish sp.; tremendous (followed by *ina*).
R 1 **lahilahianga.** *n.* —.
RE **hagalahilahi.** *v.* —.
RE1 **hagalahilahinga.** *n.* —.
ID **daane dee lahilahia.** A very special one (rarely seen).
ID **dee lahilahia.** Big (and therefore good), strong, tremendous.

LAHI$_a$
B **daballahi.** *a.* Thin (of long flat object) [sing.].
BE **hagadaballahi.** *v.* —.
R **dabadaballahi.** *a.* More-or-less thin.
RE **hagadabadaballahi.** *v.* —.

LAHI$_b$
E **llahi$_2$.** *n.* Fish sp. (= small *hagaudalolo*).

LAHO
B **laho.** *n.* Aerial root of the pandanus tree.

LAHU
B **lahu.** *v.* Investigate (to prove one's suspicions).
B 1 **lahunga.** *n.* —.
B 2 **lahua.** *v.* —.
BE **hagalahu.** *v.* —.
BE1 **hagalahunga.** *n.* —.
BE2 **hagalahua.** *v.* —.
R **lahulahu$_1$.** *v.* —.
R **lahulahu$_2$.** *n.* Bird sp.: wandering tattler? (*Heteroscelus incanus*).
R 1 **lahulahunga.** *n.* —.
R 2 **lahulahua.** *v.* —.
RE **hagalahulahu.** *v.* —.
RE1 **hagalahulahunga.** *n.* —.
RE2 **hagalahulahua.** *v.* —.
ID **lahu me.** Inclined to be suspicious.

LAI
R **lailai.** *n.* Fish sp. (= *lae*?).

LALA
B **lala.** *v.* To roast.
B 1 **laalanga$_1$.** *n.* —.
B 2 **laangia.** *v.* —; heat up on an open flame (as in shaping wood).
B 2 **lalaa.** *v.* Sizzling noise (as in frying).
BC **malala.** *n.* Charcoal.
BE **hagalala.** *v.* —.
BE1 **hagalalaanga.** *n.* —.
BE2 **hagalaangia.** *v.* —.
BE2 **hagalalaa.** *v.* —.
R **lallala.** *v.* Warm oneself by the fire.
R 2 **laalangia.** *v.* —.
RE **hagalallala.** *v.* —.
RE2 **hagalaalaangia.** *v.* —.
ID **gaa de malala.** There is sufficient [a conventional expression]; an argumentative and

stubborn person; argumentative.
ID **lala gaadinga.** To heat copra (to dry it).
CF **massagalala.** Burned (food).

LALE
B **lale.** *n.* Fish sp. (The native term is applied to many spp.).
CF **duulale.** A type of game.

LALO
B **lalo.** *nl.* Down, under.
BE **hagalalo.** *v.* Angling (a fishing method).
XCO **gailalopoli.** *a.* Stingy.
ID **aagonga i lalo.** Social class of those who know the black arts.
ID **basa hagamao lalo.** Speak humbly.
ID **boo i lalo o tangada.** The last days of a person's life.
ID **buni lunga ma lalo.** A pitch black night.
ID **daane i lalo.** A person who fails at everything he tries.
ID **dagodo lalo.** Seriously ill and not improving.
ID **dahea gi lalo.** Sink (completely).
ID **dama lalo.** A person who has visited other far-away lands.
ID **doo lalo.** Unsuccessful.
ID **dua hagalalo.** Fishing line of a size appropriate for the *hagalalo* method of fishing.
ID **gidigidi laa lalo.** A very short person, midget; miniature, diminutive.
ID **goloa lalo.** Gear obtained from foreign lands.
ID **hadu lalo.** A stone on which hermit crabs are crushed (to use for bait).
ID **hagadugu lalo.** Self-deprecatory, downgrade.
ID **hagamao lalo.** Humble, modest.
ID **henua i lalo (alodahi).** World (lands other than Nukuoro).
ID **hoa lalo.** Anvil; or other hard object (such as a stone) on which something can be struck hard; mortar stone.
ID **hulo gi lunga ma lalo.** Argue heatedly, fight.
ID **lalo ade.** Solar plexus (considered the seat of feeling).
ID **lalo de langi.** Beyond the horizon, far away from the atoll.
ID **lodo mao lalo.** Characteristically *hagamao lalo*; self-effacing, meek in spirit.
ID **manu lalo tai.** Sea shell.
ID **mao lalo.** Deep, low (in status).
ID **musumusu laa lalo.** Whisper softly.
ID **noho lalo.** Overloaded (almost to the point of sinking).

LAMA
B **lama.** *n.* A dry coconut leaf.
E **llama.** *v.* A method of fishing (using torches of *lama* to catch flying fish).
EE **hagallama.** *v.* —.
XFL **manu-de-laama.** *n.* Any of the small flying insects which swarm near a light.
ID **gau lama.** Rachis of the coconut leaf.
CF **malama.** Month, moon.

LAMU
B **lamu.** *v.* Do some bad deed suddenly or by surprise.
B 1 **lamunga.** *n.* —.
B 2 **lamua.** *v.* —.
R **lamulamu.** *v.* —.
R 1 **lamulamunga.** *n.* —.
R 2 **lamulamua.** *v.* —.
ID **lamu dada.** A jerk (e.g., of a line).

LANEA

B **lanea.** *a.* Much, plenty.
BE **hagalanea.** *v.* Cause to increase in quantity; greedy.
XCO **dagilanea.** *a.* Each having a lot.

LANIBENE

B **lanibene.** *a.* Separation in coconut oil (when it is aging).
B 1 **lanibeneanga.** *n.* —.
BE **hagalanibene.** *v.* —.
BE1 **hagalanibeneanga.** *n.* —.

LANU

BE **hagalanu.** *v.* Rinse off salt water from the body (with fresh water).
BE1 **hagalanuanga.** *n.* —.
BE2 **hagalanumia.** *v.* —.

LANGA

B **langa.** *v.* Lift, raise up; copy out (by hand); ship from one place to another.
B 1 **laanganga.** *n.* Way of plaiting.
B 2 **laangaa.** *v.* To plait completely.
B 2 **langaa.** *v.* — (ex. 'plait' meaning).
B 2 **langadia.** *v.* Able to remain afloat with a load.
BC **malanga.** *a.* Lifted up; departed (as a ship); separate from [intrans]; separated from.
BE **hagalanga —.** *d.* —.
BE2 **hagalaangaa.** *v.* Teach to plait (mats, etc.).
BE2 **hagalangaa.** *v.* —.
BE2 **hagalangadia.** *v.* —.
BF **hagamalanga.** *v.* —.
E **llanga.** *a.* Float (on the surface of the water); plait (mats).
EE **hagallanga.** *v.* —.
PC **maalanga.** *a.* —.
PF **hagamaalanga.** *v.* —.
R **langalanga.** *v.* —.
R 2 **langalangaa.** *v.* —.
RC **malangalanga.** *a.* Repeatedly (or becoming) *malanga.*
RE **hagalangalanga.** *v.* —.
RE2 **hagalangalangaa.** *v.* —.
RF **hagamalangalanga.** *v.* —.
T **laalanga$_2$.** *n.* The quality of the weave (of mat plaiting).
XCO **malaangahu.** *n.* Feast held for a newly launched canoe.
XCO **vaalanga.** *n.* Made-up (of a story only).
XFL **huaalanga.** *n.* A type of coconut tree.
ID **gili malanga.** A type of skin disease.
ID **hadu me llanga.** Lay out plaited work.
ID **hala langa goobai.** A form for plaiting hats.
ID **langaa lodo.** A sudden access of emotion.
ID **langa de gauanga.** To lift up the leg of an opponent in wrestling [considered unfair].
ID **langa de gubenga.** To pull up a *gubenga* to store it away.
ID **langa de ivi.** A method of repositioning the bones of the ribcage.
ID **langa de moana.** Becoming stormy (of the sea).
ID **malanga age.** Lifted up from; come up (e.g., weeds).
ID **vaalanga a kai.** A story which is not true, a made-up story.

LANGA$_a$

B **aalanga.** *n.* Member (of the body, a house, etc.).
ID **dili aalanga.** Exhausted (physically or mentally).
ID **tili aalanga.** Exhausted (physically or mentally); discouraged; completely relaxed.
ID **holahola aalanga.** Calisthenics, exercises.
ID **magi ssae aalanga.** Sore muscles (not associated with strain).
ID **mmade aalanga.** Exhausted (physically or mentally).
ID **mmade ange aalanga.** Completely exhausted;

completely discouraged.

ID **ssae aalanga.** Sore in the muscles.

$LANGA_b$

XCO **langadala.** *n.* (A piece of) thatch made from coconut palm frond.

ID **hale langadala.** Thatch-roofed house (of palm frond thatch).

ID **langadala tohi.** A dead coconut leaf torn by the wind [poor for making palm frond thatch].

$LANGI_1$

B **$langi_1$.** *v.* Start or begin (singing or fighting only).

B 1 **laanginga.** *n.* —.

B 2 **langia.** *v.* —.

BE **hagalangi.** *v.* —.

BE1 **hagalaanginga.** *n.* —.

BE2 **hagalangia.** *v.* —.

R **langilangi.** *v.* —.

R 1 **langilanginga.** *n.* —.

R 2 **langilangia.** *v.* —.

RE **hagalangilangi.** *v.* —.

RE1 **hagalangilanginga.** *n.* —.

RE2 **hagalangilangia.** *v.* —.

$LANGI_2$

B **$langi_2$.** *n.* Rain, heaven, sky.

XFL **iillangi.** *n.* Mollusk sp.: *Conus litteratus.*

XFL **maanga-de-langi.** *n.* Worm sp. (makes a spider-like thread).

ID **baasi e haa o de langi.** The four quadrants of the sky.

ID **bala langi.** Rain.

ID **pala de langi.** It's raining!

ID **dango de langi.** Downpour (of rain).

ID **dau langi.** Rainy season.

ID **dee madaladala de langi.** Raining without let-up.

ID **tea age langi.** The light before daybreak.

ID **gili langi.** A type of cloud (not associated with rain).

ID **kano de langi.** A blue and cloudless sky.

ID **hagalulu de langi.** Attract rain (by making certain noises).

ID **hagasaalunga de langi.** A member of the Christian Endeavor Society.

ID **lalo de langi.** Beyond the horizon, far away from the atoll.

ID **langi haanau.** A certain kind of rain [an omen of an impending childbirth].

ID **langi maadolu.** Heavy rain.

ID **langi maakau.** The sort of rain which is an omen of death.

ID **langi moni.** The sort of rain which is an omen that a ship will come.

ID **vaenga o de langi.** Milky Way.

ID **vai langi.** Rainwater.

CF **hagailangi.** A type of prepared food (made from breadfruit).

CF **hagailangi daahaa.** A type of prepared food (like *dalogo*, but without *somo* or *mugamuga*).

$LANGO_1$

B **$lango_1$.** *v.* Support (e.g., the weight put upon —).

B 1 **langonga.** *n.* —.

B 2 **langoa.** *v.* —.

B 2 **$langona_1$.** *v.* —.

BE **hagalango.** *v.* —.

BE1 **hagalangonga.** *n.* —.

BE2 **hagalangoa.** *v.* —.

BE2 **hagalangona.** *v.* —.

R **langolango.** *v.* —; inclined to throw one's legs over those sleeping nearby (when sleeping).

R 1 **langolangonga.** *n.* —.

R 2 **langolangoa.** *v.* —.

R 2 **$langolangona_1$.** *v.* —.

RE **hagalangolango.** *v.* —.

RE1 **hagalangolangonga.** *n.* —.

RE2 **hagalangolangoa.** *v.* —.

RE2 **hagalangolangona.** *v.* —.

ID **lango beau.** A method of lashing the outrigger float to the outrigger struts.

$LANGO_2$

B **$lango_2$.** *n.* Insect sp.: fly,

flying ant, wasp; or other similar flying insect.
ID **dau lango.** The season during which flies are most numerous [coincides with the breadfruit season].

LAO$_1$
B **lao$_1$.** *d.* —.
B 1 **laonga.** *n.* —.
B 2 **laoa.** *v.* —; be stuck in the throat (esp. fish bones).
BE **hagalao —.** *d.* —.
BE1 **hagalaonga.** *n.* —.
BE2 **hagalaoa.** *v.* —.
E **llao.** *v.* Gouge out (with the hand only); take out of a hole.
R **laolao.** *v.* —.
R 1 **laolaonga.** *n.* —.
R 2 **laolaoa.** *v.* —.
RE **hagalaolao.** *v.* —.
RE1 **hagalaolaonga.** *n.* —.
RE2 **hagalaolaoa.** *v.* —.
ID **lao gau-me.** To grasp a fish by inserting one's fingers in both gills.

LAO$_2$
B **lao$_2$.** *n.* The posterior portion of the coconut crab.

LAOHIE
B **laohie.** *a.* Dry weather (no rain).
BE **hagalaohie.** *v.* —.
R **laolaohie.** *a.* —.
RE **hagalaolaohie.** *v.* —.
ID **dau laohie.** Dry season.
ID **laohie age.** Improving condition (of weather).
ID **laohie de me.** Good weather (dry).

LAOSEDI
B **laosedi.** *n.* Sea water.
ID **manu laosedi.** Sea animal; marine invertebrates.

LASO
B **laso.** *n.* The posterior portion of the hermit crab.
ID **laso paava.** Skinny (of people).

LAU$_1$
B **lau$_1$.** *a.* Hooked, caught fast on.
B 1 **laudanga.** *n.* —.
B 1 **launga.** *n.* —.
B 2 **laudia.** *v.* —.
BE **hagalau$_1$.** *v.* —; able to catch many (esp. fish).
BE1 **hagalaudanga.** *n.* — (ex. 'good at fishing' meaning); way of being hooked.
BE1 **hagalaunga.** *n.* —; way of being hooked.
BE2 **hagalaua.** *v.* —.
BE2 **hagalaudia.** *v.* —.
P **llau$_1$.** *a.* —; to have one's forward motion impeded (as when walking through the surf).
P 1 **llaunga.** *n.* —.
PE **hagallau.** *v.* —.
PE1 **hagallaunga.** *n.* —.
PE2 **hagallaua.** *v.* —.
PE2 **hagallaudia.** *v.* —.
R **laulau$_1$.** *a.* —; good for hooking.
R 1 **laulaudanga.** *n.* —.
R 1 **laulaunga$_1$.** *n.* Able to be hooked.
R 2 **laulaudia.** *v.* —.
RE **hagalaulau$_1$.** *v.* —.
RE1 **hagalaulaudanga.** *n.* —.
RE1 **hagalaulaunga$_1$.** *n.* —.
RE2 **hagalaulaua$_1$.** *v.* —.
RE2 **hagalaulaudia.** *v.* —.
T **lalau.** *a.* One after another becoming *lau$_1$*.
T 1 **lalaunga.** *n.* —.
TE **hagalalau.** *v.* —.
TE1 **hagalalaunga.** *n.* —.
TE2 **hagalalaua.** *v.* —.
ID **lau de alelo.** Be unable to speak clearly, owing to a stuttering problem.
ID **lau me.** Adjacent (of taro plots only).
CF **laulau$_2$.** A type of basket.

LAU$_2$
B **lau$_2$.** *n.* Leaf, or any similar thin, flat thing.
BE **hagalau—$_2$.** *d.* Cause to have leaves which —.
XCO **laubalabala.** *a.* Slack (of rope); soft (of skin or

paper); pliable (of hair); flexible.

XCO **lausamua.** *v.* Untidy in appearance (esp. unshaven, with one's hair in disorder); unkempt.

XCO **laussoe.** *a.* Having straight hair (not kinky or wavy).

XCO **lauvinivini.** *v.* Having kinky hair.

XFL **gaalau-ango.** *n.* Plant sp.: tumeric plant (*Curcuma* sp.).

XFL **lau-gadaha.** *n.* Plant sp.: bird's-nest fern (*Asplenium nidus* L.).

ID **daula mada lau nui.** A rope for tying palm fronds together to make a *belubelu* seine.

ID **dohi lau.** To strip pandanus leaves (to make mats, etc.).

ID **goobai lau.** A hat made from pandanus leaves.

ID **hagallongo de lau nui.** To obtain oracular information by listening to the sounds made by coconut leaves.

ID **hale lau.** Thatch-roofed house (of pandanus leaf thatch).

ID **lau kena.** Leaves (or hair) which have lost their natural healthy color.

ID **lau kohu.** Growing well (of plants) [lit., 'having dark green leaves'].

ID **lau hadihadi.** Having wavy hair.

ID **lau ligi.** Having small leaves.

ID **lau maalie.** Neat-appearing hair or feathers.

ID **lau makaga.** Stiff.

ID **lau manu.** Leaf of a plant.

ID **lau ngago.** The fatty tissue of a fish or animal.

ID **lavalava lau manu.** A sarong of material with a flowered pattern.

ID **malo lau manu.** Cloth with a flowered pattern.

ID **me ssalu lau.** A scraper for leaves.

CF **lauali.** Immature leaves.

CF **lauasaasa.** Skinny.

LAU_{2a}

R **laulau₂.** *n.* A type of basket.

XG **laulau a sogo.** A type of basket.

XG **laulau dao gai.** A wrapping (like a basket) for food cooked in the earth oven.

XG **laulau hai daonga.** A type of basket [used for allocating portions at a feast].

ID **laulau gai.** A canoe used to transport food to a feast.

ID **laulau hoe.** The blade of the canoe paddle.

LAU_3

B **lau₃.** *n.* The size of something.

XCO **laudodole.** *n.* Smallness.

XE **hagalaudodole.** *v.* Cause to grow small.

ID **lau de ava.** A tuna of large size.

ID **lau de madila.** A tuna of fair size.

ID **lau tulugi.** A tuna of the size next largest to *lau de ava.*

ID **lau henua.** Waves of sufficient size to wash over all land on the atoll; tidal wave.

ID **lau iho laa.** Those of small size.

LAU_{3a}

B **laumalie.** *a.* Big, great.

BE **hagalaumalie.** *v.* —.

LAU_4

B **lau₄.** *an.* Hundred.

BE **hagalau₃.** *v.* Make a total of one hundred.

P **llau₂.** *a.* Hundreds.

R **laulau₄.** *an.* Hundreds and hundreds.

RE **hagalaulau₃.** *v.* Make many hundreds.

LAUALI

B **lauali.** *v.* Immature leaves.

BE **hagalauali.** *v.* —.

LAUASAASA

B **lauasaasa.** *v.* Skinny.

B 1 **lauasaasaanga.** *n.* —.
BE **hagalauasaasa.** *v.* —.
BE1 **hagalauasaasaanga.** *n.* —.

LAULAU
R **laulau**$_3$. *a.* Overripe coconut apple.
R 1 **laulaunga**$_2$. *n.* —.
R 2 **laulaua.** *a.* —.
RE **hagalaulau**$_2$. *v.* —.
RE1 **hagalaulaunga**$_2$. *n.* —.
RE2 **hagalaulaua**$_2$. *v.* —.

LAUMELE
B **laumele.** *n.* Fish sp.: tang (2 sorts).

LAUSEDI
B **lausedi.** *n.* [var. of *laosedi*].

LAVA
B **lava.** *a.* Finished [sing.]; wealthy [sing.]; wrap—[dp].
B 1 **lavaanga.** *n.* —.
BE **hagalava.** *v.* —.
BE1 **hagalavalavaanga.** *n.* —.
P **llava.** *v.* Finished [pl.]; wealthy [pl.]; wrap [independent form]; meat or fish (for a meal).
P 1 **llavaanga.** *n.* —.
PE **hagallava.** *v.* —.
PE1 **hagallavaanga.** *n.* —.
R **lavalava.** *v.* Becoming finished or wealthy; keep wrapping; sarong [a recently introduced usage].
RE **hagalavalava.** *v.* —.
ID **daumaha hagalava.** Evensong (last service of the day).
ID **gaa lava.** And then.
ID **lava ai donu huu.** Forget it!
ID **lava hadu.** Leader (between fishing line and hook).
ID **lava i de goloa.** Having many *goloa.*
ID **lavalava lau manu.** A sarong of material with a flowered pattern.
ID **lava sili.** Good enough!; stop!
ID **llava ai.** Wrapped (tied) around; eat fish or meat with a meal.
ID **naa gaalava.** So what?

LAVA$_a$
B **lavasi.** *n.* A leader (between the hook and the fishing line).

LAVE
B **lave.** *a.* Be caught on, stuck on.
B 1 **laavenga.** *n.* —.
B 2 **laavea.** *v.* Stumble on.
BE **hagalave.** *v.* —.
BE1 **hagalaavenga.** *n.* —.
BE2 **hagalaavea.** *v.* —.
P **llave.** *a.* —.
R **lavelave.** *a.* —.
RE **hagalavelave.** *v.* —.
RE1 **hagalavelavenga.** *n.* —.
RE2 **hagalavelavea.** *v.* —.

LEA
E **llea.** *a.* Say loudly [with both sing. and pl. subjects].
E 1 **lleaanga.** *n.* —.
EE **hagallea.** *v.* —.
EE1 **hagalleaanga.** *n.* —.
R **lealea.** *a.* —.
R 1 **lealeaanga.** *n.* —.
RE **hagalealea.** *v.* —.
RE1 **hagalealeaanga.** *n.* —.
CF **leo.** A voice, a sound, an intonational pattern.

LEAALA
ID **longolongo i leaala.** Rumor.

LEANGA
B **leanga.** *n.* Bad person.

LEANGI
ID **hai me a leangi.** Bad-mannered.

LEBA
B **leba.** *v.* Flap in the wind (like a flag).
B 1 **lebaanga.** *n.* —.
BE **hagaleba.** *v.* —.
P **lleba.** *v.* —.
P 1 **llebaanga.** *n.* —.
PE **hagalleba.** *v.* —.
R **lebaleba.** *v.* —.
R 1 **lebalebaanga.** *n.* —.
RE **hagalebaleba.** *v.* —.

LEBAa

B daleba. *v.* Flap briskly in the wind.
B 1 **dalebaanga.** *n.* —.
BE **hagadaleba.** *v.* —.
BE1 **hagadalebaanga.** *n.* —.
R **dalebaleba.** *v.* —.
R 1 **dalebalebaanga.** *n.* —.
RE **hagadalebaleba.** *v.* —.
RE1 **hagadalebalebaanga.** *n.* —.

LEBE

R **lebelebe.** *n.* Fish sp.: jack.
CF **ssuilebelebe.** Completely wet all over.

LEBELEBE

ID **ssuilebelebe.** Completely wet all over.

LEBIDI

B **lebidi.** *n.* Bird sp.: white tern?

LEBU

B **lebu.** *v.* Paint (something); put color on, color (something).
B 1 **leebunga.** *n.* —; a color (of something).
B 2 **lebua.** *v.* —.
BE **hagalebu.** *v.* —.
BE1 **hagaleebunga.** *n.* —.
BE2 **hagalebua.** *v.* —.
R **lebulebu.** *v.* —.
R 1 **lebulebunga.** *n.* —.
R 2 **lebulebua.** *v.* —.
RE **hagalebulebu.** *v.* —.
RE1 **hagalebulebunga.** *n.* —.
RE2 **hagalebulebua.** *v.* —.
ID **hano de leebunga.** Run (of a color); fade (of a color).
CF **dalebu.** Turbulent (air or seas).
CF **dangalebu.** Rough or choppy sea condition.

LEDE

B **lede.** *n.* Penetrating cold.
ID **uluhia e de lede.** Become freezing cold (of a person).

LEGA

R **legalega.** *n.* Smallness.
ID **dama legalega.** Baby, infant.
ID **tama legalega eidu.** Pupil of the eye; a cry of a bird or human that sounds like the cry of a baby; the name of a ghost.
ID **mada legalega.** A small hole; having small openings.

LEGIA

B **legia.** *n.* Bird sp.: white-capped noddy (*Anous minutus*).

LEGUNGA

BE **hagalegunga.** *a.* Show off (esp. in front of members of the opposite sex).
ID **galo hagalegunga.** To look at a member of the opposite sex in a presumptuous way.

LEHU

B **lehu.** *v.* Ashes.
B 1 **lehunga.** *n.* —; way of being blurred.
B 2 **lehua.** *v.* Blurred; covered with ashes.
BE **hagalehu.** *v.* —.
BE1 **hagalehunga.** *n.* —.
BE2 **hagalehua.** *v.* —.
RE **hagalehulehu.** *v.* —.
RE1 **hagalehulehunga.** *n.* —.
RE2 **hagalehulehua.** *v.* —.
XCO **Hadu-lehu.** *nn.* The name of a ghost in Nukuoro legend.
ID **umu lehu.** An earth oven for making coral lime [for masonry] from coral.

LEIDI

ID **ngudu leidi.** Be the object of continual gossip; scorned.

LELE

B **lele.** *v.* To fly; jump.
B 1 **leelenga.** *n.* —.
B 2 **leengia.** *v.* Jump on; be flown into.
B 2 **leia.** *v.* Be jumped upon; be landed upon.

BC malele. *a.* Completed.
BC1 maleleanga. *n.* —.
BE hagalele. *v.* —; do suddenly.
BE1 hagaleelenga. *n.* —.
BE2 hagaleengia. *v.* —.
BE2 hagaleia. *v.* —.
BF hagamalele. *v.* Complete (something); kill (someone).
BF1 hagamaleleanga. *n.* —.
P llele. *a.* —.
P 1 lleleanga. *n.* —.
PE hagallele. *v.* —.
R lellele. *v.* —.
R 1 lelleleanga. *n.* —.
ID **boo hagalele mouli.** A night on which the making of noise is permitted (i.e., on certain holidays).
ID **daa hagalele.** Unscheduled, unplanned.
ID **dua lele.** To throw one's back out of joint.
ID **tuu hagalele.** Stop suddenly; cut suddenly.
ID **hagalele mouli.** Startle; surprise (someone).
ID **leia togo mouli.** Hiccough.
ID **lele age.** Regain consciousness; epilepsy; surfacing (of flying fish).
ID **lele biho.** Dive head first.
ID **lele tua.** To pull a back muscle (or pinch a nerve?) and thus collapse.
ID **lele tuli.** Parturition.
ID **lele mouli.** Surprised [often this expression occurs with a possessive pronoun between the words].
ID **lele sseni.** Insomnia (after sleeping for a short while).
ID **lele vae.** Jump feet first.
ID **lima lele.** Quick to fight, short-tempered.
ID **llele age** + PRONOUN—. (My/his, etc.) — has returned.
ID **manu lele.** A bird.
ID **moni lele.** Airplane.
ID **muli lele.** The rear tip of the turtle shell.
ID **ngudu leelee.** Talkative, loquacious.
ID **ngudu leia.** Be the object of continual gossip; scorned.
CF **dele.** Move from one place to another; to sail (a canoe); be transmitted; slip out of one's hands (e.g., a line on which a big fish has been caught).
CF **galele.** A method of fishing (casting with a pole)for tuna).

LELEa
B **helelei.** *a.* Fly at the same time.
B 1 **heleleinga.** *n.* —.
B 2 **hagaheleleia.** *v.* —.
BE **hagahelelei.** *v.* —.
BE1 **hagaheleleinga.** *n.* —.

LENA
B **lena.** *d.* —.
B 1 **leenanga.** *n.* —.
B 2 **leenaa.** *v.* —.
BC **malena.** *a.* Stretched, stretchable.
BC1 **malenaanga.** *n.* —.
BF **hagamalena.** *v.* —.
BF1 **hagamalenaanga.** *n.* —.
E **llena.** *v.* Stretch; raise one's eyebrows.
PC **maalena.** *a.* —.
PC1 **maalenaanga.** *n.* —.
PF **hagamaalena.** *v.* —.
PF1 **hagamaalenaanga.** *n.* —.
R **lenalena.** *v.* —.
R 1 **lenalenaanga.** *n.* —.
R 2 **lenalenaa.** *v.* —.
RC **malenalena.** *a.* —; stretchable.
RC1 **malenalenaanga.** *n.* —.
RF **hagamalenalena.** *v.* —.
RF1 **hagamalenalenaanga.** *n.* —.
ID **llena luu mada.** Raise both eyebrows [a sign of assent].

LENGA
B **lenga.** *n.* A preparation made from *ango* and *doi doi* (q.v.).
ID **hulu i de lenga.** To paint

one's body with tumeric.

LENGI

B	**lengi.** *a.* Bloated, inflated, swollen up, bulging.
B 1	**leenginga.** *n.* —.
BE	**hagalengi.** *v.* —.
BE1	**hagaleenginga.** *n.* —.
BE2	**hagalengia.** *v.* —.
P	**llengi.** *a.* —.
P 1	**lleenginga.** *n.* —.
PE	**hagallengi.** *v.* —.
PE1	**hagalleenginga.** *n.* —.
PE2	**hagalleengia.** *v.* —.
R	**lengilengi.** *a.* —.
R 1	**lengilenginga.** *n.* —.
RE	**hagalengilengi.** *v.* —.
RE1	**hagalengilenginga.** *n.* —.
RE2	**hagalengilengia.** *v.* —.

LENGISI

B **lengisi.** *n.* Insect sp.: moth spp.

LEO

B **leo.** *n.* A voice, a sound, an intonational pattern.
BE **hagaleo.** *v.* To produce sound.
PE **hagalleo.** *v.* To produce many sounds.
R **leoleo.** *d.* The making of sounds repeatedly.
RE **hagaleoleo.** *v.* —.
ID **dee masae de leo.** Lose one's voice (from straining one's vocal cords).
ID **madaladala de leo.** A clear and high-pitched singing voice.
ID **sao de leo.** Clear in elocution or in one's singing voice.
ID **ssae de leo.** To project one's voice better (e.g., after clearing one's throat).

LEU

B **leu.** *a.* The yellow color or softness of fruit (indicating ripeness); ripe.
B 1 **leunga.** *n.* —.
BE **hagaleu.** *v.* —; allow to become *leu*, as when fruit is picked and left to ripen.
BE1 **hagaleunga.** *n.* —.
BE2 **hagaleua.** *v.* —.
P **lleu.** *a.* —.
P 1 **lleunga.** *n.* —.
PE **hagalleu.** *v.* —.
PE1 **hagalleunga.** *n.* —.
PE2 **hagalleua.** *v.* —.
R **leuleu.** *a.* Becoming *leu.*
R 1 **leuleunga.** *n.* —.
RE **hagaleuleu.** *v.* —.
RE1 **hagaleuleunga.** *n.* —.
RE2 **hagaleuleua.** *v.* —.
XCO **bualeu.** *n.* Ovaries and fallopian tubes.
ID **haa leu.** A leaf which has turned yellowish-brown.
ID **hua leu.** Fish eggs (mature—yellowish).
ID **lleu luu mada.** Swelling of the eyes (after crying).
ID **lleu luu malau ngudu.** Swollen lips (from eating spicy foods or foods to which one is allergic).

LEVA

B **leva.** *a.* To sail through the air.
B 1 **leevanga.** *n.* —.
BE **hagaleva.** *v.* —; to swing.
BE1 **hagalevaanga.** *n.* —.
P **lleva.** *a.* —.
P 1 **lleevanga.** *n.* —.
PE **hagalleva.** *v.* —.
PE1 **hagallevaanga.** *n.* —.
R **levaleva.** *a.* —.
R 1 **levalevaanga.** *n.* —.
RE **hagalevaleva.** *v.* —.
RE1 **hagalevalevaanga.** *n.* —.
ID **daula hagalevaleva.** A swing (made of rope).
ID **leva saele.** Vagrant (having no fixed abode).

LEVANGO

B **levango.** *a.* Fight.
BE **hagalevango.** *v.* —.

LIAGI

B **liagi.** *v.* Dump, throw out (discard).
B 1 **liaginga.** *n.* —.
B 2 **liagina.** *v.* —.

BE hagaliagi. *v.* —.
BE1 hagaliaginga. *n.* —.
BE2 hagaliagina. *v.* —.
R **liiliagi.** *v.* —; a status level [N]; having a close kin relationship [archaic].
R 1 **liiliaginga.** *n.* —.
R 2 **liiliagina.** *v.* —.
RE **hagaliiliagi.** *v.* —.
RE1 **hagaliiliaginga.** *n.* —.
RE2 **hagaliiliagina.** *v.* —.
ID **duu i de liiliagi.** Equal in status [owing to having the same skills and being of common descent].
ID **liiliagi daudahi.** Be of the same status.

LIBI
B **libi.** *v.* Do rapidly (esp. a repeated action done energetically).
B 1 **libinga.** *n.* —.
B 2 **libia.** *v.* —.
BC **malibi.** *a.* Fast.
BC1 **malibinga.** *n.* —.
BE **hagalibi.** *v.* —.
BE1 **hagalibinga.** *n.* —.
BE2 **hagalibia.** *v.* —.
BF **hagamalibi.** *v.* Rush, speed up.
BF1 **hagamalibinga.** *n.* —.
BF2 **hagamalibia.** *v.* —.
PC **maalibi.** *a.* —.
PC1 **maalibinga.** *n.* —.
PF **hagamaalibi.** *v.* —.
PF1 **hagamaalibinga.** *n.* —.
PF2 **hagamaalibia.** *v.* —.
R **libilibi.** *v.* —.
R 1 **libilibinga.** *n.* —.
R 2 **libilibia.** *v.* —.
RC **malibilibi.** *a.* Crack (of a whip).
RC1 **malibilibinga.** *n.* —.
RC2 **malibilibia.** *a.* Sharp (esp. something which causes sharp pain like a whip).
RE **hagalibilibi.** *v.* —.
RE1 **hagalibilibinga.** *n.* —.
RE2 **hagalibilibia.** *v.* —.
RF **hagamalibilibi.** *v.* —.
RF1 **hagamalibilibinga.** *n.* —.
RF2 **hagamalibilibia.** *v.* —.
ID **mada libia.** A very sharp point.

LIBO₁
B **libo₁.** *a.* Turn end over end; turn in place (of a person).
B 1 **liibonga.** *n.* —.
BE **hagalibo.** *v.* —.
BE1 **hagaliibonga.** *n.* —.
BE2 **hagaliboa.** *v.* —.
P **llibo.** *a.* —.
P 1 **lliibonga.** *n.* —.
PE **hagallibo.** *v.* —.
PE1 **hagalliibonga.** *n.* —.
PE2 **hagalliboa.** *v.* —.
R **libolibo.** *a.* —.
R 1 **libolibonga.** *n.* —.
RE **hagalibolibo.** *v.* —.
RE1 **hagalibolibonga.** *n.* —.
RE2 **hagaliboliboa.** *v.* —.
ID **libo ange de henua.** Feel dizzy or faint, vertigo.
ID **libolibo ange.** Drunk, dizzy, crazy.
ID **llibo ange luu vae.** Run.
ID **magi libolibo.** Dizziness or vertigo (as a chronic condition or illness).

LIBO₂
B **libo₂.** *n.* Fish sp.: jack.

LIE
B **lie.** *n.* Lice eggs.
E **llie.** *n.* The throat of the flying fish net.

LIGI
B **ligi.** *d.* Small — [ds].
E **lligi.** *a.* Fine (in grain, of hair, etc.); little, small [pl.].
EE **hagalligi.** *v.* Make very small.
RE **hagaligiligi.** *v.* To speed up (to get over with).
RE2 **hagaligiligia.** *v.* —.
XCO **dagaligiligi.** *a.* Broken into small pieces.
XFL **manu-ligi.** *v.* Lice (immature); louse (immature).
ID **amu ligi.** Fine threads or hairs or fibers (in feather or leaf, etc.); fine-feathered.
ID **dolodolo manu ligi.** The physical sensation (like

	bugs crawling on one) after one's leg, etc., has been asleep.
ID	**dua lligi.** Thin (line or rope, etc.); fine (thread, etc.); tenderly.
ID	**hua ligi.** Having small fruit or nuts (of trees).
ID	**lau ligi.** Having small leaves.
ID	**mada ligiligi.** Having small eyes or holes.
ID	**me-e-ligi.** Taro corm (small).
CF	**dangaligi.** A type of basket.
CF	**madaligi$_1$.** Skillful at craft work, craftsmanlike; craftsman.
CF	**nooligi.** A small knife.
CF	**vaaligi.** Small [pl.]; little [pl.]; immature taro corm.

LIHO

R	**liholiho.** *n.* String twirled from coconut fiber, sennit.

LII

B	**lii.** *n.* Bird sp. (seen only over the ocean).

LILI$_1$

B	**lili$_1$.** *v.* Rippling (of the surface of the sea).
B 1	**lilinga$_1$.** *n.* —.
B 2	**lilia$_1$.** *v.* —.
BE	**hagalili$_1$.** *v.* —.
BE1	**hagalilinga.** *n.* —.
BE2	**hagalilia.** *v.* —.
R	**lillili$_1$.** *v.* —.
R 1	**lillilinga.** *n.* —.
RE	**hagalillili$_1$.** *v.* —.
RE1	**hagalillilinga.** *n.* —.

LILI$_{1a}$

BE	**hagalili$_2$.** *n.* A type of prepared food (like *dalogo* but without the immature coconut meat).
XCO	**bolili.** *n.* A type of prepared food [small taro, prepared for the cult priests].

LILI$_2$

B	**lili$_2$.** *v.* A method of lashing.
B 1	**lilinga$_2$.** *n.* —.
B 2	**lilia$_2$.** *v.* —.

LILI$_3$

B	**lili$_3$.** *a.* Mad at, angry.
B 1	**lilianga.** *n.* —.
BE	**hagalili$_3$.** *v.* —; anger (toward someone).
BE1	**hagalilianga.** *n.* —.
P	**llili.** *a.* —.
P 1	**llilianga.** *n.* —.
PE	**hagallili.** *v.* —.
PE1	**hagallilianga.** *n.* —.
R	**lillili$_2$.** *a.* Easily angered, short-tempered.
R 1	**lillilianga.** *n.* —.
RE	**hagalillili$_2$.** *v.* —.
RE1	**hagalillilianga.** *n.* —.
ID	**lili baasi gee.** Accuse someone (in an argument, usually between spouses) of taking sides with another family member.
ID	**lili mahangahanga.** Mad as the devil.

LILO

B	**lilo.** *a.* Disappear, vanish; sheltered (from the elements).
B 1	**liilonga.** *n.* —.
B 2	**lilongia.** *v.* —.
BE	**hagalilo.** *v.* Take shelter, to shelter (something from the elements); block out (from sight).
BE1	**hagaliilonga.** *n.* —.
BE2	**hagalilongia.** *v.* —.
P	**llilo.** *a.* Able to be hooked.
P 1	**lliilonga.** *n.* —.
P 2	**llilongia.** *v.* —.
PE	**hagallilo.** *v.* —.
PE1	**hagalliilonga.** *n.* —.
PE2	**hagallilongia.** *v.* —.
R	**lilolilo.** *a.* In a sheltered place.
R 1	**lilolilonga.** *n.* —.
R 2	**lilolilongia.** *v.* —.
RE	**hagalilolilo.** *v.* —.
RE1	**hagalilolilonga.** *n.* —.
RE2	**hagalilolilongia.** *v.* —.
ID	**basa lilo.** Speak indirectly (so that the meaning is vague).

ID **lilo bule.** Covered up completely.
ID **llilo mai.** Decreasing (in number); becoming less.

LIMA
B **lima₁.** *n.* Arm, hand.
R **limalima.** *a.* Dexterous (esp. in fighting).
R 1 **limalimaanga.** *n.* —.
RE **hagalimalima.** *v.* —.
RE1 **hagalimalimaanga.** *n.* —.
XCO **dugilima.** *n.* Elbow.
XCO **limamalie.** *a.* Good at massaging.
ID **alohi lima.** Palm (of the hand).
ID **baabaa luu lima.** Clap hands.
ID **bigi lima.** Hold hands.
ID **dahido lima.** Upper arm.
ID **dili de lima.** To swing one's arms (when walking).
ID **doonga a lima.** One's own tools, or tools with which one is familiar.
ID **gai lima dahi.** To eat taro without fish (or fish without taro).
ID **gai lima lua.** Eat greedily (with both hands).
ID **gubu lima.** Hand, wrist.
ID **hagadibadiba de lima.** To wiggle one's hand [a signal that the speaker is lying].
ID **heboohagi lima.** Fist fight.
ID **lima dangada ina.** A patient of one healer who has been treated by another healer.
ID **lima lele.** Quick to fight, short-tempered.
ID **lima ma vae ange.** Work for as a servant.
ID **magau de lima.** A paralyzed arm.
ID **sisi lima.** Longhand (writing).
ID **sugi lima.** Forearm.

LIMAa
B **lima₂.** *an.* Five.
BE **hagalima (ina).** *v.* Make a total of five.
XCO **Diba-lima.** *nn.* The name of a person in a traditional story.
XCO **Lima-laangi.** *nt.* Friday ('fifth day').
XCO **Lima-malama.** *nt.* May ('fifth month').
ID **lima-pilo.** The fifth number of a counting game played to determine who is "it".

LIMADI
B **limadi.** *v.* Do fast or quickly.
B 1 **limadinga.** *n.* —.
B 2 **limadia.** *v.* —.
BE **hagalimadi.** *v.* —.
BE1 **hagalimadinga.** *n.* —.
BE2 **hagalimadia.** *v.* —.

LIMI
R **limilimi.** *n.* Coral sp.: brain coral?

LIMU
E **llimu.** *n.* A small *honu.*
ID **hidu-limu.** The seventh number of a counting game played to determine who is "it".

LINGA
XCO **gailingalinga.** *a.* Continually wanting to eat.
CF **malingalinga.** Sideburns (of hair).

LINGI
B **lingi.** *d.* —.
B 1 **liinginga.** *n.* —.
B 2 **liingia.** *v.* —.
BC **malingi.** *a.* Spilled, poured out.
BC1 **malinginga.** *n.* —.
BF **hagamalingi.** *v.* —.
BF1 **hagamalinginga.** *n.* —.
BF2 **hagamalingia.** *v.* —.
E **llingi.** *v.* Pour out, spill out (sand).
PC **maalingi.** *a.* —.
PC1 **maalinginga.** *n.* —.
PF **hagamaalingi.** *v.* —.
PF1 **hagamaalinginga.** *n.* —.
PF2 **hagamaalingia.** *v.* —.
R **lingilingi.** *v.* —.

R 1 **lingilinginga.** *n.* —.
R 2 **lingilingia.** *v.* Pour little by little.
RC **malingilingi.** *a.* Spill out little by little.
RC1 **malingilinginga.** *n.* —.
RF **hagamalingilingi.** *v.* —.
RF1 **hagamalingilinginga.** *n.* —.
RF2 **hagamalingilingia.** *v.* —.
ID **honu malingilingi.** Fill to overflowing.

LLAI
XCO **ulimagallai.** *a.* Jet black.

LLIDI
B **llidi.** *a.* Dress up (esp. in new or very fancy clothes).
B 1 **lliidinga.** *n.* —.
BE **hagallidi.** *v.* —.
BE1 **hagallidianga.** *n.* —.
ID **lodo llidi.** A dandy (always wanting to *llidi*).

LLONGA
B **llonga.** *v.* Muscle fatigue.
BE **hagallonga.** *v.* —.

LLUU
B **lluu.** *a.* Mad or angry (but not showing it).
BE **hagalluu.** *v.* —.

LOA$_1$
B **loa$_1$.** *d.* Long— [ds].
BE **hagaloa.** *v.* Groove; a path (lengthwise) in the taro bog.
P **lloa.** *a.* Long [pl.].
P 1 **lloaanga.** *n.* —.
PE **hagalloa.** *v.* —.
PE1 **hagalloaanga.** *n.* —.
R **looloa.** *a.* Long [sing.].
R 1 **looloaanga.** *n.* —.
RE **hagalooloa.** *v.* Lengthen, prolong.
RE1 **hagalooloaanga.** *n.* —.
XFL **dagua-loa.** *n.* Fish sp.: tuna sp.
XFL **dangaloa$_2$.** *n.* Earthworm.
ID **gau looloa gaadinga.** A bunch of fully mature coconuts.
ID **gave hua loa.** [var. of *gave ua loa*].
ID **gave ua loa.** A long-distance footrace.
ID **ginigini looloa.** A game played by children.
ID **mada looloa.** Longer in comparison with; extending farther than appears to be the case.
ID **mahi loa.** Tireless.
ID **sao de looloa.** Rectangular (not square), oval.

LOA$_2$
B **loa$_2$.** *n.* Ant.

LOADA
B **loada.** *n.* Sputum.
ID **ubu loada.** A coconut shell used for expectoration.

LOADU
B **loadu.** *a.* Go (toward the hearer) [pl.].

LOAGE
B **loage.** *a.* Go (up or toward the village, or land) [pl.].

LOANGE
B **loange.** *a.* Go (to the place away from both the speaker and hearer) [pl.].

LOBA$_1$
E **lloba.** *a.* Fluttering rapidly (of a sail in the breeze); [also pl. of *lobaloba*].
E 1 **llobaanga.** *n.* —.
E 2 **lobadia.** *v.* —.
EE **hagalloba.** *v.* —.
EE1 **hagallobaanga.** *n.* —.
EE2 **hagalobadia.** *v.* —.
R **lobaloba.** *v.* Flapping (of a sail in the breeze) [sing.].
R 1 **lobalobaanga.** *n.* —.
R 2 **lobalobadia.** *v.* —.
RE **hagalobaloba.** *v.* —.
RE1 **hagalobalobaanga.** *n.* —.
RE2 **hagalobalobadia.** *v.* —.
ID **hagalloba ange.** To slacken the boom sheet (of a sailing canoe).
ID **lobadia mai.** To have the

sail and mast blown down (because the wind came from the side away from the outrigger).

LOBA$_2$

B **loba.** *n.* A type of mat.

LOBO

B **lobo.** *d.* —.
B 1 **loobonga.** *n.* —.
B 2 **lobodia.** *v.* —.
B 2 **looboa.** *v.* —.
BE1 **hagaloobonga.** *n.* —.
BE2 **hagalobodia.** *v.* —.
BE2 **hagalooboa.** *v.* —.
E **llobo.** *v.* To put something in something else.
EE **hagallobo.** *v.* —.
R **lobolobo.** *v.* —.
R 1 **lobolobonga.** *n.* —.
R 2 **loboloboa.** *v.* —.
R 2 **lobolobodia.** *v.* —.
RE **hagalobolobo.** *v.* —.
RE1 **hagalobolobonga.** *n.* —.
RE2 **hagaloboloboa.** *v.* —.
RE2 **hagalobolobodia.** *v.* —.

LODO$_1$

B **lodo$_1$.** *nl.* Inside of; lagoon [*te lodo*].
T **loolodo.** *n.* Deep holes in the lagoon reef.
XCO **teungaalodo.** *nl.* Middle (of something round); center.
XCO **loimada.** *n.* Tears.
ID **anga gi lodo.** An adze blade which is set at less than a right angle to its handle.
ID **dangada lo te gohu.** Unenlightened person.
ID **dohu lodo.** Full to capacity.
ID **dugi de lodo.** To fish in various places (in the lagoon) in order to catch as many fish (of any kind) as possible.
ID **haa lodo.** The inner coconut palm frond.
ID **hale i lodo.** Rib cage, thoracic cavity.
ID **hhali lo te laagau.** A depression in a log (an abnormal growth).
ID **lodo gapua.** Seaward part of a *gapua.*
ID **lodo kabi.** Filled to capacity.
ID **lodo henua.** Inland, bush (uncleared) land, wilderness.
ID **lodo laanui.** Large in volume or capacity, spacious inside.
ID **lodo lanea$_1$.** Large in volume.
ID **lodo me muimui.** In the bush (uncleared area).
ID **lo te.** [a contraction of *lodo de...*].
ID **lo te dege.** Inside the corner of.
ID **lo te gelo.** In the deepest part.
ID **lo te hebagi.** During the war.
ID **lo te logunga.** Inside the corner of.
ID **lo te vvela.** The hottest part (of the day, of a fire, etc.).
ID **mada gi lodo.** A point which is bent inward (toward its handle).
ID **mada loolodo.** A depression in the reef (where water accumulates).
ID **madannia i lodo.** Middle finger.
ID **me de lodo.** A fishing place (in the lagoon).
ID **ngu te lodo.** The edge of the lagoon reef.
ID **soaa lodo.** The paddlers of a canoe which is engaged in catching flying fish.
ID **soe lodo modu.** To remain (or sit, or stand) motionless (as when praying).
ID **ssave de loolodo.** Flying fish inside the lagoon.
ID **ungaa lodo.** Middle part (of something round).
CF **daelodo.** Number, figure; the outrigger boom between the *giado madua* and the *giado manu.*
CF **lo gunga.** Inside the corner of.

CF **loo.** About it, concerning it, in it, for it.

$LODO_2$

B **$lodo_2$.** *a.* Want, desire.
BE **hagalodo.** *v.* To stimulate a desire for.
P **llodo.** *a.* —.
PE **hagallodo.** *d.* —.
R **lodolodo.** *a.* To be desirous continually.
RE **hagalodolodo.** *v.* Hope for (want).
ID **bebe de lodo.** Anxiety state (psychological condition).
ID **bili i de lodo.** Unforgotten.
ID **bonabona age lodo.** Feel fearful.
ID **buni ange lodo.** Paralyzed by fear; acute anxiety attack.
ID **dae de lodo.** Be satisfied completely.
ID **dahuli de lodo.** Change of heart, change one's mind, repent.
ID **dalodalo i de lodo.** Pray silently.
ID **daudali i lodo.** Follow another's will.
ID **diinei de lodo.** Become calmer (after being angry).
ID **doo lodolodo.** Risky, unreliable.
ID **tali hagalodolodo.** Hopeful expectation.
ID **e lodo goe.** Watch out!
ID **gave lodo.** Attract attention.
ID **gohu de lodo.** Ignorant.
ID **golomagi lodo.** Self-controlled.
ID **haangaa lodo i de gai.** Be continually hungry, owing to having a distended stomach from regularly eating too much.
ID **haangoda de lodo.** To fish in the lagoon.
ID **hagahonu age lodo.** Feel uncomfortably sated with food and unable to eat.
ID **hagamaamaane de lodo.** Cheer up (someone).
ID **hagammae lodo.** Insult (someone).
ID **hai lodo.** Resentful.
ID **halehale dagodo lodo.** Nauseated.
ID **labua gee lodo.** To have an upset stomach (being on the point of nausea).
ID **langaa lodo.** A sudden access of emotion.
ID **lodo a gauligi.** Immature (in personality); vulnerable to having one's feelings easily hurt.
ID **lodo aheahe.** Unstable temperamentally, inconstant.
ID **lodo baageaa.** Weak-willed, easily tempted; excited easily by the opposite sex.
ID **lodo baba.** Calmness, tranquility, freedom from worries.
ID **lodo bale.** Helpful (sort of person).
ID **lodo basa.** Talkative.
ID **lodo baubau.** Unhappy, upset, sad.
ID **lodo bigede.** Feel cowardly.
ID **lodo daemaha.** Feel unhappy or sad.
ID **lodo dagidahi.** Have differing views (within a group of people).
ID **lodo dama.** Immature in affect.
ID **lodo danuaa.** Contented, happy.
ID **lodo degi.** Having a forgiving nature.
ID **lodo gaiaa.** Competitive, envious, desirous of retaliating.
ID **lodo gilimalali.** Pureness of heart, innocence.
ID **lodo gi lunga.** Ambitious for a superior position.
ID **lodo gi me.** Acquisitive, covetous.
ID **lodo hagamau me.** Selfish with one's possessions, ungiving.
ID **lodo hinangalosaa.** A

feeling of *hinangalosaa*; depression (feeling).

ID **lodo lagolago.** Indecisive, undecided.

ID **lodo lanea$_2$.** Indecisive, confused.

ID **lodo llidi.** A dandy (always wanting to *llidi*).

ID **lodo malangilangi.** Happy.

ID **lodo manege.** Stubborn (esp. in maintaining one's own superiority); be a poor loser.

ID **lodo mao lalo.** Characteristically *hagamao lalo*; self-effacing, meek in spirit.

ID **lodo mao lunga.** Characteristically *hagamao lunga*; egotistical, self-centered, arrogant in spirit.

ID **lodo mmahi.** Persistent, patient, persevering.

ID **lodo senga.** To have unrealistic self-confidence (e.g., in one's capacity to do something impossible); to be foolishly desirous (of the impossible).

ID **lo taane.** Daring, brave, manly.

ID **lua lodo.** Undecided.

ID **magau donu i de lodo.** Want desperately.

ID **makaga lodo.** Stubborn.

ID **moolau lodo.** Having a short temper.

ID **sui de lodo.** Change one's mind.

ID **vage i de lodo.** To occur to one that someone else is doing something to affect one's mood (favorably or unfavorably).

ID **valaai hagasili lodo.** A medicine taken to reduce one's anger, or any other strong emotion.

ID **velosia de lodo.** Shocked.

LOEAA

B **loeaa.** *n.* A type of game.

LOGO

EE **hagallogo.** *n.* Chant (in the old religious ceremony).

EE1 **hagallogoanga.** *n.* —.

ID **daa de hagallogo.** Perform certain old religious ceremonies or chants.

LOGU

CF **ngalogu.** Push in, crumple up; bend out of shape (temporarily); easily changed in shape (esp. by pushing).

LOGUNGA

ID **lo te logunga.** Inside the corner of.

LOHA

B **loha$_1$.** *v.* Fathom (the span of one's outstretched arms).

B 1 **lohaanga.** *n.* —.

B 2 **lohaa.** *v.* —.

R **lohaloha.** *v.* Measure off in fathoms.

R 1 **lohalohaanga.** *n.* —.

R 2 **lohalohaa.** *v.* —.

CF **iloha.** Fathom (the span of one's outstretched arms) [var. of *loha*].

LOHA$_a$

B **loha$_2$.** *n.* Bird sp. (never seen live).

LOHI

B **lohi.** *d.* —.

B 1 **loohinga.** *n.* —.

B 2 **llohia.** *v.* —.

BE1 **hagaloohinga.** *n.* —.

E **llohi.** *v.* Erosion of sand or soil (esp. of the beach by wave action).

EE **hagallohi.** *v.* —.

EE2 **hagallohia.** *v.* —.

R **lohilohi.** *v.* —.

R 1 **lohilohinga.** *n.* —.

R 2 **lohilohia.** *v.* —.

RE **hagalohilohi.** *v.* —.

RE1 **hagalohilohinga.** *n.* —.

RE2 **hagalohilohia.** *v.* —.

LOI

XCO **loigulu.** *n.* A type of prepared food (made from breadfruit).

LOIHO

B **loiho.** *a.* Go or come down (or toward the lagoon) [pl.].

LOLO

B **lolo.** *n.* Oil.
B 2 **loongia.** *v.* To lose one's appetite after eating oily food.
BE **hagalolo.** *v.* To add oil (esp. coconut cream) to food.
BE1 **hagaloloanga.** *n.* —.
R **lollolo.** *v.* Oily.
R 1 **lolloloanga.** *n.* —.
RE **hagalollolo.** *v.* Lubricate.
RE1 **hagalolloloanga.** *n.* —.
XCO **lolomango.** *n.* To clear oil (which is separated from crude coconut oil by heating).
XCO **naamulolo.** *n.* Ramrod; [the etymology of this word is totally obscure].
ID **doo de lolomango.** Separated (of crude coconut oil).
ID **hagasii lolo.** Wheel.
ID **hudaa lolo.** Flood-like waves on the reef; tidal wave.
ID **lolo hai haahine.** A love potion (applied to the clothes or body).
ID **lolo manu-de-boo.** A type of medicine (made from coconut oil and centipedes).
ID **me hagalolo.** A type of prepared food (made from taro and coconut cream).
ID **ua lolo.** A disturbance in the sea caused by schools of big fish feeding on little fish.

LOMA

B **loma.** *a.* Very calm, silent.
BE **hagaloma.** *v.* —.
ID **hagaloma de me.** Calm weather, with no noise.

LONGO₁

B **longo.** *a.* Hear, feel; news.
B 2 **langona₂.** *a.* Heard, felt.
BE2 **hagalaangona.** *v.* —.
EE **hagallongo.** *v.* Listen to, pay attention to; be aware of.
R **longolongo.** *a.* —; acuity of hearing.
R 2 **langolangona₂.** *a.* Repeatedly heard or felt.
RE **hagalongolongo.** *v.* —; do carefully.
XCO **longoduli.** *a.* Deaf.
ID **adi longo.** To tattle.
ID **deai me hagalongolongo.** Do unhesitatingly.
ID **dele de longo.** Spread news or rumors.
ID **tangada adi longo.** Gossipy person, tattletale.
ID **gai hagalongolongo.** Eat sparingly (to save some for others).
ID **hagallongo de lau nui.** To obtain oracular information by listening to the sounds made by coconut leaves.
ID **hagallongo i muna.** Obey.
ID **hagalongolongo ngadaa.** Slow to respond to suggestions or commands (because resisting).
ID **langona iho maahana.** Feel punished or victimized.
ID **longo iho.** Be aware of, experience, perceive, feel (in one's mind or body).
ID **longolongo i adamagi.** To pick up information by asking others, who have lied (so that one's information, therefore, is false).
ID **longolongo iho dalinga.** Pick up information from others' conversation.
ID **longolongo i leaala.** Rumor.
CF **heloongoi.** Fit together with (match) each other; have an understanding with one another (e.g., as do lovers); understand one another.

LONGO₁a

B **longaa.** *a.* Annoyed by noise.
B **longoaa.** *a.* [= *longaa*].

BE **hagalongaa.** *a.* [= *hagalongoaa*].
BE **hagalongoaa.** *a.* —.

LONGO$_2$
B **longosaa.** *a.* Small around, thin.
BE **hagalongosaa.** *v.* —.

LONGO$_{2a}$
B **longohie.** *a.* Big around, fat.
BE **hagalongohie.** *v.* —.

LOO
B **loo.** *mv.* About it, concerning it, in it, for it.
ID **aahee loo.** When? (distant future).
ID **alaa ai loo.** Those there then are.
ID **alaa loo.** Those (there) were the ones.
ID **alaa naa loo.** Those there seem to be.
ID **anaa ai loo.** Those then are.
ID **anaa loo.** These (there) were the ones.
ID **anaa naa loo.** Those seem to be.
ID **anei ai loo.** These then are.
ID **anei loo.** These (here) are the ones.
ID **anei naa loo.** These seem to be.
ID **au e dee gai naa loo.** I'll bet you can't!
ID **danuaa loo.** OK! (good).
ID **deai ange loo soo savaa.** Now i've got you!
ID **deai loo me.** I doubt it!
ID **delaa ai loo.** That was it at last!
ID **delaa loo.** That was it.
ID **delaa naa loo.** That there could be it.
ID **denaa ai loo.** That is it (which has been decided upon).
ID **denaa loo.** That was the one.
ID **denaa naa loo.** That seems to be it; that could be it.
ID **denei ai loo.** This then is —.
ID **denei loo.** This is it at last.
ID **denei naa loo.** This seems to be.
ID **dogoisi loo huu.** Very few.
ID **gu hagaola loo.** Just missed catching.
ID **kaba ai loo.** Wait until —!
ID **hano muhuu loo.** Let's see...
ID **maakau laa loo dangada.** What a shame!
ID **magau loo au.** Now I'm really in trouble!
ID **maingaa ange loo.** Feel really *maingaa* about —.
ID **momo loo huu.** Just a very little.
ID **muli mai loo.** Much later.
ID **odi ai loo.** That's the end! That's all!
ID **sogoisi loo huu.** [var. of *dogoisi loo huu*].
ID **vaasuu ai loo.** I like it (or him or her) very much.
ID **vakaa laa loo.** Too bad for him (I don't care)!

LOOMAI
B **loomai.** *a.* Come or go (toward the speaker) [pl.].

LOOMOSI
B **loomosi.** *v.* Kill someone by holding him under the water until he is drowned.
B 1 **loomosinga.** *n.* —.
B 2 **lomosia.** *v.* —.
R **lomolomosi.** *v.* Repeatedly or frequently *loomosi.*
R 1 **lomolomosinga.** *n.* —.
R 2 **lomolomosia.** *v.* —.

LOONAA
B **loonaa.** *v.* The sticking of food in the throat (which is cleared by washing it down with liquid).
B 1 **loonaanga.** *n.* —.
BE **hagaloonaa.** *v.* —.
BE1 **hagaloonaanga.** *n.* —.
R **looloonaa.** *v.* —.
R 1 **looloonaanga.** *n.* —.
RE **hagalooloonaa.** *v.* —.
RE1 **hagalooloonaanga.** *n.* —.

LOOSI
BE **hagaloosi.** *v.* Guard, watch, keep an eye on.
BE1 **hagaloosinga.** *n.* —.

BE2 **hagaloosia.** *v.* —.
ID **vaga loosi.** A canoe used by the guardians of the island (in olden times) to meet canoes coming to the island.

LOSE
XFL **loselose-ganoanga.** *n.* Fish sp.
XFL **loselose-uli.** *n.* Fish sp.: trumpet fish.

LOU
B **lou.** *v.* A pole with a hook at the end, used to pick breadfruit; pick (breadfruit), pull down.
B 1 **lounga.** *n.* —.
B 2 **loua.** *v.* —.
BE **hagalou.** *v.* —.
BE1 **hagalounga.** *n.* —.
BE2 **hagaloua.** *v.* —.
E **llou.** *v.* Hang down or bent down (of branches, palm fronds, or fishing poles).
E 1 **llounga.** *n.* —.
EE **hagallou.** *v.* —.
EE1 **hagallounga.** *n.* —.
EE2 **hagalloua.** *v.* —.
R **loulou.** *v.* To repeatedly use a breadfruit picker; pull (a trigger).
R 1 **louloungа.** *n.* —.
R 2 **louloua.** *v.* —; constipated.
RE **hagaloulou.** *v.* —; constipating.
RE1 **hagaloulounga.** *n.* —.
RE2 **hagalouloua.** *v.* —.
RE3 **hagaloulouaanga.** *n.* —.
ID **lou aama.** The submerging of the outrigger float.
ID **loua ama.** To sail with the outrigger float partially submerged.
ID **lou de gaugau dalinga.** Pull the trigger (of a gun).
ID **lou gulu.** Pick breadfruit.

LUA
B **lua.** *an.* Two.
BE **hagalua (ina).** *v.* Make a total of two.
XCO **Diba-lua.** *nn.* The name of a person in a traditional story.
XCO **lua-aligi.** *a.* Chief mate (of a European ship).
XCO **Lua-laangi.** *nt.* Tuesday ('second day').
XCO **Lua-malama.** *nt.* February ('second month').
ID **duu lua.** To have the strength or capacity of two persons; to take on two persons in a fight.
ID **gai lima lua.** Eat greedily (with both hands).
ID **kangi baasi lua.** Double-edged.
ID **hhanga lua.** Split in two.
ID **lua-baaua.** The second number of a counting game played to determine who is "it".
ID **lua lodo.** Undecided.
ID **madohi lua.** Middle (of something long and thin), halfway.
ID **momme hai lua.** A fishing spot (beyond the seaward reef) where either reef or ocean fish can be found.
ID **sii bido lua.** Vomiting and having diarrhea at the same time ('flowing from both ends').
CF **duulua.** Fish sp.: jack (= large *alaala*).
CF **maaguluaa.** Dislocated (joint of the body).
CF **malua.** Vagina.

LUBE
CF **ngalubelube.** Tremble or vibrate in the air.

LUDU
B **ludu.** *d.* —.
B 1 **luudunga.** *n.* —.
BE **hagaludu.** *d.* —.
BE1 **hagaluudunga.** *n.* —.
E **lludu.** *v.* Take all (of something).
E 2 **lludua.** *v.* —.
EE **hagalludu.** *v.* —.
EE2 **hagalludua.** *v.* —.
R **luduludu.** *v.* Trembling.
RE **hagaluduludu.** *v.* —.
RE1 **hagaluduludunga.** *n.* —.
RE2 **hagaluduludua.** *v.* —.
ID **magi luduludu.** The tremor (as though chilled) of a sick person.

LUEI
B **luei.** *v.* Spit out (esp. food).
B 1 **lueinga.** *n.* —.
B 2 **lueia.** *v.* —.
BE **hagaluei.** *v.* —.
BE1 **hagalueinga.** *n.* —.
BE2 **hagalueia.** *v.* Vomit, vomitus.
R **lueluei.** *v.* —.
R 1 **luelueinga.** *n.* —.
R 2 **luelueia.** *v.* —.
RE **hagalueluei.** *v.* —.
RE1 **hagaluelueinga.** *n.* —.
RE2 **hagaluelueia.** *v.* Repeatedly *hagalueia.*
ID **luei todo.** Cough up blood.

LUGU$_1$
B **lugu.** *v.* Take or obtain something by force.
B 1 **lugunga.** *n.* —.
B 2 **lugua.** *v.* —.
R **lugulugu$_1$.** *v.* —.
R 1 **lugulugunga.** *n.* —.
R 2 **lugulugua.** *v.* —.
ID **lugu me.** Having a tendency to take by force.

LUGU$_2$
R **lugulugu$_2$.** *n.* Fish sp.

LUHE
E **lluhe.** *n.* Plant sp.: sword fern (The native term applies possibly to several spp.).

LUHI
E **lluhi.** *a.* An access (of emotion or sensory impression).
E 1 **lluhianga.** *n.* —.
EE **hagalluhi.** *v.* —.
EE1 **hagalluhianga.** *n.* —.
EE2 **hagalluhia.** *v.* —.
R **luhiluhi.** *a.* —.
RE **hagaluhiluhi.** *v.* —.
RE1 **hagaluhiluhinga.** *n.* —.
RE2 **hagaluhiluhia.** *v.* —.

LUI$_1$
B **lui$_1$.** *v.* Turn (something in direction); change course; reverse, transpose.
B 1 **luinga.** *n.* —.
B 2 **luia.** *v.* —.
BC **malui.** *a.* Turned (in direction), reversed, transposed.
BC1 **maluinga.** *n.* —.
BD **helui.** *a.* Diminution of.
BD1 **heluinga.** *n.* —.
BE **hagalui.** *v.* —.
BE1 **hagaluinga.** *n.* —.
BE2 **hagaluia.** *v.* —.
BF **hagamalui.** *v.* —.
BF1 **hagamaluinga.** *n.* —.
BF2 **hagamaluia.** *v.* —.
BG **hagahelui.** *v.* —.
BG1 **hagaheluinga.** *n.* —.
BG2 **hagaheluia.** *v.* —.
P **llui.** *v.* —.
P 1 **lluinga.** *n.* —.
P 2 **lluia.** *v.* —.
PC **maalui.** *a.* —.
PC1 **maaluinga.** *n.* —.
PE **hagallui.** *v.* —; to flip over (as in diving a sommersault).
PE1 **hagalluinga.** *n.* —.
PE2 **hagalluia.** *v.* —.
PF **hagamaalui.** *v.* —.
PF1 **hagamaaluinga.** *n.* —.
R **luilui.** *v.* —; turn (something) end over end.
R 1 **luiluinga.** *n.* —.
R 2 **luiluia.** *v.* —.
RC **maluilui.** *a.* Turned this way and that way, turned over and over.
RC1 **maluiluinga.** *n.* —.
RE **hagaluilui.** *v.* —; to flip over and over (as in diving a sommersault).
RE1 **hagaluiluinga.** *n.* —.
RE2 **hagaluiluia.** *v.* —.
RF **hagamaluilui.** *v.* —.
RF1 **hagamaluiluinga.** *n.* —.
RF2 **hagamaluiluia.** *v.* —.
ID **dao malui.** A spear with a hinged barb.
ID **laagau lui.** A cross (e.g., of wood).
ID **luilui togo.** A measurement of land along the shore [in which the chief had rights] using a punt pole.
CF **ului.** Turn inside out.

LUI_2

B **lui_2.** *n.* The water which has accumulated in a canoe.

ID **taa de lui.** To bail water from a canoe.

LULU

B **lulu.** *v.* To shake (something) rapidly.

B 1 **lulunga.** *n.* —.

B 2 **lulua.** *v.* —.

BE **hagalulu.** *v.* —; to attract fish (or animals) by feeding them; a type of old chant [sung by a priest at daybreak to chase ghosts from the village, and wake up people to work].

BE1 **hagalulunga.** *n.* —.

BE1 **hagaluulunga.** *n.* —; a good fishing spot (where fish are accustomed to take the bait).

BE2 **hagalulua.** *v.* —.

BE2 **hagalulungia.** *v.* —.

T **luuluu.** *v.* To shake (something) back and forth.

T 1 **luuluunga.** *n.* —.

T 2 **luuluua.** *v.* —.

T 2 **luuluuia.** *v.* —.

TE **hagaluuluu.** *v.* —.

TE1 **hagaluuluunga.** *n.* —; a place to which fish have been attracted by bait.

TE2 **hagaluuluua.** *v.* —.

XFL **gailulu.** *n.* Bird sp.: booby?

ID **gai hagalulu.** Habituated to taking bait (fish); feed on bait.

ID **hagalulu de langi.** Attract rain (by making certain noises).

ID **hagalulu de madangi.** To attract the wind (by making certain noises).

ID **luuluu haha.** Wash one's mouth out, gargle.

CF **luungagi.** To be in a place protected from the wind, lee.

$LULU_a$

B **ngaalulu.** *a.* A rattling or sloshing around inside (of something shaken).

B 1 **ngaaluluanga.** *n.* —.

BE **hagangaalulu.** *v.* —.

BE1 **hagangaaluluanga.** *n.* —.

R **ngalullulu.** *a.* Shaky.

R 1 **ngalulluluanga.** *n.* —.

RE **hagangalullulu.** *v.* —.

RE1 **hagangalulluluanga.** *n.* —.

ID **biho ngaalulu.** Headache.

LUNGA

B **lunga.** *nl.* Up, above, over.

ID **aagonga i lunga.** Social class of chiefs and priests.

ID **basa gi lunga.** Speak loudly.

ID **basa hagamao lunga.** Speak arrogantly.

ID **buni lunga ma lalo.** A pitch black night.

ID **daelodo gi lunga.** A large number of.

ID **dua gi lunga.** Thicker (line or rope, etc.).

ID **ea gi lunga.** To ride high in the water (e.g., of a canoe).

ID **hadu lunga.** A stone used to crush hermit crabs (for bait).

ID **hagamao lunga.** Arrogant, haughty, overbearing, proud.

ID **hagaoanga gi lunga.** Good wages; a good price.

ID **hulo gi lunga ma lalo.** Argue heatedly, fight.

ID **lodo gi lunga.** Ambitious for a superior position.

ID **lodo mao lunga.** Characteristically *hagamao lunga*; egotistical, self-centered, arrogant in spirit.

ID **lunga age.** Up a little.

ID **lunga ange.** Up more.

ID **manava i lunga.** Sigh (an intake of air) [a sign of emotion].

ID **mao lunga.** High, high-ranking.

CF **luungagi.** To be in a place protected from the wind, lee.

$LUNGA_a$

B **elunga.** *n.* Top of, the

position over (something).

LUU

B **luu.** *ma.* The two.

ID **hakohu luu mada.** Squint (eyes), frown.

ID **hano i luu moana.** Die (a person).

ID **hhadi iho luu vae.** Take a short break (in work involving standing).

ID **hhanga luu vae.** Spread one's legs.

ID **ili luu bongaa usu.** To dilate one's nostrils [a mannerism which is taken as a sign of emotion].

ID **llena luu mada.** Raise both eyebrows [a sign of assent].

ID **luu baasi.** Both sides (of).

ID **luu bido.** Both ends (of).

ID **luu duu.** Covers (of books), two halves.

ID **luu duu de maduu.** Castes (two) of aboriginal Nukuoro society.

ID **luu gili.** Labia minora.

ID **luu hua.** Labia majora.

LUUNGAGI

B **luungagi.** *v.* To be in a place protected from the wind, lee.

B 1 **luungaginga.** *n.* —.

B 2 **luungagina.** *v.* —.

BE **hagaluungagi.** *v.* —.

BE1 **hagaluungaginga.** *n.* —.

BE2 **hagaluungagina.** *v.* —.

R **luuluungagi.** *v.* —.

R 1 **luuluungaginga.** *n.* —.

R 2 **luuluungagina.** *v.* —.

RE **hagaluuluungagi.** *v.* —.

RE1 **hagaluuluungaginga.** *n.* —.

RE2 **hagaluuluungagina.** *v.* —.

M-

B **m-.** *mp.* For (always followed by *o* or *a*$_1$).

MA$_1$

B **ma$_1$.** *mi.* And, and so, and thus, and then; with, including.

ID **doo ma gu....** Fall into the bad habit of; do something which is difficult to rectify.

ID **hai me ma —.** Sort of —.

ID **hilohilo ma eidu.** A sorcerer able to take human or non-human shapes.

ID **ma ai.** And who?

ID **ma de hia e doe.** A chanted expression, on the last word of which a work group chanting it lifts a heavy object.

ID **ma tua.** Besides.

ID **mage.** [var. of *ma gi*].

ID **ma gi.** In order to.

ID **ma gu.** And then.

ID **ma hee.** Where else?

CF **madali.** With, along with, as well as; at the same time as; in addition to.

MA$_{1a}$

B **ama$_2$.** *mi.* And, among other things,...

MA$_2$

B **ma-.** *mf.* RESULTATIVE PREFIX.

B **ma$_2$.** A measure of the quantity of flying fish (*ssave*) caught (by hundreds): e.g., *dolu ma* 'three hundred flying fish'.

MAA$_1$

BE **hagamaa$_1$.** *v.* To rinse off salt water from the body (with fresh water).

BE1 **hagamaanga.** *n.* —.

MAA$_2$

B **maa$_2$.** *n.* A sibling's spouse or spouse's sibling (brother-in-law or sister-in-law) of the same sex.

BE **hagamaa$_2$.** *v.* To treat (someone) as *maa$_2$*.

ID **hai maa.** The relationship of spouse's sibling to sibling's spouse.

MAA$_3$

R **maamaa.** *v.* Chew thoroughly, masticate (soft foods which do not make noise).

R 1 **maamaanga.** *n.* —.
R 2 **maamaalia.** *v.* —.
RE **hagamaamaa.** *v.* —.
RE1 **hagamaamaanga.** *n.* —.

MAA$_4$
B **maa$_1$.** *u.* ...and the others [after personal names and pronouns]; approximately — [after expressions of quantity].
XCO **duumaa.** *u.* Remainder (less than the preceding number); about, approximately.
ID **aahee maa.** About when? (future); about how much?
ID **alaa maa.** Those there were about (approximately).
ID **anaa maa.** Those were about (approximately).
ID **anei maa.** These were about (approximately).
ID **daha de hia maa.** About what time is it?
ID **delaa maa.** That there was about (approximately).
ID **denaa maa.** That is about (approximately).
ID **denei maa.** This is about (approximately).

MAA$_5$
P **maa-$_3$.** *mf.* [pl. form of *ma-*].

MAADAI
B **maadai.** *n.* A cult official (who looked after the cult-house).
BE **hagamaadai.** *v.* —.
ID **noho maadai.** Sit quietly.

MAADAU
B **maadau.** *n.* Hook, fishhook.
BE **hagamaadau$_1$.** *n.* Barb.
XG **maadau belubelu.** A type of fishhook (small, for *belubelu* fishing).
XG **maadau daabasi.** A type of fishhook.
XG **maadau dae ssae.** A type of fishhook.
XG **maadau dagi.** A type of fishhook.
XG **maadau daodao.** A type of fishhook (large, for using a piece of fish as bait).
XG **maadau duiagi.** A fishhook of a special type (for *duiagi* fishing).
XG **maadau gina.** A type of fishhook (for *gina* fishing).
XG **maadau hholu.** A fishhook made of wire.
XG **maadau iganibongi.** A type of fishhook (biggest, for *iganibongi* fishing).
XG **maadau mada bodobodo.** A type of fishhook.
XG **maadau mangoo.** A type of fishhook (for sharks).
XG **manu solo maadau.** File (for filing metal).
ID **dagaa de maadau.** To tie a leader to a fish hook.
ID **dao hagamaadau.** A spear with a barb.
ID **duudae maadau.** [= *duudae baa*, q.v.].

MAADOLU
B **maadolu.** *a.* Thick (object); heavy or dense (of rain).
BE **hagamaadolu.** *v.* —.
R **maamaadolu.** *a.* Becoming more and more *maadolu.*
RE **hagamaamaadolu.** *v.* —.
ID **langi maadolu.** Heavy rain.
ID **malo maadolu.** Heavy clothing.

MAADU
XFL **hadu-maadau.** *n.* Coral sp. [used for polishing pearl shell fish hooks].

MAATOGO
B **maatogo.** *v.* Discourage someone (verbally).
B 1 **maatogoanga.** *n.* —.
BE **hagamaatogo.** *v.* —.
BE1 **hagamaatogoanga.** *n.* —.
BE2 **hagamaatogolia.** *v.* —.
R **maamaatogo.** *v.* —.
R 1 **maamaatogoanga.** *n.* —.
RE **hagamaamaatogo.** *v.* —.
RE1 **hagamaamaatogoanga.** *n.* —.
RE2 **hagamaamaatogolia.** *v.* —.

MAAGILA

B maagila. *v.* To appear to be barely separated (as islets on the atoll when seen from a distance); parted slightly.
B 1 maagilaanga. *n.* —.
BE hagamaagila. *v.* —.
BE1 hagamaagilaanga. *n.* —.
R maamaagila. *a.* Becoming slightly parted.
R 1 maamaagilaanga. *n.* —.
RE hagamaamaagila. *v.* —.
RE1 hagamaamaagilaanga. *n.* —.

MAAGODA

B maagoda. *a.* Jealous (sexual jealousy).
B 1 maagodanga. *n.* —.
BE hagamaagoda. *v.* —.
BE1 hagamaagodanga. *n.* —.
R maamaagoda. *a.* —.
R 1 maamaagodanga. *n.* —.
RE hagamaamaagoda. *v.* —.
RE1 hagamaamaagodanga. *n.* —.

MAAGULUAA

B maaguluaa. *a.* Dislocated (joint of the body).
B 1 maaguluaanga. *n.* —.
BE hagamaaguluaa. *v.* —.
BE1 hagamaaguluaanga. *n.* —.
ID me maaguluaa. Dislocated joint (of the body).

MAAI

B maai. *a.* Ripen (to become yellow and soft—of breadfruit only).
B 1 maainga. *n.* —.
BE hagamaai. *v.* —.
BE1 hagamaainga. *n.* —.
BE2 hagamaaia. *v.* —.
R maamaai. *a.* Ripening (of breadfruit only).
R 1 maamaainga. *n.* —.
RE hagamaamaai. *v.* —.
RE1 hagamaamaainga. *n.* —.
RE2 hagamaamaaia. *v.* —.

MAAILABA

B maailaba. *n.* Axis (or long thing through the center of something).
ID kano maailaba. The wood next to the core of a tree.

MAAILEELE

B maaileele. *a.* Die, dead (persons or animals).
B 1 maaileelenga. *n.* —.
BE hagamaaileele. *v.* —; commit suicide.
BE1 hagamaaileelenga. *n.* —.

MAAIONGI

BE hagamaaiongi. *a.* Depressed (mentally); unable to think, move, or talk (as a result of psychic depression or trauma).
BE1 hagamaaionginga. *n.* —.
RE hagamaamaaiongi. *a.* Continually *hagamaaiongi.*
RE1 hagamaamaaionginga. *n.* —.
ID noho hagamaaiongi. To sit as though stunned (i.e., as though *hagamaaiongi*).

MAALAMA

B maalama. *v.* Light (not dark), bright.
B 2 maalamangia. *v.* Illuminated (by having light shined upon it).
BE hagamaalama. *v.* Brighten, illuminate.
BE2 hagamaalamangia. *v.* —.
R malamalama. *v.* Shiny (reflects light).
RE hagamalamalama. *v.* Shine.
RE2 hagamaamaalamangia. *v.* —.
S maamaalama. *v.* —.
S 2 maamaalamangia. *v.* Continuously *maalamangia.*
SE hagamaamaalama. *v.* Shine on continuously.
ID tili de maalama. Shoot out a light into the distance.
ID gili maalama. Light-skinned.
ID kano maalama. A phosphorescent flash in the water.
ID hano gi de maalama. Transfiguration of ghosts

or spirits into human form.

ID **maalama dua de laa.** The light remaining after sunset.

MAALAVA

B **maalava.** *v.* The fatty part of the turtle.

MAALIE

B **maalie.** *mv.* Exactly; slowly; carefully, gently, softly.

ID **alaa ange maalie.** Those there are exactly right.

ID **anaa ange maalie.** Those are exactly right.

ID **anei ange maalie.** These are exactly right.

ID **basa maalie.** Speak moderately.

ID **delaa ange maalie.** That there is exactly right!

ID **denaa ange maalie.** That is exactly right!

ID **denei ange maalie.** This is exactly right!

ID **iai maalie.** Just about right.

ID **lau maalie.** Neat-appearing hair or feathers.

ID **maalie ange.** A little later.

ID **maalie loo.** Much later.

MAALIOSO

B **maalioso.** *a.* Die, dead (persons or animals).

BE **hagamaalioso.** *v.* —.

R **maamaalioso.** *a.* —.

RE **hagamaamaalioso.** *v.* —.

MAALISA

B **maalisa.** *n.* An overhanging reef shelf.

ID **hai maalisa.** Having an overhanging reef shelf.

MAALO

B **maalo.** *a.* Energetic, eager, wide-awake; waiting.

B 1 **maaloanga.** *n.* —.

BE **hagamaalo.** *v.* —.

BE1 **hagamaalonga.** *n.* —.

R **maaloolo.** *a.* Refreshed (e.g., after a rest, or a shower).

R 1 **maalooloanga.** *n.* —.

RE **hagamaaloolo.** *v.* —.

RE1 **hagamaaloolonga.** *n.* —.

S **maamaalo.** *a.* Becoming more and more *maalo.*

S 1 **maamaaloanga.** *n.* —.

SE **hagamaamaalo.** *v.* —.

SE1 **hagamaamaalonga.** *n.* —.

ID **maalo age.** Have become *maalo.*

MAANADU

B **maanadu.** *v.* Think, think about; decide; idea, thought.

B 1 **maanaduanga.** *n.* —.

B 2 **manadua.** *v.* —; remembered.

BE **hagamaanadu.** *v.* Remember, remind.

BE1 **hagamaanaduanga.** *n.* —.

BE2 **hagamanadua.** *v.* —.

R **maamaanadu.** *v.* Keep thinking about.

R 2 **manamanadua.** *v.* Keep remembering.

RE **hagamaamaanadu.** *v.* Keep reminding or keep remembering.

RE1 **hagamaamaanaduanga.** *n.* —.

RE2 **hagamaamaanadua.** *v.* —.

RE2 **hagamanamanadua.** *v.* —.

ID **bulubulu maanadu.** Incomplete idea.

ID **kangi de maanadu.** A quick-witted person (who realizes his goals fast).

ID **hai de hagamaanadu.** Remembrance, observance of (e.g., a holiday).

ID **maanadu age.** Decide (arrive at a decision), make up one's mind; think up.

ID **maanadu bodobodo.** Limited in intelligence.

ID **maanadu bolo.** "Assume that —".

ID **maanadu gelo.** Profound thoughts.

ID **maanadu iho.** Think about oneself.

ID **madagabubu de maanadu.** Slow-witted.

CF maanetonu. Act cautiously.
CF maanessala. To mistake something (or someone) for something (or someone) else.

MAANE$_1$
R **maamaane.** *a.* Light (in weight).
R 1 **maamaaneanga.** *n.* —.
RE **hagamaamaane.** *v.* Make lighter; choose the easiest work (rather than the more difficult).
RE1 **hagamaamaaneanga.** *n.* —.
ID **hagamaamaane de lodo.** Cheer up (someone).

MAANE$_2$
XCO **maanessala.** *a.* To mistake something (or someone) for something (or someone) else.

MAANE$_{2a}$
B **maanegabo.** *a.* Energetic.
B 1 **maanegaboanga.** *n.* —.
BE **hagamaanegabo.** *v.* —.
BE1 **hagamaanegaboanga.** *n.* —.

MAANE$_{2b}$
XCO **maanetonu.** *a.* Act cautiously.

MAANIHA
B **maaniha.** *a.* Strongly desirous of.
B 1 **maanihaanga.** *n.* —.
BE **hagamaaniha.** *v.* —.
BE1 **hagamaanihaanga.** *n.* —.
R **manihaniha.** *a.* Inclined to be *maaniha.*
R 1 **manihanihaanga.** *n.* —.
RE **hagamanihaniha.** *v.* —.
RE1 **hagamanihanihaanga.** *n.* —.
CF **maahia.** Want to —.

MAANU
B **maanu.** *a.* To float in place (not drifting) on the surface of the water (with no anchor).
B 1 **maanunga.** *n.* —.
BE **hagamaanu.** *v.* —.
BE1 **hagamaanunga.** *n.* —.
R **maamaanu.** *a.* —; remain stationary in the air (like a bird or a helicopter).
R 1 **maamaanunga.** *n.* —.
RE **hagamaamaanu.** *v.* —.
RE1 **hagamaamaanunga.** *n.* —.
XFL **manu-solo-maanu.** *n.* A jellyfish-like animal in the shape of a flower (burrows into the sand when touched).
ID **hagamaanu age.** Pull oneself up by one's arms.
ID **maanu iho.** To begin to fish while *maanu.*

MAANUGA
B **maanuga.** *v.* A wound or large sore (on the body).
B 1 **maanugaanga.** *n.* —.
BE **hagamaanuga.** *v.* —.
BE1 **hagamaanugaanga.** *n.* —.

MAANGA
B **maanga.** *n.* Mouthful or spoonful of food.
XFL **maanga-de-langi.** *n.* Worm sp. (makes a spider-like thread).
ID **maanga booi.** A fingerful of *booi.*
ID **maanga dalogo.** A handful of *dalogo.*
ID **mmala dana (dagu) maanga.** Lose his (my) appetite.

MAANGALO
B **maangalo.** *v.* Sweet.
B 1 **maangaloanga.** *n.* —.
BE **hagamaangalo.** *v.* —.
BE1 **hagamaangaloanga.** *n.* —.
R **maamaangalo.** *v.* Becoming more and more sweet.
R 1 **maamaangaloanga.** *n.* —.
RE **hagamaamaangalo.** *v.* —.
RE1 **hagamaamaangaloanga.** *n.* —.

MAANGI
B **maangi.** *a.* Soar or glide in the air.
BE **hagamaangi.** *v.* —.
BE1 **hagamaanginga.** *n.* —.
BE2 **hagamaangia.** *v.* —.
R **maamaangi.** *a.* Repeatedly or continually *maangi.*
RE **hagamaamaangi.** *v.* —.

RE1 **hagamaamaanginga.** *n.* —.
RE2 **hagamaamaangia.** *v.* —.

MAANGOA
B **maangoa.** *a.* To be dry.
B 1 **maangoaanga.** *n.* —.
BE **hagamaangoa.** *v.* —.
BE1 **hagamaangoanga.** *n.* —.

MAASEI
B **maasei.** *a.* Small [sing.].
B 1 **maaseinga.** *n.* —.
BE **hagamaasei.** *v.* —; reduce in size.
BE1 **hagamaaseinga.** *n.* —.
BE2 **hagamaaseia.** *v.* —.
CF **uaasei.** A type of small knife.

MAASINA
B **maasina.** *v.* Moon, light (not darkness).
B 1 **maasinaanga.** *n.* —.
BE **hagamaasina.** *v.* —.
BE1 **hagamaasinaanga.** *n.* —.
R **maamaasina.** *v.* Repeatedly lighted (esp. by moonlight).
R 1 **maamaasinaanga.** *n.* —.
RE **hagamaamaasina.** *v.* —.
RE1 **hagamaamaasinaanga.** *n.* —.
ID **pala boo maasina.** The time of the month when rain is most likely to occur (1st quarter).
ID **danu de maasina.** The setting of the moon.
ID **masulu de maasina.** "A person has died.".
ID **ssui de maasina.** The rising of the moon after the setting of the sun (i.e., when the moon is still below the water when the sun sets).

MAAUA
B **maaua.** *a.* Poisoned (by food).
B 1 **maauaanga.** *n.* —.
BE **hagamaaua.** *v.* —.
BE1 **hagamaauaanga.** *n.* —.
R **maamaaua.** *a.* Frequently *maaua.*
R 1 **maamaauaanga.** *n.* —.
RE **hagamaamaaua.** *v.* —.
RE1 **hagamaamaauaanga.** *n.* —.

MAAUI
B **maaui.** *v.* Give birth to, born.
B 1 **maauinga.** *n.* —.
BE **hagamaaui.** *v.* —.
BE1 **hagamaauinga.** *n.* —.
BE2 **hagamaauia.** *v.* —.

MAAVA
B **maava.** *a.* Yawn, belch.
B 1 **maavaanga.** *n.* —.
BE **hagamaava.** *v.* —.
BE1 **hagamaavaanga.** *n.* —.
R **maavaava.** *a.* —.
R 1 **maavaavaanga.** *n.* —.
RE **hagamaavaava.** *v.* —.
RE1 **hagamaavaavaanga.** *n.* —.
S **maamaava.** *a.* —.
S 1 **maamaavaanga.** *n.* —.
SE **hagamaamaava.** *v.* —.
SE1 **hagamaamaavaanga.** *n.* —.
ID **maava age.** Belch.

MABU
B **mabu.** *a.* Rested.
B 1 **maabunga.** *n.* —.
BE **hagamabu.** *v.* Rest, relax, quit (a job).
BE1 **hagamaabunga.** *n.* —; resting place.
BE2 **hagamabua.** *v.* Cause to *hagamabu.*
BE2 **hagamabulia.** *v.* Cause to *hagamabu.*
BE2 **hagammabulia.** *v.* —.
P **mmabu.** *a.* —.
PE **hagammabu.** *v.* —.
PE2 **hagammabua.** *v.* —.
R **mabumabu.** *a.* —.
R 1 **mabumabunga.** *n.* —.
RE **hagamabumabu.** *v.* —.
RE1 **hagamabumabunga.** *n.* —.
RE2 **hagamabumabua.** *v.* —.
RE2 **hagamabumabulia.** *v.* —.
ID **hagamabu age.** Return to land from sea (esp. of birds).
ID **hagamabu iho.** Rest for a short time.

MADA$_1$
B **mada$_1$.** *a.* Uncooked, raw.
R **madamada$_1$.** *a.* Half-cooked.
XCO **moomada.** *a.* Half-cooked.

MADA$_2$

B mada$_2$ + NUMBER. *mc.* Tens of.

BE **hagamada—$_3$.** *d.* Make a total of — tens.

XCO **madaangahulu.** *an.* Ten (objects).

XCO **madahaa.** *an.* Forty.

XCO **madahidu.** *an.* Seventy.

XCO **madalima.** *an.* Fifty.

XCO **madalua.** *an.* Twenty.

XCO **madaono.** *an.* Sixty.

XCO **madavalu.** *an.* Eighty.

XCO **matolu.** *an.* Thirty.

XCO **massiva.** *an.* Ninety.

ID **dunu madamada.** Rare (not cooked thoroughly).

MADA$_3$

B **mada$_3$.** *nl.* Front part of, face, beginning (of a thing); tip (of); point, blade.

BE **hagamada—$_1$.** *d.* —; look as though.

R **madamada$_2$.** *v.* Compete (as between individuals); front of.

R 1 **madamadaanga.** *n.* —.

RE **hagamadamada.** *v.* —; share equally; cause to compete.

RE1 **hagamadamadaanga.** *n.* —.

XCO **daumada.** *v.* Stare at, observe closely.

XCO **ganomada.** *n.* Eye.

XCO **loimada.** *n.* Tears.

XCO **madaala$_2$.** *a.* Able to remain awake for a long time.

XCO **madaangudu.** *a.* Converse with.

XCO **madaaolo.** *n.* Capital of.

XCO **madadaagodo.** *a.* Gradual slope or inclination [form *daagodo* only occurs with *mada*].

XCO **mada-galisi.** *v.* The stem of the coconut.

XCO **madagauhala.** *n.* The lower abdomen, crotch, pubic area.

XCO **mada-umanga.** *n.* The bud of a Cyrtosperma taro corm.

XCO **sugimada.** *n.* The outer corner of the eye.

XFL **mada-galadi.** *n.* Fish sp.: jack.

XFL **mada-givi.** *n.* Fish sp.

XFL **mataodao.** *n.* Fish sp.: cornetfish.

ID **bagi mada lagolago.** Machine gun.

ID **bangi mada aasanga.** A certain way of pinching with the fingers.

ID **pula luu mada.** Excited with joy.

ID **daahaa mada balabala.** The stage of development of the coconut between *mugamuga* and *daahaa.*

ID **daahaa mada giigii.** The stage of development of the coconut between *daahaa mada makaga* and *modomodo.*

ID **daahaa mada makaga.** The stage of development of the coconut between *daahaa* and *daahaa mada giigii.*

ID **daane mada daua.** Bravest in war.

ID **datada de galomada.** Twitching of an eye.

ID **dahido mada.** Inner corner of the eye.

ID **dalaa mada.** [= *dalaa umada*].

ID **dalaa umada.** Prow spray of a ship.

ID **daula mada lau nui.** A rope for tying palm fronds together to make a *belubelu* seine.

ID **tau ange luu mada.** Have noticed.

ID **tili mada.** Go at top speed.

ID **galo sugi mada.** Glimpse.

ID **gannui mada balabala.** *gannui* which is soft and mushy.

ID **gannui mada makaga.** *gannui* which is firm.

ID **haangoda mada aasanga.** To fish for *labelabe.*

ID **hadu mada.** Eyeball.

ID **hagadige de madaangudu.** A prolonged conversation (on subjects of little importance).

ID **hagamadamada ngaadahi.**

Share equally among.

ID **hagasiilangaa mada.** The appearance of fish or edible animals in great numbers (an omen of death).

ID **hakohu luu mada.** Squint (eyes), frown.

ID **hegide mada.** Early morning, before daybreak (when one can just barely recognize a person).

ID **hiihii mada.** Eyelashes.

ID **huluhulu mada.** Eyebrows.

ID **llena luu mada.** Raise both eyebrows [a sign of assent].

ID **lleu luu mada.** Swelling of the eyes (after crying).

ID **luu mada.** Face (of a person).

ID **madaa gai.** Firstfruits.

ID **mada agamu.** The essential design features of *tuai.*

ID **madaa gamu.** The measurements and special techniques used in manufacturing *duai.*

ID **mada age (iho).** Take from the bottom (top); take the worst or smallest (best or biggest).

ID **madaa hadu.** Grater (metal) attached to a board for grating taro.

ID **mada ahodo.** Any place where seawater seeps into the taro bog.

ID **madaa moni.** Prow of a canoe.

ID **madaa sele.** Loop of a lasso or noose.

ID **mada baabaa.** = *daogili.*

ID **mada baubau.** Flirtatious.

ID **mada dahi.** Having a single point or blade.

ID **mada dangada ina.** A person of importance (who is liked by the people).

ID **mada dao.** Prow of a fast ship.

ID **mada dotodo.** An abrasion of the skin (red but not bleeding).

ID **mada duulanga.** An important position (spatially).

ID **mada tea gee.** White as a sheet (of a person).

ID **mada gapua.** Lagoonward part of a *gapua.*

ID **mada galava.** Spear foreshaft.

ID **mada gelegele.** Male child.

ID **mada gi daha.** Having the point bent outward (away from its handle).

ID **mada gide.** Sharp-eyed, good at finding things.

ID **mada giivia.** Dim light.

ID **mada gi lodo.** A point which is bent inward (toward its handle).

ID **mada hoodanga.** A depression on the windward reef.

ID **mada hoou.** Brand new.

ID **mada lahalaha.** Appear to be wide.

ID **mada legalega.** A small hole; having small openings.

ID **mada libia.** A very sharp point.

ID **mada ligiligi.** Having small eyes or holes.

ID **mada looloa.** Longer in comparison with; extending farther than appears to be the case.

ID **mada loolodo.** A depression in the reef (where water accumulates).

ID **mada luu mada.** In the presence of someone.

ID **madamada a me.** A miscellaneous assortment.

ID **mada madangi.** Able to point (into the wind) well (of a sailing canoe).

ID **madamada o dangada.** In public.

ID **mada mmea.** Dark red.

ID **mada nnui.** Having big holes (or entrances, etc.).

ID **mada nuui.** Dark green in color.

ID **mada saosao.** Sharp-pointed.

ID **mada sua hadu.** Storm

beach (on the seaward reef).

ID **mada udua.** The point of a promontory or peninsula (esp. if large).

ID **ma te.** [a contraction of *mada de*...].

ID **ma te hakii.** The uvula and the adjacent portions of the oral cavity.

ID **ma tuai.** Coconut grater blade.

ID **mmala luu mada.** Stinging of one's eyes (e.g., from salt water).

ID **oha de ganomada.** To work on a craft item (e.g., a canoe) with a model in mind of the finished product which is different from that of the person who began the work.

ID **sii mada daahaa.** A fine jet of water.

ID **ssili mada.** To faint, be unconscious.

ID **sugimada ina.** Catch a glimpse of.

CF **daamada.** Start; the beginning (of an event).

CF **maadau.** Hook, fishhook.

CF **madabiebie.** Fish sp.: sea bass (2 sorts: 1 large, 1 small).

CF **madaligi$_1$.** Skillful at craft work, craftsmanlike; craftsman.

CF **madaoaligi.** A type of string figure.

CF **mataia.** Soreness of the eyes after a fishing expedition (from the glare of the sun).

CF **umada.** Rainbow.

MADA$_{3a}$

B **mada$_4$.** *n.* Common ascendents who are *daina* or other connecting links of kin relationship.

BE **hagamada—$_2$.** *d.* Basis (with respect to common ascendents)for a relationship of —.

ID **hai mada dabu.** An avoidance relationship (between kin).

ID **mada dabu.** Affinal relatives who are *maa* or *saulaba* to each other [and therefore between whom respect and avoidance are enjoined]; avoidance relationship.

MADA$_{3b}$

B **madaala$_1$.** *a.* Loosely braided; good at twirling sennit.

B 1 **madaalanga.** *n.* —.

BE **hagamadaala.** *v.* —.

BE1 **hagamadaalanga.** *n.* —.

MADA$_{3c}$

ID **bii o madahasi.** A certain kind of phosphorescence in seawater at night.

MADA$_{3d}$

B **madahuuhua.** *v.* Pimple.

B 1 **madahuuhuaanga.** *n.* —.

BE **hagamadahuuhua.** *v.* Cause to have pimples.

BE1 **hagamadahuuhuaanga.** *n.* —.

MADA$_{3e}$

B **madaniiga.** *v.* Ingrown callus.

BE **hagamadaniiga.** *v.* —.

BE1 **hagamadaniigaanga.** *n.* —.

MADA$_{3f}$

B **madannia.** *n.* Finger.

ID **angaanga madannia.** Fingernail.

ID **madannia i lodo.** Middle finger.

ID **madannia madua.** Thumb.

ID **madannia sisi.** Little finger.

MADA$_{3g}$

XCO **madavaivai.** *n.* A type of knot used in net-making.

MADA$_{3h}$

B **madabuunou.** *a.* Dull (of an edge or point).

B 1 **madabuunounga.** *n.* —.

B 2 **madabuunoua.** *a.* Become dull.

BE **hagamadabuunou.** *v.* —.

BE1 **hagamadabuunounga.** *n.* —.

BE2 **hagamadabuunoua.** *v.* —.

MADA$_{3i}$

B **madaviiga.** *v.* The needle-like spines on *daudu* fish.

MADAAGI

B **madaagi.** *v.* The scout in *belubelu* fishing.
B 1 **madaagianga.** *n.* —.
B 1 **madaaginga.** *n.* —.
BE **hagamadaagi.** *v.* To teach someone to *madaagi.*
BE1 **hagamadaagianga.** *n.* —.
BE1 **hagamadaaginga.** *n.* —.

MADAALI

B **madaali.** *a.* Lacking in oil (of a ripe coconut).
BE **hagamadaali.** *v.* —.
ID **me madaali.** A ripe coconut (= *gaadinga*) of poor quality.

MADAGU

B **madagu.** *a.* Afraid, scared.
B 1 **madaguanga.** *n.* —.
BE **hagamadagu.** *v.* Scare (someone); frighten (someone).
BE1 **hagamadaguanga.** *n.* —.
BE2 **hagamadagudia.** *v.* —.
BE2 **hagamadagulia.** *v.* —.
P **maatagu.** *a.* —.
P 1 **maataguanga.** *n.* —.
PE **hagamaatagu.** *v.* —.
PE1 **hagamaataguanga.** *n.* —.
PE2 **hagamaatagudia.** *v.* —.
PE2 **hagamaatagulia.** *v.* —.
R **madagudagu.** *a.* Cowardly (concerning others or supernaturals).
R 1 **madagudaguanga.** *n.* —.
RE **hagamadagudagu.** *v.* —.
RE1 **hagamadagudaguanga.** *n.* —.
RE2 **hagamadagudagudia.** *v.* —.
RE2 **hagamadagudagulia.** *v.* —.

MADALI

B **madali.** *mi.* With, along with, as well as; at the same time as; in addition to.
E **matali.** *mi.* —.

MADALIGI$_1$

B **madaligi$_1$.** *a.* Skillful at craft work, craftsmanlike; craftsman.
B 1 **madaligianga.** *n.* —.
BE **hagamadaligi.** *v.* —.
BE1 **hagamadaligianga.** *n.* —.
P **madaaligi.** *a.* —.
P 1 **madaaligianga.** *n.* —.
PE **hagamadaaligi.** *v.* —.
PE1 **hagamadaaligianga.** *n.* —.

MADALIGI$_2$

B **Madaligi$_2$.** *n.* January.
ID **hagadubu o madaligi.** The name of a certain type of string figure.

MADANGI

B **madangi.** *v.* Wind, gas, flatus.
BE **hagamadangi.** *v.* —.
ID **baa i de madangi.** Be hit (usually forcefully) by wind.
ID **dahuli de madangi.** A change of wind direction.
ID **dau de madangi.** Be hit by (usually a strong) wind.
ID **diinei de madangi.** A decrease of wind velocity.
ID **geu de madangi.** A change of wind direction.
ID **hagalulu de madangi.** To attract the wind (by making certain noises).
ID **hagasau madangi.** To be exposed to the wind.
ID **hai madangi.** Pass wind (flatus).
ID **mada madangi.** Able to point (into the wind) well (of a sailing canoe).
ID **madangi danuaa.** Fresh air.
ID **muli madangi.** Sailing downwind.
ID **sau makaga de madangi.** The blowing of wind steadily (for a long time) from one direction.

MADAU

B **madau.** *n.* Right (side).
B 1 **maadaunga.** *n.* —.
BE **hagamaadau$_2$.** *n.* A current which flows to the right.

ID **baasi madau.** Right side, right-handed.
ID **hilo hagamaadau.** To braid sennit with the right hand; [the result is considered inferior to sennit made with the left hand].

MADE$_1$
B **made$_1$.** *v.* Look at in an effort to identify or recognize.
B 1 **maadenga$_1$.** *n.* —.
B 2 **madea.** *v.* Identify, recognize.
BE **hagamade$_1$.** *v.* Do as hard or fast as possible.
BE1 **hagamaadenga$_1$.** *n.* —.
BE2 **hagamadea.** *v.* —.
R **mademade$_1$.** *v.* —.
R 1 **mademadenga.** *n.* —.
R 2 **mademadea.** *v.* Identify tentatively; to think that one recognizes but not be sure.
RE **hagamademade$_1$ —.** *d.* Work as little as possible; tarry in order to avoid.
ID **agu made.** Perhaps, maybe;.
ID **dagu made.** Perhaps, maybe.
ID **delaa tee madea.** Hard to tell apart from; resemble closely.
ID **made sala.** Mistaken (in identifying); mistake someone for another.

MADE$_2$
B **made$_2$.** *a.* Dead (of plants only); numb, paralyzed; go out (of a fire).
B 1 **maadenga$_2$.** *n.* —.
BE **hagamade$_2$.** *v.* —.
BE1 **hagamaadenga$_2$.** *n.* —.
BE2 **hagamadelia.** *v.* —.
P **mmade.** *a.* —.
PE **hagammade.** *v.* —.
PE1 **hagammadenga.** *n.* —.
PE2 **hagammadelia.** *v.* —.
R **mademade$_2$.** *a.* —.
RE **hagamademade$_2$.** *v.* —.
RE1 **hagamademadenga.** *n.* —.
RE2 **hagamademadelia.** *v.* —.
ID **tangada made.** Now you've done it!
ID **kano made.** Slightly aged meat.
ID **kino made.** Hate vehemently, completely disgusted.
ID **hagamademade gaiaa.** Cringe to deceive one's opponent into thinking one is afraid (when one is not).
ID **hale maadenga.** Mortuary house.
ID **hasi made.** To cut a taro corm from its stalk so far up the stalk that it won't grow a new corm when it is planted.
ID **hulu made.** The fading of one's hair color (becoming white).
ID **mademadea ange.** Feel sleepy.
ID **mmade aalanga.** Exhausted (physically or mentally).
ID **mmade gimoo.** To die in great numbers.

MADI
B **madi.** *v.* To add organic material to the taro bog.
B 1 **maadinga.** *n.* —.
B 2 **madia.** *v.* —.
BE **hagamadi.** *v.* —.
BE1 **hagamaadinga.** *n.* —.
R **madimadi.** *v.* —.
R 1 **madimadinga.** *n.* —.
R 2 **madimadia.** *v.* —.
RE **hagamadimadi.** *v.* —.
RE1 **hagamadimadinga.** *n.* —.

MADIA
BE **hagamadia.** *a.* Show-off.
BE1 **hagamadiaanga.** *n.* —.
ID **hai me hagamadia.** Behave in a more-or-less show-off manner.

MADILA
B **madila.** *n.* Bamboo [not native, but drifts ashore].
ID **gubu madila.** A joint of bamboo.
ID **lau de madila.** A tuna of fair size.
ID **madila diadia.** Bindings

wound around a fishing pole to give it extra strength.

MADU

E **mmadu.** *n.* Fish sp.: mojarra fish (= small *sugimanga*).

XFL **maduilau.** *n.* Fish sp.: goatfish.

MADUA

B **madua.** *a.* Old (persons), mature, full-grown; parent, elder (senior relative).

BE **hagamadua.** *v.* Act like a grown-up (when still a child).

P **maadua.** *a.* Parents, elders.

P **maatua.** *a.* — (ex. meanings covered by *maadua*).

PE **hagamaadua.** *v.* Be oldest among.

PE **hagamaatua.** *v.* —; [pl. of *hagamaadua*].

R **madumadua.** *a.* Very old (persons); fully mature and then some.

RE **hagamadumadua.** *v.* To act as though very old.

XCO **uumadua.** *a.* Desirous of suckling when past nursing age, to breast-feed beyond infancy.

ID **au madua.** A type of ocean current far from land in which drifting objects collect.

ID **basa madua.** Speak as an elder (treating the hearer as a child).

ID **dabuvae madua.** Big toe.

ID **dama madua.** Eldest child.

ID **dangada madua.** Old person, adult.

ID **giado madua.** Main outrigger booms.

ID **hai maadua.** Mention of one's elders by others.

ID **hai me madua.** Act grown up.

ID **madannia madua.** Thumb.

ID **muna madua.** Words used only by elders (which are not normally part of a child's vocabulary).

MADUU

ID **dae maduu.** A method of pulling flying fish into the canoe with a hand net.

ID **hagadubu maduu paa.** The name of a certain type of string figure.

ID **luu duu de maduu.** Castes (two) of aboriginal Nukuoro society.

MATAIA

B **mataia.** *v.* Soreness of the eyes after a fishing expedition (from the glare of the sun).

B 1 **mataianga.** *n.* —.

BE **hagamataia.** *v.* —.

BE1 **hagamataianga.** *n.* —.

R **madamataia.** *v.* Inclined to be (or easily) *mataia.*

RE **hagamadamataia.** *v.* —.

RE1 **hagamadamataianga.** *n.* —.

ID **mataia mai.** Seen being *mataia.*

MAE

B **mae.** *a.* Withered; [also, D form of *mmae*$_1$].

B 1 **maenga.** *n.* —.

BE **hagamae.** *v.* —.

BE1 **hagamaenga.** *n.* —.

E **mmae.** *a.* Pain, hurt; withered (of a plant).

E 1 **mmaenga.** *n.* —.

EE **hagammae.** *v.* —.

EE1 **hagammaenga.** *n.* —.

R **maemae.** *a.* —; pain, hurt (children's language).

R 1 **maemaenga.** *n.* —.

RE **hagamaemae.** *v.* —.

RE1 **hagamaemaenga.** *n.* —.

ID **hagammae lodo.** Insult (someone).

ID **hagammae manava.** Tease cruelly.

ID **mmae tinae.** Convulsed with laughter.

MAEA

B **maea.** *n.* A type of rope (the thickest sort).

MAEVA

B	**maeva.** *a.* Move from one place to another.
B 1	**maevaanga.** *n.* —.
BE	**hagamaeva.** *v.* —.
BE1	**hagamaevaanga.** *n.* —.
R	**maevaeva.** *a.* —.
R 1	**maevaevaanga.** *n.* —.
RE	**hagamaevaeva.** *v.* —.
RE1	**hagamaevaevaanga.** *n.* —.
S	**mamaeva.** *a.* —.
S 1	**mamaevaanga.** *n.* —.
SE	**hagamamaeva.** *v.* —.
SE1	**hagamamaevaanga.** *n.* —.
ID	**dee maeva.** Not present, absent.

MAGA$_1$

B	**maga$_1$.** *v.* Throw; donate (to a collection being made).
B 1	**maaganga$_1$.** *n.* —.
B 2	**magaa.** *v.* —.
BE	**hagamaga$_1$.** *v.* —.
BE1	**hagamaaganga$_1$.** *n.* —.
BE2	**hagamagaa.** *v.* —.
R	**magamaga.** *v.* —.
R 1	**magamagaanga.** *n.* —.
RE	**hagamagamaga.** *v.* —.
RE1	**hagamagamagaanga.** *n.* —.
ID	**maga de gau dogi.** Masturbate (of males only).
ID	**maga de hoe.** To paddle vigorously.
ID	**maga tau hoe.** To paddle (a canoe) vigorously.
CF	**maaguluaa.** Dislocated (joint of the body).

MAGA$_2$

B	**maga$_2$.** *v.* Callus.
B 1	**maaganga$_2$.** *n.* —.
BE	**hagamaga$_2$.** *v.* —.
BE1	**hagamaaganga$_2$.** *n.* —.
P	**mmaga.** *v.* —.
PE	**hagammaga.** *v.* —.
XCO	**ulimagallai.** *a.* Jet black.
ID	**maga ahi.** Glowing embers (without a flame).

MAGALILI

B	**magalili.** *a.* Feel cold, shivering (from cold); flow (of tide).
B 1	**magalilianga.** *n.* —.
BE	**hagamagalili.** *v.* —.
BE1	**hagamagalilianga.** *n.* —.
P	**magaalili.** *a.* —.
P 1	**magaalilianga.** *n.* —.
PE	**hagamagaalili.** *v.* —.
PE1	**hagamagaalilianga.** *n.* —.
R	**magamagalili.** *a.* Frequently *magalili.*
R 1	**magamagalilianga.** *n.* —.
RE	**hagamagamagalili.** *v.* —.
RE1	**hagamagamagalilianga.** *n.* —.
S	**magalillili.** *a.* Frequently *magalili.*
S 1	**magalillilianga.** *n.* —.
SE	**hagamagalillili.** *v.* —.
SE1	**hagamagalillilianga.** *n.* —.
ID	**magalili tai.** Flow (of tide).
ID	**magalili mai.** Flow (of tide).
ID	**moana magalili.** A cold underwater current.

MAGAU

B	**magau.** *a.* Die, dead, unconscious.
B 1	**magaunga.** *n.* —.
BE	**hagamagau.** *v.* —; commit or attempt suicide.
BE1	**hagamagaunga.** *n.* —.
BE2	**hagamagaua.** *v.* —.
BE2	**hagamagaulia.** *v.* —.
P	**maakau.** *a.* —.
P 1	**maakaunga.** *n.* —.
PE	**hagamaakau.** *v.* —.
PE1	**hagamaakaunga.** *n.* —.
PE2	**hagamaakaua.** *v.* —.
PE2	**hagamaakaulia.** *v.* —.
R	**magaugau.** *a.* Easily faint or lose consciousness; mortality-prone (e.g., of a family).
R 1	**magaugaunga.** *n.* —.
RE	**hagamagaugau.** *v.* —.
RE1	**hagamagaugaunga.** *n.* —.
RE2	**hagamagaugaua.** *v.* —.
RE2	**hagamagaugaulia.** *v.* —.
ID	**dau maagau.** A period during which many people die.
ID	**langi maakau.** The sort of rain which is an omen of death.
ID	**maakau laa loo dangada.** What a shame!
ID	**magau baubau.** Die in

agony (owing to having led a bad life).
ID **magau danuaa.** Die peacefully [as shown by a beatific facial expression on the corpse and the calmness of the weather].
ID **magau de laa.** Weakness of the sun's rays (for drying) [usually referring to the late afternoon].
ID **magau de lima.** A paralyzed arm.
ID **magau donu i de lodo.** Want desperately.
ID **magau i de hiigai.** Ravenous.
ID **magau i togaa.** Die of shame [figuratively].
ID **magau loo au.** Now I'm really in trouble!
ID **seni magau.** Sleep soundly (owing to exhaustion).

MAGAVAA
B **magavaa.** *nl.* Between; the time when; [var. of *masavaa*].
ID **hagadanuaa magavaa.** Make peace between people, conciliate.
ID **laa magavaa.** In between.

MAGI
B **magi.** *a.* Sick, sickness; ill, illness; disease (physical or mental).
B 1 **magianga.** *n.* —.
BE **hagamagi.** *v.* —.
BE1 **hagamagianga.** *n.* —.
BE2 **hagamagilia.** *v.* —.
P **mmagi.** *a.* —.
P 1 **mmagianga.** *n.* —.
PE **hagammagi.** *v.* —.
PE1 **hagammagianga.** *n.* —.
PE2 **hagammagilia.** *v.* —.
R **magimagi.** *a.* Prone to illness.
R 1 **magimagianga.** *n.* —.
RE **hagamagimagi.** *v.* —.
RE1 **hagamagimagianga.** *n.* —.
RE2 **hagamagimagilia.** *v.* —.
ID **dau magi.** Epidemic.
ID **hale magi.** Hospital, dispensary.
ID **magi dabeo.** Menstruation.
ID **magi dee manava.** Asthma.
ID **magi eaea.** An eruption in a child's mouth, said to result from improper feeding [acute herpes infection?].
ID **magi gobegobe.** Cold (sickness).
ID **magi kino.** Loss of appetite.
ID **magi haahine.** Menstruation.
ID **magi hai dama.** Morning sickness (of pregnancy).
ID **magi hanohano.** Diarrhea.
ID **magi hongagelegele todo.** To have bloody stools [dysentery?].
ID **magi i de malama.** Menstruation.
ID **magi ilihia.** Gastritis (having one's stomach full of gas).
ID **magi iviivi.** Any illness characterized by wasting of the body (esp. t.b.), consumption.
ID **magi labua gee.** Upset stomach (nausea).
ID **magi libolibo.** Dizziness or vertigo (as a chronic condition or illness).
ID **magi luduludu.** The tremor (as though chilled) of a sick person.
ID **magi nngahu.** Asthma.
ID **magi nngali.** Any sickness leading to emaciation (e.g., t.b.); a wasting illness (terminal).
ID **magi o de henua.** Cold (sickness), flu.
ID **magi sali usu.** Headcold, runny nose.
ID **magi ssae aalanga.** Sore muscles (not associated with strain).
CF **magiaa.** Envious, jealous (non-sexual jealousy).

MAGIAA
B **magiaa.** *a.* Envious, jealous (non-sexual jealousy).
B 1 **magiaanga.** *n.* —.
BE **hagamagiaa.** *v.* —.
BE1 **hagamagiaanga.** *n.* —.

R magimagiaa. *a.* Frequently *magiaa.*
R 1 magimagiaanga. *n.* —.
RE hagamagimagiaa. *v.* —.
RE1 hagamagimagiaanga. *n.* —.

MAGO
B **mago.** *a.* Bad weather (high wind or rain, or rough seas).
BE **hagamago.** *v.* —.
R **magomago.** *a.* —.
RE **hagamagomago.** *v.* —.
ID **mago de henua.** Monsoon winds (from the southwest).
ID **mago de me.** A worsening condition of the weather.

MAGUA
B **magua.** *a.* Thieving.
B 1 **maguaanga.** *n.* —.
BE **hagamagua.** *v.* To cause someone to steal.
BE1 **hagamaguaanga.** *n.* —.
ID **hai me magua.** Sort of steal.

MAGULU
B **magulu.** *a.* Defeated.
BE **hagamagulu.** *v.* —; reluctant to do or initiate (through fear of failure).
P **maakulu.** *a.* —.
PE **hagamaakulu.** *v.* —.
R **magulugulu.** *a.* To despair (of attaining success).
RE **hagamagulugulu.** *v.* —.
ID **magulu mai ange.** Less — than.

MAKAGA
B **makaga.** *a.* Hard (solid).
B 1 **makagaanga.** *n.* —.
BE **hagamakaga.** *v.* —; to persist in maintaining the truth of a falsehood.
BE1 **hagamakagaanga.** *n.* —.
BE2 **hagamakagalia.** *v.* —.
E **maagaga.** *a.* Industrious.
E 1 **maagagaanga.** *n.* —.
EE **hagamaagaga.** *v.* —.
EE1 **hagamaagagaanga.** *n.* —.
EE2 **hagamaagagalia.** *v.* —.
R **magakaga.** *a.* Firmly attached.
R 1 **magakagaanga.** *n.* —.
RE **hagamagakaga.** *v.* —.
RE1 **hagamagakagaanga.** *n.* —.
RE2 **hagamagakagalia.** *v.* —.
ID **bili makaga.** Love.
ID **daahaa mada makaga.** The stage of development of the coconut between *daahaa* and *daahaa mada giigii.*
ID **tangada maagaga.** Industrious person.
ID **gannui mada makaga.** *gannui* which is firm.
ID **lau makaga.** Stiff.
ID **maagaga dua.** To walk with one's shoulders unnaturally thrown back.
ID **makaga lodo.** Stubborn.
ID **saiolo duli magaga.** A type of string figure.
ID **sau makaga.** Blow steadily (of wind).
ID **sau makaga de madangi.** The blowing of wind steadily (for a long time) from one direction.

MAHA
R **mahamaha.** *a.* Pretty, beautiful; look as though appropriate, seemly.
R 1 **mahamahaanga.** *n.* —.
RE **hagamahamaha.** *v.* —; keep silent, pray.
RE1 **hagamahamahaanga.** *n.* —.
RE2 **hagamahamahalia.** *v.* —.
XCO **daumaha.** *v.* Church (services); religious observance; religion.
ID **dagodo mahamaha.** Nice, pleasing.
ID **tilo mahamaha.** Having a good appearance.
ID **ngadi mahamaha —.** Beautiful but otherwise useless.

MAHEDUA
B **mahedua.** *n.* Sneeze.
ID **paa de mahedua.** Sneeze loudly.

MAHI
B **mahi.** *d.* —.
B 1 **mahianga.** *n.* —.
E **mmahi.** *a.* Strong, strength, force, power, energy.

E 1 **mmahianga.** *n.* —.
EC3 **maahiaanga.** *n.* —.
EE **hagammahi.** *v.* Persevere, try hard to.
EE1 **hagammahianga.** *n.* —.
EF2 **hagamaahia.** *v.* —.
EF3 **hagamaahiaanga.** *n.* —.
R **mahimahi.** *d.* —.
R 1 **mahimahianga.** *n.* —.
RE **hagamahimahi.** *v.* —.
RE1 **hagamahimahianga.** *n.* —.
ID **gai gi de mahi.** Eat as much as possible.
ID **kave gi de mahi.** Obtain by force.
ID **hai gi de mahi.** Do or take by force, rape.
ID **lodo mmahi.** Persistent, patient, persevering.
ID **mahi bodo.** Easily tired.
ID **mahi loa.** Tireless.
ID **mmahi age de —.** Feel like —.
ID **mmahi i de gai.** Eat more than seems appropriate to one's body size.

MAHU
B **mahu.** *a.* Healed (of a sore).
B 1 **maahunga.** *n.* —.
B 1 **mahuanga.** *n.* —.
BE **hagamahu.** *v.* —.
BE1 **hagamaahunga.** *n.* —.
BE1 **hagamahuanga.** *n.* —.
BE2 **hagamahulia.** *v.* —.
P **mmahu.** *a.* —.
P 1 **mmahuanga.** *n.* —.
PE **hagammahu.** *v.* —.
PE1 **hagammahuanga.** *n.* —.
PE2 **hagammahulia.** *v.* —.
R **mahumahu.** *a.* Becoming *mahu.*
R 1 **mahumahuanga.** *n.* —.
R 1 **mahumahunga.** *n.* —.
RE **hagamahumahu.** *v.* —.
RE1 **hagamahumahuanga.** *n.* —.
RE1 **hagamahumahunga.** *n.* —.
RE2 **hagamahumahulia.** *v.* —.

MAI$_1$
B **mai.** *mv.* Toward the speaker; less; nearer.
XCO **adamai.** *v.* Recollect or recall past events or persons, etc.
ID **baalasi mai (adu).** Shine a flashlight toward me (you).
ID **bangabanga mai.** Become skinny, become shrunken.
ID **boaa ina mai.** Prevented from coming by being caught in a storm.
ID **boogia mai.** Be caught doing something wrong.
ID **boo mai ange laa.** The second night following.
ID **poo mai.** A unit of measurement (from the end of the extended thumb to the other side of the clenched fist).
ID **daabeduge mai.** Bring a lot of.
ID **dagodo mai.** Appear from yonder.
ID **danuaa mai i hee.** Good according to whom?
ID **dangada mai i daha.** Relatives by marriage or adoption, etc.
ID **dee ahe mai.** Incurably ill.
ID **dee ngado mai.** Forever, eternally.
ID **diinei mai.** Make smaller; decrease.
ID **diinei mai dege.** To round off a sharp edge.
ID **dogoisi mai.** Decreasing (in number).
ID **doo mai de malino.** Completely calm.
ID **tuu mai.** Limit, discontinue, shorten (by cutting off one end).
ID **gabaea mai.** Found hanged (suicide).
ID **galeve maimai.** Fresh (unfermented) *galeve.*
ID **gauligi mai ange.** The one next younger still.
ID **gau mai moni.** Foreigners (lit., 'people who came in canoes').
ID **gau mai vaga.** [= *gau mai moni*].
ID **gidee mai.** Found out (or be found out).
ID **godi mai.** A certain type of manipulation in playing with string figures.

ID **gu odi mai ogu.** I have done all I could!
ID **gu oo ina mai.** Shout to announce important news (e.g., to announce the arrival of a ship).
ID **kii mai.** Decreasing.
ID **hagaahe mai.** Return to the fold.
ID **hagadaga mai.** Decrease in —; travel toward speaker.
ID **hagatulu mai.** Ooze out.
ID **hagamaasei mai.** Make smaller (toward one).
ID **hagausi mai.** The appearance of rain clouds.
ID **heboohagi mai.** Found fighting.
ID **hhola mai saiolo.** To allow the sail to fill with wind, holding on to the boom sheet (after luffing).
ID **hhui mai tai.** Flow of the tide.
ID **iho mai.** I feel like —.
ID **ilaage mai.** Free from.
ID **iloo mai.** Know that someone —.
ID **llilo mai.** Decreasing (in number); becoming less.
ID **lobadia mai.** To have the sail and mast blown down (because the wind came from the side away from the outrigger).
ID **madala mai.** Get free, be loose; in bloom.
ID **mataia mai.** Seen being *mataia*.
ID **matili mai.** Remember vividly (after having forgotten); the sprouting of plants, etc., in great numbers.
ID **magalili mai.** Flow (of tide).
ID **magulu mai ange.** Less — than.
ID **mahamaha mai.** To appear beautiful (that thing over there) to me (i.e., from where I am).
ID **mai ange laa.** The next (one) following the one in question.
ID **mai i daha.** From outside.
ID **maimai mai.** Become *maimai*.
ID **mai moni.** A type of fishhook (made from pearl shell).
ID **mmenengia mai.** Discourage (someone) about something.
ID **modu mai (adu, ange).** Become one's (your, their) exclusive possession.
ID **noho mai (adu, ange).** Resist me (you, them), oppose me (you, them).
ID **ngalue mai.** Decrease.
ID **ngani mai.** *ngani* toward oneself; fit (of clothes).
ID **ngaue mai.** To reduce (in price, etc.).
ID **odi mai (adu, ange).** All (e.g., have come).
ID **oho mai.** Come early.
ID **sae mai.** Break through the bush (toward one).
ID **salu mai.** Make smaller by planing or scraping.
ID **sigisigi mai (adu, ange).** Say bad things about one to one's face.
ID **singa mai (adu, ange).** Come carrying.
ID **soe mai.** Decided for one by the will of God.
ID **suasua mai (adu, ange).** To row a canoe (with a paddle).
ID **ua mai.** The rising of the tide.
ID **vvela mai (adu, ange).** I (you, he, or she) want to — very badly.
CF **loomai.** Come or go (toward the speaker) [pl.].

MAI$_2$

R **maimai$_1$.** *a.* Sweet.
R 1 **maimainga$_1$.** *n.* —.
RE **hagamaimai.** *v.* Sweeten.
RE1 **hagamaimainga.** *n.* —.
RE2 **hagamaimaia.** *v.* —.
ID **gulu maimai.** A type of prepared food (ripe breadfruit which has been cooked in an *umu*).

ID maimai de ngudu. Sweet-talker.
ID maimai sseni. To sleep especially well or restfully.
ID me maimai. Candy.
ID muna maimai. [= *ngudu maimai*].
ID ngudu maimai. Flattery or other communication by which one attempts to ingratiate oneself; unctuous, cloying, winsome.

MAIDIGI
B **Maidigi.** *n.* August.

MAIDO
B **maido.** *n.* Fish sp.
ID **senga maido.** Stupidly unafraid of danger (like *maido*).

MAILABA
B **Mailaba.** *n.* September; [uncapitalized] the hollow core of the tree trunk.

MAILE
B **maile.** *n.* Plant sp.: maile-scented fern (*Polypodium scolopendria* Burm. F.).

MAIMAI
B **maimai**$_2$. *a.* To dull a point or sharp edge by striking it against something hard.
B 1 **maimainga**$_2$. *n.* —.
B 2 **maimaia.** *a.* —.
ID **maimai ange.** To have been dulled (from having been struck on a hard object).

MAINU
B **mainu.** *n.* Bait (on the hook).
BE **hagamainu.** *v.* Provide with bait.
ID **hai mainu.** Collect bait.
ID **mainu daodao.** Bait for *daodao* fishing [a shiny side strip of the tuna or *daodao*].

MAINGAA
B **maingaa.** *a.* Miss, feel the loss of, or the uselessness of, something of great value.
B 1 **maingaanga.** *n.* —.
BE **hagamaingaa.** *v.* Cause one to feel *maingaa.*
BE1 **hagamaingaanga.** *n.* —.
R **maimaingaa.** *a.* —.
R 1 **maimaingaanga.** *n.* —.
RE **hagamaimaingaa.** *v.* —.
RE1 **hagamaimaingaanga.** *n.* —.
ID **maingaa ange nei gi.** To wish one has —.
ID **maingaa ange loo.** Feel really *maingaa* about —.

MALA
R **malamala.** *n.* Small bits of things (e.g., sawdust).

MALAIA
B **malaia.** *a.* Have luck which is unexpected (esp. bad, in which case considered retribution for past deeds).
B 1 **malaiaanga.** *n.* —.
BE **hagamalaia.** *v.* —.
BE1 **hagamalaiaanga.** *n.* —.
P **maalaia.** *a.* —.
P 1 **maalaiaanga.** *n.* —.
PE **hagamaalaia.** *v.* —.
PE1 **hagamaalaiaanga.** *n.* —.
ID **basa hagamalaia.** To curse (someone).
ID **gu malaia donu.** To have been lucky.

MALALI
B **malali.** *a.* Smooth; cleared (of brush or obstructions).
B 1 **malalianga.** *n.* —.
BE **hagamalali.** *v.* —.
BE1 **hagamalalianga.** *n.* —.
P **maalali.** *a.* —.
P 1 **maalalianga.** *n.* —.
PE **hagamaalali.** *v.* —.
PE1 **hagamaalalianga.** *n.* —.
R **malamalali.** *a.* Becoming more and more *malali.*
R 1 **malamalalianga.** *n.* —.
RE **hagamalamalali.** *v.* —.

RE1 **hagamalamalalianga.** *n.* —.
ID **dahi-malali.** The first number of a counting game played to determine who is "it".
ID **gili malali.** Clean [adj.]; neat.
ID **lodo gilimalali.** Pureness of heart, innocence.

MALALIa
B **malalidage.** *a.* Used up or cleaned out completely.
B 1 **malalidageanga.** *n.* —.
BE **hagamalalidage.** *v.* —.
BE1 **hagamalalidageanga.** *n.* —.

MALAMA
B **malama.** *n.* Month, moon.
XCO **Tahi-malama.** *nt.* January ('first month').
XCO **Tolu-malama.** *nt.* March.
XCO **Haa-malama.** *nt.* April [lit., the 'fourth month'].
XCO **Hidu-malama.** *nt.* July ('seventh month').
XCO **Lima-malama.** *nt.* May ('fifth month').
XCO **Lua-malama.** *nt.* February ('second month')
XCO **Madaangahulu-ma-dahi-malama.** *nt.* November ('eleventh month').
XCO **Madaangahulu-ma-lua-malama.** *nt.* December ('twelfth month').
XCO **Madaangahulu-malama.** *nt.* October ('tenth month').
XCO **ONO-malama.** *nt.* June ('sixth month').
XCO **Ssiva-malama.** *nt.* September ('ninth month').
XCO **Valu-malama.** *nt.* August ('eighth month').
ID **boo hagadanu malama.** The nights on which the quarter moon is obscured by rain.
ID **galogalo malama.** The last quarter of the moon (rising in the east just before sunrise).
ID **gelegele malama.** Sand with disk-like particles.
ID **magi i de malama.** Menstruation.

MALANGIANGI
ID **lodo malangilangi.** Happy.

MALANGILANGI
B **malangilangi.** *a.* Happy, laugh (as a sign of happiness), cheerful.
BE **hagamalangilangi.** *v.* Please (someone), cheer up (someone); cheerful by nature, joyous.
ID **boi malangilangi.** Laugh abnormally.
ID **malangilangi ai.** Happy with, pleased at; appreciative.

MALAU$_1$
B **malau**$_1$. *a.* Free from (esp. hardship or illness after having had it).
B 1 **malauanga.** *n.* —.
B 1 **malaunga.** *n.* —.
BE **hagamalau.** *v.* —.
BE1 **hagamalauanga.** *n.* —.
BE1 **hagamalaunga.** *n.* —.
R **malamalau.** *a.* Repeatedly or continuously *malau*$_1$.
R 1 **malamalauanga.** *n.* —.
R 1 **malamalaunga.** *n.* —.
RE **hagamalamalau.** *v.* —.
RE1 **hagamalamalauanga.** *n.* —.
RE1 **hagamalamalaunga.** *n.* —.
ID **malau age.** Free of hardship (after having had it).

MALAU$_2$
ID **lleu luu malau ngudu.** Swollen lips (from eating spicy foods or foods to which one is allergic).
ID **malau ngudu.** Lips.

MALAU$_3$
B **malau**$_2$. *n.* Fish sp.: squirrelfish (The native term is applied to many spp.).

MALE
R **malemale.** *n.* Areola of the breast; a boil on the body.

MALEASA
B **maleasa.** *n.* Fish sp.?: tang?

(a kind of *igauli?).*

MALEMO
B malemo. *a.* Drown.
B 1 malemoanga. *n.* —.
BE hagamalemo. *v.* —.
BE1 hagamalemoanga. *n.* —.
P maalemo. *a.* —.
PE hagamaalemo. *v.* —.
PE1 hagamaalemoanga. *n.* —.
R malemalemo. *a.* [var. of *malemolemo*].
R malemolemo. *a.* A careless diver (who is frequently almost drowned).
RE hagamalemalemo. *v.* To swim with one's nose barely out of the water (as do small children).
RE hagamalemolemo. *v.* [var. of *hagamalemalemo*].
RE1 hagamalemalemoanga. *n.* —.
RE1 hagamalemolemoanga. *n.* [var. of *hagamalemalemoanga*].

MALEVA
B maleva. *a.* Present (not absent).
BE hagamaleva. *v.* —.
P maaleva. *a.* —.
PE hagamaaleva. *v.* —.

MALIE
B malie. *mv.* Good at; good (of food or certain activities only); of exceptional quality.
XCO alo-malie. *a.* Coconut meat (fully mature) of good quality for eating.
XCO gaimalie. *a.* Good at food preparation (not wasteful).
XCO kanamalie. *a.* Tasty (especially of taro).
XCO laumalie. *a.* Big, great.
XCO limamalie. *a.* Good at massaging.
XE hagaalo-malie. *v.* Cause to become *alomalie.*
ID gide malie. Get in the habit of.
ID kano malie. A tasty tuber of good quality.
ID ngudu malie. Eloquent (of a person).
CF hinangalomalie. Feel happy or contented or at peace with the world.
CF umalie. Delicious (of pandanus only).

MALIE$_a$
B lamallie. *a.* Bearing big nuts (of coconut trees).
BE hagalamallie. *v.* —.
R lamalamallie. *a.* —.
RE hagalamalamallie. *v.* —.
ID gaadinga lamallie. A coconut with an unusually large-sized kernel.

MALIE$_b$
B gamalie. *a.* Do attentively.
ID dee gamalie. Do very attentively.
ID deengaa gamalie. Let's do it attentively!

MALILI$_1$
B malili$_1$. *a.* Fall out little by little (as hair, or sand when it is poured); powdered (soap, etc.).
B 1 malilianga. *n.* —.
BE hagamalili. *v.* —.
BE1 hagamalilianga. *n.* —.
P maalili. *a.* —.
P 1 maalilianga. *n.* —.
PE hagamaalili. *v.* —.
PE1 hagamaalilianga. *n.* —.
R malillili. *a.* Easily made *malili*; to feel the nibbling of fish on a fishing line.
R 1 malillilianga. *n.* —.
RE hagamalillili. *v.* —.
RE1 hagamalillilianga. *n.* —.
ID malili gelegele. Producing hard crumbs when eaten or broken.

MALILI$_2$
B malili$_2$. *n.* Fish sp.: goatfish.

MALINO
B malino. *v.* Calm (weather), still (wind).
B 1 malinoanga. *n.* —.

B 2 **malinongia.** *v.* Be calmed (e.g., seas).
BE **hagamalino.** *v.* —; smooth seas.
BE1 **hagamalinoanga.** *n.* —.
BE2 **hagamalinongia.** *v.* —.
P **maalino.** *v.* —.
P 1 **maalinoanga.** *n.* —.
P 2 **maalinongia.** *v.* —.
PE **hagamaalino.** *v.* —.
PE1 **hagamaalinoanga.** *n.* —.
PE2 **hagamaalinongia.** *v.* —.
R **malimalino.** *v.* Becoming more and more *malino.*
R 1 **malimalinoanga.** *n.* —.
R 2 **malimalinongia.** *v.* —.
RE **hagamalimalino.** *v.* —.
RE1 **hagamalimalinoanga.** *n.* —.
RE2 **hagamalimalinongia.** *v.* —.
S **malinolino.** *v.* [= *malimalino*].
S 1 **malinolinoanga.** *n.* —.
S 2 **malinolinongia.** *v.* —.
SE **hagamalinolino.** *v.* —.
SE1 **hagamalinolinoanga.** *n.* —.
SE2 **hagamalinolinongia.** *v.* —.
ID **dau malino.** An area of the sea which is dead calm.
ID **doo mai de malino.** Completely calm.

MALINGALINGA
B **malingalinga.** *n.* Sideburns (of hair).

MALO
B **malo.** *n.* Clothes, cloth.
BE **hagamalo.** *v.* Provide clothes for.
XFL **malo-ngiso.** *n.* Driftwood sp. [used for making planks].
ID **ahi malo.** A mat wrapping for clothes.
ID **bulubulu malo.** Rag.
ID **dala malo.** Change clothes.
ID **hhuge age malo.** Lift up one's skirts (to expose one's genitals).
ID **malo diadia.** Mending holes in clothes by running threads crisscross across the hole.
ID **malo gahu.** Shirt.
ID **malo gahu de boo.** Sheet, blanket.
ID **malo gulu.** Barkcloth [made from the inner skin of the breadfruit].
ID **malo haahine.** A dress (female clothing).
ID **malo huna.** Breechclout.
ID **malo lau manu.** Cloth with a flowered pattern.
ID **malo maadolu.** Heavy clothing.
ID **malo sabo.** Breechclout.
ID **vai malo.** Perfume.

MALOGU
B **malogu.** *v.* [= *ngalogu*].
B 1 **malogunga.** *n.* —.
BE **hagamalogu.** *v.* —.
BE1 **hagamalogunga.** *n.* —.
P **maalogu.** *v.* —.
P 1 **maalogunga.** *n.* —.
PE **hagamaalogu.** *v.* —.
PE1 **hagamaalogunga.** *n.* —.
R **malogulogu.** *v.* —.
R 1 **malogulogunga.** *n.* —.
RE **hagamalogulogu.** *v.* —.
RE1 **hagamalogulogunga.** *n.* —.

MALU
B **malu.** *v.* Shade (under trees); lee (of wind).
B 1 **maalunga.** *n.* —.
BE **hagamalu.** *v.* —.
R **malumalu.** *v.* —.
RE **hagamalumalu.** *v.* —.
XCO **malumalu-tangohi.** *a.* The light after sunset; twilight (in the evening).
ID **malu gohu.** Becoming darker (as when the sky becomes overcast).
ID **malumalu de me.** Cloudy day (not bright).

MALUA
B **malua.** *n.* Vagina.

MALUU
B **maluu.** *v.* Soft.
B 1 **maluunga.** *n.* —.
BE **hagamaluu.** *v.* —.
BE1 **hagamaluunga.** *n.* —.

MALUULU
B **maluulu.** *a.* Cool.
B 1 **maluulunga.** *n.* —.
BE **hagamaluulu.** *v.* —; to

water (plants).
BE1 **hagamaluulunga.** *n.* —.
ID **maluulu de me.** The weather is cold!

MAMA
B **mama.** *n.* Dust, gas, steam, vapor, fumes, spray (e.g., of waves).
ID **buu de mama.** Air filled with *mama.*
ID **hano de mama.** Escaping fumes (from a poorly sealed container).

MAMI
B **mami.** *v.* Taste (of something).
B 1 **maminga.** *n.* —.
B 2 **mamia.** *v.* —.
BE **hagamami.** *v.* —; add flavor to.
BE1 **hagamaminga.** *n.* —.
BE2 **hagamamia.** *v.* —.
R **mammami.** *a.* Delicious.
R 1 **mammamianga.** *n.* —.
RE **hagamammami.** *v.* —.
RE1 **hagamammamianga.** *n.* —.
ID **mami age.** Taste (something) a little bit.
ID **mami ange.** Taste (food).

MAMU
B **mamu.** *n.* Fish (the generic term — cf. Ponapean *mam*).
R **mammamu.** *n.* Fish (in children's speech only).
XFL **mamu-duagaa.** *n.* Fish sp.: stingray?
XFL **mamu-honga-dai.** *n.* Fish sp.: anchovy?, silversides (small)?
XFL **mamu-lalo-beau.** *n.* Fish sp.: wrasse.
XFL **mamu-madohi-lua.** *n.* Fish sp.: parrot fish.
ID **bae mamu.** Fish weir.
ID **dada mamu.** An impatient fisherman.
ID **dau mamu.** The season in which fish are abundant.
ID **dui mamu.** A string of fish.
ID **gai mamu dua nnui.** To eat fish up (not saving any for later).
ID **hadu o de mamu.** The hard stomach-like organ of certain fish.
ID **hidi de mamu dunu.** Curling up of fish (when cooked).
ID **mamu de lagi.** The fish which live beyond the outer reef.
ID **siga de mamu.** An escape of fish from a fishing net (through its holes).
ID **ulungaa mamu.** A pair of copulating fish, (or turtles, or whales, or stingrays).
ID **ungaa mamu.** A school of fish.

MANA
B **mana.** *n.* Supernatural power.

MANAUNAU
B **manaunau.** *v.* Act crazy or insane.
B 1 **manaunaunga.** *n.* —.
B 2 **manaunaua.** *v.* Crazy, insane.
BE **hagamanaunau.** *v.* —.
BE1 **hagamanaunaunga.** *n.* —.
BE2 **hagamanaunaua.** *v.* —.

MANAVA
B **manava.** *a.* Breath, breathe; having a good lung capacity (able to remain under water for a long time).
B 1 **manavaanga.** *n.* —.
BE **hagamanava.** *v.* —.
BE1 **hagamanavaanga.** *n.* —.
PE **hagamaanava.** *v.* —.
PE1 **hagamaanavaanga.** *n.* —.
R **manamanava.** *a.* [= *manavanava*].
R 1 **manamanavaanga.** *n.* —.
RE **hagamanamanava.** *v.* —.
RE1 **hagamanamanavaanga.** *n.* —.
S **manavanava.** *a.* Breathing.
S 1 **manavanavaanga.** *n.* —.
SE **hagamanavanava.** *v.* —.
SE1 **hagamanavanavaanga.** *n.* —.
ID **pono age de manava.** Be unable to breathe.

ID **dee manava age.** Do earnestly.
ID **gabe manava.** Eat sparingly (just enough to maintain one's strength), have a snack.
ID **hadu manava.** Heart.
ID **hagammae manava.** Tease cruelly.
ID **magi dee manava.** Asthma.
ID **manava bodo.** Shortness of breath.
ID **manava duuia.** Nervous, apprehensive (suddenly).
ID **manava i lunga.** Sigh (an intake of air) [a sign of emotion].
ID **manavanava gimoo.** Panting (as when short of breath).
ID **ssae de manava.** Struggle to breathe.

MANAVA$_a$
B **manavasaa.** *a.* Worried, apprehensive, fearful.
B 1 **manavasaanga.** *n.* —.
BE **hagamanavasaa.** *a.* Risky, dangerous.
BE1 **hagamanavasaanga.** *n.* —.

MANENGA
B **manenga.** *n.* Fish sp. (= a very large *balagia*, 3-4 feet long).
ID **huluhulu-manenga.** The tenth number of a counting game played to determine who is "it" (= the person who becomes "it").

MANIDA
BE **hagamanida.** *v.* Lift (something) up.
BE1 **hagamanidaanga.** *n.* —.

MANIGANGI
B **manigangi.** *a.* Satisfied completely in sexual intercourse.
B 1 **manigangianga.** *n.* —.
BE **hagamanigangi.** *v.* —.
BE1 **hagamanigangianga.** *n.* —.

MANINI
B **manini.** *n.* Fish sp.: convict tang.

MANO
B **mano.** *an.* Thousand.
BE **hagamano.** *v.* Make a total of one thousand.
P **mmano.** *a.* Thousands.
PE **hagammano.** *v.* —.
R **manomano.** *an.* Thousands and thousands.
RE **hagamanomano.** *v.* Make many thousands.

MANOGO
B **manogo.** *n.* Fish sp.: goby.

MANONGI
B **manongi.** *a.* Fragrant; fragrance (esp. of flowers or perfume).
BE **hagamanongi.** *v.* —.
P **maanongi.** *a.* —.
PE **hagamaanongi.** *v.* —.

MANU
B **manu$_1$.** *v.* Animal, plant (flora); coral head; throat spacer of a flying fish net.
B 2 **manua.** *v.* Diseased.
BE **hagamanu.** *v.* Cause to have disease.
BE2 **hagamanua.** *v.* —.
E **mmanu.** *v.* Do (something).
EE **hagammanu.** *v.* —.
R **manumanu.** *v.* Insect sp.
RE **hagamanumanu.** *v.* —.
RE2 **hagamanumanua.** *v.* —.
XFL **damaa-manu.** *n.* Bird sp.: sharp-tailed sandpiper (*Erolia acuminata*).
XFL **manu-a-tababa.** *n.* Plant sp.: cycad plant [indigenous?] (*Cycas circinalis* L.).
XFL **manu-alioo.** *n.* Plant sp.: a variety of taro.
XFL **manu-a-luga.** *n.* Insect sp.: fruit fly.
XFL **manu-a-madaligi.** *n.* Bird sp.: short-tailed shearwater (*Puffinus tenuirostris*).
XFL **manu-daa-uga.** *n.* [= *goehau*].
XFL **manu-de-boo.** *n.* Centipede.
XFL **manu-de-bua.** *n.* Bird sp.: sacred kingfisher (*Halcyon sancta*) (The

native term applies possibly to several spp.).

XFL **manu-de-hala.** *n.* Insect sp.: walkingstick (a very large grasshopper-like insect).

XFL **manu-de-laama.** *n.* Any of the small flying insects which swarm near a light.

XFL **manu-gaba-aasanga.** *n.* Plant sp.: beach naupaka shrub (*Scaevola taccada* (Gaertn.) Roxb.).

XFL **manu-gadi-niho.** *n.* Plant sp. [used to make loose teeth firm].

XFL **manu-gili-maau.** *n.* Plant sp.: heliotrope (*Tournefortia argentea* L., = *Messerschmidia argentea* L.).

XFL **manu-kono$_1$.** *n.* Bird sp. [probably the original Nukuoro name for the *ginuede*].

XFL **manu-kono$_2$.** *n.* Pigeon [an imported sp.].

XFL **manu-hagadigedige.** *n.* Mollusk sp.: cone shell.

XFL **manu-hai-hagahoa.** *n.* Millipede.

XFL **manu-hai-hau.** *n.* Mollusk sp. [a recently coined name, = spp. of *sisi*].

XFL **manu-lalo-de-gelegele.** *n.* Mantis shrimp.

XFL **manu-ligi.** *v.* Lice (immature); louse (immature).

XFL **manu-manga-lua.** *n.* Insect sp.: scorpion.

XFL **manu-mangamanga$_1$.** *n.* Starfish.

XFL **manu-mangamanga$_2$.** *n.* Plant sp.: paco fern (*Athyrium* sp.).

XFL **manu-mangamanga-i-lote-aasanga.** *n.* Serpent cucumber.

XFL **manu-mmala.** *n.* Plant sp.: glory bower (*Clerodendrum inerne* (L.) Gaertn.).

XFL **manu-solo-maanu.** *n.* A jellyfish-like animal in the shape of a flower (burrows into the sand when touched).

XG **manu solo laagau.** File (for filing wood).

XG **manu solo maadau.** File (for filing metal).

ID **abo manu.** To correct someone without justification.

ID **bongaa manu.** Large, exposed roots (e.g., of the breadfruit tree).

ID **boo manu.** To weed (a garden).

ID **dada manu.** To snare birds (with a loop on the end of a pole).

ID **dalaa manu.** Piece of broken glass.

ID **daumaha de manu.** Christmas Eve fete in the church at which "Santa Claus" appears.

ID **dau manu.** Flock of birds (feeding on a school of fish).

ID **diinei de manu.** To kill off plants.

ID **doga de manu.** Nesting of *gadada*, or *gaalau*, or *gailulu*.

ID **dolodolo manu ligi.** The physical sensation (like bugs crawling on one) after one's leg, etc., has been asleep.

ID **dui manu.** A line of flying birds.

ID **duuduu manu.** A diving platform (made from a tree stuck in a coral head).

ID **giado manu.** The smaller outrigger booms at the ends of the canoe.

ID **gini manu.** Pick flowers.

ID **goli manu.** Pick flowers.

ID **haa manu.** The young (of an animal) born at the same time (e.g., a litter, etc.); the offspring of (sharing the characteristics of).

ID **hagadubu manu baabaa.** The name of a certain type of string figure.

ID **hagadubu o manu.** The name of a certain type of string figure.

ID **hai be se manu.**

Promiscuous (especially if indiscreet or known to have sexual relations with one's own relatives).
ID **hau manu.** A garland of flowers, headdress, necklace.
ID **(de) hine hai be.** Whore.
ID **hua manu.** Fruit.
ID **hulu manu.** Feathers.
ID **labu manu.** To pet (pets, children, or a member of the opposite sex).
ID **lau manu.** Leaf of a plant.
ID **lavalava lau manu.** A sarong of material with a flowered pattern.
ID **lolo manu-de-boo.** A type of medicine (made from coconut oil and centipedes).
ID **malo lau manu.** Cloth with a flowered pattern.
ID **manu aabi.** Kite.
ID **manu dabeo.** Trees and shrubs which grow as weeds.
ID **manu de gabadanga.** The bird leading a flock (of *ngongo*) to a school of fish [the one fisherman watch].
ID **manu de henua.** Nukuoro varieties of swamp taro (*Cyrtosperma*).
ID **manu dolodolo.** Land animal.
ID **manu dudu dangada.** Insect sp. (= *manu-de-laama*) [poisonous].
ID **manu ea.** Coral head (at or broaching the surface of the water).
ID **manu gaugau.** Plant sp.: a variety of taro.
ID **manu hagadigedige.** Top (toy).
ID **manu hale moni.** A pottery bottle or jar.
ID **manu hao vai.** A bottle (of glass).
ID **manu ina.** [= *manua*].
ID **manu lalo tai.** Sea shell.
ID **manu laosedi.** Sea animal; marine invertebrates.
ID **manu lele.** A bird.
ID **manu noodagi.** A plant which has been *noodagi*.
ID **senga manu.** Stupid (like an animal).
ID **sigi manu.** To transplant a plant.
ID **ulu manu.** Coral head (submerged).
CF **dalabaimanugadele.** Sharp (as a knife).
CF **hoimanu.** Fish sp.: eagle ray.

MANU$_a$
B **aamanu.** *v.* Coral (growing live on the reef); coral head.
ID **mulumulu aamanu.** Moss (on rocks or coral).

MANU$_b$
B **Manu$_2$.** *n.* March (month of).

MANUGIA
B **manugia.** *a.* To appear from time to time on the surface of the water.
B 1 **manugiaanga.** *n.* —.
BE **hagamanugia.** *v.* —.
BE1 **hagamanugiaanga.** *n.* —.
R **manumanugia.** *v.* —.
R 1 **manumanugiaanga.** *n.* —.
RE **hagamanumanugia.** *v.* —.
RE1 **hagamanumanugiaanga.** *n.* —.

MANUHI
B **manuhi.** *a.* Hemorrhage.
B 1 **manuhianga.** *n.* —.
BE **hagamanuhi.** *v.* —.
BE1 **hagamanuhianga.** *n.* —.
P **maanuhi.** *a.* —.
P 1 **maanuhianga.** *n.* —.
PE **hagamaanuhi.** *v.* —.
PE1 **hagamaanuhianga.** *n.* —.
R **manumanuhi.** *a.* Frequently *manuhi.*
R 1 **manumanuhianga.** *n.* —.
RE **hagamanumanuhi.** *v.* —.
RE1 **hagamanumanuhianga.** *n.* —.

MANUIA
B **manuia.** *a.* Fortunate, lucky, blessed.
B 1 **manuiaanga.** *n.* —.

BE hagamanuia. *v.* —; bless (someone).
BE1 hagamanuiaanga. *n.* —.

MANGA
B **manga.** *n.* A branch, part of (something having coordinate parts).
R **mangamanga.** *a.* Having many *manga.*
RE **hagamangamanga.** *v.* —; to move with the extremities spread out (as in trying to scare a child).
RE2 **hagamangamangalia.** *v.* —.
XCO **mada-umanga.** *n.* The bud of a Cyrtosperma taro corm.
XCO **umanga.** *n.* A bunch of *Cyrtosperma* taro corm buds planted together.
XFL **manu-manga-lua.** *n.* Insect sp.: scorpion.
XFL **manu-mangamanga$_1$.** *n.* Starfish.
XFL **manu-mangamanga$_2$.** *n.* Plant sp.: paco fern (*Athyrium* sp.).
ID **manga lua tae.** Cleft in the buttocks.

MANGALI
XCO **dilimangali.** *v.* To catch flying fish [from the Ponapean *indilmenger*?].

MANGEO
B **mangeo.** *v.* A large sore (on the body); a blemish (on the skin).
BE **hagamangeo.** *v.* —.
R **mangemangeo.** *v.* Covered with *mangeo.*
RE **hagamangemangeo.** *v.* —.
XFL **hadu-mangeo.** *n.* Cushion starfish.

MANGILA
B **mangila.** *n.* Plant sp. (a type of *ngaungau*).

MANGO
XCO **lolomango.** *n.* To clear oil (which is separated from crude coconut oil by heating).

MANGOO
B **mangoo.** *n.* Shark (the generic term).
XFL **mangoo-biho-lua.** *n.* Fish sp.: shark sp.
XFL **mangoo-dahola.** *n.* Fish sp.: blacktip shark.
XFL **mangoo-senga.** *n.* Fish sp.: shark sp.
ID **hagadubu mangoo.** The name of a certain type of string figure.

MAO
B **mao.** *d.* —.
B 1 **maoanga.** *n.* —.
BE **hagamao —.** *d.* —.
BE1 **hagamaonga.** *n.* —.
BE2 **hagamaoa.** *v.* —.
E **mmao.** *a.* Far, distant.
E 1 **mmaoanga.** *n.* —.
EE **hagammao.** *v.* —.
EE1 **hagammaonga.** *n.* —.
EE2 **hagammaoa.** *v.* —.
R **maomao.** *a.* More and more; diminishing rainfall.
RE **hagamaomao.** *v.* —.
RE1 **hagamaomaonga.** *n.* —.
RE2 **hagamaomaoa.** *v.* —.
ID **basa hagamao lalo.** Speak humbly.
ID **basa hagamao lunga.** Speak arrogantly.
ID **hagamao lalo.** Humble, modest.
ID **hagamao lunga.** Arrogant, haughty, overbearing, proud.
ID **lodo mao lalo.** Characteristically *hagamao lalo*; self-effacing, meek in spirit.
ID **lodo mao lunga.** Characteristically *hagamao lunga*; egotistical, self-centered, arrogant in spirit.
ID **mao denga ssave.** A scarcity of *ssave.*
ID **mao lalo.** Deep, low (in status).
ID **mao lunga.** High, high-ranking.

MAOLI
B maoli. *n.* A suspicion which proves to be true.

MASA
B masa. *a.* Empty, low (tide).
B 2 masaia. *v.* Trapped by low water (e.g., canoes, or fish on the reef at low tide).
B 2 masalia. *v.* Empty of water.
B 3 masaiaanga. *n.* —.
BE1 hagamaasanga$_1$. *n.* —.
BE2 hagamasaia. *v.* —.
BE2 hagamasalia. *v.* —.
BE3 hagamasaiaanga. *n.* —.
E mmasa. *a.* To be dry.
E 1 mmasaanga. *n.* —.
E 2 mmasalia. *a.* —.
EE hagammasa. *v.* —; dry (something).
EE1 hagammasaanga. *n.* —.
EE2 hagammasalia. *v.* —.
PE hagamaamasa. *v.* —.
PE1 hagamaamasaanga. *n.* —.
PE2 hagamaamasalia. *v.* —.
R masamasa. *a.* —.
R 3 masamasaiaanga. *n.* —.
RE hagamasamasa. *v.* —.
RE2 hagamasamasalia. *v.* —.
RE3 hagamasamasaiaanga. *n.* —.
T maamasa. *a.* [pl. of *masa*].
ID dau masa. The season during which tides are lowest.
ID masa bagubagu. Dry reef (at very low tide).
ID masa boo. Mornings following nights during which the tide has gone out (which are good for looking for fish trapped on the reef).
ID mmasa bagubagu. Hard and curled up owing to dryness.
CF massagaila. Incompletely cooked.
CF massagalala. Burned (food).

MASA$_a$
B massaganga. *v.* To be very dry.
BE hagamassaganga. *v.* —.

MASAALA
B masaala. *v.* Clear-headed.
B 1 masaalanga. *n.* —.
BE hagamasaala. *v.* —.
BE1 hagamasaalanga. *n.* —.

MASAGAGE
B masagage. *a.* Good at fighting.
B 1 masagageanga. *n.* —.
BE hagamasagage. *v.* —.
BE1 hagamasagageanga. *n.* —.
P masaagage. *a.* —.
PE hagamasaagage. *v.* —.
PE1 hagamasaagageanga. *n.* —.

MASAGI
B masagi. *n.* A dance (an ancient type).

MASALABA
B masalaba. *a.* Clear (not opaque or blurred); shiny (translucent).
B 1 masalabaanga. *n.* —.
BE hagamasalaba. *v.* —.

MASANA
B masana. *v.* Good (quality).
B 1 masanaanga. *n.* —.
BE hagamasana. *v.* —.
BE1 hagamasanaanga. *n.* —.
ID daane masana. Good one.

MASAUSAU
B masausau. *v.* Good at fighting.
B 1 masausaunga. *n.* —.
B 2 masausaua. *v.* Be *masausau*
BE hagamasausau. *v.* —.
BE1 hagamasausaunga. *n.* —.
BE2 hagamasausaua. *v.* —.

MASAVAA
B masavaa$_2$. *nl.* [var. of *magava*].
ID daa de masavaa. Time's up! It is time for...
ID honga de masavaa. At the time of.
ID masavaa alodahi. Always.
ID masavaa danuaa. A time of peace.
ID masavaa de gauligi. Childhood.
ID odi de masavaa. Having

insufficient time remaining for (something).
CF **savaa.** Soon (will happen).

MASI$_1$
B **masi.** *v.* To scrape or peel breadfruit when the breadfruit is ripe.
B 1 **maasinga.** *n.* —.
B 2 **masia.** *v.* —.
BE **hagamasi.** *v.* —.
BE1 **hagamaasinga.** *n.* —.
BE2 **hagamasia.** *v.* —.
R 1 **masimasinga$_1$.** *n.* —.
R 2 **masimasia.** *v.* —.
RE **hagamasimasi$_1$.** *v.* —.
RE1 **hagamasimasinga$_1$.** *n.* —.
RE2 **hagamasimasia.** *v.* —.

MASI$_2$
E **mmasi.** *a.* The ripened condition of the fruit of the pandanus (when the keys begin to fall).
E 1 **mmaasinga.** *n.* —.
EE **hagammasi.** *v.* —.
EE1 **hagammaasinga.** *n.* —.
R **masimasi$_1$.** *v.* —.
R **masimasi$_2$.** *a.* —.
R 1 **masimasinga$_2$.** *n.* —.
RE **hagamasimasi$_2$.** *v.* —.
RE1 **hagamasimasinga$_2$.** *n.* —.

MASI$_3$
R **masimasi$_3$.** *n.* Dolphin.

MASOASOA
B **masoasoa.** *a.* Spacious.
B 1 **masoasoaanga.** *n.* —.
BE **hagamasoasoa.** *v.* —.
BE1 **hagamasoasoaanga.** *n.* —.

MASOLE
B **masole.** *a.* Abraded (skin), scratched.
B 1 **masoleanga.** *n.* —.
BE **hagamasole.** *v.* —.
BE1 **hagamasoleanga.** *n.* —.
P **maasole.** *a.* —.
P 1 **maasoleanga.** *n.* —.
PE **hagamaasole.** *v.* —.
PE1 **hagamaasoleanga.** *n.* —.
R **masolesole.** *a.* *masole* in several places.
R 1 **masolesoleanga.** *n.* —.
RE **hagamasolesole.** *v.* —.
RE1 **hagamasolesoleanga.** *n.* —.
ID **masole ange.** Barely scratched.

MASSAA
B **massaa (ina).** *v.* Despised by others.
B 1 **massaanga.** *n.* —.
BE **hagamassaa.** *v.* —.
BE1 **hagamassaanga.** *n.* —.

MASSAGAILA
B **massagaila.** *v.* Incompletely cooked.
B 1 **massagailaanga.** *n.* —.
BE **hagamassagaila.** *v.* —.
BE1 **hagamassagailaanga.** *n.* —.

MASSAGALALA
B **massagalala.** *v.* Burned (food).
B 1 **massagalalaanga.** *n.* —.
BE **hagamassagalala.** *v.* —.
BE1 **hagamassagalalaanga.** *n.* —.

MASUI
B **masui.** *n.* Left (side).
B 1 **maasuinga.** *n.* —.
BE **hagamaasui.** *n.* A current which flows to the left.
ID **baasi masui.** Left side, left-handed.
ID **hilo hagamaasui.** To braid sennit with the left hand; [which is considered to give the best result].

MAU$_1$
B **mau$_1$.** *a.* To finish defecating.
B 1 **maunga$_1$.** *n.* —.
BE **hagamau$_1$.** *v.* —.
BE1 **hagamaunga$_1$.** *n.* —.
BE2 **hagamaua$_1$.** *v.* —.
BE2 **hagamaulia$_1$.** *v.* —.
P **mmau$_1$.** *a.* —.
P 1 **mmaunga$_1$.** *n.* —.
PE **hagammau$_1$.** *v.* —.
PE1 **hagammaunga$_1$.** *n.* —.
PE2 **hagammaua$_1$.** *v.* —.
PE2 **hagammaulia$_1$.** *v.* —.
R **maumau$_1$.** *a.* —.

R 1 **maumaunga₁.** *n.* —.
RE **hagamaumau₁.** *v.* —.
RE1 **hagamaumaunga₁.** *n.* —.
RE2 **hagamaumaua₁.** *v.* —.
RE2 **hagamaumaulia₁.** *v.* —.

MAU₂
B **mau₂.** *a.* Usual [sing.]; usually [sing.].
B 1 **maunga₂.** *n.* Way of becoming accustomed to.
BE **hagamau₂.** *v.* To strive to become acquainted with.
BE1 **hagamaunga₂.** *n.* —.
BE2 **hagamaua₂.** *v.* —.
BE2 **hagamaulia₂.** *v.* —.
E **mmau₂.** *a.* Mastered, memorized, known by heart; [pl. of *mau₂*].
E 1 **mmaunga₂.** *n.* Way of memorizing, (way of having memorized).
EE **hagammau₂.** *v.* Memorize.
EE1 **hagammaunga₂.** *n.* —.
EE2 **hagammaua₂.** *v.* —.
EE2 **hagammaulia₂.** *v.* —.
R **maumau₂.** *a.* —.
R 1 **maumaunga₂.** *n.* —.
RE **hagamaumau₂.** *v.* Study, attempt to memorize.
RE1 **hagamaumaunga₂.** *n.* —.
RE2 **hagamaumaua₂.** *v.* —.
RE2 **hagamaumaulia₂.** *v.* —.
ID **mau ange huu.** Usually.

MAU₃
B **mau₃.** *a.* Get, obtain, caught.
B 1 **maunga₃.** *n.* —.
B 2 **maua.** *a.* Able to, obtained, gotten, caught.
BE **hagamau₃.** *v.* —; tie up (by winding a rope around a pole).
BE1 **hagamaunga₃.** *n.* —.
BE2 **hagamaua₃.** *v.* —.
R **maumau₃.** *a.* —.
R 1 **maumaunga₃.** *n.* —.
RE **hagamaumau₃.** *v.* —.
RE1 **hagamaumaunga₃.** *n.* —.
RE2 **hagamaumaua₃.** *v.* —.
ID **lodo hagamau me.** Selfish with one's possessions, ungiving.
ID **maua laa.** Never mind!
ID **mau goloa.** Rich in material possessions.
ID **mau haahine.** Attractive to women (for some inexplicable reason).
ID **mau me.** Successful in obtaining what one wants (things).
ID **mmau gava.** Known by heart, memorized, know (how to do something) well.
ID **nnoo hagamau me.** Insatiably acquisitive.

ME
B **me.** *v.* Thing [a word which can substitute for any nominal, adjectival, or verbal notion].
BE **hagame (ange).** *a.* Move a little way toward —.
BE1 **hagameanga.** *n.* —.
RE **hagameme (iho).** *a.* Gradually decreasing (in noise level, force of wind, etc.).
RE1 **hagamemeanga.** *n.* —.
XCO **hagadau-me.** *a.* Enemy; dispute (with someone), argue.
XCO **ngudu-me.** *n.* Boundary of a taro plot.
XFL **gau-me.** *n.* Gill (of a fish).
ID **ago i me.** Copy, imitate.
ID **aloalo me.** The current nearest to the (seaward) outer reef of the atoll.
ID **ao de me.** Daytime.
ID **bagibagi de me.** All of a sudden (violent actions).
ID **booboo me.** Massage (as a medical treatment).
ID **boo gi me.** Acquisitive (and acting on acquisitive impulses).
ID **dada me.** To obtain taro (by pulling up the tubers).
ID **damaa me.** Small [sing.]; little; tiny.
ID **dangada hagao me.** Storekeeper.
ID **dangalebu de me.** Bad weather.
ID **dau me.** The sheath of the

flower of the coconut tree.

ID **deai loo me.** I doubt it!

ID **deai me ao ai.** Useless.

ID **deai me hagalongolongo.** Do unhesitatingly.

ID **deledele hainga a me.** Rush because of an emergency.

ID **doo ai me.** [= *doo me ai*].

ID **doo de gai me.** Miss a meal or meals (leading to nausea when eating is resumed).

ID **doo halehale me.** Risky, unreliable.

ID **doo i hainga a me.** Wait for a long time (beyond the time expected).

ID **doo me.** Plant things.

ID **doo me (ai).** Make fun of, ridicule.

ID **tangada dee doo gi de me.** Uncouth person.

ID **tangada hai me dabu.** Cult priest.

ID **tangi gi de me.** All of a sudden (an action not violent).

ID **gadagada doo me.** Laugh at.

ID **gai me.** Eat food.

ID **gai me hagadau doa.** Eat as though competing against other eaters in a test of manliness (e.g., to eat fish with the scales and all).

ID **gohu de me.** Become dark (with no natural light).

ID **golo me.** Unforgiving.

ID **kave huaame.** Take the whole thing.

ID **haahaula age de me.** Become bright (with morning sunlight).

ID **hagabudu me.** Selfish.

ID **hagadau hai me ai.** Use jointly or collectively.

ID **hagaduu me.** Miserly.

ID **hagatubu me.** Exaggerate matters.

ID **hagaloma de me.** Calm weather, with no noise.

ID **hagame ange laa.** A little later.

ID **hagangadi me.** Treat as unimportant; to sacrifice (not thinking of oneself).

ID **hagausiusi de me.** A sky covered with rain clouds.

ID **hagi me.** Pick coconuts.

ID **haihai me.** Be doing something suspicious.

ID **hai huaame.** Punctilious, be particular.

ID **hai huuhuaa me.** Sorcery.

ID **hai me.** Industrious.

ID **hai me a gauligi.** A childish act.

ID **hai me a gimoo.** To act insincerely.

ID **hai me a leangi.** Bad-mannered.

ID **hai me balavini.** To conduct oneself clumsily.

ID **hai me daahea.** Search for driftwood or other beached objects.

ID **hai me dagi.** Work slowly.

ID **hai me dogaa.** Behave with embarrassment or shyness.

ID **hai me dua nnui.** Do violently.

ID **hai me gaiaa.** To be reluctant to express oneself openly (esp. to persons in certain types of relationship to one).

ID **hai me galasi.** To steal after having sort of asked for.

ID **hai me gavia.** Do crazy things.

ID **hai me hagamadia.** Behave in a more-or-less show-off manner.

ID **hai me hebagi.** Be on the point of fighting.

ID **hai me hoosenga.** Somewhat *hoosenga*.

ID **hai me ma —.** Sort of —.

ID **hai me madua.** Act grown up.

ID **hai me moolau.** An habitually fast worker.

ID **hai me mudumudu.** A habitually *mudumudu*.

ID **hai me mulegi.** To show off (esp. in front of members of the opposite sex).

ID **hai me mule me.** Habitually slow or late.

ID **hai naa hanu me.** Something will happen...
ID **haingaa me.** Work requiring a large work force.
ID **hai vaivai me.** Have sexual relations.
ID **hale hagao me.** Store.
ID **halehale me.** A developing situation.
ID **halehale me donu huu.** Surprisingly, it turned out to be possible!
ID **hanu me.** A secret friend of the opposite sex.
ID **hilohilo me.** Impure.
ID **huaa me.** A coconut (for drinking); the whole thing.
ID **huahuaa me.** [var. of *huuhuaa me*].
ID **huna me.** A habitual thief.
ID **huuhuaa me.** Sorcery (made with chants).
ID **i dahi me.** Each, apiece.
ID **iloo me.** Charlatanism.
ID **lahu me.** Inclined to be suspicious.
ID **laohie de me.** Good weather (dry).
ID **lau me.** Adjacent (of taro plots only).
ID **lodo gi me.** Acquisitive, covetous.
ID **lodo hagamau me.** Selfish with one's possessions, ungiving.
ID **lodo me muimui.** In the bush (uncleared area).
ID **mago de me.** A worsening condition of the weather.
ID **malumalu de me.** Cloudy day (not bright).
ID **maluulu de me.** The weather is cold!
ID **mau me.** Successful in obtaining what one wants (things).
ID **me abadai.** European things (gear, etc.).
ID **me abasasa.** European things (gear, etc.).
ID **me abo (donu).** Truth.
ID **me abo donu.** Real, true.
ID **me aha ai.** What for?
ID **me ange laa.** The others.
ID **me balabala.** The soft spot on an infant's head; genitals (of males or females).
ID **me boogia e de eidu.** A black spot on the skin (like a bruise) noticed after sleeping.
ID **me bouli.** The deepest part of the lagoon.
ID **me pasa.** Radio.
ID **me pilo aha.** What's the point of doing this?
ID **me dau.** Thing of importance, worthwhile.
ID **me de lodo.** A fishing place (in the lagoon).
ID **me dili dai.** Any current which flows away from the atoll.
ID **me dili uda.** An ocean current which comes towards the atoll.
ID **me duu.** Clitoris.
ID **me tao.** Dye.
ID **me-e-ligi.** Taro corm (small).
ID **me gaha dea.** A coconut which is nearly mature.
ID **me gee.** A coconut without any meat.
ID **me gu modu.** Decision.
ID **me hagaahulu.** Prepared food.
ID **me hagadaahao.** Toy.
ID **me hagalolo.** A type of prepared food (made from taro and coconut cream).
ID **me hagaodi.** Last one.
ID **me hagasaga.** A toy (made from a dried breadfruit leaf or a disk of coconut shell) which slides when thrown.
ID **me hagasahu vai.** Gutter (under the eaves of a house).
ID **me hagasengasenga.** Riddle, parable.
ID **me hagasili.** A plant which is allowed to grow extra large (for some reason).
ID **me hakadanga.** Joke, jest;

trick (a practical joke).
ID **me hai ada.** Camera.
ID **me hai dago.** Ritual acts, religious acts.
ID **me hai laangi.** Calandar.
ID **me hanga dalogo.** Ingredients of *dalogo.*
ID **me hhadu.** Falsehood, lie.
ID **me hhadu hugadoo.** It's a lie!
ID **me hholu.** Bow (for an arrow).
ID **me madaali.** A ripe coconut (= *gaadinga*) of poor quality.
ID **me maimai.** Candy.
ID **me mmala.** Bile.
ID **me mmilo.** Current (in the sea).
ID **me naa gi —.** I wish that...
ID **me ne modu.** Decision.
ID **me osi.** A coconut tree seedling.
ID **me ssalu lau.** A scraper for leaves.
ID **me ssongo aha.** Useless thing.
ID **me vae.** Shoes, slippers.
ID **mmene ono me.** To be unable to go to the toilet, owing to the approach of people.
ID **nnoo hagamau me.** Insatiably acquisitive.
ID **ngadi me.** Nothing, unimportant, useless, worthless.
ID **se me be hee.** Extraordinary or unusual (esp. in size).
ID **se me gi hee.** In which direction is the current running?
ID **ungaa me.** A section of the village; village.
ID **vaivai me.** A disgusting business; genitals (of males or females).
ID **vele me.** To weed (a garden).

MEA
B **mea.** *d.* Red.
E **mmea.** *a.* Red.
E 1 **mmeaanga.** *n.* —.
EE **hagammea.** *v.* —.
EE1 **hagammeaanga.** *n.* —.
R **meamea —.** *a.* Becoming red.
R 1 **meameaanga.** *n.* —.
RE **hagameamea.** *v.* —.
RE1 **hagameameaanga.** *n.* —.
XCO **aloalo-mea.** *a.* Becoming red (of fully mature coconut meat).
XCO **alo-mea.** *a.* Reddish color (of fully mature coconut meat).
XE **hagaaloalo-mea.** *v.* Cause to become red (of fully mature coconut meat).
XE **hagaalo-mea.** *v.* Cause to be red (of fully mature coconut meat).
XFL **anga-mea.** *n.* Fish sp. (= large *dada*).
XFL **dalia-mea.** *n.* Mollusk sp.: *Mitra mitra.*
XFL **gelemea.** *n.* A by-product of the tumeric-making process.
XFL **ua-mea.** *n.* Bird sp.: red-throated frigate bird.
ID **baalanga mmea.** Copper or brass or other reddish metal.
ID **dala mmea.** Redness or inflammation of the skin (e.g., a welt).
ID **gaha mea.** Having orange coconuts (of a coconut tree).
ID **mmea be se gaagose.** Red hot (literally).
ID **vai mea.** A reddish discharge from the genitalia (of either males or females).
CF **oomea.** Afternoon (late).

MELE[1]
B **mele**[1]. *v.* To use a word or expression idiosyncratically in speech.
B 1 **meelenga.** *n.* —.
B 2 **melea.** *v.* —.
BE **hagamele.** *v.* [var. of *haigamaiana*].
BE1 **hagameelenga.** *n.* —.

BE2	**hagamelea.** *v.* —.
P	**mmele.** *v.* —.
PE	**hagammele.** *v.* —.
R	**melemele.** *v.* —.
R 1	**melemelenga.** *n.* —.
R 2	**melemelea.** *v.* —.
RE	**hagamelemele.** *v.* —.
RE1	**hagamelemelenga.** *n.* —.
RE2	**hagamelemelea.** *v.* —.

MELE$_2$

B	**mele$_2$.** *mt.* HYPOTHETICAL ASPECT MARKER; one assumes...; it would appear that...

MENE

E	**mmene.** *a.* To contract inside of (like a marine invertebrate inside a shell); detumescence; a sudden loss of desire (e.g., to defecate when people approach).
E 1	**mmeneanga.** *n.* —.
E 2	**mmenelia.** *v.* —.
E 2	**mmenengia.** *v.* —.
EE	**hagammene.** *v.* —.
EE1	**hagammeneanga.** *n.* —.
EE2	**hagammenelia.** *v.* —.
EE2	**hagammenengia.** *v.* —.
R	**menemene.** *a.* —; male genital organ, penis.
R 1	**menemeneanga.** *n.* —.
RE	**hagamenemene.** *v.* —.
RE1	**hagamenemeneanga.** *n.* —.
RE2	**hagamenemenelia.** *v.* —.
RE2	**hagamenemenengia.** *v.* —.
ID	**hagammene dua.** Go backwards (esp. a canoe).
ID	**mmenengia mai.** Discourage (someone) about something.
ID	**mmene ono me.** To be unable to go to the toilet, owing to the approach of people.

MIDI$_1$

B	**midi$_1$.** *v.* Dream.
B 1	**miidinga$_1$.** *n.* —.
B 2	**midia.** *v.* Dream about.
BE	**hagamidi.** *v.* —; appear in a dream.
BE1	**hagamiidinga$_1$.** *n.* —.
BE2	**hagamidia.** *v.* —.
R	**midimidi$_1$.** *v.* —.
R 1	**midimidinga$_1$.** *n.* —.
RE	**hagamidimidi$_1$.** *v.* —.
RE1	**hagamidimidinga$_1$.** *n.* —.
RE2	**hagamidimidia$_1$.** *v.* —.
ID	**midia ange.** Dream about.

MIDI$_2$

B	**midi$_2$.** *d.* —.
B 1	**miidinga$_2$.** *n.* —.
BE1	**hagamiidinga$_2$.** *n.* —.
BE2	**hagamiidia.** *v.* —.
E	**mmidi.** *v.* Suck, suction (e.g., of sea current).
E 2	**miidia.** *v.* —.
EE	**hagammidi.** *v.* Suction of a sea current, undertow.
R	**midimidi$_2$.** *v.* —.
R 1	**midimidinga$_2$.** *n.* —.
R 2	**midimidia.** *v.* —.
RE	**hagamidimidi$_2$.** *v.* Having a strong undertow.
RE1	**hagamidimidinga$_2$.** *n.* —.
RE2	**hagamidimidia$_2$.** *v.* —.

MIDO

R	**midomido.** *n.* End of (e.g., a stick).
ID	**duu midomido.** An abrupt stop of a trajectory (because one end of the missile has dug into the ground, etc.).

MIILI

B	**miili.** *a.* A type of game [introduced?].
B 1	**miilinga$_3$.** *n.* —.
BE	**hagamiili.** *v.* —.
BE1	**hagamiilinga.** *n.* —.
ID	**miili aheahe.** A version of the game called *miili.*

MILI$_1$

B	**mili$_1$ —.** *d.* —.
B 1	**miilinga$_1$.** *n.* —.
B 2	**miilia.** *v.* —.
BE	**hagamili$_1$.** *v.* —.
BE1	**hagamiilinga$_1$.** *n.* —.
BE2	**hagamiilia.** *v.* —.
E	**mmili$_1$.** *v.* To crush, to pulverize; rub back and

forth in the hands (like a fire drill).

EE **hagammili$_1$.** *v.* —.
R **milimili$_1$.** *v.* —.
R 1 **milimilinga$_1$.** *n.* —.
R 2 **milimilia.** *v.* —.
RE **hagamilimili$_1$.** *v.* —.
RE1 **hagamilimilinga$_1$.** *n.* —.
RE2 **hagamilimilia$_1$.** *v.* —.

MILI$_2$

B **mili$_2$.** *a.* Fruitful, fructiferous.
B 1 **miilinga$_2$.** *n.* —.
BE **hagamili$_2$.** *v.* —.
BE1 **hagamiilinga$_2$.** *n.* —.
BE2 **hagamilia.** *v.* —.
P **mmili$_2$.** *v.* —.
P 1 **mmiilinga.** *n.* —.
PE **hagammili$_2$.** *v.* —.
PE1 **hagammiilinga.** *n.* —.
PE2 **hagammiilia.** *v.* —.
R **milimili$_2$.** *v.* —.
R 1 **milimilinga$_2$.** *n.* —.
RE **hagamilimili$_2$.** *v.* —.
RE1 **hagamilimilinga$_2$.** *n.* —.
RE2 **hagamilimilia$_2$.** *v.* —.

MILO$_1$

B **milo$_1$.** *v.* Twist, turn (something, as a faucet), wind, wring.
B 1 **miilonga.** *n.* —.
B 1 **milosanga.** *n.* The way in which current flows.
B 2 **miloa.** *v.* —.
B 2 **milosia.** *v.* —; to be taken away by a current.
BE **hagamilo.** *v.* —.
BE1 **hagamiilonga.** *n.* —.
BE1 **hagamilosanga.** *n.* —.
BE2 **hagamiloa.** *v.* —.
BE2 **hagamilosia.** *v.* —; to be carried away by a current.
P **mmilo.** *v.* —; the flow of a current.
P 1 **mmiilonga.** *n.* —.
P 1 **mmilosanga.** *n.* A confluence of currents (from below the surface of the sea).
PE **hagammilo.** *v.* —.
PE1 **hagammiilonga.** *n.* —.
PE1 **hagammilosanga.** *n.* —.
R **milomilo.** *v.* —; a whorl in the hair.
R 1 **milomilonga.** *n.* —.
R 1 **milomilosanga.** *n.* The way in which a current moves about.
RE **hagamilomilo.** *v.* —.
RE1 **hagamilomilonga.** *n.* —.
RE1 **hagamilomilosanga.** *n.* —.
RE2 **hagamilomiloa.** *v.* —.
RE2 **hagamilomilosia.** *v.* —; to be carried away by a current repeatedly or continually.
ID **laangai milo sanga.** A fishing condition in which fish are not inclined to bite.
ID **me mmilo.** Current (in the sea).
ID **milo gee.** To turn the opposite way.

MILO$_2$

B **milo$_2$.** *n.* Plant sp.: tree sp.: milo tree (*The spesiapopulnea* Sol. ex Correa).

MIMI

B **mimi.** *a.* Urinate.
B 1 **mimianga.** *n.* —.
BE **hagamimi.** *v.* —.
BE1 **hagamimianga.** *n.* —.
BE2 **hagamimia.** *v.* —.
R **mimmimi.** *a.* —.
R 1 **mimmimianga.** *n.* —.
RE **hagamimmimi.** *v.* —.
RE1 **hagamimmimianga.** *n.* —.
RE2 **hagamimmimia.** *v.* —.

MISI

B **misi.** *a.* A sound made by sucking through pursed lips [like a stage kiss].
B 1 **miisinga.** *n.* —.
BE **hagamisi.** *v.* —.
BE1 **hagamiisinga.** *n.* —.
BE2 **hagamisia.** *v.* —.
R **misimisi.** *a.* —.
R 1 **misimisinga.** *n.* —.
RE **hagamisimisi.** *v.* —.
RE1 **hagamisimisinga.** *n.* —.
RE2 **hagamisimisia.** *v.* —.

MMALA

B **mmala.** *a.* Bitter, sour; unlucky.
B 1 **mmalaanga.** *n.* —.
BE **hagammala.** *v.* —.
BE1 **hagammalaanga.** *n.* —.
XFL **manu-mmala.** *n.* Plant sp.: glory bower (*Clerodendrum inerne* (L.) Gaertn.).
ID **me mmala.** Bile.
ID **mmala dana (dagu) maanga.** Lose his (my) appetite.
ID **mmala luu mada.** Stinging of one's eyes (e.g., from salt water).

MMAU

BE **hagammau$_3$.** *a.* Poisonous.
BE1 **hagammauanga.** *n.* —.
ID **hagammau de ngudu.** Argumentative in a disrespectful way.

MMUDI

E **mmudi.** *a.* Sprinkling (of rain).
E 1 **mmuudinga.** *n.* —.
EE **hagammudi.** *v.* —.
EE1 **hagammuudinga.** *n.* —.
EE2 **hagammudia.** *v.* —.
R **mudimudi.** *a.* —.
R 1 **mudimudinga.** *n.* —.
RE **hagamudimudi.** *v.* —.
RE1 **hagamudimudinga.** *n.* —.
RE2 **hagamudimudia.** *v.* —.

MMUNI

B **mmuni.** *a.* Hidden, hide.
B 1 **muuninga.** *n.* —.
BE **hagammuni.** *v.* Hide (something) from.
BE1 **hagamuuninga.** *n.* —.
BE2 **hagamuunia.** *v.* —.
R **munimuni.** *a.* —.
R 1 **munimuninga.** *n.* —.
RE **hagamunimuni.** *v.* —.
RE1 **hagamunimuninga.** *n.* —.
RE2 **hagamunimunia.** *v.* —.
ID **duu munimuni.** Hide and seek (a game).
ID **hagammuni iho.** Keep to oneself (what one has done).

MOA

B **moa$_1$.** *n.* Bird sp.
XFL **moa-a-daila.** *n.* Bird sp. (= large *moa*).

MOAGA

B **moaga.** *n.* Fish sp.: goatfish.

MOAHULU

B **moahulu.** *n.* Fish sp.: goatfish.

MOANA

B **moana.** *n.* Open sea, the atmosphere.
ID **aadea moana.** Unobstructed.
ID **aalo lo te moana.** A disturbance (local) of air.
ID **dangalebu de moana.** Rough or choppy seas.
ID **gainga o de moana.** Fish (when abundant in the ocean nearby).
ID **gano moana.** Open sea, far away from any land.
ID **hadu de moana.** A type of string figure.
ID **hano i luu moana.** Die (a person).
ID **laangai huli de moana.** A fishing condition in which tuna are jumping (showing their white bellies) and biting.
ID **laangai ngadi moana.** A fishing condition in which tuna are biting, but do not appear in schools.
ID **langa de moana.** Becoming stormy (of the sea).
ID **moana dabeo.** Rough seas.
ID **moana dugidugi.** Far from any land, in the open sea.
ID **moana magalili.** A cold underwater current.
ID **moana ngaadai.** Far from land (the place from which the atoll is just barely visible).
ID **ngadi moana.** [= *laangai ngadi moana*].

ID siia gi moana ngaadai. Drift downwind, away from land.

MODI
R **modimodi.** *a.* Walk stealthily in a crouch.
R 1 **modimodinga.** *n.* —.
RE **hagamodimodi.** *v.* —.
RE1 **hagamodimodinga.** *n.* —.

MODO
B **modo.** *a.* Unripe.
B 1 **moodonga.** *n.* —.
B 2 **modolia.** *v.* —.
BE **hagamodo.** *v.* —.
BE1 **hagamoodonga.** *n.* —.
BE2 **hagamodolia.** *v.* —.
P **mmodo.** *a.* —.
P 1 **mmodoanga.** *n.* —.
P 2 **mmodolia.** *v.* —.
PE **hagammodo.** *v.* —.
PE1 **hagammodoanga.** *n.* —.
PE2 **hagammodolia.** *v.* —.
R **modomodo.** *a.* A nearly mature coconut; the stage in the development of the coconut between *dahaa madagiigii* and *modomodo madagii.*
R 1 **modomodoanga.** *n.* —.
RE **hagamodomodo.** *v.* —.
RE1 **hagamodomodoanga.** *n.* —.
RE2 **hagamodomodolia.** *v.* —.
ID **gai modo.** Eat when still unripe.
ID **hai modo.** Eat (or pick) when still unripe.
ID **hua modo.** Fish eggs (immature).
ID **ui modo.** To pick pandanus while it is still unripe.

MODU
B **modu.** *a.* Cut off, disconnected; an islet (on the atoll); to have been decided formally; to have been adjudicated.
B 1 **moodunga.** *n.* —.
BE **hagamodu.** *v.* —; decide formally; render a final decision.
BE1 **hagamoodunga.** *n.* —.
BE2 **hagamodua.** *v.* —.
BE2 **hagamodulia.** *v.* —.
R **modumodu.** *a.* Broken in many places (like string), easily broken (e.g., of rope).
R 1 **modumodunga.** *n.* —.
RE **hagamodumodu.** *v.* —.
RE1 **hagamodumodunga.** *n.* —.
RE2 **hagamodumodua.** *v.* —.
RE2 **hagamodumodulia.** *v.* —.
T **moomodu.** *a.* [pl. of *modu*]; collapse completely.
T 1 **moomodunga.** *n.* —.
TE **hagamoomodu.** *v.* —.
TE1 **hagamoomodunga.** *n.* —.
TE2 **hagamoomodua.** *v.* —.
TE2 **hagamoomodulia.** *v.* —.
XCO **adumodu.** *n.* Group of islets; atoll (collection of islets).
ID **dee modu.** Continually.
ID **duu modu.** Vertical cut.
ID hadi modu. Sheer drop-off (as at the edge of a cliff).
ID **me gu modu.** Decision.
ID **me ne modu.** Decision.
ID **modu taalonga.** To escape (of fish, after having been speared).
ID **modu gee.** Cut away from; separated from.
ID **modu mai (adu, ange).** Become one's (your, their) exclusive possession.
ID **modu sogosogo.** Separated from others, and by itself.
ID **soe lodo modu.** To remain (or sit, or stand) motionless (as when praying).

MOE₁
B **moe₁.** *a.* Sleep; die; not yet blossomed (of a flower).
B 1 **moenga₁.** *n.* —; bedclothes, bedding; a place for sleeping.
B 2 **moea.** *v.* A person who is able to catch many flying fish (because the fish seem not to awaken at his approach).
BE **hagamoe₁.** *v.* Put to bed.

BE1 **hagamoenga**$_1$. *n.* —.
BE2 **hagamoea**$_1$. *v.* —.
P **mmoe**$_1$. *a.* —; to close both eyes.
P 1 **mmoenga**$_1$. *n.* —.
PE1 **hagammoenga**$_1$. *n.* —.
PE2 **hagammoea**$_1$. *v.* —.
R **moemoe**$_1$. *a.* —.
R 1 **moemoenga**$_1$. *n.* —.
RE **hagamoemoe**$_1$. *v.* —.
RE1 **hagamoemoenga**$_1$. *n.* —.
RE2 **hagamoemoea**$_1$. *v.* —.
ID **bua moe.** Immature girl.
ID **dama moemoe sala.** A foetus out of the proper position (in the womb) for delivery.
ID **hagadubu o de moe.** The name of a certain type of string figure.
ID **moe baubau.** Sleep without regard to remaining decently covered; die in agony [cf. *magau baubau*].
ID **moe danuaa.** Die in peace.
ID **moe dige.** To roll away from one's bedding while sleeping (on the floor).
ID **moe dolo.** To sneak into another's house at night for the purpose of having sexual relations.
ID **moe tao.** Sleep soundly.
ID **moe iho.** Sleep for a short time, nap; sleep overnight in place other than one's usual sleeping place.
CF **moele.** A lie (an untruth).

MOE$_{1a}$
B **moeagi.** *v.* Do by stealth.
B 1 **moeaginga.** *n.* —.
B 2 **moeagina.** *v.* —.
BE **hagamoeagi.** *v.* —.
BE1 **hagamoeaginga.** *n.* —.
BE2 **hagamoeagina.** *v.* —.
R **moemoeagi.** *v.* —.
R 1 **moemoeaginga.** *n.* —.
R 2 **moemoeagina.** *v.* —.
RE **hagamoemoeagi.** *v.* —.
RE1 **hagamoemoeaginga.** *n.* —.
RE2 **hagamoemoeagina.** *v.* —.

MOE$_{1b}$
B **noebili.** *a.* To long for another's presence at bedtime.
B 1 **moebilianga.** *n.* —.
BE **hagamoebili.** *a.* —.
BE1 **hagamoebilianga.** *n.* —.

MOE$_2$
B **moe**$_2$. *a.* Round, spherical, circular ; a loop.
B 1 **moenga**$_2$. *n.* —.
BE **hagamoe**$_2$. *v.* —.
BE1 **hagamoenga**$_2$. *n.* —.
BE2 **hagamoea**$_2$. *v.* —.
P **mmoe**$_2$. *a.* —.
P 1 **mmoenga**$_2$. *n.* —.
PE **hagammoe.** *v.* —.
PE1 **hagammoenga**$_2$. *n.* —.
PE2 **hagammoea**$_2$. *v.* —.
R **moemoe**$_2$. *a.* Becoming more *moe*$_2$.
R 1 **moemoenga**$_2$. *n.* —.
RE **hagamoemoe**$_2$. *v.* —.
RE1 **hagamoemoenga**$_2$. *n.* —.
RE2 **hagamoemoea**$_2$. *v.* —.
XFL **gaba-moe.** *n.* Fish sp.: cardinal fish.

MOELE
B **moele.** *n.* A lie (an untruth).

MOGO$_1$
RE **hagamogomogo**$_1$. *v.* Take special care of, cherish.
RE1 **hagamogomogoanga**$_1$. *n.* —.
RE2 **hagamogomogoa.** *v.* —.
RE2 **hagamogomogolia.** *v.* —.
T **momogo.** *d.* Want.
T 1 **momogoanga.** *n.* —.
TE **hagamomogo.** *v.* —.
TE1 **hagamomogoanga.** *n.* —.
ID **hadu hagamogomogo.** Gem.

MOGO$_2$
R **mogomogo.** *v.* Muscles (of the body).
R 1 **mogomogoanga.** *n.* —.
RE **hagamogomogo**$_2$. *v.* Cause to be muscular.
RE1 **hagamogomogoanga**$_2$. *n.* —.

ID **hai mogomogo.** Muscular; daring (show off), bold; strong (person); active physically.
ID **mogomogo ina.** Muscular.

$MOGO_3$
B **mogo.** *n.* Coconut apple (young and edible).

$MOGO_4$
E **mmogo.** *v.* Insist upon.
E 1 **mmogoaŋga.** *n.* —.
E 2 **mmogoa.** *v.* —.
E 2 **mmogolia.** *v.* —.
EE **hagammogo.** *v.* —.
EE1 **hagammogoanga.** *n.* —.
EE2 **hagammogoa.** *v.* —.
EE2 **hagammogolia.** *v.* —.

MOGOBUNA
B **mogobuna.** *n.* Grandchild, descendant of.
ID **hai mogobuna.** The relationship between grandparent and grandchild.

MOIGAGA
B **moigaga.** *n.* Fibers of the coconut husk.

MOLI
B **moli —.** *d.* —.
B 1 **moolinga.** *n.* —.
B 2 **moolia.** *v.* —.
BE **hagamoli —.** *d.* —.
BE1 **hagamoolinga.** *n.* —.
BE2 **hagamoolia.** *v.* —.
E **mmoli.** *v.* Haul (all at once or as fast as possible).
PE **hagammoli.** *v.* —.
R **molimoli.** *v.* Haul (little by little).
R 1 **molimolinga.** *n.* —.
R 2 **molimolia.** *v.* —.
RE **hagamolimoli.** *v.* —.
RE1 **hagamolimolinga.** *n.* —.
RE2 **hagamolimolia.** *v.* —.
ID **mmoli gee.** Haul away from.
ID **molimoli ange.** Take up slack in a line with hitches in order to maintain tension on something being hauled (e.g., a ship stuck on the reef during the moments when it is floated by waves).
ID **molimoli taula.** To take hitches in a rope until it is taut (and continue to take hitches as the rope becomes slack).
ID **molimoli i tuu gaha.** To express coconut oil out of the residue (*oda*) from which some oil has already been expressed.
ID **molimoli ngaadai.** A distribution of the catch of a communal fishing expedition.

$MOLO_1$
B **$molo_1$.** *v.* To make a knot of hair.
B **$molo_2$.** *n.* A noose for fishing.
B 1 **moolonga.** *n.* —.
B 2 **moloa.** *v.* Knotted (of hair).
BE **hagamolo.** *v.* —.
BE1 **hagamoolonga.** *n.* —.
BE2 **hagamoloa.** *v.* —.
P **mmolo.** *a.* —.
R **$molomolo_1$.** *v.* —.
R 1 **molomolonga.** *n.* —.
R 2 **molomoloa.** *v.* —.
RE **$hagamolomolo_1$.** *v.* —.
RE1 **hagamolomolonga.** *n.* —.
RE2 **hagamolomoloa.** *v.* —.

$MOLO_2$
R **$molomolo_2$.** *a.* Round, clear (in outline).
R 1 **molomoloanga.** *n.* —.
RE **$hagamolomolo_2$.** *v.* —.
RE1 **hagamolomoloanga.** *n.* —.
ID **duu molomolo.** Visible clearly.
ID **molomolo de biho.** Round-headed.
ID **molomolo iho (age).** Appear clearly.
ID **noho hagamolomolo.** To sit by oneself (away from the main group).

MOMME
B **momme.** *n.* A place.

ID **momme aadea.** Clearing (e.g., in the woods).
ID **momme hagadaahao.** Playground.
ID **momme hagassoe.** Court (of law).
ID **momme hai lua.** A fishing spot (beyond the seaward reef) where either reef or ocean fish can be found.

MOMO
B **momo.** *a.* A little, a small amount of.
B 1 **momoanga.** *n.* —.
B 2 **momolia.** *a.* Decrease in quantity.
BE **hagamomo.** *v.* Reduce in quantity.
BE1 **hagamomoanga.** *n.* —.
BE2 **hagamomolia.** *v.* —.
R **mommomo.** *a.* A little at a time.
R 1 **mommomoanga.** *n.* —.
RE **hagamommomo.** *v.* Reduce a little at a time.
XCO **dagimomo.** *a.* Few for each one.
ID **kave dagi de momo.** Take a little (or few) at a time.
ID **hanu momo.** Little bit, few.
ID **momo dai sii.** A very very little (in quantity).
ID **momo loo huu.** Just a very little.
ID **ssii mommomo.** Broken up into small pieces.

MONI
B **moni.** *n.* Canoe.
BE **hagamoni.** *v.* Provide a canoe for.
XCO **muaamoni.** *n.* A song formerly sung while dancing.
ID **buu hale moni.** Mollusk sp.
ID **daane hai moni.** Sailor, seaman.
ID **dada moni.** To beach a canoe without using runners [considered bad practice].
ID **dui moni.** A fleet of canoes (in line).
ID **gau mai moni.** Foreigners (lit., 'people who came in canoes').
ID **hagaditidi mai de moni.** A canoe going so fast it rides high in water (and is planing).
ID **hai moni.** Sailor.
ID **hudaa moni.** A fleet of canoes.
ID **langi moni.** The sort of rain which is an omen that a ship will come.
ID **madaa moni.** Prow of a canoe.
ID **mai moni.** A type of fishhook (made from pearl shell).
ID **manu hale moni.** A pottery bottle or jar.
ID **moni dui.** A canoe rigged for casting for tuna.
ID **moni galele.** A canoe rigged for *galele* fishing.
ID **moni kalo.** A canoe with rounded sides (designed to ride easily in rough seas).
ID **moni hagadeledele.** Model (or toy) canoe.
ID **moni hai gubenga.** A canoe rigged for *gubenga* fishing.
ID **moni lele.** Airplane.
ID **moni sulu.** Submarine.
ID **moni velovelo.** A canoe with men going spear fishing.
ID **muli moni.** Stern.
ID **saabai moni doo.** Carry a canoe (over the reef at low tide).
ID **sai moni.** A fleet of canoes.

MONO
CF **duumono.** A type of prepared food (made from taro).

MOO
B **moa$_2$.** *n.* The blossom of the banana tree.
R **moomoa$_1$.** *n.* Balls of grated taro (for making *huaahuu*).
R **moomoa$_2$.** *n.* The shoot from a germinating coconut.
XFL **dala-dalaa-moa.** *n.* Plant sp.: *Lycopodium phlegmaria* L.

XFL **moomoa-ganoango.** *n.* Fish sp.: boxfish (yellow).
XFL **moomoa-uliuli.** *n.* Fish sp.: boxfish (dark blue).

MOOa
B **moosugia.** *v.* Ripened unevenly (of breadfruit only).
B 1 **moosugiaanga.** *n.* —.
BE **hagamoosugia.** *v.* —.
BE1 **hagamoosugiaanga.** *n.* —.
R **moomoosugia.** *v.* —.
R 1 **moomoosugiaanga.** *n.* —.
RE **hagamoomoosugia.** *v.* —.
RE1 **hagamoomoosugiaanga.** *n.* —.
ID **moosugia ange.** Somewhat *moosugia.*

MOOb
E **mmoa.** *a.* Cooked.
E 1 **mmoaanga.** *n.* —.
EE **hagammoa.** *v.* —.
EE1 **hagammoaanga.** *n.* —.
XCO **moomada.** *a.* Half-cooked.
ID **mmoa gango.** Burned food which has been overcooked.
ID **moo balabala.** Barely cooked.

MOOc
B **moomuna.** *a.* Fatty.
BE **hagamoomuna.** *v.* —.

MOOd
B **moosee.** *v.* Not quite cooked (of anything but fish).
B 1 **mooseenga.** *n.* —.
BE **hagamoosee.** *v.* —.
BE1 **hagamooseenga.** *n.* —.
R **moomoosee.** *v.* —.
R 1 **moomooseenga.** *n.* —.
RE **hagamoomoosee.** *v.* —.
RE1 **hagamoomooseenga.** *n.* —.

MOOLAU
B **moolau.** *a.* Fast, quick, early.
B 1 **moolaunga.** *n.* —.
BE **hagamoolau.** *v.* Hurry, rush.
BE1 **hagamoolaunga.** *n.* —.
BE2 **hagamoolaua.** *v.* Cause to hurry.
ID **hai me moolau.** An habitually fast worker.
ID **moolau huu.** Punctual.
ID **moolau lodo.** Having a short temper.

MOOLE
B **moole.** *n.* [var. of *moele*].

MOSO
B **moso.** *n.* Bird sp.: starling (*Apolonis opacus*).
ID **balu moso.** Constant movement of the hands and feet, as when struggling (resembling the movements of a young starling).
ID **tao o de moso.** A coconut frond spine which has fallen and stuck upright in the ground.
ID **noho moso.** Able to support one's weight (e.g., a branch of a tree).
ID **sulu moso.** Be wet all over (esp. when one's hair is dripping).

MOSONGENGE
B **mosongenge.** *n.* A name children tease each other with.
BE **hagamosongenge.** *v.* —.

MOU
B **mou.** *n.* Age grade (those reaching adolescence within a few years of each other); a mnemonic chant enumerating the names of the islets, flora, fauna, chief priests, etc.; [archaic: those born during the tenure of one chief priest].
BE **hagamou.** *v.* Include in a *mou.*

MOUGU
B **mougu.** *n.* Plant sp.: *Fleurya ruderalis* (Forst.f.) Gaud. ex. Wedd.

MOULI
B **mouli.** *a.* Living, alive; life; life-style; that on which life seems to depend

(e.g., favorite food or activity); life-principle (spirit, soul, etc.).
BE **hagamouli.** *v.* Give life to, bring back life; food (prepared for a meal).
BE1 **hagamoulinga.** *n.* —.
BE2 **hagamoulia.** *v.* —.
XCO **Laangihagamouli.** *nt.* Saturday (the day on which food is prepared for Sunday).
ID **boo hagalele mouli.** A night on which the making of noise is permitted (i.e., on certain holidays).
ID **daa mouli.** Take life away from.
ID **kano mouli.** Fresh meat (including fish).
ID **hagalele mouli.** Startle; surprise (someone).
ID **hano mouli.** Disappear alive (esp. into another world).
ID **honga de mouli.** During the lifetime of.
ID **leia togo mouli.** Hiccough.
ID **lele mouli.** Surprised [often this expression occurs with a possessive pronoun between the words].
ID **mouli age.** Regain consciousness, rise from the dead.
ID **mouli age de —.** Regain feeling in — (part of body which was numb).
ID **mouli danuaa.** Easy living, a good life.
ID **mouli dangada.** Delinquent person (periodically exhibiting bad behavior).
ID **se mouli dangada.** Rascal.
ID **uaua mouli.** Veins pulsing.
CF **mouli-o-nono.** [= *malianoono*].
CF **samouli.** The spirit of a human being after his death.

MOUMOU
B **moumou.** *v.* Wasteful, waste (something).
B 1 **moumounga.** *n.* —.
B 2 **moumoua.** *v.* —.
B 2 **moumoulia.** *v.* —.
BE **hagamoumou.** *v.* —.
BE1 **hagamoumounga.** *n.* —.
BE2 **hagamoumoua.** *v.* —.
BE2 **hagamoumoulia.** *v.* —.
ID **tili moumou.** Waste (by not using).
ID **gai moumou.** Wasteful of food.
ID **hai moumou.** Use wastefully.

MOUNU
B **mounu.** *a.* To take a cover (or other thing that fits into or on something) off.
B 1 **mounuunga.** *n.* —.
BE **hagamounu.** *v.* —; separate oneself from.
BE1 **hagamounuunga.** *n.* —.
R **mounuunu.** *a.* Easily *mounu.*
R 1 **mounounuunga.** *n.* —.
RE **hagamounuunu.** *v.* —.
RE1 **hagamounuununga.** *n.* —.

MOUNGA
ID **henua mounga.** A land where there are mountains (a high island or a continental land mass).

MOUSI
B **mousi.** *a.* Defeated, lose (battle, game, etc.).
B 1 **mousinga.** *n.* —.
BE **hagamousi.** *v.* —.
BE1 **hagamousinga.** *n.* —.
BE2 **hagamousia.** *v.* —.
R **moumousi.** *a.* Repeatedly being *mousi.*
R 1 **moumousinga.** *n.* —.
RE1 **hagamoumousinga.** *n.* —.
RE2 **hagamoumousia.** *v.* —.

MUA
B **mua.** *nl.* Front (position), before, ahead.
BE **hagamua.** *v.* Be first; get closer to.
BE1 **hagamuaanga.** *n.* —.
XCO **ganimua.** *n.* The eldest

child of a couple.

XCO **muaamoni.** *n.* A song formerly sung while dancing.

ID **de gai i mua.** Favorite food.

ID **doo mua.** Very.

ID **gogo gi mua.** Bent forward.

ID **hagatoo mua.** Take every possible precaution, insure.

ID **i mua nei.** Beforehand.

ID **ino gi mua.** Bend (one's body) forward.

ID **mua mai (adu, ange).** Next to me (you, him).

ID **mua iho (age).** Next above (below).

ID **noho mua.** Overloaded in front (of a canoe).

ID **sulu gi mua.** Fall forward.

MUA$_a$

B **aamua.** *a.* High-ranking.

BE **hagaamua$_2$.** *v.* Accord honor to.

BE1 **hagaamuaanga.** *n.* —.

U **hagaamu$_2$.** *v.* Pay respect to, honor (someone).

ID **aamua ange.** Higher.

MUDU$_1$

R **mudumudu$_1$.** *a.* Slow moving (while working), slow acting, slow thinking.

R 1 **mudumuduanga.** *n.* —.

R 2 **mudumudua.** *a.* —.

R 2 **mudumudulia.** *a.* —.

RE **hagamudumudu.** *v.* Do slowly, delay.

RE1 **hagamudumuduanga.** *n.* —.

RE2 **hagamudumudua.** *v.* —.

RE2 **hagamudumudulia.** *v.* —.

ID **hai me mudumudu.** A habitually *mudumudu.*

MUDU$_2$

R **mudumudu$_2$.** *n.* Fish sp.: damselfish.

XFL **mudumudu-dua-beau.** *n.* Fish sp.: damselfish.

XFL **mudumudu-odaoda.** *n.* Fish sp.: damselfish.

MUGA$_1$

B **muga.** *v.* Used (or done, heard, or known) over and over until bored with.

B 1 **mugaanga.** *n.* —.

B 2 **mugalia.** *v.* —.

BE **hagamuga.** *v.* —.

BE1 **hagamugaanga.** *n.* —.

BE2 **hagamugalia.** *v.* —.

P **mmuga.** *v.* —.

P 1 **mmugaanga.** *n.* —.

PE **hagammuga.** *v.* —.

PE1 **hagammugaanga.** *n.* —.

R **mugamuga$_1$.** *v.* —.

R 1 **mugamugaanga.** *n.* —.

RE **hagamugamuga.** *v.* —.

RE1 **hagamugamugaanga.** *n.* —.

RE2 **hagamugamugalia.** *v.* —.

MUGA$_2$

R **mugamuga$_2$.** *v.* The muscle of a bivalve; the first stage of development of the coconut, before *daahaa; to crackle when chewed* [*of godoi* and *madaanui* only].

ID **duu mugamuga.** Half of an unripe coconut; buttock.

ID **kano mugamuga.** A crunching noise made when masticating certain foods (like cucumbers).

MUHUU

B **muhuu.** *mv.* Please! [a request].

ID **alaa muhuu.** How about those there?

ID **anaa muhuu.** How about those?

ID **anei muhuu.** How about these?

ID **delaa muhuu.** How about that one there?

ID **denaa muhuu.** How about that one?

ID **denei muhuu.** How about this one?

ID **gi-ange muhuu.** I hope that —.

ID **kaba muhuu.** Please wait!

ID **hano muhuu loo.** Let's see...

MUI

B **mui.** *v.* Gathered around

	(something).
B 1	**muinga.** *n.* —.
B 2	**muia.** *v.* Be *mui.*
BE	**hagamui.** *v.* —.
BE1	**hagamuinga.** *n.* —.
BE2	**hagamuia.** *v.* —.
R	**muimui.** *v.* Crowded (owing to a disorder of things); dense (underbrush).
R 1	**muimuinga.** *n.* —.
R 2	**muimuia.** *v.* Be *muimui.*
RE	**hagamuimui.** *v.* —.
RE1	**hagamuimuinga.** *n.* —.
RE2	**hagamuimuia.** *v.* —.
ID	**lodo me muimui.** In the bush (uncleared area).

MULE

B	**mule —.** *d.* —.
B 1	**muulenga.** *n.* —.
BE	**hagamule —.** *d.* —.
E	**mmule.** *a.* Slow, late.
E 1	**mmuleanga.** *n.* —.
EE	**hagammule.** *v.* —.
EE1	**hagammuleanga.** *n.* —.
EE2	**hagammulea.** *v.* —.
R	**mulemule.** *a.* —.
R 1	**mulemulenga.** *n.* —.
RE	**hagamulemule.** *v.* —.
RE1	**hagamulemuleanga.** *n.* —.
ID	**hai me mule me.** Habitually slow or late.

MULEGI

B	**mulegi.** *v.* Show off (in front of members of the opposite sex).
B 1	**mulegianga.** *n.* —.
BE	**hagamulegi.** *v.* —.
BE1	**hagamulegianga.** *n.* —.
ID	**hai me mulegi.** To show off (esp. in front of members of the opposite sex).

MULI$_1$

B	**muli$_1$.** *nl.* After, end (rearward part), later.
BE	**hagamuli$_1$.** *v.* Be late, tarry.
R	**mulimuli$_1$.** *v.* Much later; the very end.
RE	**hagamulimuli$_1$.** *v.* "This is the end" (of a chant).
XCO	**ganimuli.** *n.* The second child of a couple.
ID	**dama muli bee.** The twelfth child born to a couple.
ID	**muli de huaalaangi.** Afternoon.
ID	**muli lele.** The rear tip of the turtle shell.
ID	**muli madangi.** Sailing downwind.
ID	**muli mai ange.** A little later, by and by.
ID	**muli mai loo.** Much later.
ID	**muli moni.** Stern.
ID	**muli sua hadu.** Reefward of the storm beach; beach rock.
ID	**noho muli.** Overloaded in the stern (of a canoe).

MULI$_{1a}$

B	**aamuli.** *n.* Descendants (in all inferior generations).
BE	**hagaamuli.** *v.* Treat as junior.
BE2	**hagaamulia.** *v.* —.

MULI$_{1b}$

B	**muliagi.** *b.* Afterward.
B 1	**muliaginga.** *n.* —.
B 2	**muliagina.** *a.* Last, final.
BE	**hagamuliagi.** *v.* Cause to be last.
BE1	**hagamuliaginga.** *n.* —.
BE2	**hagamuliagina.** *v.* —.

MULI$_2$

B	**muli$_2$.** *a.* Debt, owe.
BE	**hagamuli$_2$.** *v.* —.
BE2	**hagamulia.** *v.* —.
R	**mulimuli$_2$.** *a.* —.
RE	**hagamulimuli$_2$.** *v.* —.
RE2	**hagamulimulia.** *v.* —.

MULO

B	**mulo.** *v.* Roll up.
B 1	**muulonga.** *n.* —.
B 2	**muloa.** *v.* —.
BE	**hagamulo.** *v.* —.
BE1	**hagamuulonga.** *n.* —.
BE2	**hagamuloa.** *v.* —.
P	**mmulo.** *v.* —.
P 1	**mmuulonga.** *n.* —.
PE	**hagammulo.** *v.* —.
PE1	**hagammuulonga.** *n.* —.
PE2	**hagammuuloa.** *v.* —.
R	**mulomulo.** *v.* —.
R 1	**mulomulonga.** *n.* —.
R 2	**mulomuloa.** *v.* —.
RE	**hagamulomulo.** *v.* —.

RE1 **hagamulomulonga.** *n.* —.
RE2 **hagamulomuloa.** *v.* —.

MULU
B **mulu —.** *d.* —.
B 1 **muulunga.** *n.* —.
B 2 **muulua.** *v.* —.
E **mmulu.** *v.* Stroke, rub gently.
R **mulumulu.** *v.* —.
R 1 **mulumulunga.** *n.* —.
R 2 **mulumulua.** *v.* —.
ID **mulu gudu.** Grab while pulling; destroy by falling on or through; break through any obstacles in one's path.
ID **mulumulu aamanu.** Moss (on rocks or coral).

MUNA
B **muna.** *n.* Word, language, speech.
R **munamuna.** *a.* A short prayer.
RE **hagamunamuna.** *v.* —.
ID **alaa muna.** Word [= *dalaa muna*].
ID **baasanga tugi ange muna.** Talk back.
ID **dalaa muna.** Word, phrase.
ID **hagadonu muna.** Act as an interpreter.
ID **hagadoodoo denga muna.** Boast foolishly about one's ability (when it is obvious that one is inept).
ID **hagallongo i muna.** Obey.
ID **hai muna.** Public meeting.
ID **muna abo (donu).** Truth.
ID **muna pada.** Harsh words.
ID **muna daemaha.** Words which hurt.
ID **muna de henua.** The Nukuoro language.
ID **muna hai alaa.** Oh my goodness!
ID **muna hhadu.** Lie (falsehood).
ID **muna madua.** Words used only by elders (which are not normally part of a child's vocabulary).
ID **muna maimai.** [= *ngudu maimai*].
ID **muna o de henua.** A community meeting (for listening to speeches or instructions).
ID **muna o tangada.** Speak of the devil!
ID **naba i de muna.** Converse earnestly.
ID **sigo de muna.** Remember what one has heard.
ID **siilinga a muna.** Trial or formal inquiry.
ID **sili muna.** Inquisitive (prone to ask too many questions).

MUSA
B **musa.** *v.* The sound of many little school fish feeding at the surface of the water.
B 1 **muusanga.** *n.* —.
B 2 **musalia.** *a.* —.
BE **hagamusa.** *v.* —.
BE1 **hagamuusanga.** *n.* —.
BE2 **hagamusalia.** *v.* —.
P **mmusa.** *v.* [pl. of *musa* — considering each as *musa*, rather than the whole group].
PE **hagammusa.** *v.* —.
PE1 **hagammusaanga.** *n.* —.
PE2 **hagammusalia.** *v.* —.
R **musamusa.** *v.* —.
R 1 **musamusaanga.** *n.* —.
R 2 **musamusalia.** *a.* —.
RE **hagamusamusa.** *v.* —.
RE1 **hagamusamusaanga.** *n.* —.
RE2 **hagamusamusalia.** *v.* —.

MUSU
B **musu.** *v.* Whispering.
B 1 **muusunga.** *n.* —.
B 2 **musua.** *v.* —.
BE **hagamusu.** *v.* —.
BE1 **hagamuusunga.** *n.* —.
BE2 **hagamusua.** *v.* —.
P **mmusu.** *v.* —.
PE **hagammusu.** *v.* —.
PE2 **hagammuusua.** *v.* —.
R **musumusu.** *v.* Whisper (to someone).
R 1 **musumusunga.** *n.* —.
R 2 **musumusua.** *v.* —.
RE **hagamusumusu.** *v.* —.
RE1 **hagamusumusunga.** *n.* —.
RE2 **hagamusumusua.** *v.* —.

ID **dangi de musu.** Hear whispering (of others).
ID **musumusu laa lalo.** Whisper softly.
CF **musa.** The sound of many little school fish feeding at the surface of the water.

MUU_1

B **muu_1.** *a.* Utter (words or sounds), reply (to someone).
B 1 **muunga.** *n.* —.
BD **hemuu.** *a.* Talk to one another.
BD1 **hemuunga.** *n.* —.
BE **hagamuu.** *v.* —.
BE1 **hagamuunga.** *n.* —.
BE2 **hagamuua.** *v.* —.
BE2 **hagamuulia.** *v.* —.
BG **hagahemuu.** *v.* —.
BG1 **hagahemuunga.** *n.* —.
BG2 **hagahemuua.** *v.* —.
P **mmuu.** *a.* —.
P 1 **mmuunga.** *n.* —.
PE **hagammuu.** *v.* —.
PE1 **hagammuunga.** *n.* —.
PE2 **hagammuua.** *v.* —.
PE2 **hagammuulia.** *v.* —.
R **muumuu.** *a.* —.
R 1 **muumuunga.** *n.* —.
RD **hemuumuu.** *a.* —.
RD1 **hemuumuunga.** *n.* —.
RE **hagamuumuu.** *v.* —.
RE1 **hagamuumuunga.** *n.* —.
RE2 **hagamuumuua.** *v.* —.
RE2 **hagamuumuulia.** *v.* —.
RG **hagahemuumuu.** *v.* —.
RG1 **hagahemuumuunga.** *n.* —.
RG2 **hagahemuumuua.** *v.* —.
ID **dee hemuu.** Not on speaking terms.
ID **muumuu kaiaa.** To remain silent (in order to hide a misdeed of oneself or others).

MUU_2

B **muu_2.** *n.* Fish sp.: snapper (The native term is applied to many spp.).
XFL **muu-madagao.** *n.* Fish sp.: snapper?
XFL **muu-madavai.** *n.* Fish sp. (rare).

NAA_1

B **naa.** *mv.* There near you; in the future.
ID **aahee naa.** Then what? (distant future).
ID **aau ai naa.** More so.
ID **aha naa.** Let's (later).
ID **alaa ange naa.** About that [pl.] (over there) much more.
ID **alaa naa.** Those only?
ID **alaa naa loo.** Those there seem to be.
ID **anaa naa.** These (there) only?
ID **anei ange naa.** About this [pl.] much more.
ID **anei naa.** These (here) only?
ID **anei naa loo.** These seem to be.
ID **au e dee gai naa loo.** I'll bet you can't!
ID **delaa ange naa.** About that [sing.] (over there), much more.
ID **delaa naa (?).** That there will be it (will that be it?).
ID **delaa naa loo.** That there could be it.
ID **denei ange naa.** About this [sing.], much more...
ID **denei naa (?).** This will be it. (Will this be it?).
ID **denei naa loo.** This seems to be.
ID **hai naa hanu me.** Something will happen...
ID **me naa gi —.** I wish that...
ID **naa gaalava.** So what?
ID **naa huu.** When, if.
ID **se aha au naa.** You are wrong! That's not right! I don't agree!

NAA_{1a}

B **anaa.** *b.* Those (away from the speaker).
ID **anaa ai.** These (there) only.
ID **anaa ai huu.** Those only then.
ID **anaa ai laa.** Those then were those.
ID **anaa ai loo.** Those then are.
ID **anaa ange.** And these (there).

ID anaa ange huu. That [pl.] much more only.
ID anaa ange maalie. Those are exactly right.
ID anaa ange naa. About that [pl.] (here) much more.
ID anaa dagodo. Those are the circumstances...
ID anaa donu. Those only.
ID anaa huu. Those only are the ones.
ID anaa laa. These (there) which were there.
ID anaa loo. These (there) were the ones.
ID anaa maa. Those were about (approximately).
ID anaa muhuu. How about those?
ID anaa naa. These (there) only?
ID anaa naa loo. Those seem to be.
ID anaa nei. Those now.
ID anaa sili. Those were enough.

NAA$_{1b}$
B **denaa.** *b.* This one (near you); that one (near you); That's right!
ID **denaa ai.** Therefore (with respect to this, there near you, or concerning, you).
ID **denaa ai huu.** That is it then!
ID **denaa ai laa.** That was it!
ID **denaa ai loo.** That is it (which has been decided upon).
ID **denaa ange.** This there is another one!
ID **denaa ange maalie.** That is exactly right!
ID **denaa ange naa.** About that [sing.] (here), much more.
ID **denaa donu.** That is it for sure!
ID **denaa tagodo.** That is the situation...
ID **denaa huu.** That is it still.
ID **denaa laa (?).** That is it there (is that it there?).
ID **denaa loo.** That was the one.
ID **denaa maa.** That is about (approximately).
ID **denaa muhuu.** How about that one?
ID **denaa naa (?).** That will be it. (Will that be it?).
ID **denaa naa loo.** That seems to be it; that could be it.
ID **denaa sili.** That is enough!

NAA$_{1c}$
B **kinaa.** *b.* There near you.
ID **laa kinaa.** Around there near you.

NAA$_2$
BE **haganaa.** *v.* To calm down someone who is excited or unhappy.
BE1 **haganaanga.** *n.* —.
BE2 **haganaadia.** *v.* —.

NAALE
ID **dama naale.** A talkative, deceitful person.

NAAMU
XCO **naamulolo.** *n.* Ramrod; [the etymology of this word is totally obscure].

NABA
B **naba.** *a.* A slip of the tongue.
B 1 **naabanga.** *n.* —.
BE **haganaba.** *v.* —.
BE1 **haganaabanga.** *n.* —.
P **nnaba.** *a.* —.
PE **hagannaba.** *v.* —.
R **nabanaba.** *a.* —.
R 1 **nabanabaanga.** *n.* —.
RE **haganabanaba.** *v.* —.
RE1 **haganabanabaanga.** *n.* —.
ID **naba i de muna.** Converse earnestly.

NABE
B **nabe.** *v.* To hook under the waistband or belt.
B 1 **naabenga.** *n.* —.
B 2 **nabea.** *v.* —.
B 2 **nabelia.** *v.* —.
BE **haganabe.** *v.* —.
BE1 **haganaabenga.** *n.* —.
BE2 **haganabea.** *v.* —.
BE2 **haganabelia.** *v.* —.
R **nabenabe.** *v.* —.
R 1 **nabenabenga.** *n.* —.

R 2	**nabenabea.** *v.* —.
R 2	**nabenabelia.** *v.* —.
RE	**haganabenabe.** *v.* —.
RE1	**haganabenabenga.** *n.* —.
RE2	**haganabenabea.** *v.* —.
RE2	**haganabenabelia.** *v.* —.

NAGO

R	**nagonago.** *v.* The sound of sloshing water (or of sexual intercourse).
R 1	**nagonagonga.** *n.* —.
R 2	**nagonagoa.** *v.* —.
R 2	**nagonagolia.** *v.* —.
RE	**haganagonago.** *v.* —.
RE1	**haganagonagonga.** *n.* —.
RE2	**haganagonagoa.** *v.* —.
RE2	**haganagonagolia.** *v.* —.

NAMA

R	**namanama.** *n.* Fish sp. (like *ngaa*, but longer and thinner).

NAMU

B	**namu.** *n.* Mosquito.
ID	**dau namu.** Mosquito net.

NAMUAA

B	**namuaa.** *v.* A sore on the lips (believed to result from missing a meal).
B 1	**namuaanga.** *n.* —.
BE	**haganamuaa.** *v.* —.
BE1	**haganamuaanga.** *n.* —.

NANU

B	**nanu.** *a.* Grumble, complain.
B 1	**naanunga.** *n.* —.
B 1	**nanuanga.** *n.* —.
B 2	**nanua.** *v.* The object of a complaint.
B 2	**nanulia.** *v.* The object of a complaint.
B 2	**nanumia.** *v.* The object of a complaint.
BE	**haganànu.** *v.* —.
BE1	**haganànuanga.** *n.* —.
BE2	**haganànua.** *v.* —.
BE2	**haganànulia.** *v.* —.
BE2	**haganànumia.** *v.* —.
P	**nnanu.** *a.* —.
PE	**hagannanu.** *v.* —.
PE1	**hagannanuanga.** *n.* —.
PE2	**hagannanua.** *v.* —.
PE2	**hagannanulia.** *v.* —.
PE2	**hagannanumia.** *v.* —.
R	**nannanu.** *a.* —.
RE	**haganannanu.** *v.* —.
RE1	**haganannanuanga.** *n.* —.
RE2	**haganannanua.** *v.* —.
RE2	**haganannanulia.** *v.* —.
RE2	**haganannanumia.** *v.* —.

NAO

B	**nao.** *v.* To extract by gouging out with a finger.
B 1	**naonga.** *n.* —.
B 2	**naoa.** *v.* —.
B 2	**naolia.** *v.* —.
BE	**haganao.** *v.* —.
BE1	**haganaonga.** *n.* —.
BE2	**haganaoa.** *v.* —.
BE2	**haganaolia.** *v.* —.
R	**naonao.** *v.* —.
R 1	**naonaonga.** *n.* —.
RE	**haganaonao.** *v.* —.
RE1	**haganaonaonga.** *n.* —.
RE2	**haganaonaoa.** *v.* —.
RE2	**haganaonaolia.** *v.* —.
ID	**gai nnao$_1$.** Eat messily.
ID	**gai nnao$_2$.** Exaggerate (esp. in storytelling).
ID	**nao baasua.** To collect *baasua*.
ID	**nao gasi.** Eat messily (by poking at all of the food instead of touching only the portion to be eaten).

NAU

B	**nau.** *n.* Plant sp. (the archaic name of *manu-gaba-aasanga*).

NE

B	**ne.** *mt.* PERFECTIVE ASPECT MARKER; if.

NEBU

B	**nebu.** *v.* To do something so earnestly that one has no time to talk; be very busy.
B 1	**nebunga.** *n.* —.
B 2	**nebua.** *v.* Be *nebu*.
BE	**haganebu.** *v.* —.
BE1	**haganebunga.** *n.* —.
BE2	**haganebua.** *v.* —.
R	**nebunebu.** *v.* —.

R 1 **nebunebunga.** *n.* —.
R 2 **nebunebua.** *v.* Be *nebunebu.*
RE **haganebunebu.** *v.* —.
RE1 **haganebunebunga.** *n.* —.
RE2 **haganebunebua.** *v.* —.
ID **nebu ange.** To perceive that others are occupied.

NEGE
B **nege.** *v.* Move (something) a little way over.
B 1 **neegenga.** *n.* —.
B 2 **negea.** *v.* —.
B 2 **negelia.** *v.* —.
BC **manege.** *a.* —.
BC1 **manegenga.** *n.* —.
BE **haganege.** *v.* —.
BE1 **haganeegenga.** *n.* —.
BE2 **haganegea.** *v.* —.
BE2 **haganegelia.** *v.* —.
BF **hagamanege.** *v.* —; disobedient, stubborn, talk back to.
BF1 **hagamanegeanga.** *n.* —.
BF2 **hagamanegea.** *v.* —.
BF2 **hagamanegelia.** *v.* —.
P **nnege.** *v.* —.
PC **maanege.** *a.* —.
PC1 **maanegenga.** *n.* —.
PE **hagannege.** *v.* —.
PE1 **haganneegenga.** *n.* —.
PE2 **hagannegea.** *v.* —.
PE2 **hagannegelia.** *v.* —.
PF **hagamaanege.** *v.* —.
PF1 **hagamaanegenga.** *n.* —.
PF2 **hagamaanegea.** *v.* —.
PF2 **hagamaanegelia.** *v.* —.
R **negenege.** *v.* —.
R 1 **negenegenga.** *n.* —.
RC **manegenege.** *a.* —.
RC1 **manegenegenga.** *n.* —.
RE **haganegenege.** *v.* —.
RE1 **haganegenegenga.** *n.* —.
RE2 **haganegenegea.** *v.* —.
RE2 **haganegenegelia.** *v.* —.
RF **hagamanegenege.** *v.* —.
RF1 **hagamanegenegenga.** *n.* —.
RF2 **hagamanegenegea.** *v.* —.
RF2 **hagamanegenegelia.** *v.* —.
ID **daane e manege.** A person who is capable at almost anything.
ID **tama e manege.** A person who is capable at almost anything.
ID **lodo manege.** Stubborn (esp. in maintaining one's own superiority); be a poor loser.
ID **manege ma de —.** Better than (nothing, etc.).

NEHU
B **nehu.** *v.* Clear (in focus).
B 1 **nehunga.** *n.* —.
B 2 **nehua.** *v.* —.
BE **haganehu.** *v.* —.
BE1 **haganehunga.** *n.* —.
BE2 **haganehua.** *v.* —.
R **nehunehu.** *v.* —.
R 1 **nehunehunga.** *n.* —.
R 2 **nehunehua.** *v.* —.
RE **haganehunehu.** *v.* —.
RE1 **haganehunehunga.** *n.* —.
RE2 **haganehunehua.** *v.* —.

NEI
B **nei.** *mv.* Here, now.
XCO **Dai-nei.** *np.* "Islands to the west" (the Mortlocks?).
ID **aahee nei.** Then what? (immediate future).
ID **aboo nei.** Tonight (future).
ID **aha nei.** Let's (now).
ID **alaa nei.** Those now.
ID **anaa nei.** Those now.
ID **anaboo nei.** Tonight (past).
ID **anailaa (nei).** Today (in the past).
ID **de hua nei.** This size.
ID **delaa nei (?).** That there is it (is that there it?).
ID **tama nei.** [an exclamation, about = Wow!; or, no kidding!; or, watch it!].
ID **humai nei.** Next —.
ID **maingaa ange nei gi.** To wish one has —.
ID **ngaage nei.** Gilbert Islands.
CF **iainei.** Now.

NEI$_a$
B **anei.** *b.* These.
ID **anei ai.** These (here) only.
ID **anei ai laa.** These then were those.
ID **anei ai loo.** These then are.
ID **anei ange.** And these (here).
ID **anei ange huu.** This [pl.] much more only.

ID anei ange maalie. These are exactly right.
ID anei ange naa. About this [pl.] much more.
ID anei dagodo. These are the circumstances...
ID anei donu. Only these are the ones.
ID anei huu. These (here) only are the ones.
ID anei laa. These (here) which were there.
ID anei loo. These (here) are the ones.
ID anei maa. These were about (approximately).
ID anei muhuu. How about these?
ID anei naa. These (here) only?
ID anei naa loo. These seem to be.
ID anei nei. These now.
ID anei sili. These were enough.

NEI$_b$
B **denei.** *b.* This one.
ID **denei ai.** Therefore (with respect to this here).
ID **denei ai huu.** This is it still.
ID **denei ai laa.** This is that then.
ID **denei ai loo.** This then is —.
ID **denei ange.** This is another one!
ID **denei ange maalie.** This is exactly right!
ID **denei ange naa.** About this [sing.], much more...
ID **denei au.** It is I!
ID **denei donu.** This is it for sure!
ID **denei tagodo.** This is the situation...
ID **denei huu.** This is it still.
ID **denei laa** (?). This is that (is this that?).
ID **denei loo.** This is it at last.
ID **denei maa.** This is about (approximately).
ID **denei muhuu.** How about this one?
ID **denei naa** (?). This will be it. (Will this be it?).
ID **denei naa loo.** This seems to be.
ID **denei nei** (?). This is it! (Is this it?).
ID **denei sili.** This is enough!

NEI$_c$
B **kinei.** *b.* Here in this place.
ID **laa kinei.** Around here.

NENGE
R **nengenenge.** *v.* Tickle; to catch an octopus by tickling it (to dislodge it from its hole).
R 1 **nengenengeanga.** *n.* —.
R 2 **nengenengea.** *v.* —.
R 2 **nengenengelia.** *v.* —.
RE **haganengenenge.** *v.* —.
RE1 **haganengenengeanga.** *n.* —.
RE2 **haganengenengea.** *v.* —.
RE2 **haganengenengelia.** *v.* —.
XFL **anengenenge.** *n.* Mollusk sp.: *Conus chaldaeus.*

NEVE
B **neve.** *v.* Blurred (out of focus).
B 1 **neevenga.** *n.* —.
B 1 **neveinga.** *n.* —.
B 2 **nevea.** *v.* Be *neve.*
B 2 **neveia.** *v.* Be *neve.*
BE **haganeve.** *v.* —.
BE1 **haganeevenga.** *n.* —.
BE1 **haganeveinga.** *n.* —.
BE2 **haganevea.** *v.* —.
BE2 **haganeveia.** *v.* —.
R **neveneve.** *v.* —; spider.
R 1 **neveneveinga.** *n.* —.
R 1 **nevenevenga.** *n.* —.
RE **haganeveneve.** *v.* —.
RE1 **haganeveneveinga.** *n.* —.
RE1 **haganevenevenga.** *n.* —.
RE2 **haganevenevea.** *v.* —.
RE2 **haganeveneveia.** *v.* —.
ID **hale neveneve.** Spider web.

NI$_1$
B **ni$_1$.** *mp.* Belonging to.
C **nii.** *mp.* [var. of *ni$_1$*].
XCO **niaai.** *b.* Whose?
XCO **nioai.** *b.* Whose?

NI$_2$
B **ni$_2$.** *ma.* GENERAL ARTICLE

(PL.); they (things) are...
ID **dee ni dago.** Never mind!
ID **ni aha.** What are these?

NIA
CF **madannia.** Finger.

NIGO
B **nigo.** *v.* Go around in a circle; wind around.
B 1 **niigonga.** *n.* —.
B 2 **nigoa.** *v.* —.
B 2 **nigolia.** *v.* —.
BE **haganigo.** *v.* —.
BE1 **haganiigonga.** *n.* —.
BE2 **haganigoa.** *v.* —.
BE2 **haganigolia.** *v.* —.
P **nnigo.** *v.* —.
PE **hagannigo.** *v.* —.
PE1 **haganniigonga.** *n.* —.
PE2 **hagannigoa.** *v.* —.
PE2 **hagannigolia.** *v.* —.
R **nigonigo.** *v.* —.
RE **haganigonigo.** *v.* —.
RE1 **haganigonigonga.** *n.* —.
RE2 **haganigonigoa.** *v.* —.
RE2 **haganigonigolia.** *v.* —.

NIGOa
B **niigoi.** *v.* Wind around (of a rope, etc.).
B 1 **niigoinga.** *n.* —.
B 2 **niigoia.** *v.* —.
BE **haganiigoi.** *v.* —.
BE1 **haganiigoinga.** *n.* —.
BE2 **haganiigoia.** *v.* —.
R **nigonigoi.** *v.* —.
R 1 **nigonigoinga.** *n.* —.
R 2 **nigonigoia.** *v.* —.
RE **haganigonigoi.** *v.* —.
RE1 **haganigonigoinga.** *n.* —.
RE2 **haganigonigoia.** *v.* —.

NIHO
B **niho.** *n.* Tooth, teeth.
XFL **manu-gadi-niho.** *n.* Plant sp. [used to make loose teeth firm].
ID **dudu de niho.** A method of treating toothaches in which a burning root (of the *aoa* tree) is applied to the tooth (which later disintegrates).
ID **gano niho.** Gums (of mouth).
ID **hale hai niho.** Dentist's office.
ID **niho gai.** Permanent teeth (appearing after deciduous teeth).
ID **niho gaina.** Teeth with cavities.
ID **niho hagadolo.** Incisor teeth.
ID **niho ngalo.** Molar teeth, wisdom teeth.
ID **niho vaiuu.** Milk teeth, deciduous teeth.
ID **ssele i de niho.** Damn it!

NIIGA
CF **madaniiga.** Ingrown callus.

NIIVOI
ID **gai niivoi.** To eat food without washing one's hands after having prepared a corpse for burial [a traditional sign of manliness].

NNADU
B **nnadu.** *v.* To receive a shock (as when hit, or by an explosion).
B 1 **nnaduanga.** *n.* —.
B 2 **nnadulia.** *v.* —.
BE **hagannadu.** *v.* —.
BE1 **hagannaduanga.** *n.* —.
BE2 **hagannadulia.** *v.* —.
R **nannadu.** *v.* —.
R 1 **nannaduanga.** *n.* —.
R 2 **nannadulia.** *v.* —.
RE **haganannadu.** *v.* —.
RE1 **haganannaduanga.** *n.* —.
RE2 **haganannadulia.** *v.* —.

NNAGI
BE **hagannagi.** *v.* Lean against.
BE1 **hagannaginga.** *n.* —.
BE2 **hagannagia.** *v.* —.

NNAMU
B **nnamu.** *a.* Odor, smell (of something), greasy.
B 1 **nnamuanga.** *n.* —.
BE **hagannamu.** *v.* —.
BE1 **hagannamuanga.** *n.* —.
BE2 **hagannamua.** *v.* —.
BE2 **hagannamulia.** *v.* —.
R **namunamu.** *a.* —.
R 1 **namunamuanga.** *n.* —.

RE haganamunamu. *v.* —.
RE1 haganamunamuanga. *n.* —.
RE2 haganamunamua. *v.* —.
RE2 haganamunamulia. *v.* —.
ID **gaa gee de nnamu.** Having a strong odor.
ID **gai haganamunamu.** Eat sparingly (in order to save some food for later).
ID **hagannamu age.** Eat a little of.
ID **nnamu hagaduugia.** Stench.

NNOO
B **nnoo.** *a.* Covetous, envious.
B 1 **nnooanga.** *n.* —.
BE **hagannoo.** *v.* —.
BE1 **hagannooanga.** *n.* —.
ID **nnoo hagamau me.** Insatiably acquisitive.

NOA
B **noa.** *v.* Tied (as with rope).
B 1 **noaanga.** *n.* —.
B 1 **noodanga.** *n.* Bundle, knot; a set of 12 different fishing lures.
B 2 **noodia.** *v.* —.
E **nnoa.** *v.* Tie.
R **noonoa.** *v.* —.
R 1 **noonoodanga.** *n.* —.
R 2 **noonoodia.** *v.* —.
ID **hale nnoa.** Prison, jail.
ID **nnoa nounu.** Tied in such a way that pulling the end of the string will undo it.
CF **dolonoa.** [var. of *olonoa* (sea cucumber)].

NODI
B **nodi.** *v.* To tie a knot in the hair.
B 1 **nodinga.** *n.* —.
B 2 **nodia.** *v.* —.
BE **haganodi.** *v.* —.
BE1 **haganodinga.** *n.* —.
BE2 **haganodia.** *v.* —.
R **nodinodi.** *v.* —.
R 1 **nodinodinga.** *n.* —.
R 2 **nodinodia.** *v.* —.
RE **haganodinodi.** *v.* —.
RE1 **haganodinodinga.** *n.* —.
RE2 **haganodinodia.** *v.* —.

NOGANOGA
B **noganoga.** *v.* A method of plaiting mats.
B 1 **noganogaanga.** *n.* —.
BE **haganoganoga.** *v.* —.
BE1 **haganoganogaanga.** *n.* —.

NOGO
B **nogo.** *mt.* PAST PROGRESSIVE ASPECT MARKER.

NOHO
B **noho.** *v.* Stay, sit, stop; freeze, coagulate; live (at); remain (somewhere); be situated.
B 1 **nohoanga.** *n.* —; position.
B 2 **nohoa.** *v.* Occupied.
B 2 **noholia.** *v.* Occupied.
BE **haganoho.** *v.* —; stop (someone or something).
BE1 **haganohoanga.** *n.* —.
BE2 **haganohoa.** *v.* —.
BE2 **haganoholia.** *v.* —.
P **nnoho.** *v.* —.
PE **hagannoho.** *v.* —.
PE1 **hagannohoanga.** *n.* —.
PE2 **hagannohoa.** *v.* —.
PE2 **hagannoholia.** *v.* —.
R **nohonoho.** *v.* —.
R 1 **nohonohoanga.** *n.* —.
R 2 **nohonohoa.** *v.* —.
R 2 **nohonoholia.** *v.* —.
RE **haganohonoho.** *v.* —.
RE1 **haganohonohoanga.** *n.* —.
RE2 **haganohonohoa.** *v.* —.
RE2 **haganohonoholia.** *v.* —.
ID **ga noho.** After a time.
ID **noho ai.** Occupy or live in (a place).
ID **nohoanga hodooligi.** The place where the chief lives (at the moment).
ID **noho baba.** Live peacefully.
ID **noho dau donu.** Sit quietly.
ID **noho dodo.** Coagulation of blood.
ID **noho donu.** Properly situated or loaded (of a canoe).
ID **noho hagamaaiongi.** To sit as though stunned (i.e., as though *hagamaaiongi*).
ID **noho hagamolomolo.** To sit by oneself (away from the main group).
ID **noho hhanga.** Sit with one's legs spread apart.

ID	**noho iho —.** Keep secret.
ID	**noho lalo.** Overloaded (almost to the point of sinking).
ID	**noho maadai.** Sit quietly.
ID	**noho mai (adu, ange).** Resist me (you, them), oppose me (you, them).
ID	**noho moso.** Able to support one's weight (e.g., a branch of a tree).
ID	**noho mua.** Overloaded in front (of a canoe).
ID	**noho muli.** Overloaded in the stern (of a canoe).
ID	**noho senga (adu).** Be ignorant (of what is happening).
ID	**oha de nnoho paba.** Disturb the peace.
ID	**valea i de noho.** Tired of waiting for someone.

NOHU

B	**nohu.** *n.* Fish sp.: stone-fish.

NONI

XCO	**dibononi.** *n.* The youngest child of a couple.
CF	**gaanoni.** An omen of death [exact nature not known].

NONU$_1$

B	**nonu$_1$.** *v.* Filter, sift.
B 1	**nonumanga.** *n.* —.
B 1	**noonunga.** *n.* —.
B 2	**nonua.** *v.* —.
B 2	**nonumia.** *v.* —.
R	**nonnonu.** *v.* —.
R 1	**nonnonumanga.** *n.* —.
R 1	**nonnonunga.** *n.* —.
R 2	**nonnonua.** *v.* —.
R 2	**nonnonumia.** *v.* —.

NONU$_2$

B	**nonu$_2$.** *n.* Plant sp.: tree sp. (the archaic name of *bugaliaa*).

NOO$_1$

B	**noo.** *mi.* If.

NOO$_2$

CF	**hainoo.** Permitted, open to the public, secular [opposite of *dabu*].

NOO$_3$

CF	**nooligi.** A small knife.

NOOBIHO

B	**noobiho.** *a.* Be enemies (of individuals only).
B 1	**noobihoanga.** *n.* —.
BE	**haganoobiho.** *v.* —.
BE1	**haganoobihoanga.** *n.* —.
R	**noonoobiho.** *a.* —.
R 1	**noonoobihoanga.** *n.* —.
RE	**haganoonoobiho.** *v.* —.
RE1	**haganoonoobihoanga.** *n.* —.

NOODAGI

B	**noodagi.** *v.* Forbidden to use (esp. plants reserved for the owner's use by tying the trunk).
B 1	**noodagianga.** *n.* —.
BE	**haganoodagi.** *v.* —.
BE1	**haganoodagianga.** *n.* —.
R	**noonoodagi.** *v.* —.
R 1	**noonoodagianga.** *n.* —.
RE	**haganoonoodagi.** *v.* —.
RE1	**haganoonoodagianga.** *n.* —.
ID	**manu noodagi.** A plant which has been *noodagi*.

NOODALO

B	**noodalo.** *v.* Duplicate.
B 1	**noodaloanga.** *n.* —.
BE	**haganoodalo.** *v.* —.
BE1	**haganoodaloanga.** *n.* —.
R	**noonoodalo.** *v.* —.
R 1	**noonoodaloanga.** *n.* —.
RE	**haganoonoodalo.** *v.* —.
RE1	**haganoonoodaloanga.** *n.* —.

NOOGELE

B	**noogele.** *v.* To tie a knot so that it is difficult to untie.
B 1	**noogeleanga.** *n.* —.
BE	**haganoogele.** *v.* —.
BE1	**haganoogeleanga.** *n.* —.
R	**noonoogele.** *v.* —.
R 1	**noonoogeleanga.** *n.* —.
RE	**haganoonoogele.** *v.* —.
RE1	**haganoonoogeleanga.** *n.* —.

NOOMEEMEA

B	**noomeemea.** *v.* A wave of

sufficient force to wash over normally dry land; tidal wave.

B 1 **noomeemeaanga.** *n.* —.
BE **haganoomeemea.** *v.* —.
BE1 **haganoomeemeaanga.** *n.* —.

NOONOGIA

B **noonogia.** *v.* Bloated from ingesting too much fat.
B 1 **noonogiaanga.** *n.* —.
BE **haganoonogia.** *v.* —.
BE1 **haganoonogiaanga.** *n.* —.

NOUNU

B **nounu.** *v.* To tie a knot so that it is easily undone (by pulling one end of the string).
B 1 **nounanga.** *n.* —.
BE **haganounu.** *v.* —.
BE1 **haganounanga.** *n.* —.
R **noonounu.** *v.* Repeatedly *nounu.*
RE **haganoonounu.** *v.* —.
RE1 **haganoonounanga.** *n.* —.
ID **nnoa nounu.** Tied in such a way that pulling the end of the string will undo it.

NUGU

ID **nugu.** Land, islet.

NUI_1

B **nui.** *n.* Plant sp.: tree sp.: coconut tree.
R **nuinui.** *n.* A sp. of driftwood (resembling *aha-bagua*), the core of which is used for the hoop of the flying fish net.
XCO **doloinui.** *a.* A hard lump inside a female's stomach [tumor?]; a coconut of the youngest stage of development.
XCO **duaanui.** *n.* Coconut palm frond spines.
XCO **gannui.** *a.* The gelatinous layer in the kernel of the immature coconut.
ID **dao o de nui.** (Topmost) roof support poles, wall plates(from the size of which one can estimate the maturity of those below).
ID **daula duu nui.** A rope used to lower a bunch of coconuts to the ground.
ID **daula mada lau nui.** A rope for tying palm fronds together to make a *belubelu* seine.
ID **daula sele nui.** A rope used to pull a coconut tree in the desired direction when felling it.
ID **duu nui.** To lower a bunch of cut coconuts from a coconut tree with a rope.
ID **hagallongo de lau nui.** To obtain oracular information by listening to the sounds made by coconut leaves.
ID **nui hoohoa.** A coconut tree trunk incised with steps [to facilitate climbing].
ID **saalingaa nui.** The rainwater which flows down a bent coconut tree (collected for drinking).
ID **vai nui.** Coconut milk.
ID **vai nui hhoa.** Very calm seas.

NUI_2

P **nnui.** *a.* Large [pl.]; big [pl.].
P 1 **nnuinga.** *n.* —.
PE **hagannui.** *v.* —.
PE1 **hagannuinga.** *n.* —.
PE2 **hagannuia.** *v.* —.
ID **basa dua nnui.** Speak undiplomatically.
ID **dua nnui.** Violence; a type of rope (thick, with thick strands).
ID **gai mamu dua nnui.** To eat fish up (not saving any for later).
ID **hai me dua nnui.** Do violently.
ID **hua nnui.** Having large fruit or nuts (of trees).
ID **mada nnui.** Having big holes (or entrances, etc.).
CF **laanui.** Big [sing.]; large [sing.].

NUUI

B **nuui.** *a.* Green.
B 1 **nuuinga.** *n.* —.
BE **haganuui.** *v.* —.
BE1 **haganuuinga.** *n.* —.
BE2 **haganuuia.** *v.* —.
ID **gaha nuui.** Having green coconuts (of a coconut tree).
ID **mada nuui.** Dark green in color.

NGA-

CF **ngaadahi.** Both, as one.
CF **ngaadai.** Lagoonward.
CF **ngaage.** Downtown.
CF **ngaahee.** Where?
CF **ngaalulu.** A rattling or sloshing around inside (of something shaken).
CF **ngaangaa.** Not sturdy, rickety.
CF **ngaangaaulu.** —.
CF **ngadaa.** With difficulty.
CF **ngadala.** Fish sp.: sea bass (The native term is applied to many spp.).
CF **ngadau.** Year; age (of a person).
CF **ngadolo.** A landslide or similar movement of things.
CF **ngaholu.** Bent.
CF **ngahui.** Tens of coconuts [cf. *dehui*].
CF **ngaiho.** Uptown.
CF **ngalubelube.** Tremble or vibrate in the air.
CF **ngalue.** Move slightly, change position.
CF **ngaohie.** Easily.
CF **ngauda.** —.
CF **ngaue.** Move (oneself), moved.
CF **ngavali.** Bent slightly (not sharply).
CF **ngavesi.** Box, coffin, crate.

NGAA

B **ngaa.** *n.* Fish sp.
CF **deengaa.** Let's — right away!

NGAANGAA

B **ngaangaa.** *v.* Not sturdy, rickety.
B 1 **ngaangaanga.** *n.* —.
BE **hagangaangaa.** *v.* —.
BE1 **hagangaangaanga.** *n.* —.

NGADAA

B **ngadaa.** *mv.* With difficulty.
BE **hagangadaa.** *v.* Come with difficulty; a difficult delivery (of a baby).
BE1 **hagangadaanga.** *n.* —.
ID **gannui ngadaa.** A coconut which has less *gannui* than would be expected at its stage of maturity.
ID **hagalongolongo ngadaa.** Slow to respond to suggestions or commands (because resisting).
ID **hagao ngadaa.** Expensive.
ID **hai ngadaa.** Difficult.
ID **ngadaa mai.** Difficult for me; difficult to come.

NGADALA

B **ngadala.** *n.* Fish sp.: sea bass (The native term is applied to many spp.).

NGADAU

B **ngadau.** *n.* Year; age (of a person).
ID **ngadau age.** Older.
ID **ngadau iho.** Younger.

NGADI

B **ngadi—.** *mf.* Hollow, vacant, empty; nothing, worthless, useless.
BE **hagangadi —.** *v.* —.
ID **gaadinga hai ngadi ubu.** Coconut with a shell of a size appropriate for use as a cooking vessel.
ID **hagangadi me.** Treat as unimportant; to sacrifice (not thinking of oneself).
ID **laangai ngadi moana.** A fishing condition in which tuna are biting, but do not appear in schools.
ID **ngadi basa.** Small talk; idle conversation.
ID **ngadi biho.** Head.
ID **ngadi dangada.** An ordinary person, commoner; a

person of slight social value.
ID **ngadi daumaha.** Religions which are not in the Judaeo-Christian tradition, pagan cults.
ID **ngadi diinonga.** Pagan gods, idols.
ID **ngadi duu.** Naked.
ID **ngadi gai.** Eat taro without fish (or fish without taro).
ID **ngadi gavadu.** A gift (to the hearer); a present (to the hearer).
ID **ngadi hai bodu.** Common-law marriage, concubinage.
ID **ngadi hanonga.** A useless journey.
ID **ngadi humai.** Come without bringing anything (such as gifts).
ID **ngadi laangi.** A day other than Sunday; a day on which nothing is accomplished.
ID **ngadi mahamaha —.** Beautiful but otherwise useless.
ID **ngadi me.** Nothing, unimportant, useless, worthless.
ID **ngadi moana.** [= *laangai ngadi moana*].
ID **ngadi ngavesi.** An empty box.
ID **ngadi seesee.** Walk barefoot, stroll.
ID **ngadi uaa.** Assent to insincerely.
ID **ngadi ubu.** An empty coconut shell used as a container.
ID **ngadi vai.** A coconut shell used for water storage (on fishing trips).

NGADO
B **ngado.** *a.* Come to the end or limit (of something).
B 1 **ngaadonga.** *n.* —.
B 2 **ngadoa.** *v.* To have *ngado.*
B 2 **ngadolia.** *v.* To have *ngado.*
BE **hagangado.** *v.* —.
BE1 **hagangaadonga.** *n.* —.
BE2 **hagangadoa.** *v.* —.
BE2 **hagangadolia.** *v.* —.
ID **dee ngado mai.** Forever, eternally.

NGAE$_1$
B **ngae$_1$.** *n.* Head.
R **ngaengae.** *v.* To become dizzy in the water.
ID **hagaduu ngae.** Earnestly; to the limits of one's capacity; struggle (e.g., to complete work).

NGAE$_2$
B **ngae$_2$.** *n.* Mollusk sp.: giant clam sp.

NGAGO
B **ngago.** *n.* Brain; egg.
ID **baalasi ngago.** Incubation of eggs (by a hen).
ID **hagabigo de ngago.** Fool (someone), deceive.
ID **lau ngago.** The fatty tissue of a fish or animal.

NGAHEAHE
B **ngaaheahe.** *v.* Taro which is watery or gummy.
B 1 **ngaaheaheanga.** *n.* —.
BE **hagangaaheahe.** *v.* —.
BE1 **hagangaaheaheanga.** *n.* —.

NGAHU
E **nngahu.** *n.* Fish sp.: damselfish.

NGAIO
B **ngaio.** *n.* Fish sp.: needlefish.
XFL **ngaio-golai.** *n.* Fish sp.: needlefish.

NGALI
B **ngali —.** *d.* —.
B 1 **ngaalinga.** *n.* —.
B 2 **ngaalia.** *v.* —.
BE **hagangali —.** *d.* —.
BE1 **hagangaalinga.** *n.* —.
BE2 **hagangaalia.** *v.* —.
E **nngali.** *v.* To take a bite out of something held in the hand (food only).
EE **haganngali.** *v.* —.
R **ngalingali.** *v.* —.
R 1 **ngalingalinga.** *n.* —.

R 2 **ngalingalia.** *v.* —.
RE **hagangalingali.** *v.* —.
RE1 **hagangalingalinga.** *n.* —.
RE2 **hagangalingalia.** *v.* —.
ID **magi nngali.** Any sickness leading to emaciation (e.g., t.b.); a wasting illness (terminal).

NGALO
B **ngalo.** *v.* Forget.
B 1 **ngaalonga.** *n.* —.
B 2 **ngaloa.** *v.* —.
BE **hagangalo.** *v.* Forget purposely.
BE1 **hagangaalonga.** *n.* —.
BE2 **hagangaloa.** *v.* —.
R **ngalongalo.** *a.* Forgetful, absent-minded.
R 1 **ngalongalonga.** *n.* —.
R 2 **ngalongaloa.** *v.* —.
RE **hagangalongalo.** *v.* —.
RE1 **hagangalongalonga.** *n.* —.
RE2 **hagangalongaloa.** *v.* —.
ID **niho ngalo.** Molar teeth, wisdom teeth.
CF **hinangalomalie.** Feel happy or contented or at peace with the world.
CF **hinangalosaa.** Miss (someone or something); longing (for a person or place).

NGALOGU
B **ngalogu.** *a.* Push in, crumple up; bend out of shape (temporarily); easily changed in shape (esp. by pushing).
B 1 **ngalogunga.** *n.* —.
B 2 **ngalogua.** *v.* —.
BE **hagangalogu.** *v.* —.
BE1 **hagangalogunga.** *n.* —.
BE2 **hagangalogua.** *v.* —.
P **ngaalogu.** *a.* —.
P 1 **ngaalogunga.** *n.* —.
P 2 **ngaalogua.** *v.* —.
PE **hagangaalogu.** *v.* —.
PE1 **hagangaalogunga.** *n.* —.
PE2 **hagangaalogua.** *v.* —.
R **ngalogulogu.** *a.* Easily *ngalogu* in many places.
R 1 **ngalogulogunga.** *n.* —.
R 2 **ngalogulogua.** *v.* —.
RE **hagangalogulogu.** *v.* —.
RE1 **hagangalogulogunga.** *n.* —.
RE2 **hagangalogulogua.** *v.* —.
CF **malogu.** [= *ngalogu*].

NGALU
XCO **daungaangalu.** *n.* High-water mark.

NGALUBELUBE
B **ngalubelube.** *v.* Tremble or vibrate in the air.
B 1 **ngalubelubenga.** *n.* —.
B 2 **ngalubelubea.** *v.* —.
BE **hagangalubelube.** *v.* —.
BE1 **hagangalubelubenga.** *n.* —.
BE2 **hagangalubelubea.** *v.* —.

NGALUE
B **ngalue.** *a.* Move slightly, change position.
B 1 **ngalueanga.** *n.* —.
BE **hagangalue.** *v.* —.
BE1 **hagangalueanga.** *n.* —.
BE2 **hagangaluea.** *v.* —.
P **ngaalue.** *a.* —.
P 1 **ngaalueanga.** *n.* —.
PE **hagangaalue.** *v.* —.
PE1 **hagangaalueanga.** *n.* —.
PE2 **hagangaaluea.** *v.* —.
R **ngalungalue.** *a.* —.
R 1 **ngalungalueanga.** *n.* —.
RE **hagangalungalue.** *v.* —.
RE1 **hagangalungalueang.** *an.* —.
RE2 **hagangalungaluea.** *v.* —.
ID **ngalue age.** Increased, augmented.
ID **ngalue ange.** Increase.
ID **ngalue de gauvae.** Dislocated jaw.
ID **ngalue de hakii.** Dislocated larynx.
ID **ngalue iho.** Reduced, decreased.
ID **ngalue mai.** Decrease.
CF **ngaue.** Move (oneself), moved.

NGANA
E **nngana.** *a.* Loud (noise).
E 1 **ngganaanga.** *n.* —.
E 2 **nnganalia.** *v.* —.
EE **haganngana.** *v.* —.
EE1 **hagannganaanga.** *n.* —.

EE2 **haganngaoalia.** *v.* —.

EE2 **haganngaanalia.** *v.* —.
R **nganangana.** *a.* Loud (noise) repeatedly.
R 1 **ngananganaanga.** *n.* —.
R 2 **ngananganalia.** *v.* —.
RE **haganganangana.** *v.* —.
RE1 **haganganaganaanga.** *n.* —.
RE2 **hagangananganalia.** *v.* —.

NGANI
B **ngani.** *a.* Going around in a complete circle (like a belt).
B 1 **ngaaninga.** *n.* —.
B 2 **ngania.** *v.* —.
BE **hagangani.** *v.* —.
BE1 **hagangaaninga.** *n.* —.
BE2 **hagangania.** *v.* —.
P **nngani.** *a.* —.
PE **haganngani.** *v.* —.
R **nganingani.** *a.* —.
R 1 **nganinganinga.** *n.* —.
RE **haganganingani.** *v.* —.
RE1 **haganganinganinga.** *n.* —.
RE2 **haganganingania.** *v.* —.
ID **ngani adu.** *ngani* toward others; fit around one as a belt etc.
ID **ngani mai.** *ngani* toward oneself; fit (of clothes).

NGAO
E **nngao.** *v.* Loud (sound).
E 1 **nngaoanga.** *n.* —.
E 2 **nngaoa.** *v.* Noisy (a loud, individually perceived, noise).
E 2 **nngaolia.** *v.* Noise (a loud, individually perceived, noise).
EE **haganngao.** *v.* —.
EE1 **haganngaoanga.** *n.* —.
EE2 **haganngaoa.** *v.* —.
EE2 **haganngaolia.** *v.* —.
R **ngaongao.** *v.* —.
R 1 **ngaongaoanga.** *n.* —.
R 2 **ngaongaoa.** *v.* —.
R 2 **ngaongaolia.** *v.* —.
RE **hagangaongao.** *v.* —.
RE1 **hagangaongaoanga.** *n.* —.
RE2 **hagangaongaoa.** *v.* —.
RE2 **hagangaongaolia.** *v.* —.
ID **nngao dalinga.** Hurting in the ears from noise.

NGAOBO
B **ngaobo.** *v.* Easily bent out of shape.
B 1 **ngaoboanga.** *n.* —.
BE **hagangaobo.** *v.* —.
BE1 **hagangaoboanga.** *n.* —.
P **ngaaobo.** *v.* —.
P 1 **ngaaoboanga.** *n.* —.
PE **hagangaaobo.** *v.* —.
PE1 **hagangaaoboanga.** *n.* —.
R **ngaoboobo.** *v.* —.
R 1 **ngaobooboanga.** *n.* —.
RE **hagangaoboobo.** *v.* —.
RE1 **hagangaobooboanga.** *n.* —.

NGAOHEOHE
B **ngaoheohe.** *v.* Easily bent (impermanently).
B 1 **ngaoheoheanga.** *n.* —.
BE **hagangaoheohe.** *v.* —.
BE1 **hagangaoheoheanga.** *n.* —.
BE2 **hagangaoheohelia.** *v.* —.

NGAOHIE
B **ngaohie.** *mv.* Easily.
ID **hagao ngaohie.** Inexpensive.
ID **hai ngaohie.** Easy.

NGAOLO
B **ngaolo.** *a.* To make noise (irregular repeated sounds).
B 1 **ngaolonga.** *n.* —.
B 2 **ngaoloa.** *v.* Noisy (irregular repeated sounds).
BE **hagangaolo.** *v.* —.
BE1 **hagangaolonga.** *n.* —.
BE2 **hagangaoloa.** *v.* —.
R **ngaongaolo.** *v.* —.
R 1 **ngaongaolonga.** *n.* —.
RE **hagangaongaolo.** *v.* —.
RE1 **hagangaongaolonga.** *n.* —.
RE2 **hagangaongaoloa.** *v.* —.

NGAU
B **ngau₂.** *v.* Chew (e.g., to suck juice out but not swallow it).
B 1 **ngaunga.** *n.* —.
B 2 **ngaua.** *v.* —.
BE **hagangau.** *v.* —; provide food for, share food with.
BE1 **hagangaunga.** *n.* —.
BE2 **hagangaua.** *v.* —.

BE2 **hagangaulia.** *v.* —.
R **ngaungau$_1$.** *v.* —.
R **ngaungau$_2$.** *n.* Plant sp.: elephant ear (*Alocasia*).
R 1 **ngaungaunga.** *n.* —.
R 2 **ngaungaua.** *v.* —.
RE **hagangaungau.** *v.* —.
RE1 **hagangaungaunga.** *n.* —.
RE2 **hagangaungaua.** *v.* —.
RE2 **hagangaungaulia.** *v.* —.
ID **ngau hala.** Bite someone.

NGAUDA
B **ngauda$_2$.** *a.* An unenthusiastic fisherman.
B 1 **ngaudanga.** *n.* —.
BE **hagangauda.** *v.* —.
BE1 **hagangaudanga.** *n.* —.
R **ngaangauda.** *v.* Habitually *ngauda*.
R 1 **ngaangaudanga.** *n.* —.
RE **hagangaangauda.** *v.* —.
RE1 **hagangaangaudanga.** *n.* —.
ID **dangada ngauda.** A person who rarely goes fishing, landlubber.

NGAUE
B **ngaue.** *a.* Move (oneself), moved.
B 1 **ngaueanga.** *n.* —.
BE **hagangaue.** *v.* Move (something).
BE1 **hagangauenga.** *n.* —.
P **ngaaue.** *a.* —.
P 1 **ngaauenga.** *n.* —.
PE **hagangaaue.** *v.* —.
PE1 **hagangaauenga.** *n.* —.
PE2 **hagangaauea.** *v.* —.
R **ngaungaue.** *a.* —.
R 1 **ngaungauenga.** *n.* —.
RE **hagangaungaue.** *v.* —.
RE1 **hagangaungauenga.** *n.* —.
RE2 **hagangauea.** *v.* —.
RE2 **hagangaungauea.** *v.* —.
ID **ngaue age.** Increase (in rank or price, etc.).
ID **ngaue ange.** Increase (in price, etc.).
ID **ngaue iho.** Reduce (in rank, price, etc.).
ID **ngaue mai.** To reduce (in price, etc.).

NGAVALI
B **ngavali.** *a.* Bent slightly (not sharply).
B 1 **ngavalianga.** *n.* —.
BE **hagangavali.** *v.* —.
BE1 **hagangavalianga.** *n.* —.
P **ngaavali.** *v.* —.
P 1 **ngaavalianga.** *n.* —.
PE **hagangaavali.** *v.* —.
PE1 **hagangaavalianga.** *n.* —.
R **ngavalivali.** *a.* Repeatedly *ngavali* (as a diving board in use).
R 1 **ngavalivalianga.** *n.* —.
RE **hagangavalivali.** *v.* —.
RE1 **hagangavalivalianga.** *n.* —.

NGAVESI
B **ngavesi.** *n.* Box, coffin, crate.
XG **ngavesi haangoda.** Fishing tackle box.
ID **duu ngavesi.** A cover of a box.
ID **hagaduu ngavesi.** Make boxes.
ID **ngadi ngavesi.** An empty box.

NGIE
E **nngie.** *n.* Plant sp.: crepe myrtle shrub (*Pemphis acidula* Forst.).

NGII
B **ngii.** *v.* A high-pitched sound.
B 1 **ngiianga.** *n.* —.
BE **hagangii.** *v.* —.
BE1 **hagangiianga.** *n.* —.
BE2 **hagangiia.** *v.* —.
P **nngii.** *v.* —.
PE **haganngii.** *v.* —.
PE1 **haganngiianga.** *n.* —.
PE2 **haganngiia.** *v.* —.
R **ngiingii.** *v.* —.
RE **hagangiingii.** *v.* —.
RE1 **hagangiingiianga.** *n.* —.
RE2 **hagangiingiia.** *v.* —.

NGISI
B **ngisi.** *v.* A squeaking sound.
B 1 **ngiisinga.** *n.* —.
BE **hagangisi.** *v.* —.
BE1 **hagangiisinga.** *n.* —.

P nngisi. *v.* —.
R ngisingisi. *v.* —.
RE hagangisingisi. *v.* —.
RE1 hagangisingisinga. *n.* —.

NGISI$_a$
B **hedangisi.** *a.* To make noise by scraping things together (e.g., the grinding sound of jaws).
B 1 **hedangisinga.** *n.* —.
BE **hagahedangisi.** *v.* —.
BE1 **hagahedangisinga.** *n.* —.
BE2 **hagahedangisia.** *v.* —.
R **hedahedangisi.** *a.* —.
R 1 **hedahedangisinga.** *n.* —.
RE **hagahedahedangisi.** *v.* —.
RE1 **hagahedahedangisinga.** *n.* —.
RE2 **hagahedahedangisia.** *v.* —.

NGISO
XFL **malo-ngiso.** *n.* Driftwood sp. [used for making planks].

NGOLE
B **ngole.** *v.* Use up, use unwisely (not saving some for later), waste.
B 1 **ngoolenga.** *n.* —.
B 2 **ngolea.** *v.* —.
BE **hagangole.** *v.* —.
BE1 **hagangoolenga.** *n.* —.
BE2 **hagangolea.** *v.* —.
R **ngolengole.** *v.* —.
R 1 **ngolengolenga.** *n.* —.
R 2 **ngolengolea.** *v.* —.
RE **hagangolengole.** *v.* —.
RE1 **hagangolengolenga.** *n.* —.
RE2 **hagangolengolea.** *v.* —.
ID **gai ngole.** Wasteful, improvident.
ID **ngole age.** Use smallest first.
ID **ngole iho.** To use the biggest first.

NGOLO
CF **ngaolo.** To make noise (irregular repeated sounds).

NGONGO
B **ngongo.** *n.* Bird sp.: common noddy (*Anous stolidus*).
ID **haula ngongo.** To roast *ngongo* (in a fire).
ID **ivi ngongo.** Collar bone.

NGUDU
B **ngudu.** *n.* Mouth.
B **ngudu$_a$.** *nl.* Mouth of, rim of.
XCO **madaangudu.** *a.* Converse with.
XCO **ngudu-me.** *n.* Boundary of a taro plot.
ID **hagadige de madaangudu.** A prolonged conversation (on subjects of little importance).
ID **hagahebaa ngudu.** Converse (conversation).
ID **hagammau de ngudu.** Argumentative in a disrespectful way.
ID **hhanga de ngudu.** Open one's mouth.
ID **lleu luu malau ngudu.** Swollen lips (from eating spicy foods or foods to which one is allergic).
ID **maimai de ngudu.** Sweet-talker.
ID **malau ngudu.** Lips.
ID **ngudu aahua.** Islet shore (except that facing the lagoon).
ID **ngudu ai.** Act as an interpreter.
ID **ngudu gaiaa.** Charlatan.
ID **ngudu lagolago.** Lie (tell a falsehood).
ID **ngudu leelee.** Talkative, loquacious.
ID **ngudu leia.** Be the object of continual gossip; scorned.
ID **ngudu leidi.** Be the object of continual gossip; scorned.
ID **ngudu maimai.** Flattery or other communication by which one attempts to ingratiate oneself; unctuous, cloying, winsome.
ID **ngudu malie.** Eloquent (of a person).
ID **ngu te.** [a contraction of *ngudu de...*].
ID **ngu te lodo.** The edge of the lagoon reef.

ID sugi de ngudu. The corner of the mouth.
ID vaivai ngudu. Evil-tongued, lying (dishonest, foulmouthed.
ID vava de ngudu. Talkative, indiscreet.
ID vini de ngudu. A screwed up mouth (as of a child on the point of crying).

NGUNGU
B **ngungu.** *v.* Chew, masticate (solids which make noise).
B 2 **nguudia.** *v.* —.
RC **mangunngungu.** *a.* The sound of something being chewed.
RC1 **mangunngunguanga.** *n.* —.
RF **hagamangunngungu.** *v.* —.
RF1 **hagamangunngunguanga.** *n.* —.
RF2 **hagamangunngungulia.** *v.* —.

NGUU$_1$
B **nguu$_1$.** *a.* A faint sound, like humming.
B 1 **nguuanga.** *n.* —.
B 2 **nguua.** *v.* Be *nguu.*
B 2 **nguulia.** *v.* Be *nguu.*
BE **haganguu.** *v.* —; ask permission.
BE2 **haganguua.** *v.* —.
BE2 **haganguulia.** *v.* —.
P **nnguu.** *a.* —.
R **nguunguu.** *a.* —.
R 1 **nguunguuanga.** *n.* —.
RE **haganguunguu.** *v.* —.
RE1 **haganguunguuanga.** *n.* —.
RE2 **haganguunguua.** *v.* —.
RE2 **haganguunguulia.** *v.* —.

NGUU$_2$
B **nguu$_2$.** *n.* Squid (3 types).
ID **duudae nguu.** The inky excretion of the squid.

NNGAHU
ID **magi nngahu.** Asthma.

NNGOLO
B **nngolo.** *a.* A steady sound (e.g., of a machine, of rain, or of vibration).
B 1 **ngoolonga.** *n.* —.
BE **haganngolo.** *v.* —.
BE1 **hagangoolonga.** *n.* —.
BE2 **haganngoloa.** *v.* —.
R **ngolongolo.** *a.* —.
RE **hagangolongolo.** *v.* —.
RE1 **hagangolongolonga.** *n.* —.
RE2 **hagangolongoloa.** *v.* —.

O
B **o.** *mr.* RELATIONAL PARTICLE I.
ID **bii o madahasi.** A certain kind of phosphorescence in seawater at night.
ID **goloa o de hine.** Female genitalia.
ID **goloa o taane.** Male genitalia.
ID **hagadubu o madaligi.** The name of a certain type of string figure.

OA
B **oa.** *n.* Gunwales (at the top of the canoe).

OAA
B **oaa.** *a.* A sound indicating disagreement or displeasure; Oh my gosh!

OBE
B **obe.** *n.* Eye of the taro corm.
B 1 **obenga.** *n.* —.
B 2 **obea.** *v.* To have an eye (of a taro corm).
BE **hagaobe.** *v.* Cause to have *obe.*
BE1 **hagaobenga.** *n.* —.
BE2 **hagaobea.** *v.* —.
R 2 **obeobea.** *v.* Having many eyes (of the taro corm).
RE **hagaobeobe.** *v.* —.
RE1 **hagaobeobenga.** *n.* —.
RE2 **hagaobeobea.** *v.* —.

ODA$_1$
B **oda$_1$.** *v.* Eat (something) raw.
B 1 **odaanga.** *n.* —.
B 2 **odaia.** *v.* —.
B 2 **odalia.** *v.* —.
BE **hagaoda$_1$.** *v.* —.
BE1 **hagaodaanga.** *n.* —.
BE2 **hagaodaia.** *v.* —.

BE2 **hagaodalia.** *v.* —.
R **odaoda$_1$.** *v.* —.
RE **hagaodaoda.** *v.* —.
RE1 **hagaodaodaanga.** *n.* —.
RE2 **hagaodaodaia.** *v.* —.
RE2 **hagaodaodalia.** *v.* —.

ODA$_2$
B **oda$_2$.** *n.* Grated coconut meat after the oil has been expressed.
BE **hagaoda$_2$.** *n.* A type of prepared food (a kind of *dalogo* made without water).
XFL **hagaoda-lolo.** *n.* Fish sp. (= large *llahi*).
ID **hagaoda tugi.** A type of prepared food (made from mashed taro and grated coconut).
CF **badioda.** The residue remaining after coconut oil has been heated; the residue remaining after arrowroot starch-making.

ODA$_3$
R **odaoda$_2$.** *n.* Driftwood (any sort).

ODEA
B **odea.** *a.* Noon, midday.
BE **hagaodea.** *v.* The time at which it is midday.

ODI
B **odi$_b$.** *a.* Gone, finished, used up.
B 1 **odinga.** *n.* —.
BE **hagaodi.** *v.* End of (e.g., time).
BE1 **hagaodinga.** *n.* —.
BE2 **hagaodia.** *v.* Finish up, be last.
R **odiodi.** *a.* Long since finished, done, or gone.
RE **hagaodiodi.** *v.* —.
RE1 **hagaodiodinga.** *n.* —.
RE2 **hagaodiodia.** *v.* —.
ID **daelodo dee odi ange.** Odd number.
ID **daelodo odi ange.** Even number.
ID **gu odi ange ona.** He has done all he could.
ID **gu odi mai ogu.** I have done all I could!
ID **me hagaodi.** Last one.
ID **odi ai loo.** That's the end! That's all!
ID **odi ange.** Even (number); complete (none missing); reach the maximum.
ID **odi de masavaa.** Having insufficient time remaining for (something).
ID **odi iho.** Just finished.
ID **odi mai (adu, ange).** All (e.g., have come).
ID **odi sango.** Completely cleaned up or finished; all gone; each and every one all gone.

ODI$_a$
B **odi$_a$.** *mv.* Already; very.
R **odiodi$_a$.** *b.* Long since, a long time ago.
ID **baba odi.** To have been settled for some time.
ID **gona odi.** Too much.
ID **kangi odi.** Too sharp.

ODO$_1$
B **odo$_1$.** *v.* To roof (a house), to thatch (a house).
B 1 **odonga.** *n.* —; the string used for securing thatch to the roof frame.
B 2 **odoa.** *v.* —.
B 2 **odohia.** *v.* —.
B 2 **odolia.** *v.* —.
BE **hagaodo.** *v.* —.
BE1 **hagaodonga.** *n.* —.
BE2 **hagaodoa.** *v.* —.
BE2 **hagaodohia.** *v.* —.
BE2 **hagaodolia.** *v.* —.
R **odoodo.** *v.* —.
R 1 **odoodonga.** *n.* —.
R 2 **odoodoa.** *v.* —.
R 2 **odoodohia.** *v.* —.
RE **hagaodoodo.** *v.* —.
RE1 **hagaodoodonga.** *n.* —.
RE2 **hagaodoodoa.** *v.* —.
RE2 **hagaodoodohia.** *v.* —.
RE2 **hagaodoodolia.** *v.* —.

ODO$_2$
XCO **odomalie.** *a.* Delicious (of

coconut apples only).

OGA

B	**oga.** *v.* To husk (a coconut) with a sharp stick.
B 1	**ogaanga.** *n.* —; the husk of a coconut (remaining after husking).
B 2	**ogahia.** *v.* —.
BE	**hagaoga.** *v.* —.
BE1	**hagaogaanga.** *n.* —.
BE2	**hagaogahia.** *v.* —.
R	**ogaoga.** *v.* —.
R 1	**ogaogaanga.** *n.* —.
RE	**hagaogaoga.** *v.* —.
RE1	**hagaogaogaanga.** *n.* —.
RE2	**hagaogaogahia.** *v.* —.
ID	**duu de ogaanga.** Having husked many coconuts (as evidenced by the many husks lying about).

OGO$_1$

B	**ogo$_1$.** *v.* Pick up one at a time (by hand).
B 1	**ogoanga.** *n.* —.
B 1	**ogonga.** *n.* —.
B 2	**ogoa.** *v.* —.
B 2	**ogohia.** *v.* —.
B 2	**ogolia.** *v.* —.
BE	**hagaogo.** *v.* —.
BE1	**hagaogoanga.** *n.* —.
BE1	**hagaogonga.** *n.* —.
BE2	**hagaogoa.** *v.* —.
BE2	**hagaogohia.** *v.* —.
BE2	**hagaogolia.** *v.* —.
R	**ogoogo.** *v.* —.
R 1	**ogoogoanga.** *n.* —.
R 1	**ogoogonga.** *n.* —.
R 2	**ogoogoa.** *v.* —.
R 2	**ogoogohia.** *v.* —.
R 2	**ogoogolia.** *v.* —.
RE	**hagaogoogo.** *v.* —.
RE1	**hagaogoogoanga.** *n.* —.
RE1	**hagaogoogonga.** *n.* —.
RE2	**hagaogoogoa.** *v.* —.
RE2	**hagaogoogohia.** *v.* —.
RE2	**hagaogoogolia.** *v.* —.

OGO$_2$

B	**ogo$_2$.** *n.* Purlin.

OGO$_3$

B	**ogo$_3$.** *n.* The attachment of a clam to the reef.

OHA

B	**oha.** *v.* Break, break up, destroy; damage, ruin.
B 2	**ohaa.** *v.* —.
B 2	**ohalia.** *v.* —.
BC	**maoha.** *a.* Broken (as a machine), broken down.
BC1	**maohanga.** *n.* —.
BF	**hagamaoha.** *v.* —.
BF1	**hagamaohanga.** *n.* —.
P	**ooha.** *v.* —.
P 1	**oohanga.** *n.* —.
P 2	**oohaa.** *v.* —.
P 2	**oohalia.** *v.* —.
PC	**maaoha.** *a.* —.
PC1	**maaohanga.** *n.* —.
PF	**hagamaaoha.** *v.* —.
PF1	**hagamaaohanga.** *n.* —.
R	**ohaoha.** *v.* —.
R 1	**ohaohaanga.** *n.* —.
R 2	**ohaohaa.** *v.* —.
R 2	**ohaohalia.** *v.* —.
RC	**maohaoha.** *a.* Broken up (into many pieces or groupings).
RC1	**maohaohaanga.** *n.* —.
RF	**hagamaohaoha.** *v.* —.
RF1	**hagamaohaohanga.** *n.* —.
ID	**maoha saele.** Broken up (into many pieces or groupings).
ID	**oha de ganomada.** To work on a craft item (e.g., a canoe) with a model in mind of the finished product which is different from that of the person who began the work.
ID	**oha de nnoho paba.** Disturb the peace.
ID	**oha valaai.** To disobey the instructions of a healer.

OHO

B	**oho.** *v.* To do something, or go somewhere, early in the morning.
B 1	**ohoanga.** *n.* —.
BE	**hagaoho.** *v.* —.
BE1	**hagaohoanga.** *n.* —.
R	**ohooho$_1$.** *v.* —.
R 1	**ohoohoanga$_1$.** *n.* —.
RE	**hagaohooho$_1$.** *v.* —.
RE1	**hagaohoohoanga$_1$.** *n.* —.

ID **oho adu.** Go early.
ID **oho age.** The following morning.
ID **oho boo.** To *oho* while still dark.
ID **oho iho.** Come ashore early in the morning.
ID **oho mai.** Come early.

OHOOHO
B **ohooho$_2$.** *v.* Frightened by noise.
B 1 **ohoohoanga$_2$.** *n.* —.
BE **hagaohooho$_2$.** *v.* —.
BE1 **hagaohoohoanga$_2$.** *n.* —.

OHU
B **ohu.** *v.* A depression in a tree trunk.
B 1 **oohunga.** *n.* —.
B 2 **ohua.** *v.* Characterized by having *ohu.*
BE **hagaohu.** *v.* —.
BE1 **hagaohunga.** *n.* —.
BE2 **hagaohua.** *v.* —.
P **oohu.** *v.* —.
P 2 **oohua.** *v.* —.
PE **hagaoohu.** *v.* —.
PE1 **hagaoohunga.** *n.* —.
PE2 **hagaoohua.** *v.* —.
R **ohuohu.** *v.* Having many *ohu.*
R 1 **ohuohunga.** *n.* —.
RE **hagaohuohu.** *v.* —.
RE1 **hagaohuohunga.** *n.* —.
RE2 **hagaohuohua.** *v.* —.

OIA
B **oia.** *a.* A sound used to communicate the tiredness of the speaker, or that the speaker recognizes his mistake.
BE **hagaoia.** *v.* —.

OLA
B **ola.** *a.* Free, escaped; survive, safe.
B 1 **olaanga.** *n.* —.
BE **hagaola.** *v.* Save from.
BE1 **hagaolaanga.** *n.* —.
R **olaola.** *a.* —.
R 1 **olaolaanga.** *n.* —.
RE **hagaolaola.** *v.* —.
RE1 **hagaolaolaanga.** *n.* —.
ID **gu hagaola loo.** Just missed catching.

OLAA
B **olaa.** *a.* A sound expressing surprise or disapproval.
BE **hagaolaa.** *v.* —.
R **olaaolaa.** *a.* —.
RE **hagaolaaolaa.** *v.* —.

OLIOLI
B **olioli.** *v.* To put an infant to sleep by singing a lullaby.
B 1 **oliolinga.** *n.* —.
B 2 **oliolia.** *v.* —.
BE **hagaolioli.** *v.* —.
BE1 **hagaoliolinga.** *n.* —.
BE2 **hagaoliolia.** *v.* —.

OLO
B **olo.** *n.* An area in which sand has accumulated; beach, sand spit.
XCO **madaaolo.** *n.* Capital of.

OLONOA
B **olonoa.** *n.* Sea cucumber sp.

OLONGAA
B **olongaa.** *n.* Plant sp.: tree sp.: a shrubby tree sp. (*Pipturus argenteus* (Forst.f.) Wedd.).

ONO$_1$
B **ono$_1$.** *an.* Six.
BE **hagaono (ina).** *v.* Make a total of six.
XCO **Diba-ono.** *nn.* The name of a person in a traditional story.
XCO **Ono-laangi.** *nt.* Saturday ('sixth day').
XCO **Ono-malama.** *nt.* June ('sixth month').
ID **ono-samono.** The sixth number of a counting game played to determine who is "it".

ONO$_2$
B **ono$_2$.** *n.* Fish sp.: barracuda.
R 2 **onoonogia.** *v.* An overindulgence in fatty

foods, leading to a loss of appetite.

R 3 **onoonogiaanga.** *n.* —.

RE2 **hagaonoonogia.** *v.* —.

RE3 **hagaonoonogiaanga.** *n.* —.

ONODAA

B **onodaa.** *n.* Mollusk sp.: *Spondylus* sp.

ONGA

RE **hagaongaonga.** *v.* Moving one's head back and forth in time to music.

ONGE

B **onge.** *v.* Famine.

B 2 **ongea.** *v.* —.

BE **hagaonge.** *v.* —.

BE2 **hagaongea.** *v.* —.

R **ongeonge.** *v.* —.

R 2 **ongeongea.** *v.* —.

RE **hagaongeonge.** *v.* —.

RE2 **hagaongeongea.** *v.* —.

OO$_1$

B **oo$_1$.** *a.* Shout.

B 1 **oonga.** *n.* —.

BE **hagaoo$_1$.** *v.* —.

BE1 **hagaoonga.** *n.* —.

R **oooo.** *a.* —.

RE **hagaoooo.** *v.* —.

RE1 **hagaoooonga.** *n.* —.

ID **gu oo ina mai.** Shout to announce important news (e.g., to announce the arrival of a ship).

OO$_2$

B **oo$_2$.** *a.* Fit to (or into).

B 1 **ooanga.** *n.* —.

B 2 **oohia.** *v.* (For a canoe) to be able to navigate on the reef (i.e., the tide not being so low that it is too shallow).

B 3 **oohiaanga.** *n.* —.

BE **hagaoo$_2$.** *v.* —.

BE1 **hagaooanga.** *n.* —.

BE2 **hagaoohia.** *v.* —.

BE3 **hagaoohiaanga.** *n.* —.

ID **oo tanga.** Too big (clothes), spacious.

ID **oo iho (age).** Able to enter, going up (down).

OO$_3$

B **oo$_3$.** *n.* A ration of food for a long canoe voyage.

OOI

B **ooi.** *a.* A sound used in communicating at a distance (= "yes?").

B 1 **ooinga.** *n.* —.

BE **hagaooi.** *v.* —.

BE1 **hagaooinga.** *n.* —.

R **ooiooi.** *a.* —.

R 1 **ooiooinga.** *n.* —.

RE **hagaooiooi.** *v.* —.

RE1 **hagaooiooinga.** *n.* —.

OOMEA

B **oomea.** *a.* Afternoon (late).

B 1 **oomeaanga.** *n.* —.

BE **hagaoomea.** *v.* To wait until *oomea.*

BE1 **hagaoomeaanga.** *n.* —.

OSI

B **osi.** *v.* A seedling; a shoot (of another plant) set aside for planting a seedling.

B 1 **osinga.** *n.* —.

B 2 **osia.** *v.* Taken for planting.

BE **hagaosi.** *v.* —.

BE1 **hagaosinga.** *n.* —.

BE2 **hagaosia.** *v.* —.

R **osiosi.** *v.* —.

R 1 **osiosinga.** *n.* —.

R 2 **osiosia.** *v.* —.

RE **hagaosiosi.** *v.* —.

RE1 **hagaosiosinga.** *n.* —.

RE2 **hagaosiosia.** *v.* —.

ID **gaadinga osi.** A coconut selected as a seedling.

ID **me osi.** A coconut tree seedling.

OSO

B **oso.** *v.* Smell (something) by sniffing, kiss (Polynesian style).

B 1 **oosonga.** *n.* —.

B 1 **osoanga.** *n.* —.

B 2 **osoa.** *v.* —.

B 2 **osohia.** *v.* —.

B 2 **osolia.** *v.* —.

B 2 **osongia.** *v.* —.

BE	**hagaoso.** *v.* —.
BE1	**hagaoosonga.** *n.* —.
BE1	**hagaosoanga.** *n.* —.
BE2	**hagaosoa.** *v.* —.
BE2	**hagaosohia.** *v.* —.
BE2	**hagaosolia.** *v.* —.
BE2	**hagaosongia.** *v.* —.
R	**ososoo.** *v.* —.
R 1	**osoosoanga.** *n.* —.
R 1	**osoosonga.** *n.* —.
R 2	**osoosoa.** *v.* —.
R 2	**osoosohia.** *v.* —.
R 2	**osoosolia.** *v.* —.
R 2	**osoosongia.** *v.* —.
RE	**hagaosooso.** *v.* —.
RE1	**hagaosoosoanga.** *n.* —.
RE1	**hagaosoosonga.** *n.* —.
RE2	**hagaosoosoa.** *v.* —.
RE2	**hagaosoosohia.** *v.* —.
RE2	**hagaosoosolia.** *v.* —.
RE2	**hagaosoosongia.** *v.* —.

OU

B	**ou.** *a.* Yes!
R	**ouou.** *a.* Yes! Yes!
U	**ouaa.** *a.* Yes! Certainly!

OVEA

B	**ovea.** *v.* Disheveled (as the chicken feathers on a much-used trolling lure).
B 1	**oveaanga.** *n.* —.
BE	**hagaovea.** *v.* —.
BE1	**hagaoveaanga.** *n.* —.
R	**oveovea.** *v.* —.
R 1	**oveoveaanga.** *n.* —.
RE	**hagaoveovea.** *v.* —.
RE1	**hagaoveoveaanga.** *n.* —.

SAA_1

B	**saa_1.** *mv.* Bad.
BE	**hagasaa.** *a.* Quarrel (like children).
BE1	**hagasaanga.** *n.* —.
BE2	**hagasaangia.** *v.* To encounter good (or bad) fortune.
BE3	**hagasaangiaanga.** *n.* —.
XCO	**gaisaa.** *v.* Wasteful in preparing food, uneconomical.
XCO	**kanosaa.** *a.* A tasteless tuber of poor quality.
CF	**hinangalosaa.** Miss (someone or something); longing (for a person or place).
CF	**longosaa.** Small around, thin.
CF	**massaa (ina).** Despised by others.
CF	**saabudu.** Fish sp. (= large *saagahinoa*).
CF	**saagahinoa.** Fish sp. (= small *saabudu*).

SAA_2

B	**saa_2.** *n.* A share of food (esp. for children).
CF	**hagasaalunga.** —.

SAABAI

B	**saabai.** *v.* Lift up and carry; carry (a burden).
B 1	**saabainga.** *n.* —.
B 1	**sabainga.** *n.* —.
B 2	**saabaia.** *v.* —.
B 2	**sabaia.** *v.* —.
BE	**hagasaabai.** *v.* —.
BE1	**hagasaabainga.** *n.* —.
BE1	**hagasabainga.** *n.* —.
BE2	**hagasaabaia.** *v.* —.
BE2	**hagasabaia.** *v.* —.
R	**sabasabai.** *v.* —.
R 1	**sabasabainga.** *n.* —.
R 2	**sabasabaia.** *v.* —.
RE	**hagasabasabai.** *v.* —.
RE1	**hagasabasabainga.** *n.* —.
RE2	**hagasabasabaia.** *v.* —.
ID	**saabai moni doo.** Carry a canoe (over the reef at low tide).
CF	**abaabai.** Carry a canoe in shallow water; carry half lifting.

SAABINI

B	**saabini.** *v.* Wrap up, tie up.
B 1	**sabininga.** *n.* —; package, bundle (wrapped up).
B 2	**sabinia.** *v.* —.
R	**sabisabini.** *v.* Wrap up or tie up over and over.
R 1	**sabisabininga.** *n.* —.
R 2	**sabisabinia.** *v.* —.

SAAGULE

B	**saagule.** *v.* Pick head lice.
B 1	**sagulenga.** *n.* —.
B 2	**sagulea.** *v.* —.

BE **hagasaagule.** *v.* Teach how to *saagule.*
BE1 **hagasagulenga.** *n.* —.
BE2 **hagasagulea.** *v.* —.
R **sagusagule.** *v.* —.
R 1 **sagusagulenga.** *n.* —.
R 2 **sagusagulea.** *v.* —.
RE **hagasagusagule.** *v.* —.
RE1 **hagasagusagulenga.** *n.* —.
RE2 **hagasagusagulea.** *v.* —.
S **saasaagule.** *v.* —.
S 1 **saasaagulenga.** *n.* —.
S 2 **saasaagulea.** *v.* —.
SE **hagasaasaagule.** *v.* —.
SE1 **hagasaasaagulenga.** *n.* —.
SE2 **hagasaasaagulea.** *v.* —.
CF **ageli.** Pick head lice.
CF **agule.** Pick head lice.

SAAHEA
B **saahea.** *a.* Be caught (esp. fish) and secured.
B 1 **saaheaanga.** *n.* —.
BE **hagasaahea.** *v.* —.
BE1 **hagasaaheaanga.** *n.* —.

SAALI
B **saali.** *n.* A type of rope (used for climbing breadfruit trees).
ID **dua saali.** One of the lines of which *saali* is composed.
ID **gage saali.** To climb a breadfruit tree using *saali.*

SAALIBA
B **saaliba.** *a.* Rush around (of a group of people).
B 1 **saalibaanga.** *n.* —.
BE **hagasaaliba.** *v.* —.
BE1 **hagasaalibaanga.** *n.* —.

SAALOA
BE **hagasaaloa.** *v.* To encounter good (or bad) fortune.
BE1 **hagasaaloaanga.** *n.* —.

SAALOHIA
B **saalohia.** *v.* Hungry.
B 1 **saalohiaanga.** *n.* —.
BE **hagasaalohia.** *v.* —.
BE1 **hagasaalohiaanga.** *n.* —.
R **saasaalohia.** *v.* —.
R 1 **saasaalohiaanga.** *n.* —.
RE **hagasaasaalohia.** *v.* —.
RE1 **hagasaasaalohiaanga.** *n.* —.

SAALUNGA
BE **hagasaalunga$_2$.** *v.* Spirit, soul, name-group.
ID **hagasaalunga ange.** Call (someone) by the name of his name-group.
ID **hagasaalunga de langi.** A member of the Christian Endeavor Society.

SAAVA
B **saava.** *v.* Skinny, thin (lacking in flesh).
B 1 **saavaanga.** *n.* —.
BE **hagasaava.** *v.* —.
BE1 **hagasaavaanga.** *n.* —.

SAAVALE
B **saavale.** *v.* Spit, drool, sputum.
B 1 **saavaleanga.** *n.* —.
BE **hagasaavale.** *v.* —.
BE1 **hagasaavaleanga.** *n.* —.
R **savasavale.** *a.* —.
R 1 **savasavaleanga.** *n.* —.
RE **hagasavasavale.** *v.* —.
RE1 **hagasavasavaleanga.** *n.* —.
ID **saavale ina.** Fish or meat which is watery in texture and bad-tasting.
ID **sali ssaavale.** Salivate.

SABA$_1$
B **saba$_1$.** *v.* Be in a precarious position.
B 2 **sabalia$_1$.** *v.* Be in a situation in which *saba$_1$.*
BE **hagasaba$_1$.** *v.* —.
BE1 **hagasabaanga.** *n.* —.
BE2 **hagasabalia$_1$.** *v.* —.
R **sabasaba.** *v.* Unstably balanced.
R 2 **sabasabalia.** *v.* —.
RE **hagasabasaba.** *v.* —; to get into a dangerous position (as children climbing trees).
RE1 **hagasabasabaanga.** *n.* —.
RE2 **hagasabasabalia.** *v.* —.
ID **duu hagasabasaba.** To stand in a place from

which one is liable to fall.
ID **duu saba.** Unstable, poorly balanced.
CF **duusaba.** A type of musical instrument (a stretched palm leaf jiggled while blown against).

SABA$_2$
B **saba$_2$.** *v.* Capable (of a person).
B 1 **saabanga.** *n.* —.
B 2 **sabalia$_2$.** *v.* Be *saba.*
BE **hagasaba$_2$.** *v.* —.
BE1 **hagasaabanga.** *n.* —.
BE2 **hagasabalia$_2$.** *v.* —.
P **ssaba.** *v.* —.
PE **hagassaba.** *v.* —.
PE2 **hagassabalia.** *v.* —.

SABALA
B **sabala.** *a.* Willing to.
BE **hagasabala.** *v.* Talk (someone) into (something).
P **saapala.** *a.* —.
PE **hagasaapala.** *v.* —.
R **sabalabala.** *a.* Always agreeing with.
RE **hagasabalabala.** *v.* —.

SABANAANA
B **sabanaana.** *v.* A phosphorescent flash in the water.
BE **hagasabanaana.** *v.* —.

SABEELOI
B **sabeeloi.** *v.* Wrap up (something) hastily [obligatorily followed by *ina* in transitive usage].
B 1 **sabeeloinga.** *n.* —.
BE **hagasabeeloi.** *v.* —.
BE1 **hagasabeeloinga.** *n.* —.

SABO
B **sabo.** *v.* Do slowly.
B 1 **saabonga.** *n.* —.
B 2 **saboa.** *v.* —.
B 2 **sabolia.** *v.* —.
BE **hagasabo.** *v.* —.
BE1 **hagasaabonga.** *n.* —.
BE2 **hagasaboa.** *v.* —.
BE2 **hagasabolia.** *v.* —.
P **ssabo.** *v.* —.
PE **hagassabo.** *v.* —.
PE2 **hagassaboa.** *v.* —.
PE2 **hagassabolia.** *v.* —.
R **sabosabo.** *v.* —.
R 1 **sabosabonga.** *n.* —.
R 2 **sabosaboa.** *v.* —.
R 2 **sabosabolia.** *v.* —.
RE **hagasabosabo.** *v.* —.
RE1 **hagasabosabonga.** *n.* —.
RE2 **hagasabosaboa.** *v.* —.
RE2 **hagasabosabolia.** *v.* —.
ID **malo sabo.** Breechclout.

SABONEALO
ID **dahuli sabonealo.** The odor of overripe breadfruit.

SAE$_1$
B **sae$_1$.** *d.* —.
B 1 **saenga$_1$.** *n.* —.
B 2 **saea.** *v.* —.
BC **masae.** *a.* Torn, deflowered (of a virgin).
BC1 **masaenga.** *n.* —; a hole (in something torn).
BF **hagamasae.** *v.* —.
BF1 **hagamasaenga.** *n.* —.
BF2 **hagamasaea.** *v.* —.
E **ssae$_1$.** *v.* Rip, tear, deflower (a virgin).
R **saesae$_1$.** *v.* —.
R 1 **saesaenga$_1$.** *n.* —.
R 2 **saesaea.** *v.* —.
RC **masaesae.** *a.* —.
RC1 **masaesaenga.** *n.* —.
RF **hagamasaesae.** *v.* —.
RF1 **hagamasaesaenga.** *n.* —.
RF2 **hagamasaesaea.** *v.* —.
T **sasae.** *v.* —; habitually *ssae$_1$.*
ID **dee masae de leo.** Lose one's voice (from straining one's vocal cords).
ID **hagasae gili.** Pierce the skin superficially.
ID **sae de hadu.** Make a grater (by punching holes in sheet metal).
ID **sae iho.** Tear from the top down; break through the bush (coming downhill).
ID **sae mai.** Break through the bush (toward one).

ID **ssae de hine.** To deflower a girl.

ID **ssae de leo.** To project one's voice better (e.g., after clearing one's throat).

SAE$_{1a}$

B **maasae.** *a.* Hatched.

B 1 **maasaenga.** *n.* —.

BE **hagamaasae.** *v.* —.

BE1 **hagamaasaenga.** *n.* —.

BE2 **hagamaasaea.** *v.* —.

SAE$_2$

B **sae$_2$.** *a.* Suffer, be in pain; crave for, desperate.

B 1 **saenga$_2$.** *n.* —.

BE **hagasae.** *v.* —.

BE1 **hagasaenga.** *n.* —.

BE2 **hagasaea.** *v.* —.

BE2 **hagasaelia.** *v.* —.

P **ssae$_2$.** *a.* —; the sensation felt in the teeth when eating lemon.

P 1 **ssaenga.** *n.* —.

PE **hagassae.** *v.* —.

PE1 **hagassaenga.** *n.* —.

PE2 **hagassaea.** *v.* —.

PE2 **hagassaelia.** *v.* —.

R **saesae$_2$.** *a.* —.

R 1 **saesaenga$_2$.** *n.* —.

RE **hagasaesae.** *v.* —.

RE1 **hagasaesaenga.** *n.* —.

ID **magi ssae aalanga.** Sore muscles (not associated with strain).

ID **ssae de manava.** Struggle to breathe.

SAELE

B **saele.** *v.* Wander aimlessly, to walk around.

B 1 **saeleanga.** *n.* —.

B 1 **saelenga.** *n.* —; road, walkway, path (for walking).

B 2 **saelea.** *v.* Walked upon.

BE **hagasaele.** *v.* —; meeting; decide (come to a considered conclusion); thought.

BE1 **hagasaeleanga.** *n.* —.

BE1 **hagasaelenga.** *n.* —.

BE2 **hagasaelea.** *v.* —.

R **saelesaele.** *v.* To wander around continually (from past time to the present).

R 1 **saelesaeleanga.** *n.* —.

R 1 **saelesaelenga.** *n.* —.

RE **hagasaelesaele.** *v.* —; to think about something (esp. a problem) for a long time (keep turning it over in one's mind).

RE1 **hagasaelesaeleanga.** *n.* —.

RE1 **hagasaelesaelenga.** *n.* —.

RE2 **hagasaelesaelea.** *v.* —.

S **saesaele.** *v.* To wander around continually (doing so at present and likely to be doing so in the future).

S 1 **saesaeleanga.** *n.* —.

S 1 **saesaelenga.** *n.* —.

S 2 **saesaelea.** *v.* To be continually walked upon.

SE **hagasaesaele.** *v.* —.

SE1 **hagasaesaeleanga.** *n.* —.

SE1 **hagasaesaelenga.** *n.* —.

SE2 **hagasaesaelea.** *v.* —.

ID **adi saele.** Disseminate information.

ID **baalasi saele.** Shine a flashlight indiscriminately on people.

ID **daabeduge saele.** To bat around.

ID **dada saele.** Always being borrowed.

ID **daumaha hagasaele.** A meeting of church members for business.

ID **deledele saele.** Walk around aimlessly; be spread all over (of news).

ID **gabi saele.** Carry around holding.

ID **galo saele.** Look around (moving one's body about).

ID **giigii saele.** Giggle.

ID **kangi de hagasaele.** A quick-witted person (who realizes his goals fast).

ID **haahaa saele.** Search here and there.

ID **hagapigi saele.** Go around with someone constantly.

ID **hagadiingia saele.** To go about exposing oneself to

the sun's rays.
ID **hagasaele age.** Make up one's mind; lift up (in a steady motion).
ID **hagasoesoe saele.** To walk about without greeting others.
ID **hano saele.** Wander around.
ID **hilo saele.** Spread venereal disease.
ID **hulo saele.** Wander around.
ID **laagau aalo saelenga.** Thatch rafters on the ends of a house.
ID **leva saele.** Vagrant (having no fixed abode).
ID **maoha saele.** Broken up (into many pieces or groupings).
ID **saibo saele.** Rush around aimlessly (of a group of people).
ID **saugalo saele.** Search for here and there, wander around looking for.
ID **see boiboi saele.** Stagger about (from a head injury), move as though unconscious.
ID **sigale saele.** Search for.
ID **sua saele.** Search for by rooting around.
ID **sulu saele.** To throw oneself about (as children do when unhappy).

SAGA

B **saga.** *a.* Glide (in the air); to overhang (of something flat).
B 1 **saaganga.** *n.* —.
BE **hagasaga.** *v.* —.
BE1 **hagasaaganga.** *n.* —.
BE2 **hagasagalia.** *v.* —.
P **ssaga.** *a.* —.
PE **hagassaga.** *v.* —.
PE2 **hagassagalia.** *v.* —.
R **sagasaga.** *a.* —.
R 1 **sagasagaanga.** *n.* —.
RE **hagasagasaga.** *v.* —.
RE1 **hagasagasagaanga.** *n.* —.
RE2 **hagasagasagalia.** *v.* —.
ID **me hagasaga.** A toy (made from a dried breadfruit leaf or a disk of coconut shell) which slides when thrown.
ID **saga gee.** *saga* away from; extend out in space.
ID **saga gi daha.** *saga* away from; extend out in space.

SAGANA

B **sagana.** *v.* Watch carefully, keep an eye on.
B 1 **saganaanga.** *n.* —.
B 2 **saganaa.** *v.* —.
BE **hagasaganaa.** *v.* —.
BE1 **hagasaganaanga.** *n.* —.
R **sagasagana.** *v.* —.
R 1 **sagasaganaanga.** *n.* —.
R 2 **sagasaganaa.** *v.* —.
RE **hagasagasagana.** *v.* —.
RE1 **hagasagasaganaanga.** *n.* —.
ID **dai sagana iho goe.** Watch out!
ID **saganaa iho goe.** Watch out!

SAGEA

B **sagea.** *v.* To do something without regard for others (because one is excited).
B 1 **sageaanga.** *n.* —.
BE **hagasagea.** *v.* —.
BE1 **hagasageaanga.** *n.* —.
R **sagesagea.** *v.* —.
R 1 **sagesageaanga.** *n.* —.
RE **hagasagesagea.** *v.* —.
RE1 **hagasagesageaanga.** *n.* —.
ID **sagea gee.** Extremely *sagea.*

SAGISAGILI

B **sagisagili.** *v.* To say dirty words to someone.
B 1 **sagisagilianga.** *n.* —.
BE **hagasagisagili.** *v.* —.
BE1 **hagasagisagilianga.** *n.* —.

SAGO

B **sago.** *v.* Tough (like meat); stiff (like a heavy fishing pole).
B 1 **saagonga.** *n.* —.
BE **hagasago.** *v.* —; pull, move, or raise, gently.
BE1 **hagasaagonga.** *n.* —.
BE2 **hagasagolia.** *v.* —.
P **ssago.** *v.* —.

PE hagassago. *v.* —.
PE1 hagassagoanga. *n.* —.
PE2 hagassagolia. *v.* —.
RE hagasagosago. *v.* —; take a little from several different sources.
RE1 hagasagosagoanga. *n.* —.
RE2 hagasagosagolia. *v.* —.
ID **iai sago.** Having special ability (strength, power, etc.) which others do not have, a strong or powerful (person).

SAGULAA
B **sagulaa.** *n.* Fish sp.: sailfish or marlin [generic name].
XFL **sagulaa-dagua.** *n.* Fish sp.
XFL **sagulaa-saamono.** *n.* Fish sp.

SAHE
B **sahe.** *n.* Any material used to absorb a menstrual flow.

SAHOLE$_1$
B **sahole.** *n.* Fish sp.: mountain bass.

SAHOLE$_2$
ID **laangai sahole.** A fishing condition in which tuna are jumping and biting.

SAHU
BE **hagasahu.** *v.* To catch water (in something).
BE1 **hagasahuanga.** *n.* —.
BE2 **hagasahua.** *v.* —.
BE2 **hagasahulia.** *v.* —.
RE **hagasahusahu.** *v.* —.
RE2 **hagasahusahua.** *v.* —.
RE2 **hagasahusahulia.** *v.* —.
ID **me hagasahu vai.** Gutter (under the eaves of a house).

SAHUDU
B **sahudu.** *n.* Fish sp.: sea bass.

SAI$_1$
B **sai**$_1$. *v.* Wrap, cover up (with several layers).
B 1 **sainga.** *n.* —.
B 2 **saia.** *v.* —.
E **ssai.** *v.* Wrap or cover completely.
R **saisai.** *v.* —.
R 1 **saisainga.** *n.* —.
R 2 **saisaia.** *v.* —.

SAI$_2$
B **sai**$_2$. *n.* Group of (e.g., *agu sai* 'my children').
ID **sai moni.** A fleet of canoes.

SAIBO
B **saibo.** *a.* Rush around (of a group of people).
B 1 **saibonga.** *n.* —.
BE **hagasaibo.** *v.* —.
BE1 **hagasaibonga.** *n.* —.
ID **saibo saele.** Rush around aimlessly (of a group of people).

SAIDULE
B **saidule.** *v.* Wrapped up or covered up completely.
B 1 **saiduleanga.** *n.* —.
BE **hagasaidule.** *v.* —.
BE1 **hagasaiduleanga.** *n.* —.
R **saisaidule.** *v.* —.
R 1 **saisaiduleanga.** *n.* —.
RE **hagasaisaidule.** *v.* —.
RE1 **hagasaisaiduleanga.** *n.* —.

SAIOLO
B **saiolo.** *n.* A sail [from Eng. "sail"?].
ID **dada saiolo.** To hoist a sail.
ID **dinae o ssaiolo.** [= *dinae o de laa*].
ID **hhola mai saiolo.** To allow the sail to fill with wind, holding on to the boom sheet (after luffing).
ID **saiolo duli magaga.** A type of string figure.

SALA$_1$
E **ssala**$_1$. *v.* Look for, search, hunt for.
E 1 **saalanga.** *n.* —.
E 2 **saalaa.** *v.* —.
R **salasala.** *v.* —.
R 1 **salasalanga.** *n.* —.
R 2 **salasalaa.** *v.* —.
ID **dama ssala.** An adopted child.

ID **hagaduu ssaalanga.** Search intently for.

SALA$_{1a}$

B **salahagi.** *v.* An expedition to look for valuable drifting objects, either in the lagoon or in the open sea near the atoll.

B 1 **salahaginga.** *n.* —.

R **salasalahagi.** *v.* Repeatedly *salahagi.*

R 1 **salasalahaginga.** *n.* —.

SALA$_2$

B **sala.** *n.* Mistake, error, accident.

E **ssala$_2$.** *n.* —.

XCO **alasala.** *a.* Vicious.

XCO **dagosala.** *v.* Death, die (of a person).

XCO **duasala.** *a.* Hardship, difficulty.

XCO **maanessala.** *a.* To mistake something (or someone) for something (or someone) else.

ID **abo sala.** Mean (by nature), unkind.

ID **baa sala.** Be clumsy (in physical contest).

ID **bubu sala.** Move unskillfully.

ID **daadaanga sala.** Ugly-looking.

ID **dagodo hai sala.** Fornication.

ID **dama moemoe sala.** A foetus out of the proper position (in the womb) for delivery.

ID **donu sala.** Misunderstand.

ID **doo sala.** Accidentally.

ID **dulagi sala.** Bad situation; presenting a poor appearance (esp. when ill).

ID **dumanu sala.** Bad situation; poor in appearance.

ID **tala hai sala.** Confess one's sins or errors.

ID **gide sala.** Misidentify.

ID **haele sala.** Spoil (children), bring up (children) badly.

ID **hagapago sala.** Unfortunate result.

ID **hai sala.** Mistake, error.

ID **(de) hine sala daane.** Nymphomaniac.

ID **labulabu sala.** Fail to take hold of (or do) properly (leading to an accident, or other unfortunate outcome).

ID **made sala.** Mistaken (in identifying); mistake someone for another.

ID **valaai tala hai sala.** Medicine to obviate the effects of *oha valaai.*

SALAA

B **salaa.** *n.* Fish sp.: flying fish.

SALABOLI

B **Salaboli.** *n.* May.

SALANI

B **salani.** *v.* Beginning to ripen (indicated by a yellowish color—of, e.g., bananas and papayas).

B 1 **salaninga.** *n.* —.

BE **hagasalani.** *v.* —.

BE1 **hagasalaninga.** *n.* —.

BE2 **hagasalania.** *v.* —.

P **saalani.** *v.* —.

P 1 **saalaninga.** *n.* —.

PE **hagasaalani.** *v.* —.

PE1 **hagasaalaninga.** *n.* —.

PE2 **hagasaalania.** *v.* —.

R **salasalani.** *v.* Becoming *salani* in one part, but not yet *salani* all over.

R 1 **salasalaninga.** *n.* —.

RE **hagasalasalani.** *v.* —.

RE1 **hagasalasalaninga.** *n.* —.

RE2 **hagasalasalania.** *v.* —.

ID **salani ange.** Just a little *salani.*

SALAU

B **salau.** *a.* Inclined, slanting, not straight, not perpendicular to.

B 1 **salaunga.** *n.* —.

BE **hagasalau.** *v.* —; be *salau* with respect to something else.

BE1 **hagasalaunga.** *n.* —.
BE2 **hagasalaua.** *v.* —.
ID **baa hagasalau.** Make contact with while not aligned.

SALI
B **sali.** *a.* Flow, seep.
B 1 **saalinga.** *n.* —.
BE **hagasali.** *v.* —.
BE1 **hagasaalinga.** *n.* —.
BE2 **hagasalia.** *v.* —.
CF **basalia$_2$.** *v.* Seep (of water).
P **ssali.** *a.* —.
PE **hagassali.** *v.* —.
PE2 **hagassaalia.** *v.* —.
R **salisali.** *a.* —.
R 1 **salisalinga.** *n.* —.
RE **hagasalisali.** *v.* —; arm-wrestling.
RE1 **hagasalisalinga.** *n.* —.
RE2 **hagasalisalia.** *v.* —.
ID **galeve sali.** A coconut tree which produces much *galeve*.
ID **magi sali usu.** Headcold, runny nose.
ID **saalingaa nui.** The rainwater which flows down a bent coconut tree (collected for drinking).
ID **sali daadaa.** To sweat.
ID **sali de usu.** Runny nose.
ID **sali dodo.** Bleed.
ID **sali tae.** Intractable watery diarrhea.
ID **sali gee.** Flow away.
ID **sali loimada.** To tear (in the eyes because, e.g., of smoke).
ID **sali ssaavale.** Salivate.
ID **vai saalia.** A group of drifting objects on the surface of the sea (brought together by the currents).

SALIBAADAA
B **salibaadaa.** *v.* A type of low cloud.
B 1 **salibaadaanga.** *n.* —.
BE **hagasalibaadaa.** *v.* —.
BE1 **hagasalibaadaanga.** *n.* —.

SALO
XFL **diinonga-o-salo.** *n.* Fish sp.
XG **gamedi vai salo.** A type of bowl.

SALU
B **salu.** *v.* Scrape (something), plane (something), scrape off (with an object), peel (with a knife toward one).
B 1 **saaluanga.** *n.* A scratch (on the skin).
B 1 **saalunga.** *n.* —.
B 2 **saalua.** *v.* Scraped (a little taken away), scratched.
B 2 **salua.** *v.* Scraped (a lot taken away), peeled (a little amount taken off), planed.
BE **hagasalu.** *v.* —; the shaping (of something) by planing.
BE1 **hagasaalunga$_1$.** *n.* —.
BE2 **hagasaalua.** *v.* —.
BE2 **hagasalua.** *v.* —.
E **ssalu.** *v.* *salu* at one time or energetically.
EE **hagassalu.** *v.* —.
EE1 **hagassalunga.** *n.* —.
EE2 **hagassalua.** *v.* —.
R **salusalu.** *v.* —.
RE **hagasalusalu.** *v.* —.
RE1 **hagasalusalunga.** *n.* —.
RE2 **hagasalusalua.** *v.* —.
ID **baa ssalu.** Carom off violently.
ID **gai salusalu.** Prepare food wastefully (too much must be thrown away).
ID **me ssalu lau.** A scraper for leaves.
ID **salu mai.** Make smaller by planing or scraping.

SALULU
B **salulu.** *a.* The noise of an explosion or loud report (as when two things collide).
B 1 **saluluanga.** *n.* —.
BE **hagasalulu.** *v.* —.
BE1 **hagasaluluanga.** *n.* —.
P **saalulu.** *a.* —.
P 1 **saaluluanga.** *n.* —.
PE **hagasaalulu.** *v.* —.
PE1 **hagasaaluluanga.** *n.* —.
CF **samumu.** The noise of an

explosion or collision [= same meaning as *salulu*].

SAMI
B **sami.** *d.* —.
B 1 **saaminga.** *n.* —.
E **ssami.** *v.* Eat.
R **samisami.** *v.* —.
R 1 **samisaminga.** *n.* —.
ID **ssami age.** Eat a snack.

SAMONO
ID **ono-samono.** The sixth number of a counting game played to determine who is "it".

SAMOULI
B **samouli.** *n.* The spirit of a human being after his death.
XCO **Samouli-daane.** *nn.* The name of *Vave* after his death.

$SAMU_1$
B 1 **saamunga.** *a.* —; food, eat heartily.
B 2 **saamua.** *v.* —.
B 2 **samulia.** *v.* —.
E **ssamu.** *v.* Lick.
R **samusamu.** *v.* —.
R 1 **samusamunga.** *n.* —.
R 2 **samusamua.** *v.* —.
R 2 **samusamulia.** *v.* —.
XCO **lausamua.** *v.* Untidy in appearance (esp. unshaven, with one's hair in disorder); unkempt.
ID **gai samusamu.** Eat left-overs (that most people would throw out).

$SAMU_2$
B **samu.** *v.* Gossip, slander.
B 1 **samuanga.** *n.* —.
B 2 **samua.** *v.* Slandered; to have been an object of gossip.
ID **hai samu.** To gossip.

SAMUMU
B **samumu.** *a.* The noise of an explosion or collision [= same meaning as *salulu*].
B 1 **samumuanga.** *n.* —.
BE **hagasamumu.** *v.* —.
BE1 **hagasamumuanga.** *n.* —.
P **saamumu.** *a.* —.
P 1 **saamumuanga.** *n.* —.
PE **hagasaamumu.** *v.* —.
PE1 **hagasaamumuanga.** *n.* —.

SANIBA
B **saniba.** *n.* Fish sp.: silversides.

SANO
E **ssano.** *a.* Know about, be acquainted with.
E 1 **ssanoanga.** *n.* —.
EE **hagassano.** *v.* —.
EE1 **hagassanoanga.** *n.* —.
R **sanosano.** *a.* —.
R 1 **sanosanoanga.** *n.* —.
RE **hagasanosano.** *v.* —.
RE1 **hagasanosanoanga.** *n.* —.
T **sassano.** *a.* Becoming *ssano.*
T 1 **sassanoanga.** *n.* —.
TE **hagasassano.** *v.* —.
TE1 **hagasassanoanga.** *n.* —.
ID **au ga sano.** I give up!
ID **ssano i de ia.** Known by him.

SANGA
B **sanga.** *v.* Have sexual intercourse, fornicate.
B 1 **sanganga.** *n.* —.
B 2 **sangaa.** *v.* —.
B 2 **sangalia.** *v.* —.
BC1 **massanganga.** *a.* Apart, widely spaced.
BE **hagasanga.** *v.* —.
BE1 **hagasanganga.** *a.* —; to walk with one's legs apart.
BE2 **hagasangaa.** *v.* —.
BE2 **hagasangalia.** *v.* —.
BF1 **hagamassanganga.** *v.* —.
E **ssanga.** *n.* Lower longitudinal tie beam purlin.
PC **maasanga.** *n.* —; twins [triplets, etc., would also be *maasanga*, but no case of such is remembered].
PF **hagamaasanga$_2$.** *v.* —.
R **sangasanga.** *v.* —.
R 1 **sangasanganga.** *n.* —.
R 2 **sangasangaa.** *v.* —.
R 2 **sangasangalia.** *v.* —.
RE **hagasangasanga.** *v.* —.

RE1 **hagasangasanganga.** *n.* —.
RE2 **hagasangasangaa.** *v.* —.
RE2 **hagasangasangalia.** *v.* —.
XCO **dalimasanga.** *v.* Way of tying (rope, etc.).
ID **dao ssanga.** Roof support (top) poles, wall plates.
ID **laangai milo sanga.** A fishing condition in which fish are not inclined to bite.

SANGA$_a$
B **aasanga.** *v.* A watercourse between islets on the atoll.
BE **hagaasanga.** *v.* To create *aasanga.*
XFL **manu-gaba-aasanga.** *n.* Plant sp.: beach naupaka shrub (*Scaevola taccada* (Gaertn.) Roxb.).
ID **bangi mada aasanga.** A certain way of pinching with the fingers.
ID **bono aasanga.** A method of fishing (by blocking the channel at high tide).
ID **gaba aasanga.** The sides of the watercourses between islets on the atoll.
ID **gaba de aasanga.** A side of the watercourses between islets on the atoll.
ID **haangoda mada aasanga.** To fish for *labelabe.*

SANGATAI
B **sangatai.** *n.* Mollusk sp.: *Spondylus* sp.

SANGO
B **sango.** *a.* Wild (of animals scared of humans).
B 1 **sangoanga.** *n.* —.
B 2 **sangolia.** *a.* —.
BE **hagasango.** *v.* —.
BE1 **hagasangoanga.** *n.* —.
BE2 **hagasangolia.** *v.* —.
P **ssango.** *a.* —.
P 1 **ssangoanga.** *n.* —.
P 2 **ssangolia.** *v.* —.
PE **hagassango.** *v.* —.
PE1 **hagassangoanga.** *n.* —.
PE2 **hagassangolia.** *v.* —.
R **sangosango.** *a.* —.
R 1 **sangosangoanga.** *n.* —.
R 2 **sangosangolia.** *a.* —.
RE **hagasangosango.** *v.* —.
RE1 **hagasangosangoanga.** *n.* —.
RE2 **hagasangosangolia.** *v.* —.
ID **odi sango.** Completely cleaned up or finished; all gone; each and every one all gone.

SAO$_1$
B **sao$_1$.** *d.* —.
B 1 **saoanga.** *n.* —.
B 2 **saohia$_1$.** *v.* —.
BE **hagasao$_1$ —.** *d.* —.
BE1 **hagasaoanga.** *n.* —.
BE2 **hagasaohia$_1$.** *v.* —.
E **ssao$_1$.** *v.* Sweep, clean up.
E 1 **ssaoanga$_1$.** *n.* —.
EE **hagassao$_1$.** *v.* —.
EE1 **hagassaoanga.** *n.* —.
R **saosao$_1$.** *v.* —.
R 1 **saosaoanga.** *n.* —.
R 2 **saosaohia$_1$.** *v.* —.
RE **hagasaosao$_1$ —.** *d.* —.
RE1 **hagasaosaoanga.** *n.* —.
RE2 **hagasaosaohia$_1$.** *v.* —.
ID **sao gainga.** Sweep or clean up trash.

SAO$_2$
B **sao$_2$.** *a.* Get out from or through, escape.
B 1 **saonga.** *n.* —.
B 2 **saohia$_2$.** *v.* Have time for, free, available.
B 3 **saohiaanga.** *n.* —.
BE **hagasao$_2$.** *v.* Let out (something), disburse (money).
BE1 **hagasaonga.** *n.* —.
BE2 **hagasaoa.** *v.* —.
BE2 **hagasaohia$_2$.** *v.* Make oneself available.
BE2 **hagasaolia.** *v.* —.
BE3 **hagasaohiaanga.** *n.* —.
P **ssao$_2$.** *a.* —.
P 1 **ssaonga$_2$.** *n.* —.
PE **hagassao$_2$.** *v.* —.
PE1 **hagassaonga.** *n.* —.
PE2 **hagassaolia.** *v.* —.
R **saosao$_2$.** *a.* —; good at penetrating (as a canoe with a narrow prow).
R 1 **saosaonga.** *n.* —.
R 2 **saosaohia$_2$.** *v.* —; [redup. form of *saohia$_2$*].

R 3 **saosaohiaanga.** *n.* —.
RE **hagasaosao₂.** *v.* —.
RE1 **hagasaosaonga.** *n.* —.
RE2 **hagasaosaoa.** *v.* —.
RE2 **hagasaosaohia₂.** *v.* —; [causative form of *saosaohia₂*].
RE2 **hagasaosaolia.** *v.* —.
RE3 **hagasaosaohiaanga.** *n.* [BE1 form of **saosaohia**].
T **sasao.** *a.* Escape one after the other.
T 1 **sasaonga.** *n.* —.
TE **hagasasao.** *v.* —.
TE1 **hagasasaonga.** *n.* —.
TE2 **hagasasaoa.** *v.* —.
TE2 **hagasasaolia.** *v.* —.
ID **dee sao age.** Always fail or be defeated.
ID **mada saosao.** Sharp-pointed.
ID **sao de lahalaha.** More wide than long.
ID **sao de leo.** Clear in elocution or in one's singing voice.
ID **sao de looloa.** Rectangular (not square), oval.

SASA
B **sasa.** *a.* To talk or move in one's sleep, or when delerious.
B 1 **saasanga.** *n.* —.
BE **hagasasa.** *v.* —.
BE1 **hagasaasanga.** *n.* —.
BE2 **hagasasalia.** *v.* —.
P **ssasa.** *a.* —.
PE **hagassasa.** *v.* —.
PE2 **hagassasalia.** *v.* —.
R **sassasa.** *a.* —; stammer (from nervousness).
R 1 **sassasaanga.** *n.* —.
RE **hagasassasa.** *v.* —.
RE1 **hagasassasaanga.** *n.* —.
RE2 **hagasassasalia.** *v.* —.
ID **sasa gee.** Impetuous in act or movement (leading to frequent error).

SAU₁
B **sau₁.** *d.* —.
B 2 **saudia.** *v.* Be exposed to the wind (not sheltered).
B 3 **saudiaanga.** *n.* —.
BE **hagasau —.** *d.* —.
BE1 **hagassaunga.** *n.* —.
BE2 **hagasaudia.** *v.* —.
BE3 **hagasaudiaanga.** *n.* —.
E **ssau.** *v.* Blow (of the wind).
E 1 **ssaunga.** *n.* —.
EE **hagassau.** *v.* —.
EE2 **hagassaua.** *v.* —.
EE2 **hagassaulia.** *v.* —.
R **sausau₁.** *v.* —.
R 1 **sausaunga₁.** *n.* —.
R 2 **sausaudia.** *v.* Continually blown upon (by the wind).
R 3 **sausaudiaanga.** *n.* —.
RE **hagasausau.** *v.* —.
RE1 **hagasausaunga₁.** *n.* —.
RE2 **hagasausaudia.** *v.* —.
RE3 **hagasausaudiaanga.** *n.* —.
T **sasau.** *v.* Increasing in velocity (of wind).
T 1 **sasaunga.** *n.* —.
T 2 **sasaudia.** *v.* —.
ID **hagasau madangi.** To be exposed to the wind.
ID **sau aloalo.** Echo.
ID **sau alohenua.** Eddying of the wind (constantly changing direction) close to land.
ID **sau makaga.** Blow steadily (of wind).
ID **sau makaga de madangi.** The blowing of wind steadily (for a long time) from one direction.
CF **dalangasau.** Be quick-witted in an emergency.

SAU₂
B **sau₂.** *n.* [an abbreviated form of *saulaba*].

SAU₃
R **sausau₂.** *n.* Fish sp.: lion-fish.

SAUAA
B **sauaa.** *a.* Power (electrical, magical, etc.); powerful (esp. supernaturally); very much [MV].
B 1 **sauaanga.** *n.* —.
BE **hagasauaa.** *v.* —; empower; do (usually bad things) with *sauaa*; approve (as a law by higher authority).

BE1 **hagasauaanga.** *n.* —.
R **sausauaa.** *a.* —.
R 1 **sausauaanga.** *n.* —.
RE **hagasausauaa.** *v.* —.
RE1 **hagasausauaanga.** *n.* —.
ID **baalanga sauaa.** Magnet.
ID **daane sauaa.** A person of extraordinary ability; shark (euphemism).
ID **taane sauaa.** Shark (euphemism).
ID **tangada hai sauaa.** Magician, sorcerer.

SAUBALIGI
B **saubaligi.** *v.* Graceful in dancing.
BE **hagasaubaligi.** *v.* —.
R **sausaubaligi.** *v.* Always *saubaligi.*
RE **hagasausaubaligi.** *v.* —.

SAUDUU
B **sauduu.** *n.* Mermaid.

SAULABA
B **saulaba.** *n.* Parent-in-law, child-in-law, mother-in-law, father-in-law, son-in-law, daughter-in-law.
BE **hagasaulaba.** *v.* Treat as *saulaba.*
ID **hai saulaba.** The relationship of parent-in-law to child-in-law.

SAULIGI
B **sauligi.** *n.* A type of adze (with a rotatable head).

SAUNOA
B **saunoa.** *mv.* Completely, very.

SAUNGA
B **saunga.** *a.* Having an unpleasant body odor.
BE **hagasaunga.** *v.* —.
R **sausaunga$_2$.** *a.* Continually *saunga.*
RE **hagasausaunga$_2$.** *n.* —.

SAVAA
B **savaa.** *a.* Soon (will happen).
BC **masavaa$_1$.** *n.* Time when, time of; between, amongst.
R **savasavaa.** *v.* Getting closer to the time (of happening).
ID **deai ange loo soo savaa.** Now i've got you!
ID **dee savaa (naa) de —.** Soon —.

SAVALA
B **savala.** *a.* Interested in, enjoys.
BE **hagasavala.** *v.* —.
P **saavala.** *a.* —.
PE **hagasaavala.** *v.* —.
R **savasavala.** *a.* Becoming interested in; getting to enjoy.
RE **hagasavasavala.** *v.* —.
ID **dee savala.** Uninterested in; not enjoy.

SAVALI
B **savali.** *v.* Hungry.
B 1 **savalinga.** *n.* —.
BE **hagasavali.** *v.* —.
BE1 **hagasavalianga.** *n.* —.
BE2 **hagasavalia.** *v.* —.
P **saavali.** *v.* —.
PE **hagasaavali.** *v.* —.
PE1 **hagasaavalianga.** *n.* —.
PE2 **hagasaavalia.** *v.* —.
R **savasavali.** *v.* Always hungry.
R 1 **savasavalinga.** *n.* —.
RE **hagasavasavali.** *v.* —.
RE1 **hagasavasavalianga.** *n.* —.
RE2 **hagasavasavalia.** *v.* —.

SAVINI
B **savini.** *a.* Run, move fast (as fish, or a canoe).
BE **hagasavini.** *v.* —.
P **saavini.** *a.* —.
PE **hagasaavini.** *v.* —.
ID **savini dua.** Run backwards, move backwards fast.
ID **savini gee.** Run away.

SE
B **se.** *ma.* GENERAL ARTICLE [SING.]; it is a...
ID **se aha.** What is it?
ID **se gainga.** Abundant.

ID se gava. Know (how to do something) well.
ID se goo. Adept at.
ID se hagabau. Do deliberately (esp. something bad); willful, mean.
ID se hono. Fit well or properly.

SEBU

B **sebu.** *a.* Seen on the surface of the sea from time to time.
B 2 **sebua.** *v.* —.
B 3 **sebuaanga.** *n.* —.
BE **hagasebu.** *v.* —.
BE2 **hagasebua.** *v.* —.
BE3 **hagasebuaanga.** *n.* —.
R **sebusebu.** *a.* —.
R 2 **sebusebua.** *v.* —.
R 3 **sebusebuaanga.** *n.* —.
RE **hagasebusebu.** *v.* —.
RE2 **hagasebusebua.** *v.* —.
RE3 **hagasebusebuaanga.** *n.* —.

SEE$_1$

B **see$_1$.** *a.* Cry aloud.
B 1 **seeanga.** *n.* —.
B 1 **seenga.** *n.* —.
BE **hagasee$_1$.** *v.* —; scold, bawl out, chide.
BE1 **hagaseeanga.** *n.* —.
BE1 **hagaseeginga.** *n.* —.
BE1 **hagaseenga$_1$.** *n.* —.
BE2 **hagaseegina.** *v.* —.
P **ssee$_1$.** *a.* —.
PE **hagassee$_1$.** *v.* —.
R **seesee$_1$.** *a.* —.
R 1 **seeseeanga$_1$.** *n.* —.
R 1 **seeseenga$_1$.** *n.* —.
RE **hagaseesee$_1$.** *v.* —.
RE1 **hagaseeseeanga$_1$.** *n.* —.
RE1 **hagaseeseenga$_1$.** *n.* —.
ID **basa hagassee.** Speak so as to change the impression one's previous words have made.
ID **dangi see.** Cry aloud for a long time, wail.
ID **dee vaaseegina.** Hardly able to wait for.

SEE$_{1a}$

B **seevoivoi.** *a.* Cry uncontrollably (hysterically inaccessible).
B 1 **seevoivoinga.** *n.* —.
B 2 **seevoivoia.** *v.* To be in the state of *seevoivoi.*
BE **hagaseevoivoi.** *v.* —.
BE1 **hagaseevoivoinga.** *n.* —.
BE2 **hagaseevoivoia.** *v.* —.

SEE$_2$

B **see$_2$.** *a.* Barely, just barely [obligatorily followed by *loo huu*, *donu huu*, or *ma de*].
BE **hagasee$_2$.** *a.* Just barely; [same limitations of distribution as *see$_2$*].
BE1 **hagaseenga$_2$.** *n.* Way of just being able to.
P **ssee$_2$.** *a.* —.
PE **hagassee$_2$.** *a.* —.
XCO **moosee.** *v.* Not quite cooked (of anything but fish).

SEE$_3$

E **ssee$_3$.** *a.* To lurch, to move sideways; to wish to be carried (of a baby).
E 1 **sseeanga.** *n.* —.
EE **hagassee$_3$.** *v.* —; to act as though innocent (when guilty).
EE1 **hagasseeanga.** *n.* —.
R **seesee$_2$.** *v.* Walk, move slowly (as a fish).
R 1 **seeseeanga$_2$.** *n.* —.
R 1 **seeseenga$_2$.** *n.* —.
RE **hagaseesee$_2$.** *v.* —.
RE1 **hagaseeseeanga$_2$.** *n.* —.
RE1 **hagaseeseenga$_2$.** *n.* —.
ID **ngadi seesee.** Walk barefoot, stroll.
ID **see boiboi saele.** Stagger about (from a head injury), move as though unconscious.
ID **seesee haangoda saele.** Look for girls.
ID **seesee hagadaahao.** Walk (for recreation).
ID **seesee hagadibadiba.** Waddle.
ID **ssee de hiigai.** Famished, ravenous.
ID **ssee gee.** Veer from an intended trajectory.

SEEDAA

B **Seedaa.** *n.* October.

SEGE

B	**sege.** *v.* Slip, slide, to ride, to surf.
B 1	**seegenga.** *n.* —.
BE	**hagasege.** *v.* —.
BE1	**hagaseegenga.** *n.* —.
BE2	**hagasegea.** *v.* Let slip or slide.
BE2	**hagasegedia.** *v.* Let slip or slide.
BE2	**hagasegelia.** *v.* Let slip or slide.
P	**ssege.** *a.* —.
PE	**hagassege.** *v.* —.
PE1	**hagasseegenga.** *n.* —.
PE2	**hagassegea.** *v.* —.
PE2	**hagassegedia.** *v.* —.
PE2	**hagassegelia.** *v.* —.
R	**segesege.** *v.* —; slippery.
R 1	**segesegenga.** *n.* —.
RE	**hagasegesege.** *v.* —; surf-riding (for amusement).
RE1	**hagasegesegenga.** *n.* —.
RE2	**hagasegesegea.** *v.* —.
RE2	**hagasegesegedia.** *v.* —.
RE2	**hagasegesegelia.** *v.* —.
ID	**baa sege.** Carom off.
ID	**dama ssege.** A foetus which has been aborted.
ID	**eu sege.** A dislocation of the shoulder joint.
ID	**hagasegesege ange.** Allow someone to do as he pleases.
ID	**hagassege i hegau.** Procrastinate (about work); refuse to participate in work.
ID	**sege de —.** Plenty of —, a lot of —.
ID	**sege de gauanga.** Dislocated thigh bone.
ID	**sege gee.** Slip or slide away from.
ID	**ssege tama.** Miscarriage, abortion (spontaneous).

SEGOODO

B	**segoodo —.** *d.* To have just —.

SEHUA

BE	**hagasehua.** *v.* To make a total of 1000 coconuts.

SEI

R	**seisei.** *n.* Fish sp.: pipefish.

SELE$_1$

B	**sele$_1$.** *v.* Lasso, noose; to catch with a lasso or noose.
B 1	**seelenga$_1$.** *n.* —.
B 2	**selea$_1$.** *v.* —.
BE	**hagasele.** *v.* —.
BE1	**hagaseelenga.** *n.* —.
BE2	**hagaselea.** *v.* —.
R	**selesele$_1$.** *v.* —.
R 1	**seleselenga$_1$.** *n.* —.
R 2	**seleselea.** *v.* —.
RE	**hagaselesele.** *v.* —.
RE1	**hagaseleselenga.** *n.* —.
RE2	**hagaseleselea.** *v.* —.
RE2	**hagaseleseleia.** *v.* —.
XFL	**daamadaa-sele.** *n.* Insect sp.: water bug.
ID	**honu ssele.** Turtle of a size suitable for eating (not quite as big as *honu tolo*).
ID	**madaa sele.** Loop of a lasso or noose.
ID	**sele gi tonu.** Make sure of.
ID	**ulu sele dababa.** [a phrase said aloud to attract sharks].

SELE$_{1a}$

B	**daasele.** *v.* To swing a rope (in a jump rope game) so as to cause the jumper to trip.
B 1	**daaseleanga.** *n.* —.
B 2	**daaselea.** *v.* —.
BE	**hagadaasele.** *v.* —.
BE1	**hagadaaseleanga.** *n.* —.
BE2	**hagadaaselea.** *v.* —.

SELE$_2$

B	**sele$_2$.** *v.* To chop down.
B 1	**seelenga$_2$.** *n.* —.
B 2	**selea$_2$.** *v.* —.
B 2	**seleia.** *v.* To cut one's hand by a hand-held fish line, when it is taken by a fish.
BE2	**hagaseleia.** *v.* —.
E	**ssele.** *v.* Cut (something); make an incision.
E 2	**seelea.** *v.* —.
R	**selesele$_2$.** *v.* —.
R 1	**seleselenga$_2$.** *n.* —.
R 2	**seleseleia.** *v.* —.

RC **maselesele.** *a.* Straight-edged.
RC1 **maseleselenga.** *n.* —.
RF **hagamaselesele.** *v.* —.
RF1 **hagamaseleselenga.** *n.* —.
RF2 **hagamaseleselea.** *v.* —.
ID **daula sele nui.** A rope used to pull a coconut tree in the desired direction when felling it.
ID **tangada ssele.** Stupid ass!
ID **ssele i de niho.** Damn it!

SELU
B **selu.** *v.* To comb (hair).
B 1 **seelunga.** *n.* —; the manner (of an individual) of doing something.
B 2 **selua.** *v.* —.
B 2 **selumia.** *v.* —.
BE **hagaselu.** *v.* —.
BE1 **hagaseelunga.** *n.* —.
BE2 **hagaselua.** *v.* —.
BE2 **hagaselumia.** *v.* —.
R **seluselu.** *v.* —.
R 1 **seluselunga.** *n.* —.
R 2 **seluselua.** *v.* —.
R 2 **seluselumia.** *v.* —.
RE **hagaseluselu.** *v.* —.
RE1 **hagaseluselunga.** *n.* —.
RE2 **hagaseluselua.** *v.* —.
RE2 **hagaseluselumia.** *v.* —.

SEMA
E **ssema.** *n.* Jellyfish sp.

SENI
B **seni.** *a.* Sleep.
B 1 **seeninga.** *n.* —.
BE **hagaseni.** *v.* —; put to bed.
BE1 **hagaseeninga.** *n.* —.
BE2 **hagasenia.** *v.* —.
P **sseni.** *a.* —.
PE **hagasseni.** *v.* —.
PE2 **hagasseenia.** *v.* —.
R **seniseni.** *a.* —; sleepyhead.
R 1 **seniseninga.** *n.* —.
RE **hagaseniseni.** *v.* —.
RE1 **hagaseniseninga.** *n.* —.
RE2 **hagasenisenia.** *v.* —.
ID **boo seniseni.** A type of children's game (played in the water, like tag).
ID **daia e sseni.** Very sleepy.
ID **dai seni.** Sleepy.
ID **lele sseni.** Insomnia (after sleeping for a short while).
ID **maimai sseni.** To sleep especially well or restfully.
ID **seni ahiahi.** Go to bed early (in the evening).
ID **seni alaala.** Sleep fitfully (esp. because one is thinking about having to arise early); wake up repeatedly owing to anxiety.
ID **seni ange.** Rest up for (e.g., the next day's work).
ID **seni tao.** Sleep soundly.
ID **seni gi de ao.** Sleep late (into daytime).
ID **seni iho.** Take a nap, stay overnight (away from home).
ID **seni magau.** Sleep soundly (owing to exhaustion).

SENGA
B **senga.** *a.* Crazy; dumb, foolish, ignorant; senseless, drunk.
B 1 **seenganga.** *n.* —.
B 2 **sengalia.** *v.* Deceived, fooled; made dependent upon (e.g., gifts).
BE **hagasenga.** *v.* Fool (someone), deceive, trick (someone).
BE1 **hagaseenganga.** *n.* —.
BE2 **hagasengalia.** *v.* —.
E **ssenga**$_{b}$. *v.* The streamer on a trolling lure.
P **ssenga**$_{a}$. *a.* —.
PE **hagassenga.** *v.* —.
PE2 **hagassengalia.** *v.* —.
R **sengasenga.** *a.* —.
R 1 **sengasengaanga.** *n.* —.
RE **hagasengasenga.** *v.* —; to speak in parables or riddles.
RE1 **hagasengasengaanga.** *n.* —.
RE2 **hagasengasengalia.** *v.* —.
ID **basa hagasengasenga.** Speak in riddles or aphoristically or in parables.
ID **basa senga.** Speak senselessly.
ID **hagatala senga.** Foolishly

rough playing or joking.
ID **hilohilo senga.** Half-crazy.
ID **labu ssenga.** To run into trouble (owing to one's misdeeds).
ID **lodo senga.** To have unrealistic self-confidence (e.g., in one's capacity to do something impossible); to be foolishly desirous (of the impossible).
ID **me hagasengasenga.** Riddle, parable.
ID **noho senga (adu).** Be ignorant (of what is happening).
ID **senga maido.** Stupidly unafraid of danger (like *maido*).
ID **senga manu.** Stupid (like an animal).
CF **hoosenga.** Shy, embarrassed, bashful.

SEU
B **seu.** *d.* —.
B 1 **seunga.** *n.* —.
B 2 **seua.** *v.* —.
BC **maseu.** *a.* To scatter (when in a group).
BC1 **maseunga.** *n.* —.
BF **hagamaseu.** *v.* —.
BF1 **hagamaseunga.** *n.* —.
BF2 **hagamaseua.** *v.* —.
E **sseu.** *v.* Push violently.
E 1 **sseunga.** *n.* —.
PC **maaseu.** *a.* —.
PC1 **maaseunga.** *n.* —.
PF **hagamaaseu.** *v.* —.
PF1 **hagamaaseunga.** *n.* —.
PF2 **hagamaaseua.** *v.* —.
R **seuseu.** *v.* —.
R 1 **seuseunga.** *n.* —.
R 2 **seuseua.** *v.* —.
T **seseu.** *v.* Push (now and into the future) [pl. only].
T 1 **seseunga.** *n.* —.
T 2 **seseua.** *v.* —.
ID **daa sseu.** A way of forming the body of a canoe.
ID **hai sseu.** Wasteful.
ID **sseu gee.** Push away, push aside (in one direction).

SIABO
ID **kano siabo.** The meat on the side of the fish's head.

SIBA$_1$
B **siba$_1$.** *v.* Move to one side (involuntarily) while walking.
B 1 **siibanga.** *n.* —.
B 2 **sibalia.** *v.* —.
BE **hagasiba.** *v.* —.
BE1 **hagasiibanga.** *n.* —.
BE2 **hagasibalia.** *v.* —.
P **ssiba.** *v.* —.
P 2 **ssibalia.** *v.* —.
PE **hagassiba.** *v.* —.
PE2 **hagassibalia.** *v.* —.
R **sibasiba.** *v.* Walk off-balance.
R 1 **sibasibaanga.** *n.* —.
R 2 **sibasibalia.** *v.* —.
RE **hagasibasiba.** *v.* —.
RE1 **hagasibasibaanga.** *n.* —.
RE2 **hagasibasibalia.** *v.* —.

SIBA$_2$
B **siba$_2$.** *n.* Fish sp. (small flying fish).

SIGA
B **siga.** *v.* To make a fire with a fire plow; to make a net with a net needle spool [called *siga*]; to escape (of fish) from a net (through its holes); sew up a hole (in clothing).
B 1 **siiganga.** *n.* —.
B 2 **sigahia.** *v.* —.
B 2 **sigalia.** *v.* —.
BE **hagasiga.** *v.* —.
BE1 **hagasiiganga.** *n.* —.
BE2 **hagasigahia.** *v.* —.
BE2 **hagasigalia.** *v.* —.
R **sigasiga.** *v.* —.
R 1 **sigasigaanga.** *n.* —.
R 2 **sigasigahia.** *v.* —.
R 2 **sigasigalia.** *v.* —.
RE **hagasigasiga.** *v.* —.
RE1 **hagasigasigaanga.** *n.* —.
RE2 **hagasigasigahia.** *v.* —.
RE2 **hagasigasigalia.** *v.* —.
ID **gano siga.** Strands (of cloth).

ID	**siga de mamu.** An escape of fish from a fishing net (through its holes).
CF	**sigale.** Scull (a boat).

SIGALE

B	**sigale.** *v.* Scull (a boat).
B 1	**sigaleanga.** *n.* —.
BE	**hagasigale.** *v.* —.
BE1	**hagasigaleanga.** *n.* —.
R	**sigasigale.** *v.* —.
R 1	**sigasigaleanga.** *n.* —.
RE	**hagasigasigale.** *v.* —.
RE1	**hagasigasigaleanga.** *n.* —.
ID	**sigale saele.** Search for.

SIGI

B	**sigi.** *v.* Transfer (from one place to another), transplant; a technique of finishing a mat edge; to assist in the delivery of a baby (by manually extracting it from the birth canal); to tack a canoe (by transferring the mast from one end of the canoe to the other).
B 1	**siiginga.** *n.* —.
B 2	**sigia.** *v.* —.
B 2	**sigidia.** *v.* —.
B 2	**sigilia.** *v.* —.
BE	**hagasigi.** *v.* —.
BE1	**hagasiiginga.** *n.* —.
BE2	**hagasigia.** *v.* —.
BE2	**hagasigidia.** *v.* —.
BE2	**hagasigilia.** *v.* —.
R	**sigisigi.** *v.* —.
R 1	**sigisiginga.** *n.* —.
R 2	**sigisigia.** *v.* —.
R 2	**sigisigidia.** *v.* —.
R 2	**sigisigilia.** *v.* —.
RE	**hagasigisigi.** *v.* —.
RE1	**hagasigisiginga.** *n.* —.
RE2	**hagasigisigia.** *v.* —.
RE2	**hagasigisigidia.** *v.* —.
RE2	**hagasigisigilia.** *v.* —.
XCO	**sigidaumaha.** *v.* Collection (in church), offering (in church), sacrifice, tithe.
ID	**sigi de hagahala.** A technique of finishing a mat edge.
ID	**sigi manu.** To transplant a plant.
ID	**sigisigi mai (adu, ange).** Say bad things about one to one's face.

SIGO

B	**sigo.** *v.* To catch (e.g., a ball); pull in a line; move a canoe to another spot when fishing (i.e., to pull in one's lines first); to climb a tree without using climbing aids [*gaahanga*].
B 1	**siigonga.** *n.* —; a coil of rope.
B 2	**sigoa.** *v.* —.
B 2	**sigohia.** *v.* —.
B 2	**sigolia.** *v.* —.
BE	**hagasigo.** *v.* —.
BE1	**hagasiigonga.** *n.* —.
BE2	**hagasigoa.** *v.* —.
BE2	**hagasigohia.** *v.* —.
BE2	**hagasigolia.** *v.* —.
E	**ssigo.** *a.* Catch on to, understand; clever, a fast learner.
E 1	**ssiigonga.** *n.* —.
EE	**hagassigo.** *v.* —.
EE1	**hagassiigonga.** *n.* —.
EE2	**hagassigoa.** *v.* —.
EE2	**hagassigohia.** *v.* —.
EE2	**hagassigolia.** *v.* —.
R	**sigosigo.** *v.* —; juggle.
R 1	**sigosigonga.** *n.* —.
R 2	**sigosigoa.** *v.* —.
R 2	**sigosigohia.** *v.* —.
R 2	**sigosigolia.** *v.* —.
RE	**hagasigosigo.** *v.* —.
RE1	**hagasigosigonga.** *n.* —.
RE2	**hagasigosigoa.** *v.* —.
RE2	**hagasigosigohia.** *v.* —.
RE2	**hagasigosigolia.** *v.* —.
ID	**dangada ssigo.** Clever person.
ID	**sigo de muna.** Remember what one has heard.
ID	**sigo ina uavesi.** Don't forget!

SII

B	**sii.** *a.* A stream or jet of water; dysentery.
B 1	**siinga.** *n.* —.
BE	**hagasii.** *v.* —; wheel.
BE1	**hagasiinga.** *n.* —.

BE2 **hagasiia$_1$.** *v.* —.
P **ssii$_1$.** *a.* —; broken in many pieces (as glass when dropped).
P 1 **ssiinga$_1$.** *n.* —.
PE **hagassii$_1$.** *v.* —.
PE1 **hagassiinga$_1$.** *n.* —.
PE2 **hagassiia.** *v.* —.
R **siisii$_1$.** *a.* —.
R 1 **siisiinga.** *n.* —.
RE **hagasiisii$_1$.** *v.* —.
RE1 **hagasiisiinga.** *n.* —.
RE2 **hagasiisiia$_1$.** *v.* —.
ID **hagasiilangaa mada.** The appearance of fish or edible animals in great numbers (an omen of death).
ID **hagasii lolo.** Wheel.
ID **momo dai sii.** A very very little (in quantity).
ID **sii bido lua.** Vomiting and having diarrhea at the same time ('flowing from both ends').
ID **sii diidii.** Urinate
ID **sii tae.** Diarrhea which escapes without one realizing (caused by eating oily fish).
ID **sii talaa umada.** A wash of waves at the prow of a canoe, when it is sailing fast.
ID **sii mada daahaa.** A fine jet of water.
ID **sii valavala.** Spray.
ID **ssii mommomo.** Broken up into small pieces.
ID **vae hagasii.** Wheel (one only).
ID **velo de hagasii.** A type of game.

SIILI
B **siili.** *n.* A stick used in a children's game.

SILA
B **sila.** *v.* Look for.
B 1 **silaanga.** *n.* —.
B 2 **sileia.** *v.* —; look at that!
BE **hagasila.** *v.* —.
BE1 **hagasilaanga.** *n.* —.
BE2 **hagasileia.** *v.* —.
P **ssila.** *v.* —.
P 1 **ssilaanga.** *n.* —.
PE **hagassila.** *v.* —.
PE1 **hagassilaanga.** *n.* —.
R **silasila.** *v.* Look around for.
R 1 **silasilaanga.** *n.* —.
R 2 **silesileia.** *v.* —.
RE **hagasilasila.** *v.* —.
RE1 **hagasilasilaanga.** *n.* —.
RE2 **hagasilesileia.** *v.* —.
ID **hagasiilangaa mada.** The appearance of fish or edible animals in great numbers (an omen of death).
ID **sileia doo soa.** Look, your neighbor is competing against you!

SILI$_1$
B **sili$_1$.** *a.* Stopped, ended.
B 1 **siilinga$_1$.** *n.* —.
BE **hagasili$_1$.** *v.* —.
BE1 **hagasiilinga$_1$.** *n.* —.
BE2 **hagasilia$_1$.** *v.* —.
P **ssili$_1$.** *a.* —.
PE **hagassili$_1$.** *v.* —.
PE2 **hagassilia.** *v.* —.
R **silisili$_1$.** *a.* Drawing to an end.
R 1 **silisilinga$_1$.** *n.* —.
RE **hagasilisili$_1$.** *v.* —.
RE1 **hagasilisilinga$_1$.** *n.* —.
RE2 **hagasilisilia$_1$.** *v.* —.
ID **alaa sili.** Those there were enough.
ID **anaa sili.** Those were enough.
ID **anei sili.** These were enough.
ID **danuaa sili.** Good enough!
ID **delaa sili.** That there is enough.
ID **denaa sili.** That is enough!
ID **denei sili.** This is enough!
ID **lava sili.** Good enough!; stop!
ID **sili iho.** Have just stopped; calm down (of a person).
ID **ssili mada.** To faint, be unconscious.
ID **valaai hagasili lodo.** A medicine taken to reduce one's anger, or any other strong emotion.

SILI$_2$

B **sili**$_2$. *d.* —.
B 1 **siilinga**$_2$. *n.* —.
B 2 **siilia.** *v.* —.
BE **hagasili**$_2$. *d.* —.
E **ssili**$_2$. *v.* Ask.
R **silisili**$_2$. *v.* —.
R 1 **silisilinga**$_2$. *n.* —.
R 2 **silisilia**$_1$. *v.* —; ask around.
ID **goai ne siilia.** Who asked you? [an expression of recent invention].
ID **siilinga a muna.** Trial or formal inquiry.
ID **sili muna.** Inquisitive (prone to ask too many questions).

SILI$_3$

B **sili**$_3$. *a.* To pass a point (in space) or a stage of development.
B 1 **siilinga**$_3$. *n.* —.
B 2 **silia.** *a.* —.
BE **hagasili**$_3$. *v.* —.
BE1 **hagasiilinga**$_2$. *n.* —.
BE2 **hagasilia**$_2$. *v.* —.
P **ssili**$_3$. *a.* —.
PE **hagassili**$_2$. *v.* —.
R **silisili**$_3$. *v.* —.
R 1 **silisilinga**$_3$. *n.* —.
R 2 **silisilia**$_2$. *a.* —.
RE **hagasilisili**$_2$. *v.* —.
RE1 **hagasilisilinga**$_2$. *n.* —.
RE2 **hagasilisilia**$_2$. *v.* —.
ID **daane ssili dala.** Special one, important one.
ID **me hagasili.** A plant which is allowed to grow extra large (for some reason).
ID **sili gee.** Stand out from (others in a group) in distance or height.

SILI$_{3a}$

B **hesilihagi.** *v.* To pass each other on intersecting courses; dislocated (joint of the body).
B 1 **hesilihaginga.** *n.* —.
BE **hagahesilihagi.** *v.* —.
BE1 **hagahesilihaginga.** *n.* —.
R **hesilisilihagi.** *v.* Repeatedly *hesilihagi.*
R 1 **hesilisilihaginga.** *n.* —.
RE **hagahesilisilihagi.** *n.* ——.
ID **hesilihagi gee.** To have *hesilihagi* by a considerable distance.
ID **hesilihaginga haiava.** Intersection.

SILIVAAHEA

B **silivaahea.** *v.* Wander about with no fixed abode.
B 1 **silivaahenga.** *n.* —.
BE **hagasilivaahea.** *v.* —.
BE1 **hagasilivaahenga.** *n.* —.
R **silisilivaahea.** *v.* Frequently *silivaahea.*
R 1 **silisilivaahenga.** *n.* —.
RE **hagasilisilivaahea.** *v.* —.
RE1 **hagasilisilivaahenga.** *n.* —.

SINA

B **sina.** *n.* White (or grey) hair (appearing in old age).
B 2 **sinaa.** *v.* Having white hair.
B 3 **sinaanga.** *n.* —.
BE2 **hagasinaa.** *v.* —.
R 1 **sinasinaanga.** *n.* —.
R 2 **sinasinaa.** *v.* White-headed; old (of living things); big (of animals).
RE2 **hagasinasinaa.** *v.* —.
ID **velo ssina.** Beginning to show white hairs on one's head.

SINGA

B **singa.** *v.* Overhand.
B 1 **siinganga.** *n.* —.
B 2 **singalia.** *v.* Overhung.
BE **hagasinga.** *v.* —; lean over toward.
BE1 **hagasiinganga.** *n.* —.
BE2 **hagasingalia.** *v.* —.
P **ssinga.** *v.* —.
P 1 **ssiinganga.** *n.* —.
P 2 **ssingalia.** *v.* —.
PE **hagassinga.** *v.* —.
PE1 **hagassingaanga.** *n.* —.
PE2 **hagassingalia.** *v.* —.
R **singasinga.** *v.* To wave back and forth (as a coconut tree in the wind).
R 1 **singasingaanga.** *n.* —.
R 2 **singasingalia.** *v.* —.
RE **hagasingasinga.** *v.* —.
RE1 **hagasingasingaanga.** *n.* —.
RE2 **hagasingasingalia.** *v.* —.

ID **singa gee.** Lean away from.
ID **singa mai (adu, ange).** Come carrying.
ID **singa sogosogo.** Do something (e.g., work) all by oneself.

SINGANO
B **singano.** *v.* The flower of the pandanus tree.
BE **hagasingano.** *v.* Cause to bear *singano.*
ID **hau singano.** Garland of *singano.*

SIO
B **sio.** *n.* Waterspout (esp. the air causing it); whirlwind.

$SISI_1$
B **$sisi_1$.** *v.* To move one end of something long and thin by pressure on the other end; to lift a fishing pole; to write (with a pen or pencil); cut copra.
B 1 **$siianga_1$.** *n.* —; writing (on paper); a letter (of the alphabet); a character (written symbol).
B 2 **siia.** *v.* —.
BE **hagasisi.** *v.* —.
BE2 **$hagasiia_2$.** *v.* —.
R **sissisi.** *a.* Striped (having stripes).
R 1 **sissisianga.** *n.* —.
RE **hagasissisi.** *v.* —.
RE1 **hagasissisianga.** *n.* —.
T **$siisii_2$.** *v.* Fishing (with a pole); fishing pole.
T 1 **siisiianga.** *n.* —.
T 2 **siisiia.** *v.* Fished in (place).
TE **$hagasiisii_2$.** *v.* —.
TE1 **hagasiisiianga.** *n.* —.
TE2 **$hagasiisiia_2$.** *v.* —.
XCO **daasissisi.** *v.* Striped (with stripes).
XCO **dagasisi.** *v.* Scoop out by inserting a knife between the meat and the shell (e.g., in cutting copra).
ID **dabuvae sisi.** Little toe.
ID **tangada sisi.** Secretary.
ID **madannia sisi.** Little finger.
ID **siia gi moana ngaadai.** Drift downwind, away from land.
ID **sisi baalasi.** Printing (block letters).
ID **sisi gaadinga.** To cut copra.
ID **sisi galisi.** Striped (with thin lines).
ID **sisi lima.** Longhand (writing).

$SISI_2$
B **$sisi_2$.** *n.* Mollusk sp.: *Neritidae* spp.

SIVA
B **siva.** *an.* Nine.
BE **hagasiva (ina).** *v.* Make a total of nine.
XCO **Diba-siva.** *nn.* The name of a person in a traditional story.
XCO **Ssiva-malama.** *nt.* September ('ninth month').
ID **siva-dahanga.** The ninth number of a counting game played to determine who is "it".

SIVI
B **sivi.** *a.* Give up.
B 1 **siivinga.** *n.* —.
BE **hagasivi.** *v.* —; cause to not repeat an action.
BE1 **hagasiivinga.** *n.* —.
BE2 **hagasivia.** *v.* —.
P **ssivi.** *a.* —.
PE2 **hagassivia.** *v.* —.
R **sivisivi.** *a.* —.
R 1 **sivisivinga.** *n.* —.
RE **hagasivisivi.** *v.* —.
RE1 **hagasivisivinga.** *n.* —.
RE2 **hagasivisivia.** *v.* —.
XCO **duasivi.** *n.* The back of the spine.

SOA
B **soa.** *a.* A friend; many (people).
B 1 **soaanga.** *n.* —.
BE **hagasoa.** *v.* Go with someone; cause to increase in number.
BE1 **hagasoaanga.** *n.* —.
R **soasoa.** *a.* Increasing in number (people).
R 1 **soasoaanga.** *n.* —.

RE **hagasoasoa.** *v.* —.
RE1 **hagasoasoaanga.** *n.* —.
XCO **dagisoa.** *a.* Many (people) at each (time or place, etc.).
ID **daahili dau soa.** A love song.
ID **dau soa.** Boyfriend, girlfriend; couple (not married); going steady (of an unmarried couple).
ID **hagasoa ange.** Go along with others, join the crowd.
ID **hai soa.** The relationship between friends; friendship.
ID **sileia doo soa.** Look, your neighbor is competing against you!
ID **soaa lodo.** The paddlers of a canoe which is engaged in catching flying fish.
ID **soa hagaaloha.** A good friend.
CF **hiisoa.** Plant sp.: cassytha vine (*Cassytha filiformis* L.).

SOBAGA
B **sobaga.** *n.* Fish sp.: tang.

SOBALO
B **sobalo.** *n.* Fish sp.: needlefish.

SOBO
B **sobo.** *a.* Rise up (as the sun), get up, jump up.
B 1 **soobonga.** *n.* —; the direction or spot from which the sun rises; rising (of the sun, etc.).
B 2 **sobolia.** *v.* —.
BE **hagasobo.** *v.* —.
BE1 **hagasoobonga.** *n.* —.
BE2 **hagasoboa.** *v.* —.
BE2 **hagasobolia.** *v.* —.
E **ssobo.** *a.* Rise (of stars, or of the moon or sun).
PE **hagassobo.** *v.* —.
PE2 **hagassoboa.** *v.* —.
PE2 **hagassobolia.** *v.* —.
R **sobosobo.** *a.* —.
R 1 **sobosobonga.** *n.* —.
R 2 **sobosobolia.** *v.* —.
RE **hagasobosobo.** *v.* —.
RE1 **hagasobosobonga.** *n.* —.
RE2 **hagasobosoboa.** *v.* —.
RE2 **hagasobosobolia.** *v.* —.
T **soosobo.** *a.* Get up [pl.], jump up [pl.].
T 1 **soosobonga.** *n.* —.
T 2 **soosobolia.** *v.* —.
TE **hagasoosobo.** *v.* —.
TE1 **hagasoosobonga.** *n.* —.
TE2 **hagasoosoboa.** *v.* —.
TE2 **hagasoosobolia.** *v.* —.
ID **sobo de laa.** Rising of the sun.

SOE
B **soe.** *a.* Straight, not crooked; level.
B 1 **soenga.** *n.* —.
BE **hagasoe.** *v.* —; go directly, speak directly (without circumlocution).
BE1 **hagasoenga.** *a.* —; show-off; proud, abrupt in manner.
BE2 **hagasoea.** *v.* —.
BE2 **hagasoelia.** *v.* —.
P **ssoe.** *a.* —.
P 1 **ssoenga.** *n.* —.
PE **hagassoe.** *v.* Straighten out; decide an issue (by higher authority).
PE1 **hagassoenga.** *n.* —.
PE2 **hagassoea.** *v.* —.
PE2 **hagassoelia.** *v.* —.
R **soesoe.** *a.* Straight or level all over (as a playing field); somewhat level or straight.
R 1 **soesoenga.** *n.* —.
RE **hagasoesoe.** *v.* —; to level off (ground, etc.); to go about one's business without regard to others.
RE1 **hagasoesoenga.** *n.* —.
RE2 **hagasoesoea.** *v.* —.
RE2 **hagasoesoelia.** *v.* —.
XCO **laussoe.** *a.* Having straight hair (not kinky or wavy).
ID **basa soe.** Say what is on one's mind; speak directly (so that one's meaning is clear).
ID **gu soe donu.** Unmistakably, for certain.
ID **hagasoe ange.** Aim at.

ID **hagasoesoe saele.** To walk about without greeting others.
ID **hainga soe.** A just law.
ID **momme hagassoe.** Court (of law).
ID **soe age.** Straight up; decide (for oneself).
ID **soe daa dahi.** Straight as can be.
ID **soe iho.** Straight down; decided for one by the will of God.
ID **soe lodo modu.** To remain (or sit, or stand) motionless (as when praying).
ID **soe mai.** Decided for one by the will of God.

SOGO
XFL **gumigumi-o-sogo.** *n.* Plant sp.: epiphytic fern (*Vittaria incurvata* Cav.).
XG **laulau a sogo.** A type of basket.
CF **gasogo.** To have sexual pleasure (of males only) either by intercourse, or by regarding a naked woman.
CF **sogoisi.** [var. of *dogoisi*].

SOGOISI
B **sogoisi.** *a.* [var. of *dogoisi*].
BE **hagasogoisi.** *v.* [var. of *hagadogoisi*].
R **sogosogoisi.** *a.* [var. of *dogodogoisi*].
RE **hagasogosogoisi.** *v.* [var. of *hagadogodogoisi*].
ID **sogoisi loo huu.** [var. of *dogoisi loo huu*].

SOGOSOGO
B **sogosogo.** *v.* Alone, only, by oneself; each.
BE **hagasogosogo.** *v.* —.
BE2 **hagasogosogolia.** *v.* —.
ID **hai sogosogo.** Masturbate oneself.
ID **i de — sogosogo.** Apiece, each.
ID **modu sogosogo.** Separated from others, and by itself.
ID **singa sogosogo.** Do something (e.g., work) all by oneself.

SOGOSOGO$_a$
B **massogosogo.** *a.* Go or do by oneself; a one-man canoe.
B 1 **massogosogoanga.** *n.* —.
B 2 **massogosogolia.** *v.* To have been by oneself.
BE **hagamassogosogo.** *v.* —.
BE1 **hagamassogosogoanga.** *n.* —.
BE2 **hagamassogosogolia.** *v.* —.
C **mossogosogo.** *a.* —.
C 1 **mossogosogoanga.** *n.* —.
C 2 **mossogosogolia.** *v.* —.
CE **hagamossogosogo.** *v.* —.
CE1 **hagamossogosogoanga.** *n.* —.
CE2 **hagamossogosogolia.** *v.* —.

SOI$_1$
B **soi$_1$** (adu, mai, ange). *d.* Assume.
R **soisoi$_1$** (adu, mai, ange). *d.* —.
ID **soi adu —.** Expect that — but.

SOI$_2$
B **soi$_2$.** *d.* —.
B 1 **soinga.** *n.* —.
B 2 **soia.** *v.* —.
E **ssoi.** *v.* To foretell a death by words or actions (which cause death).
E 1 **ssoinga.** *n.* —.
E 2 **ssoia.** *v.* —.
R **soisoi$_2$.** *v.* —.
R 1 **soisoinga.** *n.* —.
R 2 **soisoia.** *v.* —.

SOLA
R **solasola.** *v.* Not homogenous or smooth (as lumpy dough, or the grated surface of taro).
R 1 **solasolaanga.** *n.* —.
RE **hagasolasola.** *v.* —.
RE1 **hagasolasolaanga.** *n.* —.
ID **gili solasola.** Leathery black skin (of humans).
CF **halaasola.** Mollusk sp.: clam sp. (a type of *baasua*).

SOLO

B **aasolo.** *n.* Mollusk sp.: clam sp. (a type of *baasua*).
B **solo.** *v.* To grate or file (something); to launch or beach a canoe by dragging it along the shore; a type of prepared food (made from grated taro).
B 1 **soloanga.** *n.* —.
B 1 **solonga.** *n.* —.
B 2 **soloa.** *v.* —.
B 2 **solona.** *v.* —.
BE **hagasolo.** *v.* —; take turns.
BE1 **hagasoloanga.** *n.* —.
BE1 **hagasolonga.** *n.* —.
BE2 **hagasoloa.** *v.* —.
BE2 **hagasolona.** *v.* —.
E **ssolo.** *v.* Wipe, scrub, clean up (by wiping), erase.
E 1 **soolonga.** *n.* —; spouse [rarely heard].
E 2 **sooloa.** *v.* —.
E 2 **soolona.** *v.* —.
EE **hagassolo.** *v.* —; to scrape slightly in passing.
EE1 **hagasoolonga.** *n.* —.
EE2 **hagasooloa.** *v.* —.
EE2 **hagasoolona.** *v.* —.
R **solosolo.** *v.* —.
R 1 **solosoloanga.** *n.* —.
R 1 **solosolonga.** *n.* —.
R 2 **solosoloa.** *v.* —.
R 2 **solosolona.** *v.* —.
RE **hagasolosolo.** *v.* —.
RE1 **hagasolosoloanga.** *n.* —.
RE1 **hagasolosolonga.** *n.* —.
RE2 **hagasolosoloa.** *v.* —.
RE2 **hagasolosolona.** *v.* —.
XFL **manu-solo-maanu.** *n.* A jellyfish-like animal in the shape of a flower (burrows into the sand when touched).
XG **manu solo laagau.** File (for filing wood).
XG **manu solo maadau.** File (for filing metal).
ID **duudangaa solo.** A package of *solo* (food) wrapped in coconut leaves and heated; flashlight battery.
ID **hadu solo bulaga.** A taro grater made from a certain type of coral.
ID **hagasolo age.** Keep postponing or delaying.

SOLOVAANI

B **solovaani.** *v.* Thin and straight (of a person) [e.g., having flat buttocks — considered ugly].
BE **hagasolovaani.** *v.* —.

SOMO$_1$

B **somo$_1$.** *a.* Grow, develop; coconut apple.
B 1 **soomonga$_1$.** *n.* —; build (of the body).
BE **hagasomo.** *v.* —; bed of sprouting coconuts; to stick out one's tongue.
BE1 **hagasoomonga.** *n.* —.
BE2 **hagasomolia.** *v.* —.
P **ssomo$_1$.** *a.* —.
PE **hagassomo.** *v.* —.
PE1 **hagassoomonga.** *n.* —.
PE2 **hagassomolia.** *v.* —.
R **somosomo$_1$.** *a.* Grow fast or well anywhere (e.g., as a weed).
R 1 **somosomonga$_1$.** *n.* —.
RE **hagasomosomo.** *v.* —.
RE1 **hagasomosomonga.** *n.* —.
RE2 **hagasomosomolia.** *v.* —.
ID **duu gili somo.** The coconut meat remaining in a germinated coconut after the coconut apple has been removed.
ID **gili somo.** The coconut meat of a germinating coconut (after the coconut apple has been removed).
ID **hagasomo de alelo.** Stick out one's tongue.
ID **somo boi.** Grow abnormally (having defects).
ID **somo dae.** Fully mature coconut apple.
ID **somo haahine.** A fleshy (non-muscular) man.

SOMO$_2$

B **somo$_2$.** *d.* —.
B 1 **somoanga.** *n.* —.
B 1 **soomonga$_2$.** *n.* —.
B 2 **somodia.** *v.* —.

B 2 **somolia.** *v.* —.
B 2 **soomoa.** *v.* —.
E **ssomo$_2$.** *v.* Suck one's finger.
R **somosomo$_2$.** *v.* —.
R 1 **somosomoanga.** *n.* —.
R 1 **somosomonga$_2$.** *n.* —.
R 2 **somosomoa.** *v.* —.
R 2 **somosomodia.** *v.* —.
R 2 **somosomolia.** *v.* —.

SONGAGI
B **songagi.** *n.* A bad sort of person.

SONGI$_a$
B **hesongi.** *a.* Kiss (Polynesian style), embrace.
B 1 **hesonginga.** *n.* —.
B 2 **hesongia.** *v.* —.
BE **hagahesongi.** *v.* —.
BE1 **hagahesonginga.** *n.* —.
BE2 **hagahesongia.** *v.* —.
R **hesohesongi.** *a.* Repeatedly *hesongi.*
R 1 **hesohesonginga.** *n.* —.
RE **hagahesohesongi.** *v.* —.
RE1 **hagahesohesonginga.** *n.* —.
RE2 **hagahesohesongia.** *v.* —.

SOODO
B **soodo.** *n.* Lead (metal), bullet; [the etymology of this word is obscure].

SOOSOA
B **soosoa.** *n.* Outrigger float lashings (complementary to the connecting pegs).
B 1 **soosoaanga.** *n.* —.
BE **hagasoosoa.** *v.* To put *soosoa* on a canoe.
BE1 **hagasoosoaanga.** *v.* —.
ID **dada soosoa.** To put *soosoa* on the canoe.

SOU
B **sou.** *v.* A gust of wind.
B 1 **sounga.** *n.* —.
BE **hagasou.** *v.* —.
BE1 **hagasounga.** *n.* —.
BE2 **hagasoua.** *v.* —.
ID **de gau duuli sou.** Gilbertese people.
ID **sou daane.** A sudden strong gust of wind.
ID **sou hahine.** A steady, light gust of wind.

SSABE
B **ssabe.** *a.* Leave, go away.
B 1 **ssabeanga.** *n.* —.
BE **hagassabe.** *v.* —.
BE1 **hagassabeanga.** *n.* —.
R **sassabe.** *a.* About to leave, prepare to leave.
R 1 **sassabeanga.** *n.* —.
RE **hagasassabe.** *v.* —.
RE1 **hagasassabeanga.** *n.* —.
ID **ssabe age.** Eat.

SSAHU
B **ssahu.** *a.* Inquisitive, mischievous (as a child).
B 1 **ssahuanga.** *n.* —.
BE **hagassahu.** *v.* To try one's best to do something bad or harmful.
BE1 **hagassahuanga.** *n.* —.

SSAVE
B **ssave.** *n.* Fish sp.: flying fish.
XFL **ssave-a-bao.** *n.* Fish sp.: flying fish.
ID **ilihia ssave.** The submerging of flying fish below the surface of the water (making them difficult to net).
ID **mao denga ssave.** A scarcity of *ssave.*
ID **ssave de loolodo.** Flying fish inside the lagoon.
ID **ssave haula.** To roast *ssave* (in the fire of a torch).

SSENE
ID **haanau ssene.** Yield interest.

SSEVA
B **sseva.** *a.* Scarce (applied usually only to *ssave*).
B 1 **sseevanga.** *n.* —.
B 2 **ssevalia.** *v.* —.
BE **hagasseva.** *v.* —.
BE1 **hagasseevanga.** *n.* —.
BE2 **hagassevalia.** *v.* —.

SSII
B **ssii$_2$.** *a.* A hissing sound [used to indicate

	disapproval (esp. to bothersome children, or to chase chickens)].
B 1	**ssiinga$_2$.** *n.* —.
BE	**hagassii$_2$.** *v.* —.
BE1	**hagassiinga$_2$.** *n.* —.
R	**ssiisii.** *a.* —.
R 1	**ssiisiinga.** *n.* —.
RE	**hagassiissii.** *v.* —.
RE1	**hagassiisiinga.** *n.* —.
ID	**gai hagassii.** Eat messily (letting the food fall from one's hands and mouth).

SSOGA

B	**ssoga.** *v.* [var. of *ssogo*].
B 1	**ssogaanga.** *n.* [var. of *ssogoanga*].
B 2	**ssogalia.** *v.* [var. of *ssogolia*].
BE	**hagassoga.** *v.* [var. of *hagassogo*].
BE1	**hagassogaanga.** *n.* [var. of *hagassogoanga*].
BE2	**hagassogalia.** *v.* [var. of *hagassogolia*].

SSOGO

B	**ssogo.** *v.* Grated raw taro which has dried out.
B 1	**ssogoanga.** *n.* —.
B 2	**ssogolia.** *v.* To be *ssogo*.
BE	**hagassogo.** *v.* —.
BE1	**hagassogoanga.** *n.* —.
BE2	**hagassogolia.** *v.* —.

SSONGO

B	**ssongo.** *v.* Stink.
BE	**hagassongo.** *v.* —.
R	**songosongo.** *n.* —; genitals (of males or females).
ID	**me ssongo aha.** Useless thing.

SSUNU

B	**ssunu$_2$.** *v.* Suck, smoke (cigarettes).
B 1	**suununga$_2$.** *n.* —.
B 2	**ssunua.** *v.* —.
B 2	**ssunumia.** *v.* —.
BE	**hagassunu.** *v.* —; teach to *sunu*; to give (someone) something to *sunu*.
BE1	**hagasuununga.** *n.* —.
BE2	**hagassunua.** *v.* —.
BE2	**hagassunumia.** *v.* —.
R	**sunusunu$_2$.** *v.* —.
R 1	**sunusununga.** *n.* —.
R 2	**sunusunua$_2$.** *v.* —.
R 2	**sunusunumia.** *v.* —.
RE	**hagasunusunu$_2$.** *v.* —.
RE1	**hagasunusununga$_2$.** *n.* —.
RE2	**hagasunusunua$_2$.** *v.* —.
RE2	**hagasunusunumia.** *v.* —.

SSUONIONI

B	**ssuonioni.** *v.* Sand.
ID	**ssuonioni ina.** Sandy.

SUA

B	**sua$_1$.** *v.* Root up (soil); wrestling holds; rowing motion.
B 1	**suaanga.** *n.* —.
B 2	**sualia.** *v.* —.
BE	**hagasua.** *v.* —.
BE1	**hagasuaanga.** *n.* —.
BE2	**hagasualia.** *v.* —.
R	**suasua.** *v.* —.
R 1	**suasuaanga.** *n.* —.
R 2	**suasualia.** *v.* —.
RE	**hagasuasua.** *v.* —.
RE1	**hagasuasuaanga.** *n.* —.
RE2	**hagasuasualia.** *v.* —.
ID	**sua aaleloi.** A wrestling maneuver.
ID	**sua age.** Dig up soil to uncover (something).
ID	**sua hadu umu.** Stones (dead coral) used in the earth oven.
ID	**sua iho.** To dig away soil, letting the soil slide down (e.g., from the side of a hill).
ID	**sua saele.** Search for by rooting around.
ID	**suasua mai (adu, ange).** To row a canoe (with a paddle).

SUGI$_1$

B	**sugi$_1$.** *v.* Pierce (slightly), stab (lightly), lance (e.g., a boil).
B 1	**suuginga.** *n.* —.
B 2	**sugia.** *v.* —.
BC	**masugi.** *a.* Having a hole, pierced.
BC1	**masuginga.** *n.* —.
BE	**hagasugi$_1$.** *v.* —.

BE1 **hagasuuginga.** *n.* —.
BE2 **hagasugia.** *v.* —.
BF **hagamasugi.** *v.* —.
BF1 **hagamasuginga.** *n.* —.
BF2 **hagamasugia.** *v.* —.
PC **maasugi.** *a.* —.
PC1 **maasuginga.** *n.* —.
PF **hagamaasugi.** *v.* —.
R **sugisugi.** *v.* —.
R 1 **sugisuginga.** *n.* —.
R 2 **sugisugia.** *v.* —.
RC **masugisugi.** *a.* —.
RC1 **masugisuginga.** *n.* —.
RE **hagasugisugi$_1$.** *v.* —.
RE1 **hagasugisuginga.** *n.* —.
RE2 **hagasugisugia.** *v.* —.
RF **hagamasugisugi.** *v.* —.
RF1 **hagamasugisuginga.** *n.* —.
RF2 **hagamasugisugia.** *v.* —.

SUGI$_2$

B **sugi$_2$.** *n.* Tail.
BE **hagasugi$_2$.** *v.* Shorten, abbreviate; abbreviation, acronym, nickname.
PF1 **hagamaasuginga.** *n.* —.
PF2 **hagamaasugia.** *v.* —.
RE **hagasugisugi$_2$.** *v.* Repeatedly shorten or abbreviate.
XCO **daasugi.** *v.* Struggle to get free; jerking of the tail.
XCO **sugimada.** *n.* The outer corner of the eye.
ID **galo sugi mada.** Glimpse.
ID **hagasugi ange.** To use an abbreviated name or acronym.
ID **sugi au.** A current of choppy water between other currents.
ID **sugi de ngudu.** The corner of the mouth.
ID **sugi talinga.** Piercing of the ear (for insertion of an ornament).
ID **sugi hagabolebole.** The tip of anything slender and long (e.g., the tail of an animal).
ID **sugi lima.** Forearm.
ID **sugimada ina.** Catch a glimpse of.
ID **sugi vae.** Lower leg (between the ankle and the knee).
CF **moosugia.** Ripened unevenly (of breadfruit only).
CF **sugi-daa.** Fish sp.: tang.
CF **sugi-laagoo.** Fish sp.: goatfish.
CF **sugi-manga.** Fish sp. (= large *madu*).

SUI

B **sui.** *v.* Change, replace.
B 1 **suinga.** *n.* —.
B 2 **suia.** *v.* —.
R **suisui$_1$.** *v.* —.
R 1 **suisuinga$_1$.** *n.* —.
R 2 **suisuia.** *v.* —.
ID **sui ange.** Take revenge, get even; pay back (a debt).
ID **sui de lodo.** Change one's mind.
ID **sui hagahoou.** Change of personality (for the better).
CF **masui.** Left (side).

SUI$_a$

B **hesuihagi.** *v.* Exchange, trade.
B 1 **hesuihaginga.** *n.* —.
B 2 **hesuihagina.** *v.* —.
BE **hagahesuihagi.** *v.* —.
BE1 **hagahesuihaginga.** *n.* —.
BE2 **hagahesuihagina.** *v.* —.
R **hesuisuihagi.** *v.* Repeatedly *hesuihagi.*
R 1 **hesuisuihaginga.** *n.* —.
R 2 **hesuisuihagina.** *v.* —.
RE **hagahesuisuihagi.** *v.* —.
RE1 **hagahesuisuihaginga.** *n.* —.
RE2 **hagahesuisuihagina.** *v.* —.
ID **goloa hesuihagi.** Goods which are bartered.

SULA

B **sula.** *v.* Appear (sighted); succeed.
B 1 **suulanga.** *n.* —.
B 2 **sulangia.** *v.* To have appeared or succeeded.
BE **hagasula.** *v.* —.
BE1 **hagasuulanga.** *n.* —.
BE2 **hagasulangia.** *v.* —.
P **ssula.** *a.* —.
P 1 **ssuulanga.** *n.* —.
PE **hagassula.** *v.* —.
PE1 **hagassuulanga.** *n.* —.

PE2 **hagassulangia.** *v.* —.
R **sulasula.** *v.* —.
R 1 **sulasulaanga.** *n.* —.
RE **hagasulasula.** *v.* —.
RE1 **hagasulasulaanga.** *n.* —.
RE2 **hagasulasulangia.** *v.* —.
ID **hagasula tangada.** Successfully promote the candidacy of someone (or elect or appoint him) to a coveted position.
ID **sula boo.** The appearance in early morning of a ship (or plane).
ID **sula dagidahi —.** Once in a while it happens that —.
ID **sula de hegau.** Successfully completed work.
ID **sula tumuagi.** Bald-headed.
ID **sula gi dahi henua.** To have visited abroad.

SULEGI
B **sulegi.** *a.* Work (in a group) busily.
BE **hagasulegi.** *v.* —.

SULU
B **sulu.** *v.* Dive, fall head first; anoint (hair with oil).
B 1 **sulumanga.** *n.* —.
B 1 **suulunga.** *n.* —.
B 2 **sulua.** *v.* —.
B 2 **sulumia.** *v.* —.
BE **hagasulu.** *v.* —; annoint (in baptism).
BE1 **hagasulumanga.** *n.* —.
BE1 **hagasuulunga.** *n.* —.
BE2 **hagasulua.** *v.* —.
BE2 **hagasulumia.** *v.* —.
P **ssulu.** *v.* —.
PE **hagassulu.** *v.* —.
PE1 **hagassuulunga.** *n.* —.
PE2 **hagassulumia.** *v.* —.
PE2 **hagassuulua.** *v.* —.
R **sulusulu.** *v.* —.
R 1 **sulusulumanga.** *n.* —.
R 1 **sulusulunga.** *n.* —.
R 2 **sulusulua.** *v.* —.
R 2 **sulusulumia.** *v.* —.
RE **hagasulusulu.** *v.* —.
RE1 **hagasulusulumanga.** *n.* —.
RE1 **hagasulusulunga.** *n.* —.
RE2 **hagasulusulua.** *v.* —.
RE2 **hagasulusulumia.** *v.* —.
ID **ivi sulu.** A dislocation of bones such that the ends overlap (corrected by pulling).
ID **masulu de maasina.** "A person has died.".
ID **moni sulu.** Submarine.
ID **sulu de gelo.** Diving in the area in back of the center of the communal fishing net (the deepest part, in which the fish are trapped).
ID **sulu de laa.** The setting of the sun.
ID **sulu gi mua.** Fall forward.
ID **sulu i hegau.** Busy (with work or obligations).
ID **sulumanga o de laa.** The direction in which the sun sets.
ID **sulu moso.** Be wet all over (esp. when one's hair is dripping).
ID **sulu saele.** To throw oneself about (as children do when unhappy).
ID **vai sulu.** Pomade (for hair).

SUMU$_1$
B **sumu$_1$.** *v.* A method of lashing (which is diamond-shaped) and of decorating mats (with a diamond-shaped design).
B 1 **suumunga.** *n.* —.
B 2 **sumua.** *v.* —.
B 2 **sumulia.** *v.* —.
BE **hagasumu.** *v.* —.
BE1 **hagasuumunga.** *n.* —.
BE2 **hagasumua.** *v.* —.
BE2 **hagasumulia.** *v.* —.
R 1 **sumusumunga.** *n.* —.
R 2 **sumusumua.** *v.* —.
R 2 **sumusumulia.** *v.* —.
RE **hagasumusumu.** *v.* —.
RE1 **hagasumusumunga.** *n.* —.
RE2 **hagasumusumua.** *v.* —.
RE2 **hagasumusumulia.** *v.* —.
ID **hai sumu.** Having a diamond-shaped decoration or form, etc.
ID **sumu ina.** To make diamond-shaped designs in plaiting or lashing.

$SUMU_2$

B **$sumu_2$.** *n.* Fish sp.: triggerfish, filefish (The native term is applied to many spp.).
XFL **sumu-dea.** *n.* Fish sp.
XFL **sumu-gaaleva.** *n.* Fish sp.: filefish.

SUNU

B **sunu.** *n.* An oil slick on the water's surface.
B 1 **$suununga_1$.** *n.* —; way of sucking.
E **$ssunu_1$.** *v.* —.
R **$sunusunu_1$.** *v.* Oily.
R 2 **$sunusunua_1$.** *v.* Be covered with oil.
RE **$hagasunusunu_1$.** *v.* —.
RE1 **$hagasunusununga_1$.** *n.* —.
RE2 **$hagasunusunua_1$.** *v.* —.

SUU_1

B **ssui.** *a.* Wet.
B 1 **ssuinga.** *n.* —.
B 2 **suungia.** *v.* Damp.
BE **hagassui.** *v.* —; urinate.
BE1 **hagassuinga.** *n.* —.
BE2 **hagassuia.** *v.* —.
BE2 **hagasuungia.** *v.* —.
R **$suisui_2$.** *a.* —; become wet [followed by *ange*].
R 1 **$suisuinga_2$.** *n.* —.
R 2 **suusuungia.** *v.* —.
RE **hagasuisui.** *v.* —.
RE1 **hagasuisuinga.** *n.* —.
RE2 **hagasuisuia.** *v.* —.
RE2 **hagasuusuungia.** *v.* —.
ID **doo de ssui.** Still damp (but becoming dry).
ID **hagassui age.** Eat or drink just a little bit.
ID **ssui de maasina.** The rising of the moon after the setting of the sun (i.e., when the moon is still below the water when the sun sets).
ID **ssuilebelebe.** Completely wet all over.
ID **ssui o de hine.** Amniotic fluid.

SUU_{1a}

B **sua_2.** *d.* Wet and dried [occurs only in compounds].
B 1 **suanga.** *v.* A stain (impermanent) left by something wet.
BE1 **hagasuanga.** *v.* —.
E 1 **ssuanga.** *n.* Stained in one place.
R 1 **suasuanga.** *v.* Stained all over.
XCO **suugelegele.** *v.* —.
XCO **suukaha.** *n.* The land near shore [on which the chief traditionally had some rights].
XCO **suunibongi.** *n.* A coral formation (resembling a man) at the bottom of the lagoon; a method of pole fishing at night.
ID **mada sua hadu.** Storm beach (on the seaward reef).
ID **muli sua hadu.** Reefward of the storm beach; beach rock.
ID **sua bagu.** A stain which has left a dry residue.
ID **sua hadu.** Storm beach.
CF **ssuonioni.** Sand.

SUU_{1b}

B **suuduuduu.** *v.* Defecate [children's language].
B 1 **suuduuduunga.** *n.* —.
BE **hagasuuduuduu.** *v.* —.
BE1 **hagasuuduuduunga.** *n.* —.
BE2 **hagasuuduuduua.** *v.* —.
BE2 **hagasuuduuduulia.** *v.* —.

SUU_2

B **suu.** *n.* Fishhook keeper.

SUUGUI

B **suugui.** *v.* Connect, join together.
B 1 **suguinga.** *n.* —; joint, connection.
B 1 **suuguinga.** *n.* —.
B 2 **suguia.** *v.* —.
B 2 **suuguia.** *v.* —.
BE **hagasuugui.** *v.* —.
BE1 **hagasuguinga.** *n.* —.
BE1 **hagasuuguinga.** *n.* —.
BE2 **hagasuguia.** *v.* —.

BE2 **hagasuuguia.** *v.* —.
R **sugusugui.** *v.* Connect up or join several things.
R 1 **sugusuguinga.** *n.* —.
R 2 **sugusuguia.** *v.* —.
RE **hagasugusugui.** *v.* —.
RE1 **hagasugusuguinga.** *n.* —.
RE2 **hagasugusuguia.** *v.* —.
ID **suugui ange.** Join to, connect to, connect up with.

SUULEE
B **suulee.** *n.* Fish sp. (var. *dabaduu*).

SUUNUGI
B **suunugi.** *v.* Skewer, hold something down with the end of a long implement.
B 1 **suunuginga.** *n.* —.
B 2 **suunugia.** *v.* —.
BE **hagasuunugi.** *v.* —.
BE1 **hagasuunuginga.** *n.* —.
BE2 **hagasuunugia.** *v.* —.
R **suusuunugi.** *v.* —.
R 1 **suusuunuginga.** *n.* —.
R 2 **suusuunugia.** *v.* —.
RE **hagasuusuunugi.** *v.* —.
RE1 **hagasuusuunuginga.** *n.* —.
RE2 **hagasuusuunugia.** *v.* —.
ID **hale suunugi.** A house with eaves touching the ground [an old style].
ID **velo suunugi.** To spear something and hold it against something solid with the spear.

U$_1$
B **u + NUMBER.** *mc.* NUMERAL CLASSIFIER (BY TENS) FOR LONG THIN OBJECTS, ALSO NIGHTS.
XCO **uhaa.** *u.* Forty, of days + nights.

U$_2$
XCO **mada-umanga.** *n.* The bud of a Cyrtosperma taro corm.
XCO **uduu.** *n.* A half shell, a cover (of something).
XCO **umanga.** *n.* A bunch of *Cyrtosperma* taro corm buds planted together.
ID **dalaa umada.** Prow spray of a ship.
CF **umada.** Rainbow.
CF **umalie.** Delicious (of pandanus only).

UA$_1$
B **ua$_1$.** *v.* Come in (tide).
B 1 **uaanga$_1$.** *n.* —.
BE **hagaua$_1$.** *v.* —.
BE1 **hagauaanga$_1$.** *n.* —.
R **uaua$_1$.** *v.* —.
R 1 **uauaanga$_1$.** *n.* —.
RE **hagauaua$_1$.** *v.* —.
RE1 **hagauauaanga$_1$.** *n.* —.
ID **ua mai.** The rising of the tide.

UA$_2$
B **ua$_2$.** *v.* Rain [archaic, except in compounds].
B 1 **uaanga$_2$.** *n.* —.
B 1 **uadanga.** *v.* An intermittent downpour (of rain) [considered an omen of birth, death, or the coming arrival of a ship].
BE **hagaua$_2$.** *v.* —.
BE1 **hagauaanga$_2$.** *n.* —.
BE1 **hagauadanga.** *n.* —.
R **uaua$_2$.** *v.* —.
R 1 **uauaanga$_2$.** *n.* —.
R 1 **uauadanga.** *v.* —.
RE **hagauaua$_2$.** *v.* —.
RE1 **hagauauaanga$_2$.** *n.* —.
RE1 **hagauauadanga.** *n.* —.
XCO **uaduu.** *n.* Waterspout (esp. full of water) [meterological condition].
ID **too madaaua.** Drip, fall drop by drop.
ID **madaa ua.** Drop (of liquid or rain).
ID **ua dodo.** Rain of a reddish color [an omen of death].
ID **ua lolo.** A disturbance in the sea caused by schools of big fish feeding on little fish.

UA$_3$
B **ua$_3$.** *n.* Neck.
R **uaua$_4$** (ange). *a.* Crave for (food).

R 1 **uauaanga$_3$.** *n.* —.
RE **hagauaua$_3$.** *v.* —.
RE1 **hagauauaanga$_3$.** *n.* —.
XCO **uasaa.** *n.* A good time associated with good food.
XFL **ua-mea.** *n.* Bird sp.: red-throated frigate bird.
ID **bonaa ua.** The sheath of the turtle's neck.
ID **buni de ua.** To be very thirsty.
ID **dae de ua.** Have a good time.
ID **hai uaua.** Dilated veins.
ID **ua dea.** Bird sp.: white-throated frigate bird.

UA_{3a}
R **uaua$_3$.** *n.* Vein, tendon, nerve, plastic filament.
ID **tuu uaua.** Dilated veins.
ID **uaua mouli.** Veins pulsing.

UA_4
B **ua$_4$** + NUMBER. *mc.* NUMERAL CLASSIFIER (BY TENS) FOR PIECES OF THATCH ROOFING.

UAA
B **uaa.** *a.* Yes!; assent to, agree to.
B 1 **uaanga$_3$.** *n.* —.
BE **hagauaa.** *v.* —.
BE1 **hagauaanga$_3$.** *n.* —.
R **uaauaa.** *a.* —.
R 1 **uaauaanga.** *n.* —.
RE **hagauaauaa.** *v.* —.
RE1 **hagauaauaanga.** *n.* —.
ID **ngadi uaa.** Assent to insincerely.

UAASEI
B **uaasei.** *n.* A type of small knife.

UAVESI
ID **sigo ina uavesi.** Don't forget!

UBA
B **uba.** *v.* Not level.
B 1 **ubaanga.** *n.* —.
BE **hagauba.** *v.* —.
BE1 **hagaubaanga.** *n.* —.
R **ubauba.** *v.* —.
R 1 **ubaubaanga.** *n.* —.
RE **hagaubauba.** *v.* —.
RE1 **hagaubaubaanga.** *n.* —.

UBU
B **ubu.** *n.* Kneecap, the shell of the coconut.
ID **dalaa ubu.** Charcoal from the coconut shell.
ID **doo i de ubu.** Too big in size (of clothes).
ID **duu ubu haohao.** A piece of taro cooked in a coconut shell with coconut oil.
ID **gaadinga hai ngadi ubu.** Coconut with a shell of a size appropriate for use as a cooking vessel.
ID **ngadi ubu.** An empty coconut shell used as a container.
ID **ubu aahao.** [var. of *ubu haohao*].
ID **ubu haohao.** A type of prepared food (made from taro and coconut cream).
ID **ubu hhoa.** A type of prepared food dish (made from taro cooked in a half coconut shell).
ID **ubu loada.** A coconut shell used for expectoration.

UDA_1
B **uda$_1$.** *v.* To board (a ship or canoe).
B 2 **udaia.** *v.* To have room for (on a ship or canoe); arrive on time (to board a ship or canoe).
BE **hagauda.** *v.* —; anoint (in baptism).
BE1 **hagaudanga.** *n.* —; the load or capacity (of a ship or canoe).
BE2 **hagaudalia.** *v.* —.
ID **hagauda de hau.** Put on a *hau.*
ID **hagauda de hine.** A certain method of delivering a child.
ID **hagauda i tege.** Carry a basket, etc., on one's hip.

UDA$_2$

B **uda$_2$.** *nl.* Inland.
XCO **ngauda$_1$.** *nl.* Inland of; landlubber.
XFL **bodubodu-o-uda.** *n.* Insect sp.
XFL **honu-uda.** *n.* Insect sp. (small and turtle-like).
XFL **laagau-bala-uda.** *n.* Driftwood sp. (very soft).
ID **au dili uda.** An ocean current flowing toward land.
ID **dili uda.** An ocean current which comes towards the shore (and carries in driftwood, etc.).
ID **hano laa uda.** Go on foot.
ID **me dili uda.** An ocean current which comes towards the atoll.

UDO

B **udo.** *n.* The soft wood around the center of a tree trunk.
B 1 **udonga.** *n.* —.
R **udoudo.** *v.* Having soft wood in the interior (of a tree).

UDONGI

B **udongi.** *n.* A line holding together the palm fronds used in communal net fishing.

UDU

B **udu.** *n.* Fish sp.: snapper.

UDUA

B **udua.** *n.* Promontory, peninsula.
BE **hagaudua.** *v.* —.
ID **mada udua.** The point of a promontory or peninsula (esp. if large).

UDUUDUHI

B **uduuduhi.** *v.* To do little by little or gradually.
B 1 **uduuduhinga.** *n.* —.
B 2 **uduuduhia.** *v.* —.
BE **hagauduuduhi.** *v.* —.
BE1 **hagauduuduhinga.** *n.* —.
BE2 **hagauduuduhia.** *v.* —.

UE

B **ue.** *v.* Move something from one place to another; to cause to move (as in starting a machine).
B 1 **ueanga.** *n.* —.
B 1 **uenga.** *n.* —.
B 2 **uea.** *v.* —.
BE **hagaue.** *v.* —.
BE1 **hagauenga.** *n.* —.
BE2 **hagauea.** *v.* A sleeping mat.
R **ueue.** *v.* —.
R 1 **ueueanga.** *n.* —.
R 1 **ueuenga.** *n.* —.
R 2 **ueuea.** *v.* —.
RE **hagaueue.** *v.* —.
RE1 **hagaueuenga.** *n.* —.
RE2 **hagaueuea.** *v.* —.
ID **ue age.** Raise or increase (volume of radio or price, etc.).
ID **ue ange.** Increase (speed or power, etc.).
ID **ue gee.** Move to another place.
ID **ue iho.** Lower or decrease (the volume of a radio, price, etc.).
ID **ueue ange.** Exaggerate.
CF **ngaue.** Move (oneself), moved.

UGA$_1$

B **uga$_1$.** *n.* Fishing line, rope (of a sort suitable for fishing).
XCO **ugallalo.** *a.* Fishing (angling with a line) to an unusual depth.
XFL **manu-daa-uga.** *n.* [= *goehau*].
ID **hadi de uga.** The curvature of a fish line when angling (due to underwater currents).
ID **uga de henua.** The native variety of fishing line.
ID **uga duiagi.** The fishing line used in *duiagi* fishing.

UGA$_2$

B **uga$_2$.** *n.* A disturbance of water at the mouth of the atoll's channel, due to an outflowing tide.

UGU

B ugu. *v.* Rub (with pressure, as in using sandpaper); the skin of the stingray used for sanding).
B 1 uguanga. *n.* —.
B 2 ugua. *v.* —.
B 2 uguhia. *v.* —.
BE hagaugu. *v.* —.
BE1 hagauguanga. *n.* —.
BE2 hagaugua. *v.* —.
BE2 hagauguhia. *v.* —.
R uguugu. *v.* —.
R 1 uguuguanga. *n.* —.
R 2 uguugua. *v.* —.
R 2 uguuguhia. *v.* —.
RE hagauguugu. *v.* —.
RE1 hagauguuguanga. *n.* —.
RE2 hagauguugua. *v.* —.
RE2 hagauguuguhia. *v.* —.
XCO hadiugu. *v.* A unit of linear measure (from the end of an outstretched hand to the bent elbow of the other arm).

UHADO

B uhado. *n.* Worm sp. (large, white).

UHE

B uhe. *v.* Wasteful of taro when peeling it (i.e., inclined to peel too much away).
B 1 uheanga. *n.* —.
B 1 uhenga. *n.* —.
B 2 uhea. *v.* —.
BE hagauhe. *v.* —.
BE1 hagauheanga. *n.* —.
BE1 hagauhenga. *n.* —.
BE2 hagauhea. *v.* —.
R uheuhe. *v.* —.
R 1 uheuheanga. *n.* —.
R 1 uheuhenga. *n.* —.
R 2 uheuhea. *v.* —.
RE hagauheuhe. *v.* —.
RE1 hagauheuheanga. *n.* —.
RE1 hagauheuhenga. *n.* —.
RE2 hagauheuhea. *v.* —.

UHI

B uhi. *v.* To replace the ridge pole cover of a thatch house; to cover the sides of a house with plaited green coconut leaves (as protection against ghosts) [archaic].
B 1 uhinga. *n.* —.
B 2 uhia. *v.* —.
BE hagauhi. *v.* —.
BE1 hagauhinga. *n.* —.
BE2 hagauhia. *v.* —.
R uhiuhi. *v.* —.
R 1 uhiuhinga. *n.* —.
R 2 uhiuhia. *v.* —.
RE hagauhiuhi. *v.* —.
RE1 hagauhiuhinga. *n.* —.
RE2 hagauhiuhia. *v.* —.
ID uhi daguu. Turtle ribs (used as knives in rituals).

UHUUHU

B uhuuhu. *n.* Fish sp. (var. of *huuhuu*).

UI$_1$

B ui$_1$. *v.* Pick pandanus (*ui hala*).
B 1 uinga$_1$. *n.* —.
B 2 uia. *v.* —.
BE hagaui$_1$. *v.* —.
BE1 hagauinga$_1$. *n.* —.
BE2 hagauia$_1$. *v.* —.
R uiui$_1$. *v.* —.
R 1 uiuinga$_1$. *n.* —.
R 2 uiuia. *v.* —.
RE hagauiui$_1$. *v.* —.
RE1 hagauiuinga$_1$. *n.* —.
RE2 hagauiuia$_1$. *v.* —.
ID ui modo. To pick pandanus while it is still unripe.

UI$_2$

B ui$_2$. *a.* To go past a point (in time or place), or past a certain stage.
B 1 uinga$_2$. *n.* —.
BE hagaui$_2$. *v.* —; remove (clothes, etc.), disrobe, undress; lose contact with.
BE1 hagauinga$_2$. *n.* —.
BE2 hagauia$_2$. *v.* —.
R uiui$_2$. *a.* —.
R 1 uiuinga$_2$. *n.* —.

RE hagauiui$_2$. *v*. —.
RE1 hagauiuinga$_2$. *n*. —.
RE2 hagauiuia$_2$. *v*. —.
ID **hagaui gee.** Avoid.
ID **ui age.** Pass over.
ID **ui iho.** Pass under.

UI$_{2a}$
B **uinga$_3$.** *n*. Paths in the taro bog, made from dry palm fronds.
ID **dugu de uinga.** To lay down a new cover of palm fronds on *uinga*.
ID **hagaduu de uinga.** To place stakes on the sides of *uinga*.

UILA
B **uila.** *n*. Lightning, electricity.
ID **dada de uila.** An electrical storm.

ULA$_1$
B **ula$_1$.** *a*. Flame, aflame, burning.
B 1 **ulaanga.** *n*. —.
BE **hagaula.** *v*. —.
BE1 **hagaulaanga.** *n*. —.
R **ulaula.** *a*. —.
R 1 **ulaulaanga.** *n*. —.
RE **hagaulaula.** *v*. —.
RE1 **hagaulaulaanga.** *n*. —.
ID **ula age.** Be on fire.
ID **ula de gili.** Inflammation; red in the face, flushed; sunburned.

ULA$_{1a}$
B **ulavvaa.** *a*. Burn with a high flame.
B 1 **ulavvaanga.** *n*. —.
BE **hagaulavvaa.** *v*. —.
BE1 **hagaulavvaanga.** *n*. —.
R **ulaulavvaa.** *a*. —.
R 1 **ulaulavvaanga.** *n*. —.
RE **hagaulaulavvaa.** *v*. —.
RE1 **hagaulaulavvaanga.** *n*. —.

ULA$_{1b}$
B **haula.** *v*. Set fire to (causing large flames); light (a lamp).
B 1 **haulanga.** *n*. —.
B 2 **haulasia.** *v*. —.
R **haahaula.** *v*. —.
R 1 **haahaulanga.** *n*. —.
R 2 **haahaulasia.** *v*. —.
ID **haahaula age de me.** Become bright (with morning sunlight).
ID **haula ngongo.** To roast *ngongo* (in a fire).
ID **ssave haula.** To roast *ssave* (in the fire of a torch).

ULA$_2$
B **ula$_2$.** *n*. Lobster spp.
XFL **ula-dai.** *n*. Rock lobster sp.: longusta.
ID **daga ula.** Go lobster catching.

ULAHI
B **ulahi.** *n*. Fish sp.: parrot fish.

ULALO
B **ulalo.** *v*. Not level (esp. a person when sleeping).
B 1 **ulaloanga.** *n*. —.
BE **hagaulalo.** *v*. —.
BE1 **hagaulaloanga.** *n*. —.

ULI$_1$
B **uli$_1$.** *a*. Dark (in color), blackened; covered with (people, flies, etc.).
B 1 **ulianga.** *n*. —.
BE **hagauli.** *v*. —; become dark (in color).
BE1 **hagaulianga.** *n*. —.
BE2 **hagaulia.** *v*. —.
R **uliuli.** *a*. Black.
R 1 **uliulianga.** *n*. —.
RE **hagauliuli.** *v*. —.
RE1 **hagauliulianga.** *n*. —.
RE2 **hagauliulia.** *v*. —.
XCO **aloalo-uli.** *a*. Becoming dark (of fully mature coconut meat).
XCO **alo-uli.** *a*. Dark color (of fully mature coconut meat).
XCO **ulimagallai.** *a*. Jet black.
XE **hagaaloalo-uli.** *v*. Cause to become dark (of fully mature coconut meat).
XE **hagaalo-uli.** *v*. Cause to be dark (of fully mature coconut meat).

ID **baalanga uli.** Cast iron.
ID **gaha uli.** Having brown (ripe) coconuts (of a coconut tree).
ID **gelegele uli.** Black soil [soil with high organic content].
ID **uli bela.** Jet black.

ULI$_2$
B **uli$_2$.** *n.* A sprout of a plant suitable for planting.

ULI$_3$
B **uli$_3$.** *n.* Fish sp. (several spp.).

ULU$_1$
B **ulu$_1$.** *v.* Enter, join (a group), get in; wounded (by something which has pierced); level (an area); remove all fruit from a coconut tree.
B 1 **uulunga.** *n.* —.
B 2 **ulua$_1$.** *v.* —; entered.
B 2 **uluhia.** *v.* —; a sudden access of hostile feeling; interfered with; entered.
BE **hagaulu$_1$.** *v.* —; to put oneself between others (as children do).
BE **hagaulu$_2$.** *n.* Fish sp.: shark sp.
BE1 **hagaulunga$_1$.** *n.* —.
BE2 **hagaulua.** *v.* —.
BE2 **hagauluhia.** *v.* —.
R **uluulu.** *v.* —.
R 1 **uluulunga$_1$.** *n.* —.
R 2 **uluulua.** *v.* —.
R 2 **uluuluhia.** *v.* —.
RE **hagauluulu.** *v.* —.
RE1 **hagauluulunga$_1$.** *n.* —.
RE2 **hagauluulua.** *v.* —.
RE2 **hagauluuluhia.** *v.* —.
XCO **deleulu.** *v.* Good at catching tuna.
XFL **ulu-dugi.** *n.* Fish sp.: hawk fish.
XFL **ulu-dugi-lalo-beau.** *n.* Fish sp.: hawk fish.
XFL **ulu-hai-bogo-lua.** *n.* Fish sp. (resembles *hoimanu*, but much bigger).
ID **dangada ulu.** Companions or friends who share the same interests, and who get along well.
ID **daumaha hagaulu.** The church service at which new members are accepted.
ID **uluhia e de lede.** Become freezing cold (of a person).
ID **ulu i daane.** Boy-chaser, boy-crazy.
ID **ulu i haahine.** Ladies' man, girl-crazy.
ID **ulungaa iga.** A pair of copulating fish (or turtles, or whales, or stingrays.
ID **ulungaa mamu.** A pair of copulating fish, (or turtles, or whales, or stingrays).
ID **ulu sele dababa.** [a phrase said aloud to attract sharks].

ULU$_{1a}$
B **uludino.** *a.* Shed skin (as does a reptile).
B 1 **uludinoanga.** *n.* —.
BE **hagauludino.** *v.* —.
BE1 **hagauludinoanga.** *n.* —.
R **uluuludino.** *a.* —.
R 1 **uluuludinoanga.** *n.* —.
RE **hagauluuludino.** *v.* —.
RE1 **hagauluuludinoanga.** *n.* —.

ULU$_{1b}$
B **ului.** *v.* Turn inside out.
B 1 **uluinga.** *n.* —.
B 2 **uluia.** *v.* —.
BE **hagaului.** *v.* —.
BE1 **hagauluinga.** *n.* —.
BE2 **hagauluia.** *v.* —.
R **uluului.** *v.* —.
R 1 **uluuluinga.** *n.* —.
R 2 **uluuluia.** *v.* —.
RE **hagauluului.** *v.* —.
RE1 **hagauluuluinga.** *n.* —.
RE2 **hagauluuluia.** *v.* —.

ULU$_{1c}$
B **ulumagi.** *v.* Put on (clothes), wear.
B 1 **ulumaginga.** *n.* —.
B 2 **ulumagina.** *v.* —.
BE **hagaulumagi.** *v.* —.

BE1 **hagaulumaginga.** *n.* —.
BE2 **hagaulumagia.** *v.* —.
BE2 **hagaulumagina.** *v.* —.
R **uluulumagi.** *v.* —.
R 1 **uluulumaginga.** *n.* —.
R 2 **uluulumagia.** *v.* —.
R 2 **uluulumagina.** *v.* —.
RE **hagauluulumagi.** *v.* —.
RE1 **hagauluulumaginga.** *n.* —.
RE2 **hagauluulumagia.** *v.* —.
RE2 **hagauluulumagina.** *v.* —.
ID **ulumagi age.** Cover or put on from the bottom up.
ID **ulumagi iho.** Cover or put on from the top down.

ULU$_2$
B **ulu$_2$.** *nl.* Topmost part.
XFL **ulu-davage.** *n.* Plant sp.: tree sp.: Indian coral tree (*Erythrina variegata* L.).
ID **de ulu hagabolebole.** Topmost part of any standing object.
ID **ulu age.** Take from the bottom upward.
ID **ulu de henua.** To cover the land (such as do the branches of breadfruit trees).
ID **ulu hudi.** Young girl.
ID **ulu iho.** Take from the top downward.
ID **ulu i lalo.** Bottom part.
ID **ulu i lunga.** Top part.
ID **ulu laagau.** Medicine (from a plant).
ID **ulu manu.** Coral head (submerged).

ULU$_{2a}$
B **dauulu.** *v.* Verdant (indicating growing well).
B 1 **dauulunga.** *n.* —.
BE **hagadauulu.** *v.* —.
BE1 **hagadauulunga.** *n.* —.
BE2 **hagadauulua.** *v.* —.

ULUA
B **ulua$_2$.** *n.* Fish sp. (resembles *gada*, but bigger).
XFL **ulua-gabugabu-tai.** *n.* Fish sp.: round herring?, goby?

ULUMONU
B **ulumonu.** *n.* Porpoise.

ULUNGA
B **ulunga.** *v.* Pillow, lie with one's head on a pillow.
B 1 **ulungaanga.** *n.* —.
BE **hagaulunga$_2$.** *v.* —.
BE1 **hagaulungaanga.** *n.* —.
R **uluulunga$_2$.** *v.* Repeatedly *ulunga.*
RE **hagauluulunga$_2$.** *v.* —.
RE1 **hagauluulungaanga.** *n.* —.
ID **gili ulunga.** Pillowcase.
ID **ulunga hala.** A pillow made from a pandanus log (having various magical uses).

ULUNGI
B **ulungi.** *v.* Steer (a canoe).
B 1 **ulunginga.** *n.* —.
B 2 **ulungia.** *v.* —.
BE **hagaulungi.** *v.* —.
BE1 **hagaulunginga.** *n.* —.
BE2 **hagaulungia.** *v.* —.
R **uluulungi.** *v.* —.
R 1 **uluulunginga.** *n.* —.
R 2 **uluulungia.** *v.* —.
RE **hagauluulungi.** *v.* —.
RE1 **hagauluulunginga.** *n.* —.
RE2 **hagauluulungia.** *v.* —.
ID **tama ulungi.** Coxswain of a canoe rigged for the pole fishing of tuna [he also handles the pole].

UMA
B **uma.** *n.* The chestbone of a bird (used as a tool).

UMADA
B **umada.** *n.* Rainbow.
ID **duu de umada.** A rainbow appearing in the sky.
ID **sii talaa umada.** A wash of waves at the prow of a canoe, when it is sailing fast.

UMALIE
B **umalie.** *a.* Delicious (of pandanus only).
BE **hagaumalie.** *v.* —.
R **umaumalie.** *v.* Constantly bearing delicious fruit (of a pandanus tree only).

RE hagaumaumalie. *v.* —.

UMIDI

B **umidi.** *a.* Hungry for fish or meat.
B 1 **umidianga.** *n.* —.
BE **hagaumidi.** *v.* —.
BE1 **hagaumidianga.** *n.* —.
R **umiumidi.** *a.* Like (someone or something), feel affection for.
R 1 **umiumidianga.** *n.* —.
RE **hagaumiumidi.** *v.* —.
RE1 **hagaumiumidianga.** *n.* —.

UMOLO

B **umolo.** *n.* Fish sp. (two kinds).

UMU

B **umu.** *n.* Cook house, earth oven.
ID **goloa hai umu.** Implements and supplies needed in connection with use of the earth oven.
ID **sua hadu umu.** Stones (dead coral) used in the earth oven.
ID **umu lehu.** An earth oven for making coral lime [for masonry] from coral.

UNA

B **una.** *n.* The carapace of the hawksbill turtle.
ID **una dabu.** The part of the turtle shell nearest to the neck.
CF **unahi.** Scale (of a fish).

UNAHI

B **unahi.** *n.* Scale (of a fish).

UNU$_1$

B **unu.** *v.* Drink; pull in the mast stay sheet (on a canoe).
B 1 **unumanga.** *n.* Drinking party.
B 1 **ununga.** *n.* —.
B 2 **unumia.** *v.* —.
BE **hagaunu.** *v.* —.
BE1 **hagaunumanga.** *n.* —.
BE2 **hagaunumia.** *v.* —.
R **unuunu.** *v.* —; suck on the breast, nurse (at the breast).
R 1 **unuunumanga.** *n.* —.
R 1 **unuununga.** *n.* —.
R 2 **unuunumia.** *v.* —.
RE **hagaunuunu.** *v.* —.
RE1 **hagaunuunumanga.** *n.* — ['drink' meaning only].
RE2 **hagaunuunumia.** *v.* —.
ID **dai hieunu.** Thirsty.
ID **haau unuunu.** Breast-feed.
CF **ssunu.** — —.

UNU$_{1a}$

B **hakaunuunu.** *v.* To nurse (an infant at the breast).
B 1 **hakaunuunuanga.** *n.* —.
B 2 **hakaunuunumia.** *v.* —.

UNU$_{1b}$

B **haunu.** *v.* [= *hagaunu*].
B 1 **haunumanga.** *n.* —.
B 1 **haununga.** *n.* —.
B 2 **haunua.** *v.* —.
B 2 **haunumia.** *v.* —.
BE **hagahahaunu.** *v.* —.
BE **hagahaunu.** *v.* Cause to drink alcoholic beverages.
BE1 **hagahaunumanga.** *n.* —.
BE1 **hagahaununga.** *n.* —.
BE2 **hagahaunua.** *v.* —.
BE2 **hagahaunumia.** *v.* —.
R **hahaunu.** *v.* —.
R 1 **hahaunumanga.** *n.* —.
R 1 **hahaununga.** *n.* —.
R 2 **hahaunua.** *v.* —.
R 2 **hahaunumia.** *v.* —.
RE1 **hagahahaunumanga.** *n.* —.
RE1 **hagahahaununga.** *n.* —.
RE2 **hagahahaunua.** *v.* —.
RE2 **hagahahaunumia.** *v.* —.

UNU$_{1c}$

B **hieunu.** *a.* Thirsty.
B 1 **hieununga.** *n.* —.

UNU$_2$

B **Unu.** *n.* The name of a star; the name of a folk tale character.
ID **usubee o unu.** Foam (from the sea) on shore.

UNUDI

B **unudi.** *n.* Prow or stern

cover (of a canoe).

UNUSAAGI

B	**unusaagi.** *v.* Deception.
B 1	**unusaaginga.** *n.* —.
BE	**hagaunusaagi.** *v.* —.
BE1	**hagaunusaaginga.** *n.* —.
R	**unuunusaagi.** *v.* —.
R 1	**unuunusaaginga.** *n.* —.
RE	**hagaunuunusaagi.** *v.* —.
RE1	**hagaunuunusaaginga.** *n.* —.

UNUSI

B	**unusi.** *v.* Pull out (e.g., a sword from its scabbard).
B 1	**unusinga.** *n.* —.
B 2	**unusia.** *v.* —.
BC	**maunusi.** *a.* Pulled out, removed (by pulling out).
BC1	**maunusinga.** *n.* —.
BE	**hagaunusi.** *v.* —.
BE1	**hagaunusinga.** *n.* —.
BE2	**hagaunusia.** *v.* —.
BF	**hagamaunusi.** *v.* —.
BF1	**hagamaunusinga.** *n.* —.
BF2	**hagamaunusia.** *v.* —.
R	**unuunusi.** *v.* —.
R 1	**unuunusinga.** *n.* —.
R 2	**unuunusia.** *v.* —.
RC	**maunuunusi.** *a.* [pl. of *maunusi*].
RC1	**maunuunusinga.** *n.* —.
RE	**hagaunuunusi.** *v.* —.
RE1	**hagaunuunusinga.** *n.* —.
RE2	**hagaunuunusia.** *v.* —.
RF	**hagamaunuunusi.** *v.* —.
RF1	**hagamaunuunusinga.** *n.* —.
RF2	**hagamaunuunusia.** *v.* —.

UNGA

B	**unga.** *n.* Hermit crab (lives on dry land).
XFL	**unga-goo.** *n.* Mollusk sp.: vermetid gastropod sp.
XFL	**unga-lausdi.** *n.* Hermit crab (lives in water).
ID	**buu unga.** An empty seashell; one of (a pair of) diving goggles.

UNGAA

B	**ungaa.** *d.* Portion of, group of (fish or animals).
XCO	**teungaalodo.** *nl.* Middle (of something round); center.
ID	**se ungaa husi gee.** Do something different from that which was intended.
ID	**ungaa husi.** [the generic name for] sections of the taro patch.
ID	**ungaa lodo.** Middle part (of something round).
ID	**ungaa mamu.** A school of fish.
ID	**ungaa me.** A section of the village; village.

USE

X 1	**useahinga.** *n.* —.
XCO	**useahi.** *v.* Smoke, steam.
ID	**buu useahi.** Blurred.
ID	**useahi ina.** To be annoyed by smoke.
ID	**valaai hagauseahi.** Medication administered in steam or smoke.

USEGI

B	**usegi.** *n.* A type of song [archaic].

USI

BE	**hagausi.** *v.* Darkening of the sky or clouds (a sign of impending rain).
BE1	**hagausinga.** *n.* Rain cloud (includes all cumulus types).
BE2	**hagausia.** *v.* —.
RE	**hagausiusi.** *v.* Becoming darker (of sky or clouds).
RE1	**hagausiusinga.** *n.* —.
RE2	**hagausiusia.** *v.* —.
ID	**hagausi age.** Appearance of rain clouds on the horizon.
ID	**hagausi mai.** The appearance of rain clouds.
ID	**hagausiusi de me.** A sky covered with rain clouds.

USO

B	**uso.** *n.* Umbilical cord.
XCO	**vaiuso.** *n.* Good-tasting, cooked *Cyrtosperma* taro; the gummy remainder when *dagadaga* is grated.

USU_1

B	**usu₁.** *v.* (For a bird) to catch with its beak.
B 1	**usunga₁.** *n.* —.
B 2	**usua₁.** *v.* —.
B 2	**usuhia₁.** *v.* —.
R	**usuusu₁.** *v.* —.
R 1	**usuusunga₁.** *n.* —.
R 2	**usuusua₁.** *v.* —.
R 2	**usuusuhia₁.** *v.* —.

USU_2

B	**usu₂.** *v.* Push.
B 1	**usunga₂.** *n.* —.
B 2	**usua₂.** *v.* —.
B 2	**usuhia₂.** *v.* —.
B 2	**usulia.** *v.* —.
R	**usuusu₂.** *v.* —.
R 1	**usuusunga₂.** *n.* —.
R 2	**usuusua₂.** *v.* —.
R 2	**usuusuhia₂.** *v.* —.
R 2	**usuusulia.** *v.* —.
ID	**usuusu ange.** Encourage, egg on (e.g., to fight); try to talk into.

USU_3

B	**usu₃.** *n.* Nose.
ID	**bongaa usu.** Nostril.
ID	**gaigai a usu.** Flatus.
ID	**hhoa de usu.** To encounter unexpected misfortune as a result of one's evil deeds.
ID	**ili luu bongaa usu.** To dilate one's nostrils [a mannerism which is taken as a sign of emotion].
ID	**magi sali usu.** Headcold, runny nose.
ID	**mahaa de usu.** To have encountered unexpected misfortune.
ID	**sali de usu.** Runny nose.

USU_{3a}

B	**usubee.** *a.* Blow one's nose; mucus (blown from the nose).
B 1	**usubeeanga.** *n.* —.
BE	**hagausubee.** *v.* —.
BE1	**hagausubeeanga.** *n.* —.
R	**usuusubee.** *a.* —.
R 1	**usuusubeeanga.** *n.* —.
RE	**hagausuusubee.** *v.* —.
RE1	**hagausuusubeeanga.** *n.* —.
ID	**usubee o unu.** Foam (from the sea) on shore.

UU_1

B	**uu₁.** *v.* The presentation of a foetus at birth (e.g., head first).
B 1	**uuanga.** *n.* —.
BE	**hagauu₁.** *v.* —.
XCO	**uubiho.** *v.* Head-first presentation of a foetus at birth.
XCO	**uuvae.** *a.* A feet-first presentation of the foetus in delivery.

UU_2

B	**uu₂.** *a.* Yes!
B 1	**uunga.** *n.* —.
BE	**hagauu₂.** *v.* —.
BE1	**hagauunga.** *n.* —.
R	**uuuu.** *a.* —.
R 1	**uuuunga.** *n.* —.
RE	**hagauuuu.** *v.* —.
RE1	**hagauuuunga.** *n.* —.

UU_3

B	**uu₃.** *n.* Milk.
BE	**hagauu₃.** *v.* Suckle, nurse (feed milk).
XCO	**uumadua.** *a.* Desirous of suckling when past nursing age, to breast-feed beyond infancy.
ID	**vai uu.** Milk.

UU_4

B	**uu₄.** *n.* A fish trap (of wood); a bundle (e.g., of sticks); a cigarette-holder, made from a coconut leaf.
ID	**uu dogo.** A bundle of sticks.
ID	**uu duaa nui.** Broom.

UVADA

B	**uvada.** *n.* Penis.

VAA_1

B	**vaa₂.** *v.* To make noise (in a group); the sudden jumping of a school of flying fish (when they are scared by the light).

B 1	**vaanga$_1$.** *n.* —.
BE	**hagavaa.** *v.* —.
BE1	**hagavaanga.** *n.* —.
R	**vaavaa.** *v.* —.
R 1	**vaavaanga.** *n.* —.
RE	**hagavaavaa.** *v.* —.
RE1	**hagavaavaanga.** *n.* —.

VAA$_2$

B 1	**vaaginga.** *n.* —.
B 2	**vaagia.** *v.* Found or caught doing something wrong.
B 2	**vaagina.** *v.* [var. of *vaagia*].
BE1	**hagavaaginga.** *n.* —.
BE2	**hagavaagia.** *v.* —.
BE2	**hagavaagina.** *v.* —.
R 1	**vaavaaginga.** *n.* —.
R 2	**vaavaagia.** *v.* Repeatedly being *vaagia.*
R 2	**vaavaagina.** *v.* [var. of *vaavaagia*].
RE1	**hagavaavaaginga.** *n.* —.
RE2	**hagavaavaagia.** *v.* —.
RE2	**hagavaavaagina.** *v.* —.
ID	**ga vaa laa dangada.** Oh dear (that's not good)!

VAA$_3$

B	**vaa—$_1$.** *mf.* Able to.
B 1	**vaanga$_2$.** *n.* Manner of doing things.
XCO	**vaalanga.** *n.* Made-up (of a story only).
ID	**vaalanga a kai.** A story which is not true, a made-up story.

VAA$_{3a}$

XCO	**vaadagidahi.** *v.* Scattered (not in a cluster).

VAA$_{3b}$

B	**vaaligi.** *a.* Small [pl.]; little [pl.]; immature taro corm.
BE	**hagavaaligi.** *v.* —.
R	**vaaligiligi.** *a.* Very small [pl.]; very little [pl.].
RE	**hagavaaligiligi.** *v.* —.

VAASUU

B	**vaasuu.** *a.* Like (someone or something), feel affection for.
B 1	**vaasuunga.** *n.* —.
BE	**hagavaasuu.** *v.* —; healed, well (after sickness), recuperated; good (not bad, but not the best), OK; appropriate.
BE1	**hagavaasuunga.** *n.* —.
P	**vaassuu.** *a.* —.
P 1	**vaassuunga.** *n.* —.
PE	**hagavaassuu.** *v.* —.
PE1	**hagavaassuunga.** *n.* —.
R	**vaavaasuu.** *a.* Steadily *vaasuu.*
R 1	**vaavaasuunga.** *n.* —.
RE	**hagavaavaasuu.** *v.* —.
RE1	**hagavaavaasuunga.** *n.* —.
ID	**hagadau vaasuu.** Be attracted to or like each other (of members of the opposite sex).
ID	**vaasuu ai loo.** I like it (or him or her) very much.

VADU

B	**vadu.** *a.* Give (to hearer).
R	**vaduvadu.** *a.* —.

VAE$_1$

B	**vae$_1$.** *v.* Separate, divide; treat differently, sort out, part (e.g., hair).
B 1	**vaenga.** *n.* —; portion, share, division (e.g., of a tract); district, precinct (electoral); a measure (from the end of the outstretched arm to the center of the chest).
B 2	**vaea.** *v.* —.
B 2	**vaelia.** *v.* —.
BE	**hagavae.** *v.* —.
BE1	**hagavaenga.** *n.* —.
BE2	**hagavaea.** *v.* —.
E	**vvae.** *v.* —.
EE	**hagavvae.** *v.* —.
EE2	**hagavvaea.** *v.* —.
EE2	**hagavvaelia.** *v.* —.
PC	**maavae.** *a.* Separated (two things), divorced.
PC1	**maavaenga.** *n.* —.
PF	**hagamaavae.** *v.* —.
PF1	**hagamaavaenga.** *n.* —.
PF2	**hagamaavaea.** *v.* —.
PF2	**hagamaavaelia.** *v.* —.
R	**vaevae.** *v.* —.
R 1	**vaevaenga.** *n.* —.
R 2	**vaevaea.** *v.* —.
R 2	**vaevaelia.** *v.* —.
RC	**mavaevae.** *a.* Scattered.

RC1 **mavaevaenga.** *n.* —.
RE **hagavaevae.** *v.* —.
RE1 **hagavaevaenga.** *n.* —.
RE2 **hagavaevaea.** *v.* —.
RE2 **hagavaevaelia.** *v.* —.
RF **hagamavaevae.** *v.* —.
RF1 **hagamavaevaenga.** *n.* —.
RF2 **hagamavaevaea.** *v.* —.
RF2 **hagamavaevaelia.** *v.* —.
XCO **vaedama.** *a.* Play favorites amongst one's children.
XCO **vaeunga.** *v.* A method of lashing.
ID **vaenga o de langi.** Milky Way.
ID **vvae ange.** Divide into portions.
ID **vvae de biho.** Part one's hair.
ID **vvae gee.** Isolate, separate from, set aside (from a group).

VAE$_2$
B **vae$_2$.** *n.* Foot (including leg), leg.
XCO **dabuvae.** *n.* Toe, footprint.
ID **alohi vae.** Sole (of the foot).
ID **dahido vae.** The back of the thigh.
ID **dahuli de vae.** Dislocated ankle.
ID **gubu vae.** Foot, ankle.
ID **hagaditidi vae dahi.** Hop on one foot.
ID **hhadi iho luu vae.** Take a short break (in work involving standing).
ID **hhanga luu vae.** Spread one's legs.
ID **lele vae.** Jump feet first.
ID **lima ma vae ange.** Work for as a servant.
ID **llibo ange luu vae.** Run.
ID **me vae.** Shoes, slippers.
ID **sugi vae.** Lower leg (between the ankle and the knee).
ID **vae hagasii.** Wheel (one only).

VAELO
B **vaelo.** *n.* A long, thin appendage (e.g., barbel or streamer rays of a fish); the alleged cords in the body connected to the genitalia [massaged to alleviate illness].
XFL **udu-hai-vaelo.** *n.* Fish sp.

VAGA$_1$
B **vaga.** *n.* A big ship or canoe.
ID **gau mai vaga.** [= *gau mai moni*].
ID **vaga loosi.** A canoe used by the guardians of the island (in olden times) to meet canoes coming to the island.

VAGA$_2$
RE **hagavagavaga.** *v.* Punishment of a person by confinement (without food or drink) until his death.
RE1 **hagavagavagaanga.** *n.* —.
ID **dali hagavagavaga.** [= *hagavagavaga*].

VAGE$_1$
B **vage$_1$.** *v.* Bring up, put up, take up.
ID **vage i de lodo.** To occur to one that someone else is doing something to affect one's mood (favorably or unfavorably).

VAGE$_2$
B **vage$_2$.** *v.* To be aware of vaguely (e.g., the presence of a person when one is almost asleep).
B 1 **vagenga.** *n.* —.
B 2 **vagea.** *v.* —.
B 2 **vagelia.** *v.* —.
BE **hagavage.** *v.* —.
BE1 **hagavagenga.** *n.* —.
BE2 **hagavagea.** *v.* —.
BE2 **hagavagelia.** *v.* —.
R **vagevage.** *v.* —.
R 1 **vagevagenga.** *n.* —.
R 2 **vagevagea.** *v.* —.
R 2 **vagevagelia.** *v.* —.
RE **hagavagevage.** *v.* —.
RE1 **hagavagevagenga.** *n.* —.
RE2 **hagavagevagea.** *v.* —.
RE2 **hagavagevagelia.** *v.* —.

VAKAA
B **vakaa.** *v.* Be in trouble, in

danger, or in a precarious situation.
B 1 **vakaanga.** *n.* —.
BE **hagavakaa.** *v.* —.
BE1 **hagavakaanga.** *n.* —.
ID **vakaa laa loo.** Too bad for him (I don't care)!
ID **vakaa loo dangada.** See what happened! (the hearer having been forewarned).

VAI
B **vai.** *n.* Liquid, water.
B 2 **vaia.** *v.* Abounding in water.
B 3 **vaiaanga.** *n.* Way of being watery.
BE2 **hagavaia.** *v.* —.
BE3 **hagavaiaanga.** *n.* —.
R **vaivai.** *a.* Watery; bad— [when followed by another word].
RE **hagavaivai.** *v.* Cause to become watery, or less viscous.
RE1 **hagavaivainga.** *n.* —.
RE2 **hagavaivaia.** *v.* —.
XCO **dulivai.** *n.* A type of coconut (reddish in color).
XCO **vaigelegele.** *a.* Filthy, very dirty.
XCO **vaiuso.** *n.* Good-tasting, cooked *Cyrtosperma* taro; the gummy remainder when *dagadaga* is grated.
XCO **vaivaidagodo.** *a.* Unscrupulous, immoral, evil.
XG **gamedi vai salo.** A type of bowl.
ID **dangada vai gelegele.** A person of filthy appearance or habits.
ID **hai vaivai me.** Have sexual relations.
ID **manu hao vai.** A bottle (of glass).
ID **me hagasahu vai.** Gutter (under the eaves of a house).
ID **niho vaiuu.** Milk teeth, deciduous teeth.
ID **ngadi vai.** A coconut shell used for water storage (on fishing trips).
ID **vai ango.** A yellowish discharge from the genitalia (of either males or females).
ID **vai dea.** A whitish discharge from the genitalia (of either males or females).
ID **vai diadia.** A covered coconut shell which fishermen used to use for a drinking water container and (in emergencies) as a shark foil.
ID **vai doo.** Waterfall.
ID **vai geli.** Well (for water, in the ground).
ID **vai langi.** Rainwater.
ID **vai malo.** Perfume.
ID **vai mea.** A reddish discharge from the genitalia (of either males or females).
ID **vai nui.** Coconut milk.
ID **vai nui hhoa.** Very calm seas.
ID **vai saalia.** A group of drifting objects on the surface of the sea (brought together by the currents).
ID **vai sulu.** Pomade (for hair).
ID **vai uu.** Milk.
ID **vaivai adamai.** Remember poorly.
ID **vaivai basa.** Dirty or obscene language; foulmouthed, swear.
ID **vaivai daahili.** A dirty song.
ID **vaivai hai.** Do badly, abuse.
ID **vaivai hanonga.** An excursion for an evil purpose (esp. involving a sexual quest).
ID **vaivai me.** A disgusting business; genitals (of males or females).
ID **vaivai ngudu.** Evil-tongued, lying (dishonest, foulmouthed.
CF **madavaivai.** A type of knot used in net-making.

VAIDUU
B **vaiduu.** *a.* Lazy.
B 1 **vaiduunga.** *n.* —.

BE hagavaiduu. *v.* To act as though one were lazy.
BE1 hagavaiduunga. *n.* —.
BE2 hagavaiduua. *v.* —.

VALAAI
B **valaai.** *n.* Medicine.
ID **gai valaai.** Take medicine.
ID **oha valaai.** To disobey the instructions of a healer.
ID **valaai buliaamou.** Medicine to cure longing (homesickness or longing for a person).
ID **valaai de henua.** Native medicine.
ID **valaai tala hai sala.** Medicine to obviate the effects of *oha valaai.*
ID **valaai tao.** Dye.
ID **valaai kino.** Medicine taken to regain one's appetite.
ID **valaai hagasili lodo.** A medicine taken to reduce one's anger, or any other strong emotion.
ID **valaai hagauseahi.** Medication administered in steam or smoke.
ID **valaai hai haahine.** A love potion (to attract women).

VALAGEI
B **valagei.** *n.* Coral sp.: whip black coral.

VALE
B **vale.** *n.* Mold (fungus); any slippery jelly-like substance.
B 2 **valea.** *v.* Moldy; to have been in a place for a long time.
B 3 **valeaanga.** *n.* —.
BE2 **hagavalea.** *v.* —.
BE3 **hagavaleaanga.** *n.* —.
ID **valea i de noho.** Tired of waiting for someone.

$VALO_1$
B **daavalo.** *a.* Make a great deal of noise (vocal).
B 1 **daavaloanga.** *n.* —.
BE **hagadaavalo.** *v.* —.
BE1 **hagadaavaloanga.** *n.* —.
R **daadaavalo.** *a.* —.
R 1 **daadaavaloanga.** *n.* —.
RE **hagadaadaavalo.** *v.* —.
RE1 **hagadaadaavaloanga.** *n.* —.

$VALO_{1a}$
B **sauvalovalo.** *v.* Echo.
B 1 **sauvalovalonga.** *n.* —.
BE **hagasauvalovalo.** *v.* —.
BE1 **hagasauvalovalonga.** *n.* —.

$VALO_2$
B **valo.** *n.* Mollusk sp.: *Pinnidae* spp.

$VALO_3$
R **valovalo.** *n.* Plant sp.: tree sp.: a small tree sp. (*Prenna obtusifolia* R.Br.).

$VALU_1$
B **$valu_1$.** *v.* To grate (esp. coconut) on a stool grater (*duai*).
B 1 **vaalunga.** *n.* —.
B 2 **valua.** *v.* —.
B 2 **valusia.** *v.* —.
BE **hagavalu.** *v.* —.
BE1 **hagavaalunga.** *n.* —.
BE2 **hagavalua.** *v.* —.
BE2 **hagavalusia.** *v.* —.
R **valuvalu.** *v.* —.
R 1 **valuvalunga.** *n.* —.
R 2 **valuvalua.** *v.* —.
R 2 **valuvalusia.** *v.* —.
RE **hagavaluvalu.** *v.* —.
RE1 **hagavaluvalunga.** *n.* —.
RE2 **hagavaluvalua.** *v.* —.
RE2 **hagavaluvalusia.** *v.* —.

$VALU_2$
B **$valu_2$.** *an.* Eight.
BE **hagavalu (ina).** *v.* Make a total of eight.
XCO **Diba-valu.** *nn.* The name of a person in a traditional story.
XCO **Valu-malama.** *nt.* August ('eighth month').
ID **valu-dangau.** The eighth number of a counting game played to determine who is "it".

VALU$_3$
B **valu$_3$.** *n.* Fish sp. (= large *dangii*).

VANEI
B **vanei.** *mi.* Suspect that — (wouldn't be surprised if)...; I wonder how much...?
ID **vanei ai.** (E.g., I) wonder how —?
ID **vanei naa.** (E.g., I) wonder if...?

VANGANI
B **vangani.** *n.* Bad person.

VANGE
B **vange.** *a.* Give to (him, her, or them).
R **vangevange.** *a.* —; exaggerate; extremely show-off in manner.
ID **vange gi de hainga.** Sue (in court), complain about (to the authorities).

VAO
B **vao.** *n.* Wilderness, uninhabited place; the skin of the *ngaungau* plant, which contains an irritating substance.
B 2 **vaolia.** *v.* Still having some of the irritating substance within (of *ngaungau* skin).
CF **huaalavao.** A strong wind.

VASEGA
B **vasega.** *a.* Apprehensive (e.g., about a public appearance); nervous (only in a social context); anxious (in a social situation).
B 1 **vasegaanga.** *n.* —.
BE **hagavasega.** *v.* —.
BE1 **hagavasegaanga.** *n.* —.
P **vaassega.** *a.* —.
P 1 **vaassegaanga.** *n.* —.
PE **hagavaassega.** *v.* —.
PE1 **hagavaassegaanga.** *n.* —.
R **vasevasega.** *a.* —.
R 1 **vasevasegaanga.** *n.* —.
RE **hagavasevasega.** *v.* —.
RE1 **hagavasevasegaanga.** *n.* —.

VASU
B **vasu.** *v.* Timid, shy.
B 1 **vasunga.** *n.* —.
BE **hagavasu.** *v.* —.
BE1 **hagavasunga.** *n.* —.
P **vvasu.** *v.* —.
P 1 **vvasunga.** *n.* —.
PE **hagavvasu.** *v.* —.
PE1 **hagavvasunga.** *n.* —.
R **vasuvasu.** *v.* —.
R 1 **vasuvasunga.** *n.* —.
RE **hagavasuvasu.** *v.* —.
RE1 **hagavasuvasunga.** *n.* —.
ID **dee vasu.** Fearless (socially); inconsiderate.

VAVA
B **vava.** *a.* Leaky.
B 1 **vaavanga.** *n.* —.
BE **hagavava.** *v.* —.
BE1 **hagavavaanga.** *n.* —.
P **vvava.** *a.* —.
P 1 **vvavaanga.** *n.* —.
PE **hagavvava.** *v.* —.
PE1 **hagavvavaanga.** *n.* —.
R **vavvava.** *a.* Leaking in many places.
R 1 **vavvavaanga.** *n.* —.
RE **hagavavvava.** *v.* —.
RE1 **hagavavvavaanga.** *n.* —.
ID **aude vaavaa.** Don't talk about this to anyone!
ID **kano avaavaa.** Porous.
ID **vava de gede.** Forgetful (esp. with increasing age).
ID **vava de ngudu.** Talkative, indiscreet.
CF **avaava.** Full of holes.

VAVA$_a$
R **masavavvava.** *a.* Having many holes (like a screen).
R 1 **masavavvavaanga.** *n.* —.
RE **hagamasavavvava.** *v.* —.
RE1 **hagamasavavvavaanga.** *n.* —.

VEDE$_1$
B **vede$_1$.** *d.* —.
B 1 **veedenga.** *n.* —.
B 2 **veedea.** *v.* —.
BE1 **hagaveedenga.** *n.* —.
BE2 **hagaveedea.** *v.* —.

E vvede. *v.* To massage.
EE **hagavvede.** *v.* —; to teach to massage.
R **vedevede.** *v.* —.
R 1 **vedevedenga.** *n.* —.
R 2 **vedevedea.** *v.* —.
RE **hagavedevede.** *v.* —.
RE1 **hagavedevedenga.** *n.* —.
RE2 **hagavedevedea.** *v.* —.

VEDE$_2$
B **vede$_2$.** *n.* Fish sp.: goatfish.
XFL **vede-mea.** *n.* Fish sp.: goatfish.

VELA
B **vela.** *a.* Burned.
B 1 **velaanga.** *n.* —.
BE **hagavela.** *v.* —.
BE1 **hagavelaanga.** *n.* —.
P **vvela.** *a.* —; hot (of an object).
P 1 **vvelaanga.** *n.* —.
PE **hagavvela.** *v.* —; hot (of the weather).
PE1 **hagavvelaanga.** *n.* —.
R **velavela.** *a.* —.
R 1 **velavelaanga.** *n.* —.
RE **hagavelavela.** *v.* —.
RE1 **hagavelavelaanga.** *n.* —.
ID **lo te vvela.** The hottest part (of the day, of a fire, etc.).
ID **vvela de aloha.** Feel very sorry for.
ID **vvela mai (adu, ange).** I (you, he, or she) want to — very badly.

VELE
B **vele.** *v.* To weed (a garden); to clear bush (overgrowth); to pluck (feathers).
B 1 **veelenga.** *n.* —; a garden.
B 2 **velea.** *v.* —.
BE **hagavele.** *v.* —.
BE1 **hagaveelenga.** *n.* —.
BE2 **hagavelea.** *v.* —.
R **velevele.** *v.* —; to clear land (or a path, etc.) of weeds and underbrush.
R 1 **velevelenga.** *n.* —.
R 2 **velevelea.** *v.* —.
RE **hagavelevele.** *v.* —.
RE1 **hagavelevelenga.** *n.* —.
RE2 **hagavelevelea.** *v.* —.
ID **vele de henua.** Win over all comers (esp. in an athletic contest).
ID **vele duli.** Pull by the hair (in fighting).
ID **vele me.** To weed (a garden).

VELI
B **veli.** *n.* Sea urchin sp.: *Echinometra* spp.
XFL **veli-daubulebule.** *n.* Sea urchin sp.: *Diadema* sp.
XFL **veli-tea.** *n.* Burrowing heart urchin.
XFL **veli-uli.** *n.* Sea urchin sp.: *Diadema* sp.

VELO
B **velo.** *v.* To spear (someone); stab, pierce; jab, poke; inject, insert.
B 1 **veelonga.** *n.* —.
B 2 **veloa.** *v.* —.
B 2 **velosia.** *v.* —.
BE **hagavelo.** *v.* —.
BE1 **hagaveelonga.** *n.* —.
BE2 **hagaveloa.** *v.* —.
BE2 **hagavelosia.** *v.* —.
R **velovelo.** *v.* —.
R 1 **velovelonga.** *n.* —.
R 2 **veloveloa.** *v.* —.
R 2 **velovelosia.** *v.* —.
RE **hagavelovelo.** *v.* —.
RE1 **hagavelovelonga.** *n.* —.
RE2 **hagaveloveloa.** *v.* —.
RE2 **hagavelovelosia.** *v.* —.
ID **damaa velo.** Good at spearing fish.
ID **tigi velo ono aga.** Not firmly situated or settled, unsettled conditions.
ID **moni velovelo.** A canoe with men going spear fishing.
ID **velo aga.** To sprout roots.
ID **velo age.** Go up straight.
ID **velo daohi.** To spear (something) without releasing the spear.
ID **velo de baledilo.** To sprout (of plants).
ID **velo de hagasii.** A type of game.

ID **velo tili.** Throw a spear; go directly.
ID **velo huu —.** Inclined to do —.
ID **velo iho.** Come down straight.
ID **velo mai (adu, ange).** Come (go) straight.
ID **velosia de lodo.** Shocked.
ID **velo ssina.** Beginning to show white hairs on one's head.
ID **velo suunugi.** To spear something and hold it against something solid with the spear.

VEVE
B **veve.** *v.* To line an earth oven (*umu*) with stones, logs, or coconut husks.
B 1 **veevenga.** *n.* —.
B 2 **vevea.** *v.* —.
B 2 **vevelia.** *v.* —.
BE **hagaveve.** *v.* —.
BE1 **hagaveevenga.** *n.* —.
BE2 **hagavevea.** *v.* —.
BE2 **hagavevelia.** *v.* —.

VII
B **vii.** *a.* Fermented, spoiled (of cooked food left too long).
B 1 **viinga.** *n.* —.
BE **hagavii.** *v.* —.
BE1 **hagaviinga.** *n.* —.
BE2 **hagaviia.** *v.* —.
ID **galeve vii.** Fermented *galeve*, palm toddy.

VIIGA
CF **madaviiga.** The needle-like spines on *daudu* fish.

VIIVII
B **viivii.** *v.* Put to sleep (esp. a child) by rocking in the arms or singing to.
B 1 **viiviinga.** *n.* —.
B 2 **viiviia.** *v.* —.
BE **hagaviivii.** *v.* —.
BE1 **hagaviiviinga.** *n.* —.
BE2 **hagaviiviia.** *v.* —.

VIIVII$_a$
B **siiviivii.** *v.* A way of singing a child to sleep.
B 1 **siiviiviinga.** *n.* —.
B 2 **siiviiviia.** *v.* —.
BE **hagasiiviivii.** *v.* —.
BE1 **hagasiiviiviinga.** *n.* —.
BE2 **hagasiiviiviia.** *v.* —.

VILI
B **vili.** *v.* Do rapidly.
B 1 **viilinga.** *n.* —.
B 2 **vilia.** *v.* —.
BE **hagavili.** *v.* —.
BE1 **hagaviilinga.** *n.* —.
BE2 **hagavilia.** *v.* —.
R **vilivili.** *v.* —.
R 1 **vilivilinga.** *n.* —.
R 2 **vilivilia.** *v.* —.
RE **hagavilivili.** *v.* —.
RE1 **hagavilivilinga.** *n.* —.
RE2 **hagavilivilia.** *v.* —.
XCO **vilidogi.** *v.* Chatterbox, a person who speaks fast.

VINI
B **vini.** *v.* Wound around, tangled up, confused; equal in skill and strength (in a wrestling contest — so no one wins).
B 1 **viininga.** *n.* —.
B 2 **vinia.** *v.* —.
BE **hagavini.** *v.* —.
BE1 **hagaviininga.** *n.* —.
BE2 **hagavinia.** *v.* —.
P **vvini.** *v.* —.
PE **hagavvini.** *v.* —.
R **vinivini.** *v.* Really *vini*; kinky (of hair); wrinkled (of skin or clothes).
R 1 **vinivininga.** *n.* —.
R 2 **vinivinia.** *v.* —.
RE **hagavinivini.** *v.* —.
RE1 **hagavinivininga.** *n.* —.
RE2 **hagavinivinia.** *v.* —.
XCO **huevini.** *n.* A type of string figure.
XCO **lauvinivini.** *v.* Having kinky hair.
XCO **vinigoso.** *v.* Entangled in apparent disorder.
ID **hagadubu hue vini.** The name of a certain type of string figure.
ID **vini de ngudu.** A screwed up mouth (as of a child on the point of crying).

VOGI$_1$

B	**vogi$_1$.** *v.* To shame (someone) by teasing or insulting him.
B 1	**voginga.** *n.* —.
B 2	**vogia.** *v.* —.
BE	**hagavogi$_1$.** *v.* —.
BE1	**hagavoginga.** *n.* —.
BE2	**hagavogia.** *v.* —.
R	**vogivogi$_1$.** *v.* —.
R 1	**vogivoginga$_1$.** *n.* —.
R 2	**vogivogia.** *v.* —.
RE	**hagavogivogi$_1$.** *v.* —.
RE1	**hagavogivoginga$_1$.** *n.* —.
RE2	**hagavogivogia.** *v.* —.

VOGI$_2$

B	**vogi$_2$.** *a.* Whistling (with the lips).
B 1	**vooginga.** *n.* —.
BE	**hagavogi$_2$.** *v.* A whistle (made with the lips).
BE1	**hagavooginga.** *n.* —.
P	**vvogi.** *a.* —.
PE	**hagavvogi.** *v.* —.
R	**vogivogi$_2$.** *a.* —.
R 1	**vogivoginga$_2$.** *n.* —.
RE	**hagavogivogi$_2$.** *v.* —.
RE1	**hagavogivoginga$_2$.** *n.* —.

VOI

B	**voi.** *n.* Plant sp.: tree sp. (Mammea odorata (Raf.) Kost.).

VVALA

B	**vvala.** *a.* A piercingly bright light; the cutting of a fast canoe through water.
B 1	**vvaalanga.** *n.* —.
BE	**hagavvala.** *v.* —.
BE1	**hagavvalaanga.** *n.* —.
ID	**sii valavala.** Spray.

VVALE

BE	**hagavvale.** *v.* Spirit possession.
BE1	**hagavvaleanga.** *n.* —.

VVALO

B	**vvalo.** *v.* The noise of, e.g., a sail flapping, or the vibration of an airplane propeller, or the splashing of a canoe cutting through the water.
B 1	**vvaalonga.** *n.* —.
BE	**hagavvalo.** *v.* —.

?

B	**aduisiisi.** *n.* One's first spouse.
B	**aigimea.** *n.* Plant sp.: wedelia creeper (*Wedelia biflora* (L.) DC.).
B	**dalabaimanugadele.** *a.* Sharp (as a knife).
B	**daubeemala.** *v.* A method of braiding flower headdresses or necklaces made from *manu-mala.*
B	**gabetili.** *n.* Parent-in-law.
B	**gabinivali.** *n.* A kind of ancient song.
B	**gabuibui.** *n.* A type of prepared food (made with dried taro).
B	**hagadania.** *n.* A type of prepared food (made from breadfruit).
B	**hagailonga$_1$.** *v.* Sign, mark, signal, omen.
B	**hainamanilaluoo.** *n.* Secret friend of the opposite sex.
B	**hiehie.** *n.* A type of prepared food (made from breadfruit).
B	**ialona.** *n.* A type of string figure.
B	**lipaidonga.** *n.* Mollusk sp.: *Turbo petholatus.*
B	**maadoogini.** *n.* Harmonica.
B	**maduupaa.** *n.* A type of string figure.
B	**sasaanimadava.** *n.* Fish sp.: shark sp.?
B	**saulolua.** *n.* Fish sp.: triggerfish.
B	**sebaga.** *an.* Tens of billions.
B	**sebugi.** *an.* Billions.
B	**seguli.** *an.* Hundreds of thousands.
B	**seloo.** *an.* Millions.
B	**semada.** *an.* Tens of thousands.
B	**semuna.** *an.* Hundreds of millions.
B	**sengaa.** *an.* Tens of millions.
B	**sussunubega.** *n.* Fish sp.: wrasse.

BE **hagadalabaimanugadele.** *v.* [BE form of *dalabaimanugadele*].

BE **hagasebaga.** *v.* Make a total of ten billion.

BE **hagasebugi.** *v.* Make a total of one billion.

BE **hagaseguli.** *v.* Make a total of one hundred thousand.

BE **hagaseloo.** *v.* Make a total of one million.

BE **hagasemada.** *v.* Make a total of ten thousand.

BE **hagasemuna.** *v.* Make a total of one hundred million.

BE **hagasengaa.** *v.* Make a total of ten million.

XCO **galababa.** *n.* A type of prepared food (made from breadfruit skin).

XCO **ganimuumuni.** *n.* A type of string figure.

XFL **pula-laalaa.** *n.* Fish sp.: shark sp.?

XFL **dauleelage.** *n.* Fish sp.: blenny.

XFL **dotonogaa.** *n.* Fish sp.: goby.

XFL **gadagada-a-vaga.** *n.* A very small tuna.

XFL **gavaausu.** *n.* Plant sp.: tree sp.: Barringtonia tree (*Barringtonia asiatica* (L.) Kurz).

XFL **ginuede.** *n.* Bird sp.: [Ponapean? — see *manu kono*].

XFL **gulunieli.** *n.* Plant sp.

XFL **hagailonga$_2$.** *n.* Fish sp.?: damselfish?

XFL **malianoono.** *n.* Fish sp.: lizard fish.

XFL **ngudula.** *n.* Fish sp.: snapper.

XFL **umalei.** *n.* Fish sp. (rare).

XFL **uumolo.** *n.* Fish sp. (rare — like *huhu* — about 2 feet long with dark rust-colored skin).

APPENDICES

APPENDIX 1.
THE SEMANTIC INTERPRETATION OF DERIVATIVE-TYPE CODES

A. INTRODUCTION

In compiling this Lexicon each Nukuoro root form was tested for all possible stem forms (i.e., the various forms of reduplication), and each of these stem forms was tested for its compatibility with certain common affixes.*

Most of these derived forms are not glossed, since their meanings are easily inferable from the meanings of their respective base forms, as typically modified by the type of derivation in question (indicated by the derivative-type code).

The information below provides the information needed to make these inferences about the semantic interpretation of unglossed derivatives. The codes in each column of the "derivative-type code" are discussed column by column.

B. STEM TYPES

Nukuoro roots may have the following stem forms:

Column One (stem type)

B · ·** Base form: the form of a word closest to its root form. Compound words which take affixes other than *haga-* or *-nga* (or both) are also listed as B for convenience in listing, as are those forms which appear to contain a fossil affix. Some B · · are probably polymorphemic, but all forms whose constituents are not clear have been left unanalyzed.

*The absence of any particular derived form in the Root List is therefore an assertion that such a form does not exist.

**Raised dots indicate columns. Therefore, this is to be read as "A *B* in the first (of three) columns."

All B · · are glossed, except some of those of word class D (see under D in Appendix 4).

C · · A variant of the base form. The listing of variants is arbitrary in that either could be listed as the B · · form.

E · · Emphatic form: words identical in form to P · · forms, (see below) but singular, or emphatic in meaning; frequently this form refers to a single action completed at one time as opposed to many actions, or to the same act repeated or extended over some time).

All E · · are glossed. No root is listed with both E · · and P · · forms.

P · · Plural concord form: forms which contrast (usually minimally) with B · · forms and are used when the subject is plural. E.g., *llodo* 'want (pl.)', contrasting with *lodo* 'want (sing.)'. Under this heading are also listed some words which are *inherently* plural (and thus are not true "concord" forms):e.g., *haahine* 'women'; *llaau* 'hundreds'; *mmano* 'thousands'.

P · · forms are generally not glossed in this Lexicon unless their meanings cannot be inferred from the above statements. PC (or PF) forms are plural forms of the corresponding BC (or BF) forms.

R · · Reduplicated form: words reduplicated according to the rules given in Appendix 2. The general sense of such words, in comparison with the corresponding B · · form, is frequentative (or, intensive). Any or all of the following modifications of the meaning of the base form (whose position is located by a dash) may be appropriate:

'— again and again', 'always —', 'continually —',
'continuously —', 'constantly —', 'frequently —',
'habitually —', 'keep —', 'often —', 'repeatedly —',
'steadily —', 'tending to —'.*

*Other meanings (usually glossed) are as follows:
(1) 'become —', 'becoming —', '(be) increasingly —', 'getting —', 'increasing in —'; (2) 'really —', 'very —'; (3) '— all over', '— a lot', 'be extensively — (in coverage, etc.)', 'covered with —', 'full of —', 'having lots of —', 'having many —'; (4) '— by nature', 'disposed to have —', 'easily —', 'easily made —', 'given to —', 'having a — nature', 'having a tendency to —', 'inclined to (be) —', '(be) prone to —', 'tend(ing) to —'; (5) '— ish (as in 'ticklish'), 'barely formed —', 'more-or-less —', '— somewhat'; (6) '— (in, into, among, etc.) many', — 'one after another'.

N.B.: An "intensification" of meaning may result in a diminutive sense: e.g., *adaadamai* 'recall slightly (someone)' [cf. *adamai* 'remember'].

R · · forms are glossed only when their meanings cannot be inferred from the above instructions. An R · · form is never "grammatically plural" in meaning (in the sense in which the plural concord form is plural). Exception: *hoohoa*.

S · · Second reduplicated form: a few roots have two R · · forms. For convenience in listing, the second such form is given the designation S · · .

If not glossed an S · · form is interpreted as is R · · above.

T · · Partially reduplicated form: a reduplicated form of a root differing from that root's R · · form and not identical in meaning with it. Some T · · forms are, in effect, plural concord forms related either to a B · · form, or to an R · · form that is "grammatically singular" in meaning; others have the meanings associated with E · · forms.

All T · · forms are glossed in this Lexicon.

X · · Compound word: the following subtypes of compound words are listed (for convenience):

XCO: Compound words. The constituents of such words are written together, except that the constituents of names of persons and places, of compounds containing numerals, and of a few compounds which might otherwise be mispronounced, are separated by hyphens.

XE: An XCO plus the prefix *haga-*.

XFL: The name of an animal or plant. The constituents (wherever identifiable) are separated by hyphens.

XG: A designation for types of native equipment. The constituents of these expressions are written as separate words.

All X · · are glossed.

U · · Unclassified. All U · · are glossed.

C. PREFIXES

Column Two (prefixes).

· C · Resultative prefix. Forms which contain the 'resultative prefix' *ma-* are listed as · C · , unless preceded by *haga-* (in which case they are listed as · F ·). A plural concord form containing the plural form of the resultative prefix (*maa-*) is indicated by a P in column one (thus: PC ·).

All BC · are glossed in this Lexicon. The meaning of further affixation can be predicted by reference to the BC · form.

· D · Reciprocal prefix. Forms compounded with the reciprocal prefix *he-* are listed as · D · , unless preceded by *haga-* (in which case they are listed as · G ·). Where *he-* is followed by the fossil suffix *-i* 'reciprocal' the [*he-* . . .+*i*] form is listed as B · · and further affixation is coded on the B · · form.

All BD · forms in this Lexicon are glossed. The meaning of further affixation can be predicted by reference to the BD · form.

· E · Causative prefix. Forms componnded with the 'causative prefix' *haga-* are listed as · E ·, unless *haga-* is followed by the resultative prefix *ma-* (in which case · F · is used) or the reciprocal prefix *he-* (in which case · G · is used).

Haga- adds to any stem the increment 'cause to —'; 'cause to have —', 'create a —', 'encourage to —', 'make a —'; 'to teach how to —', 'help to —', 'instruct in —', 'show —'; 'allow to —'; 'provide a — for', 'furnish —', 'give —'; 'install as —', 'become —', 'cause to be —'; 'treat as —', 'be made from —'. Only cases departing from this rule are glossed.

· F · *Haga* + *ma-* [see above, under · C ·].

· G · *Haga* + *he-* [see above, under · D ·].

A blank space in column two of the DTC (derivative-type code) indicates the absence of any prefix.

D. SUFFIXES

Column Three (suffixes)

· · 1 Nominal suffix. Forms compounded with the 'nominal suffix' *-nga* (or allomorphs — see Appendix 3) are listed as · · 1.

-nga adds the increment 'way of —' to any stem.* Exceptions to this rule are glossed.

· · 2 Perfective suffix. Forms compounded with the 'perfective suffix' *-a* (or any of its allomorphs, which are given in Appendix 3) are listed as · · 2.

The increment of meaning which this suffix adds to the stem is that it proposes that the action denoted by the stem has been or will be definitely accomplished. Thus, it is this form which is used in commands; and in statements where

*Other meanings (usually glossed) are as follows: 'method of —', 'manner of —', 'conformation of —', 'that which is —', 'be in the condition of —'.

definiteness, thoroughness, and similar notions are expressed. It is the form which is usually (but not always) employed in passive constructions.

-a adds the semantic increment 'do — completely' to its stem.* Exceptions to this rule are glossed.

· · 3 A form construed as having a perfective suffix followed by a nominal suffix is coded as · · 3

The increment of meaning to the stem is 'way of — completely'; unless the · · 3 form is otherwise glossed.

A blank space in column three of the DTC indicates the absence of any suffix.

E. AN ILLUSTRATION OF THE DERIVED FORMS OF A ROOT, AND THEIR SEMANTIC INTERPRETATION

No root takes all the derivatives provided by the coding scheme. *LUI* takes as many as any other and will be used to exemplify the interpretation instructions just given.

LUI,

(Appears in the Lexicon as:)			Interpret as:
B	*lui*	Turn (something . . .)	Turn (something [singular]**)
B-1	*luinga*	—	Way of turning (something [singular])
B-2	*luia*	—	Turn (something [singular]) completely
BC	*malui*	Turned . . .	Be turned [singular]
BC1	*maluinga*	—	Way of being turned [singular]
BD	*helui*	Diminution of . . .	Diminution of (something)
BD1	*heluinga*	—	Way of being a diminution of (something)
BE	*hagalui*	—	Cause to turn (something [singular])

* Other meanings (usually glossed) are as follows: 'do — thoroughly', 'do — for certain', 'characterized by —', 'covered with —'.

** Singular, because there are P · · forms listed.

(Appears in the Lexicon as:)			Interpret as:
BE1	*hagaluinga*	—	Way of causing to turn (something [singular])
BE2	*hagaluia*	—	Cause to turn (something [singular]) completely
BF	*hagamalui*	—	Cause to be turned [singular]
BF1	*hagamaluinga*	—	Way of causing (something [singular]) to be turned
BF2	*hagamaluia*	—	Cause to be completely turned
BG	*hagahelui*	—	Cause to be a diminution of
BG1	*hagaheluinga*	—	Way of causing to be a diminution of
BG2	*hagaheluia*	—	Cause to be a diminution of, completely
P—	*llui*	—	Turn (some things [plural])
P-1	*lluinga*	—	Way of turning (some things [plural])
P-2	*lluia*	—	Turn (some things [plural]) completely
PC-	*maalui*	—	Be turned [plural]
PC1	*maaluinga*	—	Way of being turned [plural]
PE	*hagallui*	Flip over . . .	Cause (some things [plural]) to flip over
PE1	*hagalluinga*	—	Way of causing (some things [plural]) to flip over
PE2	*hagalluia*	—	Cause (some things [plural]) to flip over completely
PF	*hagamaalui*	—	Cause to be turned [plural]

(Appears in the Lexicon as:)			Interpret as:
PF1	*hagamaaluinga*	—	Way of causing to be turned [plural]
R	*luilui*	Turn (something) end over end	Turn (something) end over end
R-1	*luiluinga*	—	Way of turning (something) end over end
R-2	*luiluia*	—	Cause (something) to turn end over end completely
RC	*maluilui*	Turned over and over	Be turned over and over
RC1	*maluiluinga*	—	Way of being turned over and over
RE	*hagaluilui*	Flip over and over	Flip over and over
RE1	*hagaluiluinga*	—	Way of flipping over and over
RE2	*hagaluiluia*	—	Flip over and over completely
RF	*hagamaluilui*	—	Cause (something) to be turned over and over
RF1	*hagamaluiluinga*	—	Way of causing (something) to be turned over and over
RF2	*hagamaluiluia*	—	Cause (something) to turn over and over completely

APPENDIX 2. REDUPLICATION

A. STEM TYPES

The derivative-type codes used in this Lexicon distinguish four main stem types (see Appendix 1):

1. Base form: the form closest in shape to the root.
2. Fully reduplicated form: a form generated (except as noted below) by full repetition of the base form; e.g., *saosao* (base form: *sao*).
3. Concord form: a form derived from the base form (except as noted below) by doubling its initial consonant or vowel.
4. Partially reduplicated form: a form generated by *partial* repetition of the base form, resulting in a form different from forms (2) and (3) above (see below).

A discussion of the formal interrelationships among these sorts of reduplication follows.

B. CONCORD FORMS

In general, a concord form is derived from its corresponding base form by doubling the initial sound of the base form; e.g.,

base form	concord form
abo	*aabo*
lodo	*llodo*

The main exceptions to the above rules are base forms of the shape: $(CV) \cdot C \cdot V_a \cdot C \cdot V \cdot (V)$ or (CV)*. In such words the *a*-vowel is doubled; also the ensuing consonant if it be *b, d,* or *g*; E.g.,

base form	concord form
badai	*baatai*
dalea	*daalea*
hahine	*haahine*
sabala	*saapala*

The only additional exceptions are *dookaa* (← base form *dogaa*); and *maadua*** (← *madua*).

C. FULL REDUPLICATION

In general, a fully reduplicated form is derived from the corresponding base form by simple repetition of the entire base form *if* the entire base form is short enough (not longer than two syllables); viz.; VV (V), VCV, CVV,† CVCV.‡

Base forms longer than two syllables are fully reduplicated by repeating only the first two syllables (and adding the remainder). Thus:

base form	examples
V V: C V§	*ianga* ~ *iaianga*
V C V: V	*ovea* ~ *oveovea*
V C V: C V	*abongi* ~ *aboabongi*
V C V: V C V	*ilaage* ~ *ilailaage*
V C V: C V V	*adamai* ~ *adaadamai*

*In symbol strings such as this one, C stands for any consonant, V for any vowel; a subscripted letter further specifies the shape of the consonant or vowel (e.g., V_a means "an *a* vowel"); parentheses denote optional increments; and a raised period indicates conjunction.

**In addition to another plural form; *maatua.*

† Exceptions: CV_oV_a reduplicate by changing the V_a to V_o :*hoa* ~ *hoohoa; loa* ~ *looloa; moa* ~ *moomoa; noa* ~ *noonoa;* also *baa*$_{4a}$ ~ *baapaba; hua* ~ *huuhua* (in addition to *huahua*).

‡ CVCV of the form $C_1V_1C_1V_{(1,2)}$ lose the final vowel of the base form in full reduplication:

$C_1V_1C_1V_1$: *bobo* ~ *bopobo; bubu* ~ *bupubu; dada* ~ *datada; didi* ~ *ditidi; dodo* ~ *dotodo; dudu* ~ *dutudu; lala* ~ *lallala; lele* ~ *lellele; lili* ~ *lillili; lolo* ~ *lollolo; mimi* ~ *mimmimi; momo* ~ *mommomo; sasa* ~ *sassasa; sisi* ~ *sissisi; vava* ~ *vavvava.*

$C_1V_1C_1V_2$: *babu* ~ *bapabu; dodi* ~ *dotodi; gage* ~ *gakage; mami* ~ *mammami; mamu* ~ *mammamu; nanu* ~ *nannanu; nonu* ~ *nonnonu.*

§ A colon indicates that the preceding part (only) is repeated in the reduplication process.

C V V: V	*haau ~ haahaau; luei ~ lueluei*[*]
C V V: V V	*gaaui ~ gaagaaui; sauaa ~ sausaua*
C V V: C V	*baasi ~ baabaasi*[**]
C V V: V C V	*dauagi ~ daudauagi*
C V V: C V V	*diinei ~ diidiinei*[†]
C V V: C V C V	*saidule ~ saisaidule*[‡]
C V V: C V V C V	*maalioso ~ maamaalioso*
C V V: C V C V V	*saalohia ~ saasaalohia*
C V V: C C V C V	*maatogo ~ maamaatogo* (one example only)
C V V: C V C V C V	*saubaligi ~ sausaubaligi*
C V C V: V	*badai ~ badabadai*[§]
C V C V: V V	*magiaa ~ magimagiaa*
C V C V: C V	*dagahi ~ dagadagahi; hesongi ~ hesohesongi*[#]
C V C V: V C V	*holiage ~ holiholiage*
C V C V: C V V	*gilisau ~ giligilisau*
C V C V: V C V V	*hedaadoi ~ hedahedaadoi*

[*] Exceptions: *baoa ~ baabaoa; heui ~ heeheui.*

[**] Exceptions: *daohi ~ daadaohi; duagi ~ duuduagi; duuli ~ duuduli; haula ~ haahaula; haunu ~ hahaunu; liagi ~ liiliagi; maalo ~ maaloolo* (in addition to *maamaalo*); *maava ~ maavaava* (in addition to *maamaava*); *maeva ~ maevaeva; mounu ~ mounuunu; nounu ~ noonounu; ngauda ~ ngaangauda; ngaobo ~ ngaoboobo; saele ~ saelesaele* (in addition to *saesaele*).

[†] Exceptions: *buulou ~ bulobulou; haangai ~ hangahangai; saabai ~ sabasabai; suugui ~ sugusugui.*

[‡] Exceptions: *baalasi ~ balabalasi; buuludi ~ bulubuludi; doolohi ~ dolodolohi; loomosi ~ lomolomosi; maalama ~ malamalama* (also *maamaalama*); *maaniha ~ manihaniha; saabini ~ sabisabini; saagule ~ sagusagule* (also *saasaagule*); *saavale ~ savasavale* [All of the preceding could be interpreted as not contrary to rule if it be reckoned that the listed base form is in fact a plural or emphatic form, and that the underlying (singular) base form has a single vowel.]; also *vaaligi ~ vaaligiligi*, and *buusagi ~ buusagisagi* (in addition to *buubuusagi*).

[§] Exceptions: *magau ~ magaugau; ngalue ~ ngangalue.*

[#] Exceptions: *badodi ~ badotodi; hagahi ~ hagaagahi;* and a large subclass (17 of a total of 37 words of this shape) which derive a duplicated form by repeating the *last* two syllables: *dahuli ~ dahulihuli; daleba ~ dalebaleba; dalebu ~ dalebulebu; galava ~ galavalava; galeva ~ galevaleva; madagu ~ madagudagu; magulu ~ magulugulu; malili ~ malillili; malino ~ malinolino;* (in addition to *malimalino*); *malogu ~ malogulogu; manava ~ manavanava* (in addition to *manamanava*); *masole ~ masolesole; ngaholu ~ ngaholuholu; ngalogu ~ ngalogulogu; ngalulu ~ ngalullulu; ngavali ~ ngavalivali, sabala ~ sabalabala.*

C V C V: C V C V	*balavini* ~ *balabalavini; dagasala* ~ *dagadagasala*[*]
C V C V: V V C V V	*buliaamou* ~ *bulibuliaamou* (one example only)
C V C V: V C V C V	*heboohagi* ~ *hebooheboohagi*[**]
C V C V: C C V C V	*daballahi* ~ *dabadaballahi*
C V C V: C V C V C V	*hebaledage* ~ *hebahebaledage*[†]

To the rule stated at the beginning of this section there are the following exceptions (not yet noted). All involve double consonants.

C C V V → C C V V C C V V: *hhuu* ~ *hhuuhhuu; kaa* ~ *kaakaa; ssii* ~ *ssiissii*

C C V C V → C V C V C V C V: *pago* ~ *bagobago*[‡]

C V C C V C V → C V C V C C V C V: *makaga* ~ *magakaga* (one example only)

C V C C V V V → C V C V C V C V V V: *mataia* ~ *madamadaia* (one example only)

C V C V C C V V → C V C V C V C V C V V: *lamallie* ~ *lamalamalie* (one example only)

D. PARTIAL REDUPLICATION

Partially reduplicated forms fall into three main classes:

1. $C\ V_1\ V_1 \rightarrow C\ V \cdot C\ V\ V$: *bee* ~ *bebee; baa*$_2$ ~ *babaa.*[§]
2. $C\ V_1\ V_2 \rightarrow C\ V_1 \cdot C\ V_1\ V_2$: *dau* ~ *dadau; gai* ~ *gagai; láu* ~ lalau; seu ~ seseu.
3. C V C V → C V V · C V C V: *bada* ~ *baabada; hadi* ~ *haahadi; langa* ~ *laalanga; sobo* ~ *soosobo.*[#]

The forms listed above in this section comprise an exhaustive list of all words in this Lexicon that are classified as "partially reduplicated."

[*] But *magalili* ~ *magalillili* (in addition to *magamagalilili*).

[**] Exception: *hesuihagi* ~ *hesuisuihagi.*

[†] Exception: *hesilihagi* ~ *hesilisilihagi.*

[‡] Exception: *ssabe* ~ *sassabe.*

[§] Exception: *hoo* ~ *hohho.*

[#] Exceptions: *lulu* ~ *luuluu; hango* ~ *haahaango; sisi* ~ *siisii;* also, *sano* ~ *sassano.* A small class of additional exceptions does not double the first vowel: *dangi* ~ *dadangi; dango* ~ *dadango; geli* ~ *gegeli; gono* ~ *gogono.*

APPENDIX 3.
SUFFIXES

There are two classes of highly productive suffixes in Nukuoro: the "nominal suffix" and the "perfective suffix." The forms of these classes are not listed in the main body of this Lexicon.

A. NOMINAL SUFFIX

The nominal suffix is added to any stem type (see listing in Appendix 2) with the increment of meaning noted in Appendix 1.

The forms of this suffix are as follows: *-nga* or *-anga* (one or both of which is selected by every root but two); also (occurring rarely, see below) *-danga,* or *-hanga,* or *-langa,* or *-manga,* or *-sanga.*

No rule was discovered by which the specific form of the nominal suffix (i.e., the particular allomorph) could be predicted from the shape of the stem, or from knowledge of the form of the perfective suffix which the stem selects.

In general, (C)VCV base forms lengthen their first vowel when they select *-nga* (but not when other forms of this suffix are selected); E.g.;

base form	nominal form
anu	*aanunga*
bole	*boolenga*

but there are many exceptions to this generalization.*

*E.g., *adi* ~ *adinga; ago* ~ *agonga; ahe* ~ *ahenga; bigi* ~ *biginga; dagi* ~ *daginga; dahi* ~ *dahinga; hodu* ~ *hodunga; lugu* ~ *lugunga; lulu* ~ *lulunga; nebu* ~ *nebunga; nehu* ~ *nehunga; nodi* ~ *nodinga; etc.*

Except as noted above, base forms which select a nominal suffix do not, in general, change form.*

Emphatic forms (stem type E) without prefixes do not generally change when a nominal suffix is added, except that $C_1C_1V_1C_2V_2$ forms with *-nga* (but not *-anga*) generally lengthen the first vowel (V_1). In addition the initial consonant cluster may be shortened (from C_1C_1 to C_1), although in half the cases it is not shortened.**

E form	E-1 form
pigi	*biiginga*
tuhi	*duuhinga*
kosi$_1$	*goosinga*
hhadu	*haadunga*
llaga	*laaganga*
ssala$_1$	*saalanga*
ssolo	*soolonga*

but

tegi$_1$	*teeginga*
teve	*teevenga*
togo	*toogonga*
tugu	*tugunga*
mmasi	*mmaasinga*
mmudi	*mmuudinga*
ssigo	*ssiigonga*

Similarly with unprefixed plural concord stem forms (P), except that such forms *never* shorten the initial consonant cluster (i.e., $C_1C_1V_1C_2V_2 \rightarrow C_1C_1V_1V_1C_2V_2$).†

Fully reduplicated stem forms (R, S) and partially reduplicated stem forms (T) are invariant when the nominal suffix is affixed.

It is not the case that a stem selects only one or another of the nominal suffix forms. Many stems select both *-nga* and *-anga* (e.g., *amo, solo, ue*); in such cases there is never a difference in meaning between the two forms.

* Exceptions: *daamada* ~ *damadanga; gumi*$_2$ ~ *guumanga; hao*$_2$ ~ *haaonga; hoa*$_1$ ~ *hooanga; holiage* ~ *huliaginga; hua* ~ *huudanga* (also, *huuanga*); *hudi*$_1$ ~ *huudanga; neve* ~ *neveinga* (also, *neevenga*); *noa* ~ *noodanga; saagule* ~ *sagulenga; sisi*$_1$ ~ *siianga; sungui* ~ *suguinga* (also, *suuguinga*).

** There is one anomalous case: *hhau* ~ *haadunga.*

† A single P-1 form does not lengthen its initial vowel: *vvasunga.*

Occasionally a suffix consisting of a consonant +*anga* (C + *anga*) is the only nominal suffix form selected by a root (*alu* and *duu*$_1$ are the only examples). More usually, such a form is selected in addition to a -*(a)nga* ending. In the latter case, the two resulting forms may have exactly the same meaning: E.g., *launga* ~ *laudanga; nonunga* ~ *nonumanga*. More usually, the C + *anga* form conveys a specialized meaning: e.g., *unu* 'drink'~ *ununga* 'way of drinking'~ *unumanga* 'drinking party'.

The following is a complete list of stems that select C + *anga* forms of the nominal suffix:

C + *anga* suffix	root	other nominal suffixes selected
-*danga*	*duu*$_1$	none
	hua$_1$	-*anga*
	lau$_1$	-*nga*
	noa	-*anga*
	ua$_2$	-*anga*
-*hanga*	*alo*$_1$	-*nga*
-*langa*	*daga*$_1$	-*nga*, -*manga*
	duu$_2$	-*anga*
-*manga*	*alu*	none
	anu	-*nga*
	daga$_1$	-*nga*, -*langa*
	danu	-*nga*
	holo	-*nga*
	nonu	-*nga*
	sulu	-*nga*
	unu	-*nga*
	unu$_B$	-*nga*
-*sanga*	*milo*	-*nga*

B. PERFECTIVE SUFFIX

The second class of productive prefixes is composed of the various forms of the "perfective suffix."*

The forms of this suffix are: -*a*, -*aa*, -*e* (two examples only: *gaavee*, *gidee*), -*ea*, -*ia*, -*dia*, -*gia*, -*gina*, -*hia*, -*lia*, -*mia*, -*na*, -*ngia*, -*sia*. Except as noted, all of these forms are quite common.

*The name we have chosen for this suffix follows the usage of George Milner, and is chosen for exactly the same reasons he adduces in his *Samoan Dictionary* (London: Oxford University Press, 1966), p. xxxii.

The form of the perfective suffix that a stem selects is not predictable. Frequently a stem selects more than one form of the perfective suffix. In such cases, there is ordinarily no difference in meaning among the resulting forms (e.g., *amoa* ~ *amoaa* ~ *amoea; dogoa* ~ *dogona* ~ *dogolia; osoa* ~ *osohia* ~ *osolia* ~ *osongia*). Occasionally, however, the various perfective endings are used to differentiate meanings: *basa* 'talk' ~ *basalia* 'be talked into' ~ *basaa* 'be talked about'; *samu* 'slander' ~ *samulia* ~ 'slander (someone) thoroughly' ~ *samua* 'be slandered'.

Many (but not all) (C)VCV base forms lengthen the first vowel when the *-a* (or, rarely, *-na*) form of the perfective suffix is added (e.g., *alo* ~ *aaloa; dohi* ~ *doohia; hango* ~ *haangona; golu* ~ *goolua; vede* ~ *veedea*). Otherwise, the stem is invariant when a suffix of this sort is added to it.*

E forms to which a perfective suffix form have been added are invariant, except that $C_1C_1V_1C_2V_2$ forms taking *-a* or *-na* tend to lengthen their first vowel and shorten the initial consonant cluster (becoming $C_1V_1V_1C_2V_2$).**

All other stem forms (P, R, S, T) are invariant.

* Exceptions: *daa*$_1$ ~ *daia* (also, *daaia*); *daamada* ~ *damadaa; dada*$_1$ ~ *daangia**; *dudu* ~ *duungia; dunu* ~ *duunaa; hao*$_2$ ~ *haaoa**; *hau* ~ *haaua** (also, *haulia, hausia*); *hoa* ~ *hooia; holiage* ~ *holiagina; hua* ~ *huudia; lala* ~ *laangia* (also, *lalaa*); *lele* ~ *leia* (also, *leengia*); *lolo* ~ *loongia; noa* ~ *noodia; ngungu* ~ *nguudia; saagule* ~ *sagulea; sila* ~ *sileia; sisi*$_1$ ~ *siia; suugui* ~ *suguia* (also, *suuguia*). [*The lengthened vowel is shortened when *haga-* is affixed.]

** Exceptions: *togoa* (also, *togolia*), *lludua, mmogoa* (also, *magolia*), *nngaoa* (also, *nngaolia*).

Note that all of these except *lludua* have an alternative perfective form which does not (according to rule) lengthen the first vowel. A principle of "stem invariance" is suggested by these data.

APPENDIX 4.
WORD CLASS DEFINITIONS

A. TYPES OF WORDS

A "word" is either a "base," a "pronoun," or a "minor morpheme." Pronouns and minor morphemes are defined by listing (see Appendices 5 and 6). A "base" is interpreted as a "derivative" of a "root." A root (morpheme) is simply the minimum form which makes sense — any portion of it being nonsense. Each base that is considered a single word (as opposed to a "compound word") is construed as divisible into two parts: one part consists of "affixes" (prefixes and/or suffixes, or neither), and the other part is the "stem." Stem types are discussed in Appendix 2, suffixes in Appendix 3, and prefixes and patterns of derivation in Appendix 1.

Entries in the Lexicon are either "words" (in the above sense) or "compounds," or "idioms." Compounds act like words in that they may take some or all of the affixes associated with words,* but they are composed of independent words and do not reduplicate. Idioms are conventional phrases consisting of two or more words which do not take both prefixes and suffixes.**

B. WORD CLASS CODES

The word class codes used in this work refer to word classes defined as follows:

*Any compound (XCO) in this Lexicon may take *haga-* or *-nga*, or both, if there is no semantic incompatibility — although the listing of such forms has been avoided. Any expression which has more derivatives then *haga-* and *-nga* is treated herein as a base.

** Most idiomatic expressions (ID) in this work may take *haga-* or *-nga* (but not both); however, the routine listing of such forms has been avoided.

A Adjectives (or "statives" in the terminology of some Polynesian linguists) — bases which occur in the following frames:

(*se* + Base/ /)*
and (*gu* + Base/ /),
but not (*gu* + Base + *ina*/ /).

AN Numerals: words of class A that can be preceded by numeral classifiers.

B Base surrogates: single words (usually composed of minor morphemes) that are not A or N or V, but that can occupy the frame (/ / . . . / /).

D Dependent words: bases that are obligatorily followed by another base. Many D contrast minimally with an "emphatic" or a "plural concord" base form.** Missing glosses for such D words are listed under the corresponding emphatic or plural concord form.

I Interjections: words that occur in the frame (/ / . . . ! / /).

M . . . Minor morphemes: defined by listing (see Appendix 5 for a complete list). Words not listed as minor morphemes or pronouns are, by definition, bases.

Subtypes:

MA Articles
MC Numeral Classifiers
MF Prefixes
MI Introductory Words
MP Prepositions
MR Relational Particles
MT Tense-aspect Markers
MV Adverbs
MZ Suffixes

N Nouns: bases which occur in the following frames:

(*se* + Base/ /),
but not (*gu* + Base/ /),
nor (*gu* + Base + *ina*/ /).

* A double slant (/ /) following a string of symbols indicates the obligatory termination of a final contour (see Carroll 1965), equivalent in English to sentence-final juncture.

** See Appendix 1 under "P" (Plural concord form) and "E" (Emphatic form).

- NA Adjectival nouns: N that do not take the particle *de*, and occur only following another N.
- NL Locational words: bases that occur in the frame (*i* + NL + *de* + Noun).
- NN Names of persons (mostly excluded from the Lexicon): words that take the personal article (a_2).
- NP Place names (mostly excluded from the Lexicon): N that cannot be preceded by *de, luu,* or *denga,* and that are not NA, NT or NN.
- NT Time nouns: days of the week; months of the year; ordinal numbers in counting games.
- P . . . Pronouns: defined by listing (see Appendix 6 for a complete list).

  Subtypes:

  - PI Independent Pronouns
  - PP . . . Possessive Pronouns
  - PD . . . Dependent Pronouns
  - PT . . . Distributive Pronouns

- U Unclassified words.
- V Verbs (or "universals" in the terminology of some linguists): bases which occur in the following frames:

  (*se* + Base/ /)
  and (*gu* + Base + *ina*/ /)
  and (*gu* + Base/ /).

APPENDIX 5.
A LISTING OF MINOR MORPHEMES

The following minor morphemes are found in the Nukuoro Lexicon:

MA Articles:

	singular	dual	plural
specific	*de*		*denga(a)*
definite	*dahi*$_1$		*hanu*$_1$
general	*se*	*luu*	*ni*$_2$
personal	*a*$_2$		

MC Numeral classifiers: *dagi*$_2$, *dino*$_2$, *dogo*$_2$, *hua*$_2$, *mada*$_2$, *matogo (or motogo)*, *u*$_1$, *ua*$_4$.
MF Prefixes: *a-*$_3$, *aa-*$_2$, *ada-*$_2$, *ana-*$_1$, *haga-*, *he-*, *hii-*, *ma- (pl: maa-)*, *ngadi-*, *vaa-*.
MI Introductory words: *abe*, *adigai*, *agai*, *ama*$_2$, *be*, *bolo*$_1$, *gai*$_3$, *hidinga*, *ma*$_1$, *madali (or matali)*, *noo*, *vanei*.
MP Prepositions: *e*$_1$, *ee*, *gi*$_1$, *go*, *i*, *m-*, *ni*$_1$ *(or nii)*.
MR Relational particles: *a*$_1$, *o*.
MT Tense-aspect markers: *aude (or audee)*, *dai*$_2$ *(or tai*$_2$ *or dahi*$_3$*)*, *dee*, *(or tee)*, *tigi*, *e*$_2$, *ga (or gaa*$_1$*)*, *gi*$_2$, *goi*, *goodo*, *gu*, *kana (or ana*$_2$*)*, *mele*$_2$, *ne*, *nogo*.

The foregoing minor morphemes precede the base; the following minor morphemes follow the base.

MV Adverbs: *adu*$_1$, *age*, *agina*, *ai*, *ange*, *angeange*, *donu*$_1$, *gee*, *geegee*, *hee*, *hogi*, *huu*$_1$, *iho*, *ina*$_2$, *laa*$_1$, *loo*, *maalie*, *mai*$_1$, *malie*, *muhuu*, *naa*$_1$, *nei*, *ngadaa*, *ngaohie*, *odi*$_A$, *saa*$_1$, *sauaa*, *saunoa*.

MZ Suffixes

Nominal: *-nga*, *-anga*, *-danga*, *-hanga*, *-langa*, *-manga*, *-sanga*.
Perfective: *-a*, *-aa*, *-e*, *-ea*, *-ia*, *-dia*, *-gia*, *-gina*, *-hia*, *-lia*, *-mia*, *-na*, *-ngia*, *-sia*.

APPENDIX 6.
PRONOUNS

A. CONSTITUENTS

The following tables analyze the constituents of the various classes of pronouns, all of which are listed in the next section of this Appendix. Pronoun constituents are not listed in the main body of the Lexicon.

(1) Independent Pronouns (PI)

SINGULAR FORMS

1) *au*
2) *goe*
3) *ia*

PLURAL FORMS

Articles	Person Markers	Number Markers
(1, 3) *gi-*	*-daa-* (lst incl.) *-maa-* (1st excl.) *-laa-* (3rd)	*-u* (dual) *-deu* (plural)
(2) *goo-*	∅	*-luu* (dual) *-dou* (plural)

DISTRIBUTIVE PRONOUN

*gida**

*This form is possibly composed of the *gi-* listed in the first table and the *-da* of the second table below.

(2) Distributive Pronouns (PT)

<table>
<tr><th>Prepositions</th><th>Articles</th><th>Relational Particles</th><th>Pronoun Markers</th></tr>
<tr><td>maa-, moo-[1]
nii-
∅</td><td>(sing. specific) d-
(plural) ∅</td><td rowspan="2">-a-, -aa-[2]
-o-, -oo-[2]</td><td rowspan="2">-da, -do[1]</td></tr>
<tr><td></td><td>(dual) lu-
(sing. general) s-</td></tr>
</table>

1. The allomorph is selected to agree with the relational particle that follows it. Also, °*moododo* > *maadodo*.
2. The long allomorph is selected by all preceding morphemes ending in a vowel (*lu-*).

(3) Possessive Pronouns (PP) and Dependent Pronouns (PD)

Prepositions	Articles	Relational Particles	Pronoun Markers
	(sing. specific)[1] *de-*, *d-* (sing. general)[1] *se-*, *s-* (plural) *lu-*	*-a-*, *-aa-*[2] *-o-*, *-oo-*[2] ∅[7]	*Singular* *-gu* (1) *-u* (2)[3] *-no*, *-na* (3)[4] *Plural* *First and Third Person* *-daa-* (lst incl.) + { *-u* (dual) / *-deu* (plural) } *-maa-* (lst excl.) + { *-u* (dual) / *-deu* (plural) } *-laa-* (3rd) + { *-u* (dual) / *-deu* (plural) } *Second Person* *-luu* (2nd dual) *-dou* (2nd plural)
ma-, *mo-*[5] *nii-* ∅	(plural) ∅[6]		

1. If the next following bound morpheme begins in a consonant, select *de-* (*se-*); if the next following bound morpheme begins in a vowel, select *d-* (*s-*). Also, *de-* + *d-* > *t-*.
2. If the preceding morpheme ends in a vowel, select the long vowel allomorph; otherwise select the short variety. 2nd person plural selects only *-oo-*.
3. *ou* > *oo*; *ooo* > *oou*.
4. If the vowel preceding is *-o-*, then select *-no;* if the vowel preceding is *-a-*, then select *-na*. *Except*, *-ono* in contour final position becomes *-ona*.
5. Allomorph selected to agree with following relational particle.
6. Not with following ∅.
7. Not following *lu-* and only preceding *plural* pronoun markers.

B. LIST OF PRONOUN FORMS

PI Independent Pronouns

	sing	dual	plural	
'I', 'we'	*au*$_2$	*gidaau*	*gidaadeu*	inclusive
	(or *ngau*)*	*gimaau*	*gimaadeu*	exclusive
'you'	*goe*	*gooluu*	*goodou*	
	(or *koe*)**			
'he', 'she' 'it', 'they'	*ia*	*gilaau*	*gilaadeu*	
'each one'	*gida*			

PP . . . Possessive Pronouns

PPA PP formed with the relational particle a_1.

	sing	dual	plural	
'my (1)†:'	*dagu*$_2$	(PP)‡	(PP)	inclusive
		(PP)	(PP)	exclusive
'my (2)'	*luaagu*	*luaadaau*	*luaadaadeu*	inclusive
'our (2)'		*luaadaau*	*luaamaadeu*	exclusive
'my (3)'	*agu*$_3$	*adaau*	*adaadeu*	inclusive
'our (3)'		*amaau*	*amaadeu*	exclusive
'your (1)'	*dau*$_6$	(PP)‡	(PP)	
'your (2)'	*luaau*	(PP)	(PP)	
'your (3)'	*au*$_3$	(PP)	(PP)	
'his (1)'	*dana*	(PP)	(PP)	
'his (2)' 'their (2)'	*luaana*	luaalaau	*luaalaadeu*	
'his (3)' 'their (3)'	*ana*$_1$	*alaau*	*alaadeu*	

*Following a verbal ending in *a*, to avoid ellision: e.g., *daalia ngau!* 'wait for me!'

** Emphatic form.

† Numbers in parentheses indicate the number of things possessed: e.g., 'my (1) shoe', 'my (2) shoes'.

‡ See the listing of PP below.

PPO PP formed with the relational particle *o*.

	sing	dual	plural	
'my (1)'	*dogu*	(PP)*	(PP)	inclusive
		(PP)	(PP)	exclusive
'my (2)'	*luoogu*	*luoodaau*	*luoodaadeu*	inclusive
'our (2)'		*luoomaau*	*luoomaadeu*	exclusive
'my (3)'	*ogu*	*odaau*	*odaadeu*	inclusive
'our (3)'		*omaau*	*omaadeu*	exclusive
'your (1)'	*doo_3*	(PP)	(PP)	
'your (2)'	*luoo*	(PP)	(PP)	
'your (3)'	*oo*	(PP)	(PP)	
'his (1)'	*dono*	(PP)	(PP)	
'his (2)' 'hers (2)' 'theirs (2)'	*luoono*	*luoolaau*	*luoolaadeu*	
'his (3)', 'hers (3)' 'theirs (3)'	*ono_3* (*ona/ /*)	*olaau*	*olaadeu*	

PP Indeterminate for *o*, a_1.

	dual	plural	
'our (1)'	*taau*	*taadeu*	inclusive
	demaau	*demaadeu*	exclusive
'your (1)'	*dooluu*	*doodou*	
'your (2)'	*luooluu*	*luoodou*	
'your (3)'	*ooluu* (or *oluu*)	*oodou* (or *odou*)	
'their (1)'	*delaau*	*delaadeu*	

PD . . . Dependent Pronouns: pronominal forms incorporating other preposed minor morphemes besides the relational particles *o* and a_1. The stems of all such forms are isomorphic with the plural forms of PP.

PDM . . . PD forms built on the particle *m*-.

PDMA PD formed with $m + a_1$.

*See the listing of PP in the next section.

	sing	dual	plural	
'for me,' etc.	*maagu*	*maadaau*	*maadaadeu*	inclusive
		maamaau	*maamaadeu*	exclusive
'for you'	*maau*	(PDM)*	(PDM)	
'for him,' etc.	*maana*	*maalaau*	*maalaadeu*	

PDMO PD formed with *m* + *o*.

	sing	dual	plural	
'for me,' etc.	*moogu*	*moodaau*	*moodaadeu*	inclusive
		moomaau	*moomaadeu*	exclusive
'for you'	*moou*	(PDM)*	(PDM)	
'for him,' etc.	*moono* (*moona*/ /)	*moolaau*	*moolaadeu*	

PDM PDM forms indeterminate for a_1, *o*.

	dual	plural
'for you'	*mooluu*	*moodou*

PDN . . . PD forms built on the particle *nii*.

PDNA PD formed with *nii* + a_1.

	sing	dual	plural	
'belonging to me,' etc.	*niiagu*	*niiadaau*	*niiadaadeu*	
		niiamaau	*niiamaadeu*	exclusive
'belonging to you'	*niiau*	(PDN)**	(PDN)	
	niiana	*niialaau*	*niialaadeu*	

PDNO PD formed with *nii* + *o*.

	sing	dual	plural
'belonging to me,' etc.	*niiogu*	*niiodaau*	*niiodaadeu*
		niiomaau	*niiomaadeu*
'belonging to you'	*niioo*	(PDN)**	(PDN)
'belonging to him,' etc.	*niiono*	*niiolaau*	*niiolaadeu*

*See the listing of PDM below.

**See the listing of PDN forms below.

PDN PDN forms indeterminate for a_1, *o*.

	dual	plural
'belonging to you'	*niioluu*	*niiodou*

PDS . . . Pronominal forms which incorporate the general article *se* and which are followed by a base. In contour-final position the forms are *se*+PD stems.

PDSA PD formed from *se* + a_1.

	sing	dual	plural
'my,' etc.	*sagu*	(PDS)*	(PDS)
'your'	*sau*	(PDS)	(PDS)
'his,' etc.	*sana*	(PDS)	(PDS)

PDSO PD formed from *se* + *o*.

	sing	dual	plural
'my,' etc.	*sogu*	(PDS)*	(PDS)
'your'	*soo*	(PDS)	(PDS)
'his,' etc.	*sono*	(PDS)	(PDS)

PDS PDS forms indeterminate for a_1, *o*.

	dual	plural	
'my,' etc.	*sedaau*	*sedaadeu*	inclusive
	semaau	*semaadeu*	exclusive
'your'	*sooluu*	*soodou*	
'his,' etc.	*selaau*	*selaadeu*	

PT . . . Distributive Pronouns.

PTA PT forms with a_1.

'each person's (1)'	*dada*$_3$
'each person's (2)'	*luaada*
'each person's (3)'	*ada*$_3$

*See the listing of PDS forms below.

PTO PT forms with *o*.

'each person's (1)'	*dodo*$_2$
'each person's (2)'	*luoodo*
'each person's (3)'	*odo*$_2$ (*ooda*/ /)

PTMA PT forms with *m*- + a_1.

'for each person's one'	*maadada*
'for each person's several'	*maada*

PTMO PT forms with *m*- + *o*.

'for each person's one'	*maadodo*
'for each person's several'	*moodo*

PTMB PTMA in contour final position (. . . / /).

(sing. or pl.)	*maada*

PTMP PTMO in contour final position (. . . / /).

(sing. or pl.)	*mooda*

PTNA PT forms with *ni(i)* + a_1

'belonging to each person's one'	*niidada*
'belonging to each person's several'	*niiada*

PTNB PTNA in contour final position (. . . / /).

(sing. or pl.)	*niaada*

PTNO	PT forms with *ni (i)* + *o*.	
	'belonging to each person's one'	*niidodo*
	'belonging to each person's several'	*niiodo*
PTNP	PTNO in contour final position (. . . / /).	
	(sing. or pl.)	*niooda*
PTSA	PT forms with *se* + *a*.	
	(sing.)	*sada* (*seada/ /*)
PTSO	PT forms with *se* + *o*.	
	(sing.)	*sodo* (*seoda/ /*)

APPENDIX 7.
A LISTING OF LOCATION WORDS

The following location words (NL) are found in the Nukuoro Lexicon: *aloalo*$_3$, *baasi*, *bido*, *daha*, *dahido*$_A$, *daho*, *dai*$_1$, *dege*, *dua*$_2$, *duaahaho*, *tagelo*, *tagudai*, *teungaalodo*, *gaba*$_1$, *gabugabu*, *gaogao*, *haho*, *hiihii*, *honga*, *lalo*, *lodo*$_1$,* *lo gunga*, *lo te dege*, *lo te logunga*, *lunga*, *luu baasi*, *luu bido*, *mada*$_3$,** *magavaa*, *masavaa*$_2$, *mua*, *muli*, *ngaadai*, *ngaage*, *ngaiho*, *ngauda*$_1$, *ngudu*$_A$,† *uda*$_2$, *ulu*$_2$.

**lodo de* . . . becomes *lo te* . . .
** *made de* . . . becomes *ma te* . . .
† *ngudu de* . . . becomes *ngu te* . . .

APPENDIX 8.
IRREGULAR PARADIGMS

The relationship between singular and plural forms is not always as suggested in Appendix 2. In particular, the following forms are irregular:

singular	plural	gloss
hano	*hulo*	'go'
hanage	*loage*	'go up'
hano iho	*loiho*	'go down'
hanadu	*loadu*	'go toward you'
hanange	*loange*	'go toward them'
humai	*loomai*	'come'
laanui	*nnui*	'large'
maasei	*lligi* or *vaaligiligi*	'small'
daballahi	*llahi*	'thin'

In addition, the following paradigm is irregular in another way

gave	'take'
gamai	'give (to me)'
(ga)vadu	'give (to you)'
(ga)vange	'give (to them)'
(ga) vage	'give (upward)'

APPENDIX 9. CONVENTIONS FOR WRITING NUKUORO

The following conventions have been established in consultation with Nukuoro educational and administrative authorities.

A. SPELLING

1. Nukuoro words. Nukuoro words are spelled as rendered in this Lexicon, and are rendered here as pronounced (i.e., phonemically).

2. Foreign loan words. Foreign loan words in common use on Nukuoro should be spelled as pronounced by most Nukuoro, unless they are more intelligible when spelled as in their language of origin. In the latter case, quotation marks should be added around the word to indicate that it is foreign (e.g., "taxes," "HICOM"). Names of persons and places are also treated in the fashion just described, except that quotation marks are omitted.

The question to be asked in translation work is: in what form will this word be most intelligible to Nukuoro readers? If there is any doubt, render the foreign word as pronounced on Nukuoro, then add the foreign spelling in parentheses.

3. Abbreviations. There are no recognized abbreviations in Nukuoro.

B. WORD DIVISION

1. Space. Individual words in this Lexicon (excepting part-words, whose incompleteness is indicated by an added hyphen) are always separated by spaces.

2. Hyphenation. The use of hyphens is to be avoided, except under the conditions listed in Appendix 1 (under X · ·) concern-

ing compound words. Hyphens should not be used to indicate continuation of a word on the next line.

C. PUNCTUATION

1. Capitalization. The initial letter of a sentence is capitalized, as are the initial letters of personal names, place names, references to the Deity, days of the week, and months — but not otherwise. E.g., *De-hine-aligi* 'name of an important spirit'; *de-hine-aligi* 'cockroach'.

Personal names incorporated within compound words (i.e., words written together or hyphenated) are not capitalized. E.g., *bulaga-a-leo* '(type of) taro belonging to (i.e., introduced to the island by) Leo (a person)'. Similarly, *hakai-a-bagila* is the name of mollusk species, presumably so called because a man named Bagila was the first to use them for ornamentation; *gumigumi-o-sogo* is the name of a plant species, which translates literally as 'Sogo's beard'.

Proper names occurring within idioms are capitalized; e.g., *bolobolo a Sogo.*

2. Sentence final punctuation. A period (or question mark, or exclamation point — depending on the intonation) is placed at the end of the sentence. This point is marked by falling intonation and the possibility of long pause (i.e., at the point of "final juncture"). Commas are therefore not needed in written Nukuoro; if used at all, they should be inserted only where final juncture is *possible.*

3. Quotation marks. Quotation marks are used only in citing words, or when using foreign words (see paragraph A.2. (above), or in using Nukuoro words in an unfamiliar sense. There is no need to use them in quotations. There is never a use for single quotes.

4. Underlining. Underlining is used only for emphasis. There is no point in using italics in printed Nukuoro, as their use is not generally understood.

5. Other marks of punctuation. No apostrophes, colons, semicolons, dashes, parentheses, or brackets are ever required in written or printed Nukuoro. Avoid also the use of all other typographic conventions that are intended to convey some specific meaning (such as the indentation of long quotes, footnoting conventions, suspension points, or any symbols not mentioned above), since such conventions will not be generally understood. In printed translation work, this restriction may necessitate the interpolation of extraneous words to substitute for the omitted conventions.

APPENDIX 10.
PREVIOUS WORK ON THE NUKUORO LANGUAGE

The following are the only known sources for information about the Nukuoro language. Text material is limited to two printed gospels (Mark and Matthew) and several elementary school readers printed by the Trust Territory Department of Education.

Carroll, Vern

1965 "An outline of the structure of the language of Nukuoro." *Journal of the Polynesian Society* 74: 192 - 226; 451 - 472. Reprinted as *Polynesian Society Reprints*, no. 10.

Christian, F. W.

1898 "Nuku-oro vocabulary." *Journal of the Polynesian Society* 7: 224 - 232.

Eilers, Annelise

1934 *Inseln um Ponape: Kapingamarangi, Nukuor, Ngatik, Mokil, Pingelap.* Hamburgische Wissenshaftliche Stiftung. Ergebnisse der Südsee-Expedition 1908 - 1910, series 2, subseries B, vol. 8. G. Thilenius, series editor. Hamburg: Friedrichsen, De Gruyter & Co.

Elbert, Samuel H.

1946 "Kapingamarangi and Nukuoro word-list." Mimeographed. U.S. Navy Department.

Kubary, J. S.

1900 "Beitrag zur kenntniss der Nukuoro oder Monteverde Inseln (Karolinen Archipel)." *Mitteilungen der Geographischen Gesellschaft in Hamburg* 16: 71 - 137.

Stone, Benjamin C.
1966 "Some vernacular names of plants from Kapingamarangi and Nukuoro Atolls, Caroline Islands." *Micronesica* 2: 131 - 132.